CATHOLICISM
FAITH · HISTORY · SAINTS · POPES

CATHOLICISM
FAITH · HISTORY · SAINTS · POPES

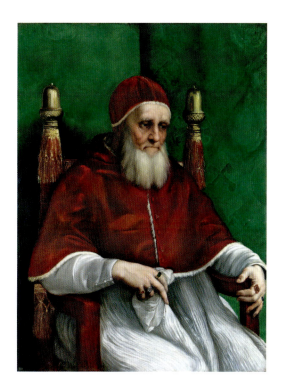

A comprehensive account of the philosophy and practice of Catholic Christianity, a guide to the most significant saints, and a history of the lives and works of 266 popes

CHARLES PHILLIPS

MARY FRANCES BUDZIK · MICHAEL KERRIGAN · TESSA PAUL
CONSULTANT: REVEREND RONALD CREIGHTON-JOBE

LORENZ BOOKS

Contents

Introduction   10
Timeline   20

Catholic History   22

THE EARLY CHURCH   24
In the Days of King Herod   26
And It Came to Pass...   28
"You are my Son, the Beloved..."   30
"Blessed are the Poor in Spirit"   32
The Way of the Cross   34
He Has Risen   36
The Disciples   38
St Paul the Convert   40
A Faith in Fear   42
New Life among the Dead: The Catacombs   44
The Church of Rome   46
The First Popes   48
The Church Fathers   50
A Church Divided   52

THE MIDDLE AGES   54
Medieval Catholicism   56
The Crusades   58
Monasticism   60
Shrines and Relics   62
Pilgrimage   64
Gothic Glory   66

RENAISSANCE & REFORMATION   68
Rival Popes   70
Indulgences   72
The Franciscan Revolution   74
Church Music   76
Heretics   78
The Inquisition   80
The Church in Transition   82
Powerful Popes   84
The Pope and the Painter   86
New Horizons   88
The Reformation   90
The Counter-reformation   92
Ecstatic Art   94
Temporal Authority   96
Political Ramifications   98

A WORLD RELIGION   100
Missions to the East   102
Missions in the Americas   104
The Gospel in Africa   106
The Enlightenment Assault   108
Holding Back the Tide   110
Dark Times   112
The Modernizers   114
The Church Militant   116
Reaching Out to Other Faiths   118
New Challenges   120
Facing Competition   122

Catholic Doctrine   124

THE MYSTERY OF FAITH   126
God in Three Persons   128
Christ the Redeemer   130
The Eucharist   132
The Classic Creeds   134
The Catechism   136
In Accordance with the Scriptures   138
The Evangelists   140
Our Lady   142
Marian Apparitions   144
All Saints   146

A STATE OF GRACE   148
The Soul Redeemed   150
The Nature of Sin   152
The Seven Deadly Sins   154
Judgement Day   156
Visions of Heaven   158
Purgatory   160
Visions of Hell   162
Visions of Damnation   164
Limbo   166

Practising Catholicism   168

INSTITUTIONS OF THE CHURCH   170
The Holy Father   172
The Vatican: A Place Apart   174
Hierarchy of the Church   176
The Path to Priesthood   178
Married to the Church   180
Called to Serve   182
Under Orders   184
Brothers in Christ   186
A Contemplative Christianity   188
Working in the World   190
Brides of Christ   192
Living for Others   194
The Missions   196
Lay Groups   198

LIVING THE SACRAMENTS	200
God's House	202
Great Churches	204
The Altar of God	206
Vestments	208
"Gathered Together in My Name"	210
The Most Holy Sacrament of the Altar	212
Baptism	214
Confirmation	216
Holy Matrimony	218
"What God Has Joined…"	220
The Sanctity of Life	222
Penance and Reconciliation	224
Anointing of the Sick and the Last Rites	226
Dust to Dust	228
Prayer	230
The Sacred Heart	232
Stations of the Cross	234
The Rosary	236
The Blessing	238
THE CATHOLIC YEAR	240
Holy Days	242
The Festive Calendar	244
A Child Is Born	246
Carnival!	248
Ash Wednesday and Lent	250
Holy Week	252
The Resurrection and Easter	254
Religious Orders	256

SAINTS & SAINTHOOD 258

SAINTHOOD	260
What is a Saint?	262
Saints in the Early Church	264
Doctors of the Church	266
Eastern Saints	268
Canonization	270
Mysteries and Miracles	272
Medieval Pilgrimage	274
Important Feast Days	276

Holy Relics	278
Heroes and Martyrs	280
New Worlds	282
Modern Pilgrims	284
The Blessed	286
Patron Saints	288
All Saints and All Souls	290
DIRECTORY OF SAINTS	292
Archangel Raphael and Archangel Michael	294
Archangel Gabriel	295
The Holy Family	296
Mary, the Virgin	298
Joseph	300
Anne	301
Joachim	302
Elizabeth and Zachary	303
John the Baptist	304
Dismas and Veronica	306
Joseph of Arimathea	307
Mary Magdalene	308
The Apostles	310
James the Great	312
James the Less and Philip	313
Bartholomew and Jude	314
Thomas	315
Peter	316
Simon and Barnabas	318
Andrew	319
Paul	320
Matthew and John	322
Mark	323
Luke	324
Stephen and Eustace	325
Polycarp	326
Justin	327
Irenaeus of Lyons and Cosmas and Damian	328
Perpetua and Felicitas	329
Denys of Paris	330
Valentine and Victor of Marseilles	331
Cecilia	332
George	333
Vitus and Dympna	334
Christopher	335
Child Saints	336
Eulalia of Mérida	338
Justus of Beauvais and Pancras of Rome	339
Dorothy and Vincent of Saragossa	340
Lucy	341
Patron Saints of Professions	342
Pantaleon	344
Lucian of Antioch	345
Helen	346
Pachomius	347
Religious Orders	348

Antony of Egypt	350
Basil the Great	351
Barbara and Cyril of Jerusalem	352
Gregory of Nazianzus	353
Ambrose	354
Agatha	355
Martin of Tours	356
Pelagia the Penitent	357
Nicholas of Myra	358
Blaise	359
Jerome	360
John Chrysostom	362
Augustine of Hippo	363
Catherine of Alexandria	364
Ursula	365
Leo the Great	366
Simeon Stylites and Genevieve	367
Celtic Saints	368
Patrick and Brigid of Ireland	370
Brendan the Navigator	371
Benedict	372
David of Wales	374
Leander and John the Almsgiver	375
Gregory the Great	376
Isidore of Seville	378
Cuthbert and The Venerable Bede	379
Rupert	380
Boniface	381
Cyril and Methodius	382
Wenceslas and Odo of Cluny	383
Ulric and Edward the Martyr	384
Wolfgang of Regensburg and Olaf	385
Stephen of Hungary and Edward the Confessor	386
Stanislaus of Cracow and Canute	387
Patron Saints of Nations	388
Margaret of Scotland and Benno of Munich	390
Anselm	391
Stephen Harding and Norbert	392
Bernard of Clairvaux	393
Henry of Finland and Eric of Sweden	394
Thomas Becket	395
Hildegard of Bingen	396
Laurence O'Toole and Dominic	397
Holy Beasts	398
Francis of Assisi	400
Antony of Padua	402
Elizabeth of Hungary	403
Clare of Assisi	404
Hyacinth of Cracow and Albert the Great	405
Fourteen Holy Helpers	406
Alexander Nevski	408
Bonaventure	409
Thomas Aquinas	410
Agnes of Bohemia and Nicholas of Tolentino	412
Elizabeth of Portugal and Roch	413
Catherine of Siena	414
Bridget of Sweden and John of Nepomuk	415
Warrior Saints	416
Joan of Arc	418
Rita of Cascia	420
Fra Angelico	421
The Martyrs of Otranto	422
Casimir of Poland and Nicholas of Flue	424
Thomas More	425
The Saints in Art	426
Angela Merici and Cajetan	428
John of God and Thomas of Villanova	429
Ignatius of Loyola	430
Francis Xavier	432
Pius V	433
Teresa of Ávila	434
Luis Bertran and John of the Cross	436
Peter Canisius and Philip Neri	437
Royal Saints	438
Turibius of Lima and Francis Solano	440
Rose of Lima	441
Robert Bellarmine	442
Francis of Sales	443
Roque Gonzalez	444
Lorenzo Ruiz and Martin de Porres	445
Peter Claver	446
Joseph of Copertino	447
Vincent de Paul	448
Saintly Popes	450
Marguerite Bourgeoys	452
Louis Grignion de Montfort	453
John-Baptist de La Salle	454
John Joseph of the Cross	455
Jeanne Delanoue and Francis Serrano	456
Leonard of Port Maurice	457
Gerard Majella	458
Margaret d'Youville	459
Vincent Liem	460
Paul of the Cross and Benedict Joseph Labre	461
Alphonsus Liguori	462
Elizabeth Seton	463
Antônio de Sant'Anna Galvão	464

Magdalena of Canossa and Joseph Cottolengo	465
Incorruptibles	466
Jean-Baptiste Vianney	468
Gaspar Bertoni and Catherine Labouré	469
Madeleine Sophie Barat	470
Kuriakose Elias Chavara	471
Antony Claret and Clelia Barbieri	472
Bernadette of Lourdes	473
Joseph Mkasa	474
Charles Lwanga and Marie Adolphine Dierks	475
John Bosco	476
John Henry Newman	477
Houses of God	478
Theresa of Lisieux	480
Raphael Kalinowski and Miguel Cordero	482
Frances Cabrini	483
Teresa of Los Andes	484
Bertilla Boscardin and Giuseppe Moscati	485
The Cult of Mary	486
Maria Faustina Kowalska	488
Maximilian Kolbe	489
Edith Stein	490
Josephine Bakhita and John Calabria	491
Katharine Drexel	492
Father George Preca	493
Padre Pio	494
Josemaría Escrivá	495
Paul VI	496
Teresa of Calcutta	497
Dulce of the Poor	498
John Paul the Great	499

GAZETTEER OF OTHER SAINTS   500

THE FIRST POPES   512

UPON THIS ROCK...: PETER TO SYLVESTER I, c.30/40–335   514
Timeline	516
St Peter, the First Pope	522
Linus to Pius I, 66–155	524
Anicetus to Urban I, 155–230	526
Pontian to Stephen I, 230–57	528
The Pope and the Bishops of the Church	530
Sixtus II to Eusebius, 257–310	532
Miltiades and Sylvester I, 311–35	534

FALL OF THE WESTERN EMPIRE: MARK TO PELAGIUS II, 366–590   536
Mark to Liberius, 366–66	538
Damascus I, 366–84	540
Siricius and Anastasius, 384–401	542
Innocent I, 401–17	544
Zosimus to Sixtus III, 417–40	546
Leo I, 440–61	548
Hilarius to Silverius, 461–537	550
Rome and the Acquisition of the Papal States	552
Vigilius to Pelagius II, 537–90	554

ENTER THE FRANKS: GREGORY THE GREAT TO HADRIAN I, 590–795   556
Gregoy I "the Great", 590–604	558
Sabinian to Boniface V, 604–25	560
Honorius I to Martin I, 625–53	562
Eugene I to Agatho, 654–81	564
Leo II to Constantine 682–715	566
Gregory II to Zacharias, 715–52	568
Stephen II to Stephen III, 752–72	570
Hadrian I, 772–95	572

CONFLICT IN THE CHURCH: LEO III TO LEO IX, 795–1054   574
Leo III, 795–816	576
Stephen IV to Sergius II, 816–46	578
Leo IV to Leo V, 847–903	580
Sergius III to Gregory V, 904–99	582
Sylvester II, 999–1003	584
John XVII to Damasus II, 1003–48	586
The Great Schism of the Two Churches	588
Leo IX, 1049–54	590

CRUSADING POPES & THE REFORMATION   592

BIRTH OF THE CRUSADES: VICTOR II TO CLEMENT III, 1055–1191   594
Victor II to Alexander II, 1055–73	596
Gregory VII, 1073–85	598
Victor III and Urban II, 1086–99	600
Paschal II and Gelasius II, 1099–1119	602
Callistus II, 1119–24	604
Honorius II, 1124–30	606
Innocent II to Lucius II, 1130–45	608
Eugenius III, 1145–53	610
Hadrian IV, 1154–9	612
Alexander III to Clement III, 1159–91	614

THE MENDICANT ORDERS: CELESTINE III TO BENEDICT XI, 1191–1304   616
Celestine III, 1191–8	118
Innocent III, 1198–1216	620
Crusades Against Enemies of the Papacy	622
Honorius III, 1216–27	624

Gregory IX, 1227–41	626
Celestine IV to Clement IV, 1241–68	628
Gregory X, 1271–6	630
Innocent I to Benedict XI, 1276–1304	632

AVIGNON EXILE AND PAPAL SCHISM: CLEMENT V TO EUGENE IV, 1305–1447 — 634

Clement V, 1305–14	636
John XXII, 1316–34	638
Exile of the Papacy to Avignon	640
Benedict XII to Urban V, 1334–70	642
Gregory XI, 1370–8	644
Urban VI to Martin V, 1379–1431	646
Eugenius IV, 1431–47	648

RENAISSANCE AND REFORMATION: NICHOLAS V TO CLEMENT VII, 1447–1534 — 650

Nicholas V and Callistus III, 1147–58	652
Pius II, 1458–64	654
Paul II, 1464–71	656
Sixtus IV, 1471–84	658
Innocent VIII, 1484–92	660
Alexander VI and Pius III 1492–1503	662
Julius II, 1503–13	664
Leo X and Hadrian VI, 1513–23	666
The Papacy and the Protestant Reformation	668
Clement VII, 1523–34	670

POPES IN THE MODERN ERA — 672

THE COUNTER-REFORMATION: PAUL III TO INNOCENT X, 1534–1655 — 674

Paul III, 1534–49	676
Julius III, 1550–5	678
Marcellus II to Pius V, 1555–72	680
Papacy and the Counter-Reformation	682
Gregory XIII, 1572–85	684
Sixtus V, 1585–90	686
Urban VII to Gregory XV, 1590–1623	688
Urban VIII, 1623–44	690
Innocent X, 1644–55	694

PAPAL POWER AND INFLUENCE: ALEXANDER VII TO CLEMENT XIII, 1655–1769 — 696

Alexander VII, 1655–67	698
The Papacy and Baroque Art and Architecture	700
Clement IX to Innocent XII, 1667–1700	702
Clement XI, 1700–21	704
Innocent XIII to Clement XII, 1721–40	706
Benedict XIV, 1740–58	708
Clement XIII, 1758–69	710

POPES IN AN AGE OF REVOLUTION: CLEMENT XIV TO LEO XIII, 1769–1903 — 712

Clement XIV and Pius VI, 1769–99	714
Pius VII, 1800–23	716
Leo XII, 1823–9	718
Papal Missions to Spread the Gospel Around the World	720
Pius VIII and Gregory XVI, 1829–46	722
Pius IX, 1846–78	724
Leo XIII, 1878–1903	726

PEACE FOR A TROUBLED WORLD: PIUS X TO FRANCIS, 1903–TODAY — 728

Pius X, 1903–14	730
Benedict XV 1914–22	732
Piux XI, 1922–39	734
Pius XII 1939–58	736
John XXIII and Paul VI, 1958–78	738
The Second Vatican Council to Revitalize the Church	740
John Paul I, 1978	742
John Paul II, 1978–2005	744
Benedict XVI, 2005–13	746
Francis, 2013	748
Glossary	750
Index	752
Acknowledgements	766

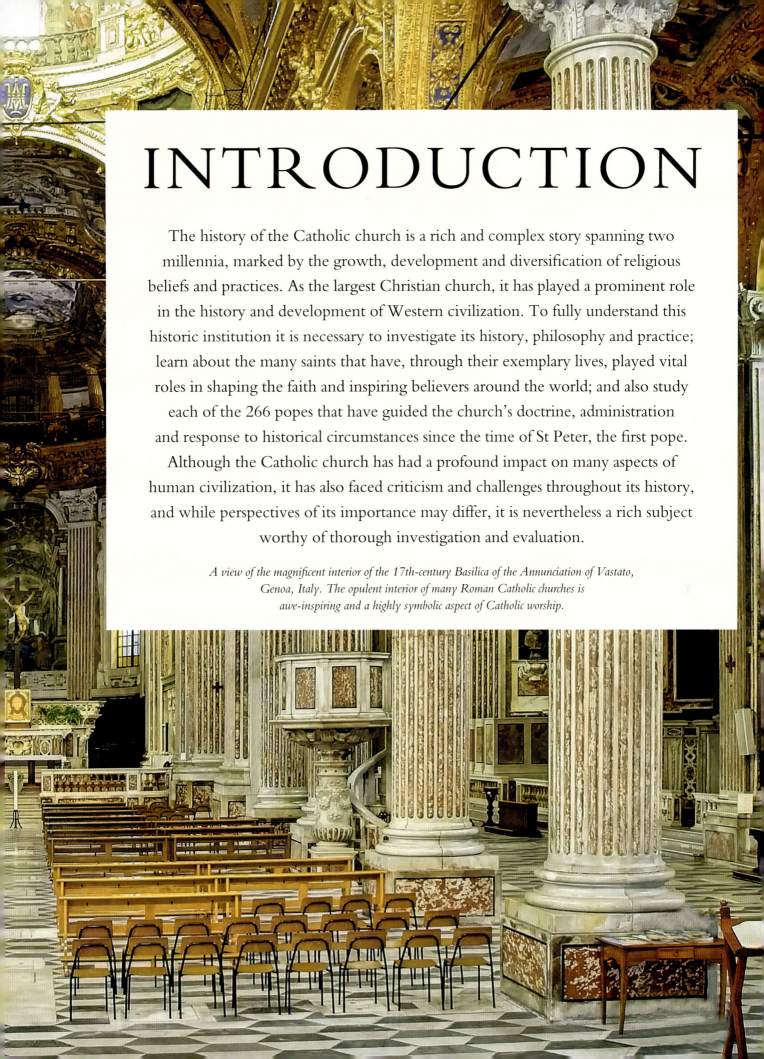

INTRODUCTION

The history of the Catholic church is a rich and complex story spanning two millennia, marked by the growth, development and diversification of religious beliefs and practices. As the largest Christian church, it has played a prominent role in the history and development of Western civilization. To fully understand this historic institution it is necessary to investigate its history, philosophy and practice; learn about the many saints that have, through their exemplary lives, played vital roles in shaping the faith and inspiring believers around the world; and also study each of the 266 popes that have guided the church's doctrine, administration and response to historical circumstances since the time of St Peter, the first pope. Although the Catholic church has had a profound impact on many aspects of human civilization, it has also faced criticism and challenges throughout its history, and while perspectives of its importance may differ, it is nevertheless a rich subject worthy of thorough investigation and evaluation.

A view of the magnificent interior of the 17th-century Basilica of the Annunciation of Vastato, Genoa, Italy. The opulent interior of many Roman Catholic churches is awe-inspiring and a highly symbolic aspect of Catholic worship.

INTRODUCTION

The thousands of pilgrims huddled beneath umbrellas in St Peter's Square in Rome on 13 March 2013 knew they would be witnessing history when the new pope was announced: the election of every new pope by the Catholic church is an historic occasion. But when French Cardinal Jean-Louis Tauran pronounced the famous words *Habemus papam* ("We have a pope!") and then revealed the identity of the new leader of the Roman Catholic Church, the event was doubly exceptional, for the election of Argentinian Cardinal Jorge Maria Bergoglio, former Archbishop of Buenos Aires, as Pope Francis was the first of its kind in no fewer than three ways: Francis is the first Latin American pope, the first Jesuit pope and the first pope from the southern hemisphere.

Pope Francis began his pontificate in light-hearted vein. His first words were: "Brothers and sisters, good evening. You all know that the duty of the conclave was to give a bishop to Rome. It seems that my brother cardinals have gone almost to the ends of the earth to get him ... But we're here." He subsequently declared he was taking his name in honour of St Francis of Assisi (1182–1226), founder of the Franciscans, and because he was especially concerned for the poor; before becoming pope he had praised St Francis: "He brought to Christianity an idea of poverty against the luxury, pride, vanity of the civil and ecclesiastical powers of the time... He changed history." As pope he declared "How I would like a Church which is poor, and for the poor."

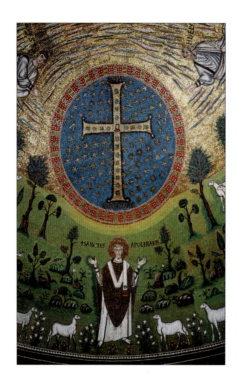

Above: Moses and Elijah look on as St Apollinare tends his flock. Ravenna's first bishop was buried in the 6th-century basilica that contains this painting.

Below: This demographic map illustrates the percentage of the Roman Catholic population around the world today.

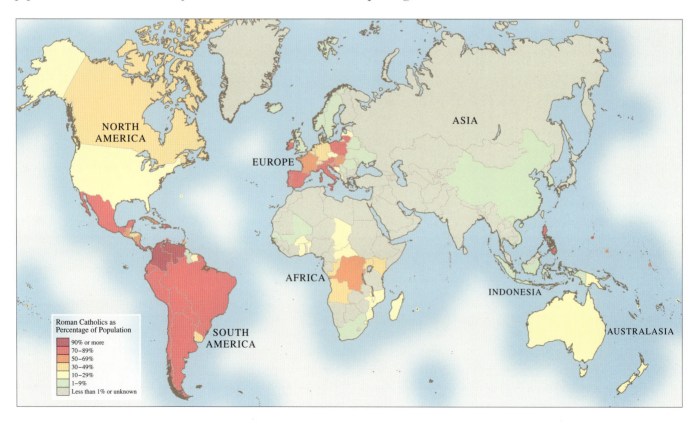

INTRODUCTION

THE CATHOLIC CHURCH
Francis's authority to lead the Church depends on his status as a successor of the first pope, the Apostle St Peter. Francis is the 266th pope in direct line from St Peter. With its spiritual, cultural and historical heritage, spanning more than 2,000 years, the Catholic religion has a great influence across the globe and has a special place in the hearts and minds of millions. Catholicism is the oldest and the largest of the Christian churches, and has become one of the world's largest religions. More than half of the world's Christians take their leadership from the pope in Rome. The number of Catholics in the world stands at around 1.34 billion people – 17.7 per cent (about one-sixth) of the planet's population. (Islam, if all its branches are taken together, just tops that total; none of the other creeds comes close.) Currently, just under half of the world's Catholics live in the Americas.

This book provides a detailed historical insight into the world of Catholicism, including a visual directory of more than 300 saints, plus a fascinating survey of the two thousands years of papal history. The book discusses Catholic doctrine and religious practices, unravels the myths, looks at how places became holy sites, the significance of relics and the purposes of pilgrimage.

One of the world's biggest and most highly organized institutions, the Catholic Church can call on around 414,000 priests (diocesan and religious order) and around 630,000 nuns, along with a multitude of loyal lay supporters. Catholicism is too important a force to be ignored, and

Right: St Peter's Basilica, in the Vatican within Rome, Italy, is both the historic centre of an ancient Catholic Church and at the heart of the modern world. Catholicism continues to flourish amid changing times.

is capable of exerting an influence on public policy and international affairs. Its religious teachings have shaped many millions of lives.

HEAVEN AND EARTH
Saints are an integral part of Catholicism. They are recognized all over world, and the Catholic church is responsible for investigating and confirming their status. The Catholic Church would be nothing if it were only an earthly institution – "My kingship is not of this world," its founder Jesus stated (John 18: 36). Looking beyond this life to the hereafter, the Church views humankind's existence in an eternal perspective: the living and departed come together in the Communion of Saints. As this book sets out to demonstrate, Catholicism offers its followers an account of God's Creation, of life and death – along with the possibility of salvation for devout Catholics, with everlasting joy in heaven.

AN EVENTFUL HISTORY
The book's first section, Catholic History, shows how eventful the story of the Church has been – and sometimes how complex, even contradictory. Catholicism's truths might be eternal, yet they took many centuries to articulate. Although Catholicism's inspirations might be divine, many of its practitioners have been all too human.

At key turning points in its history, the Church was able to grow in strength even through suffering and struggle; however, at other moments, it persecuted those who stood against it. An inspiration to creativity, Catholicism has played a central role in the Western artistic tradition, if at times it has arguably been too involved in acquiring these splendours. The papacy has provided vital leadership, yet the absolute authority it was endowed with by Christ himself has not always been wielded as conscientiously as it should have been.

13

INTRODUCTION

Right: St Paraskeva (Byzantine icon, 15th century).

Centre: Archangel Michael, the divine messenger of God (Demetrius Matthiosi, 20th century).

Left: St Menas, a Roman soldier martyred in Egypt c. AD 300. Miracles were attributed to him and his grave is believed to have curative powers (Palestinian icon, 17th century).

DIVINE DOCTRINES

The second section of the book, Catholic Doctrine, looks at the various teachings that constitute the Catholic faith. It considers beliefs about the eternal truths of existence as well as those that govern the everyday dilemmas of social and personal morality. From the status of the Scriptures and the significance of the saints, to the holy Trinity and transubstantiation, the full range of the Church's teachings are examined here. Among the questions explored are: What is sin? What does Christ's redemption mean? How are we to understand the concepts of salvation and damnation?

LIVING THE FAITH

The third section, Practising Catholicism, shows how these doctrines find expression in the everyday life of the Church: its institutions, its rituals and its celebrations and festivities. The structures of the Church are also examined, from the Vatican down to parish level, and the functions of its different offices are explained. The varieties of religious life are looked at: the contemplative, the charitable and the missionary vocations; the duties performed by the different sorts of priests and nuns; and the vows such men and women take, along with the reasoning behind them.

The seven sacraments – baptism, confirmation, holy communion, confession, marriage, holy orders and the anointing of the sick – are at the heart and soul of the Catholic church. Each is described in detail, with its rituals and what they mean. These seven sacraments mark out the landmark moments in the life of the believer, from birth to death: the development of reason, full communion with God and, of course, the partnership of marriage – which is a sacred state in the Catholic scheme. The Church has attracted both great admiration and much controversy for its stance on a number of issues of sexual morality and medical ethics.

THE IMPORTANCE OF SAINTS

The fourth section of the book, Saints & Sainthood, explores the importance of saints in the Roman Catholic Church and charts the progression of sainthood from the early Church to modern times. The section looks at what it means to be a saint, what individuals and groups have achieved or suffering they have endured to be conferred this title and honour, and what characteristics single out an individual as deserving of sainthood. The text will clearly set out answers to all of these questions, and present accurate explanations about the mysterious company of saints while largely avoiding the distraction of complex theological debates.

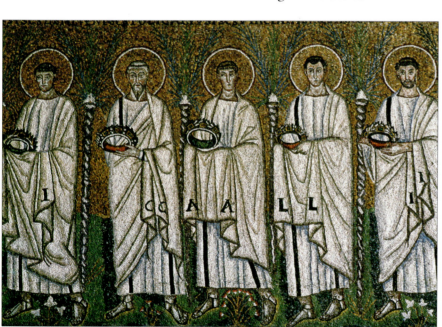

Above: Mosaic of martyrs in the Basilica Sant'Appolinare Nuovo, Ravenna, Italy (5th and 6th centuries).

INTRODUCTION

Throughout the long history of Christianity, sainthood has been invested with a great many different meanings. There are, however, many characteristics of sainthood that are agreed upon. Whether a saint devotes their life to God, or demonstrates holiness in secular life, they must be a person of great faith and religious devotion. A saint can be born in grace, or be a reformed character, but whatever path their life has traced, they must show certain characteristics that make them "heroic", such as piety, fortitude, humility and courage.

Saints, having been awarded a privileged place in heaven, are thought to be close to God and are able to function as intermediaries between the human and the divine. This combines with the human achievements of the saints to make them exemplars of virtue that the faithful can turn to in times of need.

The importance of saints for people, professions and countries is seen in the adoption of "patron" saints by these groups. Aspects of sainthood are also discussed, such as miracles, martyrdom and relics, and the diverse ways in which the qualities of sainthood have changed and manifested over time are described.

The response of believers to the company of saints is described and the official attitudes of both the Roman Catholic and the Orthodox Churches are examined. However, the focus here is on Roman Catholic saints and feast days, because the complex subject of Orthodox saints deserves its own study. Modern readers may dismiss the extravagant legends of the early saints as untrue, but the number of new saints that have been created may also surprise those outside the Roman Catholic Church. As of 2022 Pope Francis has created 911 saints during his pontificate since 2013 – though 813 of these, the martyrs of Otranto, were created in one fell swoop in 2013. Even the sceptical must applaud the shining example of devotion and sacrifice made by the recently canonized.

The range of people who have achieved sainthood is a fascinating area of study, for this special company does not recognize wealth, social status or professional achievement, and thus the canon includes peasants, merchants and kings.

Below: The Virgin in Prayer *(Sassoferrato, c.1645–50) shows Mary, the blessed virgin, who is univerally recognized as a symbol of purity and motherhood.*

INTRODUCTION

DIRECTORY OF SAINTS

A directory of saints tells the story of sainthood through the biographies of selected saints. The saints are listed in chronological order, from the Apostles and early Christian martyrs through to 21st-century saints. This is interspersed with essays on special groups who have been accorded saintly status, such as the Holy Family, Patron Saints and martyrs, taken to represent much larger groups whose tragic sacrifices have left no trace in the historical record.

The life and work of each saint is described. There are dozens of well-known and much-loved saints such as St Teresa of Avila, St Francis of Assisi, St Christopher, but entries also include 1st-century martyrs and recent additions such as St Kuriakose Elias Chavara, St Teresa of Calcutta and St John Henry Newman.

Below: "Thou art Peter, and upon this rock I will build my church." Italian Baroque painter Bernardo Strozzi painted this vision of Christ granting authority to Peter.

The Gazetteer of Other Saints deals briefly with a number of more obscure, but interesting saints. It features short accounts of saints who have not been included in the main directory but nevertheless deserve to be mentioned.

There are over 4,000 saints in the Roman Catholic canon and the selection made here is not intended to be complete or exclusive. Instead, the intent of this work is to bring an understanding of the Church's theology, teachings, and achievements, and to also show that while all saints share a devotion to God, each one has their own talent, personality, and their own story of struggle.

TWO THOUSAND YEARS OF POPES

The pope's authority to lead the Church depends on his status as a successor of St Peter. The current pope, Francis, stands at the end of almost two millennia of history of the Church in Rome, since the time of Jesus Christ. The fifth section of this book, The First Popes, explores the early popes from St Peter to Leo IX.

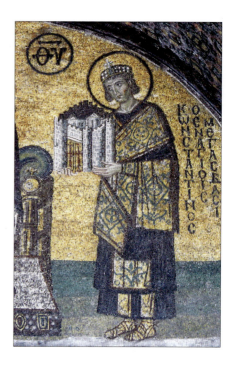

Above: A mosaic in the Hagia Sophia in Istanbul honours Emperor Constantine, founder of the city as Constantinople in 330.

Witness to the events of Jesus's life and the leader of his disciples, Peter was established by him in Rome as leader of the Christians there. After he died a martyr in Rome in c.64 AD, Christians faced persecution for more 200 years until the Roman Empire recognized their faith with the Edict of Milan of 313. Peter's successors in Rome attempted to establish their pre-eminence over other bishops and centres of the faith – notably Constantinople (modern Istanbul), the city founded by Emperor Constantine in 330 as a new, eastern capital for the Roman Empire.

Following the collapse of the Roman Empire in the West in 410, Rome struggled to escape the heavy hand of Constantinople until in the 8th century popes aligned themselves with the new European power of Charlemagne and the Franks, and in 1054 the Western and Eastern Churches of Rome

INTRODUCTION

and Constantinople – in a dramatic exchange of excommunications – brought about a split that has endured to the 21st century.

Over the early centuries the papacy acquired territory in central Italy known as the Patrimony of St Peter. This was significantly expanded with grants of land made by the Frankish kings to create the papal states. As ruler of the papal states, the pope was effectively a temporal prince. He was drawn into worldly disputes, and faced the challenge of a series of rival powers, including the Holy Roman Emperor, the Normans in Sicily and the kings of France.

CRUSADING POPES
For 500 years from 1096 onwards, pontiffs beginning with Urban II (1088–99) used crusades or holy wars to fight Muslims and heretic Christians – and also to further the

Below: Pope Clement V moved the seat of the papacy from Rome to Avignon, southern France, in 1309 – and it remained there for the 67 years of the "Avignon Exile". Clement VI (1342–52) lived in the style of a prince at the Palais des Papes.

Above: In the 11th century Pope Gregory VII clashed with Holy Roman Emperor Henry IV in the celebrated "Investiture Controversy" over the right to invest or appoint abbots and bishops.

papacy's territorial and political interests. The sixth section explores the importance of these crusades to the papacy. The wars were fought under crusade indulgences, which promised those who took part freedom from all temporal punishment for their sins. Nine crusades from 1096–1272 were directed largely towards the holy places of Palestine and Syria, and alongside years of bitter military conflict in which great suffering was caused on both sides, opened up communications between Christian Europe and the Muslim Middle East – which greatly enriched European culture.

Under French influence, Pope Clement V moved the seat of the papacy to Avignon in southern France for 68 years, 1309–77, and these years of the "Avignon Exile" were followed by the Great Papal Schism of 1378–1417, in which rival popes in Rome and Avignon set themselves up against one another and the reputation of the papacy was badly damaged. In the Italian Renaissance, however, many learned popes developed canon law and founded enduring universities, while others such as Julius II (1503–13) were

> **THE PAPACY IN FIGURES**
> Of the 266 popes to date, around 100 have been Italian-born – although in the modern era we have not had an Italian pope since John Paul I in 1978. There have been 14 French popes (the last being Gregory XI, 1370–78), 11 Greek (the last, Zacharias in 741–52), seven German (the last, Benedict XVI in 2005–13), six Syrian (the last, Gregory III in 731–41), three Sicilian (the last, Stephen III in 768–72), two Portuguese (the last, John XXI in 1276–7), two Spanish (the last, the notorious Alexander VI in 1492–1503) and two African (the last, Miltiades in 311–14). Four nationalities can claim only one pope: English (Hadrian IV, 1154–9), Dutch (Hadrian VI, 1522–3), Polish (John Paul II, 1978–2005) and Argentina (Francis 2013–present).

great patrons of the arts, responsible for funding such masterpieces as Michelangelo's Sistine Chapel ceiling and the frescoes by Raphael in the Vatican. The financial extravagance this involved – and the licentiousness that accompanied it – fuelled increasingly urgent calls for reform of the Church and led to the Protestant Reformation, launched by German pastor Martin Luther in 1517.

REFORMING PAPACY
The final section, Popes in the Modern Era, explores papal history from the Counter-Reformation up until the present day. Under Pope Paul III the papacy and the Church fought back against Protestantism, launching the Counter-Reformation with the calling of the Council of Trent (1545–63), the establishment of the teaching order of the Society of Jesus (Jesuits) in 1540 and in 1542 the creation of the Holy Office of the Inquisition to stamp out heresy. In addition, popes such as Urban VIII (1623–44) and Innocent X (1644–55) were great patrons influencing the rebuilding of the churches, streets and squares of Rome in the intensely appealing baroque style that sought to capture the drama of religious encounter.

Thereafter, however, a succession of pontiffs were unable to stem the rising tide of materialism in the "Age of Reason" while politically the papacy became increasingly marginalized on the European map. After the establishment of the Kingdom of Italy in 1861 and the choice of Rome as its capital in 1870, the popes were temporal rulers no more – save for in the enclave of Vatican City. This situation was formalized under the Lateran Treaty of 1929.

VOICE FOR PEACE
Popes increasingly concentrated on their roles as spiritual leaders and teachers. Through the terrible violence and ideological conflict of the 20th century, pope after pope called for peace and reconciliation.

The leaders of the Church tried to lead humanity away from violence towards negotiation. Benedict XV (1914–22) denounced the First World War as "horrible butchery" and "the suicide of Europe" and circulated – without success – a detailed peace plan in 1917. At the height of the Cold War between

Above: The Sistine Chapel at the heart of the Vatican in Rome is one of the greatest treasure-houses of art in the world, with a fresco ceiling by Michelangelo.

East and West, John XXIII (1958–63) issued a celebrated encyclical on 11 April 1963, *Pacem in Terris* ("Peace on Earth"), which called on people to solve disputes by negotiation rather than through recourse to arms and began "Peace on Earth – which man throughout the ages has so longed for and sought after – can never be established, never guaranteed, except by the diligent observance of the divinely established order."

John Paul II (1978–2005) declared that "War… is always a defeat for humanity," and in 1995 said in an address to the General Assembly of the United Nations that a moral law common to all could help the world progress from "a century of violent coercion" to "a century of persuasion". He supported and encouraged people working for justice and freedom but always stressed that those seeking change should do so peacefully.

In his 2020 encyclical *Fratelli Tutti* ("Brothers All") Francis declared

Below: The faithful flock to Easter Sunday Mass at St Peter's Square in the Vatican. Pope Francis led his first Easter Sunday Mass on 31 March 2013.

INTRODUCTION

"Never again War!", and on the Church's annual World Peace Day (1 January) 2021 he called for "a common, supportive and inclusive commitment to protecting and promoting the dignity and good of all, a willingness to show care and compassion, to work for reconciliation and healing", and said "there can be no peace without a culture of care".

Many modern popes have taught that people need to turn away from sterile, secular thinking and the obsession with money. John Paul II criticized materialism and the effects of untamed capitalism in the West; he also identified a "culture of death" in which people accepted abortion, euthanasia and capital punishment. In his encyclical *Caritas in veritate* ("Charity in Truth"), Benedict XVI (2005–13) taught that the prevailing economic system showed "the pernicious effects of sin" and declared that people should seek to use ethics in business. He called on people to leave "the dead-end streets of consumerism" in order to find happiness. In *Fratelli Tutti* Francis urged a return to kindness, saying "Consumerist individualism has led to great injustice. Other persons come to be viewed simply as obstacles to our own serene existence; we end up treating them as annoyances and we become increasingly aggressive".

PAPACY AND SCANDALS

From the mid-1980s onwards, the Roman Catholic Church and wider society were shocked by a series of allegations of sexual abuse of young people by diocesan priests and members of the religious orders. There were major scandals in the United States, Ireland and Australia; in some cases, members of the church hierarchy were accused of trying to silence the accusations and even of moving abusers on from one scandal into a position where the person might

Above: Pope John Paul II made nine visits to his native Poland, the first in 1979 and the last in 2003.

commit a similar offence. In 2001 John Paul II, at the urging of his friend Cardinal Ratzinger (the future Pope Benedict XVI), transferred the main responsibility for handling cases of sexual abuse by priests from dioceses to the Congregation for the Doctrine of the Faith. As its prefect, before becoming pope, Cardinal Ratzinger had made a number of changes to improve the Church's handling of the problem.

As pope, during a visit to the United States in 2008 he met victims of priestly sexual abuse and spoke out condemning perpetrators. In a pastoral letter to Irish Catholics of March 2010 he addressed victims of sexual abuse by priests: "You have suffered grievously and I am truly sorry … Your trust has been betrayed and your dignity has been violated … I openly express the shame and remorse that we all feel." Changes to canon law promulgated on 1 June 2021 tightened sanctions against priests in sexual abuse cases.

SAINTLY POPES

After Pope John Paul II's death, approximately four million people attended his Mass of Requiem, on 8 April 2005 by Cardinal Joseph Ratzinger (soon to be Pope Benedict XVI). At the Mass several cried out "Santo Subito!" ("Make him a saint at once!"). No fewer than 83 popes have posthumously been declared saints. This process is known as canonization becase a person raised to sainthood is added to the canon of saints. The most recent saints canonized by Pope Francis were John XXIII and John Paul II in 2014, and Paul VI in 2018.

ABOUT THIS BOOK

Catholicism is a complex creed and the Church a vast and venerable institution, and the purpose of this book is to offer an account of the history, philosophy and practice of Catholic Christianity including the most important saints and a history of over 2,000 years of papal leadership. Illustrated throughout, this guide aims to inform readers interested in discovering more about the Catholic faith, its history and its traditions and practices.

Timeline

The Catholic Church has a long history. The timeline below lists some of the major events that have affected it since the first century BC.

100BC–1BC
Romans conquer Judaea, 63 BC.
Herod the Great begins renovations on the Temple of Jerusalem, c.19 BC.

1–100AD
Anno Domini – by tradition, the year of Christ's birth.
c.AD 35 Saul witnesses the martyrdom of St Stephen.
c.AD 50 Council of Jerusalem convened by St Peter, the first pope.
AD 64 Nero launches the first persecution of Rome's Christians.
AD 64 Pope Peter dies a martyr.

101–200
c.150 Monumental shrine erected around St Peter's tomb in Rome.

201-300
253-60 Persecution of Valerian.

301-400
303–11 Diocletian's "Great Persecution".
312 Emperor Constantine converts to Christianity.
325 Constantine calls the Council of Nicaea.
381 Proclamation of the Nicene Creed.
382 St Jerome begins work on his Latin "Vulgate" Bible.

401–500
440–61 St Augustine starts writing his great work, *The City of God*.
Leo the Great centralizes power in the papacy.

501–600
St Benedict of Nursia establishes his monastic rule.
590 Reforming papacy of Gregory the Great begins.

Above: Detail from a fresco showing Pope Gregory the Great (540–604), from Vezzolano, Italy.

601–700
610 Muhammad begins receiving his revelations of Islam.
638 Arab armies occupy Jerusalem.

701–800
754 The Church is given temporal authority over Rome and its environs under the "Donation of Pepin".

801–900
853 The legendary "Pope Joan" supposedly succeeds to the papacy.

901–1000
910 The reformist abbey of Cluny is founded in eastern France.

1001–1100
1054 The Cistercian order tries to take monasticism back to its first Benedictine principles.
The Eastern Orthodox Church formally parts company with Rome.
1095 Urban II calls the First Crusade. Jerusalem is taken four years later.

1101–1200
The beginning of the Gothic movement in religious architecture.
The Second Crusade of 1145 breaks down in chaos.
1179 The Third Lateran Council begins.
1187 Saladin recaptures Jerusalem

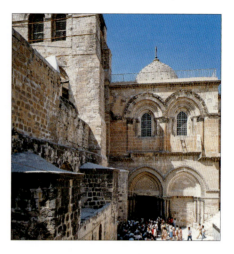

Above: Worshippers gather outside the entrance to the Church of the Holy Sepulchre, Jerusalem, Israel.

for the Muslims. The Third Crusade that follows is a failure.
1177 Peter Waldo denounces the wealth of the Church.

1201–1300
The forces of the Fourth Crusade (1202–4) sack Christian Constantinople.
Innocent III proclaims the 1208
1208 Albigensian Crusade against the heretical Cathars.
1209 St Francis of Assisi begins his ministry.
1266–74 Thomas Aquinas writes the *Summa Theologica*.

1301–1400
1309 Clement V transfers the papacy to Avignon in France.
Gregory XI makes Rome the centre of papal power again in 1377 – but rival popes continue in opposition in Avignon after his death in 1378.

1401–1500
The Council of Pisa (1408) fails to resolve the Western Schism. A solution is found in 1417.
1415 Czech heretic Jan Hus is burnt at the stake.
The Spanish Inquisition is at its height, encouraged by the "Catholic Monarchs", Ferdinand and Isabella.
The Reconquista is complete, with

TIMELINE

the expulsion of the Moors from Granada in 1492. That same year Columbus starts opening up an empire for Spain in the Americas.

1501–1600
1505 The reconstruction of St Peter's Basilica, Rome, begins.
1527 Martin Luther nails his "95 Theses" to the door of the cathedral in Wittenberg, Germany. Clement VII is taken prisoner by Germany during the Sack of Rome.
1529 The Ottoman Siege of Vienna is successfully repulsed.
1534 Henry VIII announces that he and his successors will henceforth be heads of the Church of England.
534 Ignatius Loyola founds the Society of Jesus.
1543 Copernicus' theories are published after his death.
1542–52 St Francis Xavier undertakes his mission to the East.
1545 The Council of Trent gets under way. Church leaders resist the Reformation.
1571 Turkish naval power is defeated by the Christian fleet at the Battle of Lepanto.

1601–1700
Galileo is forced to recant his claims for Copernican astronomy.
1622 A Congregation for the Evangelization of Peoples is founded to co-ordinate missionary endeavours.
1648 The Thirty Years' War ends, with Europe divided along religious lines.

1701–1800
1750 Denis Diderot and friends begin work on their secularizing *Encyclopédie*.
1789 Revolution convulses France.

1801–1900
1864 Pius IX denounces modern liberalism in his *Syllabus of Errors*. Papal infallibility will be proclaimed six years later.
1868 The "White Fathers" begin work evangelizing in Africa.
1871 Papal rule in the city of Rome is brought to an end.
1891 Leo XIII throws the Church's weight behind the cause of workers' rights in *Rerum Novarum*.

1901–2000
The Lateran Treaty of 1929 sees the Church enter into partnership with Mussolini's Fascist state.
1933 A Concordat is signed with Nazi Germany.
1937 Pius XI condemns anti-semitic violence in Germany.
1962 John XXIII calls the Second Vatican Council.
1968 Pope Paul VI's encyclical *Humanae vitae* ("On Human Life)", rejected the use of contraception, including sterilization as directly opposing God's will.
Liberation theology takes root in Latin America from the 1960s. Its followers play a leading role in the Nicaraguan Revolution of the 1980s.
1999 Pope John Paul II travelled to Romania, the first pope since the Great Schism to visit an Eastern Orthodox country.

2001–present day
Protestant Pentecostalism is on the rise in Latin America.
2000 Pope John Paul II makes the first papal visit to Israel. That same year he becomes the first pope to pray in a Muslim mosque.
2013, 12 Mar, Pope Benedict XVI abdicates, the first pope to resign since Gregory XII in 1415.
2013, 12 Mar, Pope Francis is elected, the first Latin American pope and first Jesuit pope.
2021, 6 Mar, Pope Francis makes the first papal visit to Iraq. He met with Shiite cleric Grand Ayatolla Ali al-Sistani; the two urging their communities to work for peace.

Above: The striking Gothic façade of the 14th-century Duomo di Milano, or Milan Cathedral.

Above: An 18th-century Peruvian painting of St Francis Xavier. He is the patron saint of all missions.

Above: John Paul II (served 1978–2005), an influential pope, was the second longest-serving pope to rule in Rome.

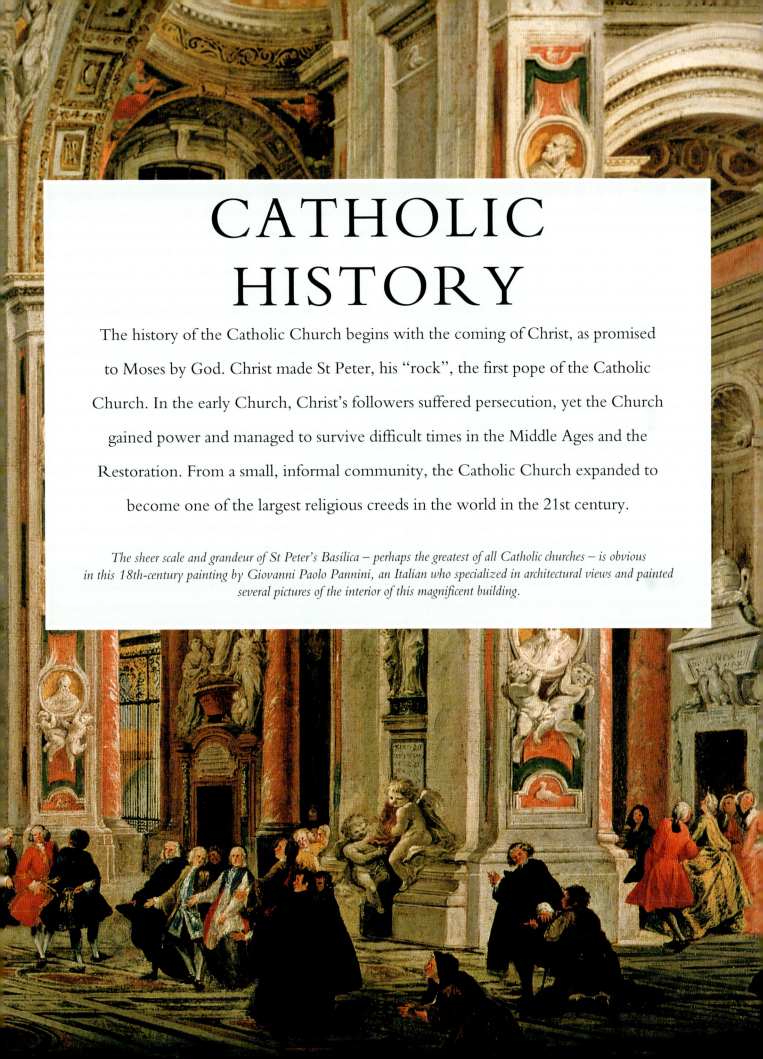

CATHOLIC HISTORY

The history of the Catholic Church begins with the coming of Christ, as promised to Moses by God. Christ made St Peter, his "rock", the first pope of the Catholic Church. In the early Church, Christ's followers suffered persecution, yet the Church gained power and managed to survive difficult times in the Middle Ages and the Restoration. From a small, informal community, the Catholic Church expanded to become one of the largest religious creeds in the world in the 21st century.

The sheer scale and grandeur of St Peter's Basilica – perhaps the greatest of all Catholic churches – is obvious in this 18th-century painting by Giovanni Paolo Pannini, an Italian who specialized in architectural views and painted several pictures of the interior of this magnificent building.

THE EARLY CHURCH

The gospels tell an inspirational story. "The word became flesh," says John's Gospel, "he lived among us and we saw his glory." The coming of Christ was the fulfilment of a promise. His remarkable life and death, and above all his Resurrection, made good God's undertaking to both Moses and Abraham. It realized the predictions of the prophets and renewed humanity's hope.

However, inspiration was not enough: as Christ incarnated the word of God, so his message had to be embodied in the institutions and practices of a living, working Church. Catholicism's structures evolved slowly, sometimes painfully, over centuries. Tried in the fire of persecution and torn by dissension – and, ultimately, division – the Church faced many difficulties as it developed. Christian theology was still comparatively new and unexplored, and it had to be systematized by learned scholars.

There were also the difficulties that come with success. The bigger and more secure Catholicism became as a worldwide institution, the greater the political pressures. The emergence of the papacy as a seat of spiritual authority and political power was a temptation as well as a triumph for the Church. Even so, as the 1st millennium came to an end, the faith was the dominant spiritual and cultural force across much of Europe. Catholicism had come a long way in its first thousand years.

Left: In this 1485 painting The Life of Mary *by the Master of Aachen, the old priest Simeon blesses the baby Jesus on his presentation in the Temple.*

IN THE DAYS OF KING HEROD

THE COUNTRY IN WHICH THE CHRISTIAN STORY STARTED WAS A TERRITORY OF THE ROMAN EMPIRE, ALTHOUGH THE ROMANS WERE JUST THE LATEST IN A LONG SUCCESSION OF INVADERS.

Jesus' birthplace, Bethlelem, and the surrounding regions have an ancient history. Christ was born among the Jews, who saw themselves as the "Chosen People" of Jehovah. However the "Holy Land" that was so important to the Jews was one of the less significant corners of the world at the beginning of the first millenium.

Judaea and Israel, its neighbour to the north, had been brought together under King David from c.1007 BC. The state he created, with its capital in Jerusalem, had come to prominence under his son, Solomon, in the 10th century BC. Though known for his legendary wisdom, Solomon had in reality all but ruined his kingdom; the construction of his celebrated Temple had bankrupted the state. Eventually, the country disintegrated and was conquered by the Assyrians in 841 BC.

UNDER OCCUPATION

The Jews never accepted their subject status, despite being sub-jugated for centuries, first under the rule of the Assyrians, then the Babylonians. In the 6th century BC, leading Jews were taken from their country to the imperial capital in what is known as the "Babylonian Captivity", but this failed to break their spirit of resistance.

Persian power proved more benign: after conquering Babylon in 539, Cyrus the Great of Persia let the exiles return to Israel. (He even ordered the reconstruction of the Temple, which had been sacked by Babylon's King Nebuchadnezzar after a Jewish up-rising in 587 BC.) The Persians, however, were swept aside by the eastward march of Alexander the Great, who came with his Greek army in 332 BC. After Alexander's death, his vast empire was fought

Above: A Bedouin tends his flock in the rocky Judaean Desert, just as Jewish shepherds would have done 2,000 years ago.

over by his surviving generals. Along with much of the Middle East, Israel fell to Seleucus, a boyhood friend and comrade-at-arms of Alexander. His descendants reigned after him, in what is known as the Seleucid line.

A TASTE OF FREEDOM

Attempts by the Seleucid ruler Antiochus IV to suppress the religious rituals of the Jews sparked a revolt in 167 BC. Simon

---

HEROD..."THE GREAT"?

Herod's honorific title, "the Great", strikes modern Christians as strange, given his client-king status – and the part he played in the Gospel account of Jesus' birth. The Magi, wise men who had journeyed from the east by following a star to where they had been told a new king of the Jews would be born, went to Herod and sought his assistance in finding the infant. He was horrified to hear of a rival's birth. However, he begged his visitors to tell him when they found the boy, so that he, too, could pay him homage. Warned by an angel not to tell Herod anything, the Magi instead returned home by another route, whereupon the enraged king had all the infant boys in Israel – the "Holy Innocents" – massacred. This is a cruel and ignominious role in the Christian Scriptures, but Jewish tradition and mainstream history have judged Herod more kindly. He is called "Herod the Great" on account of his reconstruction of the Temple.

Below: A 14th-century Italian mosaic shows King Herod enjoying a lavish banquet.

IN THE DAYS OF KING HEROD

Above: Herod lives in Jewish memory as the rebuilder of the Temple, shown here in a 19th-century painting by James Jacques Tissot (1836–1902).

Maccabaeus' Hasmonean Dynasty took power and Jewish sovereignty was restored. Jewish rule lasted until 63 BC, when the country was conquered once again – this time by the Roman general Pompey. He let the Hasmoneans stay in office, but as client-kings of what was now named Judaea. They reigned at the beck and call of the Roman emperors, but in return their subjects could still find some comfort in the fact that their country was a kingdom, rather than a mere province.

That the Jews were allowed this degree of autonomy indicates the strength of their identity – however, it also reflects the comparative irrelevance of a people living on the margins. The main centres of wealth and civilization in the ancient world were to the east in Mesopotamia (modern-day Iraq) and Persia, and to the west in the Mediterranean. Palestine was peripheral to both these spheres. Regardless, as insignificant as they were, the Jews had been allowed considerable freedom to live and worship God in the way they had for generations. This freedom was a dangerous thing: many Jews were in no way reconciled to their subjection and were eager to shake off the Roman yoke.

KING OF THE JEWS

For the moment, Rome was firmly in charge and King Herod was the Empire's servant. He had been appointed by the Romans as King of Judaea in 37 BC and was given the title "King of the Jews". In return for his loyalty, Herod won certain privileges for the Jews, and the Romans made no objections to his request when, in 19 BC, he renovated the Temple.

Above: "No foreigners shall enter…" reads the tablet King Herod placed in the Temple. Christ, by contrast, was to reach out to all people.

27

THE EARLY CHURCH

AND IT CAME TO PASS…

THE JEWS HAD BEEN EXPECTING A MIGHTY KING AS A SAVIOUR, BUT INSTEAD CHRIST WAS BORN IN A LOWLY STABLE IN BETHLEHEM. COULD THIS REALLY BE THE MESSIAH THEY HAD BEEN WAITING FOR?

Jewish scriptural tradition had long foreseen the coming of a "Messiah" – whom the Book of Daniel (9:24) referred to as the "anointed one" or "prince". "The people who lived in darkness have seen a great light," prophesied Isaiah (9:2–9). As a king descended from the House of David, it was believed that the Messiah would introduce an eternal era of justice and peace.

Most Jews expected a king to come in glory, but there were Old Testament writers with another vision. Zachary's Messiah (9:9) was envisaged as "lowly, and riding on a donkey". In a chapter of Isaiah (53:3–6), there is a foreshadowing of how the Christian servant-saviour was received: "despised, and rejected by men… he was wounded for our transgressions…and with his stripes we are healed."

A VISIT FROM AN ANGEL

"Behold, a virgin shall conceive," promises Isaiah (7:14), "and bear a son, and shall call his name Immanuel." That prophecy found fulfilment in the gospel account (Luke, Chapter 1) in which the archangel Gabriel announced to the astonished Virgin Mary the miraculous part she had been appointed to play as the Messiah's mother. The angel's words were later to form the first line of the prayer that is still repeated daily by many Catholics: "Hail Mary, full of grace, the Lord is with thee."

The angel also told Mary that her much older relative Elizabeth was pregnant, despite years of childlessness, so the Blessed Virgin went to see her in the "Visitation". Elizabeth greeted Mary with the words that became the second line of the Hail Mary: "Blessed art thou amongst women, and blessed is the fruit of thy womb."

Above: The Messiah was expected to renew the reign of King David, writer of the Psalms, shown in this c.1500 painting by the Master of Riofrio.

THE ANGELUS

Although the custom has fallen victim to the mounting pressures of modern life, for centuries, throughout the Catholic world, the rhythm of the day was set by the sound of the angelus bell. Three sets of three slow, solemn strokes rang out at 6 a.m., 12 noon and 6 p.m. as a signal to the faithful to stop whatever they were doing to meditate on the Annunciation and what it meant. The call-and-response devotion that followed re-enacted the abrupt arrival of the angel in the Virgin Mary's presence and Christ's conception by the power of the Holy Spirit.

Below: "Behold the handmaid of the lord…", begins the Latin inscription beneath this Annunciation by the Italian painter Filippo Lippi, c.1440.

Mary's reply ("Behold the handmaid of the Lord…Be it done to me according to thy word") is also recollected in the angelus, as are John's words (1:14) on the Incarnation of Our Lord ("And the word was made flesh, and dwelt amongst us").

THE NATIVITY

Mary, though a virgin, was betrothed to Joseph, whose occupation as a carpenter has made him the patron saint of working men. However, the Gospels of Matthew and Luke are at pains to make the point that he is also a descendant of the House of David: as his son, then, Christ is from Israel's royal line. Yet his is anything but a kingly birth.

At the time when Mary was due to deliver her child, she and her husband were in Bethlehem. The Romans were conducting a census in Judaea and all families had been ordered to go to the ancestral home of the father to be counted. There was no room for them at the inn, so Mary had to give birth in a stable and lay her baby in a manger.

The baby was attended, not by great Jewish dignitaries, but by shepherds from the surrounding hillsides. Although the Magi, "kings" or "wise men", had come to honour the newborn, they were outsiders, summoned from afar. The manner of Jesus' arrival in the world anticipates his later remark (Matthew 13:58) that "a prophet is not without honour except in his own country". By the same token, the coming of the Magi may be seen as a signal that Christ will ultimately find most of his followers abroad.

Above: The most momentous of events, Christ's Nativity in the stable was painted by Hans Leonhard Schaufelein in the 16th century.

Below: The Holy Family fled to Egypt when they learned that Herod had ordered the slaughter of all male babies, as shown here in this late 15th-century manuscript.

ANNO DOMINI

The "Year of the Lord" – from the Latin *anno domini* (which is commonly abbreviated to AD) – has been taken as a chronological starting point in western tradition. Supposedly, it was the year in which Christ was born. But was it really? Luke's account has the holy family travelling to Bethlehem to take part in a census ordered by the Romans. This could only refer to the survey conducted by Quirinius, Rome's governor in Syria, which is known to have taken place in AD 6–7. However, Matthew implies an earlier date, and some scholars believe that the Nativity might have taken place in 8 BC.

THE EARLY CHURCH

"YOU ARE MY SON, THE BELOVED..."

JESUS GREW UP QUIETLY IN NAZARETH, A LITTLE TOWN IN GALILEE. NO ONE GUESSED THAT THE BOY THEY SAW HELPING OUT IN HIS FATHER'S WORKSHOP WAS ACTUALLY THE MORTAL SON OF GOD.

Above: The adolescent Jesus is shown astonishing the elders of the Temple with his knowledge in this early 19th-century Russian icon.

Christ may have been born, but "Christianity" was as yet unheard of, and Jesus was raised by his parents in the traditions of Judaism. Like any other Jewish baby boy, he was circumcised at eight days old and, on the 40th day after his birth, Jesus' mother took him to the Jewish Temple for his presentation. Tradition demanded not only that the mother herself should be ritually "purified" after giving birth but that the baby should be formally presented. Jewish law decreed that the Temple had the right to claim any firstborn boy for the priesthood, unless he was redeemed with a token payment.

SEEING SALVATION

The Gospel of Luke (2:29–31) describes how Simeon, an old priest who had prayed to God to let him live long enough to see the Messiah, finally saw the infant saviour during his presentation and realized that God had answered his prayers. "Now master you are letting your servant go in peace," he said in gratitude, "for my eyes have seen the salvation which you have made ready in the sight of the nations." The child was destined to be the deliverance of his people, though he would also face great opposition from them and others. Simeon also warned Mary, "a sword will pierce your soul, too" (2:35).

A SPECIAL BAPTISM

At 12 years old, Jesus disappeared during a pilgrimage his family was making to Jerusalem. His frantic mother found him in the Temple talking to the elders. These experienced scholars were in raptures at his knowledge and insight.

Below: Simeon, an elderly priest, sees the Messiah during his presentation in this 15th-century painting by Giovanni Bellini.

30

"YOU ARE MY SON, THE BELOVED..."

Above: Jesus is determined to be purified through baptism, like any sinner, in this early 14th-century painting entitled The Baptism of Christ *by Giotto.*

> **THE INFANCY GOSPELS**
> The gospels say little about Jesus' boyhood, so perhaps it is inevitable that popular folklore has made up the shortfall. Among the many Apocrypha (purported scriptural writings of dubious origin) produced in the early centuries after Christ's death and Resurrection were what is known as the Infancy Gospels. These offer more details on Jesus' boyhood, but they view him like a fairytale hero with "magical" powers. Some of his supposed deeds, indeed, could hardly be seen as Christ-like. In one story he reacted to an insult by cursing the boy who delivered it so he died; then when the boy's parents complained, Jesus blinded them.

The boy – a little impatiently – dismissed his mother's reproaches: "Why were you looking for me?" he asked (Luke 2:49). "Did you not know that I must be in my father's house?" Though his parents did not understand what their son was saying, this is a clear indication that Jesus' own mind was already on his heavenly kingdom and his earthly mission.

The gospels agree that it was not until many years later, when Jesus was about 30 years of age, that he left home and made his way into the desert beside the River Jordan. There he found John – Elizabeth's son and his relative. Known by the title John the Baptist, he had already embarked on his own sacred ministry, living simply in the wilderness and preaching to the people, calling on them to change their lives. He baptized the repentant and prophesied the coming of a saviour.

When Jesus appeared, John pointed him out as the one who was to come. John was perplexed when the man he regarded as the Messiah asked to be baptized like any sinner, but Jesus was adamant, and John agreed. As Christ arose from the water, the heavens parted and the Holy Spirit descended in the form of a dove. A voice rang out, saying "You are my Son, the Beloved; my favour rests on you" (Mark 1:11).

THE TEMPTATION

After his baptism, Matthew tells us, Jesus went into the wilderness alone to fast and pray in preparation for the task that awaited him. He spent 40 days and 40 nights in the desert, with his solitude being interrupted only by the devil, who had come to test his resolve.

Satan appeared three times to tempt Jesus. First he offered Jesus all the kingdoms of the world if he would bow down and worship Satan. Then he challenged Jesus to turn stones into bread to satisfy his hunger. Finally, Satan took Jesus to the highest point on the Temple and dared him to jump off (the angels will make sure you are not hurt, he said). Christ refused to rise to these provocations. Dismayed, the devil left and angels arrived with bread to ease Jesus' hunger.

Right: Christ is tempted by the devil in the desert, shown here in this c.1225 stained-glass scene in Troyes Cathedral, in France.

"BLESSED ARE THE POOR IN SPIRIT"

IT IS UNCLEAR WHETHER CHRIST'S MINISTRY LASTED FOR WEEKS OR YEARS. EITHER WAY, HE HAD TIME TO PERFORM MIRACLES AND PROCLAIM THE MOST REMARKABLE MESSAGE EVER HEARD.

Jesus first performed a miracle at his mother's urging during the Wedding Feast at Cana. Supplies were running low, so he turned jars of ordinary water into wine. Once his ministry got under way in earnest, Jesus cast out demons and healed the sick – and, in the case of Lazarus, he even gave life back to the dead.

From a modern perspective, the early miracles appear to have established Christ's credentials as the Messiah. Certainly, when the apostles saw him walking across the waters of the Sea of Galilee toward their boat, they were left in no doubt of his divinity (but Peter's own faith faltered as he attempted to walk out to meet his Lord).

A DIVINITY KEPT SECRET

Jesus himself did not necessarily want his divinity known to others. At a number of points, in the Gospel of Mark especially, he urged his hearers to keep what is called the "Messianic Secret". Even when his apostles witnessed him standing on a high mountain in the episode known as the "Transfiguration", blazing forth in all his godly radiance, they were urged to not tell others what they had witnessed.

After one of his first miracles, the healing of a leper (Mark 1), Christ gave the man strict orders that he should tell no one of his cure. However, in his exhilaration, the man ignored this injunction and told everyone he met what Jesus had done for him. Crowds came from far and wide to see this marvellous miracle worker. Some came in hopes of being cured themselves; some to witness miracles or to hear what this new prophet had to say.

THE BEATITUDES

Christ's teachings have their single, most sustained exposition in the extraordinary episode known as the Sermon on the Mount – although on which particular mount the discourse was delivered is unclear. Wherever it occurred, it was during this sermon that Jesus formulated the Beatitudes (literally, Blessednesses), as is recorded in Matthew 5:3–12:

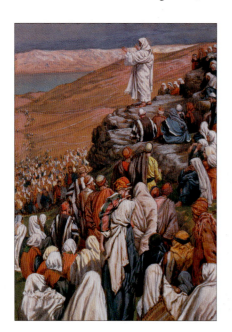

Left: Jesus is surrounded by his followers as he gives his Sermon on the Mount. He is standing in this painting by James Jacques Tissot, but traditionally Jesus is shown sitting – rabbis often sat while teaching.

Above: Christ cures a blind man in this warm and intimate scene by an 11th-century Italian artist.

- *How blessed are the poor in spirit; the kingdom of heaven is theirs.*
- *Blessed are the gentle; they shall have the earth as inheritance…*
- *Blessed are the merciful; they shall have mercy shown them…*
- *Blessed are the peacemakers; they shall be recognized as children of God…*

These blessings gave encouragement to his listeners. However, there were many other components to this thought-provoking sermon, including the Lord's Prayer and what are considered by many people to be the central tenets of Christianity. The convention is that Jesus' life and death created a "new covenant" between God and humankind. This was a merciful reaching out, a second chance for the fallen descendants of Adam and Eve.

This interpretation is true enough, but at the same time, for all the generosity and love it represented, the "deal" Jesus offered was extremely exacting. Those who followed his way, he warned, could expect to endure abuse and persecution. Harder than the insults and violent treatment they were to expect, would be the

"BLESSED ARE THE POOR IN SPIRIT"

duty they would have to respond to their oppressors with friendship and forgiveness: rather than retaliate if anyone hit them, they must offer them the other cheek (Matthew 5:39). They should love their enemies, do good to those who wish them harm, and treat others as they would hope to be treated themselves.

NOT ONLY FOR THE JUST
Jesus found his first followers when, walking by the Sea of Galilee, he met the fishermen Simon (whom Jesus promptly renamed Peter) and his friend Andrew, along with two brothers, James and John. Other "apostles" followed: 12 in all, including Philip, Bartholomew and Thomas. None was rich or learned; they represented the working poor rather than the priestly elite. Matthew, a tax collector, was a member of a despised class. But Christ had come to call sinners, he said. His later friendship with Mary Magdalene, the repentant prostitute, underlined his concern that his redemption was for all, not just the traditionally pious.

Right: Jesus dismisses the disapproving stares of his pious companions as Mary Magdalene prostrates herself at his feet in this 16th-century painting attributed to the French School.

TEACHING TALES

Arriving as he did to bring God's Word to the poor and uneducated, Christ made his message as vivid as he possibly could. Rather than setting out an abstract code of instructions, he expressed his teachings in strikingly human terms. He spoke of the Sower whose seed fell largely on stony ground; the Samaritan who remembered his charitable duty when his "betters" forgot theirs; and the Prodigal Son, welcomed home from his wanderings by his joyful father. Such parables demonstrated, more strongly than any com-mandments could, what it might mean to follow in the way of Christ.

Right: Christ's parable of fishermen making an abundant catch but only keeping the best fish is recalled in this c.1530 illustration for medieval readers.

33

THE WAY OF THE CROSS

CHRIST MAY HAVE COME TO BRING HUMANITY EVERLASTING LIFE, BUT FIRST HE HAD TO SUFFER AND DIE. THE AGONIES OF HIS CRUCIFIXION WERE THE PRICE HE PAID FOR MAN'S REDEMPTION.

The climax of Christ's ministry occurred when he made his triumphal entrance into Jerusalem. He did not do so in a chariot or on a noble stallion but mounted on a donkey. This is kingship in the humble spirit of the Beatitudes. The huge crowd cheered the Messiah through the streets, scattering palm leaves before him as he went. The crowd cried out the words of Psalm 118, "Hosanna! Blessed is he who is coming in the name of the Lord!"

However, he received a decidedly cooler welcome from his country's religious establishment. The Christ who had come to call sinners had already alienated both the learned scribes and the self-consciously pious Pharisees. Their devotion, he said, was to the letter of the law, while his was to its spirit. In Jerusalem, it became clear just how radical a reformer he was prepared to be. He was even willing to violate the peace of the Temple, driving out the moneychangers from its sacred precincts. For Jesus, they had turned the house of God into a den of thieves.

THE LAST SUPPER

Jesus had journeyed to the capital to join the celebrations for the Passover feast. As a good Jew, he wanted to take the traditional supper of lamb and unleavened bread with his apostles, but he gave the occasion a new and very special slant. Breaking the bread, he gave it to his friends, telling them solemnly, "This is my body". He offered them wine, telling them to drink it and saying, "This is my blood". What was to be his "Last Supper" with his apostles thus became a foreshadowing of the sacrifice he was so soon to be making on Calvary, and, of course, the Catholic sacrament of the Eucharist.

When the meal was over, Jesus and his apostles withdrew to the Garden of Gethsemane to pray in seclusion. Jesus felt all-too-human fear and panicked at the thought of what he was about to face. Men sent by the Sanhedrin – the sacred judges of the Jews – arrived to arrest him, away from the public eye. He was pointed out by his own apostle Judas, who betrayed him for 30 pieces of silver.

ON TRIAL

Jesus' captors accused him of blasphemy, although the evidence against him proved exasperatingly slight, until he told them that he was Christ, the son of God. His guilt established to their own satisfaction, the judges handed

Above: Christ's entry into Jerusalem, with palm leaves spread before him, has been captured in this 15th-century fresco by an unknown artist.

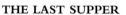

Above: The Crucifixion, and the sign of the Cross, became emblematic of Catholicism. This 13th-century Italian painted cross was an object of devotion.

Below: Jesus feared death, as any mortal would. In the Agony in the Garden, *painted by Giovanni Bellini c.1465, he prays for help.*

him over to the Roman governor Pontius Pilate, claiming that he had been scheming against the state. Pilate was unconvinced, but the clamour of the Sanhedrin and their supporters was so great that in the end he called for water and literally "washed his hands" of the problem. Christ's accusers could have their way, he said.

THE EXECUTION
Jesus was scourged at a pillar before being made to carry a heavy timber cross to his place of execution. He was mocked and spat upon as he made his slow, painful way through the streets of Jerusalem. Outside the city, on Mount Calvary, he was placed on the Cross, attached to it by nails through his hands and feet, and set up on the hilltop between two condemned thieves. "Father forgive them; they do not know what they are doing," he said of those who tormented him. Only after hours of agony did he die. On that day, a Friday, darkness fell upon the earth, which was convulsed by tremors; the curtain that screened the holiest part of the Temple ripped down the middle.

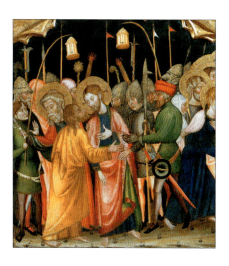

Above: Judas betrayed Jesus with the sign of love, a kiss, as captured in this 14th-century Spanish painting by the Master of Rubio.

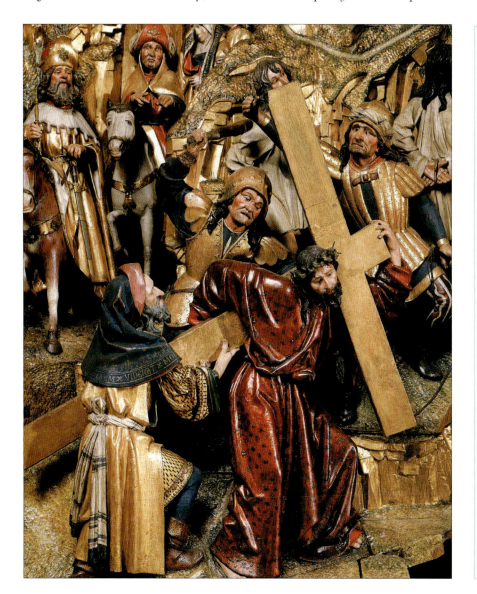

Below: Jesus staggering under the weight of his heavy Cross is depicted in this sumptuously carved, c.1460 wooden altarpiece from Antwerp.

> **PASCHAL PAST**
> The feast of Passover dates back to the deliverance of the Jews from Egyptian enslavement, as told in the Old Testament's Book of Exodus. God had sent nine plagues to afflict the Egyptians, but they still refused to let Moses and his people go. At last God sent an angel down to kill the firstborn of every family. So no Jews should be punished, Moses was instructed that each Israelite household should kill a lamb and mark their doorpost with its blood.
>
> Christ was going to his own death, sacrificing himself to atone for all of humanity's sins. Where the Jehovah of the Old Testament had meted out punishment to the Egyptians for their wickedness, now the "lamb of God" was going to take on the sins of all the world. His death and Resurrection marked the beginning of a "new covenant" in which justice would be tempered with mercy and in which sins might be forgiven.

HE HAS RISEN

CHRIST'S DEATH WAS THE ULTIMATE EXPRESSION OF LOVE, BUT IT WAS HIS RESURRECTION THAT GAVE IT MEANING. STRIVING HUMANITY HAD A WAY BACK TO GOD, A CHANCE AT LIFE IN HEAVEN.

Numbed by shock and stunned by disbelief, Jesus' friends took him down from the Cross, and his mother cradled him in her arms for the last time. One of his followers, Joseph of Arimathea, had a burial chamber already prepared for himself in a cave nearby. He got Pontius Pilate's permission to lay Christ to rest inside.

With that done, fear for their own physical safety being the least of their problems, Jesus' followers turned to despair. What were they to do? Where were they to go? They had been left emotionally and spiritually bereft by the death of their saviour, the one who had promised them eternal life. The darkness that still enveloped the earth matched their complete disorientation and their utter gloom.

AN EMPTY TOMB
But life had to go on, and part of life is the ritual responsibility of the living to the dead. So on Sunday morning, Mary Magdalene and "the other Mary", mother of the apostle James the Less, made their way to the tomb. (The gos-

Above: Christ cuts an awe-inspiring figure as he floats triumphantly above his open tomb in The Resurrection of Christ, *painted c.1502 by Raphael.*

pels differ, but Mark's Gospel mentions a third woman, another friend and follower, Salome.) There, they found that the stone protecting the entrance had been rolled aside. In the doorway, an angel greeted them, informing them that they had made a wasted journey: "He is not here, for he has risen, as he said he would."

In Matthew's account, as the astonished women ran to tell their friends the news, they met Jesus himself nearby. He asked them to tell the disciples to meet him in Galilee. Just hours later, two disciples walking along the road to Emmaus joined a stranger and went to an inn to eat with him. Only when this "stranger" blessed the bread before handing it to them did they realize who he was.

THE ASCENSION
The risen Christ then revealed himself to a number of disciples at various points, although these tended to be fleeting encounters. The apostles themselves were frightened and demoralized, and

Below: Christ appears to two travellers on the road to Emmaus in this 15th-century fresco from the Church of the Trinity, Piedmont, Italy.

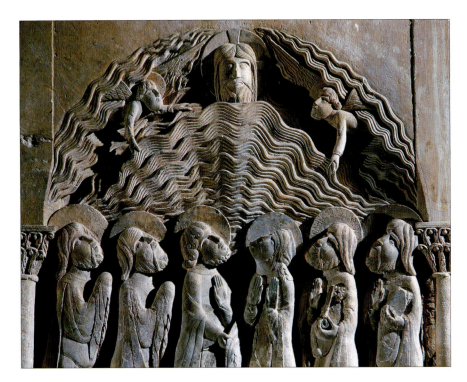

Above: The apostles gaze up as Jesus is borne aloft on a cloud by angels in this 12th-century Spanish stone relief.

Thomas was at first reluctant to believe that the sightings had even taken place. Finally, 40 days after the Resurrection, Jesus appeared before them in a room where they were all gathered. He urged them to carry his message to all the nations of the world. He told them not to fear: the Holy Spirit would protect them. He also said they would be able to pick up serpents and not be harmed, and they would have the power to cast out demons and heal the sick.

What happened next is unclear because the gospels differ on the details. However, there is agreement among the gospel writers that Jesus ascended to heaven: "a cloud took him from their sight", says the Acts of the Apostles (1:9).

PENTECOST

Left behind again, the apostles withdrew with Mary, the mother of Jesus, and other supporters to an "upper room" – the same one in which the Last Supper was celebrated. For the next few days they prayed together until, on the Jewish feast of Pentecost, the house was suddenly filled with a roaring noise, "as of a violent wind". Tongues of fire came to rest above their heads as the Holy Spirit descended upon them. With this inspiration, they ventured out into the streets to start spreading the word. Miraculously, those who listened, no matter what country they came from, could hear them speaking in their own native language.

> **THE GOSPELS AND THE GRAIL**
>
> Joseph of Arimathea is referred to in the gospels for the part he played in the burial of Christ, where he had a limited role in the event. However, he was given a more important role in a later legend. The tradition, most recently popularized by Dan Brown's novel *The Da Vinci Code,* has him carrying Christianity to Britain, along with the Holy Grail. This sacred vessel (widely assumed to be a chalice, although some sources see it as a serving dish) is said to have been used by Christ at the Last Supper. It is a colourful story, but no more than that. The earliest accounts of Christianity in Britain make no mention of Joseph of Arimathea, and it is not until the 9th century that we hear of his involvement. As for the Holy Grail narrative, that is even later in its origins, first appearing in French romances of the 12th century.

Below: Mary takes pride of place among the apostles in this representation of Pentecost, painted in Florence by Jacopo Orcagna (active 1368–98).

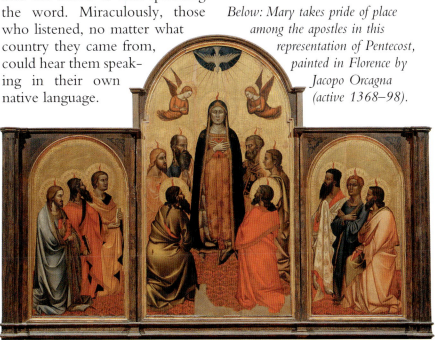

THE DISCIPLES

"Come after me," Christ had told the fishermen beside the Sea of Galilee, "and I will make you into fishers of men." His words came to pass in the early days of the Church.

Pentecost is a day of inspiration, marking the day of the descent of the Holy Spirit on the apostles. The disciples' joy was all but intoxicating – although cynics claim that they had, indeed, been drinking. Yet their euphoria, born of the Holy Spirit, is only heightened when they find ordinary people in the streets receptive to the message of Christ. As predicted by Jesus, these disciples became the "fishers of men". On that first day alone, the Acts of the Apostles assures us (2:41) some 3,000 converts were made, and more were recruited daily in the weeks that followed. Christianity, it seems, was gathering momentum. This was a mass movement, no longer a community – but a Church.

A NEW WAY OF LIFE

At the time, the disciples' religion was more fervent than thoughtful; Christian doctrine and ritual were works in progress. However, one thing is clear: at this stage the Christians were still emphatically Jewish. At the heart of their ritual, we are told (Acts 2:46), were their daily visits to the Temple together; afterwards, they adjourned to the homes of the community members for the "breaking of bread". This appeared to be both a eucharistic ritual and an act of sharing. The same verse tells us that they "shared their food gladly and generously". We are told, too, that they sold their possessions and divided up the proceeds so that everybody had what they needed. It is said that they were "looked up to by everyone", and were joined by a steady stream of new recruits.

Like Jesus before them, the apostles worked miracles, but they were careful that the glory went to God, not themselves. They fell foul of the Sanhedrin (the sacred judges of the Jews, who did not believe in resurrection), but they had no grounds on which to condemn them – nor could they explain how the Christians cured the sick and lame.

A FAITH FOR ALL

These Christians were indeed still scrupulous in their Jewish observance, worshipping regularly and

Above: The apostles were soon finding many ordinary people willing to convert to Christianity, as shown in this late 15th-century illumination by Jean Poyet.

Below: Jesus sends his followers to "make disciples of all nations" in a 20th-century stained-glass window by Gabriel Loire.

THE DISCIPLES

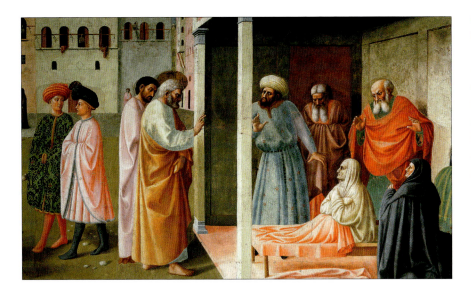

Above: St Peter continued the ministry of his departed Lord. In this Italian fresco, by Masolino da Panicale, he raises Tabitha from the dead.

maintaining all the dietary laws. However, that was soon to change. St Peter had a dream in which God instructed him that from now on no animal or bird should be deemed "unclean" (Acts 10:10–15). Additionally, there was news that an angel had appeared to a Roman centurion, Cornelius, and this persuaded Peter that God wanted Christianity to be open to all, regardless of nationality.

For hundreds of years, the Jews had prided themselves on being God's "chosen people", so what Peter was saying was a complete departure. As he was addressing Cornelius and his Roman friends and relatives, the Holy Spirit descended upon them – just as it had earlier on the disciples at Pentecost. Peter's Jewish companions were shocked, but their leader explained that this was a sign that "God has no favourites" (Acts 10:34).

The historical record shows that this principle was ratified at the Council of Jerusalem, held around AD 50 under Peter's guidance. The Council also agreed that gentiles (non-Jews) could be baptized without circumcision. This was the start of the divergence of Christianity and Judaism. So, too, was St Peter's transfer of his ministry from Jerusalem to Antioch in Syria (modern-day Turkey), and later to Rome, where he was to take his message to the centre of the ancient world.

> ### A CHRISTIAN CAPITAL
>
> Antioch, or Antakya, now in modern-day Turkey, is not an attractive place to visit. It is a noisy, congested city. However, behind this façade hides a historic and spiritual centre of extraordinary importance. The beautiful buildings may have been swept away, but the legacy of this past has endured in the people, in its small but active Christian community. Today, Antakya's Christians are in an often uncomfortable position: they are caught between the aggressive secularism of the Turkish state and the Islamic devotion of the majority of the population. Yet, they feel strengthened by their sense of 2,000 years of continuous Christian worship here. Under its old name, Antioch, this was a major metropolis. More than that, for a crucial period in the 1st and 2nd centuries, it was the capital of Christianity. St Peter himself is said to have made it his headquarters, and by the 3rd century, according to St John Chrysostom, there were 100,000 Christians in the city.

Left: St Peter preaches in a street that has the distinct look of 15th-century Florence. The painting is from the Linaiuoli Triptych *by Fra Angelico (c.1387–1455).*

THE EARLY CHURCH

ST PAUL THE CONVERT

SAUL STARTED OUT AS AN IMPLACABLE PERSECUTOR OF THE NEW RELIGION, BUT REBORN AS PAUL HE BECAME A TIRELESS EVANGELIST. HE PLAYED AN IMPORTANT ROLE IN BUILDING THE EARLY CHURCH.

Above: Saul was stopped on the road to Damascus, as seen in this 19th-century stained-glass window from Lincoln Cathedral, England. His conversion greatly influenced the course of Christianity.

Saul was born in Tarsus, in what is now the south of Turkey. In the 2nd century BC, this country had been conquered by the Romans. Tarsus had been given an unusual amount of say over its own affairs, and Saul's well-born Jewish family had been granted citizenship. This set Saul apart from the Jews of his time and made him doubly suspicious of Christ's followers, who were a potential threat to Judaism and the Roman Empire.

According to the Acts of the Apostles (Chapters 7–8), Saul first came into contact with Christianity as a witness to the martyrdom of St Stephen, who was stoned in Jerusalem around AD 35. Saul appeared as a mere bystander: those about to kill the young man placed their cloaks at his feet for safe keeping. The man from Tarsus did not remain detached for long. Oddly enough, it does not seem to have been either Stephen's proclamations of Christian faith or his criticisms of the Jews that upset Saul. What got his attention was the serenity with which the first martyr met his death and the magnanimity with which he asked God to forgive his killers.

Saul, in anything but magnanimous mood, hurled himself into the task of hunting down and destroying the rest of Stephen's fellow Christians. It was with the aim of rounding up the Christian community in the Syrian city that Saul was on the road to Damascus.

THE LIGHT OF GOD
As he travelled, a dazzling light appeared. Felled by its force, Saul pitched forward, falling on the stony road. "Saul, Saul, why are you persecuting me?" thundered God from the sky. Saul, in his shock, lay cowering and helpless. "Who are you, Lord?" he said. "I am Jesus, whom you are persecuting," came the reply. This was a revelation for Saul, and his conversion on the road to Damascus was to be a defining moment for Christianity. Saul had never set eyes on the living Christ, yet, as Paul, he did much to shape the development of Christ's Church.

SIGHT RESTORED
Having been blinded by the light, Saul was taken on to Damascus by his companions. A disciple named Ananias was told in a dream to go to the house where Saul was staying and restore his sight. Having heard what type of man Saul was, Ananias questioned this instruction. To his amazement, the Lord told him that Saul had to be cured because he was central for his plans for his Christian Church.

The restoration of Saul's sight was of course a symbolic as well as a physical cure: he had been morally blind before but was now enlightened. He became as eager a proselytizer as he had been a persecutor, dedicating his life to the spreading of the gospels.

Below: Paul preaches Christ's message in Luca di Tommè's 14th-century representation. The disciple believed the gospels should be spread to all people.

ST PAUL THE CONVERT

THE LETTERS OF THE LAW

Paul covered thousands of miles in the course of his ministry. He took his duty to the gentiles very seriously. Never satisfied with simply making converts, he kept in touch with the communities he had come to know in a series of letters. Part personal greetings, part sermons, part theological arguments with himself, the Epistles were to be incorporated into the Christian Scriptures. Paul's opinions, as set down in his Epistles, had an incalculable influence not only on his various congregations around the ancient world but on the way Christianity was to develop in modern times.

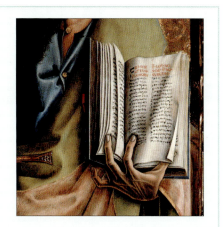

Right: A page of Paul's Epistles can be seen in this detail from a 1473 polyptych (a many-panelled altarpiece) in Ascoli Piceno's Sant' Emidio Cathedral, Italy.

APOSTLE TO THE GENTILES

The Holy Spirit, we are told (Acts:13), specifically chose Saul for the task of taking the divine word to the gentiles, or non-Jews. It is no surprise, then, that he changed his name to the Roman "Paul" during his first mission to Cyprus, Greece and Asia Minor – or that he took sides with Peter in discussions at the Council of Jerusalem, which were to open the new religion to non-Jews. In subsequent missions, Paul crisscrossed the eastern Mediterranean and Middle East regions, making new converts and revisiting existing Christian communities.

Arrested in Jerusalem, allegedly for bringing gentiles into the Temple in defiance of Jewish law, Paul was accused of blasphemy – just like Christ had been before him. However, because of his background, Paul could appeal to his rights as a Roman citizen, which meant that he was eventually transported to Rome for trial there. His arrival coincided with the first major persecution of the Christians in AD 64. He died a martyr, though the exact date and circumstances are unknown.

Right: Masaccio's 15th-century painting of St Paul shows the disciple armed with the sword of the fighter (and the martyr) and the Bible.

41

THE EARLY CHURCH

A FAITH IN FEAR

"Blessed are you when people abuse you and persecute you," Christ said. His followers were to find out what that felt like as they braved torture for the sake of their beliefs.

Toward the end of AD 64, Nero, Emperor of Rome, launched the first "Great Persecution". In these early days of Christianity, its disciples could pose no conceivable threat. By this time, the numbers in their community in the capital could have been only in the low hundreds at the most.

However, Nero had an agenda. He was widely blamed for the Great Fire of Rome, which had swept through the city that year. There were reports that the emperor's own household slaves had been seen intentionally setting the fire so that Nero could advance his redevelopment plans for parts of the city centre. As things turned out, the conflagration gutted 10 of the capital's 14 districts. Under the circumstances, Nero was only too eager to have someone else to blame, and the Christian community made the perfect scapegoat.

Above: A man is attacked by wild beasts in the arena in this 2nd-century mosaic from North Africa.

CRUEL DEATHS

On his orders, Christians were taken prisoner by the score. Some were tossed on to fires – alive – thrown to savage dogs to be torn apart or, notoriously, cast into the arena to be killed by wild animals as a public spectacle. Others were crucified, a common form of execution at the time, but also a sneer at the way the Christians' Messiah had been killed. Peter, who had arrived in Rome at the start of Nero's Great Persecution, was one of those crucified in Rome during this period. One tradition has it that he was hung upside down, at his own request, pre-sumably because it would be presumptuous to be executed in the same manner as his saviour.

PROLONGED REPRESSION

In many places and for long periods, Christians were tolerated. Yet, sometimes, persecution came

Left: St Peter is often depicted being crucified upside down, such as in this 16th-century French manuscript.

not from the state but from the general public. Christians were harassed – even physically attacked – by their pagan neighbours. Sometimes there were also more serious and sustained outbreaks of mob violence against Christians, with or without the connivance of the authorities.

As is generally the way with such things, hostility increased at times of political uncertainty or economic crisis. There were significant crackdowns during the reigns of Domitian, Trajan, Septimius Severus and Decius. Many priests and bishops were martyred in the reign of Valerian (253–60), including St Laurence, reputedly burnt on an iron grill.

In fairness, part of the problem was the Romans' incomprehension of what was motivating the Christians to resist. As far as they were concerned, they had given the Christians every chance to save themselves by abjuring their religion. They simply could not understand that this new creed could be worth dying for.

ANOTHER PERSECUTION

In 303, Emperor Diocletian issued his "Edict Against the Christians", ordering that churches should be demolished and Christians enslaved. This would have been bad enough even if it had not been the signal for the start of another Great Persecution. Again, Christians were given a chance to save themselves by offering sacrifices to the pagan gods. Some were intimidated into compliance. Some sources say (though others deny this) that even the pope of the day, Marcellinus, had been persuaded to burn incense before Roman idols. However the pope repented his weakness, reasserted his Christian faith and died a martyr some time in 304.

Left: St Sebastian, who was martyred in 287, is shown gazing stoically heavenward as arrows pierce his body in this 1480 painting by Mantegna.

Many others were killed during the eight years of the Great Persecution, but some modern scholars are sceptical about claims by contemporary sources that 10,000 martyrs were crucified on the first day of Diocletian's crackdown. Yet even the conservative estimates are in agreement that thousands were martyred and many thousands more had suffered harassment and torture. Again, the persecution appears to have been prompted by an economic crisis brought on by Diocletian's financial mismanagement. The emperor was also a religious conservative, concerned at what he saw as the abandonment of the traditional Roman gods in favour of new faiths, such as Christianity.

Above: The grisly manner of St Catherine's execution in Alexandria around 305 has clearly caught the imagination of this late medieval painter, whose work appeared in the 1280 History of Four Saints.

THE EMPEROR AND THE ANTICHRIST

After being driven underground by Nero's persecution, the Christians communicated using a code based on what was known as "gematria". This was a type of numerological theory that attributed mystical properties to different numbers and saw significance in their relations to the letters of the Hebrew alphabet. Some scholars have studied all the infinite subtleties of gematria for many years, but at its crudest level it can be used to make a straightforward cipher. For Nero, the figures came to 666: the "Number of the Beast" in the Book of Revelation. Many early Christians did, indeed, see this Roman ruler as the model for the "Antichrist".

New Life among the Dead: The Catacombs

BENEATH ROME, MEN, WOMEN AND CHILDREN CAME TOGETHER IN SECRET WORSHIP. THEY FOUND A SANCTUARY IN THE DOMAIN OF THE DEAD, WHERE THEY HAD BURIED THEIR LOVED ONES.

In the face of persecution in the world above for their adherence to the creed of Christ, early Roman Christians ventured deep into the earth to the homes of the dead to give their thanks and praise to the living God.

A PRACTICAL SOLUTION

The catacombs were first and foremost a place to bury the dead, but for the Christians, and perhaps others, they became a place of refuge in times of persecution. As many as 40 of these underground burial complexes existed around the periphery of Rome; construction had begun in pre-Christian times. The pagan Romans, while revering the dead and making offerings at their graves, had also viewed them with fear and banished them beyond the city limits. Burial grounds had sprung up along the main routes out of town. Many people were cremated and their ashes stored in special columbaria ("dovecots"), so-called because the regular niches in which the urns were placed in their hundreds resembled the pigeonholes in which the birds nested in the dovecots of the day.

With pressure growing on space around the city, these facilities were tucked discreetly away underground. More subterranean complexes were built in Christian times, and these had to be more spacious. Burial had replaced cremation for the Christian faithful, who looked forward to the resurrection of the body. Fortunately, the soft and porous "tuff" (volcanic ash) on which much of Rome is founded made excavation easy, and these underground cemeteries quickly grew.

Above: The catacombs were primarily a way of warehousing the dead: floor-to-ceiling niches line this passage.

SAN CALLISTO

Rome's biggest catacombs, the San Callisto, are named after an early pope, St Callistus (although he was

Below: Ancient skulls seem to survey the scene in a chamber at the heart of Rome's San Callisto catacombs.

44

Above: Inside the Roman church of San Callisto, the "Crypt of the Popes" houses the relics of Church leaders from the 3rd and 4th centuries.

actually one of the few 3rd-century pontiffs not to have been buried in its rectangular "Crypt of the Popes"). They were rediscovered in 1849 by the Italian Giovanni Battista de Rossi, and while more than 20km (12½ miles) of tunnels and chambers have been mapped, there are large areas of labyrinthine passages that have yet to be explored. Tunnels were often created one on top of another, in up to four separate layers.

SACRED AND SECRET
For decades at a time the Christians had been left alone, and during these settled periods the catacombs appear to have been nothing more than burial places. It was only natural, though, that during periods of official crackdowns, when worshipping in public basilicas or homes was too hazardous, families that had grown used to visiting these underground passages to honour and pray for their dead thought of seeking a sanctuary here. The tombs of martyrs put to death in the persecutions became sacred sites in themselves, and their fellow Christians would visit them later to gather for worship and prayers.

Even in times of toleration, then, the catacombs were a powerful focus for Christian faith. And then, of course, there was the symbolic resonance: the sense of life and affirmation flourishing in the midst of death. It is inconceivable that this could have been lost on the men and women of the early Church.

MODERN INSPIRATION
Today we can marvel at the courage of these early Christians and see their story as exemplifying hope. The vanquishing of death, the triumph of new life – even in the grave itself – Christianity can hold out no greater promise to the believer. Hence, perhaps, the continuing hold the catacombs exercise over the imagination of the faithful.

UNDERGROUND ART
Areas in the catacombs were crudely customized as churches, and frescoes were painted showing what appear to be eucharistic scenes. The fish often crops up as a symbol – not just because Christ and his apostles had been fishermen but because the letters of the Greek word *Ichthus* ("fish") spelled out the secret slogan *Iesu Christos Theou* (or "Jesus Christ Saviour"). Old Testament scenes are represented as well, such as Moses striking the rock and sending water gushing forth and Jonah being swallowed by the whale.

San Callisto's "Gallery of the Sacraments" has some fascinating paintings. There are more in the San Domitilla catacombs, where key saints of the 4th century were laid to rest in an underground basilica. One side room has a ceiling adorned with a 3rd-century fresco of the Good Shepherd; in nearby niches and passages are paintings of Jesus, his apostles and the Magi.

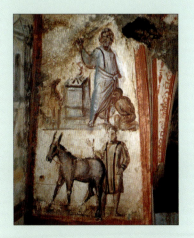

Above: Abraham prepares to sacrifice Isaac, his son, in this fresco. The catacombs hold some of the earliest Christian art.

THE CHURCH OF ROME

INCREASINGLY, CHRISTIANITY WAS EASING AWAY FROM ITS JEWISH ROOTS. ROME, THE CENTRE OF THE 1ST-CENTURY WORLD, WAS THE NATURAL HEADQUARTERS FOR THIS NEW RELIGION.

Why, despite its Middle Eastern origins, did this new religion become known as the "Roman" Catholic Church? To some extent, the development might seem accidental. The scene of so many martyrdoms had acquired strong emotional and spiritual associations for the early Christians. As early as the 2nd century – long before the age of persecutions had run its course – men and women were making pilgrimages to the tombs of St Peter and St Paul.

WORLD CAPITAL
There were other reasons that were also important. Rome was the capital of a vast empire: to all intents and purposes the centre of the world. Important decisions were all made there, and Rome ruled in many subject nations. The city was the centre of a web of well-made roads and busy shipping lanes.

Below: Tertullian was a pagan who converted to Christianity c.AD 197. His writings covered many issues in the theological field, providing a picture of religious life and beliefs in his time.

These advantages would not always have been of interest to the Church, of course. To begin with, Christianity had been influenced by Judaism. In fact, debate had raged over whether gentiles should be baptized at all, and many had been resistant to this change. However, Peter and Paul had prevailed with their literal interpretation of Christ's words, "Go…and make disciples of all nations" (Matthew 28:19).

LATIN TAKES OVER
Significant, too, was the decision of Tertullian, the Church's leading thinker, to write his works in Latin, the Roman language. Until now, there had been two languages of Christianity: Hebrew, the tongue of the Jews, and Greek, the language of the Seleucid kingdom and the Middle East. The word "Christ" came from the Greek *Christos* ("the Anointed"). Tertullian's decision in *c*.AD 200 made clear the ambition of the Church to reach out beyond its territories of origin to the rest of the known world.

CONSTANTINE'S CROSS
In 312, the Church found an unexpected supporter in Emperor Constantine I. At noon, in the hours before an important battle with a rival for imperial power, Constantine the Great had been praying to the sun – as Sol Invictus, the supreme deity of his religion. Suddenly, he and his army were astonished to see the blazing face of the sun overlain by the figure of the cross. The unmistakable symbolism was spelled out by an

Above: Rome is revealed to St Augustine as the "City of God", as shown here in a 15th-century French manuscript.

inscription written across the face of the heavens: *in hoc signo vinces* ("in this sign prevail").

Constantine's conversion at the Battle of Milvian Bridge and his patronage gave the Church a welcome boost. With the threat of persecution lifted, its members could meet and worship openly; its clergy could conduct its affairs in public. What had been – necessarily – a low-profile faith, with its adherents meeting quietly, was able to establish a presence in the world. Constantine advanced this process, endowing the Church with resources and working hard to build up its institutions. It was he who called the Council of Nicaea in 325, where important doctrinal questions were debated and resolved. While some felt that Constantine's patronage made Catholicism too "official", it allowed access to the structures of the imperial establishment that helped the Church to grow.

Constantine's Christianity was what the Church had needed at a tricky time. Even if the emperor himself was at times less than wholehearted in his commitment to his new faith, his mother St Helena ensured that he stayed loyal to its cause. Having converted following her son's example, she became his religious guide.

THE NEW CAPITAL

At the same time, Constantine took steps that were to lead to one of the saddest developments in the Church's history: he transferred the empire's capital to Byzantium, or Constantinople as he called it. In the centuries that followed, Constantinople became the real centre of the "Roman" world, while Rome itself sank into stagnation and decline. In time it was to recover, but by then the Eastern Church had broken away and Christ's followers were divided.

Above: Constantine I is depicted in this 16th-century fresco with his mother, St Helena, the traditional finder of the relics of the "True Cross". She ensured her son never wavered in his beliefs.

Below: In this 13th-century fresco, Pope Sylvester I baptizes Constantine – a breakthrough for the Church. In fact, the emperor postponed this sacrament until his deathbed.

A DOUBTFUL DONATION

Constantine gave Christianity his generous backing, building (among numerous other things) the original Basilica of St Peter's in Rome. However, the one thing the Roman does not appear to have given the Church is the rumoured "Donation of Constantine", in which he supposedly gave Pope Sylvester I and his successors temporal authority over Rome and many of its possessions in Europe and North Africa. Most of these realms fell to a variety of invaders and other rulers, but the popes held on to power in parts of central Italy into modern times. Even today, the Vatican remains a sovereign nation, its status sanctioned by custom, if not by legal title. In fact, the "Donation of Constantine" was revealed as a forgery in the 15th century. It is believed to have been created in the 8th century.

Below: A colossal head of Emperor Constantine from the Roman Forum. It was once the topmost part of a 4th-century full-length statue.

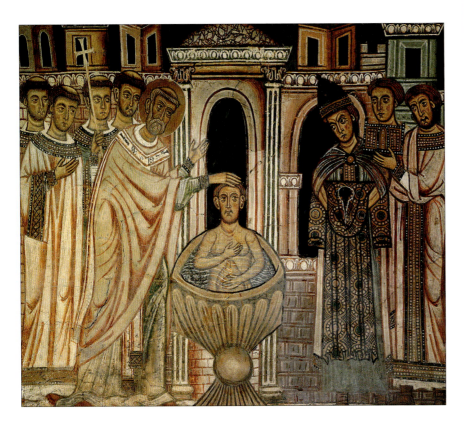

THE FIRST POPES

THE INSTITUTION OF THE PAPACY BEGAN WITH CHRIST'S COMMISSION TO PETER, "I WILL GIVE YOU THE KEYS OF THE KINGDOM OF HEAVEN: WHATEVER YOU BIND ON EARTH WILL BE BOUND IN HEAVEN…"

The papacy started to take shape as an institution over time, but the first pope was Peter. His name had been Simon, but Christ gave him a new name to go with his new and crucial role. "You are Peter," he says (Matthew 16:18), punning on the Greek word *petros*, or "stone", "and on this rock I will build my community." The Church over which he presided would be proof against the powers of Satan, Jesus promised, and its leader would have complete spiritual authority on Earth.

CHRIST'S SUCCESSORS
The "apostolic succession" is key to Catholicism's claims to be the one true Church of God. According to this theory, authority has been transmitted via an unbroken line of pontiffs from Christ and Peter down to the present day.

Below: Christ hands the keys of heaven to Peter, who becomes the first pope, as depicted by Pietro Perugino in this 15th-century fresco.

That authority is embodied in the office of the pope, who has as his emblem the crossed keys that recall the "keys of heaven" that Christ promised to Peter.

In its early days, of course, the Church was small and less structured, so to be its bishop would not have been a great honour in worldly terms. Christianity was often – due to Roman persecution – a furtive faith, forced to operate underground or on the run. There was no point in its bishops attracting attention to themselves, and they did not need to. Peter had no palace, no Vatican. Even so, his pre-eminence as "Prince of the Apostles" was acknowledged by Christ's followers. He was the Saviour's anointed successor here on earth, and no Christian would have dreamt of questioning his command.

A CHANGING CHURCH
In the Edict of Milan (313), the Roman state recognized the legitimacy of the Church. Larger and no longer persecuted, the Church had become a very different kind of institution. Leadership in what was now a big and international organization became not just a spiritual challenge but also an administrative one. Maintaining doctrinal discipline was proving to be more difficult as well. Individual teachers started striking out in their own directions and, by the end of the 4th century, theological anarchy was threatening the integrity of the Church.

This, moreover, occurred at a time when Rome was in steep decline, beset by both barbarian invasions and by instability that came from within. The centre of political power had shifted to the East, where Constantinople was booming as the capital of a more Asian-orientated "Roman" state. Rome had become a backwater in its own empire. All the indications were that, as the Western Empire declined, the Church was going to go down with it. It seemed that its brief history was going to end in oblivion.

Above: The keys of heaven have been incorporated in Pope Leo X's coat-of-arms, which were carved in this Roman stone relief of 1513–20.

A POWERFUL PAPACY

Pope Leo I, the Great, was influential in the development of the Church. His approach was far from subtle. He was unashamedly tough in his response to opposition. Democracy was a luxury he felt the Church could not afford. He was confronted with an organization that was in disarray, so he exercised dictatorial powers and centralized all power and doctrinal authority in himself. He formulated the view that the pope was heir to the powers of Peter, as stated in Matthew 16:18. Earlier generations of Christians had looked up to their popes, had valued the apostolic succession and had read and been inspired by Jesus' words to Peter, but they had not necessarily thought of the popes as heirs to Peter. Through these actions Leo the Great helped to strengthen the Church.

Below: When Pope Fabian was elected in 236, the Church was a large organization. In this depiction of his coronation by an artist of the 15th-century Spanish School, a dove (symbolic of the Holy Spirit) is perched on his head.

A PERSUASIVE POPE

Leo the Great may have been a masterful pontiff, however he was not a tyrant. He could compel people by his kindness, and won people over with his warmth. That he had a gift for getting his own way could hardly be denied: however, this was, after all, the man who managed to talk Attila the Hun out of attacking Rome. Their meeting, in 452, came after the Asiatic warlord and his army had invaded Italy and were poised to sweep down and sack the capital. Despairing of defending their city against such a ferocious enemy, the military and civic leaders of Rome approached the Pope to ask for his help. Taking two officials with him, Leo went to meet Attila and ask for peace. The latter "was so impressed with the presence of the high priest," wrote one chronicler of the day, "that he ordered his army to give up warfare and, after he had promised peace, he disappeared beyond the Danube".

Below: Leo the Great saved Rome from attack by Attila's forces when he met the Hunnish leader in 452. This c.1860 woodcut was inspired by a fresco in Munich.

THE EARLY CHURCH

THE CHURCH FATHERS

MANY SCHOLARS HAVE HELPED IN DEVELOPING THE DOCTRINAL DETAILS OF CATHOLICISM – BUT FOUR IN PARTICULAR STAND OUT AS THE "DOCTORS" OF THE EARLY CHURCH.

The Church owes an immeasurable debt to the great "doctors", or teachers, of the early Middle Ages, who helped shape not just its rituals but its faith. Clear though they were in essence, Christ's teachings had implications that had to be explored and examined, principles to be drawn out and systematized. The Church existed in the real world: Christians looked to it not just for inspiration but also for explanations, for moral guidance and for help in dealing with their doubts and fears. At first, it was ill equipped for this task. Its theology was undeveloped, and its institutional structures were limited.

AN UNBAPTIZED BISHOP

Just how disorganized it was is clear from the fact that, when the Bishop of Milan died in 374, his successor, Ambrose, had not been baptized or ordained as a priest, and he had not received any serious schooling in theology. Yet Ambrose understood the need for

Above: St Jerome had reputedly taken the thorn from a lame lion's paw, hence the cat with which he is traditionally shown, as here in this 15-century painting by an unknown Swiss artist.

Below: Gregory, Ambrose, Jerome and Augustine: the four Church Fathers attend the Virgin and Child in this 15th-century altarpiece.

THE CHURCH FATHERS

THE CONFESSOR
Today, St Augustine is best known for his autobiography, *The Confessions* (397) and for his youthful cry, "Lord make me chaste, but not yet!" However, in his eagerness to underline the fact that humanity was, from the beginning of existence, in a "fallen" state, he belaboured himself about offences that far predated this. As a boy, he lamented he had stolen fruit that he did not need; even as a baby, he believed that he had cried deliberately to unsettle the adults around him. This is a strange book in some ways, yet Augustine's self-examination is today admired far beyond the Church for its striking insights into what we would call psychology.

Right: The Devil holding up the Book of Vices to St Augustine *is the title of this work by Michael Pacher (c.1435–98). St Augustine saw evil and its temptations as a constant threat.*

theological rigour. His first move on his appointment was to give his possessions to the poor; his second was to embark on a programme of self-education. It was a spiritual and intellectual journey in which – thanks to the books he wrote – his fellow Christians were able to accompany him. Ambrose's courage was exemplary (his refusal to be bullied by Emperor Theodosius set the standard for subsequent pontiffs); so too was his piety. He was influential in his emphasis on the role of Mary, the Blessed Virgin.

LATIN WORDSMITHS
Ambrose benefited from his ease with the Greek sources in which much theological writing until that time had been set down. Writing in Latin, Ambrose can be seen as part of that same process of westernization that Tertullian had begun two centuries before. Jerome continued the process with his translation of the Bible into Latin, which he began in 382. Jerome was a Dalmatian-born scholar who worked from Greek editions because it was recognized that the finest scholarship was to be found in that language. At the same time, the Church was starting to define itself as Western. Greek, since Alexander's day, had been the language not just of Greece itself but of Asia, the home – in the Church's eyes – of heresy.

FIGHTER FOR ORTHODOXY
St Augustine of Hippo refuted two powerful heresies. As a young man, he held Manichaean views. These views were a product of Persian tradition that pitted the powers of light and virtue against darkness and sin. Manichaeism had exerted a strong influence over Christianity in the East. Augustine rejected this phase of his development, just as he did the dissolute lifestyle of his youth, and became a staunch defender of Western orthodoxy.

Augustine also defended the Roman Christians against the comforting creed of the Pelagians. Pelagius, a 4th-century monk, had argued that humanity had not irrevocably fallen in the Garden of Eden, so had no need of Christ's redemption. Individuals could choose to be good themselves, unaided. It was Augustine who helped to formulate the doctrine of original sin.

A GREAT REFORMER
Gregory I, the Great, was elected pontiff in 590. His reforms were tireless and far-reaching. From the celibacy of the clergy to the idea of the remission of time in Purgatory for acts of public and private penance, they touched just about every area of religious life. The clamour for his canonization had begun in his own lifetime, though critics claimed he had practically bankrupted the Church with his charitable giving.

Right: At "St Gregory's Mass", the Saviour appeared with his wounds bleeding and poured his blood into the chalice of the pope, as depicted in this c.1490 illumination.

THE EARLY CHURCH

A CHURCH DIVIDED

"Rome has spoken, the case is closed" are strong words attributed to St Augustine. The Church's insistence on orthodoxy came about after a lack of doctrinal discipline.

Rome was the centre of the world in the 1st century AD, but the power and control of this empire didn't last. The Dark Ages, from c.500 to the 11th century, were not as black as some popular histories claim, but it was an era in which the Church struggled. The Roman Empire was under relentless attack from invaders, and Rome itself was imploding politically, so the survival not just of the state but also of a civilization was at stake – as was the Church. Yet, at a time when Christian unity was all-important, rivalry threatened to tear the faith apart.

A CITY UNDER SIEGE

Augustine saw the danger. Rome had just been sacked by the Visigoths when, in the latter part of 410, he started writing *The City of God*. Many Romans believed the fall of their capital had been a judgement of the gods on its

Above: The Church, a fortress, is defended against heresy and sin in this illumination from a 15th-century French manuscript.

toleration of the Christian religion. However, Augustine's vision was of the city of Rome and the Church as parallel states, beset by barbarism and paganism respectively. Hence the impassioned urgency with which he strove to secure the spiritual integrity of his Church.

DIFFERENCES OF OPINION

Augustine thought the heretics were the enemies within. There was no shortage of them at this time, and they were often powerful. The adherents of Arianism followed the teaching of Arius, an Egyptian monk who had claimed that Christ, though saintly, was not divine. St Ambrose had led the fight against this heresy as Bishop of Milan in the 4th century, but it flourished and was believed in by many within Europe's ruling class. This heresy was halted when Emperor Theodosius I spoke out against it at the Constantinople Conference of 381. That year's

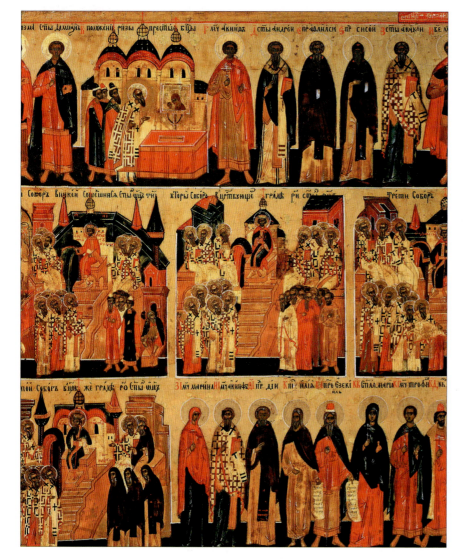

Left: A series of Nicaean Councils in the 1st millennium allowed important doctrinal issues to be thrashed out. It is represented in this Russian calendar dating from the mid-18th century.

52

revised Nicene Creed (*see below*) clearly rejected Arianism's claims. Yet its influence persisted in outlying regions of the West.

The 5th century brought the Nestorian Schism. An Archbishop of Constantinople, Nestorius asserted that Christ as God and Christ as man were not two different aspects of the same being but two distinct persons. This heresy was taken up in the East, leading to the breaking away of what became known as the Assyrian Church. Monophysitism, by contrast, held that Christ had only one aspect, the divine. Its supporters were fiercely at odds with the Nestorians in the East.

OUT OF IRELAND

Augustine's fears for the Church under barbarian attack were by no means exaggerated. Within a century of the Sack of Rome, Christianity had been almost wiped out throughout western Europe. Only in the remotest reaches of Ireland's Atlantic coast were Christianity and its culture holding out. However, in the 6th and 7th centuries, missionaries from these far-flung monasteries fanned out across western and central Europe (even Italy), reintroducing the Church of Christ.

THE EAST–WEST SCHISM

With its own bustling capital at Constantinople, the centre of a thriving empire, the Church in the East was flourishing, and it was increasingly going its own way. Cultural and linguistic differences caused the two halves of the old Roman Empire to diverge: the West was European and Latin; the East Asiatic and Greek. The West was in apparently terminal crisis, while the fortunes of the East were buoyant, so the eastern patriarchs saw no reason to bow before the popes. They owed allegiance to the Byzantine emperors, who had the right of appointing them. Their loyalty to the pontiff took second place. The authority of Rome was recognized formally, but deference was offered more grudgingly as time went on.

In 1054, Rome placed a papal bull denouncing the patriarch, Michael Kerullarios, upon the altar of Constantinople's great basilica, Hagia Sophia. Kerullarios responded in kind. Pope and patriarch had excommunicated one another – expelled each other from their Church community. The East–West Schism was under way, and the "Orthodox" Church of the East often existed separately from the Catholic Church.

Left: Heretical books are consigned to the fire in this illustration from a manuscript of the 9th century.

THE NICENE CREED

We believe in one God,
the Father, the Almighty,
maker of heaven and earth,
of all that is, seen and unseen.

We believe in one Lord,
 Jesus Christ,
the only Son of God,
eternally begotten of the Father,
God from God, Light from Light,
true God from true God,
begotten, not made,
of one Being with the Father.
Through him all things were
 made.
For us men and for our salvation,
he came down from heaven:
by the power of the Holy Spirit
he became incarnate of the Virgin
 Mary,
and became man.
For our sake he was crucified
 under Pontius Pilate;
he suffered death and was buried.
On the third day he rose again

in accordance with the Scriptures;
he ascended into heaven
and is seated at the right hand of
 the Father.
He will come again in glory
to judge the living and the dead,
and his kingdom will have no end.

We believe in the Holy Spirit,
the Lord, the giver of life,
who proceeds from the Father and
 the Son.
With the Father and the Son he
 is worshipped and glorified.
He has spoken through the
 Prophets.
We believe in one holy Catholic
 and apostolic Church.
We acknowledge one baptism for
the forgiveness of sins.
We look for the resurrection of
 the dead,
and the life of the world to come.

Amen.

THE MIDDLE AGES

The Church's second millennium could hardly have begun with a less auspicious start, split by the East–West Schism. What was really striking, though, was the easy assurance with which Catholicism shook off what should have been a catastrophic blow.

So-called in retrospect because it came between the classical period (Greece and Rome) and the Renaissance, the *medium aevum*, or Middle Ages, marked a breakthrough for the Church. Quite simply, in the West at least, there was no higher human institution: its teachings shaped the way men and women thought. The Church led the reconstruction of the West in the chaotic centuries that followed the fall of the Roman Empire in the 5th century, forming its institutions and culture and influencing architecture, music, literature and every area of learning. Catholicism had left its mark on all of these. The people saw the Church as the source of all their spiritual and moral laws, and rulers looked to it for their legitimacy.

Even so, there would be challenges. As early as the 7th century, Islam had emerged from Arabia. By the 11th century, the rapid expansion of its empire was seen as so great a threat to the West that a series of Crusades were mounted against the Muslims. Yet the existence of such a threat also gave Christendom an enemy against which it could define itself, and the Church continued to go from strength to strength.

Left: St Bridget of Sweden issues the rule for the Brigettine Order (Giovannantonio di Francesco Sogliani, 1522). Monasticism flourished in Europe during the Middle Ages.

MEDIEVAL CATHOLICISM

THE MIDDLE AGES IN EUROPE WAS A HIGH POINT FOR THE CHURCH: EVERY ASPECT OF LIFE – FROM HOW PEOPLE FELT TO HOW THEY WERE GOVERNED – WAS SHAPED BY CATHOLICISM.

As the main religion throughout Europe, the sect that had hidden itself away in the catacombs was no more. No monarchy could match its pervasive power. Kings consulted closely with its prelates and its pope, and ordinary men and women looked to their priests with all the deference due to God's representatives on Earth. Its teaching set the tone – morally, intellectually and culturally. Its monasteries were repositories of learning, driving forces in literature and science, and its cathedrals displayed the latest and the best in art and architecture.

FEUDALISM AND FAITH

The Church's power and authority were not just awesome, they were integral to the way in which medieval Europe viewed the world. In the Middle Ages, along with the idea of "faith" went that of "fealty" (from the Latin *fidelitas*, or "faithfulness"). It defined the bond of obedience and loyalty the man had to his overlord. Just as the serf owed fealty to his lord, who in turn acknowledged the overlordship of his king, so the Christian obeyed his or her priest, who was directed by the religious hierarchy.

Medieval Europeans implicitly believed that God had created an orderly cosmos and everything in the universe had its place. It was the responsibility of those entrusted with power, both spiritual and temporal, to ensure that order prevailed here on Earth. The power of the Church and State were thus regarded as two sides of the same coin. Despite their differences – there were disputes between popes and kings – it would

Above: This 12th-century golden orb, surmounted by a jewelled cross, was part of the crown jewels of imperial Germany.

never have occurred to a king to question the divine authority of the pope or his hierarchy any more than it would have occurred to the Church to undermine the power of the king. It was in neither's interest to jeopardize that principle of order on which the entire worldview of the Middle Ages rested.

POWER AND WEALTH

In truth, the Church wielded a great deal of power over secular affairs as well, and few temporal rulers dared defy its will. None would have dreamt of taxing its wealthy monasteries. Whether in a spirit of piety or in fear for their fate in the afterlife, wealthy magnates bequeathed lavish gifts in land and treasures to their local religious foundations.

Left: Serfs who worked the land used the crop to pay their tithe to the aristocracy and the Church. Late 15th-century Playfair Book of Hours.

Meanwhile, year in and year out, poor peasants and craftsmen had to pay a "tithe" (one-tenth) of their income to the Church. Although priests at village level lived pretty much as modestly as their parishioners, things were different further up the hierarchy. In time, the ethics of this would come to be questioned, but, in the meantime, senior churchmen often lived like lords.

THE ARTS AND LEARNING

At the same time that these senior church members wined and dined stupendously, they also bestowed their patronage freely. As a result of their conspicuous consumption, art lovers today can appreciate what are considered the greatest masterpieces of Western art. Giotto, Cimabué and countless anonymous artists worked under the auspices of the Church. Church buildings were often also filled with the exquisite work of master woodcarvers and sculptors, whose works brought the stories of the Bible to the illiterate.

Education and learning were to all intents and purposes the monopoly of the Church, and intellectual discussion and debate all took place within the terms of reference established by the great Catholic teachers of the day. Pre-eminent among these was Thomas Aquinas, born in Sicily c.1225. His *Summa Theologica* (1266–74) was literally a "theological summary", setting out in a single vast and coherent plan all the Church's teachings about God, the universe and the place of man within it. Aquinas' work is valued in its own right by philosophers today, but it was also an important conduit for earlier thought: the ideas of Aristotle, of Arabic thinkers such as Ibn Rushd (Averroës) and Ibn Sina (Avicenna), and of Jewish doctors such as Maimonides all found their way into Western tradition through his work.

Above: With Plato and Aristotle on either side, St Thomas Aquinas is shown with the Arab philosopher Averroës in the foreground in this 15th-century painting by Benozzo di Lese Gozzoli.

DANTE

Born in Florence *c*.1265, Dante Alighieri has been revered in modern times as the poet who envisioned hell. His *Inferno* is indeed awe-inspiring, striking in its dreadful beauty but also in the sympathy it shows for the sufferings of the damned. Yet Dante would have been surprised to see it abstracted from his *Commedia* ("Comedy") as a whole.

Hell's torments could make no sense for him except as aspects of a universal order. His *Inferno*, like his *Purgatorio* and his *Paradiso*, is founded in the love of God. He can weep for the sinner while still giving thanks for the overall scheme.

Below: Dante enlightens the citizens of Florence with his vision of the universe in this 1465 painting.

THE CRUSADES

Soon after Islam arose in the East, victorious Arab armies spread their faith to the very doors of Rome. For nearly 500 years, Christians fought back in a series of crusades.

Roughly at about the same time that Catholicism had established itself as the dominant religion in Europe, Islam was on the rise in the East. This new expansionist religion posed a threat to Catholic authority, and the Church felt urgent pressure to try to stop its growth.

THE RISE OF ISLAM

The prophet Muhammad's mission to spread his Islamic religion began about 610. Arab armies carried his message to both the East and the West. By 638, less than three decades later, these armies were occupying Jerusalem.

Spilling across North Africa, the forces of Islam crossed the Straits of Gibraltar into Spain in the early 8th century. By 720 they were pushing into France. Although they had been turned back at Tours in 732 Christian rulers in northern Spain had embarked on a long-term Reconquista, or "reconquest", but the south of the peninsula seemed securely established as al-Andalus, a Muslim kingdom. With the borders of the Islamic world expanding at an incredible speed, Christendom was in fear for its survival.

A CALL TO ARMS

In November 1095, Pope Urban II gave an electrifying speech at the Council of Clermont. The armies of Islam stood on the very doorstep of Christian Europe, he warned. His words were recorded by the chronicler Fulcher of Chartres, and

Above: Pope Urban II proclaims the First Crusade during the Council of Clermont in 1095 in this 14th-century illustration.

he finished his speech with a desperate appeal:

> For this reason I beg and urge you – no, not I, but God Himself begs and implores you, as the messengers of Christ, the poor and the wealthy, to rush and drive away this mob from your brothers' territories, and

Below: The crusaders travelled to the Middle East by both land and sea.

Right: Crusaders storm Constantinople – a Christian city – in this 16th-century painting of the Fourth Crusade by the Italian painter Jacopo Tintoretto.

to bring swift assistance to those who also worship Christ.

In response to Pope Urban II's plea, a mass mobilization took place across Europe, involving not just knights and soldiers but also ordinary men and women – and children. Thousands were inspired by what they saw as their sacred duty. Others were drawn for secular reasons: the prospect of plunder or the promise of adventure.

TO JERUSALEM!

The Crusade had a difficult start. The army that arrived in Constantinople – ready to march through Anatolia (modern-day Turkey) and on to the Holy Land – was big, but it was poorly equipped. Of the 100,000 crusaders, only 40,000 survived the journey over the mountains to Antioch. It then took a seven-month siege to take the Syrian city. Afterward, the crusaders pushed on to Jerusalem. Amid ferocious fighting, the city fell on 13 July 1099, and thousands of its inhabitants were massacred.

CONTINUED CRUSADES

Jerusalem was soon under threat again from the resurgent "Saracens", as the Christians called the Arab forces. A Second Crusade occurred in 1147 but ended in an undignified rout. In 1187, the Kurdish leader Salah al-Din al-Ayyubi, or "Saladin", recaptured Jerusalem. The English king, Richard I, the Lionheart, and other Christian kings mounted a Third Crusade in 1189, but they fought in vain.

The Fourth Crusade (1202–4) was short of funds, so the crusaders sacked Constantinople, massacring thousands. This was followed by another tragedy: in 1212, thousands of young French and Germans enlisted in the Children's Crusade, but before they reached the Holy Land they starved or were sold into slavery in North Africa.

The Fifth Crusade (1217–21) approached Jerusalem from the south but proved no more successful than its predecessors. In 1228, Holy Roman Emperor Frederick II negotiated Jerusalem's return diplomatically, but it fell into Muslim hands again. Two further crusades were mounted in 1248 and 1270: both were catastrophic failures.

Retaking Jerusalem was out of the question after the Ottoman Turks took Byzantium in 1453, but the struggle against Islam went on. In Spain, the Reconquista was coming to a conclusion, which came with the capture of Granada in 1492. In 1529, the Ottomans besieged Vienna, but were finally repulsed. The West's decisive victory came at sea, at the Battle of Lepanto (1571). Christendom had been locked in conflict with Islam for five centuries. The struggle had been very costly in terms of lives and money, but it had done much to shape the Church.

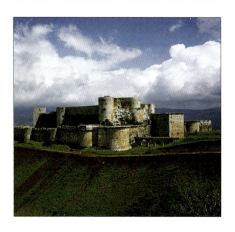

Left: Even now an intimidating sight, the 12th-century fortress of Krak des Chevaliers in Syria was built by crusaders.

MONASTICISM

THE MONASTERIES WERE IMPORTANT CULTURAL AND ECONOMIC CENTRES THAT HELPED SET THE TONE OF MEDIEVAL LIFE. THEY BROUGHT MEN TOGETHER IN COMMUNITIES OF WORK AND PRAYER.

Above: The great pioneer of the monastic movement St Benedict of Nursia delivers the Rules of the Order to St Maurus in this 1129 illumination, produced at the Monastery of St Gilles, Nîmes.

From the beginning, Christians had met in informal communities, with sharing and co-operation being fundamental to their faith. For a beleaguered, sometimes persecuted, minority, the community provided comfort. However, as time went on, organized communities of Christians were established, often living far away from the distractions and temptations of society at large. St Benedict of Nursia (c.480–543) founded at least 12 such communities in the early 6th century.

THE RULE OF ST BENEDICT

One community in particular – the Benedictines, established about 430 at Monte Cassino, south of Rome – was to have enduring importance. This was where St Benedict first formulated his "Benedictine Rule", a regime prescribing set times for collective worship, private prayer and study. It also allowed time for daily stints of manual work, which Benedict saw as an important way of suppressing personal pride and of giving praise to God. The Rule also put clear structures in place. One monk was to be elected "abbot" by his companions; he was to be in charge, though he had to consult with his community on key decisions and was not exempted from the general routines of work and prayer. With 73 points in all, the Rule gave detailed instructions about everything from forms of worship to food and clothing – it stipulated a lifestyle that was simple, but not punitively harsh.

MONASTIC LIFE

The Rule of St Benedict soon became the basis for an extensive network of monasteries across medieval Europe. Young men flocked to join these communities. They flung themselves into the monastic life in all its aspects, not just prayer and contemplation but also study and work. As beacons of learning, these monasteries soon commanded the respect of the wider communities in which they were based.

Run as they were by a well-motivated and educated workforce, their farms and market gardens

Left: Monks work in the fields, as depicted by Breu the Elder (c.1475–1537) on this panel from an Austrian altarpiece.

Above: The Cistercian Abbey of Sénanque, located in southern France, was founded in the mid-12th century.

thrived. So did their other economic ventures: some monks brewed beer or other drinks while others prepared medicines from herbs they had grown themselves. The monasteries rapidly became important centres of industry and trade – and their abbots used their influence on local rulers.

MONASTICISM REINVENTED

But soon some people were asking whether this success had not come at too high a price. Were the monasteries losing their way, becoming too "worldly" in their concerns? In 910, William the Pious, the Duke of Aquitaine, founded a new community at Cluny, in eastern France. His idea was that its members would return to the founding principles of monasticism, as originally set down in the Benedictine Rule. William had read the mood of the times and his call for a new kind of monasticism had struck a chord. Though, if anything, the code at Cluny was even stricter than St Benedict's, young men flocked to join the community. They were drawn by the possibility of a purer, more wholly dedicated religious life. Cluny subsequently became a major monastic centre.

Monasteries elsewhere begged the new community to send out teachers to instruct them in the new rule. The Cluniac Reform quickly spread throughout western Europe. Even where the Cluniac Rule was not explicitly adopted, its influence was felt. Its effects filtered beyond the monasteries and into the wider Church. Catholicism's conscience had been awakened, and individual believers, clergy and institutions all set about reforming themselves and the way they lived.

However, Cluny was a victim of its own success. It became so powerful and influential that some began to feel that it had become too worldly in its turn. In 1098, St Robert of Molesme and St Stephen Harding founded the Cistercian Order – so-called because it was established at the Abbey of Cîteaux. It too set out to restore the Benedictine Rule as originally ordained, and it did so with considerable success. From 1113, under the leadership of St Bernard of Clairvaux, it became an important force for monastic reform.

MONASTIC MYSTICISM

If the idea of community is as old as Christianity itself, so too is that of solitary contemplation. Christ's sojourn in the desert was emulated by a long tradition of hermits. Others wandered inward, deeper and deeper into their own minds, to find a peaceful place in which they could commune with God.

Some mystics, such as Julian of Norwich and Mechtilde of Magdebourg, can be seen as a kind of counterbalance to the monastic movement, pursuing the same aims as these religious communities but using contrary methods. The less these mystics attended to the world, they felt, the closer they could draw to God. In blindness to the world and its concerns, they could glimpse the truth that really mattered. Enlightenment, wrote one mystic, was to be found in a "Cloud of Unknowing".

Right: Mother Julian of Norwich was one of the great mystics of the Middle Ages.

SHRINES AND RELICS

TANGIBLE TESTAMENTS TO HEROIC LOVE AND SACRIFICE, HOLY SHRINES AND SACRED RELICS HAVE REMINDED BELIEVERS THROUGHOUT HISTORY WHAT THEIR FAITH IS ALL ABOUT.

A shrine is considered a sacred place, usually one that has been specially blessed by the presence of a holy person, who carried out an important act, or who lived, died or was buried there. A relic is an item once associated with a saintly personage, anything from a fragment of bone to a scrap of shroud, or a possession of some sort. Catholics believe that shrines and relics have been sanctified by their associations to these holy people, so shrines have often become places of pilgrimage, while holy relics have become objects of veneration.

Even Catholics today find it hard to imagine the transporting spiritual excitement their medieval forebears experienced in the presence of holy shrines and sacred relics. Though the Catholic Church continues to encourage the veneration of genuine relics, this is often misunderstood outside the Church. There is discomfort with it among modern believers, and Catholics are still sensitive to any suggestion of superstition.

OPEN TO ABUSE

During the Middle Ages, there was undoubtedly an element of the grotesque in the cult of certain relics, and, indisputably, there was at times an air of opportunistic showmanship about their presentation. Much of their fascination for the faithful may well have been as much about vulgar curiosity as about faith. At the time, businesses linked to the pilgrimages were thriving, and the possession of

Above: St Veronica wiped Christ's face as he carried his cross to Calvary. Miraculously, an imprint of Jesus' face was left on the cloth, as shown in this 15th-century painting by Hans Memling.

holy relics did not merely confer prestige, it could also bring (sometimes spectacular) earning potential. Pride of place in Venice's St Mark's Basilica was the tomb of the apostle – the Venetians had actually stolen St Mark's remains from their original resting place in Alexandria. In England, Canterbury was quick to cash in on the martyrdom of St Thomas, with entrepreneurially minded priests selling what was purported to be vials of his blood and scraps of his clothing.

A VALID TRADITION

So many churches had parts of the True Cross or the bones of various saints that not all of them could have been genuine. Yet even if not all relics were what they claimed to be, over the centuries millions of Catholics have derived great comfort and inspiration from them. Relics were of value not least as a subject for meditation. A

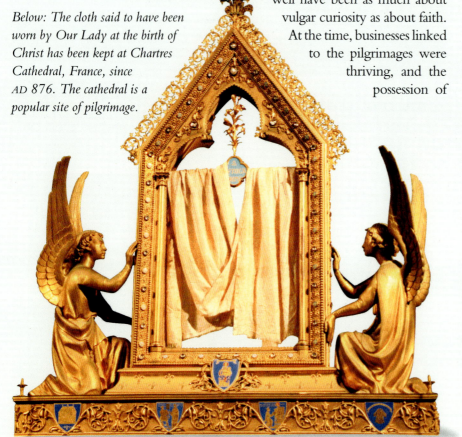

Below: The cloth said to have been worn by Our Lady at the birth of Christ has been kept at Chartres Cathedral, France, since AD 876. The cathedral is a popular site of pilgrimage.

Above: Reputed to be the last resting place of the apostle St James the Great, Santiago de Compostela is an important place of pilgrimage.

visitor to St Thomas à Becket's tomb in Canterbury could wonder at the courage of one who had stood up to his own king for what he knew was right. German visitors to the shrine of St Sebaldus in Nuremberg could reflect on what his early mission to Rome and preaching in Nuremburg had meant for their country. Several successive German emperors visited the shrine to pay him homage.

CONTACT WITH THE SAINTS

There is no doubt that the sense of being able to touch the saintly was part of the reason behind making a pilgrimage. Accordingly, a certain amount of tension arose between the instinct to present sacred relics in what would be appropriate magnificence and the pilgrims' desire for up-close contact. As monuments for these relics grew in size and splendour, they were built with open cavities, or "squeezing places", left in the tomb surround so the faithful could feel they were getting as close as possible to the source of grace.

DISTRUST FROM OTHERS

This need for contact would eventually be viewed by non-Catholics as somewhat grotesque. Protestant reformers, like many other modern intellectuals, distrusted Catholicism's instinct for the concrete – what can be seen and touched – an instinct revealed in everything from crucifixes and rosaries to statues and stained-glass windows. To them, the desire to touch a fragment of the "True Cross" or a visit to a saint's tomb could be compared to the time when Jesus told St Thomas to put his fingers in his wounds (John 20:25–9) before the doubting man would finally believe in his Resurrection.

In the 18th century, the philosophers of pre-revolutionary France had denounced Catholicism as a conspiracy to prop up corrupt institutions. Voltaire was one of these philosophers, and among his anti-religious comments was a sneer about the veneration of Christ's foreskin and the Virgin's milk, designed to humiliate Catholics.

For believers, though, the desire for contact with Christ and his saints was not rooted in weakness of faith. Contact was made for love, like that of the woman who touched the hem of Jesus' garment (Luke 8:40–8).

Below: Sacred shrines, such as the one in this 15th-century painting by the Master of San Sebastian, have sometimes been linked to miraculous healings, making them popular pilgrimage sites.

MIRRORS REFLECTING THE RELICS

In Aachen, Germany, in 1440, so many pilgrims flocked to see an exhibition of sacred relics that there was little prospect of anybody actually touching the reliquaries. The most the pilgrim could hope for was glimpses of these sacred treasures through the crush of the crowd. This situation led to the selling of metal-framed "pilgrim mirrors". These mirrors were designed to be clipped to the cap. They supposedly allowed the radiance emitted by the sacred relics to be captured, which the pilgrims could even take home to share with their family and friends.

PILGRIMAGE

EVERY YEAR, ALONG EUROPE'S HIGHWAYS, TRAVELLERS MADE THEIR WAY, SINGLY OR IN GROUPS, CRISS-CROSSING THE CONTINENT TO SEEK OUT THE MOST SACRED SHRINES OF THE CATHOLIC FAITH.

The idea of the medieval pilgrimage is still well known today to students of literature, thanks to Geoffrey Chaucer's *The Canterbury Tales*. This 14th-century poem tells the story of a group of pilgrims from different walks of life, who travel from London to Canterbury in England. There they intend to offer their devotions at the tomb of St Thomas à Becket, who lies buried in the cathedral where he met his martyr's death. Like many Christians in the Middle Ages, Chaucer's pilgrims hoped to acquire grace in the eyes of God by the commitment they were showing in making a sacred journey.

AN OLD TRADITION

By this time, the tradition of pilgrimage, or spiritual journey, was already an old one. Since the 2nd century, believers had been travelling to Jerusalem to visit the scenes of their Saviour's ministry and sufferings and to think about what they meant in their own lives. The pilgrimage is by no means a uniquely Christian custom. By the 5th century BC, Buddhists had been trekking to the birthplace of their teacher, the Buddha, at Kapilavastu, Nepal.

Pilgrimage became embedded in the traditions of Catholicism. It was a gesture, a declaration of spiritual intent. Forsaking family, friends and everyday routines, the Catholic set out on what he or she hoped would be a new direction. The pilgrimage itself was just the start, but it could be a profoundly significant start. Removed from the rhythms of daily work and home life, the pilgrim could reflect on that life and how it might be led better. Arriving at the holy place itself, the pilgrim might meditate on the religious drama that had taken place there, or on the life of the saint whose mortal remains had sanctified the spot.

Some made their pilgrimages in

Above: The Clerk of Oxenford, one of Chaucer's fictional pilgrims, is shown in The Canterbury Tales *(1400–10).*

hopes of saving a sick relative, or to help secure their salvation in the life beyond. Others were motivated by piety, a desire to perfect themselves; still others went as penitential pilgrims. They might have made their own decision to make a pilgrimage in expiation of some great wrong they had done. Or they might have been ordered by a court to make the journey, or else face a far harsher punishment. There were also those who were actuated by less pious

---

HOUSES OF HOSPITALITY

With thousands of pilgrims on the move, often travelling long distances, a considerable infrastructure was needed to feed, accommodate and protect them. It had to cope with such normal activities as treating their ailments, shoeing their horses and even mending their clothes. Every bit as important in its own time as the tourist industry is to travellers today, the pilgrimage acted as a powerful economic engine. Rather than the desire for leisure, however, it was harnessing Christian piety and spreading prosperity far and wide.

In Jerusalem, and on the great pilgrimage routes such as the road to Santiago de Compostela, monasteries and other religious houses created special hospices, where the pilgrims could stay overnight in safety. These hospices were not like today's hospices, used as places for the sick. The original hospices took their name from the Latin word *hospes*, or "host", which is the root of our modern word "hospitality".

Right: A hospice for pilgrims, one of many established across medieval Europe, is shown in this 15th-century illustration from Antoine de la Sale's Les Cent Nouvelles Nouvelles.

motives: a yen for travel or adventure or simply a desire for change.

SACRED PLACES

The Holy Land, though the ultimate place of pilgrimage, was beyond most people's reach, geographically, financially, and often politically, given that Jerusalem was so long in Muslim hands. Even when it was not, Muslim pirates from Turkey and from North Africa's Barbary Coast preyed on Christian shipping, leaving no alternative to a long, costly and hazardous overland journey through the Balkans. Rome, as both the centre of the Church and with its shrine of St Peter, was another popular place of pilgrimage. However, pilgrims from northern Europe had to find their way over the Alps on foot to get there, and many could not make their way across this treacherous mountain range.

There were less hazardous destinations, such as St Andrews in Scotland, reputedly the apostle's final resting place. In Galicia, Spain, the cathedral at Santiago de Compostela was supposed to house the remains of the apostle St James the Great. Another popular site in Spain was Zaragoza, where Our Lady had appeared atop a pillar before St James. Walsingham in Norfolk, England, had been the site of a different Marian apparition (appearance of Mary) in 1061, and it became an important place of pilgrimage.

Left: A pilgrim badge was worn to show that a person had made a particular pilgrimage. This pewter badge of St Thomas à Becket was worn by a person who had travelled to Canterbury Cathedral.

SAFETY IN NUMBERS

Even short journeys could be hazardous, and pilgrims often felt obliged to travel in groups in order to avoid attack. According to tradition, pilgrims gathered in their local town centre to receive a blessing from their priest before setting out on their journey together. On longer trips, these groups might join others, forming great congregations hundreds, sometimes thousands, strong.

Below: A 17th-century French map shows the main pilgrimage routes to Santiago de Compostela in Spain.

GOTHIC GLORY

BUILT TO CELEBRATE THE GLORY OF GOD AND AS HOUSES OF WORSHIP, EUROPE'S IMPRESSIVE GOTHIC CATHEDRALS ARE SPECTACULAR MONUMENTS TO AN AGE OF FAITH.

Imagine how a medieval peasant might have felt on seeing a great cathedral such as Chartres for the first time. Dumbstruck with amazement as far across the fields on the horizon, shimmering slightly in the haze of the August heat, the gigantic structure appeared to be rising out of the ground. They had heard of Chartres' new cathedral, of course – how its spire seemed to soar to heaven, how the clear lines of its solid stone structure dissolved into a riot of statuary figures as you approached. As for its vast interior, its wood carvings and statues bathed in the otherworldly light of a hundred stained-glass windows: that was a promise of paradise on earth. Even so, nothing had prepared them for their first actual experience of one of the great Gothic architectural monuments of the medieval age.

THE GOTHIC STYLE

Similar to most artistic movements, Renaissance architecture sought to better its predecessors. The term "gothic" was employed pejoratively by the Italian architects of the Renaissance to describe the architecture of the Middle Ages, which they had mistakenly attributed to the Germanic tribes known as the Goths. These tribes had sacked Rome in the 5th century AD, and thus had earned a reputation for barbarism.

Above: Stained glass, such as this one from a window in Chartres Cathedral showing Noah and his ark, gave the illiterate vivid access to the Bible stories.

They were seen as the destroyers of classical civilization, which the Renaissance had set out to reinstate. But although the term "Gothic Style" is still in use, it no longer has a negative connotation, and the medieval period is now generally seen as a golden age of European architecture. In fact, the Gothic style enjoyed a major revival in the 19th century.

REACHING FOR THE SKY

One striking feature of the Gothic style was its thrilling emphasis on verticality. However, for all its aesthetic and symbolic resonances, the style was reliant on advances in engineering. The old Romanesque churches had been held up by the massive masonry of their walls, their rounded arches suitable for only small windows. Now pointed arches distributed the weight, replacing a great deal of outward thrust with downward thrust. This allowed constructions to be taller, and walls and columns to be more slender. The liberal use of pointed pinnacles and spires underlined the accent on the vertical, which made even the grandest Romanesque monuments look squat and stubby.

Since the walls no longer had to bear such a load, they could afford to be less solid and could be fitted with huge, decorative windows filled with stained glass. Chartres Cathedral has more than a hundred of these. All kinds of biblical scenes were presented, creating a stunning pictorial scripture for the

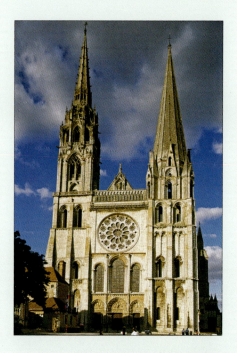

Above: Built mainly in the 13th century, Chartres Cathedral in France is one of the great masterpieces of Gothic architecture (its second spire, on the left, was added on top of a previous tower in the 1500s).

illiterate. No longer dark and gloomy, the inside of the Gothic church could be turned over to the best craftsmen to express themselves in paint and metalwork, carved wood and stone: they created statues and fonts, ornate wooden pulpits, pews and screens.

To go to church in such a setting was to be bombarded with sensory impressions. In many ways it was an experience of wonder and delight. Given the enthusiasm with which medieval artists represented devils and hell's torments, it might also be an experience of fear – but it would always be an experience to be remembered. Demons bedecked the outside, too, with waterspouts turned into hideously decorative gargoyles. Chartres' exterior offers a crash course in medieval culture. Along with religious scenes, the door surrounds are lined with figures of famous kings and queens, prophets and even philosophers.

COLLECTIVE EFFORTS

The creators of these stunning works were content to remain anonymous, though at the same time it is clear that they were given an astonishingly free hand in determining the design of their works. Where in a modern building the sense of unified, overall design is all-important, Gothic churches seem somehow to have grown organically.

All things considered, this should not be surprising. Such vast and ambitious edifices were beyond the capacity of any one man to construct or even oversee. These churches took years, decades, to build – longer than an artisan's working life – so it was not realistic to expect any continuity of craftsmanship, and generations of workers were involved in their construction. Skilled builders, masons, joiners, woodcarvers and glaziers accordingly went from place to place through the cities of Europe. On any given project, within rough parameters, they would have free rein in producing their work.

It was haphazard, but it worked. The great Gothic churches were essentially communal projects. Apart from that of praising God, and impressing and educating the public, their main purpose was to announce the wealth and prestige of the communities that built them. In that, they were triumphantly successful.

Right: Satan stokes the fire, while demons plunge the souls of the damned into a cauldron in this 12th-century relief from England's York Minster Cathedral.

Below: The Last Supper is represented in beaten gold in this stunning 11th-century relief from Aachen, Germany.

RENAISSANCE AND REFORM

The Renaissance was the age of undisputed Catholic supremacy in Europe, but it ended in dissension and strife. Outside the Church, the conventional view of modern historians has been of a papacy growing in corruption as it grew in power, with its hierarchy becoming increasingly remote from the people – even from parish priests. Although there is truth in this narrative, it tells no more than half the story of a great institution struggling to negotiate a time of extraordinary upheaval. Social, political, economic and intellectual life – all these were being transformed during this period. Great epidemics had ravaged the communities of Europe; the printing press was democratizing learning; Columbus' voyage had opened the door to the New World.

Martin Luther's stand at Wittenberg in 1517 was one reaction and the creed of Calvin another. In England, King Henry VIII's refusal to obey the pope marked a severing of the old accord between Church and State. However, there were changes within the Church, too. These had been gathering momentum for centuries, but they gained new impetus in the growing ferment.

The Reformation was a period of trauma for the Church, and in several countries it found itself driven back underground. All of Europe suffered from the wars the crisis brought, with martyrs on both sides. At the same time, in forcing a far-reaching process of reappraisal and renewal upon the Church, the Reformation also became a moment of rebirth.

Left: Religion was the inspiration for much of the greatest Renaissance art, as in this early 15th-century painting, The Resurrection of Christ, *by Mariotto di Cristofano.*

RIVAL POPES

During part of the early Renaissance, the Roman Catholic Church was based in France. There was a short-term papacy in Avignon and much conflict within the Church.

The Church was not only a religious institution but was also an extremely powerful and prominent social organization. Inevitably, it was involved in political affairs. As the Middle Ages concluded and the Renaissance began, the Church was finding its independence increasingly difficult to maintain, with secular rulers seeking to harness its influence to their own ends.

POPES AND POLITICS

The 13th century had already seen the supposedly transcendent authority of the papacy called into question by the growing interference of kings and aristocratic clans. Pope Nicholas IV had created added difficulties for the papacy when he bought the support of the Colonnas – an important Roman family – by granting them favours, and when he agreed to crown the French Prince Charles of Anjou, making him King of Naples and Sicily in 1289. The family was in no mood to surrender its special status under Nicholas' successor, Celestine V. In deference to King Charles, he had established his papal court at Naples. However, Celestine was ignominiously out of his depth and abdicated just five months after his election in 1294, making way for the more formidable Boniface VIII, who moved the papacy back to Rome.

Boniface could not be frightened into submission by Charles – or by the French ascendancy he represented – but his confrontational manner served only to precipitate a crisis. From the first, Boniface had both the King of Naples and Sicily and the Colonna family against him.

Above: Pope Boniface VIII is illustrated drafting canonical law in this 14th-century manuscript from the Decrees *of Boniface VIII.*

Years of harassment culminated in an assassination attempt in 1303. Although Boniface survived the attempt, he died of natural causes only a few weeks later.

THE AVIGNON PAPACY

Boniface's successor, Benedict XI, was pulled one way and then the other by Charles and the Colonnas. The French won after Benedict's death with the election of Clement V, who as Bertrand de Got had been the Archbishop of Bordeaux.

Clement had never visited Rome, and four years into his reign, in 1309, he transferred the seat of papal power to Avignon, in southern France. This was just one of the most obvious of Clement's concessions to King Philip IV. A host of new French cardinals were created in an intiative urged by Philip, and Clement outlawed the Order of the Knights Templar in 1307 throughout Europe. Their immense wealth in France was confiscated by the king.

Below: Built by Benedict XII and enlarged by Clement VI, the Palais des Papes in Avignon, France, was the home of a papacy in exile.

POPE AND "ANTIPOPE"

It almost seemed the move to Avignon had done the papacy good: it was growing in institutional splendour and in wealth. However, behind the scenes, the French crown was wielding unprecedented power. After Clement's death in 1314, six successive popes reigned from Avignon. The arrangement worked – but at a considerable cost to the Church's autonomy.

The transfer to France had left the Church in Italy in a rebellious mood; Rome was bereft, its purpose of so many centuries gone. There was unease in the wider Catholic Church as well. Queen Bridget of Sweden joined St Catherine of Siena in lobbying for a return. In 1376, Pope Gregory XI removed his court from Avignon to Rome. But the rejoicing was cut short by his death just a few months later.

The French had not finished with the papacy – their possession, as they now saw it. When an Italian, Urban VI, was named as pope in Rome in 1378, the French created their own "pope", Clement VII. In the decades that followed, four "antipopes" were elected as French counters to the popes of Rome. Called to arbitrate in the dispute, the Council of Pisa (1408) made matters worse: for a time the Church boasted not two popes but three, because the French cardinals could not agree among themselves. Finally, in 1417 Pope Martin V (a member of the Colonna family) received the recognition of the entire Catholic Church, with the papacy back in Rome.

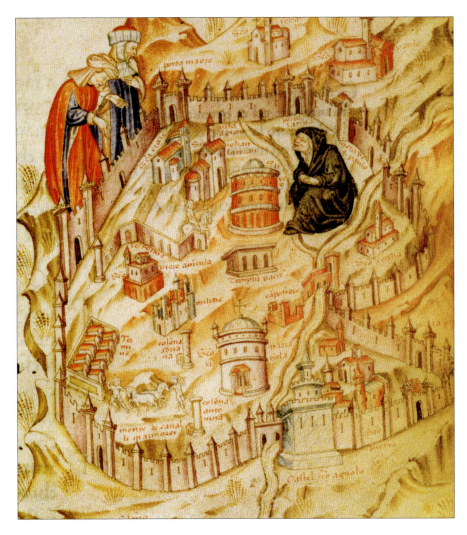

Above: In Roma La Veuve, *an Italian manuscript produced in the Renaissance, the allegorical "Widow of Rome" is illustrated mourning her bereavement after the departure of the papacy, shown outside the city walls.*

THE WESTERN SCHISM

So-called to differentiate it from the earlier separation, which had seen the Orthodox Church established in 1054, the Western Schism had consequences far beyond the papal courts. Secular rulers had to decide which side to acknowledge: the Roman pontiff or the French-backed Avignon pope. Because both papal courts appointed their own bishops, the lower clergy and the people were left confused – and spiritually adrift. Each side had excommunicated the other's supporters, so ordinary people had no way of knowing whether the sacraments their priests were administering were valid; whether their marriages, or their loved ones' funerals, were acceptable to God.

Right: Clement VII, the first "antipope" of the Western Schism, was enthroned at Avignon in 1378, shown here in the Chroniques de France ou de St Denis.

INDULGENCES

THE PAPACY HAD INITIALLY INTRODUCED INDULGENCES TO MEET A SPIRITUAL NEED. THESE REMISSIONS GAVE MILLIONS OF CATHOLICS THE HOPE TO STRIVE FOR THEIR SALVATION.

The Catholic Church is generally seen as being dogmatic in its teachings. It is easy to forget, then, that for much of the first millennium, its teachings in several areas were to some extent a work-in-progress in the development of doctrine. One issue that had from early on caused concern among Christians and their clergy was that they felt perilously poised between salvation and damnation. Surely, theologians reasoned, there must be a middle ground for those whose lives had been virtuous, though flawed?

PURIFYING THE SOUL

By the 5th century AD teachers were talking of a place of temporary chastisement, in which the soul would be purged or purified by the fire, but from which it would eventually be released into heaven, for eternity. The idea had been taken up and developed by Pope Gregory the Great in the 6th century. He had proposed that prayerful observance or good works in this life might lead to "indulgence".

An indulgence gives a period of remission to the sufferings of the soul in Purgatory after death, granted in return for some act of commitment – a pilgrimage, a programme of prayer, for example. It was a radical step, but it re-energized Christianity, giving ordinary men and women new grounds for hope. Few could hope to be saints in the hereafter, but anyone free of mortal sin could strive to do better in their daily lives, to throw themselves into their regimes of prayer and charitable works. The other great thing about the system was that, since people could earn "indulgence" not just for themselves but for their departed loved ones, it fostered a sense of solidarity between the living and the dead.

THE PLENARY INDULGENCE

As time went on, what had been an inspirational idea became a fully articulated system, with periods of indulgence established for certain observances or acts. In particularly special circumstances, a "plenary indulgence" might be granted, with a complete remission of temporal punishment for sin. If the receiver died in that moment, his or her soul could avoid going to Purgatory.

So far, this was nothing exceptional: the system may have seemed mechanistic, but it gave people a

Left: The good are lofted heavenward by flights of angels, while the wicked are carried down into hell in a burning river in Jean Colombe's 14th-century painting.

Above: Michael the archangel weighs souls, separating out the saved from the damned in this c.1450 Last Judgement, painted by Rogier van der Weyden.

spiritual incentive to which they could respond. However, at the same time, it was open to abuse: the temptation was always there for the Church to harness it to meet its worldly ends. When Pope Boniface VIII proclaimed a jubilee year for 1300, for example, he promised a plenary indulgence to those who made the pilgrimage to Jerusalem that year. Two million people heeded his call. The suspicion that he was putting on a show of strength for his political enemies in Rome must be set against the wider benefit his jubilee did in reinvigorating the whole Church.

A FINANCIAL TRANSACTION

More problematic was the financial note, which may have been innocent to start with but became corrupt over time. It began with the payment of fees for masses offered for the souls of the dead, another way of gaining them remission. The token sums paid were a welcome supplement to the incomes of poor parish priests. However, the practice spread as the Church first relied on the contributions it gained in this way and then exploited its people's piety. The poor were bullied into paying for prayers, the wealthy bribed with offers of an easy afterlife. Soon high prelates and great religious houses were growing rich on the proceeds.

The perception spread that indulgences existed not for the sake of fallen humanity but for the Church's monetary enrichment. However, this was not always the case. When Jesus gave Peter his papal power, he gave him the keys of heaven; he also promised him that the "powers of death" would not prevail against his Church. Purgatory wasn't mentioned, but by giving his pope authority to "bind" and "loose" the laws of earth and heaven, he gave him, and the popes who followed him, the right to ordain these things as he decided through God's grace.

Above: A bull of Julius II, issued in 1505, announces the indulgences that had been conferred on a group of wealthy benefactors.

SALVATION FOR SALE

In 1245, when England's King Henry III set out to rebuild Westminster Abbey, the venture won Pope Innocent IV's approval. More than this, it won his promise that any individual who made a contribution of money to this reconstruction would receive 20 days' indulgence from the sufferings of Purgatory. This was a clear cash transaction, even if it was for a good cause. By the 14th century, indulgences were being openly bought and sold. In Chaucer's *The Canterbury Tales*, the Pardoner carried a sheaf of printed "pardons" in his saddlebag. In 1344, Clement VIII issued 200 plenary indulgences in England alone, which were "earned" entirely by financial endowments to the papacy.

Below: England's King Henry III is shown with Westminster Abbey, which he rebuilt, in this c.1253 illustration from History of the English.

THE FRANCISCAN REVOLUTION

St Francis is among the most beloved of saints. To his spiritual ardour and love of nature, he allied a tactful radicalism that was to have a far-reaching impact on the Church.

Francesco di Pietro di Bernardone (*c*.1181–1226) was one of Assisi's most fashionable young men, known for his love of all things French. He was devoted to music, poetry, fashion and flirtation. However, he also had a more serious side. In the 1200s, when he was a young man in his twenties, a series of spiritual crises caused him to question his worldly preoccupations. He left behind his old pursuits and his old friends to care for lepers. The romantic enthusiasm of old was evident in the way he hurled himself into this new life, though now the mistress of his heart, he said, was "Lady Poverty".

BEGGARS IN CHRIST
This was a huge transformation, but the change in Francis was by no means done. In 1209, he was in a church in Assisi when a priest gave a sermon on Matthew's Gospel, Chapter 10.

Take no gold, nor silver, nor copper in your belts, no bag for your journey, nor two tunics, nor sandals, nor staff; for the labourer deserves his food…Do not be anxious how you are to speak or what you are to say; for what you are to say will be given to you in that hour; for it is not you who speak, but the Spirit of your Father through you.

Above: Christ officiates as St Francis takes Lady Poverty as his bride, depicted in this 13th–14th century allegorical scene by Giotto.

Francis would need no further encouragement to live the words of the gospels. He took to the roads as a beggar – with no money, no bag, no spare clothing, no sandals and no staff. However, he did soon have a companion: Bernard of Quintavalle, another wealthy young man from Assisi, and the first recruit to Francis' order of Friars Minor. Unlike the monks who lived in monasteries – and so, however hard they tried to avoid it, had worldly ties – the friars would have only the air they breathed and the food and water strangers gave them.

A NEW ORDER
This "mendicant" lifestyle could clearly be seen as an implicit criticism of the religious establishment at a time when its institutions had grown enormously in power and wealth. Already, there had been signs of restlessness, with certain

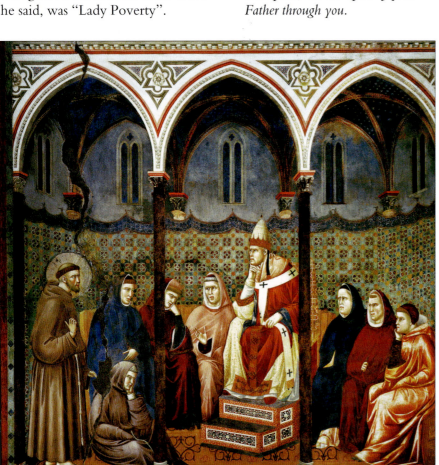

Left: St Francis maintained good relations with the papacy. In this 13th–14th century painting by Giotto, he preaches before Innocent's successor, Honorius III.

THE FRANCISCAN REVOLUTION

Above: The Dominicans, shown in this 16th-century painting by the Spanish School, were writers and teachers.

heretics attacking the Church for its close relations with wealthy, worldly interests. The hierarchy could be forgiven for feeling defensive in the face of Francis' apparent challenge.

For his own part, however, Francis showed no interest in taking the hierarchy to task. On the contrary, he defended the institutions of the Church against all detractors and sued humbly to Pope Innocent III for his support. The Pope appears to have found Francis a perplexing character. One story claims that the Pope initially ordered the ragged, dirty vagabond before him to be sent away to tend swine; however, he then relented when Francis agreed without demur.

Whatever reservations he might have had, Innocent came to the conclusion that Francis should be encouraged: that decision itself showed a certain vision on the pontiff's part. A movement that might have been profoundly destabilizing was accommodated by a Church already making conscious efforts to reform itself.

THE DOMINICANS

St Dominic was a teacher trying to hold back the rising tide of heresy in southern France. He founded his own order in 1214, which also took up mendicant proverty. Dominic saw that the poor were increasingly out of reach of the Church, not just in the scattered hamlets of the countryside but in the fast-growing cities. He wanted an order of young men to carry the Word to these lost sheep. Since Dominic had been placed in charge of a convent as early as 1206, these Dominican nuns actually predated the Dominican friars.

> **THE POOR CLARES**
>
> The daughter of a noble house, destined by her parents for an aristocratic marriage, Clare of Assisi (1194–1253) dreamt of a more meaningful religious life. She was inspired by St Francis, who had come from a background similar to her own, and in 1212 she went to him for help. With Francis' assistance, she started her own order, the Poor Ladies (also called the Poor Clares). They could not realistically travel the roads as the friars did, but had their own small convents. Despite the efforts of the established orders to absorb them into the monastic system, the Poor Ladies worked hard to maintain their independence and uphold their guiding principle of poverty.
>
> *Below: St Francis is shown with his disciple St Clare in this 14th-century painting by Memmo di Filipuccio. With his advice, she founded an order of her own.*
>
>

CHURCH MUSIC

FROM THE AUSTERE GRACE OF GREGORIAN CHANT TO THE GLORIOUS POLYPHONIES OF THE BAROQUE AND BEYOND, MUSIC HAS PLAYED ITS PART IN THE LITURGIES OF THE CHURCH.

Both solemn and spare, the sound of plainsong (also called "plainchant") as it echoes through the aisles and cloisters is for many people the quintessential sound associated with the Catholic Church. For others, however, it will be the thunderous chorus of the Lourdes pilgrims' "Ave Maria!", or the graceful harmonies of Haydn's *The Creation* or James MacMillan's *Mass*.

AN ORDERLY COSMOS
It seems likely that music formed part of the Christian liturgy from early on in its establishment, though in the absence of written notation from that time we have no real way of knowing for certain. Music had an almost theological significance for the people of the ancient and medieval worlds. The way in which the different notes could resonate harmoniously was seen as analogous to the relations between the earth and the planets and stars – all set in their own rotating spheres within the overall order of God's universe. Hence the phrase, "the music of the spheres", and therefore the importance attached to music – which went far beyond the aesthetic pleasure it provided.

SONG OF ST GREGORY
It was natural, then, that music would have its place in the monastic order, at the services offered by monks each day to mark the passage of the hours. The emphasis was on austerity: plainsong was indeed plain, involving no accompanying instruments and just a single sustained melodic line. Even so, its eerie beauty must have been an inspiration to the monks, reminding them each day of the mysterious majesty of God.

Pope Gregory the Great had encouraged the practice of singing plainsong, which, its inestimable beauties apart, helped foster the monastic virtues of co-operation and discipline. His support lent impetus to a musical genre that grew rapidly in scale and sophistication, and a rudimentary form of notation was developed during the 9th century.

Gradually, over the centuries that followed, moves were made toward simple two- and eventually more complex three- and four-part compositions – toward polyphony ("many voices"), in other words.

Left: Whether a little pipe-and-bellows affair or an elaborate one such as this from the Chapel at Versailles, the organ is the standard instrument for church music.

Above: Much early music was performed by voice alone, as shown in this 15th-century illumination from the Bible of Borso d'Este.

The organ added yet another voice: it is thought to have been in use since the time of Pope Vitalian in the 7th century. The organ's pure tones were the perfect complement to the human voice, and it has been the mainstay of church music ever since. As the Middle Ages gave way to the Renaissance, other instrumental sounds were introduced to church music.

INFLUENCES ON MUSIC
Secular music was nourished by the church tradition. Though Claudio Monteverdi is famous for having composed the first operas in the 17th century, he was also a priest, and in this role brought baroque complexity to sacred music.

In his footsteps came fellow Italians, such as Antonio Vivaldi (1678–1741), a priest who wrote many of his great works for the orchestra of the Ospedale della Pietà, a church-run orphanage for girls. The kapellmeisters (or "chapel masters"), who wrote liturgical music for services at Austria's and

Germany's courts, also found time to write secular concerti, keyboard music and orchestral suites.

By this time, of course, the Reformation had swept Europe, and several of the great Baroque composers were Protestants. However, music was an ecumenical art: Catholic creativity was stimulated by the works of Bach and Handel, while the great Protestant geniuses themselves drew on the traditions of the Catholic past.

CLASSICAL TRADITION

Religion remained an important influence into music's classical heyday of the 18th and 19th centuries. Joseph Haydn was a committed Catholic. While he wrote many explicitly sacred works – such as his wonderful oratorio, *The Creation* (1798) – he saw the whole process of composition as an act of prayer, writing "Praise be to God" at the end of every completed piece.

His younger contemporary, Wolfgang Amadeus Mozart, may have been famously flawed as an individual, but his profound faith came through in the great *Requiem* he was working on when his own life was cut short in 1791. Franz Liszt, the great piano virtuoso and romantic composer of the 19th century, was notorious for his scandalous private life. Yet this intensely emotional man was also passionate in his attachment to Catholicism. He even took minor orders in the Church in 1865.

SONGS OF PRAISE

What might be called the elite culture of sacred music has endured in 20th-century works by several noted composers, from France's Olivier Messiaen to Scotland's James MacMillan. For most modern Catholics, though, Church music has taken the less sophisticated form of hymn singing. This has been more about participation than polished performance, but regardless it has been profoundly important to its participants. Communal singing can be crucial in bringing a congregation closer together, instilling in its members a sense of common purpose and common faith.

Right: With such inspiring works as the Requiem, *Mozart created some of the most sublimely spiritual harmonies ever heard, enjoyed by Catholics and non-Catholics alike.*

Right: Many of Vivaldi's works were premiered by the girls of the orphanage he served, seen here in this 18th-century painting entitled The Orphans' Cantata, *by Gabriele Bella.*

HERETICS

SINCERE BELIEVERS WERE QUESTIONING THE AUTHORITY OF THE CHURCH. THE HIERARCHY HAD TO DECIDE WHICH CRITICISMS TO ACCEPT, WHICH TO IGNORE AND WHICH TO BRAND AS "HERESY".

An institution as far-reaching as the Church – and one with so many deeply thoughtful, idealistic individuals – was inevitably bound to have differences of opinion, even disputes, among its followers. To some extent these disputes could be contained and passionate debates took place with the Church's tacit acceptance – even its encouragement. However, some ideas were so wildly at variance with normal Catholic teaching that they could not be accommodated without the integrity of the Church being threatened. These contentious views became known as "heresies".

St Augustine had led the fight against heresy as early as the end of the 4th century, condemning the Pelagian view that humankind could earn salvation by its own efforts, without God's intervention. His view that humankind was dragged down so drastically by original sin that salvation came only and exclusively from the intervention of God

Above: Although members of a Christian faith, Waldensian followers were linked to witchcraft in this 15th-century illustration from the Book of Occult Sciences.

was to be taken to heretical extremes in the 16th century, when it was known as Jansenism. However, the late Middle Ages turned out to be a period of particular ferment, and in hindsight we can see this as the beginnings of the Reformation.

THE WALDENSIANS

In 1177, Peter Waldo, a prosperous merchant from Lyon, France, had undergone a spiritual crisis. Like St Francis, he had given away all his possessions and become a mendicant preacher. However, unlike the Franciscans, the "Waldensians" confronted the Church, denouncing it as representing only the richest and most powerful in society. Ultimately, they rejected the authority of its priests when Pope Lucius III banned Waldo from preaching in 1184. He and his followers set up their own Church, which survived prosecu-

*Left: Cathar books are consigned to the flames, for figurative damnation and literal destruction (*Santo Domingo y los Albigenses, *Pedro Berruguete, 15th century).*

HERETICS

tion during the following years. In 1848 the Catholic Church granted the Waldensians religious freedom.

THE CATHARS

Southern France had by this time become the centre of another great heresy: that of Catharism. This had its roots in the Manichaeism of earlier centuries, which preached a form of duelism that combined elements from several religions. A version of the heresy had been brought West through the Balkans by Pop Bogomil and his adherents, probably dispersed along the Mediterranean trade routes. Catharism carried to extremes the Manichaean opposition between good and evil, light and darkness, the spiritual and material. For its followers, the entire earthly Creation – the material world, the body and its desires – were evil. The aim of the godly was to transcend these things.

If the Word had been "made flesh" in Christ, that could only go to show that it, too, was evil – a fact the Cathars felt was confirmed by the wealth and power of the Church. Thousands flocked to the Cathar cause, despite the arguments of the Dominicans – newly formed to defend the faith. The violence of the official crackdown that followed (*see The Albigensian Crusade, below right*) has been condemned, but it is hard to imagine a more potent threat to the medieval order.

THE LOLLARDS

The teachings of John Wycliffe, an English priest and scholar of the 14th century, struck a chord with many of his country's less educated people. Like Waldo, Wycliffe thought the Church had no business being rich or involving itself with the concerns of temporal government. Even in religious affairs, he argued, the Church had made too much of its own role. He wanted a scaled-down hierarchy and translations of the Bible from Latin so that people could read the Word of God themselves. He denied the doctrine of "transubstantiation". The bread and wine, he said, remained bread and wine even as they took on the nature of Christ's body and blood. Wycliffe's followers, known as "Lollards", were seen as a threat to both secular and religious authority. Their ideas were spread into Europe by Jan Hus (or John Huss), the Czech reformer who campaigned against the sale of indulgences in the 15th century. The Lollards were a short-lived group, but their ideas were taken up by the Protestants.

THE ALBIGENSIAN CRUSADE

Named after Albi, a town in the Languedoc, a region in southern France, where Catharism was officially denounced in 1178, the "Albigensian Crusade" was proclaimed by Pope Innocent III in 1208. By calling it a crusade, he equated the challenge of heresy within the Church with the threat of Islam in the Middle East and Spain. In the years that followed, the forces of the French Crown and powerful northern nobles attacked the southern peasantry and the local lords who supported them. As many as a million people may have been killed.

Below: An extravagant depiction of the persecution of the Lollards was illustrated in the fiercely Protestant John Foxe's Acts and Monuments, *16th century.*

*Above: Many atrocities were committed in the Albigensian Crusade. Here, Cathars are expelled from the city of Carcassonne (*Chronicle of France, *15th century).*

THE INQUISITION

FEW INSTITUTIONS OF CATHOLICISM HAVE BEEN MORE FEARED THAN THE "INQUISITION", OR SO WIDELY MISUNDERSTOOD. YET THE EXCESSES OF THE "HOLY OFFICE", AS IT WAS KNOWN, CANNOT BE DENIED.

Above: Jan Hus is burnt at the stake for his heretical beliefs in this illustration from Ulrich von Reichenthal's Council Chronicle, *15th century.*

Throughout its history, the Catholic Church has fought against heresy, but it was not until the Renaissance that it formed an official institution against such preaching. The Albigensian Crusade, set up in France in 1208 in the hope of stemming the rising tide of Catharism, could be seen as a precursor to the official Inquisitions that followed. First ordered by Pope Gregory IX in 1232, an Inquisition was a tribunal ordered by the Catholic Church to suppress and punish heresy. The first inquisitors were chosen from the Dominicans and Franciscans, who were living mendicant lifestyles and therefore not influenced by worldly gains, and who were well educated in theology.

At about the same time an anti-Waldensian Inquisition followed in Italy, but then the Inquisition waned, to be revived in Spain and Portugal (and their overseas colonies) from the late 15th century. More of these ecclesiastical courts for suppressing heresy were constituted in France and Italy during the Reformation. The Congregation of the Holy Office, which is often shortened to the Holy Office, was formed to oversee the Inquisitions in 1542.

Although administered by the Church, the Inquisition worked with the temporal authorities. Generally, the state took the lead. Monarchs always had an interest in enforcing conformity and were happy enough to claim divine sanction for doing so. After the Reformation, religion took on a political aspect. A Protestant was no longer just a heretic but a dangerous subversive – potentially, an agent from another state in Europe.

SPANISH ACTS OF FAITH
It was in this febrile political context that the *Leyenda Negra* (or "Black Legend") was born. Spain, the Catholic superpower at the time, was demonized by the propagandists of northern Europe's Protestant powers. Books and pamphlets were printed, describing in lurid detail the supposed excesses of the Spanish, from their American colonies to the torture chambers of the Inquisition. However, modern scholarship has shown that many of these accounts were mere fabrications, created by over-excited pamphleteers.

However, some of the accounts, though sensationalized, cannot be dismissed. Recent research has shown the scrupulous thoroughness with which the Holy Office sought to document its cases, avoiding prosecutions based on malicious denunciations. At the same time it

Below: The Inquisition was especially active in the Netherlands and Ghent, where it was an arm of the Spanish occupation, as shown in this 16th-century engraving of the Flemish School.

Above: Spain's Grand Inquisitor, Tomás de Torquemada, was widely feared (Spanish School, 19th century).

THE SPANISH INQUISITION

The Inquisition in Spain had first been established in Aragon in the 13th century, but it came into its own in the 15th century under Ferdinand and Isabella, the "Catholic Monarchs". They bore that title, not because they staunchly defended Catholicism (though they did), but because by their marriage they had brought together the realms of Navarra, Aragon and Castile to form a single Spain. (The word "Catholic" originally meant "universal", "all-embracing" – hence its use for the Church of Rome.)

Ferdinand and Isabella saw the Holy Office as a way of using ecclesiastical structures as the basis for what we would now call a police state. Since the Reconquista was only recently completed, and many of the kingdom's Jews and Muslims had been converted by force, there was considerable fear that these alien groups were secretly upholding their old beliefs and practices in private meetings. Hence the drawing up of laws of *limpieza* ("cleanliness", "purity"), which anticipated the race laws of Nazi Germany. They were imposed with terrifying thoroughness by the infamous Grand Inquisitor, Tomás de Torquemada, who was appointed to the position by the pope.

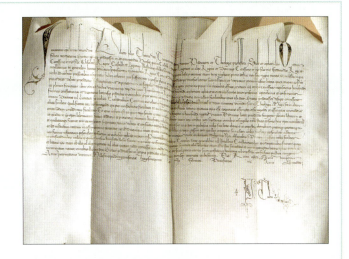

Above: Torquemada received a bull of 1487 from Pope Innocent VIII, appointing him Inquisitor General of Spain.

confirms the integral role of torture in the proceedings (after its explicit authorization by Pope Innocent IV in 1252). Although their frequency has been exaggerated, *autos-da-fé* ("acts of faith") assuredly took place. These rituals, in which there was a public penance for the guilty, were symbolic representations of the Last Judgement acted out before large crowds. An *auto-da-fé* ended with the accused being burnt at the stake.

OUTRAGEOUS ACTIONS

The readiness of the Church to consign its critics to the flames is easily exaggerated: the wilder claims of Reformation propaganda have proved obdurately persistent. The armies of the Albigensian Crusade did embark on a spree of slaughter, but the extent of the Church's blessing is unclear. Outraged though it was by Wycliffe's teachings, the Church spent so long debating them that he had died of natural causes before he was denounced as a heretic.

However, Jan Hus, the Czech preacher who campaigned against the sale of indulgences, was burnt at the stake in 1415 (an act for which Pope John Paul II apologized in 1999). Nor was he alone in suffering this fate at the hands of the Church, which, with criticism mounting, was increasingly on the defensive – and all too ready to attack.

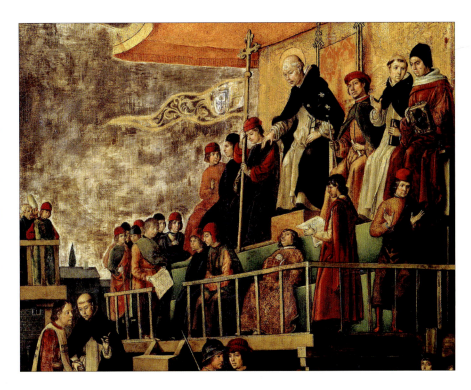

Right: St Dominic was committed to teaching – but when all else failed, the fear of death was used to persuade the people. Here, St Dominic presides over an auto-da-fé *(Pedro Berruguete, c.1495).*

THE CHURCH IN TRANSITION

THE HISTORICAL HEADLINES MAY HAVE BEEN ABOUT THE STIFLING OF DISSENT, BUT QUIETER DEVELOPMENTS WERE TAKING PLACE BEHIND THE SCENES AS CATHOLICISM REFORMED ITSELF.

The Church in the Middle Ages had been very much the establishment. Secure in its position, it had no real interest in changing. However, this does not mean that the spiritual status quo had gone unquestioned. The heresies of the time had only been the most extreme manifestation of a ferment of debate. This concerned not just the finer points of Christian doctrine but also the place that Catholicism occupied within society, and the developing relationship between Church and State.

COUNCILS FOR CHANGE

These issues were explored by the Church hierarchy at such gatherings as the Third Lateran Council of 1179 and the Fourth, which followed in 1215. These conclaves were held in the vast council chamber of the Lateran Palace, which was the pope's official residence in Rome. Leading clerics came together to discuss the changes the Church would have to make to adapt to a changing world while at the same time staying true to its original principles.

The great emphasis of the communiqués agreed by the Third Lateran Council was on the maintenance of orthodoxy, while the Fourth is today known chiefly for its decree that Jews and Muslims should have to wear distinctive garb to set themselves apart from Christians.

Yet the small print tells a slightly different story. Most of the Council's energies had gone into the attempt to get the Church's house in order. New measures were introduced to make the clergy more accountable for its actions and to control the activities of religious foundations.

THE RISE OF HUMANISM

At the end of the 15th century, the Italian scholar Giovanni Pico Della Mirandola advanced the views that became known as "humanism". God's greatest gift to us as humans, he argued, was the capacity to reason for ourselves. It was not just our right but our duty to use that gift. Traditional Catholic scholarship, he suggested, had seen its role as essentially a passive one of interpreting and implementing the will of God. Scholars had seen that will represented in the doctrinal judgements handed down over generations within the Church, which had come to have the force of legal precedent in Catholic thought.

Above: Convened in 1215, the Fourth Lateran Council, shown in this 9th-century engraving, introduced far-reaching reforms in the running of the Church.

Instead, Pico Della Mirandola claimed, people should be thinking for themselves and bypassing tradition to consult the ancient sources. In this view, he was reflecting the contemporary attitudes of the artists and writers of the wider Renaissance (rebirth), which was taking place in Italy at the time.

Inspired by the artwork of classical Greece and Rome, men such as Leonardo da Vinci saw the human form as the highest achievement of God's Creation. Scientists, too, were finding inspiration in the writings of the Greeks and Romans, gaining the confidence to set aside the perceived assumptions of centuries and to try out new theories and experiment with new ideas.

COUNCIL OF TRENT

Humanism, as then understood, did not dispute the greatness of God – still less his existence – but it did raise radical questions as to how he should be served. Church leaders were unsettled – not surprisingly, since humanist thinking did tempt some scholars toward the new Protestant theologies then emerging. However, in the works of writers such as St Thomas More and Erasmus, humanism offered a reinvigoration of a Catholic tradition, which had, to some extent, become fossilized over the passing years.

Below: Figures representing the Seven Liberal Arts – Arithmetic, Music, Geometry, Astronomy, Logic, Rhetoric and Grammar – are shown in a 1503 publication on humanism from Gregor Reisch, Margarita Philosophica Nova.

THE CHURCH IN TRANSITION

That the Church was capable of flexibility was to be demonstrated at the Council of Trent. Opening in 1545, when Europe was at the height of the Reformation, its sessions continued for several years until 1563. Its main conclusions were uncompromising, with the Church rejecting the theological heresies proposed by the Protestant rebels. At the same time, it tacitly acknowledged the justice of many of the criticisms of its own institution. It was these criticisms that caused the Church to institute root-and-branch reform. Measures were introduced to combat corruption, including regulation of the issuing of indulgences to prevent their sale. Diocesan seminaries were created to provide better training for priests, and disciplinary structures were formed to handle wrongdoers.

A CHRISTIAN JOKER

Desiderius Erasmus ("Erasmus of Rotterdam") was one of the most serious thinkers of the Renaissance, but it was with a joke that he caught the mood of an amazing time. His treatise, *Praise of Folly* (1511), was a masterly exercise in irony; among the absurdities it satirized were those of the Church. Its scholars' slavish reverence for tradition, its superstitions and its corruption: all these are ridiculed in its pages. However, this only makes the more moving the book's final reaffirmation of a Catholic faith whose truth transcends the earthly limitations of the Church.

Above: Erasmus of Rotterdam, painted in 1523 by Hans Holbein the Younger, was a brilliant scholar and thinker. He published many works and led the humanist movement within the Church.

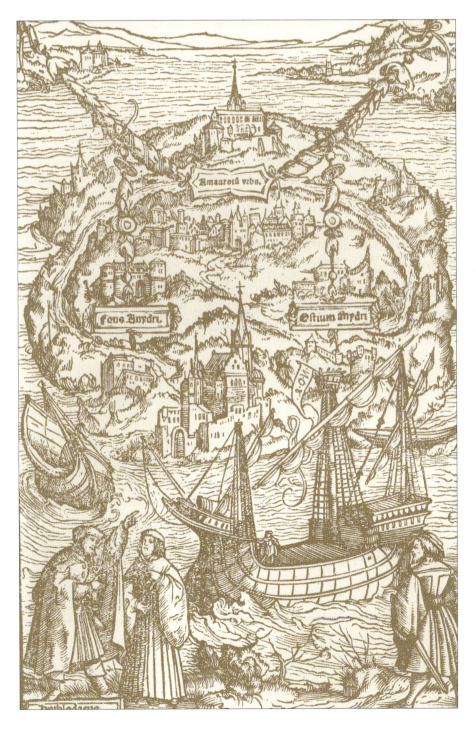

Left: The Island of Utopia, as imagined by the great English humanist St Thomas More, was illustrated by Ambrosius Holbein and published in 1518 in the book of the same title.

POWERFUL POPES

THE RENAISSANCE SAW THE PAPACY AT ITS HEIGHT AS A POLITICAL FORCE – AND ITS MORAL REPUTATION AT ITS LOWEST EBB, RESPONSIBLE FOR SOME DISREPUTABLE CHAPTERS IN THE CHURCH'S HISTORY.

Above: Pope Sixtus IV appoints a new prefect to preside over his library, another monument to the majesty of his reign, in Melozzo da Forlì's painting (1477).

Today the idea of a "Renaissance Pope" suggests magnificence and political power. However, it also implies corruption on a huge scale. This is a stereotype, of course, but one that many pontiffs of the 15th and 16th centuries appear to have lived up to. To expect otherwise would perhaps have been unrealistic. The Church was the greatest institution of the day, and its leader commanded untold wealth and incalculable influence. At the same time it was very much a human institution. The meek and innocent might be blessed in heaven, but here on earth they were pushed aside by the ambitious, the unscrupulous and the ruthless.

A FAMILY BUSINESS

Among the Church's hierarchy, favours were exchanged, inducements were offered and friends and relations were taken care of. It was no surprise when the nephew of Pope Eugene IV followed him on to St Peter's throne as Pope Paul II in 1464.

Pope Sixtus IV followed in 1471. He made no fewer than six of his nephews cardinals during his papacy, on top of which he gave them benefices that brought in colossal wealth. (The Church had a vast income from a range of sources, including rents, donations, bequests and burial fees, all of which were a temptation to the corrupt.) Sixtus IV also married his nieces into Italy's leading aristocratic houses, building up a powerful network of familial connections, which he was ruthless in defending. He is believed to have been complicit in a plot carried out in 1478 in which two Medici brothers were attacked with daggers while attending Mass in the cathedral in Florence. One of them, Giuliano de' Medici, died of his wounds.

A strong sense of "family" was creeping in – of dynastic continuity and of bitter feuding – alien as this should have been to a Church with a celibate clergy. Some popes were far from chaste. Pope Alexander VI (1492–1503) fathered nine children by an unknown number of different women. His most notorious son, Cesare Borgia, was a murderous wheeler-dealer; he became a cardinal before leaving the clergy to make an advantageous marriage.

PAPACY AND PATRONAGE

However far they may have fallen short of the principles they were supposed to serve, the Renaissance popes undoubtedly left us in their debt as the patrons of some of the most impressive Western art. It may have been extravagance, driven too much by human vanity, but their patronage had an impact on the whole history of Western culture.

Pope Sixtus IV spent a fortune beautifying the centre of Rome, which involved widening streets and constructing new churches and other buildings. His bridge, the Ponte Sisto, still spans the River Tiber.

Pope Julius II was also a great patron of the arts. It was this pope who asked Donato Bramante to design a replacement for the old

Below: Building the new St Peter's took many years. Antoine Lafréry's engraving (1575) shows a papal blessing being given beneath its uncompleted dome.

POWERFUL POPES

POPE IMPRISONED

In modern times, we have tended to think of the papacy as "above" politics, in part protected by their holy status. However, given the political power they wielded, the popes of the Renaissance could hardly claim to be simply men of God. Clement VII paid the price for this: though a member of the Medici family, ironically, he was innocent and unworldly by the standards of the times. His attempts to steer a safe diplomatic course between the great powers ruling Europe led to a dispute between him and Charles V, King of Spain and Emperor of Germany. In 1527, Charles' forces invaded Italy and sacked Rome. Pope Clement was held prisoner at Castel Sant' Angelo, from which he escaped.

Above: The massive walls surrounding Rome offered the city some protection, but it lacked defensive troops, as shown in The Sack of Rome, *a 1527 painting by Johannes Lingelbach.*

St Peter's Basilica, and work on the greatest church built for Christendom began only two years into his papacy, in 1505. (That the astronomical costs were to be met by the greatest granting of indulgences yet seen was a fact that would not be lost on the Church's critics.) Julius was also responsible for commissioning Michelangelo to paint the ceiling of the Sistine Chapel.

The Medici family were already famous for their artistic patronage when the son of Lorenzo (the Magnificent) de' Medici became Pope Leo X in 1513. "God has given us the papacy," Leo X is said to have commented to a friend. "Now let us enjoy it." Fortunately for posterity, his greatest indulgence was art, including history-making works by the Italian artists Michelangelo and Raphael. He encouraged music, too, and writers such as Erasmus.

Right: Peter Paul Ruben's c.1616 portrait of Pope Leo X captures the power and authority of the man.

85

THE POPE AND THE PAINTER

THE CEILING OF THE SISTINE CHAPEL IS UNIVERSALLY ACCLAIMED AS A MASTERPIECE. IT HAS ALSO BECOME THE ARCHETYPE FOR THE DIFFICULT RELATIONSHIP BETWEEN THE ARTIST AND HIS PATRON.

If its ceiling had never been painted by Michelangelo, art lovers would still flock to see the Sistine Chapel for its frescoes by other great artists, which include Raphael, Botticelli, Perugino and Ghirlandaio. (The chapel is in the Apostolic Palace in the Vatican City, the official residence of the pope.) Some splendid tapestries, designed by Raphael, formed part of the plunder during Charles V's sack of Rome in 1527, but they were later restored and replaced. Although named after Pope Sixtus IV, who had built the structure, the chapel really found its role under Pope Julius II, who made it a magnificent showcase for the creativity of Renaissance art.

MICHELANGELO'S TASK

Today too many tourists look past the myriad wonders that line the walls, with eyes only for the ceiling, 20m (65ft) above. Admittedly, it is an astonishing sight: the whole sweep of human existence, from Creation to Last Judgement, in crowded scenes that seem to boil over in their energy. Yet if the artist had his own way, this masterpiece would not have existed.

Above: The Deluge and the Drunkenness of Noah *illustrates transgression and punishment, important themes for the ceiling as a whole.*

Born outside Arezzo in Tuscany in 1475, Michelangelo had never doubted his artistic genius, but he saw himself as a sculptor first and foremost. When, in 1505, Julius II asked him to design his tomb, it seemed to Michelangelo to be the dream commission. He dedicated himself to the creation of his life's masterpiece. However, he was not to be left to his work for long. To his growing annoyance, Julius enlisted his help for various odd artistic jobs – and began to talk to him about a commission for painting frescoes on the ceiling of the Sistine Chapel.

A CONTEMPORARY REPORT

Giorgio Vasari, gossipy chronicler of the ins and outs of the Italian Renaissance art scene, says that this idea was not Julius' own. Raphael and Bramante talked him into it

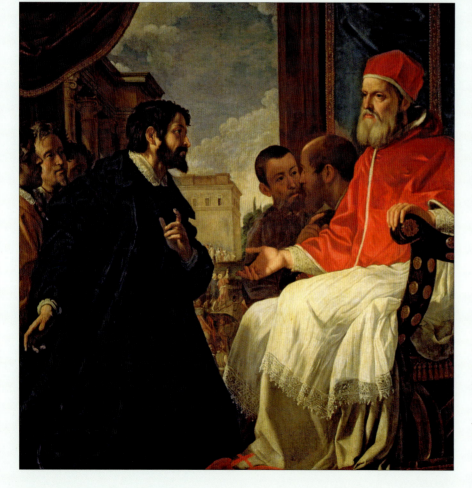

Left: Michelangelo and Julius II had a fractious – but finally fruitful – working relationship. The artist and patron are shown together in this 16th-century painting by Anastasio Fontebuoni.

mischievously, he maintained. The former was the leading painter of the time, the latter, the star architect – and both were feeling threatened by Michelangelo's prodigious talents. The pope's preference for sculpture was well known to his contemporaries, and Michelangelo's supremacy in that arena was undisputed. By getting the artist weighed down in what appeared an impossibly ambitious task for such a comparatively inexperienced and reluctant painter, his rivals saw an opportunity to level the playing field. There was even the chance that Michelangelo would blunder the job so severely that his artistic credibility would become fatally compromised.

In truth, this version of events is unlikely, but Vasari was possibly briefed by Michelangelo himself, and his account may well reflect the workings of the artist's extravagantly suspicious mind.

A GRUDGING LABOUR

Suffice it to say that Michelangelo tried every means to avoid taking on the project. In the end, when it became clear that he was not going to be able to do so, he decided to get it over and done with as quickly as he could. It took him four years in all, which is an astonishingly short time considering the enormous scale of the work – and the fact that Michelangelo seems to have worked largely alone, apart from an assistant who mixed his colours. Even so, the pope apparently asked him constantly about his progress. *The Agony and the Ecstasy* was the name given to the famous film about this episode in the artist's life – *The Irritability and the Impatience* might have been a more accurate title.

However, if these frescoes were not a labour of love, this hardly shows in a spectacular work that takes the continuity of Christian faith and worship as its theme. Seen in the artist's all-encompassing view, the

Above: An uncompromising Christ makes his appearance as Judge of the World: *the climactic, culminating scene of the Sistine Chapel ceiling.*

Old Testament is the prefiguring of Christ's New Covenant; Christ and his Church the fulfilment of what the prophets promised. However, Michelangelo is undoubtedly a man of the Renaissance in the way he places humanity at the centre of God's Creation and in his depiction of the beauty of the human form as the ultimate expression of God's greatness. These values are summed up in the outstretched hands in *The Creation of Adam*, where we see the moment in which God transmits life to man.

A RICH LEGACY

Michelangelo never did get the opportunity to finish Julius' tomb – a mausoleum was built when the pope died in 1513, but it was placed in the Church of San Pietro in Vincoli, rather than St Peter's Basilica. Little of it is Michelangelo's work – although the one piece that is, an awe-inspiring Moses, confirms that this would indeed have been a special work. It is hard, though, to feel that humanity has been the loser, as the Sistine Chapel ceiling is one of the most famous and most visited artworks in the world.

Below: The ceiling's most celebrated scene is The Creation of Adam, *where God reaches out to Adam, giving him life.*

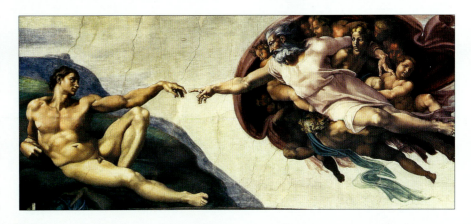

RENAISSANCE AND REFORMATION

NEW HORIZONS

WITH OVERSEAS EXPLORATIONS AND SCIENTIFIC DISCOVERIES BEING MADE IN SUCH QUICK SUCCESSION, RENAISSANCE EUROPE WAS AN EXCITING – BUT ALSO CONFUSING – PLACE TO BE.

As the ideological certainties of the preceeding centuries were dissolving, the Church was facing an uphill struggle to maintain its old intellectual authority. The medieval period was the "Age of Faith", when men and women never questioned their duty of subservience in God's order; but then neither did they doubt their centrality in his cosmos. Paradoxically, even as Renaissance humanism proclaimed the pre-eminence of humanity, that centrality was coming under threat.

As the voyages of the great navigators pushed back the boundaries of the world known to the Europeans, astronomers explored an expanding universe – which might not actually be revolving around the earth as had been thought.

THE AGE OF DISCOVERY

Europeans were aware that their continent did not encompass the entirety of the world: Africa lay just beyond the Mediterranean, after all. Spices and other luxuries were brought along the Silk Route from the East: moreover, Marco Polo had brought back tidings from China in the late 13th century. However, few Europeans had followed him. The Crusades had left the Middle East a hostile environment, and the trade that continued in this region was conducted mostly by middlemen.

The soaring costs of luxuries imported overland helped motivate the search for a sea route, which receieved a boost when Prince Henry the Navigator of Portugal established a naval academy c.1450. Portuguese navigators made great progress with

Above: Despite hurricanes and mutiny, the Portuguese navigator Vasco da Gama was the first European to reach Asia by going around Africa's Cape of Good Hope in 1497/8.

Bartolomeu Diaz finding his way down the coast of Africa to the Cape of Good Hope in 1487, while Vasco da Gama pushed on to India a decade later.

Christopher Columbus, sailing for Spain's "Catholic Monarchs", had reached the Americas, making landfall on 12 October 1492. However, he remained convinced until he died that he had found the westerly route to East Asia. The Europeans came to realize that he had instead stumbled on a "New World" – and the Old World would never be the same.

"Who is my neighbour?" Jesus had been asked by the lawyer in Luke 10:29. That question was looking harder to answer now. Difficult as it had always been to live up to Christ's injunction to love one's neighbour as oneself, now it was a conceptual challenge, too. As Gomes Eanes de Zurara, the Portuguese chronicler, put it, how could those naked "savages", of whom navigators were now bringing home reports, really be "of the generation of Adam"? Yet, shaped as they were, how could they

Below: Columbus' discoveries opened up a New World – and its peoples – to the Europeans, such as these Native Americans from Virginia, in this late 16th-century engraving by Theodore de Bry.

Above: Christopher Columbus prepares to set out from the port of Palos, Spain, in August 1492, in this 19th-century fresco by Antonio Cabral y Aguado Bejarano.

not be? Were these strangers to be our neighbours? The European idea of the world was being challenged.

REVOLUTIONS
Things got worse. In 1543, Nicolaus Copernicus died. Only then was his great work *De revolutionibus orbium coelestium* (On the Revolution of the Heavenly Spheres) published. Copernicus, a priest himself and one of a family of priests and nuns, had received encouragement in his astronomical researches from fellow churchmen. However, he had been nervous about releasing his conclusions and no wonder: the Church had always followed the view of Aristotle and Ptolemy that the Sun and planets revolved around a stationary Earth. Copernicus believed the Earth and planets went around the Sun in what is called a heliocentric system.

The Church has since accepted this view, but at the time there were fears that it overturned scriptural accounts of the Creation and the cosmos – or that, if it did not, it would appear to do so. When, later in the century, another priest showed support for the Copernican theory, he was tried by the Roman Inquisition. Giordano Bruno faced a range of charges, from blasphemy to heresy: he was burnt at the stake in 1600.

Below: Copernicus revealed that the true "harmony of the spheres" was produced by planets' concentric orbit around the Sun, shown in an illustration from Andreas Cellarius' Scenographia, *c.1660.*

GALILEO'S HERESY

In the early 17th century, another Catholic astronomer, Galileo Galilei, found his own observations lending fresh support to the Copernican case. For this backing he was tried by the Church for heresy in 1633 and was forced to recant his claims. In fairness, Galileo had found discreet support among leading clergy. Several members of the Church hierarchy had acknowledged their support for both the strength of Galileo's observational evidence and the force of his argument that Old Testament cosmology should be regarded more as poetry than as science. Cardinal Caesar Baronius spoke up for Galileo's ideas, joking that "The Bible teaches the way to go to heaven, not the way the heavens go." Officially, though, the Catholic Church had condemned such views.

Above: Galileo, shown in a 17th-century painting by the Flemish Justus Sustermans, fell foul of the Roman Inquisition with his public espousal of Copernican astronomy.

THE REFORMATION

IN THE EARLY 16TH CENTURY, MANY BELIEVERS TOOK THEIR STAND WITH THE REFORMER MARTIN LUTHER. IN ENGLAND, KING HENRY VIII PROCLAIMED HIMSELF HEAD OF THE CHURCH OF ENGLAND.

The great indulgence sale in which Pope Julius II set out to fund the rebuilding of St Peter's Basilica in 1505 caused outrage among many people across Europe. Indulgences had been around for centuries, of course, and, so too, had abuses of the system, which was widely satirized throughout the Middle Ages. It would be hard to claim that Julius' behaviour was much worse than anything that had occurred beforehand, yet it came after centuries of supposed reform – and at a time when the Church's overall authority was being questioned. In this climate, cleaning up such abuses within the Church's hierarchy was not going to be enough for the dissenters.

AUTHORITY IN QUESTION

In 1517, Martin Luther, priest and university professor, nailed his "95 Theses" to the door of the cathedral in Wittenberg, Germany, as a protest against the sale of indulgences. His arguments addressed the theology that allowed such indulgences to be awarded. The Church soon found itself under sustained attack from several sides. The scientific and intellectual tumults of the age had not left the Church unscathed. Moreover, the advent of the printing press had for the first time created what might be described as a reading public – before the press, few books were available, and they could often be read only by the clerical elite, educated in Latin.

Above: The pope acts as a moneychanger in the sale of indulgences and religious dispensations, as shown in this 1521 German woodcut by Lucas Cranach.

There was a growing sense that men and women might want to judge things for themselves. So Luther found a receptive ear when, questioning whether or not the Church hierarchy should even exist, he argued that every Christian believer should be his or her own priest. To further that end, he took an interest in making the Scriptures more accessible to the common people. The Church released a bull in 1520, proclaiming Luther's teachings as heretical, and only a few months later he was ex-communicated by the Church.

In 1522, Luther published his German translation of the New Testament, and William Tyndale's English Bible came out in 1525. The Church condemned both of these works: its fear was that the uneducated would be led astray without the interpretative assistance of their priests. However, to an increasing number of the educated middle class now emerging, especially in northern Europe, such thinking simply reeked of condescension.

Below: Martin Luther's famous protest is seen as the start of Protestantism. Ferdinand Pauwels' 19th-century painting shows the reformer nailing his "95 Theses" to the cathedral door.

KING HENRY VIII BREAKS AWAY

British coins still carry the abbreviation "F.D." after the name of the monarch: it means *Fidei Defensor*, or "Defender of the Faith". Ironically, this title was awarded by Pope Leo X to England's King Henry VIII in gratitude for his pamphlet, "A Defence of the Seven Sacraments" (1521), an eloquent response to Luther's criticisms. However, the failure of Henry's queen, Catherine of Aragon, to bear him a male heir led to a conflict between the king and Rome. Henry requested the annulment of their marriage, so he could wed Anne Boleyn, but it was rejected by Pope Clement VII. The king responded in 1532 by announcing that the monarch of England would also be head of the Church of England. He also confiscated the wealth in England's Catholic churches.

Right: King Henry VIII puts Pope Clement VII in his place in an approving English satirical engraving of the 16th century.

A SPLIT FROM THE CHURCH

These Christians became known as "Protestants", which is from the Latin word *protestari*, or "to protest". Another meaning for *protestari* is "to affirm" or "to avow", which can also be seen as appropriate for a group whose members sought to seek guidance from the Scriptures, not from the Church's teachings. They believed that the individual person should have his or her own relationship with God. Catholicism never had the right to claim proprietorship over the "keys of heaven". What mattered was the divine Word, as revealed in the Scriptures, which it was the duty of every man and woman to read.

It could be argued that they took more moral responsibility for themselves, and there was no prospect of buying indulgences, or of pattering mechanically through a set of prayers. However, there was a tendency for a self-selecting community to feel that simply by proclaiming their belief they showed themselves to be "saved" and that there could be justification by faith instead of by works.

CALVINISM

In Geneva, John Calvin drew a distinction between the "Elect", marked out for salvation, and the rest, "pre-destined" for damnation by God himself even before they were created. That Calvin rejected Rome and all its works was just the start of his offence, as far as the Catholic hierarchy was concerned. His doctrines affronted their sense of Christian mercy and forgiveness. The way in which Calvin and his followers accepted the consignment of so many to eternal suffering seemed not just ungodly to them but inhuman.

Catholics believed that God, though indeed all-knowing, did not actually pre-ordain the sins of the souls he created, compromising their free will. This meant that the door to salvation would always be left open.

Below: The Calvinist chapel contrasted starkly with the ornate Catholic churches of old. Such a chapel is shown in this c.1565 painting by Jean Perrissin.

THE COUNTER-REFORMATION

IF THE REFORMATION THREW DOWN A CHALLENGE TO CATHOLICISM, IT WAS ONE TO WHICH THE CHURCH WAS ABLE TO RESPOND. AN URGENT EXAMINATION OF CONSCIENCE RESULTED IN FAR-REACHING CHANGES.

While the leaders of the Church were debating its institutional reform at the Council of Trent, a book was causing a stir in Italy. The story of *The Miraculous Life and Doctrine of St Catherine of Genoa* seemed somehow to speak to Catholicism in its crisis. It was hard to see why this should be so. Catherine had died half a century before, and she had barely registered on the consciousness of the Church in her own lifetime. Although nobly born, she had lost any status she had once enjoyed in a loveless, violent marriage; she had never taken orders as a nun. However, she had given her life to God, tending the sick and helping the poor. She had bravely faced the agonies of her last illness.

While Catherine's biography was being read in many hundreds of European homes, a very different life was unfolding far away in a Spanish convent. There, Teresa of Ávila was experiencing visions of Christ that seemed to take possession of her whole being, body and soul. She described these visions in an autobiography in the 1560s.

PIETY AND PASSION

The experiences of Catherine and Teresa were their own, but they can still be seen as the products of their time. The Church had been ready for two such figures. Both were comparative outsiders and women, and were remarkable not for their services to the Church establishment but for the intensity – the drama, even – of their spiritual lives. Although Catherine's path to God had been arduous and difficult, it was one that many ordinary Catholics could imagine themselves following. Moreover, the passion shown in Teresa's faith proved to be deeply moving to the many people who had been finding themselves increasingly unmoved by a religious life that had become routine.

The Catholics who embraced these women might never have dreamt of turning to Protestantism – any more than Catherine or Teresa would have done – but they were responding to some of the same underlying discontents. Luther's call to Christians was based on rejecting a Catholicism of empty forms for

Above: Convened in 1545, the Council of Trent instituted wide-ranging reforms within the Church. The members of the council are depicted in this 18th-century copy of a contemporary painting.

Left: St Teresa of Ávila came to represent a new kind of spirituality – impassioned and intense – as shown in the Ecstasy of St Teresa, *sculpted by Gian Lorenzo Bernini in 1645–52.*

a deep and authentic spirituality, which was founded in the faith of the individual.

THE JESUITS

Among St Teresa's inspirations had been the Spiritual Exercises, written in the 1520s by Ignatius Loyola. This Spanish thinker is now famous as the founder of a great religious order, the Society of Jesus *(see The Society of Jesus, opposite page)*, but he always saw faith as being rooted in the individual. His Spiritual Exercises could be seen as a sort of self-help course in Christian devotion, a regime of daily meditations and guided prayer. However, for Loyola, faith had to exist within the framework of the Church: his Exercises had to be followed under the guidance of a spiritual director.

The interconnection between the Church and its followers was perhaps the crucial insight that fuelled the Counter-Reformation. Personal faith, for all its passion, was ultimately

THE COUNTER-REFORMATION

Above: Pope Urban VIII takes part in celebrations marking the Jesuits' centenary, shown in this c.1640 painting by Andrea Sacchi, Filippo Gagliardi and Jan Miel.

directionless; at the same time, a large institution could have no soul without developing a fruitful relationship with the individual. What was called for, and what Loyola's Jesuits were able to provide, was a Catholicism in which these two components went together hand in hand.

The same impulse can be seen in the life and work of St Francis of Sales who, in the early 17th century, decided to tackle the Reformation head on. As Bishop of Geneva, St Francis had his seat in the very headquarters of Calvinism, but he made it his mission to convert Protestants back to the Catholic Church.

THE SOCIETY OF JESUS

Ignatius Loyola had been born into a noble family in the Basque country and grew up with an exaggerated sense of what that meant. Like the Spanish writer Cervantes' comic hero Don Quixote, he had been addicted to the chivalric romances of the Middle Ages, with their stirring stories of gallantry. On growing up, Loyola enlisted in the army, resolved to win renown in battle, but he found soldiering had changed over the centuries. Instead of exchanging courtesies with fellow aristocrats whom he fought with sword and lance, he lost a leg to a cannonball at the siege of Pamplona. However, even then, Loyola was not disillusioned: recuperating in hospital, he asked for romances to read. Since none were available, he had to make do with reading about the lives of the saints. They inspired him to fight spiritually for Christ instead – but, a true romantic to the last, Loyola conceived of his Society of Jesus, known as the Jesuits, as a chivalric company.

Above: Ignatius Loyola thought of himself as a knight in the cause of Christ. This 1556 portrait of him is by Jacopino del Conte.

ECSTATIC ART

THE COUNTER-REFORMATION GAVE RISE TO A NEW – AND INTENSELY EMOTIONAL – AESTHETIC. ARTISTS AND ARCHITECTS LOOKED FOR WAYS TO DRAMATIZE THE PASSION AND FERVOUR OF RELIGIOUS FAITH.

Art had been one of the issues at the heart of the Reformation controversy. Protestants tended to regard the Church's display of wealth with suspicion. While secular art was one of the vanities that the Christian should be forsaking, "religious art" was really a contradiction in terms. What mattered was the Word of God: sacred pictures and statues were seen as "graven images" that had been prohibited by the Bible, evidence of a heathen adoration of Our Lady and the saints. The Church's collection of artistic treasures was considered one of the trappings of the "Whore of Babylon", their worldly beauties temptations to the struggling soul.

So strongly did Protestants feel about this that some extremists went on sprees of iconoclasm (literally, "breaking images"), smashing statues and stained-glass windows and whitewashing over frescoes. Many English churches still bear the scars – the disfigured statues and blank replacement glass of Ely Cathedral's Lady Chapel are just one example.

Above: Flamboyant expressiveness was key to the Counter-Reformation aesthetic, as seen in this 17th-century painting, The Virgin Appearing to St Peter Damian, *attributed to Pietro da Cortona.*

ON THE OFFENSIVE
The Catholic Church responded by redoubling its efforts and launched what amounted to a major artistic offensive. At the same time, religious art took on an altogether different emphasis. Where once the architect had been content to suggest the grandeur of God and the splendour of his Church, the feelings involved in religious faith were now incorporated into the designs. While the artist had previously been content to commemorate worthy piety and honest service, the new spirituality was passionate and intense. Agony, ecstasy, tragedy, triumph: all of these dramatic human sensations were harnessed by artists, designed to both arrest the attention and engage the emotions.

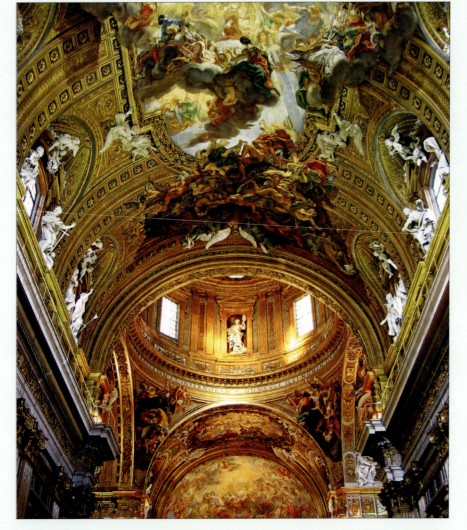

Left: Bernini's assistant, Giovanni Battista Gaulli, nicknamed "Baciccia", painted the Il Gesù ceiling, with much of his master's flair, in 1672–85. His work can be seen continuing past the boundaries normally created by barrel vaulting.

The element of surprise was exploited: artists and architects of this period showed an unabashed instinct for showmanship. Rome's Church of the Gesù is a case in point. Its dazzling white façade is elegant in its symmetries, but the overall effect is simple, even chaste. This only heightens the shock (no other word would be appropriate) when the visitor pushes through the doors to be assaulted by the ravishing beauty – and riotous exuberance – that can be found within.

There are frescoes, columns, statues, pilasters and so much ornamentation in marble and gilt that the scene seems to dissolve into a single disorientating vision, with every line and plane being thrown into doubt. The previously used boundaries disappear, with artwork spilling spectacularly across the demarcations made by the barrel vaulting in the ceiling overhead. Christ and his angels appear to waft heavenward through the ceiling itself.

The overall effect is staggering. Whereas the statues and stained glass of the Gothic churches had been visual "books" for instructing the unlettered, this interior was intended to take the senses – and hence the soul – by storm.

HIGH DRAMA

Built toward the end of the 16th century, the Church of the Gesù is the spiritual headquarters of the Society of Jesus, whose founder St Ignatius has his tomb in a side chapel. Beside the altar there is an allegorical sculpture that stands almost 3m (10ft) in height, representing *Religion Overthrowing Heresy and Hatred*. This is the work of Pierre Le Gros the Younger, a French sculptor based in Rome. With the cross of Christianity in one hand and thunderbolts of heavenly anger in the other, Lady Religion stands slightly off balance as she kicks out at Heresy, represented as an ugly old man.

Above: What might have been a stagey and schematic scene becomes a powerful human drama in the c.1696 statue Religion Overthrowing Heresy and Hatred *by Pierre Le Gros the Younger.*

Sent sprawling, he appears to be falling over the edge of the sculpture's pedestal: the rules of gravity do not seem to apply. Hatred, a withered old woman, flinches away in fear before Religion's righteous anger. At bottom left, a little angel busily tears up books by the Protestant writers Ulrich Zwingli and Martin Luther.

TOO SENSATIONALIST?

Le Gros' impressive creation is all but overwhelming in its impact. The technical accomplishment involved is also awe-inspiring. It is hard to believe that so obviously schematic a work could be so powerful or that such dynamism could be captured in a lump of cold stone. Yet the miraculous transformation of marble to moving drapery, warm flesh and breathing life seen in this statue was achieved even more astonishingly in Gian Lorenzo Bernini's famous *Ecstasy of St Teresa* (1645–52), another great sculpture of the period.

Inevitably, there have been some criticisms that such sculptures are shallow and sensationalist, being no more than exhibitionistic tours de force by artistic virtuosos. However, these objections miss the real point of the works. They were created by an avowedly evangelizing aesthetic that used sheer emotional force to compel an intensely personal engagement between God and the followers of the faith.

Below: Talented Renaissance sculptors could coax strong emotion out of cold stone. The 1674 Beatified Lodovica Albertoni, *by Gian Lorenzo Bernini, is a stunning example of the artist's work.*

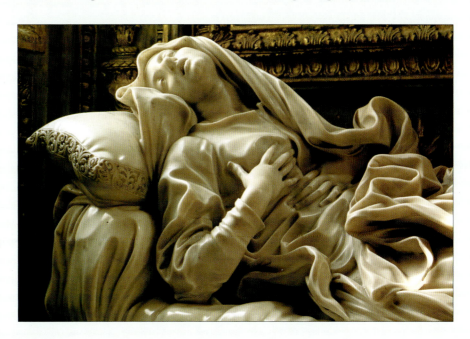

TEMPORAL AUTHORITY

Although the Catholic Church was growing in power and majesty at its centre in Italy, elsewhere in Europe anarchy and war made it harder for the Church to gain primacy.

The Church was a powerful force in Rome partly due to two donations. Although it was exposed as a forgery in the 15th century, for several centuries it was thought that the Donation of Constantine had given temporal authority over Rome and its possessions to the papacy. This misconception enabled the Catholic Church to wield an impressive political authority in Rome.

A different donation, made by the Merovingian king Pepin I, was genuine. He reigned over most of France and also over the western part of Germany and northern Italy. In 754, he had given the Church temporal authority over the Duchy of Rome and adjacent regions. Under the Holy Roman Empire, which was established by Pepin's son Charlemagne, these privileges had been upheld and even increased. By the time of Pope Innocent III in the 13th century, the Papal States embraced the whole of central Italy and much of the north-east.

These possessions brought the papacy not just great wealth but also considerable political power: great Renaissance popes such as Alexander VI and Julius II stood on an equal diplomatic footing with Europe's greatest monarchs. However, this was not always such a comfortable place to be, as Clement VII was to discover in 1527, when he was imprisoned during the sacking of Rome. Any idea that the Church was somehow spiritually removed, above politics and the grubby machinations of international diplomacy, could not credibly be maintained when the pope was practically a king.

Above: Posing with a miniature Aachen Cathedral in an 1825 painting by J.P. Scheuren, Emperor Charlemagne did much to build the bond between sacred and secular power in Europe.

CONFLICTS OF INTEREST

Tensions between these secular and religious roles were inevitable. In the early 17th century, for instance, the papacy found itself in dispute with Venice. The city-state had remained Catholic in its allegiances; but, because its economy was based on trade, it was important it kept open its commerce with the Protestant states of central Europe. Also, as a republic, it did not see why it had to be in the control of an external authority.

In 1606, Pope Paul V placed the city under an "interdict", which excommunicated all its people, denying them the sacraments. This inflicting of a spiritual punishment for what amounted to a rejection of temporal authority was extremely unpopular, not just in Venice but elsewhere, too. While the modern opposition of Church and State had

Below: Fought in 1634, the Second Battle of Nördlingen was one of many such encounters in the Thirty Years' War. The battle is depicted in a mid-17th-century painting by Pieter Meulener.

yet to be formulated explicitly, it is clear that, at some level, the pope was seen to be abusing his power.

THE THIRTY YEARS' WAR

Such goings on in southern Europe soon became parochial when the centre of economic power shifed to the north. Since Charlemagne had founded the Holy Roman Empire, Germany and Italy had been associated, but Germany was now emerging as the greater force. However, as far as the Church was concerned, it was a country that could no longer be relied on, because many of its rulers had embraced the Lutheran cause. The Peace of Augsburg in 1555 had only delayed the showdown struggle between the Catholic and Protestant principalities of what had been the Holy Roman Empire. By the time Pope Gregory XV was enthroned in 1621, war was under way in Germany. Emboldened by the spirit of the Counter-Reformation, the Catholic princes, supported by the Church, had seen their chance to sweep away the Protestant presence in their midst. However, power politics is never so simple: individual rulers pursued their own agendas, and peripheral states were drawn into a rapidly escalating conflict.

The war continued for 30 years, turning the heart of Europe into an inferno. Civilians bore the brunt as mercenary armies embarked on sprees of rape and pillage. One-fifth or more of Germany's people were killed, some slaughtered in the carnage, others caught up in the famines and plagues precipitated by the war and the large-scale population movements it brought with it.

A HOLLOW TRIUMPH

The Catholic powers won, having made significant territorial gains, especially in France. Humanity had, of course, been the loser. Paradoxically, so too had the Church. Under the terms of the Treaty of Westphalia (1648), the principle of *cuius regio, eius religio*, or "whose region, his religion", was set in stone. Protestantism became embedded in several states and even Calvinism was protected.

The Catholic rulers, meanwhile, were ceasing to side automatically with Rome. They had their own strategic aims: France, for instance, had seen the war less as a religious crusade than as a way of containing the expansion of (Catholic) Spain. To thwart the Habsburgs, it had chosen to form an alliance with Protestant Sweden, ignoring the outrage of the pope. This, it seemed, was the shape of things to come: Catholic kings would support their Church when it suited them – and only then.

Above: Urban VIII was pope through the most difficult period of the Thirty Years' War. A sculpture of the pope by Gian Lorenzo Bernini sits by his tomb in St Peter's Basilica, Rome.

Below: Signed at Münster on 24 October 1648, the Treaty of Westphalia finally brought the hostilities of the Thirty Years' War to a close.

POLITICAL RAMIFICATIONS

THE REFORMATION REPRESENTED A SEISMIC SHOCK FOR THE CATHOLIC CHURCH, BUT ITS REPERCUSSIONS CERTAINLY DID NOT STOP THERE. ITS POLITICAL CONSEQUENCES WERE ALSO PROFOUND.

There was no separating the religious sphere from the political world in Renaissance Europe. The stability of the social order rested on the unquestioning respect for authority that the Catholic Church had previously enshrined. With division between the European states, the Church was losing ground.

SECULAR REACTION
Such a blow to the Church's standing compromised the security of the state as far as the Spanish establishment saw it. The Crown in Spain linked its authority explicitly with that of the Church: to be a Protestant was not just to be ungodly but also to be un-Spanish. Given the extent of the country's empire in the Americas and the Pacific, the sponsorship of Spain was not to be dismissed lightly. Meanwhile, demands from French Protestants, known as Huguenots, for religious toleration were met with blunt refusal. In 1572, with an explosion of ferocity, thousands were murdered in the St Bartholomew's Day Massacre. While Henri IV had allowed the Protestants to practise their faith in peace, announcing the Edict of Nantes in 1598, that measure was rescinded by Louis XIV in 1685. The Huguenots saw their property confiscated and their churches closed down; more than 200,000 left the country to live in exile.

Northern Europe, which was the Reformation's heartland, was also a place of political division. In the Netherlands, which was a Spanish territory at the time, the people embraced Protestantism partly in a spirit of nationalist resistance.

REACHING A COMPROMISE
Germany, Luther's homeland, was in theory a single entity under the Holy Roman Empire, but it was actually a patchwork of smaller states. Protestantism had been embraced with genuine enthusiasm in many of these areas. Several local rulers aligned themselves with the new religion to build up their own political power. A compromise was reached in 1555, when the Peace of Augsburg originally agreed the principle *cuius regio, eius religio* ("whose region, his religion"). Where a ruler was Catholic, in other words, Catholicism should hold sway; but where the king was a Lutheran, that religion would prevail in his country.

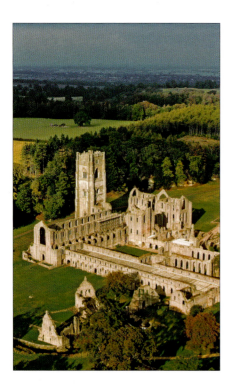

Below: Half a millennium's Catholic culture came to an end with the Dissolution of the Monasteries. These ruins are all that is left of Fountains Abbey in Yorkshire, England.

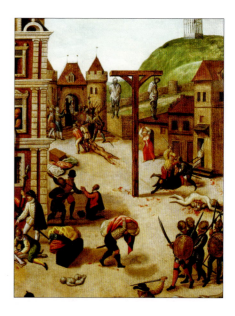

Above: Huguenots are being killed in the St Bartholomew's Day Massacre in this 19th-century painting by François Dubois.

Instead of a recipe for tolerance it was one for systematic persecution, as rulers cleansed their countries along sectarian lines. Catholic kings were by no means innocent, but in the Protestant states of Germany and in Switzerland, home of Calvinism, priests were burnt at the stake and Catholicism was suppressed.

DISSOLVED IN ENGLAND
The English Reformation had been opportunistic in its origins. King Henry VIII had not disagreed doctrinally with the Church; his conflict was based on his marriage status. Yet Catholicism quickly became identified as a threat to the country and its Crown, and its adherents punished its followers without mercy. Under the Act of Supremacy (1534), Henry became official head of the Church of England, and this allowed him to close Catholic foundations and confiscate their wealth. The Dissolution of the Monasteries shattered an ecclesiastical infrastructure that had been built up over centuries.

The Dissolution had opposition: 1536 saw the Pilgrimage of Grace – an uprising in Yorkshire (where there was to be a second rebellion, the Rising in the North, in 1569). Catholicism was reprieved in 1553, when Henry's daughter, Mary I, succeeded him and sought to turn the clock back. In the event, the wave of counter-repression she ordered against Protestantism succeeded only in seeing her branded with the nickname "Bloody Mary".

In 1593, Queen Elizabeth I, a non-Catholic, introduced legislation against "recusants" who refused to accept the authority of the Church of England. Those who remained Catholic included many of the country's leading families, especially in the north and the West Country. The father of William Shakespeare is believed to have been a recusant, and there has been speculation that England's greatest playwright was one as well.

King Philip II of Spain, Mary's widower, had supported his wife's mission to re-convert England. It

Below: The Michelade was a massacre of Catholics in Nîmes, after St Michel's Fair in September 1567. Franz Hogenberg captured it in this 16th-century painting.

Above: Protestant Elizabeth I sits in splendour before her Parliament. To her left stands Sir Francis Walsingham, a ruthless hunter of "recusants".

was with the intention of restoring Catholicism to England that, in 1588, he dispatched the Spanish Armada, hoping to invade the country. In the event, the *Armada Invencible* ("Invincible Fleet") was stopped by the English navy and dispersed by a "Protestant wind".

UNDERCOVER CLERICS

English priests were trained in continental seminaries and then smuggled back into the country. They slipped in disguise from one private house to another around the country to give Mass. It had to be held in secret because participants never knew when they might be denounced by a suspicious neighbour or a servant with a grudge.

Although a number of these houses had hiding holes for visiting priests, many were caught and executed. Typically, they were hanged, drawn and quartered. Ordinary Catholics were killed, too, but they were often tortured first in hopes that they would give up the whereabouts of other Catholics, particularly their priests. The missionaries were feared by the authorities, not just as religious dissidents but as enemy agents. It hardly helped that the headquarters of English Catholicism were abroad, at Douai in France, and Valladolid in Spain.

Above: A number of English houses had hiding holes, so priests could quickly be concealed from the authorities. This hiding hole is in the King's Room in Moseley Old Hall, Staffordshire.

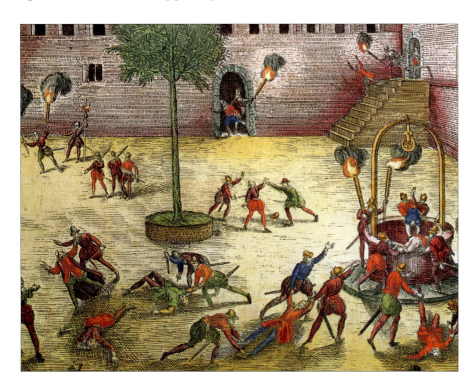

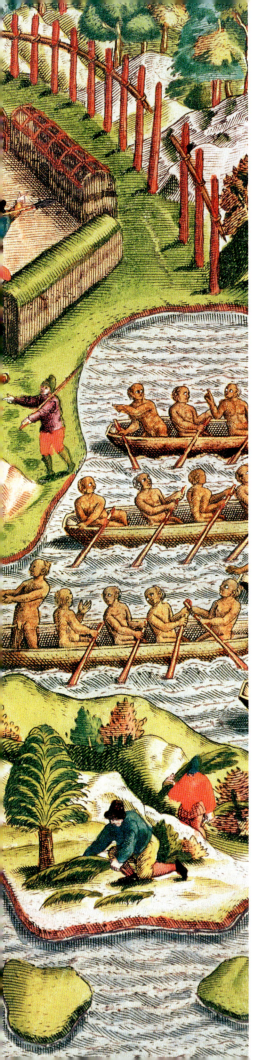

A WORLD RELIGION

The Catholic religion underwent a major cultural and geographical shift when a Middle Eastern sect became the European Church of Rome. As horizons widened, missionaries ventured out into the farthest reaches of Asia, the Americas and Africa, bringing the Word of God to some of the millions who had not yet heard it.

For a long time in Europe the idea of a godless universe had been – quite literally – unthinkable. In the 17th, 18th and 19th centuries, intellectuals, scientists and politicians began to place their faith in "reason". Christianity was so much superstition, said the rationalists, an instrument of oppression; the Church was a reactionary force. When two secularist ideologies – fascism and communism – plunged the world into chaos in the 20th century, the Church was caught up in the accompanying conflicts. Peace did return, at least for Western Europe and North America, where a new generation grew up in affluent societies. In the consumerist society, everything was a matter of choice – including religious belief and personal morality. Yet most of the world still lived in poverty and the Church had a duty to those people, too.

In the new millennium, Catholicism finds itself facing huge challenges, as it has throughout its history. Time and again, it has shown its capacity to recover from its setbacks and learn from its mistakes while holding firmly to its founding principles to be a guiding light of faith for a struggling world.

Left: European explorers introduce the Cross – and Christianity – as they come into contact with previously unknown civilizations in the New World. Théodor de Bry illustrated scenes of these meetings in his 1592 Americae Tertia Pars....

A WORLD RELIGION

MISSIONS TO THE EAST

The apostles were the first Christians to spread the gospels. From the 15th to 17th century, Europeans began to travel farther East, where they spread the message of the Church.

"Go therefore and make disciples of all nations…" was Christ's command (Matthew 28:19). To the apostles the missionary impulse was part of Christianity. They spread Christ's message through Syria and Asia Minor, and westward to Rome, the centre of an extensive empire. There was even a tradition that St Thomas carried the gospels to India. Christian communities thrived in Iraq and Iran, too, but in the 5th century their Church no longer recognized the authority of Rome when it embraced Nestorianism, a heresy that believes Christ is divided into two: the divine and the human. It was now time for missionaries to carry the gospels to the farthest corners of Asia.

CENTRAL ASIA

The willingness of the Mongols to adopt Nestorianism may have contributed to the rise of the legend of Prester John *(see right)*. In 1289, Pope Nicholas IV dispatched John of Montecorvino to take messages to Kublai Khan of China and other Mongol leaders. He was the first Roman Catholic missionary in China and translated the New Testament and Psalms into the Mongol language. Missionary work appealed to the enterprising spirit of the new Franciscan and Dominican orders, who sent missions to western and central Asia from the 13th century.

Above: St Francis Xavier (1506–52) did more than anyone else to carry the Christian message to the East. This 17th-century portrait is by an unknown painter.

PRESTER JOHN

By the 12th century, the failure of the Crusades and the growing strength of the Islamic world had left western Christendom in a state of demoralization. People were prepared to clutch at straws – even the legend that, somewhere in the East, there was a powerful empire ruled by a Christian king. Prester John had even written a letter, it was said, promising to come to Europe's rescue, attacking the Muslim enemy from the rear. So vague were the stories, and so inexact the geographical knowledge of Europe at this time, that Prester John's realms were variously reported as lying in Ethiopia and Central Asia. In 1177, Pope Alexander III went as far as writing a letter to Prester John seeking his assistance, but his messenger appears to have been lost somewhere in the vastness of Asia.

Below: China's Mongol emperor Kublai Khan greets the Polo brothers on their visit to China. In this c.1412 illustration from the Book of the World's Marvels, *they receive a letter to deliver to the newly elected Pope Gregory X.*

SPREADING OUT

The missions into Asia were bold but small-scale ventures. Anything more was unrealistic, given Christendom's political and geographical situation. Europe was effectively "boxed in": by Islam on its eastern frontier, by Africa's Sahara to the south and by an apparently infinite Atlantic Ocean to the west. However, the Age of Discovery changed all that, opening a door upon a much wider world. This was a period between the early 15th century and the 17th century in which Europeans explored the oceans, seeking new trading routes. As these great voyages broadened horizons, they brought Christians into contact with nations which had never heard the Gospel Word.

The evangelizing impulse was never lost and found fresh impetus in the 16th century. The Counter-Reformation brought a new spiritual energy, with the Jesuits leading the way. St Francis Xavier founded a mission in Goa, on the coast of India, in 1542. The "Apostle of the Indies" went on to preach Christianity in Indonesia and, from 1549, Japan. The other orders were not idle: the Franciscans were by now well-established in Malacca and Malaysia, and Augustinian friars had a mission in the Philippines from 1565.

THE CHINESE ENDEAVOUR

The greatest challenge for the missionaries at the time was China, a vast and complex country that had an ancient history and strong religious traditions of its own. In 1552, St Francis Xavier was preparing to embark on another mission, this time to China, when he died on an island off Guangdong, on its southern coast. However, 30 years later, his fellow-Jesuits, Michele Ruggieri and Matteo Ricci, established their own mission in Beijing.

The Jesuits were under no illusions about the huge scale of the task that awaited them, and not merely

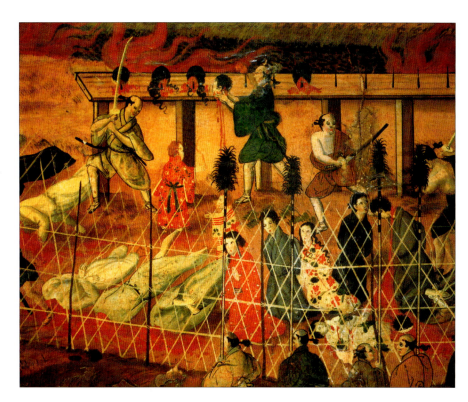

Above: Many missionaries paid the ultimate price for their devotion to their religion. An unknown 17th-century Japanese artist illustrated Jesuits being martyred in Japan in 1622.

Below: Jesuit missionary Matteo Ricci and scholar Li Paul Xu Guangqi became friends, shown together in this 17th-century engraving. They translated key works of Western science into Chinese.

because of the enormous population of the country. Chinese society was sophisticated and its sense of cultural identity secure. There could be no pretence that these were "savages" in need of civilization.

A CULTURAL EXCHANGE

The Westerners sought out the Chinese scholarly elite and, addressing them as equals, opened up a dialogue on just about every aspect of life and thought. In the process, they introduced the Chinese to the whole range of Western culture, from art and literature to mathematics and science. They earned the respect and trust of China's rulers – and several Jesuits were even given posts in the imperial administration. Many Chinese intellectuals willingly converted to Christianity.

Sadly, as time went on, dissension between the Jesuits and Franciscans ended up hampering the effectiveness of both. In 1644, moreover, Manchu invaders swept away the old Qing dynasty in China and inaugurated a new order that was far less tolerant toward foreign faiths.

A WORLD RELIGION

MISSIONS IN THE AMERICAS

The discovery and exploration of the New World during the 16th to 18th centuries brought with it the discovery of new nations and cultures – and another wave of missions.

The newly discovered peoples of the Americas were the subject of an important debate held in Valladolid, at that time the capital of Spain, in 1550–1. Two Dominicans, Juan Ginés de Sepúlveda and Bartolomé de Las Casas, argued the burning question of the day. Were the native peoples of "New Spain" really men and women, like Europeans? They looked like humans, but they apparently went unclothed, like animals,

Below: After Columbus' first landfall in the Caribbean, Christianity soon spread down through South America.

and their customs were alien to Europeans. Should they be treated as equals, or put under subjection?

There were good grounds for taking the latter view, Sepúlveda said. Had not Aristotle himself written that some peoples were by their very nature slaves, and needed to be subjected for their own good? On the contrary, Las Casas maintained. He believed that the "Indians" were entitled to exactly the same treatment as Europeans, but these rights were being scandalously ignored. Both in his Valladolid address and in a series of polemical writings on

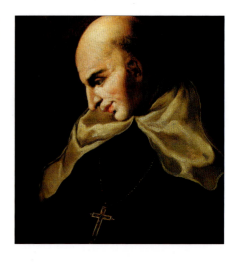

Above: Fray Bartolomé de Las Casas (1484–1566) became Catholicism's conscience in the Americas, with his impassioned pleas for humanity toward the native peoples (artist unknown).

the subject, Las Casas catalogued every kind of exploitation and abuse that the native peoples were being subjected to. From Columbus' voyages to the Caribbean islands to the conquests of Mexico and Peru, by Cortès and Pizarro respectively, the native peoples, including the Taino, Aztec, Maya and Inca, were harshly treated by the Spaniards.

NEW WORLD, NEW WAYS
Both sides of the debate claimed victory, but the controversy went on for years. The Church was divided:

Below: Spanish conquistadors massacre the Inca after capturing their capital, Cuzco, in 1532. The event is captured in this 1602 engraving by Théodor de Bry from the Historia Americae.

104

in some places it had become an arm of oppression, while elsewhere it had become a fighter for the indigenous peoples and their rights. An encomienda system was established, in which Europeans took land for themselves, in effect enslaving its indigenous occupiers.

In theory expropriation came with a duty of guardianship. Some took this obligation seriously: the Society of Jesus led the way in trying to make the New World a better one. The Jesuits reigned over *reducciones* ("reductions") that covered most of what is now Paraguay, along with vast tracts in Uruguay, Brazil, Bolivia and Argentina. There they had the rights of the representatives of the colonial power. However, instead of enslaving the indigenous peoples, they settled them around their mission stations, giving them schools and establishing farms to teach skills in agriculture.

The Jesuits' approach could be accused of high-handedness, but their paternalism was preferable to the outrageous exploitation going on elsewhere. The indigenous peoples made it clear where their preferences lay, flocking to the *reducciones* in large numbers. Neighbouring colonists had no alternative but to improve conditions radically if they were to have any hope of hanging on to their subject Indians. As Bishop of Michoacán, Mexico, from 1537, Bishop Vasco de Quiroga introduced a system of his own. Along with a foundation in Christian education, he had "his" indigenous people taught craft skills, each village being given a different speciality, from weaving and metalwork to pottery. His subjects even had a degree of political autonomy.

Not surprisingly, such utopias sparked controversy and other Europeans lobbied against them. There, lobbying was so successful that in the middle of the 18th century the Jesuits were formally expelled from Spanish and Portuguese America.

Above: Made for Aztec offerings, this casket cover found a new role in the Christian liturgy. It is now kept in the Templo Mayor Museum, Mexico City.

NORTHERN MISSIONS

Along North America's eastern sea coast, the main colonial power was Protestant England – with the exception of the colony of Maryland, which was founded by Catholic refugees from the same country in 1633. Farther north, in Canada, the French were in charge. Their intrepid priests played a major part in exploring the interior, venturing up the St Lawrence River to the Great Lakes.

The west coast, though nominally Spanish-ruled, saw little sign of European settlement at first. It was not until the 18th century that encroachments were made down the coast by Russian traders, which created nervousness at home.

In 1769, Father Junípero Serra set out from San Diego with the Spanish soldier and official Gaspar de Portola to build a chain of missions. They founded 21 missions in total, up and down what became known as the *Camino Real*, or "Royal Road". Junípero Serra set up nine of them personally, travelling an estimated 38,000 km (23,600 miles) in the 15 years before he died.

Below: A figure of founder Junípero Serra stands before the Mission Church of San Diego de Alcalá, San Diego – California's first church, established in 1769.

THE HURON CAROL

In 1643, the Jesuit priest and explorer Jean de Brébeuf wrote his "Huron Carol", referring to God as Gitchi Manitou – the great deity of the Algonquin people – and giving the Christmas story a new setting in Canada.

Twas in the moon of wintertime when all the birds had fled
That mighty Gitchi Manitou sent angel choirs instead;
Before their light the stars grew dim, and wondering hunters heard the hymn:
Jesus your King is born, Jesus is born, in excelsis gloria…

Within a lodge of broken bark the tender babe was found;
A ragged robe of rabbit skin enwrapped his beauty round
But as the hunter braves drew nigh, the angel song rang loud and high:
Jesus your King is born, Jesus is born, in excelsis gloria.

A WORLD RELIGION

THE GOSPEL IN AFRICA

THE STORY OF CATHOLICISM IN AFRICA IS TIED UP WITH THAT OF COLONIALISM IN THE 16TH TO 19TH CENTURIES. TODAY'S CHURCH MUST LOOK BACK ON A RECORD THAT IS DECIDEDLY MIXED.

Exploration of sub-Saharan Africa by Europeans came late. Prior to the 19th century, Africa was for the most part considered only as a place for buying slaves. Sea captains of different nations sailed down the hazardous coast, but generally stopped for only as long as it took to load up with their helpless human cargo. Then the ships set off again – some sailing to the plantations of British North America, but many to the New World colonies founded by Catholic Portugal, Spain and France.

Although this slave trade was a monstrous business, at the same time it was immensely profitable, and the American venture was central to the strategic aims of these great powers. So closely were the clergies of these conquering countries involved in this project that few seem to have questioned its moral implications for Christians. Although a succession of popes did condemn the trade – such as Gregory XIV in 1591, Urban VIII in 1639 and Benedict XIV in 1741 – with so much at stake they failed to make their message heard.

Above: To many Africans, such as these slaves photographed in Zanzibar in the 1880s, the Christian message could give meaning to a downtrodden life.

AFRICAN CATHOLICISM?

Some efforts were made to preach the gospel: indeed, Portuguese priests made great strides in the Kingdom of Kongo (which included much of what is now Angola, as well as parts of the modern Republic of the Congo and Democratic Republic of the Congo). However, in a spirit of tolerance, the Church allowed the incorporation of elements of African religion, and soon Kongolese Catholicism was barely recognizable as Catholicism at all. At the start of the 18th century, for example, a woman named Kimpa Vita mobilized the masses, claiming to be the reincarnation of St Anthony of Padua. She insisted that Christ had been Kongolese, and that St Anthony was a deity alongside him.

Left: A contemporary cartoonist addressed the imperial ambitions of the wealthy businessman Cecil Rhodes: Europeans were tripping over one another in their "Scramble for Africa".

106

A SPIRITUAL SCRAMBLE

The exploration of Africa's vast interior began in real earnest in the 19th century, when it was still seen as a "dark continent" by many Catholics. Nevertheless, the Church was equipped: a wealth of missionary experience had been acquired in the Americas and Asia, and in 1622 a co-ordinating Congregation for Propagation of the Faith had been founded. (In the 20th century this was renamed the Congregation for the Evangelization of Peoples.)

The Catholic Church had competition. The most famous British traveller in Africa, David Livingstone, though today generally thought of simply as an explorer, was just one of many highly motivated Protestant missionaries. Livingstone's explorations, moreover, are difficult to disentangle from the wider British effort to colonize the African interior. Cecil Rhodes' boastful ambition to build a railway "from the Cape to Cairo" typified the colonialists' view of Africa as a blank canvas on which to capture their grand designs. Catholic and Protestant missionaries had brought with them, along with the gospels, an unmistakable message of European supremacy.

> ### ABUSIVE RULERS
> The presence of the French Archbishop Charles Lavigerie in Tunisia, a French statesman once remarked, "is worth an army to France". Lavigerie had once said, "as missionaries we also work for France". Where Catholic powers prevailed, the Church often acted as an arm of the colonial administration. Terrible atrocities were committed when the French ruled in what is now the Republic of the Congo.
>
> Still worse was the holocaust committed by Belgium's King Leopold II in the south in his so-called Congo Free State, now the Democratic Republic of the Congo. Mass rape and mutilations were carried out by troops to discourage dissent and boost productivity on the plantations and in the mines. By 1908, up to ten million citizens had been killed by the troops.

These missionaries were fighting a (sometimes unseemly) turf war, analogous to the great colonial "Scramble for Africa" itself, where Europeans competed to claim African territories as their own in the late 19th century until World War I. In some places this had tragic consequences. In Buganda, the main kingdom of what is now Uganda, the local king – a despot of hideous cruelty – kept himself in power by playing Protestant and Catholic missionaries off against one another.

The Catholic missionaries at work in Africa belonged to the Society of the Missionaries of Africa, which was better known as the "White Fathers". The society was founded in 1868 by the Archbishop of Algeria, Charles Lavigerie, who was originally sent to work in French North Africa. The distinctive white garb for which its members were named was modelled on the robes of the desert nomads. Also in the van-guard were the priests of the Society of African Missions, which was founded in 1850 by Bishop Melchior de Marion-Brésillac.

Below: French White Fathers pose amid a congregation of local converts outside their traditionally built mission in Urundi (now Burundi) in the years before World War I.

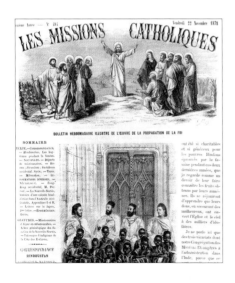

Above: A French missionary bulletin of 1878 sends an uplifting message to encourage generosity from back home.

THE ENLIGHTENMENT ASSAULT

From the scientific, intellectual and political communities came trenchant criticisms of Catholicism: soon the Church was struggling to hold its own.

The Copernican revolution, in which the 16th-century astronomer claimed that the Earth revolved around the Sun – which meant that the Earth was not, as the Church believed, the centre of the universe – had been only a foretaste of the formidable challenges to come. In 1687, the English scientist Sir Isaac Newton published his *Philosophiae Naturalis Principia Mathematica* ("Mathematical Principles of Natural Philosophy"). While Newton was not an atheist, it was hard to resist a feeling that his far-reaching theories could be suggesting a universe that was governed not by God but instead by mathematics and science.

Below: Sir Isaac Newton's theories transformed perceptions of the universe – and, inevitably, of God. This 1687 frontispiece is from the Philosophiae Naturalis Principia Mathematica.

The English poet Alexander Pope, a Catholic, had no difficulty in reconciling his fellow countryman's new science with his deeply felt religious views on the Creation:

Nature and Nature's laws lay hid in night,
God said "Let Newton Be!" and all was light.

In a perverse sort of way, it probably helped that the poet was living in a Protestant country in which anti-Catholic feeling was rife. Catholics had even been blamed for the Great Fire of London of 1666. Under the Penal Laws then prevailing, the poet was not allowed to live in London, but had been forced to take a house outside the city, at Twickenham. Pope's faith was almost certainly steeled by the humiliations he had to undergo.

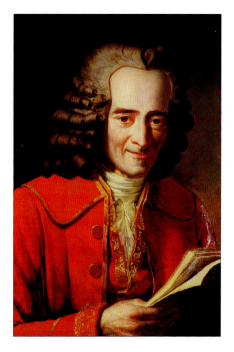

Above: Brilliant in his thinking, vicious in his satire, Voltaire became the scourge of the Catholic Church. This 1811 portrait is by Jacques Augustin Pajou.

THE FRENCH "INFAMY"

In Catholic France, the situation was different: there the Church was closely identified with a monarchical establishment that oppressed the poor and repressed all freedoms. In such circumstances, young intellectuals were more predisposed to regard religion as superstition and to dismiss the liturgy and sacraments as mumbo-jumbo. These intellectuals, and soon the general French public, were quick to adopt anything that seemed to offer a rational explanation for the wonders of creation. *Écrasez l'Infâme* ("Crush the Infamy") became the war cry of François-Marie Arouet, who is much better known today by his pseudonym Voltaire. The infamy he was referring to was the alliance of the Church and Crown against freedom, justice and the rule of reason.

Voltaire was the most famous of the 18th-century *philosophes*, whose work extended far beyond the realm of philosophy as normally understood into just about every area of

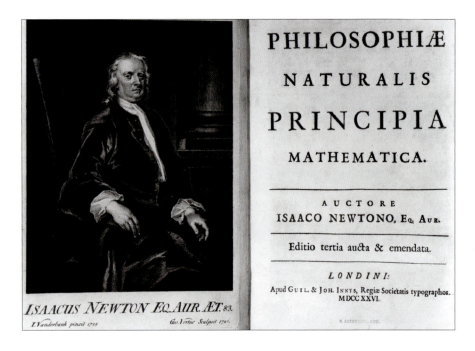

THE ENLIGHTENMENT ASSAULT

life and politics. Other prominent *philosophes* included Jean Jacques Rousseau, who said "Man was born free, but he is everywhere in chains". These metaphorical chains were not just those of tyranny but of public institutions, even of morality: children were born innocent, he said, then corrupted by their education. He also claimed that no institution did more to blight the pure soul than the Catholic Church, which was steward of a morality that destroyed the very virtue it claimed to save.

COMPREHENSIVE CRITIQUE

By 1750, under the leadership of Denis Diderot, a group of scholars worked on a great, multi-volume *Encyclopédie*. This was to be a "systematic dictionary of the sciences, arts and crafts", and it was to be drawn up, said Diderot, "without regard to anybody's feelings". They wanted to include every branch of human knowledge.

The Encyclopedists questioned Christianity's most fundamental tenets, arguing that theology was just another branch of philosophical investigation, and that religious doctrine should be submitted to the same sort of scientific testing as anything else.

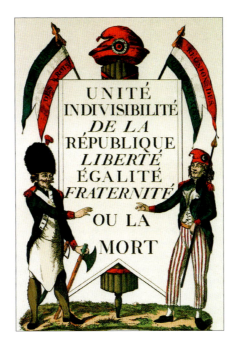

Above: An intimidating late 18th- century French illustration shows an army sapper and a revolutionary exhorting "Liberty, Equality and Fraternity…Or Death".

REVOLUTION

The *Ancien Régime* was finally swept away in 1789. Although the French Revolution did bring a sort of freedom, it also brought its own infamy, too, in the Reign of Terror. The new Republic was defiantly secular in its approach. The idea of *laïcité* was established: France was to be run by and for lay people, not the clergy. Christian values were to be replaced by those of *Liberté*, *Egalité* and *Fraternité* ("Liberty", "Equality" and "Fraternity").

Religion was not actually outlawed (as it would be later in some communist countries), but it was restrained and no longer enjoyed special favours from the state, and it was certainly not allowed to set the tone for ruling the country. Catholicism was given the same slightly grudging tolerance as the Protestants: gone were the days when its cardinals and bishops were active participants in the government of the state.

In the absence of any real understanding developing between the state authorities and the Church hierarchy, the concept of "Ultramontanism" soon grew among the Catholics in opposition to *laïcité*. *Ultramontane* literally means "beyond the mountains": the range in question was the Alps, on the other side of which lay Italy and Rome. French Catholics were told by their clergy that, whatever their state might try to tell them, its authority was trumped by that of their Church.

THE IMPERIAL CATECHISM

In 1804, Napoleon Bonaparte overthrew the revolutionary state, installing himself as Emperor Napoleon I. However, any hopes that the Church might find its old authority restored were cruelly dashed. On the contrary, the ultimate ignominy came in 1806 with the "Imperial Catechism", rewritten by the emperor himself and imposed on France's Catholic educators:

What are the duties of Christians toward those who govern them, and in particular toward Napoleon I, our emperor?

Christians owe the princes who govern them – and we in particular owe Napoleon I, our emperor – love, respect, obedience, fidelity, military service, and the taxes levied for the preservation and defence of the empire and of his throne…

Right: Pope Pius VII and his legates suffered the indignity of being obliged to be present during Napoleon's Coronation in 1804. The pope is the subject of this 1807 painting by Jacques Louis David.

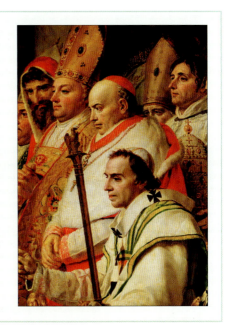

HOLDING BACK THE TIDE

THE 19TH AND 20TH CENTURIES SAW THE CHURCH ENGAGED IN AN INCREASINGLY FRANTIC REARGUARD ACTION TO DEFEND ITSELF AGAINST FREE-THINKING LIBERALISM AND REFORM.

The Church's identification with its conservative causes was to leave a lasting legacy that would be difficult for Catholicism to live down. It has always insisted that it was no enemy of science or reason – only to the "rationalism" that makes an idol out of human thought. Although Catholicism would come to terms with the discoveries of Newton and his successors, during the 19th and early 20th centuries the clergy often found itself acting as apologists for scientific backwardness, which only seemed to confirm the charge that the Church stood for superstition.

CONSERVATIVE VIEWS

It hardly helped that the most obvious product of the "Enlightenment" had been bloody revolution in Catholic France. The ferment there was viewed with consternation in other countries, whose rulers saw their own authority under threat. Rome's unease at the rise of *laïcité* may have been understandable, but it also placed the Church firmly in the camp of the conservatives.

Under the guise of resisting revolution, the Habsburg rulers of Austria, for instance, set themselves against every kind of social change. Backed by the state chancellor and Emperors Francis I and Ferdinand I, they refused the ambitions expressed by subject populations for national sovereignty – not just in Hungary and the Balkans but also in Italy.

THE *RISORGIMENTO*

In 19th-century Italy, a resurgence of national feeling, known as the *Risorgimento*, arose among a people who had for too long lived under Austrian domination. The movement received no encouragement from the Church, which saw any attack on authority as corrosive of its own. Conservatives in Italy shared

Above: Giuseppe Garibaldi led the Italians in their 19th-century struggle for nationhood. Most could not understand why the Church opposed this movement.

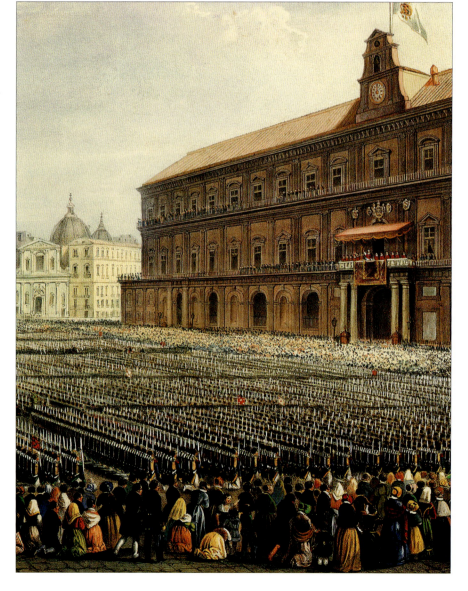

Left: By the 1860s, Pope Pius IX was completely dependent on French backing. He blesses Bourbon troops outside the Royal Palace in Naples in this 19th-century painting by Achille Vespa.

this view, but as time went on and the ferment rose, theirs became an increasingly unpopular position. Because the Vatican identified itself more closely with despotic rulers in Vienna than with the overwhelming will of the Italian people, it severely damaged the Church's reputation.

Pope Pius IX still insisted that, as pope, he was temporal ruler of the Papal States, the central Italian territories traditionally under the rule of the Vatican. Increasingly, the Italians disagreed and, in 1849, Pius IX needed military intervention by France's Emperor Napoleon III to secure his position. Repeatedly, he had to rely on the support of foreign imperialists – sometimes the French, sometimes the Austrians – against the Italian freedom fighter Giuseppe Garibaldi and his patriotic Red Shirt army. Finally, in 1871, papal rule in the city of Rome came to an end. The tiny enclave of the Vatican apart, the former territories were annexed by the state. Rome was now the capital of a unified Italy.

SET AGAINST CHANGE

The episode left a bad feeling behind. Liberals saw the Catholic Church not as a champion but as the foe of freedom; workers saw it as the enemy of change. The Church itself had been wounded and it lashed out, responding to threats to its authority with a flurry of authoritarian pronouncements. Already, in 1864, Pius IX had issued his Syllabus of Errors, a catalogue of new liberal ideas that he felt were damaging. He summed up by rejecting any notion that the Church should take steps to accommodate "progress…liberalism, or recent civilization". (Called in 1869 to ratify the Syllabus, the First Vatican Council sprang another surprise when, in a statement of 1870, Pius IX proclaimed the dogma of papal infallibility, claiming that popes are divinely guided, so infallible.)

In Protestant-dominated countries, the Church's political position might be more subtly nuanced. For the most part, though, it was identified with conservatism. In Spain, the poor knew better than to look to the Church for support in bettering their situation. They had learned to see the black-garbed priests as scavenging, flesh-eating *corvos* ("crows"). When Civil War broke out in the country in 1936, priests and nuns were massacred in their hundreds.

Below: General Franco greets some of his clerical supporters with studied courtesy: relations were not quite so warm between Spain's working people and the Church.

THE WORKERS' POPE

Despite the conservative stand taken by the Church, there was one pope who held a different view. Pope Leo XIII's proclamations on behalf of the world's workers would put many a socialist to shame. He himself was anything but a democrat, putting down one dissenting adviser with an unceremonious *Ego sum Petrus* ("I am Peter") but he saw the need for radical change, if only to rescue the status quo.

In his 1891 encyclical *Rerum Novarum* ("Of New Things"), he addressed the condition of the working classes as one of the great issues of the age. Reasoning that failure to reform would lead to revolution, he called for far-reaching changes in the way modern economies were organized. Denouncing the glaring gulf between rich and poor, he spoke out in support of workers' rights and trade unions, expressing his sympathy for those who went on strike to ensure the welfare of their families.

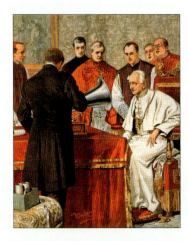

Above: Addressing the Church – and looking to the future – Pope Leo XIII is shown recording his blessing by phonograph in this 1903 print by Achille Beltrame.

DARK TIMES

WITH FASCISTS MARCHING ON ROME ITSELF, NAZISM ON THE RISE IN GERMANY AND COMMUNISTS IN EASTERN EUROPE, THE FIRST HALF OF THE 20TH CENTURY WAS A TUMULTUOUS TIME FOR THE CHURCH.

In 1922, cheering crowds turned out to welcome Benito Mussolini and his "Blackshirts" – the nickname given to members of his Fascist paramilitary – as they made their triumphal entrance into Rome. However, Italy's senior churchmen were rather more muted in their welcome: they had little in common with the young thugs who were following *Il Duce* ("The Leader").

Even so, there was something in Fascism to which these churchmen found themselves able to respond: its reverence for authority, its avowed respect for old traditions. Years of liberalism, with its vaunted freedoms, had brought the country only incessant labour unrest and public immorality – and a press that held the Church and all its values in clear contempt. Worse still, there was evidence everywhere in Europe of the advances made by the Communists, who had already established an atheistic state in the Soviet Union.

SENT BY PROVIDENCE
The Holy See had refused to acknowledge Italy's annexation of Rome in 1871, spending the next six decades in denial – and in endless wrangling with successive governments. Under the terms of the Lateran Treaty of 1929, Mussolini agreed compensation for the loss of the old Papal States. Mussolini had discarded the Catholicism of his upbringing, and privately despised it, but he also recognized its importance to the conservative Italians he wanted on his side. He made Catholicism the state religion, made criticism of the Church a crime, outlawed divorce and made religious education mandatory in all schools. All state legislation would be reviewed to ensure that it conformed with canon law. Pope Pius XI declared that *Il Duce* was "a man sent by providence": there were some who did not question the moral price the Church would have to pay for this arrangement.

Both Mussolini and Hitler were lapsed Catholics. Like Mussolini, Hitler saw Christianity as a weaklings' creed, but he recognized the value of good relations with the Church. Pius XI signed a Concordat – an agreement between pope and secular ruler on religious matters – with Hitler's government in 1933, eager to have another ally in resisting the Communist advance.

However, the Nazis made more uncomfortable bedfellows than the Italian Fascists, especially when the ugliness of their anti-semitism became evident to all. In 1937, the pope sent out a letter to be read in German churches. *Mit Brennender Sorge* ("With Burning Sorrow") contained a forthright condemnation of the Nazis' attacks on the Jewish population as well as their attempts to establish control over the Catholic Church within Germany.

STANDING BY?
The ensuing Holocaust was one of the darkest episodes of modern history, and the Church is one of many institutions that emerged with its reputation tarnished. Pope Pius XII, who succeeded Pius XI in 1939, has rightly been condemned. Broadly speaking, any good he did

Above: At the height of his power, Benito Mussolini visits the Vatican in 1932 to meet Pope Pius XI and his officials.

Below: Cardinal Pacelli, the future Pope Pius XII, signs the infamous Concordat with Germany in 1933 on behalf of Pope Pius XI.

was done by stealth; he was guarded in his public denunciations. He had a love for Germany and its culture (earlier in his career he had been Papal Nuncio – akin to a Vatican ambassador – in the country) and held Hitler's populism in deep disdain. Yet the uncomfortable fact remains that what really excited his moral ardour was the threat represented by Communism in the East. Nazism appeared to him to be the lesser of two evils.

While acknowledging Pius XII's attempts to relieve the plight of World War II's victims, including Jews, some critics charge him and the Catholic Church with a failure of moral leadership. Although there were heroic efforts made by individual priests and nuns, these critics saw the institution as being weak during the war. There was general approval within the Church when, on a visit to Jerusalem in 2000, Pope John Paul II made a heartfelt apology to the Jewish community.

AFTER THE WAR

Fascism had been all but vanquished by the end of World War II, though authoritarian governments endured for a few decades in Spain and Portugal. The Communists gained a strong hold in Eastern Europe, putting the Church there in a weak position. After the lessons of the Nazi era, the Church became outspoken critics of Communist oppression. Yet the Church's earlier links with Fascism meant some Western liberals remained sceptical that the Church's opposition to Communism was truly rooted in principle.

CATHOLICS UNDER COMMUNISM

The Soviet Union had been among the victors of World War II in 1945. With Communism's avowedly materialist principles, there was no place in the Communist scheme for the religious institution. In Russia itself, the established Church had been Orthodox, and its more independent-minded clergy was quickly hounded out by the Soviet authorities. A collaborationist congregation was created in its place. In the Ukraine, Romania and Czechoslovakia, Catholics were forced to join this officially sanctioned pseudo-Church in the tens of thousands, though many of the faithful continued their accustomed worship underground. In Poland, too, a "silent Church" clung on precariously in a mutually uncomfortable co-existence with the Communist state.

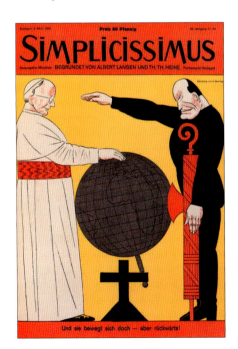

Above: Pius XI and Mussolini agree upon the Lateran Treaty, as illustrated on the cover of the March 1929 edition of Simplicissimus, *a liberal satirical magazine published in Germany.*

Above: Pope John Paul II visited the "Hill of Crosses" in 1993. On several previous occasions the Soviet authorities had attempted to remove this massive memorial to the Lithuanians' faith.

THE MODERNIZERS

THE 20TH-CENTURY POPES BROUGHT ABOUT RELIGIOUS CHANGES, AND THEIR REFORMS TRANSFORMED BOTH THE PROFILE OF THE CHURCH AND THE EXPERIENCE OF BEING CATHOLIC.

Though Pope Pius XII's pontificate is considered controversial now, in the 1950s his authority seemed impregnable. The pope who had brought the Church through World War II was naturally regarded with gratitude – his own personal role, and that of his Church, were as yet unexamined. In the Cold War climate, moreover, his uncompromising stand against Communism had won him respect well beyond the boundaries of his Church. As the first "media Pope", he became known to the world through newspaper pictures, television appearances and radio broadcasts. Within the Church, his power was immense, even by papal standards, because he had surrounded himself with elderly and like-minded cardinals.

A CONVENTIONAL CHOICE

Pius XII's unabashedly conservative Church was a frustrating place for the young and the radical. When he died in 1958, some saw a chance to advance reforms. However the cardinals elected Angelo Roncalli, Patriarch of Venice, to serve as Pope John XXIII. The new pontiff was already 77 years of age, and in a long career he had shown himself a meek and unquestioning servant of his superiors. He was not the breath of fresh air the progressives had been wanting. All the evidence indicated that this was what had recommended him as Pius' replacement: he could be relied upon not to rock the boat.

Above: Pope John XXIII blesses the crowd as he is carried in to officiate at the opening of the Second Vatican Council in 1962.

The only issue that appeared to stir up any passion in the new pope was that of Christian unity. John mourned the gradual disintegration of Jesus' Church down the centuries and longed to build bridges with Catholicism's "separated brethren". Hence, he arranged meetings with England's Archbishop of Canterbury and had talks with representatives of other churches. This, though clearly a worthy cause, was hardly an exciting one. There was no immediate prospect of real change.

SECOND VATICAN COUNCIL

John XXIII's dream of Christian unity has remained elusive to this day. However, it was to have one very real and immediate consequence.

Left: The scene inside St Peter's Basilica at one of the climactic moments of the Vatican Council. Pope John is enthroned beneath the baldacchino in the distance.

THE MODERNIZERS

In 1962, the pope called together the Second Vatican Council, and from then onward the Catholic Church would never be the same.

Although some critics might see the changes as superficial, the Council re-emphasized (in some ways reinforced) the hierarchical nature of the Church. At the same time, it acknowledged the need for "top-down" directives to be supplemented by "bottom-up" reform. There was a new tone of openness, and a genuine receptiveness to criticism – lay observers, including women, were encouraged to be involved. Ordinary Catholics were to play a fuller part in the conduct of their faith, and there was to be a drive to make the Scriptures more widely available in the vernacular (people's own languages).

Measures were also taken to give lay Catholics a greater role in the Mass, and in the liturgy, too, there was to be a vernacular component. This process was completed under Pope Paul VI in 1969 when, along with a full transition to the vernacular, the practice of having the priest face the congregation when saying Mass was introduced. Previously, he had faced the altar, which was typically at the eastern end of the church, in the direction of Jerusalem (just as Muslims orientate themselves toward Mecca for daily prayers). Worshippers might feel a sense of wonder at being present for such a sacred ritual, but the new Catholicism wanted to draw parishoners in to make them feel involved.

Above: In 1976 the reactionary Archbishop Marcel Lefebvre defiantly celebrated the traditional Tridentine Mass. This celebration has been encouraged by recent popes.

THE BACKLASH

The Second Vatican Council was in many ways less far-reaching than has since been assumed. Issues that were already becoming controversial, such as contraception and divorce, were mostly unaddressed. Yet Catholicism now had a completely different feel, and Pope John XXIII's critics were in no doubt that there was substance in the changes.

The French Archbishop Marcel Lefebvre led a movement within the Church to return to the old ways and the Tridentine Mass, the Latin liturgy approved by the Council of Trent in the 16th century. Ultimately, he had to lead it from outside the Church. In 1988, he was excommunicated by Pope John Paul II (himself a conservative) after the archbishop consecrated four new bishops without official sanction.

POP RELIGION

The new-look Catholicism was taken up with great enthusiasm, its advent corresponding with that of the 1960s' pop culture. Guitars strummed, children acted out scriptural scenes and kisses of peace were freely exchanged at self-consciously informal "folk masses". This occurred nowhere more so than in Liverpool, England, home of the Beatles and, from 1967, of a thoroughly modern "Metropolitan Cathedral of Christ the King". Although shaped like a stylized crown with a spectacular stained-glass lantern, its circular ground plan was inclusive and democratic. Poet Roger McGough caught the mood with his poem of dedication: "O Lord on Thy New Liverpool Address". The poem has a reference to a priest wearing the cassock, concluding that if it is worn, "Then let's glimpse the jeans beneath".

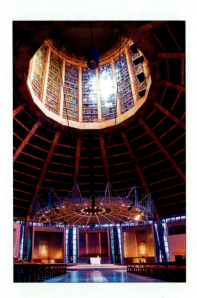

Above: In the modern design of the Liverpool Metropolitan Cathedral, stained-glass windows in the roof complement the colourful lighting that highlights the altar.

A WORLD RELIGION

THE CHURCH MILITANT

The Christian's duty to help the poor is clear, but just how far the Catholic Church should be prepared to go was a question raised by Liberation Theology.

In the 20th century, many South Americans lived in deprivation and from this arose Liberation Theology. It challenged the Church to make the spirit of the Beatitudes prevail by helping to overthrow established political and economic systems.

> *He has put down the mighty from their thrones and exalted those of low degree;*
> *He has filled the hungry with good things, and the rich he has sent empty away.*

This is one of the most remarkable passages in the gospels, from Mary's "Magnificat" (Luke 1:46–55). Our Lady's words celebrate the Christ who, for all his divine greatness, would keep company with prostitutes and lepers. He is the Christ who, for all his gentleness and his injunction to "turn the other cheek", was moved to violence by the sight of the moneychangers in the Temple.

MARX'S "GOSPEL"
Was Jesus not just a saviour but also a revolutionary? It is easy to see why many should have thought so, although it is harder to see what form a real-world Christian revolution would actually take. Especially given that, from the 18th century onward, the revolutionary orthodoxy has seen religion not as an aid to humanity but as a great part of the problem. Karl Marx, the renowned founder of Communism, notoriously saw religion as "the opium of the people" – though to put this into context, it should be noted that he was writing at a time that was lenient toward taking recreational drugs. His suggestion that religion was "the sigh of the oppressed creature", "the heart of a heartless world" showed at least a degree of sympathy for those who sought religious comfort. However, he saw that comfort as illusory.

Marx's later followers took a less nuanced view and settled into the conviction that religion was a cruel hoax designed to reconcile the people to their oppression. In the false hope of salvation hereafter, they would accept their lot on the earth: a dismal status quo was thus perpetuated.

20TH-CENTURY RADICALS
That the Church might be letting down the poor had, of course, occurred to many in its history. Even in the 19th century, Pope Leo XIII had met the labour movement halfway with his *Rerum Novarum*, a letter that addressed the condition of the working classes. However, in the 1960s, radicalism was present around the world: this was a time of student sit-ins and anti-war demonstrations. African Americans (as well as Catholics in Protestant-dominated Northern Ireland) marched in the thousands to demand their civil rights; there were general strikes and student riots in France. The aims of the activists might have been vague, but the mood of rebellion was infectious, and many Catholics – the young in particular – felt they should be making their own contribution to the "struggle".

SOUTH AMERICAN LIBERALS
In Latin America, many millions were living in abject poverty while a helpless Church hierarchy looked on. By contrast, the leftists were able to report real achievements. In 1959, Fidel Castro, Che Guevara and their guerrilla army overthrew a repressive regime in Cuba. As proclaimed by Gustavo Gutiérrez, a priest from Peru, Liberation Theology called for a Catholicism that, not content with promising salvation in the next life, would do whatever it took to bring about revolutionary change in this one on earth.

Above: Russia's Bolsheviks expressed their antagonism to religion in no uncertain terms, shown in this 1930 print by Achille Beltrame, from the Italian newspaper La Domenica del Corriere.

Below: Óscar Romero, Archbishop of San Salvador, was an advocate for the poor and victims of the country's civil war. He was killed in 1980 while celebrating Mass and was canonized by Pope Francis in 2018.

There is no doubting the movement's sincerity in trying to improve the living conditions of the South American people – or, for a time, its real significance. Thousands of priests, nuns and lay Catholics were inspired by the Liberationist message, and several important Catholic figures died for their beliefs. Archbishop Óscar Romero, who had led the popular opposition to El Salvador's oppressive military regime, was gunned down at the altar as he was saying Mass on 24 March 1980. Catholic clerics were well represented among the Sandinistas, who came to power in Nicaragua in the 1980s, including the famous poet-priest Ernesto Cardenal.

However, it seemed inevitable that the hierarchy of the Church would look askance at such developments, and not only through ingrained conservatism. Despite certain common aims, the marriage

Above: Many Catholics reasoned that Christ would have approved of the Nicaraguan Literacy Campaign run by the Sandinistas, but the Church took issue with the Sandinistas' wider aims.

of Communism and Christianity was always going to be problematic given the former's refusal to acknowledge the existence of a spiritual dimension.

REHABILITATION
The election of Pope Francis in 2013 changed the situation. Before he became pope, as Father Bergoglio in Argentina, he was critical of its liberal Marxist version of Liberation Theology, but his statements when he became pontiff that he wanted "a Church which is poor and for the poor", and his denunciations of consumerism and capitalism rehabilitated the movement to a certain extent.

At the start of his pontificate he was a key player (with Canada) in negotiations that led to the restoration of full diplomatic relations between Cuba and the United States. In 2015, he invited Gustavo Guiérrez to speak at the Vatican, and in 2018 Francis canonized Óscar Romero. He said that Romero's "ministry was distinguised by his particular attention to the most poor and marginalized". Then, in February 2020, Francis approved the beatification of Romero's friend and another key figure in the movement, El Salvadoran Jesuit priest Rutilio Grande, who was assassinated by the country's security forces in 1977.

Below: Pope John Paul II listened to a speech made by Daniel Ortega, leader of the Sandinistas, when the pontiff visited Nicaragua in 1983.

> **CAMILO TORRES**
> "If Christ were alive today, he would be a guerrilla," claimed Camilo Torres. Born in 1929, and a priest since the early 1950s, he had become disillusioned with the Church's failure to relieve the sufferings of the poor. Deciding that radical action was needed – even violent action if need be – he went as far as enlisting with his country's Marxist guerrillas. The ELN (*Ejército de Liberación Nacional*, or National Liberation Army) was engaged in open war with the Colombian government. However, Torres was killed in 1966 during his first operation with the ELN, becoming the Liberation Army's most famous martyr.

REACHING OUT TO OTHER FAITHS

IN THE 20TH AND 21ST CENTURIES, THE CATHOLIC CHURCH HAS BEEN EXCHANGING VIEWS WITH OTHER CHRISTIAN COMMUNITIES – AS WELL AS WITH LEADERS OF THE DIFFERENT GREAT WORLD FAITHS.

With the exception of Poland, the Christians of Eastern Europe have historically looked to the Orthodox Church rather than to Rome. The Polish people have always defined themselves against their Russian neighbours (who were often also their oppressors). Their Catholicism was a matter not just of religious faith but of patriotic pride. Yet the Poles were Slavs as well, and Pope John Paul II, who always remembered his Polish origins, was mindful of that ethnic inheritance. The desire for reconciliation with the Eastern Church ran as deep in his heart as, so many years before, it had run in that of Pope John XXIII.

Above: An ecumenical service at Paris' Notre-Dame Cathedral is celebrated by leading Catholic prelates alongside an Orthodox metropolitan bishop (centre) and a Protestant minister (right).

A DIVISIVE DIPLOMAT?

In more than a quarter of a century as pope, John Paul II accomplished much for the Catholic Church, but his particular dream of reconciliation had to be deferred. It has been suggested by his critics that the pope himself had created part of the problem: his own instinctive authoritarianism rendered impossible the soft approach that would have been required. It was the same, some critics believe, with his approach to the Church of England, whose doctrine was not so far removed from that of Rome's. Although the decision of the Anglican Church to ordain women priests caused dissension between the two communities, liberal critics have claimed it was a matter in which a less stubborn pope would have found some type of accordance.

On the other hand, John Paul II's charisma propelled Christianity back on to the front page of many of the big newspapers, reminding many jaded Westerners that religion could still hold relevance in a modern society. Elsewhere, adherents of the other world religions could find evidence

Left: In 2000, Pope John Paul II visited Jerusalem and the Western ("Wailing") Wall, where he begged forgiveness on behalf of the Catholic Church for centuries of anti-semitic persecution.

in his energy and enthusiasm that the Christian West was not entirely sunk in cynicism and apathy.

Ultimately, his love of humanity – and the love that humanity felt for Pope John Paul II – made him a more effective bridge-builder than anyone might have expected. His impetuous style certainly helped his cause. A more cautious man might never have dreamt, for example, of making his historic (and, at the time, controversial) visit to the Auschwitz concentration camp in 1979. The first-ever papal visit to Israel followed in 2000, where John Paul II's heartfelt apology for centuries of Christian persecution of Jews opened the way to a new era of discussion and co-operation.

COMMON CAUSE

There are, of course, limits to how much progress can be made between different communities. The Catholic creed professes that it is the "one" true Church. John Paul II's successor, Pope Benedict XVI, maintained that, while other Christian Churches and non-Christian religions may offer aspects of the truth and may thereby be instruments of salvation,

Above: In 2006, Pope Benedict XVI met the Orthodox Patriarch in Istanbul, Turkey. It was his first official visit to a Muslim country.

the whole truth is to be found only in Catholicism. If anything unified the world's religions, as far as Benedict XVI was concerned, it was their rejection of modern secularism and the culture it had fostered.

On his election in 2013, Pope Francis met with leaders of other faiths and Christian denominations and urged all to come together to work for peace and justice. He called those without religious faith "precious allies in our commitment to defend human dignity, build a more peaceful coexistence among people and protect nature". With regard to different religions, he said in April 2019, "What God wants is fraternity among us... we must not be frightened by difference. God has allowed this."

THE POPES AND THE IMAMS

When the Ayatollah Khomeini died in 1989, Pope John Paul II called for his achievements to be reflected upon "with great respect and deep thought". There have been more effusive eulogies, perhaps, but the pope's was still strikingly cordial in the circumstances. John Paul II had refused to lend his authority to other Christian leaders who earlier that year had expressed sympathy with the leader of Islam in Iran. The Ayatollah had issued a *fatwa* – a religious decree – calling for the killing of author Salman Rushdie for writing his novel, *The Satanic Verses*, which was said to be blasphemous. In the years that followed the papacy continued its dialogue with Islam's leaders, with John Paul II becoming the first pope to pray in a Muslim mosque.

Under Benedict XVI, in 2008, Muslim scholars were invited to a joint seminar with Catholic thinkers held in Rome. Over three days they vowed to work together to combat violence and terrorism. In 2019, Francis visited Abu Dhabi in the United Arab Emirates and became the first pope to visit and conduct a papal mass on the Arabian peninsula. In March 2021, he visited Iraq, the first pope to do so, and met with Shiite cleric Grand Ayatolla Ali al-Sistani; the two urged Christian and Muslim communities to work for peace.

Above: Ayatolla Ali al-Sistani receives Pope Francis at his residence in the holy city of Najaf, Iraq, 2021.

A WORLD RELIGION

NEW CHALLENGES

THE NUMBER OF CATHOLICS DECREASED IN MANY WESTERN SOCIETIES DURING THE LAST CENTURY. THE INFLUENCES OF CAPITALISM AND CONSUMERISM ARE PERHAPS PARTLY TO BLAME.

In recent years, the Church has seen its support ebb away in the advanced industrialized societies. In the mostly Protestant and Anglo-Saxon countries of Europe, Catholicism was long regarded as a peasant creed that was associated with "backward" regions: southern Italy, Spain, remote parts of France – and pre-eminently with Ireland. Yet Christ had always loved the poor, and the poor had always reciprocated, offering their sons and daughters into his service.

CHANGING SOCIETIES

When a previously poor region begins to thrive, no one mourns the passing of mass poverty – however, economic development often brings problems as well as benefits. In some places, historical tendencies can be traced. For example, that most Spaniards say they no longer bother to go to Church may reflect resentments dating back to the Franco era and beyond. Italy is another country in which the Church's most visible adherents recall an authoritarian past. Although comparatively few Italians have rejected the Church outright, it is for many now no more than a part of their cultural rituals – baptisms, marriages and funerals – and is otherwise ignored.

Increased wealth has resulted in population shifts, which have created their own impact. The old overcrowded communities of the cities have been dispersed to suburbs, where more secular attitudes have prevailed. One example can be seen in St Anthony's parish in Jersey City in New Jersey, USA. In the 1950s, a typical Sunday Mass was attended by around 10,000 Christians; today, less than 300 people turn out.

The problem has partly been that there is so much more to do at weekends for families with cars and money to spend – but who have precious little quality time together. Although Christ was clear in his insistence that material wealth was not spiritually enriching, Catholics are not immune to the attractions of material consumerism. Nor are they immune to the consumeristic attitude that encourages people toward the various spiritual options available these days, from yoga and meditation to New Age practices.

A DECLINE IN CLERGY

Something is clearly wrong with the Church when Ireland is running out of priests. In 2018, just five men started training for the priesthood at St Patrick's College, Maynooth, Ireland's principal seminary. In addition, the priests constitute an ageing population: the average age in

Above: Falling levels of attendance and reduced collections have sent parochial incomes tumbling, a formidable challenge for the Church in the new century.

Below: Sardinians process through their village as they have done for so many centuries, but can Catholicism offer more than history and local colour?

120

2019 was about 70 years old. This is because as societies prosper, life expectancy increases and families feel more secure. With this security, families tend to have fewer children. This has happened in many industrialized countries, regardless of religious culture. It has certainly occurred in Ireland, which has enjoyed great economic success in recent decades. The youths who would once have gone into the Church no longer exist in such abundance, and they have other life choices and distractions. Ireland faces the kind of administrative adjustments with which Catholics in the United States and Great Britain have become familiar, with small groups of priests and lay helpers taking charge of sprawling parish clusters.

NEW OPPORTUNITIES

The difficulties can hardly be denied, yet given the age of the institution, talk of doom and gloom is misplaced. In 2,000 years, Catholicism has come through many more challenging times. Despite all its claims for apostolic continuity, the Church has shown the capacity to reinvent itself again and again down the centuries. That it will have to do so again has become clear, with its great structures perhaps learning to accommodate a more administratively flexible, "small is beautiful" community-based system. There could be scope for lay Catholics to play a far greater role in their local communities, which has been an official goal ever since the time of the Second Vatican Council.

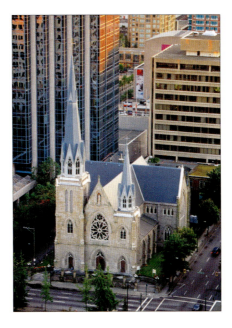

Left: Once Vancouver's Holy Rosary Cathedral dominated the skyline. Today, the Christian message risks being lost amid the pressures and distractions of modern life.

Below: A businessman finds comfort confiding with his priest in the confessional, something that many middle-class Westerners have decided is not for them.

THE SINS OF THE FATHERS

The Church has admitted it has not always been worthy of its members' trust. Catholics have been rocked in recent years by allegations of the clergy's sexual impropriety. From the mid-1980s, scandals in the United States, Ireland, Australia and other countries focused attention on alleged sexual abuse of young people by diocesan priests and members of the religious orders. In some cases, the Church hierarchy was accused of attempting to cover up accusations, and even of moving sexual abusers away from one scandal and into a position where he or she could offend again.

In the United States, the Church made financial settlements of $2 billion to victims of sex abuse in the past 60 years.

In 2018, in the US, a grand jury report said more than 1,000 children had been abused by "predatory priests" in Pennsylvania over many decades. Pope Francis issued an apology, expressing "shame and repentance". He went on to say "We showed no care for the little ones; we abandoned them." On 21–24 February 2019, he convened a summit on clerical sexual abuse at the Vatican and called for concrete and effective measures to be put in place. Then, on 1 June 2021, he promulgated changes to canon law that tightened sanctions against priests in sexual abuse cases.

A WORLD RELIGION

FACING COMPETITION

IN TODAY'S SOUTH AMERICA AND AFRICA, THE CATHOLIC CHURCH IS BEING CHALLENGED BY OTHER CREEDS THAT MAY APPEAR MORE ENERGETIC, AND MORE IMMEDIATELY RELEVANT TO PEOPLE'S LIVES.

As recently as a generation or so ago, South America was one of the bastions of world Catholicism, a region consecrated to Christ and the Virgin Mary, utterly loyal to the pope. The idea of a Protestant Brazil or Chile was practically unthinkable. Catholicism was in the culture, in the air the people breathed.

Nevertheless, Pentecostalism has spread like wildfire throughout the region in recent decades. This new form of Christianity first appeared in the United States at the beginning of the 20th century. Rooted in a range of different Protestant churches, Pentecostalism is a faith of enthusiastic evangelism that demands that the believer be born again in the Holy Spirit – just like the disciples at the first Pentecost.

AN ALTERNATIVE CREED
The explanations given for such a quick expansion in South America vary. Pentecostalism is strongly emotional in its emphasis, which offers the individual Christian a spiritual (or, perhaps, merely psychological) high. Catholicism has always tended to distrust this type of extravagant emotionalism. Yet the importance of the ecstatic sense of self-worth it brings to the Pentecostalist convert can hardly be exaggerated. However, in some ways, it is the logical outcome of the attentions given by dedicated missionaries, hard at work for decades among poor people who may well feel that their traditional religious leaders have often taken them for granted.

Some South Americans have pointed to the remoteness of a conservative clergy, reluctant to involve itself with the problems of the masses. Others have seen the failure of ideologically driven Liberation Theology to see the poor as real people. Either way, the Protestant missionaries have made huge strides.

By 2005, an estimated 13 per cent of Latin America's huge population had embraced Pentecostalism; that is, 75 million out of 560 million people. This overall figure conceals the fact that there are areas in which Catholicism has been in headlong retreat. In some of Rio de Janeiro's poorest districts, Protestant chapels now outnumber Catholic churches in a ratio of seven to one.

Above: A worshipper is energetically welcomed to a Pentecostal congregation in Rio de Janeiro. Latin Americans have been flocking to the new chapels in their thousands.

A PLACE OF SAFETY
In some areas, politics have certainly played a part. For example, through the many long years of vicious state repression in Guatemala, courageous priests and nuns made a stand against the military, which also made them targets. The conspicuously apolitical stand of (overwhelmingly American) Pentecostalist missionaries made their church a refuge from the violence and turmoil of the time. Middle-class Guatemalans, who were instinctively uneasy at the thought of any association with the leftists, have turned to Pentecostalism in large numbers. Today, about 42 per cent of the population now considers itself Protestant.

COMPETITION FROM ISLAM
In West and Central Africa, the main competition is not from Pentecostalism but from Islam. This is not surprising since Islam's history in the region is at least as long as Catholicism's. Muhammad's faith was first brought south across the Sahara by desert traders; nomadic tribes thereafter carried it farther to the south.

Left: Pentecostalism is not just for the poor. These bourgeois Brazilians have crossed the ocean to be baptized in the sacred waters of the River Jordan.

FACING COMPETITION

A kind of frontier has long existed across this part of the continent, with – broadly speaking – Islam to the north, Christianity to the south. There are roughly twice as many Christians as Muslims in sub-Saharan Africa. In reality, this border has been highly porous, with any number of communities to be found on the "wrong" side, and with close contacts, even family relations, between the two.

MODERN RADICALS

Peaceful co-existence has until recent history been maintained, but the emergence of Islamic fundamentalism has altered the dynamics. With an agenda that is as much political as religious, radical Islamic groups have engaged in direct competition for converts with Catholics, and their evangelisation has to some extent paid off. Conflict has flared as well, most famously in the Sudan, whose Islamic Khartoum government has for years been at war with the Catholic communities of the south. Elsewhere, too, there has been trouble, most notably perhaps, in parts of Nigeria, where attempts have been made to introduce the full rigour of Sharia law.

RESPONDING TO CHANGE

Ultimately, the only way for the Catholic Church to respond to such changes will be to change itself, while staying true to the central principals of so many centuries. Rome may remain its centre, but a Eurocentric Church will hardly be able to provide Catholicism with the worldwide guidance and support it needs. The ethnic mixture of the hierarchy has already been transformed by the addition of new African, Asian and South American faces, and more changes may occur in the years to come. It would seem strange indeed if the first great world religion were unable to meet the challenge of globalization. Despite its past difficulties, the Catholic Church appears well placed to face the future.

Right: Théodore-Adrien Sarr celebrates Mass after being made a cardinal by Pope Benedict XVI in 2007. Senegalese Muslims also joined in acclaiming the new Cardinal.

Right: Followers of Islam gather to pray outside the main mosque in Asmara, Eritrea. Islam is on the rise across much of North and Central Africa.

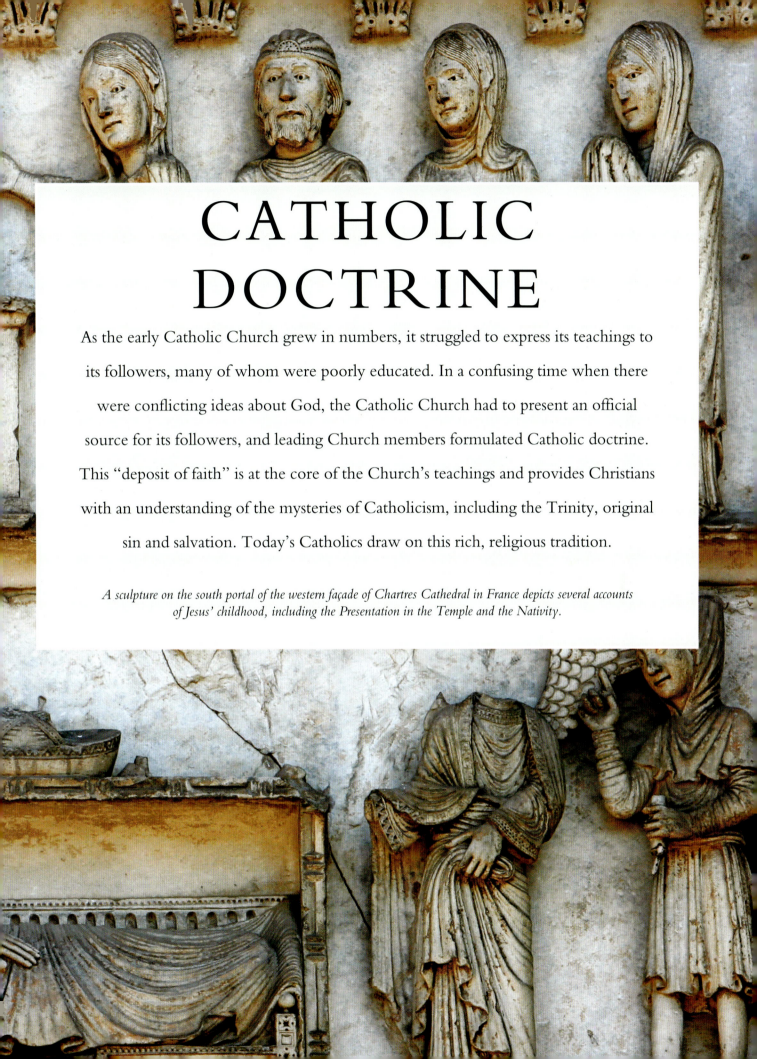

CATHOLIC DOCTRINE

As the early Catholic Church grew in numbers, it struggled to express its teachings to its followers, many of whom were poorly educated. In a confusing time when there were conflicting ideas about God, the Catholic Church had to present an official source for its followers, and leading Church members formulated Catholic doctrine. This "deposit of faith" is at the core of the Church's teachings and provides Christians with an understanding of the mysteries of Catholicism, including the Trinity, original sin and salvation. Today's Catholics draw on this rich, religious tradition.

A sculpture on the south portal of the western façade of Chartres Cathedral in France depicts several accounts of Jesus' childhood, including the Presentation in the Temple and the Nativity.

THE MYSTERY OF FAITH

As the nascent Catholic Church began to develop its doctrines in the first centuries after Christ's death, it was faced with many challenges, including persecution, the difficulty of communicating abstruse concepts, such as the Trinity, to an uneducated and superstitious populace, and the constant threat of heretical beliefs and teachings. Such challenges forced early ecclesiastics and Catholic theologians to be vigilant and proactive as they formulated and disseminated Church doctrine.

The early Church councils acted as both the universities and the senates of the Church to standardize beliefs and promulgate them as law. The early Church was blessed with a number of brilliant early thinkers such as Sts Augustine, Athanasius, Jerome and Thomas Aquinas, whose devotion to understanding Christ and his teachings, as well as to the development of the Church, was absolute. As Catholic beliefs developed into officially disseminated teachings and practice, they became part of the "deposit of faith", the vast bulwark of accepted Church tradition that had its genesis in the earliest oral apostolic teachings, the canons of the New Testament and in the decisions and decrees of the Church councils.

At the core of Church doctrine are the Trinitarian nature of God, the Incarnation of Christ as God-Man, his real presence in the Eucharist, his suffering and death, and his resurrection for our salvation. All other Catholic beliefs and teaching are nourished from the deep wellspring of these particular articles of faith.

Left: The three persons of the Trinity – Christ, the Holy Spirit (in the form of a dove) and God – are the focus of this 17th-century painting by Pierre Mignard. Christ's bare chest alludes to his crucifixion, when he was stripped of his garments.

THE MYSTERY OF FAITH

GOD IN THREE PERSONS

CATHOLICS BELIEVE IN THE TRINITY OF GOD, OFTEN TRADITIONALLY PORTRAYED WITH THE FATHER AS A REGAL OLDER MAN, THE SON AS A YOUNG, SORROWFUL MAN AND THE HOLY SPIRIT AS A DOVE OR FLAME.

Belief in the Trinity is an absolutely central tenet of the Roman Catholic faith, but it is also an item of doctrine that has a controversial past among Christians. It is a paradox that is difficult to understand rationally. The doctrine states that there is only one eternal, almighty God, who exists without beginning or end, and who is the creator of all that exists. However, there are three "persons" – the Father, the Son and the Holy Spirit – existing "one in being" as that God. The three are equal and eternal, each existing without beginning or end.

THE SAME BUT DIFFERENT
As stated in the Nicene Creed, which deals specifically with the nature of Christ, the Son is said to be "eternally begotten" of the Father, but "not made", emphasizing that there was never a time when he did not exist and that he partakes of the substance of the Father even while he is another person. The Holy Spirit "proceeds" from the Father and the Son – this is an active verb that emphasizes a continuous being, a kind of eternally advancing horizon of existence. The Greek word for

Above: In this 13th-century French image, the "Creator of heaven and earth" takes the measure of his raw materials with a compass. This image may have influenced William Blake's 1794 Ancient of Days.

proceed emphasizes "movement out of". The Greek word *perichoresis*, meaning "permeation without confusion", is also used by theologians to express how the persons of the Trinity interpenetrate each other, yet remain distinct.

DIVINE BEINGS
The three persons of the Trinity are perceived by most Catholics as having particular, appropriate divine aspects. The Father is the Creator, the maker of all and the interlocutor with Adam and Eve. The Son's defining attribute is that he was made man. He demonstrated the infinite depth of divine love by becoming human, walking among us and acceding to a sacrifice of his simultaneously human and divine self as an

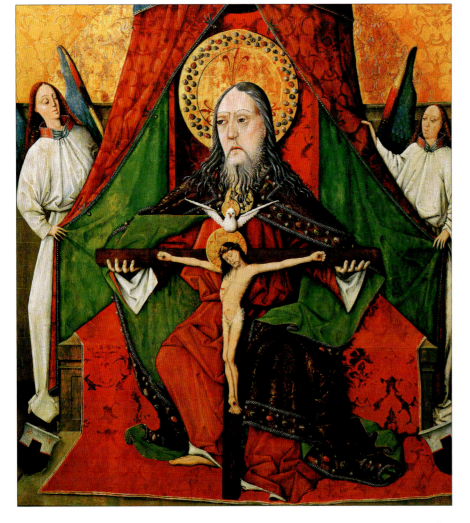

Left: The Catholic mystery of the Trinity is shown in this 15th-century European painting. They are intimately connected yet distinct, with God the Father holding his crucified Son, while the Holy Spirit as a dove rests on Christ's halo.

offering to re-open the possibility of man's freedom from Adam and Eve's original sin.

The Holy Spirit, as implied by his name, is the only divine persona without a human form in traditional Catholic iconography. He is usually artistically represented as either a dove or a tongue of flame, the form in which, ten days after Christ's ascension to heaven, he descended to inspire the apostles as teachers of the Word of God (the day now known as Whitsunday, or more commonly in Catholic theology, Pentecost). Metaphorically, in his role as bringer of grace and an inspirer of wisdom, he is spoken of as a mighty wind or as the inspiration or breath of God. He is also known as the "Paraclete", or advocate, which refers to his role as a spiritual teacher or guide.

A CONTROVERSIAL TIME

The doctrine of the Trinity was fiercely debated by the bishops and Church fathers in the early days of Christianity. The 4th-century controversy surrounding Arianism – a heresy that claimed the Son of God

Above: The Holy Spirit is the only person of the Trinity who never speaks, but we can almost hear the whirr of his wings in this graceful French c.1490 illumination by Jean Colombe.

Above: At Jesus' baptism, the heavens opened, the Holy Spirit descended and the Father spoke, "This is my beloved son…" Giovanni Guercino's 17th-century painting shows a powerful God the Father.

was not truly God but was created by God – in particular, served as a spur to bishops to set and define the immanent divinity of the three persons of the one God as a crucial and defining Catholic doctrine.

Arianism argued that Christ was inferior to the Father in that "there was a then when he was not" – in other words, there was a time when Christ did not exist. Christ was described as the first of the Father's created beings, not "eternally begotten", but simply "begotten", thus denigrating his divine nature as a being without beginning or end.

The Council of Nicaea was convened in AD 325 by Constantine, Emperor of Rome, in large part to counteract Arianism. The Nicene Creed that was formulated at the council, then finalized at the Council of Constantinople in AD 381, is still the familiar creed recited in Roman Catholic churches today.

Even more contentious was the relationship of the Holy Spirit to the Father and the Son. The Nicene Creed of AD 325 merely stated "we believe in the Holy Spirit". In AD 381, the "filioque" ("and the son") clause was added, stating that the Holy Spirit "proceeds from the Father and the Son". It was disagreement about this "dual procession" doctrine that caused the Eastern Christian Church to split from the Roman Church in the Great Schism of 1054.

THE TRINITY

The term "Trinity", from the Latin noun *trinitas*, meaning "three at once", does not occur in the Bible, but the gospels do contain references to the divinity of the Father, Son and Holy Spirit. For example, after Christ rose from the dead, he bid the apostles to "go forth and teach all nations, baptizing them in the name of the Father, and of the Son and of the Holy Spirit" (Matthew 28:20). The term Trinity in relation to the Godhead was first used by Tertullian, the 3rd-century son of a Roman centurion and an early convert to Christianity, who was a prolific writer and contributor to evolving Christian theology in the early centuries after Christ's death.

CHRIST THE REDEEMER

IN CATHOLIC THEOLOGY, ORIGINAL SIN IS THE METAPHORICAL "STAIN" ALL HUMAN BEINGS ARE BORN WITH – AND IT IS THE REASON WHY CHRIST SACRIFICED HIMSELF TO REDEEM THE HUMAN RACE.

Original sin is inherited, like a genetic disease, from the first man – our ancestor Adam – and all humans have inherited it. The Catholic catechism says, "The whole human race is in Adam". This does not mean that original sin is a sinful action of Adam that we imitate or recreate. It is, rather, our tragic patrimony, meaning that we have been born deprived of the original grace that was God's initial endowment to our ancestral parents, Adam and Eve. The poet John Milton (although not a Catholic himself) expressed it well:

> Of man's first disobedience,
>   and the Fruit
> Of that Forbidden Tree,
>   whose mortal taste
> Brought Death into the World,
>   and all our woe…

FORBIDDEN FRUIT

The actual sin, described in Genesis, was eating the fruit of the Tree of Knowledge of Good and Evil, the only tree in paradise prohibited by God to Adam and Eve. Eve was tempted by Satan in the guise of a serpent, who told her she would be like a god and understand good and evil. Adam then took the fruit from Eve and ate as well.

As a result of Adam and Eve's wilfully disobedient act, Catholicism teaches that we are born fallen, with our souls deprived of sanctifying grace, not fully and freely open and receptive to God's love. The fall of the first man infused not just humanity but the entire world – the originally harmonious world made by God became discordant. Instead of every type of fruit tree, God prophesied that the earth would bring forth thorns and thistles. Instead of being blissfully unaware of their nakedness, Adam and Eve perceived it as shameful and hid. Original sin set man against himself and the earth – first intended to be our garden of delight – against man.

Catholics believe that death became part of life with original sin. As a direct response to Adam and Eve's disobedience, God pronounced, "In the sweat of thy face shalt thou eat bread till thou return to the earth out of which thou wast taken: for dust thou art, and into dust thou shalt return" (Genesis 3:19).

Left: Eve, having already eaten from the forbidden fruit, colludes with the serpent, who places the apple in her waiting hand as she draws Adam close. This detail is from a 16th-century German triptych.

Above: Because of original sin, death gained power over us and took us from the garden of paradise. In Evelyn de Morgan's 1890 The Angel of Death, *death has wings.*

BODY AND SOUL

Although the concept of original sin already existed, it was first defined as a doctrine in the 5th century AD by St Augustine of Hippo. Augustine had lived a dissolute life before his conversion from Manichaeism (a type of gnostic religion) to Catholicism, so he was particularly alert to man's sinful nature. The Second Council of Orange in AD 529 specified that while death of the body was the punishment for original sin, death of the soul was the sin itself.

Death of the soul is emphasized because original sin is responsible for destroying our first intimate union with God. Adam and Eve's action deprived them of the original grace that was their birthright, and this loss introduced the tendency toward corruption into the world, as though the previously perfect fabric of Creation was rent with a fatal flaw, weakening it so that it easily became tattered. Original sin is also responsible for allowing our

CHRIST'S CRUCIAL SACRIFICE

At both the Council of Orange in AD 529 and the Council of Trent in 1546, the Church fathers defined the doctrine of justification. This emphasized that our redemption was not possible without Christ's mediation, or the merit that he obtained for us by his obedient death, to make restitution for our disobedience. Redemption is not possible by human good works and good behaviour alone. The Church fathers pronounced anathema (a kind of doctrinal condemnation) on anyone who believed humans could save themselves without Christ – specifically, Pelagius, an Irish monk whose heretical beliefs triggered the Council of Orange's pronouncements.

Pelagius believed we could save ourselves by our good works and he de-emphasized the role of God's Grace. The Catholic Church teaches that we need the grace that Christ first obtained for us by his sacrifice. Additionally, we also require the sanctifying grace that fills our soul in baptism, the educating aid of the Holy Spirit that comes to us through participation in the sacraments, and continuous obedience to God's commandments in order to avoid damnation and find eternal life with God.

Above: Pelagius (AD 355–425) believed that original sin was not every man's inheritance, and that man could save himself without Christ's sacrifice.

inferior worldly and carnal desires, known as "concupiscence", to prevail over our reason.

SEEKING REDEMPTION

The counterpoint to this tragic fall from grace is our ability to essentially re-enact our first parents' temptation and choice – but this time, individually, because we still retain the free will with which they were endowed by God, to choose to turn toward God, or *conversio ad deum*. The possible redemption of each individual is a direct result of the offering Christ made of himself to the Father: as man out of his own free will chose to turn away and reject God's love (*adversio ad deum*) and instead act to satisfy his own egotistical desire, Christ out of his own free will did not resist actual torture on the Cross to pay the price to redeem man. The Latin word *redemptio* is related to Hebrew and Greek words meaning "a ransom price".

Right: Our first defence against original sin comes through the grace of baptism. In this late 16th-century painted stone, St Augustine, once a libertine, and his illegitimate son Adeodatus are baptized by St Ambrose.

THE EUCHARIST

LIKE THE HOLY TRINITY, THE DOCTRINE OF THE EUCHARIST, WHICH CELEBRATES JESUS' LAST SUPPER WITH HIS APOSTLES, IS ONE OF THE MOST IMPORTANT, CENTRAL BELIEFS OF THE CATHOLIC CHURCH.

The Roman Catholic catechism calls the Eucharist "the source and summit of the Christian life". Most Catholics would probably agree that the Eucharist is a particularly special doctrine. It is one that each practising Catholic is introduced to at an early age, and it continues through the years, becoming a customary thread of the faith drawing together generations of families.

Almost any person brought up in the Catholic faith will have specific memories of their first Holy Communion, because it is a joyful day that has delightful worldly celebrations

Above: The most sacred moment of the Mass is the consecration, when the bread and wine are transubstantiated into the body and blood of Christ, as seen in this 15th/16th-century image by Giovanni di Giuliano Boccardi.

surrounding it. It is also the first time that a child is called to participate in one of the central mysteries of the faith, the Eucharist. This is a particularly special occasion, when the child is first asked to try to extend his or her perception to encompass a numinous dimension of the infinite by participation in a very specific individual act.

THE LORD'S SUPPER

The word "Eucharist" comes from the Greek *eucharistein*, or "grateful, thankful". It is the name given to the communion that has been repeated through the centuries at every Catholic Mass. Its origin lies in the Last Supper, the story of which is engraved on the consciousness of every Catholic. The Last Supper is described in almost the same words in Matthew 26:26–28, Mark 14:22–24 and Luke 22:17–20. Celebrating the paschal meal with his apostles, and well aware that he was about to be betrayed and put to death, Christ took bread, broke it and offered it to his apostles, saying,

THE LAST SUPPER

Leonardo da Vinci's renowned mural painting, *The Last Supper* (1495–8), depicts the paschal supper at which Christ broke bread and offered wine. The painting dramatizes the moment described in the gospels when Jesus, "troubled in spirit", announces "Amen, amen, I say to you, one of you shall betray me." The disciples therefore looked upon one another, doubting of whom he spoke.

Despite the press of the apostles around the table and the apparent furor caused by Christ's words, there are two figures who remain alone with their thoughts. Judas' hand hovers slightly above a dish, illustrating Christ's words, "he that dippeth his hands with me in the dish, he shall betray me". All the other apostles lean toward Christ or toward each other, exchanging glances. Judas leans away from Christ without touching anyone else, and while the others look at Christ beseechingly, Judas simply stares. Christ's arms extend down with his palms turned upwards in a gesture that is one of submission, yet he also seems to be gathering power from the heavens toward which his hands open. Although Christ's gaze is directed away from Judas, the entire side of his face is angled toward him, almost as if he were offering a cheek to be kissed – and, of course, it is with a kiss on Jesus' cheek that Judas will betray him to his captors on the following day.

Above: Da Vinci's late 15th-century painting The Last Supper *not ony recalls the last meal between Jesus and his apostles but is also full of symbolism, referring to the momentous event that will occur when Judas betrays Christ.*

"Take ye, and eat. This is my body." Taking the chalice, he gave thanks, and gave it to them, saying, "Drink ye all of this. For this is my blood of the new testament, which shall be shed for many unto remission of sins." During this supper, Christ spoke the simple words, "Do this in memory of me." This quiet command is the genesis of the Eucharistic sacrifice around which a great world religion has been formed. In allusion to the Last Supper, communion is sometimes called the Lord's Supper.

Christ prefigured these actions before his death when he fed a crowd of people that had come to hear him preach and who were hungry, yet with little food. In the hands of Jesus, on that day the five loaves and two fishes available miraculously became enough to feed the multitude. When preaching in the synagogue at Capharnaum soon after performing this miracle, Jesus said, "I am the bread of Life…. He that eateth my flesh and drinketh my blood have everlasting life: and I will raise him up in the last day."

BREAD AND WINE

Through the centuries, the central act of Mass has been the priest's consecration of wheaten bread and grape wine into Christ. The Council of Trent in 1546 defined the Eucharist as "the Body and Blood, together with the Soul and Divinity of our Lord Jesus Christ, and therefore the whole Christ, is truly, really and substantially contained in the sacrament of the Holy Eucharist."

Various theologians over the years have attempted to define the Holy Eucharist as a symbol of the body and blood of Christ (16th-century Zwinglians), or as a dynamic trans-

Right: A literal interpretation of the doctrine that the host is transubstantiated into the entirety of the body and blood of Christ can be seen in this 14th-century painting by Ugolino di Prete Ilario.

ferral of the efficacy of Christ's body and blood to the souls of the elect at the moment of reception of the host (Calvinists), but the Church declared all such limitations on the definition of the Eucharist to be heresies.

THE CONSECRATION

Catholic doctrine is specific regarding the holiest moment of Mass. This is known as the consecration, when the priest repeats the words of Christ at the Last Supper. "This is my body" is spoken when the priest raises the

Left: The first Holy Communion is an inspiring milestone in the lives of Catholic children. In this late 19th-century painting by Carl Frithjof Smith, a young girl proudly wears her new crucifix.

bread and "This is my blood" is uttered with the wine, and at each and every Mass a miracle occurs and the bread and wine are changed, or "transubstantiated", into the body and blood of Christ. How the change occurs when the priest speaks the words is a mystery known only to God. What is changed is the entire substance – the being – of the bread and wine into the entirety of the substance, or being, of Christ, with only the "species", or appearance, of bread and wine remaining.

The Church holds that, in essence and in actuality (not symbolically), Christ is present in the Eucharist. In order to skirt an association with cannibalism, the Church does not usually emphasize (but it would not deny) that Christ is physically present (like the person sitting next to you in Church, for example), but that he is substantially present, which is known as the "Real Presence".

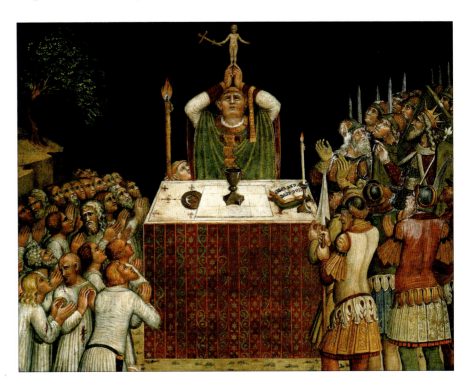

THE CLASSIC CREEDS

THERE ARE THREE CLASSIC CREEDS OF THE CATHOLIC CHURCH: THE APOSTLES', NICENE AND ATHANASIAN CREEDS. EACH WAS DEVELOPED TO SHIELD THE CHURCH FROM A SPECIFIC HERESY.

Many modern Catholics can usually repeat by rote the Nicene Creed, imprinted on their memory since childhood. However, they may not realize that in the early centuries after Christ's death, when Christianity was still seeking to define and establish itself in the face of uncertainty, danger and opposition, creeds were developed and perceived as true badges of faith. They were developed to fight heresies, to establish, teach and promote right doctrine, and, in the words of the Catholic catechism, to be "the spiritual seal, our heart's meditation."

THE FIRST SYSTEM OF BELIEF
The Apostles' Creed is the oldest. It originated in the first century after Christ's death and sets forth the teachings of the Church under the leadership of St Peter, the first pope. During the Middle Ages it was believed that the first 12 apostles had composed the Creed on Pentecost, the day that the Holy Spirit descended to inspire them; however, this is probably a legend.

About two-thirds of the Apostles' Creed sets forth in straightforward language beliefs about the identity of Jesus Christ. This is because, during the first five centuries of the Church's existence, when the Apostles' Creed was formulated, Gnosticism was an influential heresy. Followers of this faith believed that the material world was completely corrupt (beyond the "tendency to sin" of the doctrine of original sin) and, therefore, although they were willing to believe that Jesus was God, the Gnostics denied that he had ever been a true man, a flesh and blood corporeal man who had died, as well as being divine.

Above: St Athanasius, shown in this 18th-century Greek icon, was an Egyptian theologian known as the Father of Orthodoxy. His fight against Arianism was influential in the development of the doctrine of the Trinity.

Below: The ravaged body of Christ, showing he was flesh and mortal, stands out in a contemporary landscape, an attempt by a 16th-century French artist to help refute the Gnostic doctrine that Christ had never been truly mortal.

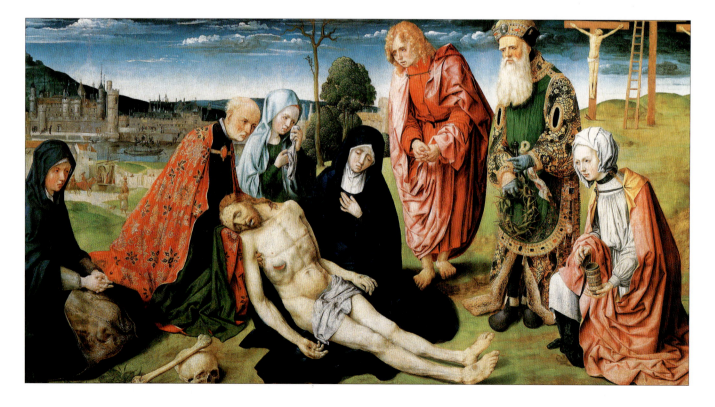

By denying Jesus' humanity, the followers of Gnosticism were also denying that he died for us, which was a blatant contradiction of a bedrock Catholic doctrine. The Apostles' Creed refutes this Gnostic heresy by dwelling on the corporeal history of Christ on earth, stating that he "suffered, died and was buried". This creed may have been used as a profession of faith for early Christians about to be baptized, and even today the Apostle's Creed is part of the baptismal rite.

ONE IN BEING

The second of the classic creeds, the Nicene Creed, which is also known as the Niceno-Constantinopolitan Creed, clarified Jesus' standing. It was developed in the 4th century and endures today in both the Roman and Eastern Catholic Churches. During the 4th century, Arianism – essentially the belief that Jesus, while divine, was an inferior divinity to the Father – became such a widespread and contentious issue that it threatened the stability of the Roman Empire itself. In the Edict of Milan (AD 313), Constantine declared that Christians were free to practise their religion, so the disputes over Catholic doctrine, freed from the earlier need for secrecy, became even more acrimonious than before.

Constantine ordered a council of bishops to be convened in Nicaea (in present-day Turkey) to make a ruling on the heated issue. The Nicene Creed, which was developed at that conference, declared in its

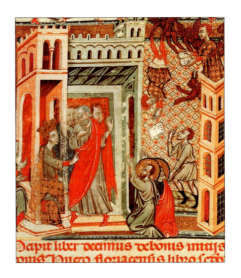

Above: Simon Magus, shown in this 14th-century French manuscript, was a Gnostic teacher and magician known as the "first heretic". Legend says he fell to his death from the Roman Forum while trying to prove to St Peter that he could fly.

most significant line that Jesus was "one in being with the father". The most significant Greek term used in this phrase was *homoousios*, or "consubstantial", meaning of the same substance, not *homoiousios*, which means "similar" (but not the same) substance.

In AD 381, the creed was revised to expand its definition of the Holy Spirit. The earlier AD 325 version had only noted "We believe in the Holy Spirit", somewhat short-changing the third person.

THE STERNEST CREED

The newest of the three classic creeds, the Athanasian Creed, is a resolute profession of doctrines on the nature of the Trinity and of the Incarnation (particularly with regard to the divinity and humanity of Jesus). It also declares the absolute necessity of belief in these doctrines in order to achieve one's salvation.

The creed was written in a series of declarations that were clearly and inclusively formulated in an obvious attempt to stifle all the various heresies on the Trinity and the nature of Christ that plagued the Catholic Church, among them being Arianism, Modalism, Sabellianism, Apollinarianism and Eutychianism. To emphasize that this was a serious matter, the creed contains a series of clauses that outline two stark choices: belief, or the road to damnation. It concludes: "This is the Catholic faith, which except a man believe faithfully and firmly, he cannot be saved."

Below: The large hands of the Madonna protectively enfold the Christ child in this 15th/16th-century painting by Giovanni Bellini. He grasps his mother's thumb, even as he asserts his divinity by offering a blessing.

OF UNKNOWN ORIGIN

The Athanasian Creed is also known as the Symbol Quicunque for its first Latin words, "*Quicunque vult salvus esse…*" ("Whosoever wishes to be saved…"). Tradition has ascribed the Athanasian Creed to Athanasius, the 4th-century Bishop of Alexandria, but this has been proved untrue. Although many plausible theories have been put forward as to its origin, none have been conclusive. However, scholars tend to agree that it was written in France *c.* mid-5th century.

THE MYSTERY OF FAITH

THE CATECHISM

TO HELP THE FAITHFUL LEARN THE BELIEFS OF THE CATHOLIC CHURCH, ALL ITS GREAT THEOLOGICAL TEACHINGS HAVE BEEN SUMMARIZED IN WHAT IS POPULARLY KNOWN AS THE CATECHISM.

"Catechetics" comes from the Greek *katechesis*, meaning instruction by word of mouth. A "catechumen" is the person being instructed in religious doctrine. The New Testament portrays the 12-year-old Jesus as an exceptional catechumen:

> And it came to pass, that, after three days, they found him in the temple, sitting in the midst of the doctors, hearing them and asking them questions. And all that heard him were astonished at his wisdom and his answers. (Luke 2:46)

THE WORDS IN WRITING

A catechism is doctrinal instruction provided in written form. It is in a question and answer format because the Church considers it the best method for ensuring that the doctrine being taught is correct and uniform – which is important in a religion where shades of meaning are crucial and confusion can unwittingly lead to heresy.

In Catholicism's early history, written doctrinal instruction was generally sparse, a deficiency that contributed to the Church's

Above: A youthful Jesus turned the usual catechetical order inside out by teaching the rabbis. In this 15th/16th-century painting by Albrecht Dürer, Jesus amazed them with his preternatural wisdom.

vulnerability to the Reformation. Fifteenth-century parish priests, who were often poorly educated in abstruse Church doctrines themselves, were usually unable to help their confused parishioners. Poor instruction and misunderstanding of the complexities of the doctrines, including the plenary indulgence, enabled corrupt practices, such as selling indulgences for money. Martin Luther was one of the reformers who pounced on these practices, and many left the Church to join the reformers as a result.

The first-ever Catholic catechism was published in Vienna in 1555 by Peter Canisius, a Dutch Jesuit. Canisius compiled a single volume

Left: Peter Canisius (1521–97), shown in this 17th-century Flemish painting, wrote three Latin and German catechisms and helped to found the University of Fribourg, Switzerland, still an influential school of Catholic theology.

136

that contained 222 questions and 2,000 scriptural quotations. This catechism is still a favourite of theologians and historians centuries later; however, at the time it was first published, it was too sophisticated to be of much help to the ordinary priest and parishioner.

EDUCATING THE CLERGY

The Church recognized the need for, in the words of the 16th-century Council of Trent, "...a formulary and method for teaching the rudiments of the faith, to be used by all legitimate pastors and teachers". This was to take the shape of a simpler catechism that would be helpful for ordinary priests as they cared for the souls of their flocks. The resulting Roman catechism was published in 1566 and translated into the vernacular languages used by all Catholic countries.

The Roman catechism was intended to educate the clergy, and parish priests were ordered by their bishops to memorize it and to pass on that rote knowledge to their parishioners. It was the work of a number of distinguished theologians and cardinals of the day, and the authority of the Roman catechism was considered unimpeachable.

> ### THE DISCIPLINE OF THE SECRET
>
> In the early centuries of the Church, during and just after the Roman persecutions, admission to the mysterious doctrines and rites of the new religion called Christianity was treated with great reserve. Scriptural support for a gradual revelation of the mysteries was provided by Matthew 7:6: "Give not that which is holy to dogs; neither cast ye your pearls before swine, lest they trample them under their feet, and turning upon you, they tear you."
>
> The gradual revelation of the doctrines and rituals of the Church was known as the Discipline of the Secret. In particular, early Christians considered that the teachings of the Trinity and the Eucharist should be revealed to postulants only after careful preparation, because the doctrines imparted to the poorly prepared could easily be misconstrued as tritheism (the Trinity) or cannibalism (the Eucharist). As Christianity became more established, the practice of the Discipline of the Secret began to diminish and it was for the most part finished by the 5th century AD.

MODERN VERSIONS

New catechisms continue to be developed. The catechism familiar to Americans is the Baltimore Catechism. In 1829, American bishops asked for a catechism adapted to the needs of the diverse American Catholic audience. *A Catechism of Christian Doctrine, Prepared and Enjoined by Order of the Third Council of Baltimore*, was issued in 1855 and became the standard United States catechism. A modernized edition of the Baltimore Catechism is still available today.

Another new catechism, entitled *Compendium of the Catechism of the Catholic Church*, was started on the 20th anniversary of the Second Vatican Council, brought to completion by Pope John Paul II and published by Pope Benedict in 2005.

Below: Founded in 1253 by the Chaplain of Louis V, the Sorbonne was an institution of education, famed for its influential, but conservative, school of theology.

Below: A nun from the Missionaries of Charity, the order founded by Mother Teresa, is engaged in the traditional catechetical method of oral instruction.

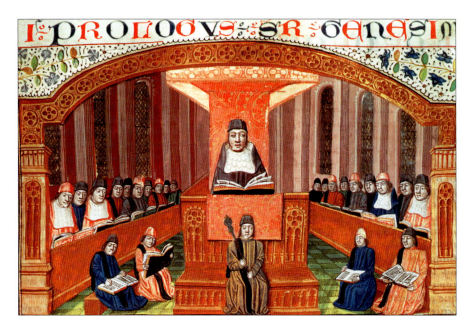

IN ACCORDANCE WITH THE SCRIPTURES

CATHOLICISM VIEWS THE SCRIPTURES AS THE WORD OF GOD, PASSED ON BY WRITERS INSPIRED BY THE HOLY SPIRIT. THEY ARE CONSIDERED DIVINE REVELATION IN WRITTEN FORM.

The Scriptures that form the sacred canon are the biblical books accepted by the Church as genuine. Catholicism sees the Old Testament, which existed years before the birth of Christ, as part of a divine plan, calling the Old Testament an "active and steady preparation" for the revelations of Christ in the New and credited with tilling the ground for the coming of the Messiah. According to the Catholic catechism, this is a covenant that is "strikingly fulfilled" in the New Testament. It says the Old Testament books:

> …give expression to a lively sense of God, contain a store of sublime teachings about God, sound wisdom about human life, and a wonderful treasury of prayers, and in them the mystery of our salvation is present in a hidden way.

"Typology" is the term that describes seeing the revelations of the New Testament prefigured in the books and stories of the Old.

THE DEPOSIT OF FAITH

Unlike Protestant Christianity, the Catholic Church does not view Scripture as the sole source of divine revelation. This was a major issue during the Reformation, with the Protestant reformers claiming that all belief required specific evidence or *sola scriptura* ("scriptural proof"). The Catholic Church, in contrast, argued that scripture should be read from the perspective of a sacred tradition, and that it should include the non-scriptural compendium of teachings and traditional beliefs – referred to by the Church as the "deposit of faith". These teachings and beliefs were revealed by Jesus to the apostles and passed down through the apostles and early Church fathers to become Catholic customary belief and practice through the centuries.

At the same time, the Church does not encourage individualistic interpretations of Scripture, especially when they are not supported by valid study and scholarship. Instead, the ultimate authority for scriptural interpretation is the magisterium, or the teaching authority of the Church comprised of the pope and the bishops of the Church. The magisterium's scriptural interpretations, according to Church doctrine, are infallible because they are inspired by the Holy Spirit. That said, the Catholic Church does encourage serious biblical study, so that readers will not react to the Bible only according to their own subjective emotional responses.

Above: Moses keeps a protective arm around the second tablets of law written by the hand of God in this 17th-century painting by Laurent de la Hyre. Moses had smashed the first tablets when he saw his people worshipping a golden calf.

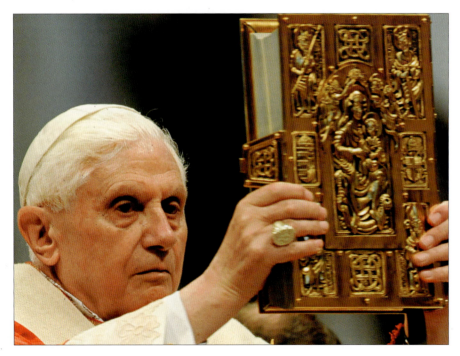

Left: Pope Benedict XVI provided an extensive commentary on modern methods of Biblical exegesis in his 1988 Erasmus lecture, "Biblical Interpretation in Crisis".

THE BACKGROUND

In "The Interpretation of the Bible in the Church", a 1993 document written by Cardinal Joseph Ratzinger (who became Pope Benedict XVI in 2005), the cardinal freely asserted that the Bible would be more fully appreciated if its readers had a working knowledge of the society, history, languages and geography that influenced its writers. Of this "historical-critical" approach, Cardinal Ratzinger pointed out that the "eternal word" of God, the Bible, was brought into being during specific historical periods, and that readers of the Bible must necessarily be grounded in the cultural and social details of those eras for proper and accurate comprehension of the text.

However, an overemphasis on these methods could obscure what the Church refers to as the "spiritual sense", a dimension of the Scriptures that extends far beyond the reality of other human texts. Benedict warned that modern historical-grammatical methods of interpretation can lead to the distancing of God's original words if too much emphasis is put on the human dimension of the words.

Benedict went on to assert that while approaching biblical exegesis (or interpretation) with the proper respect for the texts, as God's Word requires, all the possible methods of interpretation – historical, philological, sociological – should also be given their due. It is essential for Catholics to keep in mind that the principal aim of their studies should be the deepening of their faith.

DIFFERENT TESTAMENTS

The Protestant and Catholic Bibles differ in the number of canonical books contained in their respective Old Testaments. Catholic Bibles have 46 books, Protestant Bibles, 39. The reasons for the discrepancy go back to ancient political and religious history. Early Christians accepted as divinely inspired the *Septuagint* (Greek for 70, referring to the 70 translators from Hebrew into Greek) version of the Jewish Old Testament. When the *Septuagint* was translated from Hebrew into Greek, it contained seven newer Greek books that had never been in the Hebrew language, but they were still considered part of the divinely inspired canon by Jews at the time of Jesus.

In AD 100, Jews purged their canon of these non-Hebrew books, known as the Deuterocanonical (for second canon, because they were newer) books. Christians chose to keep the seven, because at the time of Christ, they had been considered inspired texts. However, in 1517 during the Reformation, Martin Luther advocated the old Hebrew canon, partly because he objected to references to Purgatory in some of the Deuterocanonical Books. Even today, many Protestant Bibles include the seven disputed books only at the back of the volume and refer to them as the Apocrypha (hidden) books. The Seven Books of the Apocrypha are Baruch, Maccabees I and II, Tobit, Judith, Ecclesiasticus (or Sirach) and Wisdom.

Below: The English translation of the New Testament by William Tyndale (1494–1536) was the first based on Hebrew and Greek texts.

Above: Biblical exegesis – the critical explanation of the text – takes many forms. This medieval French Bible Moralisée from c.1230 features brief biblical passages interspersed with moral or allegorical lessons.

THE EVANGELISTS

THE "FOUR EVANGELISTS" – MARK, MATTHEW, LUKE AND JOHN – ARE CREDITED IN THE TRADITION OF THE CATHOLIC CHURCH AS THE AUTHORS OF THE GOSPELS IN THE NEW TESTAMENT.

"Evangelist" is from the Greek for "one who proclaims good news", so the title when referring to the gospel writers emphasizes they are spreading the word of Jesus' life to inspire others to believe in Jesus as God. The earliest Gospel, Mark, was written about 40 years after Jesus' Resurrection. In that intervening time, accounts of Jesus were passed on orally, and all the Evangelists used this oral tradition for the content of their gospels. The four gospels were composed from about AD 65 to 100.

AUTHOR UNKNOWN

Secular biblical scholars generally agree that the actual authorship of the gospels is anonymous; the titles "according to..." (not "by") Matthew, Mark, Luke or John, were added in the late 2nd century. Secular scholars also believe that the gospels were written according to the oral tradi-tions of, rather than written by, the particular Evangelists. Yet the Church, while acknowledging the likely accuracy of the historians' position, has essentially declared that

Above: A portrayal of the four Evangelists eschews symbology and shows the four as reverent scholars, each cradling his precious gospel (Greek school, 18th century).

scholarly debate over the specific human authorship of the gospels is beside the point. In *Dei Verbum* (or "Word of God"), a "dogmatic constitution on divine revelation" issued by Pope Paul VI in 1965, the Church stated that as whoever "wrote" the gospels was inspired by the Holy Spirit, the real author of the gospels is God – and as such, the Church accepts them in their entirety as sacred and canonical. In other words, the authors, no matter who, were divinely inspired.

THE ORATORS

Tradition describes the Evangelists as four distinct people: Mark was a missionary with Paul, and Peter's follower. Matthew, one of the apostles, was a tax collector from Galilee. Luke, another missionary with Paul, was a Greek doctor, and is also believed to be the first Christian

Left: Tradition says that St Luke painted some of the earliest icons of the Virgin Mary. This has become a popular subject in art, as in this 16th-century painting by Maerten van Heemskerck.

THE EVANGELISTS

FOUR CREATURES BOUND TOGETHER IN SPIRIT

For centuries, the four Evangelists have been magnificently illustrated in Christian iconography and art as the "four living creatures" that flank God's throne in Revelation and Ezekiel. Described as six-winged and "full of eyes", the living creatures are fierce testaments to God's majesty and power. Traditionally, the first living creature, a lion, symbolizes Mark; the second, an ox, Luke; the third, a man, Matthew; and the fourth, an eagle, John. Each creature encompasses certain virtues: Mark's lion is royal and courageous; Luke's ox represents endurance and sacrifice; Matthew's man suggests the primacy of human intellect; and John's eagle, spirit and aspiration.

The Book of Kells, the superb 9th-century illuminated manuscript produced by Irish monks on the island of Iona, devotes a full page to the four living creatures. They frequently guard the portals of medieval cathedrals and glow in the light of ancient stained-glass windows. The symbols of the Evangelists are most often seen together, reflecting the beautiful words of St Irenaeus of Lyons (AD 120–202), "He who was manifested to men, has given us the gospel under four aspects, but bound together by one Spirit."

Right: The symbols of each of the four Evangelists are shown in this introductory page to the Gospel of St Matthew, from The Book of Kells.

painter (he is often portrayed holding a brush and is said to have painted the Black Madonna of Czestochowa, now the centrepiece of a Polish shrine). John was the beloved youngest apostle of Jesus.

THE "SYNOPTIC GOSPELS"

The first three gospels, Mark, Matthew and Luke, which are similar in content, are known as the "Synoptic Gospels", meaning they "see with the same eyes". Scholars believe the Synoptics have a common, lost source document, which is referred to as "Q" (from the German *Quelle*, or "source"). The Gospel of John, which is notably different, is known as the "maverick" gospel.

Each gospel was developed with unique characteristics. Mark is referred to as the "action" gospel, because it contains the most miracles and has a quick narrative pace – in fact, the word "immediately" appears 39 times. Luke contains more parables, and, as befitting a doctor, has a somewhat scientific tone. Its opening words state that it is intended as an orderly account for attaining knowledge. Matthew opens with a genealogy of Jesus, with frequent references to the Old Testament, and it emphasizes that Jesus is the prophesied Messiah. His work appears to have been written for a Jewish audience.

John opens with the famous passage, "In the beginning was the Word: and the Word was with God: and the Word was God." John is the most spiritual of the four gospels and the only one to state an evangelical purpose, "that ye might believe that Jesus is the Christ, the son of God; and that believing ye might have life through his name". John is also the only Gospel not to describe Jesus offering bread and wine at the Last Supper (the acts that instituted the Eucharist). In its place is the account of Jesus washing the apostles' feet.

Right: Christ walking on water, as depicted in this 20th-century painting by Frederic Montenard, is described in the gospels of Matthew, Mark and John. The miracle is prefigured in the Old Testament when the River Jordan parts for Joshua. "Jesus" is Latin for the Hebrew name Joshua.

OUR LADY

MANY OF TODAY'S CATHOLICS GROW UP SURROUNDED BY IMAGES OF THE VIRGIN MARY, BUT IT WAS NOT UNTIL THE 5TH CENTURY AD THAT MARY'S UNIQUE STATUS AS GOD-BEARER WAS EVEN RECOGNIZED.

Mary's eminent position in the Catholic pantheon was slow to develop. St Paul does not mention Mary, mother of Jesus, in any of his epistles. The Bible does not mention Mary's ultimate fate after Christ's death on the Cross. The last mention of Mary is in Acts 1:14, when she was present with the apostles as they persevered in prayer after Jesus' Ascension and just before Pentecost. We do not know where, how or even if Mary actually died. The Scriptures are silent on all of these things.

THE GOD-BEARER

Mary's status in the Church began to develop after she was declared *Theotokos* (Greek for "God-bearer") by the Council of Ephesus in AD 431. As was their wont, the early Church fathers debated for a long time before endowing Mary with this title. Its ultimate conferral was yet another means for the Church fathers to promulgate the concept of Christ as God-man, indivisibly true man and true God. By officially proclaiming Mary "God-bearer", it meant that she did not give birth to just the "man" aspect of God, as believed by Nestorius, the 3rd-century Bishop of Constantinople. Calling Mary *Theotokos* was just one more way to affirm the indivisible divine-human nature of Christ.

A PRAYER FOR MARY

It was only after the Council of Ephesus that liturgical feasts were held in Mary's honour, though the earliest known prayer to Mary, the *Sub Tuum Praesidium* ("Beneath Thy Compassion"), dates from *c.* AD 250. The prayer is a plea to Mary in her role as an intercessor for humanity with God. Pope John Paul II mentions this important mediatory role of Mary in *Redemptoris Mater*, his 1987 encyclical letter concerning Mary, noting that she intercedes "…not as an outsider, but in her position as mother". Mary, as both mortal woman and mother of the God-man, has a special attentiveness to the needs of mankind as well as a unique intimacy with her son. As a suffering mother, she has earned the right to be an adviser – even to God.

CONCEIVED WITHOUT SIN

There are three Catholic doctrines regarding Mary. The Immaculate Conception claims that alone among human beings, Mary was conceived without the inherited stain of original sin. It states "…the most Blessed

Above: As he hung on the Cross, Christ placed Mary under the protection of the apostle John, shown in this painting by Rogier van der Weyden. Christ spoke words to each in turn, "Woman behold thy son…Behold thy mother."

Virgin Mary, from the first moment of her conception, by a singular grace and privilege from Almighty God and in view of the merits of Jesus Christ, was kept free of every stain of original sin."

This dogma sets forth the utter singularity of Mary. No other human being received this privilege from God. Besides the logic that the woman who was to bear and raise God would be free of a fallen nature, this doctrine also endows Mary with a special role, if not of our Redeemer, as is Christ, then as the one who made redemption possible through her obedience.

PERPETUAL VIRGINITY

Mary was a virgin at Christ's conception and remained so despite his gestation and birth and indeed for the rest of her life. Known as Perpetual Virginity, in the words of the Lateran Council (AD 649), Mary conceived

Below: Mary spreads her cloak in a gesture of protection in this detail from a c.1422 painting by Jean Miralhet. The Sub Tuum Presidium, *a hymn dating from the 3rd century, begins, "Beneath thy compassion, we take refuge, O Theotokos".*

"without any detriment to her virginity, which remained inviolate even after his birth". Mary's lasting virginity was accepted by most of the early Church fathers, although Tertullian disagreed with it.

The doctrine provided a prototype for the monastic movement as it gained strength in the Church, starting *c.* the 4th century with St Anthony. Mary's celibacy is also representative of the metaphor of being "wedded to Christ", or so devoted to Christ that this relationship subsumes all others. The Church is known as the Bride or Spouse of the Lamb, nuns are brides of Christ and the Church continues to insist on the celibacy of priests, so that their devotion to God remains completely unchallenged by earthly vows.

THE ASSUMPTION

Celebrated by Catholics each year on 15 August, the Assumption is the doctrine that "…at the end of her earthly course, Mary was assumed into heavenly glory, body and soul". This is the 1950 definition given by Pope Pius XII, in a decree (*Munificentissimus Deus*) whose solemnity is apparent from the fact that it is the only ex-cathedra invocation by a pope since the doctrine of papal infallibility was established in 1870.

Pius XII's decree leaves vague the question of whether or not Mary actually died before she was raised by God into heaven. A variety of early non-scriptural accounts of the Assumption exist, some written by early saints, such as Gregory of Tours and John of Damascus.

Eastern Orthodox Catholics tend to favour more explicit stories concerning Mary's actual death, stating that she was surrounded by 11 of the apostles at the moment of her death. They refer to this death as Mary's Dormition, but believe along with Western Catholics that she was bodily assumed into heaven after her burial; the Dormition is also celebrated on 15 August. In any case, the Assumption is viewed by most Catholics as prefiguring the final redemption of all observant Catholics on the Last Day.

MOTHERLY LOVE

Despite all the unusual doctrines that surround Mary, the Catholic fascination with this figure seems to be related to something intimate and simple: her motherhood. The familiar enveloping motherly relationship and the idea that Jesus had a special fondness for Mary were illustrated when he did favours for her (turning water into wine at the wedding at Cana). Some of his last words as a living man were spoken to her as he hung from the Cross, where he appointed his apostle John to care for his mother. These actions seem to simplify Jesus' humanity into something that we can understand, even while he maintains his godliness. A simple emotion in powerful people is always resonant, and through Mary we can find this in Christ.

Below: The Eastern Catholic tradition of the Dormition (falling asleep) of Mary teaches that she died a natural death, surrounded by all of the apostles except Thomas, who was late. The scene is shown in this 14th-century Byzantine mosaic.

Above: Mary rests her cheek on the head of her thriving son, whom she closely resembles. This early 16th-century Madonna and Child *by Raphael emphasizes the natural maternal bond.*

MARIAN APPARITIONS

APPARITIONS OF THE BLESSED VIRGIN MARY HAVE BEEN REPORTED FOR MANY CENTURIES. THE CATHOLIC CHURCH REFERS TO SUCH VISIONS AS "PRIVATE REVELATIONS".

Probably the earliest of the Marian revelations dates back to AD 40. It occurred before Mary's Assumption into heaven, when the apostle James, who was in Spain trying to spread the gospel, had a vision of the Virgin atop a marble pillar. She instructed him to build a church on the site, and that church today is said to be the first of the thousands of churches that have been dedicated to and named for the Blessed Virgin.

GUADALUPE

The three most influential Marian apparitions occurred at Guadalupe in Mexico, Lourdes in France and Fatima in Portugal. Guadalupe is notable because the visionary, Juan Diego, was an Aztec and a recent convert to Christianity. Mary appeared to him in 1531 at the site of a former temple to the Aztec gods, and as a proof of her appearance she left her image mysteriously imprinted on Juan Diego's tilma, a type of cactus-fibre cloak. The image and the cloak have never decomposed and even today, more than four centuries later, the cloak (protected by bullet-proof glass) can still be seen at the basilica that was built in Guadalupe. Juan Diego's vision was influential in converting many indigenous Mexicans to Christianity, although these people were initially disinclined to do so because of their subjugation by the Spanish.

LOURDES AND FATIMA

Probably the best-known Marian vision occurred at Lourdes in 1858. The lady who appeared to a poverty-stricken and sickly shepherd girl said very little, mainly directing her supplicant to pray the rosary and to do penance. Yet the simple, intense, committed (and lifelong) piety and certainty of Bernadette Soubirous so impressed the clergy who examined her that Bernadette remains today the exemplary believable visionary in the eyes of the Church. Lourdes is also known for Massabielle, the spring blessed by the Virgin that has been responsible for dozens of otherwise inexplicable cures.

Fatima is remarkable for both the number of the visions and the loquacity of the Virgin Mary. Appearing six times in 1917 to three young children, Mary foretold the end of World War I but warned of a worse war to come. She provided the children with a brief vision of hell and requested that Russia (this was during the Russian Revolution) be consecrated to her Immaculate Heart. Pope John Paul II, who felt that Our Lady of Fatima was

Above: Our Lady, atop a pillar carried by angels, is illustrated in a c.1629 painting by Nicolas Poussin. She appeared to the apostle James as he prayed by the banks of the Ebro River in Zaragoza, Spain.

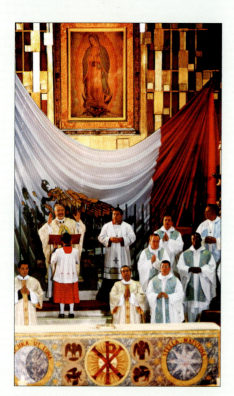

Left: The Basilica of Guadalupe in Mexico is the most visited Catholic shrine in the world; on the feast of Our Lady of Guadelupe, millions make the pilgrimage – some on their knees.

THE PRINCIPAL REVELATIONS

At least 75 visions, or private revelations, have been reported over the centuries, but the Church has deemed "worthy of belief" perhaps 30 of them. Of these, there are nine principal, approved Marian apparitions:

Guadalupe (Mexico, 1531)
Rue du Bac (France, 1830)
La Salette (France, 1846)
Lourdes (France, 1858)
Pontmain (France, 1871)
Knock (Ireland, 1879)
Fatima (Portugal, 1917)
Beauraing (Belgium, 1932)
Banneux (Belgium, 1933)

responsible for his own survival from an assassination attempt that occurred on the feast of the Lady of Fatima, did perform such a consecration in May 1984. As a gesture toward Russia, he mentioned the nations that "particularly needed to be… consecrated" in the consecration.

THE DEPOSIT OF FAITH
The Church teaches that even the private revelations they dub "worthy of belief" do not constitute part of the "deposit of Faith" (the approved doctrines) of the Catholic Church, and that Church members are not bound to believe even the "approved" apparitions. The Church holds that the sum total of crucial Catholic revelations was given in apostolic times and, in particular, is contained in the doctrines of Christ's birth, death and Resurrection. Cardinal Ratzinger (who is now Pope Benedict XVI) commented in 2000 that the "…mystery of Christ as enunciated in the New Testament" was the utter, complete revelation of God to humanity, and that the Church neither needs nor expects anything more. There is no need for further divine manifestations. The Church feels that revelation is complete and that "secrets" revealed by visions cannot add to it.

MODERN REVELATIONS?
The attitude of the Catholic Church to Marian apparitions is cautious. The amount of attention paid to contemporary apparitions (such as the "disapproved" manifestations in Bayside, Queens, New York City) can quickly get out of hand due to the speed and widespread nature of modern publicity and ease of travel for pilgrims. The Church is concerned

Right: Our Lady of Fatima asked the three shepherd children to whom she appeared to pray the rosary daily; today there are nightly candlelight processions to the shrine, where the participants pray.

that such charismatic phenomena will spread false doctrine and corrupt its magisterial authority. In essence, the devotees of particular Marian visions run the risk of developing into cultists.

Catholic doctrine also teaches that private revelation is not something to aspire to. St Teresa of Ávila (though

Left: A personal supplication to St Bernadette of Lourdes (1844–79) is inscribed on this little holy card, together with an image of Bernadette (shown with a halo) after the pious woman entered the Sisters of Charity.

she herself had visions) reflected the sentiments of the Church when she said, "They desire to see; faith holds on without seeing." In other words, you should not need visions to believe. Christ himself said, "More blessed are they who have not seen and have believed."

Modern-day investigations of Marian apparitions are instituted by the bishop of the relevant diocese. If the messages being relayed by the apparition to the visionary are in any way contrary to the accepted doctrine of the Church, that alone is enough to have the apparition declared invalid. Investigations will also probe the mental, physical and spiritual health of the visionary and consider whether the messages being conveyed by the apparition are considered beneficial to the spiritual health of the faithful.

ALL SAINTS

THE MOST FAITHFUL SERVANTS OF GOD WHILE THEY WERE ON EARTH ARE KNOWN AS SAINTS, AND CATHOLICS BELIEVE THEY ARE REWARDED WITH A PARTICULAR INTIMACY WITH GOD IN HEAVEN.

The word "saint" comes from the Latin *sanctus*, or "holy, consecrated". In the general sense, the Catholic Church believes that anyone who has died and been accepted into heaven has earned the status of saint. However, there are also people who have been judged worthy of canonization by the Church hierarchy here on earth because of their exemplary behaviour as Christians. These saints are considered to have an especially intense beatific vision of God.

THE FIRST SAINTS

In the early centuries of Christianity, saints came from the ranks of the martyrs, those who in Roman times chose death rather than renounce their faith. After Christianity was legalized by the Edict of Milan in AD 313, the learned of the faith such as bishops or theologians ("doctors") were often considered for sainthood. Anchorites, or hermits, were also likely to achieve the designation by popular reputation. A saint chosen by reputation would be venerated by the people, who might visit the person's tomb or celebrate the day of his or her death.

After many years, the ecclesiastical authorities became involved and eventually created an official process for declaring someone a saint. The first saint for whom official canonization documents exist is St Udalricus, who was canonized in AD 973. In the early days of canonization, it was part of the practice to exhume the presumed saint's body and place it under an altar, apparently to facilitate the practices of veneration and pilgrimage that often resulted. An alternate way to express canonization is "to

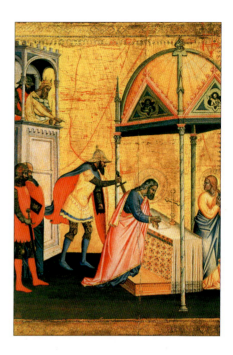

Above: St Matthew was stabbed in the back by a hired assassin while saying Mass in the church he built in Ethiopia. He is a saint by virtue of being an apostle and a martyr. This 14th-century illustration is from an altarpiece of St Matthew showing scenes from his life.

Left: In this 15th-century painting, the bones of King Louis IX of France are disinterred (for reburial under an altar) by Pope Boniface VIII, who later canonized Louis.

THE LONG ROAD TO CANONIZATION

There is a set procedure to follow for a person to be made a saint. First there is The "Opening of the Cause", which occurs when the diocesan bishop agrees that there is enough evidence to initiate an investigation into the life of a deceased resident of his diocese, by popular opinion known as outstandingly holy. Usually, there is a five-year waiting period after the candidate's death, but in the case of Pope John Paul II, Pope Benedict XVI waived this waiting period. At this point the candidate can be called "a servant of God". The report that results from the investigation is sent to the Congregation for the Causes of Saints, the Vatican investigative body that vets saintly nominees. If the Vatican agrees the report profiles a saint in waiting, the candidate is called "Venerable".

A posthumous miracle, evidence of the candidate's intercessory influence with God, must be verified. After verification, the candidate is beatified and afterwards called "Blessed". The Congregation for the Causes of Saints must verify that a second miracle occurred after the beatification, before the candidate can be called a "Saint". This can take years. Mother Teresa was beatified in 2003 and canonized as Saint Teresa of Calcutta in 2016.

Above: The widely held conviction that Pope John Paul II was an exceptionally holy man caused Pope Benedict XVI to open the cause for canonization only weeks after John Paul's death.

be raised to the full honours of the altar". Even today, saintly bodies reside under altars in some of the most surprising places – the body of St Mother Mary Frances Cabrini, for example, is under the altar of the chapel at Mother Cabrini High School in New York City.

VENERATION OR WORSHIP?

The modern Church recognizes saints as people of exemplary holiness who are worthy of veneration, which is not the same as worship. The act of worshipping a saint would violate the first commandment – "thou shalt not have strange gods before me". Catholicism is emphatically a monotheistic religion. The Church makes a specific distinction between *latria*, or "worship", due only to God, and *dulia*, which is "honour or veneration", due to saints. The Blessed Mother has her own intermediate category, known as *hyperdulia* – a very high degree of veneration due only to her.

Right: St Anne's status as grandmother of the Holy Family means that she is asked to intercede on family matters. Shown here in this 17th-century French painting, she is patroness of expectant mothers, women in labour and of the sick.

Worship and veneration can seem similar, since their practices (prayers to the worshipped or venerated, for example, or kneeling before statues, and feast days) are alike. However, the difference between worship and veneration is found in the believer's heart. When he or she worships, he or she is recognizing that the object of worship is divine. There is an element of awe rather than respect. When you venerate or honour, you are recognizing that the object of your veneration is due your respect – in the case of the Blessed Mother, the highest respect – but there is no awe and no intent to confer or recognize divinity.

Catholics who pray to saints do so not to obtain grace or favour straight from the saints themselves, but to ask the saint to intercede with God. This is because the saint is so close to God that their intercession is likely to smooth the way of the prayers of the petitioner.

A STATE OF GRACE

An individual's state of grace (whether or not he or she will receive sanctifying grace from God) depends on his or her efforts to gain salvation by turning to God through free will. Yet, one has to only briefly consider contemporary scandals that fill the newspapers' headlines to realize that humankind's sinful nature has not changed much over the centuries since early ascetic monks and doctors of the Church, such as Thomas Aquinas, created the Christian vocabulary to talk about sin. The seven "deadly" categories still apply – pride, avarice, greed, lust, gluttony, envy and sloth – leading men and women into both public and private trouble and strife. What has changed over the centuries is the emphasis that the Church places on forgiveness rather than punishment, and most particularly on the manner in which it defines not only punishment, but reward.

Also enduring is the human metaphysical longing for answers to ultimate questions and the craving to put our faith in something that is unified, peaceful and eternal. Catholicism defines this as the Trinity, the ultimate end of our seeking. The emphasis that the modern Church places on our personal relationship with God and on our eventual either beatific union with or desolate divorce from him is evidence that the Church has shifted the promise of heaven's glory and the threat of hell's fires and mutilations from the pointedly physical to the ineffably spiritual. The Church offers the heaven of rest and union with God.

Left: In contrast to many paintings of the Harrowing of Hell, Giotto di Bondone portrays Christ as a tender and kind, rather than glorious and triumphant, liberator in his c.1320–5 painting, Descent into Limbo.

A STATE OF GRACE

THE SOUL REDEEMED

Catholics have disagreed on what people need to do to gain redemption from original sin. In addition to Christ's sacrifice, individuals must also contribute to their own salvation.

Debates between Christians on what sinful humans need to do to attain salvation involved some of the most divisive issues of the 16th century, leading to the Protestant Reformation. Shuffled around in the debates were issues of grace, faith and the relative significance of human good works, along with the role of Christ's sacrifice on the Cross. The Catholic Magisterium, or teaching authority, and Martin Luther – the Catholic priest responsible for starting the Protestant Reformation by nailing his influential 95 Theses to the door of a church in Wittenberg – agreed on one important issue: that Christ's ultimate sacrifice on the Cross was the absolutely necessary prerequisite for human redemption.

Above: Faithful Catholics pray before The Way of the Cross, *a sculpture that emphasizes the physical reality of Christ's sacrifice. The weight of the Cross seems to drive Christ into the ground, with only the help of Simon of Cyrene keeping him from falling.*

GOD'S GIFT

As a result of original sin, humans are viewed as helpless to effect their redemption on their own. (Pelagius, a 5th-century theologian, disagreed and thought that people could handle their redemption without God's intervention; the Catholic Church declared him a heretic.) Both Catholics and Lutherans also agreed that salvation is a gift from God. God has no obligation or need to save sinful humanity.

Fortunately, even the grievous fact of original sin was not enough to destroy God's love for humanity – his Creation – and his infinite goodness is displayed in the mystical balance of Christ's redemptive sacrifice. As the 20th-century theologian Jaroslav Pelikan has noted, Christ's obedient passion and sacrifice on the tree of the Cross undid the damage that humankind had done next to the tree of disobedience.

Left: The Catholic Church recognizes seven sacraments, while the Lutheran Church practises only two – baptism and the Eucharist. In this detail from a 1561 altar front from Torslunde, Denmark, Martin Luther, who was once a Catholic monk, performs both.

150

HAVING FAITH

Luther believed that *sola fide* (or "faith alone") was the sole active principle in humankind's salvation. People would be saved by their faith in Christ's life, death and Resurrection. Christ basically earned redemption that is "imputed", or credited, to us if we have faith. Although Luther agreed that due to their faith in Christ, people develop a disposition to do good works, known as the process of sanctification, he thought that these human good works would never be enough to have any active effect on our redemption. Christ's sacrifice, and our faith in it, are all that matter. Luther is said to have declared, "Good works are useless."

CATHOLIC BAPTISM

In contrast, Catholicism teaches that not only can we be active contributors to our own salvation, but in fact, we must be so, in order to be saved. Faith alone will not be sufficient. Catholics view salvation as a process, so unlike Protestants they do not say, "I've been saved". Their ultimate salvation will be decided on their particular Judgement Day.

Catholicism teaches that we are redeemed through the progressive and co-operative interactions of first (and most crucially) Christ's initial sacrifice, the prerequisite that has made our personal redemption possible. Next we need to participate in a baptism, which is like our first purifying bath to cleanse us of original sin and infuse us with an initial dose of sanctifying grace. This act of baptism can be seen as an introductory step toward the process necessary for spiritual salvation.

JUSTIFICATION

Catholic theologians call what happens at baptism "initial justification". Justification is defined as making a person righteous in the eyes of God. However, to keep the spiritual introduction received at baptism vigorous, Catholicism teaches that we need to participate actively in the Church and its sacraments, especially attendance at Mass, reception of the Eucharist and good works. Through these sincere acts of participation in the Catholic community, we become more immune to sin – and we also turn into more vigorous spiritual beings. This level of participation is known as "progressive justification".

Above: On the day of the final judgement, Catholic tradition declares that soul and body will be reunited. This 15th-century fresco by Giovanni Canavesio shows bodies rising from their graves on this ultimate day.

Above: The scallop shell is the traditional Catholic symbol of baptism. John the Baptist is said to have baptized Christ with water poured from a scallop shell. Here Pope John Paul II baptizes a child in the Sistine Chapel in 2001.

THE NATURE OF SIN

CATHOLICISM RECOGNIZES DIFFERENT TYPES OF SIN, FROM THE ORIGINAL SIN OF ADAM AND EVE TO THE UNFORGIVABLE SIN. IT IS OUR CHOICE TO TURN TO GOD AND NOT SIN OR TO TURN AWAY FROM HIM.

To understand how sin is viewed in Catholic doctrine, one needs to consider the concept of *aversio ad deo*, or "turning away from God". Sin is an insult to God, an almost unimaginable rudeness when considering that, in the Catholic view, God has offered us the most superb gift, his love. Sin is perverse, in that it says "no" to the love of God; the Catholic catechism says that sin contradicts the love of God.

Sin is the refusal to accept this priceless love and to choose instead to turn down the blind alley of self-love or toward a false attraction to worldly objects or persons. It is a dis-ordered perception (as a result of original sin) of the value of attractions of the temporal world that we mistakenly define as

Below: Man's fallen nature leaves him vulnerable to the attractions of the temporal world, including riches, corporeal delights and secular power, shown in Jean de Gerson's 1462 Mirror of Humility.

love. The more complete the degree of turning away from God, the more distance we put between ourselves and the grace we receive in his presence, and thus the more likely we are to continue to sin.

PERSONAL SIN

When we resist or turn away from God's love for us, we cannot receive his grace, and without God's grace we lose the most effective means to avoid our tendency toward personal sin. While original sin is inherited from our ancestral parents, personal sin is our own production (though we can blame Adam and Eve for the fact that we were born imperfect). Regardless of excuse, Catholic doctrine teaches that after Adam and Eve's fall from grace, humanity retained, in weakened form, its free will. Since we still have free will, even in a fallen world we can choose to "turn toward God", or *conversio ad deo*, and not sin.

Above: A 15th-century Italian illustration shows Jesus uttering the famous words, "He that is without sin among you, let him cast the first stone at her".

VENIAL VERSUS MORTAL

Catholics classify sins as either venial or mortal (theologians break these sins down into smaller categories, but for most of us the mortal/venial distinction is sufficient). To continue the metaphor of turning away from God, a venial (from the Latin word *venia*, or "forgiveness, pardon") sin would be a slight acknowledgement, and a mortal (from Latin *mortalis*, or "death") sin would be turning one's back, which is the rudest of cuts that would sever all social ties (*see Before the Mortal Blow, opposite*). Biblical reference to the venial versus mortal sin distinction can be found in 1 John 5:16–17:

> He that knoweth his brother to sin a sin which is not to death, let him ask, and life shall be given to him, who sinneth not to death. There is a sin unto death: for that I say not that any man ask.

Venial sins (those little rudenesses to God) do not in and of themselves sever all ties and destroy our hope for eternal life with God. However, like any rudeness, they can damage the relationship between us and him and lead in time to the final rift unless

BEFORE THE MORTAL BLOW

Unconfessed and therefore unforgiven mortal sins cause the death of the soul and consign the sinner to hell – eternal punishment. However, God is fair and just, so mortal sins are not easy to commit. You cannot "accidentally" commit a mortal sin. Before you turn away from God and choose the devil, three ominous conditions must be present:

Grave Matter: The act, to any person of normal reason, would be understood as evil.

Full Knowledge: The potential sinner must know that the act is evil. A person with a mental illness, such as schizophrenia, for example, may not have full knowledge that an act he is about to commit is heinous.

Deliberate Consent: It is up to us. The choice is ours, because God endowed us with free will. We can choose to turn toward the Dark or the Light. If you hit someone with your car accidentally and kill him or her, that is not a mortal sin; but if the accident happened because you drank alcohol at a party, knowing that you planned to drive home, then the accident is a mortal sin because you acted irresponsibly.

Right: St Augustine thought one of the most terrible results of the fall of man was libido dominandi, *or "the lust for dominance". Cain, son of Adam, enacts a tragic result of that lust – fratricide – in* The Killing of Abel, *a detail from the 1379–83 Grabower Altarpiece by Master Bertram of Minden.*

we mend our ways. As this particular passage makes clear, mortal sin leads to the death of the soul.

THE UNFORGIVABLE SIN

The New Testament refers to an eternal, or unforgivable, sin. In Mark 3:22–30, Christ says, "All sins will be forgiven the sons of men, and whatever blasphemies they may utter; but he who blasphemes against the Holy Spirit never has forgiveness, but is subject to eternal condemnation." Christ also refers to unforgivable sin in Matthew 12:3–32, when Pharisees, who witness Christ cast out demons, claim Christ had the power of Beelzebub (the devil).

The unforgivable sin is connected to a wilful rejection of God in the face of all the manifest good that is clearly vouchsafed to us. This sin consists of seeing good and perversely calling it evil. It blasphemes against the Holy Spirit in his role as a "convincer of sin", which is what Pope John Paul II called the Holy Spirit in the 1986 encyclical, *Dominum et Vivificantem*. John Paul pointed out that the Holy Spirit's role is to purify humankind's consciences, so that they are able to call good and evil by their proper names. When we radically reject the Holy Spirit, we are no longer able to see our good and our salvation even when they stare us in the face. This is the unforgivable sin.

Right: A 14th-century biblical illumination shows the fool who said, "There is no God" (Psalm 53). The sin of apostasy, or rejecting God, is called the unforgivable sin.

THE SEVEN DEADLY SINS

SINCE THE 5TH CENTURY, CATHOLIC THEOLOGIANS HAVE DISCUSSED A LIST OF PARTICULAR SINS FOR THE FAITHFUL TO AVOID, BUT IT WAS ONLY IN THE 12TH CENTURY THAT A CREED LISTED THE SEVEN DEADLY SINS.

Although the list of the seven deadly, or cardinal, sins has traditionally been paired with a list of virtues, it is the sins that are remembered. The seven deadly sins (and the corresponding virtues), in the order of descending gravity, are: pride (humility), avarice (generosity), envy (kindness), wrath (patience), lust (chastity), gluttony (temperance) and sloth (diligence).

The Catholic catechism refers to these sins as capital vices, noting that they are capital because they produce other sins. In fact, the seven deadly sins are actually categories of sin, and sins falling within those categories are not always mortal. For example, eating two desserts when you really needed only one – or none – would be a sin classified as gluttony, but it would not be enough to send you to eternal punishment (unless it was a symptom of a much larger problem).

EARLY MENTIONS
The tradition of the seven deadly sins originated in the writings of John Cassian, a 5th-century monk and ascetic. In his book *Collationes*, he provided a list of eight vices that were particularly tormenting to ascetic monks, as follows: gluttony, impurity, covetousness, anger, dejection, accidia (or boredom), vainglory and pride. Pope Gregory the Great included a similar list in his book *Moralia on Job*. Cassian and Gregory may have been influenced in turn by *Psychomachia*, an allegorical poem by the 4th-century Roman Christian poet Aurelius Prudentius Clemens. His poem featured a battle between personified virtues and vices in the style of the *Aeneid*. Prudentius may have influenced later authors who made specific use of the deadly sins in their writing, in particular, Geoffrey Chaucer and Dante Alighieri. Of the church fathers, Thomas Aquinas in his *Summa Theologiae* (1265–73) paid attention to the seven deadly sins, for example, analysing multiple manifestations of gluttony, such as *studiose*, or "eating too daintily", and *laute*, or "eating too expensively".

BY COUNCIL DECREE
The wide dissemination and subsequent popularity in public discourse of the seven deadly sins can be traced back to the Church's Fourth Lateran Council (1214). One of the decrees of the council was the

Above: The virtue of flourishing generosity is seen in opposition to the deadly vice of avarice in this 1945 illustration, Allegory of Generosity and Avarice, *by Rémy Hetreau.*

Below: Hieronymus Bosch's 15th-century Tabletop of the Seven Deadly Sins and the Four Last Things *shows the deadly sins balanced with four medallions of the four last things: death, judgement, heaven and hell.*

Above: St Thomas Aquinas, one of the Church's most erudite theologians, provided an exhaustive analysis of the seven deadly sins in his Summa Theologiae. *This portrait of Aquinas is by Alessandro Botticelli (1445–1510).*

requirement that Catholics attend yearly confession. In order to make a good confession – or any confession at all – the ordinary communicant needed to be educated in the concept of sin and given a vocabulary to talk about it. Parish priests as well had to learn the language of sin. In the Lambeth Constitutions of 1281, Archbishop of Canterbury John Peckham provided the clergy with a syllabus that included the seven deadly sins (as well as the seven virtues and the seven sacraments).

THE NUMBER SEVEN

Many Christians have asked why there are only seven deadly sins and have noted some considerable omissions from the list, such as cruelty to others. This is because seven was considered a number of significance in the Old Testament, starting with the creation of the world in seven days, and it has reappeared in many other guises as an important ordering principle in Scripture, in particular, in the "Book of Sevens", Revelation. Seven is generally considered a number of high sacred significance.

SEVEN SINS OF THE 21ST CENTURY

In 2005, the Church published a "Compendium of the Social Doctrine of the Church", which reasserted the humanist position of the Catholic Church on all social issues. The widely publicized list of the seven "social sins" derived from this compendium. The social sins of the 21st century are:

1: Bioethical violations, such as birth control
2: Morally dubious experiments, such as stem cell research
3: Drug abuse
4: Polluting the environment
5: Contributing to the widening gap between rich and poor
6: Excessive wealth
7: Creating poverty

The compendium states that social sin falls into two categories: "On the one hand, the all-consuming desire for profit, and on the other, the thirst for power, with the intention of imposing one's will upon others." Bishop Gianfranco Girotti also stated that, "While sin used to mostly concern the individual, today it has mainly a social resonance, thanks to the phenomenon of globalization."

Above: The oil industry often displays social sin. It pollutes the Earth in its desire for great wealth.

JUDGEMENT DAY

ACCORDING TO CATHOLICISM, EACH PERSON IS JUDGED AT DEATH (PARTICULAR JUDGEMENT). CHRIST WILL RETURN ON JUDGEMENT DAY TO JUDGE THE LIVING AND THE DEAD (GENERAL JUDGEMENT).

The Catholic vision of Judgement Day is a particularly specific one. Catholic tradition teaches that there are two separate and specific judgements: the particular and the general. The particular judgement, as the name implies, has more significance for the fate of each person, while the general judgement is the Judgement Day that will see the Second Coming of Christ and the end of the world as we know it.

AT DEATH

Particular judgement happens at the exact moment of individual death, when the soul separates from the body. Catholic sacred tradition teaches that the particular judgement is instantaneous, so that the soul will simply know, immediately, what the verdict is and go on its own in the right direction. The choices are heaven, which is reserved for the perfectly pure; Purgatory, for the vast group of the imperfectly pure (those with venial sins that are still unconfessed and unforgiven); and hell, for the definitely not pure (those with mortal sins that remain unconfessed and unforgiven).

A PAPAL BULL

This belief in the prompt fulfilment of the sentence was a controversial one within the early Church. Some Church fathers argued that either the bliss of the beatific vision (for example, the intuitive knowledge of God) or the suffering of the tormenting fires of hell would be postponed until the general judgement. Pope Benedict XII convened a commission to decide the question, and after four months of testimony from various theologians, he issued the 1336 papal bull, *Benedictus Deus*. This bull proclaimed, once and for all, that your fate was indeed determined right away.

Above: Aided by its guardian angel, this soul is slipping away to its judgement (fresco detail from the Last Judgement, *Voronet Monastery, Moldavia, Romania). The soul will be reunited to the body it leaves behind at the general judgement.*

GENERAL JUDGEMENT

The judgement that has been traditionally depicted in Western art – full of angels, demons, writhing naked bodies and a just Christ sitting on a throne with a group of saints in attendance – is known as the general judgement. It is a popular theme of medieval and Renaissance paintings.

Church tradition teaches that at the general judgement, all bodies, both the saved and the damned, will be rejoined to their immortal souls. The wicked, unfortunately, will not be happy to meet their bodies again, as noted in Revelation 9:6, "The wicked shall seek death, and shall not find it, shall desire to die, and death shall fly from them…"

Scripture specifically assigns the general judgement as a role for Christ. In John 5:28, it states, "…for the hour cometh wherein all that are in the graves shall hear the voice of the Son of God." This is why the general judgement is also referred to as Christ's Second Coming.

Below: During the Second Coming of Christ, saints will be rewarded with the beatific vision of Christ, implied in this early 15th-century German painting by his larger size in relation to the others and the blissful expression of the saints.

JUDGEMENT DAY

It will be during the general judgement that the Godhead's ultimate purpose for mankind will finally be fulfilled.

The general judgement appears to have the same function as a public trial: although a particular judgement has already been pronounced, the general judgement is needed so that all may witness the justice of the final decrees. General judgement features an aspect of public proclamation, as described in the Athanasian Creed, "at whose coming all men must rise with their bodies and are to render an account of their deeds". The general judgement is the day of public accounting and is a final judgement.

THE FINAL JUDGEMENT

Catholicism teaches its followers that when Christ returns, it will be for the final judgement and that the resulting reign will be eternal and in heaven. Over the centuries, however, Christians have held different views on what will happen during the final judgement (*see* Final Judgement and the Millennium, *below*). Pre-millennialism describes this as an actual return of Christ for a thousand years, before the final judgement. However, post-millennialism prefers to describe an achieved perfection on earth due to the preaching of the gospel, as a result of which the entire earth will be Christianized. After the thousand years of earthly Christian perfection, then Jesus returns to conduct the final judgement. Pre-millennialism posits a return and reign of Christ on earth prior to the final judgement, whereas post-millennialism believes in a period of achieved perfection on earth prior to the final judgement.

The Catholic Church refutes pre-millennialism and also rejects the post-millennial view that there will ever be a period of perfection on earth prior to the final judgement (this view would contradict the doctrine of original sin).

Above: A phalanx of saints are in attendance above, the mouth of hell gaping is on the right and delight or dismay (as applicable) are shown on earth in The Last Judgement *by Bartholomaeus Spranger (1546–1611).*

Below: Weighing souls after death, shown in this 12th-century Catalan fresco, was an ancient belief of Egypt and Greece as well as early Christianity. Traditionally, the archangel Michael escorted souls to God on Judgement Day and weighed them.

FINAL JUDGEMENT AND THE MILLENNIUM

The Book of Revelation, and Chapter 20 in particular, is problematic for Catholics. This difficult chapter describes a thousand-year period when Satan will be bound with chains in a pit, after which he will be "loosed for a little while" and emerge to deceive again. This thousand-year period when Satan will be bound is known as the millennium. There are many gradations of opinion (much of it Protestant evangelical) on the millennium, but most understand it as a thousand-year "golden age" of the triumph of Christianity, a reign of Christ himself (pre-millennialism) or of the Christian religion (post-millennialism) on earth that will be distinct from the final judgement and distinct from eternity.

A STATE OF GRACE

VISIONS OF HEAVEN

THE WRITERS OF THE BIBLE REFERRED TO HEAVEN AS A PHYSICAL PLACE, GOD'S FIRMAMENT. HOWEVER, TODAY'S CATHOLIC CHURCH DESCRIBES HEAVEN AS A STATE OF BEING.

The Bible uses several descriptive phrases when referring to heaven, including a kingdom, a crown, the city of God, a reward and even an inheritance. This metaphorical variety on the part of biblical writers shows that the early Christians felt a certain liberty in their attempts to imagine heaven, as long as it provided a good image.

In the popular imagination, both in the past and present, heaven is often seen as being palatial, expressed in the term "pearly gates", which derives from the opulent description of heaven as the "New Jerusalem". In Revelation 21:21, its gates "are twelve pearls, one to each: and every several gate was of one pearl". In paintings and movies, heaven is dreamy, awash in clouds that are often shot through with pastel rays of effulgent light. In common usage, "heavenly" is the adjective of choice for anything highly pleasurable, from pizza ("a slice of heaven") to relaxing in a hot bubble bath.

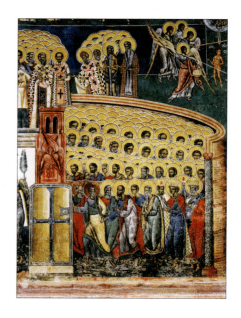

Above: Orderly groups of saints approach the fortified portal of paradise in this 1480 detail from the Last Judgement, *Voronet Monastery, Moldavia, Romania.*

GOD'S FIRMAMENT

Despite these images, the etymology of the word "heaven" derives from words referring to "a roof or covering", confirming the majority view that heaven is above us. Genesis 7:10 describes God making the "firmament", which serves as a vast buttress that divides the elemental regions of the earth: "And God made a firmament, and divided the waters that were under the firmament, from those that were above the firmament… And God called the firmament heaven…".

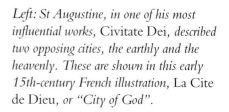

Left: St Augustine, in one of his most influential works, Civitate Dei, *described two opposing cities, the earthly and the heavenly. These are shown in this early 15th-century French illustration,* La Cite de Dieu, *or "City of God".*

158

This soaring support of the world came to be associated with the abode of God, "…a building of God, a house not made with hands, eternal in heaven" (2 Corinthians 5:1). Medieval cathedrals aspired to represent in earthly architecture the inspiring span and lofty height of heaven.

A STATE OF BEING

Catholic doctrine, however, is circumspect in describing heaven as an actual physical place. No doctrine of the Church has ever attempted to establish the latitude and longitude of heaven, and although it is the traditional concept, the modern Church is even cautious in describing heaven as the dwelling place of God. This is because by doing so, it would imply that God can be contained in a particular place.

Instead, the Church describes heaven as a state of being achieved only by those who are pure of all sin. The Catholic catechism says that when we enter into the state of being of heaven, we will have a "beatific vision" of God. Unless God makes himself open to an individual for contemplation, God cannot be seen. If this contemplation takes place, our spiritual and intellectual perceptive capacity will be unbound from its earthly limitations so that we will be able to perceive and receive God – this is a beatific vision. Such an encounter "is what the perfect happiness of heaven will consist of".

In 1336, Pope Benedict XII defined belief in the beatific vision (for those who attain heaven) as a dogma of the faith. Theologians, however, put limits on even the beatific vision. They state that while we will see God (such as in the Trinity) entirely, our vision will not have the absolute and infinite clarity with which God perceives himself. The Church also believes that there are degrees of beatitude granted to the Blessed; saints have a more extensive vision of God.

Above: New residents, borne on the backs of obliging angels, are welcomed to heaven with open arms in this 15th-century work from Hastings Book of Hours.

BEING REUNITED

There is also a more homely aspect to heaven. The Church teaches that in heaven we will be reunited with our beloved family and friends who have gone there before us, and the language of some of the prayers for the dead in the Church emphasizes that heaven is the true home of the righteous and that our arrival in heaven will actually be a homecoming. In the service that is given for the dead, the Prayer of Commendation states:

> *May you return to [your Creator] who formed you from the dust of the earth.*
> *May holy Mary, the angels, and all the saints come to meet you as you go forth from this life…*
> *May you see your Redeemer face to face.*

The sense is of a family's loving, eager greeting to one of its members who has been too long away. Heaven is also a homecoming in that we return to our first home, paradise, redeemed from a long sojourn in the fallen world. St Augustine said, "Thou hast made us for Thyself (O God) and our heart is troubled till it rests in Thee."

Below: The Madonna and saints contentedly work, read and play in a walled garden in this c.1410 German painting, Paradise Garden. *The garden is the earthly mirror of paradise, which is from the old Persian word for "a walled garden" or "park".*

PURGATORY

CATHOLICS BELIEVE THAT AFTER DEATH THERE ARE MANY SOULS THAT ARE NOT DESTINED FOR HELL BUT THAT ARE NOT READY TO ENTER HEAVEN WITH GOD – THEY GO TO PURGATORY TO BE CLEANSED OF SIN.

The Catholic doctrine regarding the concept of Purgatory has developed from the Catholic belief that God is both merciful and just. Because God is merciful, sinners can atone for their non-mortal sins even after death, but because he is just, this atonement is a requirement that must be met.

Purgatory (from the Latin word *purgare*, "to make clean, to purify") is where that atonement happens. The Church teaches that Purgatory is where those who die without mortal sin on their soul, but also without making full satisfaction to God for their sins, must suffer for a time to purify their souls and to make recompense to God. Purgatory is different from hell because it is temporary. Souls suffering in Purgatory know that eventually they will be with God. In traditional teaching, Purgatory is a place; however, in more contemporary teaching it is a state of being.

A DEVELOPING CONCEPT

The early church Councils of Lyons (1274), Florence (1438–43) and Trent (1545–63) all made statements describing, with varying degrees of specificity, the Church's developing concept of Purgatory. In *The City of God*, St Augustine expressed his belief that there would be temporal punishment after death, and Pope (later St) Gregory the Great, influenced by Augustine, was principally responsible for refining the idea of *purgatorius ignis*, or the "cleansing fire", into doctrine.

Going to Purgatory is not completely inevitable. The pure do not go to Purgatory, and Catholics also believe that those who, through no fault of their own, have suffered terribly in life (say an unjustly convicted prisoner), essentially pay recompense for their sins by experiencing Purgatory here on earth. However, those who have been less than pure will go to Purgatory.

PURGING OUR SINS

Purgatory is necessary, in most cases, even if you have made an appropriate confession of your sins and have been forgiven. The Catholic concept of penance is that temporal punishment is required to discharge our debt

Above: Few theologians were as aware of the struggle between good and evil as St Augustine. In this 15th-century French woodblock print, he focuses on his work despite the clamour of demonic distractions around him.

Above: Purgatorial punishments match the earthly sin. In an illustration in Le Trésor de Sapience *by Jean de Gerson (1363–1429), the prideful are pushed into the ground and trodden on, expiating their arrogance by being forced to grovel in flames.*

of sin as a necessary condition of absolution. The Church makes the point that Purgatory is necessary not because God is vengeful but because our sins, like a stain, have worked into our essence. Only the spiritually clean can truly see God, and being spiritually cleansed is difficult work, a sense expressed by the early Church father, Gregory of Nyssa, in his reflections on Purgatory:

…we may figure to ourselves the agonized struggle of that soul which has wrapped itself up in earthy material passions, when God is drawing it, his own one, to himself, and the foreign matter, which has somehow grown into its substance, has to be scraped from it by main force, and so occasions it that keen intolerable anguish.

INTERCEDING SAINTS

Catholicism also teaches that the prayers of the faithful still residing on earth can help the souls in Purgatory. The Communion of Saints refers to the belief that all faithful members of the Church, whether living or dead, are united as members of a single spiritual community and can help one another; therefore, the saints in heaven can intercede with God to help us on earth, and by offering suffrages – our prayers, fasting and works of charity on earth – we can obtain divine mercy for the souls in Purgatory, perhaps even hastening the time that they will be released into heaven.

Above: Part of a larger panoramic 15th-century French painting by Enguerrand Quarton, The Coronation of the Virgin, *this detail depicts Purgatory in an unexpected location – just beneath the walled city of Rome. It includes a few fortunate penitents who have completed their time in Purgatory and are rising from the depths, with the aid of angels.*

HEAVEN SHOULD NOT BE FOR SALE

Indulgences, or remission of time spent in Purgatory, became a hot trading commodity during the early 16th century. The trade in indulgences reflected the extreme concern with the afterlife during this era when the Black Death (plague) had decimated Europe's population. Pope Leo X took advantage of this situation to enrich the Church coffers by selling indulgences – though selling them is a mortal sin (Leo, a member of the Medici family, was extremely corrupt). Leo was selling plenary indulgences, a particular type of indulgence that provides total remission of the temporal punishment (time in Purgatory).

Indulgences are legal in the Church, but because of this earlier history they are often misunderstood as being a kind of coupon for time off from Purgatory that the Church offers in exchange for cash. However, what many do not understand is that even forgiven sins may result in some time in Purgatory after death, before an individual is in acceptable spiritual shape for heaven. Plenary indulgences can free you from that prospect, but there are conditions attached. First, they should never be offered solely in exchange for money. Sins must be forgiven by confession; the person receiving the indulgence must go to confession and receive Communion for a week, and the person must perform charitable works prescribed by the Church.

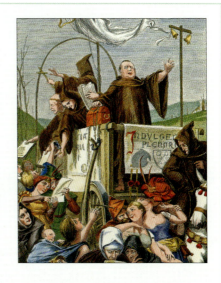

Above: Johann Tetzel, a Dominican prior, sells indulgences in Germany in this 18th-century woodblock print.

VISIONS OF HELL

MODERN CHURCH DOCTRINE ON HELL IS RELATIVELY TAME IN COMPARISON TO THE LURID VISION OF ETERNAL DAMNATION THAT HAS GRIPPED THE POPULAR IMAGINATION SINCE THE MIDDLE AGES.

The Scriptures contain a number of references to a hell with a fearsome aspect, describing it as a place of fire and darkness. Among these are: "pool of fire" (Revelation 19:20), "everlasting fire (Matthew 18:8; 25:41; Jude 7), "unquenchable fire" (Matthew 3:12), "furnace of fire where they will weep and gnash their teeth" (Matthew 13:42, 50), "exterior darkness" (Matthew 7:12; 22:13; 25:30) and "mist" or "storm of darkness" (2 Peter 2:17; Jude 13).

ETERNAL DAMNATION

These are all arresting descriptions, particularly when coupled with the concept of being never ending, because hell, of course, is eternal. Contemporary Catholic clergy are

Above: The license allowed in portraits of Satan is evident in this 15th-century rendition, which depicts him with belled horns, wings like ribbed leaves and tusks.

unlikely to dwell for long on these descriptions. However, in medieval times and up to the Second Vatican Council (1962–5), priests and nuns often invoked the grim spectre of hell in an effort to scare their congregations into good behaviour. The Church considered meditation on the "Last Things," which are death, judgement, heaven and hell, as salutary to spiritual health.

We are indebted to the medieval period for many of our images of hell as a place of gruesome punishments and apocalyptic landscapes. The vision literature of the Middle Ages featured an entire genre of texts that recounted personal tours of hell, featuring horrible retributions that were tailor-made to suit the sin. This early vision literature influenced the great Florentine poet Dante, who in his *Inferno* described hell as a series of nine concentric circles, with limbo, the least severe, at the outer rim and Satan confined at the centre.

Left: A 14th-century image from Dante's Divine Comedy *shows stars in paradise, terraces in Purgatory and fire in hell.*

VISIONS OF HELL

Right: A demon delivers a new soul to hell to join eternally tormented souls in this detail from a 15th-century painting by Enguerrand Quarton.

HELLFIRE

The fires of hell are supernatural: they do not require fuel and they do not consume those they burn, but blaze eternally. Traditional Catholic theology describes hellfire as *poena sensus*, meaning the "pain of sense". *Poena sensus* is considered a corporeal pain, because Scripture specifies that after the last judgement, the damned will be rejoined to their bodies. Some have noted that *poena sensus* was an appropriate pain, because mortal sin is often allied to excessive desire for physical and material pleasures.

THE CHURCH'S VIEW

The Second Vatican Council did not mention hell, but the gentling of Church rhetoric on hell dates from then. The current Catholic definition of hell, as noted by Pope John Paul II, states that the ultimate punishment for sin itself is hell, and that it is "more than a physical place". Hell represents the state of those who have chosen freely and completely to "separate themselves from God".

The Catholic catechism describes hell as a state of being where the individual chooses to reject God's love, thereby dying in mortal sin. By choosing to exclude him or herself from God, and by not repenting, he or she will be separated from God for eternity – this is hell.

To older Catholics whose lifetime spans the expositions of both the older eternal, infernal physical punishment vision of hell from before the Second Vatican Council and today's metaphysical "eternally separated from God" hell, the difference can be striking. This is a situation in which the Catholic Church has exercised its magisterial authority to interpret Scripture. Here we see the evolution of Church tradition at work.

John Paul II also went on to say that we need to understand the meanings presented by the images of hell in Scripture, which illustrate an empty and frustated life if living without accepting God. The Pope calls the scriptural words on hell "images" and says, not that they "are" hell, but that they "show" a state of being. So, heaven is unity with God and hell is separation from God. Although John Paul II did not repudiate the old concept of hell, he did go so far as to redefine the terms of the discussion.

Above: The damned make their way to hell and the pure to heaven in Rogier van der Weyden's 15th-century painting of the Last Judgement.

THE PAIN OF LOSS

Poena damni, or the "pain of loss", refers to psychic pain. The Church describes *poena damni* as a real, intense pain, rooted in the loss of the beatific vision. The damned still retain the human need for God, even if they have rejected this desire, and so are tormented eternally by the unquiet described by Augustine in his *Confessions*, "…You have formed us for yourself, and our hearts are unquiet until they find rest in you." The disquiet of the damned can never be stilled, so they burn with eternal despair. It is the *poena damni* that Pope John Paul II emphasized in his definition of hell. "Damnation" comes from the Latin word *damnum,* which means "loss", emphasizing that the essence of hell is in the pain of loss.

Visions of Damnation

THE ARTISTIC REPUTATION OF PAINTINGS OF HELL HAS ALWAYS ECLIPSED THOSE OF HEAVEN. BLISS SEEMS TO LEAVE ARTISTS AT A LOSS, BUT THEY APPEAR TO HAVE A PASSION FOR PAINTING ETERNAL PUNISHMENT.

Hell was by no means an unusual subject in religious art. Two popular themes are of "The Harrowing of Hell", when Christ descended into hell after his Crucifixion, before his Resurrection, and the Last Judgement. Numerous artists, including Giotto di Bondone (c.1267–1337), Fra Angelico (c.1387–1455), Hans Memling (c.1440–94) and Michelangelo (1475–1564), have depicted hell. Giotto's hell is a fiery nether region dwarfed by a conquering Christ who was en-throned in an orderly heaven with the righteous in attendance.

Memling's triptych *The Last Judgement* depicts hell as a flaming pit into which the undifferentiated bodies of the damned tumble, superintended by colossal and well-armed demons. Jesus holds centre stage as the archangel Michael weighs the souls. The left panel shows the pure being led to heaven, while the right panel shows the damned.

Fra Angelico's hell is honey-combed with flaming caverns where bleeding, naked people are bound, speared and burnt by gleeful demons resembling diabolical monkeys, or the unfortunate occupants are eaten in great gulps by Satan himself, looking like a great ape.

THE MASTER OF HELL

Pre-eminent among all the painters of the horrors of hell is Hieronymus Bosch (c.1450–1516). He was an unassuming Dutchman who never travelled far from 's-Hertogenbosch, his village in the duchy of Brabant (modern-day Netherlands). In a small house on the market square, besides making devotional wood-cuts, he painted hell and its countless demons in endlessly inventive, startlingly modern, gruesome detail.

In contrast to many of the other illustrations of hell, Bosch's chaotic, brightly coloured depictions are typically overrun with life, albeit in monstrous forms: strange demons that resemble insects or sea creatures, monstrous birds, odd plants with pod-like excrescences, enormous ears, mussel shells, eggs, unusual ice skaters and odd little bathyspheres with grilles for doors. One representative Bosch monster is a fish swallowing another fish, with lobster legs and a spiny tail.

Bosch's demons tend to have long whip-like tails resembling the stingers on stingrays. The damned are not simply burnt or bound, but are tortured in an indescribable variety of obscene manners by a wealth of phantasmagoric creatures. Hellfire burns on the outskirts of Bosch's canvases, in dark regions shot with red light; unlike the typical painting of hell, the flames are not the principle torture of the damned.

THE FIRST SURREALIST

Because he married an heiress, Bosch did not depend on the Church hierarchy for commissions of his work, unlike many other artists. Free from the need to submit his compositions to the censorship of the Church, he was able to produce beautifully painted works featuring imagery not found in any Scripture.

Bosch's technique came to him naturally: several of his relatives were also painters, including his grandfather, father, brother and three uncles. The Flemish style of slender, restrained human bodies

Above: The damned are subjected to various forms of torture applied by tiny demons, from being suspended by the hair to the racking of bare skin, in this detail from Giotto di Bondone's c.1303 painting, The Last Judgement.

Above: The descent into the mouth of hell was a standard subject of medieval "doom" paintings. In a detail from Hans Memling's 15th-century version, the damned souls tumble with arms and legs extended in almost balletic poses.

Right: Looking at Hieronymus Bosch's imagery, such as The Garden of Earthly Delights *(c.1500), it is hard to believe that he lived and painted in the 15th century. His imagery and technique still look startlingly modern today.*

and of meticulous attention to detail is evident in his work. However, Bosch's iconography is like no other religious painter's and is a precursor in its hallucinatory specificity to the early 20th-century work of the Surrealists, artists that were hailed as "revolutionary" more than five centuries after Bosch.

A DEVOUT BROTHER
Surprisingly, the little-known story of Bosch's life suggests that he participated in the conventional pious observances of society: he was a sworn member of the Society of Our Lady, a devout brotherhood founded in 1318. The society was a powerful but exclusive group, and Bosch was allowed to become a member upon marriage because his wife was already one. The studies of the brotherhood may have contributed to Bosch's obsession with hell: they were said to conduct daily readings of accounts of hell.

Despite his deeply unconventional work, during his lifetime Bosch became enormously popular among the laity, if not the Church itself. King Philip II (1527–98), the Spanish monarch known for his collection of saintly relics, was a particular admirer of Bosch. He was a keen collector of his works and kept Bosch's painting of a wheel depicting the seven deadly sins in his bedroom at the Escorial Palace.

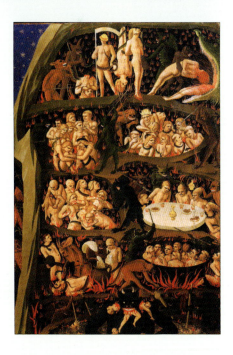

Left: Only in the hell of Bosch would one find what resembles a penguin on ice skates, as seen in this 1503–4 detail from Die Hölle. *The horror of Bosch's hell is its complete lack of logic and reason – all the universe is askew.*

Above: Fra Angelico's vision of hell exemplifies the "cooking and eating" motif, with a cauldron of unfortunates being boiled, Satan gorging on their flesh and lesser demons contemplating bodies massed for their delectation.

Limbo

A REGION ON THE EDGE OF HELL, LIMBO WAS RESERVED FOR THOSE WHO DIED FREE FROM SERIOUS PERSONAL SIN, YET, THROUGH NO FAULT OF THEIR OWN, WERE STILL IN A STATE OF ORIGINAL SIN.

The name "limbo" derives from the Latin *limbus*, meaning "hem", "border" or "edge", reflecting its juxtaposition with hell. The concept of limbo was developed as an extension of the doctrinal importance that the Church ascribes to original sin and baptism, added to its belief that only those who are free of all vestiges of sin will be worthy of the beatific vision of God.

There are two categories of candidate that can go to limbo. These are either virtuous people who died before Jesus redeemed them from original sin, or babies who died before being baptized.

GOD'S GIFT

Original sin is an inescapable fate for all humans, with only the Virgin Mary being conceived without it. Romans 5:18 says, "Therefore, as by the offence of one, unto all men condemnation; so also by the justice of one, unto all men justification of life." This scriptural syllogism makes clear the direction of the Church's thinking: if salvation, that gift of God, is going to apply to all people, then so must the unfortunate predecessor to salvation: the hereditary stain that marks all the unbaptized as exiles from God. In other words, the unbaptized are at risk.

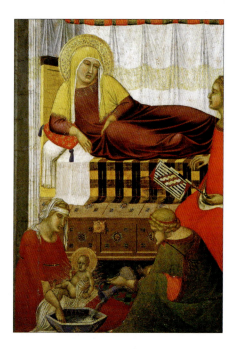

Above: The halo over Mary in Pietro Lorenzetti's 14th-century painting, The Birth of the Virgin Mary, *is a clue that she was conceived without original sin.*

THE TWO LIMBOS

Catholic tradition originally taught that there were two limbos: *limbus patrum*, for virtuous but unbaptized adults (*patrum* refers to "fathers"), reflecting the belief that the Old Testament patriarchs – including Abraham – would go there, and *limbus infantium*, for unbaptized infants. The two limbos were required because *limbus patrum* would end with the Second Coming, whereas *limbus infantium* was permanent. The fathers could not be baptized because Jesus Christ had not yet redeemed man. The babies were not baptized because they had died before anyone had baptized them.

In fact, this is why the Church teaches that in an emergency, anyone can baptize a baby by making the sign of the cross over the infant

Left: Abraham holds the souls of the righteous in this 12th-century French manuscript. Because he lived before Jesus was born, Abraham was not redeemed before he died and went to limbo.

and speaking the words, "I baptize thee (NAME) in the name of the Father and of the Son and of the Holy Spirit." Many doctors, nurses and midwives have performed such baptisms over newborns they feared would not survive.

INNOCENT BUT IN LIMBO
The ultimate fate of the innocent but unbaptized was controversial, as were so many theological issues before their applicable doctrines were established. St Augustine was the most severe: this 4th-century theologian believed that the innocently unbaptized would be punished, though more mildly than the truly damned. The theologian Peter Abelard (1070–1142) believed that the innocent but unbaptized suffered no physical pain, only the pain of the loss of God, and Pope Innocent III (1160–1216) agreed.

St Thomas Aquinas held an even more soothing concept, stating that limbo was a place of "natural happiness", but with the crucial exception that its residents were deprived of the transcendent joy of true union with God (known as supernatural happiness). However, the Council of Florence (1438–43) seemed to backtrack, stating, "the souls of those dying in actual mortal sin or in original sin alone go down at once into hell, to be punished, however, with widely different penalties". Yet the teaching of Aquinas remained the somewhat equivocal general Church position – crucially, it was never a definitive doctrine – right up until the 21st century and the pontificate of Pope Benedict XVI.

> **A 21ST-CENTURY DEBATE**
> Centuries of debate about limbo continue. In April 2007, the International Theological Commission, an advisory panel to the Vatican (previously headed by Cardinal Ratzinger, later Pope Benedict XVI) published a report endorsing the belief that *limbus infantium* was too limiting when it came to salvation. The report affirmed the superabundance of God's Grace over sin, noting that Christ's relationship with humankind must be stronger than any links with Adam. In a contest between original sin and salvation where no personal guilt is involved, the power of Christ's mercy vanquishes the power of Adam's sinfulness. The report, however, does not repudiate the Church's doctrine of original sin or the need for baptism. Instead, it theorizes that in the case of unbaptized infants, God can give his Grace without the need of the sacrament being given in baptism.

Above: The theologian Peter Abelard, shown in this 19th-century engraving, supported the idea of limbus infantium. *Pope Innocent III accepted his view.*

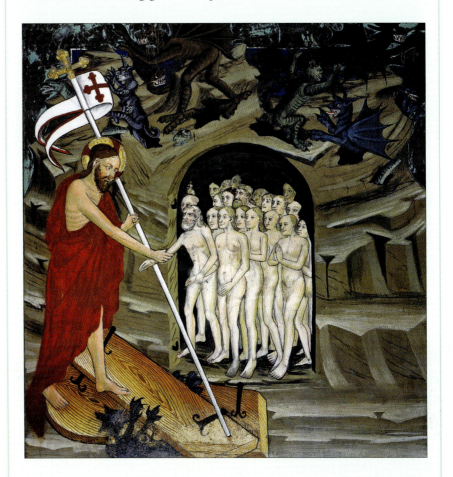

Above: In the Harrowing of Hell, between death and Resurrection, Christ went to limbo to free the just who died before him. It is depicted in this 15th-century fresco.

PRACTISING CATHOLICISM

One of the world's biggest institutions, the Catholic Church has a huge hierarchy. As leader of the Church, the pope rules from the Vatican, the centre of the Church's government. From there, the pope provides guidance to the bishops in their dioceses, the priests in their parishes, the monks and nuns in their monasteries and missionaries, and ordinary lay people in their everyday activities. People from all these walks of life seek inspiration from the Church as they practise their faith and celebrate the holy days that occur throughout the liturgical year.

The Eucharist, along with baptism and confirmation, is a sacrament of initiation into the Catholic Church. These girls are taking their first Holy Communion in Charlotte, North Carolina, in the United States.

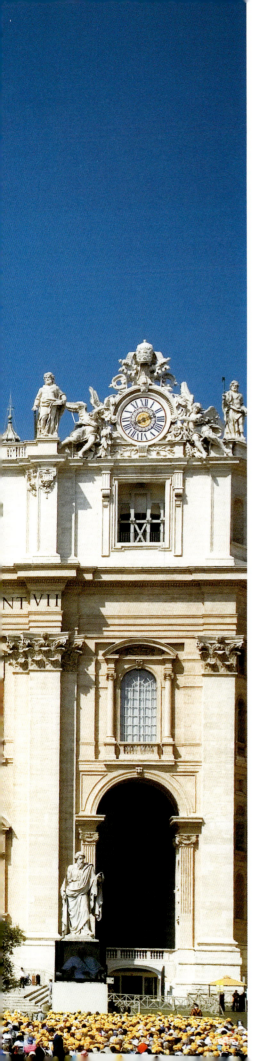

INSTITUTIONS OF THE CHURCH

On Easter Day, tens of thousands of Roman Catholics pack into St Peter's Square in Vatican City, Rome, to hear the pope celebrate Mass and give his Easter address. The event is broadcast live around the world: the address and the Apostolic blessing that follows it are termed *Urbi et Orbi* ("to the City [of Rome] and to the World").

As spiritual leader of the Roman Catholic Church, the pope heads a vast global organization. Pope Benedict XVI's third Easter address, delivered on 23 March 2008, was televised in 57 countries, and he followed it by giving Easter greetings in no fewer than 63 languages. In February 2022, the Vatican released statistics showing that in 2020, more than one in six people worldwise – 17.7 per cent of the global population – was Roman Catholic. This percentage is equal to around 1.36 billion people.

For these people the pope's authority is supreme. As well as being Europe's only absolute monarch, ruler of Vatican City (the world's smallest independent state), he stands at the head of the Holy See, the Church's machinery of government, and its administrative structure, the Roman Curia. He is at the peak of the great Church hierarchy of cardinals and archbishops, bishops, priests and deacons that also includes the many thousands of priests, monks, friars, nuns and religious sisters in the Church's religious orders. He is nothing less than the Vicar of Christ, his representative on earth. Yet in all these roles, the pope is called to humility and service: among his official titles is "Servant of the Servants of God", in line with the passage in St Matthew's Gospel (20:27) where Christ declares "whoever would be first among you must be your slave".

Left: A vast crowd of the Roman Catholic faithful attend open-air Mass in St Peter's Square at the Vatican on Easter Sunday.

INSTITUTIONS OF THE CHURCH

THE HOLY FATHER

THE POPE HAS ULTIMATE AUTHORITY OVER ROMAN CATHOLICS AND OVER THE CHURCH. HE IS ONE OF A LONG SUCCESSION OF POPES, ELECTED TO THIS POSITION BY THE COLLEGE OF CARDINALS.

The title "pope" derives from the words in Late Latin (*papa*) and Greek (*pappas*) meaning "father", and his position is similar to that of a father in a patriarchal family. The pope is addressed as "Your Holiness" and "Holy Father". In addition, the pope has eight formal titles listed in the official directory of the Holy See (the central government of the Catholic Church): Bishop of Rome, Vicar of Jesus Christ, Successor of the Prince of the Apostles, Supreme Pontiff of the Universal Church, Primate of Italy, Archbishop and Metropolitan of the Roman Province, Sovereign of the State of Vatican City and Servant of the Servants of God.

SUCCESSOR OF ST PETER

Bishop of Rome and Successor of the Prince of the Apostles are two titles that reflect the fact that for Roman Catholics the pope is a spiritual descendant of the apostle St Peter. Pope Benedict XVI, who has been pope from 19 April 2005, is said to be the 265th pope in an unbroken succession of popes from St Peter.

According to biblical accounts, Christ renamed Simon, son of John, Peter, based on the Greek *petros*, or "rock", because the Church was to be built with his strength. In later tradition, Peter was recognized as the leader of the 12 disciples who established the Christian Church in Italy, becoming the first Bishop of Rome. He was also buried in Rome, in the place where the high altar in St Peter's Basilica now stands.

CHRIST'S REPRESENTATIVE

The pope is also called the Vicar of Christ, meaning his representative – a person acting in his place.

Below: Under rules introduced in 1970 by Pope Paul VI, only cardinals aged 80 or below can vote for a new pope. In 2005, 117 cardinals were eligible to vote when Pope Benedict XVI was elected.

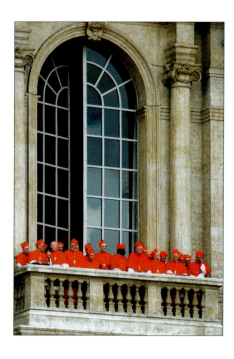

Above: The name conclave comes from the Latin cum clave *("with a key"). At one time the cardinals were locked away until a new pope was elected.*

For Roman Catholics, the pope serves as Christ's officer, with supreme authority over the Church, because he occupies the place of St Peter, who was originally given the authority to serve in this way. Pope Gelasius I (served AD 492–6) was the first to assume the name "Vicar of Christ"; before his time Christians had reserved the title for the Holy Spirit and popes were referred to as "Vicar of St Peter". The other titles reinforce the pope's position as supreme ruler of both the Catholic Church and the Vatican.

Roman Catholics believe that – just as the pope is the successor of St Peter – the archbishops and bishops of the Church are the successors of the apostles. The archbishops, bishops and the pope receive from the Holy Spirit the gift of infallibility – the capacity to discern what is right, and to be free from mistakes in morals and matters of faith when they jointly proclaim a doctrine. By this remarkable gift they share a part of Christ's own infallibility.

THE HOLY FATHER

> **A BURNING ISSUE**
> After each vote the ballot papers are burnt. Crowds gathered in St Peter's Square watch for the smoke to see the result: when a new pope has been elected white smoke is sent up, but when the vote has been unsuccessful black smoke rises. In the past, the cardinals used damp straw to colour the smoke but today they use more reliable chemicals.

The pope as leader of the bishops possesses a unique infallibility that makes it possible for him to make a definitive decree on doctrine that concerns matters of faith or morals.

RITUALS OF ELECTION

The pope is elected by the College of Cardinals in a series of closed sessions called a papal conclave, held in the Sistine Chapel in the Vatican Palace. The cardinals vote by writing the name of their preferred candidate on ballot papers beneath the words *Eligo in Summum Pontificem* ("I Elect as Supreme Pontiff"). They carry on voting until one man has the votes of two-thirds of the cardinals plus one. However, if the process becomes prolonged, the cardinals can agree to elect by simple majority.

When one name is agreed, the cardinal in question is asked if he accepts election as Supreme Pontiff. If he replies yes, he then gives the papal name by which he will be known, and the other cardinals pay him their respects.

The pope blesses the crowd and is then ceremonially installed in a service a few days later. At one time this was a grand coronation, but since the time of Pope John Paul I (served for 33 days in 1978), this has been replaced with a simpler ceremony in which the pope is invested with the papal robe, called the pallium, during a Papal Inauguration Mass.

Above: During a conclave in the Sistine Chapel at the Vatican to appoint a new pope, ballot papers are placed in these ballot boxes by the cardinals.

Below: Pope John Paul II greets the faithful during his first public appearance at the Vatican after his election to the papacy on 16 October 1978.

173

THE VATICAN: A PLACE APART

THE ROMAN CATHOLIC CHURCH'S CENTRE OF GOVERNMENT, GENERALLY KNOWN AS "THE VATICAN", IS IN VATICAN CITY. IT HAS ITS OWN MILITARY CORPS, GOVERNMENT AND INFRASTRUCTURE.

Vatican City is a city-state set within the Italian capital Rome. The world's smallest independent state, the Vatican covers about 44 hectares (109 acres) and has a population of between 800 and 1,000 people. The city-state is mostly enclosed by high stone walls that separate it from Rome. It is the sovereign territory of the Holy See (the Church's central government), and heads the Church's machinery of spiritual and pastoral rule.

While the Holy See has a history dating to the time of St Peter, Vatican City was created only in 1929 under the Lateran Treaty signed by the Kingdom of Italy and the Holy See. Its official name is *Stato della Città del Vaticano* ("the State of Vatican City").

Below: St Peter's Basilica looks down on St Peter's Square. The basilica's majestic 45m (150ft)-high façade was built by Carlo Maderno in the 17th century.

Vatican City is run as an elected monarchy that is ruled by the pope. One of the pope's formal titles is Sovereign of the State of Vatican City. Roman Catholic clergymen serve as the city-state's chief functionaries. The official state flag is the yellow and white papal banner.

MOUNT VATICAN

Vatican City takes its name from the hill in north-western Rome on which it stands. This area was known as *Mons Vaticanus* ("Mount Vatican") by the Romans in the pre-Christian era. The city contains the magnificent domed church of St Peter's Basilica, which by tradition stands over the burial place of St Peter, as well as the vast Vatican Palace (also known as the Apostolic Palace). With more than 1,000 rooms, this is an impressive structure that contains the pope's apartments, the

Above: Indoors, the vast scale of St Peter's Basilica impresses upon worshippers the power and grandeur of God – Father, Son and Holy Spirit.

Church's government offices and several chapels, as well as the Vatican Museum and the Vatican Library.

Within the complex is the Sistine Chapel, famed for its ceiling frescoes of scenes from the book of Genesis that were painted by Michelangelo in 1508–12. It also has a papal reception suite decorated with frescoes by Raphael and the artists of his studio, from 1508 onward, and the Borgia Apartment, a suite decorated with frescoes by Pinturicchio in 1492–5 for Rodrigo Borgia, Pope Alexander VI. The Vatican Museum contains a wealth of statuary, including the ancient Roman statues of *Apollo Belvedere* (350–325 BC) and of *Laocoön and His Sons* (160–20 BC).

Adjacent to the museum, the Vatican Archive houses religious and historical documents dating back over centuries, including the report on the Church trial in 1633 of mathematician and astronomer Galileo Galilei, whose promotion of the theory that Earth and other planets revolve around the Sun

was condemned by the Church on the grounds that it conflicted with Scripture. The complex also holds the Vatican Library, which has one of the world's most valuable collections of manuscripts and early books.

A number of other buildings belong to Vatican City but are situated beyond the city walls. These include the pope's summer villa in Castle Gandolfo, 24km (15 miles) south of Rome, as well as the churches of St John Lateran, St Mary Major and St Paul's Outside the Walls, all in Rome. The Church of St John Lateran is Rome's Cathedral Church and the ecclesiastical seat of the Bishop of Rome – that is, of the pope.

PROTECTING THE CITY

Vatican City has its own military corps known as the Pontifical Swiss Guard. The guardsmen, who are all Swiss and Roman Catholics, maintain a 24-hour watch over the pope and the Apostolic Palace. The Swiss Guard's role in protecting the pope dates back to the time of Pope Sixtus IV in the late 15th century. The guardsmen wear a Renaissance-style uniform that is sometimes said to have been designed by Michelangelo, but in fact was created in 1914. Technically, the Swiss Guard is a unit of the Holy See, not Vatican City.

The city has its own security and civil defence services department. It encompasses a police and security force called the Gendarme Corps of Vatican City-State, as well as its own fire brigade.

RUNNING THE CITY

The Vatican has the infrastructure and machinery of government necessary to run an independent country: a diplomatic corps; a court system; its own bank and independent postal,

Right: The elaborate Vatican Library was established by Pope Nicholas V in 1448. It holds some of the most important books from the earliest days of the Church.

Above: As well as protecting the pope and the Apostolic Palace, the Pontifical Swiss Guard are responsible for controlling access into and out of Vatican City.

telephone and telegraph services; its own water supply; street-cleaning and lighting; and a railway system. The railway is a stretch of track about 270m (885ft) in length, used for carrying freight. There is even a Vatican jail and a printing plant.

The Pontifical Commission for the State of Vatican City, a group of cardinals appointed by the pope, has responsibility for the state's domestic administration, while foreign relations are handled by the Secretariat of State of the Holy See.

The Vatican City newspaper *L'Osservatore Romano* (The Rome Observer) has been published since 1 July 1861. It was initially independently run, but since 1885 it has been owned by the Holy See.

HIERARCHY OF THE CHURCH

From papacy to parish, the Catholic Church's hierarchy is a vast pyramid connecting the pope at its summit through priests and deacons to members of the faithful at the base.

As Vicar of Christ on Earth, the pope holds supreme and universal power over the Roman Catholic Church. As Bishop of Rome and successor to St Peter, he is foremost among, and leader of, the bishops of the Church.

THE UPPER HIERARCHY
Bishops, archbishops and cardinals are at the top of the hierarchy. The pope has ultimate authority for the appointment of bishops. With them he shares what is termed "collegiate" responsibility for leading the Church.

Below: On ordination a bishop becomes a member of the College of Bishops and takes on his share of responsibility for governing the Church.

The bishops together form the College of Bishops. They are viewed as the successors of Christ's apostles and have a duty to teach the faithful.

Each bishop is in charge of an ecclesiastical area known as a diocese, which contains several individual parishes. His principal task is to care for the faithful in his area, like a shepherd cares for sheep. The main church of the diocese is known as a cathedral and is the ecclesiastical seat (base) of the bishop. In some metropolitan areas, an "ordinary bishop" is the principal bishop and is assisted by a team of auxiliary bishops.

The pope appoints some bishops as archbishops. They have control of an even larger area known as an

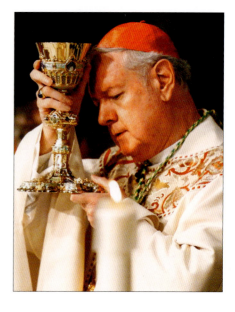

Above: Archbishop Egan leads his first service as archbishop in St Patrick's Cathedral, New York, on 19 June 2000. Archbishops are responsible for presiding over Mass in their ecclesiastical seat.

archdiocese, which contains a number of dioceses. The pope is also responsible for appointing some senior bishops as cardinals. They form the College of Cardinals. Some care for dioceses, while others serve the pope as advisers and administrators in Rome. When a pope dies or if a pope abdicates, the cardinals meet in closed session (conclave) to elect one of their number as the next pope.

PRIESTS AND DEACONS
Beneath the bishops are two further ranks in the ordained orders: priests and deacons. Priests have the same principal responsibility as a bishop, which is to care for the faithful in the area. Priests proclaim the gospels, lead community prayer and worship, celebrate Mass and the other sacraments for their congregation and teach the faith. Some are members of religious orders, while others are diocesan priests devoted to service in a particular diocese. Most serve in parishes but some instead serve as chaplains in hospitals, universities, prisons or the armed services.

HIERARCHY OF THE CHURCH

Both priests and bishops are assisted by deacons. In the early Church, deacons also held a special responsibility for charitable work, but as the role of deacon evolved, it became no more than a stage in training to become a priest. However, reforms introduced in 1967 by Pope Paul VI have re-established a group of permanent deacons in the Church. These deacons are men not called to be priests. They often have full-time jobs outside the Church, and whereas priests must be celibate, some deacons may be married.

WITHIN THE RANKS

Ecclesiastical duties are restricted by rank. Only bishops can perform ordination – that is, make others a bishop, a priest or a deacon through the sacrament of Holy Orders, which is centred on the laying on of hands and a prayer of consecration. Only bishops or priests can say Mass or hear confession.

Deacons have a special responsibility for reading the gospel in Church and for working with the poor. Deacons can preach, perform baptism and conduct marriage services – in the latter case they technically act as witnesses, because the bride and groom administer the sacrament of Holy Matrimony to one other.

CHURCH GOVERNMENT

The pope is the head of the Holy See, the Church's central machinery of government. The Holy See's administrative structures are collectively known as the Roman Curia. The Roman Curia is divided into several departments, the most important of which is the Secretariat of State, which performs political and diplomatic work for the Holy See.

Right: Pope Benedict XVI presides over the Roman Curia at the Vatican. Curia (from medieval Latin) means "court" – as in "royal court".

CANON LAW

The Roman Catholic Church has its own legal system, complete with its courts, judges, lawyers and legal code. The code derives its authority from the council of bishops as descendants of the apostles and the pope as successor of St Peter and Vicar of Christ.

The code has its original source in canons (rules) adopted by Church councils, supplemented by papal decretals or letters that state legal decisions, and input from Celtic, Saxon and other legal traditions. The material was formulated as a code and promulgated by Pope Benedict XV in 1917, then revised in the 1960s to 1980s and repromulgated by Pope John Paul II in 1983. On 1 June 2021, Pope Francis promulgated changes that tightened sanctions against priests involved in sexual abuse cases.

Parts of the code were adapted from Roman Law as codified on the order of Byzantine emperor Justinian I in AD 529–34. Church courts follow the Roman law style practised in continental Europe, with panels of judges and inquisitorial or investigative proceedings, as distinct from the adversarial proceedings with a single judge and a jury followed in law courts in the United Kingdom and the United States.

Above: A canon law tribunal hears a case. Roman Catholic canon law is the world's oldest continuously used legal system.

The Secretariat is split into the Section for General Affairs, which holds responsibility for appointments, documents and so on, and the Section for Relations with States. The latter is responsible for interacting with governments of countries from around the world as well as with international bodies, such as the United Nations.

THE PATH TO PRIESTHOOD

A MAN CALLED TO THE PRIESTHOOD UNDERGOES TRAINING THAT OFTEN TAKES SEVEN OR MORE YEARS AND INCLUDES STUDY IN A SEMINARY AND PASTORAL WORK IN A PARISH.

The journey to the priesthood starts by receiving a call from God to serve as a priest. The calling is known as a vocation (from the Latin *vocatus*, which is the past participle of *vocare*, or "to call"). The call to become a priest is only one of four possible vocations that are recognized by the Roman Catholic Church.

The other three are the calls to life as a brother or sister in a religious order; the call to marriage, with husband and wife sharing faithful love; and the call to single life, embracing celibacy and living either alone, with family or with other single faithful.

These four vocations are viewed as being equal but different. Each faithful Catholic will receive a call by God to one of the four forms of life. The task is to discern the calling and then test it to be sure that a person is truly being called to that particular pathway. The training to become a priest is known as his formation. The details of the training vary from place to place, but the process typically encompasses several stages.

PASSING THE TEST

If a young man acts upon a calling to become a priest, he must be willing to embrace a life of celibacy and prayer. He must be ready to commit to proclaiming the gospel, teaching the Catholic faith and doing his utmost to build his faith community. This is a lifelong commitment, so first the young man will need to test his vocation during a period of enquiry and preparation.

He is expected to pray to God for guidance and to be open and patient in waiting for a response. He will discuss his vocation with his local priest and either through him or independently can make contact with the specialist vocations director of the diocese or of a religious order if he feels called to join one.

Above: Young men training for the priesthood pray in a seminary chapel. The word "seminary" comes from the Latin seminarium *("bed of seeds").*

EARLY EDUCATION

If he is convinced that he has a vocation, the next stage is to apply to a seminary, a theological college specializing in training priests. A young man who wants to become a diocesan priest applies to a seminary through his local diocese. If he wants to become a priest in a religious order, such as the Franciscans, he applies directly to the order. The application process for a seminary generally includes academic assessment, interviews and psychological tests.

If the young man is accepted into the seminary, he begins his priestly education. The amount of time this takes depends on many factors, including the level of his previous education. His studies will include philosophy, theology, history and Scripture. The training will usually encompass a pre-pastoral stage of study for a year or two, followed by a pastoral stage in which the student serves in a working parish – perhaps returning to his own parish.

TRANSITIONAL DEACON

The next stage is to train as a deacon. For many years being a deacon was a stage in training to be a priest, but following Pope Paul VI's reforms there has been a return to the practice – common in the early Church – of maintaining a group of permanent deacons who are not destined to

Below: During an ordination service, ordinands prostrate themselves to symbolize their personal unworthiness, humility and reliance on the Grace of God.

THE PATH TO PRIESTHOOD

be priests. For this reason, students training to be priests who become deacons are now referred to as transitional deacons to distinguish them from permanent deacons.

After training the student is ordained a deacon. He will then serve for some time – at least six months, but often longer than that – as a transitional deacon before being ordained as a priest.

CALLED AS A PRIEST

At the completion of his training a student is called to be a priest by his bishop. If the bishop makes the decision not to call a student to become a priest, his action establishes that the young man did not truly have a vocation to the priesthood.

Young men must normally be at least 25 years old to become priests. Bishops have the authority to lower this age limit by one year, but only the Holy See can authorize the ordination of anyone younger than 24 years old.

Below: Transitional deacons become familiar with the priestly functions they will perform once they have completed their ordination.

TAKING VOWS

At ordination priests take vows of celibacy and of obedience to their bishop. Priests in religious orders take a vow of poverty in addition to those of obedience and celibacy. Before they can actively serve, priests have to be "incardinated" by a bishop or certain other religious superiors, such as the head of a religious order. This word derives from the Latin word for "a hinge", and when a priest is incardinated it means he is attached to and subject to a religious superior.

In practice, the priest will promise obedience to the bishop during his ordination service. However, if the priest has already made a vow of obedience to the superior of a religious order, then he will also acknowledge this pre-existing vow during his ordination.

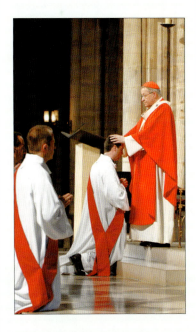

Above: After a priest takes his vows of celibacy during his ordination, the bishop will practise laying on of hands – this is a symbolic gesture that has been used since the Old Testament.

179

INSTITUTIONS OF THE CHURCH

MARRIED TO THE CHURCH

A PRIEST IS EXPECTED TO EMBRACE A CELIBATE LIFE. BEING CELIBATE ENABLES HIM TO AVOID WORLDLY DISTRACTIONS AND CONCENTRATE ON DEDICATING HIS LIFE TO SERVING GOD.

Roman Catholics believe that a priest's celibate life is a reflection of heaven. Priests are said to be married to the Church. The catechism declares that priests who embrace celibacy are "called to consecrate themselves with undivided heart to God…and give themselves entirely to God and to men" and that when it is accepted "with a joyous heart", "celibacy radiantly proclaims the Reign of God". Celibacy is a gift from the priest to God and to the people, to be made in a spirit of service.

The Church stresses that requiring celibacy in priests does not devalue the sacrament of marriage.

Below: Both brothers and sisters in Christ make sacrifices in adapting their lives to harmonize with the Church's teachings.

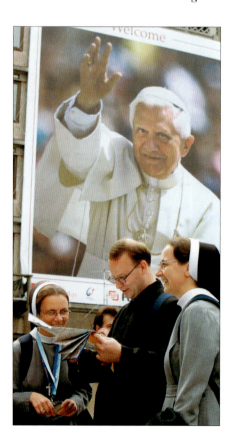

Being a priest or entering married life are among the four vocations recognized by Catholics – and no one vocation is said to be superior to any of the others.

BIBLICAL JUSTIFICATION
There is a principal source often cited by the Church in support of a call for clerical celibacy, a biblical passage found in Matthew, Chapter 19. In this passage Christ gives a description of marriage as a divinely ordained union between man and woman, and declares that any man who divorces his wife on grounds other than "unchastity" and then takes another is committing adultery. The disciples then say that if this is true it is surely better not to marry. In his response Christ apparently agrees, saying "Not all men can receive this saying, but only those to whom it is given" – that is, not everyone can accept this. He then adds, in the key verse (Matthew 19:12) that is generally cited by Roman Catholics:

> *For there are eunuchs who have been so from birth, and there are eunuchs who have been made eunuchs by men, and there are eunuchs who have made themselves eunuchs for the sake of the kingdom of heaven. He who is able to receive this, let him receive it.*

By the word that is translated as "eunuchs", Christ is thought to mean men who are celibate, who have freely chosen not to have sexual relations. Priests are an example of those in Christ's third category, who are celibate "for the sake of the kingdom of heaven".

Above: A priest consecrates himself to a new life and adopts celibacy, as stated in the catechism, "for the love of God's kingdom and the service of men".

Another key biblical justification for the celibacy requirement can be found in the writing of St Paul in the First Letter to Corinthians (7:32-4): "The unmarried man is anxious about the affairs of the Lord, how to please the Lord; but the married man is anxious about worldly affairs, how to please his wife, and his interests are divided." These verses clearly support the Church's position that a celibate life frees a priest to concentrate on serving God and man.

PRESSURE ON THE CHURCH
In the late 20th and early 21st centuries, critics inside and outside the Church have questioned the requirement of celibacy in priests. In an era of sexual liberation through much of Western society, the vow of celibacy has apparently made it more difficult to attract young men to the priesthood. There has been a mounting crisis in vocations, with the Church unable to replace priests who die and a number of parishes being left without priests.

180

THE CHURCH HOLDS FIRM

Nevertheless, the requirement of sexual abstinence by priests has been repeatedly reaffirmed by the Church hierarchy. The Second Vatican Council's Decree on the Ministry and Life of Priests in 1965 addressed the issue and claimed that celibacy was a charitable act of the priest, one that provided "a source of spiritual fruitfulness in the world".

In 1967, Pope Paul VI expressed in his encyclical *On Priestly Celibacy* that when a priest dedicates himself to God through celibacy, he can form a more profound relation with God, and this would benefit humankind. The priest would be better prepared to devote himself to his parishioners. In 1979, Pope John Paul II declared in a letter to priests that in order to serve their fellow humans, the priests must be free in their hearts – and that celibacy is a sign of this freedom.

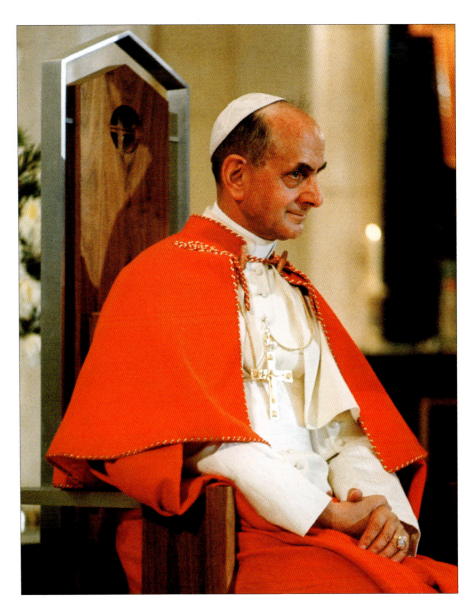

Right: Pope Paul VI called celibacy a special kind of asceticism that is more exacting than the sacrifices demanded of other Christians.

Below: Pope Paul VI, enthroned, opens the Second Vatican Council in 1965. In its deliberations, the Council made notable pronouncements on celibacy.

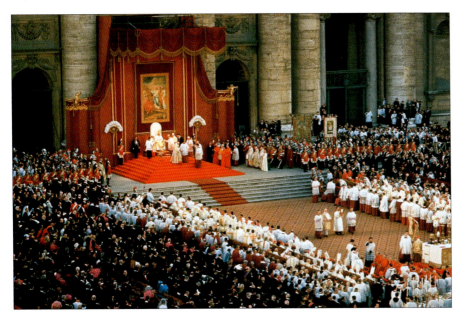

MARRIED PRIESTS?

There are some exceptions to the strict requirement of celibacy. Certain Protestant ministers who are married and then convert to Catholicism are allowed to serve as priests while married if they are given authority by the pope. Men of mature age who are married may be ordained and serve as permanent deacons – that is, they may be deacons but may not become priests. Men who have been ordained deacons while single may not later marry.

CALLED TO SERVE

IN THE SACRAMENT OF HOLY ORDERS, CANDIDATES ARE ORDAINED AS BISHOP, PRIEST OR DEACON. THE PROFOUND, BEAUTIFUL CEREMONIAL CONTAINS MOMENTS OF POWERFUL VISUAL THEATRE.

There are three types of ordination: as bishop, priest or deacon. On his ordination the candidate will join the relevant order – of bishops, priests or deacons. The word "ordination" means the incorporating of an individual into an order.

Only bishops have the power to perform ordinations. The essential rite of the sacrament is when the bishop lays his hands on the head of the candidate, or ordinand, and pronounces the prayer of consecration. It is traditional, but not required, for

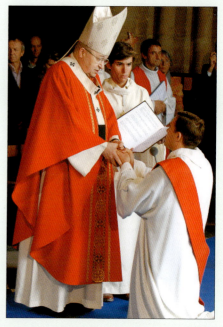

Above: An ordinand puts his clasped hands between those of his bishop as a sign of faithfulness to his ecclesiastical superior.

the ordination to take place during a Mass; ordinations are often held on a Sunday in the cathedral of the presiding bishop.

THE ORDINAND'S EXAM
In the usual service of ordination, the ordinands are called forward to the altar after the reading of the gospel. The presentation follows, when the bishop asks a series of questions to establish that the candidates have passed through the necessary levels of training in their formation as priests and that they are worthy to become priests. The bishop then "elects" – that is, chooses – each candidate and offers the prayer: "We rely on the help of the Lord God and our Saviour Jesus Christ and we choose this man, our brother, for priesthood in the presbyteral order." The congregation present then signals its support by applauding.

Left: Prostrating himself while the bishop prays the Litany of the Saints, the ordinand shows his reliance on the Holy Spirit and the support of the faithful.

The candidates sit while the bishop delivers a homily (sermon) on the nature of priesthood and the role of the priest. The candidates then come forward to the altar once more for the examination, in which the bishop asks whether they are willing: to discharge the office of the priest-hood; to celebrate Christ's mysteries; to exercise the ministry of the Word; and to consecrate their lives to God through Christ the High Priest. They reply each time "I am".

VOW OF OBEDIENCE
Each ordinand goes forward and, putting his hands in those of the bishop, promises to respect and be obedient to the bishop and his successors. (In some forms of the ordination service, when the candidates are being ordained as priests in a religious order, rather than as diocesan priests, they instead make a vow of obedience to the superior of the religious order to which they belong.) The bishop prays, "May God who has begun the good work in you bring it to fulfilment."

Next the ordinands lie prostrate on the floor while the bishop and assembled faithful recite the Litany of the Saints. The ordinands lie face down to symbolize their unworthiness to be a priest (or bishop or deacon, depending on the service) and the fact that to take on and succeed in the job they depend on the grace of God, and the prayers both of the saints and martyrs and of the Christian Community on Earth.

LAYING ON OF HANDS
The ordinands kneel. The ordaining bishop places his hands on the head of each ordinand in silence. The already ordained priests helping at the service do likewise. The laying

Right: The laying on of hands is a principal ritual that symbolizes the granting of priestly authority and the descent of the Holy Spirit.

on of hands is an ancient ritual going back to Old Testament times, when it was used by Jews to install their priests. The gesture is symbolic of the bishop's prayer to the Holy Spirit to descend on the candidate, and also of the long tradition of sacerdotal, or priestly, authority running right back to the time of the apostles.

The bishop says the Prayer of Consecration. He prays to the Holy Spirit to descend on the priest-to-be, to give him gifts needed for the ministry to which he is called.

THE NEW PRIEST
Priests who are newly ordained now put on the stole and chasuble, the vestments worn by priests when celebrating Mass. The bishop anoints the hands of each new priest with chrism (consecrated oil), which is symbolic of Christ himself as High Priest. The newly made priests then wipe the chrism from their hands on cloths. (They usually give these to their mothers in recognition of the women's sacrifice in giving their sons to the service of the Church.)

The new priests are given patens and chalices that have been brought forward by the people. The bishop prays: "Accept from the holy people of God the gifts to be offered to

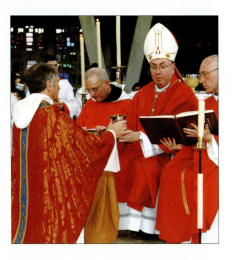

Above: A newly ordained priest receives from the bishop the chalice and paten he will use to celebrate his first Mass.

Him. Know what you are doing, and imitate the mystery you celebrate: model your life on the mystery of the Lord's Cross."

The bishop makes the sign of peace to the newly ordained priests. They then join with the bishop in celebrating the Eucharist. At the close of the Mass service the bishop will kneel before the altar and the priests will give him their blessing. The priests can now share in Christ's own eternal priesthood: they have now been ordained to serve the Church as Christ did many centuries earlier.

INSTITUTIONS OF THE CHURCH

UNDER ORDERS

MEMBERS OF RELIGIOUS ORDERS UNDERTAKE TO FOLLOW A RELIGIOUS RULE OR WAY OF LIFE UNDER THE LEADERSHIP OF A SUPERIOR. THEY MAKE A FORMAL DEDICATION OF THEIR LIVES TO GOD.

Religious orders are also known as Institutes of Consecrated Life. Their members take solemn public vows of chastity, poverty and obedience under Church law. Some members of religious orders are also ordained as priests or deacons, but if they are not they are considered to be members of the laity rather than clergy.

Within a religious order, authority is centralized in a superior or general house, which holds jurisdiction over geographically distributed dependent houses. However, a major exception to this general rule is the Order of St Benedict, in which there is no single superior house with overall authority and each of the individual abbeys is autonomous.

THE RELIGIOUS ORDERS

Some members are known as monks and nuns, or simply monastics, and live in enclosed communities. They devote their lives primarily to prayer and devotions. Others are known as friars and religious sisters, or mendicants, and live in a more open context and engage in social, medical or educational work. Historically, the monastics are self-supporting, while the mendicant orders rely on alms for their upkeep.

There is also a distinction between canons regular and clerks regular. Those known as canons regular live in either a closed community or as secular canons in open society. Although they are first and foremost monks, some of them are priests. They devote themselves primarily to the monastic life, which is centred on celebration of the liturgy and on contemplation. Conversely, clerks regular are first and foremost priests, but they choose to live in a community following a religious rule, in a similar manner to monks. Clerks regular devote themselves primarily to the ministry of the priesthood.

TAKING OF VOWS

Members of religious orders take what are known as solemn vows of obedience, chastity and poverty. Under solemn vows they renounce

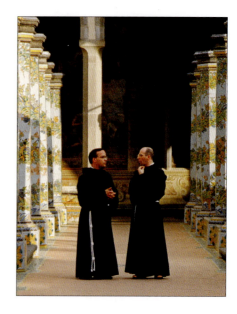

Above: Franciscan friars confer in the cloisters of Santa Chiara in Naples, Italy. They share the complex with nuns of the Poor Clares.

the right to own property. Members of another type of order, called religious congregations, take "simple" vows. In practice, those who swear simple vows retain the right to own material possessions, but they hand over the administration of the possessions to the congregation. Simple vows can be for a limited period, whereas solemn vows are for life. Those serving as novices, who are in the process of becoming

---

RULE OF LIFE

The "rule of life" is a set of guidelines that govern all aspects of behaviour by members of a religious order. Major examples in the Roman Catholic tradition include:

- The Rule of St Francis of Assisi, which is followed by those in the Franciscan tradition, such as the Order of the Friars Minor
- The Rule of St Benedict, followed by the Benedictines
- The Rule of St Augustine, which is traditionally followed by the Augustinians.

Right: Benedictine monks harvest flowers in the grounds of the 11th-century Abbey of Santa Maria Assunta at Praglia, near Padua, Italy.

Above: Jesuits are led from Rome by the Superior General, who holds the office for life. Spanish father Adolfo Nicolas was appointed in 2008 but resigned the position in 2016. He is succeeded by father Arturo Sosa.

a monk or nun, swear simple vows for a limited period before professing solemn vows for life.

There is another kind of religious community in which members do not take any vows. This is called a Society of Apostolic Life. A bishop grants this kind of society authority to operate in his diocese. An example is the Catholic Foreign Missionary Society of America.

SOCIETY OF JESUS

Jesuits are an important example of clerks regular. They are members of the Society of Jesus, which was established in the 1530s by Spaniard Ignatius Loyola in Paris. Today the society is governed from its headquarters in Rome, the General Curia, by the Superior General (also known as Father General), who is confirmed in his position by the pope. The Father General is assisted by an advisory council in Rome; around the world, the order is split into geographic provinces, each one led by a Father Superior.

The Society is the largest religious order of priests in the Catholic Church. About 13,500 of its 20,000 members are priests, with around 1,800 brothers, 3,000 students and almost 1,000 novices. From its early days the society combined strong central authority with mobility. Jesuits place emphasis on obedience to the pope – they are said to take a "fourth vow" (in addition to those of poverty, obedience and chastity) of particular obedience to the pope. Because Loyola had a military background, and due to this particular reverence for the papacy's authority, the Jesuits are sometimes referred to as the "Foot soldiers of the pope".

Right: A statue of Father John Carroll sits in front of the Jesuit university of Georgetown. He founded the private university in 1789.

JESUIT EDUCATION

Priests and brothers engage in many kinds of evangelical work, including missions and social work in less developed countries, but they are associated with education. Their first university, the Pontifical Gregorian University, or Gregorianum, in Rome, has been providing education since its foundation in 1551.

The Jesuits staff and run many schools, colleges, seminaries, universities and theological colleges. They work in more than 112 different countries around the world, and their education work is particularly important in India and the United States. In India, the Jesuits maintain colleges and schools in Mumbai, Calcutta, Delhi and Goa. In the United States, the Jesuits run more than 50 universities, colleges and schools, including the celebrated Georgetown University, which was founded in Washington, D.C., and Fordham University, which is located in New York City.

BROTHERS IN CHRIST

ONE BRANCH OF THE RELIGIOUS ORDERS STRESSES THE SPIRITUAL BENEFITS OF COMMUNITY LIVING. MONKS FOLLOW A RELIGIOUS RULE CENTRED ON CELEBRATING THE LITURGY OF THE HOURS TOGETHER.

St Benedict of Nursia, author of the *Rule of St Benedict*, is often celebrated as being the founder of Western monasticism. Modern Benedictines are the successors of the 6th-century monks for whom Benedict, founder of the monastery at Monte Cassino in Italy, wrote his rule of life in *c.* AD 535–40.

In a prologue and 73 chapters, the *Rule of St Benedict* directs monks to divide their time mainly between common prayer, prayerful meditative reading and manual work. The monks are expected to work six hours a day with their hands. The Rule, which St Benedict calls "a school of the Lord's service", also gives detailed guidance on acceptable sleeping arrangements, food and drink, clothing and caring for the sick, as well as hospitality for guests and recruitment. Although modern Benedictines do not follow the rule so strictly, they do still use it to guide their lives.

THE ORGANIZATION

From early on the Benedictines were organized to allow for local decision-making. Each monastery or "house" is autonomous, and the houses are grouped in 21 congregations. In 1893, Pope Leo XIII established the Benedictine Confederation of the Order of St Benedict, which is a confederation of the autonomous congregations, and appointed an abbot primate as its head. The abbot primate does not have direct jurisdiction in Benedictine monasteries but has a general concern for the wellbeing of Benedictines worldwide. The headquarters of the confederation is in Rome.

A LIFE GOVERNED BY VOWS

Benedictine monks take three vows: of obedience, that they promise to live according to the Rule of St Benedict; of stability, that they will endeavour to remain in the Benedictine order for life; and of conversion, that they will seek to follow Christ's example in all things, and will transform their life by adopting poverty and chastity.

In a typical Benedictine house, the monk's day is structured around six church services in the Liturgy of the Hours, with intervening periods of work and private prayer with meditative reading (known as *lectio*

Above: St Benedict's great legacy was his inspired and moderate Rule for monastic life. He wears a plain cloak in this 15th-century illustration by Andrea di Bartolo.

Below: The brothers of Bec Abbey at Le Bec-Hellouin, a Benedictine abbey in France, are joined for Mass by the sisters of the nearby Monastère de Ste Françoise Romaine.

divina). The typical day includes four hours in liturgical prayer, five hours in private prayer and spiritual reading, six hours of labour and eight hours of sleep. The remaining hour is set aside for eating.

A monk is required to attend the liturgical services. The first service is the "night office" of matins, which is prayed while still dark, and this is followed by the "morning office" of lauds at dawn. The monks work in the morning, and meet for midday prayer. They then work again in the afternoon, and celebrate Mass together in the late afternoon. The evening services are vespers (evening prayer) and compline (night prayer), which is said and sung before the monks retire to sleep.

The monks view their times of prayer and reading as their true work, but they are also required by the Rule of St Benedict to work. It warns that idleness can be dangerous to the life of the soul and urges brothers to keep themselves busy, sometimes at manual labour and at other times, in spiritual reading. The Rule specifically calls on the monks to work with their hands, but in modern monasteries the work done varies according to circumstance. Many Benedictine houses run schools in which monks work as teachers and administrators; there is also a good deal of practical work in and around the monastery: in the gardens, kitchens and laundry. In some houses, the monks also run a parish and keep a retreat house. They also often perform social work with local people.

BECOMING A MONK
A young man who wants to become a monk typically starts by staying in the monastery for a period as a visitor, then progresses to being a

Right: The Rule of St Benedict encourages brothers to work with their hands each day. A monk works prayerfully in his pottery studio.

postulant. As a postulant he commits to living in the monastery alongside the monks for three to six months.

He may leave after six months, or commit to being a novice. As a novice he is "clothed": this means he is given his monk's habit or cloak. After one or two years as a novice, the young man may be asked to renew his simple (temporary) vows for three years. After three years he may take solemn (life) vows and become

Above: Brothers share a meal. Their communal life is known as cenobitic monasticism, from the ancient Greek words koinos *and* bios *("common" and "life").*

a monk. He can continue as a novice for six or nine years, but after that period he must take life vows or leave the monastery. At any point when the applicant is free to leave, he may also be asked to leave if the abbot thinks he is not suited to monastic life.

DECLINING NUMBERS
Membership of the Roman Catholic Church is on the rise, but the number of those living a monastic life is in decline. Figures released in March 2021 showed that the number of members of the consecrated life fell in 2018–19. Women in religious orders far outnumber their male counterparts. The number of women in religious orders fell 1.8% from 541,661 in 2018 to 630,099 in 2019. Brothers in religious orders fell from 50,941 in 2019 to 50,295 in 2019. Men and women in monastic communities follow different rules of life.

A CONTEMPLATIVE CHRISTIANITY

IN THE TRADITION OF CONTEMPLATIVE MONASTICISM, MONKS LIVE IN AN ENCLOSED COMMUNITY AND COMMIT TO A LIFE OF SELF-DISCIPLINE AND PRAYER ON BEHALF OF THE CHURCH AND THE WORLD.

Above: St Bruno was a brilliant theologian and teacher. In this detail from a 17th-century painting by Nicholas Regnier, he is receiving the order.

Contemplative monks have no active ministry in terms of pastoral or missionary work or charitable enterprises, and they have little social interaction except through prayer. They generally live under strict rules governing their interaction. They spend large parts of the day alone and endeavour to live largely in silence. They usually work to produce goods by which they wholly or partially support themselves.

Members of the Carthusian Order (or the Order of St Bruno) live a life of this kind. The order was founded by St Bruno of Cologne in 1084 and takes its name from Chartreuse in France, where Bruno established his first hermitage with six companions. Carthusian monasteries are headed by a prior. They contain a community of cloister monks (sometimes called fathers), who commit to greater solitude, and brothers (or lay brothers), who have a less solitary life and take on the material tasks necessary to the running of the house.

In England, Carthusian monasteries are called charterhouses. The order is open to women as well as to men. There are currently 24 charterhouses worldwide – 19 monasteries, holding 370 monks, and 5 nunneries, holding 75 nuns.

LIFE IN A HERMITAGE

In a typical charterhouse, each of the cloister monks has his own hermitage, or living quarters, which usually has two storeys. Below is a workshop and wood for the wood-burning stove that is the hermitage's source of heat. The main room, above, is the cubiculum. The hermitage also has its own water supply and lavatory.

In the cubiculum, the monk prays, studies, sleeps and eats. He follows most of the Liturgy of the Hours, using full ceremony as if in public, although three daily services are celebrated communally in the chapel attached to the monastery. The monk enters the cubiculum through a small antechamber, which is known as the Ave Maria. This symbolizes the fact that in prayer the monk comes to Christ by way of the Blessed Virgin Mary. He begins all his offices and other prayers with intercessions to the Virgin. In the workshop area, the monk performs work for at least two hours a day.

The hermitage adjoins a walled garden in which the cloister monk meditates and grows vegetables and flowers. Each of the hermitages gives

Below: The mother house of the Carthusian Order is the remote monastery of La Grande Chartreuse, which is based in the Chartreuse Mountains of eastern France.

A CONTEMPLATIVE CHRISTIANITY

Above: A documentary film Into Great Silence *(2005) provided an insight into the lives of Carthusian monks at La Grande Chartreuse.*

on to a communal cloister through a turnstile: food and other materials can be left in this area without disturbing the cloister monk, which allows the contemplative monk to maintain absolute solitude.

Unlike the monks, the brothers of the community spend less time in prayer and more maintaining the monastery. They are responsible for managing food and other supplies, preparing meals, organizing the library and delivering books to cloister monks, carrying out repairs around the charterhouse and so on.

SILENCE

The monks attempt to live in silence. Although they do not take a vow of silence, they try to speak only when strictly necessary. They aim by this discipline to cultivate inner serenity.

Each cloister monk leaves his hermitage three times a day for services in the main chapel. These are the night offices (matins), the morning Eucharist and vespers in the evening. Occasionally, he meets his superior for a conference. On feast days and Sundays, all the monks meet for a community meal, held in silence. Once a week the brothers participate in a four-hour walk in the countryside around the charterhouse. They are permitted to speak on the walk: they walk in pairs, and change partners every 30 minutes. Two times a year the monks join in a community day of recreation and once annually they receive a visit from family.

THE SOLITARY LIFE

The Carthusian motto is the Latin *Stat crux dum volvitur orbis* ("The Cross holds steady while the world turns"). It celebrates the idea that silent contemplation and solitary prayer can create a place of sacred stillness amid change. The place of stillness serves to sanctify the wider world.

The monks endeavour to interiorize the silence amid which they live. They report that by a spiritual paradox, in solitude they can experience unity with all God's Creation. Through this experience their hearts are expanded to the dimensions of the love felt by Christ himself, for all people and all creatures.

The Carthusians live by a rule known as the Statutes. It declares that the hermitage is on holy ground and is a place where the monks can talk to God, where "earth meets heaven, and the divine meets the human". Carthusians aim to live in a state of constant and pure prayer, to exist in the presence of God and to maintain their hearts as an altar from which prayer rises constantly to God.

TRAPPIST MONKS

Another well-known group of contemplative monks is the Order of Cistercians of the Strict Observance. Its members are known as Trappists, from the name of La Grande Trappe (La Trappe Abbey) in Normandy, France, where the order was established in 1664. Trappists are contemplative monks who follow the Rule of St Benedict. Like the Cistercians, they divide their day between prayer and work. Trappist monasteries are known particularly for their production of celebrated ales, such as Chimay, which is made in Scourmont Abbey in Forges, Belgium, and Orval, made in the Abbaye Notre-Dame d'Orval monastery, also in Belgium. The order is open to women as well as to men. There are currently about 2,100 Trappist monks and 1,800 Trappist nuns (known as Trappistines) housed in about 170 monasteries worldwide.

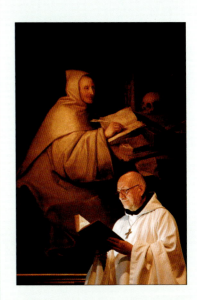

Above: A monk at La Trappe Abbey in Normandy, France, reads in front of a 1692 portrait of Father de Rancé, who was the founder of the Trappists.

WORKING IN THE WORLD

ANOTHER BRANCH OF THE RELIGIOUS ORDERS, KNOWN AS THE MENDICANTS, MAKES IT A PRIORITY TO PREACH THE WORD OF GOD AND TO PERFORM GOOD WORKS IN SOCIETY.

The mendicant orders are distinct from the monastic orders. The calling of monastic orders, such as the Benedictines or the Carthusians, is to live a life of self-disciplined routine and devotion in a monastery. While many monastic orders minister to the world through schools, parishes and retreat houses attached to their monasteries, the mendicant orders follow a call to engage directly with the wider world. They traditionally rely on the charity of others for support as they administer their work.

The mendicant orders also have a different organization. Brothers are attached to a province rather than to an individual monastery. They are answerable to a provincial superior general instead of to the abbot or prior of their own religious house.

Brothers and priests in the mendicant orders are known as friars, which distinguishes them from their counterparts in the monastic orders, who are called monks. "Friar" comes from the French *frère* and the Latin *frater* (both meaning "brother").

THE FOUR GREAT ORDERS

Of the mendicant orders, four of them in particular are referred to as the "great orders": the Franciscans, the Dominicans, the Carmelites and the Augustinians. They were recognized as the four Great Orders at the Second Council of Lyon (the Fourteenth Ecumenical Council of the Roman Catholic Church) in 1274. There are other mendicant orders, which are generally known as the lesser mendicant orders (*see Catholic Mendicant Orders, left*).

The Franciscans were founded in about 1209 by St Francis of Assisi. They are sometimes called the Friars Minor because Francis called his followers *fratres minores* ("lesser brothers") to place stress on their humility. They are traditionally called the Grey Friars because they wear a grey habit. The Dominicans were established in around 1215 by St Dominic; they are often called the Black Friars because they wear a

Above: Franciscan friars gather to follow the Via Dolorosa ("Way of Grief") in Jerusalem on Good Friday. Devotions are the ground from which good works grow.

Below A Carmelite friar from Aylesford Priory in Kent, England, leads local children in learning and worship. The priory was founded in the 13th century.

> **CATHOLIC MENDICANT ORDERS**
>
> The great and lesser mendicant orders are listed below, with the year they were established:
> - Franciscans, founded in 1209
> - Dominicans, founded *c.*1214
> - Carmelites, founded *c.*1155, mendicant order from 1245
> - Augustinians, founded in 1256
> - Minims, founded in 1474
> - Conventual Franciscans, founded in 1517
> - Capuchins, founded in 1520
> - Third Order Regular of St Francis, founded in 1521
> - Discalced Carmelites, founded in 1568
> - Discalced Trinitarians, founded in 1593
> - Order of Penance, founded in 1781

Right: Children orphaned by the tsunami disaster of 2004 can attend a new nursery that has been set up by the Salesians of Don Bosco in Sri Lanka.

black *cappa*, or "cloak", over a white habit. The Carmelites were founded in about 1155, originally as a contemplative order, but they became mendicants in 1245. They are also called the White Friars because they wear a white cloak over a brown habit. In 1255, the Augustinians were founded as a mendicant order from various groups of hermits by Pope Alexander IV and follow a rule based on the writings of St Augustine. They wear black garments too.

THE FRIARS' WORK

Many thousands of friars in the mendicant orders engage with needs across the world. Augustinian friars work as teachers, missionaries and also as parish priests; there are more than 2,700 Augustinian friars serving in about 40 countries. Franciscan friars work in virtually every country in the world. They have a special calling to work with the poor, in shelters, hospitals, schools and in programmes supporting justice and peace.

Dominican friars have a special calling to preach the gospel – indeed their official title is the Order of Preachers. They are also strongly committed to communal religious life, which they see as an essential support for their preaching work. According to their constitutions, they commit themselves to study assiduously, to celebrate the liturgy and especially the Eucharist together, to persevere and "to live with one mind the common life".

Dominican friars live in priories under an elected prior, where they

Right: Street children from Nairobi enjoy working the land at a youth centre founded in 1994 by the Salesians of Don Bosco in Langata, Kenya.

sing the Mass and Holy Liturgy together and share their meals and times of recreation. They commit to spreading the gospel wherever their work takes them, whether it is in hospitals, prisons, universities or schools. They see publishing books and dissemination of the gospel on the Internet as part of their work. These friars aim to emulate their founder, of whom it was said that he was always either talking to God or about God.

TEACHING ORDERS

Some religious orders are devoted particularly to teaching in schools and colleges. The De La Salle brothers, which was founded in 17th-century France by St Jean-Baptiste de La Salle, a canon at Rheims Cathedral, runs schools in 80 countries teaching more than 900,000 students.

The Salesians of Don Bosco, which was founded in 19th-century Italy by St John Bosco, are committed to working with young people in need. The Salesians number more than 16,000 priests and brothers who work with the young in 128 countries.

The Salesians run a large number of secondary or high schools, including: in London, Farnborough and Bolton in England; in Los Angeles and Richmond, California, and New Rochelle, New York, in the United States; at Imphal and Calcutta in India; and one in Hong Kong. They also run college-level educational establishments, which include DeSales University in Pennsylvania.

INSTITUTIONS OF THE CHURCH

BRIDES OF CHRIST

WOMEN ENTER RELIGIOUS ORDERS TO SERVE GOD THROUGH PRAYER, DEVOTIONS AND GOOD WORKS. WOMEN CALLED TO RELIGIOUS SERVICE ARE CALLED "BRIDES OF CHRIST".

When women commit themselves to religious life they can choose to become nuns or religious sisters. The words "nun" and "sister" are often not distinguished in common usage, but strictly speaking a nun is a woman who has taken vows, committing herself to an enclosed life of prayer and contemplative devotions within a convent, while a religious sister has chosen a much more actively engaged life of service, caring for the sick, starving, poor and otherwise needy.

LIFE IN A CONVENT
Nuns live in a monastery or a convent. A monastery is normally thought to be a community of monks and a convent to be a community of nuns, but some communities of monks are also called convents and some communities of nuns are referred to as monasteries, especially in the Benedictine tradition. (Religious communities of nuns were once also called nunneries, but this word is now archaic.)

Nuns live an enclosed life. They are not generally permitted to leave the convent or to receive visitors, although some do carry out teaching or other ministries as permitted by the constitution or rule of their particular community. Strictly, convents should be built so that the inner courtyards and gardens cannot be seen from without and the windows do not open on to public roads.

The convents are independent of one another, with each community headed by a Mother Superior. She is usually elected for life, but in some constitutions the Mother Superior is subject to re-election every three years.

If the community is an abbey, she is known as an abbess, and if it is a priory she is a prioress. The distinction made between abbey and priory depends on differences in the particular religious orders and in the community's level of independence.

STEPS TO SISTERHOOD
If a young woman feels she has a calling to the religious life as a nun or sister, she becomes a postulant for six months to a year. During this time she usually lives in the community, following the life of the nuns and sisters closely, but takes no vows. If she and the order then determine that she has a vocation, she is generally given the habit (clothing) of the order and lives for one to two years as a novice; at this point she still takes no vows. The next stage is to take temporary vows for one year or

Above: Today's nuns still follow the advice of the 16th-century nun St Teresa of Ávila, who taught sisters that Christ "has no hands on earth but yours".

Below: Sisters of contemplative orders work tirelessly and devotedly through prayer to bring peace and God's love to a troubled world.

192

Right: Work is a form of prayer for nuns, such as for these English Benedictine sisters attentively labouring over the ironing.

more, up to six years. The last stage is to take final vows and make perpetual profession.

The vows the nuns take will vary from one order to another. In the Benedictine tradition nuns, such as Trappistines and Cistercians, take a threefold vow of stability (to remain a member of the community), of obedience to the Mother Superior and of conversion of life (to adopt poverty and chastity). Franciscan and Dominican nuns take a vow of poverty, chastity and obedience. Some nuns take an extra vow specific to the kind of work they do or the character of their order.

TYPES OF ORDERS

There are contemplative orders and charitable orders. Most of the strictly enclosed congregations of nuns are members of contemplative religious orders who are devoted to seeking union with God through prayer and contemplation. The Carmelite nuns, the Redemptoristines and the Poor Clares (or Order of Poor Ladies) are all examples of contemplative orders. They sometimes undertake enclosed ministries by supporting a particular type of work through prayer in the convent: for example, the Redemptoristines pray for the work of the Redemptorist friars. They often support themselves by labour in the convent – for example, by making liturgical items, such as church candles and vestments.

Women in the charitable orders are committed to performing works of charity and mercy, teaching and caring for the sick or aged. Examples include the Little Sisters of the Poor, Ursulines and the Sisters of Charity.

THE DEVOTION OF ST THERESA

St Theresa of Lisieux was a French Carmelite nun of the late 19th century whose spiritual autobiography, *L'histoire d'une âme* ("Story of a Soul"), published in 1898, inspired great popular devotion. She was canonized in 1925 by Pope Pius XI and in 1997 Pope John Paul II declared her a Doctor of the Universal Church. She is one of four women among the 33 Doctors of the Church.

Theresa, who is today popularly known as "the Little Flower of Jesus", became a Carmelite novice in April 1888 at the tender age of 15, following her sisters Pauline and Marie into the order. She died of tuberculosis on 30 September 1897 when just 24 years old. Theresa is celebrated for her "Little Way" of devotion and love, which promotes the need for trust and absolute surrender. She wrote:

Love shows itself in deeds....Great deeds are beyond me. The only way I can show my love is by throwing out flowers and these flowers are each a small sacrifice, each look and word, and doing of the very least thing simply for love.

Right: St Theresa was a teenage novice when she posed for this picture at the Carmelite house in Lisieux, c.1890.

LIVING FOR OTHERS

WOMEN IN THE RELIGIOUS ORDERS DEDICATE THEIR LIVES TO GOD IN CHRIST AND TO PRAYING FOR AND SERVING THOSE IN NEED BECAUSE OF POVERTY, SICKNESS OR IGNORANCE OF THE GOSPEL.

Whether nuns or religious sisters are members of a contemplative or charitable order, their religious life is intended to reach out to help other people. Enclosed orders seek to ease suffering in the world through devoted prayer, while charitable orders provide care, shelter, education and love to the needy.

IN AN ENCLOSED ORDER
The Poor Clares, which was established in 1212 by St Clare of Assisi and St Francis of Assisi, is an enclosed contemplative order of Franciscan nuns who are committed to a life of prayer without possessions. These nuns pray the Holy Liturgy and

Below: Sisters in the Poor Clares dedicate themselves to service through prayer. Some undertake strict acts of penance, fasts and other austerities.

celebrate Mass together. They see intercessionary prayer as an important part of their calling, and they accept prayer requests from outside the convent and pray daily for the Church and the world.

Some houses keep retreat centres in the grounds of the convent. They also work in their convent to maintain the community as well as to support themselves. To this aim, they might make candles, vestments, greeting cards or religious pictures. The nuns follow a rota for cooking, gardening, cleaning and so on.

The nuns view the enclosed life they live as a vital spiritual discipline that expresses their love for God. They leave the enclosed community only when it is absolutely necessary – perhaps to visit the doctor or dentist or to see a parent who cannot travel. They are permitted to receive visits

Above: A sister distributes medicine at an Ursuline orphanage in Guyana, South America. The Ursulines have a special calling to education and healthcare.

by close family members as allowed by the abbess.

CARING FOR THE POOR
Among many orders of nuns dedicated to charitable work in the world, the Missionaries of Charity, a religious order with a special calling to serve the extremely poor, is one of the most celebrated in modern times. The order was established in 1950 by Mother Teresa of Calcutta, and today it includes 5,200 nuns working in 133 countries.

These nuns care for orphans, lepers, victims of AIDS, refugees, former prostitutes, street children, the mentally ill and those suffering in the wake of famine and natural disasters. In Calcutta, the place of their foundation, they maintain no fewer than 19 homes, including ones for the dying, for lepers and a school for street children. The nuns in this order take the conventional vows of poverty, chastity and obedience. They also take a fourth vow to offer "wholehearted and free service to the poorest of the poor".

CARING FOR THE OLD
The Little Sisters of the Poor is a religious order with a particular calling to care for the elderly. The order was established in 1839 in France

JEANNE JUGAN

Born in 1792 in Cancale, Brittany, Jeanne Jugan – also known as Sister Mary of the Cross – worked as a shepherdess and a nurse in a hospital, becoming an associate of the Congregation of Jesus and Mary. In 1837, she founded a community of prayer dedicated to caring for the elderly poor that developed into the Little Sisters of the Poor, established two years later. By the end of the 1840s they had five houses and more than 100 women had joined. The Little Sisters opened their first house in England in 1851 and in 1886–71 established five communities in the United States. Jugan died in 1879. She was canonized by Pope Benedict XVI on 11 October, 2009. He said, "In the Beatitudes, Jeanne Jugan found the source of the spirit of hospitality and fraternal love... which illuminated her whole life."

Right: Jeanne Jugan's mission was to care for the poor and elderly. Her feast day is 30 August.

by Jeanne Jugan, but they have a strong presence in many cities in the United States. Today the order has approximately 2,000 sisters caring for more than 13,000 elderly people in 31 countries, including India, Hong Kong, Taiwan and the United Kingdom. In the United States alone, the Little Sisters of the Poor are responsible for running 22 homes for the elderly, including houses in San Francisco, Washington D.C., Chicago, New York and Pittsburgh.

The Little Sisters of the Poor put into practice their founder's instuctions to always show kindness toward others, but particularly to those who are sick. Jeanne Jugan had stressed that the calling to serve the sick was a great sign of God's Grace, and she declared that because the infirm were God's creatures, when the sisters cared for the sick they were serving God himself.

The nuns rely on charitable contributions to support their work, and they generally tour the area around their home in a "begging van", in which they collect gifts not only of food but also of medical and other important supplies.

Right: The Benedictine sisters care for the sick in this early 18th-century French painting by Louise Madeleine.

In addition to vows of obedience, chastity and poverty, the sisters take a fourth vow of hospitality. They endeavour not just to give their residents shelter, food and comfort, but also to cater for their spiritual, psychological and social needs.

PRAYER AND DEVOTION

Sisters in charitable orders, such as the Missionaries of Charity and the Little Sisters of the Poor, anchor their active life in a routine of prayer and contemplative devotions. The Little Sisters of the Poor, for instance, will typically start the day with meditation and morning prayer, and then hold a daily Mass at the end of the morning. Residents in their homes are welcomed to this service. The sisters also take time for regular prayer throughout the day and they engage in meditative religious reading, or *lectio divina*. In addition, they meet for evening prayer at the end of the day.

THE MISSIONS

A NUMBER OF ROMAN CATHOLIC RELIGIOUS ORDERS ARE DEDICATED TO MISSIONARY WORK. THEY WORK ACROSS THE WORLD IN BOTH DEVELOPED AND DEVELOPING COUNTRIES TO SPREAD THE GOSPEL.

There are many Catholic missionary orders, but the Missionaries of the Sacred Heart, an order founded in France in 1854 by French priest Jules Chevalier, is particularly notable.

WORLDWIDE MISSION
The Sacred Heart has about 1,700 brothers and priests working around the world in more than 50 countries from Senegal to Venezuela, inspired by their founder to find opportunities to serve Christ in the depths of the world's need. Chevalier was convinced that Christians could have as profound an experience of God's Grace in the world as they would in an enclosed religious community, and he declared that when brothers were helping the poor, the great power of God's love and of the Sacred Heart of Jesus would flow forth as needed. The greater the difficulties the brothers encountered in doing God's work, the greater the help God would provide.

The brothers, who are sometimes better known as "MSC" from the initials of their name in Latin, *Missionarii Sacratissimi Cordis*, declare that they see their work as "to be on Earth the heart of God", to meet need in whatever form they encounter it. In Venezuela, MSC priests spread the gospel in the impoverished barrios through work in parishes and seminaries and as hospital chaplains, caring for the sick and poor and dying. In Russia, the mission has grown from the work of three MSC priests who travelled there in 1995 to try to rebuild the Catholic Church in an area where religious life had been suppressed under the communists. In Africa, the MSC run missions in Senegal, Namibia, South Africa and the Democratic Republic of Congo, running schools and agricultural training and operating pastoral and spiritual centres. In missions in England, Wales and Ireland they work with migrants and refugees in ecumenical interfaith initiatives and widely in education and parishes. Their motto is: "May the Sacred Heart of Jesus be everywhere loved."

On 1 September 2004, Pope John Paul II wrote to the Sacred Heart to mark its 150th anniversary, praising its founder and its work. He said that the organization's founder, Father Chevalier, established the Sacred Heart as a place for God to meet humankind, and expressed his wish that the community continue to inspire and have strength for its spiritual work. He also declared that they had a wonderful history worth remembering, but also "a great history still to be accomplished".

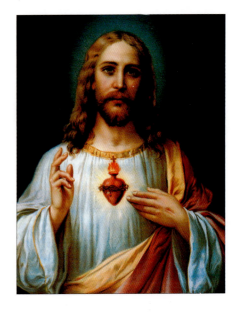

Above: The Sacred Heart of Jesus provides spiritual inspiration to the brothers of the Missionaries of the Sacred Heart.

Below: The brothers of some missionaries are active in helping the poverty-stricken, such as these from the Missionaries of the Poor, repairing roofs in Kingston, Jamaica.

THE MISSIONS

Right: A priest from the Catholic Foreign Missionary Society of America (Maryknoll) greets those attending a wedding Mass in Kibera, Nairobi, Kenya.

MARYKNOLL

Formerly known as the Catholic Foreign Missionary Society of America, Maryknoll sends around 470 priests and brothers to work around the world, especially in Africa, Latin America, Korea, Japan and China. The order was founded in 1911 in the United States by Fathers James Anthony Walsh and Thomas Frederick Price.

In their mission statement, the brothers declare that, wherever they have travelled, they have been touched by the strength of human perseverance and greatly empowered by their experience of Christian faith in times of need. They work with them in declaring their faith in Jesus. The Maryknoll brothers commit themselves to standing in solidarity with the poor, to entering inter-religious dialogue, to serving as witnesses of Christ, to celebrating the Church's liturgy and to proclaiming the gospel and teaching the faith.

The society is linked to the Maryknoll Sisters of St Dominic, a group of religious sisters founded in 1912, in the United States. Around 300 Maryknoll Sisters work in 18 countries, including Albania, Panama, Nepal, Sudan and Hong Kong. The sisters are associated with setting up convent schools. Widely known examples are Maryknoll Convent School in Kowloon Tong, Hong Kong, and Miriam College in Quezon City, Manila, the Philippines.

OTHER MISSIONS

The larger religious orders, while not formed primarily to carry out missionary outreach, do a great deal of work of this kind. Among many examples, Capuchin Franciscans maintain missions in Central America (Panama and Nicaragua) and in South Africa. In Pretoria, South Africa, for example, they run the Damietta Peacemaking Initiative to promote non-violence and peace.

The Jesuits spread the gospel through their outreach work in educational establishments, orphanages, hospitals and community centres as part of their overseas missions – notably in Guyana, Zimbabwe and South Africa. The Carmelites also maintain several missions, including ones in Kenya, Mozambique, Indonesia, East Timor, Burkina Faso, Cameroon and the Democratic Republic of Congo. In Kenya, for instance, the Carmelites have established an enclosed monastery in Machakos and a house of formation in Ngong diocese.

Another notable order is the Missionaries of La Salette, which was founded in 1852 in La Salette, near Grenoble, France, where a shrine to the Blessed Virgin Mary was established. The order has around 1,000 nuns, priests and lay members working in support of healing and reconciliation in North America and Europe, as well as performing missionary work in countries such as Madagascar, the Philippines, Bolivia, Myanmar, Namibia and Angola.

Right: Franciscan sisters demonstrate God's love for the helpless by running an orphanage school in northern Egypt.

LAY GROUPS

THE CHURCH ENDORSES THE WORK OF SEVERAL ORGANIZATIONS THAT WERE ESTABLISHED TO HELP LAY CATHOLICS FOLLOW THE GOSPEL IN THEIR RELIGIOUS WORK AND FAMILY LIVES.

The largest lay group, Opus Dei (Latin for "God's work") is a Roman Catholic organization of predominately lay people who seek to grow closer to God and achieve sanctity through work and everyday activities, including family life. There are around 93,000 members worldwide, in 90 countries; 98 per cent are lay people and only around 2,100 are priests. Approximately 30 per cent of lay members (called numeraries) are celibate and live in Opus Dei centres, while roughly 70 per cent (called supernumeraries) are married and serve God in family life.

The movement was founded in 1928 in Spain by Roman Catholic priest Josemaría Escrivá and received approval in 1950 from Pope Pius XII. In 1982, Pope John Paul II declared the organization a personal prelature within the Church, under the name the Prelature of the Holy Cross and Opus Dei. This means that it functions like a religious order. The Church governs Opus Dei members through a prelate, who is appointed by the pope, and has a status equivalent to that of a superior general in a religious order. The members remain part of local church congregations.

As an organization, Opus Dei runs high schools, colleges, university halls of residence, business and agricultural schools, and it also does charitable work. In Spain, it founded and runs the University of Navarre at Pamplona. It also runs a university at Piura in Peru.

Above: Pope John XXIII stands between St Josemaría Escrivá and Msgr Álvaro del Portillo, another leading Opus Dei figure, in 1960.

A SECULAR ROUTINE

Josemaría Escrivá encouraged people to try to "convert their work into prayer". He described a dream in which God's children could sanctify themselves although they lived as ordinary citizens. It was through regular work and the mundane routine of everyday life that people could find God's love.

Escrivá died in 1975. Pope John Paul II beatified him in 1992 and proclaimed him a saint in 2002. John Paul II declared Escrivá the "saint of ordinary life", adding that he disseminated through society the awareness that a calling to holiness is received by all, with no distinctions of culture, racial identity, social class or age.

SPIRITUALITY

Opus Dei members are expected to follow a set form of personal devotions every day, including Mass, and to attend a weekly confession. They should also attend an annual spiritual retreat of three weeks for numeraries and one week for supernumeraries.

Left: The Church of Our Lady of Peace in Rome is the headquarters of Opus Dei. Many pray at the crypt of St Josemaría Escrivá.

Spiritual practice for a member of Opus Dei often includes an element of sacrifice by voluntarily offering discomfort or pain to God. This can simply involve self-sacrifice in terms of self-denial and charity in dealing with others. However, some celibate numeraries are said to practise physical mortification by either wearing a spike metal chain known as a cilice on the upper thigh or by flailing themselves with a woven cotton strap known as a discipline.

A CRITICIZED PRACTICE

Self-mortification is one of many areas in which Opus Dei has been criticized. Opponents attack the practice as being akin to masochism and even liable to undermine spiritual development by fostering pride.

IN RECOGNITION FOR CHRISTIAN SERVICE

The Association of Papal Orders is an organization for people who have been awarded papal knighthoods. These awards are made at five levels to people who have provided a great service to the Catholic Church. The five levels are:
- Supreme Order of Christ
- Pontifical Order of the Golden Spur
- Pontifical Order of Pius IX
- Pontifical Order of St Gregory the Great
- Pontifical Order of Pope St Sylvester.

Notable recipients of the awards include Prince Rainier III of Monaco (Pontifical Order of the Golden Spur), former German Federal Chancellor Helmut Kohl (Pontifical Order of St Gregory the Great) and the Hollywood entertainer Bob Hope (Pontifical Order of Pope St Sylvester).

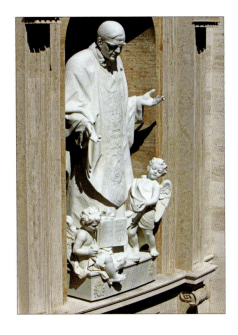

Above: A statue of St Josemaría Escrivá, founder of Opus Dei, stands in an alcove of the basilica façade within the Vatican.

However, defenders of the practice respond that it is a valued way of identifying with Christ's physical suffering, has been used by Christians for centuries and is more used today in the Roman Catholic Church than is generally known.

A SECRETIVE SOCIETY

Opus Dei has been accused by some of being both secretive and manipulative. They claim that a number of leading politicians around the world are members of the society, although few make public statement of their membership. Some people suggest that the organization dominates members and uses overly aggressive recruitment techniques. Opus Dei, however, states that members are not coerced into joining and people are free to leave if they want to.

OTHER LAY GROUPS

Many of the major religious orders also support lay associates: for example, the Dominican laity have their own rule, the Rule of the Lay Fraternities of St Dominic, first issued in 1285, while Franciscan lay followers are members of the Secular Franciscan Order and follow a rule established for secular followers by St Francis himself in 1221. Secular Franciscans have a novitiate and formal profession, but they are not bound by their religious vows, and can be married and live ordinary lives in the community.

Among the other Catholic lay bodies is the Catenian Association, which is an international brotherhood of Catholic professionals and businessmen. It was established in 1908 in Manchester, England, and now has about 10,000 members in Australia, Ireland, South Africa, Malta, Zimbabwe and Zambia, as well as in the United Kingdom.

Their aims are to develop social bonds and foster brotherly love among members. The association grants bursaries to provide partial support for young Catholics who are performing community work. The Catenians also maintain a Public Affairs Committee that monitors and speaks out on any proposed legislation that would contradict Catholic teaching.

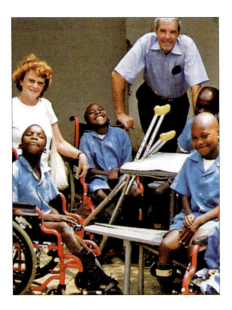

Above: The Catenian Association has sponsored projects to help the needy in Mexico and Africa, such as at this children's home in Zambia.

LIVING THE SACRAMENTS

There are seven sacraments through which practising Catholics receive God's Grace. These are baptism, confirmation, the Eucharist, penance and reconciliation (popularly known as confession), "the anointing of the sick", holy orders and Holy Matrimony. According to the *Catechism of the Catholic Church*, the sacraments were "instituted by Christ and entrusted to the Church". They are stages in the spiritual life – from new birth as a Christian in baptism and confirmation, through to the anointing of the sick, often administered at the end of earthly life before the final journey into eternal life. The sacraments help individual Catholics make spiritual progress and grow in holiness.

Most people do not receive all seven sacraments: only some have a priestly vocation and receive holy orders, for example, and all who receive holy orders (except already married deacons) cannot receive Holy Matrimony. Individuals must be prepared to receive the sacraments. God's Grace may be blocked from working if someone is not disposed to receive it. For a sacrament to be effective, a person must have faith in it, although at the same time the sacraments in themselves strengthen and give expression to a person's faith.

Particular objects used by the clergy, including the special robes or vestments that a priest or bishop wears when celebrating the Eucharist or the Liturgy of the Hours, are termed "sacramentals". They are material things blessed or set apart to summon the respect believers should have for the sacraments of the Church – in the words of the *Baltimore Catechism* (a Catholic school text in the United States) "to excite good thoughts and increase devotion".

Left: The Eucharist is central among the sacraments. All seven sacraments are connected to Christ's paschal mystery – his redemptive sacrifice that is re-enacted in the Eucharist.

GOD'S HOUSE

THE FIRST CHRISTIANS WORSHIPPED IN PRIVATE HOUSES, BUT OVER TIME CHURCHES HAVE DEVELOPED INTO SUBSTANTIAL PUBLIC BUILDINGS THAT SERVE AS THE CENTRE OF ROMAN CATHOLIC LIFE.

The earliest public churches were built after Christianity was adopted as the state religion of the Roman Empire in the 4th century AD. They were based on the Roman basilica, a large roofed public building often used as a courthouse or market. Like the basilica, the early churches had a central hall, known as the nave, with a timber roof and an aisle on each side, which were separated from the nave by a line of columns.

A wooden altar was established toward one end of the nave. In the first churches, the altar was typically at the west end of the nave, in imitation of the arrangement in the Jewish Temple in Jerusalem. The bishop or priest celebrating the Eucharist faced east – on the grounds that it was the direction of the heavenly Jerusalem and thus it was from this direction that Christ would return in glory – and so he always looked toward the congregation. For unknown reasons, in about the 6th century the arrangement was reversed, with the altar at the east end of the nave.

Beyond the altar was the apse, basically a semicircular or sometimes rectangular recess, usually vaulted, occupied by the bishop and priests during services. When celebrating the Eucharist, the bishop or priest, who continued to face east, looked toward the apse and away from the worshippers in the nave. The area around the altar, which was set aside for the clergy, became known as the presbytery or sanctuary.

Above: The Jewish Temple in Jerusalem, shown in this c. 1728 Jewish manuscript, was an inspiration to early Christians, who based part of their church layout on it.

Left: The west front of Lincoln Cathedral in England incorporates elements dating from 1072. The main part of the cathedral is 13th-century, in the Gothic style.

At the west end, a long entrance porch called the narthex ran across the full width of the nave and led into the nave. Unbaptized believers and penitents generally remained in the narthex, where they were separated from clergy and other believers.

THE BEMA AND THE CHOIR

There were many variations of these areas. In some churches, a wooden platform called the bema was built in the centre of the nave. The clergy sat in this area and read lessons and delivered sermons from the lectern on the bema. In some large churches, the eastern end of the nave began to be fenced off with a small railing to form an area for the choir, and sometimes the choir area was attached to the bema. This arrangement survives to this day in the Basilica di Santa Maria Maggiore (AD 430–40) in Rome. More typically, the choir area became a separate architectural feature connecting the nave and sanctuary.

CRUCIFORM PLAN

In some churches, a transept was added on a north–south axis, perpendicular to the nave, to form a church shaped like a cross. The point at which the transept cuts across the nave was known as "the crossing": the nave usually extended to the west of the crossing and the choir and sanctuary lay to the east. The arms of the crossing were called north

Above: The altar stands at the centre of the Metropolitan Cathedral of Christ the King, Liverpool, England, surrounded on all sides by seats. The designer was aiming to help the congregation feel more linked to the liturgy.

transept and south transept: at each end of these, additional altars were added in honour of particular saints. Often a dome was built above the crossing. A good example of this design is the magnificent 11th-century Basilica of San Michele Maggiore in Pavia, Italy. In some cathedrals – for instance at Lincoln (built 1092–1311) and Salisbury (1220–58), both in England – a second, smaller transept was built to the east of the main one.

HALL CHURCH

In Italy in the 15th and 16th centuries, the hall church design was developed to reduce the long distance between entrance and altar. At this time, during the Counter-Reformation (the Catholic Church's response to the rise of Protestantism), Church authorities wanted to promote the importance of preaching: a pulpit was introduced halfway down the nave and large side chapels were built nearby. A fine example of this design is the Church of the Gesù in Rome, the mother church of the Society of Jesus, or Jesuits, built in around 1568 by Giacomo da Vignola and Giacomo Della Porta.

GREEK CHURCH DESIGN

From early times, many Eastern churches were built on the plan of a Greek cross – a cross with four arms of equal length. Rather than have the crossing toward one end of a long nave, these churches had four equally sized wings meeting at a central crossing. The crossing point was generally square and domed. One good example is the 6th-century Church of Hagia Sophia in Istanbul (which eventually became a mosque and is now a museum).

This design returned to relevance in Western churches of the late 20th century, many of which put the altar toward the centre of the church to symbolize the centrality of the Mass in Catholic life. Two examples include the Metropolitan Cathedral of Christ the King in Liverpool, England (1958–70), and the Cathedral of Saint Mary of the Assumption, which was built in San Francisco, California (1967–71).

THE ROOD SCREEN AND REREDOS

In many medieval churches, a wooden screen separated the faithful in the nave from the clergy and other celebrants in the choir and sanctuary. The screen consisted of a large carved cross (or "rood") with an image of Jesus upon it, often flanked by carvings of the Blessed Virgin Mary and St John looking on. The structure was called the rood screen or choir screen. Many churches also had decorated screens behind the altar in the east. This often profoundly beautiful structure was called an altar piece or reredos.

Right: The intricately carved rood screen in the Gothic church of Saint-Etienne-du-Mont in Paris, France, has spiral staircases on either side.

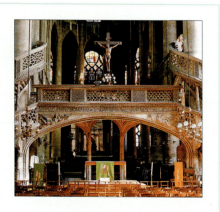

GREAT CHURCHES

FROM ROME TO LOS ANGELES, FROM THE 4TH TO THE 21ST CENTURY, THE BASILICAS AND CATHEDRALS OF THE ROMAN CATHOLIC CHURCH ARE AMONG THE WORLD'S MOST INSPIRATIONAL BUILDINGS.

Traditionally, the apostle Peter went to Rome and became the Church's first bishop. He was martyred in Rome and was buried in a Christian cemetery on *Mons Vaticanus*, where the Vatican now stands. Emperor Constantine built a basilica on the site in AD 326–33. However, by the end of the 15th century this building was in poor condition.

ST PETER'S BASILICA
The Basilica di San Pietro di Vaticano, better known as St Peter's Basilica, was built on the same site as the original basilica over more than a century, 1506–1626, and was consecrated in 1628. Among its many architects were Donato Bramante, Michelangelo and Gian Lorenzo Bernini. It stands within Vatican City – reputedly with St Peter's grave beneath its altar – and is considered the most holy church for Catholics worldwide. Many popes, including John Paul II in 2005, have been buried in this basilica.

MEDIEVAL CATHEDRALS
In the Middle Ages, the pope was often at odds with the Holy Roman emperor. During this time the great St Peter's Basilica in Rome was rivalled by the imperial church at Aachen (which is now part of western Germany), the most historic cathedral in northern Europe. At the heart of this church is the Palatine Chapel, which was founded by Charlemagne, King of the Franks, in 792 and consecrated to the Blessed Virgin Mary in 805 by Pope Leo III. German kings (and later emperors)

Below: Filippo Brunelleschi's breathtaking dome at Florence Cathedral contains 4 million bricks. With the lantern at its top, it is 114.5m (375ft) high.

Above: The throne of Charlemagne on which Holy Roman emperors were crowned stands in the upper gallery of the Palatine Chapel in Aachen, Germany.

were crowned in the Palatine Chapel for more than 600 years, between 936 and 1531.

Charlemagne himself was buried in a vault beneath the cathedral on his death in 814, and the cathedral became an attraction for pilgrims throughout the Middle Ages, when it was known as the Royal Church of St Mary at Aachen. The golden Shrine of St Mary was built in the choir in 1220–39 to contain four sacred relics: Christ's swaddling cloth, his loincloth, Mary's cloak and the beheading cloth of John the Baptist. Every seven years to the present day the relics are removed from the shrine and put on display for pilgrims.

There are other great European cathedrals of the Middle Ages and Renaissance, including the grand 13th-century Gothic cathedral of Chartres in France, celebrated for its magnificent stained-glass windows, and the Basilica di Santa Maria del Fiore, also known as Florence Cathedral, with its glorious 14th-century campanile (bell tower) partly designed by Giotto, the bronze doors of 1403–24 on the

Above: The Basilica of Our Lady of Peace in Yamoussoukro, Ivory Coast, was built with the finest Italian marble as well as 7,000sq m (75,350sq ft) of stained glass.

Above: Light falling through the glass roof creates striking patterns in the Catedral Metropolitana Nossa Senhora Aparecida.

baptistery by Lorenzo Ghiberti and the octagonal dome that was built in 1420–36 by Filippo Brunelleschi.

MODERN RIVALS

The cathedral at Florence was built to rival St Peter's Basilica in size and grandeur, and this desire survived into the late 20th century. The Basilica of Our Lady of Peace in Yamoussoukro, Ivory Coast, Africa, was modelled on St Peter's, built in 1985–90 and consecrated by Pope John Paul II on 10 September 1990. It was designed to be the greatest Catholic church in the world: it covers a slightly larger area than St Peter's – 3 hectares (7.4 acres) compared to 2.3 hectares (5.7 acres). However, critics point out that the area includes a villa and rectory, which are not part of the church, and that the Ivory Coast basilica has a smaller capacity at 18,000 people, compared with 60,000 for St Peter's.

In Liverpool, England, the Metropolitan Cathedral of Christ the King was built in the 1960s to a design by Sir Frederick Gibberd. Its circular plan was drawn up in response to the call by the Second Vatican Council for increased participation by the laity in the sacred liturgy. The cathedral was consecrated on the Feast of Pentecost, 14 May 1967. Another strikingly modern, circular cathedral is the Catedral Metropolitana Nossa Senhora Aparecida in Brasilia, Brazil. It was designed by Oscar Niemeyer, built from 1958 onward and was consecrated on 31 May 1970.

OUR LADY OF THE ANGELS

The greatest Roman Catholic church dedicated in the early 21st century is surely the outwardly austere, inwardly beautiful Cathedral of Our Lady of the Angels in downtown Los Angeles, California. It was begun in 1997 to designs by Spanish architect José Rafael Moneo, and opened in September 2002. It incorporates a plaza of 1,860sq m (20,000sq ft) and a main sanctuary 100m (333ft) in length and up to 30m (100ft) high. It has superb bronze doors, created by artist Robert Graham, which pay homage across the centuries to Ghiberti's bronze doors in the Florence baptistery.

Right: The Cathedral of Our Lady of the Angels is 12 storeys high and is specially designed to resist earthquake damage.

LIVING THE SACRAMENTS

THE ALTAR OF GOD

THE ALTAR, AT WHICH THE PRIEST CELEBRATES THE EUCHARIST, IS THE FOCAL POINT OF THE SANCTUARY. IT IS REVERED BY CHRISTIANS AS THE *MENSA DOMINI* ("TABLE OF THE LORD").

The sanctuary itself is the area set aside for the priest celebrant, deacons and other ministers. It is usually raised above the rest of the church, with its area demarcated by a low rail. Within the sanctuary, the altar is the principal furnishing. The altar represents the table at which Christ shared the Last Supper with his apostles and instituted the Eucharist.

The Church teaches that the altar also stands for Jesus himself and for the Cross on which his sacrifice was made: for these reasons, it is honoured with incense. Numbers are often symbolic to Catholics, and

Above: The altar stands in for the table used at the Last Supper by Christ and the apostles, which is shown in Domenico Ghirlandaio's 15th-century painting.

the five crosses carved on it represent Jesus' Five Sacred Wounds.

The table or horizontal top of the altar is normally made of natural stone because it embodies Christ, described in the First Letter of Peter as "that living stone, rejected by men but in God's sight chosen and precious" (1 Peter 2:3–4). Although the support of the tabletop can be of any material, the altar should honour Christ by being simple and beautiful.

SANCTIFIED BY RELICS

The altar stands on a raised platform called the predella. This is often made of wood. For symbolic reasons, the steps leading up to it are normally an uneven number – three, five or seven – and each about 15cm (6in) high. The steps may be of stone, wood or brick. If there are three steps, they are used to distin-

Left: Three steps mount to the main altar in St Patrick's Cathedral, New York City. The sanctuary was renovated in the 1930s to 1940s, when the elegant baldacchino (canopy) was added.

206

guish between ranks of ministers at the Eucharist: the celebrant will stand on the predella, the deacon on the second step and a subdeacon or another lower-ranking minister on the third step.

Beneath the altar is a box called the sepulchrum, used for containing a holy relic and other specific objects. The box has a gold, silver or lead reliquary to hold part of the bodily remains of a saint, together with three grains of incense and a parchment certifying that the altar has been consecrated. If possible, the relic is of the saint in whose name the church was built. The relics were traditionally placed within the altar, but they are now set beneath it. Catholics do not worship the relics or saints. The saints are honoured as men and women of great holiness, exemplars of the Christian life. The relics remind believers that the Eucharist celebrated on the altar is a source of God's Grace, the grace that enabled the saints to live such holy lives.

MARKING A CELEBRATION

For a celebration three white cloths are laid on the altar. Two candles are lighted to celebrate a Low Mass, one spoken by a priest without incense or the presence of a deacon or subdeacon; but six candles are required for a High Mass, a solemn celebration with music.

THE TABERNACLE

The gifts of the bread and the wine are consecrated during the Mass and distributed to the people. Some consecrated bread and wine – the blessed sacrament – is reserved in the tabernacle, a small carved metal container. The tabernacle is usually kept within the sanctuary, on the altar or at the side, but in some churches it is kept in a separate side chapel. It is sometimes kept beneath a small canopy or conopaeum.

A candle must always be kept burning above the tabernacle. This is called the altar lamp, or sanctuary light. The light reminds the faithful of the presence of Christ in the blessed sacrament and it embodies Christ, called in the Gospel of John "the true light that enlightens every man" (John 1:9). The light is an expression of the burning love of the faithful for their Lord. Although more than one light may be on the tabernacle, there are always uneven numbers lit: three, five, seven and so on.

GOSPEL AND SERMONS

In many churches, a raised pulpit stands at the front of the sanctuary, on the left-hand side of the church as you face the altar. The gospel and sermons or homilies are traditionally delivered from this pulpit. On the right-hand side of the sanctuary as you face the altar is usually a lectern, from which the Epistle is generally read. Although lay people can use the lectern, only members of the clergy can use the pulpit. Some churches do not have pulpit and lectern. Instead, they have a single podium, called an ambo, in the space otherwise occupied by the pulpit.

PRIESTLY CHAIR

The sanctuary also contains a chair for the priest celebrant. Although this chair should not be grandiose, it should reflect the dignity of the priest's role in administering the sacrament of the Eucharist. In a cathedral, the bishop has a permanent chair called the cathedra and another chair is placed alongside for other priest celebrants. Additional chairs are provided for deacons and other ministers.

Above: The sanctuary of the 13th-century St Asaph Cathedral in Denbighshire, North Wales, contains the bishop's seat.

Below: A burning candle marks the presence of the blessed sacrament within the tabernacle (centre). Its presence further sanctifies the altar as the table of the Lord.

VESTMENTS

WHEN CELEBRATING THE LITURGY OF THE CATHOLIC CHURCH, MEMBERS OF THE CLERGY WEAR SPECIAL ROBES OR VESTMENTS THAT SYMBOLIZE ASPECTS OF A PRIEST'S SPIRITUAL ROLE.

The celebrant's vestments distinguish him from the people and remind him of his vocation and duties, and the holiness of the acts he undertakes. The wearing of priestly vestments has historical roots going right back to the early days of Christianity – and even beyond to the Old Testament age, when the Jewish priests of Aaron wore ritual garb.

To celebrate the liturgy and in processions, clerics traditionally wear a cassock, a long, close-fitting cloak with buttons down the front, so-called from the Italian *casacca* for "greatcoat". Priests generally wear a black cassock, while bishops wear a purple one and cardinals a red one (or a black one with red piping). The pope's cassock is always white.

VESTMENTS FOR EUCHARIST
To celebrate the Eucharist, a priest also wears an alb, a cincture, a stole and a chasuble. An alb is a full-length white linen gown worn over the priest's cassock. It is a descendant of the white toga worn by the ancient Romans and takes its name from the Latin word *albus*, meaning "white". The alb's colour symbolizes purity. Around the waist the priest secures the alb with a braided linen or woollen cord called the cincture, from the Latin *cinctura*, meaning "girdle". It is usually white, like the alb. The cincture is worn to symbolize the priest's chastity.

Around his neck and across his shoulders, the priest wears a long decorated strip of material called a stole. It should be approximately 200cm (80in) long and 5–10cm (2–4in) in width. The stole generally has a cross embroidered at each end and in the middle (the part worn behind the neck); the middle cross is required because the priest must

Above: Many priests still wear a black cassock for day-to-day duties, but some wear a suit with shirt and clerical collar.

kiss this when putting on the stole. Bishops wear the stole in the same manner as priests; deacons wear it over the left shoulder and diagonally across the chest.

The priest wears a decorated outer garment called the chasuble over his vestments. The chasuble is usually made of silk or velvet and often has a large cross on the back. Its name derives from the Latin *casula*, which means "little house", because the over garment provides prote-ction or shelter for the priest. The chasuble symbolizes the yoke of Christ and the virtue of charity.

Below: Kneeling deacons wear the alb (full-length white gown), cincture (cord belt) and stole (strip across shoulder and chest).

208

THE AMICE AND MANIPLE
Beneath the alb the priest can choose to wear an amice over his shoulders. The amice is a rectangular white cloth, marked with a cross and attached to two long ribbon-like strings, which are used to secure it. It takes its name from the Latin *amictus*, meaning "cloak" or "mantle". Wearing an amice was once compulsory for priests celebrating the Eucharist, but when liturgical reforms were introduced in 1972 wearing an amice became voluntary. Today many priests choose to wear one in honour of tradition.

The priest may also choose to wear a maniple. This is a long and narrow embroidered strip of material traditionally worn over the left arm. For most priests the maniple is an optional vestment, but those who celebrate the Extraordinary Form of the Roman Rite (the Tridentine Mass) are required to wear it when celebrating the Eucharist.

OTHER VESTMENTS
In liturgical settings other than the Mass, a priest may wear the cope, humeral veil and surplice. The cope is a very long and often heavy embroidered mantle or cloak worn over the shoulder, reaching to the ankles, and fastened at the chest with an often highly decorated clasp called a morse. The cope, which takes its name from the Latin *cappa* ("cape"), is often worn in processions and at benedictions (a service in which the blessed sacrament is exposed on the altar in a monstrance, or vessel, for the adoration of the faithful), as well as for many other solemn liturgical offices other than the Mass.

The humeral veil is also traditionally worn at benediction: it is a long piece of usually richly ornamented material worn over the shoulders and covering the hands of the priest. Priests also wear it when carrying sacred vessels containing the reserved sacrament in a procession.

LITURGICAL COLOURS
Priests celebrate Mass in vestments of different colours according to the season of the church year or to mark a particular saint's day or festival. The four main colours are white, red, green and purple; in addition, on more solemn days festive silver and gold vestments can also be worn – silver in place of white, and gold in place of white, red or green.

White symbolizes purity and the glory of the Resurrection and is the colour for the Easter season; it is also worn on major feast days, such as Christmas Day and Easter Day, feasts of the Blessed Virgin Mary and of saints who were confessors or virgins. Purple symbolizes repentance and is worn for Lent and Advent. Red, as the colour of blood, is worn on the feast days of saints who were martyred; as the colour of fire, it is worn on Pentecost, the festival commemorating the descent of the Holy Spirit as tongues of fire (Acts 2:3). Green is worn on ordinary days – that is, times of the year that are not part of a particular church season and not feast days. Green stands for the growth of the Church.

Above: Clergy in procession at Lourdes, France, prior to a Mass for the sick wear the cope or long clerical cloak.

The surplice is basically a half-length tunic usually made of cotton or linen and sometimes featuring an embroidered hem and sleeves. It is worn over the cassock when administering sacraments other than the Eucharist and when saying the Liturgy of the Hours, as well as during processions.

Right: Because this priest is celebrating the Eucharist, he is wearing a chasuble (the heavy, ornately decorated outer garment), which is worn over his alb, cincture and stole.

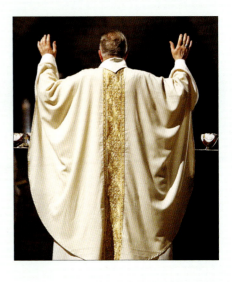

LIVING THE SACRAMENTS

"GATHERED TOGETHER IN MY NAME"

IN THE FIRST PART OF THE SACRAMENT OF THE EUCHARIST, READINGS AND A HOMILY FORM THE LITURGY OF THE WORD, WHICH PREPARES THE FAITHFUL TO RECEIVE HOLY COMMUNION.

The Catholic celebration of the Eucharist is known as the Mass, from the word *missa*. This is used as a form of dismissal at the close of the traditional Latin form of the service: *Ite, missa est* ("Go, it is finished"). The Mass is a sacramental re-enactment of the death and Resurrection of Jesus, in which bread and wine become the body and blood of Christ and are offered to God again, just as they were on the Cross. In this sacrament, the community of believers makes symbolic expression of its unity and is nourished by receiving Jesus' body and blood.

Mass was originally said in Latin, but the Second Vatican Council (1962–5) allowed conferences of bishops to make their own judgement on the extent to which English

Below: The bread that Jesus broke during the Last Supper with his apostles can be seen in Girolamo di Romano's 16th-century painting The Last Supper.

or other local vernacular languages could be used. The great majority of Masses are today celebrated in approved vernacular translations, but Latin is still used occasionally and in some places is used regularly.

ENTRANCE AND GREETING
On entering, the priest kisses the altar and, when incense is used, he censes it. All present make a large sign of the Cross, using the fingertips of the open right hand to touch forehead, chest, left shoulder, then right shoulder, while the priest says "In the name of the Father, and of the Son, and of the Holy Spirit: Amen."

The priest extends both hands and, facing the people, welcomes them with one of a series of greetings based on the beginnings of the Epistles of St Paul. They respond. In the simplest form of the greeting, the priest says "The Lord be with you", and the people respond "And also with you".

Above: Pope John Paul II censes the altar during a Mass in Switzerland in 1984. He uses a thurible (metal censer).

ACT OF PENITENCE
The priests call on those present to take part in the act of penitence. The most common form is the Confiteor, or Mea Culpa, said by all. It begins:

I confess to Almighty God, and to you, my brothers and sisters, that I have sinned through my own fault in my thoughts and in my words…

When the congregation says together "through my own fault", it is customary for them to strike themselves on the chest. The act of penitence concludes with the priest praying, "May almighty God have mercy on us, forgive us our sins, and bring us to everlasting life."

All present then usually say or sing the Kyrie Eleison, either in English ("Lord have mercy, Christ have mercy, Lord have mercy") or the original Greek (*Kyrie Eleison, Christe Eleison, Kyrie Eleison*). The threefold repetition is in veneration of the Trinity of Father, Son and Holy Spirit. Afterward, all join in singing or saying the ancient hymn of *Gloria in Excelsis Deo*, which begins "Glory to God in the highest, and peace to his people on earth…"

LITURGY OF THE WORD
The priest invites all to pray and after a period of silent prayer, he reads the set collect (a collection of short prayers)

for the day. Biblical readings follow with three on Sundays and solemn occasions, two on other days. The first is from the Old Testament and is usually followed by a psalm. The second is from the New Testament, generally one of the Epistles to early Christians. On both occasions, the reader declares on finishing "This is the Word of the Lord" and the congregation responds "Thanks be to God".

THE HOLY GOSPEL

The third reading is from the Holy Gospel. This is read by a deacon, or by the priest if no deacon is present. Before the Gospel an hallelujah, or expression of praise to God, is sung or said. The deacon or priest declares "The Lord be with you", to which the people respond, "And also with you"; he announces "A reading from the Holy Gospel according to…" and makes a sign of the cross over the Bible and on his own forehead, lips and chest; the people do likewise and make the response "Glory to you, Lord". When incense is used, the priest or deacon censes the book. At the end of the reading he declares "This is the Gospel of the Lord", and the congregation responds "Praise to you, Lord Jesus Christ". The priest or deacon then kisses the book.

ENDING WITH A PRAYER

A bishop, priest or deacon usually delivers a homily or sermon, then all present recite the Nicene Creed, which begins: "We believe in one God, the Father, the Almighty…" The liturgy of the Word concludes with the Prayers of the Faithful: a deacon, cantor or member of the congregation leads all in prayer requests before the priest declaims a concluding prayer.

Left: As the high point of the liturgy of the Word, a priest delivers a reading from the Holy Gospel.

HOLY WATER

On Sundays, and especially during the Easter season, the rite of asperges – the blessing and sprinkling of holy water – is sometimes used in place of the act of penitence and the Kyrie. The priest explains that the water is to remind all present of their baptism.

One of several prayers available includes the phrase "Lord in your mercy give us living water, always springing up as a fountain of salvation: free us, body and soul, from every danger…". The priest then takes the aspergil (silver water sprinkler) and sprinkles first himself, then the other clergy and then the people present with the holy water. While he does this, an antiphon or hymn is sung.

Above: A priest pours out water prior to blessing and sprinkling it in the rite of asperges.

Left: Priests sing "We praise Thee, We bless Thee, We worship Thee, We glorify Thee" as they lead the gloria during Mass.

LIVING THE SACRAMENTS

THE MOST HOLY SACRAMENT OF THE ALTAR

THE SECOND PART OF THE MASS IS THE LITURGY OF THE EUCHARIST, IN WHICH THE BREAD AND WINE ARE CONSECRATED AND DISTRIBUTED TO THE COMMUNICANTS AS THE BODY AND BLOOD OF JESUS CHRIST.

In the first section of the liturgy, the bread and wine that will be used in the Eucharist are brought to the altar, usually by members of the congregation in a formal procession. They usually sing an offertory hymn.

The priest prays over the gifts of bread and wine. He places the bread on a small silver or gold plate called the paten and mixes water and wine in a precious cup, referred to as the chalice. When incense is being used, the priest censes the offerings and the altar, and a deacon or other minister censes the priest and the people. The priest then washes his hands, symbolizing his desire for inner purification.

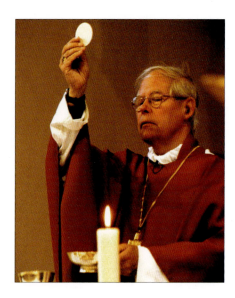

Above: At the sacred climax of the Eucharist, a bishop holds the consecrated Host aloft to show it to the congregation.

EUCHARISTIC PRAYER

The Eucharistic Prayer leads the congregation through the sacred climax of the Eucharist, in which the bread and the wine are consecrated and become Christ's body and blood. There are variations of the prayer. The key elements, found in all versions, are when making a sign of the Cross over the bread and the wine, the priest blesses the offerings on the altar and recalls how Christ instituted the Eucharist at the Last Supper.

The priest copies Christ's actions as he recounts how Christ took the bread in his sacred hands, looked to heaven, gave thanks and praise to God the Father, and then broke the bread, giving it to his disciples, and said, "Take this, all of you, and eat it", then referring to it as his body, "which will be given up for you". At this point, the bread is made holy and becomes the consecrated Host, the very body of Christ. An acolyte often rings a bell to signal the holy moment, and if incense is being used

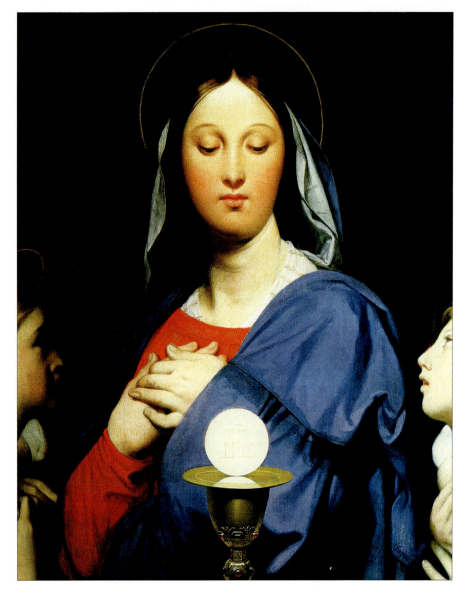

Left: In Ingres' 1866 painting, Virgin of the Eucharist, *the Blessed Virgin Mary contemplates the divine mystery of her son's presence in the Host.*

he censes the priest and the paten. The priest lifts the Host and then places it back on the paten on the altar and kneels in adoration.

The priest raises the chalice and recounts Christ's actions in taking a cup of wine, giving thanks and praise to the Father in heaven, then giving it to the disciples, stating, "Take this all of you and drink from it". The priest refers to the contents in the cup as "the blood of the new and everlasting covenant" and continues by stating that blood was shed for humankind so that its sins will be forgiven. At this point, an acolyte once again rings a bell to signal the moment of consecration, and if incense is being used, he will cense the priest and chalice.

COMMUNION RITE

Before the congregation receives the Eucharist, all join in repeating the Lord's Prayer, then they share a sign of peace according to local custom. The priest breaks the Host and puts a piece in the chalice in what is called the rite of fraction, and prays: "May this mingling of the body and blood of our Lord Jesus Christ bring eternal life to all who receive it."

Below: In today's Mass, communicants receive the consecrated Host when the priest places it on the tongue.

Above: Incense signifies the sanctity of the altar and of the gifts of bread and wine that become the Lord's body and blood.

The priest says a prayer of personal devotion, then presents the Host (consecrated bread) to the congregation with the words, "This is the Lamb of God who takes away the sins of the world. Happy are those who are called to his supper." All present respond with the words, "Lord I am not worthy to receive you" and finish off with "say the word and I shall be healed".

The priest receives Communion himself and distributes it to other ministers and deacons, and then to the congregation, who usually come forward in procession. Each communicant bows, then receives the Host on the tongue (in the past it was sometimes received in the hand); the priest declares "the body of Christ" and the communicant responds "Amen". The communicant is offered the chalice and the priest declares "the blood of Christ".

It is possible for communicants to receive only the Host, and for the priest to dip the Host into the wine and present it in that form, laying it on the communicant's tongue; this is called intinction. Usually, the congregation sings a Communion song throughout this period.

Afterward, the chalice, paten and other vessels are washed and dried and placed on the altar and the priest declaims a prayer after Communion. At this point notices are read out, then the priest gives one of a choice of blessings on the people and pronounces one of a choice of dismissals. All include the phrase "Go in peace"; the variant based on the original Latin dismissal (*Ite, missa est*), which gives the Mass its name, is "The Mass is ended. Go in peace". The congregation responds, "Thanks be to God." Then the priest kisses the altar, makes a customary reverence with other ministers and leaves. A hymn is often sung at the close of the service.

BAPTISM

IN THE SACRAMENT OF BAPTISM, AN INDIVIDUAL IS REBORN AS A CHRISTIAN AND GAINS A SANCTIFYING GRACE THAT ENABLES HIM OR HER TO SHARE IN THE LIFE OF GOD – FATHER, SON AND HOLY SPIRIT.

Most Catholics are baptized as infants, but those who convert to Catholicism can be baptized as an adult if they have not previously been baptized in another Christian denomination. With confirmation and Holy Communion, baptism is listed as one of three sacraments of initiation that prepares an individual for life as a Christian.

According to the *Catechism of the Catholic Church*, baptism is the backbone of the complete Christian life, "the gateway to life in the spirit"; through baptism people are united with Christ and are "incorporated into the Church and made sharers in Her mission". In baptism, people join the priesthood of believers.

A NEW BIRTH
One of the key biblical texts that supports baptism is from Jesus' words to Nicodemus, "Truly, truly, I say to you, unless one is born of water and the Spirit, he cannot enter the kingdom of God" (John 3:5). Baptism is a symbolic rebirth: and only through baptism can believers come to the other sacraments of Christian life.

According to Catholic doctrine, baptism frees an individual from original sin (the mark of human sinfulness with which all are tainted, and which derives from the disobedience to God's commandments of the first people, Adam and Eve, in the Garden of Eden). For this reason, practising Catholics believe they must baptize their children as infants; should the children die unbaptized, they would remain tainted by original sin and their salvation would be prevented. Baptism also liberates people from their own sins and from any punishment deriving from these.

Above: When Jesus was baptized by John the Baptist, the Holy Spirit descended upon him. Perugino captured the scene in this c.1500 painting, Baptism of Christ in the Jordan.

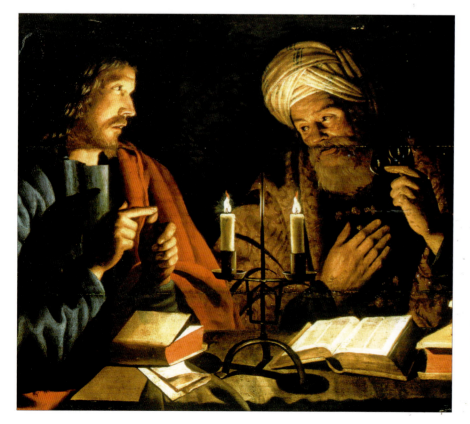

Below: Our Lord explains the necessity of being "born of water and the Spirit" to Nicodemus, depicted in this 17th-century painting by Crijn Hendricksz Volmarijn.

RITE OF BAPTISM
In normal circumstances, the rite of baptism involves friends or relatives of the child's parents as "godparents"; they hold a responsibility to help the parents in raising the baptized child as a Christian. The bishop, priest or deacon greets both the parents and godparents and reminds them of the responsibilities attendant on bringing an infant to baptism, which include training the infant "in the practice of the faith" and keeping God's commandments "as Christ taught us, by loving God and our

BAPTISM

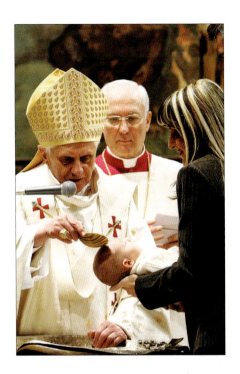

Above: An infant is baptized by Pope Benedict XVI. The catechism teaches that by being baptized "we are freed from sin and reborn as sons of God".

holy Church. The prayers also call on God to "renew the grace of our baptism in each one of us".

The celebrant invokes the Blessed Virgin and the saints, and proceeds to a prayer of exorcism and anointing before baptism in which he calls on God to free the child from original sin and "make him (or her) a temple of your glory". He then anoints the infant with oil in Christ's name.

SACRED WATERS

At the font, the celebrant recites an introductory prayer. The priest blesses the water in the font, then once again reminds the parents and godparents of their responsibility to raise the infant in the Catholic faith. He asks them to make three professions of their faith: in God the Father; in Jesus Christ; and in the Holy Spirit. As he says this he refers to the Catholic Church and the communion of saints, as well as Jesus' Resurrection and everlasting life. All present then announce their belief in these things: "This is our faith. This is the faith of the Church." They then declare that they are proud of their profession.

Then the celebrant baptizes the infant, saying the child's name and declaring, "I baptize you in the name of the Father and of the Son and of the Holy Spirit." At each naming of God, he either pours water over

Above: A Catholic convert leans over a font as she is baptized in the Cathedral of Notre-Dame de Paris – the celebrant is using a traditional scallop shell.

neighbour". He then leads the parents (and godparents if desired) in tracing the Cross of Christ on the infant's forehead.

Readings from the Holy Gospel and a homily or sermon follow. The celebrant leads the prayer of the faithful that calls on God to "bathe this child in light" and give the child "new life of baptism" and asks that the child is welcomed into the

the infant's forehead or immerses the child in the water of the font. The celebrant anoints the infant with chrism, or holy oil, and clothes him or her in a white garment as an "outward sign of Christian dignity". The baptism usually concludes with the celebrant reaffirming that the infant has been reborn in baptism, leading the congregation in the Lord's Prayer, then giving a blessing.

SYMBOLIC WATER

When the main baptism takes place at the font, the celebrant's introductory prayer identifies water as a symbol of God's grace and a "wellspring of holiness". The waters of baptism are likened to those that existed before the Creation and on which God breathed, to those of Noah's flood, to the waters of the Red Sea that parted as the Israelites were led out of Egypt, to those of the Jordan in which Christ himself was baptized and to the waters mixed with blood that flowed from his side on the Cross.

Right: A font holds holy water used for baptism – this 12th-century Belgian font depicts Jesus' own baptism.

215

CONFIRMATION

PEOPLE WHO RECEIVE THE SACRAMENT OF CONFIRMATION ARE ANOINTED WITH HOLY OIL. THE RITE CONFIRMS AND STRENGTHENS THE GRACE THEY DERIVED FROM BAPTISM.

Confirmation is the second of the three sacraments of initiation, and is traditionally delivered after baptism and before the Eucharist. In the early Church and the Eastern Church today, these three sacraments are delivered in a single occasion in early childhood, but in the Western Church (in the Latin Rite) confirmation is delayed until late childhood, at a time when the recipient can understand the significance of the sacrament. When adults are baptized, they usually receive the three sacraments at the same time and in the traditional order.

In most cases in the Western Church, only a bishop can administer the sacrament of confirmation, but priests have been authorized to confirm adult converts and children who are at risk of death; the priest uses chrism or holy oil blessed by the bishop. The chrism is blessed in a special service, the Chrism Mass, on Holy Thursday during Easter Week.

THE GIFT OF THE SPIRIT

The Church places an emphasis on the connection between confirmation and the Feast of Pentecost, when the Holy Spirit descended on Christ's apostles. Bishops, as successors to the apostles, administer confirmation. There is also a biblical precedent for the practice of bishops imparting the Holy Spirit to others through the laying on of hands. Acts 8:15–17 describes when the apostles Peter and John went to the Christians in Samaria and "prayed for them that they might receive the Holy Spirit, for it had not yet fallen upon any of them; they had only been baptized in the name of the Lord Jesus. Then they laid hands on them and they received the Holy Spirit."

In the Latin Rite used by the Western Catholic Church, the confirmation service begins with those ready for confirmation, known as confirmands, renewing their baptismal vows and professing their faith. The bishop extends his hands over them and prays: "All-powerful God, Father of our Lord Jesus Christ, by water and the Holy Spirit you freed your sons and daughters from sin and gave them new life…". Then he anoints each confirmand with chrism. The bishop says, "Be sealed with the gift of the Holy Spirit." The anointing is accompanied by a laying on of hands by the bishop. The phrase "be sealed" signifies that the newly confirmed belongs to Christ in God. The seal marks the Christian as being enrolled in Christ's service and also provides a promise of divine protection. At the close of the service the bishop makes the sign of peace over the newly confirmed Christians.

In the Eastern Catholic Church, a priest generally administers the sacraments of baptism, confirmation

Above: A bishop anoints candidates for confirmation with chrism, signifying the mark of the Holy Spirit, in this 15th-century painting by Rogier van der Weyden.

Below: The laying on of hands is a key part of confirmation. As descendants of the apostles, bishops perform the rite.

(usually referred to as Chrismation) and Communion in a single ceremony. The priest will use chrism blessed by the bishop, anointing the recipient on the forehead, eyes, nose, ears, lips, breast, back, hands and feet, each time, declaring "The seal of the gift that is the Holy Spirit".

ITS BENEFITS

The sacrament is called confirmation in the Western Church because it confirms, completes, strengthens and deepens the grace imparted by baptism. In confirmation, according to the catechism, baptized members of the faithful are "more perfectly bound to the Church", "enriched with a special strength of the Holy Spirit" and thereby "more strictly obliged to spread and defend the faith by word and deed".

The sacrament connects believers "more firmly to Christ" and unites the faithful in "divine filiation" (the condition of being a child of God). While baptism brings Christians into the priesthood of believers, confirmation perfects this priesthood and, according to St Thomas Aquinas, "The confirmed person receives the power to profess faith in Christ publicly and as it were officially (*quasi ex officio*)."

FIRST COMMUNION

In the Western Church, the occasion on which a young person receives Holy Communion (when he or she participates in the Eucharist) for the first time, is often celebrated with a family party. Especially in the United States and Ireland, these celebrations can be lavish: boys dress in a suit and girls wear a special white dress with a veil and gloves. In some countries, a girl wears a dress handed down from her mother or sister; in others, she will take First Communion in school uniform plus veil and gloves. In many Latin American countries, boys dress in a uniform with military-style aigullettes (braided cords) for the ceremony. It is also traditional for the young person to receive a present to mark the occasion – perhaps a prayer book, icon or rosary.

> **CONFIRMATION AFTER FIRST COMMUNION**
>
> The traditional order in which the three sacraments of initiation were received was: baptism, confirmation, Communion. However, in the early 20th century, Pope Pius X encouraged Catholics to allow children to receive the Eucharist as soon as they reached the age of reason (generally understood to be about the age of seven years). As a result, many young people received Communion before they were confirmed. However, in the late 20th and early 21st centuries, there has been a return to the traditional order.
>
>
>
> *Above: Girls wear white dresses, sometimes with veils and gloves, for first Communion. The colour symbolizes their purity.*

Below: The Eastern Catholic Church emphasizes the Christian initiation by delivering baptism, Chrismation (confirmation) and the Eucharist together.

LIVING THE SACRAMENTS

HOLY MATRIMONY

THE SACRAMENT OF HOLY MATRIMONY GIVES A COUPLE THE DIVINE GRACE THEY NEED TO ACHIEVE HOLINESS IN THEIR MARRIED LIFE. THE "AUTHOR" OF THE MARRIAGE IS GOD.

In marriage, husband and wife receive the Holy Spirit, which helps the married couple to keep their vows. As the *Catechism of the Catholic Church* puts it, "The Holy Spirit is the seal of their covenant, the ever available source of their love and the strength to renew their fidelity."

WITNESS TO THE UNION
In the Latin Rite of the Western Church, the wedding ceremony takes place before a priest and at least two witnesses: strictly speaking, the ministers of Christ's Grace in this sacrament are the husband and wife, and the priest is a witness. However,

Above: In the Eastern Catholic Church, the sacrament is called the "Crowning". The crowns worn by bride and bridegroom are a sign of the marriage covenant.

in the Eastern Catholic Church, the minister of the sacrament will be the presiding bishop or priest, who crowns husband and wife. There are two variants of the Latin Rite Catholic marriage ceremony: one with Mass, lasting about one hour, and one without Mass, which lasts around 20 minutes.

RITE OF MARRIAGE
When both husband and wife are Catholics, they are encouraged by the Church to have a wedding Mass. The priest usually meets the couple at the door of the church and leads them to the altar. The next stage is to celebrate the liturgy of the Word, in the course of which the priest delivers a homily on the mystery of marriage, the responsibilities of husband and wife and the dignity of love between a married couple.

Then the priest begins the rite of marriage. He addresses the couple: "You have come together in this church so that the Lord may seal and strengthen your love in the presence of the Church's minister and this community." He will question the

Left: Catholic marriages are usually celebrated during Holy Mass. In their marriage, bride and bridegroom are inspired by Jesus' self-sacrifice. They become one body in Christ.

218

couple's condition and intentions, asking them to confirm that they are joining "freely and without reservations", that they will "love and honour each other as man and wife for the rest of [their] lives" and that they will accept children from God and bring them up in the law of Christ and his Church.

Then the couple exchange vows, each promising "to be true…in good times and in bad, in sickness and in health" and declaring, "I will love and honour you all the days of my life". The words of the vows may vary. The priest blesses the couple, asking Jesus to strengthen their consent and fill them with blessings. The priest then blesses the rings and the couple exchange rings, which are worn as a sign of mutual love and fidelity.

NUPTIAL BLESSING

The service proceeds by way of general intercessions into the liturgy of the Eucharist. After the Lord's Prayer the priest proclaims the nuptial blessing, calling on Jesus to bless bride and groom individually and as a couple joined in a holy bond and married in Christ to one another. The priest reminds all that marriage is a holy mystery that symbolizes the marriage of Christ to his Church, the one blessing of those given to Adam and Eve that was not "forfeited by original sin or washed away in the flood", and asks that the husband trust his wife and recognize that "she is his equal and heir with him to the life of grace". The priest prays, if the woman is of childbearing age, that the couple be blessed with children and have a long life, and after happy old age achieve fullness of life with the saints in heaven.

Then the couple receive Holy Communion. At the end of the service the priest blesses them once more before husband and wife kiss. All sing a hymn as the couple process out of the church. When a couple chooses a marriage service without Holy Communion it largely follows the outline above, but omits the celebration of the Eucharist.

Above: Joseph and Mary exchange rings in this 14th-century detail of Wedding of the Virgin Mary *by Bartolo di Fredi. From early on, the Catholic Church has taught that couples should love with a "supernatural…and fruitful love".*

Below: God blesses married love; its purpose is for procreation. A married couple receive a child from God in this 15th-century French miniature.

> **SPECIAL DISPENSATION**
>
> Those who come forward for marriage should normally be baptized Catholics. However, a dispensation, usually granted by the priest himself, is possible for a "mixed marriage" between a Catholic and a baptized non-Catholic (a Christian of another denomination) as long as the couple have chosen freely to marry, have the intention of remaining together for life and being faithful to one another, and are planning to have children if the bride has not passed the childbearing age.
>
> If one partner is Catholic and the other is not baptized (perhaps a non-Christian or a person of no religion), a church dispensation for disparity of cult is required from the local bishop.

"WHAT GOD HAS JOINED..."

FOR CATHOLICS, HOLY MATRIMONY CREATES A PERMANENT AND INDISSOLUBLE BOND BETWEEN HUSBAND AND WIFE. GOD CREATED MARRIAGE AS THE FULFILMENT OF LIFE FOR MOST MEN AND WOMEN.

As part of the blessing of the married couple during the sacrament of Holy Matrimony, the priest may state, "What God has joined together, let no man put asunder", which is a direct quotation from Christ's own teaching on marriage (Mark 10:9). The *Catechism of the Catholic Church* is also unequivocal, stating that once a marriage between a baptized couple has been consummated, it "can never be dissolved".

Like the other sacraments, Holy Matrimony has both outward and inward signs: the outward sign is the marriage contract, which is the agreement made verbally between both husband and wife when they exchange vows before the priest and witnesses; the inward sign is the grace it delivers. The Church's teaching accepts that marriage can bring many challenges; however, it also stresses that God's Grace is sufficient to help husbands and wives overcome their difficulties.

DIVINE INSTITUTION

The Church teaches that God created man and woman for one another and that married love is in the image of God's love. Christ attended the wedding at Cana in Galilee, where he performed the first of the many signs that confirmed his status as the Son of God by turning water into wine (John 2:1–11). The Church interprets this event as confirmation of the goodness of marriage and a proclamation that marriage is a sign of Christ's presence.

For Catholics, marriage is both a natural and a divine institution. It is a natural institution because it has existed in the form of a lifelong union between a man and a woman in all societies and cultures through history. Yet it is also a divine institution created by God, sanctified by Christ at Cana, and sealed through the sacrament of Holy Matrimony by the action of the Holy Spirit.

IN PREPARATION

The Church instructs that both parties to a marriage must have a clear understanding of what they are doing when they take their marriage vows. Husband and wife are required to attend preparatory meetings with the priest who will witness their marriage. These meetings are known as pre-Cana meetings – a reference to the wedding at Cana.

A course of pre-Cana meetings can be held over a single weekend or be spread over six months or so.

Above: A blessing is given to both man and woman in this 15th-century detail from Engagement of the Virgin *by Michael Pacher. Both must freely give their consent to be married.*

Below: By participating in the wedding at Cana in Galilee, shown in this 14th-century painting, The Marriage Feast at Cana, *by Duccio di Buoninsegna, Jesus confirmed the holiness of the marriage bond.*

ANNULMENT OF A MARRIAGE

The key condition for a marriage is that husband and wife give their consent to be married freely and are free to give their consent. In cases where the parties to a marriage can show that either of these conditions were not met, a Church tribunal can grant an annulment of the marriage. Annulment is not the same as divorce: the judgement does not dissolve the marriage, for marriage is an indissoluble bond; it determines that the marriage did not ever take place.

The two parties must understand what they are doing and must have given the matter some consideration; they must have a genuine intention to keep the vows they swear – to form a permanent and faithful union, inclusive of sexual acts intended for the purpose of procreation. Various impediments to the marriage are grounds for annulment. Examples include husband and wife being close blood relatives, one partner being already married at the time of the wedding or one partner being in a psychological state that precludes an ability to give free consent.

Right: Henry VIII's wife Catherine of Aragon is shown in The Divorce of Henry VIII, *by Eugene Deveria. Theirs was one of several marriages Henry had annulled.*

The priest and the married couple discuss the sanctity of marriage, their faith and life in the Church, plans for children and so on; they may be asked about financial matters. Nearer to the time, husband and wife, if both are baptized Catholics, are expected to receive the sacrament of penance and reconciliation in preparation for their wedding. With these preparations, both husband and wife should enter marriage prepared to maintain their vows – married life should present no surprises.

WHEN A MARRIAGE FAILS

The Church recognizes that in some cases a marriage can deteriorate so badly that husband and wife can no longer live together. In this situation, they should live separately and the members of the Church should help them live as best they can in a Christian fashion. The estranged husband and wife are not free to divorce or remarry, and they should remember that the preferred solution in the eyes of the Catholic Church would be for the couple to reconcile their differences.

If a Catholic divorces and makes a second (civil) marriage, the Church views the person as committing adultery against the first marriage partner. He or she is in contravention of God's law and cannot receive the Eucharist. Nevertheless, that person should be welcomed to church if he or she wants to come: priests and the whole Church community should be attentive toward that person.

Right: God intends man and woman to join permanently in marriage; once joined, they should not seek separation. A 19th-century engraving, The Ages of Life, *shows how a married couple honour their vows throughout life.*

THE SANCTITY OF LIFE

CHURCH TEACHINGS ON MARRIAGE, SEX AND CONTRACEPTION, ABORTION AND HOMOSEXUALITY ARE UNDERPINNED BY BELIEF IN THE SANCTITY OF ALL LIVES CREATED BY GOD.

The Catholic faithful believe that sex has a divinely ordained place within a couple's marriage: its purpose and function is for the procreation of children. Married love is blessed by God and meant to be fruitful. This teaching is based on verses in Genesis, Chapter 1:

> *So God created man in his own image, in the image of God he created him; male and female he created them. And God blessed them, and God said to them, "Be fruitful and multiply, and fill the earth and subdue it."*
> *(Genesis 1:26–29).*

AT THE SERVICE OF LIFE
Parents are called not only to procreate but also to educate: having brought children into the world, they must give them instruction in moral and spiritual matters. Parents should serve their children in love. The *Catechism of the Catholic Church* states that one of the main functions of marriage and family is "to be at the service of life".

There are some married couples who have not had children, but this does not devalue their marriage in any way. They can still aim to live a life of service through hospitality, self-sacrifice and charity. Other people are called to chastity. This does not devalue marriage, either. The vocation to chastity and the vocation to married life both come from God, and both should be equally valued. The two ways of life reinforce one another.

CONTRACEPTION
The Church's teachings on contraception arise from the understanding that Catholics should only have sex within marriage and that the main function of sex is for procreation. Using contraceptives, such as a condom or the contraceptive pill, is directly against Catholic teaching. This is because these methods interfere with the natural law of God's Creation and split sex from its proper procreative role.

However, Catholics are allowed to use natural methods of birth control – chiefly by having sex only when the wife is at a low-fertility part of her cycle. Natural birth control is allowed because it is in harmony with the natural law of God's Creation and uses God-given powers, such as self-control, rather than chemical interference (as with the pill) or a physical barrier (such as a condom). Catholics must be responsible and correctly motivated in using this method: for example, it would be acceptable to use the method to space out children in a

Above: In this 14th-century detail from The Creation of Adam *by Master Bertram of Minden, God is shown instructing Adam about his duty to procreate and father children.*

HOMOSEXUALITY
The Church recognizes that some men and women have deep-seated homosexual tendencies: the catechism calls these tendencies "intrinsically disordered" and "contrary to natural law". Sexual relations between people of the same sex are not approved because they "close the sexual act to the gift of life" and "do not proceed from a genuine affective and sexual complementarity". The Church believes that homosexual people are called to chastity: they are required to develop self-mastery and they are expected to pray for support. In these circumstances, they can rely on God's sacramental grace to help them reach Christian perfection.

Below: The pope holds a fatherly position to Catholics. Married couples entrust their children to the care of God and his Church.

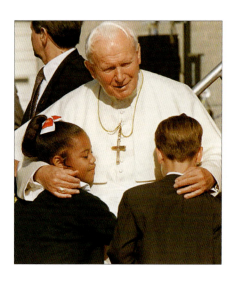

222

THE SANCTITY OF LIFE

Right: Catholic parents bring their children to Christ in Lucas Cranach the Elder's Christ Blessing the Children *(c.1540). Parents are responsible for teaching their children the Catholic faith.*

family, but to do so to avoid having children in order to have more spending money would be immoral.

The Church also teaches that sex has a unifying function – it brings the husband and wife into a close spiritual, mental and physical union. By using artificial contraception, according to the teaching, the couple are violating this function and preventing themselves from giving completely to each other.

In addition, according to the Church, the use of contraception has a number of negative effects. Among these it promotes immoral behaviour, damages marriage as an institution, makes men respect women less, and gives people the idea that they can achieve total control over bodily processes of reproduction when this control rightly belongs to God.

Opponents of the Church's position argue that contraception has benefits for people both as individuals and collectively. The Church's response is that using contraception is evil and that it is never the correct approach to do evil, even if you believe good may come of it.

RIGHT TO LIFE
The Church takes a very strong position against the use of abortion. Catholics believe that a new life begins at the moment in which a woman's egg is fertilized by a sperm. The fertilized egg is a human being independent of mother and father. According to Pope John Paul II in his 1995 encyclical *Evangelum Vitae* ("The Gospel of Life"), abortion is

Right: The catechism teaches that God's Grace helps married couples "attain holiness in their married life and in welcoming and educating their children".

"a grave moral disorder" because it involves the intentional killing of an innocent person. Church teaching states that every individual, including a foetus, has an inalienable right to life – and this right extends from the moment of conception until the person's physical death. In canon law, a person who procures an abortion is excommunicated.

223

LIVING THE SACRAMENTS

PENANCE AND RECONCILIATION

DURING THE SACRAMENT OF PENANCE AND RECONCILIATION, WHICH IS OFTEN REFERRED TO AS CONFESSION, CATHOLICS CONFESS ANY WRONGDOINGS TO THEIR PRIEST AND RECEIVE ABSOLUTION.

Confession provides spiritual healing for people who have been distanced from God by their sins and restores to them the Grace of God. The sacrament has two effects or aspects: outer and inner – the outer aspect is that the penitent believer receives absolution from his priest, either by remission of sin or the punishment due to sin; the inner aspect is that through repentance and confession the believer is reconciled to God.

In addition to being known as confession, penance and reconciliation can also be called the sacrament of conversion (because, according to the *Catechism of the Catholic Church*, it "makes sacramentally present Jesus' call to conversion") and the sacrament of forgiveness. Along with the anointing of the sick, confession is one of two sacraments of healing. Through these two sacraments, according to the catechism, the Church continues Christ's work of "healing and salvation, even among Her own members".

Christ instituted the sacrament of confession on Easter Day, when after rising from the dead following his Crucifixion he appeared to the apostles and said, "Receive the Holy Spirit. If you forgive the sins of any, they are forgiven; if you retain the sins of any, they are retained" (John 20:22–23).

There is another biblical precedent for this sacrament, found in the episode described in the Gospel of Matthew (9:2–8) in which Jesus publicly forgave the sins of a paralytic man brought to him for healing and cured him of his paralysis.

Above: The penitent admits any wrongdoing, but also humbly confesses (acknowledges and honours) God's profound holiness and great mercy.

WHEN TO CONFESS
Catholics must receive the sacrament of confession when they are aware that they have committed a mortal sin and in any case at least once a year. They are encouraged to go to confession once a month. (Mortal sins are distinct from venial sins. Mortal sins are those that condemn a soul to hell because they cannot be forgiven without repentence; lesser venial sins, if unconfessed and so not absolved, cause separation from God but not eternal damnation.)

Catholics are also required to receive the sacrament of confession before they receive the Eucharist for the first time. In Lent, the Church urges believers to receive the sacrament of confession as part of their preparation for Easter. Catholics are generally keen to receive confession

Below: After his Resurrection, Christ tells his disciples that they have the power to forgive sins, as seen in this 14th-century panel by Duccio di Buoninsegna.

224

PENANCE AND RECONCILIATION

Right: Sin is straying from God, while penance, such as the confession shown in this 15th-century painting by Domenico di Niccolò dei Cori, is a return to the Father.

because, as one of the seven sacraments instituted by Christ, it delivers God's Grace to those who receive it and so is a vital aid in living a good Christian life.

There are four key elements to the sacrament. Firstly, penitent individuals are required to be contrite; that is, to feel sincere remorse for their sins. They must have a genuine intention not to commit the sins again. Secondly, they must confess the number and kind of their sins to a priest. Thirdly, they need to receive absolution from the priest. Lastly, they must perform satisfaction or the acts of penance that were prescribed by the priest.

ABSOLUTION FROM SIN

A priest (or bishop) does not himself have the power to forgive sins. However, he exercises the power on behalf of Christ through the sacrament of penance if he is ordained validly and has proper jurisdiction over the penitent who makes confession. In administering the sacrament, the priest acts in *persona Christi* ("in the person of Christ").

Below: In delivering absolution, a priest acts on Christ's behalf. As well as receiving God's pardon, the penitent is reconciled with the Church.

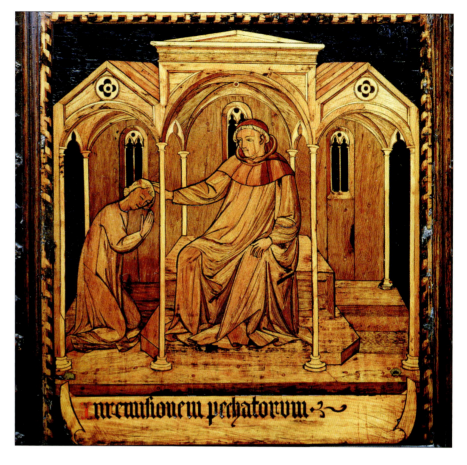

The priest hears the confessions of his parishioners or other members of the faithful at set times, and the normal form of confession is for the penitent individual to say, "Bless me Father for I have sinned" and then to specify the period that has elapsed since his or her last confession. The penitent has to confess all mortal sins committed in that period and is encouraged to confess venial sins, too. The prayer of confession begins, "O My God I am heartily sorry…"

The priest then delivers absolution. One form describes a merciful God, who "through the death and resurrection of his Son" has become reconciled to humankind and has sent the Holy Spirit among people "for the forgiveness of sins". It goes on to state that through the Church's ministry God may pardon the person and give him or her peace. The priest ends by absolving the person from his or her sins in the three names of the Holy Trinity.

SEAL OF THE CONFESSIONAL

The priest is bound by the absolutely inviolable seal of the confessional – he cannot reveal what he has been told in confession, even under threat of death. A priest who does so is automatically excommunicated from the Church. In criminal matters, for example, if a person admits to murder in the confessional, the priest cannot tell the police or other authorities, but he can encourage the penitent to give himself or herself up and can withhold absolution as a means of leverage.

ANOINTING OF THE SICK AND THE LAST RITES

God's Grace is delivered to the severely ill through the anointing of the sick and last rites, which help them cope with sickness or death and resist the feeling of discouragement.

In the sacrament of the anointing of the sick, a priest anoints a seriously ill Catholic person with holy oil. Along with penance and reconciliation (or confession), the anointing of the sick is one of the Catholic Church's two sacraments of healing. Through the anointing of the sick, an ill person is united with the suffering of Christ, and even permitted to share in the redemptive work performed by Christ's Passion. The sacrament will bring spiritual and sometimes physical healing – and also forgiveness of sins.

All the sacraments draw on biblical precedent. The central text in support of the anointing of the sick is in James 5:14–15:

Is any among you sick? Let him call for the elders of the Church, and let them pray over him, anointing him with oil in the name of the Lord; and the prayer of faith will save the sick man, and the Lord will raise him up; and if he has committed sins, he will be forgiven.

RECEIVING THE SACRAMENT

Only a priest or bishop can administer the sacrament of the anointing of the sick. According to canon law, he can give the sacrament to any member of the faithful who has reached the age of reason and is in danger of death either though illness or old age. If a person receives the sacrament when close to death, then recovers, he or she can receive this sacrament a second time if the illness strikes again. Equally, a person can receive the sacrament a second time if a continuing illness worsens. A person about to have serious surgery can also receive the sacrament.

The priest can also use his pastoral judgement to determine whether or not it is appropriate to administer the sacrament a second time or even more often when a person is chronically ill or very old and weak. He can administer the sacrament to a person at home, during Mass or while in a hospital and may give it to a group of the seriously ill if desired.

ADMINISTERING THE SACRAMENT

The priest uses olive or vegetable oil that has been blessed by the bishop in the Chrism Mass on Holy Thursday (the Thursday of Holy Week). In the Latin Rite of the Western Church, the priest usually anoints the sick person on the forehead, marking the shape of the Cross, and says: "Through this holy anointing may the Lord in his love and mercy help you with the grace of the Holy Spirit. May the Lord who frees you from sin save you

Above: Christ comforted and healed the sick, as illustrated by James Tissot in his 19th-century painting, In the Villages the Sick Were Brought unto Him.

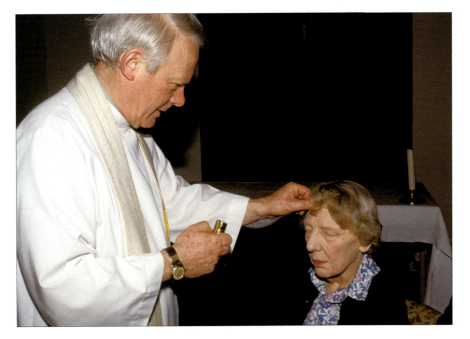

Below: The sacrament delivers grace to strengthen the ill person, bringing courage, peace of mind and, subject to God's will, physical healing.

ANOINTING OF THE SICK AND THE LAST RITES

Above: A priest visiting a seriously ill person will carry all the equipment he needs to perform anointing and to celebrate the Eucharist.

sacrament of the earthly journey, the *viaticum* for 'passing over' to eternal life." The sacrament of the anointing of the sick is also called *sacramentum exeuntium* ("the sacrament of those departing"). It is the last of the holy anointings of the Christian life, and follows on from the anointings of baptism and con-firmation. "This last anointing," according to the catechism, "fortifies the end of our earthly life like a solid rampart for the final struggles before entering the Father's house."

> **EXTREME UNCTION**
>
> When given among the last rites, the anointing of the sick was traditionally known as extreme unction, meaning "a last anointing". In the modern Church, the sacrament is called the anointing of the sick, but some traditional Catholics, who usually adhere to the practice and terminology in use before the Second Vatican Council (1962–5), still use the name extreme unction.

and raise you up." He may anoint other parts of the body, without using the verbal formula.

LAST RITES

When the sick person is in immediate danger of death the anointing is considered to be one of the "last rites", which also includes penance and reconciliation and the Eucharist. The normal procedure is for the priest to hear the person's confession, then anoint him or her, before giving him or her the Eucharist. In some cases, when a person is too ill to confess, the priest can pronounce absolution – but this is believed to be effective only if the dying person inwardly feels contrition for the sins.

The Eucharist given to a seriously ill person is called *viaticum*, a Latin word meaning "provision for the voyage" and referring to the final journey of this earthly life – through death into eternal life. In the words of the *Catechism of the Catholic Church*, "As the sacrament of Christ's Passover, the Eucharist should always be the last

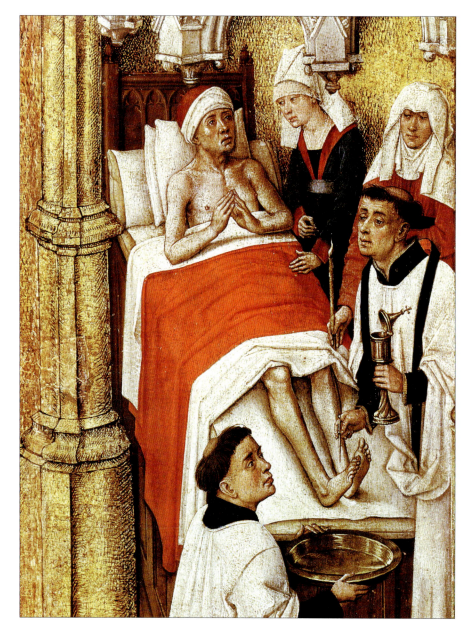

Right: In addition to anointing, those near to death confess their sins and receive the Eucharist, as in this 15th-century painting by Rogier van der Weyden.

LIVING THE SACRAMENTS

DUST TO DUST

WHEN A PERSON DIES, CATHOLICS GIVE THANKS FOR THE GRACE OF GOD EVIDENCED IN HIS OR HER LIFE. CATHOLIC FUNERAL SERVICES COMPRISE A VIGIL, A MASS AND A BURIAL OR COMMITTAL.

The three forms of funeral service have been authorized in the *Ordo exsequiarum* ("Order of Christian Funerals") of the Catholic Church's Roman Rite. Each form has its proper place: the vigil is usually held at home; the funeral or requiem Mass in the Church; and the committal in the cemetery. All three forms express what the catechism calls the "paschal character" of death. This refers to a Catholic's understanding of death in terms of Easter, in the light of Jesus' death and Resurrection.

VIGIL, MASS, COMMITTAL

The vigil is a gathering for prayers and biblical readings, with a sermon, that is held before the day of the funeral Mass and committal, often at the home of the deceased person. One or more eulogies on the dead person's life are shared. These should not praise the individual but concentrate on the workings of God's Grace in his or her life. The vigil is often held as part of a wake.

Below: After the funeral Mass, a priest blesses the coffin before it is transported to the cemetery for the committal.

The funeral Mass is often called a requiem Mass. Those gathered pray for the forgiveness of sins and the salvation of the soul of the departed. The service takes the name *requiem* from the Latin wording at the beginning of the first section, the Introit: *Requiem aeternam dona eis, Domine, et lux perpetua luceat eis* ("Grant them unending rest, O Lord, and may light perpetual fall on them"). Requiem Masses can also be held as a memorial for a deceased person and to mark an anniversary of a person's death.

The rite of committal consists of prayers and Bible readings as the body is buried in a cemetery, or before cremation. In the committal the faithful bid farewell to the deceased person; the Church commends him or her to the care of God.

FULFILMENT OF A LIFE

Catholic teaching views death as the end and fulfilment of a devout person's sacramental life. His or her religious life has been structured to lead to this end: death is the fulfilment of the new birth of baptism, of the new life that was confirmed and strengthened by the anointing

Above: During a funeral Mass, the presiding priest censes and blesses the coffin as the Church expresses its communion with the departed.

of the Holy Spirit at confirmation, and the participation in the heavenly feast anticipated every time he or she received the Eucharist. During the funeral, the Church, which has carried the devout person through life, like a mother would care for a growing child, now offers him or her to God the Father, in Christ.

The liturgy and ceremonial of the requiem Mass generally follows that of the standard Mass, but omits its more joyful expressions, including the gloria and the Creed and certain doxologies, or hymns of praise. A key element of the Mass in this setting is the funeral homily, which must be delivered by a bishop, priest or deacon, and which explicates the meaning of death in the context of Christ's own death and his triumphant Resurrection.

Celebrating Mass is central to the funeral because the Eucharist lies at the very heart of a Catholic's understanding of death. In the Eucharist, a member of the faithful will have communion with Christ and with the departed person. The gathered faithful will then pray for the forgiveness of the deceased person's sins, and ask that he or she enjoy the heavenly feast to which the Eucharist looks forward: in doing this, and in

Right: The funeral, followed by burial or cremation, is illuminated by belief in "the resurrection of the dead, and the life of the world to come".

receiving the Eucharist, the faithful at the Mass will learn to exist in communion with the departed.

ATTITUDE TO CREMATION

For many centuries the Catholic Church did not allow cremation because it held the practice to be counter to belief in the resurrection of the body. The official position was that cremation was a pagan practice. However, in 1963 the Vatican began to permit the use of cremation as long as the reason for choosing it did not go against Catholic beliefs.

The initial requirement was that all funeral services had to be carried out in the presence of the dead body, which would then be cremated afterward. This was changed in 1997 and since then the funeral liturgy can be used in the presence of cremated remains of the body. The Church does not permit the scattering of ashes after cremation; it teaches that the ashes should be entombed in a grave or mausoleum.

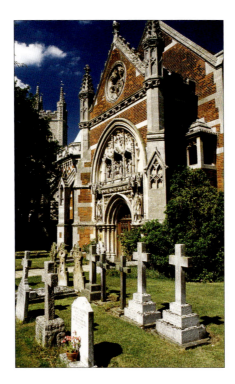

DRESSED FOR A MASS

Bishops or priests that celebrate requiem Masses were traditionally expected to wear black vestments and ornaments. Black is considered to be the colour of the most profound grief, and is also worn for services on Good Friday. Today, clergy often wear white to symbolize the glory of the Resurrection.

MUSICAL HERITAGE

Requiem Masses are often sung, and there is a very rich heritage of musical settings of requiem Masses, including works by the notable composers Wolfgang Amadeus Mozart, Hector Berlioz and Gabriel Fauré.

The revised form of the Latin Rite for the requiem Mass, which was introduced following the Second Vatican Council (1962–5) and is used generally today, does away with a number of elements of the traditional requiem that are familiar to people who know the service chiefly through these magnificent musical settings.

One example is the sequence beginning *Dies irae, dies illa, Solvet sæclum in favilla* ("Day of anger, day when the world turns to ashes…"). This is a powerful part of classical requiems by Mozart and Verdi, but was made optional and then dropped from the requiem Mass following the Second Vatican Council as part of changes designed to tone down elements suggestive of despair and fear of judgement while emphasizing hope and belief in the Resurrection. The *Dies irae* was part of the requiem Mass in the Roman Missal 1962 (prior to the Second Vatican Council) and so is still heard in churches that celebrate the Tridentine liturgy in use before the Council.

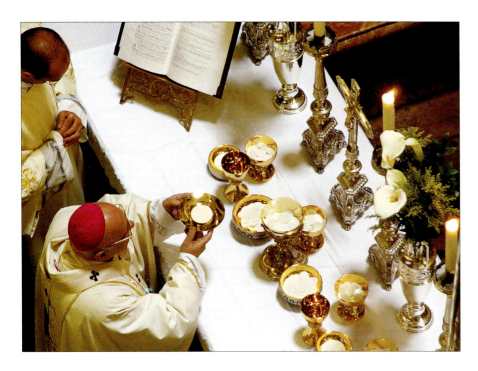

Left: A memorial Mass for Pope John Paul II was held in the Church of the Holy Sepulchre (the church in which Jesus is traditionally believed to be buried), in Jerusalem, on 6 April 2005. Latin Patriarch Michel Sabbah presided, and some 200 heads of state, heads of government and royalty gathered to attend the pope's funeral.

LIVING THE SACRAMENTS

PRAYER

IN PRAYER, CATHOLICS CAN COMMUNICATE WITH THEIR CREATOR. BELIEVERS CAN BUILD AND MAINTAIN A LIVING AND PERSONAL RELATIONSHIP WITH GOD THE FATHER, SON AND HOLY SPIRIT.

Prayer can be public or private: it can be a shared communal experience or a personal and solitary formal rite, spoken aloud or a more fluid, silent interior activity. Public forms of prayer include the Mass and the Liturgy of the Hours. Among private forms are the use of the rosary and the practice of *Lectio Divina*, which is a meditative reading of the Scriptures developed as a form of devotion by medieval monastics. The Catholic Church teaches that the chief sources of and inspirations to prayer are the Word of God in the Bible, the liturgy of the Church and the virtues of faith, hope and charity.

HOW TO PRAY

Catholic authorities stress that it is essential to pray but that the kind of prayer does not matter. Pope John Paul II, in writing about how to pray, said that it was a simple thing to do and recommended that you pray "any way you like, so long as you do pray". Prayer may be a very personal outpouring. The catechism quotes St Thérèse of Lisieux:

For me prayer is a surge of the heart; it is a simple look turned towards heaven, it is a cry of recognition and of love, embracing both trial and joy.

Prayer is not just self-expression. Elsewhere, the catechism states that prayer is not something to be turned into a "spontaneous outpouring of interior impulse". The Holy Spirit instructs the faithful in how to pray through "a living transmission" (Sacred Tradition) within the Church.

Above: In Jacob Cornelisz van Oostsanen's 1523 painting, Adoration of the Trinity, *a Christian (right) prays with hands clasped together.*

Prayers of all kinds must be made in the name of Jesus, for these have access to God the Father through Christ. The Holy Spirit teaches believers to pray to God the Father through the Son, and that through the many different kinds of prayer the one Holy Spirit acts.

BENEFITS OF PRAYER

The Church teaches that prayer leads the faithful away from sin toward salvation. In prayer, a believer turns to God and receives direction from the Holy Spirit; without this guidance the believer is trapped in sin. According to the Church, people who pray with eagerness and call on God cannot sin, therefore they are saved; those who do not pray are trapped in sin and are in the way of damnation.

Praying by repeating the name of Jesus in the Jesus Prayer has the effect of summoning Christ within the believer. Whereas in the Old

THE JESUS PRAYER

The catechism states, "There is no other way of Christian prayer than Christ." St Paul exhorted Christians to "pray constantly" (1 Thessalonicans 5:17), to attempt to keep one's life in God's presence and under his eye: a favoured way of doing this is through "prayer of the heart". One example used for centuries by Christians in both the Eastern and Western Churches is the Jesus Prayer, an invocation based on repetition of the Lord's name. The Jesus Prayer developed in a variety of forms, the most common of which is "Lord Jesus Christ, Son of God, have mercy on us sinners". Praying this prayer while being active in the world sanctifies every action.

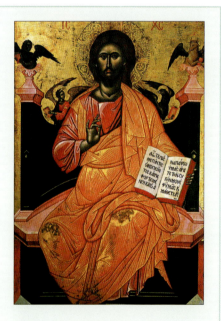

Above: Catholics are encouraged to pray in Jesus' name, who spread the Word, as shown in this 17th-century Greek icon.

Testament, the Jews were forbidden to utter the name of God, in Jesus, God adopted human form and delivered his name to humanity: the name Jesus contains the divine presence. The catechism explains: "The name 'Jesus' contains all: God and man and the whole economy of creation and salvation…whoever invokes the name of Jesus is welcoming the Son of God who loved him [or her] and who gave himself up for him [or her]."

PRIVATE PRAYER
The Church also teaches that private meditative prayer complements and sustains the public prayer of the liturgy. In his apostolic letter *Rosarium Virginis Mariae* ("Rosary of the Virgin Mary"), which was witten on 16 October 2002, Pope John Paul II described the rosary as a good introduction and an accurate echo of Church liturgy. He added that praying the words of the rosary as taught by the Church involves carrying on an inner meditation on the glories and hidden meanings of Christ's life and this lets the believer take part in a deep study of Christian mystery that amounts to a profound and practical training for a holy life.

Above: A prayer book, shown in this 16th-century detail from Portrait of the Artist's Sister in the Garb of a Nun *by Sofonisba Anguissola, is an indispensable aid for some Catholics.*

Pope Benedict XVI emphasized the fact that private prayer, contemplation and religious devotions do not distract from loving service in the world but in fact provide an essential underpinning and support for that service. He used the example of Mother Teresa of Calcutta and the work of her order, the Missionaries of Charity, as an example. In his first encyclical, *Deus Caritas Est*, written in December 2005, he declared that the example of Teresa of Calcutta illustrates the fact that when we devote time to God in private or public prayer, it does not distract us from serving our neighbours in love, but rather is a limitless source of loving service.

Left: In prayer, the believer reaches out to God. The Church teaches that calling on the name of Jesus summons his presence within us.

THE SACRED HEART

CATHOLICS USE THE SACRED HEART OF JESUS AS A FOCUS FOR THEIR INTENSE DEVOTIONS IN WHICH THEY SEEK TO MAKE REPARATIONS TO JESUS FOR THE SINS OF HUMANKIND.

The Sacred Heart of Jesus is a symbol of God's love for humanity. God's love was expressed in Christ's suffering, and the Sacred Heart is pierced by human sins. Through prayer and contemplation, Catholics can consecrate themselves to the Sacred Heart.

In Catholic art, the Sacred Heart is usually shown to be aflame and shining with light, injured by the lance that stabbed Jesus' side on the Cross, with a crown of thorns around it and blood falling from it. This image is often superimposed on Jesus' chest, with his wounded hands pointing to the heart. The light and flames represent the power of divine love.

Above: Many Catholic homes, churches and other institutions contain Sacred Heart statues to remind the faithful of Jesus' profound love and suffering.

DEVOTION TO THE HEART

Those who want to express their devotion to the Sacred Heart usually seek to receive Communion often. They commit to establish a "first Friday" routine – to go to confession and then receive the Eucharist on the first Friday of the month for nine months consecutively. They also partake of Holy Hour devotions on Thursdays. The Holy Hour is an hour-long prayer vigil, usually conducted in the presence of the Holy Sacrament. It is intended to make amends to Jesus for the hour in the garden of Gethsemane when he prayed alone, and returning to his disciples found them asleep. He reproached Peter: "So, could you not watch with me one hour? Watch and pray that you may not enter into temptation; the spirit indeed is willing, but the flesh is weak" (Matthew 26:40–41).

Sometimes the devout partake in a ceremony at home known as the enthronement of the Sacred Heart. A priest visits the home to set up ("enthrone") an image or statue of Jesus bearing his Sacred Heart: it reminds those living in the house that they have been consecrated to the Sacred Heart.

PAPAL TEACHINGS

In his encyclical *Annum Sacrum* (On Consecration to the Sacred Heart) of 25 May 1899, Pope Leo XIII

Below: The apostles showed human frailty when they failed to keep watch with Jesus. They are asleep in Barna da Siena's 14th-century painting, Christ in the Garden of Gethsemane.

THE SACRED HEART

Above: The Sacred Heart Cathedral at Bendigo in Victoria, Australia, is one of many Catholic institutions named after the Sacred Heart.

consecrated all humans to the Sacred Heart of Jesus. He described the Sacred Heart as a comprehensible symbol of Christ's endless love and declared that it was right that Catholics should dedicate themselves to the Sacred Heart; when the faithful do this, he added, they offer and bind themselves to Jesus. Many Catholic organizations, including churches, colleges and missionary and teaching orders, are dedicated to the Sacred Heart.

Pope Pius XII delivered a teaching on the mystical aspects of revering the heart of Jesus in his encyclical *Haurietis Aquas* (On Devotion to the Sacred Heart) in 1956. He declared the heart of Jesus to be a symbol of God's threefold love in the Father, Son and Holy Spirit; he wrote that believers should look devoutly upon the divine Redeemer's heart as an image of Jesus' love and a witness of our salvation in the events of Easter, and as a kind of mystical pathway along which we climb upward to be embraced by our Saviour.

Pius XII also declared in this letter that devotion to Jesus' Sacred Heart was the foundation on which individual believers, their families and whole nations could construct the kingdom of God.

FEAST DAY
The feast of the Sacred Heart was established in the church calendar in 1856 by Pope Pius IX and is celebrated 19 days after Pentecost. Because Pentecost falls on a Sunday, the feast of the Sacred Heart takes place on a Friday. On this feast day, devout Catholics will meditate on the devotional aspects of the Sacred Heart of Jesus.

They say the prayers laid out in the Act of Reparation to the Sacred Heart, which begins "Most sweet Jesus, whose overflowing charity for men is requited by so much forgetfulness, negligence and contempt, behold us prostrate before Thee, eager to repair by a special act of homage the cruel indifference and injuries to which Thy loving Heart is everywhere subject…"

ORIGINS OF SACRED HEART RITUALS
Medieval mystics were the first to develop the practice of revering Jesus' heart. The devotion then became popular among the Jesuits during the 16th and 17th centuries. The modern form of the devotion derives in particular from the 17th-century French mystic and nun St Marguerite Marie Alacoque, who had several revelations of the Sacred Heart in 1673–5. She declared that Jesus called on believers to offer prayers of expiation for his suffering, to take Communion frequently, especially on the first Friday of the month, and to observe the Holy Hour.

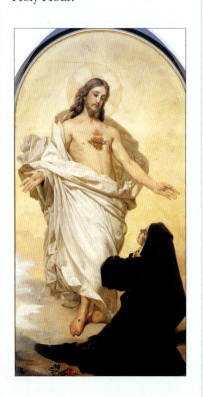

Above: As a nun, St Marguerite Marie Alacoque had an intense mystical experience of Christ's suffering, captured in this 1888 painting, Beatified Marguerite Marie Alacoque's Vision of Jesus' Heart, *by Antonio Ciseri.*

STATIONS OF THE CROSS

THE STATIONS OF THE CROSS IS A SET OF 14 PENITENTIAL MEDITATIONS ON CHRIST'S PASSION, WHICH ARE OFTEN PERFORMED DURING LENT, ESPECIALLY ON FRIDAY EVENINGS.

The 14 meditations are each linked to a specific scene that illustrates one of the series of events that included Christ's condemnation to death, passage to Calvary and his Crucifixion. They are performed before paintings or statuary that represent the scene in question. The paintings or statues are usually carefully arranged around the walls of a church or chapel; however, they can also be laid out as a series of images along a pathway, for example, near a shrine.

By praying at the Stations of the Cross, the Catholic believer can make a spiritual pilgrimage. The Church teaches that the prayers and meditations before the Stations of the Cross should be performed in a spirit of reparation – in an attempt to clear away humanity's sins.

In 1928, Pope Pius XI wrote in his encyclical *Miserentissimus Redemptor* that Catholics had a duty to offer reparation to Christ for the sins that have been committed against him. In 2000, in a letter marking the 50th anniversary of the Benedictine Sisters of Reparation of the Holy Face, Pope John Paul II called the effort to make reparation for the sins committed every day against Jesus an attempt to place oneself alongside the infinite number of crosses on which the son of God is still crucified. The meditations made at these Stations often seek to focus on the positive effects of the acts of atonement that Christ performed, as well as consider the grave sins of humankind that have been the reason for Christ's suffering.

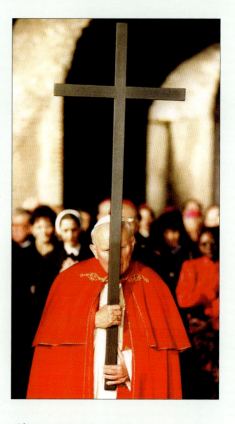

Above: Pope John Paul II bears a cross during the first part of the Stations of the Cross in the Colosseum in Rome on 5 April 1996.

Above: The 5th station: Jesus is judged by Pilate. These images are from a fresco by an unknown artist of the 15th century.

Above: The 6th station: Jesus is mocked, beaten, blindfolded and crowned with thorns by enemies.

THE OLD SEQUENCE

The traditional sequence of the Stations of the Cross was used by Catholics for centuries. It was as follows: Jesus is condemned to death (1), is given the Cross (2), then falls for the first time under the weight of the Cross (3); Jesus encounters his mother, the Blessed Virgin Mary (4), and Simon of Cyrene is forced to carry the Cross (5); Veronica (Berenice), a pious Jerusalem woman, gives Jesus her veil to wipe his face (6); Jesus falls down for a second time (7); he addresses the daughters of Jerusalem (8); he falls for a third time (9), then he is stripped of his garments (10); Jesus is nailed to the Cross (11); Jesus dies on the Cross (12); his body is removed from the Cross and laid in the arms of his mother (13), and then laid in the tomb (14).

This sequence was altered by Pope John Paul II in 1991 because the traditional sequence included six scenes (3,4,6,7, 9 and 13) not backed by Scripture. The first five of these do not appear at all in biblical accounts, while station 13 – the scene of Jesus laid in his mother's arms, represented so famously and beautifully in the many Pietà statues of art history – is a misrepresentation, for in biblical accounts Joseph of Arimathea was working alone when he took down Jesus' body and laid it in a tomb.

THE REVISED SEQUENCE

John Paul II devised a new (though not obligatory) sequence called the Scriptural Way of the Cross. The 14 scenes of this sequence are as follows: Jesus prays in the Garden of Gethsemane (1), then is betrayed by Judas Iscariot and arrested (2); he is condemned by the Jewish judicial body, the Sanhedrin (3); St Peter denies Jesus (4), then Jesus is judged by Pontius Pilate (5) and is whipped and given a crown of thorns (6); Jesus takes the Cross (7), then Simon of Cyrene carries it (8); Jesus speaks to the women of Jerusalem (9); he is crucified (10); he promises the "good thief" being crucified with him, "Truly, I say to you, today you will be with me in Paradise" (11), entrusts his mother to his disciple John with the words, "Woman, behold, your son!" and to the disciple, "Behold your mother!" (12); he dies on the Cross (13); his body is put in the tomb (14).

GOOD FRIDAY

Catholics are generally encouraged to pray and meditate at the Stations of the Cross on Good Friday. John Paul II made a practice of performing public devotions at Stations of the Cross set up in the Colosseum, Rome, each Good Friday. In 1991 and thereafter, he prayed the new scriptural sequence outlined above. Initially, the Holy Father himself carried the Cross from station to station, but in later life his age made it necessary for him to watch the devotions from a stage while others carried the Cross. In 2007, Pope Benedict XVI approved the new sequence of the Stations of the Cross for use by Catholics.

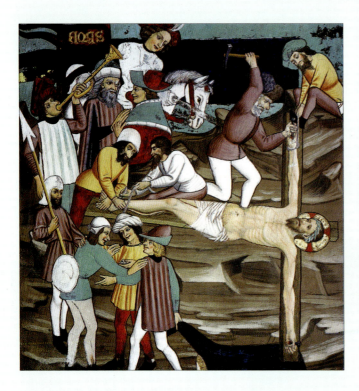

Above: The 10th station: Jesus is bound and nailed to the Cross during his Crucifixion.

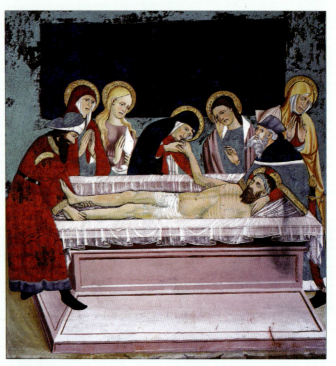

Above: The 14th station: Jesus' body is placed in the tomb with the help of Joseph of Arimathea.

LIVING THE SACRAMENTS

THE ROSARY

FOR CENTURIES DEVOTED CATHOLICS HAVE USED THE ROSARY — A ROUND OF PRAYERS THAT ARE CENTRED ON THE BLESSED VIRGIN MARY — IN BOTH PUBLIC AND PRIVATE DEVOTIONS.

The rosary is also a physical object that enables believers to keep track of their prayers. It consists of a small crucifix on a circular string with a medal and a series of beads of various numbers. The beads are divided into groups of ten beads called decades, each group preceded by an individual bead set apart slightly from the others. It is used to say the prayers that form the rosary. The central prayer of the rosary is the Hail Mary:

Hail Mary, full of Grace, the Lord is with thee; blessed art thou amongst women, and blessed is the fruit of thy womb, Jesus. Holy Mary, Mother of God, pray for us sinners now and at the hour of our death.

The other key prayers used in the rosary to complement the Hail Mary are the Lord's Prayer beginning "Our Father, who art in Heaven…" and the Apostles' Creed beginning "I believe in God, the Father Almighty, creator of heaven and earth…"

PRAYING THE ROSARY

The usual pattern of prayers is an introduction, then five decades of the rosary and a conclusion. During the introduction, believers hold the crucifix as they pray the dedication "In the Name of the Father, and of the Son and of the Holy Spirit: Amen" and the Apostles' Creed. Then they progress along the four beads after the crucifix, saying one Our Father and three Hail Marys.

Then they begin on the five decades. At each bead they say one Our Father and at each decade one Hail Mary. At the conclusion they hold the medal as they pray one of many other prayers to Mary, then return to the dedication "In the Name of the Father, and of the Son and of the Holy Spirit: Amen".

THE MYSTERIES

While praying the decades of the rosary, believers meditate inwardly on the mysteries of the lives of the Virgin Mary and Jesus. These

Above: A Luminous Mystery: Peter, James and John see Jesus in his true light in Pietro Perugino's 15th–16th century The Transfiguration.

meditations were divided into three groups of five: the Joyful Mysteries (of Jesus' birth), the Sorrowful Mysteries (of Jesus' Crucifixion) and the Glorious Mysteries (of Jesus' Resurrection). However, in 2002 Pope John Paul II proposed a new set of mysteries, the Mysteries of Light, or Luminous Mysteries, following key events in Christ's ministry.

In each group, one mystery is aligned to one decade of the rosary, so when praying the entire rosary once, believers can meditate on one set of five mysteries. There is a pattern for meditating on the mysteries: the Joyful Mysteries are considered on Monday and Saturday, the Sorrowful Mysteries on Tuesday and Friday, the Glorious Mysteries on Wednesday and Sunday and the Luminous Mysteries are optional for Thursdays.

Left: Pope John Paul II declared that the rosary prayer encompasses in its words the depth of the Holy Gospel's message.

Right: A Glorious Mystery: The Virgin is carried to heaven and crowned in this c.1500 Flemish illustration, Assumption and Coronation of the Virgin.

ORIGINS AND REVIVAL

The Hail Mary is also known as the Ave Maria, which comes from its first words in Latin *Ave Maria, gratia plena, Dominus tecum*. The prayer combines three main parts, the first being the salutation delivered by the archangel Gabriel to the Blessed Virgin at the Annunciation. The second part, "Blessed is the fruit of thy womb, Jesus", derives the greeting of Elizabeth to Mary (Luke 1:42); and the third part, the prayer "Holy Mary, Mother of God…" was, according to the *Catechism of the Catholic Church*, developed by the Church.

By tradition, the rosary was developed by St Dominic when combating the heresies of the dualist Cathars in 13th-century France. It has been refined over many years, but it reached its modern form by the 15th century when the Dominican preacher Alan de la Roche promoted its use. In 1520, Pope Leo X gave the rosary his official papal backing.

In 1858 in Lourdes, France, Marie-Bernarde Soubirous (St Bernadette) saw apparitions of the Blessed Virgin Mary, who urged her to say her rosary, and to tell others to pray, perform penances and say the rosary for the salvation of sinners. Lourdes is now a centre of pilgrimage for Catholics.

Below: A Joyful Mystery: the Virgin Mary gives her consent to God's planned Incarnation at the Annunciation in Melchior Broederlam's 14th-century Annunciation and Visitation.

> **THE WORDS OUR SAVIOUR GAVE US**
>
> Also known as the paternoster and the Our Father from its initial words in English and Latin, the Lord's Prayer is based on the one taught by Jesus to the apostles. According to the accounts in Matthew 6:9–15 and Luke 11:2–4, it runs:
>
> *Our Father who art in heaven,*
> *Hallowed be thy name.*
> *Thy kingdom come,*
> *Thy will be done,*
> *On earth as it is in heaven.*
> *Give us this day our daily bread.*
> *And forgive us our trespasses,*
> *As we forgive those who*
>   *trespass against us.*
> *And lead us not into temptation,*
>   *but deliver us from evil.*
>
> The Catholic version does not include the doxology or hymn of praise "For the kingdom the power and the glory are yours, now and forever" that appears in some other versions.

LIVING THE SACRAMENTS

THE BLESSING

THERE ARE CENTURIES OF TRADITION AND LAYERS OF SYMBOLISM BEHIND CATHOLIC PRACTICES, SUCH AS THE BLESSING GIVEN BY THE CLERGY, MAKING THE SIGN OF THE CROSS AND USING HOLY WATER.

When Roman Catholic priests are ordained, their hands are anointed with chrism, holy oil that has been blessed by a bishop. After receiving the sacrament of Holy Orders through this and other related rituals, priests are able to share in Christ's own priesthood: their hands have the power to bless people and objects. In the act of blessing, the clergy can sanctify both people and objects, and dedicate them to God's service.

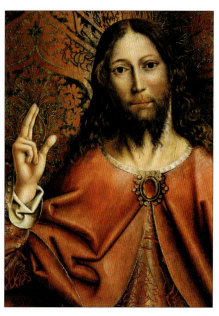

Above: Jesus gave numerous blessings, as shown in Fernando Gallego's 15th-century Christ Blessing, *and with a gesture of his hands worked many miracles.*

The long-held practice of sanctifying both people and objects through the act of blessing has many biblical precedents. God blessed his Creation and after the Flood blessed Noah, while priests of the Jewish faith delivered blessings on their people. Christ himself and the apostles gave blessings to the sick and needy and to their followers. The Church teaches that blessing is the chief sacramental, a rite or object through and with which the sacraments are administered.

THE POWER TO BLESS
In general, only bishops and priests can deliver blessings, except in one exception under which a deacon is empowered to bless the paschal candle on Holy Saturday. Certain types of blessing are reserved for more senior clergy. Only the pope

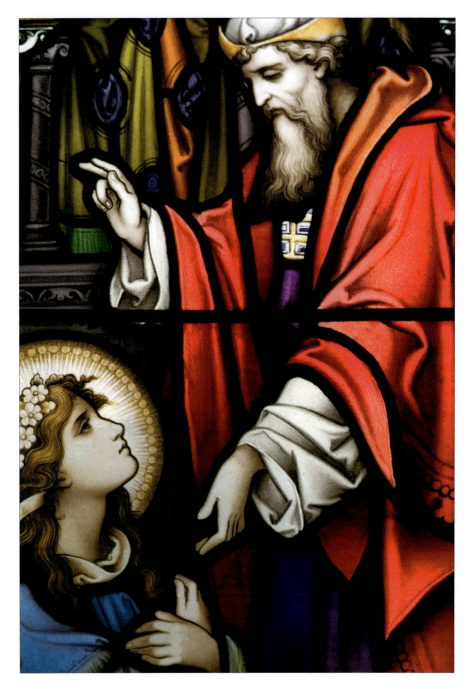

Left: A stained-glass window in a Catholic church in Dublin shows a priest giving his blessing to a young child. The stained-glass windows are by the famous artist, William Early, who died during the commission.

238

can deliver some blessings – for example, those to which are attached an indulgence or remission of temporal punishment due to sin.

The pope's *Urbi et Orbi* blessing to the city of Rome and to the world, which is delivered every year on Easter and Christmas, has an indulgence attached for all Catholics who hear it in person, on television or on radio. Only bishops can deliver another class of blessings – for example, blessings on churches, cemeteries, chalices and vestments.

PRIESTLY BLESSINGS

There is a wide range of blessings that can be made by priests. They include blessings for the sick or for women due to deliver a baby and for people at various stages of Church life. There are also blessings for sanctifying objects used in religious devotions, such as crosses, images of Jesus, bells, medals, candles, rosaries and so forth. There are blessings for animals, food, buildings, such as schools or hospitals, and public objects, such as bridges, ships, stores, planes and so on.

Above: Pope Benedict XVI delivers the papal Urbi et Orbi *blessing. He prays that God's blessing should settle on the listening faithful and be with them always.*

> ### DIMINUTIVE CROSSES
> A variant form of the ritual is to use the thumb to make a small sign of the Cross three times over forehead, lips and chest, sometimes while praying quietly "May Christ's words be in my mind, on my lips and in my heart". This is the normal usage when the gospel is proclaimed during Mass. A third kind of Cross made by the clergy is a small sign, traced with the thumb, for example, on the forehead of a baby in the sacrament of baptism or on the Holy Gospel during the liturgy of the Word in the Mass.

Above: A priest makes the sign of the Cross on a child's forehead using his thumb. The sign assures the child of God's protection.

The Church teaches that blessing is necessary and efficacious because people, animals and objects are all part of the Creation touched by sin after the Fall and therefore vulnerable to evil spirits. The blessings counter this effect by invoking the name of God, Father, Son and Holy Spirit and usually also by using the sign of the cross, a symbol of God's mercy and of Christ's victory over sin.

THE SIGN OF THE CROSS

When Catholics make the sign of the cross, they are honouring the Cross of Calvary and the redemptive sacrifice of Jesus. The Cross is a symbol of both God's mercy and his victory through Christ over sin.

Individual believers make the sign of the Cross on their own bodies as an expression of devotion. The most common form is to touch forehead, breastbone or stomach, left shoulder and then right shoulder in sequence. Usually the believer prays "In the Name of the Father" when touching the forehead, "And of the Son" when touching the stomach, "And of the Holy Spirit" when touching the left and right shoulders in sequence.

HOLY WATER

Sometimes a person will touch his fingers in holy water before making the sign of the Cross. When the faithful arrive at church for Mass, they dip their fingers in the bowl of holy water that is kept in a font near the entrance and make the sign of the Cross on head and torso.

The holy water has been blessed by a priest, and in this action the faithful bring to mind their baptismal promises as they seek to purify themselves before preparing to receive the Eucharist. Holy water is sometimes used to bless the faithful by sprinkling them with an aspergil (silver water sprinkler) during the Mass, especially during the Easter season. It is also used in blessings to sanctify places, objects and people.

THE CATHOLIC YEAR

The Catholic liturgical year has been shaped by events in the life of Christ. Although the actual historical dates of these events are uncertain, over the centuries a chronology has evolved that reflects the principal milestones of Christ's life as described in the Scriptures. However, at the same time it considers the manner in which human progress through time has fluctuated with the seasonal cycles. Thus "Christ our Light" was born after the deep night of the winter solstice, and our redemption from despair and damnation came in spring, after the full moon of the equinox. In the Catholic calendar, these natural cycles have assumed a religious dimension as they are allied to the life of the God-man who Catholics believe died for humankind's eternal salvation.

Just as in the life of each individual, "ordinary time" is also a component of the liturgical year. During ordinary time, no specific events in Christ's life are celebrated, although holy days of obligation such as All Saints' and the Assumption of Mary do fall within ordinary time. Strictly speaking, "ordinary" here refers to ordinal, or numbered, time; it encompasses the period from the evening of Candlemas (2 February) until Shrove Tuesday, and again from the Monday after Pentecost until vespers the night before Advent. Ordinary time pays homage to the simpler days that Christ spent on earth and reminds us to consider, even now, how we go about our normal daily lives.

Left: Youthful Christians bear a massive wooden cross in Jerusalem's Church of the Holy Sepulchre, built at the site of Christ's Crucifixion. The original 4th-century church was built by Constantine; the present structure dates from the Crusades of the 12th century.

HOLY DAYS

ROMAN CATHOLICS CONSECRATE EACH DAY OF THE YEAR TO REMEMBRANCE OF AN EVENT IN THE LIFE OF CHRIST OR THE BLESSED MOTHER, OR TO ONE OF THE SAINTS.

There are around 10,000 Catholic saints, and in the Catholic year, which is known as the liturgical year, each day has some sacred significance relating to a saint. Catholics nourish their spiritual consciousness by meditating on the particular virtues and mysteries that are invoked by the history of the saint on each new feast or saint's day.

THE FIRST HOLY DAYS

The tradition of saints' days dates back to the first centuries of the Catholic Church during the Roman persecutions. The first saints were the Christian martyrs, and early Christians often honoured their sacrifice by celebrating the day of their death, also known as their "birthday into heaven". During the Middle Ages, saints' days were a common method of dating, so "St Martin's Tide", or "Martinmas", referred to a date near 11 November, the feast day of St Martin of Tours; "Bartholomew Tide" meant a date in the waning days of summer, on about 24 August (commemorating St Bartholomew, patron of printers).

The Church classifies the daily liturgical observations as solemnities, feasts, memorials and commemorations. Solemnities, as their name implies, are the most important, but of the 13 yearly solemnities, only 6 are classified as holy days of obligation in the United States and 10 in Europe. (This group of six does not include ordinary Sundays, when Catholics are obliged to attend Mass each week, in honour of the day Christ rose from the dead.)

The Catholic Church mandates that Catholics must attend Mass on holy days of obligation, and refrain from "unnecessary servile work", often defined as physical labour. This prohibition is the genesis of today's word "holiday", which is an obvious contraction of "holy day". In feudal times serfs were freed on holy days of obligation so they could attend Mass.

MEDIEVAL HOLY DAYS

By the Middle Ages, holy days were so numerous and engrained in the observances of society that in some quarters they came to be considered a nuisance. The prohibition against servile work was taken up by the populace with enthusiasm, and soon medieval lawmakers found themselves having to issue stern decrees to make "exemptions" from the command not to work on holy days so that crucial work, such as harvesting, did not come to a standstill. The *Catholic Encyclopedia* notes that from the 13th to the 18th century, some dioceses observed more than 100 feast days – days in which no work was done. Celebrations of the "octaves" of major Catholic holy days, such as Easter, could cause work to stop for more than a week. Complaints reached a crescendo

Above: St Bartholomew is associated with books, as in this 14th-century illustration by Andre Beauneveu, because of a printers' celebration, the Wayzgoose. It is held on 24 August, the time of year printers began to work by candlelight.

Below: Farm labourers, such as the one in this 15th-century image from the Historia Naturalis, *often stopped working on the many holy days in medieval times, so holy days were unpopular among landowners.*

EARLY "FAIRS"

Not all Catholics abstaining from work on holy days were involved in reverent contemplation. The Latin *feria*, meaning "religious holiday", evolved to become "fair", a word that is still used to refer to a leisure activity, not to religious observance. One prelate suggested that while holy days gave Catholics a chance to "...receive the food of the Word of God, which they sorely need", they were instead using their holy days to relax or set up impromptu markets – and some of these were held within the churchyards themselves.

242

in the 16th century, and finally in 1642 Pope Urban VIII bowed to the inevitable and issued an encyclical, *Universa per Orbem*, that reduced the number of holy days to 36 (not including Sundays).

Even priests are subject to normal human nature, and in 1858 Pope Pius IX had to issue a second encyclical – this time to order priests to offer Mass on the "suppressed" holy days. This was issued because some priests had decided to take a holiday of their own and had ceased to celebrate Mass on feasts that were no longer holy days of obligation, although to do so was still their responsibility.

EUROPEAN HOLY DAYS

Holy days of obligation vary from country to country and year to year. In Europe, holy days are often celebrated with opulence. In Rome, for example, the Feast of Sts Peter and Paul (29 June) is a general holiday for the entire city, marking the day in AD 64 when both saints were martyred for their faith (Peter by being crucified upside down and Paul by beheading). Today, Romans observe the holy day with extravagant decoration of the 4th-century basilicas dedicated to each saint, and each year the pope presents palliums (from the Latin for "stole") to the city's bishops. The palliums are newly woven from wool shorn from lambs, and they symbolize the lamb carried over the shoulders of the good shepherd, reminding the bishops they are the shepherds of their pastoral flock, just as was Peter, Rome's first bishop.

AMERICAN HOLY DAYS

The holy days of obligation in the USA are fewer than in Europe. This is, in part, because the tradition of their celebration is shorter than in many European countries, where Catholicism has been the majority religion for many centuries. In the early years of the United States, Catholics were a minority, widely scattered in a vast country, and victims of prejudice. Puritans did not celebrate holy days because they had been offended by the excesses that they had observed in Europe. American bishops took such realities into account and reduced the number of holy days.

In the United States, if All Saints' Day or Ascension falls on a Saturday or Monday, the obligation to attend Mass is rescinded. The American Conference of Bishops has also suppressed certain holy days that are still active in Europe: the observances for Epiphany (6 January), Corpus Christi (the Thursday after Trinity Sunday), St Joseph (19 March) and the apostles Sts Peter and Paul (29 June) have been moved to the next following Sundays.

American holy days of obligation, with the exception of Christmas, are normally celebrated in a low-key manner simply by going to Mass. However, in certain American ethnic enclaves, old traditions of celebration on a saint's day still endure; for example, the feast of San Gennaro is usually celebrated with a street fair in Manhattan's Little Italy.

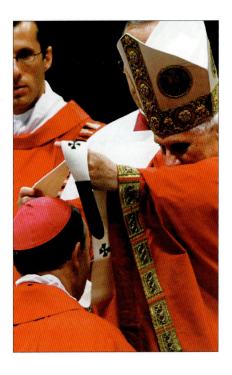

Above: On the feast of Sts Peter and Paul in Rome, Pope Benedict XVI drapes a pallium made of new woven wool over the shoulders of an archbishop.

Below: The September feast of San Gennaro, here celebrated in New York's Little Italy neighbourhood, home of many Italian-Americans, honours the 4th-century martyrdom of Januarius, the patron saint of Naples.

THE FESTIVE CALENDAR

THE FEASTS OF THE CATHOLIC CALENDAR HAVE MARKED THE DAYS OF THE YEAR FOR CENTURIES. SOME FEASTS OCCUR ON THE SAME DAY EACH YEAR, BUT OTHERS MOVE DEPENDING ON THE LUNAR CYCLE.

Like the saints that they honour, Catholic feast days have been ranked and classified. Solemnity is the highest ranking of the holy days, but depending on the country it is not always a holy day of obligation. A feast day is the next highest rank of holy days, with celebrations that honour Jesus, Mary and the saints. A memorial is the lowest rank of holy days, a way of honouring saints without giving them fully fledged feast days. Below is a key to symbols that indicate if the feast has a fixed or moveable date, and when a day of obligation is celebrated by most countries or only those in Europe.

KEY
✝ moveable feast
⌘ fixed feast
✢ Holy Day of Obligation
❖ Additional European Holy Day of Obligation

Above: A calendar of saints' days from a 14th-century French Bible highlights the numerous days that were celebrated.

JANUARY
1 Solemnity of Mary Mother of God ⌘ ✢
6 Solemnity of Epiphany ⌘ ❖
13 Feast of Baptism of Jesus ⌘
25 Feast of the Conversion of St Paul ⌘

FEBRUARY
2 Feast of Candlemas (Presentation) ✝ ⌘
5 Shrove Tuesday ✝
6 Ash Wednesday ✝

MARCH
2 Laetare Sunday ✝
16 Palm Sunday ✝
19 Spy Wednesday ✝
19 St Joseph ✝
20 Maundy Thursday ✝
21 Good Friday ✝
23 Easter ✝
25 Solemnity of the Annunciation ⌘

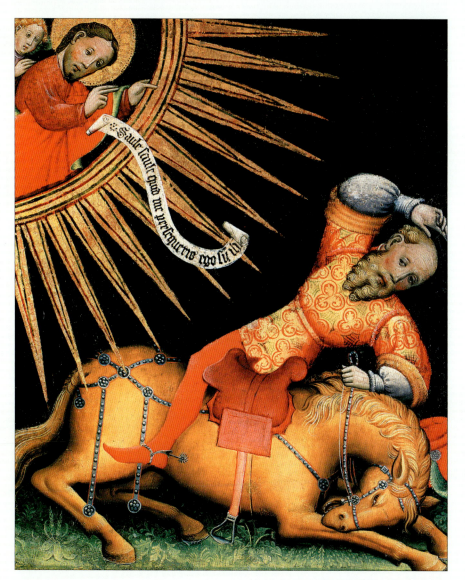

Left: St Paul's conversion to Christianity, captured in this 15th-century painting by Hildesheim, is celebrated on 25 January.

244

Above: Many feast days celebrate Jesus and the Virgin Mary, depicted together in this Byzantine painting.

Above: The holy days of All Saints and All Souls are celebrated in Mexico with graveside offerings, including pan de muertos *– bread made for the dead.*

JUNE
29 Solemnity of Sts Peter and Paul ❖

MAY
1 Ascension ✝ ✤
11 Pentecost ✝
18 Feast of Trinity Sunday ✝
22 Solemnity of Corpus Christi ✝ ❖
30 Sacred Heart of Jesus ✝
31 Immaculate Heart of Mary ✝

AUGUST
15 Solemnity of Assumption of Mary ⌘ ✤

SEPTEMBER
18 Birth of the Virgin Mary ⌘
29 Mass of archangels Michael, Raphael and Gabriel ⌘

NOVEMBER
1 All Saints' Day ⌘ ✤
2 All Souls' Day ⌘
23 Feast of Christ the King ⌘
30 First Sunday of Advent ✝

Above: Michael, Raphael and Gabriel, the only archangels in the Scriptures, share a feast day in September. They are shown in this 15th-century image by Domenico di Michelino with Tobias, an encounter described in the Book of Tobit.

DECEMBER
7 Second Sunday of Advent ✝
8 Feast of the Immaculate Conception ⌘ ✤
14 Gaudete Sunday (Third Sunday of Advent) ✝
21 Fourth Sunday of Advent ✝
25 Christmas Day ⌘ ✤
28 Solemnity of the Holy Family ✝

Above In Valencia, Spain, the feast of Corpus Christi is marked with processions of rocas, *carts decorated with holy statues.*

Left: Christmas in midwinter, lights against the darkness – despite the debate and uncertainty about the true date of Christ's birth, it is celebrated around the world on 25 December.

245

A CHILD IS BORN

CHRISTMAS, A SEASON THAT CATHOLICS DEVOTE TO THE CELEBRATION OF JESUS' BIRTH, ENCOMPASSES TWO PERIODS IN THE CATHOLIC CHURCH: ADVENT AND CHRISTMASTIDE.

Advent is a season of preparation that is about four weeks long, although it is sometimes a little shorter, depending on the day of the week the 25th falls on. It will always include four Sundays. Christmastide is the period from Christmas Day to the feast of the Epiphany on 6 January – the traditional 12 days of Christmas.

CELEBRATING ADVENT

Like the secular Christmas, the Catholic Christmas (from Old English *Cristes Maesse*, or "Mass of Christ") involves weeks of preparation. However, unlike the frenzied weeks of shopping promoted by the worldly media, the four weeks of Advent (from the Latin *Adventus*, or

Above: The Magi, probably Persian kings, visited Christ when he was nearly a year old – not in the stable, as some traditions suggest. Gerard David captured the visit in his Adoration of the Kings, *c.1515.*

"coming") involve steady spiritual preparation, marked by a certain amount of sober sacrifice and longing in the beginning, but as Christmas Day approaches, a mounting sense of joy. On the third Sunday of Advent, known as Gaudete (or "Rejoice") Sunday, the heightened anticipation is symbolized by a change in the colour of the priest's vestments from purple to rose.

Celebration of Advent originated in the 5th century, when Bishop Perpetuus of Tours decreed a fast, known as "St Martin's Lent", from St Martin's Day (11 November) to Christmas. In the 6th century, Pope Gregory the Great shortened Advent to four weeks, its modern duration, and strict fasting gave way to a less rigorous abstinence from meat and dairy. The liturgy of Advent emphasizes that preparation for Christ's first coming at his birth prefigures the preparations that Christians should make for his Second Coming.

THE NATIVITY

One of the most widely known and beloved stories is that of Christ's Nativity. The tradition of the divine birth in a primitive stable in the depth

---

DOMESTIC RITUALS

The domestic rituals of Advent evolved as expressions of the longing and expectation that characterize the season. The colourful family ceremonies are particularly attractive to children, helping them to focus on the spiritual rather than the commercial meaning of the season. The Advent wreath is a circular wreath of evergreens with four evenly spaced candles, three violet and one rose, to represent the four weeks of Advent. The violet symbolizes penitence, and the rose, lit on the third Sunday known as Gaudete Sunday, represents joy at the imminent approach of the Nativity. Families gather at a weekly Sunday dinner to light the candles, a new candle as each week passes, and dine by their light in the December evening. Some modern wreaths also include a white candle, symbolic of Jesus, that is lit on Christmas Eve. The familial ritual reminds Catholics of the intimate scene of the Holy Family within the snug stable.

Nativity scenes are usually small enough to fit on a table or mantelpiece. Some are simple and homemade, others are heirloom sets crafted by old world-artisans. The stable, the barn animals and the manger are arranged before Christmas, and Mary and Joseph are allowed to set up housekeeping, but the infant Jesus and the Magi must await the day appointed for their arrival in Scripture. Meanwhile, each day children add a few wisps of straw to the manger. By Christmas Eve, the manger will be comfortable for the infant figure, who arrives on time and with ceremony – gently placed in the manger at midnight on Christmas Eve. On Epiphany, the royal visitors from the East arrive, and the three kings are added to the stable scene.

Right: The weekly ritual of lighting the Advent wreath in church or at home helps children understand the spiritual significance of the Advent season.

A CHILD IS BORN

Right: Although born in a humble setting, the Christ child seems to transfix the gaze of all in this 15th-century illustration by Rosello Franchi and Filippo Torelli.

of winter concentrates the sense of mystery and delight that Catholics experience during this season. However, despite the hold that the Nativity story has on the popular imagination, the date of Jesus' birth is still unknown, and the only gospel to describe the Nativity is Luke, Chapter 2, in just a few words that have echoed down the centuries:

And she brought forth her first born son and wrapped him in swaddling clothes and laid him in a manger: because there was no room for them in the inn.

Around this quiet description, combined with the telling in Matthew, Chapter 2 of the wise men from the East who saw the star of the King of the Jews and travelled to seek and adore him, has arisen the vast tradition of the Christian Nativity in story and especially in art.

A DATE IN QUESTION
In the early centuries of the Church, Christmas was not celebrated; some early theologians, such as Origen (AD 185–254), viewed celebrating the birthday of Christ with disfavour, calling it a pagan custom. The actual date of Christ's birth was also much disputed. Scriptural evidence for the date of the Nativity is inconclusive, and many scholars have argued that shepherds would not have kept their flocks in the fields at night in winter. The choice of 25 December was a compromise. Because the Church identified Christ with the coming of the light of redemption, it seemed most natural to celebrate the birth of "Christ Our Light" at a time when light was reborn after the solstice on 21 December. The date also takes advantage of a deep-rooted human urge to celebrate at this time; the Roman holiday of *Sol Invictus*, or the birth of the Unconquered Sun, and the birthday of Mithras, the Persian God of Light, were both celebrated in December. By the 4th century, Christ's birth was celebrated in Rome on 25 December; early celebrations of Christmas were often combined with the older celebrations of Epiphany on 6 January.

Right: The birth of Christ Our Light, after the winter solstice, reached its fruition at the Transfiguration, when Christ shone before his apostles. Fra Angelico painted the scene in The Transfiguration, *1436–45.*

CARNIVAL!

THE MOST JUBILANT OF ALL OF THE CATHOLIC FESTIVALS, CARNIVAL IS INEXTRICABLY LINKED TO LENT, THE MOST AUSTERE. CARNIVAL HAS BEEN CELEBRATED BY CATHOLICS FOR SEVERAL CENTURIES.

As the predecessor to Lent in Catholic countries, carnival is a riotous indulgence of role reversal and licentious behaviour that has occurred for centuries. The word "carnival" probably derives from the medieval Latin phrase *carnem levare*, meaning "to remove meat". The linking of carnival and Lent in the calendar expresses an apparently innate human desire for cycles of feast and famine.

Some historians suggest that the Catholic Church was aware that carnival, which originated in southern European countries, was simply the ancient Roman pagan festival of Saturnalia under another name, yet tolerated the festival in order to smooth the transition from old pagan observances to those of the new religion. However, it is also true that the Catholic Church, especially when compared to the more sober Christian sects, such as Puritans or Quakers, has always had an appreciation of festival and pageantry.

EARLY CELEBRATIONS

Contemporary carnivals are often associated with Rio de Janeiro – which mixes the European tradition with native American and African cultures: Venice, New Orleans and the Caribbean – and they almost always include vast costume parades with elaborate floats. However, carnival celebrations in Catholic countries have a long history – the Venetian carnival is mentioned in documents from 1092. In ancient times, carnival is said to have begun just after Epiphany (6 January) and lasted until Shrove Tuesday (*see* Shrove Tuesday, *below*), but in Rome the carnival was permitted to last for eight days, from the Monday of the week before Lent until Shrove Tuesday.

Above: Like carnival, the Roman festival of Saturnalia was officially approved and served as an antidote to a more solemn time – Saturnalia was held in mid-winter; and carnival before Lent.

THE POPE AND CARNIVAL

Right up through the 19th century, Rome held a famous carnival that was supported, sometimes implicitly and sometimes explicitly, by the popes. No Roman carnival could begin without a papal edict, and depending on the reigning pope, that edict might be withheld.

Some popes, such as the 15th-century Pope Paul II, were involved in planning for carnival. Paul II ordered the Jewish people of Rome to pay a yearly tax of 1,130 gold florins

---

SHROVE TUESDAY

The British version of carnival, which is held on the day before the first day of Lent, is Shrove Tuesday. It takes its name from the verb "to shrive", meaning to absolve of sin and give penance. Medieval custom was to confess and receive penance just before Lent in order to approach the austere week in a state of penitent purity.

A more whimsical name for Shrove Tuesday is Pancake Day because fasting was practised during Lent, and pancakes were a convenient way to use up any remaining eggs, milk and butter. This particular Tuesday has many aliases and is also known as Mardi Gras, which is French for another common name, Fat Tuesday. New Orleans is renowned for its Mardi Gras, its carnival celebrations that culminate on Fat Tuesday.

Right: A 19th-century vignette by Basile de Loose shows the making of pancakes, enjoyed by young and old.

Above: The pre-Lenten celebration of carnival reaches its apotheosis in Rio de Janeiro's sambodrome, a custom-built parade ground for carnival extravaganzas.

(the 30 added to recall Judas and the 30 pieces of silver), and the money was spent on carnival. Paul II also paid, straight from the papal treasury, for races for the elderly, children, asses and bulls. Conversely, Pope Sixtus V (elected in 1585) directed that gibbets and whipping posts be erected on the piazzas as a warning not to let carnival licentiousness to verge to the criminal.

In the 16th century, the Church attempted to steal carnival's thunder by holding a 40-hour prayer service on Monday and Shrove Tuesday – however, the 40 hours of prayer did not have a lasting negative effect on carnival's popularity.

RACES AND CANDLES

The high points of the Roman carnival, popular from the 17th century onward, were the race of Berber horses and the Race of the Candles, both held in the Via del Corso. The riderless horses were released, wearing balls full of sharp pins hanging from their sides to goad them on down the crowded Corso. In 1882, 15 people were killed when the horses charged into the crowd, and that put an end to this tradition.

The Festa dei Moccoletti (candles) was held on the last night of carnival, when the people dressed in costume, and carrying candles and lanterns, swarmed through the streets trying to put out others' candles while keeping their own lit. The custom also ended in the 19th century, but children in Rome still celebrate it by going to school in costume.

Above: The Race of the Candles involved three wooden pillars – representing Sts George, Ubaldo and Anthony – raced to the basilica. They seem ready to topple in this 19th-century Italian illustration.

ASH WEDNESDAY AND LENT

Lent is an austere period of spiritual preparation leading up to Easter. It starts on Ash Wednesday, and devout Catholics fast during this 40-day period.

Lent is a period of penitence and self-denial. It developed as an adaptation of an ascetic period of study and prayer followed by early postulants converting to Christianity. They undertook this period before being baptized on Easter eve. Pre-baptism instruction in these early centuries also included exorcism; descriptions of such initiation preparations are found in the 3rd-century *Apostolic Tradition*, a written collection of early Christian practices attributed to St Hippolytus. The word "Lent" derives from Middle English *Lenten*, or "spring", and is related to the German root for "long", because the days in spring get longer.

Below: A 16th-century Flemish artist has portrayed carnival as a corpulent figure among revellers. He is armed with a spitted fowl, ready to do battle with the opposing force of Lent, who thrusts a baker's paddle bearing fish toward him.

THE PERIOD OF LENT

Lent lasts for a total of 40 days, in imitation of the number of days Christ was in the wilderness, fasting and withstanding the temptations of Satan (Matthew 4:1–2, Mark 1:12–13, Luke 4:1–2). Until the 600s, Lent always began on Quadragesima Sunday, 40 days before Easter, but Pope Gregory the Great moved the start to Ash Wednesday to achieve 40 days without counting Sundays, which are feast days, when fasting is relaxed. During Lent, fasting was general: law courts were closed (in AD 380, the Roman emperor Gratian decreed that all legal proceedings be suspended for 40 days); theatres were shuttered; and hunting and military manoeuvres were all forbidden.

THE START OF LENT

On Ash Wednesday, priests smear the foreheads of penitents with ash (made by burning the palms used

Above: Jesus' 40-day fast in the desert, when he was tempted by the devil, is captured in this 19th-century painting by Ivan Nikolaevich Kramskoy. It is the model for the 40-day period of Lent.

in the previous year's Palm Sunday celebration) in the shape of a cross, saying "Remember that you are dust, and to dust you shall return" (Genesis 3:19), a reminder to those who have revelled in the excesses of Mardi Gras. Expressing penitence by using ashes is a custom inherited from ancient Jewish observance. In the Old Testament, Job expresses penitence to God with the words, "Therefore I despise myself and repent in dust and ashes" (Job 42:6).

Right: Lent's sobriety is represented by this stark composition of ash and palm, invoking the two celebrations of Ash Wednesday and Palm Sunday.

In the early days of Christianity, ashes were used for those who had declared serious sins and asked to be shriven; the penance imposed began on Ash Wednesday and exiled the penitents from society for the 40 days of Lent; this custom is the genesis of the word "quarantine". The ashes were not smeared in a cross but sprinkled on the heads of the sinners. Over time, a public display of humility and penitence by the mark of the ashen cross became widespread.

FASTING DURING LENT

Lent has always been associated with fasting; there is a scriptural basis for this, as in Matthew 9:15, Christ, when questioned why his disciples, unlike the Pharisees, did not fast, commented, "Days will come, when the bridegroom shall be taken away from them, and then they shall fast." It was after Jesus' departure that Christians began fasting. By the 12th century, St Bernard of Clairvaux noted that Lenten fasting was general: "kings, and princes, clergy and laity…" all fasted. When King Wenceslaus of Bohemia needed to eat meat during Lent due to ill health, he first sought dispensation from the pope. The "Black Fast" referred to one meal, taken in the evening, consisting of bread, herbs and water. Rules for fasting have become more lenient over time, but devout Catholics will still fast on Lenten Fridays.

MODERN FASTING

For today's Catholics, 40 days of Lenten fasting in imitation of Christ's trial and temptation in the wilderness can be a particularly instructive experience, as we are so accustomed to relative plenty. A strict fast today is defined as only one meal, with two smaller meals that taken together would not equal a full meal. Animal foods, except fish, are avoided. As Christ lay in the tomb for 40 hours, the devout undertake a total fast for 40 hours just prior to Easter.

Catholics often undertake fasting as a family affair (although children under 14, according to canon law, are not required to fast), with the entire family choosing to give up meat, dessert, television or video games, then donating the money saved by this abstinence to charity, following the ancient Lenten tradition of almsgiving. Catholics are also encouraged to allow a sort of spiritual plenty to fill the space no longer occupied by temporal delights – Lent is a time of prayer and meditation. For this little time, Catholics follow the rigorous practice of monks, hoping to achieve some of the same religious insight.

Participating in fasting and other forms of abstinence are understood to be physical self-control that mirrors spiritual discipline. The Catholic catechism describes fasting as an "interior penance" and "spiritual preparation" that prepares Catholics for the arrival of Christ in the Eucharist, at his Resurrection and at the Second Coming.

Below: On Ash Wednesday, the first of Lent's 40 days, Catholics wear a cross of ash on the forehead, a symbol of penitence since Old Testament times.

HOLY WEEK

THE WEEK LEADING UP TO EASTER IS A PERIOD IN WHICH CATHOLICS REMEMBER AND MOURN THE SUFFERING OF JESUS, WHEN HE WAS SACRIFICED ON THE CROSS TO REDEEM HUMANKIND.

The week before Easter begins with Palm Sunday and extends to the vigil of Easter at sunset on Holy Saturday; it is known as Holy Week. During Holy Week devout Catholics follow along with Christ in a respectful attempt to take on the burden of the agony that he accepted as the price for their redemption.

Before the agony in the garden, anticipating the trial about to come, Christ said to Peter and the sons of Zebedee, "I am sorrowful even unto death….Stay you here and watch with me" (Matthew 26:38). The apostles, though, fell asleep, leaving Christ alone; he reproached them with, "Could you not watch one hour with me?" (Matthew 26:40). The liturgy and customs of Holy Week draw Catholics along with Christ's Passion, so that they "watch" with Christ and try to make reparation for that original abandonment.

IN MOURNING

The stark and mournful tone of Holy Week is marked in many churches by obscuring all statues and crucifixes in purple veiling. The custom derives from the European tradition of hiding the altar crucifix behind a

Above: Judas was paid 30 pieces of silver to betray Christ. He is shown with the apostles' money bag in this 16th-century fresco by Eglise St Sébastien Plampinet.

hanging that would be dropped to the ground during Palm Sunday, and reading from Matthew 27:51: "And behold the veil of the temple was rent in two from the top even to the bottom." This was one of the cataclysms that followed Christ's death. The liturgical atmosphere is of a community in mourning: the altar is not decorated with flowers, and the Te Deum and gloria are not sung.

FROM PALM SUNDAY

In Scripture, Holy Week begins with the entry of Jesus into Jerusalem, his way strewn with palms and lauded with the Hosannas of the multitude, an event described by all four Evangelists. However, the triumph was short-lived; by Friday, Jesus would hang from the Cross. Today the entry into Jerusalem is commemorated as Palm Sunday. Palms are distributed at Mass, and some palms are saved to burn to make ashes for the next year's Ash Wednesday, symbolically linking

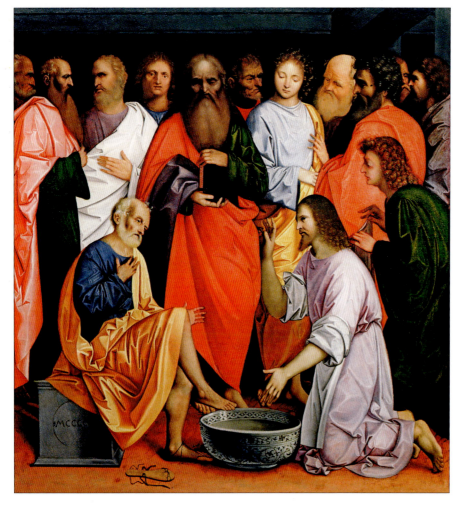

Left: After the Last Supper, Christ washed the apostles' feet. The ritual of washing feet, shown in Giovanni Agostino da Lodi's painting, 1500, symbolizes repentance.

triumph (palms) and penitence and death (ash). Wednesday of Holy Week is also known as "Spy Wednesday", referring to Judas and his agreement to betray Christ for 30 pieces of silver.

THE HEART OF THE WEEK

Easter Triduum (*triduum* is Latin for "three days") refers to the three days at the heart of Holy Week: Maundy Thursday, Good Friday and Holy Saturday. In Anglo-Saxon times, the Triduum was called "The Still Days", referring to the sorrow Catholics feel at this time, as well as to the time Christ lay in the tomb.

Maundy Thursday has tremendous significance for the Catholic Church, because it is on this day, at the paschal meal of the Last Supper, that Christ instituted the Eucharist. "Maundy" from the Latin *Mandatum*, or "commandment", refers to Christ's injunction to the apostles at the Last Supper, "A new commandment I give unto you, That ye love one another; as I have loved you" (John 13:34).

In John's Gospel, there is also a description of Christ humbly washing the apostles' feet on this day, and some churches commemorate Holy Thursday by a ritual in which the diocesan bishop washes the feet of 12 parishioners. In monasteries, the tradition was for the abbot to wash the feet of an ordinary monk.

After Thursday evening Mass, known as the Mass of the Lord's Supper, the altar is stripped of all cloths and candles, and the Eucharist in its chalice is removed from the tabernacle on the central altar and set in an unobtrusive side altar, known as the "altar of repose". The central altar remains bare and desolate of the sacred presence for all of Good Friday, the day marking Christ's Crucifixion and his death. Many churches remain open so that their parishioners can stay and pray quietly, "watching" with Christ in his time of need.

Above: A cross is borne through the streets in Corsica, France, on Good Friday.

No masses are celebrated on Good Friday – the only day of the liturgical year on which it is forbidden to celebrate the Mass. Good Friday observances often include the Way of the Cross. Parishioners and clergy assemble in the late afternoon (Scripture notes that Christ died at the ninth hour, or 3 p.m.) at some public meeting place outdoors and carry a large cross in procession through the streets, stopping at designated points along the route to recite the Stations of the Cross. This public ritual is another example of the effort Catholics make during Holy Week to share and make reparation for the agony that Christ experienced for their sake.

THE TENEBRAE SERVICE

Although the events commemorated by Holy Week occurred around 2,000 years ago, the Tenebrae is designed to help Catholics bridge the emotional distance and experience Christ's Passion as though they were there. "Tenebrae" means "shadows or darkness", and the service makes its participants feel as though a dark cloud has just passed over the sun.

The elements of the Tenebrae date from the 5th century. The original Tenebrae services were held in monasteries in the earliest morning hours. Today the service is held on either Maundy Thursday or Good Friday, usually at dusk. The church is in semi-darkness, the only light source a triangular candelabra known as the hearse, from the Middle English *herse*, or "harrow" (the two were similar in shape). As the service of sorrowful psalms, chants and lamentations is read, the candles are extinguished one by one until only a single lit candle remains. Then the celebrants, making no sound, leave the altar, marooning the congregation in the dark, silent church. Suddenly, a rough, clattering noise, known as the *strepitus* (Latin for "wild din" or "crash") is heard. It represents the convulsion of the earth at Christ's death. The congregation file from the church in silence, their way lit only by a few candles as they depart.

Right: Since the 13th century, the hearse has held candles during the Tenebrae service. "Hearse" later came to refer to a candle frame over a coffin, and from that to the vehicle that carries a coffin.

THE RESURRECTION AND EASTER

AFTER THE SOMBRE HOLY WEEK, CATHOLICS AROUND THE WORLD CELEBRATE EASTER, A JOYOUS OCCASION COMMEMORATING THE RESURRECTION OF CHRIST OUR LIGHT.

To Catholics, Easter is the greatest Catholic celebration and completes the meaning of all that came before and all that followed and is to come in Christian history. Without Easter, Catholic doctrine has no point, but all of Christianity is enlivened by the Resurrection of Christ on Easter.

The name "Easter" in Germanic languages is derived from old English and Germanic root words referring to the East and dawn. *Eastre* or *Ostara* was also the Anglo-Saxon Teutonic goddess of spring and fertility. In France, Easter is known as *Pâques*, and all Romance language names for Easter are from *Pascha*, for "Passover".

HE IS RISEN

The Easter story can be simply told: two days after Christ was placed in the tomb of Joseph of Arimathea and a big stone rolled across the entrance, Mary Magdalene, Mary, the mother of James and Salome, and "the other women" (the gospels differ on who was with Mary Magdalene) visited the tomb to anoint the body with spices, only to find the stone rolled away and the sepulchre empty. An angel sitting on the stone informed them that Jesus had risen (*see Easter: The Quem Quaeritis, opposite*).

A DATE IN DISPUTE

Easter was first known as "Pasch", and the earliest references to it date from the 2nd century. Easter is a moveable feast, meaning that its date varies each year according to the lunar calendar (all of the other major Christian holidays follow the solar calendar). During the first centuries of Christianity, the correct date was disputed, but the First Council of Nicaea in AD 325 finally decreed that Easter was to be celebrated the first Sunday after the 14th day of the moon (approximately the full moon) following the date of the spring equinox (assumed to be 21 March). Therefore, Easter can come as early as 22 March or as late as 25 April. The dates of other holy days, such as Pentecost, depend on the Easter date. Easter's date is linked to the Jewish celebration of Passover, because the Last Supper, three days before Christ's Resurrection, was a Passover Seder.

CHRIST OUR LIGHT

After the darkness of the events of Holy Week, Catholics express their jubilation at the Resurrection in the traditional Easter vigil service. Near midnight on Easter eve, Catholics gather in a dimly lit church, symbolizing the darkness of Christ's tomb, and wait. Outside the church, a new fire is kindled and blessed. At midnight, priests light the paschal candle, marked with the Cross and the alpha and omega, symbols of Christ, from the new fire and process

Above: The unleavened bread of Passover has become in Catholicism the unleavened bread transubstantiated into the Eucharist. The bread is being made in this 15th-century detail from the Schocken Bible.

Left: Andrea Mantegna's dramatic 15th-century painting of Christ's Resurrection is scripturally inaccurate – according to the Bible no man or woman witnessed Christ coming forth from the tomb.

THE RESURRECTION AND EASTER

EASTER: THE QUEM QUAERITIS

Four lines of dialogue beginning in Latin *Quem Quaeritis*, or "Whom do you seek?" were the genesis of the theatrical tradition of miracle and mystery plays that began in the 10th century. The Quem Quaeritis is a trope, or elaboration, of the part of the Easter liturgy that describes Mary Magdalene and "the other women" finding Jesus' tomb empty, with an angel sitting on the great stone.

Whom do ye seek in the sepulchre, O followers of Christ?
Jesus of Nazareth, the Crucified, O heavenly ones.
He is not here; he is risen, just as he foretold.
Go, announce that he is risen from the sepulchre.

The original adapted dialogue has come down to us in manuscripts from the monks at the 10th-century Abbey of St Gall and in actual stage directions written *c.*AD 965 by Bishop Ethelwold for Benedictine monks at Winchester. The original four-line vignette was performed, in Latin, by priests in the church sanctuary. Such dramatic renditions by the clergy of parts of the Easter liturgy were so popular that the subject matter was expanded to dramatize episodes from the New Testament and the lives of the saints. Responsibility for productions was removed from the clergy and taken over by the guilds of medieval towns, who performed the plays in English, with non-reverent elements.

Above: Mystery plays, adaptations of biblical scenes, were produced in public squares on moveable stages known as pageant wagons, as depicted in this 16th-century English illustration.

into the dark Church, symbolizing the Resurrection of Christ our Light. Easter is also traditionally associated with the baptism of new converts to Christianity, and Easter vigil services often incorporate baptisms of new Catholics on this auspicious day. The custom of wearing new clothes at Easter derives from the fresh white robes worn by the newly baptized.

The association of light with Christ's Resurrection is also the symbolic basis of the sunrise services, a variation of the Easter vigil. Often held on a hilltop, the faithful wait to see the new light of dawn pierce the dim sky; after dawn, a mass is celebrated outdoors. Joyful Catholics may be greeted by their priest with the ancient traditional Easter greeting, "Christ is risen indeed!" The one greeted then replies with "And hath appeared unto Simon!"

Right: An Easter vigil opens with the kindling of a new paschal candle, a large white candle symbolizing the return of the light of Christ, which is relit throughout the year to mark sacred rites.

255

THE CATHOLIC YEAR

RELIGIOUS ORDERS

THERE ARE A GREAT MANY DIFFERENT ORDERS WITHIN THE CATHOLIC CHURCH. BELOW IS A LIST OF THE MAJOR RELIGIOUS ORDERS AND THEIR FOUNDERS, ARRANGED CHRONOLOGICALLY.

BENEDICTINES
The first great order of monks, founded by St Benedict of Nursia in 529.

CARTHUSIANS
Enclosed order, including both monks and nuns, established by St Bruno of Cologne, 1084.

CISTERCIANS
Reformist monastic order, founded by Robert of Molesme in 1098 and greatly expanded by St Bernard of Clairvaux.

CARMELITES
The Brothers (and Sisters) of Our Lady of Mount Carmel, founded in the 12th century on Mount Carmel, Israel.

TRINITARIANS
Order of the Holy Trinity, an order of priests, monks and nuns that was founded by St John de Matha in France in 1198.

FRANCISCANS
Friars (Mendicant Brothers), founded by St Francis of Assisi in 1209.

POOR CLARES
The Order of Poor Ladies, founded in Assisi, Italy, by St Clare with the help of St Francis in 1212.

DOMINICANS
Friars, predominantly a teaching order; established by St Dominic in southern France in c.1215.

AUGUSTINIANS
A group of monastic orders, incorporated as a "Grand Union" in 1256.

CAPUCHINS
The Order of Friars Minor Capuchin, following a back-to-first-principles re-foundation of the Franciscans, started by Matteo di Bascio in 1520.

THEATINES
The Congregation of Clerks Regular of the Divine Providence, known as the Theatines from their foundation in Chieti (Theate), Italy, founded in 1524 by St Cajetan.

Above: St Benedict of Nursia can be seen teaching his Rule to his monks in this 13th-century French illustration.

JESUITS
The Society of Jesus, founded by St Ignatius Loyola in 1534.

URSULINES
Order of nuns, devoted mainly to the teaching of girls, established in Italy by Ste Angela de Merici in 1535.

SISTERS OF LORETO
Order of nuns founded by Mary Ward, an Englishwoman in French exile, in 1609.

Above: St Bruno, founder of the Carthusian order, prays in the wilderness at Chartreuse, France, in this 17th-century painting by Nicolas Mignard.

Right A 14th-century sculpture shows St Bernard of Clairvaux, a leading Cistercian, carrying the chapel of Clairvaux, the abbey that he founded.

256

RELIGIOUS ORDERS

Above: St Ignatius Loyola presented the rule book for his newly established Society of Jesus to Pope Paul III (1534–49), shown in this anonymous painting.

CONGREGATION OF THE MISSION
Also known as the Lazarists or Vincentians, this order of priests was established by St Vincent de Paul in 1624.

DAUGHTERS OF CHARITY
Often referred to as Sisters of Charity, a congregation of nuns formed by St Vincent de Paul in 1633.

TRAPPISTS
An order of monks and nuns, a Cistercian offshoot named for France's La Trappe Abbey, where their famous rule of silence was first introduced in 1664.

LOVERS OF THE HOLY CROSS
Order of nuns, founded in 1670 in Vietnam and centred in the Far East.

REDEMPTORISTS
The Congregation of the Most Holy Redeemer, who are missionaries to the poor; the order was founded in Italy by St Alphonsus of Ligouri in 1732.

CONGREGATION OF CHRISTIAN BROTHERS
Commonly known as Christian Brothers, a congregation of lay brothers within the Roman Catholic Church, dedicated to educating poor boys worldwide; it was established by Edmund Ignatius Rice in Waterford, Ireland in 1808.

Above: Trappist monks perform their religious office at the Abbey Notre-Dame d'Aiguebelle, France. Prayer is an important part of their routine.

Above: An Indian nun from the Missionaries of Charity ministers to Calcutta's poor. Founder Mother Teresa won international renown for the charity's work with the destitute.

SOCIETY OF MARY
The Marist Fathers (the Marist Brothers are an offshoot), an order of teachers and workers dedicated to the poor, founded by William Joseph Chaminade in France, 1817.

LITTLE SISTERS OF THE POOR
Order of nuns dedicated to the care of the poor – especially the elderly – founded in France by Jeanne Jugan in 1839.

SOCIETY OF AFRICAN MISSIONS
Founded by Melchior de Marion Brésillac in 1850.

WHITE FATHERS
More formally, the Society of the Missionaries of Africa, founded in Algeria by the French cardinal Charles Lavigerie in 1868.

MISSIONARIES OF CHARITY
An order of nuns established in 1950 by Mother Teresa of Calcutta to help the poor.

SAINTS & SAINTHOOD

For hundreds of years, starting with the first martyrs of the early Church, saints were chosen by public acclaim. Gradually the bishops, and finally the Vatican, took over authority for approving saints, using a process known as Canonization. Being given the title of saint tells us that the individual lived a holy life, is in heaven, and is to be honoured by the Church. Canonization does not make a person a saint; it simply recognizes what God has already done.

The Last Supper (Leonardo da Vinci, c. 149–98) is a mural painting that represents a scene from the final days of Jesus with his apostles – 12 men chosen to be ambassadors of his teachings around the world. Eleven of the apostles later died cruel deaths for their faith, and many churches are dedicated to them.

SAINTHOOD

The company of saints is filled with souls from all walks of life. These former human beings have been granted the highest accolade that their fellow Christians can give in honour of their holiness and worldly achievements.

In this section, Sainthood, there is a clear explanation of the qualities a person must show before they are officially recognized as a saint. Many have devoted their lives to spreading the word of God, others have sacrificed their own well-being for the welfare of their fellow men, women and children. Believers choose candidates for sainthood from a spontaneous understanding of their superior qualities as humans, but the Church is more circumspect in granting this status.

Official and non-official attitudes within the Church are given a full history, and the religious beliefs surrounding saints are clearly described. Also covered is the alteration of custom and religious practice brought by the religious wars of the Reformation, a change that affected the regard in which saints are now held. Ritual expressions of faith, such as pilgrimages and the veneration of shrines and relics, are analysed in both historic and modern expressions. Feast days and the festivals that have developed around these occasions are discussed. The reasoning behind certain saints being selected as patrons of nations, professions and causes is explained. This is not a history of the Church, but a revelation of the role saints play in art and the prayers of the faithful.

Left: Detail of Procession in St Mark's Square *(Gentile Bellini, c.1500).*

SAINTHOOD

WHAT IS A SAINT?

A SAINT IS A DEAD INDIVIDUAL WHOSE EXCEPTIONAL HOLINESS CHRISTIANS BELIEVE HAS EARNED HIM OR HER A PLACE IN HEAVEN. THERE, SAINTS ACT AS CELESTIAL AGENTS. THE FAITHFUL MAY PRAY TO THEM AND BESEECH THEM TO CONVEY THEIR PRAYERS TO GOD.

Above: Detail from the Communion of the Apostles, *a 15th-century fresco at Platanistasa in Cyprus.*

Saints are not gods, they are not worshipped. But they are believed to exist so close to God in heaven that they fulfil a key role as intermediaries for the Roman Catholic and Eastern Orthodox Churches.

Lacking the temerity to approach God directly, worshippers call upon these holy souls for assistance. In 1545, the defining Council of Trent stated that the saints, who "reign" with Christ, offer people's prayers to God to obtain his benefits.

A Christian mystic once described the feelings of all believers when he said, "We worship Christ, as the Son of God; as to the saints, we love them as the disciples and imitators of the Lord."

CULT FOLLOWING

From the earliest days of the Church, the cultus (cult) of veneration developed to include figures besides Jesus who were deemed to be holy. Their lives, which showed great piety and humility, served as inspiration to the inchoate community of believers.

On the day of their death, these holy individuals were believed to have been reborn into God's presence. Possessing this elevated status, the saints quickly developed cult followings. Their death was commemorated with a feast day, at which time typically the faithful would gather at the saint's tomb. The bodily remains, or relics, were believed to possess power. Not only were saints in a privileged position to get prayers answered, but they could also work fabulous miracles.

MARTYRS

The judgement of an individual's imitation of Christ in this early period of Christianity was concerned as much with the manner of their death as with the conduct of their life. A martyr – he or she who dies for the Christian faith – became an automatic choice for the company of saints. As the Church grew, especially once the pope became the sole authority in conferring such status in the 2nd millennium, other factors became as important, if not more so, in determining a saint.

HEROIC VIRTUE

Those who did not die a martyr had to be shown by their cultus to have led a life of "heroic virtue", as it is defined by the Vatican. In Christian terms, this means they

Right: From the early Renaissance, Madonna Enthroned with Saints *(Domenico Ghirlandaio, 1484).*

262

WHAT IS A SAINT?

must have abandoned worldly interests. Whatever their station in life, whether prince(ss) or pauper, their devotion to faith in Jesus had to be manifest in their humility, charity and prayer.

As bureaucracy and suspicion played ever greater roles in the assessment process, so fewer saints were created. The late John Paul II did much to rationalize and clarify the procedure of canonization (literally, adding a name to the canon of saints).

SINNERS REDEEMED
Not all saints led virtuous lives from beginning to end. Some were formerly tyrants, thieves or prostitutes before they turned to Christ. Even St Paul once cheered the stoning of the martyr St Stephen. St Pelagia was a harlot.

But these lives inspire believers, who feel hope when they learn that anyone might be redeemed through devotion. Perhaps St Paul summed up the quality of sainthood best when he said, "I live, yet not I, but Christ liveth in me."

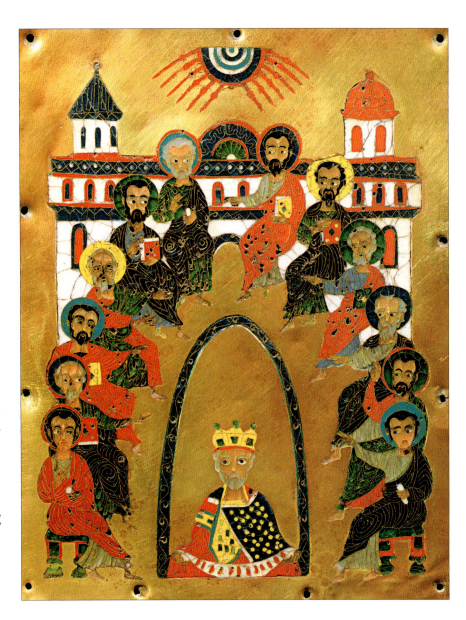

Right: A panel showing Christ and the apostles at Pentecost (Georgian School, 12th century).

SAINTS IN OTHER FAITHS

Veneration of holy people, as messengers of the Almighty, has a place outside the Christian faith, too. Judaism refers to a category of holy figures known as Tzadikkim. In Islam, certain holy men, known as *Sufis*, are remembered with festivals. Thousands of Muslims in Pakistan, for example, commemorate the life and death of a 12th-century Sufi, Lal Shahbaz Qalandar, with sacred songs and dances performed by dervishes (followers of Sufism).

In Hinduism, *Sadhus*, or holy men, are considered to have reached saintly status while still alive. Likewise, in Buddhism, *Arhats* are monks who are considered to have reached a state of nirvana.

Although there are some similarities in concept between the faiths, each has its own meaning. None are identical with that of Christian sainthood, which constitutes a unique doctrine of heavenly community.

Right: Dancing dervishes from a Persian miniature (c.1650).

SAINTHOOD

SAINTS IN THE EARLY CHURCH

THE FIRST CHRISTIANS WERE FORBIDDEN TO PRACTISE THEIR FAITH AND WERE CRUELLY PERSECUTED BY THE ROMANS. MANY EVEN DIED FOR THEIR BELIEFS. THESE MARTYRS WERE HONOURED AS SAINTS BY THEIR FELLOW BELIEVERS IN THE EARLY CHURCH.

There has never been any argument over the saintly status of the Holy Family, or the apostles and friends of Jesus on earth, but other saints have had slower recognition, or their status has been disputed. The earliest figures chosen for sainthood were usually those who died as martyrs.

Christianity was born in Palestine, a land that was then part of the Roman Empire. The Roman authorities who had condemned Jesus to death forbade any practice of his faith. Periodic state persecutions of Christians were merciless.

Whole communities who refused to abandon their faith were massacred, and some individuals suffered hideous torture. Some, dressed in rags with no weapon, were pitted against well-armed Roman gladiators, or fierce beasts. Thousands were murdered. While the names of many survive, we know few details beyond the date, and perhaps the place, of their death.

Records of these martyrs, the first Christians, can be read in the grave inscriptions found in the catacombs of Rome where the dead were laid to rest.

EARLIEST MARTYRS

The first martyr (protomartyr) known to us was murdered about five years after the death of Christ. St Stephen was carried to the outskirts of Jerusalem and stoned to death. As he fell to his knees, he cried out, "Lord, lay not this sin to their charge." Thus, in his dying, he showed his belief in

Above: St Agnes, fellow virgins and singing angels in an altarpiece from the Upper Rhine (c.1460).

Jesus' message of love and forgiveness towards the wrongdoer. Many of the early martyrs showed a similar courage in their deaths. St Catherine of Alexandria endured the cruel spikes of a wheel. St Lucy refused to forsake her faith, even under torture, and was savagely beheaded.

It must be accepted that many legends grew up around the martyrs. For instance, although Lucy's tormentors had gouged out her eyes, it was said that she could fit them back into their sockets. Likewise, it was said that divine intervention broke Catherine's wheel, rescuing her from pain. Sebastian survived being tied to a column and shot through by a shower of arrows. And, when Januarius was thrown to the lions, the beasts refused to attack him, instead laying quiescent at his feet. There are accounts of saints being thrown into vats of boiling oil and

Below: The martyrdom of St Erasmus as illustrated in the Golden Legend, *a 13th-century hagiography of saints written by Jacobus de Voragine.*

264

emerging unscathed. Others who suffered a beheading were said to have merely replaced their heads.

BLESSED VIRGINS
Many of the earliest female saints were chosen not only for their status as martyrs, but also for their purity in imitation of the Blessed Virgin. The importance of virginity has always been a strong (but not essential) consideration in the sainthood of women. As late as the 15th century, when St Joan of Arc claimed this status, she was given humiliating physical inspections to test the truth of her words.

During the Roman persecutions, St Agnes, at the age of 13, consecrated her virginity to Christ. She refused marriage, and both her faith and innocence were put to the sword. St Irene, a young girl, was forced by the Romans to go naked into a brothel, but she radiated such purity that no man dared go near her. She was martyred in AD 305. In the same century, the most extravagant legend of proud virgins involves the British St Ursula and her 11,000 virgin companions. Forced to flee their homelands to avoid "violation" through marriage, they finally reached Germany. There they were martyred for their beliefs, yet they died joyously.

TRUTH IN LEGEND
Sceptics tend to dismiss these tales. But Christians honour them because they symbolize the superhuman courage and piety of the persecuted, and confirm that all suffering is eased by faith in Christ. As the novelist Sir Arthur Conan Doyle once said, "a legend however exaggerated upon fact is its own fact, witnessing belief". Although in many cases these stories are embellishments of a terrible reality, they still hold a certain truth for believers.

THE CATACOMBS OF ROME
Beneath the city of Rome lies a great labyrinth of caves and tunnels. Probably first used by pagans as burial grounds, the early Christians tunnelled into this underground world to lay their dead. Some of the catacombs had been dug out to form large halls with connecting chapels. Recesses were hollowed out to hold three or four bodies apiece. They were sealed with slabs of marble or tiles bearing inscriptions and motifs. The labyrinth was also used as a place of refuge to escape Roman persecutors. By the late 4th century AD, the catacombs were no longer burial vaults but pilgrimage sites, which are still visited today.

Above: The interior of a catacomb in Rome dating from the 3rd century AD.

Left: One of the 40 martyrs of Sebaste being killed in AD 320, during the Roman persecution of Christians under the rule of Emperor Licinius (Byzantine, 12th century).

SAINTHOOD

DOCTORS OF THE CHURCH

Leaders emerged from the early Christian communities to help develop the structure of the Church. Learned writers and thinkers among them who made significant contributions were called "Doctors of the Church".

A landmark change in the fortunes of the Church occurred early in the 4th century AD, when Emperor Constantine I converted to Christianity. His edict permitting the worship of all faiths meant saints were no longer chosen primarily for their martyrdom. More important was the purity of a life dedicated to Christ. Some did so by renouncing the world; others played key roles in developing the Church for the benefit of the flock.

Scholarly writers and thinkers worked on formulating doctrine for the Church. Some helped develop new forms of prayer and

Above: St Augustine of Hippo *(Piero della Francesca, 15th century).*

ritual. The greatest among these learned Christians were the early "Doctors of the Church", a term meaning great teachers. Unlike other saints who are championed by the people, the Church authorities alone decide who is worthy to receive this title.

GREAT TEACHERS

To be recognized as a Doctor, the saint must formulate a special doctrine. Alternatively, he or she may make a profound interpretation of the faith, as well as having a "remarkable holiness" of life.

St Jerome (c. AD 341–420), who started his life as a monk, translated the Bible from Greek into Latin. St Ambrose interpreted the significance of the sacraments, and

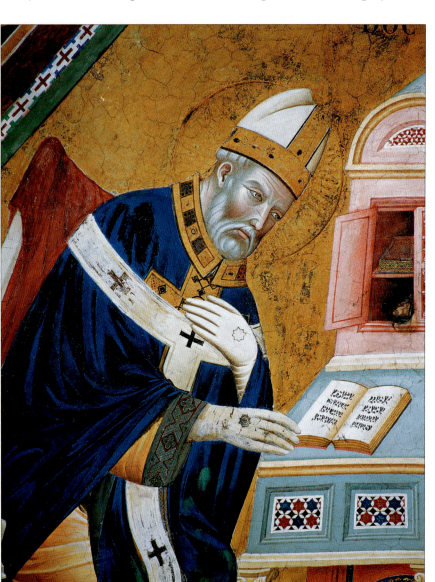

Left: Detail of St Ambrose from the fresco Doctors of the Church *(Giotto di Bondone, 13th century).*

266

DOCTORS OF THE CHURCH

defended the authority vested in the office of the pope. St Gregory the Great (c.AD 540–604) was a successful missionary, notably directing the conversion of the English. St Augustine of Hippo's interpretation of Christ's message profoundly influenced Christian moral principles.

MODERN DECLARATIONS
Recognition as a Doctor of the Church could be a long process, sometimes taking centuries to complete. Sts Ambrose, Jerome, Augustine of Hippo and Gregory the Great all lived before the 8th century, but they were not declared Doctors until Pope Benedict XIV came to office in 1740.

The tradition of creating doctorships still continues today. St Theresa of Lisieux (1873–97) was declared a Doctor by John Paul II in 1997 for her simple but inspirational devotion. She is now one of the most popular of saints.

Above: St Gregory in the Golden Legend *(Jacobus de Voragine, c.1370).*

DESERT FATHERS
Christ said, "If any man will follow me, let him deny himself, take up his cross and follow me" (Mark 8:34). In the first centuries of Christianity, there were believers who took these words as a direction to forsake all earthly pleasure. They followed the example of John the Baptist in hoping that hardship would wash away their sinful selves, and isolated themselves from society by living in deserts and other uninhabited places.

They led harsh lives, with little food. Legends say they were fed by ravens or wolves, and that water gushed from stony wastelands. The genuine humility and devotion shown by these ascetics attracted others, and soon groups of hermits chose to inhabit huts and caves close to each other.

From these loose communities, particularly those in Egypt, emerged teachers known as the "Desert Fathers". First among them was St Pachomius, who lived alone on the banks of the Nile until other ascetics gathered around him. Some were so fanatical in their contempt for their own bodies they risked starvation and madness. To impose some constraints, Pachomius set up a community of 100 followers who committed to abide by his "Rules". To vows of chastity, poverty and obedience, he added orders of prayer and routine.

By his death, c.AD 346, Pachomius had founded ten monasteries, among the first such Christian institutions. Another popular Egyptian hermit of the 4th century, St Antony, also organized a monastic community. Over the centuries many other founders have established similar orders.

Above: This 12th-century wall painting from Macedonia depicts St Antony, sometimes referred to as "the eremite" for his desert life.

SAINTHOOD

EASTERN SAINTS

THE CHURCHES OF RUSSIA, EASTERN EUROPE AND THE MIDDLE EAST DEVELOPED THEIR OWN THEOLOGY, VARYING FROM THAT OF ROMAN CATHOLICISM. EASTERN SAINTS FORM A DISTINCT COMPANY AND EVOKE A PARTICULAR KIND OF VENERATION.

The Eastern Church treats its saints in a slightly different way from that of Rome. Saints are not approached primarily as a means of conveying prayers to God, but rather to bring the believer closer to the reality of God. The reason for this difference lies in the Eastern Church's separate development in history from the West.

A formal schism between Western and Eastern Christians in 1054 led to the formation of a branch of Christendom known as the Eastern Orthodox Church. The two branches of Christianity had different beliefs about the dual nature of Christ, as both man and God.

The Roman Catholic and Orthodox Churches both believe that Christ is the Son of God who nevertheless assumed human form. The Orthodox interprets this to mean humans can attain the spiritual

Left: An icon of St Gregory Palamas (Russian School, 19th century).

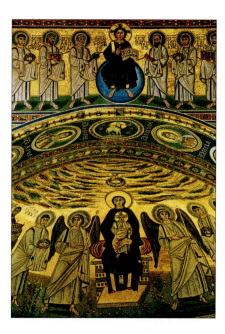

Above: Mosaic detail in the apse of the Basilica Eufrasiana in Poreč, Croatia (4th century). The work draws the eye to focus on the Blessed Virgin and the Christ child.

qualities of God; the Roman Church believes humans can only strive for these qualities.

The Orthodox Church has not altered its dogma or ritual since the 8th century. So tradition is paramount, and the saints form a key part of their worship.

EARLY HOLY FIGURES
Pre-eminent among the Eastern saints is the Blessed Virgin. But everyone who is in heaven is a saint for the Orthodox, including pre-Christian Jews such as Moses. Popular early saints, such as John, Nicholas of Myra, George and Christopher, are common to both branches, but post-medieval saints are not.

The Orthodox categorize their saints according to type: prophets (those who foretold the coming

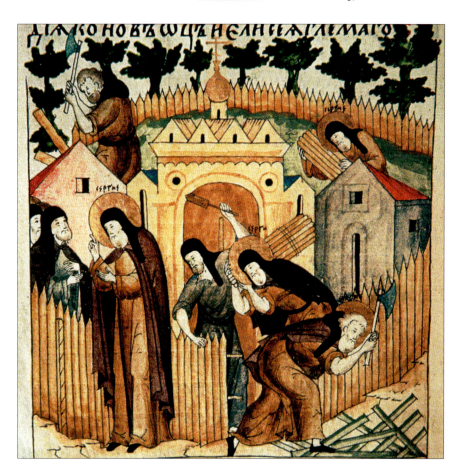

Left: Detail from a manuscript showing St Sergius of Radonezh overseeing the building of a church (Andrei Rublev, 15th century).

268

EASTERN SAINTS

of Jesus), the apostles, martyrs, Church Doctors (or Fathers), monastics (Desert Fathers) and the just (those who imitate Christ).

St John Chrysostom is highly honoured as a preacher and teacher. In AD 398, he was elected as Archbishop of Constantinople (now Istanbul) and is recognized as a Doctor of the Church.

Another Doctor is St Basil the Great (c.AD 330–79), who laid down rules of organization for monastic life. His friend, St Gregory of Nazianzus, also ranks high among Orthodox saints.

BYZANTINE MYSTICS

St Gregory's spiritual theology was developed by Simeon the New Theologian (d.1022) to reach a high point in Byzantine mysticism. Another Gregory, of Sinai (d.1346), devised new methods of meditation that influenced Orthodox practice. Other saints include Sergius of Radonezh (c.1315–92), monastic founder beloved of the Russians.

Mount Athos in Greece has a tradition of saintliness. Here the monk St Gregory Palamas (d.1359) founded an ascetical order, Hesychasm. Controversially it claimed visions of God's "uncreated light", an idea later accepted.

Below: The transfiguration of Christ in an Armenian manuscript (1362).

WINDOWS INTO HEAVEN

The Eastern Orthodox Church regards images of the holy saints as "windows of perception". It is believed these images open a vista leading to God. By so doing, they convey the message of the gospels.

Images of saints often appear on icons and architectural mosaics, rarely as statues. Depictions are lavishly decorated, with details worked in gold. In following the traditional Byzantine style of art, these images reflect the conservative nature of the Orthodox Church.

The icons are portable, being painted on three folding panels, and are designed as objects of meditation. By creating "a window into heaven", their contemplation and prayer increases the spirituality of the believer, bringing them closer to a knowledge of God.

Whether in church or at home, the icon is positioned with reverence. It may be surrounded by candles or placed near a crucifix, creating the appearance of a small altar. But the icon is never an object of worship. It is a symbol and an aid to spiritual awareness.

CANONIZATION

AS THE CHURCH GREW, ITS COMMUNITIES REVERED MORE AND MORE DEVOUT FIGURES AS SAINTS. THE NEED TO CONTROL THE CREATION OF SAINTHOOD RESULTED IN THE ESTABLISHMENT OF A SYSTEM OF UNIVERSAL RECOGNITION IN A CANON OF HOLY SOULS.

Although some living people are described as saints, to be a real saint, the person must be dead. Up until the 4th century AD, when Christianity was adopted as the official religion of the Roman Empire, the devout were made saints only if they had died for their faith for example, were martyrs.

In the early, unstructured Church, groups began to identify individuals who, in their life and particularly in their death, imitated Christ. Such a group, known even today as a "cult" or "cultus", acknowledged the saintly qualities of the individual at their death.

The cultus prepared a joyous burial at which the death was celebrated with the eucharist. The earthly remains, or relics, of the saint were carefully wrapped in an effort to preserve them. Every anniversary of the death called for a reunion of followers, and this day came to be known as the saint's "feast day".

GROWTH OF CULTUSES

The proclamation of these devout members of local communities as saints was based on no established criteria in the early period. Vague ideas of holiness based on manner of life and death were frequently supported by claims of miracles and visions.

By the 4th century AD, local priests or bishops were being drawn into debate on the worthiness of these decisions. In some cases, for instance, there was suspicion that a person had committed suicide in the hope of being granted the glory of a martyr

Above: The Canonization of St Catherine of Siena by Pope Pius II *(Pinturicchio, 16th century).*

saint. This was a particular problem among the desert hermits of North Africa. So priests began to assess the claims of the cultuses.

Bishops saw formal procedures of investigation as the best way to tackle the growth of false cultuses. Priests kept records of saints and the reasons for their sanctification.

PAPAL SAINTS ONLY

At last, in the 12th century, the right to confer, or "canonize", sainthood was reserved for the Holy See, the office of the pope.

The official implementation of this development was attributed to Pope Alexander III (1159–81), though recent scholarship prefers Innocent III (1199–1216). From the 13th century, papal commissions were ordered to investigate claims to sainthood. The cultuses continued to select an individual, but the commission required evidence that the candidate had lived a life worthy of Christ. Any claims

Below: Pope John Paul II canonized 120 Chinese martyrs in a ceremony held in St Peter's Square, Rome, on 1 October 2000.

to miracles were to be thoroughly investigated by the Church. These rules are followed to this day, although in 1983 Pope John Paul II streamlined the regulations, making them more precise.

MAKING A SAINT

Step One: The cultus makes its choice of saint, but the local bishop does not automatically accept it. For five years after the candidate's death, he conducts research into his or her virtues, or the circumstances of martyrdom. This allows time for a calm assessment of the candidate's life and death.

Then, the bishop's approval is submitted to the Congregation for the Causes of Saints, a panel made up of theologians and cardinals of the Church. If the panel

approves, the name is submitted to the pope, who then declares the candidate "Venerable".

Step Two: Martyrs will be canonized by the pope, but the Venerable must now be supported by a written claim from the recipient of a purported miracle performed by the holy candidate.

This miracle must occur after the death of the candidate. The believer must avow that they prayed to the Venerable, who then interceded with God in answer to that prayer. This is seen as proof that the dead one's spirit is close to God. The pope approves the beatification of the candidate,

Above: Detail from a fresco showing the canonization of St Francis by Pope Gregory IX (Giotto di Bondone, c.1295).

who can now be venerated by his or her cultus as "Blessed". Blessed Carlo Acutis is an example.

Step Three: The third and last step towards sainthood needs evidence of one more miracle. When the pope has this, he agrees to canonize the beatificd, who is then named a saint. This status identifies the person as one who lived and died in imitation of Christ, and is officially in heaven. He or she can be honoured by all.

DECANONIZATION

The Holy See knows the early saints have poor records, if any, to support their status. But it generally accepts the situation.

However, the Holy See did de-canonize St Barbara in 1969 and Simon of Trent in 1965 because they were purely legendary characters. St Brigid of Ireland was accused of being a pagan figure, and so she too was decanonized.

Official announcements are often ignored. Cultuses can remain attached to saints, despite formal abolishment. In recognition of this loyalty, the Church has allowed certain cultuses to venerate "their" saint, but has withdrawn universal recognition.

Some decanonized saints in history include: Barbara, Brigid of Ireland, Christopher, George, Philomena, Simon of Trent, Valentine and William of Norwich.

SAINTHOOD

MYSTERIES AND MIRACLES

LEGENDS OF MIRACLES AND EXTRAORDINARY BRAVERY ARE WELL-KNOWN ATTRIBUTES OF THE SAINTS, BUT SOME WERE WITNESSED MANIFESTING MYSTERIOUS POWERS AND PHYSICAL CHANGES THAT DEFY SCIENTIFIC EXPLANATION.

Saints were so named because they led lives in imitation of Christ. It followed therefore that, like Jesus, they might be capable of performing miracles. The early saints were credited with having all sorts of supernatural powers. Evil spirits, disease, mortal enemies and wild animals were all claimed to be overcome. The perceived holiness of saints and their closeness to God led the faithful to believe that their prayers might be answered, and in miraculous fashion, too. Once a devout Christian had been declared a saint, their life

Above: St Denys is said to have carried his severed head to his burial place, as shown in this stained glass window in St Aignan Church, Chartres, France.

often became embellished with events of the miraculous, such as inexplicable cures or angelic assistance.

VOICES AND VISIONS

St Joan of Arc claimed she had heard the voices of three saints instructing her to save France. The mystic and writer St Hildegard of Bingen described heavenly visions she experienced during her life. Crowds of people in Milan heard a unearthly child's voice calling out repeatedly, "Ambrose for bishop." The divine message persuaded them to elect Ambrose, despite him being unbaptized.

Another account of a divine apparition involved St Isidore the farmer, a humble, browbeaten peasant. He was so tired, and in

Left: St Januarius Visited in Prison by Proculus and Sosius *(Francesco Solimena, c.1700).*

such pain from beatings, he could not work, but two angels appeared and ploughed the fields for him.

St Clement was said to have experienced a vision of Jesus while suffering extreme thirst digging a quarry under Roman coercion. The vision which came in answer to the saint's prayers was accompanied by a spring of water gushing suddenly from the rocks.

HEALING

The more obvious imitation of Christ involves miraculous cures reminiscent of his ministry, such as healing disease. St Odile, for example, was said to have been born blind, but was given sight after her baptism. During her life, she restored the sight of others.

Saints' relics were believed to have the power to effect miraculous cures. Pilgrims travelled great distances to be in the presence of a saint's tomb, so that they might receive the healing power believed to reside within the corpse.

The relics of St Martin, for instance, were said to ooze curative oil and the faithful would flock to his tomb for a mere dab. Likewise, in the 7th century, oil was said to weep from the tomb of St John the Baptist and bore the odour of the honey upon which he had survived.

RESCUE

Miraculous cures save the body from physical peril. Closely associated in terms of salvation are the rescues of individuals or whole communities from evil, frequently in the shape of a human enemy.

A painting of Our Lady of Częstochowa, commonly referred to as the Black Madonna, became the focus of Polish nationalism in the 14th century. When the Hussites overran the monastery of Jasna Gora (Mount of Light) in 1430, the painting was said to resist all attempts to destroy it. Every subsequent siege failed and Our Lady of Częstochowa was officially named Queen of Poland.

In times of war, saints are invoked for their protection, especially in great peril. And, when victory comes against all odds, guardian angels and patron saints often receive the credit.

The blood of St Januarius has been revered in Naples ever since 1631, when Mount Vesuvius erupted. Subsequent prayers to the saint are believed to have prevented any repetition of such a disaster. Every year the vial containing the blood is displayed. If it liquefies, the year will be free from disaster.

THE STIGMATA

The appearance of wounds on the hands, feet and in the ribs, in imitation of those made by the nails that pinned Christ to the Cross, are a phenomenon known as the stigmata. St Francis of Assisi was the first Christian to manifest the marks, in 1224, which remained on his body for two years until his death. Since then, the Catholic Church has recognized 62 men and women as stigmatics. Listed below are the best-known sufferers, some saints, others Blessed.

St Angela of Foligno
Blessed Baptista Varani
Blessed Carlo of Sezze
St Catherine of Genoa
Blessed Catherine of Racconigi
St Catherine de' Ricci
St Catherine of Siena
St Clare of Montefalco
St Colette
St Frances of Rome
St Francis of Assisi
St Gertrude
St John of God
St Lidwina
Blessed Lucy of Narni
St Lutgardis

St Margaret of Cortona
Blessed Marguerite-Marie Alacoque
St Marie de l'Incarnation
Blessed Mary Anne of Jesus
St Mary Frances of the Five Wounds
St Mary Magdalene de' Pazzi
Blessed Osanna of Mantua
Padre Pio (*St Pius of Pietrelcina*)
St Rita of Cascia
St Veronica Giuliani

Right: St Francis of Assisi receiving the stigmata on the mountain of La Verna in Italy (School of Bonaventura Berlinghieri, 13th century).

MEDIEVAL PILGRIMAGE

A JOURNEY TO VISIT THE SACRED RELICS OF A SAINT WAS AN IMPORTANT ACT OF DEVOTION IN THE MIDDLE AGES. THE HEALING POWER BELIEVED TO RESIDE IN THEM, AND THE SPIRITUAL ENERGY ASSOCIATED WITH THEIR SHRINES, DREW HORDES OF PILGRIMS.

Early Christians believed it an important act of piety to pray at the places where the Saviour and his company of saints had lived and died. A pilgrimage involved hardship. It was a form of penance, a humble mission to offer prayers of contrition, and call on the saints to intercede with God. From as early as the 2nd century AD, records tell of Christians travelling great distances on foot to the Holy Land in order to visit Bethlehem and Jerusalem.

They would have had a hard job, for these sites in Palestine were lost after AD 132, when the Roman Emperor Hadrian demolished Jerusalem and rebuilt the city with temples dedicated to Roman gods. Only in AD 326, when Emperor Constantine I ordered Christian bishops to find the sites of Christ's passion, were shrines and churches built there.

One such site, the Holy Sepulchre, built by Constantine himself, stands to this day, albeit with some modification. The emperor's mother, St Helen, also a convert, founded churches in the Holy Land, which drew yet more pilgrims.

HEART OF THE EMPIRE
Outside the Holy Land, the most significant destination was Rome. Here the tombs and relics of the Holy Martyrs, including Sts Peter and Paul, were located. In AD 326,

Above: The chapel at Aachen Minster was built AD 788–805 for Emperor Charlemagne to house his huge collection of relics.

St Helen brought to the city a marble staircase taken from the judgement hall of Pontius Pilate in Jerusalem. Purported to be the very steps upon which Christ had trodden as he went to his trial, these Holy Stairs were installed in the church of St John Lateran, and are said to be stained with Christ's blood. To this day, pilgrims climb the 28 stairs on their knees.

ROADS THROUGH EUROPE
In England, thousands trekked to Canterbury to see the relics of St Thomas Becket, or made their way to Norfolk to pray before the holy shrine of Our Lady of Walsingham. Pilgrims took the Via Francigena, a popular route from Canterbury to Rome.

On the way was Paris, with Christ's crown of thorns, and Chartres, which held the holy tunic of the Virgin Mary. Pilgrims

Left: An illustration from John Lydgate's The Siege of Thebes, *shows pilgrims leaving Canterbury for London (1412–22).*

flocked to Tours, where the relics of St Martin were kept. And Cologne, in Germany, possessed the relics of the Magi, the three wise men who visited the stable to pay homage to the baby Jesus.

Once in Italy, pilgrims could glimpse the Holy Shroud of Jesus in Turin. And, travelling on southwards, they would throng the streets of Assisi, where St Francis was buried. From all over Europe, devout Christians journeyed to Santiago de Compostela in Spain, where the relics of St James the Great lay in his tomb.

IMPACT OF REFORM
Pilgrimage had become so popular, even hysterical in its folksy enthusiam, that the whole activity invited disdain in some quarters. The bishop of Salisbury was moved to describe the veneration of relics as "abominable idolatry".

In 1517, the German priest Martin Luther introduced a radical idea. He argued Christians could approach God for forgiveness, without the intercession of the saints. So began the great division in the Church, the Reformation, which separated Christians into Roman Catholics and Protestants.

As Christendom became a battlefield, shrines were destroyed and relics burnt. In England, the shrine of St Thomas Becket was melted down to enrich the king's coffers, and the beautiful shrine in Walsingham violated.

Even Luther, the angry reformer, was distressed at such destruction wrought by the mobs. After these calamitous events, relics no longer gripped the religious mind. Pilgrimages, too, lost their worldly appeal and were not the major social events they were in the pre-Reformation period.

Instead, pilgrimages reverted to being the pious causes of penance they had once been. Modern believers still honour relics, even venerate them, especially on feast days. Some recently canonized saints, such as the Aztec peasant Juan Diego, command huge followings of pilgrims, who come to witness their relics.

Above: The Church of the Holy Sepulchre in Jerusalem, c.AD 335, commemorates the tomb of Christ and is a special place of pilgrimage.

> **NEW MARTYR SAINTS**
> A major consequence of the Reformation (1517–1648) was that new martyrs joined the company of saints. Hundreds of Welsh and English Roman Catholics were burnt, crushed between milling stones or beheaded by Protestants during the religious strife.
>
> Some deaths were political in intent, and since then 200 have been named as martyrs. In 1970, Pope Paul VI found 40 to be worthy of canonization. They are known as the Forty Martyrs of England and Wales. Of these, 13 were priests, 20 monks and friars, and the remaining 7 consisted of lay-men and -women.

IMPORTANT FEAST DAYS

FEAST DAYS, TRADITIONALLY SET TO MARK THE DAY OF THE SAINT'S DEATH, ARE A CELEBRATION OF BIRTH INTO HEAVEN. CHURCHES CONDUCT SPECIAL MASSES, AS WELL AS PUBLIC EVENTS OUTDOORS. PROCESSIONS, MUSIC AND DANCE INVOLVE THE WHOLE COMMUNITY.

Roman Catholics and members of the Orthodox Churches venerate the saints' feast days in their liturgy. Important saints are celebrated on these days with special processions, particularly when the church houses their relics and images.

JANUARY
Gregory of Nazianzus, Basil the Great 2
Genevieve 3
Elizabeth Seton 4
Sava 14
Antony of Egypt 17
Sebastian 20
John the Almsgiver 23
Thomas Aquinas 28

FEBRUARY
Brigid of Ireland 1
Agatha 5

Below: Russian priests celebrating the feast day of St Cyril and St Methodius, known as "apostles to the Slavs", in 2007.

Jerome Emiliani 8
Valentine, Cyril and Methodius 14
Martyrs of China 17

MARCH
David of Wales, Gregory of Nyssa 1
Katharine Drexel 3
Patrick, Joseph of Arimathea 17
Joseph (husband of Mary) 19
Cuthbert 20

APRIL
Isidore of Seville 4
John-Baptist de La Salle 7
Teresa of Los Andes 12
Bernadette of Lourdes 16
Anselm 21
George 23
Mark 25
Catherine of Siena 29

MAY
Joseph (husband of Mary) 1
Pachomius (West) 9
Helen with Constantine (East) 21
Rita of Cascia 22

Above: Thomas Aquinas Being Received into the Dominican order *(German School, 16th century). His feast day is 28 January.*

Madeleine Sophie Barat, Bede 25
Philip Neri, Augustine of Canterbury 26
Bernard of Montjoux 28
Joan of Arc 30

JUNE
Justin 1
Martyrs of Uganda 3
Boniface 5
Martha (East) 6
Columba of Iona 9
Antony of Padua 13
Thomas More 22
John the Baptist 24
Peter and Paul 29

JULY
Thomas 3
Athanasius the Aconite 5
Benedict 11
Mary Magdalene 22
Bridget of Sweden 23
Christopher, James the Great 25

Anne (West) 26
Martha (West) 29
Ignatius of Loyola 31

AUGUST
Jean-Baptiste Vianney 4
Fourteen Holy Helpers,
   Dominic 8
Edith Stein 9
Clare of Assisi 11
Maximilian Kolbe 14
Mary, the Blessed Virgin
   (Assumption) 15
Stephen of Hungary 16
Rose of Lima 23
Augustine of Hippo 28

SEPTEMBER
Gregory the Great 3
John Chrysostom (West) 13
Hildegard of Bingen 17
Matthew 21
Padre Pio 23
Sergius of Radonezh, Fermin 25
Wenceslas 28
Archangel Michael, Raphael 29

Below: The running of the bulls in Pamplona takes place on 7 July, the day the relics of St Fermin, a popular local saint, came to the town.

Above: St Athanasius the Aconite, a Greek Father of the Church (print, 16th century). His feast day is 5 July.

OCTOBER
Theresa of Lisieux 1
Francis of Assisi 4
Denys of Paris 9
Edward the Confessor 13
Teresa of Ávila 15
Luke 18
Crispin and Crispinian 25
Simon, Jude, Martyrs of the Spanish
   Civil War 28

NOVEMBER
All Saints 1
All Souls 2
Malachy 3
Vincent Liem 7
Leo the Great (West) 10
Martin of Tours (West) 11
John Chrysostom (East) 13
Albert the Great 15
Elizabeth of Hungary 17
Cecilia 22
Alexander Nevski 23
Andrew 30

DECEMBER
Francis Xavier 3
Nicholas of Myra 6
Ambrose (West) 7
Eulalia of Mérida 10
Lucy 13
John of the Cross 14
Thomas 21
Stephen (West) 26
John 27
Holy Innocents (West) 28, (East) 9
Thomas Becket 29

Below: The Feast of St Lucy (Carl Larsson, 20th century). On 13 December, the oldest girl in a Scandinavian family wears a crown of candles.

SAINTHOOD

HOLY RELICS

WHETHER SKELETON OR MERE SCRAP OF CLOTHING, RELICS WERE BELIEVED TO REPRESENT A SAINT'S PRESENCE ON EARTH. FOR THE DEVOUT, THEIR POWER WAS SUCH THAT EVEN SIGHT OF THESE ARTEFACTS WAS SAID TO EFFECT MIRACULOUS CURES.

From the earliest period of Christianity, the bodily remains of saints were venerated. A custom developed in which the saint's relics were no longer buried or laid in catacombs, but placed beneath church altars.

Churches sheltering relics were perceived by St Augustine of Hippo to be "as tombs of mortal men, whose spirits live with God". To this day, in the Roman Catholic Church, altars upon which mass is celebrated must contain the relics of a saint, according to canon law.

Gradually, the term "relic" embraced lengths of bone, scraps of burial wrappings, jewellery. Indeed, it could mean any little thing that had once belonged to the saint. The Church accepted this development because in the 1st century AD in Ephesus, Turkey, tradition held that God had performed miracles through the handkerchiefs and aprons of St Paul. The sick believed they had been cured simply through their proximity to Paul's clothing.

The faithful believed that their prayers for forgiveness were more likely to be heard when uttered before relics or tombs. Other believers claimed the very sight of the relic summoned forth the saint who, through God, might perform miraculous cures of any ailment, from warts to infertility.

COLLECTORS' ITEMS

Holy sites were not limited to the saints' burial places but included any site where a relic was housed. Their bodily relics became valuable, some fetching large sums, and were often plundered by clergy and believers who

Above: A reliquary of the hand of St Thomas Becket kept at Burgos Cathedral, Spain.

THE HOLY HOUSE

The story attached to the "Holy House" of Loreto in Italy indicates the crazed, but profound, attachment medieval Christians had for their greatest saints.

According to the extravagant legend, an angel lifted the house in Nazareth where Joseph and the Virgin Mary had once lived, and carried it away. The house landed in random places before finally coming to rest in Loreto. The event was precisely recorded as ending on 7 September 1295. So many pilgrims flocked to see this wondrous relic, coined the "Holy House", that the authorities constructed an imposing church on the site. It continues to attract visitors.

Right: The Basilica (Holy House) of Loreto, Italy, is one of the most revered sites in the Christian world. It was built in 1469 to house what is believed to be the miraculously transported home of the Virgin Mary.

278

strove to build up collections. In the process relics were moved – "translated" – from one place to another. There could be a finger at one church, a shinbone elsewhere, while a third might claim to have a saint's sandal or cloak.

The faithful might ideally have wished to visit tombs, but a relic would serve just as well. It held the power of the saint. Even the churches of Jerusalem, whose significance rested on their association with the sites of Jesus' passion, boasted ownership of the relics of the True Cross upon which the Saviour had suffered crucifixion.

Every Christian pilgrim longed to visit the shrine of a saint, and many collected relics. The more precious items were kept in beautiful caskets, known as reliquaries, shaped like small tombs.

These containers were wrought in precious metals and adorned with jewels and enamelled images. Many are treasured to this day in Roman Catholic and Eastern Orthodox churches, although most are housed in museums across Europe and the USA.

STRANGE AND BIZARRE
Some of the more interesting relics include a small carving of St Foy (also known as St Faith), from the 9th century. The figure is covered in gold plate and, over the centuries, believers bedecked the surface with precious emeralds, pearls and amethysts. This martyr was just 12 years old when she died. In the back of the carving there is a cavity containing her tiny wrapped skull.

Pope Urban V had the head of St Cassian encased in an elaborate casket. But Charlemagne (Charles the Great AD 747–814), emperor of the Holy Roman Empire, did better than that. He built a cathedral to house his huge collection of relics.

Among them, he claimed, were the cloth that once wrapped the decapitated head of John the Baptist, the tunic of the Virgin Mary, and swaddling cloths of the Infant Jesus. His collection of relics was displayed every seven years for a week in July. Vast crowds visited the church in Aachen, formerly Aix-la-Chapelle. The custom is still followed, revealing 200 relics every seventh year.

Right: A reliquary of St Foy (also known as St Faith) made of gold and jewels, held in the church in Conques, France (9th century).

Above left: This reliquary depicts the martyrdom of the Roman St Candidus. It is made of nutwood and covered in gold and silver (c.1165).

Above: Reliquary of St Stephen with enamel work from Limoges (12th century).

SAINTHOOD

HEROES AND MARTYRS

REVERENCE FOR RELICS AND DEEP ATTACHMENT TO THE SAINTS DID NOT SIT WELL WITH ALL BELIEVERS. PROTESTANTS REGARDED THESE PASSIONS AS IDOLATRY, AN AFFRONT TO THE TRUE FAITH, AND THREW OUT THE SAINTS. YET THE IDEA OF HONOURING HEROES REMAINS.

Above: A portrait of Martin Luther, the priest who started the Protestant movement (Lucas Cranach, the Elder, 1529). He is greatly honoured for his brave and radical reforms.

For more than a thousand years, Christendom guarded and reigned over Europe, Russia and eastern Europe. The pope, his bishops, archbishops and clergy played a major role in economic and political life. The vast majority of the people recognized the authority of the Church. Even kings and queens, believed to be anointed by God to rule, formed an integral part of the system.

Below: The Protestant priest and theologian Martin Luther (is shown here in triumph over Catholic Pope Leo X (woodcut, 1568).

But, by the 14th century, the Church was not the fervent, disciplined institution it once had been. Popes lived in splendour and priests were corruptible. The Reformation started as a call to return to the "purity" of early Christianity, and was not intended to create a major rift. However, great differences of opinion arose, and during the 15th and 16th centuries Christendom became a realm of war and disorder.

CRY FOR REFORM
Reformers insisted the individual was important to God and no person needed the intercession of saints or priests to reach him. They insisted that veneration of the saints was contrary to the teachings of the Bible. As a result,

the Protestants, as reformers came to be known, refuted the need for saints as intermediaries, and dismissed the rule that priests be ordained by the pope. In acts of rebellion against the Roman Church, Protestants in countries across northern Europe forbade all worship relating to saints: relics, statues, shrines and pilgrimages were all considered unnecessary and banned. Even images of the Blessed Virgin were now prohibited.

EVENTS IN ENGLAND
However, the Church of England was born out of political need rather than religious fervour. Henry VIII (1491–1547) chafed under papal rule and rejected the authority of Rome.

A period of killings and torture of Roman Catholics under Henry was followed by a similar persecution of Protestants by Mary Tudor (1516–58). By the death of Elizabeth I in 1603, most English subjects had learnt to accept that their monarch, and not the pope, was the head of their Church. However, English Protestants did not reject all the practices of the Roman Church. Indeed, in the Preface to their new Book of Common Prayer, the English Church emphasized the continuation of "the main essentials".

Saints who had been canonized before the Reformation generally continued to be viewed as saints by English churches after the split from Rome. Some people who had suffered through their opposition to the Catholic Church, such as John Wycliffe and Thomas Cranmer, were commemorated by Anglican churches as martyrs.

In addition, some post-Reformation Christians are viewed as heroes of the Christian Church by Anglicans. Examples include John Bunyan (1628–88), author of *The Pilgrim's Progress*; the Quaker George Fox (1624–91); Elizabeth Fry (1780–1845); and John Wesley (1703–91), the founder of Methodism. Some individuals, such as Carinnal Newman (1801–90) and Arch-bishop Oscar Romero (1917–80), are viewed by Anglicans as heroes of the faith and have also been canonized as saints by the Catholic Church.

On 9 July 1998, Queen Elizabeth II, who was the Supreme Head of the Church of England, was accompanied by the highest priestly officer of her Church, the Archbishop of Canterbury, to unveil ten new statues of 20th-century martyrs. The list was cross-denominational, and in fact none of the men and women so honoured were members of the Church of England.

20TH-CENTURY MARTYRS
Instead of saints, the Church of England recognized heroes and martyrs. Statues of ten heroes and martyrs were erected on the façade of Westminster Abbey in London.

Grand Duchess Elizabeth of Russia: Murdered in 1918 during the Russian Revolution.
Manche Masemola: Killed in 1928 by her parents in South Africa for converting to Christianity.
Maximilian Kolbe: Polish priest murdered in 1941 in a Nazi concentration camp.
Lucian Tapiedi: Peasant from Papua New Guinea murdered in 1942 by Japanese troops.
Dietrich Bonhoeffer: German pastor murdered in 1945 by the Nazis.
Janani Luwum: Teacher murdered in 1977 by Idi Amin in Uganda.
Esther John: Indian missionary martyred in 1960.
Dr Martin Luther King Jr: Civil rights campaigner assassinated in 1968 in the USA.
Wang Zhiming: Chinese pastor killed in 1973 by the government.
Archbishop Oscar Romero: Murdered in 1980 in San Salvador.

Above: The martyrs' statues at Westminster Abbey: Martin Luther King Jr, Oscar Romero, Dietrich Bonhoeffer, Esther John and Lucian Tapiedi.

NEW WORLDS

EXPLORATIONS BEYOND EUROPE HELPED SPREAD THE CHRISTIAN FAITH TO THE AMERICAS, AFRICA, INDIA AND THE FAR EAST. MISSIONARIES AND THEIR CONVERTS FACED HARDSHIP, EVEN MARTYRDOM, AND INEVITABLY THE COMPANY OF SAINTS EXPANDED.

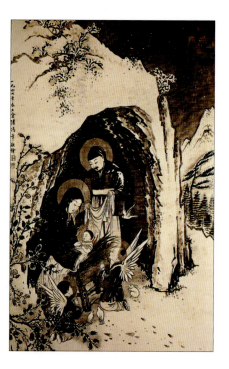

Above: A Chinese representation of The Nativity *(Lu-Hang-Hien, 19th century).*

The apostles set a pattern of evangelism, making it a duty for Christians to spread the Gospel. Whether Roman Catholic, Eastern Orthodox or Protestant, churches have always treated this duty as a serious commitment.

The faith of these missionaries was tested during the widespread explorations of the Europeans in the 17th and 18th centuries. Adventurers and merchants first traded with, then colonized, far-flung lands, and Christian evangelists followed in their wake. A number became martyrs or saints.

MISSIONARY MARTYRS

Modern secular opinion asserts that these missions forced their faith on people for mere political purpose or to exploit natural resources. This may be true of ambitious leaders, but thousands of lowly religious gave their lives to the service of the indigenous people of these lands. Frequently, the missionaries protected their flock from both colonial masters and local warlords.

In remote, uncharted parts of the world, nuns and monks from Ireland, France, Portugal and Spain suffered the same hardship as their flock. They also filled non-religious roles as nurses and educators. Many paid the ultimate price of martyrdom and were canonized for their faith.

St Francis Xavier was among the first to be venerated for his life as an evangelist beyond the bounds of old Christendom. He travelled through the Far East, spreading the gospel, and was martyred. As other Europeans followed his example through the Americas, Asia and Africa, so the company of saints expanded.

NATIVE CONVERTS

The legends of the saints were told to inspire converts and it mattered not that the Blessed Virgin was depicted with Chinese or Mexican features. With the infant in her arms, she became a universal symbol. Regardless of ethnic features, St Francis was recognized with his stigmata, and St Roch with the dog at his feet.

One of the earliest New World converts to inspire a cultus was Blessed Kateri Tekakwitha, a Native American who died in 1680 and was canonized in 2012. Similarly, a cultus developed after the death of the Spanish Dominican St Joachim Royo, who died in China in 1748.

In Japan, Paul Miki and his companions, converts of St Francis Xavier, suffered relentless persecution before finally being tortured and crucified in 1597. Survivors venerated the bloodstained clothes of these 26 victims who were all canonized.

In Uganda, Charles Lwanga and his 21 companions, all under the age of 25, were burnt alive for their faith in the 1880s. As they faced their horrific deaths, "their exemplary courage and cheerfulness were comparable with those of the early Christians". They were canonized in 1964.

The first native saint of the USA, Elizabeth Seton, died in 1821, and was canonized only in 1971 for her charity towards deprived children.

St Josephine Bakhita was taken into slavery in Africa, but found

Below: A Catholic nun in Africa teaches children how to use knitting needles in the 1920s.

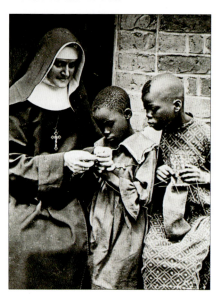

Right: Missionaries and their catechumens experience floodwater in Hindustan, north India, in 1910.

refuge in a convent in Italy. Her work as a nurse, together with her humility, attracted a cultus after she died in 1947. She was canonized in 2000.

MASS CANONIZATION

Pope John Paul II recognized the neglected martyrs of the New and Developing Worlds. Tireless in visiting Catholic communities and in reinforcing the Universal Church, the late pope created more than 480 new saints. Through this pope's concern for his global flock, victims of mass persecution have been sanctified. He canonized 117 martyrs of Vietnam, all of whom gave their lives between 1745 and 1862. The Martyrs of Mexico, 25 Christians killed between 1915 and 1937, were also made saints in 2000. Furthermore, he initiated the process of sanctification of the estimated 6,832 priests and religious put to death during the Spanish Civil War (1936–39). In 2017, Pope Francis canonized the Martyrs of Tlaxcala, three Mexican youths slain for refusing to revert from Catholicism to indigenous beliefs in 1527/29, and the Martyrs of Natal, 30 Catholics slain by members of Dutch Calvinism, in 1645.

Above: A painting of the Madonna on animal hide, made by Pueblo Indians in a traditional style (1675).

Left: An armed ship carrying missionaries under the monogram of Jesus off the coast of New Granada, modern-day Colombia (artist unknown, 18th century).

MODERN PILGRIMS

THE MODERN ERA HAS SEEN A REVIVAL IN PILGRIMAGE AS A CHRISTIAN DUTY. NOT SINCE THE 16TH-CENTURY REFORMATION OF THE CHURCH HAVE SO MANY PILGRIMS UNDERTAKEN THE LONG JOURNEYS TO SHRINES FOR CURES, PENANCE AND PRAYER.

Above: Pope John Paul II celebrated mass with a million believers in front of a statue of the Virgin in Fátima, Portugal, on 12 May 1991.

The pious duty of pilgrimage, although never abandoned by Roman Catholics, regained some of its former popularity during the Victorian era. The Ottoman Islamic hold on Palestine had weakened, and in 1855 a cross was borne through Jerusalem for the first time since the Crusades.

Pilgrims began visiting again the holy sites of Jerusalem, Bethlehem and Nazareth – and others made holy by their association with the lives of the saints. By 1900, the traveller Gertrude Bell described a hostelry in the Holy Land "packed with pilgrims tight as herrings sleeping in rows on the floor".

VISIONS OF MARY

In 1876, more than 100,000 pilgrims attended the dedication of the church at Lourdes, in southwest France, where St Bernadette received a vision of the Virgin Mary. Three years later, at Knock in Ireland, 15 people saw a vision standing on the village chapel roof of the Virgin accompanied by St Joseph, St John and a lamb. A shrine there now attracts more than a million pilgrims every year.

In 1917, the Blessed Virgin was said to have visited three children at Fátima in Portugal and entrusted them with three secrets. Now five million pilgrims a year visit their shrine. Believers claim that the Virgin told the children about forthcoming mass death in a second world war and an attempted assassination of a pope

Below: Catholic pilgrims during the Holy Week praying at the first Station of the Cross on the Via Dolorosa in Jerusalem (Erich Matson, c.1900).

– both of which prophecies have come true.

ECHOES OF THE PAST

Modern pilgrims, in imitation of the difficult conditions of their medieval counterparts, and also to show penitence, may choose to walk the "pilgrim's way" to particular shrines.

A popular route is the trek to Santiago de Compostela on the Atlantic coast of Spain. During their journey, they may pass other places of pilgrimage, such as the

shrine to the Virgin Mary in Vézelay and at Conques, and can see the relics of the martyr, St Foy.

The main aim of the pilgrimage is to visit the tomb and relics of St James the Great at Santiago de Compostela. The Church gives a certificate to those pilgrims who have walked the last 100km/ 60 miles or cycled the last 200km/ 120 miles of the route. These awards echo the medieval habit of rewarding successful pilgrims with distinctive clothes and badges.

RECENT DEVELOPMENTS

Ever since 1717, the most devout have walked about 110km/70 miles from Warsaw to the Jasna Gora monastery in Poland to see the miraculous icon of Our Lady of Czestochowa, reputedly painted by St Luke. But, since the ending of Communist rule in the late 20th century, many more throng the route. An estimated million pilgrims a year now go to the site.

The biggest crowds are found at Zihuatanejo in Guadalupe, Mexico, where St Juan Diego had a vision of the Virgin. Ten million pilgrims pay homage to Our Lady of Guadalupe at this shrine every year. And seven million people travel to the tomb of the humble stigmatic, St Padre Pio, at San Giovanni Rotondo in south Italy.

PERSONAL JOURNEYS

Other holy sites and shrines draw those seeking a significance particular to themselves. The pilgrim might be named after the saint, or be seeking one who is patron of a disease or other affliction.

Many visit Assisi, Italy, for St Francis, although an earthquake has left this site damaged. Pilgrims travel to abbeys at Montserrat in Spain, or Trier in Germany, to seek intercession from the saints and wonder at the glorious holy buildings. Today, pilgrimages to the Holy Land can be almost as dangerous as they were during the Crusades.

Many aspects of modern pilgrimage resemble the medieval experience, as Chaucer described in his poetic work *The Canterbury Tales*. Hostelries proliferate along the routes, especially near the shrines, just as they did in the Middle Ages. Translators and guides find work, while merchants are busy selling souvenirs, often facsimiles of medieval relics.

Right: Souvenir of the pilgrimage to Lourdes, made for the International Exhibition in Paris in 1867.

BEING A PILGRIM

Modern Roman Catholic and Orthodox pilgrims are serious in their intent when they undertake journeys to the places associated with the saints. This is often the site where their relics are enshrined. Pilgrims seek penance and offer prayers of gratitude, or request their intercession.

Walking the route to a shrine, the faithful will take time to pray or undergo some physical hardship in penance. They venerate those shrines they pass as they head toward their final destination. If that is Rome, they will climb, on hands and knees, the hard marble steps of the Holy Stairs of St Peter's Cathedral.

Popular pilgrimages are those to Assisi, the shrine of St Francis, or to places that honour St James the Great in South America, or visits to sacred sites of the Holy Land. But, in the 21st century, the sites and festivals that attract most visitors are those associated with the Virgin Mary, the one figure from the company of saints who seems to have sustained an imaginative hold on believers – and non-believers.

Above: Pilgrims kneel with crosses at the pass of Roncesvalles, Spain, on their way from south-west France to Santiago de Compostela.

THE BLESSED

THE CHURCH DOES NOT GRANT SAINTHOOD LIGHTLY. HOLY SOULS MAY REMAIN FOR DECADES, EVEN CENTURIES, IN THE RANKS OF THE BLESSED OR THE VENERABLE, WHILE THE CLAIMS MADE ON THEIR BEHALF ARE CAREFULLY SCRUTINIZED BY THE VATICAN.

Above: A photo of Blessed Father Joseph Damien de Veuster in 1873.

Mary of the Divine Heart, a Roman Catholic nun who played a key role in influencing Pope Leo XIII to consecrate the world to the Sacred Heart of Jesus – the measure he called "the greatest act of my pontificate" – might be considered an obvious candidate for sainthood. Born a German noblewoman, Maria Droste zu Vischering, she became Mother Superior of the Convent of the Good Shepherd Sisters in Porto, Portugal, where she received mystical messages from Christ telling her to contact the pope to ask for the consecration of the world to the Sacred Heart of Jesus. Leo XIII commissioned an inquiry based on her revelations and commanded the consecration of the human race to the Sacred Heart in his 1899 encyclical *Annum sacrum*. After Sister Mary died three days before the world consecration took place, her body proved to be incorruptible and it can be venerated at the Church of the Sacred Heart of Jesus in Ermesinde, northern Portugal. However, the path to sainthood is long, and to be declared a saint a person must be shown to have been the source of two miracles. Mary of the Divine Heart was declared Blessed in 1975 by Pope Paul VI after the cure, in December 1952, of a girl of tubercular peritonitis and meningitis following intercession to Sister Mary was accepted as miraculous. She is yet to be canonized. Until a second miracle is officially attributed to her, she remains among the Blessed.

CAREFUL RESEARCH

Sometimes clarification of the history surrounding venerated figures prevents their proceeding to canonization. This is the case with Blessed Clare of Rimini (1282–1346), who according to tradition was an Italian noblewoman who

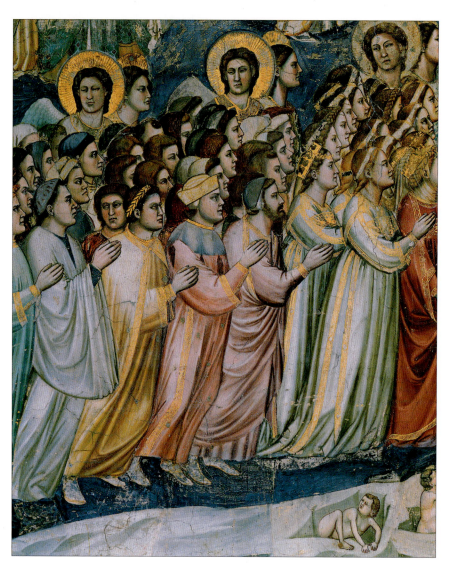

Left: The procession of the Beatified in The Last Judgement *(Giotto di Bondone, 1303).*

THE BLESSED

Left: A watercolour portrait of Pierre Toussaint, fondly known as the "Barber Saint" (c.1825).

gave up a life of luxury to join the Poor Clares and established the monastery of Santa Maria degli Angeli in Rimini. However, in 1751 Giuseppe Garampi, Prefect of the Vatican Archives, had demonstrated after careful research that details of the accepted life of Clare were inaccurate and she had probably never taken vows or founded the monastery in question; she was probably not a nun but a beguine, a laywoman who dressed in a religious habit. She is still celebrated as Blessed Clare of Rimini. She was declared Blessed in 1784 by Pope Pius VI and her feast day is 10 February. But, due to the work of Garampi, her elevation to sainthood, which appeared inevitable, now seems very unlikely.

UNKNOWN BUT HOLY

Many individuals considered Blessed do not have national or global recognition. Cultuses have sometimes asked for obscure, private individuals to be named as saints. One such is Pierre Toussaint, who was born a slave in Haiti in 1776 and taken by his master, John Berard, to live with him in New York. There Berard taught Pierre to read and write.

When Berard died, Pierre continued to care for the family of his late master by working as a barber. When Mrs Berard married again, Pierre set up his own home and, with his wife, cared for the homeless and destitute.

They purchased the freedom of many slaves, opened a school, and set up a religious order for black women. After his death in 1853, Toussaint became the only layman to be buried in the grand precincts of St Patrick's Cathedral in New York. He was recognized as Venerable by the Church in 1996, but in the local community people know him fondly as the "Barber Saint".

PATRONS OF CAUSES

In some cases, the Blessed have been allowed by the pope to become patrons of causes. Maria Teresa Ledóchowska, who was born into a 19th-century noble Polish family, nevertheless devoted herself to mission work, especially to the abolition of slavery. The countess founded a community, first called the Sodality, now known as the Institute of St Peter Claver. Having taken vows as a nun, Maria worked tirelessly against slavery. She was beatified in 1976 by Pope Paul VI, who declared her the patron of Polish missions.

Many saints are honoured for giving to the poor, but Blessed Bernardino of Feltre (d.1494) helped those too proud to accept welfare. He took over the Church's faltering pawn shops, started in 1462 by Barnabas of Terni. Under Bernardino's care, the pawnshops charged very low rates of interest and profits were used for charity. For centuries the shops could be found all over western Europe. His cultus was approved in 1728.

BLESSED CARLO ACUTIS

Carlo Acutis (1991–2006) was a devout teenager with a great interest in computers who established a website cataloguing the world's Eucharistic miracles before his tragically early death from leukaemia aged just 15 in 2006. Born in London in 1991 to Italian parents, he was raised in Italy after his parents relocated to Milan in the year of his birth. Among his models for living was St Francis of Assisi. When he developed leukaemia, he dedicated his suffering to the then pope, Benedict XVI, and the Catholic Church. He has been credited with the miraculous healing of a young Brazilian boy born with a pancreatic defect, and he was beatified on 10 October 2020.

He is likely to become the first millennial saint and some are suggesting he should be made the patron saint of the internet. Presently however, that position is held by St Isidore of Seville (560–636), who attempted to record the origins of all things in a twenty-volume work.

Below: Carlo Acutis, who died of leukaemia, aged 15.

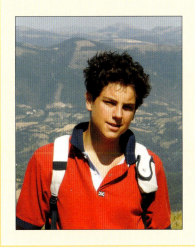

PATRON SAINTS

EACH BELIEVER NURSES A PARTICULAR AFFECTION FOR ONE OR MORE SAINTS, AND TURNS TO THESE HOLY SOULS FOR HELP AND PROTECTION. EVERY ASPECT OF LIFE IS UNDER SAINTLY GUARDIANSHIP, WHETHER IT IS BABYHOOD, COURTSHIP, DOG BITES OR LOST POSSESSIONS.

Early Christians, believing the saints to be alive in heaven, found it logical to see them as patrons for mortals on earth. Saints were thought to look after certain sectors of society, as well as support themes or activities with resonance in their personal story.

Above: St Jerome Emiliani, the patron saint of lost children, with a young orphan boy (Giovanni Domenico Tiepolo, 1780).

Abandoned children – Ivo of Brittany, Jerome Emiliani
Alpine travellers – Bernard of Montjoux
Asylums for the mentally ill – Dympna
Babies – Holy Innocents, Maximus, Nicholas of Tolentino, Philip of Zell
Beggars – Giles
Birds – Gall
Blind people – Thomas the Confessor, Cosmas and Damian, Archangel Raphael
Blood donors – Mary, the Blessed Virgin, Our Lady of the Thorns
Booksellers – John of God
Boys – Dominic Savio
Breastfeeding – Basilissa, Giles
Brides – Dorothy
Cemeteries – Michael, Anne
Childbirth – Margaret of Antioch, Raymund Nonnatus, Leonard of Noblac, Erasmus
Children, longing for – Rita of Cascia
Children, lost – Jerome Emiliani
Criminals – Dismas
Degree candidates – Joseph of Copertino
Dentists – Apollonia
Difficult situations – Eustace
Dog bites – Ubaldo

Left: Ferdinand III ruled as a king in Spain in the 13th century (illuminated manuscript, c.1250). He is the patron of prisoners and the poor.

288

Doubters – Joseph (husband of Mary)
Drought – Genevieve
Emigrants – Frances Cabrini
Epilepsy – Dympna, Vitus
Falling – Venantius Fortunatus
Flying – Joseph of Copertino
Geese – Martin of Tours
Girls – Maria Goretti
Harvests – Antony of Padua
Heart patients – John of God
Hermits – Giles, Hilarion
Homeless – Benedict Joseph Labre
Horses – Eloi, Martin of Tours, Hippolytus
Hospitals – Camillus of Lellis, John of God
House hunting – Joseph (husband of Mary)
Housewives – Martha
Infertility – Rita of Cascia
Invalids – Roch
Journeys – Christopher, Nicholas of Bari, Archangel Raphael, Joseph (husband of Mary)
Kings – Edward the Confessor, Louis IX, Henry II
Knights – George, James the Great
Learning – Catherine of Alexandria
Lost causes – Jude
Lost things – Antony of Padua
Lovers – Valentine
Marriage – John Francis Regis
Married women – Monica
Motherhood – Nicholas of Tolentino
Motorists – Christopher
Mountaineers – Bernard of Aosta
Music – Cecilia, Gregory the Great
Navigators – Brendan the Navigator, Erasmus, Nicholas of Myra
Old people – Teresa of Jesus Jornet y Ibars
Orphans – Ivo of Brittany, Jerome Emiliani
Paralysed – Osmund
Pets – Antony of Egypt
Pilgrims – Christopher, Nicholas of Myra
Poison sufferers – Benedict, John, Pirmin
Poor people – Antony of Padua, Ferdinand III

Pregnant women – Margaret of Antioch
Prisoners – Leonard of Noblac, Roch, Vincent de Paul, Ferdinand III
Rabies – Hubert, Ubaldo
Race relations – Martin de Porres, Peter Claver
Radio – Archangel Gabriel
Repentant prostitutes – Mary Magdalene, Mary of Egypt, Margaret of Cortona
Restaurants – Martha
Retreats – Ignatius of Loyola
Rheumatism sufferers – James the Great, Philip Neri
Shortsightedness – Clarus (abbot)
Shepherds – Cuthbert, Bernadette
Sleepwalkers – Dympna

Above: St Giles, patron saint of beggars and invalids, was a hermit who probably lived in France in the 9th century (high altar of the Pacher School, c.1500).

Spas – John the Baptist
Stamp collectors – Archangel Gabriel
Teenage girls – Maria Goretti
Television – Clare of Assisi
Throat infections – Blaise
Toothache sufferers – Apollonia, Médardus, Osmund, Cunibert of Cologne
Tourists – Francis Xavier
Unhappily married women – Wilgefortis, Rita of Cascia
Workers – Joseph (husband of Mary)
Youth – Aloysius Gonzaga

SAINTHOOD

ALL SAINTS AND ALL SOULS

THE CHURCH CREATED TWO UNIVERSAL FEAST DAYS TO HONOUR THOSE WHO HAVE LEFT THIS WORLD. CATHOLICS COMMEMORATE ALL SAINTS ON 1 NOVEMBER, AND ALL THE DEVOUT SOULS WHO HAVE NOT YET REACHED HEAVEN THE FOLLOWING DAY.

Above: A man lights a candle at the All Saints Memorial, to celebrate fallen soldiers on Hungarian territory.

Below: All Souls' Day in the Churchyard at Glendalough *(Joseph Peacock, 19th century).*

Precisely when the Roman Catholic Church adopted the practice of commemorating all the saints is unknown. However, it is known that the earliest believers left inscriptions of general prayers for the dead in the catacombs of Rome. Two later saints, St Ephrem (d.AD 373) and St John Chrysostom (d.AD 407), describe in vague terms prayers for "the martyrs of the whole world". Yet, whether these prayers referred only to officially sanctified individuals or more generally to all devout souls who reside in heaven is unclear.

A 7th-century-AD manuscript states that not only unknown martyrs but unnamed saints, too, were remembered in prayers and rituals. Catholics believe, to paraphrase St Paul's words, that many of the faithful live not as themselves but through Christ, who lives within them. These

souls, it is believed, reside in heaven but they are unknown. By the 9th century, the practice of praying to unknown saints had become widespread, and an official feast day was established on 1 November as All Saints, which in England is known also as All Hallows.

ALL SOULS' DAY

Believers pitied the faithful dead who might not be in heaven. Naturally, the living prayed for their dead relatives, priests and friends, in the belief that their prayers would help accelerate the passage of their beloved up to heaven. The faithful prayed for the purification of the souls of their beloved ones and their quick passage through purgatory. According to Roman Catholic belief, this is a transitionary abode where those souls who are not saints wait for redemption before passing to heaven. They depend for that redemption on the prayers of the living.

The origin of offering prayers for the unredeemed may date to before the 7th century. Certainly during the lifetime of Isidore of Seville (*c.*AD 560–636), prayers for this purpose were offered in churches. However, the Roman Church was reluctant to dedicate a liturgical place to those who hover on the edge of heaven.

It was not until the 10th century that the liturgy became fixed. According to tradition, a pilgrim returning from the Holy Land encountered a beggar who pointed to flames issuing from a fissure in the earth, believed to emanate from hell. Despairing moans of the dead were said to be audible. The pilgrim reported his terrible experience to St Odilo, abbot of Cluny, who immediately decreed that a day should be marked for "all the dead who have existed from the beginning of the world to the end of time". The feast day was set on 2 November to commemorate all dead souls.

CAKES FOR THE DEAD

Some have interpreted All Souls' Day in a more sinister light. They see the occasion as a time when the souls of the unredeemed return, briefly, to haunt the living. The angry dead, unsupported by prayers from their relatives and friends, turn into toads or witches to punish the living.

In parts of Catholic Italy, the dead are placated with alms in the form of food left on windowsills or the kitchen table, and bunches of flowers are heaped at gravesides in honour of the dead. In Poland, candles are lit on graves in the cemeteries and bread is left shaped in the figure of a body. In Ireland, the devout celebrate the eve of All Souls with a big feast, but the next day is spent fasting, with flowers laid on graves at cemeteries.

All Souls' Day has developed to become a time for feeding the poor and giving to charity. For centuries, believers in the Church of England used to offer alms to the poor on this day. Children would make lanterns from root vegetables, such as turnips, and go "souling" at the doors of friends and neighbours, asking for spiced buns known as soul-cakes.

The modern, secular world has added its own "spin" on these occasions. Halloween, a hybrid of All Saints and All Souls, has become a time for children to dress up in costumes and act as spooks, with rewards of sweets and money replacing traditional soul-cakes. These particular celebrations originated in the USA, but they have spread to areas where the Church is not as influential as it once was.

THE DAY OF THE DEAD

Catholics in Mexico have turned the period between 31 October and 2 November into a bizarrely festive occasion. A once pre-Hispanic festival merged with the Christian calendar to produce what is known as the "Day of the Dead". On this public holiday, people have picnics in the cemeteries, where graves are festooned with flowers, such as marigolds, and candlelight illuminates the scene.

Everywhere on display are skeletons – not real ones, but puppets made of plastic or metal; even cakes are shaped as ornamental skulls. This is not a sad occasion, because the devout believe that the dead are all together. It is thought the spirits of the dead may even be hungry when they visit earth on this day, so food is laid at the graves among the flowers for them to eat.

Above: At a cemetery in La Digue, Seychelles, visitors bring gifts and flowers to dress the gravestones of their loved ones on All Souls' Day.

DIRECTORY OF SAINTS

The first Christian saints were recognized soon after Christ's death over two thousand years ago and new names have been added ever since. This Directory lists a selection of major saints chronologically in order of their deaths. A strong historical sense emerges from studying these biographies, while changing cultural systems form a background to their stories.

Many saints are surrounded by myths of super human strength and startling powers of endurance. These legends can be viewed as entertaining tales, yet they linger in the mind because these impossible acts are underwritten by a sincere faith. But, generally, the lives show the humanity of the saints. Some were short-tempered, some had brilliant minds, while others were confused and bewildered. We see kings becoming humble, scullery maids honoured for their integrity, and pious illiterates making an impact on the world.

The difficulties and problems encountered in their lives mirror the political and social worlds they inhabited. The persecution of Christians during the Roman Empire is reasonably familiar to most readers, but perhaps less well known is the persecution of later times that proved equally horrific.

The company of saints is varied and complex, filled with eccentric personalities, but all are alike in their pious attachment to God.

Left: St Francis Expels the Devils from Arezzo *(Giotto di Bondone, c.1297–99).*

ARCHANGEL RAPHAEL

This Archangel is the hero of a legend in which he helps a poor, blind man. His name means "God heals", and he is traditionally seen as both a healer and protector.

> **KEY FACTS**
> *Divine messenger of God*
> Dates: *Not human but a manifestation of God*
> Patron of: *Travellers, young people leaving home, sad people, health inspectors, the sick, the blind and against eye disease*
> Feast Day: *29 September*
> Emblem: *Holding a bottle, carrying a fish or a staff, accompanied by a boy*

The Gospel of John tells us that in Jerusalem there was once a pool called Bethesda where, at a certain time every year, "an angel" stirred its waters. The first people to enter the pool after this visit would be cured of their illness or disability. By tradition, Raphael is credited as this very angel.

In the Apocryphal Book of Tobit, there are many stories about Raphael. Disguised as a man, he takes a journey with a boy, Tobias, and his dog. They travel to recover a debt owed to the boy's blind grandfather, and have many adventures. On their return home, Raphael restores the old man's sight by asking him to eat a particular fish. Most paintings of this archangel show him with a fish, the boy and the dog, and he is a patron of travellers.

Above: Tobias and the Angel *(Andrea del Verrocchio, c.1470–80).*

ARCHANGEL MICHAEL

The Archangel Michael saved heaven by vanquishing the devil, who was intruding while disguised as a dragon.

> **KEY FACTS**
> *Divine messenger of God*
> Dates: *Not human but a manifestation of God*
> Patron of: *Ambulance drivers, bakers, mariners, paramedics, soldiers and battles*
> Feast Day: *29 September*
> Emblem: *Frequently dressed in armour carrying a gatekeeper's staff, sword, scales, banner, dragon*

The Old Testament describes Michael as the protector of Israel, "always interceding for the human race". He was the angel who spoke to Moses on Mount Sinai. The New Testament says he "has authority over the people" and "gave them the law".

Archangel Michael fought the devil when war broke out in heaven. Michael defeated the beast and the angels siding with it, so he was given the right to judge souls seeking entry into heaven.

Many medieval images show Michael weighing human souls brought before him for judgement. He is very often pictured fighting the dragon. Michael is the patron of battles and soldiers, as well as those believed to be "possessed by the devil".

Archangel Michael appeared in visions at Monte Gargano in Apulia, Italy, in the 5th century AD. Many churches worldwide, especially those built on hilltops, are dedicated to him, such as Mont-St-Michel in France.

Above: The Archangel Michael Defeating Satan *(Guido Reni, c.1600–42).*

ARCHANGEL GABRIEL

THE ARCHANGEL GABRIEL DELIVERS SOME OF GOD'S MOST IMPORTANT MESSAGES TO MAN. HE INFORMED BOTH ELIZABETH AND MARY THAT THEY WOULD SOON GIVE BIRTH.

> **KEY FACTS**
> *Divine messenger of God*
> DATES: *Not human but a manifestation of God*
> PATRON OF: *Communications, postal workers, journalists, broadcasters*
> FEAST DAY: *29 September*
> EMBLEM: *Trumpet, often carries a lily, shield or spear*

In the Old Testament, Gabriel was present at the burial of Moses and at an Israelite victory over the Assyrians. He visited the prophet Daniel to warn him of the coming of the Messiah, saviour of the Israelites. He also helped Daniel interpret a dream that rescued the Israelites.

In the New Testament, the Archangel Gabriel was charged with telling Zachary that his wife Elizabeth would bear a son who would play an important role in the Messiah's life. This son was John the Baptist.

THE ANNUNCIATION

The most important message Gabriel delivered was to the Virgin Mary. He appeared before her to announce she had been chosen, above all women, to give birth to Jesus, the Son of God. His greeting to Mary, reported in the Gospel of Luke, has become the start of the "Hail Mary".

The Annunciation, Gabriel's visitation to the Virgin Mary, has been the subject of hundreds of paintings. The archangel always has wings and often wears a courtier's clothes, or a white tunic covered by a cloak.

Some traditions hold that, accompanied by "a multitude of heavenly hosts", Gabriel appeared above the hills of Bethlehem where shepherds were tending their flock. He announced the birth of Jesus to them.

In an ancient chapel on the Appian Way in Rome, there is an early image of Gabriel. Some medieval depictions show him carrying the staff of a doorkeeper to show that he is a guardian of the Church.

His feast day used to be 24 March, date of the Annunciation. In 1969, the pope decided he should share a feast day with Archangels Michael and Raphael.

Below: The Archangel Gabriel appears before Mary for the Annunciation *(Sandro Botticelli, c. 1489–90).*

> "HAIL MARY, FULL OF GRACE.
> THE LORD IS WITH THEE.
> BLESSED ART THOU AMONGST WOMEN,
> AND BLESSED IS THE FRUIT OF THY WOMB, JESUS.
> HOLY MARY, MOTHER OF GOD,
> PRAY FOR US SINNERS, NOW AND AT THE HOUR
> OF OUR DEATH."
>
> GABRIEL'S GREETING TO MARY MAKES UP THE FIRST TWO LINES OF THE "HAIL MARY" PRAYER

THE HOLY FAMILY

JOSEPH, MARY AND THE INFANT JESUS MAKE UP THE HOLY FAMILY. THE GOSPEL OF MATTHEW SAYS THAT THE MESSIAH WILL BE DESCENDED FROM THE HOUSE OF DAVID. THE SPIRITUAL RELATIVES OF THE HOLY FAMILY ARE THE HOLY TRINITY.

Joseph and Mary were humble and loving parents of the infant Jesus. They brought up their son in the Jewish faith and Jesus was taught to be a carpenter by his earthly father, Joseph.

OF ROYAL DESCENT?
In the first 16 verses of his gospel, Matthew demonstrates a direct line of descent from King David of the Israelites to Joseph and Jesus. Such an ancestry was essential if the Jewish prophecy that the Messiah would come from the House of David was to be fulfilled. The same royal connections are ascribed to Mary, although nothing is known of her origins. Details of the lives of her mother, Anne, and of her father, Joachim, come only from apocryphal sources.

THE BIRTH OF JESUS
When the Roman authorities held a census of the population, Joseph was obliged to travel to

Above: The Holy Family *(Luca Signorelli, 1486–90). Christ is shown as a diligent child.*

Below: A fresco depicting The Flight into Egypt, *from the Lower Church at Assisi in Italy (Giotto di Bondone, 14th century).*

Bethlehem, the city of David, to record his name. The journey was slow because of his young wife's pregnancy. Mary was very close to giving birth, but as Joseph hurried round Bethlehem at nightfall all he heard was the cry, "No room at the inn". Many other people had crowded into the town to fulfil the Romans' demands.

At last, a kindly innkeeper led him to the stables and told the tired girl that she could rest there. It was here in the stable, alongside cows and donkeys, that Mary gave birth to Jesus and laid him in a manger for lack of a cradle.

Shepherds arrived because angels had told them to visit the new Messiah. A bright star hung over the stable and guided the shepherds who brought the baby the gift of a lamb. The Holy Family received more guests with the arrival some time later of the three Magi, or wise men. They had read signs and warnings that told them where to find the new "King of the Jews". They brought him costly gifts of gold, frankincense and myrrh.

Below: Stained glass showing the holy family in the carpenter's shop, Steeple Aston, England (19th century).

Above: A Nativity scene from the Bellieu Orthodox Church in Samokov, Bulgaria (16th century).

After Jesus was born, Joseph received a warning that Herod was planning to kill the baby, so the Holy Family fled to Egypt. Herod carried out his threat, killing all male infants in Bethlehem under two years, but the Holy Infant was not among them.

NO ORDINARY CHILD

Because the archangel Gabriel had appeared to both Mary, at the Annunciation, and to Joseph to explain the importance of their son, they knew that Jesus was a special child. In spite of this they were still horrified to find, a day into their return journey from the annual trip to Jerusalem for Passover, that the 12-year-old Jesus could not be found among the family group.

Joseph and Mary returned immediately to the city and after searching for three days found him in the temple in the midst of doctors and rabbis, listening to the teachings and asking questions. Jesus calmly asked his mother why she had been so worried when she knew that he would be "about my Father's business".

THE CRUCIFIXION

We know from St John's Gospel that the Blessed Virgin was accompanied by her sister, Mary of Cleophas during her vigil at the foot of the cross. As Jesus hung from the cross, he asked the apostle John to care for his mother. This implies that she had no other sons or a husband to care for her after Jesus' death. By tradition, ary became surrogate mother to John, and travelled with him on missionary work abroad.

Below: Twelve-year-old Jesus debating with the rabbis in the temple (Adolph Friedrich Erdmann von Menzel, 1851).

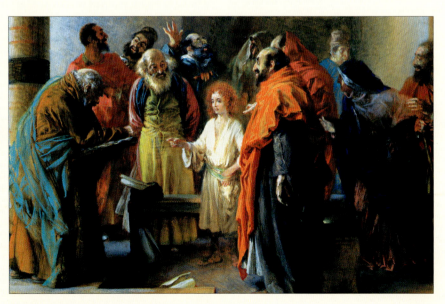

297

MARY, THE VIRGIN

MARY IS THE UNIVERSAL SYMBOL OF PURITY AND MOTHERHOOD. MANY CHRISTIANS BELIEVE SHE WAS FREE OF SIN FROM THE MOMENT SHE WAS CONCEIVED, A DOCTRINE KNOWN AS THE IMMACULATE CONCEPTION.

> **KEY FACTS**
> *Mother of the Son of God*
> DATES: *1st century BC*
> BIRTH PLACE: *Unknown*
> PATRON OF: *Motherhood, virginity*
> FEAST DAY: *15 August*
> EMBLEM: *Blue robes, crown, lily*

The image of Mary, the Blessed Virgin, is instantly recognizable, whether as a mother with her child in her arms or with her dead son laid across her lap. A mother nurtures her child, and her suffering for the sake of that child is intense. Mary, in the role of the Holy Mother, represents feelings understood by everyone. No saint can match the mother of the Son of God.

EARLY LIFE

Little is known about Mary's early life. There are no dates for her birth or her death, and mention of her parents Anne and Joachim is only found in the apocryphal 2nd-century AD Gospel of James.

We do know, from the Bible, that the Blessed Virgin was a young Jewish girl, and that, like her future husband Joseph, she was said to be descended from the family of the great Israelite king, David.

MOTHER OF CHRIST

It was the angel Gabriel who told Mary that she was to be the mother of Christ, an event known as the Annunciation. The angel said that the child would be the Son of God, not of a man. Mary accepted this extraordinary fate with great faith and courage.

The Roman population census obliged Mary and Joseph to travel to the home of their ancestor, David. Mary gave birth to Jesus in a stable in Bethlehem, surrounded by animals. Shepherds and later three wise men, the Magi, came to worship the young Messiah.

After the Nativity, Mary is mentioned only a few times in the gospels. Mary and Joseph took Jesus for his presentation at the Temple of Jerusalem, as was the custom. With Joseph and Jesus she fled to Egypt to save their child from slaughter by Herod's men.

Left: Mary and the baby Jesus are depicted as playful and loving in this stained glass from Eaton Bishop, England (14th century).

At the marriage feast at Canaan, Mary asked Jesus to intervene when the wine ran out. And, when Jesus hung dying on the cross, Mary kept vigil close by.

The Blessed Virgin was also with the apostles at Pentecost, the time after Christ's Ascension, when the Holy Spirit is believed to have descended upon them. There is no mention of Mary living with Jesus and his apostles or teaching during this time.

Left: A sculpture of Mary cradling the body of her dead son (I. Günther, 18th century). Artistic images of this moment are known as "Pietàs".

> **LEVELS OF VENERATION**
> Mary, the Mother of God, is universally admired by Catholic believers. The Catholic Church accords different levels of honour. The highest level is adoration, or *latria*, and is reserved for God and the Trinity (God the Father, God the Son and God the Holy Ghost). Veneration of the Blessed Virgin is granted the Church's second highest honour and is known as *hyperdulia*, as theorized by Thomas Aquinas. Veneration of the company of all other saints is known as *dulia*.

DIRECTORY OF SAINTS

Right: Mater Dolorosa, *or Our Lady of Sorrows. The Seven Sorrows (or* Dolors*) are events in the life of Mary that are a popular devotion and are often depicted in art. (Aelbert Bouts, c. 1495).*

A MOTHER'S PLACE

Although nothing is known of her death, members of the Catholic and Eastern Orthodox Churches hold that Mary was lifted body and soul into heaven. This event is celebrated as the Assumption. Her role as the mother of Jesus placed her very close to God in heaven.

Many believers think that if a person asks Mary to intercede on their behalf, her great influence is bound to bring God's forgiveness and redemption of their sins.

MARY IN ART

In earlier times Mary's image could be seen widely throughout Christendom. During the early medieval era, depictions of the Virgin Mary and the infant Jesus were generally richly decorated with gold. They were portrayed as formal, grand and majestic.

Images from the late medieval and early Renaissance periods show a tender young woman with a baby. She is often clothed in a heavenly blue gown and the child is naked. More sorrowful depictions are paintings of Mary with tears running down her face (*Mater Dolorosa*), standing at the foot of the cross during the Crucifixion of Christ (*Stabat Mater*), or sculptures of the Virgin Mary cradling the dead body of Jesus (*Pietà*).

In today's Catholic and Orthodox worlds, Mary is still remembered when many other saints are neglected. Holy icons and festivals held in Mary's honour continue to attract millions of believers across the globe.

Left: The Assumption of the Virgin Mary *(Peter Paul Rubens c. 1616–18).*

> "OH MOTHER OF GOD, IMMACULATE MARY, TO THEE DO I DEDICATE BY BODY AND SOUL, ALL MY PRAYERS AND DEEDS, MY JOYS AND SUFFERINGS, ALL THAT I AM AND ALL THAT I HAVE."
>
> PRAYER TO THE BLESSED VIRGIN MARY

JOSEPH

THRUST INTO THE UNIQUE ROLE OF EARTHLY FATHER TO THE SON OF GOD, JOSEPH PROVED A KINDLY HUSBAND AND CARING PARENT. HE PROTECTED HIS YOUNG FAMILY BY FLEEING FROM KING HEROD.

> **KEY FACTS**
> *Husband of the Virgin Mary*
> DATES: *1st century BC*
> BIRTH PLACE: *Palestine*
> PATRON OF: *Canada, Peru, Mexico, families, fathers, manual workers (especially carpenters), the homeless, exiles, travellers*
> FEAST DAY: *19 March and 1 May*
> EMBLEM: *Bible, branch, carpenter's tools, ladder, lamb, lily*

Joseph, husband of the Virgin Mary, was a godly man. He is most often portrayed as both honourable and compassionate.

He makes few appearances in the New Testament. The Gospels of both Mark and Luke describe his royal descent from the House of David, although a carpenter by trade. According to the Jewish prophets, the Messiah would come from this House.

Joseph's age is unknown. As the betrothed of a young woman, it may be fair to assume he was also relatively young at the time of his engagement. An indication of his noble character is given by the nature of his reaction when he learnt Mary was pregnant. Not wishing to shame her, he decided to end the betrothal quietly. His distress was dispelled when an angel appeared and explained the intervention of the Holy Spirit.

THE FLIGHT INTO EGYPT
After the Nativity and the visit of the Magi, an angel interpreted one of Joseph's dreams, warning him of Herod's order to murder all the small boys in Bethlehem. This led Joseph to flee his home to save his wife and the baby Jesus. Numerous paintings depict Joseph as very protective of his family.

Later in Egypt, an angel let Joseph know when it was safe to return to Palestine, and he settled in Nazareth. He followed Jewish custom when he took his wife to the purification ceremony that all women underwent after giving birth. The scribes do not record Joseph's death, but it is assumed he died sometime before the crucifixion of Jesus, as Joseph is not mentioned as present on this day.

OTHER INTERPRETATIONS
Joseph's actions show him worthy of his role as protector of the Son of God. Despite this, some apocryphal writings represent him as an old man and parent of other children. The travelling players of medieval theatre liked to present him as a clownish old fool.

Veneration for Joseph grew, however, and in 1870 he was declared patron of the Roman Catholic Church. A special day, 1 May, was dedicated to him as patron of manual workers.

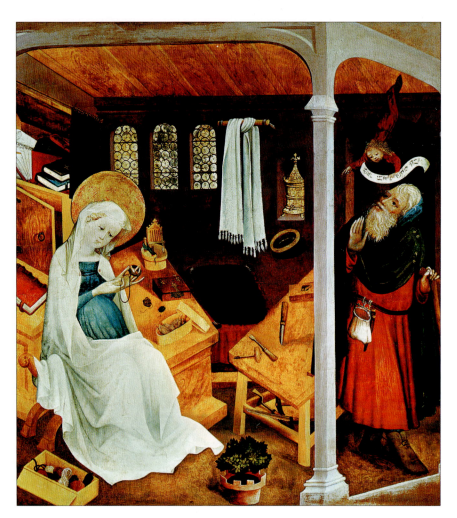

Left: A small angel reassures Joseph in The Doubt of Saint Joseph *(French School, c.1410–20).*

ANNE

The mother of the Blessed Virgin is not mentioned in the canonical gospels, but apocryphal sources praise her, and she has a loyal following nonetheless.

> **KEY FACTS**
> *Mother of the Virgin Mary*
> Dates: *1st century BC*
> Birth Place: *Unknown*
> Patron of: *Childless women, horsemen and miners*
> Feast Day: *26 July (West)*
> Emblem: *Basket, door*

There is no firm evidence to determine the parentage or place of origin of the mother of the Virgin Mary. Yet believers longed to have information about the earthly grandmother of Jesus. There is an apocryphal text, the *Gospel of James*, that mentions her as a saint. Gregory of Nyssa, the brother of St Basil the Great and a saint in his own right, also refers to her with reverence.

In the Gospel of James, Anne is described as childless, and she "mourned in two mournings, and lamented in two lamentations". Her desperate prayers were answered when an angel visited her house to tell her she would bear a child.

Anne responded with the words, "As the Lord my God liveth, if I beget either male or female I will bring it as a gift to the Lord my God; and it shall minister to Him in holy things all the days of its life." So the Virgin Mary was consecrated to God even before her birth.

In the *Golden Legend*, stories of the saints from the 13th century, Anne's husband Joachim dies shortly after the birth of Mary. Anne remarries twice. She has a daughter by each of these new husbands, and both these girls are given the name of Mary. The girls grow up to produce many cousins for Jesus, and two boy cousins become apostles. Despite the fictitious nature of both these sources, Anne became sufficiently important in the Church for her relics to appear at the church of Santa Maria Antiqua in Rome.

Above: A young Mary is shown reading to her mother in this manuscript drawing (15th century).

Below: The story of Mary's birth is here imagined within a contemporary Venetian domestic setting (Vittore Carpaccio, 1504–8).

LATER INFLUENCE

The figure of Anne remained in the public mind and artists favoured her as a subject. Paintings and stained-glass illustrations show Anne as a tender mother to her little girl. Other images depict Anne teaching Mary how to weave and read.

An unexpected cultus grew in Constantinople (Istanbul) during the 6th century AD when Emperor Justinian I dedica,ted a shrine to St Anne. She was venerated in Europe from the 13th century. When England's King Richard II (1367–1400) married Anne of Bohemia in 1382, the English bishops petitioned the pope to grant a feast day for St Anne. Later, the official status of such an unsubstantiated figure aroused great anger in Martin Luther.

JOACHIM

JOACHIM IS HONOURED AS THE HUSBAND OF ANNE AND THE FATHER OF MARY. HIS POPULARITY GREW IN THE WEST IN THE MIDDLE AGES AS THE CULTUS OF THE BLESSED VIRGIN FLOURISHED.

> **KEY FACTS**
> *Father of the Virgin Mary*
> DATES: *1st century BC*
> BIRTH PLACE: *Unknown*
> PATRON OF: *Fathers, grandfathers*
> FEAST DAY: *26 July (West)*
> EMBLEM: *Elderly man holding doves, lamb*

This man became a saint by virtue of being the husband of St Anne and the father of the Blessed Virgin. In Hebrew, his name means "the Lord will judge". The sources of information for him are entirely fictitious, as they are for his wife.

In the *Golden Legend*, Joachim is given a picturesque history. This book tells how he was expelled from the Jewish temple because, after 20 years of marriage, he and his wife remained childless.

Desolate and believing God had cursed him, Joachim went to seek refuge with a band of shepherds. He decided to fast for 40 days. An angel visited and comforted him with the news that his wife would bear a child. Excited, Joachim hurried home.

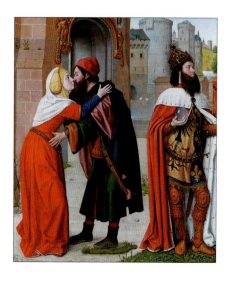

Above: Charlemagne, and the Meeting of Saints Joachim and Anne at the Golden Gate *(the Master of Moulins, c.1500).*

Below right: Presentation of the Virgin at the Temple *(Philippe de Champaigne, 1639–40). Mary would have been taken to a synagogue, but this image depicts a Christian setting.*

But Anne, his worried wife, was wandering through Jerusalem looking for her husband. An angel appeared and advised her to go to the Golden Gate. There, Anne found her husband. After this happy reunion, she conceived the child who would become the Mother of God.

LATER RECOGNITION

The cultus of St Joachim began in the East and was more popular there than in the West. For several centuries, the Eastern Orthodox Church has celebrated his feast day on 9 September. The Roman Catholic Church was less eager to grant him sainthood, but the large cultus could not be ignored. Pope Gregory XV (1554–1623) allowed him status as a saint, and Joachim shares a feast day with his wife.

Below: A fresco scene showing Joachim among the shepherds (Giotto di Bondone, c.1303–10).

ELIZABETH

ELIZABETH WAS ELDERLY AND GENERALLY ASSUMED TO BE BARREN WHEN SHE BECAME PREGNANT WITH THE BOY WHO WOULD BECOME JOHN THE BAPTIST. THE ARCHANGEL GABRIEL DELIVERED THE NEWS.

It is assumed that Elizabeth was close to menopause when Gabriel announced that she was carrying a child. She was known to be childless, and the news must have brought her great joy.

Elizabeth, a descendant of the patriarch Aaron, is said to have been related to the Blessed Virgin. Their friendship was cemented by their fates as well as by blood.

> **KEY FACTS**
> Wife of Zachary, mother of John the Baptist
> DATES: *1st century BC*
> BIRTH PLACE: *Probably Palestine*
> PATRON OF: *Pregnancy*
> FEAST DAY: *5 November*
> EMBLEM: *Elderly woman*

Numerous paintings show these women together. Elizabeth was the first person to recognize Mary as the mother of the future Lord.

Left: A detail of St Elizabeth from the church of Santa Maria di Porto Fuori, Italy (Ercole de' Roberti, c.1480–81).

ZACHARY

INITIALLY DOUBTFUL, ZACHARY WAS JOYFUL AT THE PROMISE OF A CHILD AND NAMED HIM JOHN.

The father of John the Baptist was a Jewish priest. He and his wife Elizabeth had long been married, but had no children.

Zachary was visited in the temple of Jerusalem by the archangel Gabriel, who announced that Elizabeth was to give birth to a child who would "make ready a people prepared for the Lord". Zachary doubted the words of the angel and was struck dumb.

At the baby's circumcision, Elizabeth insisted that he was to be called John, going against the Jewish tradition that a child should be given a family name. Zachary supported her by writing on a tablet, "His name is John." Immediately, he regained his voice and began praising God. His words, known as the Benedictus, form part of the Church liturgy.

> **KEY FACTS**
> Father of John the Baptist
> DATES: *1st century BC*
> BIRTH PLACE: *Probably Palestine*
> FEAST DAY: *5 November*

> "AND THOU, O CHILD, SHALL BE CALLED THE PROPHET OF THE MOST HIGH; FOR THOU SHALT GO BEFORE THE LORD TO PREPARE HIS WAYS, TO GIVE HIS PEOPLE KNOWLEDGE OF SALVATION THROUGH FORGIVENESS OF THEIR SINS . . ."
>
> THE BENEDICTUS (CANTICLE OF ZACHARY)

Left: In this Flemish early Renaissance painting, Zachary is displayed in the fine clothes of a medieval baron to indicate his high status as the father of John the Baptist (Jan Provost, 1510).

JOHN THE BAPTIST

JOHN THE BAPTIST DEVOTED HIS LIFE TO WARNING PEOPLE TO "REPENT, FOR THE KINGDOM OF GOD IS AT HAND". HE DECLARED THAT THE MESSIAH WOULD SOON APPEAR AMONG THEM.

> **KEY FACTS**
> *Baptized Jesus*
> DATES: *d.c. AD 30*
> BIRTH PLACE: *Nazareth*
> PATRON OF: *Pilgrims to the Holy Land, Knights Hospitallers, hoteliers, birdwatchers*
> FEAST DAY: *24 June, 29 August*
> EMBLEM: *Lamb, cross, a scroll*

The writings of Sts Jerome and Augustine of Hippo suggested that John the Baptist was sanctified in the womb and never committed a sin. He certainly chose a "heroic" life of hardship and poverty, dressing only in animal skins and living on food he could scavenge.

John devoted his life to telling people to prepare for the coming of the Messiah and his kingdom. He must have had a charismatic personality with great energy and determination, for he attracted a large following.

BY THE JORDAN

His youth was spent as a hermit, surviving on a diet of locusts and wild honey, a lifestyle that closely resembled that of some of the prophets of the Old Testament. Crowds came to hear him preach, and John began to baptize them by dipping them in the River Jordan. When Jesus came through the crowd, a dove hovered over his head.

John took this bird to be a sign of the Holy Spirit, so he knew Jesus was the Messiah. He then baptized Jesus, saying he was "the Lamb of God who takest away the sins of the world". In paintings, John is often shown pointing at a lamb and holding a cross.

John the Baptist was later put in prison for denouncing an incestuous marriage between the governor of Galilee, Herod Antipas, and his niece, Herodias. His stepdaughter, Salome, pleased Herod so much with her dancing that he offered her anything she wanted. At her mother's prompting, the girl requested the head of John the Baptist. It was delivered to her on a platter.

TEACHINGS

The teachings of John the Baptist prepared the way for the work of Jesus. John preached about the presence of a "messianic kingdom" and the need for all to repent their sins. His lessons were

Left: Saint John the Baptist in the Wilderness *(Hieronymus Bosch, c.1504–5). John the Baptist is shown in a landscape of strange plants with a lamb, one of his emblems.*

DIRECTORY OF SAINTS

rooted in the Jewish belief that one day the Almighty would send a messiah to lead the people to righteousness. Many Jews who heard John speak were therefore sympathetic to the arrival of Jesus and accepted him as their long-awaited leader.

A large number of disciples followed John and imitated his severe ascetic mode of life. He taught them methods of prayer and meditation. Many ordinary, humble families were moved by his message, too.

Historians believe that John the Baptist's wanderings took him to the Dead Sea. Lessons similar to his message are recorded in the Dead Sea Scrolls – papyrus writings dating from the early Christian era. In Samaria, there is evidence of a community, the Mandaeans, or Sabaeans, who defined themselves as "Christians according to John". It seems these people preserved ideas and traditions that confused John the Baptist with Jesus.

Below: Salome with the Head of Saint John the Baptist (Bernardino Luini, c.1525–30). Salome is shown as a young woman with a sly and cunning expression.

Medieval Christians prayed to John the Baptist, believing that, through him, Christ would enter their souls. He is reputedly buried in Sebaste, Samaria. Alone among the saints, his feast day is held on his birthday. However, the date of his death is also celebrated in the West on 29 August.

An important saint, some of his relics are claimed to be held in St Sylvester's Church in Rome, and in Amiens, France. Many churches in Britain and Europe have been dedicated to him.

Left: Saint John the Baptist (Titian, c.1540). John may be dressed in skins and rags, but he is here presented as a powerful man and leader. The lamb lies at his feet.

THE MEANING OF BAPTISM

Baptism is a religious purification ceremony in which a person is either immersed in water, or has water poured over their head. Baptism is part of the Christian tradition, but can be seen to have a precursor in the Jewish tradition of undergoing a *mikvah*, or cleansing ritual – for instance, on conversion to Judaism.

Baptism has been subject to many interpretations by different Christian churches, and as a result has varied meanings. It can be seen as a path to salvation and a process by which a person is cleansed of their sins. In this way, baptism may help a convert to Christianity put their past behind them and start afresh.

Similarly, baptism may be seen as a symbolic death and rebirth, an interpretation put forward in the Bible by Paul, who says that we share in the death, burial and re-birth of Jesus Christ through baptism. Baptism can also function as a symbol of conversion, through which a believer declares their faith and their membership of a particular church.

Right: Mosaic in the dome of the Arian Baptistry in Ravenna, Italy (5th century AD). It depicts the Holy Spirit, visible as a dove, hovering above the head of Christ during his baptism by John.

DISMAS

JESUS COMFORTED DISMAS, THE "GOOD THIEF", AS TOGETHER THEY SUFFERED DEATH BY CRUCIFIXION. DISMAS FELT THAT UNLIKE JESUS HE DESERVED HIS PUNISHMENT AS HE HAD COMMITTED A CRIME.

KEY FACTS
Crucified next to Christ
DATES: *d.c.AD 30*
BIRTH PLACE: *Probably Galilee*
PATRON OF: *Thieves, condemned criminals, undertakers*
FEAST DAY: *25 March*
EMBLEM: *Tall cross, naked on cross*

Dismas, a common thief, was nailed to a cross next to Jesus on the day of the Crucifixion and spoke with him. The Eastern Orthodox Church has put in their litany the words that Dismas uttered to Jesus. "Lord," he said, "remember me when you come into your kingdom." Jesus gave the reassuring answer, "Today thou shalt be with me in Paradise."

Luke records the story in his gospel. Dismas reprimands the other thief, Gestas, who asks Jesus, as the Messiah, to prove it and save all three of them from death. According to a medieval story, some time previously, Dismas, in awe of the infant Jesus, had even ordered his fellow bandits to leave the Holy Family unmolested as they made their escape to Egypt.

In the Middle Ages, Dismas came to be seen as the patron saint of prisoners and thieves.

Right: The Crucifixion *(Francesco Botticini, c.1471).*

VERONICA

AN ORDINARY WOMAN WITH A KIND HEART TRIED TO SOOTHE CHRIST AS HE CARRIED HIS CROSS ON THE WAY TO HIS CRUCIFIXION AT CALVARY. THE VEIL SHE USED BECAME AN IMPORTANT RELIC.

KEY FACTS
Wiped the brow of Christ
DATES: *1st century AD*
BIRTH PLACE: *Probably Galilee*
FEAST DAY: *12 July*
EMBLEM: *Veil with Christ's image upon it*

There is a strong possibility that Veronica is a legendary figure. Even her name is likely to be a combination of *vera*, meaning "true" in Latin, and *icon*, meaning "image" in ancient Greek. However, she figures in the Stations of the Cross, the 14 events that mark the journey of Christ carrying his cross to the Hill of Calvary.

Veronica was a woman in the mob who followed Jesus on his last earthly trip. The crowds pushed and shoved to catch a glimpse of this man, the so-called "King of the Jews", and many yelled insults in bloodthirsty tones. But scattered among the crowds were frightened, anxious and distressed

Christians. Veronica was one of these. Pitying Jesus as he sweated and struggled under his burden, she took off her veil and wiped his brow.

An imprint of his face was left on the veil and it was taken to St Peter's Basilica in Rome in the 8th century. The veil became a popular relic in the 14th and 15th centuries. Claims that Jesus had once cured Veronica of a blood illness remain unproven.

Left: St Veronica's veil is clearly imprinted with the image of Jesus Christ (the Master of Saint Veronica, Germany, c.1420).

JOSEPH OF ARIMATHEA

A SECRET BUT WEALTHY CONVERT TO CHRISTIANITY RESCUED THE BODY OF CHRIST AFTER THE CRUCIFIXION. HE LAID IT TO REST IN THE TOMB HE HAD PREPARED FOR HIMSELF.

> **KEY FACTS**
> *Cared for the dead body of Jesus*
> DATES: *1st century AD*
> BIRTH PLACE: *Jerusalem*
> PATRON OF: *Grave diggers, burial, cemetery keepers and caretakers*
> FEAST DAY: *17 March*

Joseph was a wealthy Israelite who had secretly converted to Christianity. He did not take part in the Jewish condemnation of Jesus, nor did he speak against it.

Following the arrest of Jesus, the situation in Jerusalem was tense. Jewish leaders were calling for the punishment of this person who claimed to be the Messiah. But Pontius Pilate, the Roman governor, was reluctant to sentence Jesus to death.

To mark the Jewish festival of Passover, Pilate offered to pardon one prisoner, giving the Jews a choice between Jesus and the common thief, Barabbas. Pilate was shocked by their choice and washed his hands to indicate his innocence. "Let his blood be upon us," the irate crowd replied. No doubt many Christians, like Joseph of Arimathea, did not dare face the mob.

Below: Joseph of Arimathea preaches to the inhabitants of Britain (William Blake, 18th century).

THE TOMB OF CHRIST
Overwhelmed by shame at his cowardice after the Crucifixion, Joseph went to Pontius Pilate and asked for the body of Jesus. It was the custom to throw the bodies of criminals as carrion for animals to devour. But Joseph bought the mutilated body before this happened, and took it to a garden he owned, close to Calvary, where Jesus had died. Here, Joseph had carved out a rocky sepulchre intended as his own burial place. He wrapped the body in clean linen, pushing a huge rock against the opening to close the tomb.

LEGENDARY TRAVELS
It is said that the apostle Philip sent Joseph on a mission to England, where he founded a church at Glastonbury and grew a tree that is said to flower on Christmas Day. Joseph is included in the Arthurian legends.

DIRECTORY OF SAINTS

MARY MAGDALENE

LOVED FOR HER DEVOTION TO JESUS, MARY MAGDALENE IS THE GRAND EXAMPLE OF THE REFORMED SINNER. HER LIFE SHOWS THAT ANYONE MAY BE TRANSFORMED IF THEY TRULY REPENT.

> **KEY FACTS**
> *First witness to the risen Christ*
> DATES: *1st century AD*
> BIRTH PLACE: *Possibly Magdala, Palestine*
> PATRON OF: *Repentant sinners, hairdressers, perfume-makers, contemplatives*
> FEAST DAY: *22 July*
> EMBLEM: *Jar of ointment, loosened hair*

Mary Magdalene was one of the many women who accompanied Jesus and the apostles on their travels, caring for them and supporting them. She was close to Jesus and played a major role in the events surrounding his death and resurrection.

CONTROVERSIAL FIGURE
Over the centuries, Mary Magdalene has aroused much controversy among theologians.

In Western Christianity, she is often identified both as the sister of Martha of Bethany and as the sinner who dried Christ's feet with her hair. But, in Eastern Christianity, Mary Magdalene, Martha of Bethany and the sinner are three different women.

Despite these problems, the existence of Mary Magdalene is not questioned. She is known for her sincere conversion, generous heart and contemplative mind.

Above: Detail of Mary kissing Jesus' feet from Life of Saint Mary Magdalene *(attr. to Giotto di Bondone, Palmerino di Guido and others, 14th century).*

REPENTANT SINNER
The story of the sinner is perhaps the most significant of the earlier accounts thought to relate to Mary Magdalene.

While Jesus was dining at the home of a Pharisee called Simon, a woman crept in and knelt before him. Simon was angered by this interruption from a woman who was a known sinner.

The woman began to kiss Jesus' feet and weep, begging to be forgiven for her transgressions. She dried his feet with her long hair and rubbed them with expensive

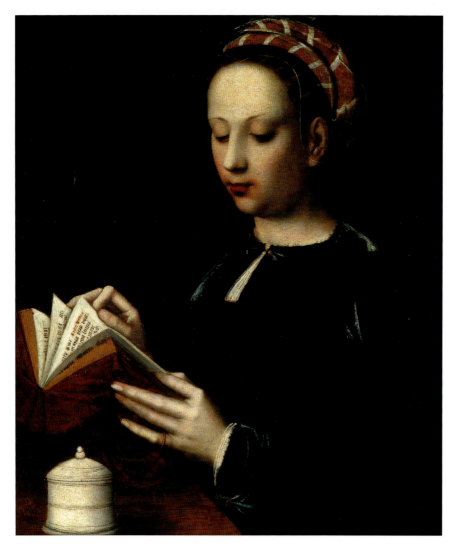

Left: Mary Magdalene Reading *(attr. to Ambrosius Benson, 1540).*

308

DIRECTORY OF SAINTS

Above: Christ on the Cross with Saints *(Luca Signorelli and Pietro Perugino, 1482).*

perfumed ointment. Jesus told the distraught woman that all her sins were forgiven.

MESSENGER OF CHRIST
To modern Christians, both Orthodox and Catholic, Mary Magdalene is important because she was a devoted and committed follower of Christ who witnessed some of the most significant moments of his life. She accompanied Jesus on his last journey to Jerusalem and was present at the Crucifixion, keeping vigil.

Three days after his death, Mary went to his burial cave, intending to anoint his body. When she arrived she found the rock that closed the cave opening had been rolled away and the body was gone. Mary ran to question a gardener nearby. But when he spoke she realized that he was the risen Christ. Jesus gave her the glory of telling the disciples that he had been resurrected.

PREACHER AND HERMIT
Eastern legend claims that, after the Resurrection, Mary Magdalene travelled to Ephesus with the Blessed Virgin and the apos-

> "SAINT MARY MAGDALENE, TEACH US TO FORGIVE OURSELVES, AND THEN TO FORGIVE OTHERS."
>
> PRAYER TO ST MARY MAGDALENE

Above: Mary Magdalene carried by angels (Simon Vouet, 17th century).

tle John, where she later died and was buried. According to a Western legend, however, Mary, along with her sister Martha and brother Lazarus, travelled by boat to France. They landed in Provence and proceeded to Marseilles, where they preached the gospel. Mary is said to have retired to a nearby cave to live as a hermit. When she died, angels carried her to the oratory of St Maxim near Aix-en-Provence.

MARTHA

Martha was either the sister of Mary of Bethany or, as in the Western Christian tradition, the sister of Mary Magdalene. Jesus was said to enjoy visiting Martha's house and loved her and her siblings. It was Martha's brother, Lazarus, whom Jesus raised from the dead.

A popular story reveals Martha's busy nature. On one of Jesus' visits to their home, she bustled about preparing food, while Mary sat in rapt attention at the feet of Christ. When Martha expressed irritation at her sister's idleness, Jesus rebuked her. He told her that Mary had made the better choice; the contemplative life is preferable to an active one that allows no time for thought or prayer.

Above: The Raising of Lazarus *(the Coetivy Master, c.1460). Martha was chief among the mourners to witness the miracle.*

309

THE APOSTLES

THE 12 MEN CHOSEN BY JESUS TO AID HIM IN HIS WORK WENT OUT TO PREACH THE GOSPEL WITH AUTHORITY AFTER HIS DEATH. IT WAS EACH APOSTLE'S DUTY TO LIVE IN IMITATION OF CHRIST.

Above: A very early fresco of Jesus Christ and his apostles, found in a church in Cappadocia, Turkey.

Jesus had at least 120, possibly thousands, of disciples. They were ordinary men and women who followed him wherever he went, learning from his teachings. He selected 12 special men to be his apostles (derived from the Greek word for "ambassador") from among these people. They became his closest companions and were witness to some of the most significant moments of Christ's life and resurrection.

FOLLOWERS OF JESUS

The earliest followers of Christ were two pairs of brothers – Peter and Andrew, and James and John – fishermen who worked along the coast of the Sea of Galilee. Tax collectors were generally despised at the time, and yet that was the profession of Matthew, the next apostle to be called.

It is thought that 11 of these 12 men were Galileans. Judas Iscariot, their treasurer and the man who betrayed Jesus, was the only non-Galilean. After the Crucifixion, Peter oversaw the replacement of Judas by Matthias.

FISHERS OF MEN

When Jesus called Peter and Andrew, he said that if they followed him he would make them "fishers of men". Many Christians consider these words to be a metaphor for the apostles' role: to bring people to Jesus as a fisherman catches fish.

In the years of persecution, cautious Christians used the image of a fish, scratched on walls and rocks, as a secret sign. *Icthys*, the Greek word for "fish", is an acrostic, or word puzzle, consisting of the initial letters for five other words that described Christ to his believers: *Iesous Christos, Theou Yios, Soter* (Jesus Christ, Son of God, Saviour).

ROLE OF THE APOSTLES

Jesus defined the purpose of the work of his chosen few. They were to teach his message, to baptize, to rule by guiding the faithful, and to sanctify the grace of God through prayer. These roles were to be passed on to successors when an apostle died or became frail.

Roman Catholics believe that Jesus appointed these "men of the apostolate" to administer his Church. He put the organization into their hands with Peter, the first pope, as his chief. Peter was to rule the whole Church, make judgements and name his successor. This division of duties has remained the basis of the administrative structure of the Church ever since. All popes are believed to be Peter's successors.

Above: Christ calming a storm and saving fishermen, in stained glass from Exeter Cathedral, England.

310

JUDAS ISCARIOT

This apostle is infamous for betraying Christ to the Jewish authorities. But it was his method of identifying his leader, Jesus, that is perceived as particularly repugnant. Judas knew that Jesus and the apostles had spent the night praying in the Garden of Gethsemane. At dawn, he and the temple guards approached the group, and Judas told the guards, "The one I kiss is the man you want." For the sum of 30 pieces of silver, he kissed Jesus, who was then led to his death.

It was said that Judas, crazed with remorse, threw the "blood money" into the temple and then hanged himself. The kind of tree to which he tied his noose is still known as a Judas tree, and the field where Judas died is called "Aceldama" – the field of blood. His name is given to traitors, while any act of betrayal is often termed "the kiss of Judas".

Right: The traitor's kiss is hewn from stone on this church wall in France.

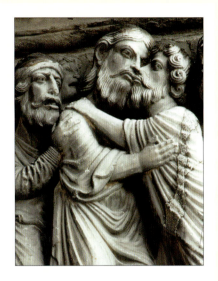

Protestants were, and are, more ambivalent about the role of the individual apostles. Some credit them with divine authority. Other sects say they are simply the first evangelists or preachers. They are seen as early missionaries who were given significant qualities to fulfil their role as heralds of the gospel message.

SPREADING THE WORD

Soon after he had chosen the 12, Jesus gave his apostles the power to cast out evil spirits and cure disease. He sent them out in pairs to preach and use their gifts in the towns of Galilee, instructing them to "take nothing for their journey, except a mere staff".

After the Resurrection, the apostles dedicated themselves to spreading the teachings of Jesus around the known world. Peter was the first of them to perform a miracle and was also one of the first apostles to set out into the world as a missionary.

All the apostles undertook arduous journeys to fulfil their appointed roles. They set high standards of obedience, poverty and chastity, avoiding all worldly pleasures that might distract them from their mission.

DYING FOR THEIR FAITH

Such was the conviction of these men that they were prepared to die cruel deaths for their faith. A total of 11 apostles were martyred. The work of these brave men proved productive. After 300 years of continued apostleship, the Emperor Constantine I made Christianity the religion of the Roman Empire, and from then on the "new" religion spread rapidly.

Below: All the apostles were present with Jesus at the Last Supper (Justus van Gent, 1473–74).

JAMES THE GREAT

ABANDONING HIS FISHING NETS IN ORDER TO BECOME A "FISHER OF MEN", JAMES WAS ONE OF THE EARLIEST DISCIPLES TO FOLLOW JESUS, AND THE FIRST APOSTLE MARTYR.

> **KEY FACTS**
> *Apostle*
> DATES: *d.AD 44*
> BIRTH PLACE: *Galilee*
> PATRON OF: *Spain, Guatemala, Nicaragua (with Philip), Uruguay*
> FEAST DAY: *25 July*
> EMBLEM: *Shell, sword, pilgrim's staff, pilgrim's hat*

There were two apostles that were named James. One became known as James the Less, and the other, James the Great – so-called because he was the elder of the two. James the Great was one of the leading apostles.

James and his brother John were fishermen who abandoned their nets to follow Jesus. Both brothers were known to be very quick-tempered, hence their nickname "sons of thunder".

James also had qualities of reliability, leadership and loyalty. He witnessed the major events of Christ's life. He was one of those present at the Transfiguration, and was in the Garden of Gethsemane to comfort his master during his most despairing moments.

The details of James' life after the Crucifixion are uncertain. He may have gone to Judea and Samaria to spread the Christian message. But it is known that he was beheaded by Herod Agrippa in Jerusalem.

Above: The shell and pilgrim's staff identify St James the Great (Hans Klocker, c.17th century).

Below: Apostles Philip and James are often portrayed as men of learning (School of Fra Bartolomeo, c.1400).

His body, it is said, was carried to the shore where a boat suddenly materialized. His disciples placed the body in this miraculous vessel and it floated to the coast of Spain. There, Christians found the relics and buried them in a forest where the city of Santiago de Compostela now stands.

The shrine containing his relics in Compostela was of great importance during the Crusades, because soldiers believed St James could grant military prowess. Santiago de Compostela remains a major site of modern pilgrimage.

GROWTH OF HIS CULTUS
According to Spanish tradition, James appeared to fight the Moors when they invaded Spain in AD 844. He rode through the sky on a white horse, holding a shield bearing a red cross and a sword. With his help, the Spanish vanquished their enemy.

In the 16th century, sailors allegedly saw St James resting on a cloud. It hovered protectively over the galleons carrying early Spanish explorers across the Atlantic to the Americas. He inspired them to convert the American people they encountered. The feast day of St James the Great is celebrated in major national festivals in South America to this day.

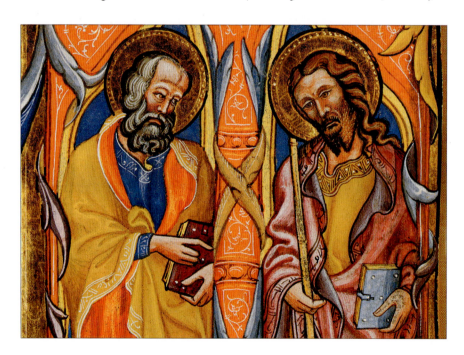

JAMES THE LESS

This apostle is identified as "the son of Alphaeus", but he slips quietly, almost anonymously, through the Christian story. Some sources identify him as Christ's brother.

KEY FACTS
Apostle
DATES: *d.AD 62*
BIRTH PLACE: *Galilee*
PATRON OF: *The dying*
FEAST DAY: *3 May*
EMBLEM: *Fuller's club*

There is little mention of James the Less during Jesus' ministry. But, after the Crucifixion and Resurrection, this James communicated closely with Jesus before his Ascension into heaven.

James became an important figure in the new Christian community in Jerusalem, where St Paul relied on his leadership. During the Council of Jerusalem (*c*.AD 50), James supported Paul in the call to accept Gentiles as Christians without demanding that these converts be circumcised. This decision caused much controversy at the council. As men brought up in the Jewish tradition, the apostles tended to regard circumcision as an important symbol of faith.

James was stoned or possibly clubbed to death. Another version says James was thrown from a temple top, but as he lay dying, he forgave his tormentors. Even Jewish leaders of the time believed the city faced calamity after the death of this fine man. James is often linked with the apostle Philip, and many churches are dedicated to "Philip and James".

Right: The Communion of the Apostle James the Less *(Niccoló Bambini, 1720).*

PHILIP

This practical-minded apostle helped in the feeding of the 5,000, and the searching questions he asked Jesus clarified important points of faith.

KEY FACTS
Apostle
DATES: *1st century AD*
BIRTH PLACE: *Bethsaida*
PATRON OF: *Uruguay*
FEAST DAY: *3 May (West)*
EMBLEM: *Loaf of bread, large cross, a dragon*

Philip heard John the Baptist preach and then sought out Jesus. Philip seems to have been an energetic and practical man. He arranged appointments, and introduced Nathanael, later St Bartholomew, to Christ.

When Jesus wanted to feed a crowd of 5,000 people who had gathered to hear his message, Philip commented, "Two hundred pennyworth of bread is not sufficient for them." But when a small boy offered five loaves and two fishes, Philip helped distribute the food, believing this would feed everyone as Jesus said.

Above: The Apostle Philip *(Georges de La Tour, 1620).*

At the Last Supper, Philip asked, "Lord, show us the Father." The answer came from Jesus, "I am in the Father and the Father is in me."

Philip preached in Phrygia and is thought to have killed an evil dragon brought by the Scythians. He possibly died a martyr in Hierapolis (in Syria), but his relics are held in Rome. He is closely associated with James the Less. The two apostles share a feast day.

DIRECTORY OF SAINTS

BARTHOLOMEW

BEST KNOWN FOR THE CRUEL MANNER OF HIS DEATH FROM BEING FLAYED ALIVE, THIS SINCERE AND LOYAL APOSTLE IS THOUGHT TO HAVE PREACHED AS FAR AFIELD AS INDIA.

> **KEY FACTS**
> *Apostle*
> DATES: *1st century AD*
> BIRTH PLACE: *Probably Galilee*
> PATRON OF: *Tanners*
> FEAST DAY: *24 August*
> EMBLEM: *Butcher's knife*

When Jesus first met Bartholomew, also known as Nathanael, he observed a man "in whom there is no guile". Bartholomew never doubted the truth of Jesus' teachings and was one of the early apostles. He was present at the Pentecost and then travelled to spread the message.

Bartholomew is said to have preached in Armenia and India, where he may have left behind a copy of the Gospel of St Matthew. Tradition says he defeated demons in India that encouraged idol worship. He converted the local king Polemius and his family. This action enraged the king's brother, Astrages, who captured him and ordered Bartholomew to be flayed alive and then beheaded.

Michelangelo shows Bartholomew holding his own flayed skin in *The Last Judgement*, in the Sistine Chapel, Vatican City. His relics were enshrined on an island in the River Tiber in Rome.

Left: A curved butcher's knife forms part of this statue of Bartholomew, in San Gennaro in Italy, referring to his cruel death.

JUDE

TRADITIONALLY BELIEVED TO BE THE AUTHOR OF THE EPISTLE OF JUDE, THIS APOSTLE IS NOW BEST KNOWN AS THE PATRON SAINT OF LOST CAUSES. HE IS OFTEN TURNED TO BY THOSE IN DESPAIR.

> **KEY FACTS**
> *Apostle*
> DATES: *1st century AD*
> BIRTH PLACE: *Palestine*
> PATRON OF: *Hopeless causes*
> FEAST DAY: *28 October (West)*
> EMBLEM: *Club, holding a boat*

The apostle Jude is not mentioned with any great frequency in the gospels, but he has a large modern cultus. For uncertain reasons, this apostle gained a reputation for offering sympathy and hope to those in despair. Worshippers turn to him when they are in dire trouble.

His name is often followed by the words "not Iscariot", so that he is not confused with Judas. He is also known as Thaddaeus.

It is claimed he wrote the Epistle of Jude. This tells of a mission to Persia with another apostle, Simon, who apparently was his cousin. Jude was martyred by being clubbed to death, although there is little evidence to verify how he died.

Sometimes Jude is pictured holding a ship while his cousin clutches a fish. These signs indicate that the men were both former fishermen.

Left: A detail of The Apostle Thaddeus *from Siena Cathedral (Duccio di Buoninsegna, 1308).*

314

THOMAS

CHIEFLY REMEMBERED AS "DOUBTING THOMAS", THIS APOSTLE NEEDED PROOF BEFORE ACCEPTING ANY TRUTH. HE WAS THE FIRST TO ACKNOWLEDGE CHRIST'S DIVINITY AFTER THE RESURRECTION.

> **KEY FACTS**
> *Apostle*
> DATES: *1st century AD*
> BIRTH PLACE: *Probably Palestine*
> PATRON OF: *Architects, carpenters, surveyors, builders, sculptors*
> FEAST DAY: *3 July (West)*
> EMBLEM: *Incredulity, holding T-square as a builder*

Thomas questioned things but, once he was given a satisfying answer, remained firm in his belief. He asked Jesus, "Where are you going? How can we know the way?" Jesus answered, "I am the way, the truth, and the life." Fiercely loyal, Thomas was ready to die with Jesus.

The apostle is most famously known as "Doubting Thomas", because he could not believe the Resurrection of Christ. When he met the Lord after his death, Thomas asked to touch the wounds left by a soldier's lance as he hung on the cross. Christ allowed him to do so and, now convinced of the reality, Thomas became ardent in his belief. Indeed, he was the first to publicly acknowledge the divinity of Christ by calling him "My Lord and my God."

A legend says that because Thomas did not witness the Blessed Virgin's Assumption to heaven, she appeared in person to reassure him. As a token of proof, she gave him her belt.

His life after the Pentecost is mysterious. There are claims that he travelled to India, where he

Below: A patient Christ offers proof of his resurrection in the painting Doubting Thomas *(Gian Francesco Barbieri, 1621).*

preached and built a cathedral for a prince. Such stories are perhaps confirmed by a community of Christians in Kerala, south India, who identify themselves as the "St Thomas Christians".

In 1522, Portuguese travellers claimed to have seen his grave in Mylapore near Madras. The *Acts of Thomas*, a document from the 3rd or 4th century, says he was killed by a lance. His relics ended up in Persia (Iran), but Ortona, in Italy, also laid claim to them.

PETER

CHRIST DESCRIBED PETER AS THE "ROCK OF THE CHURCH". AS THE LEADER OF THE APOSTLES, HE IS THE EARTHLY FATHER OF THE FAITH, AND IS SAID TO HOLD THE KEYS TO THE KINGDOM OF HEAVEN.

> **KEY FACTS**
> Leader of the apostles; called the "rock of the Church" by Jesus
> DATES: *d.c.AD 64*
> BIRTH PLACE: *Bethsaida, Sea of Galilee*
> PATRON OF: *Fishermen, papacy*
> FEAST DAY: *29 June*
> EMBLEM: *Keys, ship, fish, cockerel*

Peter was warm and impetuous by nature, yet also rather cautious. He needed reassurance that Jesus was indeed the Messiah.

To his eternal shame, he was so overwhelmed by fear during the trial of Jesus that three times he denied his friendship with him. But Peter's passion and general boldness made him leader of the apostles. His name in Aramaic, Cephas, means "rock", and Jesus chose him as the "rock" upon which the Church was built.

Known as Simon Peter, he fished with his brother Andrew on the Sea of Galilee. Jesus came to them one day when they had failed to catch any fish. He told them to lower their nets and to their surprise they hauled up an enormous catch. "Come with

Above: A mural showing Peter's denial of Christ and the cock crowing (from the Church of the Holy Cross at Platanistasa, Cyprus, 15th century).

me," Jesus said, "and I will make you fishers of men." After this, Peter began his ministry with Jesus, and he is mentioned frequently throughout the gospels. He was very close to Christ and became the leader of the 12 apostles. He was with Jesus during the Agony in the Garden, the night Christ spent in tormented prayer before his arrest and death. And when Judas came with soldiers and some officials that dawn to make the arrest, Peter was so enraged that he drew a sword and sliced off the ear of Malchus, the high priest's servant.

Peter was one of three apostles to witness the Transfiguration, when Jesus was surrounded by light with the prophets, Moses and Elijah, on either side. A voice said, "This is my beloved Son… Listen to Him." And, after Pentecost, when the Holy Spirit gave the apostles the gift of tongues, Peter was the first to speak to the crowds.

FIRST CHURCH LEADER

Peter took administrative control of the apostles after Christ's death and chose Matthias to replace Judas Iscariot. He sent Paul and Barnabas to the Mediterranean as disciples and evangelists.

Peter cured a beggar who had suffered all his life from a lame leg, thus becoming the first apostle to perform a miracle. More significantly, he was ready to sit at a meal with a non-Jew, or Gentile. Peter converted a Roman centurion, Cornelius, who was the first Gentile to become a Christian believer.

The admittance of Gentiles caused controversy among the other apostles who had preached

Below: Peter enthroned, and six scenes from the lives of Jesus and St Peter (the Master of St Peter, 1280).

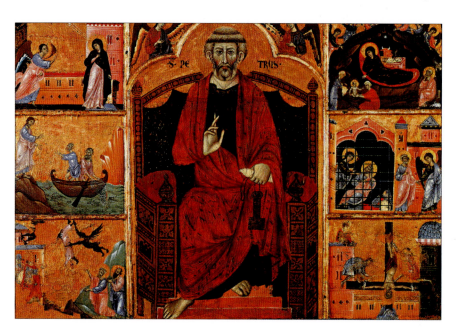

only to other Jews. They regarded the diet of non-Jews as unclean. But Peter had the support of Paul, who, like him, was determined to spread Christianity to everyone. Peter's frequent public preaching led to his arrest by Herod, who imprisoned him under heavy guard. But the apostle escaped, helped – it was said – by an angel who broke his chains and opened the prison doors.

This convinced Peter that he had truly been chosen to lead. He wrote letters and preached unceasingly, while organizing from Jerusalem the appointment and missions of evangelists.

Some authorities credit Peter with introducing the concept of "episcopal succession". In finding a replacement for Judas Iscariot, he began a system of choosing leaders from men who were familiar with the first apostles. This gave rise to the tradition that bishops and priests had a special closeness to Christ, and ensured that the status of priests remained separate from their flock.

When Peter visited Rome, he was arrested for his Christian activities and tried by the Emperor Nero, who condemned him to death by crucifixion. Legend has it that Peter asked to be hung upside down on the cross because he was not worthy of dying in the same way as Christ.

Some claim that he died on the same day as Paul, and they share a feast day. For two centuries after Peter's death, letters which were supposedly written by him were distributed in order to revive his lessons and maintain his influence.

He was buried in a tomb beneath the Vatican. Believers consider him the keeper of the gates to heaven, the saint who can let them enter the kingdom, or deny them entry when they die. Peter's enduring popularity is shown by the dedication of 1,129 churches to him in England alone.

Below: Peter is dressed in papal splendour as he observes the Crucifixion (Ottaviano di Martino Nelli, 1424).

Below: Peter was the first apostle to perform a miracle. In this painting St John and St Peter heal a lame man (Masolino da Panicale, 1425).

CORNELIUS

Cornelius (not to be confused with the Gentile Roman centurion) was an heir to Peter, who became "bishop" of Rome in 251. He followed Peter in teaching that the Church must be conciliatory in its embrace. He favoured a lenient approach towards Christians who had lapsed. Another priest, Novatian, thought those who committed adultery, murder or even made a second marriage, should be expelled from the Church. Cornelius asserted that the Church had the power to forgive and welcome the repentant back to the community. The inscription "Cornelius martyr" inscribed on his tomb can be seen in the crypt of Lucina, in Rome.

Right: This reliquary of St Cornelius, dating from 1350–60, is made of gold and silver.

> "YOU ARE PETER AND UPON THIS ROCK I WILL BUILD MY CHURCH."
>
> JESUS SPEAKING TO PETER

DIRECTORY OF SAINTS

SIMON

SIMON LIVED TO A GREAT OLD AGE AFTER A SUCCESSFUL LIFE AS A WELL-TRAVELLED MISSIONARY.

Above: The Apostle Simon *in a chiaroscuro drawing (Mair von Landshut, 1496).*

> **KEY FACTS**
> *Apostle*
> DATES: *1st century AD*
> BIRTH PLACE: *Probably Galilee*
> FEAST DAY: *28 October (West)*
> EMBLEM: *Boat, sometimes the weapon of his murder, a falchion – a short sword bent like a sickle*

Simon is featured in a number of legends and has long been venerated, especially in the East. He is also known as the Zealot or the Canaanite, possibly because he had belonged to a strict Jewish sect. He appears in the New Testament as one of the apostles, but is not much mentioned after the Pentecost, when the Holy Spirit granted Christ's followers the gift of tongues.

One story says he travelled with Jude and that they took their mission as far as Persia (Iran). Here, pagan priests slaughtered both men. Some sources say Simon was sawn in two; others, that he was stabbed to death.

A further interpretation has Simon dying in battle when he was bishop of Jerusalem, while others claim that the apostle trekked across North Africa until he reached the age of 120 years and was finally martyred.

BARNABAS

CHRIST DID NOT CHOOSE BARNABAS AS AN APOSTLE. HOWEVER, HIS MISSIONARY WORK OUTSIDE PALESTINE, FIRST WITH PAUL, THEN ALONE, BROUGHT HIM THE TITLE OF HONORARY APOSTLE.

> **KEY FACTS**
> *Apostle*
> DATES: *1st century AD*
> BIRTH PLACE: *Unknown*
> FEAST DAY: *11 June*
> EMBLEM: *Sometimes associated with a type of thistle that flowers on his feast day (in England)*

Barnabas was a Cypriot Jew who took the newly converted Paul to meet the other apostles in Jerusalem. Though not one of the 12 apostles, Barnabas was one of the earliest evangelists.

Peter described Barnabas as "a good man, full of the Holy Ghost and of faith", and sent him to Antioch. From there Barnabas sailed with Paul to Cyprus, where Barnabas showed the people what "wonders God had wrought".

He is believed to be the founder of the Church in Cyprus. He may have been martyred at Salamis in AD 61. *The Epistle of Barnabas* carries his name, but its authorship is uncertain.

Below: Paul and Barnabas (attr. to Rombout van Troyen, 17th century).

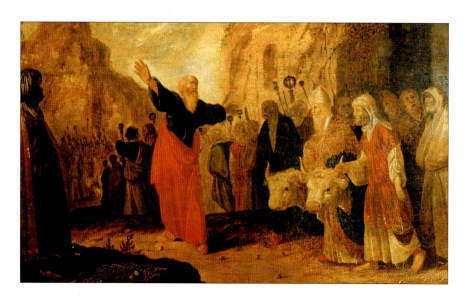

318

ANDREW

Peter's brother Andrew was the first of the disciples Jesus called. The cruel manner of his reputed martyrdom on a saltire cross is commemorated on the Scottish flag.

> **KEY FACTS**
> *Apostle*
> Dates: *d.c.AD 60*
> Birth Place: *Bethsaida, Galilee*
> Patron of: *Scotland, Greece and Russia, fishermen*
> Feast Day: *30 November*
> Emblem: *Small saltire cross*

Andrew heard John the Baptist preach and longed to meet Jesus. He and his brother Peter (then called Simon), worked as fishermen on the Sea of Galilee.

Initially, the brothers only joined Jesus at his preaching from time to time. But finally they abandoned their families and their work to follow him. The Greek Orthodox Church calls Andrew the "Protoclete", meaning "first-called". They venerate him highly, as do the Roman Catholic and Russian Orthodox Churches.

Jesus granted the Miraculous Draught of Fishes to Andrew and Peter. This occurred when, after a day of poor fishing, the presence of Jesus produced a great haul for the two men. Andrew also played a part in the feeding of the 5,000 with loaves and fishes. Being an intense believer, he encouraged Gentiles to meet the Messiah, too.

MISSION AND DEATH

After the Crucifixion, it seems much of Andrew's mission work was in Greece, but he also went to Constantinople (Istanbul), a key place in the history of the early Church. Medieval worshippers claim he founded the Church there. Some believe he preached as far as Kiev in Ukraine before moving on to Scotland, but there is no evidence for this.

Legend gives Andrew a brave martyrdom at Patras. With dignity, he disrobed himself and knelt before the cross as his persecutors prepared him for crucifixion. He was bound to the wooden beams of the saltire (X-shaped) cross. Even in his agony, Andrew is said to have carried on preaching. The crowd begged the consul to show mercy and take the dying man down. This he did after two days.

In 1204, Crusaders seized Constantinople and took St Andrew's supposed relics to Amalfi, Italy. However, some say that St Regulus journeyed "to the ends of the earth" carrying his relics. Then an angel led him to Scotland, to the place now named after him, St Andrews.

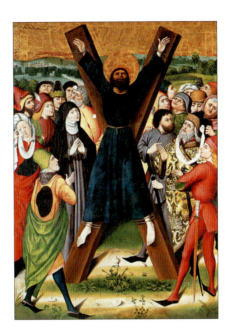

Above: Martyrdom of the Apostle Andreas *from Westphalia (artist unknown, c.1500).*

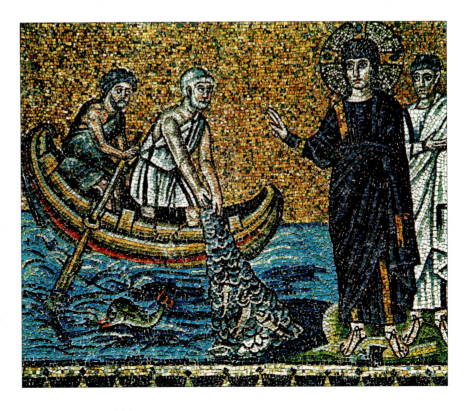

Below: St Andrew and St Peter Responding to the Call of Jesus, Byzantine mosaic (6th century).

PAUL

INITIALLY A PERSECUTOR OF CHRISTIANS, AFTER HIS DRAMATIC CONVERSION PAUL BECAME THE CHURCH'S FIRST MISSIONARY. HIS LETTERS DEVELOPED AND EXPOUNDED CHRISTIAN THEOLOGY.

> **KEY FACTS**
> Great missionary and theologian
> DATES: *d. AD 64–65*
> BIRTH PLACE: *Tarsus in Cilicia*
> PATRON OF: *Malta, Greece, Catholic missions and lay teachers*
> FEAST DAY: *29 June*
> EMBLEM: *Sword and book; generally portrayed as elderly and balding with a long beard*

On meeting Paul, a Roman centurion was struck by the apostle's air of nobility and courage. Others described him as having the spirit of a strong man who was generous and eager to create a cheerful atmosphere.

Paul was born in Tarsus to a strict Jewish family and was named Saul. His upbringing was steeped in strict Jewish law. Although he applauded the killing of the Christian martyr, St Stephen, Saul was confused. How could this man find the strength to defy the law, simply through the love of Jesus Christ? Even so, Saul decided that no one should break the laws that bind society.

CONVERSION
Saul tried to find Christians and deliver them to possible death. On one such , Saul was travelling along the road to Damascus when suddenly he was blinded by a great light and overcome by the presence of Jesus. He understood from this vision that his mission was to spread the Christian faith to Gentile, non-Jewish people.

His sight was miraculously restored three days later, and shortly afterwards he was baptized. He then spent several years in Arabia living as a hermit.

He returned to Damascus and began to preach about Jesus, and took the name of Paul as a mark of his change. His preaching, however, aroused the fury of local Jews. Paul was forced to escape with the help of fellow disciples, who lowered him in a basket over the city wall.

He travelled to Jerusalem to meet Peter who chose him and Barnabas as travelling evangelists.

APOSTLE TO THE GENTILES
Paul's first journey took him to Cyprus and Syria before he returned to take part in what came to be called the Council of Jerusalem in about AD 50. Here, he found Peter and others in dispute over the rules of conversion.

The apostles, all born as Jews, had tended to preach only to other Jews about Jesus the Messiah. Peter wanted Gentiles, or non-Jews, to be brought into the fold. Paul, who agreed Christ brought redemption to all

Above: This portrait of St Paul captures the expression of a noble man (Etienne Parrocel, c. 1740s).

Below: Paul travelling on the road to Damascus with his troops in search of Christians to persecute in The Conversion of St Paul *(Pieter Bruegel the elder, 1567).*

of humanity, managed to find a compromise. The Church, he argued, should be as catholic (universal) as the Roman Empire.

The disciples agreed that Gentiles must adopt certain Jewish rules, especially those regarding food. But they decided that the Gentiles must never be denied access to the Lord's message. Paul's diplomacy possibly saved Christianity from remaining a mere sect of Judaism, and opened the way for a whole new religious belief system.

Paul spent years travelling around the Middle East and the Mediterranean coast preaching the gospel. He was shipwrecked, mocked, arrested, but never deterred. While travelling, he wrote numerous letters, which are included in the Epistles of the New Testament. These letters were read at gatherings so people might be inspired by his words to convert to the new faith.

His teaching was intimate and personal, related to his own experience of the vision of Jesus. His writings say that Jewish Talmudic Law teaches knowledge of sin, provoking people to dwell on evil thoughts. But the message of Jesus, said Paul, is one of love, "written on the heart". Jesus works inwards and outwards on people's thoughts, and Christians are "inspired to God-likeness".

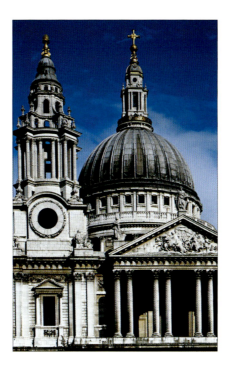

Above: St Paul's, Christopher Wren's magnificent cathedral in London, is dedicated to the man regarded as the greatest apostle of the Church.

ARREST AND DEATH

While visiting Jerusalem, Paul's preaching enraged the Jews, who handed him over to the authorities. As a Roman citizen, he was able to claim trial in that city, though shipwrecked in Malta on the way. He was placed under house arrest and, after some years, he was put on trial. Sources vary, and it was possibly on a later visit to Rome after further travels that he was found guilty of "anti-imperial activities" and beheaded.

It was claimed that his head bounced three times, and at each bounce a spring gushed from the earth. The place of his beheading is called Tre Fontane, in Rome. Tradition claims he died on 29 June in AD 64 or 65, the same day as Peter's martyrdom (also in Rome), and thus they share their feast day.

Paul is the first great missionary and theologian of Christianity. He is regarded as second only to Jesus in inspiring Christian faith.

> "For I am persuaded that neither death, nor life nor angels, nor principalities, nor powers, nor things present, nor things to come, nor height, nor depth, nor any other creature, shall be able to separate us from the love of God, which is Jesus Christ our Lord."
>
> ROMANS 8

SAINT TITUS

St Paul's importance is confirmed by the enormous church dedicated to him in London. Yet little is heard of his close disciple, Titus, the Gentile who attended the decisive Council of Jerusalem where the apostles agreed that Gentiles should be accepted into the faith.

Titus travelled with Paul as secretary and companion on a mission and was entrusted with setting up a community in Crete. Paul warned him to be firm in converting the surly Cretans. Titus was to spend most of his life there, although he lived for a while in Dalmatia. He is recognized as the first bishop of Crete and was buried there in Gortyna. His head was taken as a relic to Venice in AD 823.

Above: Titus helped Paul to escape the city walls of Damascus in a basket.

MATTHEW

THE PRESUMED AUTHOR OF THE FIRST GOSPEL WAS A FORMER TAX COLLECTOR.

There are few stories about Matthew, also known as Levi. Little is known, too, about his life as an evangelist. He is presumed to be the author of the First Gospel, written in an easy style for public reading.

Matthew was a tax collector, one of the hated class of Jews who collected money on behalf of the Roman authorities. His fellow Jews not only regarded this close contact with Gentiles as unclean, but also distrusted tax men and believed they were corrupt. When Jesus approached Matthew,

Above: Saint Matthew *from* The Book of Kells, *an illuminated manuscript, c.AD 800.*

and was even prepared to eat with him, he immediately rose from his counting table and followed him.

KEY FACTS
Author of the First Gospel
DATES: *1st century*
BIRTH PLACE: *Capernaum*
DEATH PLACE: *Possibly Ethiopia*
PATRON OF: *Bankers, accountants, tax collectors, bookkeepers*
FEAST DAY: *21 September*
EMBLEM: *An angel or man with wings, money bag, spear or sword*

After Christ's Ascension to heaven, Matthew became a missionary like the other apostles, but his journeys are not recorded.

An apocryphal story says that Matthew was martyred in Ethiopia defending an abbess. His reputed relics were transported to Salerno in Italy via Brittany. Others say he died in Persia.

JOHN

THE DISCIPLE WHOM JESUS LOVED AND ENTRUSTED HIS MOTHER TO AFTER HIS DEATH IS THOUGHT TO BE THE AUTHOR OF THE FOURTH GOSPEL, THREE EPISTLES AND THE BOOK OF REVELATION.

John and James the Great were two fiery-tempered brothers, sons of Zebedee. Both were called from mending their fishing nets to follow Jesus.

John's ardour could turn him to brave and reckless endeavours. However, Jesus' faith in John was apparent at the Crucifixion. When he was facing death, Jesus put his mother, Mary, the Blessed Virgin, into John's care rather than choose anyone else.

The belief that he was a favourite disciple is confirmed by the facts of John's life. He was with Jesus at the Miracle of the Loaves and Fishes. With Peter and James, he witnessed the Transfiguration, and he was by the side of Jesus during the Agony in the Garden of Gethsemane.

John was placed at the right hand of Christ at the Last Supper, and he was the only disciple not to desert Jesus during the horrors

Left: This woodcarving depicts John's anguish and horror during Christ's crucifixion at Calvary (Ferdinand Maximilian Brokof, 18th century).

KEY FACTS
Author of the Fourth Gospel and the Book of Revelation
DATES: *1st century AD*
BIRTH PLACE: *Galilee*
PATRON OF: *Booksellers, writers, artists, knights, theologians, typesetters*
FEAST DAY: *27 December (West)*
EMBLEM: *Eagle, chalice, sometimes a book*

of the Crucifixion. He kept vigil at the foot of the cross, and then showed no hesitation in accepting Jesus had risen from the dead.

After the Ascension, John worked with St Peter organizing the early Christian Church. After some years, he was exiled to Patmos, a Greek island. One of the greatest Christian evangelists, it is thought he died at a great age in Ephesus, Turkey.

MARK

THE AUTHOR OF THE SECOND GOSPEL INTERPRETED AND RECORDED PETER'S TEACHING.

Mark was young when he first met Jesus. His mother's house was a favourite meeting place for the apostles and Jesus often visited.

Although Mark was not an apostle, he seems to have been charming and affectionate, though not brave or confident. It was rumoured that he ran away from the Roman soldiers who arrested Jesus. And he abandoned a difficult mission with St Peter to Cyprus. But, when older, he gave St Paul much support during his arrest in Rome. St Peter even referred to him fondly as his son.

Mark travelled widely as an evangelist, visiting Jerusalem, Rome and Egypt. He may have travelled to Alexandria and become the first bishop of that city. Mark's gospel incorporates many of Peter's teachings and memoirs, so it is likely it was written in Rome, where the two men spent long periods together.

Despite Mark's important role in the Christian story as the writer of the Second Gospel, his place and manner of death are uncertain. He is thought to have died sometime after Jerusalem was destroyed in AD 70. A legend claims he was tied round the neck and dragged through the streets of Alexandria. His bodily relics were carried by the Venetians to Venice, where they were placed in the basilica named after him, St Mark's Basilica.

Right: St Mark's famous emblem, the winged lion, sits at his feet (the Ulm Master, 1442).

The relics survived a fire in the church in AD 976, and were installed in the new building. A series of mosaics in the church tell the story of St Mark and the translation of his relics.

KEY FACTS
Writer of the Second Gospel
DATES: *d.c. AD 74*
BIRTH PLACE: *Jerusalem*
PATRON OF: *Notaries, translators, opticians, glass workers, Venice*
FEAST DAY: *25 April*
EMBLEM: *Winged lion*

Left: A statue of St Mark by the early Renaissance sculptor Donatello (1411–15). St Mark's image appears widely in Italy.

His emblem is a winged lion. This refers to the inspiration Mark derived from John the Baptist, who lived in the wilderness with animals. Mark became the patron saint of Venice. His lion emblem can be found on the façades of many buildings across the Greek Ionian islands, where medieval Venice held dominion.

LUKE

THE PHYSICIAN AND WRITER OF THE THIRD GOSPEL WAS A MOST SYMPATHETIC MAN WHO, UNUSUALLY FOR THE TIME, INCLUDED IN HIS WORK THE WOMEN WHO WERE IMPORTANT IN THE LIFE OF JESUS.

> **KEY FACTS**
> *Writer of the Third Gospel*
> DATES: *1st century AD*
> BIRTH PLACE: *Antioch, Syria*
> PATRON OF: *Surgeons, doctors, painters and glass artists*
> FEAST DAY: *18 October*
> EMBLEM: *Winged ox*

St Luke was a Greek doctor. His writings contain observations of women and human suffering, and reveal him to be gentle and sensitive. St Paul probably converted Luke, a Gentile of Antioch, and persuaded him to travel with him on evangelical voyages around the Mediterranean.

More than any other New Testament writer, Luke shows us the women in Jesus' life. Thanks to him, we know more about Mary Magdalene and about the widow whose son Jesus restored to life.

Luke tells the story of Mary and the Annunciation, and also mentions Elizabeth, mother of John the Baptist. He is deeply respectful of the Virgin Mary and apparently knew her. The words he puts into her mouth when he describes the Annunciation are known as "Mary's Prayer", and have become part of the liturgy.

Above: This enamel plaque showing St Luke was made in the workshop of the Kremlin (17th century).

Below: St Luke Drawing the Virgin *(Rogier van der Weyden, 15th century). Luke was a talented painter, as well as a writer.*

A HUMANE APPROACH

Luke emphasizes gentle aspects of the faith. He repeats the most moving parables that Jesus told to show examples of goodness and kindness. However, his gospel does open with the story of the bull sacrificed by Zachary to celebrate the birth of his son, John the Baptist. This accounts for Luke's emblem, a winged ox.

He also wrote *The Acts of the Apostles*, a mixture of history and prophecy describing the spread of Christianity. He explains how the faith broke with Judaism, and extended beyond Jerusalem to Rome in the West.

Luke also has a reputation as a painter. There are many portraits of the Virgin attributed to St Luke in the Christian world, though unfortunately none are authenticated. The church of St Augustine in Rome has several such portraits. It is said Luke lived to a great age and never married.

> "MY SOUL DOTH MAGNIFY THE LORD, AND MY SPIRIT HATH REJOICED IN GOD MY SAVIOUR."
>
> LUKE 1:46

STEPHEN

THE FIRST CHRISTIAN MARTYR WAS CRUELLY STONED TO DEATH IN JERUSALEM FOR HIS BELIEFS.

The first ever Christian martyr was a learned Jew and one of the first deacons. After his conversion, Stephen took control of almsgiving to elderly widows in his community. When he began to preach, he often criticized some aspects of Jewish Mosaic law.

After Stephen had made some particularly hostile allegations, his Jewish listeners became outraged. He accused them of resisting the true Spirit and being responsible for the death of Christ.

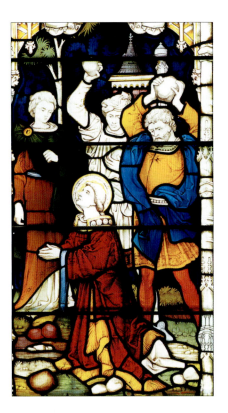

KEY FACTS
First martyr
DATES: *d.c. AD 35*
BIRTH PLACE: *Jerusalem*
PATRON OF: *Bricklayers, stonemasons, builders, deacons*
FEAST DAY: *26 December (West)*
EMBLEM: *Stones, the palm of martyrdom, a book*

The mob stoned him to death with the consent of a man called Saul, a Roman Jew. Saul later converted and became Paul, the great Christian leader.

Left: The stoning of St Stephen as depicted in a stained-glass window (St Edmundsbury Cathedral, Suffolk, England, 19th century).

EUSTACE

THE HERO OF THIS LEGEND CHASES A STAG THAT BEARS THE CROSS OF CHRIST WITHIN ITS ANTLERS. THIS EXPERIENCE LEADS TO HIS CONVERSION AND HIS UNTIMELY DEATH.

Fabulous stories surround the figure of St Eustace. Named Placidas at birth, he became a high-ranking Roman soldier and was a keen huntsman.

One day he stalked a stag deep in the forest. As he lifted his bow, the stag turned. A gleaming crucifix grew between its antlers. Then the stag said, "I am Jesus, whom you honour without knowing."

Placidas, his wife and children converted to Christianity, and he was baptized as Eustace. They suffered many misfortunes and Eustace's faith was tested to the limits. His wife was seduced (or raped) and his children sold into slavery. Later, their luck changed for the better when Eustace was

KEY FACTS
Miracle appearance of the crucifix
DATES: *Unknown*
BIRTH PLACE: *Unknown*
PATRON OF: *Hunters and those in difficult situations*
FEAST DAY: *2 November (West; officially de-canonized)*
EMBLEM: *Stag bearing a crucifix*

reunited with his family in Rome. He was honoured for a military victory, but unfortunately this good luck did not last, and when he refused to make a pagan sacrifice, he and his family were thrown to the lions in the arena. The beasts refused to attack, so the entire family was burnt inside a brazen bull – a form of execution devised by the ancient Greeks, akin to being boiled alive.

Left: The Vision of Saint Eustace (Albrecht Dürer, 16th century).

POLYCARP

A TRUE SHEPHERD TO HIS FLOCK, THE BISHOP OF SMYRNA WAS ONE OF THE APOSTOLIC FATHERS OF THE CHURCH. HE GUIDED IT THROUGH DANGERS OF HERESY AND INTERNAL DISPUTES IN ROME.

KEY FACTS
Apostolic Father of the Church
DATES: *c.AD 69–155*
BIRTH PLACE: *Possibly Syria*
FEAST DAY: *23 February*

Polycarp knew the apostles, particularly St John. He was the living link between those who had known Christ in the flesh and the next generation of believers. This made him an Apostolic Father, and with this authority he played a significant role in the early Church.

During a wave of paganism in Asia in the 2nd century AD, Polycarp kept an strong hold on the essentials of Christ's teaching. He fought heretical or radical interpretations and practices, and his firm stand strengthened the spread of the Church in the East.

A heretical sect leader who wished to have a debate with Polycarp was rebuffed with the phrase, "I recognize you as the first-born of Satan." In his own writing, Polycarp explained, "For every one who shall not confess that Jesus Christ has come in the flesh is the antichrist."

St Irenaeus of Lyons was a child when he first heard Polycarp preach and recount his memories of the apostles. Irenaeus left letters mentioning Polycarp, who was the bishop of Smyrna for almost 50 years. These letters give glimpses of his life and his high standing in the Church. Ignatius of Antioch, awaiting martyrdom in Rome, trusted Polycarp to receive and forward secret letters on his behalf.

In old age, Polycarp was called to Rome to discuss the timing of feast days, especially that of Easter. He met Anicetus, bishop of Rome. They agreed to disagree, and Polycarp returned to Smyrna, believing his community could now peacefully use the calendar that it preferred.

Left: Saint Sebastian and Saint Polycarp Destroying the Idols *(Pedro Garcia de Benabarre, 15th century). Broken idols litter the floor.*

MARTYRDOM

He was over 80 when a mob bayed for his blood. Excited by pagan festivities that included lions attacking Christians, they shouted, "This is the father of the Christians." The Roman consul refused to throw Polycarp into the arena, but conceded to a death by burning. At the stake, Polycarp said, "May I be received among the martyrs in your presence today as a rich and pleasing sacrifice." A soldier stabbed him in order to spare him the pain of burning. Christians gathered relics from the ashes, and wrote an account of the trial and death of this martyr saint, giving evidence of an early cultus.

Left: St Polycarp spread the Christian faith in the sometimes rugged terrain of Palestine (left) and Syria.

JUSTIN

THIS CHRISTIAN PHILOSOPHER EXPLAINED THE MESSAGE OF CHRIST IN HIS WRITINGS.

KEY FACTS
Apologist (vindicator) of the faith
DATES: *c.AD 100–65*
BIRTH PLACE: *Flavia Neapolis (now Nablus, Palestine)*
PATRON OF: *Philosophers*
FEAST DAY: *1 June*
EMBLEM: *Philosopher's clothes*

Justin was well educated and sought answers to life's problems through philosophy. But the teachings of Pythagoras, Plato and the Stoics brought him no closer to the Almighty.

CONVERSION
A chance encounter with a stranger directed him to look for meaning in the message of Christ. When Justin converted to the faith, he was about 30 years old. The Christians he met were reluctant to discuss their rituals with an outsider. Justin said, "It is our duty to make known our doctrine, lest we incur the guilt and the punishment of those who have sinned through ignorance."

Justin wrote the *Apologies* and *Dialogues*, important fragments of which have survived. In these writings, he sets out the moral values of the faith and presents a philosophical proof of its truth.

He is recognized as the first Christian apologist. Dressed as a philosopher, he preached and taught throughout Palestine, Syria and other regions.

TRIAL AND DEATH
In Rome, he had a public debate with another philosopher, named Crescens. Justin presented the more convincing argument, and his adversary is believed to have later instigated his arrest. A record of his trial survives. The martyr confessed his faith unhesitatingly, and gave courage to six other Christians who were also on trial. Justin was decapitated, in accordance with Roman law.

Left: A stained-glass window depicting St Justin preaching to fishermen in stormy weather.

Below: A Sailor Offering a Model Boat to Saint Justin (Domenico Robusti Tintoretto, son of Jacopo, c.17th century).

327

DIRECTORY OF SAINTS

IRENAEUS OF LYONS

THE BISHOP OF LYONS WAS AN INFLUENTIAL THEOLOGIAN WHO HELPED THE CHURCH TO CLARIFY THE ARTICLES OF CHRISTIAN FAITH, IN PARTICULAR THE UNITY OF THE FATHER AND THE SON.

KEY FACTS
Venerated as a martyr
DATES: *c.AD 130–200*
BIRTH PLACE: *Possibly Smyrna*
FEAST DAY: *28 June (West)*
EMBLEM: *Bishop's clothes*

As a theologian St Irenaeus was not only able to defend and explain Christianity theoretically, he could also preach it to laymen.

Irenaeus worked as a priest in Lyons. He was sent to Rome on a peacemaking mission by his bishop, Pothinus, in AD 177. He took a message to the pope to show leniency towards the North African Church, whose practices differed from those of Rome. He also brokered a compromise between the East and Pope Victor III who wanted Rome to decree the dates for Easter.

On his return, Irenaeus became Bishop of Lyons, as his predecessor had been killed. Under his care the faith spread through this rich merchant city. He was the first to make a systematic organization of Catholic beliefs. His writings distinguished faith from the then popular heresy, Gnosticism, and he enhanced the unity of the faithful.

He wrote the "rule of faith" that encompasses all "the riches of Christian truth", still delivered at baptisms. He died at Lyons, but unfortunately his shrine was destroyed in the Reformation.

Above: St Irenaeus resurrects and baptizes a girl in this Belgian tapestry.

COSMAS AND DAMIAN

THE TWIN DOCTORS WHO NEVER CHARGED FOR THE MEDICAL CARE THEY GAVE HAVE LONG BEEN VENERATED FOR THEIR HEALING SKILLS AND THEIR KINDNESS. AS SUCH, THEY ARE PATRONS OF DOCTORS.

KEY FACTS
Doctors, miracle cures
DATES: *Unknown*
BIRTH PLACE: *Syria*
PATRON OF: *Doctors, dentists, barbers, chemists, hairdressers*
FEAST DAY: *26 September (West)*
EMBLEM: *Ampoules and medicine jars*

A widespread cultus followed Sts Cosmas and Damian in the 5th century AD. They practised as doctors in Cyrrhus, Syria, where a famous basilica was erected.

With wonderful powers of healing, aided by the Holy Spirit, they were known as the "holy moneyless ones", because their medical care was free. They also looked after sick animals.

Although Cosmas and Damian were persecuted by the Romans, it was said that rocks thrown at the twins simply flew backwards. Neither did the torture rack function. A further account says that, after their eventual deaths by beheading, the twins returned to earth to save Justinianus, deacon of their church. He lost a leg and they replaced the pale limb with another one from a black-skinned Ethiopian man. Differing versions of this story have been depicted by artists over the years.

Sick believers took to sleeping in the twins' church, hoping this "incubation" would cure them – a practice known also to occur in other religions.

Right: Healing of the Deacon Justinianus by the Saints Cosmas and Damian *(Fra Angelico, 1440). The new black leg is clearly visible.*

328

PERPETUA

A YOUNG MOTHER RECORDED HER EXPERIENCES AND VISIONS WHILE AWAITING MARTYRDOM.

KEY FACTS
Martyr
DATES: *d.AD 203*
BIRTH PLACE: *Carthage*
FEAST DAY: *7 March*

The daughter of a wealthy pagan in Carthage, Perpetua was arrested during a Roman persecution of newly converted Christians. Perpetua was first placed under house arrest, then imprisoned, even though she was the mother of a young baby.

She was 22 years old when she wrote about her extraordinary experiences. The work, finished anonymously, is an authentic record of Christian martyrdom.

Above: The shrine of St Perpetua is transferred to the church of Bouvignes after the Siege of Dinant in 1466 (Flemish School, 15th century).

She mentions her worries about her father and baby, and describes vivid dreams of ladders to heaven and her dead brother, but the most inspiring vision was one of herself, changed into a man, fighting the devil.

Perpetua was allowed to send her baby home before her death. Some say she entered the arena at Carthage singing joyfully. She was wounded by a mad heifer, then dispatched by the sword.

FELICITAS

ST PERPETUA'S HANDMAIDEN RISKED HER OWN LIFE AND THAT OF HER UNBORN CHILD WHEN SHE ACCEPTED THE CHRISTIAN FAITH. SHE WAS MARTYRED AT THE SAME TIME AS HER MISTRESS.

KEY FACTS
Martyr
DATES: *d.AD 203*
BIRTH PLACE: *Carthage*
FEAST DAY: *7 March*

This young woman was a slave of St Perpetua in the Roman colony of Carthage. When her mistress was arrested, Felicitas (or Felicity) went with her to prison.

Felicitas was heavily pregnant at the time of their detention. Her husband, Revocatus, and two other slaves, Saturninus and Secundulus, were also caught up in the persecution. While under house arrest, they were all baptized before their transfer to prison.

Incarcerated in a filthy cell, Felicitas went into a difficult labour and brutal warders jeered at her pain. She knew her fate and that of her husband was death in the arena, so was grateful to give birth beforehand. A free Christian adopted the baby girl.

Above: The ancient Punic city walls of Carthage in present-day Tunisia. For the saints' martyrdom in the city's arena, leopards and bears were prepared to attack the men, and a mad heifer directed towards the two women.

DENYS OF PARIS

CREDITED WITH THE FOUNDING OF THE CHRISTIAN CHURCH IN PARIS, THIS VIRTUOUS MAN WENT ON TO BECOME A BISHOP AND WAS LATER MARTYRED FOR HIS FAITH.

> **KEY FACTS**
> *Early mission to France*
> DATES: *d.c. AD 250*
> BIRTH PLACE: *Italy*
> PATRON OF: *Paris and France, headaches*
> FEAST DAY: *9 October*
> EMBLEM: *Head held in his hands*

Said to be a fearless preacher, the Italian-born St Denys (or Dionysius) of Paris was sent on a dangerous mission to revive the persecuted Church of Gaul (France) in AD 250. Together with the deacon Eleutherius and the priest Rusticus, he established a Christian community on an island in the River Seine, close to Roman Paris.

St Denys' mission led to countless conversions, arousing the anger of the local pagan priests

Below: The interior of the 12th-century monastery dedicated to St Denys, built on the site of his death in Paris. It is a fitting tribute to the patron saint of the city and France.

Above: This Baroque statue of St Denys is one in a group of the Fourteen Holy Helpers. Denys is shown carrying his severed head, still preaching, in accordance with the story.

who pushed for the missionaries to be stopped. The saint and his companions were eventually imprisoned and tortured before being beheaded on Montmartre (Martyrs' Hill) where the church of the Sacré Coeur now stands.

According to legend, a great miracle then occurred: St Denys picked up his head and walked two miles, preaching as he went. He eventually lay down and was buried with his fellow martyrs by a pious woman named Catulla.

Another version of events states that, after they had been murdered, the bodies of the martyrs were thrown into the Seine and retrieved and buried by converts. In both accounts, a shrine was built over the burial place, to be covered years later (*c.*AD 630) by a great abbey and church. This building, the Basilica of St-Denis, later became the burial place of the kings of France.

A NATIONAL FIGURE

St Denys had become a figure of national devotion by the 9th century. This was partly due to a great medieval mix-up. The Emperor Louis I of France had been given the writings of a certain Dionysius (or Pseudo Dionysius), in which the author claimed to know the apostles. To the people of the time, this would have identified the author as Dionysius the Areopagite, who was converted to Christianity by St Paul.

When Louis commissioned Hilduin, Abbot of St-Denis, to write a biography of St Denys in 835, he asked the abbot to use the works of Pseudo Dionysius as his source. In Hilduin's book, Dionysius the Areopagite and St Denys became the same man. This fiction persisted for 700 years, until it was discovered that Pseudo Dionysius was actually a 5th-century theologian and philosopher, and St Denys was a significant figure in his own right.

VALENTINE

Two different Valentines were martyrs during the Roman period, and it was only during the 14th century that the saint's name became associated with lovers.

> KEY FACTS
> Representative of hidden love and courtship
> DATES: *3rd century AD*
> BIRTH PLACE: *Unknown*
> PATRON OF: *Lovers, betrothed couples, greetings*
> FEAST DAY: *14 February*
> EMBLEM: *Heart, birds, roses*

There seem to be two saints with this name. One was a 2nd-century bishop of Terni, Italy, the other a 3rd-century priest in Rome; both were martyred. Some hagiographers claim they were one and the same person.

The 3rd-century Valentinus was reportedly imprisoned for helping Christians, then tried to convert the Emperor Claudius II, cured his jailer's daughter of blindness, and was beheaded outside Rome's Flaminian Gate.

No one is sure why Valentine is associated with lovers. It may follow Lupercalia, an old pagan festival, celebrated in mid-February. On the eve of the Lupercalia, all the young women's names would be put into a container, and each young man would draw out a name. He would then be paired with the woman he had chosen for the remainder of the festival.

Another theory associates the courtship with a line by the English medieval poet Chaucer, who observed that birds choose their mates on 14 February.

Right: St Valentine (painted glass, Hungarian School, 19th century).

VICTOR OF MARSEILLES

This convert, a soldier, was severely punished for his faith and had a strong cultus in the medieval era. His tomb became a popular pilgrim shrine.

> KEY FACTS
> Venerated as a martyr
> DATES: *3rd century AD*
> BIRTH PLACE: *Marseilles, France*
> PATRON OF: *Millers, lightning, torture victims, cabinet-makers*
> FEAST DAY: *21 July*
> EMBLEM: *Windmill, millstone*

Archaeological evidence points to the burial of a total of three martyrs beneath the abbey of St Victor in Marseilles. Tunnels and caves show early habitation, probably of monks.

Victor may have been a Moor in the Roman army who was converted. His fellow soldiers, fearing for his life, begged him to return to traditional Roman beliefs, but he refused. Legend says he was betrayed by other militia.

He was thrown into prison but his profound faith converted the two military wardens charged with guarding him. These two men were executed, and legend describes the cruel treatment meted out to Victor. He was put on the rack, and burnt. His foot was hacked off and then he was crushed and ground between two large millstones.

Many miracles were claimed in his name and he developed a wide cultus in the medieval era. His tomb became one of the most visited pilgrim centres in what was then Gaul, and the abbey of St-Victor can still be visited today.

Below: Victor of Marseilles is shown as a brave soldier of the faith destroying false idols (Hermen Rode, 1481).

CECILIA

Angels and heavenly music helped Cecilia to convert her husband and others.

Above: A terracotta statue of Cecilia in the cathedral in Le Mans, France (Charles Hoyau, 17th century).

When she was a young woman, Cecilia's family refused to accept that she had taken a vow of virginity and forced her to marry a pagan. During the wedding, Cecilia sang silently to the Lord, "My heart remains unsullied, so that I may not be confounded." The bride vowed that her marriage would never be consummated.

Cecilia kept strong in her faith and told her husband, Valerian, that an angel was guarding her. She said God would be angry if Valerian touched her, but, if he desisted, God would love him. Furthermore, if her husband were baptized, he would see this angel.

Valerian converted and angels appeared and placed flowers on the heads of the young couple. Cecilia's brother Tiburtius chose to become a Christian after this incident. In fact, the two men became so ardent in their faith that the Romans beheaded them, as Christianity was proscribed. Cecilia buried the two martyrs at her home. She, too, attracted anger from the State, but officials sent to arrest her were so overwhelmed by her faith that they converted.

Cecilia converted 400 people, who were later baptized by Pope Urban in her home, which was later dedicated as a church.

The authorities did not abandon their persecution of Cecilia. They tried locking her in her own bathroom and burning the furnaces high. She lived through this ordeal, and then survived for three days after a soldier hacked at her neck with a sword.

There is little firm evidence for Cecilia's story. Her patronage of music comes from the heavenly sound she heard in her head while the organs played at her wedding.

KEY FACTS
Virgin martyr
DATES: *3rd century AD*
BIRTH PLACE: *Rome*
PATRON OF: *Musicians, singers, composers*
FEAST DAY: *22 November*
EMBLEM: *Organ or lute*

ANASTASIA

Virgin martyrs such as Ursula and Cecilia have attracted legends of heroism and miracles. Other martyrs give their names to churches, or else linger in the religious folk memory.

One such figure is St Anastasia. Nothing is known about her. It is possible she was martyred at a place now known as Sremska Mitrovica, Serbia. Her name is in the Roman Canon. A prayer is said to her at Mass, and a few antique Byzantine churches carry her name. She was a "matron", not a "maiden", so she is not counted as one of the virgin martyrs.

Below: A stained-glass window depicting the martyrdom of St Anastasia (20th-century copy from a 13th-century original).

Left: St Cecilia's tomb. Her body was found lying in this position in 1599, and the statue copies it exactly.

GEORGE

The potency of his story ensures that St George holds a place in the company of saints, but the Church suspects that this chivalrous knight may be merely a legend.

> **KEY FACTS**
> *Knight martyr*
> DATES: *d.c.AD 303*
> BIRTH PLACE: *Cappadocia, Turkey*
> PATRON OF: *England, Istanbul, boy scouts, soldiers, and many other groups*
> FEAST DAY: *23 April*
> EMBLEM: *Red cross on white background, dragon*

In the 6th century, St George was described as good in so many ways that all his "deeds are known only to God". Sadly, most things about this saint remain known only by his maker, because evidence of his life is so sparse.

It seems certain, however, that George was a real martyr, a knight who came from Cappadocia in Turkey and died in Lydda (site of modern-day Lod) in Palestine.

GEORGE AND THE DRAGON
In what is undoubtedly his most famous legend, George was riding through Libya when he heard cries of mourning. Townspeople told him that they were being tyrannized by a dragon that they had to feed with two lambs a day. Now they had no lambs left and the dragon was demanding a human meal. They had drawn lots from the maidens and the king's daughter had been chosen. Dressed in a beautiful bridal gown, the princess had gone forth to meet her doom. St George dashed into action and crippled the monster by thrusting his lance into it. Tying her girdle round the dragon's neck, the princess led it limping to the town. The terrified citizens prepared to run, but George told them that, if they would be baptized, the dragon would be slain. They all agreed. It was alleged that approximately 15,000 people were baptized. Four ox carts moved the beast's body to a distant meadow.

Right: Saint George and the Dragon *(Paolo Uccello, c.1439–40).*

Above: St George as depicted in a fresco in the Church of our Lady of the Pasture, Asinou, Cyprus (late 12th century).

CULTUSES AND CRUSADES
There are signs that St George's cultus was widespread early in Christian history. He was venerated across Europe and known in England before the Norman Conquest of AD 1066. His image can be found all over the Middle East, the Balkans and Greece.

During the Crusader battle of Antioch in AD 1098, Frankish (German) knights were blessed with a vision of George and another knight, St Demetrius. Possibly on his return from the Third Crusade a century later, Richard I promoted the veneration of St George in England.

PATRONAGE
St George is now the patron saint of England, as well as of boy scouts and soldiers, and many churches bear his name. In 1914, together with St John Chrysostom and St Roch, St George was declared a patron of Constantinople (Istanbul).

Because so little is actually known of St George, the Church downgraded him in 1960, and today his feast day is reduced to prayers during Mass. But his name and his story of chivalry are loved across the world. His flag, a red cross on white background, was well known by the 14th century and is the national flag of England.

VITUS

A CHILD WHO DEFIED HIS PARENTS TO BECOME A CHRISTIAN, VITUS CURED SUFFERERS OF MENTAL ILLNESS AND EPILEPSY. FOLLOWERS DANCED ON HIS FEAST DAY TO ENSURE A YEAR OF GOOD HEALTH.

> **KEY FACTS**
> *Miracle worker*
> DATES: *d.c.AD 303*
> BIRTH PLACE: *Sicily*
> PATRON OF: *St Vitus' dance, actors, comedians, against lightning and storms, against epilepsy, protection against dangerous animals, Sicily*
> FEAST DAY: *15 June*
> EMBLEM: *Dog or cockerel*

It is said that Vitus was a young boy when he elected to be baptized without his parents' knowledge. His angry parents beat him and threw him into a dungeon when he refused to give up his faith.

Above: The façade of the neo-Gothic Cathedral of St Vitus in Prague.

Angels, dancing in a dazzling light, came to comfort him. His furious father visited him and tried to persuade Vitus to abandon the faith. But the angry man was blinded by the light and flitting movements of the dancing angels. He restored his father's sight, but this did not bring Vitus any peace.

As various other miracles were attributed to him, he found that officials became suspicious of him. Fearing for his safety, he fled from his birthplace in Sicily. He landed with two companions at Lucania in Italy, where they stayed a while, preaching to the people. Finally they reached Rome, where Vitus cured Emperor Diocletian's son by expelling evil spirits that possessed the child.

But, after this healing, Vitus was expected to make a thanksgiving sacrifice to the Roman gods who, it was presumed, had given him the power. Vitus refused, and so was branded a dangerous sorcerer.

Vitus and his companions were subjected to various unsuccessful tortures and were reputedly lifted to safety by an angel during a great storm. The site of their death or martyrdom remains unclear. Both St-Denis in Paris and Corvey in Saxony claim to hold his relics.

DYMPNA

A PRINCESS WHO FLED FROM HER OBSESSED FATHER BECAME PATRONESS OF THE INSANE.

Above: This intricate decorated altar is found in the St Dympna Church in Gheel, Belgium (c.1490–1500). It is called the Passion Altar, and it depicts the last days of Christ on earth.

> **KEY FACTS**
> *Virgin, miracle worker*
> DATES: *c.7th century*
> BIRTH PLACE: *Possibly Celtic Britain*
> PATRON OF: *The mentally ill, against epilepsy and possession by the devil, sleepwalkers*
> FEAST DAY: *30 May*

Legend explains that Dympna was a princess, the daughter of a Celtic king. She grew up to be beautiful, but she also bore an uncanny resemblance to her dead mother.

Her father developed a perverted passion for his daughter, and so she fled with her confessor or teacher, St Gerebernus. The two fugitives made their way to Gheel, near Antwerp, in Belgium. They lived as hermits, but the king traced them and demanded her return. When the king's request was refused, he ordered his guards to murder Gerebernus and he beheaded his own daughter. Years later, the bones of the victims were discovered. After visiting these relics, numerous epileptics and lunatics claimed to be cured.

CHRISTOPHER

THE PATRON SAINT OF TRAVELLERS DERIVES HIS NAME FROM A GREEK WORD MEANING "ONE WHO CARRIES CHRIST". CHRISTOPHER IS LOVED FOR THIS HONOURABLE TASK.

> **KEY FACTS**
> *Carried the child Jesus across a river*
> DATES: *Unknown*
> BIRTH PLACE: *Unknown*
> PATRON OF: *Wayfarers, travellers and motorists*
> FEAST DAY: *25 July*
> EMBLEM: *Pole to aid walking through the river, carrying a child on his shoulder*

One of the best-known saints, Christopher is now deemed legendary and no longer included in the Roman calendar. However, this "de-canonization" has not stopped the popular veneration of St Christopher, whose image adorns cars and key rings. Travellers everywhere continue to pray for his intercession.

According to some stories, Christopher was a tall, muscular man. He is described in the *Golden Legend* as having a "fearful face and appearance".

Below: This image from a German illuminated manuscript gives a realistic view of the agony St Christopher endured as he carried the small, but extraordinarily heavy, infant Jesus across the river (15th century).

BECOMING A CHRISTIAN

Christopher found "a right great king" to serve, but soon observed he made the sign of the cross whenever hearing the word "devil". Christopher felt that needing such help was hardly fitting for a great monarch. So instead, he sought this powerful devil and worked for him.

With the devil leading him, Christopher travelled through the desert. The discovery that a cross, thrust into the sands, frightened the devil prompted Christopher to seek an explanation. A holy hermit told him about the power of this cross, and then converted him to Christianity.

Because of his size, Christopher dreaded fasting. Nor could he accept long hours of prayer and short periods of sleep. The hermit asked if Christopher could carry travellers across the river. In this way, the *Golden Legend* explains, he found a way to serve the Lord.

CARRYING CHRIST

A child once asked Christopher to carry him, so he hoisted the little boy on to his shoulders and stepped into the water. The child grew heavier, but Christopher persevered. On reaching the other bank, he felt "all the world upon me; I might bear no greater burden". The boy replied, "Thou hast not only borne all the world upon thee, but thou hast borne Him that made all the world, upon thy soldiers. I am Jesus Christ."

Christopher went to Lycia (southern Turkey) to preach, but was arrested. He survived burning by iron rods, and when they shot him, the arrows stopped in mid-air. Finally they beheaded him.

The truth about Christopher is sparse. He was martyred in the Middle East, honoured in the 3rd century AD, and a church was dedicated to him in the 4th century AD. Early Christians prayed to his image to ensure safe travel, which has led to the practice today.

Below: St Christopher is gaunt but noble in this sensitive wood-carving (Gothic-style winged altar in the Kefermarkt, Austria, c.1490).

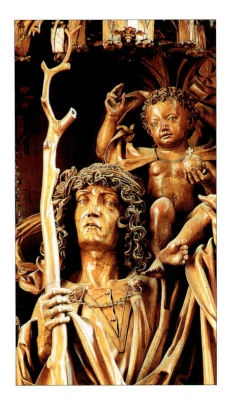

CHILD SAINTS

THOUSANDS OF CHILDREN HAVE DIED ALONE OR WITH THEIR CHRISTIAN FAMILIES IN DEFENCE OF THEIR FAITH. YET FEW NAMES SURVIVE FROM THIS GROUP OF YOUNG MARTYR SAINTS.

Many children were named as saints not only for the purity and innocence of their youth, but for the horrible deaths they suffered as martyrs.

It is safe to assume that many thousands of unnamed children, together with their families, were slaughtered by the Roman authorities. Some attracted a cultus and their names live on. These child saints mostly come from the early years of the Catholic faith when its members were subject to horrific, intermittent persecution.

EARLY MARTYRS

Legend describes St Foy (or Faith) as a defiant child who is said to have lived in Agen, Gaul (France) in the late 3rd century. Legend states that she was roasted alive and beheaded for her belief. Her bravery was venerated and thousands made the journey to visit her relics in Conques, France. Crusader soldiers, especially, pleaded for her protection.

The story of St Irene tells that this brave Macedonian girl was about 13 when she was arrested with her sisters in c.AD 303. While her sisters were killed, Irene was spared because she was so young. She was sent naked into the soldiers' brothel where no man dared approach her. She was eventually burnt alive in AD 304.

Although the 4th-century St Pelagia of Antioch is named in the church litany, all we know about her is that, when she was 15, soldiers invaded her home. To escape from them and avoid dishonour, the young virgin sacrificed her life by jumping off the roof of her house.

St Philomena's history is also obscure, but even now pilgrims visit her shrine in Naples. Her relics were unearthed in 1802 near an inscription bearing her name in the Roman catacombs. Her relics were subsequently moved to Naples, and miracles began to occur.

Because of controversy surrounding the relics of St Philomena, in 1961 the Holy See removed her from the liturgical calendar of saints and wanted to dismantle her shrine, yet she continues to attract pilgrims.

Son of Coenwulf, King of Mercia (AD 796–821), Prince Kenelm was next in line for the throne. But, according to legend, his sister Quendreda was jealous of the seven-year-old Christian prince and ordered the boy's tutor to murder him so she would inherit the throne. It was said that a dove carried a document to Rome telling of his death, and his relics were translated to Winchcombe in Gloucestershire. His wicked sister's eyes fell out and she was blind for the rest of her life.

Above: The Abbey church of St Foy in Conques, France, which holds her gorgeous relics.

Left: A sculpture of St Philomena made out of gilded wood (1890).

CHILD MARTYRS

Names with age at death; those in bold refer to martyrs described on these two pages:

Agape (Charity), 9
Agnes, 13
Christodoulos, 14
Dominic Savio, 15
Elpis (Hope), 10
Eulalia Mérida, 12
Foy (or **Faith**), unknown
Gabriel Gowdel, 7
Irene, 13
Justus of Beauvais, 9
Kenelm, 7
Kizito, 13
Maria Goretti, 12
Niño de Atocha, unknown
Pancras of Rome, 14
Paul Lang Fu, 9
Pelagia of Antioch, 15
Philomena, unknown
Pistis (Faith), 12
Rais, 12

Right: Maria Goretti was canonized by Pope Pius XII at St Peter's in Rome in 1950.

19TH AND 20TH CENTURIES

There are only a few known child saints from the 19th and 20th centuries. They are symbols of the bravery of the thousands of unnamed children who suffered for their faith during this time.

One such child is Dominic Savio. He was only 12 when he entered a Turin monastery. A cheerful, peaceful child, he was famous for the hours he spent in prayer. Dominic suffered from tuberculosis and, during a fever, experienced a vision. Before his death in 1857 he cried out, "I am seeing the most wonderful things!" He was 15.

During the Boxer Rebellion in 1900, thousands of Christians were murdered for playing a part in the foreign domination of China. One of the youngest was Paul Lang Fu, just nine years old. He ran to his mother's side as soldiers tied her to a tree, but they hacked off his arm and burnt him to death.

Maria Goretti (1890–1902) was a martyr for chastity and the Christian life. She was only 12 years old when she was murdered by a man who tried to rape her. Before she died, she forgave him his sin. He was imprisoned, and after eight years he became a Christian; he was present at her canonization in 1950.

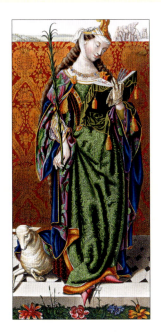

AGNES

Agnes is probably the best-known child saint. Some stories claim she was 13 when she died in Rome around AD 305. She was buried on the Via Nomentana, and a church was built over her grave soon after her death.

This young Christian girl refused to marry the son of a Roman prefect because she had dedicated herself to Christ. When the son complained, the father tried to force the marriage. Agnes remained steadfast in her refusal. According to legend, she was then dragged naked through the streets to a brothel, but her hair grew and hid her body. One man who tried to rape her was blinded, but Agnes prayed for him and his sight returned. The Romans finally put her to death by piercing her throat with a sword after flames would not burn her.

Agnes is often painted with a lamb to symbolize her purity, and every year, on her feast day, two lambs are blessed inside her church in Rome. Their wool is woven by the nuns of St Agnes' convent into bands, which the pope confers on bishops as a sign of authority. The superstitious believe virgins who go without supper on the eve of the feast of St Agnes will dream of the man who will become their true love.

Left: St Agnes holding the palm of martyrdom (Lucas van Leyden, 1510).

EULALIA OF MÉRIDA

This young Spanish girl dared to confront a Roman judge, boldly reproving him for his persecution of Christians. She was accompanied at her death by a white dove.

KEY FACTS
Virgin martyr
DATES: *d.c. AD 304*
BIRTH PLACE: *Mérida, Spain*
FEAST DAY: *10 December*
EMBLEM: *Oven*

Eulalia is widely venerated in Spain for being a courageous virgin, a martyr – and a child.

Early in the 4th century AD, under the Roman Emperor Maximian, the persecution of Christians was widely enforced. In Mérida, local believers were rounded up and arrested. The judge Dacian was presiding over their trials when a young girl confronted him. Her wealthy family were apparently austere and frugal, and it must be assumed they were among the persecuted. She was only 12 years old, but Eulalia was courageous and loyal to her faith and family. She informed the judge that he was wrong to condemn and oppress the Christians.

She said that his prisoners were following the way of the one true God, so the Romans should not

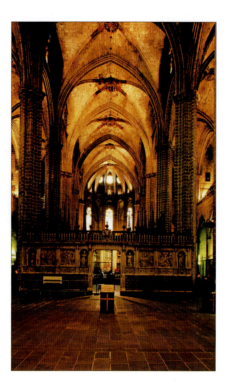

Above: The interior of the Cathedral of Santa Eulalia, Barcelona (13th–15th century). The saint commemorated by this building may be merely legendary.

punish them. He tried to divert the child with bribes, but Eulalia became angry and stamped on the sacrificial pagan cake he offered her. Then she delivered a deadly insult. Eulalia spat at the judge.

Dacian gave orders that she be tortured by being torn with iron hooks. Finally, she was bound and burnt to death in an oven. Spectators said that, just as she was thrust into the flames, a white dove fluttered from her mouth and soared into the air. Then a short and unexpected snow fell,

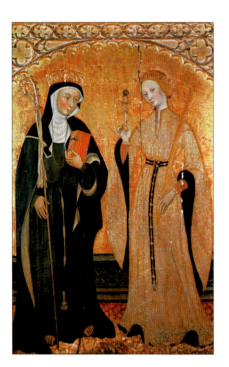

Left: Sts Eulalia and Clare (Pedro Serra, 14th century).

soothing her burns and covering her body. Christians dug her body from the icy mound and buried her remains with the oven in which she had died. The burial site is in Mérida.

THE CULT OF EULALIA

Thousands of medieval pilgrims visited the young saint's shrine, and many sites claimed to house her relics during the 6th and 7th centuries. Numerous churches and monasteries were dedicated in her name.

Artists favoured her gruesome death as a subject. The cathedral of Palma and the Catalonian art gallery in Barcelona have paintings of Eulalia. The Venerable Bede refers to this childmartyr in one of his hymns, saying, "scorched by fierce flames, Eulalia endures." The Spanish poet Prudentius describes the flight of the white dove from Eulalia's mouth.

FALSE CLAIMS

From time to time, it seems the longing to proclaim sainthood for a friend or relative overwhelms a community. There are examples of "duplicate saints" being given the name, and even the legend of a known saint.

For instance, another girl named Eulalia, from Barcelona, has also been claimed as a saint. She has been accorded similar legends and status by false cultuses. Scholars have decided that the young girl from Mérida is the person who probably did exist, whereas the other girl never did.

JUSTUS OF BEAUVAIS

DURING ONE OF THE MOST SEVERE PERSECUTIONS OF THE CHURCH BY THE ROMAN AUTHORITIES, SOLDIERS CAME TO TAKE AWAY A CHRISTIAN FAMILY, BUT WERE GREETED BY A DEFIANT SMALL BOY.

KEY FACTS
Child martyr
DATES: *3rd or 4th century AD*
BIRTH PLACE: *Beauvais*
FEAST DAY: *18 October*

The persecution of Christians by edict of the Roman Emperor Diocletian in AD 303 was one of the worst in the history of the early Church.

It was possibly during this violent period that soldiers came to the family home of the young Justus demanding the arrest of his Christian father and brother. The boy, just nine years old, showed no fear, although he must have known that the soldiers were dangerous and brutal men. He refused to reveal where his family were hiding. Ignoring his youth and bravery, his persecutors lifted their swords and swiftly sliced off the boy's head.

According to legend, Justus' head continued to speak after his decapitation. The words remained defiant. Justus had a large cultus in France, Belgium and Switzerland.

Above: The grave of a martyr from the 2nd or 3rd centuries AD, the fish was a secret symbol among Christians.

PANCRAS OF ROME

THIS SAINT'S HISTORY IS OBSCURE, YET HIS NAME LIVES ON BOTH WITHIN THE CHURCH AND IN THE SECULAR WORLD, NOTABLY AS A PARISH AND RAILWAY TERMINUS IN LONDON, ENGLAND.

KEY FACTS
Child martyr
DATES: *Early 4th century AD*
BIRTH PLACE: *Phrygia*
FEAST DAY: *12 May*

There is no hard evidence about St Pancras. A martyr of that name was buried in the Aurelian Way in Rome. Legend has it that St Pancras was only 14 when he was killed.

In about AD 500, Pope St Symmachus built a church in Rome over the tomb of St Pancras. Miracles in his name were claimed at the site. The great St Augustine of Canterbury built a church in his honour in that city. This building, too, carried an atmosphere of great spirituality.

After their conquest of England in 1066, centuries later, the Normans dedicated a church in London to the boy saint. His name was given to a parish and a railway station in London. These facts make it easier to believe that the boy did exist, and that once upon a time his bravery and the circumstances of his death were well known.

Below: An etching of St Pancras Church at Euston in London, designed by H.W. Inwood (Thomas Kearnan, 19th century).

DIRECTORY OF SAINTS

DOROTHY

FEARLESS IN THE FACE OF TORTURE AND DEFIANT IN DEATH, DOROTHY RETURNED TO WORK A MIRACLE, DELIVERING A GIFT FROM PARADISE TO A MAN WHO HAD TAUNTED HER FOR HER FAITH.

> **KEY FACTS**
> *Virgin martyr*
> DATES: *d.c. AD 304*
> BIRTH PLACE: *Caesarea, Cappadocia*
> PATRON OF: *Florists, gardeners, brewers, bridal couples*
> FEAST DAY: *6 February*
> EMBLEM: *Basket of flowers, especially roses, and of fruit*

Despite coming from a noble Roman family in Caesarea in Cappadocia, Turkey, Dorothy would not pay homage to her family's pagan gods. Punished for her Christian faith and refusal to marry, she experienced frightful torture. But the weapons used against her felt as mere feathers.

At the place of execution, Dorothy showed no fear and instead announced to the crowd around her that she was glad to leave this cold world for one that knew neither ice nor snow. A young man called Theophilus, taunted her for both her virginity

and her faith. He then challenged her to send him roses and fruit when she reached her paradise.

In the winter after Dorothy's martyrdom, an angel delivered a basket filled with roses and fruit to Theophilus. He converted, but the young man, too, was executed.

Left: Theophilus taunts Dorothy in The Flower Miracle of Saint Dorothy *(Hans Baldung, 1516).*

VINCENT OF SARAGOSSA

SPAIN'S FIRST MARTYR SAINT WAS REVERED FOR HIS COURAGE AND STAMINA IN THE FACE OF REPEATED TORTURE. SYMBOLIC OF THIS RESISTANCE IS HIS SUPPOSED POWER AGAINST WINTER FROST.

> **KEY FACTS**
> *Spain's first martyr*
> DATES: *d. AD 304*
> BIRTH PLACE: *Saragossa, Spain*
> PATRON OF: *Wine-growers, wine- and vinegar-makers, Portugal*
> FEAST DAY: *22 January*
> EMBLEM: *Dressed as a deacon holding a palm tree or on a gridiron*

There is little evidence about this early martyr saint, yet St Vincent of Saragossa was venerated across the Roman Empire. Every Christian community associated his name with Christ.

He is the protomartyr of Spain and his fate was horrible. Taken prisoner, Vincent was thrown into jail. He was kept on a starvation diet so that his body, and resolve, might weaken. Still he refused to recognize the pagan gods.

The authorities put him in the stocks, stretched him on the rack and roasted him on a gridiron. After that he was returned to his

miserable prison and left to starve. Vincent endured all this brutal violence with defiance and took a long time dying.

Vincent is credited with the power to fight winter frost hence his patronage of wine.

Left: A depiction of the Martyrdom of Saint Vincent *(French manuscript illumination, 15th century).*

LUCY

Yet another victim of the Diocletian persecution, Lucy was believed to have been rescued by the Holy Spirit. She is remembered for the miraculous recovery of her eyes.

> **KEY FACTS**
> *Virgin martyr*
> DATES: *d.AD 304*
> BIRTH PLACE: *Syracuse, Sicily*
> PATRON: *Against eye afflictions and throat infections*
> FEAST DAY: *13 December*
> EMBLEM: *Disembodied eyes, usually on a platter*

Lucy lost her father when she was a child but was, by all accounts, a resolute, devout young Sicilian. She had a loving mother, yet Lucy kept secret her Christian faith and her vow of virginity.

Her mother, Eutychia, was a wealthy noblewoman from Syracuse. She followed tradition by betrothing her adolescent daughter to a local youth. This expectation made Lucy confess her faith and she invited her mother to accompany her on a pilgrimage to the tomb of St Agatha. The two women prayed at this shrine and Eutychia was cured of the haemorrhages from which she suffered. Grateful and convinced of Lucy's faith, she released the girl from the betrothal. But the young man was furious at the rejection of his marriage proposal, and reported Lucy to the authorities, who promptly arrested her.

MARTYRDOM

The persecution by the Emperor Diocletian was famous for its zeal in attacking Christianity, with many of its followers perishing.

The emperor sentenced Lucy to be taken to a brothel. However, it was said that the girl became immovable. Neither a gang of strong men nor a team of oxen could shift her. She had been filled by the Holy Spirit, making her miraculously heavy.

Her wardens could not lift her to take her to the stake for burning. So instead, it is claimed, they tore out her eyes and threw them on a platter. Lucy calmly

Above: St Lucy displays her eyes on a platter (A. Colza, 1513).

took hold of them and put them back in their sockets. Her sight was magically restored. Frustrated by the failure of their cruel methods in persuading the saint to abandon her faith or her virginity, the soldiers beheaded the girl.

In many paintings, Lucy holds the platter bearing her eyes. Otherwise, her eyes are dangling from a sprig of leaves or on her clothes. She has long been connected with light, partly because of the story of her eyes, and also because her name is linked to the Latin word for "light", *lux*.

Lucy is remembered in Sweden on the shortest day of the year with festivals at which young girls carry candles in her memory. She is likewise venerated in her birthplace, Sicily.

Below: Detail of St Lucy resisting a team of oxen in front of Judge Paschasius (Bartolo di Fredi, c.1380).

PATRON SAINTS OF PROFESSIONS

In the world of work, some saints are patrons by custom, others by papal concession. Some helped particular professions; others are chosen for the lives they led.

Accountants – Matthew
Actors – Genesius of Arles, Vitus
Actresses – Pelagia the Penitent
Advertisers – Bernardino of Siena
Air crew – Joseph of Copertino, Theresa of Lisieux
Anaesthetists – René Goupil
Apothecaries – Nicholas of Myra, Cosmas and Damian
Archaeologists – Jerome, Helen
Architects – Thomas, Barbara
Art dealers – John
Artists – Luke, Catherine de' Vigri of Bologna
Astronauts – Joseph of Copertino
Astronomers – Dominic
Athletes – Sebastian
Authors – John, Paul, Lucy, Francis of Sales
Bakers – Elizabeth of Hungary, Zita, Nicholas of Myra, Agatha
Bankers – Bernardino of Feltre, Matthew
Bar staff – Amand
Basket-makers – Antony of Egypt
Beekeepers – Ambrose, Bernard of Clairvaux, Valentine, Modomnoc
Bishops – Charles Borromeo
Blacksmiths – Dunstan, Eloi
Bookkeepers – Matthew
Brewers – Amand, Wenceslas, Augustine of Hippo, Boniface
Bricklayers – Stephen of Hungary
Broadcasters – Archangel Gabriel
Builders – Barbara, Blaise, Louis IX, Vincent Ferrer
Bus drivers – Christopher
Butchers – Adrian of Nicomedia, Luke
Cab drivers – Christopher, Eloi, Fiacre, Frances of Rome
Cabinet-makers – Anne, Joseph, Victor of Marseilles
Carpenters – Joseph, Thomas
Civil servants – Thomas More

Above: St Bernardino of Siena *(Giovanni di Paolo, 1450). He is patron of advertisers.*

Clergy – Gabriel Possenti
Clowns – Genesius of Arles, Julian the Hospitaller
Cobblers – Crispin and Crispinian, Bartholomew
Cooks, chefs – Laurence, Macarius the Younger, Martha, Paschal Baylon
Craftspeople – Eloi, Catherine of Alexandria

Customs officers – Matthew
Dancers – Vitus, Genesius of Arles, Philemon
Dentists – Apollonia
Dietitians – Martha
Diplomats – Archangel Gabriel
Doctors – Blaise, Cosmas and Damian, Pantaleon
Domestic workers – Adelelmus, Martha, Zita
Ecologists – Francis of Assisi
Editors – John Bosco, Francis of Sales
Engineers – Ferdinand III
Farm-workers – Benedict, Isidore the Farmer, Eloi, Phocas of Sinope, George
Firefighters – Agatha, Laurence, Catherine of Siena
Fishermen – Andrew, Peter, Simon, Zeno, Magnus of Norway
Florists – Dorothy, Rose of Lima
Funeral directors – Joseph of Arimathea, Dismas, Sebastian

Above: St Fiacre *(illumination, 15th century). Cab drivers in Paris plied their trade from the Hôtel St Fiacre and the saint has become their patron.*

Above: St Ivo of Brittany is patron of judges because he mediated in church disputes (Gaudenzio Ferrari, 1520).

Goldsmiths – Dunstan, Eloi
Grocers – Archangel Michael, Leonard of Noblac
Gunners – Barbara
Hairdressers – Louis IX, Martin de Porres, Mary Magdalene
Hoteliers – Amand, Julian the Hospitaller, Martha
Housewives – Martha, Zita, Anne
Huntsmen – Eustace, Hubert
Jewellers – Eloi, Agatha, Dunstan
Journalists – Francis of Sales, Paul, Maximilian Kolbe
Judges – Ivo of Brittany
Labourers – Eloi, Isidore the Farmer, Guy of Anderlecht, Lucy
Lawyers – Ivo of Brittany, Thomas More, Robert Bellarmine
Leather-workers – Crispin and Crispinian, Bartholomew
Librarians – Jerome, Catherine of Alexandria, Laurence of Rome
Locksmiths – Dunstan, Eloi, Peter, Leonard of Noblac
Magistrates – Ferdinand III
Mechanics – Catherine of Alexandria
Merchants – Nicholas, Homobonus
Midwives – Dorothy of Myra, Brigid of Ireland, Peter of Verona, Raymund Nonnatus
Miners – Barbara
Musicians – Cecilia, Gregory the Great
Naval officers – Francis of Paola
Nurses – Agatha, Camillus of Lellis, John of God, Catherine of Siena
Obstetricians – Raymund Nonnatus
Painters – Catherine de'Vigri of Bologna, Benedict Biscop
Paramedics – Archangel Michael
Paratroopers – Archangel Michael
Pawnbrokers – Nicholas of Myra
Perfumers – Nicholas of Myra, Mary Magdalene
Philosophers – Albert the Great, Justin, Catherine of Alexandria, Thomas Aquinas
Photographers – Veronica
Poets – Columba of Iona, John of the Cross, Brigid of Ireland, Cecilia
Police officers – Archangel Michael, Sebastian
Politicians – Thomas More
Priests – Jean-Baptiste Vianney
Printers – Augustine of Hippo, John of God

Right: Limestone statue of St Maurice, the patron of soldiers and armies (Magdeburg Cathedral, c.1240).

Above: St Vincent of Saragossa is surrounded by vines and grapes to indicate his patronage of wine-makers.

Publishers – John of God
Sailors – Nicholas of Myra, Francis of Paola, Phocas of Sinope
Scholars – Jerome, Brigid of Ireland, Catherine of Alexandria
Scientists – Albert the Great, Dominic
Secretaries – Genesius of Arles, Catherine of Alexandria
Silversmiths – Andronicus, Dunstan
Social workers – John Francis Regis, Louise de Marillac
Soldiers – Martin of Tours, George, Maurice, Foy, James the Great
Surgeons – Cosmas and Damian, Luke, Roch
Surveyors – Thomas
Tailors – Boniface, Homobonus
Tax collectors – Matthew
Teachers – John-Baptist de La Salle, Catherine of Alexandria, Francis of Sales, Gregory the Great, Ursula
Veterinarians – Eloi, Blaise, James the Great
Waiters – Martha, Notburga, Zita
Weavers – Maurice
Wine-makers – Amand, Vincent of Saragossa, Martin of Tours

PANTALEON

Once ambitious and worldly, Pantaleon abandoned a successful career in medicine to live "in imitation of Christ" and was eventually martyred for his faith.

> **KEY FACTS**
> *Martyr saint*
> DATES: *d.c. AD 305*
> BIRTH PLACE: *Nicomedia (now Izmit, Turkey)*
> PATRON OF: *Doctors, midwives, a Holy Helper*
> FEAST DAY: *27 July*
> EMBLEM: *Olive branch*

The Eastern Orthodox Church honours this saint as the "Great Martyr and Wonder Worker". (In the Greek language, *Pantaleon* means "all compassionate".) However, although his cult was well established in the East and West from an early date, there are no surviving authentic particulars of Pantaleon's life, which has become the subject of legends.

It is thought that he was the son of a pagan father, but was brought up as a Christian by his mother. He studied medicine and later practised as a doctor in Nicomedia (now Izmit) in Turkey, eventually gaining the important position of physician to the Emperor Galerius Maximianus.

However, being young and carefree, as well as ambitious and successful, Pantaleon abandoned his faith to enjoy the worldly pleasures of the royal palace. Fortunately, one of his friends from his former Christian life, Hermolaos, persistently reminded him of the truth of the Christian faith. When Emperor Diocletian came to power and started his fierce campaign of terror against Christians, Pantaleon realized where his feelings and loyalties lay. He distributed his wealth among the poor, treated the sick without receiving payment, and changed his life to one of discipline and austerity in imitation of Christ.

CAPTURE AND TORTURE

Other doctors, who had long envied Pantaleon for his success at court, took the opportunity to denounce him to the authorities.

Above: The church of St Pantaleon (AD 966–80) in Cologne, Germany.

He was arrested with Hermolaos and two other friends. The other three men were all executed, but the emperor, reluctant to lose a good doctor, begged Pantaleon to deny his faith. He refused, and his statement of faith was reinforced when he miraculously cured a cripple during his trial.

According to the stories, six types of torture were devised for Pantaleon. He was thrown into deep water to drown, then burning lead was poured over him. They tried to burn him, and they set wild beasts upon him. Then they turned him on a wheel and thrust a sword through his throat. But, no matter what mode of torture was employed, Pantaleon was miraculously protected from harm, suffering no wounds and feeling no pain. When at last his tormentors beheaded him, it is said that milk flowed from his veins and the olive tree to which he had been tied burst into fruit.

In Ravello, southern Italy, a reputed relic of St Pantaleon's blood allegedly liquefies every year on his feast day.

Above: A fresco of St Pantaleon from Macedonia (12th century). Scarcely remembered now in the West, St Pantaleon is still venerated in the East, and many legends and miracles are associated with this martyr.

LUCIAN OF ANTIOCH

THE MAN WHO ESTABLISHED THE IMPORTANT SCHOOL OF THEOLOGY IN ANTIOCH MADE AN AUTHORITATIVE TRANSLATION OF THE OLD TESTAMENT INTO GREEK BEFORE HIS MARTYRDOM.

> **KEY FACTS**
> *Martyr saint*
> DATES: *d. AD 312*
> BIRTH PLACE: *Samosata, Syria*
> FEAST DAY: *7 January (West)*
> EMBLEM: *Bishop's vestments, dolphins*

Orphaned at the age of 12, Lucian had Christian parents, who it is thought may have been martyred. He became the student of a famous teacher, Macarius of Edessa. After baptism, Lucian adopted a strictly ascetic life.

TEACHER AND SCHOLAR

His routine of disciplined habits allowed Lucian to write and study. He became a teacher, and is believed to be the man who established the school of theology in Antioch, which at that time was a significant Christian centre. One of his students was Arius, whose followers were sometimes known as Lucianists and who became the founder of Arianism.

Lucian is also known to have made an important translation of the Old Testament from Hebrew into Greek. His version, which corrected misleading translations in common use at the time, stressed the importance of maintaining the literal sense of the texts. His complete edition of the Bible, known as the Lucian Recension, was used by St Jerome during his work on the Vulgate, and St John Chrysostom also regarded it as an authoritative text. Surviving manuscripts confirm this respect, and one such text, the Arundelian, is in the British Museum.

ORTHODOXY OR HERESY?

Lucian lived at a time of conflict within the Church in Antioch. Three successive bishops were hostile to his teachings, and for some years he was excluded from major meetings of Christian leaders. However, it seems that he otherwise enjoyed wide popular support. The people respected him for his great learning as well as admiring his noble character. He was later restored to office.

PRISON AND MARTYRDOM

During an outbreak of Christian persecution, Lucian was arrested and taken to Nicomedia, where he faced the Roman official Maximinus Daza. He was thrown into prison, but, despite brutal treatment, his reputation for dignity and courage grew during the nine years he spent there. When dragged before the authorities for interrogation, he would always reply simply "I am a Christian."

At last, because he would not renounce his faith, his diet was reduced to sacrificial cake that had been dedicated to pagan idols. This he refused to eat. Some say he starved to death, but others relate that he was tortured and then beheaded. One legend even claimed he was flung into the sea and drowned, but that dolphins carried his body to shore where it was collected by his follow,ers.

Lucian's relics were taken to Drepanum, where on the first anniversary of the saint's death, St John Chrysostom preached a tribute to this much-admired scholar and martyr.

Left: The remains of the Roman Emperor Diocletian's palace at Nicomedia (now Izmit) in Turkey. Lucian suffered during Diocletian's persecution of Christians.

DIRECTORY OF SAINTS

HELEN

THE MOTHER OF EMPEROR CONSTANTINE WAS AN ELDERLY WOMAN WHEN SHE CONVERTED. AN ANGEL IS SAID TO HAVE HELPED HER IDENTIFY THE TRUE CROSS WHILE SHE WAS VISITING THE HOLY LAND.

> **KEY FACTS**
> *Mother of Constantine, finder of the True Cross*
> DATES: *c.AD 250–330*
> BIRTH PLACE: *Drepanum (later Helenopolis, in modern-day north-west Turkey)*
> PATRON OF: *Archaeologists*
> FEAST DAY: *21 May (West)*
> EMBLEM: *Crown, cross*

Helen came from humble origins, but she made a grand marriage and gave birth to a great son. According to tradition, she was born in Drepanum (later renamed Helenopolis after her, by her son Constantine) and her father was an innkeeper. Her husband, Constantius Chlorus, a Roman general, divorced her when he became Emperor of Rome in AD 292, but their son greatly honoured her.

FINDING THE TRUE CROSS
When in her sixties, Helen made a pilgrimage to Jerusalem. She had converted to Christianity by this time. Her son, who was by then emperor, had organized diggings to uncover the holy sites of Jesus and the apostles.

It is told that Helen was at the hill of Calvary, where foundations were being dug for the church of the Holy Sepulchre, when

Left: St Helen *(Altobello Meloni, 15th century).*

three crosses were excavated. A woman with a terminal illness was touched by each of the crosses, and the True Cross cured her, thus revealing its sacred nature.

Relics of the Cross were taken to Rome, where they were housed in the Basilica of Santa Croce, built for the purpose. The Holy Stairs – allegedly the marble steps excavated from the hall of Pontius Pilate, where Christ's trial was held – were also moved to Rome.

Helen was renowned for her generosity and work among prisoners and the poor, and she founded churches in both Palestine and Rome.

CONSTANTINE THE GREAT
Some biographies of Constantine claim his mother, Helen, was his father's paramour, not a wife. Though his father was emperor, Constantine still had to fight hard to win leadership of the Roman Empire. His cause was doubtless helped by his diplomatic skills. Although he promoted Christianity after his conversion, he was reluctant to cause strife in a predominantly pagan Rome. As emperor, he founded Constantinople (now Istanbul) on the site of the old city of Byzantium, which in time became the centre of the Christian world.

Right: Emperor Constantine and St Helen with the True Cross *(fresco, c.8th century).*

Above: Saint Helena and the Miracle of the True Cross *(attr. to Simon Marmion, 15th century).*

PACHOMIUS

A COMPETENT ADMINISTRATOR, THIS FORMER ROMAN SOLDIER WAS HIGHLY INFLUENTIAL IN ESTABLISHING ORDERLY COMMUNAL LIFE FOR HERMITS IN THE REGION OF UPPER EGYPT.

> **KEY FACTS**
> Founder of the first monasteries
> DATES: c.AD 290–346
> BIRTH PLACE: *Esna, Upper Egypt*
> FEAST DAY: *9 May (West)*
> EMBLEM: *Appearance of a hermit*

Life in the Roman army prepared Pachomius well for the path he chose to follow. Born to heathen parents in Egypt, he was conscripted into the Roman army, where he fought under Constantine the Great. He became a Christian after his return home, and immediately went to live in the wilderness, there putting himself under the guidance of an old hermit named Palemon.

Pachomius lived near the River Nile and became part of a small community of other ascetics committed to the austere life of a recluse. An angel is said to have visited Pachomius after a few years and told him to establish a monastery in the desert. It seems this Desert Father preferred the life of the community to that of the solitary. He was concerned, too, that some of his fellow hermits were extreme in their behaviour and that they were running the risk of madness from starvation and hardship.

FOUNDING MONASTERIES
His life in the army had taught Pachomius about the organization of a dedicated community, and he also had a flair for administration. After his first monastery was founded in AD 320, he established nine others for men and two nunneries for women, and wrote rules for living in these communities.

Above: This Byzantine mosaic includes Pachomius' name in Latin in the design (12th century).

The monks and nuns took vows of chastity, poverty and obedience, and regulations regarding diet and prayer were strict but humane. Fanaticism was outlawed and meditation and prayer were supervised. Members learnt by heart passages from the Psalms and other books of the Bible. Pachomius acted as an army general might do in running the monasteries. Monks were commanded to move from one house to another, superiors were put in charge of each house and accounts were presented every year.

The order he founded was known as the Tabennisiots, after a place near his first monastery. Pachomius' manuscripts have not survived, but his Rule was translated into Latin by St Jerome, and this influenced Sts Basil the Great and Benedict, both of whom founded great monastic orders based on St Pachomius' methods.

St Athanasius the Aconite, patriarch of Alexandria, was a friend of Pachomius and visited the monk in his monastery at Dendera, near the Nile, where Pachomius lived out his life. The Eastern Orthodox Church holds this remarkable man in high veneration.

Right: St Pachomius (16th century). The saint, remembered for building the first monasteries, is shown in this fresco to be casting his saintly light on the construction of a grand tower.

RELIGIOUS ORDERS

MONASTERIES AND CONVENTS SUSTAIN COMMUNITIES DEVOTED TO A STRICT RELIGIOUS LIFE. THESE RELIGIOUS ORDERS HAVE A ROLE IN ROMAN CATHOLIC AND EASTERN ORTHODOX CHURCHES.

Although Christianity does not regard ownership of property or marriage as sinful, the Church recognizes that some people have a special calling to dedicate their lives to prayer and to God.

Those called to this religious life fall into two categories. The first are the eremites, who choose to pursue a life of solitary meditation, following the precepts formulated by St Antony of Egypt and other Desert Fathers. The second group, the coenobites, share a communal life of prayer that is influenced by the ideas of St Pachomius. Founders of the various orders laid down rules for monastic life, which continue to apply in Roman Catholic and Eastern Orthodox Churches.

The lives of all monks and nuns are guided by the primary disciplines of prayer, spiritual development, inner contemplation and physical labour.

EARLY MODELS

The earliest monasteries were self-supporting and independent of papal authority. Many monks were not even ordained as priests.

Some early founders, such as Martin of Tours and Cassian, maintained harsh regimes. But St Benedict, who established a monastery at Monte Cassino, Italy, rejected this military-like austerity. His rules were those of a well-ordered household with routine and sympathetic discipline. He encouraged labour to sustain the community and literacy to provide an understanding of the scriptures. By the 10th century, his rule was accepted throughout Western Christendom.

The Rule of St Augustine of Hippo was also influential. He stipulated that monks should be ordained clerics, living within an order but going into the world to work as priests.

Above: Saint Zeno *(Francesco Bonaza, 17th century). St Zeno founded the earliest nunneries and encouraged women to take vows.*

Above left: Saint Hugo of Grenoble in the Refectory of the Carthusians *(Francisco Zurbarán, 1633). St Hugo helped establish their house in Grenoble, France.*

Over time, monastic orders lost their independent status and were required to obtain papal blessing and authorization.

LATE MEDIEVAL TIMES

During the Crusades, monastic rules of prayer and preaching were extended to include military and medical duties. The Knights Hospitaller of St John, which was founded in 1113, and the Knights Templar, established in 1119, both consisted of fighting men or soldier-nurses.

Above: The monastery of Monte Cassino, originally established by St Benedict, had to be rebuilt after severe bombing by the Allies in World War II.

Other religious orders were established in the 13th century, which returned to the asceticism of the early Desert Fathers. They included the Franciscans, founded by St Francis of Assisi, the Dominicans of St Dominic, the Carmelites, and the Augustinian Hermits. These were all mendicant orders, relying on charity for survival. Although the monks were attached to a community, they functioned as individuals.

Nuns generally lived in their enclosed communities, isolated from the outside world. They followed the Rule of St Francis through St Clare, or that of the Dominicans or Benedictines.

COME THE REFORMATION

During and after the Reformation, orders developed to strengthen the faith. Priests concentrated on teaching, nursing, leading retreats or missions. Most famous were the Jesuits, a missionary order founded by Ignatius of Loyola in 1534.

The Reformation reinforced eremitical orders. The Capuchins evolved from the Franciscans in 1525, the Trappists from the Cistercians in 1664, and the Maurists from the Benedictines in 1621. In 1562, St Teresa founded the first the Discalced Carmelite community in Ávila, Spain.

Below: A 15th-century drawing of monks wearing the distinctive habits of their orders. The Carmelites wore white, the Franciscans brown or grey, the Benedictines black, and the Dominicans black and white.

KNIGHTS HOSPITALLER OF ST JOHN

For centuries, a nursing order ran a hospital in Jerusalem. Then, in the 1120s, Raymond du Puy turned the order into a military community known as the Knights Hospitaller of St John. Nursing was not abandoned, but during the Crusades, the monks became much-feared soldiers. Expelled from Jerusalem by the Turks in 1291, they went to Rhodes.

Later, in the 16th century, the order was forced to move to Malta, where it remained until 1798. In 1834, after demonstrating that they had left their military past behind them, the order was allowed to settle in Rome.

Above: Order of Saint John of Jerusalem, a woodcut dating from the 14th century.

DIRECTORY OF SAINTS

ANTONY OF EGYPT

THIS SAINT IS OFTEN REGARDED AS THE FATHER OF MONASTICISM, AND WAS KNOWN FOR HIS HEALINGS, BUT IT IS HIS LIFE OF SOLITUDE, PRAYER AND GENTLENESS THAT HAS HAD THE MOST LASTING IMPACT.

> **KEY FACTS**
> *Desert Father, ascetic*
> DATES: *AD 251–356*
> BIRTH PLACE: *Coma, Egypt*
> PATRON OF: *Skin diseases, domestic animals and pets, basket-makers*
> FEAST DAY: *17 January*
> EMBLEM: *Pig, bell*

The popular view of saintliness is embodied by St Antony of Egypt. He was not tempted by worldly goods or comfort, he did no harm to others, he was not too proud to undertake humble work, and he spent his life in prayer.

SOLITUDE AND PRAYER

Born into a respectable Christian family in Coma in Upper Egypt, Antony was given a narrow education. When his parents died, he was 20 and heir to a considerable estate. But he recalled the words of Christ, "Go, sell what thou hast,

Left: St Antony in a stained glass from Suffolk, England (17th century). He was once a swineherd and St Antony's cross can be seen on his cloak.

and give it to the poor, and thou shalt have treasure in Heaven." He gave away his land and wealth, keeping only enough for the care of his younger sister, and lived among local ascetics. Then for 20 years, from AD 286 to AD 306, he took to the desert, where he lived a life of complete solitude and extreme austerity, seeking the love of God in prayer and meditation.

When he was 54, Antony was asked to leave his hermitage and organize some nearby ascetics into a monastic order. Back on his mountain, the hermit cultivated a garden and wove baskets. A follower, Marcarius, guarded him from curious onlookers.

Towards the end of his life, Antony visited Alexandria to comfort persecuted Christians and refute Arianism. He was, by now, famous for his wisdom and miracles; crowds rushed to see him and many were converted.

Sufferers from ergotism (also known as "St Antony's Fire") visited his shrine at La Motte in France, where the Order of Hospitallers of Saint Antony was founded, c.1100, to seek a cure.

Left: The central panel of The Temptation of Saint Anthony *(Hieronymus Bosch, c.1505).*

BASIL THE GREAT

VENERATED FOR HIS ROBUST DEFENCE OF THE FAITH, THIS DOCTOR OF THE CHURCH WAS ALSO AN IMPORTANT FIGURE IN ESTABLISHING MONASTIC RULES DEDICATED TO CHARITABLE WORK AND POVERTY.

KEY FACTS
Doctor of the Eastern Church
DATES: *c.AD 330–79*
BIRTH PLACE: *Cappadocia, Turkey*
PATRON OF: *Russia, monks of the Eastern Churches*
FEAST DAY: *2 January (with St Gregory of Nazianzus)*
EMBLEM: *Bishop's vestments, often pictured with other early Doctors of the Church*

Basil's extensive writings reveal a humorous, tender person, yet he proved unyielding in his fight for orthodoxy.

He was born in Cappadocia, one of ten children in an extraordinary family: his grandmother, both parents, and three siblings were all destined for sainthood.

On returning from studies in Constantinople and Athens, where he had become good friends with Gregory of Nazianzus, he travelled widely, to Palestine, Egypt, Syria and Mesopotamia, studying the religious life, before taking up life as a hermit in Cappadocia. His brother joined him there in a life of contemplation and preaching.

Basil established the first monastery in Asia Minor, instigating a brotherhood of hard labour, charitable work and communal routine, a system that he believed better served God and his faithful than did solitary asceticism. His rule, unchanged, is followed by monks today in the Eastern Orthodox Church, and forms the basis of orders dedicated to him.

BATTLING ARIANISM
During Basil's lifetime, a schism threatened the Church, caused by the popular teachings of Arius, which denied the divinity of Jesus.

The harsh activities of the Arian Emperor Valens against traditionalism brought Basil back to Caesarea to protect his community from attack. Valens was too afraid of Basil's reputation to act against him, and withdrew from Caesarea, but he continued

Above: An icon from Moscow shows St Basil wearing the omophor vestment of an Eastern Orthodox bishop and holding a copy of the gospels.

to promote Arianism elsewhere. Basil preached daily to huge crowds and produced numerous texts on belief that remain in use in the Eastern Orthodox Church.

During a period of drought, he built hospitals and soup kitchens ,where his monks served the poor. But, anxious that the faith might be waning in the East, he increased his preaching, emphasizing the Church's beliefs. His lessons were conveyed everywhere both by texts and through word of mouth.

In AD 378, Valens died and was succeeded by his nephew, Gratian, who discouraged Arianism. As Basil himself lay dying the following year, he was confident that, with the emperor on his side, orthodoxy would prevail.

Christians, pagans and Jews all mourned the "father and protector" of Caesarea, while the Church honoured St Basil for keeping the faith alive. He is one of the great Doctors of the Church.

Below: An 18th-century altarpiece in St Peter's Basilica in Rome shows St Basil defiantly celebrating Mass in the presence of the Emperor Valens.

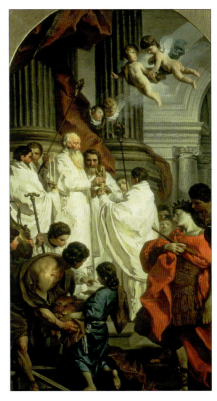

BARBARA

THE LEGEND OF ST BARBARA IS A ROMANTIC ONE ABOUT A BRAVE AND BEAUTIFUL GIRL WHO REFUSES ALL SUITORS FOR CHRIST. HER CULTUS WAS POPULAR IN FRANCE DURING THE MIDDLE AGES.

KEY FACTS
Virgin martyr
DATES: *Unknown*
BIRTH PLACE: *Unknown*
PATRON OF: *Gunners, artillery, dying people, miners*
FEAST DAY: *Formerly 4 December, but removed from Roman calendar in 1969*
EMBLEM: *Tower*

It is highly unlikely that this saint ever existed: although she allegedly lived in the 3rd century, nothing was written about her until the 7th. She was officially de-canonized in 1969.

According to the *Golden Legend*, Barbara was the daughter of a pagan, who locked her in a tower so that no man could see her. But her beauty was so renowned that men still came to court her. When Barbara became a Christian, her father was so furious that he tried to kill her, but she miraculously escaped.

Above: St Barbara (Flemish manuscript illumination, 1475).

Eventually she was handed over to a judge, who condemned her to death and ordered her father to carry out the deed. This he did, but he was immediately struck by lightning and died.

This is the reason that Barbara is regarded as a patron of those in danger of sudden death, originally from lightning, later from cannonballs, gunfire or mines.

CYRIL OF JERUSALEM

THE LESSONS OF ST CYRIL FOR THOSE SEEKING BAPTISM ARE SO PROFOUND, AND HIS FIGHT FOR THE TRUE FAITH SO EARNEST, THAT HE IS HONOURED AS A DOCTOR OF THE CHURCH.

KEY FACTS
Doctor of the Church
DATES: *c.AD 315–86*
BIRTH PLACE: *Jerusalem*
FEAST DAY: *18 March*
EMBLEM: *Bishop's gown*

St Cyril was a clear thinker and an excellent teacher. But it was his misfortune to live during a time of schism among the Eastern Christian communities, when the ideas of the unorthodox Arians were gaining ground against the traditionalist concept of the Holy Trinity – the threefold godhead of Father, Son and Holy Spirit.

Cyril was born and educated in Jerusalem. After becoming a priest, his first assignment, from St Maximus, was to train converts preparing for baptism. His lessons of faith were – and indeed still are – much admired, and they brought him prestige and high office.

When he first became Bishop of Jerusalem in AD 349, strange lights were said to fill the sky over the city. But, during the 35 years Cyril served as a bishop, he spent

Left: The Church of the Holy Sepulchre in Jerusalem where St Cyril was bishop during the 4th century AD. This scene has scarcely changed since.

much of his life in hot dispute with the dominant Arians. He was first exiled in AD 357, and, although he was recalled two years later, he was banished twice more and spent a total of 16 years in exile.

However, in AD 381, Cyril took part in the First Council of Constantinople, which gave official endorsement to the concept of the Trinity. St Cyril was made a Doctor of the Church in 1882.

GREGORY OF NAZIANZUS

The inspired preaching and writing of St Gregory helped to unify the Eastern Orthodx Churches in times of strife. As a result, he was made a Doctor of the Church.

KEY FACTS
Doctor of the Eastern Orthodox Church
DATES: AD 329–89
BIRTH PLACE: Arianzus, south-west Cappadocia, Turkey
FEAST DAY: 2 January
EMBLEM: Bishop's gown

This shy, diffident poet-priest was the son of wealthy parents, Gregory, Bishop of Nazianzus, and his wife Nonna, who were able to give him the best education. He attended the renowned theological school at Caesarea and continued his studies first at Alexandria and then at the University of Athens, where he rekindled his youthful friendship with St Basil the Great.

RELUCTANT PRIEST
Together, the two friends formed a common resolve to live a contemplative life, and when Basil set up a retreat in Pontus (now Turkey) Gregory joined him. Together they wrote the Monastic Rules.

After two years of the contemplative life, Gregory returned to Nazianzus. His father, now elderly, was not happy with his son's decision to live as a monk, and resolved to have him home. In AD 361, the bishop forced his son to be ordained as a priest.

Neither did his friend leave him in peace. Basil, who had by then become Archbishop of Caesarea, had Gregory consecrated as Bishop of Sasima, most probably to maintain his own influence in what was a disputed area. The place, however, was a hostile border settlement and Gregory spent little time there. The whole affair brought about a quarrel between the pair, from which their friendship never fully recovered.

After the death of his parents, Gregory, who had always desired the contemplative life, escaped briefly to a monastery in Seleucia.

Above: These four images depict some of the visions of the Old Testament prophet Ezekiel, and are part of The Homilies of Saint Gregory, *an illuminated manuscript held in Paris (9th century).*

AGAINST HERESY
Five years later, in 379, Gregory was recalled to serve the Christian community of Constantinople in their battle for orthodoxy. Church officials were determined to use Gregory's oratorial talents in their dispute with Arianism.

The heresy had been so successful in Constantinople that there was no longer an Orthodox Church active there, and Gregory was obliged to use his house to hold meetings. Here, he preached five discourses on the Holy Trinity. These teachings helped ensure that orthodoxy was confirmed at the First Council of Constantinople in AD 381. For a brief, unhappy period, he was Bishop of Constantinople, but differences of opinion with the Eastern bishops led him to resign.

PEACE AT LAST
Gregory spent his last years in priestly duties in Nazianzus and in retreat. Many of his letters survive, as does an autobiography and some religious poetry.

After his death aged 60, St Gregory's relics were translated to Constantinople and later to Rome. He is one of the great Eastern Doctors of the Church alongside Sts John Chrysostom and Basil the Great.

Above: St Gregory of Nazianzus, overseen by an angel while working at his desk, in a mosaic in the second dome of the Basilica San Marco, Venice (c.1350).

AMBROSE

This popular Bishop of Milan became a key combatant in the struggle against the Arian heresy. He also wrote important texts on Christian ethics and interpretation of the Bible.

> **KEY FACTS**
> One of the four great Latin Doctors of the Western Church
> DATES: *AD 339–97*
> BIRTH PLACE: *Trier, Germany*
> PATRON OF: *Bees, beekeepers and those who work with wax*
> FEAST DAY: *7 December (West)*
> EMBLEM: *Whip, to symbolize his fight against heresy*

A vigorous intellect, energy and charm helped Ambrose in the murky political world he encountered as Bishop of Milan.

He was the son of a noble Roman family, and legend tells that, when he was child, a swarm of bees settled on him, which was deemed to symbolize his future eloquence (hence his patronage).

He studied law, Greek, rhetoric and poetry before becoming consular prefect of Liguria and Aemilia, with headquarters in Milan. He was a gifted administrator and diplomatic leader – and the citizens trusted him.

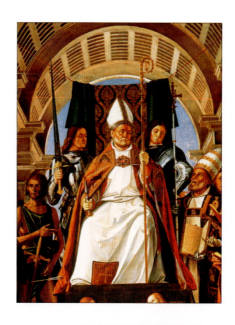

Left: Enthroned Ambrose *(Alvise Vivarini, 1503).*

Then Ambrose took to studying Christianity. In AD 374, when the Bishop of Milan died, he attended the council meeting to elect a successor. Ambrose was not a follower of Arianism, a sect that was strong in the Milan area, and gave a speech favouring orthodox beliefs. To his great surprise – he was not even baptized – he was elected bishop and was in office within a week.

TACKLING THE HERETICS

The new bishop took charge of a weak Church. The empire, too, was stricken by battles for supremacy between East and West.

The greatest demonstration of his moral strength was shown after the Massacre of Thessalonica in AD 390. The governor there had been assassinated and, in retribution, Theodosius, Emperor of the eastern Roman Empire, ordered thousands of citizens to be killed. Ambrose was horrified. He faced Theodosius and reminded him that God was more important than the State, and that even the emperor must submit to holy law. Contrite, Theodosius made a public penance for his savage act.

Left: The Emperor Theodosius and Saint Ambrose *(Peter Paul Rubens, 17th century).*

AGATHA

Although little is actually known about this saint, her alleged bravery in the face of horrific torture and death ensured her a widespread following in medieval times.

> **KEY FACTS**
> *Virgin martyr*
> DATES: *Unknown*
> BIRTH PLACE: *Catania or Palermo in Sicily*
> PATRON OF: *Protection from breast disease, volcanoes and fire; jewellers, nurses, bell founders, Catania*
> FEAST DAY: *5 February*
> EMBLEM: *Mutilated breasts, often carried on a dish*

Although there is some evidence that a virgin martyr named Agatha died in Catania in the first years of the 4th century, little is known about this saint. However, her memory persists and she is patron of Catania.

Her legend recounts that her parents were Christians from the nobility who openly refused to offer sacrifices to pagan gods. The local consul Quintinian, who tried unsuccessfully to seduce Agatha, raised a campaign against all Christians, and the young girl was arrested. As she approached the consul, she prayed, "Jesus Christ, Lord of all, Thou seest my heart… I am thy sheep: make me worthy to overcome the devil."

Her persecutors were aware that virginity was important to their Christian victims, so Agatha was sent to a brothel. It is said that her faith and piety shone from her, and no man dared approach her.

MUTILATION AND DEATH
Instead, she was taken away to be tortured. Agatha was not afraid of martyrdom, because it meant she would soon join Christ. Quintinian devised a mutilation suited to horrify a beautiful young girl. His henchman pierced and severed Agatha's breasts.

St Peter is said to have visited Agatha and restored her breasts. However, she was then forced to walk across hot coals and shards of glass. But, as she took her first step, Mount Etna erupted and an earthquake shook the earth. The watching crowd screamed for her release, convinced her that God was punishing them all. Quintinian stopped the torture, but quietly starved her to death instead.

St Agatha is often the subject of paintings illustrating her mutilation. The resemblance in shape of bells to breasts is the reason for her patronage of bell founders.

Above: This marble altarpiece portrays the coronation of St Agatha in heaven (15th century).

Below: Saint Agatha (Francesco Guarino, 17th century).

355

MARTIN OF TOURS

The son of a military man, Martin joined the army but chose instead to be a "soldier of Christ". He followed his faith with energy and conviction.

> **KEY FACTS**
> *Monk bishop*
> DATES: *c.AD 315–97*
> BIRTH PLACE: *Pannonia (present-day western Hungary)*
> PATRON OF: *Soldiers, infantry and cavalry, horses and their riders, geese, wine-makers*
> FEAST DAY: *11 November (West)*
> EMBLEM: *Armour, sword, cloak*

This saint is traditionally commemorated as having led a life of bravery as a "soldier of God". In fact, his first career was in the army – following his pagan father's footsteps – but he came to believe that war was incompatible with his commitment to Christ. When accused of cowardice, he offered to stand unarmed between the opposing sides, but was instead discharged from the army.

Martin became known for his charity as well as moral courage. One famous legend recounts that, as a soldier riding to Amiens in bitterly cold weather, he saw a poor man dressed in rags. Filled with compassion for the man's plight, he cut his heavy army cloak in two and wrapped the man in one half. That night, as he slept, Jesus appeared to him wearing that half of the cloak.

Below: Saint Martin Sharing His Cloak with a Poor Man *(Domenico Ghirlandaio and workshop, 15th century).*

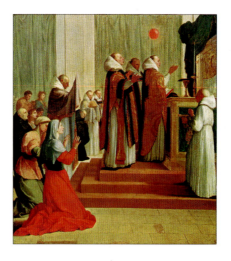

Above: The Mass of Saint Martin of Tours *(Eustache Le Sueur, 1654).*

MONK AND BISHOP

For ten years, Martin lived at Ligugé, a plot of land given to him by Hilary, the Bishop of Poitiers. Originally living a solitary life, Martin was soon joined by others, and founded a monastery there – the first one in Gaul. Then, in AD 372, at the acclamation of clergy and people, he was elected as Bishop of Tours.

After his ordination, he continued to live as a monk, moving to a solitary place, Marmoutier, where he later founded one of several other monasteries.

Martin travelled around his parish on foot and by donkey, preaching over a wide area with a desire to see the conversion of rural areas. He destroyed heathen temples and sacred trees and performed many miracles, notably healing lepers. It is said that he even raised a dead man to life.

He became involved in many doctrinal disputes. In AD 384, when some bishops appealed to the Roman authorities to execute local heretics, Martin begged (in vain) for their lives, claiming banishment was sufficient. Such a forgiving nature ensured his popularity into old age. A mausoleum marks his grave at Tours.

> **HILARY OF POITIERS**
>
> In AD 356, the Arian Roman Emperor Constantius II banished this bishop, whom he had branded a "mischief-maker". Throughout his life, Hilary was fierce in his fight against the Arian heresy.
>
> Though born (*c.*AD 315) and brought up in a pagan family, Hilary converted to Christianity in AD 350, following a long process of study. He became a bishop around three years later, and went on to produce many influential writings, particularly discourses on the Holy Trinity. He was praised by Jerome and Augustine of Hippo, and was influential in the spiritual development of Martin of Tours.

PELAGIA THE PENITENT

KEY FACTS
Penitent
DATES: *5th century*
BIRTH PLACE: *Antioch*
PATRON OF: *Actresses*
FEAST DAY: *8 October*
EMBLEM: *Hermit*

THIS BEAUTIFUL AND TALENTED ACTRESS ABANDONED HER FORMER LIFE AND WEALTH TO BECOME A CHRISTIAN. SHE LIVED THE REST OF HER LIFE AS A RECLUSIVE HERMIT, DISGUISED AS A MAN.

In the 5th century, St John Chrysostom wrote about a glamorous harlot of Antioch who repented and became a nun. The story of Pelagia the Penitent seems to follow this tale, but it comes with embellishments.

Pelagia was a beautiful and immensely wealthy woman as well as an actress, which was considered a disgraceful profession.

She liked to sway through the promenades of Antioch, dressed in marvellous clothes to flaunt her attributes. A retinue of admirers followed in her wake. One day, as she passed a solemn group of bishops attending a service given by bishop Nonnus of Edessa, a leading Christian, the men turned their backs on her. But Nonnus himself stopped preaching and admired the lovely woman. He was troubled that she was clearly so successful at her chosen yet despised profession, while he felt he had failed as bishop to his Christian flock.

PELAGIA'S CONVERSION
Nonnus prayed all through the night, then the next morning went to attend to his duties at the cathedral. Pelagia, who had heard his preaching, followed him and begged to be baptized. She was given instruction by a deaconess and accepted into the Christian community. After her baptism, she gave away all her possessions and disappeared from Antioch. She crept off and, dressed as a man, she took up the life of a hermit on the Mount of Olives in Jerusalem.

Pelagia was forgotten by all her old companions, although some Christians visited her. A deacon, known as James, was said to have sought an interview with the "beardless recluse", and afterwards wrote down her story. Only at her death did people realize that this hermit was not only a woman, but one with an infamous reputation in the city of Antioch.

The legend has been seen as a fine example of penitence. Others say it was written by a male hermit who longed for a female counterpart in his harsh life.

Pelagia's story has remained a popular one, and has been told in a number of versions over the centuries – from the fourth all the way to the thirteenth. Her name appears in many ports and villages around the Mediterranean Sea.

Right: Sts Pelagia and Euphemia in a mosaic from Sant' Apollinare Nuovo, Ravenna, Italy (AD 561).

NICHOLAS OF MYRA

Legends about the patron of Russia credit St Nicholas with being a miracle worker blessed with the virtues of kindness and generosity – especially towards children.

> **KEY FACTS**
> *Identified with Santa Claus*
> DATES: *4th century AD*
> BIRTH PLACE: *Possibly Patara, Lycia (modern-day Turkey)*
> PATRON OF: *Children, brides, unmarried girls, Russia, travellers, sailors, maritime navigators*
> FEAST DAY: *6 December*
> EMBLEM: *Three balls or bags of gold, purse, anchor, ship*

This saint is famous for his role as Father Christmas. The fact that he is patron of children may explain this status. Alternatively, the reason might lie in the legend that St Nicholas once found three dead children hidden in a brine tub and brought them miraculously back to life. There is also the story of his rescue of three young girls doomed to prostitution through poverty. As a gift, St Nicholas threw three bags of gold into their window, thus providing the girls with marriage dowries.

There is evidence that a bishop of Myra, named Nicholas, did live in the 4th century AD, but little else is known about him. Some claimed St Nicholas attended the Church's first General Council in Nicaea in AD 325. Or he may have been martyred before Constantine legalized Christianity in AD 313.

Above: This fresco shows St Nicholas saving three condemned knights from death (Giotto School, c.1300–5).

Below: Saint Nicholas Protecting the Sailors *(Vitale da Bologna, 14th century). He is patron saint of sailors.*

A PEOPLE'S SAINT
Despite his lost life story, St Nicholas has been, since early Christian history, a popular saint. His image can be found all over Russia and the Christian Middle East. Churches everywhere are dedicated in his name.

His many legends depict a strong, chivalrous man. He rescued three sailors from drowning, and saved three condemned men from execution. Sailors faced with a storm called upon his name, and it is said St Nicholas appeared at the shore and calmed the waves.

His physical strength was revealed as a newborn, when he sprang to his feet and stood firm. And, as a small boy, he showed deep devotion, listening attentively to the sermons of the local bishop, his uncle.

Italians stole his relics in 1095 and gave them to the church in Bari, where they remain to this day. Europeans carried his name to the New World. Linguists have observed that Dutch settlers in the USA called him "Sinte Klaas". Following European tradition, they would have given presents on his feast day, thus starting the Santa Claus tradition.

BLAISE

KNOWN FOR HIS KINDNESS AND FOR HIS MEDICAL SKILLS, BLAISE WAS SOUGHT BY BELIEVERS TO INTERCEDE NOT ONLY FOR THEIR OWN HEALING, BUT ALSO FOR THEIR PETS AND FARM ANIMALS.

> **KEY FACTS**
> *Martyr saint*
> DATES: *4th century AD*
> BIRTH PLACE: *Sebaste, Armenia*
> PATRON OF: *Doctors, farmers, wool trade, laryngologists, builders, veterinarians, a Holy Helper*
> FEAST DAY: *3 February*
> EMBLEM: *Wool-comb, two crossed candles*

Although no historical details of his life exist, the stories of Blaise's healings have made him popular and his feast day is still celebrated in some churches.

It is said that Blaise was born into a wealthy, Christian home in the 4th century AD. Blaise became Bishop of Sebaste in Armenia while he was still young, but he lived during the reign of Emperor Licinius, a time of severe persecution of Christians.

Warned by his brethren that his life was in danger, Blaise fled to the hills, where he remained isolated from his community, and where, allegedly, wild animals would turn to Blaise when they were ill or hurt and he would heal them.

STORIES OF HEALINGS

Among many stories is one of a countrywoman who came to the saint's cave with her small son, who was choking to death on a fishbone. Blaise touched the child's throat, the bone was dislodged, and the boy survived.

Eventually, Blaise was arrested. It is told that, as he was marched off to jail, he passed a wolf loping off with a pig in its mouth, while nearby a poor woman wept at the loss of her animal. Blaise ordered the wolf to drop its prey and was instantly obeyed. The grateful woman later brought the prisoner food, and a candle to light his cell. Indeed, different traditions have varied tales of St Blaise, but all tell of farmers calling on him for help with their sickly animals. Water with the blessing of St Blaise is given to sick cattle.

PATRONAGE

The saint is also associated with mending sore throats, and some churches celebrate the Blessing of the Throat on his feast day. The priest ties ribbons to two candles, then touches the candle ends to the throat of the sufferer, saying, "May the Lord deliver you from the evil of the throat, and from all other evil."

Perhaps Blaise's torturers knew of his bond with animals, because, before beheading him, along with numerous other tortures, they combed his flesh with an iron wool-comb. In time, the wool-comb came to be his emblem, and he became patron of the wool trade. For a long time, his feast day was celebrated with a procession in Bradford, once the centre of the English wool business.

St Blaise's cult is not known before the 8th century, but he became one of the most popular saints of the Middle Ages, most probably due to his association with miraculous cures. He was called upon to help diseased people and animals, and his name lives on in the village of St Blazey in Cornwall, England.

St Blaise also enjoys an international cultus. He is the patron saint of Dubrovnik, and in Spain he is venerated under the name of San Blas; in Italy he is known as San Biagio. He is one of the Fourteen Holy Helpers.

Above: Saint Blaise *(Giovanni Battista Tiepolo, 1740). His bishop's vestments give no hint of his hardships as a hermit.*

Below: A statue of St Blaise in Dubrovnik, Croatia (15th century).

JEROME

THE GREATEST BIBLICAL SCHOLAR OF HIS TIME WAS VENERATED FOR HIS AUTHORITATIVE TRANSLATION OF THE BIBLE FROM THE ORIGINAL HEBREW AND GREEK VERSIONS INTO LATIN.

> **KEY FACTS**
> One of the four great Latin Doctors of the Western Church
> DATES: c.AD 341–420
> BIRTH PLACE: Strido, Dalmatia (Balkans)
> PATRON OF: Scholars, students, archaeologists, librarians, translators
> FEAST DAY: 30 September
> EMBLEM: Bishop's hat, book, stone and lion

Numerous paintings of Jerome have created an abiding image of a lean old man, bent over his books in a remote cave. At his feet a large friendly lion keeps benevolent guard. But the reality was quite different.

Jerome seems to have been a man at war with himself. He longed to concentrate on his , but also sought academic debate. A quick temper and impatient manner made this saint unpleasantly aggressive and intolerant of his colleagues' ideas. Critics bemoaned his lack of Christian meekness and surfeit of sarcasm and unkindness.

Left: Saint Jerome *(Theodoric of Prague, 14th century). Often his symbol in art is a book.*

EARLY LIFE

Jerome received a classical education and went on to study further in Rome. During this time, he nursed an ambition to experience the world, and, in order to fulfil this ambition, the young man travelled widely and actively sought out teachers and further intellectual stimulation.

At this early stage in his life, Jerome was not devout, being too interested in the literature and philosophy of the Greeks. After a headstrong dispute in Rome with colleagues, he felt impelled to leave the city and travelled again, this time with two friends touring eastern Europe.

However, a chance occurrence changed his life. All three men fell dangerously ill with a severe fever. The subsequent death of both his companions had a profound impact on Jerome, who

Left: Saint Jerome in a Landscape *(Giovanni Battista Cima da Conegliano, c.1500–1510).*

turned to the Christian faith. But his commitment to Christianity caused him great anguish.

He greatly enjoyed the company of women, and found too much pleasure in reading pagan Greek texts. Believing these joys would carry him away from God, he decided to abstain from them. To this end, Jerome went to live as a hermit in the desert, where he could think and pray without distraction.

GREAT SCHOLAR

Somewhat against his will, he was ordained and sent back to Rome in AD 382. Pope Damasus I saw that this man would never do as a parish priest, but believed his scholarship could serve well.

Jerome produced important texts about traditional dogma and monasticism, and expounded the virtue of celibacy. He wrote in praise of the Virgin Mary, asserting the view that she remained a virgin throughout her life.

Posterity honours him for translating the Bible from Greek and Hebrew into Latin. His version is known as the Vulgate or Authorized Bible. Jerome was the first scholar to make the distinction between the "true" texts and the dubious, or

> "Show me, O Lord, Your mercy and delight my heart with it. Let me find you for whom I so longingly seek... I am the sheep who wandered into the wilderness — seek after me and bring me home to your fold. Amen"
>
> PRAYER OF ST JEROME

Above: Annunciation to Mary with the Saints Jerome and John the Baptist *(Francesco Raibolini, c.1448–1517).*

"apocryphal", texts. His work has proved invaluable to theologians ever since.

As was his wont, however, Jerome became embroiled in theological dispute, this time with the heretical Arians, about whom he wrote a scathing attack. And, in the process, it is possible he made one too many enemies.

SCANDAL AND FLIGHT

Jerome's promotion of a study group for girls and widows in Rome proved to be too risky. Soon rumour was rife that Jerome shared more than his religious teachings with the ladies. Despite protests of his innocence, he did not have the support of friends and was forced to flee.

Jerome travelled to Cyprus and Antioch where two Roman women, the widow Paula and her daughter, joined him. Together they went to Egypt, then returned to Bethlehem in the Holy Land.

Paula established three nunneries in Bethlehem, and she built a monastery for men which Jerome headed. Living in a cave nearby, he continued to analyse scripture. Even from this remote spot, his sharp tongue aroused fury among fellow theologians. He went into hiding again, before returning to Bethlehem in AD 418.

By then Jerome was old and sickly. It is said he died with his head resting on the manger where baby Jesus was born. Jerome was buried under the Church of the Nativity in Bethlehem.

JEROME AND THE LION

A lion had crept into the monastery in Bethlehem and its presence was frightening the monks. But the animal was limping, and Jerome, realizing its distress, and impatient no doubt with the squeals of his colleagues, strode over and removed a thorn from the lion's paw. For the rest of his days, the lion padded along next to him. Perhaps a dumb beast suited the saint's social temperament better than a human could. After Jerome's death, the lion protected the monastery's domestic animals.

Above: Saint Jerome Reading *(Rembrandt Harmenszoon van Rijn, 1634).*

JOHN CHRYSOSTOM

BOTH LOVED AND HATED FOR UPHOLDING CHRISTIAN PRINCIPLES, ST JOHN CHRYSOSTOM WAS A GREAT PREACHER, WHO ALSO PRODUCED PROFOUND INSIGHTS INTO SCRIPTURE.

KEY FACTS
Doctor, Eastern Orthodox Church
DATES: *AD 347–407*
BIRTH PLACE: *Antioch, Syria (site of modern-day Antakya, Turkey)*
PATRON OF: *Preaching, sacred oratory, Constantinople*
FEAST DAY: *13 September (West)* EMBLEM: *Bishop's gown*

A man of high intellect, John Chrysostom knew how to touch the hearts of his listeners. A committed ascetic, he aroused fury among those churchmen who preferred ease and luxury to the simplicity of a devout life.

John grew up in the major Christian centre of Antioch (in Syria). After his father died, his mother brought him up as a Christian. He studied law, but opted instead for a religious life. After his baptism, c.AD 370, he retired to the desert.

For health reasons, he returned to Antioch, where he was ordained a priest in AD 386. His eloquent preaching won him many followers in the city.

Left: Detail of Saint John Chrysostom *from the Apse Mosaic, San Paolo fuori le Mura, Rome (Edward Burne-Jones, 19th century).*

A RENOWNED TEACHER
St John Chrysostom is remembered for his preaching – his name means "golden mouth" in Greek. He emphasized literal interpretation and practical application of scripture and wrote treatises on the Psalms, St Matthew's Gospel and St Paul's Epistles. He is admired in the West, where he is one of the four Great Doctors of the Eastern Orthodox Church.

REFORM AND OPPOSITION
In AD 398, he was appointed Archbishop of Constantinople, and began to instigate moral reform. He dedicated Church money to hospitals, forbade the clergy from keeping servants, and put idle monks to work.

It was not long before he faced opposition. Empress Eudoxia took his attacks on the morals at court as a personal affront, and Theophilus, Bishop of Alexandria, demanded that John be exiled from Constantinople.

He was briefly recalled, but then banished again a year later, and eventually died of exhaustion after he was forced to travel long distances on foot in bad weather.

Right: Saint John Chrysostom Exiled by the Empress Eudoxia *(Benjamin Constant, 19th century).*

AUGUSTINE OF HIPPO

This influential thinker from North Africa was the architect of early Church doctrine. His writings, *City of God* and *Confessions*, became famous Christian texts.

KEY FACTS
One of the four great Latin Doctors of the Western Church, Bishop of Hippo
Dates: *AD 354–430*
Birth Place: *Tagaste (now in Algeria)*
Patron of: *Printers and theologians, brewers, against eye diseases*
Feast Day: *28 August*
Emblem: *Bishop's staff and mitre, dove, pen, shell, child*

As a young man of Roman Carthage, Augustine had considerable intellect and charm. His vivacity brought him, by the age of 20, a concubine and small son, Adeodatus. But he matured into a disciplined theologian and bishop, kindly towards his flock.

His pagan father ensured Augustine was well educated. His mother, St Monica, was a Christian, but her son rejected her beliefs. Driven by ambition, he moved with his family from North Africa to Rome, and then to Milan. He was a restless man, searching for a vocation. His widowed mother insisted he send the concubine, his companion of 15 years, back to Africa. Shortly after this separation, Augustine claimed to hear a heavenly child's voice bearing a divine message.

CONVERSION
His subsequent conversion to Christianity, however, was marred by the emotional conflict between, on the one hand, his love of comfort and women, and, on the other, the austerity demanded by his faith. These feelings are recorded in his autobiography, *Confessions*.

He and his son were baptized in AD 387 and, with a group of friends, retired to his estates in Africa. The group took vows of chastity, poverty and obedience, and undertook charitable work in the community. The rules that Augustine made for his monastic life formed the basis of future orders.

In AD 396, Augustine became Bishop of Hippo and never left North Africa again. From this corner of the empire, he set down his beliefs about spiritual redemption, which had a lasting impact on Church teachings.

Augustine lived in a period when the Roman Empire was crumbling under the burden of invading barbarians. Civic order was breaking down. However, Christianity was spreading, albeit haphazardly, across Europe.

Augustine believed the Church to be superior to the State, because its secular duties were based on spiritual qualities. He introduced the doctrine of man's salvation through the grace of God, and his ideas laid the foundations of a Christian political culture.

> "O God our Father, who dost exhort us to pray, and who does grant what we ask, hear me, who am trembling in the darkness, and stretch forth Thy hand to me, hold forth Thy light before me, recall me from my wanderings, and may I be restored to myself and to Thee. Amen."
>
> PRAYER OF ST AUGUSTINE

Below: Saint Augustine *(the Master of Grossgmain, c.1498).*

Above: A view of St Augustine's Cathedral at Hippo Regius (now Annaba), a Roman town in Algeria.

CATHERINE OF ALEXANDRIA

THIS COURAGEOUS AND INTELLIGENT WOMAN OUT-ARGUED LEARNED PHILOSOPHERS IN DEFENCE OF CHRISTIANITY. SHE WAS TORTURED ON TWO SPIKED WHEELS AND THEN BEHEADED.

> **KEY FACTS**
> *Virgin martyr*
> DATES: *4th century AD*
> BIRTH PLACE: *Unknown*
> PATRON OF: *Philosophers, young female students, librarians, nannies, wheelwrights*
> FEAST DAY: *25 November*
> EMBLEM: *Jagged wheel and the sword that beheaded her*

The legend of St Catherine of Alexandria is a gorgeous and romantic tale of heroism and faith.

Catherine was the beautiful young daughter of King Costus of Cyprus. She was also clever and courageous. A Christian, she confronted Emperor Maxentius about his persecution of her community. He was amused and intrigued, and challenged her to a debate with 50 philosophers. On learning that her arguments had converted these learned men, he ordered all 50 to be burnt on a pyre, and had Catherine beaten. Unfortunately for the emperor's wife, she and 200 soldiers were converted too, and also executed.

Isolated in prison, Catherine had doves come to feed her. Then she was "despoiled naked and beaten with scorpions". But no punishments affected her body or her convictions. Maxentius then tried to tempt her with wealth and status, and asked the beautiful Christian to become his wife.

CATHERINE'S DEATH
When Catherine refused, he devised a cruel death. She was to be turned between two wheels spiked with blades. But the blades broke and the splinters killed and injured the onlookers. An angel rescued Catherine. No torture could make the girl forsake her faith or her virginity. Even her beheading confounded the emperor. Instead of blood, milk flowed from her virginal veins.

Angels, or perhaps monks, are said to have lifted her body and carried it to Mount Sinai. There it remains, in a monastery built in AD 527 by Emperor Justinian.

Catherine had an early cultus in the East, possibly originating near Mount Sinai, and it seems the Crusaders brought her story to the West. Her story is featured in the *Golden Legend*.

Catherine was removed from the Church's Calendar of Saints in 1969, but people continued to venerate her as the bride of Christ (for refusing to marry) and patron of advocates and the dying. A limited recognition of her cultus and sainthood was allowed in 2001.

Left: St Catherine poses, calm and fearless, against her torture wheel (detail from a painting by the studio of Lucas Cranach, 1510).

Above: A medieval woman depicted as Saint Catherine *(Dante Gabriel Rossetti, 1857).*

URSULA

THIS BEAUTIFUL DAUGHTER OF A CHRISTIAN KING OF ENGLAND IS SAID TO HAVE TURNED DOWN AN OFFER OF MARRIAGE FROM ATTILA THE HUN ON ACCOUNT OF HER FAITHFUL VOW OF VIRGINITY.

KEY FACTS
Virgin martyr
DATES: *4th or 5th century* AD
BIRTH PLACE: *Unknown*
PATRON OF: *Girls, students, the Ursuline Order*
FEAST DAY: *21 October*
EMBLEM: *Crown, huddle of women under her opened cloak*

It is uncertain in which century St Ursula lived, or even that she lived at all. A mound of bones in a burial ground was uncovered in Germany in the 8th century, and in the 10th century an inscription bearing the name "Ursula", a 12-year-old girl, was found at the same site. From this "evidence", a medieval legend grew.

Ursula was a British princess during the 4th or 5th century. As a dedicated follower of Christ, she vowed to remain a virgin. She is said to have refused a marriage arranged by the court. In other versions, she was betrothed to a pagan and did not refuse him but, instead, set out to convert him.

PILGRIMAGE TO ROME

She requested that, before the wedding, she make a pilgrimage. Either she ran away, or was allowed to board a ship with 11,000 young women, also avowed to Christ and virginity.

This crowd reached Rome, where they venerated the saints and their relics. Ursula apparently had a meeting with the pope, one Cyriacus (unknown in papal records). Ursula and her handmaidens then turned back and sailed the Rhine to Germany.

They stopped in Cologne, but invading Huns had taken the city. These barbarians slaughtered the 11,000 Christian women, but not Ursula. The princess was spared because her beauty had been noticed by Attila, warrior leader of the Huns. He desired her, even offering marriage. But her refusal, on account of her vows, angered

Above: Saint Ursula Bidding Farewell to her Parents *(the Master of the Legend of St Ursula, before 1482).*

Below: St Ursula and her companions are martyred (16th century).

the Hun, whereupon he ordered his archers to shoot her through with arrows.

In Cologne, the romance of Ursula and her maidens was supported by old rumours of an early martyrdom of many young women in the city. The city's basilica was rebuilt to honour them. The story led to a hurried circulation of relics and forged inscriptions. Then, in the 11th century, Elizabeth of Schönau claimed visions of Ursula, and made revelations in her name.

The Roman Catholic Church removed Ursula and her companions from the Calendar of Saints in 1969.

LEO THE GREAT

Known to have been an astute diplomat, Leo I is venerated particularly for strengthening the role of the pope, and for his articulate writings on the incarnation of Jesus.

> **KEY FACTS**
> *Doctor of the Church*
> DATES: *d. AD 461*
> BIRTH PLACE: *Rome*
> FEAST DAY: *10 November (West)*
> EMBLEM: *Papal clothing*

This pope embodied the belief that the Church brings a beneficial authority to affairs of state. He was diplomatic, and his decisions were supported by a strong faith and conviction in the spiritual discipline of the Church.

Born in Rome, Leo took office as pope in AD 440, when the Church was in upheaval. Not helped by the destruction of the Roman Empire, he soon went to parley with Attila, leader of the invading Huns, who had reached the River Mincio, close to Rome.

Leo persuaded Attila to withdraw beyond the Danube. When the Vandals invaded Rome in AD 455, Leo's diplomacy once again prevailed, preventing widespread massacre of the city's citizens. Leo's strong leadership was important in Church affairs. The faith's foothold in Europe was shaky, and heresies were rife, especially monophysitism (a sect declaring "one nature" of Christ).

This doctrine held that Jesus was completely absorbed by his divinity, thus had no humanity. In contrast, Leo maintained that God had made his Son a man in order to preach the truth and to suffer in a sacrificial offering to redeem the sins of mankind.

CHAMPION OF RIGHT

Leo wrote his tome to rebut the Monophysites and presented it at the Council of Chalcedon in AD 451. His views were upheld, confirming the orthodox belief that Jesus is both man and God. Also at the Council, the balance of power in the Eastern Church was maintained because Leo refused to grant Constantinople primacy over Antioch and Alexandria.

His energy and mission work ensured the growth of the faith in Spain, France and North Africa. Leo implemented papal authority in these countries as well as in Italy. He was convinced that, for the Church to survive, believers needed to respect the spiritual guidance embodied in the papacy.

To support his conviction, Leo spoke of St Peter's role as leader. He reminded his followers that this succession had been passed in an unbroken line to every pope since St Peter. Leo's teachings, particularly those expressed in a sermon one Christmas, brought many Christians a deeper understanding of the Incarnation of the Word.

Of Leo's numerous and articulate writings, 96 sermons and 143 letters survive. It was the long-lasting influence of these texts on the Christian Church that inspired Pope Benedict XIV to pronounce St Leo as a Doctor of the Church in 1754.

Left: St Peter and St Paul can be seen floating above the scene here in The Meeting of Attila the Hun and Pope Leo I *(Raphael, 1509–11).*

SIMEON STYLITES

FOR 37 YEARS, ST SIMEON LIVED ON TOP OF A PILLAR, FROM WHERE HE PREACHED SERMONS THAT DREW CROWDS FROM FAR AND WIDE.

Right: A Byzantine mosaic of St Simeon Stylites living on top of his pillar in the Basilica San Marco, Venice.

> **KEY FACTS**
> *Stylite (pillar hermit)*
> DATES: *AD 390–459*
> BIRTH PLACE: *Cilicia*
> FEAST DAY: *5 January (West)*
> EMBLEM: *Saint on pillar*

This saint's story is as fantastic as any legend. Simeon was a shepherd's son who hated comfort and longed for solitude. His self-mortifications included tying plaited palm leaves round his body, causing a flesh infection that nearly killed him. He chained himself to a rock on a mountain, and spent the 40 days of Lent with neither food nor water. Priests usually had to rescue him.

His fame spread when he built a pillar, 3m/9ft high, and lived on it for four years. But, feeling this altitude did not give him enough solitude, he moved to ever higher pillars until eventually he climbed atop a pillar 20m/60ft high and 2m/6ft wide. There he stayed for 20 years until his death. Food and water were hauled up by rope. But still he had no solitude. Throngs of spectators came to gawp and ask questions. Unfazed, Simeon gave informal sermons about kindness, fairness, and not cheating on God.

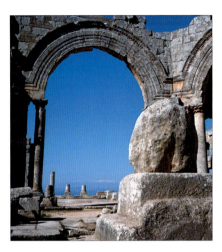

Above: A monument in a sanctuary to Simeon Stylites, on the site in Syria where he lived as a pillar hermit.

GENEVIEVE

BARBARIAN INVASIONS OF HER HOMELAND INSPIRED GENEVIEVE TO PERFORM HEROIC ACTS OF DEFENCE IN ORDER TO PROTECT THE CITIZENS OF PARIS. IN TIME, THEY ADOPTED HER AS THEIR PATRON.

> **KEY FACTS**
> *Heroic virgin*
> DATES: *c.AD 420–500*
> BIRTH PLACE: *Nanterre*
> PATRON OF: *Paris, against fever and plague*
> FEAST DAY: *3 January*
> EMBLEM: *Carries a candle, the devil at her side, shepherd's crook, bread*

As a child, Genevieve confided to Bishop Germanus that she lived only for God. In Paris, her young life was spent in prayer and caring for the poor.

When the city was threatened by a Hun invasion, Genevieve begged the frightened citizens not to flee but to pray. To everyone's relief, the Huns turned away at Orléans and Paris was saved.

Later, Genevieve ran sorties up the River Seine to fetch food for Parisians when under siege by the Franks. She also persuaded barbarian kings to show leniency to French prisoners-of-war. In 1129, her relics were paraded through Paris during a plague of the deadly disease, ergotism. The sick were said to be miraculously cured. The event is commemorated annually in Paris, but without her relics, which were burnt in the French Revolution.

Above: St Genevieve praying to save Paris (French School, 17th century).

CELTIC SAINTS

THE CELTIC CHURCH WAS THE PRODUCT OF UNCONVENTIONAL IRISH MONKS WHO, INDEPENDENTLY OF THE ROMAN CHURCH, CREATED A GOLDEN AGE OF SPIRITUALITY, ART AND LEARNING.

Christianity arrived as early as the 2nd century AD in Wales, England and Ireland, which became the Celtic branch of the Church, albeit in scattered communities. Then, in the 5th century AD, the Irish missions of two saints, Patrick and Brendan the Navigator, took the faith across the North Sea to Scotland.

These Irishmen are also thought to have introduced the austere monasticism of the Desert Fathers to the British mainland. Ascetic ideals, conceived in Egypt and Syria, might have made their way to Ireland via the distribution of religious texts, or through trade and pilgrimage in Europe.

Two other saints, Finnian of Clonard (d.AD 549) and Columba of Iona (d.AD 597), played key roles in establishing monastic life in Ireland and on the British mainland respectively. By the middle of the 6th century there were monasteries at Glastonbury and Tintagel in Cornwall. St Columba founded a community at Iona, Scotland, in AD 565. And St Aidan established the abbey of Lindisfarne, on the coast of Northumbria, in the 7th century.

Above: St Cuthbert turns water into wine, from Bede's Life of Saint Cuthbert *(English School, 12th century).*

Below: A Celtic cross outside the Iona Monastery, Scotland.

"WHAT WRETCHES WE ARE, GIVEN UP TO SLEEP AND SLOTH SO THAT WE NEVER SEE THE GLORY OF THOSE WHO WATCH WITH CHRIST UNCEASINGLY! AFTER SO SHORT A VIGIL WHAT MARVELS I HAVE SEEN. THE GATE OF HEAVEN OPENED AND A BAND OF ANGELS LET IN..."

FROM BEDE'S LIFE OF ST CUTHBERT

BEACONS IN THE DARK

These times were the Dark Ages. The old Roman Empire was in disarray. Rome herself was under constant attack from the Huns, and she neglected the distant Celtic churches.

The British Isles were wild, backward and uncivilized, except in the monasteries, where Latin and learning were kept alive. Irish monks were to become famous for the quality of their scholarship and all Celtic monasteries became beacons of study and literature.

When St Augustine of Canterbury's mission arrived in AD 597, the Celtic Church, though not heretical, was regarded with some suspicion. It had a peculiar administrative structure, with no dioceses, and bishops performing mainly ritual duties. Monasteries were built on land owned by the abbot, not the Church, and

monks were not bound by rules of a founder. They lived in monasteries, which allowed, within the usual vows of austerity and obedience, independence and individual expression.

Perhaps this freedom from a more rigorous communal routine accounts for the extraordinary flowering of art and craft among the Celtic monks. Beautiful ornamental ironwork and stone work developed to a high degree of sophistication.

Some monks wrote poetry and biographies of religious figures. Others transcribed scriptural texts into lovingly made manuscripts, adorned with intricate decoration and illustration. The writing of history and biography formed an important part of the monks' literary output. The best-known examples of this genre come from a writer who was the epitome of a Celtic monk, the Venerable Bede. Bede died in AD 735 and spent his entire life within cloisters, devoting himself to scholarship and prayer. Bede is most famous for his

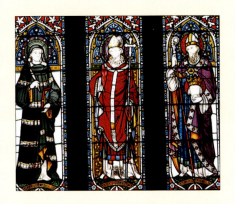

Above: The Venerable Bede, St Wilfrid and St Cuthbert in St Augustine's Chapel, Ramsgate, England.

Ecclesiastical History of the English People. Examples of biography include Bede's *Life of Cuthbert* and Eddius Stephanus' *Life of Wilfrid.*

Christianity gradually came to replace the old pagan practices. Saxon kings of the 7th and 8th centuries AD led mass conversions, strengthening the Church in England, especially in Northumbria, in the north-east.

PRESSURE FROM ROME

As the mission of St Augustine gained ground, the Celtic Church came under pressure to conform to Roman authority. The Irish tradition, with its archaic rituals and odd calculations of the Church calendar was finally rejected at the Synod of Whitby in AD 664.

The influential monk St Wilfrid (*c.*AD 633-709) approved this turn towards Rome. And, by early in the 8th century, even Iona and Lindisfarne, centres of Celtic culture in the north, had rejected the old Irish practices.

From the 9th to 11th centuries, invading Vikings destroyed many monasteries, dispersing the monks. Thus the "Golden Age" of the Celtic Church was ended, and little of its identity remained.

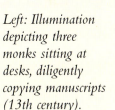

Left: Illumination depicting three monks sitting at desks, diligently copying manuscripts (13th century).

CELTIC ARTISTRY

The monks of Northumbria and Ireland produced illuminated manuscripts, the quality of which has rarely been surpassed. Until the 14th century, the material used for manuscripts in Europe and the Celtic fringe was vellum or parchment. Some of the finest early medieval artwork is found in these books. Celtic monks exhibited extraordinary skill in the art of interlacing patterns of animal and geometric designs. The text, written in a script known as *literae saxonicae*, consisted of letters inked in decorative shape and subtle hue. Little illustrations appear in the margins around the text, providing a detailed record of contemporary rural and courtly life. The finest examples are the Lindisfarne Gospels, produced in honour of St Cuthbert, and the Irish *Book of Kells.*

Right: Ornamental page from The Book of Kells *(8th century).*

369

PATRICK

THE FEAST DAY OF ST PATRICK IS CELEBRATED WITH MUCH FANFARE, NOT ONLY IN HIS NATIVE IRELAND, BUT ALSO IN THE USA AND AUSTRALIA WHERE COLONISTS AND SETTLERS SPREAD HIS CULT.

KEY FACTS
Missionary and bishop
DATES: *5th century AD*
BIRTH PLACE: *Between the Rivers Clyde and Severn*
PATRON OF: *Ireland*
FEAST DAY: *17 March*
EMBLEM: *Snake, bishop's vestments, shamrock, harp*

It is said that St Patrick alone converted Ireland, and banished all snakes from the island. His own life story is also extraordinary.

Patrick grew up somewhere between the Rivers Clyde and Severn. Irish pirates kidnapped and enslaved him. He escaped after six years of servitude.

After a long period of aimless wandering, he found his way home. Patrick studied the Latin Bible in preparation for joining the priesthood, but was criticized for his lack of scholarly education. He was ordained and, inspired by a dream, returned to Ireland as a missionary. He was appointed Bishop of Ireland in about AD 435.

Patrick divided the country into dioceses, and encouraged the setting up of monastic orders. He devoted himself to the delicate task of spreading the Christian faith across a land in which sun worship prevailed at the time. Every year, the pilgrims of Croagh Patrick commemorate his retreat for 40 days on Cruachan Aigli.

Right: St Patrick and a king (vellum, Irish School, 13th century).

BRIGID OF IRELAND

LONG VENERATED IN IRELAND, ST BRIGID WAS SO LOVED BY THE NUNS AT HER MONASTERY THAT THEY KEPT A FIRE BURNING AT HER SHRINE IN KILDARE FOR CENTURIES AFTER HER DEATH.

KEY FACTS
Founder of Kildare monastery
DATES: *d.c.AD 525*
BIRTH PLACE: *Near Kildare, Ireland*
PATRON OF: *Milkmen, poets, cows and yard animals, blacksmiths, healers*
FEAST DAY: *1 February*
EMBLEM: *Cow lying beside her, cross made of rushes, candle*

Irish Catholics have a special affection for Brigid, placing her second only to St Patrick. Although the Church has de-canonized her, Brigid's cultus continues. Her legends reflect a generous, kindly personality, but historical facts are hard to find.

She was born, it is believed, near Kildare, and St Patrick baptized her. A very young Brigid took vows as a nun. In the convent she was a milkmaid, hence the legends of Brigid giving butter to the poor, or of cows giving her milk three times a day to cope with the thirst of visiting bishops. Brigid founded the monastery of Kildare and helped spread Christianity through Ireland and beyond her shores. Churches dedicated in her name span Europe, showing her wide veneration. A brass reliquary of her shoe, set with jewels, is kept at a museum in Dublin.

Left: Stained-glass windows depicting St Patrick and St Brigid (Paul Vincent Woodroffe, 1919).

BRENDAN THE NAVIGATOR

A LEGEND CLAIMS THAT ST BRENDAN CROSSED THE ATLANTIC OCEAN IN A CORACLE. CERTAINLY, HE WAS VENERATED BY CELTIC PEOPLES FOR HIS MISSIONARY OUTREACH TO UNKNOWN LANDS.

KEY FACTS
Founder of four monasteries
DATES: c.AD 486–575
BIRTH PLACE: *Possibly Tralee, Ireland*
FEAST DAY: *16 May*
EMBLEM: *Sitting in a small boat*

Best known as the hero of an adventure legend of the 10th century, St Brendan became widely known as "the Navigator". Translated from the Anglo-Norman into several European languages, the story of his life was one of the first books to be published after Caxton's invention of the printing press in 1476.

EARLY LIFE
Brendan was fostered by Ita, a much-loved Irish nun and saint who founded a small convent, where she lived in solitude. Her nuns were encouraged to care for the sick, and Ita herself educated needy boys, instilling into them her own faith.

As a youth, Brendan studied with St Erc, the Bishop of Kerry. Brendan became a monk and later was appointed as abbot of Clonfert monastery. Some reports also claim he became abbot of Llancarfan in Wales.

He founded four monasteries in Ireland, one in Scotland, and evangelized in Wales and Brittany. In imitation of the apostles, Brendan was an indefatigable missionary. His life of extensive travel, criss crossing the Irish Sea and the English Channel to France, became the source of legends about St Brendan.

TO PARADISE
In the legend of St Brendan, he and his band of monks take to the sea in search of the Island of Promise. They sail in a traditional vessel, a coracle, made of leather stretched over a wicker frame. During the journey, unwittingly, they make camp on the back of a whale and light a fire there.

One Christmas Eve, they come upon Judas Iscariot. Every year on this night, Christ's betrayer is allowed to sit on a rock in the middle of the ocean to cool off before returning to fiery hell.

Within these stories of adventure there are hints that Brendan reached the shores of distant America. Researchers say that a close study of the text allows for an interpretation that confirms that he conducted an expedition across the Atlantic Ocean. Brendan's popularity is shown by the survival of 116 Medieval Latin manuscripts of his story.

Below: Painting on vellum depicting St Brendan and his companions meeting a siren on their travels from the Navigatio Sancti Brendani Abbatis *(German School, c.1476).*

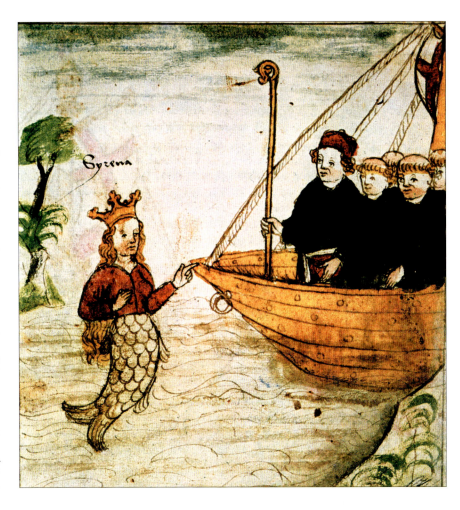

DIRECTORY OF SAINTS

BENEDICT

St Benedict created a monastic life of simplicity, work and prayer for the religious. His Rules rejected the grim hardship imposed by founders of more austere orders.

KEY FACTS
Founder of the Benedictine Order
DATES: *c.AD 480–550*
BIRTH PLACE: *Norcia, Italy*
PATRON OF: *Europe*
FEAST DAY: *11 July*
EMBLEM: *Black gown of his order, Rule book, broken cup containing poison*

The best way to appreciate the character of St Benedict is by studying his Rule. These guides to daily living reveal a man who understood the perils of power. He knew that extreme forms of discipline were unkind and could even drive men and women mad.

The system Benedict set up was inspired by his own experiences as a young man. Born into a good family in Umbria in the 5th century AD, he was sent as a student to Rome. However, he disliked the riotous living of the city and wandered off through

Left: Saint Benedict with His Monks at the Refectory *(Il Sodoma, c.1505).*

the forested valley between Lazio and Abruzzo. Finding the ruins of Nero's palace beside a lake at Subiaco, he settled in a cave there and spent most of his time in prayer and meditation.

Only one person knew of his whereabouts, a monk named Romanus, who secretly delivered him food. Gradually, knowledge of the hermit became common and his fame spread.

MONASTIC BEGINNINGS
Benedict was persuaded to join a nearby monastery, where he was disturbed by the lax, even dissolute, ways of the monks, and set about reforming them. The monks enjoyed their easy life, and determined to poison the abbot.

Legend tells that, when the deadly draught was served to Benedict, he made the sign of the cross over the cup. It immediately shattered, and a raven carried the shards away.

He returned to the life of a hermit, but he was not left alone, and soon disciples gathered about him. Benedict founded 12 small monasteries, in each placing

Left: Saint Benedict, *shown wearing the black garb of his monastic order (Pietro Perugino, c.1495–98).*

372

12 monks, over whom he served as abbot. The houses all gained a reputation for orderly, learned living, without austerity.

RULE OF THE ORDER
Benedict perceived that prayer, routine and purposeful activity were the paths to serenity and to God. Authority was to be controlled. If a monk were to commit a major transgression, the abbot must, before fixing on a punishment, seek the advice of everyone in the monastery, even the youngest.

Though the abbot's decision was final, he must be minded that his decisions would be judged by God. Benedict recommended a simple but ample diet, though no flesh should be served, and the first meal should be around noon.

Benedict allowed for sensible hours of sleep. Property was communal, and the monks had to work, either producing food, maintaining the monastery, or spending time reading and writing the scriptures. But more important than any other duty was regular communal prayer. This he called "divine work".

MONTE CASSINO
Soon Benedict's order became established and noble families sent their sons to his monasteries. These boys were destined to be monks and their training began early. It is said that Benedict saved two of these youths from drowning by walking across water to rescue them.

They became his favourite disciples, Maurus and Placid, and were also venerated as saints. When a powerful, jealous priest complained about the abbot, Benedict left Subiaco, taking with him a few disciples, including Maurus and Placid. He climbed a mountain above the village of Cassino. On a plateau he built Monte Cassino, the monastery that would become the centre of religious life in western Europe and which still operates today.

It was the kindly, humane interpretation of the monastic life that made Benedict so popular. He found a way of allowing the religious to live with an austerity suited to their calling, without risking their health or well-being.

SCHOLASTICA
Scholastica, the sister of St Benedict, followed her brother to Monte Cassino. She founded a nunnery about five miles from her brother's monastery. They met once a year, and on one visit Scholastica begged him to stay, for she longed to converse with him. But he refused, so she prayed for rain. It is said that a thunderstorm started and so he stayed the night. Alas, she died three days later, and Benedict then wrote about his conversation with Scholastica during which they discussed their faith.

Above: John the Evangelist, Scholastica and Benedict *(the Master of Liesborn, c.1470-80).*

Left: Benedictine monks walking through the monastery of Monte Cassino, Italy.

DAVID OF WALES

AN AUSTERE PRIEST RENOWNED FOR THE HARSHNESS OF THE MONASTIC REGIME HE ESTABLISHED IN WALES, HE NEVERTHELESS BECAME ONE OF THE BEST-LOVED SAINTS IN HIS COUNTRY.

> **KEY FACTS**
> *Founder of monasteries*
> DATES: *c.AD 540–601*
> BIRTH PLACE: *Possibly Ceredigion, Wales*
> PATRON OF: *Wales, poets*
> FEAST DAY: *1 March*
> EMBLEM: *Dove, later associated with a leek or daffodil*

St David is known as Dewi Sant in Wales, and his name is also sometimes translated as Dafydd. He is also given the title Dewi Dyfrwr, or David Aquaticus, meaning "David, the Water Drinker". This is attributed to the teetotal regime of his monks, who drank neither wine nor beer.

Tradition says David had a grand lineage. His father was thought to be of a princely family named Sant, and his mother, St Non, was also well connected. Possibly born in AD 540, David chose the life of a religious and went to study under the Welsh St Paulinus on a remote, unidentified island. He is said to have found the old hermit blind from weeping for the sins of the world, and restored his sight.

There is another report that David made a pilgrimage to the Holy Land, where he was consecrated as an archbishop by the patriarch of Jerusalem.

AUSTERE ORDERS
When David attended the Synod of Victory at Caerleon, he was uncompromising in his stand against the Pelagian movement. This heresy claimed it was possible to find salvation without the help of divine grace. A decisive victory for the established Church outlawed the British movement. David then focused on founding monastic orders.

He settled with his disciples in St David's (Mynyw), a remote corner of Wales, and set up the first of many monasteries. David's rule was renowned for its severity. His monks had to live by hard labour and were not even allowed oxen to help them plough the fields.

Their diet was bread, salt and vegetables, and only water could be drunk. Speech was permitted only when absolutely necessary. The monks prayed without break from Friday evening till dawn on Sundays. The monks were described as "more abstemious than Christian".

David was also a powerful preacher. Once, as he was denouncing Pelagianism to a crowd, the earth swelled into a small hill so that more people could see him. He was made head of the Church in Wales by popular acclaim, and died at Mynyw. Leeks and daffodils are worn to mark his feast day.

There are more than 50 place names and dedications to David in South Wales, with further dedications in Devon, Cornwall and Brittany. David's cult was approved by Callistus in 1120, and two pilgrimages to Mynyw in Pembrokeshire were said to equal one pilgrimage to Rome, while three were said to equal a pilgrimage to Jerusalem.

Left: Detail from a manuscript depicting St David (15th century).

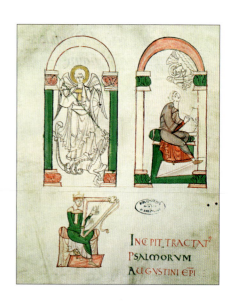

Right: Detail from a manuscript depicting St David playing the harp (French School, 11th century).

374

LEANDER

In his capacity as Bishop of Seville, the son of the duke of Carthagena became a prominent defender of orthodoxy in the Arian debate, and drew up a rule for Spanish nuns.

KEY FACTS
Bishop
DATES: c.AD 550–600
BIRTH PLACE: *Carthagena*
FEAST DAY: *27 February*
EMBLEM: *Bishop's vestments*

As a member of the Spanish aristocracy, Leander was well disposed to influence those around him. He was a man who carefully selected projects, then applied his energy to completing them successfully.

In about AD 584, he became Bishop of Seville and turned his attention to the unwelcome dominance of the unorthodox Arians in Spain. He used his position to ensure that, at the Council of Toledo, the orthodox concept of the Holy Trinity was officially confirmed. He then concentrated on converting the Arian Visigoths, a strong presence in the Seville region. Patiently, he set about convincing these people of the truth of the Church.

His third concern was for the lives of nuns, for whom he drew up a Rule that proved highly influential. Leander introduced the practice of singing the Nicene Creed at Mass. His younger brother was St Isidore of Seville.

Below: The region around Seville today, where Leander was a bishop in the 6th century AD.

JOHN THE ALMSGIVER

When St John became Patriarch of Alexandria, he applied ideals of charity and justice to the administration of the city, earning him the epithet of Almsgiver.

KEY FACTS
Bishop, Patriarch of Alexandria
DATES: c.AD 560–620
BIRTH PLACE: *Amathus, Cyprus*
PATRON OF: *Formerly patron of the Knights of Malta but replaced by John the Baptist*
FEAST DAY: *23 January*
EMBLEM: *Bishop's vestments*

Though it is known John was born in Cyprus, it is uncertain where he lived as an adult with his wife and children. At some point he moved to Egypt, where, in about AD 610, he became the Bishop and Patriarch of the archdiocese of Alexandria.

John observed that the heretical Monophysites had been busy in the city. They were persuading Christians to accept their view that Jesus had no humanity and was wholly divine.

Instead of confronting the sect, John thought to weaken them through his own example of humble but generous Christian living. His work included establishing a system of welfare reform, and

Above: Detail from a manuscript depicting St John the Almsgiver (French School, c.550–616).

the building of maternity hospitals and homes for the aged and frail. Citizens with legal or financial problems were invited to seek John's advice at twice-weekly meetings. And he organized relief for refugees after the Persians sacked Jerusalem in AD 614.

These efforts at ameliorating hardships and difficulties much endeared him to the people of Alexandria. Many were persuaded to follow his orthodox beliefs. John died soon after retiring to Cyprus in AD 619.

GREGORY THE GREAT

FACED WITH MILITARY THREATS FROM GERMANIC TRIBES AND UNEASY RELATIONS WITH CONSTANTINOPLE, ST GREGORY DID MUCH TO STRENGTHEN CHRISTENDOM AT A DIFFICULT TIME.

> **KEY FACTS**
> One of the four great Latin Doctors of the Western Church
> DATES: c.AD 540–604
> BIRTH PLACE: Rome
> PATRON OF: Music, protection against plague
> FEAST DAY: 3 September
> EMBLEM: Three-tiered papal crown, dove of the Holy Spirit

Although Pope Gregory I dreamt of a life of solitude and prayer, he was the obedient son of a wealthy family and so took up a worldly career. Self-assured and clever, he studied law and then, just 30 years of age, was appointed governor of Rome.

A year later, his father died and Gregory found himself one of the richest men in Rome. At last he revealed his true longings by giving up his position and all his wealth. His house became a monastery and he a simple monk.

The Church was reluctant to miss out on such talented leadership. First it made Gregory deacon of Rome, then an ambassador to the Byzantine court in Constantinople. He spoke no Greek and seemed to use this deficiency as a reason for living a monastic life among the monks of the city.

After a few years, in AD 586, he was recalled to Rome. Although he returned as deacon of the city, again he sought the monastic life. But when Pope Pelagius II died four years later, the people of Rome elected Gregory to succeed him. Rome was in a terrible condition when Gregory became pope. Over the previous century, the state had been conquered, sacked and pillaged many times. The city was dilapidated, without leadership or administration.

AS POPE

When Gregory took office, a plague was raging through the city. One of his first duties was to seek penitence from the citizens in order to end the disease. And so he led a great processional litany through the ruined streets.

Soon after taking office, he wrote to all his clerics, reminding them to treat their flocks with compassion and generosity. He recommended that Church money be given to those in dire straits. The granaries of Rome were filled to feed the needy in

Right: An altarpiece depicting Gregory the Great (Pedro Torres, 16th–17th century).

Below: Canterbury Cathedral, where Gregory based his English mission (Wenzel Hollar, c.1650).

> "AFTER HAVING CONFIRMED ALL HIS ACTIONS TO HIS DOCTRINES, THE GREAT CONSUL OF GOD WENT TO ENJOY ETERNAL TRIUMPHS."
>
> EPITAPH ON ST GREGORY'S TOMB

DIRECTORY OF SAINTS

Right: A detail of Saints Augustine and Gregory in The Fathers of the Church *(Michael Pacher, 1480).*

times of food shortage. Jews were allowed to practise their faith and keep their property without fear of being persecuted.

AFFAIRS OF STATE
A greater worry to Gregory was the barbarian foe. From the very outset of his papacy, Gregory had to find energy to deal with the Lombards, an extremely well-organized Germanic group intent on settling in the Roman Empire.

Their presence threatened Christianity. Gregory induced them to remain beyond the border, and arranged an uneasy truce between their leaders and the Byzantine emperor in Constantinople. However, his relationship with the Byzantines was also tense. He resented the grand titles of office assumed by

ANGELS IN SLAVERY
When wandering the streets of Rome one day, Gregory noticed three boys with golden hair and fair skin. They were Anglo-Saxons to be sold in the slave market. On inquiry, he was informed that the youths were "Angels".

Gregory observed, "They are well named, for they have angelic faces and it becomes such to be companions with the angels in heaven. And who is the king of their province?"

"Aella," came the reply.

"Then," announced Pope Gregory, "Alleluia must be sung in Aella's land."

He felt such pity for these little golden creatures that he determined to spread the gospel to their country.

---

the Patriarch of Constantinople, who he feared wanted to wrest power from the West. Gregory insisted Rome was the centre of the Church and was successful in strengthening papal authority.

MISSION TO ENGLAND
Denied a life of solitude, Gregory found other ways to serve God directly. After once saving some English boys from slavery (see box left), Gregory set his mind on converting England. To this end, he dispatched St Augustine and 40 missionaries to Canterbury. Their success among the Anglo-Saxons gave Gregory deep satisfaction.

His writings about the liturgy were of special value, and his text is still used in the Roman Missal. Gregory died in Rome and was buried in St Peter's Cathedral.

Below: Saint Gregory the Great *is visited by a dove representing the Holy Spirit as he sits writing letters (Carlo Saraceni, c.1620). The dove of the Holy Spirit is one of his emblems.*

ISIDORE OF SEVILLE

KNOWN AS THE "SCHOOLMASTER OF THE MIDDLE AGES", ISIDORE OF SEVILLE WAS FAMOUS FOR WRITING A HUGE ENCYCLOPEDIA, WHICH BECAME A STANDARD REFERENCE WORK FOR CENTURIES.

> **KEY FACTS**
> *Bishop, historian*
> DATES: *c.AD 560–636*
> BIRTH PLACE: *Carthagena*
> FEAST DAY: *4 April*
> EMBLEM: *Bishop's vestments, books*

The veneration of St Isidore of Seville rests on his scientific and historical research. For the intellectual discipline involved in academic work, he had to thank his brother Leander, who educated him.

Although not a monk, Isidore learnt the monastic habits of deep thinking and discipline of work. When he succeeded his brother as Bishop of Seville in about AD 600, he continued Leander's mission to lead the Visigoths away from the unorthodox views of Arianism. He made the Church run more efficiently, and emphasized duty of service and charity. Above all, believing in the importance of education, Isidore recommended that every diocese should have a Church school.

EDUCATIONIST
His writings were to become major texts in the education of generations of theologians, students and researchers. Isidore wrote 86 biographies of biblical figures, and a handbook on morals and theology. He also produced various liturgical analyses.

But his most important work was a massive encyclopedia, called the *Etymologies* (or *Origines*). This opus covered the arts, medicine, law, theology, history, zoology, anthropology, cosmology, agriculture, science and other subjects. Almost 1,000 medieval manu-

Above: Isidore of Seville gives a book to his sister in this Latin manuscript.

scripts of the *Etymologies* are still in existence. Isidore intentionally did not apply any original thinking when he compiled this text. He wished to present all the knowledge then available to the European world, and drew on numerous sources.

His other important writings include *On the Wonders of Nature* and *Chronica Majora,* a history from creation to AD 610, though with emphasis on Spanish history. His scholarship was admired across Christendom, and medieval intellectuals thought him equal to St Gregory the Great.

Right: Scenes from the Life of Saint Isidore, *from* Le Miroir Historial *by Vincent de Beauvais (French School, 15th century).*

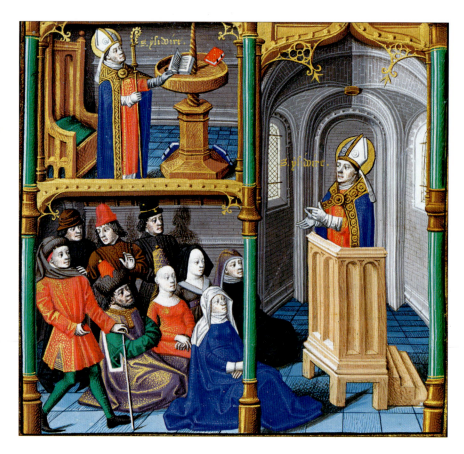

CUTHBERT

A PURPORTED PROPHET AND HEALER, THE POPULAR ANGLO-SAXON ST CUTHBERT PERSUADED HIS CELTIC FLOCK OF THE CORRECTNESS OF FOLLOWING ROMAN CHURCH CUSTOMS.

KEY FACTS
Bishop, missionary
DATES: c.AD 634–87
BIRTH PLACE: *Possibly Jarrow*
PATRON OF: *Formerly of Lindisfarne*
FEAST DAY: *20 March*

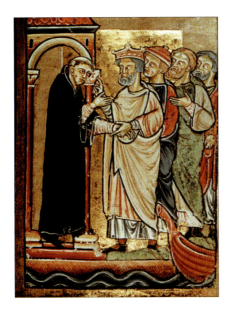

After becoming a monk in Melrose in AD 651, Cuthbert spent ten years striving to be a model ascetic. He followed the practice of the time of standing for hours waist-deep in freezing sea water, and walked miles to visit the sick, whom he was said to heal miraculously.

His appointment as abbot put him in a position of influence. His winning manner and frequent local missions laid the groundwork for replacing the ideas of the Celtic Church with those of the Roman Church. The Synod of Whitby endorsed his view.

After a spell at Lindisfarne Abbey, he retired to Inner Farne as a hermit, only to be recalled to become Bishop of Lindisfarne. The gentle monk had a special affinity with the birdlife of the Farne Islands. After he died, his body reputedly stayed incorrupt.

Left: King Siegfried visits St Cuthbert and asks him to accept the bishopric of Lindisfarne, from the Latin manuscript of Life and Miracles of Saint Cuthbert *by the Venerable Bede (English School, 12th century).*

THE VENERABLE BEDE

NO HARDY MISSIONARY OR INSPIRED LEADER, THIS HOMELY MONK SPENT HIS ENTIRE LIFE IN CLOISTERS. YET HE BECAME THE MOST RESPECTED HISTORIAN IN MEDIEVAL WESTERN CHRISTENDOM.

KEY FACTS
Writer, historian
DATES: *AD 673–735*
BIRTH PLACE: *Sunderland, England*
FEAST DAY: *25 May*
EMBLEM: *Monk with pen at a manuscript*

At the age of seven, Bede was given to a monastery in Jarrow, Northumbria, and stayed there for the rest of his life. From an early age, he loved singing, studying, reading and writing.

He produced numerous texts on many different subjects and the fame of his learning spread far beyond his native county. The best known of his works, *Ecclesiastical History of the English People*, was written in AD 731, and is still in print.

The book was compiled at a time when Christianity was still relatively new to the Anglo-

Above: Bede is shown here dictating a translation of St John's Gospel into Anglo-Saxon (James Doyle Penrose, 1906).

Saxons of Britain, and the faith is presented as a unifying force for the nation. Unusually for his time, Bede took the trouble to differentiate between fact and hearsay in writing history.

An important biography was his *Life and Miracles of St Cuthbert*. His last work was a translation into Old English of the Gospel of St John. It is said he dictated the closing sentences of this work from his deathbed.

RUPERT

KNOWN AS THE "APOSTLE OF THE BAVARIANS", ST RUPERT IS CREDITED WITH ESTABLISHING CHRISTIANITY IN LANDS BORDERING THE RIVER DANUBE AND WITH FOUNDING SALZBURG.

> **KEY FACTS**
> *Missionary, bishop*
> DATES: *d.c.AD 710*
> BIRTH PLACE: *Unknown*
> PATRON OF: *Bavaria, Austria, Salzburg*
> FEAST DAY: *27 March*
> EMBLEM: *Barrel of salt*

Little is known about Rupert's early life, including his birthplace. He may have been a Frank or an Irishman. However, having committed himself to becoming a missionary, Rupert attained high office in the Church, being elected Bishop of Worms in southern Germany.

At the invitation of the Duke of Bavaria, Theodo II, the saint went to Regensburg in Bavaria. There he founded a church near the Wallersee and dedicated it to St Peter. Rupert moved on to Salzburg and gathered disciples around him. For these followers, he founded a monastery at a site

Left: St Rupert in a detail from the Altar of St Hildegard of Bingen, Chapel of St Roch (1896).

now known as the Mönchberg, and a convent, the Nonnberg. His sister, Ermentrude, was appointed as abbess to the nuns. He built a house to accommodate clerks and dedicated another church to St Peter. It is possible that Rupert wished to emulate the great apostle in his life of fearless travel, spreading the faith.

MISSION TO THE DANUBE
Having been appointed Bishop of Salzburg, Rupert made that city his headquarters while he travelled extensively through the lands along the River Danube. This region was still a wild part of Europe. The Frankish Empire had not yet extended this far east, so Rupert was blazing a trail into hostile barbarian territory.

He must have been a charismatic preacher, for his success as a missionary was immense. He is credited, too, with opening the salt-mining industry at a place which, before his efforts, held only the crumbling ruins of an old Roman town, Juvavum. He renamed the place Salzburg. Because of this activity, paintings often depict St Rupert with a barrel of salt beside him.

Left: A statue of St Rupert located outside the Ruprechtskirche, the oldest church in Vienna.

BONIFACE

One of the great missionary saints, St Boniface played a major role in establishing Christianity in Germany, where he is said to have converted followers of Norse gods.

> **KEY FACTS**
> *Missionary martyr, archbishop*
> Dates: c.AD 680–754
> Birth Place: *Possibly Crediton, Devon, England*
> Patron of: *Germany, brewers, tailors*
> Feast Day: *5 June*
> Emblem: *Axe*

Boniface was born in England but he spent very many years in Europe, where he became known as the "Apostle to the Germans". For the first 40 years of his life he was a monk, for the main part at Nursling, near Southampton. Learned and devoted to biblical studies, Boniface was nevertheless no timid scholar.

The Church recognized his qualities of boldness and effective preaching, and sent him on a hazardous mission to lands still in heathen hands. It is said that in AD 718, armed with an axe, Boniface marched into a shrine dedicated to Thor, the Norse god of thunder.

With one mighty swing of the axe, Boniface is said to have felled the oak that was a key cultic object. The amazed onlookers were so impressed with the power of this man's God that tradition says the Germanic tribes converted to his faith en masse.

TIRELESS MISSIONARY
It is much more likely that these conversions happened over a period of time. But Boniface quickly established a reputation among the people of Bavaria, Württemberg, Westphalia and Hesse as "a man who moved with power", in the words of contemporary reports. Pope Gregory II was equally impressed and gave him the bishopric of Mainz.

Above: St Boniface is here shown in proselytizing mode with his axe (Alfred Rethel, 1832).

Boniface summoned more male and female missionaries from his native country.

In about AD 732, the pope made him archbishop. Boniface increasingly handed over the outward missionary work to his English evangelists, while he concentrated on organizing the new Church in West Germany.

Once satisfied that Christianity had taken firm root in Germany, Boniface turned to France. Many sees were vacant or poorly managed. With the help of the Frankish King Pepin, Boniface reformed those dioceses.

He then turned northwards to Frisia, where pagan communities still existed. He was over 70 when he undertook this mission. Travelling with a small band of disciples, he stopped at a place called Dokkum. Here, Boniface and his fellow missionaries were slaughtered by the very people he had hoped to convert.

St Boniface's surviving Latin correspondence reveals a man of courage and determination, who deserves as high a profile in his native England as he enjoys in Germany. The faithful continue to make pilgrimages to his shrine at Fulda, where his remains lie.

Right: Detail from a manuscript showing Germans being baptized and the martyrdom of St Boniface at Dokkum (AD 975).

CYRIL AND METHODIUS

These brothers are venerated as apostles of the southern Slavs and fathers of Slavic literature. St Cyril gave his name to the modern script Cyrillic, devised from his work.

> **KEY FACTS**
> Translators of Christian texts and apostles to the Slavs
> DATES: *Cyril AD 826–69, Methodius c.AD 815–85*
> BIRTH PLACE: *Thessalonica, Macedonia*
> PATRON OF: *Europe*
> FEAST DAY: *14 February (West)*
> EMBLEM: *Books, Cyrillic script*

In 1980, Pope John Paul II decided the brothers, Cyril and Methodius, should share the patronage of Europe with St Benedict. Together, these three saints symbolize the religious and political unity of eastern and western Europe.

Cyril and Methodius were scholarly men from Thessalonica, Macedonia. Cyril studied in Constantinople, where he earned the nickname, "the philosopher".

MISSION TO MORAVIA

His older brother, Methodius, went on a mission to the Khazars of Russia. He then returned to Greece as abbot of a monastery.

At the request of Prince Rostislav of Moravia, both men were sent on a mission to the Slavic province of Moravia (now part of the Czech Republic). The two missionaries were unique in being Greek monks sent off with the blessing of the pope in Rome. Until 1054, the Eastern and Western Churches remained in communion with each other.

Above: This icon from Bulgaria shows Sts Cyril and Methodius in their role as the inventors of the Cyrillic alphabet.

Below: A fresco depicting Cyril and Methodius meeting Pope Adrian II (Lionello de Nobili, 1886).

The brothers not only preached in Slavonic, but began translating the Bible and liturgy into the vernacular. Using Greek letters as a model, they invented an alphabet for Slavonic, later named Cyrillic, after Cyril, the younger brother.

But their mission, while finding converts, aroused much political and theological opposition. Their early supporters, Rostislav and Pope Adrian II, had died, and their replacements condemned the use of Slavonic, asserting that no vernacular language was suitable for use in the Church.

METHODIUS ALONE

After Cyril died in Rome in AD 869, Methodius continued the mission alone. But he was persecuted by Bavarian princes and forces within the Church, and imprisoned by German bishops.

After he had spent two years in a damp cell, Pope John VIII had him released and he continued his work in Moravia. He endeavoured to finish translating the Bible into Slavonic, but opposition went on, and he died of exhaustion. Cyril and Methodius are admired for their ecumenism – the desire to unite worshippers, East and West.

WENCESLAS

VENERATION OF ST WENCESLAS FOLLOWED HIS RULE AS A GOOD CHRISTIAN DUKE OF BOHEMIA. HE WAS CRUELLY MURDERED FOR HIS FAITH.

KEY FACTS
Ruler of Bohemia
DATES: *AD 907–35*
BIRTH PLACE: *Prague*
PATRON OF: *Brewers, Czech Republic*
FEAST DAY: *28 September*
EMBLEM: *Crown, dagger*

Left: St Wenceslas is depicted here in armour, bearing a banner of an eagle, oil on panel (Czech School, 16th century).

Despite the conversion of much of Bohemia (now part of the Czech Republic), pagan culture persisted and often took a political hue. When Wenceslas' father, the Duke of Bohemia, died, opposition factions mobilized. His grandmother, St Ludmilla, who had educated the boy as a Christian, was murdered and his mother was banished.

However, the people of Bohemia defeated these factions and chose Wenceslas to be their leader. He allied himself with the Christian Henry I (known as Henry the Fowler) of the Holy Roman Empire. Some nobles, including his pagan brother Boleslav, resented the power the clergy of the new court now had.

Boleslav feared his brother's marriage would produce an heir, further strengthening Christian rule and jeopardizing his own chances of power. Following celebrations at the Feast of Sts Cosmas and Damian, Wenceslas died. Boleslav was implicated in the murder, but he later repented and had his brother's relics translated to St Vitus' Church, Prague.

The popular carol "Good King Wenceslas" reflects his reputation for strength and generosity.

ODO OF CLUNY

SO ADMIRED WAS ST ODO FOR HIS LEADERSHIP THAT EVEN THE SECULAR AUTHORITIES TURNED TO HIM FOR GUIDANCE.

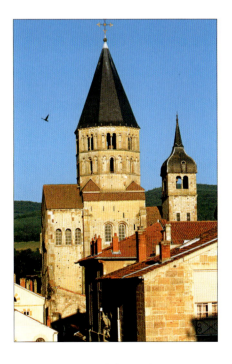

KEY FACTS
Abbot of the Benedictine monastery of Cluny
DATES: *AD 879–942*
BIRTH PLACE: *Tours, France*
PATRON OF: *Rain*
FEAST DAY: *18 November*

Reports say Odo had a good sense of fun and was a sympathetic person. Yet he was also a leader who instilled strict monastic observances across France and Italy.

Brought up by the Duke of Aquitaine, he founded the monastery of Cluny. When Odo was made abbot, he introduced the Rule of St Benedict, with its emphasis on vows of chastity, communal poverty and long periods of silent meditation. Cluny rose to become the most important monastery in Europe and Odo was instrumental in it.

He attained papal protection from secular interference for this monastery and others in western Europe. By the time he retired from the world, Odo's stature was such that Italian politicians often referred to him for help as an impartial mediator in disputes.

Above: A view of the 12th-century Benedictine monastery at Cluny in Burgundy, France.

ULRIC

BELOVED FOR HIS GENEROSITY AND CARE OF THE POOR, ST ULRIC SERVED AS BISHOP TO THE DIOCESE OF AUGSBURG, BAVARIA, FOR 50 YEARS BEFORE DYING ON A CROSS OF ASHES.

> **KEY FACTS**
> *Bishop*
> DATES: c.AD 890–973
> BIRTH PLACE: *Near Zurich, Switzerland*
> FEAST DAY: *4 July*
> EMBLEM: *Bishop's vestments*

His father placed Ulric in the care of his uncle, Bishop of Augsburg, as a child, and Ulric lived at the monastery of St Gall. He never forgot the care shown to him there.

Ulric developed a deep piety and strong sense of duty towards the poor and afflicted in the community. But his office as Bishop of Augsburg was beset with strife from constant Magyar raids on Bavaria. Ulric devoted himself to easing the hardships suffered.

He founded a number of religious houses, and built a small church where he hoped to live as a monk. However, the trappings of high office kept him from fulfilling this wish. He once caused consternation by trying to hand his bishopric to a nephew, thus infringing canonical law. As a symbol of Christian sacrificial love, Ulric died on a cross of ashes marked out on the floor. His canonization in AD 993 is the first recorded canonization by a pope.

EDWARD THE MARTYR

COMING TO THE THRONE AT A YOUNG AGE, EDWARD WAS THRUST INTO A POLITICAL HORNET'S NEST IN ENGLAND. HIS MARTYRDOM A FEW YEARS LATER WAS RECEIVED WITH HORROR BY THE NATION.

> **KEY FACTS**
> *Martyr*
> DATES: c.AD 962–79
> BIRTH PLACE: *Possibly Corfe Castle, Dorset, England*
> FEAST DAY: *18 March*
> EMBLEM: *Dagger*

Aged just 13, Edward became King of England. At such a tender age, he inherited a country troubled by disputes within the Church and faced a rival claim to the throne from his stepbrother Ethelred. His bid for the throne was supported by a rebellious party led by his stepmother, Aelfthryth. Together they plotted to overthrow the young king.

Riding home one day after hunting, Edward was greeted by Aelfthryth, who offered him a chalice of wine. As he leant to take the drink, a courtier stabbed him with a dagger. Edward slumped from his horse, but a foot caught in the stirrup and he was dragged over the ground, leaving behind a trail of blood.

Though this was not technically a martyr's death, kings were regarded as representatives of God. His murder was described as "the worst deed in English history". A pillar of light was said to hover over his abandoned body, and folk claimed their ailments were cured when they visited his grave. By common consent, he was deemed a martyr, while his stepmother retired to a convent.

Left: Edward the Martyr shown about to be murdered at Corfe Castle.

WOLFGANG OF REGENSBURG

DURING HIS LIFETIME, THE HOLY ROMAN EMPIRE EVOLVED AS A CONFEDERATION OF DUCHIES IN GERMANY. ST WOLFGANG WAS ENTRUSTED WITH EDUCATING ITS FUTURE EMPEROR HENRY II.

> **KEY FACTS**
> *Bishop*
> DATES: c.AD *924–94*
> BIRTH PLACE: *Duchy of Swabia, Germany*
> FEAST DAY: *31 October*
> EMBLEM: *Bishop's vestments*

Though content to lead a life as an abstemious monk devoted to prayer, Wolfgang was recognized for his wisdom and qualities as a teacher. He was handed the responsibility of educating the young prince and future emperor, Henry II.

Wolfgang was put in charge of the Benedictine monastery school at Einsiedeln in Switzerland before progressing to become Bishop of Regensburg in AD 972. He set about reforming the lax ways of the monks and nuns in his dio-

cese. This meant reinforcing the vows of poverty and prayer, for which Wolgang set an admirable example.

Despite Wolfgang's talents as an evangelist, his mission into Hungary was largely unsuccessful. Wolfgang's cultus remains strong, and his relics at Regensburg continue to attract pilgrims.

Left: A woodcut depicting St Wolfgang (P.M. Vogel, 1860).

OLAF

A SOLDIER KING WHO ROVED AS A PIRATE BEFORE COMMITTING TO THE FAITH, ST OLAF OF NORWAY IS CREDITED WITH INTRODUCING CHRISTIANITY TO HIS COUNTRY AT A TIME OF POLITICAL TURMOIL.

> **KEY FACTS**
> *King*
> DATES: AD *995–1030*
> BIRTH PLACE: *Norway*
> PATRON OF: *Norway*
> FEAST DAY: *29 July*
> EMBLEM: *Battle-axe, loaves of bread*

The son of a Norwegian lord, Olaf began his adult life as a Viking pirate raiding the shores of the Baltic and France. But one trip to Normandy ended with Olaf's conversion to Christianity.

His new faith inspired him to fight for the English, who were suffering invasions from the Danes. On returning to Norway, he seized power and determined to make his country Christian.

Just though his rule was, its severity spawned dissent. Olaf's erstwhile enemy, King Cnut of Denmark and England, took advantage of the situation and sponsored a rebellion in Norway.

Their combined forces succeeded in exiling Olaf in 1029. On trying the following year to regain his throne with the aid of Swedish allies, Olaf was killed in battle. After his death, Norwegians longed for his Christian rule and claimed many miracle cures from a spring issuing at his grave.

Left: The church of St Olaf in Wasdale in Cumbria is one of the smallest churches in England. Its beams are said to have come from a Viking longship.

STEPHEN OF HUNGARY

ALSO KNOWN AS STEPHEN THE GREAT, THIS NATIONAL HERO IS CONSIDERED THE ARCHITECT OF AN INDEPENDENT CHRISTIAN HUNGARY AND FOUNDER OF A CHURCH WELFARE SYSTEM.

KEY FACTS
King
DATES: *c.AD 975–1038*
BIRTH PLACE: *Esztergom, Hungary*
PATRON OF: *Hungary*
FEAST DAY: *16 August*
EMBLEM: *Crown*

Filled with reforming zeal, King Stephen was inspired by his faith and sympathy for the oppressed. As king, he reduced the power of the nobles and established a semi-feudal, but secure, social system.

If the hallmark of his rule was charity, it was also fundamentalist. Adultery and blasphemy were crimes not to be tolerated, and marriage between Christians and pagans was forbidden. On the other hand, he helped the poor through his church-building programme. By ensuring there was a church in virtually every diocese, tithes demanded from landlords could feed and clothe the underprivileged.

Stephen encouraged missions and finished building the great monastery of St Martin, begun by his father. His last years were spent in dispute over his successor, because his only son had died.

Right: The crown of St Stephen, now held at the Magyar Nemzeti Galeria in Budapest (11th century).

EDWARD THE CONFESSOR

ADMIRED FOR HIS DEVOTION TO GOD AND CARE FOR HIS POORER SUBJECTS, EDWARD WAS THE LAST NATIVE KING TO RULE ENGLAND BEFORE THE NORMAN CONQUEST.

KEY FACTS
King
DATES: *1003–66*
BIRTH PLACE: *Islip, England*
PATRON OF: *Once of England*
FEAST DAY: *13 October*
EMBLEM: *Ring*

The term "Confessor" refers to the fact that Edward lived his life as a devout follower of Christ. It was said that the king and his wife, Edith, were so holy that they did not consummate their marriage.

Edward became King of England in 1042 during a time of great political turbulence. His father-in-law, Earl Godwine, plotted against him while the Danish king threatened to invade England. Edward was generous to the poor. His subjects believed he could "touch for the king's evil", meaning that, simply through touch, the king was able to cure scrofula, a kind of tuberculosis.

Another story surrounded a ring which the king supposedly gave to a beggar. Years later, English pilgrims in the Holy Land met an old man who claimed to be John the Apostle and he gave the travellers the king's ring.

Edward started building Westminster Abbey however, he died before it was consecrated. He was canonized in 1161, and since then many sick people have visited his shrine in Westminster Abbey to pray for a cure. The worn steps to the shrine are evidence to the number of pilgrims. The shrine was dismantled during the Reformation that began under Henry VIII, and Edward's body was removed. His relics lie behind the high altar in the abbey to this day.

Left: A sculpture of Edward the Confessor in the church of San Marco, Florence (Pietro Francavilla, 1589).

STANISLAUS OF CRACOW

THE PATRON OF POLAND WAS A BRAVE REFORMER WHO WOULD NOT ALLOW SPECIAL DISPENSATION TO AN UNREPENTANT KING. ST STANISLAUS WAS MARTYRED FOR HIS UNCOMPROMISING STAND.

> **KEY FACTS**
> *Martyr saint, bishop*
> DATES: *1010–79*
> BIRTH PLACE: *Szczepanów, Poland*
> PATRON OF: *Poland, soldiers in battle*
> FEAST DAY: *11 April*
> EMBLEM: *Bishop's vestments, sword*

Born into a noble Polish family, Stanislaus was well educated, possibly studying in Paris. He was consecrated a bishop in 1072, having made a reputation as a stern reformer of lapses in Christian behaviour.

In the 11th century, Boleslav II was King of Poland and said to be violent and headstrong. Once he abducted a nobleman's wife and imprisoned her in his palace.

Refusing to repent of this demeaning act, the king incurred the wrath of Stanislaus, who publicly excommunicated him from the Church. King Boleslav II chased his bishop from the church at Cracow and cornered him in the chapel of St Michael.

The knights who hunted down Stanislaus refused to raise their swords against him, so Boleslav committed the murder himself. The king was later deposed and Stanislaus was acknowleged as a martyr saint.

Below: The Death of Saint Stanislaus *(Hungarian, 15th century).*

CANUTE

KING CANUTE OF DENMARK WAS DETERMINED TO TURN HIS NATION TO CHRISTIANITY, BUT HE PAID WITH HIS LIFE FOR IMPOSING RELIGIOUS LAWS AND TAXES THAT RILED THE NOBLES.

> **KEY FACTS**
> *Martyr king*
> DATES: *d.1086*
> BIRTH PLACE: *Denmark*
> PATRON OF: *Denmark*
> FEAST DAY: *10 July*
> EMBLEM: *Crown, dagger, lance, barefoot king with hair in a fillet*

Two passions drove this King of Denmark. He wished to impose the Christian faith on his subjects and he was determined to gain the English throne.

Twice he tried to invade England. Its countrymen, who resented the rule of French invaders brought by William the Conqueror in 1066, sided with the Danish pretender. His first attack on England was a minor raid on York, but for his second campaign, in 1085, he prepared huge numbers of men.

Not all his subjects supported the invasion. Much had been spent on church buildings, and new laws empowered priests at the expense of secular nobles. Annoyed by high taxes and heavy-handed religious laws, they sided with Canute's rebellious brother, Olaf. Under siege in the church of St Alban at Odensee, Canute took the sacrament. As he knelt before the altar, he and 18 followers were stabbed to death.

Left: Stained glass depicting King Canute, from the west window of Canterbury Cathedral.

PATRON SAINTS OF NATIONS

Nations everywhere have chosen patron saints as special guardians over their country. In times of national peril, citizens ask their saint to pray to God for them.

Above: Saint Rose of Lima *(Carlo Dolci, 17th century).*

Albania – Mary
Algeria – Cyprian
Andorra – Our Lady of Meritxell
Argentina – Francis Solano
Armenia – Bartholomew
Australia – Francis Xavier
Austria – Leopold III, Rupert
Belgium – Joseph
Bolivia – Francis Solano
Borneo – Francis Xavier
Bosnia – James the Great
Brazil – Peter of Alcantara, Antony of Padua
Bulgaria – Cyril and Methodius
Canada – Anne, George, Joseph
Chile – Francis Solano
China – Francis Xavier
Colombia – Luis Bertran, Peter Claver
Corsica – Devota
Costa Rica – Mary
Crete – Titus
Croatia – Joseph
Cuba – Mary

Cyprus – Barnabas
Czech Republic – Wenceslas
Denmark – Anskar, Canute
Dominican Republic – Dominic
Ecuador – Mary
Egypt – Mark
El Salvador – Mary
England – George
Ethiopia – Frumentius
Finland – Henry of Finland
France – Denys of Paris, Joan of Arc, Theresa of Lisieux
Georgia – George
Germany – Boniface
Gibraltar – Bernard of Clairvaux
Gozo – George
Greece – Nicholas of Myra, Paul
Guatemala – James the Great
Haiti – Mary
Honduras – Mary
Hungary – Stephen of Hungary
Iceland – Thorlac of Skalholt
India – Rose of Lima, Thomas
Indonesia – Mary
Iran – Maruthas
Ireland – Brigid, Patrick
Italy – Catherine of Siena, Francis of Assisi

Jamaica – Mary
Japan – Francis Xavier, Peter
Jordan – John the Baptist
Korea – Joseph
Kosovo – Methodius
Lithuania – Casimir of Poland
Luxembourg – Willibrord
Macedonia – Clement of Okhrida
Madagascar – Vincent de Paul
Malta – George, Paul
Mexico – Our Lady of Guadalupe, Joseph
Monaco – Devota
Montenegro – George
Moravia – Wenceslas
Netherlands – Willibrord
New Zealand – Francis Xavier
Nicaragua – James the Great
Nigeria – Patrick
Norway – Olaf, Magnus
Oceania – Peter Chanel
Pakistan – Francis Xavier, Thomas
Palestine – George
Panama – Mary
Papua New Guinea – Archangel Michael
Paraguay – Francis Solano
Peru – Francis Solano, Rose of Lima

Below: Detail from a 13th-century mosaic showing scenes from the life of St Mark.

Far Left: St Francis Xavier Blessing the Sick *(Rubens, 17th century).*

Left: Nicetas *(Giovanni Antonio Guardi, 18th century).*

Philippines – Rose of Lima
Poland – Stanislaus of Cracow, Casimir of Poland
Portugal – Antony of Padua, Francis Borgia
Puerto Rico – Mary
Romania – Cyril and Methodius, Nicetas of Remesiana
Russia – Nicholas of Myra, Andrew, Vladimir
Sardinia – Maurice
Scotland – Andrew, Margaret of Scotland
Serbia – Sava of Serbia
Sicily – Andrew Avellino
Slovakia – John of Nepomuk
Slovenia – Virgilius
South Africa – Mary
Spain – James the Great
Sri Lanka – Thomas
Sudan – Josephine Bakhita
Sweden – Bridget of Sweden, Eric of Sweden
Switzerland – Gall, Nicholas of Flue
Syria – Barbara
Tanzania – Mary
Tunisia – Mary
Turkey – John the Evangelist, John Chrysostom
Uganda – Mary
Ukraine – Josaphat
USA – Mary

Below: Stained-glass window depicting St Andrew from the church of St Neot in Cornwall (16th century).

Uruguay – James the Less
Venezuela – Mary
Vietnam – Joseph
Wales – David
West Indies – Rose of Lima
Zaire – Mary

MARY, THE BLESSED VIRGIN

Many nations around the world have adopted Mary, mother of Jesus, as their patron, often in addition to other saints. In this feature she is listed only beside those states where she is sole patron.

Mary, the Blessed Virgin, is believed to appear in symbolic and visionary form at times of national crisis. The Philippine navy, for example, was convinced Mary hovered over their ships and helped them to repulse the enemy.

Another example comes from Albania. Catholics believe a canvas painting of the Virgin, lodged on a cliff, prevented bombs in World War II falling on their land.

Above: Enthroned Madonna with Child, Angels and Saints *(Lorenzetti, c.1340).*

MARGARET OF SCOTLAND

AN ANGLO-SAXON ROYAL WHO MARRIED A SCOTTISH KING DID MUCH TO REVIVE THE FLAGGING CHURCH IN HIS COUNTRY.

KEY FACTS
Queen
DATES: *1046–93*
BIRTH PLACE: *Hungary*
PATRON OF: *Scotland*
FEAST DAY: *16 November*
EMBLEM: *Crown*

Left: A portrait of Margaret published in the Memoirs of the Court of Queen Elizabeth *(c.1825).*

This cultivated granddaughter of the English King Edmund Ironside was one of the last members of Anglo-Saxon royalty before the Norman Conquest. Indeed, at the invasion she fled northwards and took refuge at the court of Malcolm III of Scotland.

The king was beguiled by her charm and intelligence, and they married in 1069. Her Christian devotion inspired her to revive the Church in Scotland, which had declined since the Celtic heyday of St Columba of Iona and St Aidan. She reformed the abbey at Iona and encouraged pilgrimages and the building of monasteries.

Margaret built Dunfermline church to be a burial place for the Scottish royal family. Her adoring husband, who was at first rough and illiterate, grew to be proud of her generosity towards his subjects, and became as devout a Christian as she was.

Two of her sons became kings of Scotland. She died shortly after hearing of the death of her husband and son in battle.

BENNO OF MUNICH

TORN BETWEEN LOYALTIES, ST BENNO HAD TO SEARCH HIS CONSCIENCE TO MAKE THE RIGHT DECISIONS. HE WAS IMPRISONED AND CASTIGATED, BUT IN ALL HE STROVE ONLY TO SERVE HIS FLOCK.

KEY FACTS
Bishop
DATES: *d.1107*
BIRTH PLACE: *Saxony*
PATRON OF: *Munich*
FEAST DAY: *16 June*
EMBLEM: *Fish and key*

Born to a noble Saxon family at a time of political strife, Benno was frequently caught up in the agitation. Having been appointed Bishop of Meissen by the German Emperor Henry IV, Benno found himself torn between allegiances. He opted to support his fellow Saxons in their uprising against the emperor.

Henry IV promptly had Benno imprisoned, but then released him on oath of fidelity. However, he reneged on this promise, siding again with the emperor's enemies.

When, as a punishment, his bishopric was removed, Benno vowed allegiance to the anti-pope Guibert in the hope that he might

recover his position as bishop and return to his flock. When this move failed, Benno revived his loyalty to Pope Urban II.

A legend says that, when the emperor was excommunicated, Benno decided the best way to stop him entering his cathedral was to throw the key into the river. Benno later found his key miraculously stored inside a fish. The saint's relics were later moved to Munich for safekeeping.

Left: The Martyrdom of Saint Benno (Carlo Saraceni, 1618). Benno was venerated throughout Saxony.

ANSELM

Despite falling out with two kings of England, the Italian monk who became Archbishop of Canterbury was widely admired for his learning and "proof" of God's existence.

> **KEY FACTS**
> *Doctor of the Church*
> Dates: *1033–1109*
> Birth Place: *Aosta, Italy*
> Feast Day: *21 April*
> Emblem: *A ship, symbolizing spiritual independence*

As a boy, Anselm longed to be a monk. After his mother died when he was 20, Anselm left home to wander as a lone ascetic. He passed through Burgundy and found himself in Normandy, where he was inspired by the teaching of the abbot Lanfranc.

He stayed at Lanfranc's monastery of Bec and in time became its abbot. It was a wealthy establishment. Once Anselm was obliged to visit England to oversee property owned by Bec, and it was on this trip that the Italian monk first met the king.

IN AND OUT OF FAVOUR

He so impressed King William II (Rufus) that, in 1093, he made Anselm Archbishop of Canterbury. Though preferring to stay in Bec, Anselm nevertheless accepted the office.

The Italian's reluctance was soon justified when William declared his hand and demanded that he, the king, should appoint all English bishops and abbots henceforth. Anselm claimed that such power resides solely within the Church, and went to Rome to discuss the problem.

In his absence, the king took his opportunity and seized the Church revenues. Anselm condemned the action as theft and abandoned Canterbury to live as an exile in Europe.

In 1100, the new English king, Henry I, summoned Anselm back. Again monk and monarch disagreed over appointments, and again Anselm went into exile. By 1107, they finally reached a compromise and Anselm returned to office to live out his last years in relative peace.

Above: A 15th-century window in Tournai Cathedral, Belgium, shows Anselm travelling to consult the pope.

Exile had provided him with a chance to put down his ideas in writing. Unlike his predecessors, Anselm defended his faith by reason, rather than using scripture as his authority.

Anselm is famous for his "ontological argument" for the existence of God, in which he asserts that the mere idea that there is a God necessarily proves his existence.

Anselm's cult grew slowly, but was helped by a well-written and sympathetic biography of his life written by his friend and disciple, Eadmer of Canterbury. In 1734, in recognition of his position as the most influential Christian writer in the period between Augustine of Hippo and Thomas Aquinas, Anselm was named a Doctor of the Church. He is admired to this day for his steadfastness and piety, and is remembered as an intellectual and philosophical man.

Below: Scenes from the Life of St Anselm of Canterbury, *from* Le Miroir Historial *by Vincent de Beauvais (French School, 15th century).*

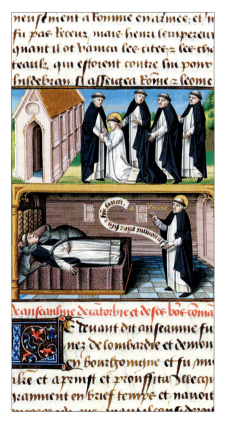

391

STEPHEN HARDING

ESTABLISHING THE MONASTIC SYSTEM OF THE CISTERCIANS WAS ST HARDING'S GREAT ACHIEVEMENT. HIS IDEAS SPREAD ACROSS WESTERN EUROPE AND REFORMED NEARLY 700 MONASTERIES.

KEY FACTS
Founder of Cistercian monastic order
DATES: *d. 1134*
BIRTH PLACE: *England*
FEAST DAY: *28 March*
EMBLEM: *Cistercian habit*

Having settled in France, Stephen Harding, who was English by birth, made a huge impact on the religious history of Europe by helping to found the great monastery of Cîteaux, south of Dijon, France. Under his 25-year leadership, this first of the Cistercian monasteries became a model for the austere religious life.

In a bid to return to a strict observance of the Benedictine Rule, Stephen demanded wholesale changes to the dissolute lifestyle of contemporary monks. Luxuries were banned. The monks could no longer enjoy the monastic income derived from their mills, serfs and tithes. They now had to farm the fields themselves and live on their produce alone. Many new monasteries were built in remote places to avoid contact with town folk.

Stephen expected each abbot to visit the monasteries under his care and report to Citeaux. Thus he maintained his high standards.

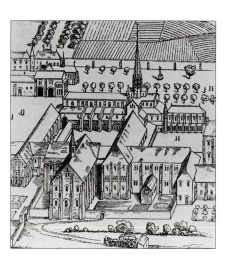

Right: A woodcut of the Cistercian monastery at Cîteaux, France, founded in 1098.

NORBERT

NORBERT GAVE UP A WEALTHY LIFE TO BECOME A MONASTIC REFORMER. HE SET UP THE SO-CALLED "WHITE CANONS", WHICH SPREAD QUICKLY OVER WESTERN EUROPE, ESPECIALLY HUNGARY.

KEY FACTS
Founder of order, archbishop
DATES: *c. 1080–1134*
BIRTH PLACE: *Xanten, Prussia*
FEAST DAY: *6 June*
EMBLEM: *Bishop's vestments*

Like St Francis of Assisi, Norbert was born into a wealthy family and then abandoned his worldly privileges. Norbert almost died in a thunderstorm in 1115. This frightening experience inspired him to give away his possessions and beg the pope for forgiveness for his past life. To atone for his sins, he became a wandering preacher in northern France and the Low Countries.

Norbert's sternness of faith and eschewing of worldly things did not endear him to all the clergy. To put his beliefs into practice, he founded a community in Prémontré in the Rhineland, where he instituted an austere regime following the rules of St Augustine of Hippo. Norbert was a friend of St Bernard of Clairvaux and shared his reforming zeal.

Although there were clergy who resented his ideas, Norbert was generally popular. In 1126, he was appointed Archbishop of Magdeburg. His monastic order, known as the Premonstratensians, or "White Canons", after their vestments, gained ground quickly.

Left: A portrait of St Norbert from an illuminated manuscript (11th–12th century).

BERNARD OF CLAIRVAUX

Under the leadership of St Bernard, the Cistercian Order greatly influenced the spiritual direction Christianity would take during medieval times.

KEY FACTS
Doctor of the Church
Dates: *c.1090–1153*
Birth Place: *Fontaines-lès-Dijon, France*
Patron of: *Gibraltar*
Feast Day: *20 August*
Emblem: *Beehive, beekeepers, candle-makers, Eucharistic host*

St Bernard was one of the most charismatic figures of the medieval Church. His powerful preaching, energy and dedication to leading a model Christian life made him an influential force in the Church, though not one that always met with approval.

Fervent in his commitment to reforming monastic life, Bernard followed the example set by Stephen Harding, and joined his monastery at Cîteaux. His clarity of vision for the developing Cistercian Order naturally led to Bernard's appointment in 1115 as abbot of the poverty-stricken Clairvaux, the third Cistercian monastery.

Critical of the gentler, parallel order at Cluny, known as the "Black Benedictines", Bernard was determined to establish an austere discipline without compromise, surviving on minimal rations and hard labour.

Starting with just 30 fellow devotees, his way blossomed despite its rigours. It is said that his charm and facility to heal the sick attracted thousands of pilgrims. By his death, the number of monks at Clairvaux alone had risen to 700, while some 400 Cistercian monasteries were established across Europe.

POLITICS AND CRUSADE
Bernard's enthusiasm, coupled with his eloquence, inevitably drew him into Church politics. At this time, the authority of the Roman Church was jeopardized by disputes over who should be pope. The princes of Europe tended to back one candidate or another. Bernard's successful promotion of Eugenius III to the papacy in 1145 did much to raise his public profile. Soon he was being asked to combat the rising Albigensian heresy in southern France, which he condemned with characteristic fervour.

Perhaps Bernard's greatest challenge was promoting the Second Crusade (1145–49) to recover the Holy Land from Muslim control. His stirring speeches inspired thousands of the virtuous, the bad, and even criminals, to "take the cross". To protect Christians travelling to Palestine, Bernard championed and endorsed the Order of Knights Templar and devised a chivalric code of conduct. Following the failure of the crusade, Bernard's esteem suffered a great deal, allowing his enemies to make capital out of the disaster.

Bernard's eloquent articulation of his faith is nowhere more evident than in his surviving letters and sermons, and in his treatise on the Love of God.

Below: Saint Bernard of Clairvaux *(Ferrer Bassa, 14th century).*

HENRY OF FINLAND

AN ENGLISH BISHOP OF UPPSALA, SWEDEN, HENRY JOINED A CRUSADE TO FINLAND IN ORDER TO CONVERT ITS WAR-LIKE PEOPLE, AND REMAINED THERE AS A MISSIONARY.

KEY FACTS
Martyr bishop
DATES: *d.1156*
BIRTH PLACE: *England*
PATRON OF: *Finland, sea fishermen*
FEAST DAY: *20 January*
EMBLEM: *Bishop's vestments*

Henry was a soldier for Christ. In 1154, he joined King Eric IX of Sweden's war against the Finns. The king saw his military expedition as a crusade and offered the Finns peace if they became Christian. They refused and were defeated in battle.

Henry stayed in Finland and he baptized many of the people. He built a church at Nousiainen, which became the centre of his missionary work. Eventually, he

was killed by a Finnish convert when he refused to grant him forgiveness for killing a Swedish soldier. His cultus spread and he became Finland's patron saint.

Left: St Henry of Finland from the Sforza Hours, *one of the most beautiful Renaissance manuscripts extant (Giampietrino Birago, c.1490).*

ERIC OF SWEDEN

ERIC HOPED TO INTRODUCE CHRISTIAN RULE TO HIS COUNTRYMEN, BUT WAS MURDERED IN DENMARK WHEN HE TRIED TO USE HIS MILITARY MIGHT TO SPREAD HIS CHRISTIAN MESSAGE.

KEY FACTS
Martyr king
DATES: *d.1160*
BIRTH PLACE: *Sweden*
PATRON OF: *Sweden*
FEAST DAY: *18 May*
EMBLEM: *Crown*

Through his marriage to Christine, of the Swedish royal family, Eric was able to claim the throne in 1156. Committed to his faith, he instituted a Christian legal system and channelled funds into the Church.

However, disgruntled Swedes opposed to his reforms sought allies abroad to back a rebellion. In 1154, one such ally arose in Denmark. Determined to spread Christianity across Scandinavia, Eric waged war against any neighbouring peoples who would not accept Christianity as their faith. He began by invading Finland. When he continued into Denmark, he was outnumbered by a united force of Danes and rebel Swedes. As Eric left Mass on Ascension Day, he was cut down by Danish soldiers. Lying humiliated at their feet, he was subjected to terrible torture and beheaded.

A cultus quickly developed around Eric. Ironically, Nordic mythology possibly played its part in raising his profile to that of national hero, residing in the heavenly abode of Valhalla.

Eric's body and kingly regalia were laid in a new cathedral built in Uppsala, and he was adopted as patron of Sweden. Until the Reformation, farmers would hold annual processions begging Eric's intercession for good harvests.

Left: The coronation of Eric of Sweden (Italian School, 19th century).

THOMAS BECKET

The tragic murder in Canterbury Cathedral of this devout priest created such a sensation that pilgrims came from all over medieval Christendom to visit his shrine.

KEY FACTS
Martyr, archbishop
DATES: *1118–70*
BIRTH PLACE: *London*
PATRON OF: *Clergy*
FEAST DAY: *29 December*
EMBLEM: *Tonsured (crown of head shaved), holding archbishop's cross, mitre*

The clever son of a wealthy family, Thomas was a man of the world in his early career as archdeacon of Canterbury. He was just the sort of pleasure-loving priest that appealed to the young King of England, Henry II.

The king soon appointed him Chancellor of England. In this capacity, Thomas entertained lavishly and travelled abroad on diplomatic missions on behalf of his friend, the king.

ARCHBISHOP
Henry ensured Thomas was made Archbishop of Canterbury in 1162, but, to his intense annoyance, Thomas repented of his former ways. Instead, he became a dutiful, austere religious, wearing a hairshirt and holding long prayer vigils.

No longer the carefree friend, Thomas began to upbraid the king on matters of taxation, reminding him of the Church's rights and privileges. Henry was further enraged when Thomas insisted God and Rome were the supreme authorities, not the King of England. Henry wished to try the clergy in the courts of England, but Thomas claimed this was unacceptable, that they had the right to appeal to Rome.

EXILE AND MURDER
The differences between the two men descended into bitter squabbles, including disputes over money. Thomas went into exile, seeking refuge in a Cistercian monastery in France. After six years, he believed reconciliation had been reached, and returned to Canterbury in hope.

To his great dismay, he discovered his land had been appropriated and his followers alienated. But Thomas continued to assert his allegiance to God over the State. Henry, demanding and quick-tempered, was exasperated. In an outburst, his uttered wish to be rid of "this turbulent priest" was taken at face value by four nearby barons.

His henchmen sped off to the cathedral in Canterbury and, after a brief altercation with Thomas, set upon him with their swords. The king did public penance for this savage murder, but the veneration of Thomas as a martyr spread fast. Hundreds of miracles were claimed in his name and his shrine became one of the most popular in all Christendom.

Above: Detail from a medieval manuscript showing the murder of Thomas Becket (English School).

Below: Henry II of England arguing with Thomas Becket (English School, 14th century).

HILDEGARD OF BINGEN

A MEDIEVAL RENAISSANCE WOMAN, HILDEGARD WAS A VISIONARY NUN, POET, PAINTER, COMPOSER AND WRITER OF BOOKS, NOT ONLY ON MYSTICAL THEOLOGY BUT ALSO ON BOTANY AND NATURAL CURES.

KEY FACTS
Abbess, theologian
DATES: *1098–1179*
BIRTH PLACE: *Bokelheim, Germany*
FEAST DAY: *17 September*
EMBLEM: *Books*

Born the tenth child of a noble German family, the "Sibyl of the Rhineland", as she was dubbed, became aware of receiving visions as early as three years of age. At eight, she was entrusted to the care of a reclusive nun, Jutta, who lived beside a Benedictine abbey at Disibodenberg in Germany.

Hildegard took vows at the age of 15, and entered a small convent established by Jutta. Under her guidance, the young nun grew in stature to eventually succeed Jutta as abbess at the age of 38.

MYSTICAL VISIONS

The depth and quality of Hildegard's mystical experiences prompted her contemporary, St Bernard of Clairvaux, to urge her to record them on paper. This she did in abundance.

The best known of her mystical works is *Scivias* (short for *Sciens vias Domini*, "Know the ways of the Lord"). In the book she describes visions as coming to

Above: An engraving of Hildegard (William Marshall, 1648).

her through "the eyes of her soul". Fully awake, she saw luminous images of figures and scripture bathed in divine light.

This bright light, she wrote, ignited a flame in her chest, "not like a burning, but like a gentle warming flame, as the sun warms everything its rays touch." The experiences deepened her understanding of scripture, and she felt impelled to write widely on whatever inspired her.

Morality plays, hymns and prayers flowed from her pen. Her illustrations to *Scivias* have been likened to those of the English visionary William Blake.

DIVERSE INTERESTS

Besides religious subjects, Hildegard compiled a survey of natural history, and a medical handbook of ailments and their treatment by natural remedy. Her breadth of knowledge prompted her to correspond with the theologian, Guibert of Gembloux, who sought her views on dogma. She gave written advice to King Henry II of England, the German Emperor Frederick Barbarossa, and even the pope himself.

Despite all this creative output, Hildegard did not neglect her duties. When it became necessary, she moved her convent to a larger building near Bingen. She founded a new house at Eibingen, and made reforms elsewhere.

Keen to pass on her spiritual insights, Hildegard preached in Germany and beyond, before finally dying of old age. In the modern feminist movement, she is lauded for her independence and creative energy.

Left: The Vision of Saint Hildegard (attributed to Battista Dossi, c.1474–1548).

LAURENCE O'TOOLE

The invasion of Ireland by English adventurers in 1170 turned Laurence's duties from tending to his famine-stricken flock to protector of the Irish Church.

> **KEY FACTS**
> *Archbishop*
> DATES: *1128–80*
> BIRTH PLACE: *County Kildare, Ireland*
> FEAST DAY: *14 November*
> EMBLEM: *Bishop's vestments*

As abbot of Glendalough monastery, one of the five suffragan dioceses to Dublin, Laurence O'Toole was mainly involved in preventing his rural congregations from starving. But, eight years after his election in 1162 as Archbishop of Dublin, O'Toole had to contend with invading Anglo-Normans led by Strongbow, Earl of Pembroke.

Two years later, the archbishop went to Rome, where he was made papal legate. He also secured the pope's protection of all Church property in Ireland. This upset the English king, who had told the Irish archbishop to remind the pope that he, Henry II of the Angevin Empire, now controlled Ireland. In a tricky meeting with the king, it is a measure of O'Toole's talents that he won the king's agreement not to threaten Irish Church property.

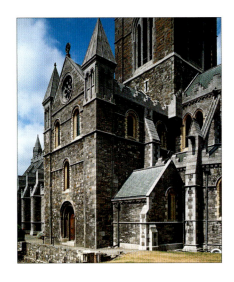

Left: Christ Church Cathedral, Dublin (built 1172–1240).

DOMINIC

The founder of the "Black Friars" order understood that leading an exemplary life of virtue was the best way to bring converts to the faith.

> **KEY FACTS**
> *Founder of an order*
> DATES: *c.1170–1221*
> BIRTH PLACE: *Caleruega, Spain*
> FEAST DAY: *8 August*
> EMBLEM: *Lily, black-and-white dog*

Of noble birth in Castile, Dominic de Guzmán led an uneventful life until he joined his bishop on a mission to the heretical Cathars of southern France. The movement was growing into a menacing force.

Though avowedly Christian, the Cathars did not regard Jesus as Saviour, but merely a teacher. Other groups joined the effort but failed. A warrior knight, Simon de Montfort, mounted a crusade against them in 1208, and caused much grief and bitterness.

But Dominic took no part in such confrontation. His bishop having left him to his own devices, Dominic discovered his gift for preaching. Direct and personal, his style appealed to the listener's heart, rather than the contemporary Franciscan friars' emphasis on creation's beauty.

Basing himself in Toulouse, Dominic founded an order in which he trained priests as itinerant preachers. His eagerness to guard the teachings of Christ meant his priests were nicknamed *domini canes*, "dogs of God".

His order multiplied rapidly. Even now, Dominican men and women play an important role in teaching and preaching the faith.

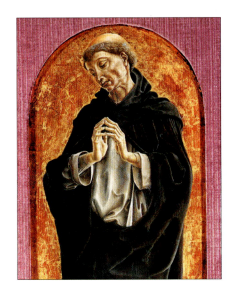

Above: Saint Dominic (Cosmé Tura, c.1430-95).

HOLY BEASTS

CHRISTIANITY HONOURS ANIMALS AS PART OF GOD'S CREATION. THE SAINTS TURNED TO THEM FOR HELP AND COMPANIONSHIP, AND STORIES TELL OF SAINTS PERFORMING MIRACLE CURES ON ANIMALS.

Above: A wooden carving showing St Roch with an angel and a dog (Antwerp School, early 16th century).

From the very beginning of the Christian story, beasts have played their role. Mary, the Blessed Virgin, was said to have given birth in a stable, witnessed by cows and donkeys. She was visited by shepherds who brought a lamb as a gift for the infant Jesus.

Legend states that Christ trusted animals. He even used one to deliver his message. When St Eustace went hunting, his prey, a stag, turned to display a crucifix between his horns, thus converting the hunter to Christianity. The cross marking the back of the donkey is also seen as Christ's legacy to this humble beast who bore him on his final entry into Jerusalem.

Above: St Bernard dogs were used by members of the St Bernard fathers to rescue Alpine travellers from the snow.

As with Christ, so the saints' lives are linked to animals. Some saints had them as companions, others were reputed to have performed miracle cures on the sick and maimed. In turn, stories tell of animals rescuing saints from hardship and mortal danger.

DIVINE SYMBOLS

Certain creatures came to symbolize human qualities. Dogs stood for loyalty and can be spotted in numerous paintings of saints. A lion represents courage and a dove symbolizes the Holy Spirit of peace.

St Bernard of Clairvaux is shown with a little dog at his feet. His mother, pregnant with her son, dreamt of a dog, which is regarded as the guardian of God's house, and security against evil. But the highest status in the Christian world is held by the lamb. The holiest of saints have a lamb as their attribute in emulation of Christ's figuration as

Left: Detail from Annunciation to the Shepherds *(attributed to Simone Martini and others, 14th century).*

> "PRAISE BE TO THEE, MY LORD, WITH ALL THY CREATURES."
>
> ST FRANCIS OF ASSISI

the Lamb of God. This symbolism is based on the Paschal Lamb, sacrificed at the Jewish Passover. John the Baptist and St Agnes are both depicted with the creature.

RESCUE AND CARE
A wolf is said to have looked after St Antony of Egypt when he lost his way in the wilderness. And St Roch was indebted to a dog. As the saint lay in a forest, dying of the plague, a little dog appeared carrying bread in his mouth and saved St Roch from starvation.

St Bernard mountain dogs, employed to track people lost in the Swiss Alps, were named after St Bernard of Aosta. In the 11th century, this saint founded a monastery in the Alps to provide shelter for crusaders trekking to the Holy Land.

As well as coming to their rescue, animals have worked closely with saints. St Antony was once a swineherd and St Brigid a dairymaid. The Welsh St Beuno worked with, and cared for, his cattle and sheep. At his death, these animals were taken to visit his tomb, and thereafter were said to produce strong offspring.

TENDING TO ANIMALS
St Francis of Assisi is famous for his empathy with wild creatures. His sermon to the birds and taming of the wolf of Gubbio illustrate the saint's appreciation of creatures, which he sees as objects of God's love. St Cuthbert also had a special affinity with birds, particularly eider ducks on the Farne Islands of northern England. It was said that birds inhabiting these barren rock stacks fell under the protection of the saint who was a sort of prototype conservationist.

Famously, St Jerome drew a thorn from the paw of a lion who became his life companion. St Blaise was said to have the power to heal animals. Farmers brought him their ailing cattle, and beasts came of their own accord. St Antony of Padua, often aloof with people, had sympathy with the animal world. He preached to fishes who were said to swarm toward him to hear his wisdom. It is said that a badly treated mule once refused its owner's choice of fodder in indignation, but knelt at the eucharist St Antony offered it.

Below: Saint Francis of Assisi Preaching to the Birds *(Giotto di Bondone, c.1295–1300).*

Below: The stag appears in The Vision of Saint Eustace *(Antonio Pisano Pisanello, 15th century).*

PATRON SAINTS OF ANIMALS
Animals – Francis of Assisi, Antony of Padua
Bees – Ambrose, Bernard of Clairvaux
Birds – Francis of Assisi
Cats – Gertrude of Nivelles
Deer – Francis of Assisi
Diseased animals – Blaise
Dogs – Hubert
Dogs, mad – Sithney
Domestic animals – Antony of Egypt
Fish – Francis of Assisi, Antony of Padua
Horned animals – Cornelius
Horses – Martin of Tours, Giles, Eloi, Hippolytus
Wolves – Francis of Assisi

FRANCIS OF ASSISI

Throughout the world today, Franciscan monks and nuns continue the charity work begun by their founder, whose pure love of creation inspired a new attitude to the world.

> **KEY FACTS**
> *First saint to receive the stigmata, in 1224*
> DATES: *1181–1226*
> BIRTH PLACE: *Assisi, Italy*
> PATRON OF: *Animals and birds, ecologists, merchants*
> FEAST DAY: *4 October*

Few saints are held in such high esteem for their spirit of devotion as is St Francis. The humble friar wished for nothing other than to imitate Christ. For him the world was an expression of God, and this conviction gave him a special affinity with nature.

REJECTING WEALTH
Francis was born into a rich Italian family, and as a youth enjoyed his privileged status. But, in the course of a war between Assisi and Perugia, he was imprisoned and began to question his spiritual life. After the war he

Left: Scenes from the life of Saint Francis of Assisi *(Bonaventura Berlinghieri, 1235). This panel is the earliest known depiction of this saint.*

started to give away money to the poor, and once, so overcome with compassion, he kissed the diseased hand of a leper.

His father was so angry at this bizarre behaviour that he demanded his son renounce his inheritance. In fact, Francis was glad to do so, for he had heard a voice telling him to live without property, and to preach the word of God. Francis left his family to take up a life of poverty.

NEW ORDER
Francis lived near the ruined chapel of St Mary of the Angels, known as the Portiuncula, near Assisi. He took shelter in a bare hut, and cared for the local lepers.

His preaching and devotion attracted followers, impressed by the simplicity and humility of Francis' faith. In 1210, Pope Innocent III authorized Francis and 11 companions to be "roving preachers of God".

Franciscans travelled in pairs preaching his philosophy of poverty and living by begging. The order soon spread across Europe as far as England.

Left: The Lower Church of San Francesco in Assisi, Italy, built in the 13th century.

Mountains, where he fasted for 40 days with his followers. While there he had a vision of an angel, who enveloped him with light.

Francis then famously received the stigmata. His hands, feet and side are said to have manifested the same wounds that Christ received at the Crucifixion. The marks stayed with him for the rest of his life. In 1226, blind yet filled with joyous faith, Francis died at Portiuncula.

Despite poor health, Francis made several journeys to convert Muslims living around the Mediterranean Sea. Once, when he was taken prisoner during a battle in Egypt between Crusaders and Muslims, the local sultan was so touched by his devotion and disdain of wealth that he was released. In 1219, he reached the Holy Land, but the following year the Franciscans recalled him to Europe.

Above: Saint Francis Prays to the Birds, *fresco from the church of San Francesco in Assisi (c.1260).*

SPIRITUAL RETREAT

The order had grown hugely in his absence and Francis handed control to the able administrator, Elias of Cortona. It was he who now maintained the Franciscan Rule, which insisted on possessing no money or property, teaching the word of Christ, and caring for the sick and needy. In 1224, Francis retreated to the Apennine

> "LORD GRANT ME THE SERENITY TO ACCEPT THE THINGS I CANNOT CHANGE, THE COURAGE TO CHANGE THE THINGS I CAN, AND THE WISDOM TO KNOW THE DIFFERENCE."
>
> ST FRANCIS OF ASSISI

> "MOST HIGH, ALL-POWERFUL, ALL GOOD, LORD!
> ALL PRAISE IS YOURS, ALL GLORY, ALL HONOUR
> AND ALL BLESSING.
>
> TO YOU ALONE, MOST HIGH, DO THEY BELONG.
> NO MORTAL LIPS ARE WORTHY
> TO PRONOUNCE YOUR NAME.
>
> ALL PRAISE BE YOURS, MY LORD, THROUGH ALL THAT YOU HAVE MADE,
> AND FIRST MY LORD BROTHER SUN,
> WHO BRINGS THE DAY; AND LIGHT YOU GIVE TO US THROUGH HIM.
>
> HOW BEAUTIFUL IS HE, HOW RADIANT IN ALL HIS SPLENDOUR!
> OF YOU, MOST HIGH, HE BEARS THE LIKENESS."
>
> THE FIRST FOUR VERSES OF THE CANTICLE OF BROTHER SUN

DIRECTORY OF SAINTS

ANTONY OF PADUA

THIS CHARISMATIC SAINT FROM LISBON, BELIEVED TO BE A GREAT MIRACLE WORKER, WAS MOSTLY REVERED FOR HIS PREACHING TO THE UNCONVERTED, TO HERETICS, AND TO THE MOORS OF AFRICA.

KEY FACTS
Doctor of the Church
DATES: *c.1193–1231*
BIRTH PLACE: *Lisbon, Portugal*
PATRON OF: *Portugal, lost articles, the poor, animals*
FEAST DAY: *13 June*
EMBLEM: *Loaves of bread*

Stout and overweight, St Antony looked an unlikely person to radiate holiness. Yet it was said that, when people heard his eloquent words, they were filled with the wonder of his faith.

Having joined an Augustinian monastery at the age of 15, Antony was impressed more by some visiting Franciscan friars. The simple modesty of the way taught by his contemporary, St Francis of Assisi persuaded him to join their order in 1221. On a dangerous mission to Muslims in North Africa, he was lucky to suffer only fever, not martyrdom.

On returning to Italy, Antony made his way to Assisi. While staying at a nearby hermitage, he attended an ordination of Franciscan monks. Speakers who were expected to give addresses failed to appear, and Antony was prompted to step up in their place. His speech was so impressive that he was asked to become a wandering preacher.

His renown as such spread beyond his province of Romagna. Soon he was preaching against the Cathars in France, and was known as the "hammer of the heretics."

MIRACLE WORKER
Many miracles were attributed to this popular figure. The most famous example causes the faithful to ask for his intercession now to find things lost or stolen.

Tradition says that a novice at his monastery stole Antony's psalter. When the saint prayed for its return, the thief was duly moved to do so, and re-joined the order, too. At Rimini, a mule was said to have refused its diet of oats for three days, then accepted the eucharist when Antony offered it.

It was also claimed that fish once swarmed a river to hear him preach; a tale symbolic of his powers as a preacher.

Left: The Vision of Saint Anthony of Padua *(Giovanni Battista Pittoni, 18th century).*

Right: St Antony is shown here holding the infant Christ *(c.16th century).*

ELIZABETH OF HUNGARY

The noble wife of a German prince was happily married before his tragic death propelled her into a life of such selfless charity and mortification that she died young.

KEY FACTS
Princess
DATES: *1207–31*
BIRTH PLACE: *Bratislava, Hungary*
PATRON OF: *Catholic charities, bakers*
FEAST DAY: *17 November*
EMBLEM: *Alms of a pitcher, basket of bread, fruit, and fish, apron of flowers*

The tragic story of Elizabeth is set in the royal society of medieval central Europe. At the birth of Elizabeth, a wandering poet-musician predicted that she would marry the German Prince Louis of Thuringia. Aged four, she was duly betrothed to Louis, and her father, Andrew II of Hungary, sent her to live with his family.

Expectations were fulfilled when the couple married when she was 14 and he 21 years old. Furthermore, the marriage was a happy one, with each partner allowing the other to be free to do as he or she wished.

Elizabeth was committed to helping the poor in her adoptive province. The couple's castle home was sited at the top of a cliff. Elizabeth built a hospital at the foot of this rock, and daily took down food and clothing.

She worked tirelessly as a nurse there, tending the sick and orphaned children, as well as the poor of the diocese. At her own expense, it is said, she fed over 900 people a day.

CHANGING FORTUNES

When she was pregnant with their third child, her husband joined the Sixth Crusade (1228–29). They parted, vowing they would never marry anyone else, should anything happen to either of them. Within months of departing, Louis died of the plague. His death proved to be a turning point in her life. His brother-in-law Henry, for some unknown reason, expelled Elizabeth and her children from the castle. The family was forced into a life of hardship, without home or protection.

At last, elderly relatives came to their rescue. An uncle, the Bishop of Bamberg, let her live in his castle and provision was made for the children.

In a state of continuing grief, she assumed the life of a Franciscan tertiary (lay member). In time, the urge to return to her former place of work prompted a move back to Marburg, where she lived in a small hut attached to the hospital she had built. Here she resumed nursing.

Although Master Conrad of Marburg offered her protection, he was alarmed by the harsh regime Elizabeth imposed upon herself. Extreme acts of self-mortification and devotion to others took a toll on her. The restrictions Conrad placed on her, and the beatings given if she disobeyed, only served to harden Elizabeth's will.

Despite an offer of sanctuary from a Magyar noble, she could not bear to leave the place where she believed the poor needed her. She died weak from lack of nutrition, and austerity, aged just 23.

Right: Saint Elizabeth of Hungary holding a basket of flowers (Ambrogio Lorenzetti, 14th century).

DIRECTORY OF SAINTS

CLARE OF ASSISI

Like her neighbour, St Francis, St Clare abandoned a life of inherited ease to serve God. Following the Franciscan way, she founded the order now known as the Poor Clares.

KEY FACTS
Founder of Poor Clares
Dates: *1194–1253*
Birth Place: *Assisi*
Patron of: *Embroiderers, television*
Feast Day: *11 August*
Emblem: *Lilies for purity, holding a monstrance, scimitar for triumph over Saracens*

Having declined two offers of marriage, Clare decided that her greatest desire in life was not to be found in the aristocratic world into which she was born, but in devotion to God. She knew that Francis in the same village of Assisi had made the same decision a few years earlier, and now she determined to emulate him.

Clare was 18 when she made her way to the chapel of the Portiuncula, where Francis based himself, two miles from Assisi. As a test of her commitment, he told Clare to don sackcloth and go and beg in the streets of her home town. Francis then asked her to dress as a bride, and in his chapel he solemnly shaved her head and received her vows.

POOR CLARE
Francis set up a house for her nearby at San Damiano. He drew up a Rule following the example he had set himself, of poverty, chastity and obedience, and in 1216 she was made abbess.

Clare added another rule, forbidding ownership of any property, personal or communal. The order, which her widowed mother and sister also joined, was known as the Second Order of St Francis, and later the Poor Clares.

The nuns survived by begging for food, but the Church disapproved of this undignified public display. At the time, nuns lived in enclosed communities,

Right: The Miracles of Saint Clare of Assisi, *fresco (Lorenzo Lotto, 1523–24).*

Above: St Clare (attributed to Simone Martini and others, 14th century).

financed by church rents. She also struggled to have her rules of austerity approved, but eventually won her way in 1253.

However, these measures of self-denial seriously affected her health. During bouts of illness, she would lie in bed embroidering religious vestments. It was said that once, when too ill to attend Christmas Mass, Clare saw the Nativity crib projected on her cell wall and heard singing as if she were in church. As a result, she has become the patron of television.

She never wavered in her belief in God's protection. When the Saracens attacked Assisi, she was said to have held up a monstrance (vessel for the Eucharist) on the city walls in defiance, and the infidel army withdrew.

For 40 years, Clare lived with poverty and prayer, guiding her nuns, who later adopted an even harsher regime than her own. The order spread through Europe, but the English convents did not survive the Reformation.

HYACINTH OF CRACOW

THE EXPANSION OF THE DOMINICAN ORDER OF FRIARS ACROSS NORTHERN AND EASTERN EUROPE WAS SPEARHEADED BY ST HYACINTH. HE ALSO FOUNDED THE CHURCH IN POLAND.

> **KEY FACTS**
> *Evangelist*
> DATES: *1185–1257*
> BIRTH PLACE: *Kammien (Grosstein), Poland*
> FEAST DAY: *15 August*
> EMBLEM: *Dominican friar's habit*

A determined missionary, he was one of the key first-generation evangelizers of the Dominican Order. He helped to establish Christianity in his native Poland, and some claim he also took the faith to Russia, Lithuania and Sweden, though the historical accuracy of this is uncertain.

Legends abound of him working miracles and travelling great distances to spread the gospel. The crucial moment in his life came during a visit to Rome accompanied by his uncle, the Bishop of Cracow. Hyacinth was already a priest, but, on meeting St Dominic, he was overwhelmed by the founder's strength of faith and compassion. Thus inspired, the young priest felt a profound conversion and was received into the order of preachers.

In 1221, he went to Cracow, where he set up five Dominican monasteries as centres of learning. However, his missions to the East were severely hampered by invasions from Tartar hordes that began in 1238.

Left: Vision of Saint Hyacinth *(Domenikos Theotocopoulos, El Greco, late 16th or early 17th century).*

ALBERT THE GREAT

THIS GERMAN DOMINICAN HELPED LAY THE FOUNDATIONS OF MODERN SCIENCE.

> **KEY FACTS**
> *Doctor of the Church*
> DATES: *1200–80*
> BIRTH PLACE: *Swabia*
> PATRON OF: *Students of the natural sciences*
> FEAST DAY: *15 November*
> EMBLEM: *Dominican friar, scientific instruments*

An inspiring teacher, Albert was the only scholar of his time to be called "Great". After joining the Dominicans in Padua, he taught in Germany, where Thomas Aquinas was his student.

After spells in Paris and Cologne, Albert was made Bishop of Ratisbon in 1260. But Albert longed to pursue his writings on geology, astronomy, chemistry, and geography, so asked to be released from office after just two years. His scientific observations filled 38 volumes. His theological texts also contain insight. Like Aquinas later, Albert asserted there was no conflict between faith and reason. The two are joined in harmony, he said, but some truth can only be grasped through faith. Albert was made a Doctor of the Church in 1931.

Left: Portrait of Saint Albertus Magnus *(Justus van Gent, c.1475).*

FOURTEEN HOLY HELPERS

IN THE 14TH CENTURY, THE BLACK DEATH STRUCK TERROR IN THE POPULATIONS OF EUROPE. AS A SOURCE OF RELIEF TO ROMAN CATHOLIC VICTIMS, THE POPE SET UP A SPECIAL GROUP OF SAINTS.

A magnificent chapel was built in the 18th century to house the statues of the Fourteen Holy Helpers. Within its Baroque interior, massed in a circle around the altar, stand 14 figures, each representing a saint. The Vierzehnheiligen Sanctuary was built in Germany in veneration of these saints, who were first grouped together during the Black Death of the 14th century.

IMMORTAL PERIL
This disease was terrifying in its symptoms and caused rapid death. People were dying before they received the last rites.

> "REMEMBER THE DANGERS THAT SURROUND US IN THIS VALE OF TEARS, AND INTERCEDE FOR US IN ALL OUR NEEDS AND ADVERSITIES. AMEN."
>
> A PRAYER OF INVOCATION TO THE FOURTEEN HOLY HELPERS

This both saddened and frightened the faithful, who believed that, without receiving this sacrament, they would forego the essential final step on the journey to heaven. To compensate in some measure for the lack of a priest available to serve the last rites, sufferers could call upon any one of these specified saints to intercede on their behalf for the absolution of their sins.

Some of the Helpers are martyrs; others are associated with certain diseases. Some, such as St Christopher, are even legendary. A collective feast day was assigned for all Holy Helpers on 8 August.

MEANING THROUGH ART
As well as the statues in the sanctuary in Germany, there are many other representations of the Fourteen Holy Helpers, particularly from the 14th and 15th centuries.

Images of the figures were usually placed near church altars, often with Mary, the Blessed Virgin, cradling the Baby Jesus, or with St Christopher carrying the Christ Child on his shoulders.

Left: Saint Roch Praying to the Virgin for an End to the Plague *(Jacques-Louis David, 1780).*

Above: View of the Town Hall of Marseilles During the Plague of 1720 *(Michel Serre, 18th century).*

Paintings and sculptures often represent these saints as distorted, or holding awkward positions to indicate the symptoms they are believed to cure. Clothes or an animal companion might give a symbolic meaning or denote their traditional significance.

Indeed, some paintings are so grotesque in their depictions of diseases and suffering that the artists seem intent on bringing home the full horror of the Black Death to the viewer.

CULTUS IN EUROPE
For centuries, these images attracted large crowds. The cultus was strong in Germany, Hungary and Scandinavia. But it never commanded much of a following in Italy, France or England.

The numbers of pilgrims decreased after the Reformation. Now this group of saints is relatively obscure to most Roman Catholic worshippers.

THE PROTECTORS
- **Acacius** and **Denys of Paris** are called upon for headaches.
- **Barbara** intercedes for fevers and sudden death.
- **George** and **Pantaleon** protect domestic animals.
- **Blaise** guards against sore throats.
- **Catherine of Alexandria** and **Christopher** are patrons of sudden death.
- **Cyricus** helps to ward off temptation.
- **Margaret of Antioch** aids women in childbirth.
- **Vitus** prevents epilepsy.
- **Erasmus** is associated with intestinal troubles.
- **Eustace** helps out in difficult situations.
- **Giles** is invoked by lepers, the physically disabled, and nursing mothers.

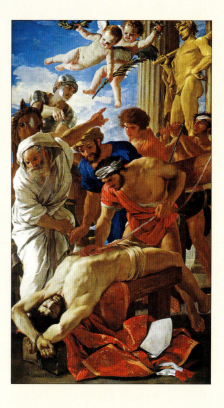

Above: Martyrdom of Saint Erasmus *(Nicolas Poussin, 1629).*

The list of saints is generally stable, but substitutions were made in some regions or cities where the veneration of particular saints was strong. The Holy Helpers were invoked to guard against specific illnesses – and these included diseases suffered by animals as well as humans.

THE BLACK DEATH
The origin of this plague remains a mystery. It was a virulent epidemic that swept across Europe in 1348. It caused rapid putrefaction of the sufferer's body, which turned black before death occurred. In Europe, 25 million died, including one-third of the English population. The numbers of victims in Asia and North Africa are unknown.

There were other outbreaks of plague in Europe, but none so devastating as the Black Death. Its cause has been attributed variously to unknown substances, germs introduced by sailors, or a predominance of rats. The lack of hygiene found in medieval cities was a major factor.

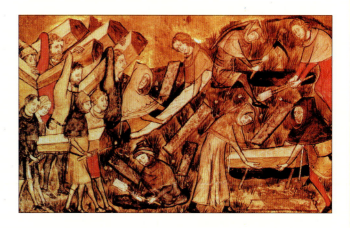

Above: Black Death at Tournai *(Gilles Le Muisit, 1349).*

ALEXANDER NEVSKI

A WARRIOR COUNT WAS CANONIZED BY THE EASTERN ORTHODOX CHURCH FOR HIS VALIANT DEFENCE OF RUSSIA, AND FOR ASSURING PEACE FOR HIS COMPATRIOTS DURING THE MONGOL OCCUPATION.

> **KEY FACTS**
> *National hero of Russia*
> DATES: *1220–63*
> BIRTH PLACE: *Novgorod, Russia*
> PATRON OF: *Russia*
> FEAST DAY: *23 November*
> EMBLEM: *Knight's armour*

As the Grand Duke of Vladimir, Alexander Nevski spent much of his early life in wars against neighbouring nations of Europe. His title "Nevski" was earned by his decisive victory over the Swedes at the River Neva in 1240.

Born a prince and patriot of Russia, military pride rode next to Nevki's devotion to God. Integrity of faith was an essential component of all Nevski's military expeditions. The belief that God was not on the side of force but on the side of truth and justice was one of the guiding maxims of his faith.

Major campaigns included repelling the Swedes from Novgorod and Pskov. Lithuanians were other foes, as were the Knights of the Teutonic Order,

Left: Alexander Nevski *(Afanasiy Yefremovich Kulikov), 20th century.*

a noble Germanic troop formed during the Crusader wars. In a triumphant battle on the banks of the frozen Lake Peipous in 1242, Nevski repelled the enemy. In so doing he put an end to all future claims of conquest by the Knights.

TARTAR OVERLORDS

Perhaps equally as important for Russia as these military conquests was the time Nevski had to spend placating the occupying Tartars. Between 1237 and 1240, these fearsome successors of Genghis Khan invaded the principalities of eastern and central Russia.

The control these menacing hordes exerted over his country posed quite a different problem, requiring careful handling. From 1240, Russia was held in servitude, paying high tribute and penalties.

Through clever diplomacy, Alexander Nevski achieved some key concessions, which boosted national morale. He persuaded the Mongols to drop compulsory military service, and negotiated reductions in the tribute demanded by these overlords.

His reputation as a national hero has grown since his death. In recognition of his national status, the Russian Orthodox Church raised a division during World War II named after this patriotic saint. Many street names in Russia are also named in his honour.

Below: The silver gilt tomb of Alexander Nevski, held in the State Hermitage Museum, St Petersburg (1747–52).

BONAVENTURE

RECOGNIZED AS THE "SECOND FOUNDER" OF THE FRANCISCANS, ST BONAVENTURE INTRODUCED REFORMS THAT EDUCATED THE FRIARS AND MODERATED AUSTERE TENDENCIES WITHIN THE ORDER.

> **KEY FACTS**
> General of the Franciscan Friars, known as the Seraphic Doctor
> DATES: *c.1218–74*
> BIRTH PLACE: *Bagnoreggio, Italy*
> PATRON OF: *Theologians, farmers, porters, weavers*
> FEAST DAY: *15 July*
> EMBLEM: *Franciscan gown, bishop's mitre; his cloak is bordered with images of seraphim, the highest order of angels*

The "Seraphic Doctor", as Bonaventure was known for his intellectual and mystical qualities, established a high reputation in the Church for his reforming theology. Choosing not to follow in his father's footsteps as a medical doctor, Bonaventure opted instead to become a Franciscan in 1243. It was an interesting choice for a clever man, since the Franciscan order discouraged intellectual pursuits. But he was happy to lead a life of frugal simplicity.

REFORMS

In 1257, Bonaventure became general of the Franciscan Order in Paris, where he had studied. Because the founder, St Francis of Assisi, was detached from formal learning, there were no books to be found in the monasteries.

Yet Bonaventure could see that, if the friars were to be effective as teachers, they needed to be educated. They would need books and libraries to house them.

Another problem was that St Francis' Rules forbade the ownership of property. So Bonaventure had to persuade his followers to accept a different model. Being a patient man with moderate views, he was prepared to travel to the many Franciscan monasteries and Poor Clare convents to convince the religious that these changes made sense.

For the reforms he thus achieved, as well as the curbs he placed on the more austere practices of some members, he is regarded as the "second founder" of the Franciscans. Disliking high office, he once refused to become Archbishop of York, but later was compelled to be Cardinal Bishop of Albano. In this role, he brokered a reconciliation with the Greek Church at Constantinople.

The peace turned out to be a temporary one, though Bonaventure never knew this, since he died shortly afterwards.

Below: Saint Bonaventure Taking the Franciscan Habit *(Francisco Herrera the Elder, 17th century).*

THOMAS AQUINAS

The "Angelic Doctor" was an intellectual giant of the medieval Church who expanded Christian thinking to establish a comprehensive doctrine of the Catholic faith.

> **KEY FACTS**
> *Theologian and writer*
> **Dates:** *c.1225–74*
> **Birth Place:** *Rocca Secca, near Aquino, Italy*
> **Patron of:** *Academics, universities, schools, students, theologians, pencil-makers*
> **Feast Day:** *28 January*
> **Emblem:** *Star shedding light, ox, books, lily*

This well-built man was dubbed the "dumb ox" for his gentle courtesy and because he was thought to be a little slow of mind. But, as his energy and output was to demonstrate, Thomas Aquinas comprehensively outstripped all his contemporaries in intellectual capacity.

One writer said that the amount of study required to produce all Aquinas' books would take several normal lifetimes. However, his aristocratic family did not share the young man's enthusiasm to join the Dominicans, a mendicant order that lived by begging.

HOUSE ARREST
His family, who regarded the mendicants' activities as shameful, had educated Thomas at the reputable Benedictine monastery at Monte Cassino, whose abbot was related to the Aquino family. When the determined prodigy nevertheless joined the Black Friars at the age of 21, his brothers kidnapped him and imprisoned him at the family home.

But Thomas would not relent. His family even sent a beautiful girl to tempt him from his chosen path. Paintings depict him brandishing a burning stick to ward away the temptress.

FAITH AND REASON
Eventually released, Thomas went to Cologne, Germany, to study under St Albert the Great. This teacher provided the groundwork for much of Aquinas' theology. Thenceforth, he was to spend

> "We should show honour to the saints of God, as being members of Christ, the children and friends of God, and our intercessors. Therefore, in memory of them we ought to honour any relics of theirs in a fitting manner."
>
> ST THOMAS AQUINAS

Left: Temptation of Saint Thomas Aquinas (Diego Rodríguez de Silva y Velázquez, 17th century).

his life moving back and forth between France and Italy as a teacher and academic.

In tandem with St Albert the Great, Thomas Aquinas believed in the harmony of faith and reason. Hitherto, theological points of debate had taken the Bible as their authority. Now Aquinas was asserting that reasoned argument was authority in itself, because God gave mankind the power of reason.

ARISTOTLE AND ISLAM

Aquinas held that everything comes from God. He said that at the end of their lives humans return to God as to their home.

A perfect life was one that combined contemplation with action, since it is only through prayer that we can know the will of God. At the time that Aquinas

Below: Saint Thomas Aquinas *(Abraham Jansz, Diepenbeeck, c.1640–50).*

lived, Islamic scholars were bringing ideas of the ancient Greek philosophers, such as Aristotle, back to Europe. In debate with Muslims, Aquinas produced an entire book responding to their writings.

His intellect aimed not only at the higher reaches of the Church. Some of the most beautiful hymns written for Mass have been ascribed to him, and he produced prayers and expositions of the Creed for the ordinary believer. He was also a preacher, giving sermons on the Ten Commandments and key tenets of the Christian faith.

SPIRITUAL END

In about 1266, Aquinas began his *Summa Theologica*, a study of all the Christian mysteries, which ran to five volumes. He never finished the work, because in 1272 he had a profound mystical experience while attending Mass.

The effect of receiving a vision of God, as he reported, was so overwhelming that he felt his intellect no longer adequate. Indeed, he is famously reputed to have said that all he had written to date was "like straw" compared to this spiritual experience.

Not long after this event, he prepared to attend the Council at Lyons, but was taken ill on the journey. He died at the abbey of Fossanova aged 49.

Left: St Thomas Aquinas wearing Dominican garb and praying at the altar, *from* Libro de Horas de Alfonso el Magnifico, *the vellum prayer book of Alfonso V of Aragon (Spanish School, c.1442).*

SUMMA THEOLOGICA

Having produced a text, *Summa contra Gentes,* that presented the faith to non-believers, Thomas Aquinas set about writing his magnum opus to instruct beginners in Roman Catholic theology. Running to five volumes, *Summa Theologica* covers a great variety of subjects.

The first volume explains all that emanates from God. The second volume explains the psychology of human activity and its organization. The third asserts that humans return to God as to their natural home. The fourth volume discusses the Holy Spirit, and a life of meditation and action. And the fifth, unfinished, summarizes faith.

Above: Title page from Summa Theologica *on vellum (French School, 14th century).*

AGNES OF BOHEMIA

PRINCESS AGNES USED HER WEALTH TO FINANCE HER LIFE AS A HUMBLE NUN WORKING WITH LEPERS. SHE WAS CANONIZED BY POPE JOHN PAUL II IN 1989.

KEY FACTS
Princess, abbess
DATES: *d.1282*
BIRTH PLACE: *Bohemia*
FEAST DAY: *6 March*
EMBLEM: *Poor Clare habit*

The daughter of the King of Bohemia (now part of the Czech Republic) was once betrothed to Emperor Frederick II of the Holy Roman Empire. However, this marriage was not one she wished to fulfil, so she wrote to the pope asking to be released from the engagement.

Frederick retreated with grace, and accepted that his fiancée preferred to "wed the king of heaven". Agnes' family were also supportive. On becoming king, her brother funded various projects of hers, including new monasteries, a hospital and the first Poor Clare convent north of the Alps, located in Prague.

Agnes became its abbess, having taken her vows in 1236. St Clare herself sent five nuns to help establish the convent. The severe rules of poverty demanded by the order were faithfully followed by Agnes for 40 years until her death.

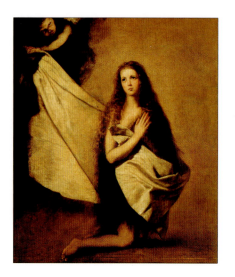

Left: Saint Agnes in Prison *(José de Ribera, 1641).*

NICHOLAS OF TOLENTINO

THIS AUGUSTINIAN FRIAR SPENT MANY YEARS AS A PREACHER AND GAINED A REPUTATION AS A MIRACLE HEALER. AT TOLENTINO HE BROUGHT HARMONY TO A TOWN TORN BY STRIFE.

KEY FACTS
Augustinian friar, miracle worker
DATES: *1245–1305*
BIRTH PLACE: *Sant'Angelo, Italy*
PATRON OF: *The dying and souls in purgatory, babies and mothers, fires, sick animals*
FEAST DAY: *6 March*
EMBLEM: *Augustinian habit, basket of bread rolls, star on his chest*

On hearing an Augustinian friar preaching that the best form of love comes from beyond the world, Nicholas became so inspired that he decided to join the order.

For some years, he lived successfully as a wandering preacher in the Italian district of Ancona, on the Adriatic coast. He gradually acquired a reputation for healing people, including, in about 1270, restoring the sight to a blind woman in Cingoli.

Shortly afterwards, he heard heavenly voices calling him to Tolentino, a town devastated by family feuds and religious schism. For the rest of his life, Nicholas devoted his energies to mending broken relations in the little town.

He fostered harmony at domestic level, caring for children and the dying and criminals. Not surprisingly, Nicholas became much loved for his kindness and sincerity of faith – it is said the entire city turned up to listen to his preaching. After a long illness, he died, and was deeply mourned.

Above: Nicholas at the Battle of San Romano *(Paolo Uccello, c.1450–60).*

DIRECTORY OF SAINTS

ELIZABETH OF PORTUGAL

A SPANISH PRINCESS, MARRIED TO A PORTUGUESE KING, BECAME A SYMBOL OF RECONCILIATION BOTH AT THE DOMESTIC LEVEL AND AT THE HIGHEST LEVEL OF INTERNATIONAL DIPLOMACY.

> **KEY FACTS**
> *Queen of Portugal*
> DATES: *1271–1336*
> BIRTH PLACE: *Aragon, Spain*
> PATRON OF: *Difficult marriages*
> FEAST DAY: *4 July*
> EMBLEM: *Crown*

The daughter of Peter III of Aragon was married at the age of 12 to King Denis of Portugal. Though her husband became cruel and abusive to Elizabeth, she followed the Christian teaching of turning the other cheek. In time, her husband converted to the faith.

Elizabeth founded hospitals and orphanages, and cared for abused prostitutes. After the death of her husband, she made a pil-

grimage to St James the Great's shrine at Compostela and became a Franciscan tertiary (lay member).

Although Elizabeth wished to live in modest obscurity, she was called upon to soothe the poor relations between Portugal and Castile. She died at Estremoz but was buried in the Poor Clares convent at Coimbra.

Left: Saint Elizabeth of Portugal *(Francisco Zurbarán, 1640).*

ROCH

THIS MYSTERIOUS SAINT, WHO WORKED HEROICALLY DURING A PLAGUE IN ITALY, WAS SAID TO HAVE MIRACULOUSLY SURVIVED THE DISEASE HIMSELF, BUT THEN PERISHED IN PRISON FALSELY ACCUSED.

Also known as Rocco or Roc, Roch is remembered chiefly for nursing plague victims in medieval Italy. It was in a time of great desperation that this young man came to do good public service. Born to a wealthy merchant family in Montpellier, France, Roch chose early in life to be a hermit and pilgrim.

It is believed he lived in Rome, but was staying in Piacenza when a plague broke out. By all accounts, he exhausted himself nursing humans, and even animals, before falling victim to the disease himself. Not wishing to become a focus of concern, Roch crawled to a wood to face

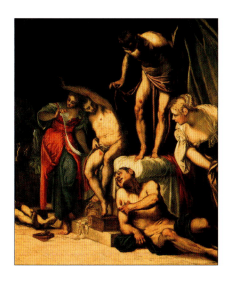

Above: Saint Roch is shown healing victims of the plague (Tintoretto, 1549).

> **KEY FACTS**
> *One of the Fourteen Holy Helpers*
> DATES: *c. 1350–80*
> BIRTH PLACE: *Montpelier, France*
> PATRON OF: *Istanbul, contagious diseases, physicians, surgeons, prisoners, cattle*
> FEAST DAY: *17 August*
> EMBLEM: *Plague sore on his thigh, dog at his feet, angel, bread*

death. But legend has it that a dog brought him bread to eat and an angel cured him of the disease.

On recovering, he returned home, whereupon his uncle did not recognize him, or refused to do so. Roch was then imprisoned, accused of being a fraud or spy.

He died behind bars in Lombardy. Miracle cures were later claimed at his grave, and believers started calling upon him for help at times of epidemic.

CATHERINE OF SIENA

CATHERINE'S AGGRESSIVE SPIRITUAL BELIEFS DIVIDED PUBLIC OPINION ABOUT HER TRUE UNDERSTANDING OF THE FAITH. SOME THOUGHT HER HYSTERICAL; OTHERS AN EXEMPLARY VISIONARY.

KEY FACTS
Dominican tertiary
DATES: *1347–80*
BIRTH PLACE: *Siena*
PATRON OF: *Italy, Italian nurses*
FEAST DAY: *29 April*
EMBLEM: *Dominican tertiary habit, stigmata, holding a cross, crown of thorns, lily*

Like Hildegard of Bingen, this remarkable woman was a mystic who experienced visions and wrote meaningful religious texts. Both also became involved in worldly affairs.

Catherine was the youngest in a family of 25 children. Her twin sister died at birth. And, aged six, she is said to have had her first vision of Jesus.

She used to say a "Hail Mary" on each step of the staircase while ascending or descending. Frightened and angered by her behaviour, her family insisted on her working incessantly, never allowing her to be alone. However, her patience and obedience convinced her father of her holiness, and he permitted her to become a Dominican tertiary.

Left: Saint Catherine of Siena *(Giovanni Battista Tiepolo, 1746).*

Below: Saint Catherine of Siena Exchanging Her Heart with Christ *(Giovanni di Paolo, 15th century). Her heart is held in her fist.*

ZEAL AND STIGMATA

She lived a solitary life of prayer until 1366, when she was said to have received a vision of Mary, the Blessed Virgin, who led her to Christ. Catherine was convinced she had received a wedding ring given by Christ, though no one else could see the jewellery.

After this experience, Catherine went out into the world and began to preach. A band of followers gathered round her, referring to her as "mama".

She was energetic as a preacher, and not all the citizens of her hometown, Siena, admired her style. Some thought her hysterical. But she won respect from the pope after admonishing people to go on a crusade to the Holy Land. In 1375, while visiting Pisa, Catherine suffered pangs of pain, and claimed she was marked by the stigmata (wounds identified with those of the Crucifixion). Again, none could see the scars, but on her death they became clearly visible.

THE AVIGNON POPES

In all her contact with the public, Catherine had developed a talent for mediation, which brought her into Church politics. For some 75 years, the popes had lived in exile at Avignon. Now Catherine became involved in persuading Pope Gregory XI to return to the papal seat in Rome. Gregory responded to her quasi-mystical call and sailed for the city in 1376.

After Gregory's death, French factions in Avignon selected a rival pope in opposition to his successor, Urban VI. Catherine tried to settle the dispute but aroused such anger in her opponents they threatened her life. In 1380, she dreamt she was being crushed by a ship that symbolized the Church. Shortly afterwards, she was paralysed for days by a stroke before her death.

BRIDGET OF SWEDEN

ROYAL ADVISER, NURSE OF THE BLACK DEATH, AND MORAL CRUSADER, BRIDGET STOPPED AT NOTHING IN PURSUIT OF RIGHT. SHE PROPHESIED DAMNATION, AND EVEN CRITICIZED THE POPE.

> **KEY FACTS**
> *Founded Bridgettines*
> DATES: *1303–73*
> BIRTH PLACE: *Uppland*
> PATRON OF: *Sweden, pilgrims*
> FEAST DAY: *23 July*
> EMBLEM: *Monogram of Christ (HIS), candle, book, pen, dressed as a widow or pilgrim*

This daughter of the governor of Uppland served in the Swedish court as lady-in-waiting, moral adviser to the feckless royal family. In 1344, Bridget (or Birgitta) went with her nobleman husband on the long pilgrimage to Compostela in Spain, but he died on their return journey.

Now widowed, though with eight children from her marriage, Bridget for a time directed her energy into founding a monastic order, called the Most Holy Saviour, or Bridgettines.

Despite the Black Death then sweeping across Europe, Bridget travelled to Rome and nursed the sick there. After reputedly receiving a vision of St Francis, she went on to Assisi and spent two years visiting Italian shrines.

It was said Bridget had the power of prophecy about political events. She is believed to have used this facility to condemn to damnation weak or corrupt heads of state. The fearless nun even dared once to criticize the pope.

Left: St Bridget in a Portuguese vellum from the 17th century.

JOHN OF NEPOMUK

A DEVOUT ADVISER TO THE ARCHBISHOP OF PRAGUE UPHELD HIS CLERICAL DUTIES TO THE POINT OF MARTYRDOM RATHER THAN COMPROMISE THE CHURCH IN THE FACE OF A POWERFUL TYRANT.

> **KEY FACTS**
> *Martyr*
> DATES: *c.1345–93*
> BIRTH PLACE: *Nepomuk, Bohemia*
> PATRON OF: *Slovakia, of confessors, bridges, protection against slander*
> FEAST DAY: *5 January*
> EMBLEM: *Seven stars*

As vicar general, John of Nepomuk (or Nepomucen) became the close aide of the Archbishop of Prague on matters of Church-State relations. When, in 1378, Wenceslaus IV became King of Bohemia, these relations took a turn for the worse.

A legend says that being a man given to violent rages, Wenceslaus became insanely jealous of his wife and harassed John to reveal her confessional secrets. The king so mistrusted priests that he planned to set up a monastery manned by his own priests. To this end, when the abbot of the rich Benedictine monastery at Kladruby died, Wenceslaus wanted to appoint his successor in order to gain control of the revenues from the land.

However, in anticipation, the priests appointed a new abbot the moment the old incumbent died. Learning this, Wenceslaus believed John to be the instigator.

He first beat the priests, then tied John up, his ankles bound to his head, and hurled him into the River Vltava at Prague. Seven stars were said to glow over the site of his drowning. John was greatly mourned when his body was found the next day.

Right: A statue of St John of Nepomuk with a halo of stars, on the Charles Bridge in Prague.

WARRIOR SAINTS

WHETHER SOLDIERS OF WAR OR FOR PEACE, MANY MEN AND WOMEN SINCE THE BIRTH OF CHRISTIANITY HAVE BEEN CANONIZED FOR DEFENDING THEIR FAITH AND GOING INTO BATTLE.

Throughout history, soldiers have often claimed that the saints have aided and protected them in battle. Many warriors have converted to Christianity and died for their faith, or fought bloody wars to protect their right to worship their God. There are others whose inspiration came from Christ himself and who took to the path of peace.

HEAVENLY INSPIRATION

The Archangel Michael, "captain of the heavenly host" and protector of Christian soldiers, has often appeared above battlefields or kept company with troops in combat. Joan of Arc identified him as helping spur her into battle.

In their long battle against Moorish invasion, the Spanish frequently called upon the apostle St James the Great, patron saint of Spain. After the miraculous victory at the Battle of Clavijo (AD 844), the soldiers claimed that James had appeared in their midst in full armour, sword in one hand and banner in the other, riding a white charger.

SOLDIER SAINTS

Since the days of the Roman Empire, there have been military men who have rejected their earthly masters and pledged to serve only Christ.

Known in the Eastern Orthodox Church as the "Great Martyr", St Demetrius was much admired as a warrior saint. He was a soldier in the Roman army in the early 4th century, who converted to Christianity and was subsequently put to death.

Above: St Maurice, fresco detail (artist unknown, 15th century).

A great soldier saint and inspiration to warriors and crusaders, St George is always depicted as a knight in armour. Although most of what we know is legendary, he is venerated throughout the Christian world. St George is thought to have been martyred at Lydda in Palestine around AD 303.

St Theodore, known as "the recruit", was a young Roman soldier. After his conversion to Christianity he refused to join his comrades in the worship of pagan gods. Tradition says that he also set fire to a pagan temple. He was martyred in the 4th century at Pontus (part of modern Turkey).

During birthday celebrations for the Roman Emperors Diocletian and Maximian, a centurion named Marcellus threw off his soldier's belt crying, "I am a soldier of Christ, the eternal king, and from now I cease to serve

Left: Camillus of Lellis rescues hospital patients during the flooding of the Tiber in 1598 (Pierre Subleyras, 1745).

you." Other Roman soldiers who converted expressed the same anti-military sentiments, such as St Julius, who chose to die by the sword rather than serve a master on earth.

There are also great leaders who are much venerated because they were soldiers in service of Christ. St Stephen of Hungary, a skilled military strategist, set out to conquer the pagans in his country and force them to convert to the Christian faith. St Vladimir of Kiev is revered throughout Orthodox Russia as the man who brought Christianity to his country, although initially he used the army to impose the new faith.

PEACEFUL PATH

Some soldier converts came to realize that the Christian life was not compatible with violence.

Martin of Tours, a young officer in the Roman army, asked for a discharge after his conversion. He announced, "I am Christ's soldier; I am not allowed to fight."

Left: Alexander Nevski (artist unknown, 1855).

Much later, in the 16th century, St Camillus of Lellis was a mercenary or "soldier of fortune" who began nursing the sick and injured after his conversion. He is credited with organizing the first field ambulance unit, going into the battlefield to care for the wounded. St John of God was another mercenary whose conversion made him seek peace. He also turned to nursing and founded the Brothers Hospitallers.

During the Spanish Civil War of 1936–39, thousands of Christians fought for a country that was guided by the faith against their fellow citizens who wanted a secular regime. Hundreds of the Catholics who died were beatified by Pope John Paul II and are known as the Martyrs of the Spanish Civil War.

Below: St Demetrius (Serbian icon, 18th century).

THE CRUSADES

In the Middle Ages, European Christian countries mounted military campaigns to oust the Muslims from Jerusalem and give support to Christians isolated in the East.

There were eight Crusades in all, lasting from 1095 to 1272 and ending with the Muslims still in control. Vast sums of money and huge numbers of men were involved. The journey to the Holy Land involved travelling great distances and was often disrupted by battles on land and sea. The Crusaders often fought while weak with hunger and ravaged by disease.

The Crusaders believed they had God on their side and often experienced heavenly visions. They adopted St George and St Demetrius as patron saints after they appeared above the demoralized soldiers and led them to victory against the Saracens at the Siege of Antioch (1097–98).

King Louis IX of France led two disastrous crusades in 1248 and 1270. Although he was not victorious, he was venerated for his zeal in fighting for the Holy Land.

Left: The archangel Michael (Greek, c.14th century).

Above: Manuscript illumination showing soldiers departing for the Crusades (c.1240–84).

JOAN OF ARC

As the girl warrior, Joan of Arc, perished in the fire prepared by Englishmen, one soldier was heard to cry out, "We are lost. We have burnt a saint."

> **KEY FACTS**
> *Visionary, military leader*
> Dates: *c.1412–31*
> Birth Place: *Domrémy, France*
> Patron of: *France, French soldiers*
> Feast Day: *30 May*
> Emblem: *Armour, battle banner*

Joan of Arc is one of the most remarkable women in history. Her life has inspired books, films, poems and paintings, yet she remains mysterious. She was courageous and indifferent to pain, a good horsewoman and deft with her sword. Yet she began as a simple illiterate peasant, at home with domestic work.

How did she convince a royal court that she could be a military leader? Where did she learn to lead an army on horseback and wield a weapon? Brought up in the Champagne area of France during the Hundred Years' War between England and France, Joan was used to living in a war-torn environment.

Her village was sympathetic to the royal house of Orléans. But across the river to the south, the peasants sided with the dukes of Burgundy and the English. When she was 13, Joan said she heard God speak to her. As a result, she vowed to remain a virgin, devoted to the will of Christ.

Below: Joan of Arc Kissing the Sword of Deliverance *(Dante Gabriel Rossetti, 1863).*

DIVINE VOICES

At 16, Joan claimed frequent visits by the Archangel Michael and two saints, Catherine of Alexandria and Margaret of Antioch. She said the saints were dressed as queens and they instructed her to save France and crown the dauphin, Charles, as King of France.

Ignoring pleas from her father to remain, Joan prepared to travel to the court of Charles. To help her cause, she dressed as a man.

Entering the royal quarters, Joan unerringly approached the dauphin. He was a frivolous youth who hid among his courtiers to trick the girl. But she was said to have had a divine recognition

> "It is better to be alone with God: His friendship will not fail me, nor His counsel, nor His love. In His strength I will dare, and dare, and dare, until I die."
>
> Words given to Joan in *St Joan* by G.B. Shaw

of him. Confounded, the young royal listened to her announcement that God had sent her to help him and his kingdom. After close questioning from religious and military leaders, Joan won permission to raise arms.

INTO BATTLE

Stealing a sword from behind a church altar, Joan prepared for battle bearing a banner painted with the words "Jesus Maria". The people of nearby Vaucouleurs gave her a horse and a man's suit of white armour.

On 7 May 1429, Joan led her soldiers into war and banished the English from Orléans. She went on to win victories in Patay and Tours as well. But her greatest moment of triumph came when she stood beside the dauphin as he was crowned King Charles VII of France, at Rheims in July of that year. However, the indolent Charles neglected Joan, who

Below: The Burning of Joan of Arc on 30 May 1431 *(lithograph of the French School, 19th century).*

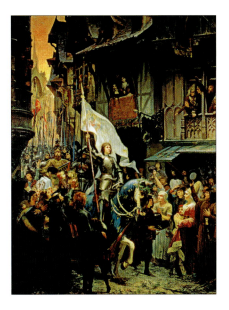

Above: The Entrance of Joan of Arc into Orléans on 8 May 1429 *(Jean-Jacques Scherrer, 1887).*

took it upon herself to continue the fight. But in Compiègne she was captured by the Burgundians, who then sold her to the English.

WITCHCRAFT

Joan suffered nine months of brutal confinement charged with witchcraft and heresy. Her decision to dress as a man was deemed to be proof of her heresy. Barely 19 years old, the transcript of her trial in Rouen, then in English hands, makes sad reading. The court found her guilty of heresy.

As she approached the scene of her dreadful punishment in Rouen's market square, she asked for a crucifix. This she kissed and was heard to cry "Jesus" as the flames licked round her. Before her body was consumed, her corpse was displayed naked to the crowd to prove she was indeed a woman who had "wickedly" paraded as a man.

To prevent any veneration of the relics, her ashes were thrown into the River Seine. Her family petitioned to clear her name. In 1456, the pope overturned the guilty verdict. For centuries she was popularly held to be a saint, but the Church waited until 1920 before granting canonization.

Joan was not a martyr, but a virgin who lived her faith. She is the first Christian patriot, her love of country entwined with her religion. Even the English went so far as to erect a statue of St Joan in Winchester Cathedral.

VOICE OF A LEGEND

There is a tradition that Margaret of Antioch, who may never even have existed, spoke to Joan. Legend claims Margaret was a Christian exiled from home by a pagan father. She lived as a poor shepherdess until the governor of Antioch tried to seduce her. When she refused him, he tortured her. A dragon is said to have swallowed her, but she burst from it and survived. She promised divine protection, safeguards against devils, and fertility to the childless.

Above: St Margaret *(Raffaello Sanzio Raphael, 16th century).*

RITA OF CASCIA

AFTER CARING FOR HER WAYWARD FAMILY, ST RITA BECAME A NUN AND SUFFERED THE PAINS OF MORTIFICATION. HER RENOWN AS A HEALER MADE HER ONE OF THE FOURTEEN HOLY HELPERS.

> **KEY FACTS**
> Widow, mystic
> DATES: *1377–1447*
> BIRTH PLACE: *Roccaporena, Italy*
> PATRON OF: *Those in desperate situations, parenthood, help for the infertile*
> FEAST DAY: *22 May*
> EMBLEM: *Crown of thorns, stigmata on forehead*

Born in a village in Umbria, Rita was brought up a pious girl. Indeed, she longed to devote herself to God. But she owed greater allegiance to her parents' wishes than to her own and so she submitted to a marriage that they arranged.

Unhappily, Rita found herself bound to a violent, unfaithful husband. Furthermore, their sons followed his example. Despite the difficulties she had to endure, she patiently cared for her family.

Rita prayed unceasingly that Jesus might be revealed to them. And in time the husband seemed to repent and convert to the faith, only to come home one day mortally wounded in a vendetta.

Her sons swore vengeance for his death, so Rita prayed for their death before they committed any dreadful deeds. They then fell ill. Inspired by their mother's gentle nursing, the two sons repented of their evil ways and were forgiven before they too died.

THORN OF GOD

Now widowed, Rita applied to join an Augustinian convent in Cascia. She was refused on the grounds of not being a virgin. But persistent entreaties on her part eventually succeeded and, at the age of 52, Rita was admitted to the convent.

She proved a devout sister who never flinched from the austere rules. Rita made it her special duty to nurse the sick and counsel sinners outside the nunnery. Her kindliness was said to inspire many converts.

At the age of 60, Rita attended a sermon centred on the crown of thorns. As she listened to the words describing Jesus as "King of the Jews", being forced to wear a mock crown, Rita suffered a dreadful stab of pain. She later found a wound, such as that which a thorn might cause, on the middle of her forehead.

The wound did not disappear but suppurated. It became so offensive that, for the last 16 years of her life, Rita lived largely as a recluse. On a pilgrimage to Rome in 1450, her wound disappeared, only to return when she was back in her convent. Rita contracted tuberculosis, and thus a life of devotion, prayer and obedience was ended in 1447.

Miracles were attributed to Rita after her death. Her body, housed in a grand tomb, has remained incorrupt to the present day. A school, a hospital and an orphanage have been built around the tomb, which forms part of the Cascia convent buildings.

Below: Detail from Three Depictions of Saint Rita of Cascia *(colour lithograph of the French School, 20th century).*

Above: Detail from Three Depictions of Saint Rita of Cascia *(colour lithograph of the French School, 20th century).*

FRA ANGELICO

THE PRIOR AT A MONASTERY IN TUSCANY BECAME KNOWN AS THE "ANGELIC BROTHER" FOR HIS BEAUTIFUL SPIRITUAL PAINTINGS. FRA ANGELICO REGARDED HIS ARTISTIC WORK AS ACTS OF PRAYER.

> **KEY FACTS**
> *Artist monk*
> DATES: *1387–1455*
> BIRTH PLACE: *Vicchio, Italy*
> PATRON OF: *Artists*
> FEAST DAY: *18 February*
> EMBLEM: *Paintbrush*

Guido di Pietro, as he was christened, was born in the mountains beyond Florence, Italy. He joined the Dominican Order in Fiesole as a young man and soon became known as Fra Angelico, or "angelic brother".

An artist who thought of painting as an act of prayer, Fra Angelico produced works entirely religious in subject. Indeed, the spirituality of his work prompted the Victorian art critic, John Ruskin, to declare that the talented monk was an inspired saint rather than an artist.

MEDICI PATRONS

Initially, the monastery trained Fra Angelico in manuscript painting under guidance from an older monk, Lorenzo Monaco. When the monks were moved to San Marco convent in Florence, the powerful and wealthy Medici family paid for enlargements of the building.

With his teacher, Fra Angelico painted the new walls with a series of murals depicting sacred scenes. He coupled the elements of medieval work with the new scientific knowledge of his own Renaissance era.

Thus his style appealed to the contemporary tastes, but did not alienate traditional viewers. It is the beauty of his work, with its mystical quality, that still inspires.

In 1445, he was called to Rome to produce wall paintings at the Vatican, in St Peter's Cathedral and the pope's private rooms. And four years later he went to decorate the vault of a chapel in Orvieto's Catherdral, though he was called to monastic office before finishing the work.

PRIOR AT FIESOLE

From 1449 to 1452, he was prior of the monastery at Fiesole. He then returned to Rome, where he died after three years.

His works, which serve a contemplative purpose, are regarded as "visual prayers". They brought him recognition from a public who would gaze at them in admiration. Many are preserved in religious buildings. Almost 600 years later, at the beatification of Fra Angelico, Pope John Paul II exclaimed, "Why do we need miracles? These are his miracles."

Above: Fresco detail from The Deeds of the Antichrist *(Luca Signorelli, c.1499–1502). In the foreground, Fra Angelico (right) is depicted standing next to Signorelli (left).*

Right: The Annunciation *(Fra Angelico, c.1440–45).*

MARTYRS OF OTRANTO

Antonio Primaldo and around 800 fellow citizens of Otranto were martyred in 1480 when Gedik Ahmed Pasha, leader of an invading Ottoman army, executed them after they refused to convert to Islam.

> **KEY FACTS**
> *Martyrs*
> Date: *1480*
> Birth Place: *Citizens of Otranto, Italy*
> Patron of: *Otranto*
> Feast Day: *14 August*

On 28 July 1480, a forbidding Ottoman fleet of 90 galleys, 15 galleasses and 40 smaller galiots made landfall at Roca in southern Italy and began to bombard the nearby fortified town of Otranto. Its commander, Gedik Ahmed Pasha, had around 18,000 troops at his disposal and orders to sweep opposition aside and march northwards to conquer Rome in the name of Islam.

Sultan Mehmet II, dubbed "the Conqueror" after leading the Ottoman capture in 1453 of Constantinople, the fabled capital of the eastern Roman Empire, had pronounced himself "Caesar of Rome" and declared his intention to conquer the Eternal City and reunite the eastern and western halves of the empire. The threat was that he would turn St Peter's Basilica into a stable for his cavalry. Alarm was spreading across Italy. In Rome, Pope Sixtus IV called for a crusade against the Ottomans and prepared to evacuate the city if necessary.

Above: Painting in the Cathedral of Naples depicting the massacre of Otranto citizens in 1480.

NO SURRENDER

The Ottomans offered mercy if Otranto surrendered, but the people refused. And, when the invaders sent a messenger to try again to urge the garrison to give up the keys of the town, the defenders shot him dead in a hail of arrows and hurled the keys into the sea. The Ottomans commenced bombardment and damage was heavy – after a day, the people and the garrison took refuge in the citadel.

The siege lasted 15 days, until 12 August. In the course of it many of the defending soldiers fled, leaving a core of around 50 troops and the townspeople who refused to be cowed. When the citadel fell, the Ottoman troops flooded through the streets. In the 11th-century cathedral they encountered Archbishop Stefano Agricolo wearing his vestments and brandishing a crucifix. They beheaded him in front of the altar, and cut garrison commander Count Francesco Largo, Bishop Stephen Pendinelli and other companions in half. Then they rounded up women and children to be sold into slavery.

There remained around 800 able-bodied men. The Ottomans demanded they convert to Islam to be spared. To a man, they refused. Only one is known by name – Antonio Primaldo, a tailor, who stood defiantly before the invaders and delivered a stirring speech to his countrymen, declaring that it was time for them to fight to save their souls, and adding that, since Jesus Christ had given his life on the cross for them, they should be willing to give their lives to honour Him. Many years later, Pope John Paul stated that Primaldo said: "We

Left: A statue commemorating the martyrs of Otranto stands by the walls of the Castello of Otranto.

believe in Jesus Christ, son of God, and for Jesus Christ we are ready to die."

Fortified by Primaldo's words and their own faith, the men gave a great cheer.

Two days later they were taken to the Hill of Minerva. Determined to honour their Lord and defiant of the Ottomans' threats, every man made it obvious that, rather than convert to Islam, they were willing to be executed for their faith in Christ. The story was later told that one Ottoman officer named Bersabei was so moved at this show of faith that he converted to Christianity on the spot. He was slain by his comrades.

Antonio Primaldo was the first to be beheaded. According to the legend of his martyrdom, he was forced to his knees to be executed, but, after the stroke severed his head, his headless body stood upright once more. The soldiers tried to knock it down or move it but it could not be shifted and stood in mute and horrible witness while the 800 men of Otranto were beheaded on that hilltop. The ground was stained red by their blood.

SAINTS – AND SAVIOURS OF ITALY?

The stiff resistance put up by the people of Otranto significantly slowed the Ottoman invasion and enabled King Ferdinand of Naples to strengthen fortifications in the area. The encounter has been credited with saving Rome and the whole Italian peninsula from falling into Ottoman hands. But the key element in terms of the martyrs' claim to sainthood was that they were said to have been executed for upholding the Christian faith – for refusing conversion.

Otranto was recaptured by Alfonso of Aragon with the help of troops in the service of King Matthias Corvinus of Hungary. The skeletal remains of the martyrs were gathered and placed in a reliquary in Otranto Cathedral. The martyrs' bodies were reputedly discovered to be uncorrupted and were moved to the Cathedral. Some were later taken to Naples and set beneath the altar of Our Lady of the Rosary in the Church of Santa Caterina a Formiello, an altar built to celebrate the final victory of the Christian West over the Ottomans at the naval Battle of Lepanto in 1571.

Below: Remains of the martyrs of Otranto rest in glass cases in the Chapel of the Martyrs, Otranto Cathedral.

> **MASS CANONIZATION**
>
> In 1771 Pope Clement XIV beatified the 800 martyrs slain for their faith on the Hill of Minerva. A miracle was attributed to them in the healing of sister Francesca Levote as a result of intercession by Blessed Antonio Primaldo and the eight hundred companions. On 11 February 2013, Pope Benedict announced the date of their canonization and the entire group were canonized by Pope Francis on 12 May 2013. They are patron saints of the city of Otranto and Archdiocese of Otranto. A certain element of controversy attached itself to the decision since some felt that the canonization could be viewed as an anti-Islamic gesture at a time in the early 21st century when relations between Christianity and Islam were arguably in need of repair. Francis did not mention Islam in his homily proclaiming the saints: "As we venerate the martyrs of Otranto, let us ask God to sustain the many Christians who, today and in many parts of the world, now, still suffer from violence, and to give them the courage to be devout and to respond to evil with good." He added: "Dear friends, let us keep the faith which we have received, and which is our true treasure; let us renew our devotion to the Lord even in the midst of obstacles and misunderstandings."

CASIMIR OF POLAND

St Casimir is claimed as patron by Poland, Russia and Lithuania, reflecting the complicated geo-politics of medieval eastern Europe.

KEY FACTS
Prince of Poland
DATES: *1458–84*
BIRTH PLACE: *Cracow, Poland*
PATRON OF: *Poland, Russia, Lithuania, the youth of Lithuania*
FEAST DAY: *4 March*
EMBLEM: *Crown*

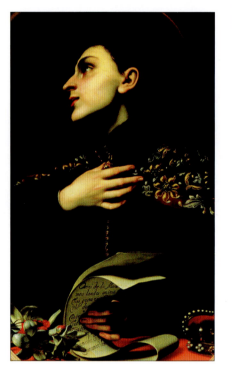

Numerous reports from the medieval period describe well-born children possessed of a deep spirituality. But Casimir is an extraordinary example. From infancy, it was said, he had a natural tendency to be ascetic.

His father was King Casimir IV of Poland, yet his small son would admit no luxury, choosing to sleep on a bare floor and spend hours at prayer. He frequently recited a long Latin hymn in praise of Mary, the Blessed Virgin. Under plain clothes, he wore a hair-shirt to mortify the flesh. He visited the poor regularly, using his royal position to gain concessions on their behalf.

When Casimir was 15, the king appointed this unworldly son to lead the Polish army in a bid to take the throne of Hungary. As both the boy's officers and the pope were opposed to this war, Casimir decided to turn back home during the campaign. His angry father imprisoned him in Dobzki Castle for months.

Yet nothing would induce Casimir to take up arms, nor would he abandon his vow of celibacy. He continued to follow his stern, simple ways, ultimately to his death. He died in what is now Lithuania, aged 26.

Left: St Casimir of Poland (Carlo Dolci, 17th century).

NICHOLAS OF FLUE

Pope Pius XII declared St Nicholas of Flue to be the Father of Switzerland, a tribute to his role in uniting the various factions that had plunged the region into civil war.

KEY FACTS
Hermit
DATES: *1417–87*
BIRTH PLACE: *Sachseln, Switzerland*
PATRON OF: *Switzerland*
FEAST DAY: *21 March (25 September in Switzerland)*
EMBLEM: *Hut, hermit's clothes*

The life of St Nicholas falls into two halves. At first, he lived as a soldier, magistrate and judge in Switzerland. His family belonged to the Friends of God, a Christian brotherhood that stressed the personal union of their souls with God.

On turning 50, the second part of his life began. Nicholas decided to become a hermit. With his wife's blessing, he set off for France, but on the way observed what he described as a fiery sign calling him back to Switzerland. So he settled on a high pasture, living under the shelter of a tree.

The faithful sought him out, and built him a hut and a chapel. At this time, Switzerland was in the grip of civil war, and delegates from both sides visited Nicholas. His words are said to have resolved the political differences and a national unity was achieved by the Edict of Stans (1481).

Left: Nicholas of Flue praying in the wilderness, with a skull by his side as a memento mori (woodcut, artist unknown, 1860).

THOMAS MORE

At his execution, the Lord Chancellor Thomas More told the crowd that he was "the king's good servant – but God's first". To the end, More would not compromise his faith.

KEY FACTS
Martyr saint
Dates: *1478–1535*
Birth Place: *London, England*
Patron of: *Politicians*
Feast Day: *22 June*
Emblem: *Lawyer's hat*

A scholar of great integrity, Thomas More was granted high office by his friend, King Henry VIII of England. He read law at Oxford University and, at the age of 23, became a Member of Parliament.

Thomas had a witty, light-hearted personality, and the king delighted in his company. When appointed Lord Chancellor, he wrote his most famous work, *Utopia*, a fantasy about an ideal community living in harmony, with equality of opportunity.

His first wife, by whom he had four children, died young but he made a happy second marriage. His family was a source of love and comfort, and Thomas drew great strength from his faith.

Much of his work was written in support of the Catholic Church and against Martin Luther's ideas of reformation. He corresponded with theologians across Europe, including Erasmus.

RUPTURE WITH THE KING
Thomas was deeply distressed by Henry VIII's decision to break with Rome and set himself up as supreme head of the Church in England. The king's reasons were not theological.

He simply wished Rome to nullify his marriage to Catherine of Aragon, but the pope refused. Henry followed fashionable ideas of reformation and revolt against Rome, and declared religious independence.

But Thomas More was a pious man and could not support his wayward king. He resigned as

Above: An engraving of Thomas More after a painting by Holbein (Francesco Bartolozzi, 1792).

Lord Chancellor in 1532. Two years later, More was called to take an oath denying papal authority over English Christians. He refused and was dispatched to the Tower of London. His lands were confiscated and his family forced into poverty.

During his imprisonment there, he wrote often to his beloved daughter, Margaret Roper. He also produced his *Dialogue of Comfort*, a moving text on the meaning of faith.

The following year he was taken to Westminster Hall, where he faced charges of treason because he refused to accept the king's authority over the pope's. Thomas More was sentenced to death and was beheaded in public on Tower Hill, London.

JOHN FISHER
A distinguished scholar-priest, John Fisher was Chancellor of Cambridge University and Bishop of Rochester. He was involved in reforming the Church, but preferred dialogue to confrontation as a means of bringing change.

Fisher was a good friend of Thomas More and, like him, was asked to accept the Act of Succession, which gave Henry VIII authority over English Catholics. John refused and was taken to the Tower. While there, the pope made him a cardinal. The infuriated king condemned John to death.

The saint was so ill, he had to be carried to the executioner's block. He died in 1535, a month before Thomas More.

Above: Portrait of Martyr and Prelate John Fisher (artist and date unknown).

THE SAINTS IN ART

PAINTINGS OF THE SAINTS INSPIRED BELIEVERS TO FEEL THAT, IN CONTEMPLATING HOLY IMAGES, THEY WOULD DRAW CLOSER TO GOD. PERSONAL ATTRIBUTES WERE ADDED TO IDENTIFY THE SAINTS.

Gregory the Great observed that paintings do for the illiterate what texts do for readers. There can be little doubt that the medieval faithful, most of whom could not read, were uplifted by illustrations of the saints' lives.

Despite the passing of centuries, believers who gazed upon these images were not dismayed by various artistic developments. Changes to the style of clothing worn by the saints or altered settings tended to cause no discomfort among the faithful. Neither did the portrayal of particular saints with different faces in successive paintings.

Above: The Martyrdom of St Catherine of Alexandria *(Lucas Cranach the Elder, 1506).*

SYMBOLS OF IDENTITY

From early in the history of Christian art, a convention arose to identify saints through symbols. These emblems served to clarify the narrative being told, and to identify the characters.

Mary, the Blessed Virgin, and infant Jesus are instantly recognizable. Likewise, Mary holding her dead son, a scene known as the Pietà, is universally understood, as is the image of the crucifix, representing the crucified Christ.

But other characters needed their individual code of identity in order to be recognized, since no one knew what the saints looked like. To modern eyes, medieval and Renaissance Christian paintings can look quaint, even bizarre.

Doves emanate rays of light, lions lie meekly on cathedral floors, and a stag might display a crucifix within its antlers. Angels have blue duck-feathered wings, and men stand, pierced by arrows or even holding their own heads. For some 1,700 years, these unlikely elements possessed a beautiful logic, easily understood by all Christians, from the bogs of Ireland to the deserts of Syria.

Above: St Lucy with her eyes on a plate (Umbrian School, c.1550).

LIONS TO ALABASTER

The medieval faithful knew the scholarly man with the lion was St Jerome. Likewise, the man with an arrow was Sebastian, who by tradition was shot in this manner.

The shepherdess, St Margaret of Antioch, carried a staff and was shown with a dragon because she escaped from such a beast. St James the Great had a seashell and pilgrim's staff near him. The shell

Below: St Jerome in the Desert (Pietro Perugino, c.1499–1502).

> "THE WORK SHINES NOBLY,
> BUT THE WORK WHICH SHINES NOBLY SHOULD CLEAR MINDS,
> SO THAT THEY MAY TRAVEL THROUGH THE TRUE LIGHTS TO THE TRUE LIGHT
> WHERE CHRIST IS THE TRUE DOOR."
>
> ABBOT SUGER (C.1081–1151)

indicated his body was found in a drifting boat, the staff that he was a journeying evangelist.

All Christendom recognized Mary Magdalene because a jar of ointment and loosened hair marked her apart. With oil of alabaster she anointed Christ's feet before drying them with her hair.

ART AS IDOLATRY

The Church regarded artistic representations as an expression of the holiness of the saints. In the Orthodox Church, they were used to concentrate the mind during meditation. But these artistic works aroused anxiety during the Reformation.

Protestant leaders forbade the erection of any kind of image in religious buildings. Images were regarded as idolatrous on the ground that the Old Testament forbids worship before idols.

Paintings, shrines and statues of saints were cleared away and frescoes were concealed behind a covering of wall paint. These zealous reformers even showed hostility toward music. The Roman Catholic Church uses music for worship. The Eastern Orthodox Church retains a sung liturgy so revered it has remained unaltered to this day.

The reformer John Calvin declared that music had no place in a church. The less stern Martin Luther, on the other hand, composed his own church hymns.

SAINTLY ARTISTS

There are saints who were artists, the first being the Apostle Luke, reported to have made studies of Mary, the Blessed Virgin. Perhaps the greatest painter is Fra Angelico whose spiritual paintings are famous, but the drawings and music of Hildegard of Bingen also carry a mystical quality.

Musicians and poets can be found in the company of saints. It is assumed Gregory the Great was a musician – one reason for this assumption is that the Gregorian Chants bear his name.

There are contemporary reports that describe Nicetas of Remesiana as a poet and composer who wrote the beautiful Latin hymn, *Te Deum*. He used music as a form of preaching.

Below: A fresco showing the popular subject of St Luke painting the Madonna (Andrea Delitio, 1477).

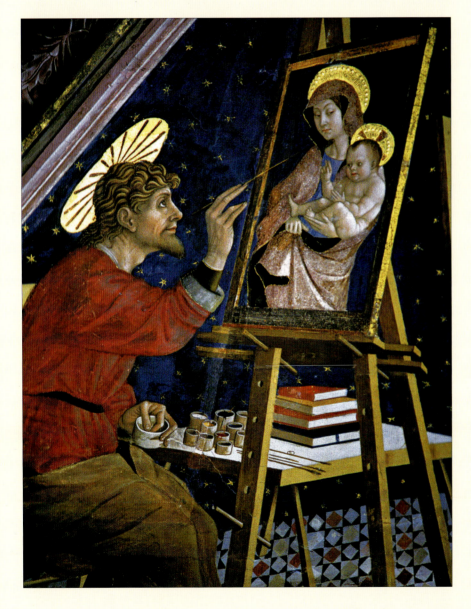

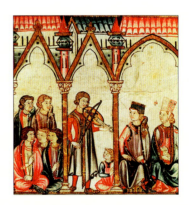

Above: Manuscript illumination from Cantigas de Santa Maria *(Alphonse Le Sage, 13th century).*

ANGELA MERICI

THE ITALIAN FOUNDER OF THE FIRST ORDER OF WOMEN DEVOTED SPECIALLY TO EDUCATING CHILDREN HAS BECOME A PATRON OF MANY CAUSES RELATED TO THE UNDERPRIVILEGED IN SOCIETY.

KEY FACTS
Founder of Ursuline nuns
DATES: *1474–1540*
BIRTH PLACE: *Lake Garda, Italy*
PATRON OF: *Disabled people*
FEAST DAY: *27 January*
EMBLEM: *Book*

As an orphan from an early age, Angela Merici suffered great deprivation and neglect. Vulnerable, malnourished and unloved, orphaned children were a pitiable class in Italian society at this time.

Forced to be independent as a child, Angela developed a special sympathy for the plight of orphans. While she could not help their loss of parentage, she could work to improve their lot.

To this end, she first joined the Franciscan tertiaries and then founded a special Christian community. Its members were women who were not cloistered but free to move among those who most needed education – children. The sisters, who went wherever it was convenient to deliver lessons, taught local children in the villages. Aged 42, Angela went to educate the children at Brescia.

The lay nun made pilgrimages to Rome and the Holy Land, where she was strangely struck blind. She recovered her sight on returning home.

Once again, Angela gathered a group of women in Brescia, who dedicated their lives to educating children. The women made no vows of chastity or obedience, and shared no communal life. But from this nucleus grew the Company of St Ursula (known as the Ursuline nuns), named after the legendary virgin martyr.

Right: Saint Angela Merici *(Moretto da Brescia, date unknown).*

CAJETAN

DEVOTING MOST OF HIS LIFE TO WORKING AMONG THE POOR IN THE SLUMS OF NAPLES OPENED ST CAJETAN'S EYES TO THE REALITY OF RENAISSANCE SQUALOR FOR LARGE SECTIONS OF THE COMMUNITY.

KEY FACTS
Founder of the Theatines
DATES: *1480–1547*
BIRTH PLACE: *Vicenza, Italy*
PATRON OF: *Job seekers*
FEAST DAY: *7 August*
EMBLEM: *Theatine habit*

Though not ordained until he was 36, Cajetan had seen enough in his working life to realize that the Church was in dire need of reform. Being an active charity worker made him acutely aware of the suffering and loss of faith in the community.

In partnership with Pietro Caraffa, a mistrusted fanatic who in fact became Pope Paul IV, Cajetan founded the Theatines (named after the diocese of Theate). This fundamentalist group of priests were trained to follow the first teachings of Christ, avoiding all sophisticated theology.

Their purpose was to preach the basics of the Christian faith in the hope of bringing back the disaffected into the Church. Cajetan also devised a system of alleviating poverty. He set up pawnshops owned by the Church to allow the poor access to loans. These non-profit organizations operated for centuries. He lived briefly in Rome, but left during an invasion by troops of the Holy Roman Emperor.

Cajetan spent most of his life in Naples, then a corrupt diocese. He died there, having tried to improve its moral culture.

JOHN OF GOD

A PORTUGUESE MADMAN RESCUED FROM AN ASYLUM TURNED ROUND HIS LIFE BY DEDICATING IT TO THE RELIEF OF SOCIETY'S OUTCASTS. A HOSPITAL SERVICE WAS FOUNDED IN HIS NAME.

KEY FACTS
Founder of the Brothers of St John of God
DATES: *1495–1550*
BIRTH PLACE: *Monte Mor il Nuovo, Portugal*
PATRON OF: *Nurses and nursing associations, bookbinders*
FEAST DAY: *8 March*
EMBLEM: *Poor clothing, cross*

John of God, a Portuguese, spent his youth as a soldier for Spain, roaming the battlefields of Europe, before working first as a shepherd in Andalusia, and later as a merchant, peddling religious images and pamphlets in Granada.

Attending a sermon given by John of Avila, the merchant went mad with remorse for his sins. He began to scream and tear at his hair. He was confined to a lunatic asylum until John of Avila visited him, asking him to serve God. John of God began to sell wood, feeding the poor with his profits. He built a house where he sheltered vagabonds, prostitutes, and nursed the ill.

He never founded an order, but his hospital service became the Order of the Brothers of St John of God. He tried to hide his ill health, but when a noblewoman insisted on nursing him, he wept, believing he was unworthy of comfort while others suffered. When John died, all Granada followed his funeral procession.

Right: Saint John of God *(School of Pedro Nolasco y Lara, 18th century).*

THOMAS OF VILLANOVA

FROM SIMPLE FRIAR TO ARCHBISHOP OF VALENCIA, ST THOMAS ENDEAVOURED TO MEET THE NEEDS OF ALL WHO CAME HIS WAY, REGARDLESS OF THEIR WEALTH OR STATUS IN SOCIETY.

KEY FACTS
Archbishop
DATES: *1488–1555*
BIRTH PLACE: *Near Villanova, Castile*
FEAST DAY: *22 September*
EMBLEM: *Franciscan habit, archbishop's crook*

A dreamy man by nature, fond of meditation, Thomas of Villanova was destined to join a religious order. When admitted to the Spanish Franciscan friary at Salamanca, he developed a deep faith and became a significant preacher for 25 years.

Somewhat against his will, Thomas was then appointed Archbishop of Valencia. What he found, on taking office, was a Church in need of inspiration.

A lazy, dissolute clergy required discipline, but Thomas knew that high-handed methods achieved nothing. Instead, he adopted patience and diplomacy. His gentle faith served many quarters of the community. Among his congregation were disturbed *Moriscos*, Moors who had been forcibly converted to Christianity. His spirituality and reputed gift for healing brought much solace to these people.

Preferring the solitary life, Thomas asked to be allowed to step down as archbishop. But his leadership was so vital the Church ignored his requests. Worn out by duties, Thomas died in Valencia and was canonized in 1658.

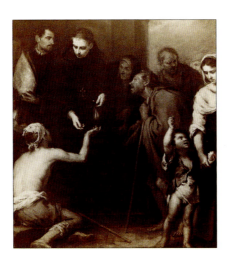

Above: The Charity of Saint Thomas of Villanova *(Bartolomé Murillo, c. 1670).*

DIRECTORY OF SAINTS

IGNATIUS OF LOYOLA

AS FOUNDER OF THE POWERFUL MISSIONARY ORDER, THE SOCIETY OF JESUS (ALSO KNOWN AS THE JESUITS), ST IGNATIUS SPEARHEADED THE COUNTER-REFORMATION IN EUROPE.

> **KEY FACTS**
> Founder of the Society of Jesus, or "Jesuits"
> DATES: *c.1491–1556*
> BIRTH PLACE: *Azpeitia, Spain*
> PATRON OF: *Spiritual exercise and retreats*
> FEAST DAY: *31 July*
> EMBLEM: *Black cassock, heart pierced by thorns, the monogram of Christ (HIS), and a crown of glory*

The youngest of 11 children of a noble Basque family, Ignatius was born in the Castle of Loyola at Azpeitia. He followed the course taken by many young men of the period and trained as a soldier in the Spanish army.

But for a severe wound to his leg while fighting the French at Pamplona, Ignatius would probably have joined the ranks of the conquistadors on their expeditions to the Americas.

Instead, he was forced to take a long convalescence, during which he is said to have had a conver-

Left: Colour engraving of Ignatius of Loyola (c.1500).

sion experience. Having no strong convictions of faith up to then, he reported suddenly having a vision of Mary, the Blessed Virgin, with Jesus beside her.

The experience inspired Ignatius to go to the Benedictine abbey at Montserrat. There he duly laid his sword and dagger upon the altar, and sought a cave nearby to take up life as a hermit.

TRAINING THE SPIRIT
Ignatius imposed a harsh lifestyle on himself, going without food for long periods, scourging his body daily, and immersing himself in prayer.

As word spread, people started visiting him to seek his advice and join him in prayer. But his life of deprivation took its toll and his health suffered. He came to realize that he should not shut himself away from people, but serve them in their spiritual needs.

At the age of 32, Ignatius walked to Jerusalem, despite a permanent limp caused by his war injury. He hoped to convert Muslims, but the Franciscan

Left: Detail of heaven and angels from The Glorification of Saint Ignatius *(Andrea Pozzo, c.1691–94).*

brothers discouraged him and, fearing for his safety, sent him home. Back in Barcelona, he took up studying and began to preach and to help the needy. However, since he was no priest, this did not endear him to the Church.

SOLDIERS OF CHRIST

In Paris to do further studies, the ambitious young man formed a brotherhood with six friends. Among them was St Francis Xavier, who would become the great missionary to the East.

Having now been ordained, Ignatius instructed the group using his own spiritual manual, *Spiritual Exercises*. This work consisted of a four-week course designed to induct new "soldiers of Christ", as Ignatius refered to the members of his brotherhood. They gave themselves to chastity and poverty, and determined to teach those without education.

Calling themselves the Society of Jesus, they also pledged to conduct missions in Europe to reclaim souls lost to the Protestant reformers. The pope gave the society his blessing in 1540, and Ignatius was chosen as its general.

RETRIEVING CATHOLICS

Ignatius spent the rest of his life in Rome. He founded a house for converted Jews and hostels for prostitutes. But it was his work in organizing foreign missions that

earned him his reputation. His writing and teaching played a pivotal role in drawing believers back to the Roman Catholic Church after the Reformation.

His conviction in the power of prayer and sympathy towards those struggling with Christian principles endeared him to believers. His influence over Church doctrine and teaching has been immense.

Yet Ignatius was criticized in some quarters for being too militaristic and authoritarian. Likewise, the Jesuits, as they were popularly known, have been attacked for their power and political meddling.

Under Ignatius' leadership, the society grew rapidly. By his death, after 16 years of development, the number of Jesuits had increased to more than 1,000 members.

Right: Detail of The Vision of Saint Ignatius of Loyola *(Peter Paul Rubens, 17th century).*

Left: Saint Francis Borgia Helping a Dying Impenitent *(Francisco José de Goya y Lucientes, 1795).*

THE SOCIETY OF JESUS

This order made the usual commitments to chastity, poverty and obedience, but added a fourth vow: absolute loyalty to papal authority. It proved an effective mission in post-Reformation Europe.

Chief among their European missions was that led by St Francis Borgia (1510–72), described as the order's "second founder". St Aloysius Gonzago (1568–91) nursed plague victims and wrote important texts. And St Stanislaus Kostka (1550–68) gained fame as a Jesuit mystic.

In the 16th century, missions were set up in Brazil, China, India, Japan and Malaysia. Two martyrs, St Francis Xavier (1506–51) and St Modeste Andlauer (1847–1900), served these missions. The society has since spread worldwide.

> "Dearest Jesus, teach us to be generous;
> To serve Thee as Thou deservest;
> To give, and not to count the cost;
> To fight, and not to heed the wounds;
> To toil, and not to seek for rest;
> To labour, and to seek for no reward,
> save that of knowing that we do Thy
> holy will."
>
> Prayer of St Ignatius of Loyola

FRANCIS XAVIER

THE JESUIT WHO DEVOTED HIS LIFE TO SPREADING THE GOSPEL TO DISTANT LANDS PLANTED THE FAITH AS FAR EAST AS JAPAN. HE EXTENDED THE CHURCH FURTHER THAN ANY OTHER MISSIONARY.

> **KEY FACTS**
> *Missionary to the East*
> DATES: *1506–51*
> BIRTH PLACE: *Xavier Castle, Navarre*
> PATRON OF: *India, Pakistan, Outer Mongolia, missions, Spanish tourism, the pelota players of Argentina and Archdiocese of Calcutta (co-patron with St Teresa of Calcutta)*
> FEAST DAY: *3 December*
> EMBLEM: *Jesuit cassock, holding a crucifix, baptism bowl, heart and pilgrim's hat*

A poor linguist and sufferer from seasickness, St Francis Xavier was nevertheless eager to carry the message of Christ to far-off lands. He was born in the Basque region and studied in Paris, where he met Ignatius of Loyola. With him and five others, they formed the Society of Jesus, popularly known as the Jesuits.

After the men were ordained as priests in 1534, Ignatius sent Francis to join Father Simon Rodriguez in Lisbon. Seven years later the young missionary set sail for Goa, western India.

After a journey lasting over a year, he landed to find a decadent Portuguese community of clerks and merchants who had abandoned their Christian ideals and virtues. Francis lived simply among the people and hoped to encourage them as converts by setting lessons to their music. Through his example as a Christian, he tried to counteract the greed of the cruel colonists.

For seven years he travelled through southern India, Ceylon (now Sri Lanka) and Malaysia, sleeping on the floor and living off boiled rice and water.

Always having a bowl to hold water for baptism, Francis converted many, especially among the Parava tribe, who still follow the faith to this day.

TO THE FAR EAST
In 1549, Francis ventured to Japan where he translated the key tenets of Christianity. By currying the favour of the ruling Mikado, he was given the use of an empty Buddhist temple to practise his faith. He established a Christian community, but it was subject to persecution in future years.

In 1552, Francis briefly returned to Goa but felt compelled to reach out to new horizons. The conviction that the unbaptized were condemned to an eternity in hell drove Francis to preach in China, then a country closed to all foreigners.

Horribly seasick during the journey, he asked to be left on a small island, Chang-Chuen-Shan, near Hong Kong. Unable to make the crossing to the mainland, he took a gamble and went with a Chinese man who promised to sneak him into China.

Alas, he was abandoned. Being exposed to bad weather and weak from malnutrition, Francis died before arriving. His coffin was packed with lime, to preserve the corpse, and taken to Goa. His body proved incorruptible and is enshrined in a church there.

Left: The missionary, St Francis Xavier (artist unknown c.1545).

Left: St Francis Xavier and his entourage in a detail from a folding screen (Japanese School, 16th century).

PIUS V

A STERN REFORMER WHO TOLERATED NO LAXITY AMONG HIS OWN KIND, PIUS V WAS JUST AS RUTHLESS IN STAMPING OUT THE MUSLIM PRESENCE IN EASTERN EUROPE.

KEY FACTS
Pope
DATES: *1504–72*
BIRTH PLACE: *Bosco, Italy*
FEAST DAY: *30 April*
EMBLEM: *Papal vestments*

St Pius V entered the Church when he was a youth of 15, and became a diligent priest. He held office as bishop, cardinal and inquisitor-general before being appointed pope in 1566.

At this time the Church was in a fragile state. Congregations had turned to the new churches of the Reformation. Morale was low among the clergy. The previous pope was infamous for his nepotism. The pope before him was the unpopular Paul IV, the fanatical priest Caraffa, who suppressed Protestantism by violent means.

PAPAL POLICY

Pius V started his reign as he meant to continue it. The Church was to be an example of discipline, modest living and charity. The usual lavish party to celebrate papal ordination was cancelled. Instead, the money went to fund hospitals and the poor.

He insisted bishops live in their own diocese, not luxuriate in Rome. Priests were commanded to teach the faith to the young within their parishes. The Roman Catechism, the statement of belief, was completed after years of preparation, and translated into different languages. The Missal was reformed, as well.

Although Pius's methods were stern, congregations approved of his reforms. During his papacy, he led the Inquisition, determined to stamp out Islam inside Europe. At a political level, he allowed papal ships to join those of Spain and Venice in an alliance that defeated the Turks at the Battle of Lepanto in 1571. This victory proved decisive in breaking Muslim power in the eastern Mediterranean region.

In England, however, Pius V disappointed Catholics by not insisting they fall under the authority of the Roman Church. Indeed, his excommunication of Queen Elizabeth I only led to further persecutions of Catholics in that country, including the destruction of their legal rights.

But, in Europe, many Catholics admired his leadership. They saw him as a hero against the Turks and Protestantism, and as a pope who strengthened the Roman Catholic Church and encouraged his flock.

Right: Pope Pius V *(Scipione Pulzone, 1570).*

TERESA OF ÁVILA

This devout nun courted controversy during her lifetime by challenging the established Carmelite Order and by claiming numerous visions and communications with Christ.

> **KEY FACTS**
> *Mystic, virgin*
> DATES: *1515–82*
> BIRTH PLACE: *Ávila, Spain*
> PATRON OF: *Spain, Spanish Catholic writers, Carmelites*
> FEAST DAY: *15 October*
> EMBLEM: *Pen and book, an angel, burning lance or arrow*

Teresa de Capeda y Ahumada was born at Ávila to a wealthy Castilian family. She was a bright, independent girl whose piety was evident from an early age. After her mother's death, her father sent her to an Augustinian convent, where she discovered her calling to the Church. Aged 20, and against her father's wishes, she entered a Carmelite convent. Within a short time, however, Teresa was taken gravely ill and left the convent to be cared for by her family. Although she never regained full health, she returned to the Carmelites, where she enjoyed the sociable, relaxed environment of the order.

Following the death of her father in 1543, Teresa became committed to a more private,

Below: Teresa of Ávila's Vision of a Dove *(Peter Paul Rubens, c.1614).*

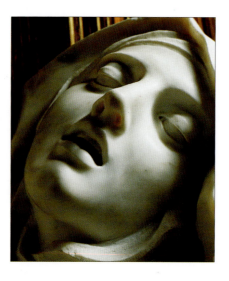

Above: Detail of the Ecstasy of Saint Teresa, *held in the Church of Santa Maria della Vittoria in Rome (Gianlorenzo Bernini, c.1645–52).*

contemplative life. One particular incident changed her life: she collapsed in front of an image of Christ, later waking and realizing she must renounce all worldly emotion and live only for Him.

VISIONARY
From the moment of her conversion, Teresa had visions and went into deep spiritual trances when she prayed. She felt misunderstood by her fellow nuns, who were dismissive of her mystic experiences. For the rest of her life she continued to have rapturous visions. In particular, she suffered a pain in her side, inflicted, she claimed, by an angel who thrust a burning lance into her heart. Her powers of contemplation developed into a deep devotion and she referred to herself as "Teresa of Jesus".

REFORMER
After meeting Peter of Alcantara, Teresa was moved to follow his example of strict penance and mental prayer. She requested permission from the pope to open a small house. The order would be named St Joseph after her patron saint. When the secret plans were revealed, the Carmelite nuns and influential people of Ávila asked the pope to stop them. Teresa appealed to Spain's King Philip II, who resented Rome's authority. This caused angry confrontation between Church and State and Teresa was imprisoned for two

> "ST TERESA, GRANT THAT MY EVERY THOUGHT, DESIRE AND AFFECTION MAY BE CONTINUALLY DIRECTED TO DOING THE WILL OF GOD, WHETHER I AM IN JOY OR IN PAIN, FOR HE IS WORTHY TO BE LOVED AND OBEYED FOREVER. OBTAIN FOR ME THIS GRACE, THOU WHO ART SO POWERFUL WITH GOD; MAY I BE ALL ON FIRE, LIKE THEE, WITH THE HOLY LOVE OF GOD."
>
> PRAYER OF INTERCESSION TO ST TERESA OF ÁVILA

DIRECTORY OF SAINTS

years before she was permitted to open a Carmelite subgroup. Her nuns, known as Discalced, or Barefoots, wore coarse brown habits and rope sandals to show their lives of poverty.

During the next few years, Teresa travelled across Spain establishing convents. Her nuns were separated from the world, lived on alms, were forbidden to eat meat, and were instructed by Teresa in meditation.

She founded 16 convents and 14 monasteries, because men, too, wanted to take the vows of the Discalced. These male orders were organized with the help of another mystic, John of the Cross.

Below: The Communion of Saint Teresa of Ávila *(Claudio Coello, 17th century).*

Left: Saint Teresa of Ávila *(Gregorio Fernandez, 1625).*

Teresa's writings are testament to her great personal devotion and her thoughts on a life of prayer and contemplation. Chief among her works are *The Interior Castle* and *The Way of Perfection*. The books, which describe the journey of the "soul toward a perfect unity with God", continue to be published in numerous languages.

Teresa of Ávila died at the convent of Alba de Tormes. The odour of violets and sweet oil emanated from her tomb. It was opened and a hand was cut off illicitly, and this was found to work miracles. Her remains were reburied in 1585 in a tomb built by the Duke of Alba. Teresa was canonized by Pope Gregory XV in 1622, and declared a Doctor of the Church in 1970, the first woman to win this recognition. Her order continues to prove the need for retreat and prayer in the modern world.

ST PETER OF ALCANTARA

St Teresa of Ávila was inspired by the life and teachings of another great mystic, Peter of Alcantara. Born Peter Garavito, he was ordained a Franciscan, but longed for a more rigorous discipline. In 1538, he became head of the strict order in Estremadura, Spain, but met with opposition when he tried to reform them further. He went on to found a small, reformed Alcantrine Franciscan order at a friary in Pedrosa. Peter encouraged Teresa to follow his rules of avoiding meat and wine, and walking barefoot. His treatise on prayer and meditation has been translated into many languages. He was canonized in 1669.

Above: St Peter of Alcantara visited by a dove *(engraving by A. Masson after a painting by Francisco de Zurbarán, c.1560).*

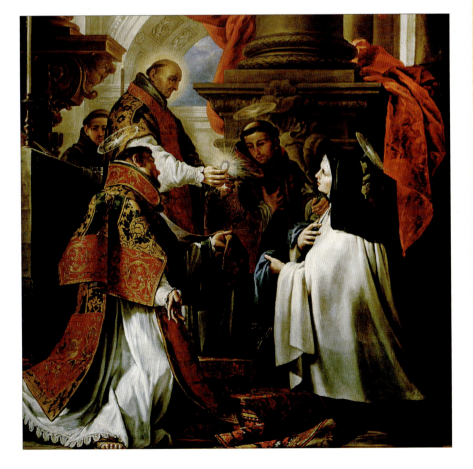

435

LUIS BERTRAN

LUIS BERTRAN WAS A GIFTED PREACHER WHO CONVERTED THOUSANDS OF SOUTH AMERICAN INDIANS AND CARIBBEAN ISLANDERS TO CHRISTIANITY.

> **KEY FACTS**
> *Missionary in the New World*
> DATES: *1526–81*
> BIRTH PLACE: *Valencia, Spain*
> PATRON OF: *Colombia*
> FEAST DAY: *9 October*
> EMBLEM: *Dominican habit*

A Dominican priest with a serious nature, Luis Bertran was a great preacher and apostle, known for his austerity. For many years, he trained Dominican novices and was admired for his teaching, profound wisdom and counselling skills. Teresa of Ávila is said to have turned to him for advice when she was reforming the Carmelite Order.

Athough he spent most of his life in his native Valencia, Luis' most significant work was carried out during his six years as a missionary to Latin America. In 1562, he was sent to a Dominican priory in Cartagena, Colombia, where he began to preach through an interpreter.

There are stories that his mission was successful because he inspired his listeners through an exhilarating combination of prophecy, miracles and talking in tongues. Certainly, his conversion rate was high – he baptized thousands of people during his travels around South America and the Caribbean Islands.

Recalled to Valencia in 1568, Louis began to train preachers for the missions. He emphasized the importance of prayer, simple Christian living and the need to reinforce words with actions.

Luis Bertran was one of the very first missionaries to speak out against the greed, cruelty and violence of many of the Spanish conquistadors. He was taken ill in Valencia Cathedral and died 18 months later.

JOHN OF THE CROSS

JOHN OF THE CROSS IS ONE OF SPAIN'S GREATEST MYSTICAL THEOLOGIANS, LOVED FOR THE BEAUTY OF HIS POETRY AND PITIED FOR THE SUFFERING THAT HE WAS MADE TO ENDURE.

> **KEY FACTS**
> *Poet and mystic*
> DATES: *1542–91*
> BIRTH PLACE: *Near Ávila, Spain*
> PATRON OF: *Mystics, poets*
> FEAST DAY: *14 December*
> EMBLEM: *Carmelite habit, book*

Born to a poor but noble Spanish family, John of the Cross attended a Jesuit college and became a Carmelite friar in 1563.

Teresa of Ávila inspired John with her reform of the Carmelite Order, the Decalced (Barefoot) Carmelites. With Teresa's help, he set up a Decalced Carmelite friary in a hovel in Duruelo.

The Carmelite Order rejected their reforms, and in 1575 John of the Cross was imprisoned. Subjected to extremely harsh treatment, John found expression for his suffering in poetry dedicated to his search for, and love of, God. After nine months he escaped and continued his spiritual work, founding a college at Baeza and working at monasteries in Granada and Segovia.

At the end of his life, John was once again harshly treated, this time by the Decalced Carmelites, who now found his views too moderate. He died in 1591 after having written some of the most moving poetry in Christian literature, such as *The Dark Night of the Soul*, *The Spiritual Canticle* and *The Living Flame of Love*.

Left: St John of the Cross *(Joaquín Vaquero Turcios, 20th century).*

PETER CANISIUS

CATHOLICS AND PROTESTANTS ALIKE ADMIRED ST PETER CANISIUS FOR HIS MODERATION DURING A PERIOD OF STRIFE AMONG CHRISTIANS IN THE 16TH CENTURY.

> **KEY FACTS**
> *Jesuit Doctor of the Church*
> DATES: *1521–97*
> BIRTH PLACE: *Nijmegen, Holland*
> PATRON OF: *Germany, Catholic press, catechism writers*
> FEAST DAY: *21 December*
> EMBLEM: *Jesuit habit*

Peter Canisius rejected a legal career and marriage in Holland to join the Society of Jesus, or Jesuits. In 1552, he was sent to revive the Roman Catholic Church in Vienna, where he found deserted monasteries and many lapsed believers.

He applied all his energy to teaching the faith and strengthening the Catholic Church. He skilfully avoided confrontation with the Protestants by emphasizing a common belief in Christ's teachings. He also won the respect of the Viennese by nursing the sick during the plague.

Canisius quickly recognized the importance of the printing presses flourishing at this time. His numerous writings persuaded thousands to return to the Church, and his Catechism (1555), was translated into 15 languages. He helped found the University of Fribourg in Switzerland, where he died in 1597.

Left: Peter Canisius the Preacher *(attr. to Pierre Wuilleret, c.1635).*

PHILIP NERI

PHILIP NERI, THE APOSTLE OF ROME, WAS A MAN OF GREAT INTUITION AND HUMOUR WHOSE PATIENCE AND GOOD ADVICE WON HIM MANY SUPPORTERS AMONG THE PEOPLE OF ROME.

> **KEY FACTS**
> *Founder of the Congregation of the Oratory in Rome*
> DATES: *1515–95*
> BIRTH PLACE: *Florence, Italy*
> FEAST DAY: *26 May*
> EMBLEM: *Bell, book*

Kindly and charismatic, Philip Neri founded a brotherhood devoted to welfare. In 1533, he abandoned business to live in poverty in Rome. His charisma drew loyal followers to him. In 1548, he set up a fraternity to care for the sick and the many pilgrims to the city.

After he was ordained in 1551, he formed the Congregation of the Oratory in San Girolamo. His followers took no vows and did not abandon their property or dedicate their lives to a monastic community. Pope Gregory XIII approved the order in 1575.

The Holy See called for Philip's advice in 1593, when it was reluctant to recognize Henry IV of France, a former Protestant. Philip told them to forgive the king for his lapse.

Philip died in 1595 and was so well loved that he was instantly recognized as a saint. The Oratory Order is found all over the Catholic world.

Left: The interior of the 19th-century Brompton Oratory in London, dedicated to Philip Neri.

ROYAL SAINTS

MANY MONARCHS ARE VENERATED FOR THEIR BRAVE DEFENCE OF CHRISTIANITY. SOME GAVE THEIR LIVES FOR THAT CAUSE; OTHERS RULED WITH ESPECIAL WISDOM AND BENEVOLENCE.

It may be difficult to reconcile the virtuous qualities of sainthood with the characteristics of the rich and mighty, but many saints were, in fact, also powerful monarchs. In their privileged positions, these holy men and women ruled with great fortitude, promoting Christianity through example and sacrifice.

Right: Edward the Confessor in stained glass from Canterbury, England (15th century).

WARRIOR SAINTS

Many kings have been involved in warfare, protecting their borders and Christianity on behalf of their countrymen. Some, including Vladimir and Alexander Nevski, were soldiers. These early rulers of Russia used arms to quell invaders but proved righteous monarchs.

Henry II, another militant man, went to war to establish the borders of Germany and became emperor in 1014. After this, he turned to his religion and prayer, built monasteries, and promoted welfare for the poor. He was said to be so pious that his marriage was never consummated. Henry II was canonized in 1146, while his wife Cunegund was canonized in 1200.

Other saintly warrior kings include Stephen of Hungary, who limited the power of the nobles, reduced tribal tensions and installed a judicial system. Stephen made Hungary a Christian country, and was a heroic leader.

SPREADING THE FAITH

As Christianity began to take root in Europe, monarchs played a vital role in imparting the faith to their subjects. English kings, such as Ethelbert of Kent and Oswald, were pioneers of the faith and venerated for encouraging the first Christian missions. Edward the Confessor was known for his visions and miraculous cures of the ill. He devoted much of his time to the establishment of the Church and the monasteries in England, and was loved for his kind and fair rule.

Norway's patron saint, King Olaf, established the Christian faith among his people and, after

Left: St Cunegund, empress and wife of Henry II, holding the model of a church (the Master of Messkirch, c.1530–38).

> "DEAR SON, IF YOU COME TO REIGN, DO THAT WHICH BEFITS A KING, THAT IS, BE SO JUST AS TO DEVIATE IN NOTHING FROM JUSTICE, WHATEVER MAY BEFALL YOU."
>
> ST LOUIS, KING OF FRANCE

Above: A statue of Stephen of Hungary near the Freedom Bridge in Budapest, Hungary.

his death in battle, was credited with miracles and a healing spring that began to flow from his grave.

MARTYRED MONARCHS

Several Christian monarchs have been martyred for their faith. One was the English boy king, Edward the Martyr, who was killed in AD 979 in a power struggle for the throne. Another, Edmund of Abingdon, was cruelly murdered by Viking invaders when he refused to deny his faith.

Two Scandinavian kings, Canute of Denmark and Eric of Sweden, also gave their lives for their Christian beliefs. Canute's murder at an altar was followed by many miracles and wonders. Sweden became a Christian country under Eric, but he was tortured and beheaded by attacking soldiers. These Scandinavian kings had large cultuses until the Reformation, when the Protestant movement began to overwhelm the Roman Catholic Church in northern Europe.

QUEENLY SAINTS

By the 11th century, the Scots had a pious queen. Margaret of Scotland was recognized for both her devotion to her family and her deep faith, as witnessed by her charitable work for the poor and for prisoners.

Elizabeth of Portugal was married to King Denis of Portugal. He was a violent man, but she converted him to the faith. She brought comfort and aid to orphans and "fallen women", and founded hospitals. Pilgrims and the very poor turned to her for hospitality and care.

Her distant relative, after whom she was named, Elizabeth of Hungary, likewise established hospitals, as well as founding the first orphanage in central Europe. The final part of her life was austere, poverty-stricken and devoted to prayer and charity. Her relics at the church of St Elizabeth at Marburg drew hordes of pilgrims until, in 1539, the Lutheran Philip of Hesse removed them and hid them in an unknown site.

Right: A portrait of St Vladimir (anonymous Russian artist, 1905).

Although many later monarchs continued to support the Catholic Church and to exercise their rule with Christian values, few European kings or queens were canonized after the Reformation.

KING LOUIS IX OF FRANCE

Louis IX took up arms for his faith, but he dedicated much of his life to spiritual causes. His subjects knew him as a man who was severe in his habits, devoting long hours to prayer. He built monasteries and a hospital for the poor. He was also admired for his efforts to show justice, even though his courtiers sometimes thwarted his good intentions. His courage in fighting for Christendom aroused great respect and he led two crusades, meeting his death at Tunis in 1270. During this last expedition, Louis tried to reconcile the Greeks to the Church of Rome.

Above: King Louis IX of France (St Louis) embarking on his first crusade in 1248 (manuscript illumination, c.1325).

TURIBIUS OF LIMA

TURIBIUS WAS A TIRELESS APOSTLE, BLESSED WITH INTELLIGENCE AND A STRONG MORAL SENSE. HE SPOKE NUMEROUS LOCAL DIALECTS, WHICH ENDEARED HIM TO THE PEOPLE OF PERU.

KEY FACTS
Archbishop and missionary
DATES: *1538–1606*
BIRTH PLACE: *Mayorga, Spain*
PATRON OF: *Bishops of Latin America*
FEAST DAY: *23 March*
EMBLEM: *Archbishop's vestments*

Turibius Alfonso de Mogrobejo was born in Spain and studied law at the University of Salamanca. His reputation as a scholar and professor led to his appointment as chief judge of the Inquisition Court, and to his becoming Archbishop of Lima. He protested his inadequacy for the latter post – an unusual appointment, as he was a layman – but took orders and was made archbishop before travelling to Peru in 1581.

As he visited the members of his vast new diocese, he found immorality and tyranny to be rife amongst the Spanish colonists. He saw that their Peruvian converts were not given the benefit of good Christian teaching and set about reforming the communities by building churches and hospitals. In 1591, he established the first seminary in the Americas.

Turibius was sensitive and considerate to his congregation, and his kindness encouraged trust. His implacable stand against tyranny was so effective that many converted to the faith. He died in Santa, Peru, having achieved considerable success in his mission.

Above: The monastery of St Turibius of Lima in Potes, Spain.

FRANCIS SOLANO

THIS DEDICATED MISSIONARY SHOWED PROFOUND COMPASSION FOR HUMAN SUFFERING AND BECAME KNOWN AS "THE APOSTLE OF AMERICA", WINNING NUMEROUS CONVERTS TO CHRISTIANITY.

KEY FACTS
Missionary
DATES: *1549–1610*
BIRTH PLACE: *Montilla, near Córdoba, Spain*
PATRON OF: *Peru, Bolivia, Paraguay, Uruguay, Chile, Argentina*
FEAST DAY: *14 July*
EMBLEM: *Franciscan habit*

Local legend has it that Francis Solano addressed his congregation in one language but was understood by everyone, irrespective of their tongue. In fact, the Franciscan priest was a gifted linguist and this talent helped him make many converts.

Ordained as a priest in Seville in 1576, Francis spent several years in the Franciscan convent before travelling to the Americas in 1589. His ship was destined for Peru, but was wrecked on the way and abandoned by the Spanish crew. Francis rescued 80 African slaves, who were on board, encouraging them to cling to a section of the ship. Inspired by his prayers, they landed in Lima after two months at sea.

Left: Seville Cathedral, Spain, where Francis Solano was ordained in 1576. It is the largest Roman Catholic cathedral in the world.

Francis spent the next 20 years evangelizing in Argentina, Chile, Colombia and Peru. He charmed his congregation by playing his lute in veneration of Mary, the Blessed Virgin, and they often joined him in song. Later, as Guardian of Lima, Francis aroused anger because of his attacks on corrupt colonists. Nevertheless, his death was the cause of widespread grief. His relics are kept in Buenos Aires and Rome.

ROSE OF LIMA

In 1671, Rose of Lima was canonized by Pope Clement X, thus becoming the first officially recognized saint of the New World. She is the patron of South America.

> **KEY FACTS**
> First saint of the New World
> DATE: *1586–1617*
> BIRTH PLACE: *Lima, Peru*
> PATRON OF: *Peru, Bolivia, Central and South America, the Philippines*
> FEAST DAY: *23 August*
> EMBLEM: *Crown of roses*

As a young woman, Rose was so mortified by her own beauty that she rubbed her face and hands with pepper and lye to ruin her complexion. This pious child was born to modest parents and christened Isabel, though she was always known as Rose. She chose to model herself on St Catherine of Siena by living a life of purity and self-denial. Though her parents were anxious for her to marry, Rose vowed to remain a virgin and became a tertiary of the Dominican Order. However, she remained a conscientious daughter, working to help her parents by growing flowers and making exquisite lace to sell at the local market.

EXTREME PENANCE
To bring herself closer to God, Rose built a hut in her parents' garden and lived there in virtual seclusion. In imitation of Christ, who was forced to wear a crown of thorns, she wore on her head a circlet of silver studded inside with small spikes. She prayed for long hours, often in spiritual despair, because she felt she was not worthy of God's love.

Throughout this time, she faced constant ridicule from her community and fierce opposition from her parents. Her self-inflicted penances were so extreme that she attracted the attention of the Church, which held an inquiry into her behaviour. Her friend, the archbishop St Turibius of Lima, defended her, and the Church eventually conceded that her visions and mystic exaltations were holy and true.

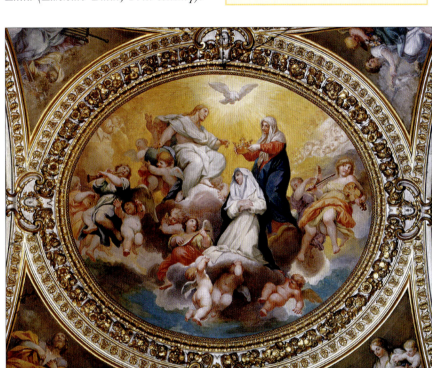

Below: A ceiling painting in Rome showing Mary crowning St Rose of Lima (Lazzaro Baldi, 17th century).

Left: A statue of Rose of Lima outside the Mission San Francisco de Asís, California (20th century).

CARE FOR THE SICK
In spite of her own suffering, Rose spent much time among the sick and needy of Lima. However, after many years of physical deprivation, her health declined and she was taken to live with the government official Don Gonzales de Massa and his wife, who nursed her through a long and painful illness. They later testified as to the words she used in prayer, "Lord, increase my sufferings, and with them increase thy love in my heart."

By the time Rose died in 1617 – still only a young woman at the age of 31 – her holiness was widely recognized. The people of Lima went into mourning. Dominicans, city dignitaries and officials took it in turn to carry her coffin to the grave. Her example still holds much power.

ROBERT BELLARMINE

AMONG HIS MANY ACHIEVEMENTS, THE BRILLIANT THEOLOGIAN ROBERT BELLARMINE WAS RESPONSIBLE FOR CORRECTING THE VULGATE BIBLE AND WRITING A CATECHISM, BOTH IN USE TODAY.

KEY FACTS
Archbishop and theologian
DATES: *1542–1621*
BIRTH PLACE: *Montepulciano, Tuscany, Italy*
PATRON OF: *Catechists and catechumens*
FEAST DAY: *17 September*
EMBLEM: *Archbishop's vestments*

This great Italian archbishop chose a life of service to God over a secular career. Despite his father's wishes that he become a politician, Robert Bellarmine entered a novitiate in Rome and went on to teach in Jesuit colleges in Rome and Florence.

GIFTED THEOLOGIAN
After his ordination in 1570, Robert became the first Jesuit professor of the University of Louvain. It was here that his writings and lectures began to stir strong feelings and debate. The Church brought him to Milan as professor of controversial theology at the Roman College. The lectures he gave there formed the basis of one of his greatest works, *Disputations on the Controversies of the Christian Faith*, which is described as "the most complete defence of Catholic teaching yet published". It was read eagerly by all Christians, although his enemies denounced it as being so clever it must have been the joint effort of several Jesuit scholars. The work was banned in England.

Above: St Robert Bellarmine, in a painting from the Church of Sant' Ignazio in Rome.

Below: The trial of Galileo by Pope Urban VIII during the Inquisition in 1633 (Italian School, 17th century).

CONTROVERSY
Robert continued to attract controversy when his stand on the power of the Church was opposed by the French and by James I of England because he insisted the pope had complete authority above that of any monarch. His *De potestate papae* on this subject was burnt by the Paris *parlement*. Then, contrary to other Church leaders at the time, Robert was gentle with Galileo, asking him only to produce better evidence about the sun's movements.

Appointed Archbishop of Capua in 1602, Robert dedicated his time to preaching and to attending to his parish. His last appointment, in 1605, was as Prefect of the Vatican Library.

SIMPLE LIFE, NOBLE DEATH
All his life, Robert Bellarmine lived on the bread and garlic diet of a peasant, denied himself fires in winter and gave his possessions to the poor. In old age, he continued to write, and his *Art of Dying* was translated into many languages. He died in Rome, but he had asked beforehand that the day of his death be marked each anniversary as a time to honour the stigmata of St Francis of Assisi. The Church granted this request.

FRANCIS OF SALES

THE FIRST SOLEMN BEATIFICATION TO TAKE PLACE IN ST PETER'S IN ROME WAS THAT OF ST FRANCIS OF SALES, A SAINT WHO WAS ADORED FOR HIS GENTLE LEADERSHIP.

KEY FACTS
Founder, Doctor of the Church
DATES: *1567–1622*
BIRTH PLACE: *Château de Sales, Savoy, France*
PATRON OF: *Journalists, editors and writers*
FEAST DAY: *24 January*
EMBLEM: *Archbishop's vestments*

Francis of Sales was physically frail from birth, but had a determined spirit and an unwavering faith. From an early age, he longed to join the Church. But his father refused his permission, instead sending Francis to study at the University of Paris. He later became a Doctor of Law at Padua in Italy. When a relative found Francis a position as provost to the Jesuit chapter in Geneva, his father finally relented and Francis was ordained.

Left: St Francis de Sales in the Desert *(Marco Antonio Franceschini, c.1700–10).*

MISSIONARY PRIEST
Francis volunteered as a missionary to Chablais, where he distributed notices explaining his work and Christ's message to attract his reluctant congregation. Trekking through isolated hamlets, he met many dangers, including a wolf attack and another by a mob. Yet, slowly, lapsed Catholics began to seek his guidance.

His success was acknowledged, and in 1602, the Church appointed him Bishop of Geneva. Francis lived in Annecy, where he was a popular preacher and began to compile his handwritten texts into books. His most famous work is the *Introduction to the Devout Life*. In addition to his writing, Francis was instrumental in the founding of the Order of the Visitation with his friend, St Jane Frances de Chantal in 1610.

In 1622, Francis accepted an invitation to join the Duke of Savoy at Avignon, hoping to gain privileges for his community. In every village he passed, people wanted him to stop and minister to them. It was bitterly cold, but Francis continued to preach throughout Advent and Christmas, before becoming ill and dying at a Visitandine convent in Lyons.

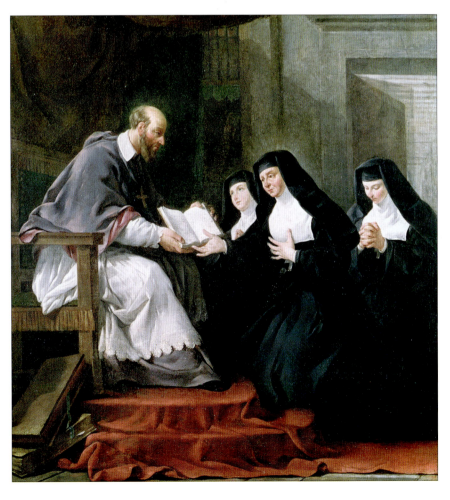

Right: St Francis of Sales *(Noel Halle, 18th century).*

ROQUE GONZALEZ

Although Roque Gonzalez spent two decades protecting the freedom of indigenous people in South America, he was martyred for his faith, along with two fellow missionaries.

> **KEY FACTS**
> *Martyr of Paraguay*
> **Dates:** *1576–1628*
> **Birth Place:** *Asunción, Paraguay*
> **Patron of:** *Posadas, Argentina, and Encarnación, Paraguay*
> **Feast Day:** *17 November*

Roque Gonzalez was born into a noble Spanish family in Asunción, Paraguay, and raised a strict Catholic. He was ordained in 1599 and ten years later joined the Jesuits to pursue his dream of becoming a missionary.

THE REDUCTIONS

Gonzalez was instrumental in founding the Reductions, an organization that created settlements for local tribes in which they could learn about Christianity. The Jesuits were passionately opposed to slavery and sought to teach, nurse and bring solace to the converts.

Without complaint, Roque endured bad weather, insects, illness and hunger, but his biggest problems came from the European "guardians". The Spanish authorities demanded that these officials be present on every mission, but they were disdainful, even brutal,

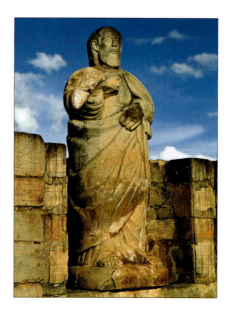

Left: A statue standing in the ruins of a Jesuit mission near Encarnación in Paraguay.

towards the indigenous people. This did not reflect on Roque, whose courtesy and simplicity won the admiration of numerous converts. He taught them valuable skills such as building and farming, and established churches and schools. After three years in the Reduction of St Ignatius of Loyola, Roque travelled east of the Parana and Uruguay Rivers, establishing six more communities.

In 1628, he was joined by Alonso Rodriguez and Juan de Castillo, also brothers of the Jesuit Reductions. They opened another Reduction near the Ijuhi River. Juan de Castillo was selected to stay there, while Roque and Alonso trekked to an even wilder area – Caaró, now part of southern Brazil.

OPPOSITION AND MURDER

Now, however, the missionaries met with hostility from the local medicine man, who incited some local tribesmen to attack the priest. Giving him no opportunity to defend himself, they brutally murdered him with their tomahawks. They killed Alonso, too, then dragged their bodies into the church the men had built and set it alight. A few days later, Juan de Castillo was beaten and murdered at the Ijuhi River mission.

Although these sad events were reported, the records were lost until the 19th century, when they were discovered in archives kept in Argentina. All three men were canonized as the Martyrs of Paraguay in 1988.

Left: A map of Brazil by a Dutch cartographer in the early 17th century.

LORENZO RUIZ

The first Filipino saint was afraid of martyrdom, but his faith sustained him so that, facing death, he proclaimed, "I am a Catholic and happy to die for God."

> **KEY FACTS**
> *Martyr of Japan*
> Dates: *1600–37*
> Birth Place: *Binondo, Manila, Philippines*
> Patron of: *Filipino youth*
> Feast Day: *28 September*

Married with three children, Lorenzo Ruiz was a member of the lay brotherhood, the Holy Rosary. In 1636, he was falsely accused of murder and, fearing an unfair trial and imprisonment, he sought refuge with the Dominicans. He sailed to Japan with Father Antonio Gonzalez and others.

On their arrival in Okinawa, the Emperor Tokugawa Yemitsu ordered the ship's Christians to be arrested. Faced by a tribunal in Nagasaki, a frightened Lorenzo asked if a denunciation of Christianity would bring release. His translator consulted the judges, but Lorenzo found his courage and cried out, "I am a Christian." His brave confession brought terrible retribution. He was burnt, hung upside down and beheaded, and his body was thrown into the sea. Lorenzo was one of 17 people martyred by the Emperor. They were canonized as Martyrs of Japan in 1987.

Left: The Franciscan Martyrs in Japan *(Don Juan Carreño de Miranda, 17th century).*

MARTIN DE PORRES

The life of Martin de Porres was one of humble devotion. He is venerated for his constant, unassuming service to the poor and his miraculous cures of the sick.

> **KEY FACTS**
> *Charity worker*
> Dates: *1579–1639*
> Birth Place: *Lima, Peru*
> Patron of: *Social justice, public education, public health service, people of mixed race, Italian barbers and hairdressers*
> Feast Day: *3 November*

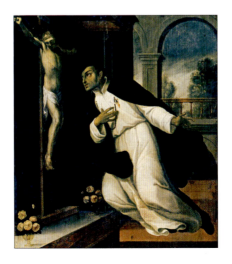

Above: St Martin de Porres (artist and date unknown).

Martin de Porres was one of two illegitimate children born to a Spanish knight and a freed black woman. His mother apprenticed the 12-year-old Martin to a barber-surgeon, from whom he learnt to care for the sick. Three years later, he was admitted to the Dominican Convent of the Holy Rosary, first as a lay brother and later as a coadjutor brother.

Here, Martin helped to establish a hospital and an orphanage. He also welcomed African slaves, who were comforted on their arrival in Lima. Animals loved him, and it was said he could feed a dog, cat and mouse from the same bowl. One of his many duties at the convent was to handle the alms for the poor, and his careful budgeting allowed him to feed and clothe hundreds of needy people in the city.

Martin was acquainted with St Rose of Lima, and when he died, as at her funeral, noblemen and Church officials were honoured to carry his coffin to its grave.

PETER CLAVER

This Spanish missionary was blessed "by God with those gifts that particularly pertain to apostles, of miracles, of prophecy and of reading hearts".

KEY FACTS
Missionary
Dates: *1580–1654*
Birth Place: *Verdu, Catalonia, Spain*
Patron of: *Colombia; missions to slaves and African Americans*
Feast Day: *9 September*

In the late 16th century, the port of Cartagena in Colombia was the centre of a thriving slave trade. Thousands of captive Africans arrived at the port every month. Here, Peter Claver baptized about 300,000 enslaved people and ministered also to traders, sailors, prisoners and others in need.

Born in Catalonia in Spain and educated at the University of Barcelona, Peter Claver's spiritual journey began at the Jesuit college in Majorca. Here, he met Alphonsus Rodriguez, who foretold that they both had a future in South America.

Peter left for Cartagena in 1610, and was ordained there by the Jesuits five years later. Inspired by working alongside Father Alfonso de Sandoval, who had been ministering to the slaves for 40 years, Claver declared himself "the slave of Negroes forever".

Below: Sts Peter Claver and Aloysius Gonzaga (St Xavier Church, Amsterdam, Holland).

Left: A stained glass showing St Peter Claver (Chapelle de la Colombière, Chalon sur Saône, France, 1930).

MISSIONARY TO THE SLAVES

Peter would meet the slave ships as they came into the harbour. Conscious of the need for immediate emotional and physical care, he comforted the slaves with his gentle manner and gave them gifts of medicines, food, brandy and lemons. He carried pictures to convey Christ's life and his promise of redemption, explaining to his helpers, "we must speak to them with our hands before we try to speak to them with our lips". He later visited the plantations and mines where these slaves were put to work. Refusing the hospitality of the owners, who were not all happy to see him, he stayed in the slaves' quarters.

In 1650, Peter succumbed to a plague, which left him weak and incapacitated. He was confined to his cell. He was neglected by everyone until Dona Isabel de Urbina, who had funded his charities, came to his rescue and, with her sister, nursed him. Four years later, Peter took Mass before falling into a coma. The people of Cartagena, realizing they were losing an extraordinary priest, were anxious to kiss his hands. Even plantation owners sensed his greatness, and after his death his cell was stripped of relics. He was canonized, along with his friend Alphonsus Rodriguez, in 1888.

JOSEPH OF COPERTINO

CREDITED WITH POWERS OF LEVITATION, AS WELL AS WITH MANY OTHER MIRACLES, THIS SIMPLE, THOUGH MISUNDERSTOOD, PRIEST GAINED THE NICKNAME THE "FLYING FRIAR".

KEY FACTS
Mystic, miracle worker
DATES: *1603–63*
BIRTH PLACE: *Copertino, near Brindisi, Italy*
PATRON OF: *Aviation, astronauts, students and students' examinations*
FEAST DAY: *18 September*
EMBLEM: *Flying in Franciscan habit*

The story of Joseph of Copertino is a sad one. His father's death left his mother penniless and she considered the slow-witted Joseph a tiresome burden. He was widely ridiculed and known for his violent temper. He seemed incapable of learning a trade and was rejected by local monasteries until Franciscans at Grottella accepted him as a servant. The young boy became serious in his devotions and performed menial tasks without complaint.

Despite his academic struggles, Joseph was ordained in 1628 and legends began to surround him. The mere sight of religious imagery or the mention of holy names sent Joseph into a state of ecstasy during which his body would rise in the air.

INQUISITION AND EXILE

In Joseph's 17 years at Grottella, witnesses recorded 70 incidents of levitation. One extraordinary occurrence reportedly took place during the construction of a cross of Calvary. The centre strut was 11m/36ft high and very heavy. Ten men couldn't lift it, but during the night, Joseph flew through the air, raised the strut and fixed it to the earth.

This behaviour so worried his superiors that he was prohibited from celebrating Mass, eating with his brethren or attending processions. As his trances continued, and the public interest in him increased, Joseph was taken for questioning by the Inquisitors in Naples. Finding no fault with him, they sent him to Rome,

Above: Pope Urban VIII *(Gianlorenzo Bernini, c.1625–30), before whom Joseph experienced a religious ecstasy.*

Below: St Joseph of Copertino levitates *in front of an image of the Virgin. The saint was known for such ecstasies.*

where, at an audience with Pope Urban VIII, Joseph fell into an ecstasy and the pope decided to send him to Assisi.

With crowds of people seeking out the "Flying Friar", Joseph was exiled to a monastery at Pietrarossa, and was forbidden to speak or write to anyone. When pilgrims continued to clamour for a glimpse of his miracles, he was sent to an even more remote monastery at Fossombrone, and then to Assisi, where he was kept in strict isolation. Although consoled by his visions, Joseph died in solitude. In 1767, he was canonized for his humility and patience.

VINCENT DE PAUL

A CLEVER AND DIPLOMATIC FRENCH PRIEST, ADEPT AT PERSUADING THE WEALTHY TO BE GENEROUS TO THE POOR. TODAY, HIS SOCIETIES CONTINUE HIS TRADITION OF CHARITY AND SOCIAL WELFARE.

> **KEY FACTS**
> *Founder of charitable orders, hospitals and orphanages*
> DATES: *1581–1660*
> BIRTH PLACE: *Landes, France*
> PATRON OF: *Charity workers, hospitals, prisoners, Madagascar*
> FEAST DAY: *27 September*
> EMBLEM: *White cloak, begging bowl*

Vincent de Paul was born in Gascony to a peasant family, but he escaped the harsh life of a farmer by studying under the Franciscans at Dax and later attending Toulouse University. He was ordained at 19 and undertook a journey to Rome, at which point he seemed to vanish for two years. Historians suspect that he obscured, or even invented, the truth about this time.

In fact, Vincent himself perpetuated the most famous account of these two years through letters he wrote to his patron, a Gascon judge called Monsieur de Comet. He claimed that, on his way from Toulouse to Narbonne, his ship was overwhelmed by Barbary pirates. He was sold into slavery at Tunis and endured two years there before, appealing to the Christian faith of one of his captors, he managed to escape to Marseilles.

Above: St Vincent de Paul *(attributed to Daniel Dumonstier, 17th century).*

Below: Saint Vincent de Paul and the Sisters of Charity *(Jean Andre, c.1729).*

Following this uncertain period, Vincent appeared in Rome, where he was given instructions by Pope Paul V to travel to the French court of Henry IV. Vincent remained in Paris as chaplain to the queen, which gave him access to the rich and powerful members of court. He was charming and kind and able to persuade many wealthy patrons to devote funds to his worthy causes.

CHARITY WORKER

Vincent's sensitivities to the suffering of others came to dominate his thinking. He met, and was profoundly influenced by, Francis of Sales, and expanded his work to found hospitals and orphanages. He also worked to improve the lives of galley slaves and gave missions to prisoners in Bordeaux.

Then, in 1625, he founded an order of priests to preach in remote villages, where they cared for convicts and the poor. From 1633, the men lived in small communal groups and became known as the Vincentians, or Lazarists. The order was so successful in its mission that the Archbishop of Paris

Above: An old people's home run by the Sisters of Charity at St Vincent de Paul's hospital in Peking (1900).

asked Vincent to train priests for parish work. For 27 years, Vincent gave weekly conferences, and his priests taught at seminaries around France. They also travelled as missionaries to Madagascar, Poland, Ireland, Scotland and countries in Africa.

Also in 1633, Vincent asked his friend, Louise de Marillac, to help him form an order of women to nurse the sick. At this time, nuns lived in enclosed houses, cut off from public lives. This new order, the Sisters of Charity, took a vow of obedience for one year only, this being the time the Church allowed noviciates to enjoy social contact. They renewed their vows yearly, but Vincent's rule allowed them to take their good works into the wider world.

INFLUENCE

Vincent de Paul had a profound effect on Church reform and was extremely popular and influential in his lifetime. He inspired countless men and women to care for the dispossessed, and the rich to fund the work. His Sisters of Charity and Vincentians continue to work all around the world, helping the homeless, the debt-ridden, orphans and prisoners. In 1833, Frederick Ozanam, a Frenchman, instituted a lay brotherhood in the name of Saint Vincent de Paul. The modern worldwide membership of SVP, as this charity is called, includes men and women, Catholics and Protestants. Vincent always insisted that Protestants be treated with courtesy and understanding.

Vincent's teaching of care and service, his gentle faith, and resolute belief in the sustaining love of God brought him many friends and admirers. He died peacefully and was buried at the church of Saint-Lazare. He was beatified in 1729 and Pope Clement XII canonized him in 1737.

Above: The Church of Saint Vincent de Paul in Paris (Rouargue Frères, 19th century).

> "IT IS OUR DUTY TO PREFER THE SERVICE OF THE POOR TO EVERYTHING ELSE, AND TO OFFER SUCH SERVICE AS QUICKLY AS POSSIBLE... OFFER THE DEED TO GOD AS YOUR PRAYER."
>
> ST VINCENT DE PAUL

LOUISE DE MARILLAC

When Louise de Marillac was widowed in 1625, she devoted herself to the charity work of Vincent de Paul. He depended on her good sense, and she helped found the Sisters of Charity, "whose convent is the sickroom; their chapel their parish church; their cloister, the city streets". She was an inspiring teacher and, under her guidance, women were committed to 40 houses of the Charity, working with the sick and giving shelter to distressed women. She was canonized in 1934. Her feast day is 15 March.

Above: Louise de Marillac distributing alms to the poor (Diogène Maillart, 1920).

SAINTLY POPES

THE FIRST POPES ARE VENERATED AS MARTYRS OF THE FAITH, BUT MANY OTHERS ARE REVERED FOR THE WISDOM, STRENGTH AND SPIRITUAL LEADERSHIP THEY DEMONSTRATED IN OFFICE.

The role of the papacy has often been fraught with spiritual and political strife. When Christianity was just beginning to be established, during persecution by the Roman Empire, a number of early popes were martyred for their faith. Later, popes struggled to unite the Church, which was being damaged by warring factions and corruption. Many of these holy men have been canonized in recognition of their faithfulness and spiritual leadership.

> "WHEN THE WORK OF GOD IS FINISHED, LET ALL GO OUT WITH THE DEEPEST SILENCE, AND LET REVERENCE BE SHOWN TO GOD."
>
> FROM THE RULE OF ST BENEDICT

Above: A fresco of Leo the Great (Italian School, 8th century AD).

THE MARTYRS

One of the first popes, Clement I, who died around AD 100, was a contemporary of Sts Peter and Paul. He was credited with miraculous powers, and some of his writings are extant, revealing him as a thoughtful theologian. His Epistle to the Corinthians is significant because it marks the first time a bishop of Rome intervened in the business of another Church. Clement I was martyred by having an anchor tied to his neck and being pushed into the sea. Allegedly, angels built him a tomb on the seabed, and this could be seen when the sea was at low tide.

Pope Callistus was born a slave and rebelled against Roman law by promoting marriage between free-born Christians and slaves. Kind and forgiving, he was thrown down a well and drowned in AD 222. Pope Cornelius was likewise resented for his policy of forgiveness to those who truly repented their sins. His attitude caused a split among churchmen, and the Romans beheaded him.

Sixtus II, who became pope in AD 257, was killed by the sword one year after he took office.

LEADERS OF THE FAITH

One of the most influential early popes was Leo the Great. During his reign, he freed Rome from the barbarians and healed a Church fractured by war and the spread of pagan beliefs. Both the people and the clergy needed clarification on Christian dogma. In a letter to the Council of Chalcedon, Leo explained that Jesus Christ is one person, in whom the divine and the human are united, but not mixed. This became a fundamental teaching of the Church.

Left: Coronation of Pope Celestine V in August 1294 (French School, 16th century).

The Church continued to strengthen under the rule of Pope Gregory the Great, an austere, devout man, who succeeded in establishing the primacy of Rome against claims from the Eastern Orthodox Church. He developed the Church liturgy and mounted a successful mission to England.

Gregory II, too, was an energetic apostle. He instigated reforms in the clergy, built churches and sustained the Church's authority against secular power. The monastery at Monte Cassino was revived under his care, and he built another in Rome, St Paul's-outside-the-Walls.

DIVISION AND REFORM

The problems between the Eastern and Western branches of the Church became urgent during the office of Pope Leo IX (1002–54). Under his rule, the Church increased its independence from secular authority, and he sent legates to confer with Michael Cerularius, Patriarch of Constantinople. Leo died before the schism between the East and West had widened into total separation. Leo was a holy man, and many miracles were attributed to him after his death.

Pope Gregory VII continued his predecessors' reformation of the Church and alienated many powerful people in the process. He was determined to stop the practice of laymen appointing officers of the Church, because these laymen were often the rich

and powerful, who used the clergy to extend their secular ambitions. The German Emperor Henry IV was infuriated by this reform and tried to depose Gregory, though he later famously repented by standing at the palace gates for three days in the snow.

Peter Celestine (or Celestine V) founded the Celestine Order, but was an unwilling and unworldly pope. He abdicated his office but was still canonized for his devout nature in 1313.

In the 16th century, while the Church was still reeling from the Reformation, Pope Pius V provided vigorous leadership. A key figure in the Counter-Reformation, he helped rid the Church of heresy and corruption, controlled excessive spending by the bishops, and reformed the liturgy, making the words and rituals accessible to ordinary worshippers.

In the 21st century, Pope Francis has canonized three popes: John XXII (pope 1958–63), John Paul II (pope 1978–2005) in 2014, and Paul VI (pope 1963–78) in 2018.

Left: St Peter's Basilica and Square, Rome, as depicted in the 18th century.

Left: Gregory the Great dictating a manuscript (illuminated manuscript, 9th century).

POPE PIUS X

Pope Pius X wanted "to renew all things in Christ". He opened the Church and her liturgy to ordinary people, encouraged daily attendance at Mass and welcomed children to partake of the Holy Eucharist. Church music was modernized, and, on Sundays, Pius X would deliver a short sermon in a Vatican courtyard, which anyone was welcome to attend. He faced problems with the French state, and was forced to sacrifice Church property in exchange for freedom from secular control. He also restated the Christian doctrine against what he saw as heretical interpretations, in what he termed the "Modernist" crisis. After his death in 1914, a cultus came quickly into being.

Above: Pope Pius X (c. 1905).

MARGUERITE BOURGEOYS

This pioneering educator, who established the first religious order in Canada and the first school in Montreal, became known as the "Mother of the Colony".

> **KEY FACTS**
> *Educator, founder of a religious order*
> DATES: *1620–1700*
> BIRTH PLACE: *Troyes, France*
> PATRON OF: *Poverty*
> FEAST DAY: *12 January*

Born into the large family of a rich merchant, Marguerite Bourgeoys enjoyed a privileged upbringing. After her mother's death in 1639, she cared for her younger siblings, but soon felt the calling of a religious vocation.

She joined a lay order of women called the Congregation of Troyes, an organization devoted to teaching the poor children of the area.

CALLED TO CANADA

In 1652, Marguerite's future took a dramatic turn when she met Monsieur de Maisonneuve, a governor in New France (now Canada). He was recruiting teachers for an outpost called Ville-Marie, and, because she was not a cloistered nun, Marguerite was able to accept the challenge.

She arrived at the fort in 1653, finding herself both teacher and nurse for the tiny community. As there was no permanent place of worship, she organized the building of the stone chapel of Notre-Dame-de-Bon-Secour in 1655. A year later, seeing an urgent need for education in this new land, she established the first Montreal school, teaching domestic, spiritual and academic subjects. The school thrived and she travelled back to France three times in the following years to enlist teachers.

Above: An engraving of a tattooed Iroquois Indian holding a snake and smoking a peace pipe (c.1701).

Below: Marguerite Bourgeoys with Canadian Indian converts (artist and date unknown).

FOUNDING EDUCATOR

Marguerite and her fellow teachers were very courageous women, spreading their schools across the wilderness of Quebec. They were resolved to educate the children of the Iroquois tribes as well as those of the French colonists, but they faced hardships of illness, hunger, fires, and violent attacks from the very people they hoped to help. In 1676, determined to persevere with her cause, Marguerite founded the Sisters of Notre Dame.

Sadly, by 1698, she had become exhausted by hardship, and chose to resign as the superior. In keeping with the selflessness of her life, she nursed a young nun who was dying. She prayed, "God, why do you not take me instead, I who am useless and good for nought!" The young nun lived and, a few days later, Marguerite died. Thousands mourned the loss of her wise, steady guidance.

Today, giving testimony to her faith and ambition, there are 200 convents and missions around the world following Marguerite's ideals of Christian education.

LOUIS GRIGNION DE MONTFORT

THIS UNCONVENTIONAL PRIEST ENRAGED CHURCH AUTHORITIES, BUT HIS MISSIONS TO THE POOR AND INSPIRATIONAL SERMONS ENSURED HIM RECOGNITION AS A FAITHFUL APOSTLE.

KEY FACTS
Missionary apostolic and founder
DATES: *1673–1716*
BIRTH PLACE: *Montfort, Brittany*
FEAST DAY: *28 April*

As a student in Paris, Louis de Montfort experienced such squalid poverty that his future course as a missionary to the poor was decided. After his ordination in Paris in 1700, he was sent to work in Poitiers. There he founded the Daughters of Wisdom, an order of nuns that nursed in hospitals, and took his own mission to the poorest quarters.

EVANGELIST TO THE POOR
He was very popular with the public, but his flamboyant speeches caused concern among his superiors. To enhance his lessons, Louis would make an effigy of the devil dressed as a rich woman, then burn irreligious books before it. Or he would act out the role of a dying sinner caught between the angels and the devil. His writing, too, was dramatic. *The True Devotion to the Blessed Virgin* gained a wide readership, except among theologians.

Banned from Poitiers for his evangelistic style, Louis was given the office of "missionary apostolic" by the pope. This allowed him to roam Brittany and Poitiers, which well suited his personality. The singing of the hymns that he wrote reinforced his intense and emotional preaching, and he encouraged the use of the rosary in prayer. Wherever he went, churches were restored and charity to the poor was revived. Lapsed believers returned to faith after attending his sermons, while, in La Rochelle, a number of Calvinists return-ed to the Roman Catholic Church.

In 1712, Louis founded an association of missionary priests called the Company of Mary. These men, and the women of his Daughters of Wisdom, were trained to follow his emotional approach to faith. The orders have both since become highly successful international apostolic and educational missions.

Louis Grignion de Montfort died in St-Laurent-sur-Sèvre and was canonized in 1947.

Right: Pope Pius XII canonized Louis Grignion de Montfort in 1947.

Above: Louis Grignion de Montfort in a church dedicated to him in St-Laurent-sur-Sèvre.

JOHN-BAPTIST DE LA SALLE

This saint made a major difference to the educational system in 17th-century France, and his influence is evident today in the continuing success of his schools.

KEY FACTS
Educator, founder of the Brothers of the Christian Schools
DATES: *1651–1719*
BIRTH PLACE: *Rheims, France*
PATRON OF: *Schoolteachers*
FEAST DAY: *7 April*

John-Baptist de La Salle, a French nobleman, became one of the most distinguished educators in Europe. He studied in Rheims and at Saint-Sulpice, in Paris, where he was ordained in 1678.

In 1679, he met Adrian Nyel, a layman hoping to start a school for poor boys. While he encouraged him, John-Baptist did not foresee the great role he himself would play in this endeavour. He later wrote, "God, who guides all things with wisdom and serenity …willed to commit me entirely to the development of the schools."

CHRISTIAN SCHOOLS
John-Baptist used his family home to house the schoolmasters. Patient and confident in his methods, he slowly gathered men dedicated to the profession. He sold his home, resigned as canon of Rheims and, with his 12 followers, drew up a Rule.

Teachers were to make a vow of obedience, renewable every year, and they agreed on a name – the Brothers of the Christian Schools. Rural congregations appealed to him to train youths who would then teach in the villages, so John-Baptist opened the first training school for teachers in Rheims in 1686, followed by others in Paris and Saint-Denis. He also opened free schools for poor boys in Paris.

He drew up statutes to govern his growing institution: no Brother of the Christian Schools should be ordained a priest, and no priest should be a teacher; classes were to be given in the vernacular, not Latin; pupils were to be silent and taught as a class, not as individuals. By 1700, there were schools across France. Today, there are more than 20,000 members, and Christian Brothers schools can be found across the French- and English-speaking worlds.

Although John-Baptist faced controversy within his brotherhood over rules and teaching methods, his contribution to the training of teachers and educational methods was significant, especially for working-class boys, who previously had been destined for manual labour. His methods of caring for delinquent boys made important advances in the rehabilitation of disturbed youth.

He died in Rheims after a short illness and was canonized in 1900. His relics lie in Rome.

Above: The interior of Saint-Sulpice in Paris, where John-Baptist de La Salle studied and was ordained.

Below: An engraving of John-Baptist de La Salle preaching (H. Jannin and P. Sarrazin, 1845).

JOHN JOSEPH OF THE CROSS

HIS SOLICITUDE FOR THE UNHAPPY, AND HIS GENTLE MANNERS AS A LEADER, BROUGHT THIS FRANCISCAN PRIEST WIDESPREAD TRUST AND ADMIRATION AMONG THE PEOPLE OF NAPLES.

KEY FACTS
Franciscan minister-provincial
DATES: *1654–1734*
BIRTH PLACE: *Ischia, near Naples*
PATRON OF: *Naples*
FEAST DAY: *5 March*

John Joseph longed to follow the teachings of Franciscan Peter of Alcantara, and to keep rules of simplicity and contemplation. He joined the order when he was 16, but the quality of his character brought him rapid promotion. He was only 21 years old when he was placed in charge of a monastery in Piedimonte di Alife, and despite his longing for seclusion, he was ordained in 1677.

Still devoted to a contemplative life, John Joseph built hermitages where his congregation could take retreats for prayer and penance. He was sensitive in his handling of penitents, guiding them through confession and meditation. However, although he was diligent in following his duties, he begged the Church to release him from his position of authority. After a short period in Naples studying as a novice-master, John Joseph returned to Piedmont, becoming a menial in 1681. His leadership qualities were such that, in 1684, his fellow friars re-elected him as guardian.

MINISTER-PROVINCIAL
In the latter part of the 17th century, the Spaniards had control of Naples, and, with the pope's agreement, they insisted Spanish priests fill all high office in the Neapolitan Church. But, when the Spaniards withdrew, John Joseph appealed to the pope to recognize Naples as an Italian province. He also requisitioned two large houses that the Spanish had claimed for

Above: A view of the island of Ischia, the birthplace of John Joseph of the Cross (English School, 18th century).

themselves. In recognition of his contribution, the pope made John Joseph minister-provincial of the new province.

John Joseph applied himself to improving the discipline and organization of the monasteries, badly needed after the Spanish era. When satisfied he had done his duty, he obtained exemption from further office. He continued to help sinners and penitents, and to offer spiritual counselling. The people of Naples adored him, and would gather round him when he went out in the streets. The more hysterical would try to tear patches from his ragged habit, seeking something of the holy old priest for their own comfort.

After he died, in Naples, a cultus arose, and he was canonized in 1839.

Left: This contemporary image of a Franciscan monk shows the austere simplicity of the garments that John Joseph of the Cross would have worn.

JEANNE DELANOUE

JEANNE DELANOUE GAVE UP A BUSY COMMERCIAL LIFE FOR ONE OF PERSONAL SQUALOR, DEVOTING HER LIFE INSTEAD TO CARING FOR THE POOR, PARTICULARLY OUTCAST WOMEN AND REFUGEES.

KEY FACTS
Founder of the Sisters of Providence
DATES: *1666–1736*
BIRTH PLACE: *Saumur, France*
FEAST DAY: *17 August*

In her earlier life, Jeanne Delanoue ran the family business, selling drapery and religious items. At the age of 26, she encountered Françoise Suchet, a religious enthusiast who claimed to have experienced visions. Inspired by this eccentric woman, Jeanne turned her home and shop into a guesthouse, transforming the cellars and caves below it into shelters for the homeless.

By 1704, Jeanne had founded an order that came to be called the Sisters of Providence. The order brought solace to homeless women, unmarried mothers, and prostitutes, and during the famine of 1709 they housed 100 starving people. Each day, having slept in a filthy old shroud, Jeanne would rise at 3 a.m., pray, then tend to the needy women.

Her nickname, "the pig of Jesus", suggests a lack of care for her appearance, but Jeanne was greatly respected for her protection of outcasts, and for her care of refugees during the frequent periods of war and famine. She founded 12 communities before her death in Saumur.

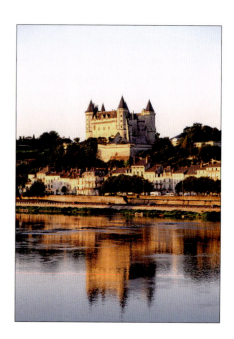

Right: The castle in Saumur, the city where Jeanne Delanoue was born and founded her religious order.

FRANCIS SERRANO

A COURAGEOUS AND FAITHFUL MISSIONARY, FRANCIS SERRANO WAS COMPLIMENTED BY A FELLOW PRIEST FOR WORKING "AS ENERGETICALLY AS A LION FOR THE BENEFIT OF SOULS".

KEY FACTS
Martyr
DATES: *1691–1748*
BIRTH PLACE: *Granada, Spain*
FEAST DAY: *17 February*

Francis Serrano was a Dominican priest who left Spain for the Philippines in 1725. Assigned to the post of Fujian, he showed great virtue as a missionary in a treacherous land.

Serrano was a hardy man, who had an abundance of energy, and was adventurous in spirit. His writings reveal him as a humorous, high-spirited character. He would journey unafraid through the night, crossing rivers and forests, determined to tend to his persecuted flock. He even disguised himself as a local peasant so that he could pass unnoticed into villages to administer the Sacraments in secret.

In 1746, he was imprisoned in Fuzhou and, during 19 months of incarceration, endured violent beatings that badly damaged his hearing. He and other missionaries were branded on their faces, and Francis wrote, "Our hearts exulted. We were branded as slaves of Jesus Christ…these heads are no longer ours, but the Lord's. He can take them whenever He wishes." Francis, who was finally suffocated to death in his prison cell, is included among the Martyrs of China canonized in 2000.

Left: A map of Indonesia and the Philippines (Charles Marie Rigobert Bonne, 18th century).

LEONARD OF PORT MAURICE

Leonard wished first, that he "might live for God and last, that he might live in God". Travelling around Italy, he used the Stations of the Cross to preach the Christian message.

> **KEY FACTS**
> *Franciscan missionary*
> Dates: *1676–1751*
> Birth Place: *Port Maurice, Italy*
> Patron of: *Missions in Catholic lands*
> Feast Day: *26 November*
> Emblem: *Franciscan habit*

Baptized as Paul Jerome Casanova in Port Maurice, Leonard joined the Franciscan Order, basing his life on the teachings of Christ as he understood them from a close reading of the New Testament, and on the Rules of St Francis of Assisi.

In 1709, Leonard instituted reforms at the friary of San Francesco del Monte in Florence, bringing its practices back into line with the strict austerity demanded by St Francis. He attracted many followers, whom he trained and sent out to preach across Tuscany. He also established a hermitage nearby, with the purpose of enabling the friars to make biannual retreats of silence and fasting. In 1730, he was sent to Rome, where he was appointed Guardian of St Bonaventura. During his time here, he made a point of ministering to soldiers, sailors, convicts and galley slaves.

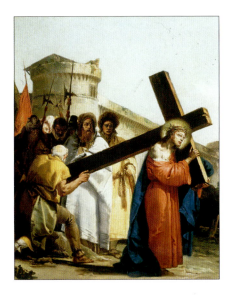

STATIONS OF THE CROSS
In 1736, Leonard asked to be released from office, and travelled around Italy, often preaching outdoors. As a tool to spread his message, and as a symbol of his devotion, he used the Stations of the Cross, teaching his listeners how to pray before each of the

Left: Leonard of Port Maurice used the Stations of the Cross to teach his listeners about the Christian faith. The Fifth Station recounts how Simon of Cyrene helped Christ carry the cross (Giovanni Domenico Tiepolo, 1749).

14 incidents that marked Christ's journey to the cross. It is said that he installed about 500 Stations of the Cross throughout Italy.

In 1744, Pope Benedict XIV sent Leonard to Corsica, where he encountered a hostile political atmosphere, and turbulent congregations who brought weapons to church services. The mountainous land was hard for a priest, who had to walk everywhere. Leonard's health suffered, and eventually, a ship had to be sent to bring him home.

Leonard returned to his Italian flock with renewed vigour and, in 1750, set up the Stations of the Cross in the Roman Coloseum, where he preached to a huge, excited crowd.

Soon afterwards, he took a mission to the south, but the weather turned against him. Refusing an offer of shelter from some friars at Spoleto, Leonard insisted on continuing to Rome. Here he took to his bed and, exhausted by the journey, he received the last rites and a message from the pope before he died.

Left: The Gulf of Porto in Corsica. Leonard was sent to the island by Pope Benedict XIV in 1744.

GERARD MAJELLA

Gerard Majella, a humble lay brother from a simple, modest background, has been described as the "most famous wonder-worker of the 18th century".

KEY FACTS
Miracle worker
Dates: *1725–55*
Birth Place: *Muro Lucano, near Naples*
Patron of: *Mothers*
Feast Day: *16 October*

Gerard Majella's widowed mother said of him that "he was born for heaven", and he demonstrated his religious calling from an early age, spending much of his childhood in prayer.

He initially turned down an apprenticeship as a tailor – his father's profession – to work as a servant in the house of the Bishop of Lacedogna. But the bishop was bad-tempered and unpredictable, and Gerard was neither sly nor subtle enough to withstand such a regime. So he returned home to take up his apprenticeship and worked to support his mother and three sisters.

A SIMPLE LAY BROTHER

In 1752, Gerard fulfilled his long-held dream to join a religious order when he was accepted as a lay brother into the Congregation of the Most Holy Redeemer, or the Redemptorists. St Alphonsus Liguori, the founder of this community, had a particular empathy with peasant and illiterate congregations and Gerard found a role as a gardener, tailor and porter. His fellow priests were puzzled by his frail appearance and shy manners, and decided that he must be "either a fool or a great saint".

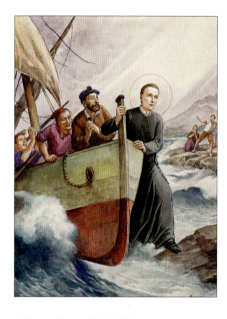

Above: Gerard Majella saving fishermen near Naples (M. Barberis, 19th century).

Below: The Market at Naples (Domenico Gargiulo, 17th century). Gerard Majella never travelled beyond the boundaries of the city.

MIRACLES AND CHARITY

Claims were soon circulating that Gerard could heal the sick, appear in two places at one time, read minds and tell the future. Perhaps most extraordinary of all, one story tells of his ability to levitate and fly half a mile through the air.

Despite Gerard's lowly position in the Redemptorists, he always found alms and food for the poor, and time and patience for the sick. Because of his purity and sensitivity, he was appointed as the spiritual director of numerous communities of nuns.

He remained unworldly and, when accused of lewd behaviour by a young woman, refused to defend or incriminate himself, believing silence to be the righteous response to dishonesty and injustice. The girl later admitted that the charges were false.

Gerard was only 29 years old when he died of tuberculosis. Although he had never travelled outside the kingdom of Naples, a cultus grew after his death. He is patron saint of unborn children and expectant mothers in particular, and was canonized by Pope Pius X in 1904.

DIRECTORY OF SAINTS

MARGARET D'YOUVILLE

Margaret d'Youville is known as the mother of universal charity. The founder of the Sisters of Charity of Montreal, she "loved greatly Jesus Christ and the poor".

KEY FACTS
Founder of a lay order
DATES: *1701–71*
BIRTH PLACE: *Varennes, Canada*
FEAST DAY: *23 December*

From a very early age, Margaret was faced with responsibility and the rigours of poverty. Born in Varennes, Canada, she was the eldest of six children. Her father died when she was seven years old and, after a brief education from the Ursuline nuns, she helped her mother to bring up her siblings.

From this difficult start in life, she made what appeared to be a good marriage to a fur trader, François Youville. The Governor-General and other grand officials attended the wedding.

Margaret's marriage brought her great unhappiness, during which her faith sustained her. Youville was not only a drunkard and a gambler, but also illicitly traded alcohol with local Indians. The effect of this was so devastating on their community that they begged the governor for protection. Margaret bore four children, of whom only two survived. When her husband died in 1730, she found he had spent her mother's legacy and left her in debt.

DEVOTION TO THE POOR
Margaret opened a shop to support her children and, despite her own hardships, found time to visit others in unfortunate circumstances. She tended to the sick and to criminals and, when her eldest son left home to enter the seminary (both sons became priests), she moved a destitute blind woman into his room. Her

female friends shared her sense of duty and faith and worked as seamstresses to raise money for the poor. But Margaret still struggled to find resources to pay for her good works. She was once forced to beg for funds to pay for the funeral of an executed criminal.

Left: The Storming of Quebec *(English School, 18th century). The "Grey Nuns" tended the wounded on both sides of the fighting.*

THE GREY NUNS
In 1737, along with three young companions, Margaret formed a lay order for the service of the poor – the Sisters of Charity of Montreal, known as the "Grey Nuns". They cared for women and prisoners, nursed the sick during a smallpox epidemic and, with an all-embracing policy that made no distinction of race or status, they tended to the wounded of both sides during the war between Quebec and England that ended in 1759. The Grey Nuns' convent was burnt down twice, but the entire community funded the rebuilding.

Margaret died in Montreal, and was canonized in 1990, the first native-born Canadian saint.

Right: Montreal on the Saint Lawrence River in 1760. *Margaret founded her order in the city in 1737.*

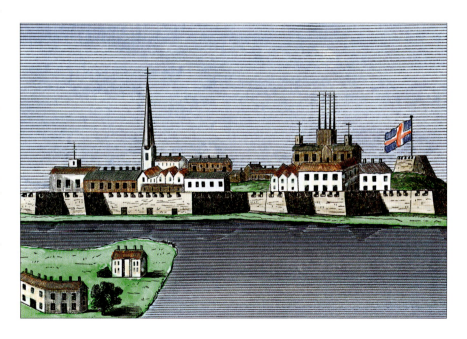

459

VINCENT LIEM

This saint took the name "Vincent Liem of Peace", yet he confronted terrible, officially sanctioned violence, and eventually martyrdom, for his Christian faith.

KEY FACTS
Protomartyr
DATES: *1732–73*
BIRTH PLACE: *Tra Lu, Vietnam*
FEAST DAY: *7 November*

In the 16th century, Christian missions from Europe entered the kingdoms of Tonkin, Annam and Cochin, now Vietnam. When Vincent Liem was born in Tra Lu in 1732, his parents were part of a well-established, but furtive Christian community that risked state persecution.

A pious child, Vincent joined the Dominican seminary when he was 12 years old. He was an intelligent and diligent pupil, and in 1753 was sent to the St John Lateran Dominican College in Manila in the Philippines, where he prepared for ordination. In 1759, he returned to his homeland and taught noviciates at the seminary of Trung Linh.

SUFFERING PERSECUTION

The persecution of Christians was remorseless during this period, perhaps as severe as anything the early Christians suffered under the Roman Empire. Documentation of the Vietnamese martyrs is rare, but it is estimated that between the 16th and 18th centuries, more than 100,000 Christians were killed. Torture was common: limbs were cut off, flesh burnt from the living body, and some Christians who escaped death were branded on the face with the words *ta dao*, meaning "false religion".

Above: A map showing the Kingdom of Tonkin in South Asia (Charles Marie Rigobert Bonne, 1780).

Faced with religious oppression similar to that endured by the first apostles, Vincent followed their example, undergoing difficult journeys to spread the faith. As Sts Peter and Paul had done, he worked among non-believers, seeking converts despite the fearful dangers he risked.

Vincent was caught and imprisoned in Trung Linh, where he met fellow prisoner Hyacinth Castaneda, a Spanish priest. He was executed in 1773, the first Vietnamese-born martyr. Vincent Liem was canonized in 1988, and is one of the named Martyrs of Vietnam, representing the thousands of anonymous Christians who have been murdered in this part of the world.

Left: A coloured engraving showing the forms of torture endured by Catholic missionaries in Tonkin, China (French School, 19th century).

PAUL OF THE CROSS

THE SON OF A NOBLEMAN, PAUL OF THE CROSS REFUSED A RICH INHERITANCE AND A WEALTHY WIFE BECAUSE OF HIS INNER DESIRE TO FOLLOW HIS SPIRITUAL VOCATION.

KEY FACTS
Founder of an order
DATES: *1694–1775*
BIRTH PLACE: *Ovada, Italy*
FEAST DAY: *19 October*

Paul Francis Danei refused a considerable inheritance and a promising marriage. Instead, he joined the Venetian army as a volunteer in 1714. This experience affected him profoundly and, within a year, he became a recluse.

In 1720, he emerged with a powerful vocation, determined to share with believers his profound awareness of the Passion of Christ, the suffering Jesus endured as he hung on the cross.

He was ordained as a priest and, with the help of his brother, founded the Passionist Congregation in 1727, with the aim of combining monastic virtue with active missionary work.

Paul wanted his followers to live monastic lives, even as they went forth to spread his message and minister to the sick, but papal authority was granted only after the severe rules of the order were modified. The order expanded throughout Paul's lifetime, and, in 1771, an enclosed convent of Passionist nuns was approved.

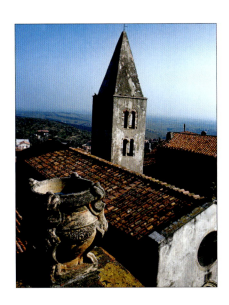

Right: The monastery of the noviciate of the Passionist friars in Italy.

BENEDICT JOSEPH LABRE

PILGRIM AND MENDICANT, BENEDICT JOSEPH LABRE WAS THE EMBODIMENT OF THOSE RARE, HOLY MEN AND WOMEN WHO ARE DESCRIBED AS "FOOLS FOR CHRIST'S SAKE".

KEY FACTS
Mendicant
DATES: *1748–83*
BIRTH PLACE: *Boulogne, France*
PATRON OF: *Tramps, the homeless*
FEAST DAY: *16 April*

All faiths produce exceptional followers, who dedicate their lives to spirituality at the expense of a conventional role in society. Benedict Joseph Labre, the eldest of 15 children of a prosperous shopkeeper, was such a man.

Both the Cistercians and the Carthusians claimed that Benedict was too young and delicate to join them, but possibly they sensed his eccentricity. Rejected by these monks, Benedict decided to become a pilgrim, walking from his birthplace of Boulogne to Rome, then visiting, again on foot, the holy sites of Italy, Switzerland and France.

Above: Nuns standing in front of the St Labre mission in Ashland, Montana (19th century).

He slept in fields and on street corners, and accepted food when offered, but gave away any money he received. In 1774, Benedict settled in Rome, spending his days praying in the churches, his nights curled up in doorways. Eventually, due to poor health, he moved into a shelter for poor men, where he gave his food to other inmates. He collapsed in church while praying, and was carried to the shop of a friendly butcher, where he died.

The Romans recognized him as a holy man, a cultus developed, and he was canonized in 1881.

ALPHONSUS LIGUORI

ALPHONSUS LIGUORI RECOMMENDED SIMPLICITY IN THE PULPIT AND CHARITY IN THE CONFESSIONAL. A BEGUILING PREACHER, HE WAS LOVED BY HIS CONGREGATION.

KEY FACTS
Founder of an order
DATES: *1696–1787*
BIRTH PLACE: *Naples, Italy*
PATRON OF: *Those who hear confessions, teachers of moral theology*
FEAST DAY: *1 August*

Alphonsus' father was ambitious for his son, propelling him into a legal career in Naples. Alphonsus became a successful barrister, but after eight years a voice prompted him to "Leave the world and give yourself to me." He studied theology privately and, after he was ordained in 1726, proved to be a priest with moderate views, sympathetic to sinners.

As a preacher, he developed a clear, intelligible style, anxious that "even the poorest old woman in the congregation" should understand him. He organized Christian clubs for the unemployed of Naples and, while dining at one, advised a member not to be overzealous in his fasting, but to eat the cutlets God had provided. These comments caused rumours of extravagant goings-on at the "Cutlet Clubs" that abounded in the city. Some members were arrested, but the clubs were allowed to continue and later evolved into the Association of the Chapels.

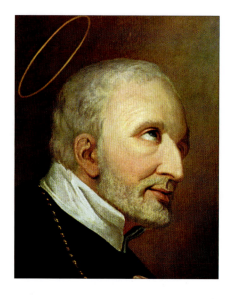

Above: Alphonsus Liguori (artist unknown, 19th century).

THE REDEMPTORISTS

In 1732, aided by his friends Thomas Falcoia and Maria Celeste, Alphonsus founded the Congregation of the Most Holy Redeemer, or the Redemptorists. Unfortunately, the order was stricken by internal dissension. This, combined with the anti-clericalism of the Italian government and the opposition of the Jansenists, left the Redemptorists in a precarious position. Despite these difficulties, however, the order survived, and Alphonsus received popular acclamation for his religious texts, *Moral Theology* and *The Glories of Mary*.

In 1762, he became Bishop of Sant' Agata dei Goti near Naples, but the congregation was corrupt and lax. Alphonsus was unbending in his reforms. During a famine, he insisted that the wealthy share food with the starving. The subsequent court actions brought against him added to his burdens.

During Alphonsus' career, he faced many professional and personal difficulties, but he never lost the support of ordinary believers. He retired from high office, in 1775, crippled with rheumatism and with his sight and hearing impaired. The Redemptorists still faced fierce opposition and, in 1780, Alphonsus was expelled from his own order when he was tricked into signing a document authorizing reforms favourable to the anti-clerical government.

Alphonsus died believing his congregation had failed, but, in 1793, the order was recognized by the Neapolitan state, and it now operates all over the world.

Left: Sant' Agatha dei Goti in Campania, Italy, where Alphonsus Liguori became bishop in 1762.

ELIZABETH SETON

Elizabeth Seton, exemplary wife, mother, widow and consecrated nun, was the first American to be canonized by the Roman Catholic Church.

> **KEY FACTS**
> *Founder, first American-born saint*
> Dates: *1774–1821*
> Birth Place: *New York, USA*
> Feast Day: *4 January*

Elizabeth Seton was born into a wealthy American family, respected in New York society. Her grandfather had been the Episcopalian Rector of Staten Island, and her father was the first public physician of the city.

When she was 19, Elizabeth married a wealthy trader, William Seton. Theirs was a happy marriage, but at the age of 28 she was left widowed, with five small children, after her husband died while they were on a trip to Italy.

CATHOLIC CONVERSION
Although she had been brought up as an Episcopalian, Elizabeth found spiritual comfort in the Roman Catholic Church. Moved by the charity of the nuns she encountered in Tuscany, she underwent a conversion on her return to New York, and was baptized a Roman Catholic.

Her conversion left her an outcast from her family and her anti-Catholic community. Her religious ardour was regarded as unseemly in her sophisticated circle, and she faced some difficult years of financial trouble during which she repeatedly tried and failed to start a Catholic school in her home city.

THE SISTERS OF CHARITY
In 1808, at the invitation of Reverend William Dubourg, she went to Baltimore to care for poor children. Here, she found her true vocation. She established a small religious community devoted to the relief of the poor, especially children, and to teaching in parish schools. From this grew her congregation, the American Sisters of Charity, based on the rules of St Vincent de Paul.

She took her vows as a nun, and her commitment to Christ was unswerving. Others perceived her dynamic conviction, and were inspired by her to join her cause. The Sisters of Charity is now an influential congregation, active not only in the United States, but also in Latin America, Italy and the developing world. Elizabeth died at Emmitsburg and was canonized in 1975 after prayers for her intercession brought about cures for leukaemia and meningitis.

Above: An engraving showing Elizabeth Seton dressed in the costume of the Sisters of Charity (Maurindel, date unknown).

Right: The shrine of Elizabeth Seton in Emmitsburg, Maryland.

ANTÔNIO DE SANT'ANNA GALVÃO

MORE THAN A MILLION PEOPLE ATTENDED THE CANONIZATION OF ST ANTÔNIO, A MAN OF PEACE AND CHARITY, AND THE FIRST BRAZILIAN TO BE MADE A SAINT.

KEY FACTS
Founder, miracle worker
DATES: *1739–1822*
BIRTH PLACE: *Guaratingueto, near São Paulo, Brazil*
FEAST DAY: *11 May*

Antônio de Sant'Anna Galvão was born into a wealthy and deeply religious family, who sent him to a Jesuit seminary at the age of 13. However, because of a strong anti-Jesuit movement in Brazil at the time, his father advised him to join the Alcantrine Franciscans.

Antônio enrolled as a noviciate at St Bonaventure near Rio de Janeiro and was ordained in 1762. In 1768, he became preacher and confessor to the laity at the St Francis Friary in São Paulo. He was also confessor to the women of the Recollects of St Teresa, where he met Sister Helena Maria of the Holy Spirit.

In 1774, inspired by this nun and her religious visions, he founded Our Lady of the Conception of Divine Providence. At this home for girls, young women could receive instruction without being required to take vows. When Sister Helena died, Antônio took sole responsibility for the Recollects, who were subsequently incorporated into the Order of Immaculate Conception.

Over the following years, Antônio achieved high office. In 1808, he became visitator in general and president of the Franciscan chapter of São Paulo. When, at one stage, the Church posted him outside the city, the bishop and churchgoers begged for his return.

In his old age, he returned to the St Francis friary, but it was the sisters from the Recollects da Luz who attended him at his death.

MIRACLE PILLS

Antônio is most famous for his "pills" – scraps of paper inscribed with prayers to Mary, the Blessed Virgin, that the faithful would swallow in hope of a miraculous cure. To this day, the pills are manufactured by the nuns of St Clare, a convent founded by Antônio in Sorocaba near São Paulo.

In 1998, the Archbishop of São Paulo tried to bring an end to what he regarded as a superstition, and ordered the nuns to stop their work. However, at the canonization of St Antônio, Pope Benedict XVI recognized the miraculous power of the saint, acknowledging two healing miracles ascribed to the pills, including a recent case of a four-year-old girl whose hepatitis had been declared incurable by the medical profession. Since the saint's canonization in 2007, the nuns have distributed as many as 10,000 pills in one day.

Above: An altar painting of Antônio de Sant'Anna Galvão in Brazil.

Below: Pope Benedict XVI canonized Antônio de Sant'Anna Galvão in front of nearly a million people in São Paulo in May 2007.

MAGDALENA OF CANOSSA

MAGDALENA OF CANOSSA HAD "A MOTHER'S HEART AND AN APOSTLE'S ZEAL". HER LIFE WAS DEDICATED TO TEACHING AND EXTENDING SPIRITUAL AWARENESS.

KEY FACTS
Virgin, founder of the Daughters of Charity
DATES: *1774–1835*
BIRTH PLACE: *Verona, Italy*
FEAST DAY: *8 May*

Although Magdalena made a vow to dedicate her life to God at the age of 17, she was compelled to take up a secular life. The third of six siblings left fatherless as children, she found herself left in charge of running the family's large estate.

Despite her worldly worries, however, she could not forget her calling, and sought out friends to join her in following Christ with chastity and obedience. In 1808, in spite of family opposition, she moved to the poorest part of town to start her religious life, and built up such a following that, in 1819, she founded the Daughters of Charity. The order was dedicated to establishing charity schools, training teachers for rural areas and supporting women patients in hospital. Later, she founded the Sons of Charity for male followers.

Magdalena died in Verona surrounded by her followers. There are now 4,000 Daughters of Charity all over the world, and the Sons are active in Italy, the Philippines and Latin America.

Above: St Mary's College in Hong Kong, founded by the Canossian Daughters of Charity in 1900.

JOSEPH COTTOLENGO

JOSEPH COTTOLENGO WILL ALWAYS BE REMEMBERED AND LOVED AS AN UNSTINTING CHAMPION OF THOSE IN NEED, WHETHER THEY BE ORPHANS, DISABLED, MENTALLY ILL OR FRAIL.

KEY FACTS
Founder of a hospital
DATES: *1786–1842*
BIRTH PLACE: *Piedmont*
FEAST DAY: *30 April*

Joseph Cottolengo was ordained in 1811 and quickly demonstrated his empathy for the unfortunate. His good works began modestly, with the founding of a hospital of five beds, the "Little House", in a Turin slum.

The hospital expanded quickly, and Joseph and his followers formed the Societies of the Little House of Divine Providence. When the authorities closed the Little House during a cholera epidemic, the brothers nursed the sick in their homes. The Little House then moved to Valdocco, a suburb of Turin, where it was soon surrounded by an assortment of care homes for the deaf and dumb, orphans, elderly people, epileptics and the mentally disabled.

Joseph also started communities of prayer to bring solace to those in mortal and moral danger. Joseph seemed carefree about finances, believing that the Lord would provide, and so it was with surprise that his successor accepted his perfectly kept account books when he retired.

Although he was only 56 years old, Joseph died of typhoid in his brother's home at Chieri only a week after his retirement.

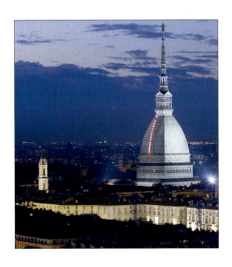

Above: The city of Turin, where Joseph Cottolengo did many great works.

INCORRUPTIBLES

ALL SAINTS ARE REVERED FOR THE WONDROUS ACTS, AND OFTEN MIRACLES, THEY PERFORM WHEN THEY ARE LIVING, BUT SOME SHOW EXTRAORDINARY PHYSICAL QUALITIES EVEN AFTER THEIR DEATH.

The words "incorrupt" and "incorruptible" are used by the Catholic Church to describe bodies that do not decompose after death. The body is considered incorrupt only if no preservation techniques, such as embalming, have been used, and it is not uncommon for the body's lack of decomposition to be accompanied by a sweet smell. The discovery of an incorrupt corpse is generally made by chance, and when the body of a holy person is found intact, it is traditionally taken as a sign of sainthood.

Alongside other miraculous phenomena associated with saints, including stigmata and the healing of the sick, the survival of a saint's corpse seems to defy any scientific explanation, and many Catholic Christians believe the holiness and piety of an incorruptible saint to be the cause of divine preservation.

EARLY INCORRUPTIBLES

A very early example of an incorruptible is the 3rd-century Saint Cecilia. When her tomb was opened in 1599, a thousand years after she was buried, her corpse showed no signs of corruption. Sadly, on exposure to the air, it quickly turned to dust.

Left: A portrait of Bernadette of Lourdes (19th century).

Above: A portrait of Rita of Cascia in the church of Santa Maria del Giglio, Venice (19th century).

There was frequent correspondence between Rome and the English clergy after the death of Edward the Confessor in 1066. A cultus grew around this king, and the campaign to have him canonized was strengthened when his body was found to be incorrupt in 1102. Monks from Westminster made enquiries and, in 1161, Pope Innocent III finally agreed with their findings and advised that the saint's relics be translated to Westminster Abbey. In 1163, a procession carried the incorrupt body to its final resting place.

THE BLOOD OF ST JANUARIUS

St Januarius, who was martyred in AD 305, is the patron saint of Naples, and his presence is believed to protect the port from harm. Twice every year – on 19 September and on the Saturday before the first Sunday in May – a solemn procession, led by representatives of the Church, progresses through the city displaying a vial of St Januarius's blood, which liquefies and bubbles in just the same way as fresh blood. Believers fear a calamity would hit Naples if the blood failed to liquefy. Other saints whose blood was said to show this quality include Pantaleon, Stephen and John the Baptist.

Right: Cardinal Crescenzio Sepe, Archbishop of Naples, looks at the glass vial holding the blood of St Januarius during the Feast of San Gennaro in 2006.

Above: The incorrupt body of Catherine Labouré, kept at 140 rue du Bac in Paris, France.

Above: The incorrupt body of Jean-Baptiste Vianney is kept in the Basilica at Ars, France.

St Rita of Cascia (1377–1447) is another incorruptible, whose face, hands and feet survive along with much of her skeleton. Her remains are on display in the Basilica of St Rita in Cascia, Italy.

THE LAST 200 YEARS

The body of John-Baptiste Vianney also remained intact after his death in 1859. He won the admiration of his congregation for his faith and goodness. They were amazed, too, by his meagre diet of boiled potatoes, and his habit of sleeping for a mere two or three hours a night. His extraordinary qualities in life were extended in death, when his body did not decompose.

Madeleine Sophie Barat was an energetic woman who travelled widely and devoted herself to the Christian education of children. The miraculous preservation of her body, which is kept in Jette in Belgium, reflects the strength and vitality that she always demonstrated in life.

Another holy woman whose body has proved incorrupt is Catherine Labouré. This modest nun, who is venerated as a mystic, was canonized in 1947. She died in 1876 and her body rests in the the convent where she lived for nearly half a century, in the chapel at 140 rue du Bac, Paris.

> "WE SHOULD SHOW HONOUR TO THE SAINTS OF GOD, AS BEING MEMBERS OF CHRIST, THE CHILDREN AND FRIENDS OF GOD, AND OUR INTERCESSORS. THEREFORE, IN MEMORY OF THEM WE OUGHT TO HONOUR ANY RELICS OF THEIRS IN A FITTING MANNER."
>
> ST THOMAS AQUINAS

An equally humble woman whose body survives without corruption is Bernadette of Lourdes, who saw visions of the Virgin and lived piously as a nun. After her death in 1879, her corpse was removed three times from its resting place to undergo scientific examination. It now resides in a glass case in the convent at Nevers, where visitors can marvel at its preserved state. Doctor Comte, who examined St Bernadette's corpse in 1925 wrote "the body does not seem to have putrefied, nor has any decomposition of the body set in, although this would be expected and normal after such a long period in a vault hollowed out of the earth."

Right: The incorrupt body of St Rita of Cascia is carried around Rome during a celebration on her feast day.

JEAN-BAPTISTE VIANNEY

JEAN-BAPTISTE FAILED HIS CLERICAL EXAMS, BUT WAS ACCEPTED INTO THE PRIESTHOOD BECAUSE THE CHURCH NEEDED MEN OF SIMPLE GOODNESS AND DEVOTION AS WELL AS MEN OF LEARNING.

> **KEY FACTS**
> *Founder*
> DATES: *1786–1859*
> BIRTH PLACE: *Dardilly, near Lyons, France*
> PATRON OF: *Patriarchal clergy*
> FEAST DAY: *4 August*

Jean-Baptiste was a shepherd boy, who, dismayed by the treatment of priests during the Revolution, applied to join the clergy. He was conscripted into the Napoleonic army but, soon after, deserted and resumed his studies for the priesthood. This was a precarious career because anti-clerical forces in control of France remained hostile even after a ban on all monastic orders was lifted in 1810.

VILLAGE PRIEST

Two years after his ordination in 1815, Jean-Baptiste was sent as parish priest to a remote village, Ars-en-Dombes. He had a genuine hatred of immorality, and a recital of sins would often reduce him to tears. This made him intolerant of simple pleasures, such as dancing, and minor transgressions, such as lewd language. But villagers forgave Jean-Baptiste's severity because he revealed supernatural talents, producing miraculous supplies of food to feed to orphans, and prophesying the future. He could also read hearts and had knowledge of things happening beyond his sight. He suffered violent assaults from the devil, who beat him and even burnt his bed.

Above: A contemporary drawing showing Jean-Baptiste Vianney being harassed by a demon.

Below: A lithograph portrait of Jean-Baptiste Vianney (1866).

Jean-Baptiste was so sympathetic to remorseful sinners that confessors queued for his pastoral care, and a special booking office was set up at Arles railway station to handle the 300 visitors travelling every day to visit the wonder worker. He started work at 11 o'clock each morning and spent long hours in the confessional. He wanted to develop his spiritual meditations and tried three times to become a monk, but returned each time to Ars.

Years of listening to the sins of penitents eventually moderated his views on frivolity and pleasure, and he turned his full attention to teaching his flock about the enduring love of God and the significance of Church liturgy.

Jean-Baptiste was a modest man. He never wore the decoration he was given when made a member of the Légion d'Honneur, and to raise money for the poor he sold the luxurious robes of office he received when he was made a canon. He died in Ars, and was canonized in 1925. The cultus for this saint is now worldwide.

GASPAR BERTONI

ALTHOUGH GASPAR BERTONI WAS DRIVEN BY POLITICAL PRESSURE TO TURN FROM MISSION WORK TO EDUCATION, THIS CHANGE OF DIRECTION BROUGHT WISDOM AND FULFILMENT.

KEY FACTS
Founder
DATES: *1777–1853*
BIRTH PLACE: *Verona, Italy*
FEAST DAY: *12 June*

When Gaspar Bertoni was born, revolutionary anti-clericalism held sway in Europe. He came from a legal family in Verona but chose to work as a parish priest after his ordination in 1800. Undeterred when the Napoleonic conquerors held Pope Pius VII prisoner, he abandoned neither his leader nor his faith.

After Napoleon's defeat in 1814, Verona fell under Austrian control and the pope was released. In 1816–17, Gaspar founded a mission that would preach on the Passion of Christ – the suffering of Jesus on the cross. However, the work was jeopardized by hostility from the new regime, and he refocused his attentions on education.

With his brotherhood, Gaspar began teaching in free schools, hoping to inspire boys into a life of service to God. His group became the Congregation of Holy Stigmatics, an educational mission that now works in Europe, Africa, the Americas and Asia. Although he was bedridden for many years, Gaspar continued to guide his congregation. He died in Verona and was canonized in 1989.

Above: Verona, the city where Gaspar Bertoni was born and died.

CATHERINE LABOURÉ

THE "MIRACULOUS MEDAL" OF CATHERINE LABOURÉ INSPIRED ALPHONSE RATISBONNE, AN ALSATIAN JEW, TO CONVERT AND FOUND THE FATHERS AND SISTERS OF SION.

KEY FACTS
Visionary
DATES: *1806–76*
BIRTH PLACE: *Fain-les-Moutiers, near Dijon, France*
FEAST DAY: *28 November*

Catherine Labouré was a peasant from Fain-les-Moutiers. She cared for her widowed father, worked in Paris as a waitress and then, in 1830, joined the Sisters of Charity at the rue du Bac.

Her superiors thought little of this plain woman who tended the convent hens, but Catherine had extraordinary visions, the most enduring of which was a picture of the Virgin standing on a globe. The vision was accompanied by the words, "Mary conceived without sin, pray for us who have recourse to thee." On the reverse of the picture was an M with a cross and two hearts.

Above: Apparition of the Virgin to Saint Catherine Labouré 31 July 1830 (Le Cerf, 1835).

THE MIRACULOUS MEDALS
The Archbishop of Paris was persuaded to sanction medals stamped with these images, and, in 1832, 1,500 were minted. After the appearance of a pamphlet describing Catherine's vision, 130,000 further medals were sold. The "Miraculous Medal" was authenticated by canonical decree, and is now distributed across the Catholic world.

Catherine's cultus was strengthened by the incorruptibility of her body after her death in the convent she had called home for more 40 years. She was canonized in 1947.

MADELEINE SOPHIE BARAT

Madeleine Sophie Barat devoted her life to the service of others, bringing a Catholic education to pupils across the world through the Society of the Sacred Heart.

> **KEY FACTS**
> *Virgin, founder, educational reformer*
> DATES: *1779–1865*
> BIRTH PLACE: *Joigny, France*
> FEAST DAY: *25 May*

From a very early age, Madeleine was placed under the harsh tutelage of her brother, Louis, who was 11 years her senior. She learnt how to deflect his unpleasant manners through patience, charm and diplomacy, traits that were to serve her well throughout her life. Her brother's stubborn, aggressive nature led to his imprisonment for two years when he refused to accept the civil constitution of the clergy.

SCHOOL TEACHER
Madeleine nursed an ambition to become a lay sister with the Carmelites, but was persuaded by l'Abbé Varin to instead join his new community, the Society of the Sacred Heart, dedicated to teaching Christian children, rich and poor alike. In 1800, she was sent to Amiens, to the Society's first convent school. Two years

later, aged just 23, she was made Superior, and soon afterwards travelled to Grenoble and Poitiers to establish other convent schools.

Her youth made her high position precarious, and, while she was away from Amiens, a chaplain and another nun tried to displace her. Madeleine responded with

Left: A portrait of Madeleine Sophie Barat (artist and date unknown).

characteristic tact and patience, and, supported by l'Abbé Varin, strengthened her role as Mother Superior, a position she was to hold for 63 years.

EDUCATIONAL REFORMER
During this time she implemented standards of education across every school of the Sacred Heart. Although these guides were uniform, they were not inflexible, with provision made for regular reviews and adjustments to meet changing needs.

The society became truly international under Madeleine's guidance, with communities established in 12 different countries during her lifetime, including foundations in the United States, orchestrated by her friend Rose Philippine Duchesne. Madeleine personally travelled to found new schools and monitor old ones in France, Switzerland and England. The Society of the Sacred Heart has since become one of the most successful institutes in the Roman Catholic educational system.

Still in office at the age of 85, Madeleine died in Paris. Her incorrupt body lies at Jette in Belgium. She was canonized in 1925.

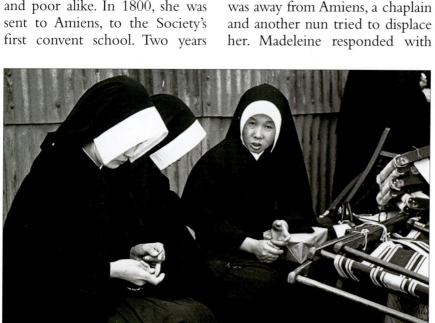

Left: The Society of the Sacred Heart operates around the world. Here, Sacred Heart nuns wait to board a ship in May 1949, during the civil war in China.

KURIAKOSE ELIAS CHAVARA

A MEMBER OF THE SYRO-MALABAR CHURCH, AN EASTERN CATHOLIC CHURCH, CHAVARA WAS AN EDUCATIONALIST, SOCIAL REFORMER AND CO-FOUNDER OF THE CARMELITES OF MARY IMMACULATE.

> **KEY FACTS**
> *First male Indian saint*
> DATES: *1805–1871*
> BIRTH PLACE: *Kainakary, Kerala, south-west India*
> PATRON OF: *Press, media, literature*
> FEAST DAY: *18 February (West), 3 January (Syro-Malabar Church)*

Kuriakose Elias Chavara was born into a family who belonged to the ancient community of "St Thomas Christians", possibly descendants of Christians baptized by the Apostle Thomas himself in the 1st century AD. St Thomas is said to have visited Kerala in AD 52 and converted local people to Christianity.

Educated in his village school, Kuriakose entered a seminary aged 13 and was ordained in 1829 at the age of 24. He was a pioneer of monastic life in the region and a great promoter of education. He founded a monastery in 1831, establishing the Carmelites of Mary Immaculate and becoming the first Prior General of the monastery at Mannanam. There he established a school for studying Sanskrit and in nearby Arpookara he also set up a school for children of the Pulaya caste (also known as Dalits or "Untouchables"). In addition, he founded a printing press at Mannanam in 1846 that launched the publication of what is today the oldest existing Malayalam newspaper, known simply as Deepika.

He pioneered giving poor children a hearty lunch at school and this became a widespread practice that greatly supported the growth of education locally. He was also a writer, who wrote ten pastoral plays. Among his many other works was an autobiographical poem, "Lamentations of a Repentant Soul", as well as prayers, and liturgical writings.

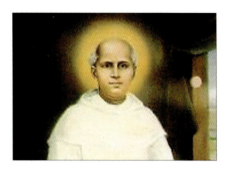

Above: Kuriakose Chavara was a Catholic priest, religious and social reformer.

PRAISING THE HOLY FAMILY

On taking his vows, he took the name Kuriakose Elias of the Holy Family, and, when he passed on in 1871 at the age of 66, he reputedly said: "Always rely on Jesus, Mary and Joseph. Let the Holy Family reign in your hearts." He was

Below: An altar at the home of Kuriakose Elias Chavara.

initially buried in St Philomena's Forane Church in Koonammavu, but his body was later moved to St Joseph's Monastery Church in Mannanam.

> **SAINT EUPHRASIA**
> When Pope Francis canonized Kuriakose Elias Chavara, on 3 April 2014, he also canonized Euphrasia Eluvathingal, another Indian Carmelite and member of the Syro-Malabar Church. Born Rose Eluvathingal, she is said to have had a vision aged 9 of the Blessed Virgin Mary, and there and then dedicated her life to God. She was admitted as a novice to the Carmelite Convent at Ambazakad in 1898 but suffered from ill health. However, after she had a vision of the Holy Family, she was permanently healed. She later became the convent's Mother Superior. She dedicated herself to prayer and devotion to the Sacred Heart of Jesus and became known as the "Praying Mother". After her death in 1952, her tomb at St Mary's Convent in Ollur in the Keralan city of Thrissur became a major pilgrimage site and she was credited with many miracles. Her feast day is 30 August.

ANTONY CLARET

ANTONY WAS A PRIEST OF GREAT INTELLECTUAL TALENT, BUT HE WAS ALSO A MIRACLE WORKER AND A GIFTED TEACHER, WHO REACHED OUT TO ALL BELIEVERS IN HIS SERMONS AND WRITINGS.

KEY FACTS
Founder of an order
DATES: *1807–70*
BIRTH PLACE: *Sallent, Spain*
PATRON OF: *Weavers, savings banks*
FEAST DAY: *24 October*

Antony was the son of a Spanish weaver, but decided to enter a seminary and was ordained in 1835. He joined the Jesuits in Rome, but ill health caused his return to Spain. He spread the message of Christianity widely and was a keen speaker and a successful and prolific writer, preaching some 10,000 sermons and writing around 200 texts during his lifetime.

In 1849, Antony founded the Missionary Sons of the Immaculate Heart of Mary (the "Claretians"), an order that still flourishes today. The following year, Queen Isabella II requested he serve as the Archbishop of Santiago in Cuba. Antony's reforms angered many, resulting in an attempt on his life.

After seven years in this post, he was recalled to be Isabella's confessor and used his powerful position to fund educational institutes. In 1868, a revolution drove Queen Isabella into exile, and Antony went with her. He died at the Fontfroide monastery near Narbonne, where he had been placed under house arrest.

Right: Antony Claret (artist and date unknown).

CLELIA BARBIERI

CLELIA BARBIERI WAS A PIOUS CHILD AND THE YOUNGEST FOUNDER IN THE HISTORY OF THE ROMAN CATHOLIC CHURCH. ALTHOUGH SHE DIED YOUNG, HER COMMUNITY HAS SPREAD TO 35 COUNTRIES.

KEY FACTS
Founder of an order
DATES: *1847–70*
BIRTH PLACE: *Budrie, near Bologna, Italy*
FEAST DAY: *13 July*

Clelia was born in Budrie, Italy. Her wealthy mother married a servant far below her station and instilled religious values in their children. Their eldest daughter, Clelia, was 11 years old when she was confirmed and had a spiritual experience that made her mourn for her sins and those of all the world.

Clelia joined the Christian Catechism Workers, a mostly male group, and encouraged other girls to follow her example of hard work and religious devotion. In 1868, she founded the Suore Minime dell'Addolorata for her followers. Though she faced public disdain, she persevered in her mission, nursing sick children and teaching the catechism. Despite her youth, the sisters and the children she cared for called her "Mother".

The poor conditions in which she lived made her vulnerable to tuberculosis and, as she lay dying, she told her followers, "I'm leaving, but I'll never abandon you." She was canonized in 1989.

Left: Clelia's order is named after the Mater Dolorosa, *the Virgin of the Sorrows, depicted here (Sassoferrato (studio of), 17th century).*

BERNADETTE OF LOURDES

BERNADETTE HAD VISIONS OF MARY, THE BLESSED VIRGIN, AND HER REMAINS PROVED INCORRUPT, BUT IT WAS HER SINCERITY AND TRUST IN GOD THAT QUALIFIED HER AS A SAINT.

> **KEY FACTS**
> *Visionary*
> DATES: *1844–79*
> BIRTH PLACE: *Lourdes, France*
> FEAST DAY: *16 April (in parts of France 18 February)*

In the tradition of other saints of devout simplicity, such as Jean-Baptiste Vianney and Joseph of Copertino, Bernadette Soubirous was deeply spiritual and blessed by heavenly visions. And, as with those great men, she bore her role with dignity.

Bernadette was a country girl, the eldest of six children born to an impoverished miller in the Basque region of France. As a child, she was thin and stunted, from lack of proper nutrition, and suffered from asthma.

VISIONS OF MARY

When she was 14 years old, Bernadette experienced her first vision at the rock of Massabielle near Lourdes. Over the next six months, the same apparition of a beautiful young woman appeared to her 18 times. No one else saw or heard the vision, but there were witnesses to her reaction. The vision informed Bernadette that the beautiful woman was Mary of the Immaculate Conception and instructed her to drink from the nearby spring and show penitence.

Church clerics and minor state officials interrogated Bernadette for months. Her answers, simple and unchanging, led some of them to label her stupid, but most were impressed by her sincerity. The resulting publicity frightened Bernadette, but she faced the jokes and cruel jibes, showing no anger. No matter how remorseless the goading became, she never denied her miraculous experience.

In 1866, she joined the Sisters of Notre-Dame of Nevers, and found merciful seclusion from the public. Her health was poor and she spent her remaining years in stoic suffering. Bernadette was canonized in 1933, in recognition of her patience, integrity, simplicity and devout trustfulness.

Above: Since Bernadette's visions at Lourdes, many ill pilgrims visit the site in the hope that they will be cured.

Below: The incorrupt body of Bernadette of Lourdes, kept at the convent in Nevers, where she lived for many years.

A PILGRIMAGE CENTRE

Secluded in the convent, Bernadette was unaware that the site where she had met the Blessed Virgin was being transformed into a pilgrimage centre, or that the basilica built there was consecrated in 1876, three years before her death.

Lourdes has become one of the great pilgrimage centres of the Christian faith, drawing to its miraculous waters those seeking spiritual healing.

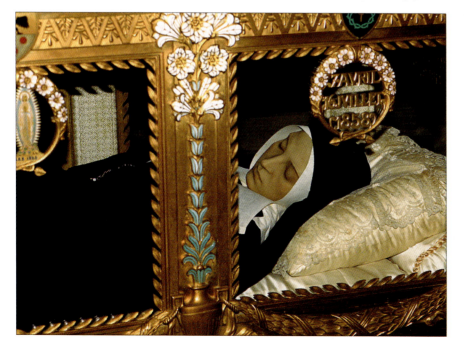

JOSEPH MKASA

JOSEPH MKASA SHOWED GREAT COURAGE AND FAITH WHEN HE DARED TO CONFRONT A TYRANT FEARED FROM ZANZIBAR TO THE CONGO. HE IS NAMED AMONG THE MARTYRS OF UGANDA.

> **KEY FACTS**
> *Martyr of Uganda*
> DATES: *c.1860–85*
> BIRTH PLACE: *Uganda*
> FEAST DAY: *3 June*

In , Mwanga, the King of Uganda, ordered the killing of the Anglican missionary bishop, James Hannington, and his companions. Joseph Mkasa, a Roman Catholic convert and adviser to the king, was outraged by the killings, and was determined to do something about it, although he was aware that King Mwanga was a dangerous man.

This had not always been the case. As prince, Mwanga had shown no untoward behaviour or aggression towards Christians, but, the moment he became king, he turned into a tyrant and a degenerate man, who treated slaves and servants cruelly, and made sexual advances towards the pages in his court. Mwanga was angered by the Christians because their loyalty to God outweighed that shown to himself, and he resolved to rid his country of Christianity.

CONFRONTING THE KING
Fearless for his own safety, Joseph Mkasa decided to make a stand and reproached the king for the murder. The bravery displayed by Joseph is even more impressive in the light of contemporary extracts from the diary of Henry Stanley, an American explorer in Africa. Stanley records the infamous reputation of Mwanga, who was feared by the British Foreign Office, the Arab authorities and merchants in East Africa. Even the infamous slave trader Tippu Tib was wary of him. Anyone travelling through Uganda needed military protection against violence from the king's men.

Above: A plaque commemorating some of the Martyrs of Uganda. In 1885 and 1886, a total of 22 Africans were martyred.

Below: A stained-glass window of the boy martyrs in St Andrew's Parish Church, Surrey, England.

On being confronted by Joseph Mkasa, the mad monarch immediately sentenced his adviser to death for being a traitorous convert. Joseph replied simply, "A Christian who gives his life for Christ is not afraid to die." He was publicly beheaded and fierce persecution of both Ca,tholics and Protestants followed.

In time, Mwanga's religious persecution succeeded in uniting Christian and Muslim Ugandans, who put aside their traditional enmity and deposed him in 1889, placing his brother on the throne.

Joseph Mkasa and other named Martyrs of Uganda were canonized by Pope Paul VI in 1964.

CHARLES LWANGA

CHARLES LWANGA, ONE OF THE NAMED MARTYRS OF UGANDA, WAS MURDERED BECAUSE HE PROTECTED THE CHILDREN IN HIS CARE AND REFUSED TO DENY HIS FAITH.

KEY FACTS
Martyr of Uganda
DATES: *1865–86*
BIRTH PLACE: *Uganda*
FEAST DAY: *3 June*

The tyrant of Uganda, King Mwanga, beheaded the bishop missionary James Hannington and the Ugandan convert Joseph Mkasa, but he did not stop there.

When Mwanga killed a page, Denis Sebuggwawo, for teaching the catechism, Charles Lwanga, who supervised the court pages, voiced his rage. That night, fearing the worst, Lwanga baptized four of the boys in his charge.

In the morning, the king called up Charles Lwanga, 15 pages and numerous other Christians captured by his warriors. He told them to deny their faith, but they said they would remain Christians "until death". They were marched to Namugongo, where they were beaten, wrapped in reed mats and burnt alive. Their joyful courage has been likened to that of the early Christians.

Mwanga murdered many more Christians, including Matthias Murumba and Andrew Kagwa. In 1964, 22 of the young men, including Charles Lwanga, were canonized as the Martyrs of Uganda. Their feast day is a public holiday in Uganda.

Above: The Martyrs Monument at Namugongo in Uganda, which commemorates the martyrdom of Christians on 3 June 1886.

MARIE ADOLPHINE DIERKS

MARIE ADOLPHINE DIERKS WAS A HUMBLE DUTCH WOMAN WHO FELT CALLED UPON AND COMPELLED BY GOD TO BECOME A NUN. SHE SAID, "I WANT TO SUFFER FOR THE LORD."

KEY FACTS
Martyr of China
DATES: *1866–1900*
BIRTH PLACE: *Ossendrecht, Holland*
FEAST DAY: *17 February*

Marie was born in Holland, one of six siblings who lost their mother at an early age and were taken in by poor but kindly neighbours. Marie was dedicated to her studies and her prayers, but soon realized that her adoptive family needed financial help. She worked as a factory hand and as a domestic servant, giving part of her earnings to her family.

However, she felt a strong call to serve God, and in 1893 she joined the Franciscan Missionaries of Mary in Antwerp. With six other nuns, she was sent to the Shanxi diocese in China. Work at the hospital and orphanage in Shanxi was hard, but Marie served with patience.

She was beheaded, along with her six Christian colleagues, in a crackdown on foreign missionaries during the Boxer Rebellion of 1900. Her name is included in the list of the 120 Blessed Martyrs of China, canonized by Pope John Paul II in 2000.

Left: A colour lithograph depicting the murder of a monk during the Boxer Rebellion in China.

JOHN BOSCO

JOHN BOSCO WAS A GREAT TEACHER WHO NEVER PUNISHED HIS PUPILS BUT, INSTEAD, GUIDED BY A CHILDHOOD VISION, USED THE "PREVENTIVE" MEASURES OF LOVE, PATIENCE AND FIRMNESS.

> **KEY FACTS**
> *Founder of an order*
> DATES: *1815–88*
> BIRTH PLACE: *Piedmont, Italy*
> PATRON OF: *Editors, young people, young workers, apprentices and youth of Mexico*
> FEAST DAY: *31 January*

John Bosco's life was given direction by a dream he had when he was very young. In this dream, he saw a group of young boys who were playing and swearing. To stop their blaspheming he punched them with his fists, but a man intervened, saying, "You will have to win these friends of yours not by blows, but by gentleness and love."

A LIFE OF POVERTY

John was born into a peasant family from Piedmont, Italy, but lost his father when he was only two years old. He was brought up by his mother, and such was their poverty that, when he decided to enter a seminary in 1831, his clothes and shoes were donated by neighbours.

After he was ordained priest in 1841, John became chaplain of a girl's school in Turin. On Sundays, a group of boys who lived on the city streets would come to the school to play and learn their catechism. John quickly realized, with the help of his guide and teacher, Joseph Cafasso, that his life's work lay with these boys.

LED BY HIS DREAM

Bosco left the school and went to live in shabby rooms in the Valdocco area of Turin, where, with his mother as housekeeper, he housed and educated the abandoned boys of the city. He set up shoemaking, tailoring and printing workshops, where the boys could learn a trade, and gave them lessons in Latin and grammar. Never forgetting his dream, Bosco

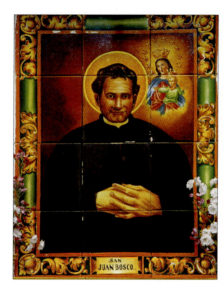

Above: A mosaic tile depiction of St John Bosco in Seville, Spain.

fostered a good relationship with his pupils through recreation, and encouraged picnics, outdoor play and a love of nature and music.

By 1856, he was housing 150 boys and he began to train like-minded people to help him in his work. He called these teachers "Salesians", after St Francis of Sales. They were approved as a religious order in 1874.

Bosco founded a similar order for women – the Daughters of Our Lady, Help of Christians – in 1872. These orders are now established across the globe, and run seminaries and technical and agricultural colleges.

John Bosco died in 1888, shortly after the completion of his church dedicated to the Sacred Heart in Rome, where he had been able to offer only one Mass. About 40,000 mourners visited his body and the people of Turin lined the streets to watch the cortège. He was canonized by Pope Pius XI in 1934.

Below: Part of an engraving from an Italian newspaper showing the canonization of John Bosco in St Peter's Basillica, Rome, on 1st April 1934.

JOHN HENRY NEWMAN

A LEADING THEOLOGIAN, SCHOLAR, AUTHOR AND CHURCHMAN WHO CONTROVERSIALLY CONVERTED FROM ANGLICANISM TO CATHOLICISM IN MID-LIFE AND WAS LATER MADE A CARDINAL.

> **KEY FACTS**
> *Founder of an order*
> DATES: *1801–90*
> BIRTH PLACE: *City of London*
> PATRON OF: *Poets, Personal Ordinariate of our Lady of Walsingham*
> FEAST DAY: *9 October*

Cardinal Newman was the first Englishman born since the 1600s to be raised to sainthood when he was canonized by Pope Francis on 13 October 2019. Born in London in 1801, in his youth he became an Evangelical Christian and then, after studying at Trinity College, Oxford University, became a fellow of Oriel College and a clergyman in the Church of England. Subsequently, he was one of the founders of the Oxford Movement, which set out to bring the Church of England back to its roots and led to the establishment of Anglo-Catholicism. In 1845, aged 44, he converted to Catholicism, and later wrote: "It was like coming into port after a rough sea." The following year he went to Rome, and then was ordained a priest on 30 May 1847 and granted the degree of Doctor of Divinity by Pope Pius IX.

Back in Britain, he settled in Edgbaston, Birmingham, and with papal approval established the Birmingham Oratory, a religious community of secular clergy following the rule established by St Philip Neri (1515–95). He subsequently created further groups in Oxford, London, York and Manchester. He also played a key role in founding the Catholic University of Ireland, which became University College Dublin.

A WRITER'S LIFE

Newman was a prolific theologian and writer, who produced the lecture series "The Present Position of Catholics in England"

Above: A painting of John Henry Newman by Sir John Everett Millais.

(1851) and the book *Apologia pro Vita Sua* (a defence of his religious opinions) in 1864, as well as the novels *Loss and Gain* (1848) and *Callista* (1855). His prose style was strongly commended by no less a figure than James Joyce, who wrote: "nobody has ever written English prose that can be compared with that of [an] Anglican parson who ... became a prince of the only true church."

Newman's 1865 poem "The Dream of Gerontius" inspired the choral work of the same name by Edward Elgar in 1900. Newman's *Collected Works* are published in 31 volumes. He wrote the hymns "Lead, Kindly Light", "Praise to the Holiest in the Height" and "Firmly I Believe and Truly". At his canonization, Pope Francis addresssed the audience, saying: "Let us ask to be like that, 'kindly lights' amid the encircling gloom."

Newman was made a cardinal by Pope Leo XIII in 1879, but at his own request was not made a bishop and was permitted to remain in Birmingham. He chose as his cardinal's motto *Cor ad cor loquitor* ("Heart speaks to heart"). In 1886, his health became poor and, after celebrating Mass for the last time on Christmas Day, 1889, he died of pneumonia on 11 August 1890 and was buried in the cemetery at the Oratory's country house, Rednal Hill in Birmingham. His remains were later removed to a closed sarcophagus at the Birmingham Oratory.

Below: Statue of John Henry Newman in front of Brompton Oratory by L.J. Chavalliaud.

HOUSES OF GOD

MEDIEVAL CHURCHES WERE DESIGNED TO CAST THE MIND TOWARD HEAVEN AND INSPIRE AWE. MODERN CHURCHES TEND TO BE MORE SIMPLE AND INTIMATE TO HELP THE VISITOR FEEL CLOSER TO GOD.

As Christianity spread across the Middle East and Europe, so churches were built to provide places of worship for believers. In small towns and villages, these buildings became the centre of community life.

The church was the house of God, and as such, money, time and talent came to be lavished on great cathedrals and grand churches. The faithful entered these wondrous buildings and were filled with awe and reverence. Statues and paintings inside confirmed the reality of the saints, and Christians were convinced that, in these surroundings, their prayers would fly to heaven, where the saints were listening.

THE GOTHIC STYLE

The medieval period saw the building of churches throughout the Christian world on an unprecedented scale. In the West, the predominant architectural style was Gothic.

The Gothic architects erected structures of great grandeur to express the majesty of God and emphasize man's insignificance. These cathedrals featured huge flying buttresses, pointed arches, rib vaults, and large windows. Enormous doors opened into interiors lit by the mysterious glow of stained glass.

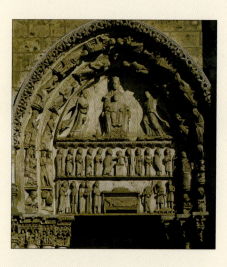

Above: The royal portal on the west front of Notre-Dame Cathedral in Chartres, France (c.1145).

> "I AM THE ETERNAL DOOR: PASS THROUGH ME, FAITHFUL ONES.
> I AM THE FOUNTAIN OF LIFE: THIRST FOR ME MORE THAN WINE."
>
> ON THE PORTAL OF THE CHURCH OF SANTA CRUZ DE LA SERÓS, SPAIN

Façades were laced with decoration and statues of saints, and to remind the faithful of hell, small devilish gargoyles flew from the buttresses or were carved into pews. One of the finest examples of the Gothic style is the 12th-century Notre-Dame Cathedral in Chartres, France.

The construction of Gothic cathedrals often took centuries to complete, so these buildings frequently incorporate a range of architectural and artistic styles.

Left: The front façade of the Cathedral of St Michel and St Gudule in Brussels, Belgium.

Construction of the Cathedral of St Michel and St Gudule in Brussels, for example, commenced in the early 13th century but the work was not completed for another 300 years. Cologne Cathedral, which has the largest façade of any church in the world, was begun in 1248 and finished 600 years later. Much of the stained glass in the cathedral is from the 19th century.

A NEW DIRECTION

When Martin Luther criticized the power and practices of the Roman Catholic Church in 1517, he began a new era for the church in northern Europe, known as the Reformation.

During the Reformation and in its aftermath, exterior carvings and statues, and the splendid interiors, walls hung with paintings, reliquaries gleaming with precious metals and jewels, and even the shrines so carefully constructed for relics were destroyed by Luther's Protestant supporters.

A new and austere style emerged, and this mood prevails in much modern northern European church architecture. Architects of Protestant churches

Left: The dome of the Hagia Sophia in Istanbul, Turkey. This magnificent Byzantine building was the mother church of the Eastern Christians for 916 years before it was turned into a mosque by the Ottomans in 1453. It is now a museum.

no longer seek to replicate heaven; neither do they wish to inspire awe in visitors. Churches are usually designed to be informal, and space is meant to promote fellowship among believers and stress a sense of community. Altar tables and light fittings are simple, and roof levels may be flattened or given low curves more in sympathy with an earthly landscape.

SURVIVAL OF DECORATION

Despite the efforts of the reformers, most medieval churches survived the Reformation. Even after the destructive Civil War in England, hundreds of examples are still relatively intact.

Where the Roman Catholic Church survived, or was unaffected by, the Reformation – in Italy, Spain, Poland, and parts of France and Germany – church architecture remained centred upon the glorification of God with beauty.

In the Balkans, Greece and the Middle East, where the Eastern Orthodox Church prevails, many ancient religious buildings can still be found, although some of these became mosques after the Islamic conquest of the East and the rule of the Ottoman Empire from Istanbul (once Constantinople).

Below: The interior of Cologne Cathedral in Germany.

STAINED GLASS WINDOWS

The origin of the stained glass window is unknown, but artists were working in this medium by 1100. Coloured sections of glass, cut to shape and held together by black lead strips, formed elaborate designs that depicted biblical stories and lives of the saints. By the 16th century, artists preferred to paint the glass, and by the 18th century, many windows had been removed. Superb examples of medieval glass can still be seen in their original setting, for example at Notre-Dame Cathedral in Chartres, France, and York Minster in England. Many stained glass windows are preserved in the world's great museums.

Above: A stained glass window at Chartres Cathedral showing St Lubin, Bishop of Chartres in the 6th century (c.1200–10).

THERESA OF LISIEUX

THERESA, THE "LITTLE FLOWER", WROTE OF HER RELATIONSHIP WITH GOD WITH AN ARTLESS SIMPLICITY THAT CONVEYED A DEEP SPIRITUALITY, QUALIFYING HER AS A DOCTOR OF THE CHURCH.

> **KEY FACTS**
> *Virgin, mystic, Doctor of the Church*
> DATES: *1873–1897*
> BIRTH PLACE: *Alençon, France*
> PATRON OF: *France, missions, florists and flower growers*
> FEAST DAY: *1 October*
> EMBLEM: *Flowers*

Theresa of Lisieux lived a very ordinary life. She did not perform great works, found a religious order or convert thousands to Christianity. And yet this young girl, who lived for such a brief time, left a rich spiritual legacy.

AN EARLY VOCATION
Although she was only four years old when her mother died, Theresa had four older sisters to look after her. The eldest, Pauline, became her surrogate mother, but, by the time Theresa was ten, her two eldest sisters had left home to enter the local Carmelite convent in Lisieux.

Theresa begged constantly to join the convent, but she was too young to take such vows. On a pilgrimage to Rome with her father, she knelt for a blessing from Pope Leo XIII. Knowing that she was forbidden to speak to him, she broke all protocol and begged him to let her be a nun. He supported the decision of the Carmelites, but, when Theresa reached the age of 15, the Bishop of Bayeux, impressed by her piety and determination, allowed the prioress to admit her.

In April 1888, the young girl began her life in the enclosed Carmelite convent, where she began to develop her spirituality by reading the Carmelite mystics and following the austere rules of the order. The abbess forbade Theresa to fast because she was not physically robust, but she sensed that the young girl was an intuitive thinker, and encouraged her to write. This wise advice allowed Theresa the time and space to produce *The Story of a Soul*, and her many other texts, which include 54 poems, 20 prayers, eight plays and more than 200 letters. In a simple poetic style, these writings describe how every "little life" can be enhanced by faith and reveal her extraordinary relationship with God.

THE "LITTLE WAY"
The young nun longed to be a saint, but, aware that, as a Carmelite, she would not be able to achieve great works, she looked for a new path that would lead her to sanctity. "I knew I was a very little soul who could offer only little things to the good God", she wrote. From this thought grew her "little way" of "the doing of the least actions for love".

A year after she had joined the Carmelites, Theresa's father suffered two strokes that left him weak and dependent. Emotionally disturbed and unhappy, he had a nervous breakdown, and in 1894, died in a lunatic asylum. Her fourth sister, Celine, who had spent her life caring for their father, joined Theresa at the Carmelite convent.

Theresa wanted to follow the example of the apostles

Above: Theresa of Lisieux (artist and date unknown). Aware she was dying, Theresa wrote that, after her death, she would "let fall a shower of roses", meaning that in heaven she would intercede for her friends.

Left: A photograph of Theresa of Lisieux in the garden of the Carmelite convent in Lisieux in France (c.1890).

480

DIRECTORY OF SAINTS

Above: The Basilica of St Theresa in Lisieux, France, is the saint's major shrine.

and longed for the opportunity to spread the love of Christ in foreign lands. She had always prayed for missionaries – it was a Carmelite discipline to pray for Christian missions abroad – but she also corresponded with the Carmelite nuns in Hanoi, Indo-China (now Vietnam), and they wanted her to join them.

QUIET SUFFERING

Then, in 1895, Theresa had a curious experience. During the night between Maundy Thursday and Good Friday, she heard "as it were, a far-off murmur announcing the coming of the Bridegroom". She seemed unaware that she was bleeding from her mouth – a symptom of tuberculosis. With her health broken, her dream of becoming a missionary would never be realized.

For 18 months, Theresa suffered pain and difficulty in breathing. She was eventually confined to the convent infirmary, where she was so ill that she was unable to receive Holy Communion. She died at the age of 24.

Pilgrims still flock to Lisieux to venerate St Theresa, who is known as the "little flower of Jesus" and Theresa-of-the-Child-Jesus, names that reflect her simple, childlike faith. Her book has been translated into 50 languages and has brought inspiration to millions of people. Theresa of Lisieux was canonized in 1925.

Below: St Theresa, from a cycle of Carmelite life made from mosaic, in the Basilica of St Theresa in Lisieux, France (Pierre Gaudin, 1958).

> "I DESIRE TO BE A SAINT, BUT I KNOW MY WEAKNESS AND SO I ASK YOU, MY GOD, THAT YOU YOURSELF WILL BE MY HOLINESS."
>
> THERESA OF LISIEUX

GEMMA GALGANI

Born in 1878, Gemma was an orphan, terribly afflicted by tuberculosis of the spine. She resembled Theresa of Lisieux in other ways, too. Hers was a "little life" without office, wealth or public recognition. Faith guided all her actions, only ill health preventing her from entering a convent. Her mysticism was expressed in ecstasies, during which she gave spiritual messages. She had visions of Jesus and stigmata appeared on her body. Heroic in enduring illness and poverty, Gemma died in 1903 and was canonized in 1941.

Above: Lucca in Tuscany, Italy. St Gemma Galgani's relics are housed at the Passionist monastery in the city.

RAPHAEL KALINOWSKI

IN HIS ROLE AS A PRIEST, RAPHAEL KALINOWSKI FOSTERED HOPES OF UNITING CHRISTIANS, THROUGH SPIRITUAL GUIDANCE, TO COMBAT THE GROWING POWER OF THE SECULAR STATE.

KEY FACTS
Carmelite
DATES: *1835–1907*
BIRTH PLACE: *Vilnius, Poland (now Lithuania)*
FEAST DAY: *15 November*

The 19th century in Europe is a story of industrialization, nationalism and secular politics. The life of Raphael Kalinowski reflects the period. Raised a devout Catholic, he became an engineer, working on the new Russian railways. While running a Sunday school at the fortress in Brest-Litovsk, where he was a captain, he became increasingly aware of the State persecution of the Church, and of his native Poles.

When the Poles rose against the Russians in 1863, Raphael joined them and was soon taken prisoner. Few survived the forced

march to slave labour in Siberia, but Raphael was sustained by his faith and became spiritual leader to the prisoners. He was released ten years later.

Left: Polish Insurrectionists of the 1863 Rebellion (*Stanislaus von Chlebowski, 19th century*).

Profoundly changed by his experiences in Siberia, Kalinowski joined the Carmelites, and, in 1882, he was ordained priest at the monastery at Czerna, near Cracow, the last Carmelite brotherhood allowed in Poland.

Raphael strove to revive the Carmelites in Poland and to bring religious freedom to his oppressed countrymen. He died in Wadowice and was canonized in 1991.

MIGUEL CORDERO

MIGUEL CORDERO OF ECUADOR WAS A GIFTED TEACHER, WHO, THROUGH HIS TEACHING AND WRITINGS, SPREAD THE WORD OF JESUS ACROSS HIS COUNTRY.

KEY FACTS
De la Sallist
DATES: *1854–1910*
BIRTH PLACE: *Cuenca, Ecuador*
FEAST DAY: *9 February*

Miguel Cordero was physically disabled but intellectually precocious. In his thinking, he was a precise theologian, but his actions showed a man concerned with the welfare of his students and fellow priests.

The De La Salle Brothers (the international teaching order founded by St John-Baptist De La Salle) accepted Cordero when he was only 14, and, a year later, sent him to Quito in Ecuador. He proved to be an outstanding teacher. At the age of 20, he published a Spanish grammar that became adopted nationwide, and later wrote other

Above: Cuenca in Ecuador, birth place of Miguel Cordero. Cordero was the first Ecuadorian to be accepted into the de la Salle teaching order.

acclaimed textbooks, and translated a life of John-Baptist de La Salle.

The Ecuadorian government despised the Church, but, in spite of the state's efforts to suppress religion, Cordero's fame as a holy teacher and writer spread.

In 1907, he was called to work in Belgium. However, the Belgian climate did not suit him and he was moved to Barcelona. When an anti-clerical revolution erupted in the city, Cordero had to be rescued by gunboat. He died in Premia del Mar, Spain, in 1910, and was canonized in 1984.

FRANCES CABRINI

A MISSIONARY AMONG ITALIAN IMMIGRANTS IN AMERICA, FRANCES IS KNOWN AS THE "MOTHER OF EMIGRANTS" FOR HER WORK TO KEEP THE FAITH ALIVE AMONG CHRISTIANS FAR FROM HOME.

> **KEY FACTS**
> Founder of schools and orphanages
> DATES: *1850–1917*
> BIRTH PLACE: *Sant' Angelo Lodigiano, near Pavia, Italy*
> PATRON OF: *Migrants and emigrants*
> FEAST DAY: *22 December*

Frances Cabrini was a missionary in the New World, but she did not work among the indigenous people. Instead, she was sent to revive the faith of Italian immigrants in America. Initially, she thought the mission unnecessary, believing all Italians to be as devout as her relatives.

Frances was the youngest of 13 children of northern Italian parents. After qualifying as a teacher, she tried to become a nun but was refused by two orders for health reasons. She was a tiny woman, barely 152cm/5ft tall, but a friendly priest, guessing at her inner strength, appealed to his bishop, who invited her to manage a small orphanage in Codogno, Lombardy. She remained there until the house closed.

Above: The body of Frances Cabrini lies in state in the chapel at the Mother Cabrini High School in New York City.

Left: A statue of St Frances Cabrini in the National Shrine of the Immaculate Conception in Washington, DC.

THE MISSIONARY SISTERS

The bishop encouraged Frances to start her own missionary congregation. She gathered seven women who had worked with her at Codogno and founded the Missionary Sisters of the Sacred Heart, dedicated to the education of Christian girls.

Frances had always wanted to work in China, but the Archbishop of New York had invited her to set up schools and orphanages for Italian immigrants. When, in 1889, she and six sisters crossed the Atlantic, they found no one had prepared for their arrival, and they had to live in poverty with the immigrants until Frances was able to find a building and open the orphanage.

SPREAD OF THE MISSION

Success followed, and Frances opened more orphanages and schools in New York. She also founded schools in Managua, the capital of Nicaragua, and in New Orleans. Over the following years, her mission spread to Italy, Costa Rica, Panama, Chile, Brazil, France and England. Her profound faith drove her, and her proudest achievement was in opening the Columbus Hospital in New York.

Before moving to the United States, Frances had never met a Protestant and had difficulty in accepting that they, too, could be Christian. Her views were stern on subjects such as illegitimacy, but her deep love of God and a sense of justice tempered her thinking and ideas.

When her Missionary Sisters of the Sacred Heart were approved in 1907, there were 1,000 members in eight countries, and they served orphans, schools, prisons and hospitals.

Frances died in Chicago in 1917. and, in 1946, was the first U.S. citizen to be canonized.

DIRECTORY OF SAINTS

TERESA OF LOS ANDES

Teresa wanted to devote her life completely to Jesus and "to love and suffer for the salvation of souls". The simple faith of this young woman has become an example to many.

> **KEY FACTS**
> *Virgin, Carmelite*
> Dates: *1900–20*
> Birth Place: *Santiago, Chile*
> Feast Day: *12 April*

The shrine of St Teresa of Los Andes at La Riconda attracts 100,000 pilgrims every year. She is among those pious young women, such as Theresa of Lisieux, whose every thought and action was directed toward God.

CALLED TO SUFFER
One of six children born in Santiago, Chile, to wealthy, unassuming Christian parents, Teresa was well educated in the sciences, music and the arts. Her parents, who named her Juanita, were pleased by the religious faith of their daughter and the happiness it seemed to bring her.

When she was 14 years old, and suffering a painful bout of appendicitis, Teresa heard the voice of Jesus telling her that her pain was in imitation of his suffering. She had been lively and athletic until then, nicknamed "the Amazon" by her brothers, but after hearing Jesus speak, she made an inner vow of chastity, took to teaching the catechism to deprived children, and read the biographies of Teresa of Avila and of St Elizabeth of the Trinity.

Above: A statue of St Teresa of Los Andes in Chile. A cultus developed after her death and she remains popular, especially with young women.

DEVOTION TO CHRIST
Teresa considered joining the Sacred Heart Sisters, who were an educational order, but was overwhelmed by the need to devote her life to Christ. Her father was reluctant to give his permission when she told him she preferred to join an enclosed order, but he and the family did support her when, at 19, she became a noviciate with the Carmelite nuns.

The Carmelite convent in Los Andes was a rough building that lacked electricity and plumbing. Here, she took the vow of Victimhood, which meant that she was prepared to suffer for the Church and for sinners. Teresa's hours were spent deep in prayer, fasting, learning methods of contemplation, and recording and sharing her spiritual experiences in letters and a diary.

She was not quite 20 years old when she died of typhus at the convent, but her piety was regarded with great respect, and slowly, the power of her "hidden life" of devotion was revealed. A cultus grew around her memory and she was canonized by Pope John Paul II in 1993.

Left: Personal messages for St Teresa of Los Andes cover a wall outside the church dedicated to her in Los Andes, Chile.

BERTILLA BOSCARDIN

BERTILLA WAS A SIMPLE PEASANT WOMAN WHO HAD BEEN BADLY TREATED AS A CHILD, BUT HER PATIENCE AND STAUNCH RELIGIOUS FAITH MADE HER A WONDERFUL NURSE.

KEY FACTS
Nun, nurse
DATES: *1888–1922*
BIRTH PLACE: *near Vicenza, Italy*
FEAST DAY: *20 October*

This saint lived a humble life, but those whom she cared for loved her, and miracles have been attributed to her intercession.

Maria Bertilla Boscardin was a peasant girl who joined the Sisters of St Dorothy in Vicenza in 1904. The other nuns, considering her dim-witted, used her as a kitchen and laundry maid until her profession in 1907, when she was sent to care for children with diphtheria at the hospital in Treviso.

During World War I, Vicenza was bombed, but Bertilla remained calm, intent only on saving her patients. When the hospital was moved away from the front line to Como, the military authorities praised her work. But, again, her simplicity was misinterpreted, and she was put to work in the laundry. Bertilla never complained, but in 1919, the superior-general of the order rescued her and placed her in charge of the children's isolation ward back at Treviso, where she nursed with compassion.

Bertilla died while undergoing surgery. Her family and some of her former patients were present at her canonization in 1961.

Above: Bertilla Boscardin worked as a nurse in Treviso, where she cared for the sick with patience and sympathy.

GIUSEPPE MOSCATI

GIUSEPPE MOSCATI BELIEVED HIS SCIENTIFIC KNOWLEDGE AND CARE OF THE SICK WERE A WAY TO REVEAL THE GLORY OF GOD, AND CONSIDERED HIS MEDICAL WORK TO BE A "SUBLIME MISSION".

KEY FACTS
Doctor of medicine
DATES: *1860–1927*
BIRTH PLACE: *Benevento, Italy*
FEAST DAY: *16 November*

Giuseppe Moscati came from a family brave in their faith. His father was a magistrate who had risked his livelihood, when he refused to deny Christianity during the anti-clerical control of Italy during the mid-19th century.

Giuseppe was a top medical student at the University of Naples, where he specialized in biochemistry. After qualifying, he began working with patients afflicted with syphilis at the Hospital for Incurables, Santa Maria del Populo.

Parallel to his hospital duties, Giuseppe conducted medical research and gave free care to the poor. This entailed visiting the swarming slums of Naples, often at night, to tend the sick. His scientific learning was underpinned by his faith, and he treated patients for spiritual as well as medical problems.

In 1911, he was appointed Chair of Physiology at Naples University, but success did not turn him from his prayers or his veneration of Mary, the Blessed Virgin. Neither did he neglect his charity work. Patients, priests and laymen appreciated the spiritual dimension he brought to medicine. He died peacefully in his home and was canonized in 1987.

Above: Pilgrims touch the hand of the Giuseppe Moscati statue at Gesù Nuovo church in Naples, Italy.

THE CULT OF MARY

Mary, the Blessed Virgin, is honoured worldwide by millions of faithful for her purity as well as for her extraordinary role as the Mother of God.

Above: A statue of the crowned Virgin and Child in Siena, Italy.

Devotion to Mary can be traced as far back as the 4th or 5th centuries AD, but the full doctrine has developed gradually. In the earliest days of the Church, Mary, the Blessed Virgin, was called "Christokos", "Mother of Christ", but this caused some wrangling among theologians because it implied that Jesus was not divine. In the 6th century AD, they agreed on "Theotokos", "Mother of God", and this more emphatic description of Mary confirmed her strong position in the faith as the mother of Jesus, the Son of God. Even the Protestant Church accepted her unique role as the virgin mother of Christ, but some Protestant sects have recently questioned this.

> "Grant we beseech Thee, O Lord God, unto us thy servants, that we may rejoice in continual health of mind and body; and, by the glorious intercession of Blessed Mary ever Virgin, may be delivered from present sadness, and enter into the joy of thine eternal gladness. Through Christ our Lord. Amen."
>
> FINAL WORDS OF THE *LITANY OF LORETO*

AN EXCEPTIONAL WOMAN

Christians who venerate Mary often call her the Immaculate Conception. This refers to the belief that her spirit was conceived free from original sin, untainted by the sins of Adam and Eve in the Garden of Eden. This has led some theologians to refer to her as the "new Eve".

Not only is Mary believed to be immune from original sin, but she was also a virgin when Jesus was born, hence the title given to her, the Blessed Virgin. Because she embodies purity and perfect motherly love, she has always held a special place in the heart of believers. Augustine of Hippo, when discussing the nature of Mary, said, "After all, how do we know what abundance of grace was granted to her who had the merit to conceive and bring forth him who was unquestionably without sin?"

When Mary had completed her life on earth, it is believed that she was received into heaven as a complete being – body and soul together. This special event is key to both Roman Catholic and Eastern Orthodox belief, but the Anglican Church also includes it in its calendar. The day of the Assumption, 15 August, occasions great celebration, as it is considered to be Mary's heavenly birthday.

THE GREATEST SAINT

Mary has long been perceived as chief among all the saints, mediating with Jesus on behalf of the world. For this reason, the faithful turn to her to resolve their most difficult problems.

In 1587, Pope Sixtus V sealed this view of Mary's role when he approved the *Litany of Loreto*.

Left: A West African woodcarving of Madonna and child (20th century).

Right: Catholics seek blessings for their child from a statue of Mary in Hyderabad, India.

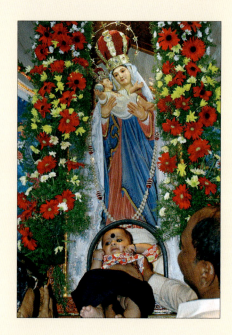

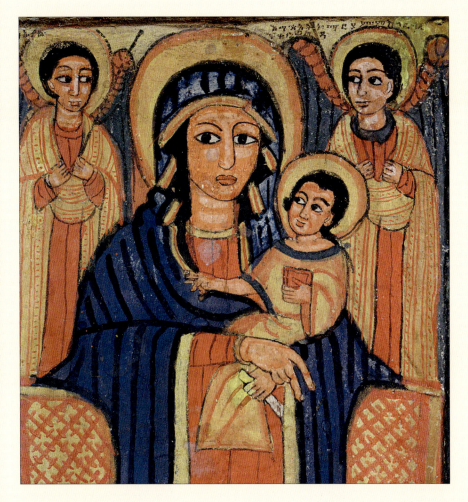

Left: An Ethiopian icon triptych depicting the Virgin and child (18th–19th century).

Catholic homes, schools and institutions display the image of the Blessed Virgin and often create small shrine-like altars in veneration of her. No Catholic church is without a statue to Mary, the Blessed Virgin, and the infant Jesus.

In modern times, Mary is firmly lodged in the Christian culture. She is a central figure in literature and popular idiom, and she is patron saint to a number of countries.

The principal Marian shrines attract huge numbers of pilgrims, millions visiting every year the sites of Lourdes in France, Guadalupe in Mexico, Fatima in Portugal, Walsingham in England and the House of Loreto in Italy.

In this long prayer, believers call upon God to heed Mary, and the text uses her many titles.

WORLDWIDE INFLUENCE

The Eastern Orthodox Church has been untouched by debate about Mary's role. There, she has always had a profound significance, and many Orthodox icons are devoted to the image of Mary as Mother with her Holy Infant.

In the Western Church, theologians have long debated her role, but since the 15th century, popular religion has developed a deep devotion to Mary. She represents motherhood and family life, one who understands the universal experiences of joy and pain. Those believers suffering tragedy meditate on the image of Mary with her dying son. The rosary is a set of prayers often recited by Christians who venerate Mary, the Blessed Virgin. A string of beads, also called a rosary, is used as an *aide-mémoire* for the correct order of the prayers.

Right: The famous Pietà *in St Peter's, Rome (Michelangelo, 1496).*

SOME TITLES OF MARY

There are numerous titles for Mary, many used in the long prayer, the Litany of Loreto. Here are a few examples:
Advocate of Grace
The Blessed Virgin
Champion of God's People
Chosen Daughter of the Father
Gracious Lady
Handmaid of the Lord
Holy Mary
Holy Mother of God
The Immaculate Conception
Joy of Israel
Most Honoured of Virgins
Mother of Christ
Mother Mary
Our Lady
Perfect Disciple of Christ
Queen of All Saints
Queen of Apostles and Martyrs
Queen of Confessors and Virgins
Queen of Mercy
Queen of Peace
Splendour of the Church

MARIA FAUSTINA KOWALSKA

Maria Faustina Kowalska was a humble lay sister, but her heavenly visions, her obedience and her deep devotion to God, recorded in her diaries, brought her sainthood.

> **KEY FACTS**
> *Visionary and Polish mystic*
> Dates: *1905–38*
> Birth Place: *Glogowiec, Poland*
> Feast Day: *25 August*

Maria Faustina Kowalska offered her own suffering to God to make amends for her sins and the sins of others. Her inspiration came from a miracle described in John's Gospel: after Jesus had healed a man who had been an invalid for 38 years, he said to him, "Sin no more, lest a worse thing come unto thee." The man went away and told others that Jesus had made him well. Maria believed that, with faith and virtue, sins would be forgiven, just as the faith of the invalid had banished his disability.

A LIFE GUIDED BY VISIONS

Born in Glogowiec, Poland, Maria was the third of ten children. She was certain that she had a vocation to the religious life, and, in 1923, she had a vision of Christ that strengthened her conviction. In 1925, she joined the Congregation of Our Lady of Mercy in Warsaw as a lay sister.

She did not aim for high office, and nursed no ambition, but, in humility and obedience, worked in the garden, the kitchen and as a porter. The compassion and patience she showed towards the poor who visited the convent impressed her fellow nuns.

DIVINE MERCY

Visions of Jesus were a frequent part of Maria's experience, and in one of these Christ is said to have asked her to keep a diary. In this, she began to record the spiritual guidance the visions brought her, primarily the message of the "Divine Mercy of God". Her diary was later published with the title *Divine Mercy in My Soul: The Diary of St Faustina*.

Her health was delicate, and in 1936 she was moved to a sanatorium in Cracow with suspected tuberculosis. Here, she was given her own cell, and in this privacy she was able to surrender herself to prayer and contemplation. Her last years were spent fighting for breath and in constant pain. She died in Cracow, still a young woman, in 1938, and was canonized by Pope John Paul II in 2000.

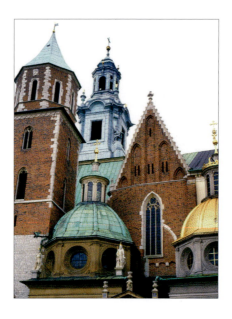

Above: Cracow, Poland, where Maria Faustina Kowalska spent the last few years of her life in contemplation and prayer while she fought off illness.

Left: The canonization of Maria Faustina Kowalska by Pope John Paul II took place in front of 100,000 pilgrims in 2000.

MAXIMILIAN KOLBE

Maximilian Kolbe made the ultimate sacrifice, giving up his life for the sake of another in a German concentration camp. He is known as the "martyr of charity".

> **KEY FACTS**
> *Martyr*
> DATES: *1894–1941*
> BIRTH PLACE: *near Łódź, Poland*
> FEAST DAY: *14 August*

Maximilian Kolbe was the son of devout, patriotic Polish parents. After Maximilian entered the Franciscan Order in 1910, his parents separated and began living religious lives. His father was hanged by the Russian government in 1914, because he was fighting with the Polish Legion for Polish independence.

In 1912, Maximilian was sent to Cracow, then to Rome, where he studied philosophy, theology, physics and mathematics. After his ordination in Rome in 1919, he founded Franciscan communities dedicated to prayer and serving the poor at Niepokalanow, near Warsaw, and at Nagasaki in Japan. He was keen to revive the faith and started up various religious publications in both Poland and Japan to accomplish this. He also took advantage of modern technology by installing a radio station at Niepokalanow.

HOUSING REFUGEES

When the Germans invaded Poland in 1939, Maximilian closed the Niepokalanow community and sent the priests home, anxious that they should not endanger themselves by joining the Resistance. Heedless of his own safety, he and the remaining brothers housed 4,500 Polish refugees, of whom 1,500 were Jewish. Maximilian's various publications continued and included articles critical of the German invaders. In 1941, he and four brothers were arrested and taken to the Nazi concentration camp at Auschwitz in Poland.

Above: An undated photograph of Maximilian Kolbe, the Franciscan priest who served, then gave up his life for fellow Poles in World War II.

GIVING HIS LIFE

Maximilian had suffered tuberculosis most of his life, so he found his duties at the camp – carrying logs and moving the bodies of dead inmates – particularly hard. He applied himself to giving his fellow sufferers religious comfort, and somehow even managed to smuggle bread and wine inside the walls so that he could offer the Holy Eucharist.

One day, the inmates from Maximilian's hut were lined up and the wardens selected several men to die. This was a reprisal for a successful escape attempt. One of the chosen, a Polish sergeant named Francis Gajowniczek, cried out, "My poor wife! My poor children! What will they do?" Maximilian stepped forward and announced, "I wish to die for that man. I am old; he has a wife and children."

The swap was approved and the condemned men were locked into Cell 18 and left to starve. Maximilian comforted them, sang psalms and prayed in preparation for their deaths. After two weeks, he was the only man still conscious. He was killed by lethal injection in August 1941.

Sergeant Gajowniczek – who himself died at the age of 94 in 1995 – attended the canonization of St Maximilian Kolbe in 1982.

Below: Francis Gajowniczek, the man saved by Maximilian Kolbe in 1941, is embraced by Pope John Paul II in St Peter's Square in 1982.

EDITH STEIN

EDITH STEIN, A JEWISH CONVERT AND PHILOSOPHER, BECAME A CARMELITE NUN, BELIEVING THAT IT WAS HER VOCATION "TO INTERCEDE TO GOD FOR EVERYONE".

KEY FACTS
Martyr
DATES: *1891–1942*
BIRTH PLACE: *Breslau, Germany (now Wrocław, Poland)*
PATRON OF: *France*
FEAST DAY: *9 August*

Edith Stein was brought up in the Jewish faith and studied philosophy at the German universities of Göttingen and Freiburg. During this time, she was profoundly affected by the writings of St Teresa of Ávila. She converted to Catholicism and was baptized in 1922. Edith did not regard her Christianity as a denial of her family's faith, but as an expansion of their Jewish beliefs. She continued to attend synagogue with her mother in order to soften the impact that her conversion would have on her devout Jewish family.

TEACHING AND STUDYING
Although Edith was not at ease in front of a class, she became a German language and literature teacher at a Dominican girls' school. As a woman, academic work in a university was closed to her. She joined the Educational Institute, but privately continued her philosophical studies, including a work on the role of women in the Christian Church. In 1932, Hitler initiated his anti-Jewish propaganda and Edith wrote, "Christ's Cross is being laid upon the Jewish people…".

In 1933, Edith entered the Carmelite Order, where a sympathetic abbess allowed her to

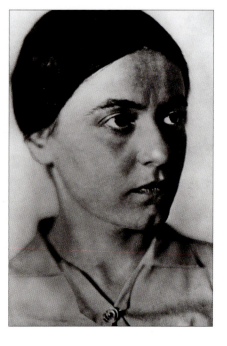

Left: The Jewish philosopher, photographed aged 39, became a Carmelite nun in 1934. Reading the autobiography of St Teresa of Ávila inspired her to convert.

continue writing on religious and scholarly topics. Edith prepared philosophical texts on prayer and the Eternal Being, and began a study of St John of the Cross.

By 1937, those of Jewish origin were no longer safe in Germany, and the Carmelites sent her to Holland. The Dutch Church campaigned against Nazi anti-Semitic policies but to no avail.

AUSCHWITZ
Edith refused to stay hidden in her convent, fearing her presence would harm the other nuns, and said on learning that she would be sent to Auschwitz in 1939, "I am going for my people."

Edith's faith brought her comfort and strength, and she ministered to her fellow prisoners. An insight into how she regarded her fate can be drawn from her own words: "Sufferings endured with the Lord are his sufferings, and bear great fruit in the context of his great work of redemption." Edith Stein was killed, with her sister Rose, in Auschwitz in 1942, and was canonized in 1998.

Left: Edith Stein was captured in the Netherlands during a persecution of Jewish converts. She was sent to Auschwitz death camp, where she was gassed in 1942.

JOSEPHINE BAKHITA

JOSEPHINE WAS SO TRAUMATIZED WHEN CAPTURED AND ILL TREATED BY SLAVE TRADERS THAT SHE FORGOT HER NAME. PROPHETICALLY, HER KIDNAPPERS NAMED HER BAKHITA – "THE FORTUNATE ONE".

> **KEY FACTS**
> *Convert, nun*
> DATES: *1869–1947*
> BIRTH PLACE: *Olgossa, Darfur, Sudan*
> PATRON OF: *the Sudan*
> FEAST DAY: *8 February*

Josephine represents all victims of oppression, and is venerated for her message of forgiveness. For many years a slave, Josephine claimed that, if she were to meet the men who enslaved her, she "would kneel to them to kiss their hands", because, without them, she would never have met Jesus.

Born in Darfur, Sudan, Josephine was only nine years old when Arab traders abducted and sold her in Khartoum. She was traded from one unpleasant owner to another until, in 1882, an Italian named Callisto Legnani bought her. He in turn gave her to his friend Augusto Michieli, who took her to Italy.

While he was away on business, Bakhita, as Josephine had been named, and Michieli's daughter stayed at the Canossian convent in Venice, where Josephine became a Christian. On her master's return, she requested permission to stay at the convent, and took her vows there in 1896.

Josephine was moved to the Canossian convent at Schio, Vicenza, where she remained for the rest of her life, apart from three years in Milan spent teaching young sisters to work in Africa. She was known and loved for her gentleness, calming voice, and ever-present smile. She died in Schio, murmuring, "Madonna, Madonna!" Pope John Paul II canonized her in 2000.

Right: A convoy of slaves in the Sudan, where Josephine Bakhita herself was traded as a slave while still a child.

JOHN CALABRIA

ON THE TOMB OF JOHN CALABRIA ARE THE WORDS: "HE SHONE LIKE A LIGHTHOUSE IN THE CHURCH OF GOD. HIS MISSION WAS 'TO PROVE TO THE WORLD THAT DIVINE PROVIDENCE EXISTS'."

> **KEY FACTS**
> *Founder of a charitable institution*
> DATES: *1873–1954*
> BIRTH PLACE: *Verona, Italy*
> FEAST DAY: *4 December*

John Calabria's holiness was recognized beyond the Roman Catholic community. During World War II, he protected persecuted Jews, disguising one woman as a nun to save her. He practised charity to everyone, regardless of faith or creed.

John was born in poverty in Verona, and was educated at the Institute for Poor Children. In 1897, he began to work with orphaned and abandoned boys, starting a "Charitable Institution for assistance to poor, sick people", which became the Congregation of the Poor Servants, and its sister house, the Poor Women Servants of Divine Providences.

John assured his followers that faith would help them in difficult situations "where there is nothing humanely possible", and he sent them to open hospitals and care homes in Italy and India. His writings and sermons encouraged people to follow God's love without prejudice. John died in San Zeno, Verona, in 1954, and was canonized in 1988.

Left: The San Zeno Basilica, the best-known church in Verona, where John Calabria spent his life.

KATHARINE DREXEL

KATHARINE DREXEL, MOTIVATED BY A PROFOUND FAITH, USED HER INHERITANCE TO IMPROVE THE SOCIAL AND RELIGIOUS WELFARE OF RACIAL MINORITIES AND DEPRIVED PEOPLES.

KEY FACTS
Founder of a university
DATES: *1858–1955*
BIRTH PLACE: *Philadelphia, USA*
FEAST DAY: *3 March*

Katharine Marie Drexel learnt the Christian virtue of charity from her stepmother, Emma Bouvier, who donated $20,000 a year to the welfare of the poor in Philadelphia. Another influence was Dr James O'Connor, a priest and family friend who campaigned for the just administration of Native Americans.

In 1878, Katharine "came out" in society, but she remained unmoved by the lavish circuit of balls and parties enjoyed by many of her peers. During a trip to Europe, she made a pilgrimage to the home of St Catherine of

Below: A statue of Katharine Drexel in the National Shrine of the Immaculate Conception in Washington, D.C.

Above: A painting of Katharine Drexel (artist and date unknown) shows her with some of the children she gave her life to serve.

Siena, and later confided to Dr O'Connor that she wished to become a nun.

By 1885, O'Connor, who had recently been appointed Bishop of Omaha, called on Katharine to help him resolve disputes between white and Native Americans in Dakota. On her return, she and her sisters, all wealthy women, founded the Drexel Chair of Moral Theology at Washington University (DC).

At an audience with Pope Leo XIII in 1887, she was encouraged by the pope to become a missionary. Taking his advice, and fulfilling her dream of a life dedicated to God, Katharine joined the Sisters of Mary in Pittsburgh.

AIDING MINORITIES
Katharine was determined to start a community devoted to helping ethnic minorities, and, in 1891, founded the Sisters of the Blessed Sacrament. In 1894, the order's first school for Native American children, St Catherine Indian School, was built in Santa Fe, New Mexico.

She established schools, missions and hospitals in Boston, Chicago, New Orleans, New York, Texas and Tennessee, and her congregation trained nearly 200 teaching sisters and 80 lay teachers. She also founded the first university for African American students, Xavier University in New Orleans.

Katharine worked until she was disabled by illness (she suffered a severe heart attack in 1935). Thereafter, she continued to pray for, and advise, her communities, who all knew her as "First Sister". She died in Philadelphia in 1955 at the age of 97. At her funeral, the pallbearers represented the groups she had helped – Native Americans, African Americans and European Americans.

Although Katharine focused on the welfare of racial minorities, her work extended to all the underprivileged. From the time she founded her order at the age of 33 until the end of her life, Katherine gave away a personal fortune of 20 million US dollars to the work of the Sisters of the Blessed Sacrament.

She also funded many convents, monasteries and chapels. Her congregation, which remains rooted in the welfare and education programmes she instituted, still has an important role within the Church. Katharine Drexel was canonized by Pope John Paul II in 2000.

FATHER GEORGE PRECA

FATHER GEORGE PRECA LOVED THE GOSPELS, WHICH HE CALLED "THE VOICE OF THE BELOVED". A HUMBLE MAN, HE DEVOTED HIS LIFE TO TEACHING THE DEPRIVED AND UNEDUCATED.

> **KEY FACTS**
> *Founder of an order*
> DATES: *1880–1962*
> BIRTH PLACE: *Valletta, Malta*
> FEAST DAY: *9 May*

The young George Preca was cured of an illness after prayers of intercession to St Joseph. Throughout his life, George heard heavenly voices and had visions, and these spiritual experiences gave him a powerful sense of his mission on earth. He was inspired, too, by the words of Jesus, "Blessed are the meek, for they shall inherit the earth" (Matthew 5:5).

MALTESE MISSION

After he was ordained in 1906, George began to seek out ordinary working people, and he set up a mission on the waterfront of Valletta, Malta. In 1907, he founded a community that came to be called the Society of Christian Doctrine. This order of laymen and -women pursued mission work throughout Malta, and Father George sent them forth with the hope that "the world would follow the gospel". These missions organized daily sessions of prayer and discussion, and taught children the Catechism.

However, the Church in Malta was displeased with George's inclusion of lay people in the Church hierarchy and his use of female missionaries. They tried to shut down the order, but encountered such uproar from believers and other priests that Father George was eventually reinstated, and the Society of Christian Doctrine was given approval in 1932. During the controversy, Father George cautioned his followers to quell their anger and forgive those who taunted them.

Above: Pope John Paul II prays at the tomb of Father George Preca in Hamrun, Malta, in 2001.

Below: The cityscape of Valletta, Malta, the birthplace of Father George Preca.

A HOLY, HUMBLE MAN

The Maltese admired Father George as a sympathetic confessor, and as a priest who welcomed the laity into the rituals of the Church. He was regarded as a holy man and saw a vision of the boy Jesus, which, he reported, brought him a sense of great spiritual sweetness. Others claimed he had cured their physical ailments.

The society's reputation spread, and it now has missions in Albania, Australia, Kenya, Peru and Sudan. Pope Pius XII made Father George a Monsignor of the Church, but the honour embarrassed him, and he dropped the title after the pope's death.

Father George Preca died at Santa Venera, Malta, in 1962, and his relics lie in Blata I-Badja. Prayers for his intercession have been known to cure the sick. He was canonized in 2007 by Pope Benedict XVI.

PADRE PIO

The humble Capuchin monk, now best known as Padre Pio, modestly tried to hide the marks of his stigmata, saying, "I only want to be a poor friar who prays."

> **KEY FACTS**
> *Stigmatist*
> DATES: *1887–1968*
> BIRTH PLACE: *near Naples, Italy*
> FEAST DAY: *23 September*

St Pius of Pietrelcina, better known as Padre Pio, first knew he belonged to God at the age of five. Throughout his childhood, he experienced visions and spoke with Jesus and Mary. He joined the Capuchin Order and was ordained at the friary of San Giovanni Rotondo, Pietrelcina, in 1910.

RECEIVING THE STIGMATA
In 1918, he became "aware that my hands, feet and side were pierced and were dripping with blood". He had received stigmata, but he covered the wounds and tried unsuccessfully to hide them.

Padre Pio may have been awed, even frightened, by this gift of holy marks, but he could not have anticipated the antagonism he met within the Church. When his secret was revealed, other churchmen claimed he was a fake and accused him of sexual licence, but

Above: Padre Pio as depicted on the front of Italian magazine La Domenica del Corriere *in 1956.*

Below: A friar bends over the coffin of Padre Pio. During his lifetime, Pio was both revered and reviled. The controversy continued after his death in 1968.

believers crowded the friary, seeking blessings and forgiveness from him. In 1923, the Church placed increasingly severe restrictions on Padre Pio, until he was virtually locked away and only allowed to take Mass in private. After Pope Pius XII lifted all these restrictions in 1933, life became easier for Padre Pio, but spiteful attacks from other clergy continued. True to Christ's teachings, Padre Pio remained meek and dedicated, despite slander and injustice.

MAN OF PRAYER
The Capuchins had built, in the friary grounds, a House for the Relief of Suffering, a place that was a hospital, hospice and retreat directed towards families in need. Pius XII encouraged Padre Pio to pray for the hospital. The saint spent long hours praying and meditating on the Way of the Cross, saying, "In books we seek God, in prayer we meet him."

In 1959, he began regular broadcasts on national radio, his sermons reinforcing his belief that "Prayer is the best weapon we possess, the key that opens the heart of God." His example inspired prayer groups across the world, and these continue today.

Padre Pio wore mittens to hide the stigmata on his hands, and remained a humble friar, who spent all his life in his friary and died there, yet more than 100,000 people attended his funeral. A mother claimed a miracle cure of her child's meningitis after prayers to Padre Pio, who was canonized in 2002.

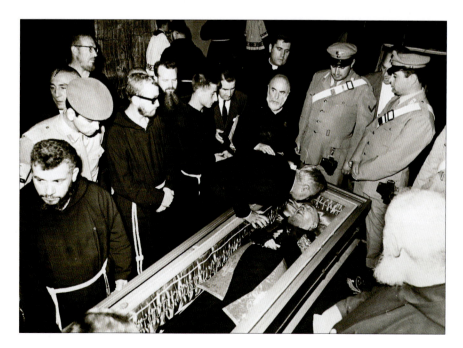

JOSEMARÍA ESCRIVÁ

THE FOUNDER OF OPUS DEI, JOSEMARÍA ESCRIVÁ, LIVED CHRISTIAN VIRTUES TO THE HIGHEST DEGREE AND HAD A MISSION TO FILL EVERYDAY LIVES WITH FAITH AND HOPE.

> **KEY FACTS**
> Founder of Opus Dei
> DATES: *1902–75*
> BIRTH PLACE: *Barbastro, Spain*
> FEAST DAY: *26 June*

As a youth, Josemaría Escrivá saw the footprints of a monk in the snow. He took this as a sign to follow the path to God and was ordained in 1925, soon after his father's death. He began a graduate law course in Madrid and supported his mother and siblings by tutoring other students. His personal experiences taught him that there was a path to God through family life, work and social duty.

OPUS DEI

In 1928, inspired by a religious experience on a retreat, Escrivá founded Opus Dei. This order of laymen lived communally, but their only rule was obedience to their founder. Josemaría taught them how to "sanctify their lives in the midst of the world", and to show how an everyday life can be enriched if it is dedicated to God.

When Spain erupted into civil war, thousands of religious were killed, and, despite support from the pro-Church side, Josemaría was forced to flee across the Pyrenees. Some of those martyred have been canonized as individuals, while others are honoured as the Martyrs of the Spanish Civil War.

After the war ended in 1939, Opus Dei grew rapidly, working largely in the world of education, establishing houses in Europe and Latin America. In 1943, Pope Pius XII gave approval for members of Opus Dei to become priests. The order now has 80,000 members, many of whom are laymen and -women, in 80 different countries. It owns radio stations and newspapers, which it uses to promote traditional faith and liturgy, to integrate faith into work and social responsibility, and to encourage religious domestic life.

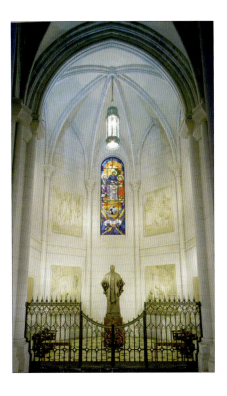

Above: Chapel of St Josemaría Escrivá at the Catedral de la Almudena, Madrid.

Alongside providing guidance for his order, Josemaría continued to study and to support his mother. When she died, he went to Rome to further his studies, and was made an honorary prelate of the Pontifical Academy of Theology.

Secularists have criticized Opus Dei for blurring the line between religion and politics. Others accuse the order of being secretive and exclusive, but few deny the goodness and spirituality of Josemaría, who died in his office in Rome, and was canonized in 2002 by John Paul II.

Left: Josemaría Escrivá with a group of his followers in Rome in 1971.

PAUL VI

As leader of the Catholic church from 1963 to 1978, Pope Paul VI oversaw the completion of the Second Vatican Council and the implementation of its decisions.

> **KEY FACTS**
> *Pope*
> Dates: *1897–1978*
> Birth Place: *Concesio, Italy*
> Patron of: *Archdiocese of Milan*
> Feast Day: *29 May*

Paul VI's papal reign saw many firsts. He was the first pope to fly by aeroplane and helicopter, the first to make a pastoral visit in Africa, and the first to celebrate Mass on American soil. His many pastoral visits and travels may have won him the nickname of "the pilgrim pope", but he is remembered above all as the pope who skilfully oversaw the main part of the Second Vatican Council initiated by John XXIII and carried through its many modernizing reforms – including the use of vernacular languages instead of Latin in the Mass and the freeing of the priest to celebrate Mass facing the congregation instead of facing East and the crucifix.

Born in Lombardy in 1897 as Giovanni Battista Montini, he studied philosophy and law before being recruited to serve in the Vatican diplomatic service and working for 30 years in the Vatican Secretariat of State. He became Archbishop of Milan in November 1954, and in this role he visited factories regularly and called himself the "Archbishop of the workers". His diplomatic skills served him well – and helped him become – as pope – a builder of bridges and a peacemaker. In 1964 he travelled to the Holy Land, where he met Ecumenical Patriarch Athenagoras I on the Mount of Olives, Jerusalem, and after which he and the Patriarch

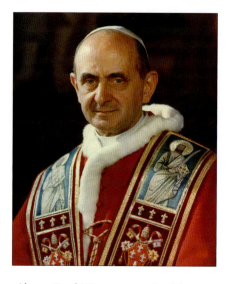

Above: Paul VI was canonized by Pope Francis on 14 October 2018.

issued a proclamation in 1965 withdrawing the excommunications that sparked the Great Schism between Roman Catholic and Eastern Orthodox Churches in 1054. During his US trip in 1965, he visited the United Nations, where he called powerfully for peace in the face of the escalating US involvement in the Vietnam War – saying "No more war, never again war. Peace, it is peace that must guide the destinies of people and of all mankind."

A WORLD LEADER

He also established a Pontifical Council for Inter-religious Dialogue and began dialogues with Communist officials in an attempt to improve the living conditions of Christians behind the Iron Curtain. Overall, he established diplomatic relations between the Holy See and no fewer than 40 countries. He issued a message on 1 January 1968 calling for a World Day of Peace each year and even reached out beyond the world, sending a goodwill message on Apollo 11 in 1969.

He was the last pope to be crowned with the papal tiara, and so the last to swear the papal oath on coronation not to change what had been handed down in Church tradition. Although he showed great skill in implementing some of the modernising decisions of the Second Vatican Council he also issued encyclicals that reaffirmed traditional values and attracted some controversy – not least *Humanae Vitae* in July 1968, which opposed the used of artificial birth control, and *Sacerdotas Caelibatus* in June 1967 that reaffirmed the need for priestly celibacy. Paul VI died at Castel Gandolfo on 6 August 1978 and was laid to rest in St Peter's Basilica.

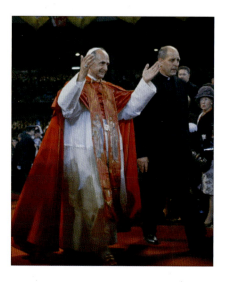

Right: Pope Paul at the Yankee Stadium, New York City, where he said Mass to a crowd of 90,000.

TERESA OF CALCUTTA

Saint Teresa of Calcutta, founder of the Missionaries of Charity, dedicated her life to caring for the sick, the poverty-stricken and the abandoned.

KEY FACTS
Founder of a mission
Dates: *1910–97*
Birth Place: *Skopje, North Macedonia*
Patron of: *World Youth Day, Missionaries of Charity, Archdiocese of Calcutta (co-patron with St Francis Xavier)*
Feast Day: *5 September*

Born Anjeze Gonxhe Bojaxhiu in Skopje, Macedonia, Mother Teresa of Calcutta initially wanted to be a missionary. She took her name from St Theresa of Lisieux, the patron saint of missionaries, after becoming a nun with the Sisters of Loreto, and for 20 years worked as a teacher in a convent school, before, on 10 September 1946, she had a vision calling on her to leave the convent and care for the sick by living among them. "It was an order," she said. She began this work in 1948, taking medical training before engaging with the destitute in the slums of Calcutta.

In 1949, her first helpers joined her, but the life was hard. She wrote in her diary that she experienced the life of the poor at first hand – "While looking for a home I walked and walked till my arms and legs ached" and she thought how much the poor must "ache in body and soul looking for a home, food and health". She felt tempted to return to the comfort of the convent, but reaffirmed her commitment: "Of free choice, my God, and out of love for you, I desire to remain and do whatever be your Holy will in my regard."

MISSIONARIES OF CHARITY
On 7 October 1950, she gained permission from the Vatican to found a diocesan congregation to care for "the hungry, the naked, the homeless, the crippled, the blind, the lepers, all those who felt unwanted, unloved, uncared for throughout society". This became the Missionaries of Charity.

Above: Teresa of Calcutta was beatified on 19 October 2003 by Pope John Paul II and canonized by Pope Francis on 4 September 2016.

She opened her first hospice for the dying, the Home of the Pure-Hearted, in Calcutta in 1952, in her words "for people who [had] lived like animals to die like angels – loved and wanted". She went on to open a home for lepers and several leprosy clinics, and then a refuge for the young, the Immaculate Heart Children's Home. Her work spread beyond Calcutta across India and around the world, the order opening its first house outside India, in Venezuela, in 1965; its first in Europe, in Rome, in 1970; and the first in the United States, in Harlem, in 1971 (it soon moved to the South Bronx). Eventually the order opened more than 500 establishments around the world. St Teresa travelled to various places of need, to help the starving in Ethiopia, care for radiation victims after the Chernobyl nuclear disaster of 1986, and to help those suffering as a result of the Armenian earthquake of 1988. Teresa was awarded the Nobel Peace Prize in 1979 and asked for the prize money to be given to the poor. She survived many years after suffering a heart attack in 1983, dying in Calcutta on 5 September 1997. Pope John Paul II, who visited the Home of the Pure-Hearted in 1986 while in India, later said of her: "Her life is a testimony to the dignity and the privilege of humble service."

St Teresa's body lay in an open casket in St Thomas, Calcutta, before her state funeral and burial at the Mother House in the city, the headquarters of her order.

Right: St Teresa's Sisters of Mercy provide food for a queue of women and children in Calcutta, India.

DULCE OF THE POOR

FRANCISCAN SISTER ST DULCE OF THE POOR FOUNDED A MAJOR CHARITABLE WORKS FOUNDATION TO CARE FOR THE DESTITUTE IN THE STATE OF BAHIA, BRAZIL.

KEY FACTS
Founder of a charitable foundation
DATES: *1914–92*
BIRTH PLACE: *Salvador, Bahia*
SHRINE: *Church of the Immaculate Conception of the Mother of God, Salvador*
FEAST DAY: *13 August*

Celebrated as the "Mother Teresa of Brazil", St Dulce of the Poor was born Maria Rita de Souza Pontes in an upper-middle-class family in Salvador, in Bahia State, in 1914. A happy child who loved flying her kite and playing soccer, she was inspired to help the poverty-stricken of Salvador after a visit to the poorer areas of the city with her aunt when was just 13. Even before that she had helped beggars and homeless people at the gate of her house, giving them haircuts and dressing their wounds. Her father wanted her to become a teacher, but on graduating high school she convinced him to allow her to follow her religious vocation and joined the Missionary Sisters of the Immaculate Conception of the Mother of God in the state of Sergipe in 1932. She took

Above: Franciscan sister St Dulce of the Poor is the first Brazilian woman to be made a saint.

the name Dulce in memory of her mother who had died when she was just seven years old.

HOUSING THE SICK
She started working as a teacher in a school associated with her order, then, with Friar Hildebrando Kruthaup, founded a Christian workers' organization, the São Francisco Workers Union, in 1933; afterwards she started work among the poor in the areas of Alagados and Itapagipe, and was dubbed the "Angel of Alagados". She began to house the sick in abandoned dwellings in an area of Alagados called "Rat Island" and then, with

Left: Founded by St Dulce in 1959, OSID's mission is "To love and serve the poorest ones, offering them free health care and education for life."

the permission of her mother superior, began to use the chicken yard of the San Antonio convent as a makeshift hostel. She housed 70 people there. In 1959, she established the Charitable Works Foundation of Sister Dulce, known by its Portuguese acronym OSID, providing educational, social and medical help for the poor, and the following year opened the Santo Antonio Hospital in Salvador.

In the later part of her life, her lung function was severely impaired, and she spent 16 months in hospital – during which Pope John Paul II visited her during a trip to Brazil in 1990 – before her death on 13 March 1992 aged 77. She was initially buried in the Basilica of Our Lady of the Immaculate Conception then moved in 2010 to the chapel of San Antonio convent. It was found that her body and even her clothes were undecayed.

Two miracles were verified as having been brought about by Sister Dulce – one in 2001, when a woman named Claudia Cristina dos Santos recovered from severe haemorrhaging after childbirth when the priest her family approached prayed for Sister Dulce's intervention; and a second in 2014, when a man blind for 14 years, Maurício, recovered his sight after praying and placing an image of Sister Dulce over his eyes. She was beatified in 2011 and canonized by Pope Francis on 13 October 2019.

JOHN PAUL THE GREAT

POPE JOHN PAUL II WAS MADE A SAINT NINE YEARS AFTER HIS 2005 DEATH – THE FASTEST CANONIZATION OF MODERN TIMES. HE WAS THE SECOND-LONGEST SERVING POPE IN HISTORY AFTER PIUS IX.

> **KEY FACTS**
> *Pope*
> DATES: *1920–2005*
> BIRTH PLACE: *Wadowice, second Polish Republic*
> PATRON OF: *World Youth Day, Poland, Archdiocese of Kraków*
> FEAST DAY: *22 October*

John Paul II, born Karol Wojtyla in Poland in 1920, was the first non-Italian pope in almost half a millennium when he was elected in 1978. In his papacy he was unrestrainedly loved, not just among Catholics but beyond the Church. This was attributable not only to his immense charisma but also to his instinctive gifts as a communicator. He visited 129 countries, taking his papacy to ordinary people around the world. His belief that ordinary Catholics should have access to his papacy was in the spirit of the Second Vatican Council.

He was an intensely serious, scholarly man whose faith had a strongly private, mystical aspect. The youngest of three children, he was afflicted in childhood by the loss first of his mother and then of a much-loved elder brother. He lost all his family members before he became a priest. In youth, Wojtyla was a brilliant student and intellectual,

Above: John Paul II was beatified in 2011 and canonized in 2014 on Divine Mercy Sunday, 27 April 2014, at the same time as Pope John XXIII.

fluent in several languages and widely read, he wrote poems and plays; he also loved sport, playing as a goalkeeper for a soccer team; and had a sociable side that he was able to draw on when making his public appearances as pope.

His early bereavements apart, the great formative experiences in Wojtyla's life were those of totalitarianism – in two different forms. As a young seminarian he lived underground for months at the time of the Warsaw Uprising against the Nazis. He pursued his vocation under Communism and rose to the position of Archbishop

Left: Pope John Paul II celebrates mass at the Knock Shrine, Country Galway, Ireland.

of Kraków in a Church that had to keep silent if it was to continue to exist. Wojtyla emerged as an individualist – not an egotist, but a firm believer in the importance of the private voice of conscience. He could never accept that this should be subordinated either to the "collective will" of the Fascists or to the "dictatorship of the proletariat" under the Communists.

A PRINCIPLED APPROACH

It might be expected that John Paul II had little time for Latin America's liberation theology. However, those who dismissed him as an old-fashioned reactionary were wide of the mark. He was generally more than ready to condemn the Western powers when the occasion demanded. He was forthright in denouncing the invasion of Iraq in 2003. He was also withering in his assessment of the capitalist system, which he considered was responsible for intolerable economic inequalities and which encouraged a consumer culture that exercised a tyranny all its own. However, he did not give ground on such issues as contraception, divorce and same-sex marriage, and resisted calls for married clergy and women priests, reforms that might seem commonsensical to others. He argued that the Church was not just an institution to be brought up to date like any other, but one that was bound by laws lain down by Christ himself.

GAZETTEER OF OTHER SAINTS

On the following pages are brief accounts of saints who have not been included in the main section of this book but who nevertheless deserve mention.

CORENTIN
dates unknown
Cornish hermit who later became a bishop in Brittany, where his cultus revived in the 1600s after he appeared to a believer in a vision.
Feast Day: 1 May

JULIAN THE HOSPITALLER
dates unknown
According to legend, he killed his parents in a case of mistaken identity, then fled and built a house for poor people. He revived a dying man who disappeared into a bright cloud, which was seen as a sign that Jesus had forgiven Julian's sins.
Feast Day: 29 January

URITH OF CHITTLEHAMPTON
dates unknown
Legend has it that her pagan stepmother arranged her death – by harvesters wielding scythes – but that, as she fell to the ground, a spring burst from the earth.
Feast Day: 8 July

ALBAN
3rd century AD
Protomartyr of Britain, this Roman citizen was converted by a priest whom he hid from persecution and helped escape. After disguising himself as the priest, he was arrested and later beheaded.
Feast Day: 2 August

CALLISTUS I
died AD 222
Born a slave and served time as a criminal before his conversion. He became Bishop of Rome and a pope, respected for his kind treatment of sinners. It is thought he died a martyr.
Feast Day: 14 October

PONTIAN AND HIPPOLYTUS
died c.AD 236
Hippolytus criticized bishops of Rome, Zephyrinus and Callistus I. He was banished to the Sardinian quarries, where he met Pontian, a former pope. Both died as prisoners and were later hailed as martyrs. Hippolytus' text, *Apostolic Tradition,* is a record of Christian worship during the Roman era.
Feast Day: 13 August

APOLLONIA
died c.AD 249
This aged deaconess of Alexandria was persecuted by an anti-Christian mob, who knocked out all her teeth. She chose to walk into the flames rather than deny her faith. Patron of toothache.
Feast Day: 9 February

BABYLAS
died c.AD 250
Antioch's most famous early bishop was martyred along with three boys whom he had converted. He is the first martyr whose relics are recorded as having been translated.
Feast Day: 24 January

LAURENCE
died AD 258
Legend claims he was a deacon of Rome and that he was roasted on a gridiron. Fra Angelico painted his life cycle in the Vatican.
Feast Day: 10 August

Above: The Martyrdom of Saint Laurence *(altar from Waldburg, c.1520).*

CRISPIN AND CRISPINIAN
died c.AD 285
It would seem these men were of Roman origin and fled the city to avoid persecution. Their relics were moved to Soissons, France, which became the centre for their cultus from the 6th century.
Feast Day: 25 October

SEBASTIAN
died c.AD 300
Roman martyr sentenced to be shot to death by arrows. Popular subject for Renaissance painters. Patron of archers; one of the Fourteen Holy Helpers.
Feast Day: 20 January

ERASMUS (ELMO)
died c.AD 300
According to legend, this bishop fled persecution in Syria to hide as a hermit in Lebanon, but was discovered, rolled in pitch and set alight. An angel rescued him.
Feast Day: 2 June

MEN(N)AS
died c. AD 300

This Roman soldier was conver-ted and martyred in Egypt, where he is still highly venerated. Miracles were attributed to him, and the water inside clay bottles made at his grave was believed to have curative powers.
Feast Day: 11 November

FLORIAN
died AD 304

A converted Roman army officer, Florian joined persecuted Christians and was tortured, then drowned in the River Enns. His body was recovered and his relics enshrined in St Florian Abbey, Linz.
Feast Day: 4 May

NINO
died c. AD 340

A slave girl credited with bringing Christianity to Georgia. She was taken to the royal court, where her powers of curing illness in Jesus' name caused the king to ask her to teach his people about Christianity.
Feast Day: 15 December

Above: The martyrdom of Crispin and Crispinian *(French glass painting, 15th century).*

PAULA
died AD 404

A young widow of noble Roman birth, Paula settled in Bethlehem, where she built a convent and monastery, helped Jerome with his studies, and gave away her wealth.
Feast Day: 26 January

MOSES THE BLACK
c. AD 330–c. AD 405

An Ethiopian servant in Egypt who became a criminal. After his conversion, he joined a community of desert monks and was ordained. He was killed by raiding Berbers.
Feast Day: 28 August

HONORATUS OF ARLES
died AD 429

Born and converted in Rome, he founded a monastic community in Greece with his brother. After the latter's death, he moved to southern France and built another monastery. He died two years after becoming Bishop of Arles.
Feast Day: 16 January

PAULINUS OF NOLA
died AD 431

Born in Bordeaux, Paulinus trained as a lawyer and poet in Italy. After their baby died, he and his wife found faith, began to give away their wealth, and moved to a large house in Nola, Spain, where they provided shelter for pilgrims and fugitives. Paulinus was ordained Bishop of Nola *c. AD* 409.
Feast Day: 22 June

CASSIAN (JOHN CASSIAN)
c. AD 360–433

Probably born in Romania, Cassian became a disciple of John Chrysostom in Constantinople. When the latter was exiled, Cassian went to Rome to plead his cause with the pope. He later founded two monasteries in Marseilles.
Feast Day: 23 July

DANIEL THE STYLITE
AD 409–93

Joined an abbey when he was only 12. An admirer of Simeon Stylites, he locked himself in an abandoned temple for nine years, and, when Simeon died in AD 459, he built a pillar and lived on it until his death.
Feast Day: 11 December

FLORENCE OF MONT GLONNE
5th century

Ordained by Martin of Tours, he lived as a hermit before founding a monastery in Saumur. His cultus lasted for centuries.
Feast Day: 22 September

CLOTILDE
c. AD 474–545

Married to Frankish King Clovis, a pagan who converted after he asked "Clothilde's God" for victory in battle and his prayer was granted. She later retired to a monastery, but, through her, northern Europe took its first steps towards Christianity.
Feast Day: 3 June

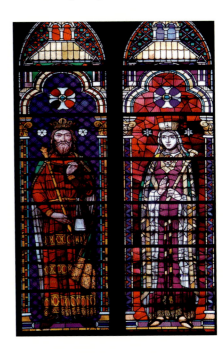

Above: Clovis and Clotilde *(French stained glass, 19th century).*

MARCOUL
died c.AD 558

Born into a rich family, Marcoul preached in Normandy before becoming a hermit. He had many disciples and founded a monastery. Kings of France used to pray before his shrine.
Feast Day: 1 May

PETROC
6th century AD

This Celtic missionary trekked Cornwall, Devon and Brittany, made pilgrimage to Jerusalem and Rome, and was briefly a hermit.
Feast Day: 4 June

VENANTIUS FORTUNATUS
c.AD 530–610

An Italian who settled in Poitiers (elected its bishop in AD 600), he became chaplain to a convent. He wrote hymns, verse to the Blessed Virgin, and biographies of saints.
Feast Day: 14 December

FINBAR
c.AD 560–610

Irish saint who made a pilgrimage to Rome with Welsh St David. Venerated in Cork as founder of its monastery and for mission work.
Feast Day: 25 September

KENTIGERN
died AD 612

Celtic monk and Bishop of Glasgow and Cumbria. Legends abound. One tells that his mother was thrown into the sea and he (her illegitimate son) was born in a coracle.
Feast Day: 13 January

THEODORE OF SYKEON
died AD 613

Child of a prostitute mother and circus-artist father, Theodore was ordained a priest at 18. He took a pilgrimage to Jerusalem, then returned to Galatia, where he was an influential preacher. For a while, he was Bishop of Anastasiopolis, near Ankara, but returned to live as a monk at Sykeon.
Feast Day: 22 April

BRAULIO OF SARAGOSSA
died AD 650

Braulio became a monk and joined St Isidore in Seville before returning to his hometown of Saragossa, where he became the city's bishop. He defended converted Jews and fought against Arianism.
Feast Day: 26 March

ELOI
c.AD 588–660

His artistry in metalwork made Eloi famous throughout western Europe. He was Bishop of Noyen and counsellor to the queen-regent, Bathilde, a freed slave. Together they forbade the export of slaves from the kingdom.
Feast Day: 1 December

FIACRE
died c.AD 670

Irish by birth, Fiacre lived as a hermit most of his life in France. He was known as a gardener and cared for those suffering from venereal diseases. His cultus flourished in France until the 1700s.
Feast Day: 30 August

Below: Eloi miraculously replaces the foreleg of a horse in this French tapestry (16th century).

AMAND
c.AD 584–675

French-born bishop who travelled as a missionary to Flanders and Carinthia, and founded monasteries near Ghent and a convent at Nivelles. His cultus spread through Flanders, Picardy and England.
Feast Day: 6 February

EBBE
died AD 683

Ebbe, the daughter of the King of Northumbria, was the first abbess of Coldingham. Despite the convent's lax reputation, she was holy and wise, and was instrumental in releasing St Wilfrid from prison.
Feast Day: 25 August

THEODORE OF CANTERBURY
AD 602–90

Born a Greek, yet became Archbishop of Canterbury, England. His devout and scholarly leadership brought much-needed unity. His canonization was supported by the Venerable Bede's writings.
Feast Day: 10 September

LAMBERT
c.AD 635–c.AD 705

A leading churchman in the Low Countries, where pagans predominated. As Bishop of Liège, he was forced into exile for a time and later died as a martyr in the city.
Feast Day: 17 September

GILES
died c.AD 710
Born in Athens, he became a hermit near Nîmes, France. A strong cultus developed after his death, penitents believing his intercession would bring forgiveness.
Feast Day: 7 September

ODILE
AD 660–720
Daughter of the Duke of Alsace, Odile was born blind, but her sight was restored at baptism. She became an abbess and founded a nunnery. Her relics were spread across Europe to give those with weak sight access to her power.
Feast Day: 14 December

JOHN OF BEVERLEY
died AD 721
A monk in Whitby, then Bishop of Hexham and later of York, he showed patience and kindness to the mentally disabled. A cultus grew quickly after his death.
Feast Day: 7 May

FRIDESWIDE
c.AD 680–727
Fleeing from a seducer, this virgin sought refuge in Oxford, where she became abbess of a monastery. Her shrine in Christ Church, Oxford, still attracts pilgrims.
Feast Day: 19 October

HUBERT
died AD 727
A missionary in the Ardennes, he became Bishop of Liège, where he built the cathedral. Many miracles were attributed to him.
Feast Day: 30 May

WILLIBRORD
AD 658–739
A Yorkshireman sent by the pope to organize a diocese in Utrecht. He seemed successful in establishing the faith, despite persecution.
Feast Day: 7 November

JOHN DAMASCENE
c.AD 657–749
A monk, then a priest, he spent his whole life under Muslim rule, first in Damascus, later at an abbey near Jerusalem. He was declared a Doctor of the Church in 1890.
Feast Day: 4 December

PIRMIN
died AD 753
Probably a Spaniard who fled Moorish rulers. He went first to Switzerland, where he rebuilt a monastery at Dissentis and, later, as abbot of Riechenau monastery, built up a library. Political unrest forced him to flee to Alsace, where he founded more monasteries.
Feast Day: 3 November

ANDREW OF CRETE
died AD 766
Eighth-century Constantinople saw fierce arguments over icons, with Emperor Constantine V torturing and killing his opponents. Andrew (from Crete), who was visiting the city, criticized the emperor for his cruelty and was beaten, scourged, then stabbed to death in the streets.
Feast Day: 20 October

Above: The Miracle of St Walburga (Peter Paul Rubens, c.1610–11).

WALBURGA
died AD 779
English-born missionary who became abbess of the monastery in Heidenheim. After her death, it is said that her shrine exuded oil believed to cure ailments. But her name became associated with witchcraft: on Walpurgisnacht in Germany, people dress as spooks, bats and witches.
Feast Day: 25 February

LIOBA
died AD 782
Educated in England, she went to Germany as a nun. As abbess of Tauberbischofsheim, she was known for being calm, cheerful and wise.
Feast Day: 28 September

ANSKAR
AD 801–65
Born near Amiens, France, Anskar devoted his life to taking the Christian message to pagans from Denmark to Sweden. Christianity was established in Scandinavia 200 years after his death.
Feast Day: 3 February

GAZETTEER OF OTHER SAINTS

LUDMILLA
died AD 921
Martyr saint and grandmother of Prince (King) Wenceslas.
Feast Day: 16 September

ADALBERT OF PRAGUE
AD 956–97
A pioneer in taking Christianity to north-eastern Europe. After being exiled twice, he became a missionary in Poland, Prussia and the Baltics, and was martyred near Königsberg. His relics lie in Prague.
Feast Day: 23 April

ABBO OF FLEURY
died 1004
A Benedictine monk, scholar and martyr saint, he visited England, where he wrote a biography of St Edmund and reformed the monastic movement.
Feast Day: 13 November

WILLIGIS
died 1011
Priest, politician and missionary in Germany and Scandinavia.
Feast Day: 23 February

VLADIMIR
AD 955–1015
Forced to convert on marrying Princess Anne of Constantinople, he is venerated for introducing Christianity to Russia.
Feast Day: 15 July

WILLIAM OF ROSKILDE
died 1070
Set up a mission in Denmark, where he became a preacher and Bishop of Roskilde, Zeeland.
Feast Day: 2 September

DOMINIC OF SILOS
c.1000–73
A peasant from Navarre, Spain, whose piety, miracles, and liberation of captives taken by the Moors made him a much-loved priest.
Feast Day: 20 December

Above: Vladimir the Saint (Ivan Yakovlevich Bilibin, 1925).

BERNARD OF MONTJOUX
c.AD 996–c.1081
As archdeacon of Aosta Cathedral in the Alps, he cleared mountain passes of robbers and established resthouses for travellers.
Feast Day: 28 May

ROSALIA OF PALERMO
12th century
Born into a noble Sicilian family, she chose to live in a cave. Pilgrimages are still made to the church built over her hermitage.
Feast Day: 4 September

BRUNO
c.1032–1101
His Carthusian Order set a benign but influential example of spirituality throughout Europe.
Feast Day: 6 October

IVES
died c.1107
In 1100, in the village of Slepe, four bodies were found: someone dreamt their unusal insignia belonged to a Persian bishop (Ives), who had lived in England as a hermit. The bodies were translated to Ramsey Abbey, and miracles occurred.
Feast Day: 24 April

ALBERIC
died 1109
Co-founder of the Cistercian Order, which insisted on poverty and labour for God. By the time of his death, there were nearly 400 Cistercian houses in Europe.
Feast Day: 26 January

ROBERT OF MOLESME
1027–1110
Spent most of his life as abbot at Molesme. Co-founder of the Cistercian Order at Cîteaux, based on the rule of St Benedict, which grew into an influential worldwide organization.
Feast Day: 29 April

LEOPOLD III
1075–1136
Reigned for 40 years as the third Duke of Austria. He reformed existing monasteries and founded new ones, strengthened Austria as a nation and promoted Christianity.
Feast Day: 15 November

WILLIAM OF NORWICH
died 1144
When the 12-year-old's body was found in a wood near Norwich, his uncle claimed Jews had tortured and murdered him. A cultus developed, but papal letters directed Norwich to stop the ghastly story, and his shrine was abandoned.
Feast Day: 26 March

MALACHY
1094–1148
Archbishop of Armagh who introduced the Cistercian Order into Ireland and was a pioneer in Ireland's early religious reform.
Feast Day: 3 November

UBALDO
died 1160

As Dean (later Bishop) of Gubbio Cathedral in Umbria, he persuaded clerics to live a communal life. Patron against rabies.
Feast Day: 16 May

GODRIC
c.1069–1170

He walked barefoot to Rome before becoming a hermit. His poems set to music are the earliest known in the English language.
Feast Day: 21 May

GILBERT OF SEMPRINGHAM
c.1083–1189

An English pastor who organized women, then men, into Benedict-ine communities, where they nursed orphans and lepers.
Feast Day: 4 February

BARTHOLOMEW OF FARNE
died 1193

A priest and monk until his vision of Christ, after which he went to Farne Island as a hermit. Miracles were attributed to him by visitors.
Feast Day: 24 June

THORLAC OF SKALHOLT
1133–93

As bishop of Skalholt, Iceland, Thorlac reformed the priesthood and founded a community. His miracles are recorded, and a cultus flourished until the Reformation.
Feast Day: 23 December

HOMOBONUS
c.1120–97

Neither priest, king nor martyr, this "good man" of Cremona, Italy, was a tailor and merchant, who cared for the sick, fed the poor and buried the dead. Patron of tailors and clothworkers.
Feast Day: 13 November

WILLIAM OF ROCHESTER
died 1201

This Scottish fisherman vowed to visit Jerusalem, but was murdered by his travelling companion near Rochester. Miracles are said to have occurred at his burial site.
Feast Day: 8 June

SAVA (SABAS) OF SERBIA
c.1173–1236

Born a prince, he became a monk. He founded a monastery on Mount Athos, Greece.
Feast Day: 14 January

RAYMUND NONNATUS
1204–40

Ordained priest who became a slave in Algiers, hoping to rescue others from this dreadful fate.
Feast Day: 31 August

LUTGARDIS
1182–1246

Cistercian nun whose contemplative life caused many to turn to her for spiritual counselling.
Feast Day: 16 June

FERDINAND III
1199–1252

Revered King of Castile and Leon who wrested Andalusia from the occupying Moors, bringing it into the Christian world.
Feast Day: 30 May

ROSE OF VITERBO
c.1235–52

The 12-year-old Rose, dressed as a Franciscan, preached in the streets and loudly supported the pope, despite hostile opposition.
Feast Day: 4 September

ZITA
1218–72

A lifelong servant, venerated for her devotion and for her care of the poor and condemned convicts.
Feast Day: 27 April

RAYMUND OF PENNAFORT
c.1180–1275

He worked in Barcelona and Bologna before becoming confessor to Pope Gregory IX. He codified laws and wrote many texts. In his old age, he tried to convert the Moors who occupied Spain.
Feast Day: 7 January

AMATO RONCONI
1225–92

An Italian penitent, he joined the Secular Franciscan Order and dedicated his life to serving the poor and pilgrims, as well as building hospitals and chapels.
Feast Day: 8 May

CELESTINE V
1210–96

A devout hermit, he founded the Celestine Order in 1274. He was appointed Pope Celestine V in 1294, but abdicated five months later, the only pope ever to do so.
Feast Day: 19 May

Above: Saint Celestine *(panel, Niccolò di Tommaso, 14th century).*

GAZETTEER OF OTHER SAINTS

Above: Louis of Toulouse *(panel, Simone Martini, 1317).*

LOUIS OF TOULOUSE
1274–97
Held for seven years as hostage after the King of Aragon captured his father, Charles II of Naples. Released in 1295 and ordained a Franciscan in 1297, he was immediately promoted to Bishop of Toulouse, but still lived in poverty.
Feast Day: 19 August

MARGARET OF CORTONA
c.1247–97
Mistreated by her stepmother, she ran off with a knight and bore him a son. When her lover died, she was destitute and became a Franciscan tertiary, famous for public acts of penance. Miracles were attributed to her, and sinners sought her help.
Feast Day: 22 February

ANGELA OF FOLIGNO
1248–1309
Known by the Catholic Church as "Mistress of Theologians", for

Right: Gospel Folios of St Sergius of Radonezh (Russian School, 14th century).

her profound mystical writings, she married young and had children, but, after a vision of St Francis of Assisi and the death of her husband and family, became a Franciscan tertiary.
Feast Day: 4 January

ALEXIS FALCONIERI
died 1310
Joined a community of hermits as a lay brother. The group (the Seven Founders) funded a mendicant order, the Servants of Mary (Servites). He also helped establish a Servite community in Siena.
Feast Day: 7 February

MARGARET OF CITTÀ DI CASTELLO
1287–1320
Born blind and with curvature of the spine, she was abandoned by her parents but was cared for by nuns until she became a secular member of the Third Order of St Dominic. She was known for her profound holiness.
Feast Day: 13 April

PEREGRINE LAZIOSI
died 1345
A Servite, recognized for his piety and dedication to the poor.
Feast Day: 1 May

CATHERINE OF SWEDEN
1331–81
Daughter of Bridget of Sweden. After nursing her husband until his death, she joined her mother in the convent of Vadstena, later becoming abbess. She worked hard to obtain approval of the Brigittines (her mother's order), and for ther mother's canonization.
Feast Day: 24 March

SERGIUS OF RADONEZH
1315–92
From a noble family who fled the Tartars and settled in Radonezh, near Moscow. He and his brother restored the monastery there and Sergius became an important figure in religious and state life.
Feast Day: 25 September

HEDWIG
1374–99
Daughter of the King of Hungary and Poland, she was used as a political pawn, but eventually married Jagiello, Grand Duke of Lithuania and Ruthenia, and together they set about converting their subjects.
Feast Day: 17 July

VINCENT FERRER
1350–1419
Dynamic preacher who converted

Jews and Muslims in his native Spain and gained a reputation for miracle cures.
Feast Day: 5 April

FRANCES OF ROME
1384–1440
A powerful, religious presence in Rome, she experienced visions and cared for plague victims and war-wounded. Other women joined her and she founded the Oblates of Tor de' Specchi, which still exists.
Feast Day: 9 March

BERNARDINO OF SIENA
1380–1444
After nursing plague victims, he became a Franciscan evangelist, attacking greed and the warmongering of Italy's city-states.
Feast Day: 20 May

COLETTE
1381–1447
The anti-pope Bernard XIII made her a Poor Clare in charge of France's Franciscan nuns. She founded 17 new convents.
Feast Day: 6 March

JOHN OF CAPISTRANO
1386–1456
A married man and governor of Perugio, he became a Franciscan. A fierce believer, keen to reform, he was appointed inquisitor-general to Vienna in 1451.
Feast Day: 23 October

ANTONINUS OF FLORENCE
1389–1459
Dominican friar who founded the convent at San Marco. As Archbishop of Florence, he lived in poverty, nursed plague victims and fed the hungry and came to win the esteem and love of his people. He wrote important texts and advised papal reforms.
Feast Day: 10 May

CATHERINE DE'VIGRI OF BOLOGNA
1413–63
Well-born and highly educated, she refused marriage and joined the Augustinian tertiaries.
Feast Day: 9 March

JOHN OF SAHAGUN
c.1430–79
He reconciled fighting factions in Salamanca, a town riven by feuds. In 1463, he joined the Austin Friars. Miracles followed his death.
Feast Day: 12 June

CATHERINE OF GENOA
1447–1510
After she helped win her husband back to faith, they ran a hospital together in Pammatone. In later life, she wrote about spirituality and experienced visions.
Feast Day: 15 September

CHILD MARTYRS OF TLAXCALA
1514–1527/29
Three Mexican teenagers from Tlaxcala state – Antonio, Juan and Cristobal – who had been converted and baptized by the Order of Friars Minor were martyred when they refused to abandon their Catholic faith and revert to indigenous traditions in 1527 (Cristobal) and 1529 (Antonio and Juan).
Feast Day: 23 September

JEROME EMILIANI
1481–1537
A priest, Jerome founded a small community (the Somaschi), where he built hospitals, orphanages and homes for reformed prostitutes.
Feast Day: 8 February

PETER FABER
1506–46
Co-founder of the Society of Jesus with St Ignatius of Loyola and St Francis Xavier, he was the first Jesuit theologian and priest. He was known for his graceful manner and gentleness with people and was acclaimed for his effectiveness as a teacher and preacher. He founded Jesuit colleges in Spain and at Cologne.
Feast Day: 2 August

JUAN DIEGO
died 1548
Born near Mexico City, he was baptized at age 50. Allegedly received an image of the Blessed Virgin miraculously printed on his cloak, signifying Jesus' rebirth.
Feast Day: 12 December

STANISLAUS KOSTKA
1550–68
Refused by local Jesuits, he walked more than 300 miles to Rome. A devout young man who experienced mystical visions.
Feast Day: 13 November

PHILIP OF MOSCOW
1507–69
As metropolitan of the Russian Church, he upbraided Ivan the Terrible for his bloodshed and cruelty. He was arrested, held in chains, and eventually martyred.
Feast Day: 9 January

Above: Stanislaus Kostka *(artist unknown, 17th century).*

GAZETTEER OF OTHER SAINTS

Above: Saint Charles Borromeo Fasting *(19th-century copy, after Daniele Crespi from 1620).*

EDMUND CAMPION
1540–81
An Anglican, scholar and founder of Trinity College in Ireland, he became a Jesuit in Rome. Arrested and executed on a false conspir-acy charge, he is one of the Forty Martyrs of England and Wales.
Feast Day: 25 October

ALEXANDER BRIANT
c.1556–81
When Catholicism was banned in England, he refused to reveal the hiding place of a family he had persuaded to convert. For this he was cruelly tortured, then executed. He is one of the Forty Martyrs of England and Wales.
Feast Day: 25 October

CHARLES BORROMEO
1538–84
Archbishop of Milan and favoured nephew of Pope Pius IV. He instituted Sunday schools and opened seminaries to train priests.
Feast Day: 4 November

MARGARET CLITHEROW
1556–86
With her Protestant husband, she hid Catholic priests during a time of persecution. One of the Forty Martyrs of England and Wales.
Feast Day: 25 October

BARTHOLOMEW OF THE MARTYRS
1514–90
Also known as Bartholomew of Braga, he took part in the Council of Trent and established hospices and hospitals in Braga, Portugal. He was a member of the Order of the Preachers and served as Archbishop of Braga.
Feast Day: 18 July

CATHERINE DE' RICCI
1522–90
Became a Dominican nun in 1535; later promoted to prioress.
Feast Day: 2 February

ALOYSIUS GONZAGA
1568–91
Despite his family's military ambitions for him, he became a Jesuit.
Feast Day: 21 June

PHILIP HOWARD
1557–95
Converted to Catholicism from Anglicanism. He would not deny his faith and spent the rest of his life in the Tower. One of the Forty Martyrs of England and Wales.
Feast Day: 19 October

JOSEPH OF ANCHIETA
1534–97
Spanish Jesuit missionary, known as the "Apostle of Brazil" for his evangelizing work in the Portuguese colony in the 16th century, he was one of the founders of São Paulo (1554) and Rio de Janeiro (1565).
Feast Day: 9 June

MARY MAGDALENE DE' PAZZI
1566–1607
She entered the Carmelite convent in Florence at the age of 17. Her writings reveal a love of the local landscape, as well as her devotion to God.
Feast Day: 25 May

ANDREW AVELLINO
1521–1608
After failing in a mission to reform a riotous house of nuns, he joined the Theatines, a new order, revealing his talent as a preacher and sensitivity toward confessors.
Feast Day: 10 November

CAMILLUS OF LELLIS
1550–1614
Founded the Servants of the Sick for priests and laymen, and opened hospitals around Italy.
Feast Day: 14 July

JOHN BERCHMANS
1599–1621
His youthful piety and theological understanding encouraged a cultus.
Feast Day: 13 August

JOSAPHAT
1580–1623
Archbishop of Polotsk in Belarus, and martyr saint. A brisk reformer who sought unity with Rome.
Feast Day: 12 November

JOHN FRANCIS REGIS
1597–1640
Jesuit priest who worked exhaustively, preaching, serving the poor and nursing plague victims.
Feast Day: 2 July

JANE FRANCES DE CHANTAL
1572–1641
Founded the Visitation Order. By the time she died, 86 convents had been established in Europe.
Feast Day: 12 December

MARTYRS OF NATAL
d. 1645
30 Portuguese Catholics were killed in 1645 in a massacre in

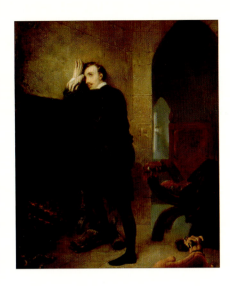

Above: Philip Howard imprisoned in the Tower of London *(Henry Barraud, 19th century)*.

Natal, northern Brazil, by Dutch Calvinists. Two were killed in an attack during Mass on Sunday 16 July and the remainder died in a second incident on 3 October.
Feast Day: 3 October

JOSEPH CALASANZ
1550–1648
He gave up his office of vicar of Andorra to teach slum children in Rome. After his death, his congregation was revived as the Piarists.
Feast Day: 25 August

ANDREW BOBOLA
1591–1657
Polish nobleman who devoted his life to God, cared for the suffering and died for his faith.
Feast Day: 21 May

MARIE DE L'INCARNATION
1599–1672
A French nun, Marie was one of a group who established the Ursuline Order in New France (French-held North America) and reputedly set up the first girls' school in the New World. She was a writer and mystic who experienced several profound visions.
Feast Day: 30 April

JOHN KEMBLE
1599–1679
Jesuit priest and one of the Forty Martyrs of England and Wales.
Feast Day: 25 October

OLIVER PLUNKET
1625–81
Jesuit Archbishop of Armagh and Primate of All Ireland. His charm won the grudging admiration of Irish Protestants, but English overlords dragged him to Newgate, London, tried him for high treason, and executed him.
Feast Day: 1 July

CLAUDE DE LA COLOMBIÈRE
1641–82
French Jesuit imprisoned in England as a Catholic. He was saved by Louis XIV of France, but he died soon after.
Feast Day: 15 February

MARGUERITE-MARIE ALACOQUE
1647–90
Entered the Visitation convent at Paray-le-Monial, where she revived the medieval cult of devotion to the Sacred Heart of Jesus.
Feast Day: 17 October

GREGORIO BARBARIGO
1625–97
Priest who founded a seminary, set up printing presses and tried to reconcile Eastern Orthodox and Roman Catholic Churches.
Feast Day: 18 June

STANISLAUS PAPCZYNSKI
1631–1701
Founded the first Polish men's religious order, the Marians of the Immaculate Conception, who wore a white habit. Before founding the order Stanislaus was a member of the Piarist Order. He was known as a preacher and writer.
Feast Day: 17 September

JOSEPH ORIOL
1650–1702
A popular ascetic priest. It is said he saw the Virgin as he lay dying.
Feast Day: 23 March

JOSEPH VAZ
1651–1711
A Portuguese Oratorian missionary and priest in Ceylon (now Sri Lanka), he is known as the "Apostle of Ceylon" for his work supporting Catholics and rebuilding the Church in the face of persecution by Dutch Calvinists. He is known also for the "Miracle of the Rain", when he reputedly brought about a miraculous rainfall to end a drought in 1696 in the kingdom of Kandy.
Feast Day: 16 January

JOSEPH TOMASI
1649–1713
Much-loved scholar and teacher, known as the "prince of liturgists".
Feast Day: 1 January

FRANCIS DE GIROLAMO
1642–1716
A Jesuit who preached in the docks and slums of Naples.
Feast Day: 11 May

JOHN BAPTIST ROSSI
1698–1764
Preached to and cared for beggars, prisoners and prostitutes in Rome.
Feast Day: 23 May

JULIE BILLIART
1751–1816
Co-founder of the Institute of the Sisters of Notre Dame, dedicated to teaching children.
Feast Day: 8 April

VINCENT STRAMBI
1745–1824
Bishop who improved education of priests. Exiled for refusing to take an oath of allegiance to Napoleon.
Feast Day: 25 September

VINCENZO ROMANO
1751–1831

He was known locally in his native region of Naples as the "worker priest" for his care of the local poor, especially orphans. Vincenzo played an important role in clearing and rebuilding areas devastated by the 1794 eruption of Mount Vesuvius.
Feast Day: 20 December

PETER CHANEL
1803–41

An early member of the Society of Mary, he was sent as a missionary to the French territory of Futuna, where he was martyred.
Feast Day: 28 April

VINCENT PALLOTTI
1795–1850

Founded the Society of Catholic Apostolate and later the Pallotine Missionary Sisters, which encouraged membership of laymen and -women. His mission is now found throughout the Catholic world.
Feast Day: 22 January

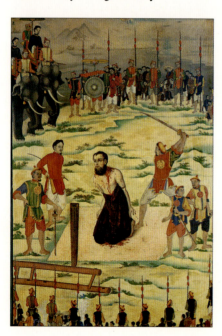

Above: Many missionaries, including Theophane Vénard, were martyred in Vietnam in the 19th century (Indo-Chinese School, 1838).

PHILIPPINE DUCHESNE
1769–1852

Born in Grenoble, she established schools for Native American children in Louisiana and Missouri.
Feast Day: 17 November

JOSEPH CAFASSO
1811–60

Ministered to young priests, prisoners and condemned men, and established an institute for boys.
Feast Day: 23 June

JOHN NEUMANN
1811–60

Bishop of Philadelphia. He supervised the building of more than 100 churches and 80 schools, and wrote several texts.
Feast Day: 5 January

THEOPHANE VÉNARD
1829–61

One of the named Martyrs of Vietnam, he was held in a bamboo cage before being beheaded.
Feast Day: 2 February

MARY ROSE MOLAS Y VALLVE
1815–76

Founded the Sisters of Our Lady of Consolation to serve the needs of deprived children.
Feast Day: 11 June

MARIAM OF JESUS CRUCIFIED
1846–78

Born Mariam Baouardy in Galilee, she was the 13th child born to her parents after the previous 12 had all died, and was born after her parents had made a pilgrimage to Bethlehem. They named her Mariam in honour of the Blessed Virgin Mary and she was raised in Palestine before she moved to France and eventually was admitted to the Sisters of the Apostolic Carmel, taking the name Mary of Jesus Crucified. She was a mystic who received the stigmata and later founded a house of the order in her birthplace, Bethlehem. In 1878, she had a vision of Jesus that helped identify the Arab village of Amwas (now within the Israeli national park of Canada Park) as the site of the biblical Emmaus.
Feast Day: 26 August

MARGUERITE BAYS
1815–79

A Swiss seamstress and member of the Secular Franciscan Order, Marguerite cared for the local poor and was reputedly cured of bowel cancer on the day, 8 December 1854, when Pope Pius IX proclaimed the dogma of the Immaculate Conception. She was a mystic who received the stigmata in 1854.
Feast Day: 27 June

LUDOVICO OF CASORIA
1814–85

Born Arcangelo Palmentieri in Naples, he took the name Ludovico on becoming a novice with the Order of Friars Minor in 1832. After a mystical experience aged 33, he dedicated himself to a life of care, founding orphanages, schools and infirmaries. He established the Gray Friars of Charity and the Franciscan Sisters of Saint Elizabeth.
Feast Day: 30 March

GIOVANNI ANTONIO FARINA
1803–88

A gifted teacher and educationalist in Vicenza known for his care of the poverty-stricken, he founded the first poor girls' school in Vicenza and the Institute of the Sister Teachers of St Dorothy, Daughters of the Sacred Heart, to provide teachers. He served as Bishop of Treviso and later Bishop of Vicenza. He ordained the future

Pope Pius X in 1858 and attended the First Vatican Council in 1869–70. He is sometimes called the "Bishop of Charity".
Feast Day: 4 March

TERESA OF JESUS JORNET Y IBARS
1843–97
Founded the Little Sisters of the Abandoned Elderly in 1872. She showed particular sympathy for the elderly.
Feast Day: 26 August

MARIA KATHARINA KASPER
1820–98
Born Katharina, she worked for many years to support her family members, especially after her father's death, but was from her youth determined eventually to become a religious sister. She took the name Maria on founding the Poor Handmaids of Jesus Christ in Dernbach, Germany, in 1851. The order now has more than 100 houses around the world.
Feast Day: 1 February

SHARBEL THE MARONITE
1828–98
A Lebanese, he joined Our Lady of Mayfug monastery before becoming a hermit. Miracles occurred after his death.
Feast Day: 24 December

MARIA GORETTI
1890–1902
A youth tried to rape the 12-year-old Maria. When she fought back, he stabbed her. She died the next day, having forgiven her attacker.
Feast Day: 6 July

ELIZABETH OF THE TRINITY
1880–1906
A Discalced Carmelite nun often associated for her similar strain of contemplative mysticism with her contemporary St Theresa of Lisieux (1873–97), Elizabeth was known for her dedication to the Trinity and joined the local Carmelite convent aged 21. She wrote of God, "no one can take us away from Him. He dwells in our souls!" She died aged just 26.
Feast Day: 6 July

MARIAM THRESIA
1876–1926
A Syro-Malabar Christian, Mariam Thresia was a mystic who had profound visions and received

Above: Pope Francis celebrates Mass in Saint Peter's Square on 14 October 2018 for pilgrims from El Salvador after the canonization of the martyred Archbishop Óscar Romero.

the stigmata in 1905/09. Born in Kerala, southern India, she was named Thresia in honour of St Teresa of Ávila and took the name Mariam after a vision of the Blessed Virgin Mary. She founded the Congregation of the Holy Family in 1914.
Feast Day: 8 June

LEOPOLD MANDIC
1866–1942
Born in Croatia, he was ordained a Capuchin Franciscan and ministered in Padua for 40 years. He showed great compassion as a spiritual adviser and confessor.
Feast Day: 12 May

ÓSCAR ROMERO
1917–80
As Archbishop of San Salvador, Romero was a staunch critic of the El Salvador military government. He took a stand against violence in the Salvadoran Civil War, and was shot by a gunman widely believed in 1980 to be in the pay of right-wing leader Roberto D'Aubuisson while celebrating Mass.
Feast Day: 24 March

Above: Marguerite Bays was canonized by Pope Francis on 13 October 2019.

THE FIRST POPES

The roll call of leaders of the Church begins with the first bishop to the Christians to Rome, founder of the papacy – Saint Peter. Peter died a martyr for his faith, as did many of his successors through more than 200 years of on-off persecution that followed until the 313 Edict of Milan that recognized Christianity in the Roman Empire. Across almost 1,000 years of history from Peter to Leo IX in 1054, almost 150 popes led the Church. Aside from Peter, the greatest must include Leo I, who in 452 persuaded Attila the Hun not to sack Rome, and Leo III, who crowned Charlemagne emperor in the West, and consolidated the relationship with the Franks that set Rome free from the heavy hand of Constantinople.

Several early popes were celebrated as saints. This detail of a 6th-century mosaic shows Clement (died c.101) and Sixtus (died c.125) – at the far left. Next to Sixtus is Saint Lawrence of Rome (died 258), another martyr, but not a pope.

'UPON THIS ROCK...'

PETER TO SYLVESTER I, *c.*30/40–335

The origin of the papacy lies in a momentous encounter between Jesus Christ and the Apostle Peter, when Jesus gave Peter authority over the community of his followers. According to the Gospel of St Matthew 16:13–20, Jesus was with his disciples in Caesarea Philippi when he asked them, "Whom do men say that I am?" and Peter made the ringing statement "Thou art the Christ, the Son of the living God". Then Jesus declared, "Thou art Peter, and upon this rock I will build my Church; and the gates of hell shall not prevail against it. And I will give unto thee the keys of the kingdom of heaven: and whatsoever thou shalt bind on earth shall be bound in heaven: and whatsoever thou shalt loose on earth shall be loosed in heaven." After Jesus' crucifixion and resurrection, Peter became leader of the fledgling Church. Each pope draws his authority from his position as a descendant of Peter.

Peter was crucified, probably in 64, in the persecution of Christians led by Roman Emperor Nero. Over the next three centuries, his successors as bishop of Rome tried to safeguard the Church's future in the face of often brutal official persecution; they worked to establish their authority as leaders of the Christian world and the pre-eminence of Rome as a centre of the faith.

In the early 4th century, under Emperor Constantine the Great, the persecution was ended and the Roman Empire itself began to become Christian. Constantine founded a new imperial capital, Constantinople. This had the effect of diminishing the status of Rome, but gave added importance to the papacy's assumed role as a unifying force, a figurehead for the Christian world.

Left: Pope Sylvester I baptizes Constantine. According to legend, Constantine gave the pope authority to govern Rome and the Western empire. This fresco (1508/9–20) by Raphael is in the Vatican Palace.

TIMELINE

64–1054 *(Bracketed italic entries are antipopes, i.e. not popes in the real succession.)*

Above: Dome of the Rock, Jerusalem.

Above: St Peter's statue, Vatican city.

Above: The first popes, Ravenna.

64–275

c.64 St Peter dies a martyr in Rome.
c.66–c.78 Pope St Linus.
c.79–c.91 Pope St Anacletus.
c.91–c.101 Pope St Clement I – ordained by St Peter?
c.101–c.109 Pope St Evaristus.
c.109–c.116 Pope St Alexander.
c.116–c.125 Pope St Sixtus I.
c.125–c.136 Pope St Telesphorus.
c.138–c.142 Pope St Hyginus.
c.142–c.155 Pope St Pius I.
c.155–c.166 Pope St Anicetus.
c.166–c.174 Pope St Soter.
c.175–c.189 Pope St Eleutherius.
c.189–c.199 Pope St Victor I – first African-born pope.
c.199–c.217 Pope St Zephyrinus.
211 Church Father Origen visits Rome.
c.217–c.222 Pope St Callistus I.
(217–35) Antipope St Hippolytus.
c.222–30 Pope St Urban I.
230–5 Pope St Pontian – first pope to resign papacy.
235–6 Pope St Anterus.
236–50 Pope St Fabian.
250–1 Election of new pope delayed due to imperial persecution of Church.
251–3 Pope St Cornelius.
(251–8) Antipope Novatian.
253–4 Pope St Lucius I.
254–7 Pope St Stephen I – emphasizes pre-eminence of Rome.
257–8 Pope St Sixtus II – early martyr.
260–8 Pope St Dionysius.
269–74 Pope St Felix I.

275–418

275–83 Pope St Eutychian.
283–96 Pope St Gaius.
296–304 Pope St Marcellinus.
301 Armenia is the first Christian state.
304–8 Severe persecution of Christians causes break in line of popes.
c.308–9 Pope St Marcellus I.
310, 18 Apr–21 Oct, Pope St Eusebius.
311–14 Pope St Miltiades.
312 Battle of Milvian Bridge – Roman Emperor Constantine I defeats rival Maxentius.
313 Edict of Milan, Christians free to practise faith in the Roman Empire.
330 Foundation of Constantinople.
314–335 Pope St Sylvester I.
325 Council of Nicaea – first ecumenical council; agrees Nicene Creed.
336, 18 Jan–7 Oct, Pope St Mark.
337–52 Pope St Julius I.
352–66 Pope Liberius – first pope not to be canonized.
(355–65) Antipope Felix II.
366–84 Pope St Damasus I.
381 First Council of Constantinople – confirms Nicene Creed.
(366–85) Antipope Ursinus.
384–99 Pope St Siricius.
399–401 Pope St Anastasius I.
397–401 St Augustine (Bishop of Hippo c.395) writes his Confessions.
401–17 Pope St Innocent I.
410 Rome sacked by Visigoths.
417–18 Pope St Zosimus.
(418–23) Antipope Eulalius.

418–608

418–22 Pope St Boniface I.
422–32 Pope St Celestine I.
431 Council of Ephesus.
432–40 Pope St Sixtus III.
440–61 Pope St Leo I the Great.
451 Council of Chalcedon.
461–8 Pope St Hilarius.
468–83 Pope St Simplicius.
476 Last Roman emperor in West, Romulus Augustulus, deposed.
483–92 Pope St Felix III.
492–6 Pope St Gelasius I.
496–8 Pope Anastasius II.
498–514 Pope St Symmachus.
(498–9) Antipope Laurence; returned to power 501–506.
514–23 Pope St Hormisdas.
523–6 Pope St John I.
526–30 Pope St Felix IV.
(530) Antipope Dioscorus.
530–2 Pope Boniface II – first pope of Germanic descent.
533–5 Pope John II – first pope to change his name.
535–36 Pope St Agapitus I.
536–7 Pope St Silverius.
537–55 Pope Vigilius.
553 Second Council of Constantinople.
556–61 Pope Pelagius I.
561–74 Pope John III.
575–9 Pope Benedict I.
579–90 Pope Pelagius II.
590–604 Pope St Gregory I the Great.
604–6 Pope St Sabinian.
607, 19 Feb–12 Nov, Pope Boniface III.

TIMELINE

Above: Monastery, County Limerick.

Above: The Temple Church, London.

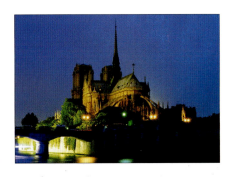

Above: Notre Dame, Paris.

608–768

608–15 Pope St Boniface IV.
615–18 Pope St Adeodatus I.
619–25 Pope Boniface V.
625–38 Pope Honorius I.
632 Death of Prophet Muhammad – birth of Islam.
640, 28 May–2 Aug, Pope Severinus.
640–2 Pope John IV.
642–9 Pope Theodore I.
649–53 Pope St Martin I.
654–7 Pope St Eugenius I.
657–72 Pope St Vitalian.
663/664 Synod of Whitby.
672–6 Pope Adeodatus II.
676–8 Pope Donus.
678–81 Pope St Agatho, said to have been over 100 years old on election.
680–81 Third Council of Constantinople.
682–3 Pope St Leo II.
684–5 Pope St Benedict II.
685–6 Pope John V.
686–7 Pope Conon.
(687) Antipope Theodore.
(687) Antipope Paschal.
687–701 Pope St Sergius I.
701–5 Pope John VI.
705–7 Pope John VII.
708, 15 Jan–4 Feb, Pope Sisinnius.
708–15 Pope Constantine I.
715–31 Pope St Gregory II.
731–41 Pope St Gregory III.
741–52 Pope St Zacharias.
752, 26 Mar–26 Apr, Stephen II – dies before consecration.
752–7 Stephen II – so named since his immediate predecessor is discounted.
757–67 Pope St Paul I.
(767–68) Antipope Constantine II.
(768) Antipope Philip.

768–914

768–72 Pope Stephen III.
772–95 Pope Hadrian I.
787 Second Council of Nicaea.
795–816 Pope St Leo III – crowns Charlemagne 'Emperor of the Romans'.
816–17 Pope Stephen IV.
817–24 Pope St Paschal I.
824–7 Pope Eugenius II.
827, Aug–Sep, Pope Valentine.
827–44 Pope Gregory IV.
(844) Antipope John.
844–7 Sergius II.
846 Muslim Saracens attack Rome.
847–55 Pope St Leo IV.
855–8 Pope Benedict III.
(855) Antipope Anastasius Bibliothecarius.
858–67 Pope St Nicholas I the Great.
867–72 Pope Hadrian II.
869–70 Fourth Council of Constantinople.
872–88 Pope John VIII – first pope to be assassinated.
882–4 Pope Marinus I.
884–5 Pope Hadrian III.
885–91 Pope Stephen V.
891–6 Pope Formosus.
896, May–Aug, Pope Boniface VI.
896–7 Pope Stephen VI.
897, Aug–Nov, Pope Romanus.
897, Nov–Dec, Pope Theodore II.
898–900 Pope John IX.
900–3 Pope Benedict IV.
903, Aug–Sep, Pope Leo V.
855–7 According to legend, reign of female Pope Joan.
(903–4) Antipope Christopher.
904–11 Pope Sergius III.
911–13 Pope Anastasius III.
913–14 Pope Lando.

914–1054

914–28 Pope John X.
928, May–Dec, Pope Leo VI.
928–31 Pope Stephen VII.
931–5/6 Pope John XI.
936–9 Pope Leo VII.
939–42 Pope Stephen VIII.
942–6 Pope Marinus II.
946–55 Pope Agapitus II.
955–64 Pope John XII.
963–5 Pope Leo VIII – sometimes listed as an antipope.
964, 22 May–23 Jun, Pope Benedict V.
965–72 Pope John XIII.
973–4 Pope Benedict VI.
(974) Antipope Boniface VII – returns to power 984–985.
974–83 Pope Benedict VII.
983–4 Pope John XIV.
985–96 Pope John XV.
996–9 Pope Gregory V.
(997–1001) Antipope John XVI.
999–1003 Pope Sylvester II – first French pope.
1003, 16 May–6 Nov, Pope John XVII.
1003–9 Pope John XVIII – abdicated.
1009–12 Pope Sergius IV.
(1012) Antipope Gregory VI.
1012–24 Pope Benedict VIII.
1024–32 Pope John XIX – first pope to grant an indulgence.
1032–44; 1045; 1047–8 Pope Benedict IX.
1045, 20 Jan–10 Mar, Pope Sylvester III.
1045–6 Pope Gregory VI.
1046–7 Pope Clement II.
1048, 17 Jul–9 Aug, Pope Damasus II.
1049–54 Pope St Leo IX.
1054 Great Schism – Western and Eastern churches split.

517

TIMELINE
1054–1534

Above: The Duomo, Florence.

Above: The Crusaders before Antioch.

Above: The Vatican in Rome, Italy.

1054–1138
1054 The Eastern Orthodox Church formally parts company with Rome.
1055–7 Pope Victor II.
1057–8 Pope Stephen IX.
(1058–9) Antipope Benedict X.
1058–61 Pope Nicholas II – made important alliance with Norman leader Robert Guiscard.
1061–73 Pope Alexander II.
(1061–4) Antipope Honorius II.
1073–85 Pope St Gregory VII – clashed with Holy Roman Emperor Henry IV in "Investiture Dispute".
(1080 and 1084–1100) Antipope Clement III.
1086–7 Pope Blessed Victor III.
1088–99 Pope Blessed Urban II – launched First Crusade.
1096–9 First Crusade.
1099–1118 Pope Paschal II.
(1100–1) Antipope Theoderic.
(1101/2) Antipope Aleric.
(1105–11) Antipope Sylvester IV.
1118–19 Pope Gelasius II.
(1118–21) Antipope Gregory VIII.
1119–24 Pope Callistus II.
1122 Concordat of Worms ends Investiture Dispute.
1123 First Lateran Council.
1124–30 Pope Honorius II.
1129 Honorius grants papal approval to Knights Templar.
(1124) Antipope Celestine II.
1130–43 Pope Innocent II.
(1130–38) Antipope Anacletus II.

1138–1217
(1138) Antipope Victor IV.
1139 Second Lateran Council.
1143–4 Pope Celestine II.
1144–5 Pope Lucius II.
1145–53 Pope Blessed Eugenius III.
1147–9 Second Crusade.
1153–4 Pope Anastasius IV.
1154–9 Pope Hadrian IV – only English pope.
1159–81 Pope Alexander III.
(1159–64) Antipope Victor IV.
(1164–8) Antipope Paschal III.
(1168–78) Antipope Callistus III.
1179 Third Lateran Council.
(1179–80) Antipope Innocent III.
1181–5 Pope Lucius III.
1185–7 Pope Urban III.
1187 Pope Gregory VIII.
1187 Saladin recaptures Jerusalem for the Muslims.
1187–91 Pope Clement III.
1187–92 Third Crusade.
1191–8 Pope Celestine III – confirms Teutonic Knights.
1198–1216 Pope Innocent III – church reformer who calls Fourth and Fifth Crusades.
1202–4 Fourth Crusade.
1208 Innocent III calls crusade against Albigensians in southern France.
1209 St Francis of Assisi begins his ministry.
1215 Fourth Lateran Council.
1216–27 Pope Honorius III – approves Dominicans and Franciscans.

1217–1285
1217–21 Fifth Crusade.
1218 Crusade against Muslims in Spain.
1227–41 Pope Gregory IX canonizes Francis of Assisi and Dominic Guzman.
1231 Gregory IX founds Dominican inquisition.
1228–9 Sixth Crusade.
1241, 25 Oct–10 Nov, Pope Celestine IV.
1241–3 Cardinals take a year and a half to elect a new pope.
1243–54 Pope Innocent IV.
1245 First Council of Lyon.
1248–54 Seventh Crusade.
1254–61 Pope Alexander IV.
1261–4 Pope Urban IV.
1265–8 Pope Clement IV.
1266–74 St Thomas Aquinas writes the *Summa Theologica*.
1268–71 On Clement's death cardinals take three years to elect successor.
1270 Eighth Crusade.
1271–6 Pope Blessed Gregory X.
1271–2 Ninth Crusade.
1274 Thomas Aquinas dies.
1275 Second Council of Lyon.
1276, 21 Jan–22 Jun, Pope Blessed Innocent V.
1276, 11 Jul–18 Aug, Pope Hadrian V.
1276–7 Pope John XXI (due to an error in numbering, there has never been a Pope John XX).
1277–80 Pope Nicholas III.
1281–5 Pope Martin IV.

TIMELINE

Above: Correggio's Madonna and Child.

Above: Michelangelo's Moses.

Above: San Jose de Laguna, New Mexico.

1285–1394

1285–7 Pope Honorius IV.
1288–92 Pope Nicholas IV.
1291 Last Christian holding in the Holy Land, at Acre, lost to army of Egyptian Mamluk Sultanate.
1294 Pope St Celestine V.
1294–1303 Pope Boniface VIII – founds University of Rome in 1303.
1297 Boniface canonizes King Louis IX of France.
1302 Boniface VIII issues *Unam Sanctam* bull – salvation depends on being subject to the pope.
1303–4 Pope Benedict XI.
1305–14 Pope Clement V.
1309–77 Avignon exile – papacy is based in city of Avignon, southern France, not Rome.
1311–12 Council of Vienne.
1312 Knights Templar dissolved.
1316–34 Pope John XXII.
(1328–30) Antipope Nicholas V.
1334–42 Pope Benedict XII.
1337–1453 Hundred Years' War between England and France.
1342–52 Pope Clement VI – purchases Avignon and surrounding area for papacy.
1352–62 Pope Innocent VI.
1362–70 Pope Blessed Urban V.
1367 Urban V attempts to return papacy to Rome but is forced by unrest to retreat to Avignon.
1370–78 Pope Gregory XI.
1377 Gregory returns papacy to Rome, ending Avignon exile.
1378–89 Pope Urban VI.
(1378–94) Antipope Clement VII.
1389–1404 Pope Boniface IX.

1394–1492

(1394–1417) Antipope Benedict XIII.
1404–6 Pope Innocent VII.
1406–15 Pope Gregory XII.
1408 Council of Pisa fails to resolve the Western Schism.
(1409–10) Antipope Alexander V.
(1410–15) Antipope John XXIII.
1417–31 Pope Martin V.
1414–18 Council of Constance.
1415 Czech reformer Jan Hus is condemned and burned as a heretic.
1431 Joan of Arc is found guilty of heresy and burned at the stake.
1431–47 Pope Eugenius IV.
1431–42 Council of Basel; moved to Ferrara and then Florence.
1447–55 Pope Nicholas V – founds Vatican Library.
1453 Constantinople sacked by Ottoman Turks.
1455–58 Pope Callistus III – first Borgia pope.
1456, Jul, In the Battle of Belgrade governor of Hungary John Hunyadi defeats the Ottomans. Pope Callistus III makes the Feast of the Transfiguration of Jesus a universal feast to celebrate victory,
1458–64 Pope Pius II.
1464–71 Pope Paul II.
1464 First printed books in the papal states.
1479 Bartolomeo Platina's *Lives of the Popes* is published.
1471–84 Pope Sixtus IV.
1473–79 Ponte Sisto built in Rome.
1478 Spanish Inquisition is established.
1483 Sistine Chapel opens.
1484–92 Pope Innocent VIII.

1492–1534

1492 End of Reconquista – Ferdinand and Isabella expel Muslims from Granada, ending 700 years of Islamic presence in Spanish peninsula.
1492 Christopher Colombus sets sail to Americas and starts opening up an empire for Spain there.
1492–94 Borgia Apartments laid out in Vatican.
1492–1503 Pope Alexander VI.
1503, 22 Sep–18 Oct, Pope Pius III.
1503–13 Pope Julius II.
1506 Julius II lays foundation stone for new St Peter's Basilica.
1508–12 Michelangelo paints Sistine Chapel ceiling.
1512–17 Fifth Lateran Council.
1506 Foundation of the Swiss Papal Guard, one of the oldest military units in the world.
1513–21 Pope Leo X.
1517 Martin Luther pins his "95 Theses" on the door of Wittenburg Cathedral – the beginning of the Protestant Reformation.
1521 Pope Leo X excommunicates Luther.
1522–3 Pope Hadrian VI.
1523–34 Pope Clement VII.
1527 Rome sacked by troops of Charles V. Pope Clement VII is taken prisoner during the Sack of Rome.
1529 The Ottoman Siege of Vienna is successfully repulsed.
1534 Henry VIII announces that he and his successors will henceforth be heads of the Church of England.
1534 St Ignatius Loyola founds the Society of Jesus, the Jesuits.

TIMELINE
1534–PRESENT DAY

Above: St Louis Cathedral, New Orleans.

Above: Statue of Mary, Santiago, Chile.

Above: In front of St Peter's Rome.

1534–1584
1534–49 Pope Paul III.
1536–41 Michelangelo paints *The Last Judgement* in the Sistine Chapel.
1540 Papal bull *Regimini militantis ecclesiae* gives official recognition to Jesuits.
1542 Paul III establishes the Holy Office of the Inquisition.
1545–63 Council of Trent.
1547 Paul III appoints Michelangelo principal architect on St Peter's Basilica.
1550–5 Pope Julius III.
1553 Catholicism restored in England.
1555, 9 Apr–1 May, Pope Marcellus II – died after 22 days.
1555–9 Pope Paul IV.
1557–8 Paul IV creates Index of Prohibited Books.
1559–65 Pope Pius IV.
1561–5 Porta Pia in Rome is built – to designs by Michelangelo.
1564 Michelangelo dies.
1566–72 Pope St Pius V – his reign is dated from 1566 because Pius IV died in Dec 1565.
1570 Pius V excommunicates Elizabeth I of England.
1571 Battle of Lepanto – victory for Catholic League against Turks.
1572–85 Pope Gregory XIII.
1572 Massacre of St Bartholomew's Day – slaughter of French Huguenots.
1580 Gregory XIII backs reform of Carmelites by Teresa of Avila.
1582 Gregorian calendar introduced to replace Julian calendar.

1584–1669
1584 The Gesù – mother church of the Jesuits – is consecrated.
1585–90 Pope Sixtus V.
1590 Dome of St Peter's completed.
1588 Spanish Armada – Sixtus V renews Elizabeth's excommunication.
1590, 15–27 Sep, Pope Urban VII – Fell ill at once and died 11 days later.
1590–1 Pope Gregory XIV.
1591, 29 Oct–30 Dec, Pope Innocent IX – 82 years old on election.
1592–1605 Pope Clement VIII.
1593 King Henry IV of France is reconciled to the Church.
1605, 1–27 Apr, Pope Leo XI.
1605–21 Pope Paul V.
1605 Paul V establishes Bank of the Holy Spirit.
1618–48 Thirty Years' War in Germany.
1621–3 Pope Gregory XV.
1622 Gregory XV canonizes Ignatius of Loyola, Francis Xavier, Philip Neri and Teresa of Avila.
1623–44 Pope Urban VIII.
1623–4 Gian Lorenzo Bernini designs the baldachin in St Peter's Basilica.
1633 Galileo is condemned by the Inquisition and forced to recant.
1644–55 Pope Innocent X.
1650 Diego Velazquez paints portrait of Innocent X.
1655–67 Pope Alexander VII.
1656–67 Gian Lorenzo Bernini design St Peter's Square.
1667–9 Pope Clement IX.

1669–1809
1669 Candia, last Christian stronghold on Crete, falls to the Ottoman Turks.
1670–6 Pope Clement X.
1673 John Sobieski defeats Turks.
1676–89 Pope Innocent XI.
1688 Catholic King James II driven from English throne and replaced by Protestant William and Mary.
1689–91 Pope Alexander VIII.
1691–1700 Pope Innocent XII.
1700–21 Pope Clement XI.
1721–4 Pope Innocent XIII.
1726 John of the Cross is canonized.
1724–30 Pope Benedict XIII.
1725 Benedict XIII opens Spanish Steps in Rome.
1730–40 Pope Clement XII.
1740–58 Pope Benedict XIV.
1758–69 Pope Clement XIII.
1751–2 French encyclopedia of Diderot and d'Alembert is published; Clement XIII has the book placed on the Index.
1762 Trevi Fountain in Rome, designed by Nicola Salvi, is completed.
1769–74 Pope Clement XIV.
1773, 16 Aug, Papal bull *Dominos ac Redemptor noster* dissolves Jesuits.
1775–99 Pope Pius VI.
1789 French Revolution.
1797 French army occupies papal states, proclaims Roman Republic and announces deposition of pope as head of state; Pius flees to Florence.
1800–23 Pope Pius VII.

TIMELINE

Above: St Patrick's Cathedral, Manhattan.

Above: Sagrada Familia, Barcelona, Spain.

Above: John Paul II, the first Polish pope.

1809–1937

1809 Napoleon annexes papal states. Pius excommunicates Napoleon, who has the pope arrested and imprisoned.
1814 After Napoleon is defeated, the Congress of Vienna returns the papal states to the papacy.
1814 Jesuits are restored.
1823–9 Pope Leo XII.
1829–30 Pope Pius VIII.
1829 Catholic Emancipation Act in Britain.
1830 In the July Revolution Louis Philippe comes to the French throne.
1831–46 Pope Gregory XVI.
1846–78 Pope Pius IX.
1849 Creation of Roman Republic abolishes pope's secular powers.
1860 Establishment of Italy, with Rome as its capital – the papal states annexed.
1864, Dec, Pius issues Syllabus of Errors.
1869–70 First Vatican Council.
1878–1903 Pope Leo XIII.
1903–14 Pope Pius X.
1914–22 Pope Benedict XV.
1914–18 First World War.
1917 Russian Revolution.
1920 Benedict XV canonizes Joan of Arc.
1922–39 Pope Pius XI.
1929 Lateran Treaty establishes the pope as sovereign ruler of an independent neutral state in Vatican City.
1931 Pius XI becomes the first pope to make a radio broadcast.
1933 Papacy signs concordat with Hitler's German Reich.
1936–9 Spanish Civil War.

1937–1989

1937 Pius XI's encyclicals denounce Nazism and communism.
1939–58 Pope Pius XII.
1939–45 Second World War.
1949 Pius condemns Soviet Union and threatens excommunication for Catholics joining Communist Party.
1950 Pius invokes papal infallibility in defining dogma of the Assumption of Blessed Virgin Mary.
1958–63 Pope John XXIII.
1962–5 Second Vatican Council.
1962 Cuban Missile Crisis.
1963–78 Pope Paul VI.
1964 Paul VI is first modern pope to visit Holy Land.
1965 Pope Paul VI and Ecumenical Patriarch Athenagoras I issue a joint statement withdrawing the excommunications exchanged in 1054.
1965 Paul VI travels to USA, meets President Johnson, and celebrates Mass in the Yankee Stadium.
1968 Paul VI's encyclical *Humanae vitae* condemns artificial birth control.
1969 Paul VI introduces revised form of Mass.
1978, 26 Aug–28 Sep, Pope John Paul I.
1978–2005 Pope John Paul II.
1981, 13 May, John Paul II survives an assassination attempt in St Peter's Square.

1989–present day

1993 The Holy See establishes diplomatic relations with the state of Israel.
2001, 11 Sep, Terrorist attacks launched by Islamic terrorists al-Qaeda hit New York City.
2003 United States-led invasion of Iraq.
2005–13 Pope Benedict XVI.
2013, 11 Feb, Benedict announces his abdication.
2013 Francis is the first Latin American, Jesuit and non-European pope for more than 1,000 years.
2013, 23 Mar, Pope Francis meets and prays with pope emeritus Benedict – the first time such a meeting has been possible since 1294.
2014, 27 Apr, Francis canonizes Pope John XXIII and Pope John Paul II.
2014, 24–26 May, Francis visits Israel, Jordan and Palestine.
2015, 24 Sep, On a visit to Cuba and the United States, Francis is the first pope to address the US Congress.
2017, 13 May, Francis visits Portugal to celebrate 100th anniversary of Our Lady of Fatima.
2018, 14 Oct, Francis canonizes Pope Paul VI.
2019, 3–5 Feb, Francis visits Abu Dhabi in the United Arab Emirates, and is first pope to visit and conduct Mass on the Arabian peninsula.
2021, 6 Mar, Francis visits Iraq, the first pope to do so, and meets Shiite cleric Grand Ayatollah Ali al-Sistani at his residence in the holy city of Najaf.
2021, 1 June, Francis promulgates major changes to canon law that includes a strengthening of sanctions on priests who commit sexual abuse.
2023, 19 Dec, Pope Francis grants his formal approval to allow the possibility for Catholic priests to bless same-sex couples so long as they do not appear to endorse their marriage.

ST PETER
THE FIRST POPE

The man Jesus singled out among his disciples and identified as the rock on which to build the community of Christians was originally a fisherman at Bethsaida on the northern shore of the Sea of Galilee (a large freshwater lake now in northeast Israel). He was roughly the same age as Jesus, having been born in c.4BC. The son of Jonas, he was originally known as Simeon (the Hebrew form; Simon in Greek) and worked alongside his brother Andrew with James and John, sons of Zebedee.

By the time Simeon encountered Jesus he had married, and was living in his mother-in-law's house further west along the shore of the Sea of Galilee, at Capernaum. With his brother Andrew he responded to Jesus's call, "Follow me, and I will make you fishers of men," and thereafter travelled with Jesus, gradually becoming the foremost disciple.

Below: A mosaic from St Peter's in Rome depicts Christ passing to Peter the key that represents papal authority over the church.

> **FACT BOX**
> **Original name** Simeon/Simon
> **Born** c.4BC, Bethsaida, Sea of Galilee
> **Origin** Jewish
> **Died** c.AD64
> **Key fact** Named by Christ as the rock on which the Church would be built

ENTRUSTED WITH CARE OF CHRISTIANS

When Simeon replied to Jesus's question, "Whom do men say that I am?" with the words "Thou art the Christ, the Son of the living God", Jesus named him the rock on which the Church would be founded (Matthew 16:13–20). He was then called Peter, from the Latin *Petrus* ("rock"). After the resurrection Jesus entrusted Peter with the care of his followers (John 21:15–17). Three times Jesus asked Peter if he loved him; and each time Peter replied, "Lord, thou knowest that I love thee." Jesus said, "Feed my lambs … feed my sheep".

Above: Leader of the early Christians, Peter is remembered as the first pope. Accounts of his life show that he had natural authority and, above all, a profound love for Jesus.

LEADER AND PREACHER

Peter was leader of the Christian community. He had the principal role in the election of Matthias to replace Judas Iscariot, who had betrayed Jesus and then hanged himself (Acts 1:15–26). He was the first to preach in explanation of the events of Pentecost when the Holy Spirit descended upon the faithful, making them speak in tongues (Acts 2: 14–40). He stood up and spoke as advocate for the Apostles before the religious authorities in Jerusalem (Acts 4:5–22).

In the early days of the Church, Peter travelled far and wide, preaching, guiding the first Christians and performing miracles – healing the sick and even raising the dead.

UNSHAKEABLE FAITH

We know that Peter was not learned – Acts 4:13 makes it clear that he was not trained in the Mosaic Law. He probably did not know Greek. However he always put his faith in the risen Christ.

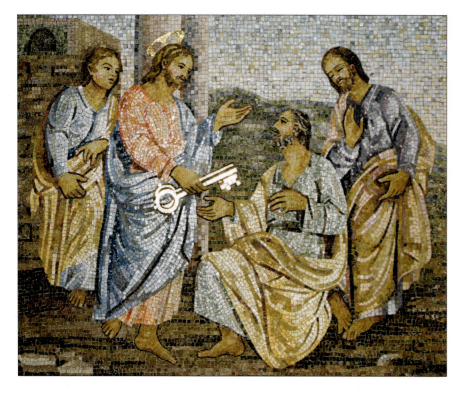

ST PETER

Above: Peter was crucified upside down since he wanted to avoid comparisons with his Lord's Passion. A cherubic angel waits to deliver the saint's heavenly reward.

In c.44 he was arrested by Herod Agrippa I, but an angel visited him in jail, making the chains fall from his hands and leading Peter past sleeping guards to freedom (Acts 12:1–8). Thereafter he departed from Jerusalem, probably leaving leadership of the Church there in the hands of James "the brother of the Lord". He seems to have gone to Antioch (near modern Antakya, Turkey), which traditionally claims Peter as its first bishop.

CRUCIFIED IN ROME

After that he may have settled in Rome. There is no firm historical evidence that Peter was in Rome but many accounts by early Christian writers place him there. According to the historian Eusebius (c.260–c.340) Peter was martyred in Rome in the time of Emperor Nero (54–69) – probably in Nero's persecution of the Christians in 64.

Tradition has it that Peter went voluntarily to his death after an encounter with the Risen Christ. Peter was leaving Rome on the Via Appia to escape Nero's persecution when he met Jesus. He declared *Domine, quo vadis?* ('Where are you going, Lord?"); Jesus replied, "To Rome, where I will be crucified once more." At once Peter turned around and went to his death. According to the Alexandrian theologian Origen (c.185–c.254), Peter asked to be crucified upside down to avoid comparison with the death of his Lord.

The crucifixion took place beside an Ancient Egyptian obelisk that then stood near the Circle of Nero and today can be seen in St Peter's Square. By tradition Peter was buried by a Christian convert named Marcellus and a tomb was raised over his grave by Pope Anacletus (c.79–c.91). The first St Peter's Basilica was built on the site under Emperor Constantine in 319 onwards.

Below: The baroque bronze canopy (baldachin) over the high altar in St Peter's Basilica, Rome, is meant to mark Peter's tomb beneath. The baldachin was designed by Bernini and built in 1623–34.

> **ST PETER'S TOMB?**
>
> During alterations made to the burial crypt beneath St Peter's Basilica as part of the burial of Pope Pius XI in 1939, the remains of a man who died in the 1st century AD were found. They were in a tomb within a wall that was seemingly covered with marks made by pilgrims visiting the grave of St Peter. The bones – those of a powerfully built man who died in his 60s and wrapped in a splendid purple cloth engraved in gold – were declared by Pope Paul VI to be those of St Peter, on 26 June 1968.

'UPON THIS ROCK...'

LINUS TO PIUS I, 66–155
THE FIRST NINE POPES AFTER PETER

Pope Linus, first in a long line of successors to St Peter as head of the Church, was reputedly appointed by saints Peter and Paul acting together. The Church Father Irenaeus (130–202) identified this pope with the Linus mentioned by St Paul in 2 Timothy 4:21. The *Liber Pontificalis* ("Book of the Popes") dates Linus to 56–67, but St Jerome (c.347–420) places him at 67–78, and if he is right Linus would have been pope when the Second Temple was destroyed in Jerusalem by the Roman army of Emperor Titus and 20,000 Jewish slaves were transported to Rome and put to work building the Colosseum.

Linus was succeeded by Pope Anacletus (c.79–c.91). Tradition has it that he was a Roman, but took a Greek name (meaning "called back", or when spelled Anencletus, "beyond reproach"). He ordained priests to work in Rome, and like Linus is said to have died a martyr for his faith.

Below: St Sixtus (pope c.116–c.125) ruled that only ministers were permitted to touch the vessels used in the Mass. He was reputedly buried near St Peter's grave on Vatican Hill. His feast day is 6 April.

PAPAL EPISTLE
The fourth pope, Clement I (c.91–c.101) – who is said to have been ordained by St Peter himself – wrote an epistle c.96 to the Christians at Corinth that is one of the oldest surviving early Christian documents beside the New Testament. In the letter he attempted to reinforce the authority of presbyters (local church leaders) who had been deposed in Corinth, arguing that they should be honoured because they had been appointed by the Apostles.

The Basilica of San Clemente in Rome reputedly stands on the site of Clement's house. Some accounts identify him as the Clement mentioned by St Paul in Philippians 4:3 as a "fellow-labourer" in Christ's service and others as a cousin of Emperor Domitian, Titus Flavius Clemens.

MARTYRED AT SEA
According to legend Clement was martyred after being exiled to the Crimean peninsula by Emperor Trajan. Sent to work in a quarry where the other labourers were desperate for water, he

Above: Linus was pope at the time of the destruction of the Second Temple in Jerusalem by Emperor Titus in 70. This view (1625–26) is by Nicolas Poussin.

knelt in prayer and was granted a vision of a lamb on a nearby hillside. When he went to the spot, he struck with his quarryman's axe and brought forth a stream of the purest water.

Witnessing this miracle, many were converted to be followers of Christ, but Clement was martyred by being tied to an anchor and thrown from a boat into the Black Sea. In images he is often shown with an anchor.

THE POPE FROM BETHLEHEM
The next three popes were Evaristus (c.101–c.109), Alexander I (c.109–c.116) and Sixtus I (c.116–c.125). The *Liber Pontificalis* identifies Evaristus as being an Hellenic Jew, born in Bethlehem, and says he appointed seven deacons to the Church in Rome and assigned churches as titles to individual priests.

According to tradition, Alexander – who seems to have been born in Rome

– introduced the narration of the events of the Last Supper into celebration of the Mass. Sixtus I (spelled Xystus in the oldest documents) reputedly introduced the custom of the priest saying the Sanctus ("Holy, Holy, Holy") with the people during the Mass. Sixtus is recorded as being Roman by birth, the son of a man named Pastor.

THE PHILOSOPHER POPE

Pope Telesphorus (c.125–c.136) was from a Greek family and was said to have been a monk before being elected pope – according to tradition on Mount Carmel, Israel, so that the religious order of the Carmelites view him as their patron saint. An unexplained gap of two years in the papal lists interrupts the succession from Telesphorus to Pope Hyginus (c.138–c.142), a Greek, born in Athens, who was a philosopher before becoming pope. Gnostic theologians

Below: A 6th-century fresco in the Basilica of San Clemente, Rome, shows Clement I (pope c.91–c.101) celebrating Mass. The basilica is said to be on the site of his house.

Above: The Gnostic Valentinus claimed to have received esoteric spiritual knowledge from his teacher Theudas, who received it from St Paul. It was said to be derived from Paul's encounter with the risen Christ.

Valentinus and Cerdo visited Rome during Hyginus's pontificate, a time of ferment and theological debate.

Pope Pius I (c.142–c.155) was according to Church tradition from Aquileia, northern Italy, and the brother of a poet named Hermas who wrote "The Shepherd", a series of visions and par-

> **GNOSTICS**
>
> Gnostics believed that people could achieve salvation through esoteric knowledge. Many Gnostics were dualists, believing there were two gods: one greater, pure and good, and one lesser, who had created the material world. The Egyptian Gnostic Valentinus, who was excommunicated by Pius I, held there were three types of people: those with a spiritual nature, who had the knowledge he taught, would at death be reabsorbed into the fullness of God, while those with a psychical nature (Christians) would achieve a lesser salvation. Those with a material nature (Jews and pagans) would simply die.

ables. He excommunicated another Gnostic, Marcion, who subsequently founded the heretical sect of the Marcionites, teaching a form of dualism (belief in two gods) under which Christ was not the Son of the God of the Jews and the Old Testament but the offspring of a different, good God.

'UPON THIS ROCK...'

ANICETUS TO URBAN I, 155–230
THE PAPACY GROWS IN CONFIDENCE

Pope Anicetus (*c.*155–*c.*166) was a Syrian by birth, from Emesa (modern Homs). The fact that he was visited by the early Christian historian Hegesippus (110–180) suggests that the pope and the Church in Rome were beginning to hold a prime position in the Christian world.

Italian-born Pope Soter (*c.*166–*c.*174) was noted for his charity to Christians in need throughout the empire. Pope Eleutherius (*c.*175–*c.*189), a Greek born in Nicopolis, continued the struggle against Gnostics and followers of Marcionism begun under his predecessors and took a stand against non-conformity in explicitly condemning Montanism, a charismatic Christian movement that had originated in Asia Minor (Anatolia). The followers of Montanism emphasized simplicity in the Church and reliance on the power of the Holy Spirit, and their meetings featured prophecies and also speaking in tongues.

EASTER ON A SUNDAY
The first African-born pope, Victor I (*c.*189–*c.*199), seems to have been a strong-willed man who set out to establish the authority of the papacy. He decided that Easter should always be celebrated on a Sunday and called synods in the major church centres in both Western and Eastern parts of the Christian world to consider the issue. By this date a tradition had been established whereby the Roman Church celebrated Easter on a Sunday since this was the day of the week on which Christ rose from

Above: Victor I (c.189–c.199) was the first African pope. This portrait is based on a medallion in the Basilica of Saint Paul Outside the Walls, Rome.

Below: Christians were traditionally said to have been martyred in the Colosseum, though modern historians doubt this – thinking the faithful were put to death at the Circus Maximus. In 1749 Pope Benedict XIV consecrated the Colosseum because of its link to early martyrs.

526

ANICETUS TO URBAN I

Above: Callistus I (pope c.217–c.222) is buried in the basilica of Santa Maria in Trastevere in Rome. He built the first sanctuary on the site of the church.

Right: Persecution at the hands of Marcus Aurelius struck fear into the hearts of the early Christians. This ancient bronze statue of the emperor stands on the Capitoline Hill in Rome.

the dead, but Christians in the East celebrated it on any day of the week according to the date of the Jewish festival of Passover – since the events of Christ's Passion took place at Passover.

The Western synods agreed with Victor's decision to fix Easter on a Sunday, but the ones in Asia Minor (Anatolia) did not; his response was to excommunicate those who challenged him. He also excommunicated Theodotus of Byzantium, who had argued that Jesus – although born of the Virgin Mary by the action of the Holy Spirit – was not divine until after his Resurrection.

PERSECUTION – AND HERESY

His successor, another Italian named Zephyrinus (c.199–c.217), ruled in difficult times.

Christians faced increasingly severe persecution under the Roman Emperor Septimius Severus, and Zephyrinus had to face down heretics including followers of the excommunicated Theodotus of Byzantium as well as the Montanists, Marcionists and Gnostics who had troubled his predecessors.

In a dialogue written by a leading Christian named Caius to refute the teachings of the Montanist Proclus, we find the first reference to the graves of St Peter and St Paul in Rome. In exerting papal authority against the heretics, Zephyrinus made enemies. Hippolytus the Martyr dismissed this pope as "ignorant" and "a receiver of bribes and lover of money".

TWICE CHEATED DEATH

Pope Callistus I (c.217–c.222) came to power by taking advantage of the weakness of Zephyrinus towards the end of a wild and colourful life in which he bankrupted several Christians and twice narrowly escaped death.

As a young man he was a slave owned by a Christian named Carpophorus. Trusted by his master with substantial amounts of money, he launched a banking operation in which other Christians, including widows, invested. When Callistus lost all the money, he fled but was caught by his master just as he was about to embark on a cargo ship. The fugitive leapt into the sea but was hauled out and set to work at the hand-mill – a punishment used for slaves. Christians called for his release, and after further adventures he was sent to Antium with a pension by Pope Victor. Under Zephyrinus he was recalled to Rome and managed to ingratiate himself with the church hierarchy.

This account of his life is from the early 3rd-century *Philosophumena* (or "Refutation of All Heresies"), probably written by Hippolytus of Rome. Callistus died a martyr, perhaps killed during an uprising in Rome; according to tradition his body was thrown down a well on the site of the Church of San Callisto in Rome that bears his name.

POWER OF PRAYER

The election of Callistus's successor, Urban I (c.222–230) was challenged and Hippolytus of Rome, author of the *Philosophumena* and a noted scholar, set himself up as a rival pope. Urban defied Hippolytus and maintained his hold on the papacy. The number of Christians in Rome increased under his rule. Legend has it that he converted many people through his sermons, and baptized the husband and brother-in-law of Saint Cecilia. It is also said that he succeeded in knocking a pagan idol over through the power of prayer alone and for this was seized and beheaded.

ANTIPOPES

Hippolytus of Rome was the first of the antipopes, the name given to the many individuals over the centuries who claimed the rights and authority of the papacy without proper authority. The term was first used in the late 12th century. Some antipopes arose because of disputes over doctrine, others when one candidate was preferred by the secular authorities but church leaders refused to give way, others as a result of papal exile. The last antipope was Felix V (1439–49).

'UPON THIS ROCK...'

PONTIAN TO STEPHEN I, 230–57
STEPHEN ASSERTS PRIMACY OF POPE OVER OTHER BISHOPS

Roman-born Pontian (230–5) was the first pope to resign the papacy. The Roman Emperor Maximinus Thrax reinstituted persecution of Christians and banished Pontian and the antipope Hippolytus into exile in the Sardinian mines. Pontian resigned to allow a new pope to be elected in Rome. He had to live in terrible conditions in Sardinia and died as a result. Before his exile he had presided over a synod in Rome that condemned the Alexandrian theologian Origen.

The reign of Pontian's successor Anterus, a Greek, lasted just under six weeks from 21 November 235 to 3 January 236. He probably died of natural causes although some sources claim he was martyred during the persecutions of Maximinus.

THE TOUCH OF THE DOVE

Pope Fabian (236–50) was singled out for election as pope by a most unusual method – the intervention of a dove, symbol of the Holy Spirit. According to the 4th-century church historian Eusebius, Fabian was both a layman and a stranger to the Christians in Rome, but when they saw the dove land on his head while they were meeting to choose a new pontiff they acclaimed him as a bishop and elected him pope. From these unorthodox beginnings, he went on to become a quietly efficient leader, an important figure in the history of the early papacy who reorganized the Church in Rome and sent seven bishops to preach the Gospel in France.

Fabian also appointed officials to record the deeds of the Christian martyrs and corresponded with the theologian Origen. He was martyred on 20 January 250 during the persecution of Christians under Emperor Decius and after his death the Church was governed by a committee in the teeth of fierce official persecution for 14 months.

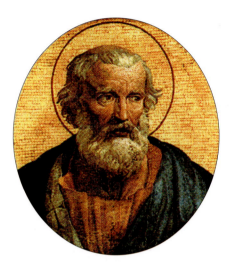

THE SECOND ANTIPOPE

Pope Cornelius finally succeeded in March 251 during a lull in the persecutions, but he was then faced by a second antipope, Novatian.

Novatian was the first Roman theologian to use the Latin language. He was consecrated by three bishops in 251. The principal disagreement between the two leaders was over whether Christians who had lapsed in the face of persecution could be readmitted to the Church: Novatian said that they could not unless they were rebaptized, but the official position of the Church was that they could, without the need for a second baptism.

Cornelius prevailed and Novatian was excommunicated. From figures quoted in Cornelius's letters, we know that there were around 50,000 Christians in Rome by this time; the letters also make the first reference to the office of exorcist. Cornelius was exiled by Decius's successor Trebonianus Gallus to Centumcellae (modern Civitavecchia, Italy), where he died as a result of the hardships he endured.

Left: Pope Fabian (pope 236–50) brought back the bodies of Pontian and the first antipope, Hippolytus, from their place of death in Sardinia for burial in Rome.

ORIGEN

Origen (c.185–c.254) was a theologian and preacher, author of many biblical commentaries including the *Hexapla*, a comparative edition of the six extant versions of the Old Testament. He was celebrated for his chastity, and according to the 4th-century church historian Eusebius castrated himself. He was head of a catechetical school first in Alexandria, Egypt (his probable birthplace) and – after he was exiled by Bishop Demetrius of Alexandria – in Caesarea, Palestine. In the persecution of Christians under Emperor Decius he was imprisoned and tortured but survived to die in Tyre, Phoenicia (modern Sur in Lebanon). Among the controversial ideas associated with him are that souls exist before bodies, that humans might endure a second Fall from Grace and that the devil was not beyond salvation.

Left: Origen was never sainted because his teaching was so controversial. Some historians hold he believed in reincarnation.

528

PATRON SAINT OF COPENHAGEN

Lucius I (253–4) seems to have been a prudent man who, although initially exiled under Emperor Trebonianus Gallus, won permission to return to Rome under Emperor Valerian. He is the patron saint of the Danish capital Copenhagen: according to tradition, his skull (within a reliquary) was taken to the area in *c*.1100 to banish local demons.

FROM THE CHAIR OF PETER

Stephen I (254–7) was a forthright exponent of the primacy of Rome. He opposed African and other churches that rebaptized heretic and lapsed Christians and threatened Cyprian, Bishop of Carthage, and other African bishops with excommunication; Cyprian wrote a spirited defence, asserting the right of each bishop to govern his own see, and sent envoys and threatened schism between Africa and Rome, but Stephen declared the primacy of the pope over other bishops, on the grounds that he followed in direct succession from Peter, the rock on whom the Church's

Below: Fabian was a surprise candidate for the papacy, elected after a dove alighted on his head, as depicted in this 15th-century image of the Spanish school.

Above: In the biblical account the Spirit of God descended to Jesus in the form of a dove after John the Baptist had baptized him in the River Jordan.

foundations were laid. He is associated with the phrase *cathedra Petri* ("The Chair of Peter") that symbolized the pre-eminence of the pope in Rome.

The Church does not celebrate Stephen as a martyr, although for many centuries he was remembered as such, following the tradition recorded in the 13th-century book the *Legenda aurea* ("Golden Legend") that he was sitting on the papal throne celebrating Mass on 2 August 257 when the Emperor Valerian's men burst in and beheaded him there and then.

THE POPE AND THE BISHOPS OF THE CHURCH

The pope and college of bishops derive their authority to teach and govern the Church from their status as direct spiritual descendants of St Peter and Jesus's other disciples.

Jesus gave the name Peter (from Greek *petros*, the translation of Syriac *cephas* – "rock") to his disciple Simon, son of John, and told him he was the rock on which the Church would be built. He said "I will give unto thee the keys of the kingdom of heaven: and whatsoever thou shalt bind on earth shall be bound in heaven: and whatsoever thou shalt loose on earth shall be loosed in heaven." The pope is regarded as the direct spiritual descendant of St Peter – Pope Francis is 266th in line from Peter – and has these keys as his emblem, signifying his authority as "Vicar" or representative of Christ.

Simon Peter became the foremost of Jesus's disciples and first leader of the Christians in Rome, where according to tradition he was martyred and buried in the spot where the high altar stands in St Peter's Basilica.

THE CHRISTIAN NARRATIVE

The profoundly inspirational narrative of the Christian Gospels taught by the pope and the Roman Catholic Church tells that the Son of God – born Jesus, son of the Virgin Mary in Bethlehem, Judea, roughly 2,000 years ago – gathered 12 disciples and for around three years was an itinerant preacher who taught in vivid parables or teaching tales and performed breathtaking miracles such as resurrecting Lazarus from the dead and calming a wild storm. He was betrayed to the Roman authorities, crucified in Jerusalem on the orders of the Roman prefect, Pontius Pilate, suffered, died and was buried, then on the third day rose again to life – and afterwards ascended into Heaven; by his death he redeemed all humankind who come to believe in Him from punishment due as a result of the sins of the first man, Adam, and the first woman, Eve.

These events fulfilled prophecies in Jewish tradition that a prince or king, the Messiah, would come to inaugurate an era of peace and justice: the name

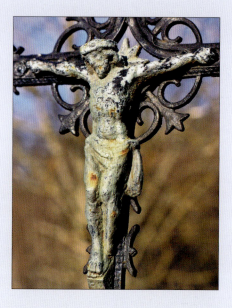

Above: Jesus Christ, the Son of God, gave himself up to die on the cross and redeem humankind from the consequences of sin.

"Christ" (Greek *Christos*, "Anointed One") is the translation of the Hebrew word (*Meshiah*) for the Messiah and was given to Jesus by his followers after his death to signify that they knew him to be the Messiah.

After Jesus ascended into Heaven, at the Jewish festival of Pentecost, the disciples led by Peter felt the inspiration of God's Holy Spirit come upon them to inspire their preaching as they set about spreading the new faith that Jesus the Christ had founded. Roman Catholics and members of most other Christian denominations believe that God exists and is experienced in a Trinity of three forms: God the Father, God the Son and God the Holy Spirit.

Disagreement over the precise nature or origin of the Holy Spirit was later a matter of controversy between Western and Eastern Christian churches

Left: This ancient mosaic is at Tabgha, Israel – sometimes identified as the site of the miracle of the Feeding of the Five Thousand.

Left: The Angel Gabriel broke the news to Mary that she was to become pregnant with the Son of God. Fra Angelico painted several versions of the "Annunciation".

> **SYNODS**
>
> Synods – from the Greek *synodos*, meaning "gathering" or "assembly" – were meetings of bishops and other leaders of the early church to decide on matters of discipline or make administrative decisions. The same word in Latin, *concilium*, is the origin of our "council". Synods of bishops in the Roman Empire were held from the mid-3rd century onwards.

for centuries: while Latin (Roman) Christians held that the Holy Spirit proceeds from the Father and the Son together, their Eastern counterparts held that the Holy Spirit proceeds from the Father alone. This was a significant factor in the Great Schism between the churches in 1054.

THE EARLY CHURCH

The first Christians carried the new faith to many places in the Roman Empire, including the capital Rome. According to church tradition, Peter became bishop or leader of the Christians in Rome and in 64 died a martyr there. The Christians faced violent persecution for more than two centuries until under the Edict of Milan in 313 the empire recognized the legitimacy of the Christian Church.

COLLEGE OF BISHOPS

After he rose from the dead, Jesus commanded the disciples to "go and make disciples of all nations" (Matthew 28:19); in Christian tradition the disciples are known as the Twelve Apostles, from the Greek word meaning one who is sent on a mission. Roman Catholics understand that, just as the pope is the spiritual successor of St Peter, so the bishops of the Church are successors of the apostles.

In the words of the Dogmatic Constitution of the Church as agreed by the Second Vatican Council (1962–5), the church is governed "by the successor of Peter and by the bishops in communion with him". The same council's Decree on the Bishops Pastoral Office identified the bishops of the Roman Catholic Church as a college that succeeded the Apostles as a group to teach and govern the Church.

At the time some scholars were concerned that this conception of the bishops' role would revive the idea that a general council of the Church should have equal or greater power than the pope himself – the "conciliar theory" that caused a good deal of conflict between pope and council in the 15th century. A preliminary explanatory note to the decree established that the college of bishops cannot challenge the pope since: "There is no such thing as the college without its head ... and in the college the head preserves intact his function as Vicar of Christ and pastor of the universal Church."

Below: Christ said to Peter: "I will give unto thee the keys of the kingdom of heaven." The pope is Peter's descendant as Christ's "Vicar".

531

'UPON THIS ROCK...'

SIXTUS II TO EUSEBIUS, 257–310
POPES ARE MARTYRED BUT THE CHURCH SURVIVES PERSECUTION

Stephen's successor Sixtus II (257–8) is one of the most celebrated martyrs of the early Church. When Emperor Valerian launched a new round of violent persecution, Sixtus was seized and beheaded with six deacons while conducting a service in the catacomb of Praetextatus on the Appian Way. Sixtus prophesied the death of his best-known deacon, Lawrence of Rome, who was killed three days after the pope.

During his reign, Sixtus repaired relations with the Eastern churches, reputedly under the influence of Bishop Dionysius of Alexandria. He may or may not have written the *Sentences of Sextus*, a collection of spiritual teachings that bears his name.

For two years the severity of Valerian's persecution made election of a new pope impossible but after the emperor's humiliating death while

Above: Pope Marcellinus. His martyr's death led to the veneration of his tomb by early Christians. He was buried in the Catacomb of Priscilla on the Via Salaria.

a prisoner of the Persian King Shapur I, Pope Dionysius (260–8) took up the reins and the new emperor, Gallienus, issued an edict of toleration towards Christians.

STATEMENT OF FAITH

Dionysius was an able administrator who reorganized the Church in Rome, sent funds to support Christians in Cappadocia (modern Turkey) and reinforced the authority of Rome and the papacy: in a dispute with Bishop Dionysius of Alexandria – known as "the affair of the two Dionysii" – the Pope clarified an orthodox position in which Father, Son and Holy Spirit were clearly seen as aspects of the Trinity rather than separate deities and the Bishop accepted the Pope's authority. This laid some of the groundwork for the statement of faith in the Nicene Creed of 325.

We know very little about popes Felix I (269–74), Eutychian (275–83) and Gaius (283–96), beyond the fact that

Left: Emperor Diocletian introduced the Tetrachy: rule by four emperors. This porphyry sculpture – now in St Mark's Basilica, Venice – celebrates the concept.

Felix issued an important dogmatic letter establishing the unity of the person of Christ and Eutychian was the last pope to be buried in the catacombs of Rome.

THE APOSTATE POPE

When Emperor Diocletian renewed violent persecution of the Roman Empire's Christians in 303, Pope Marcellinus (296–304) caved in. In an abnegation of his responsibility, the pope simply gave in to Diocletian's demands that he hand over the Scriptures. Marcellinus even offered sacrifices to the pagan gods of Rome. After this failure, Marcellinus repented and again professed his faith as a Christian – and died a martyr.

(This is the widely circulated account, although St Augustine of Hippo denied its truth.) His reign, whether or not stained by this apostasy, is also marked by a great positive: the declaration of the first Christian state, when in 301 King Tiridates III of Armenia made Christianity the official faith of his country.

EXILED FROM ROME

Several years of trouble followed Marcellinus's death – persecution eased after Diocletian abdicated in 305 and

Above: This 3rd-century fresco of The Last Supper in the Catacombs of Callixtus was rediscovered beneath Rome by Giovanni Battista de Rossi in 1854: Pius IX (pope 1846–78) visited to inspect the Crypt of the Popes.

was succeeded as emperor by Maxentius. A new pope, Marcellus I (c.308–9), was not elected for around four years. Once in office, he reorganized the administration of the Church in Rome and established a burial place on the Via Salaria. But he did not last long. The severe penalties he imposed on Christians who had lapsed under Diocletian's persecution led to rioting and Maxentius exiled the pope in an attempt to keep the peace. Marcellus died in exile. His remains were later returned to Rome where they lie beneath the altar in the Church of San Marcello.

CHURCH IN TURMOIL

Marcellus's successor Eusebius was also embroiled in violent disagreements over whether lapsed Christians needed to perform penance to be readmitted to the Church. His reign lasted just six months, from 18 April to 21 October 310. Such was the upheaval among Christians in Rome that he, too, was sent into exile by Emperor Maxentius. He died shortly afterwards, in Sicily.

CATACOMBS

In times of persecution early Christians took refuge in a network of underground cemeteries (catacombs) beneath Rome: to worship; to honour the remains of martyrs of the faith; and, when necessary, as a hiding place. The first underground cemeteries had been made by pagan Romans in pre-Christian times and these were greatly extended by the Christians. Excavation was relatively easy in the soft tuff (volcanic ash) that lies beneath much of Rome, and large complexes developed, sometimes with four layers of tunnels built on top of one another. San Callisto, the largest of the catacombs – covering 15 hectares (37 acres) and containing more than 20km (12½ miles) of tunnels – is named after and was probably built by Pope Callistus I, although he was not buried in the "Crypt of the Popes" within the complex. The origin of the word catacomb is not known; it was initially applied to the cemetery beneath the Basilica of San Sebastiano on the Appian Way and afterwards applied to other underground burial sites. Frescoes on the walls of the catacombs – treasured examples of early Christian art – represent incidents from Jesus's life as well as well as Old Testament scenes.

MILTIADES AND SYLVESTER I, 311–335
IMPERIAL CHRISTIANITY AND THE DONATION OF CONSTANTINE

The reigns of popes Miltiades (311–14) and Sylvester I (314–35) saw the birth of the Christian Roman Empire. In 312, prior to the Battle of the Milvian Bridge, Emperor Constantine had a vision of the Christian cross written in light on the midday sky, together with the words "In this sign you will triumph", and this profoundly transformative event set him on the road to victory over his rival for power, Maxentius, and conversion to the Christian faith. In 313 in the Edict of Milan, Constantine and his co-ruler Licinius declared that Christians should be free to profess their faith, removed all existing penalties for being Christian and returned Church property. Constantine also donated the Lateran Palace in Rome to Miltiades as a papal residence.

Pope Miltiades was probably North African. Towards the end of his reign he was in charge of a church synod at the Lateran Palace that condemned Donatus Magnus, leader of the Donatist sect, for rebaptizing clergy who had lapsed from their faith but who wanted to return to the Church. Miltiades died on 10 January 314 before he could attend the Council of Arles, a gathering of bishops called by Emperor Constantine. The Council rejected an appeal by the Donatists against the Rome decision and excommunicated Donatus.

COUNCIL OF NICAEA

The meeting at Arles was the forerunner of the Council of Nicaea, called by Constantine in 325 with the backing of Miltiades's successor Pope Sylvester I, to meet in Nicaea (modern Iznik, Turkey). Sylvester did not attend the council in person but sent the legates Vitus and Vincentius to represent him.

The council's principal task was to find a solution to problems in the Eastern Church caused by disagreements

Above: Arius of Alexandria, who argued that Christ was a created being and so not the equal of God the Father, was condemned by both the emperor and the pope.

over Arianism, the teachings of the presbyter Arius of Alexandria (c.250–336) – in particular, the idea that God is unique and self-existent (He exists of and in Himself) and that Christ, as God's Son, is a created being, not self-existent and therefore not fully divine.

The council condemned Arianism and issued the Nicene Creed as a statement of orthodoxy. The creed specified that Christ was "of one substance" with the Father, so could not be differentiated from God the Father as Arius had suggested. Sylvester approved the council's decision; Constantine exiled Arius from the Roman Empire. Church and secular authority stood side by side.

A NEW ROME

Another event of Pope Sylvester's reign that had major and enduring consequences was Constantine's foundation of the city of Constantinople (modern

Left: In moving the seat of imperial rule to the new capital of Constantinople the emperor, according to legend, recognized the papacy's right to Rome.

MILTIADES AND SYLVESTER I

Above: The story of Pope Sylvester and Emperor Constantine seeks to establish the supremacy of papal authority and its role in guiding imperial power.

Istanbul, Turkey) as a new capital for the Roman Empire in 330. After defeating his rival Licinius at Chrysopolis (now a district of Istanbul) in 324, so establishing himself as sole ruler of the Roman Empire, East and West, he determined to establish an Eastern imperial capital on the site of the Greek trading colony of Byzantium. The new capital undermined the importance of Rome, and of the western regions of the Roman Empire.

THE POPE AND THE EMPEROR

According to legend, Pope Sylvester baptized Constantine and in doing so cured the emperor of leprosy. As a sign of his gratitude Constantine declared that the pope had primacy over all other bishops and gave him the "Donation of Constantine".

The legend also recounts how Constantine gave up his insignia and led Sylvester's horse by the bridle, humbly acting as his groom. The pope then gave Constantine his imperial crown, and the emperor determined to give up Rome to the pope's control and move his own residence to Constantinople. The legend, probably created in the 6th century, establishes the supremacy of the pope even over the Roman emperor.

A PIECE OF JERUSALEM IN ROME

In Sylvester's reign the Basilica di Santa Croce in Gerusalemme was established in Rome, in around 325. One of the many legends surrounding this pope tells that the church was built to contain relics of Christ's passion brought from the Holy Land by Emperor Constantine's Christ-ian mother, St Helen. The floor of the basilica was covered in soil from Jerusalem, thus giving the building its name in Gerusalemme. The first St Peter's Basilica in Rome was also begun during Sylvester's reign.

"DONATION OF CONSTANTINE"

This document was supposedly a decree made by Emperor Constantine in 315 or 317 that gave Pope Sylvester and his successors imperial authority to govern Rome and the Western empire, possession of the imperial palace in Rome and primacy over the bishops of Antioch, Alexandria, Constantinople and Jerusalem and all the world's churches. It was proved by Italian humanist Lorenzo Valla to be a forgery in the 15th century. The forgery was made by a cleric at the Lateran in the 750s/760s, perhaps with the backing of Pope Stephen II (752–7). This was a time when the papacy was embarking on a close relationship with the Frankish monarchy, which led to the creation of the Holy Roman Empire in the West, and so was seeking to challenge the authority of the Byzantine Empire. Surprisingly, given the document's importance for claims of papal authority, no pope before Leo IX (1049–54) cited the Donation in any official document.

535

FALL OF THE WESTERN EMPIRE

MARK TO PELAGIUS II, 336–590

In 410 Rome was sacked for three days by the Germanic tribe of the Visigoths while Pope Innocent I took refuge in Ravenna. St Jerome, former secretary to Pope Damasus I, was aghast. He wrote: "The bright light of the whole world was put out … the Roman Empire was beheaded … The entire world perished in one city…" The status of Rome as principal city of the Western Roman Empire was in sharp decline, yet it remained the base of the papacy and arguably the centre of the Christian world. Throughout the years 336–590, the popes sought to maintain their authority over rival church leaders, and to elevate Rome above all other Christian cities.

Pope Damasus I claimed Rome as the city of saints Peter and Paul; in an epitaph on their joint shrine he declared that as the place of their martyrdom Rome had the right to claim them as citizens. Pope Leo I based his claim to a pope's absolute authority as leader of the Church on the fact that he and other popes were in direct descent from St Peter. The popes won secular backing: in 380 co-emperors Theodosius I and Gratian declared the empire's inhabitants must follow the form of Christianity "handed down by the Apostle Peter to the Romans"; in 445 Emperor Valentinian III issued an edict giving Leo I and his successors authority over all the other bishops of the Christian Church.

The struggle to establish pre-eminence met constant challenges. The Council of Chalcedon in 451 accepted as the ultimate truth Pope Leo's declaration that Christ had two natures in the course of His incarnation, one human and one divine: the bishops stated that "Peter had spoken through Leo". But they also declared that as capital of the Eastern Roman Empire, Constantinople was "the new Rome".

Left: Protector of Rome: Pope Leo I rode north to confront Attila the Hun who had invaded northern Italy; Attila withdrew – and Rome was safe. This grand vision of the event (1514) is by Raphael in the Apostolic Palace.

MARK TO LIBERIUS, 336–66
CHURCH IN TURMOIL OVER ARIAN HERESY

The most enduring legacy of Pope Mark, who reigned for less than nine months in 336, was the Basilica San Marco, which he founded in Rome in honour of St Mark the Evangelist. The church has been rebuilt several times, beginning in 792 under Pope Hadrian I (772–95), and underwent a major reconstruction in the Renaissance under Pope Paul II (1464–71).

A Roman clergyman before becoming pope, Mark was consecrated on 18 January 336. During his rule he ordained that the Bishop of Ostia would have the honour of consecrating each new pope and invested the bishop with the *pallium*, an ecclesiastical robe that served as a symbol of spiritual authority. He died of natural causes on 7 October 336.

POPE'S PRIMACY
Pope Julius I (337–52) played a key role in resurgent controversy over Arianism in the Eastern Church, in the course of

Above: Pope Mark. He was buried in the Catacomb of Balbina, although in the 12th century his remains were moved to the Basilica San Marco, where they are kept in an urn beneath the altar.

Above: Antipope Felix II, who came to power when Liberius was banished by Emperor Constantius II, was in the end ousted by Liberius and died in Porto, near Rome.

> ### ARIUS
> The man who gave his name to the heresy of Arianism was a Christian presbyter from Alexandria, born in c.250. His principal teaching was that God the Father was timeless, without beginning and without equal and that because Jesus Christ his Son was created by the Father and so had a beginning, therefore Christ had a distinct and different nature and a lesser divinity. His main work was Thalia ('Plenty') and elements of his teaching were spread in popular songs accessible to those who were not learned. Arius dropped dead while walking in Constantinople – possibly having been poisoned by his enemies – in 336, but the controversies over Arianism were to continue for many years in both Western and Eastern churches.

which he made a significant statement asserting the primacy of the pope and of Rome over other bishops and regions. Arianism – the theological teachings of Arius of Alexandria, who held that Christ was created by God the Father and therefore a lesser divinity – had been condemned and Arius declared a heretic at the Council of Nicaea of 325. The orthodox position, fervently held by churchmen such as Athanasius, Archbishop of Alexandria, was that God exists in three equal persons – Father, Son and Holy Spirit – all of one substance and therefore of equal divinity.

The controversy continued: after followers of the pro-Arian Eusebius, Patriarch of Constantinople, had succeeded in ousting Athanasius from his position, Athanasius travelled to Rome, where he was backed at a synod called by Pope Julius in 342. Julius then wrote to the Eastern bishops in an attempt to quell the dispute, declaring Athanasius reinstated and asserting that in such matters bishops should apply to Rome before making decisions so that the pope could define what was just.

COUNCIL OF SARDICA
Subsequently Julius called a church council at Sardica (modern Sofia, Bulgaria) in 343 but was unable to impose his will on the Eastern bishops, who at the rival council of Philippopolis (modern Plovdiv, Bulgaria) voted to depose the pope, along with Athanasius and other leading churchmen. However, the Council of Sardica remained in session, attended by around 300 Western bishops, and backed the pope's authority to intervene in ecclesiastical disputes.

Julius declared Athanasius restored to his bishopric and this was initially accepted by pro-Arian Roman emperor Constantius II. When Athanasius returned to Alexandria in 346, Julius wrote to the priests, deacons and people of Alexandria to congratulate them.

ROMAN CHURCH THRIVES

In Rome, Julius presided over a thriving and expanding Church, with greatly increasing numbers of the faithful, and established two churches, the first now Santa Maria in Trastevere and the second now Santi XII Apostoli. On his death on 12 April 352 he was buried in the Catacomb of Calepodius on the Aurelian Way, then later his remains were moved to Santa Maria in Trastevere.

The Arian issue came to the fore once more under Julius's successor Pope Liberius. The pro-Arian Emperor Constantius wanted to establish religious unity in the empire: he condemned Athanasius, and required all Western bishops to approve this decision. When Liberius refused to agree to the condemnation, he was exiled by Constantius while antipope Felix II took power in Rome.

Below: A veteran of the First Council of Nicaea, Patriarch Athanasius of Constantinople fought long and hard against the Arian heresy. This altar mosaic is from a Ukrainian monastery.

In exile, Liberius submitted to the emperor, agreeing to break off relations with Athanasius and accepting changes to the Nicene Creed to eliminate anti-Arian elements. Recalled to Rome, he was rapturously welcomed by the people, but ordered by Constantius to rule alongside Felix II.

FIRST POPE NOT TO BE CANONIZED

Liberius's failure to manage the controversy, and his weakness in the face of the emperor, brought the papacy's standing low. When Constantius called the Council of Ariminum (modern Rimini, Italy) in 359, Liberius and Felix II were not invited. The Western bish-

Above: The Roman church of Santa Maria in Trastevere, founded by Callistus I, was enlarged and rebuilt by Julius I. Like Callistus, Julius is buried there.

ops at Ariminum were mostly orthodox but were outmanoeuvred and ended up approving an Arian creed.

After the death of Constantius in 361, Liberius attempted to revive the papacy's flagging authority, repudiating the creed agreed at Ariminum and then patched up differences with the moderate among the Arian Eastern bishops. Nevertheless after his death on 24 September 366 he gained the unenviable distinction of being the first pope not to be declared a saint.

DAMASUS I, 366–84
POPE WHO PROMOTED PRIMACY OF CHRISTIAN ROME

Damasus I (366–84) was a ruthless operator who won the papacy by force. When he was elected pope in October 366, he immediately faced the challenge of a rival, Ursinus. The conflict was played out in the streets between mar-auding gangs, and Damasus prevailed because his supporters were more num-erous and tougher – his street fighters, who included groups of the fearsome *fossores* (diggers of catacombs) slaughtered 137 of Ursinus's supporters amid scenes of carnage at the Basilica of Sicinius (now the Basilica di Santa Maria Maggiore).

Rioting was so severe that Emperor Valentinian intervened to restore public order. The emperor backed Damasus and exiled Ursinus first to Cologne and after-wards to Milan.

TICKLER OF WOMEN'S EARS
Yet Damasus was also a charming man, an urbane priest with a particular influence among the wealthy women and heiresses of Rome – to such an extent that he was dubbed *matronarum auriscalpius* ("tickler of women's ears").

By this period Christianity was increasingly acceptable among the well-to-do in Rome who exchanged gifts that featured Christian symbols alongside pagan iconography such as pictures of Venus. Once established in the papacy, Damasus lived in great style – dressing well, travelling by carriage and enjoying lavish banquets. He was never without his enemies and faced accusations of adultery, but was cleared by a synod of 44 bishops.

CHRISTIAN ROME
Damasus may have been a worldly cleric, but he conducted an effective papacy that enhanced the prestige of the pope and the Roman Church. He set out to establish Rome as a great Christian rather than pagan city.

He was the first pope to refer to Rome as the Apostolic See – the one established by the Apostle Peter. He claimed that Christ's words to Peter in Matthew

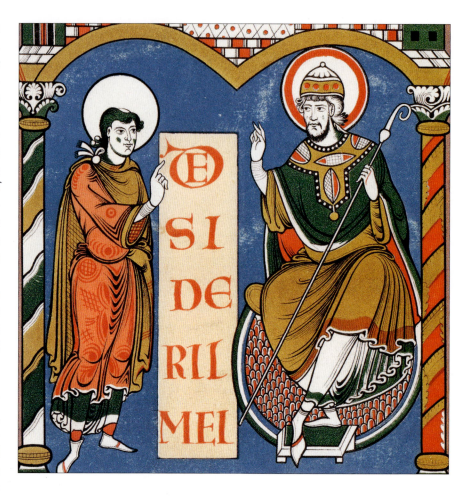

Above: An 11/12th-century French manuscript Bible shows Pope Damasus I engaging the youthful St Jerome as his secretary.

Below: Albrecht Durer shows St Jerome in his study (1521). Jerome is often shown with a lion – a legend told how he healed a lion.

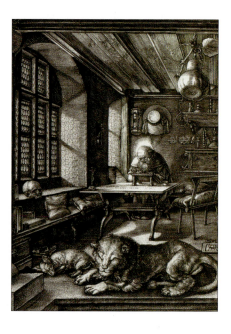

> **FACT BOX**
> **Original name** Damasus
> **Born** c.304
> **Origin** Roman
> **Date elected pope** 1 October 366
> **Died** 11 December 384
> **Key fact** First pope to refer to Rome as the Apostolic See – established by the Apostle Peter

> **THE VULGATE BIBLE**
>
> St Jerome – or Eusebius Hieronymus – was a scholar and ascetic who while secretary to Pope Damasus I made translations of the Old and New Testaments from Greek into Latin. These were the basis of the Vulgate Bible. Jerome was born in Stridon in the Roman province of Dalmatia (somewhere near the Slovenian city of Ljubljana) and from the age of about 12 studied in Rome, where he was baptized a Christian, probably by Pope Liberius. Over decades of study and spiritual searching – including two years as a desert hermit – he had become a major scholar by the time he returned to Rome to serve as secretary to Damasus in 382–5. After Damasus's death, he retired to monastic life in Bethlehem, where he died in 420.

16:18 ("thou art Peter and it is upon this rock that I will build my church") established the primacy of Rome over other centres of the faith. He promoted the veneration of Rome's Christian martyrs, restoring the catacombs, gathering and reburying the bodies of the saints beneath verse epitaphs.

For the joint shrine of saints Peter and Paul he wrote a celebrated epitaph: while acknowledging that the Apostles came from the East, he claimed them as citizens of Rome because they died as martyrs in Rome. In 384 he prevailed over non-Christian senators who wanted to maintain a pagan altar of Victory in the Senate, and had the altar abolished.

ENEMY OF HERESY

Damasus fought hard to maintain orthodoxy, writing no fewer than 24 anathemas against various heresies. At Roman synods in 368 and 369 he condemned Apollinarianism (the teaching of Bishop Apollinaris the Younger of Laodicea, according to which, while Christ had a human body and soul, He did not have a normal human mind, but the divine Logos in its place) and Macedonianism (the theories of Bishop Macedonius of Constantinople, according to which the Holy Spirit was created by Jesus and thus had a lesser divinity than the Father and the Son).

He also continued the battle against Arianism, excommunicating the Arian Bishop of Milan, Auxentius, in 369 and negotiating at length with Bishop Basil of Caesarea – but in the end to little effect. In 380 this work gained imperial sanction when Eastern Emperor Theodosius I and Western Emperor Gratian jointly decreed that the empire's inhabitants must follow the form of Christianity "handed down by the Apostle Peter to the Romans" as defined by the bishops of Rome and Alexandria.

LATIN BIBLE AND LITURGY

Another Roman synod, in 382, proclaimed the primacy of Rome. One of the delegates at the conference, Jerome, remained in Rome and became the pope's secretary. Damasus asked Jerome to revise the Latin translations of the Bible in the light of the Greek Septuagint (Old Testament) and New Testament, so creating the celebrated Vulgate version of the Bible. In Damasus's reign, Latin became established as the language of the liturgy.

Above: Western Emperor Gratian. His joint decree with Theodosius backing the form of Christianity "handed down by ... Peter to the Romans" was an important landmark.

Below: Eastern Emperor Theodosius I holds a victory laurel. This detail is from the pedestal to an Ancient Egyptian column that Theodosius erected in Constantinople.

SIRICIUS AND ANASTASIUS, 384–401
FIRST DECREES IMPOSING CLERICAL CELIBACY

The first Roman bishop to call himself "pope" in the modern sense, Siricius (384–99) was an uncompromising disciplinarian. He is celebrated above all for his surviving letters that enforce church discipline, with threats of sanctions against any who failed to abide by his decisions – notably on the celibacy of priests, penance, ordination and baptism.

FIRST PAPAL DECRETAL

Almost his first act as pope in 385 was to pen a letter to Bishop Himerius of Tarragona in Spain requiring that all priests should be celibate – this was the first statement from any pope on this matter and the letter is the first surviving papal decretal (authoritative statement on discipline or canon law).

Siricius emphasized the supremacy of Rome, exhorting Himerius to pass on his ordinances to bishops of the surrounding provinces and praising him for having consulted Rome, which he likened to the head of the Christian body. Now the pope was the supreme authority, the final arbiter and definer of the law.

When Priscillian, ascetic Bishop of Avila in the Roman province of Gallaecia, was charged with magic and executed by Emperor Magnus Maximus, Siricius and Bishop Ambrose of Milan complained to the imperial authorities and were able to limit the persecution of his followers.

Siricius sought to exercise papal authority in the Eastern as well as the Western Church. He declared that no bishop should be consecrated without papal approval and succeeded in finding a temporary solution in 393 to the Meletian Schism, a dispute over the bishopric of Antioch.

Above: Pope Anastasius I. He was succeeded by his son (Innocent I) – perhaps the only case of a pope being followed in the papacy by his offspring.

ON ST PAUL'S GRAVE

In Rome, Siricius dedicated the Basilica di San Paolo fuori le Mura in 390. The church had originally been founded on the site of the grave of St Paul by Emperor Constantine but was beautifully expanded as an elegant, five-aisled basilica by Emperor Theodosius. A column naming Siricius and commemorating the dedication still stands today in the vestibule to the side entrance of the transept.

Siricius died on 26 November 399 and was interred in the Catacomb of Priscilla on the Via Salaria. His forthright statements ruffled feathers and divided opinion on his character. French-born letter-writer and later bishop Paulinus of Nola declared Siricius to be reserved and haughty, but Emperor Valentinian III noted his piety. The former papal secretary Jerome, meanwhile, held that Siricius lacked judgement.

His successor Anastasius I (399–401) was warmly praised by Paulinus, Augustine of Hippo and Jerome, who were all his friends. Jerome celebrated Anastasius as saintly and blessed, "of very rich poverty and Apostolic solicitude".

ST AUGUSTINE

Augustine of Hippo (354–430), or Aurelius Augustinus, was one of the most important of the Church Fathers, who adapted classical ideas to Christian thinking. His essential works are his 13-book spiritual autobiography *Confessions* (397–398) and the 22-book *City of God* (413–26), which celebrates Divine Providence and justifies the Church. Born in Tagaste, Numidia (modern Souk Ahras, Algeria) in 354, the son of Patricius and Monica, a devout Christian. He converted to Christianity in 386 and was baptized alongside his son Adeodatus by Bishop Ambrose of Milan the following year. After being ordained a priest in 391 he was Bishop of Hippo (modern Anaba in Algeria) from 396 to his death in 430. He had an immense influence on Christian thought and Western philosophy and the concepts of original sin and the just war derive from his work.

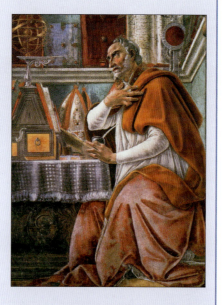

Above: St Augustine meditates on the fundamentals of Christianity in his study. Jerome said Augustine "established anew the ancient Faith". This image was made by Sandro Botticelli in 1480.

SIRICIUS AND ANASTASIUS

Above: The pope in the legend of St Ursula (shown here) is sometimes said to be Siricius. Ursula made a pilgrimage to Rome with her newly converted husband.

ORIGEN DENOUNCED

Some of this praise may be due to the pope's willingness to deliver what these friends wanted – in particular, under pressure from Jerome and Theophilus, patriarch of Alexandria, he was willing to anathemize the works of 3rd-century Alexandrian theologian Origen (c.185–c.254), whose *First Principle* had recently been translated from Greek into Latin by the monk and theologian Rufinus of Aquileia (345–410). The work is the first endeavour to present Christianity as a complete theory of the universe.

Anastasius called a council in 400 that denounced Origen, and when Rufinus wrote to defend his own work and Origen, the pope upheld the verdict despite the fact that he seems not to have read the offending work. He also wrote several papal letters denouncing Origen.

DONATIST DISPUTE

Anastasius also moved against Donatism in North Africa. He wrote to African bishops at the Council of Carthage in 401, who were struggling with a shortage of clergy, urging them not to lift the ban on Donatists (followers of Donatus Magnus, who had been excommunicated at the Council of Arles in 314 for requiring the rebaptism of clergy who had lapsed under persecution but wanted to re-enter the Church). In the end the bishops resisted papal pressure and did lift the ban.

Anastasius died on 19 December 401 after just over two years as pope. He was buried in the Catacomb of Pontian on the Via Portuensis.

INNOCENT I, 401–17
WHEN ROME WAS SACKED BY THE VISIGOTHS

Innocent I – elected to the papacy on 21 December 401 – was reputedly the son of his predecessor Anastasius, making this the only instance of a son succeeding his father as pope. In addition to being the pontiff who endured the Sack of Rome by the invading Visigoths in 410, Innocent was embroiled in the campaign led by St Augustine of Hippo to anathemize the British/Irish monk Pelagius, who argued against Augustine's concept of original sin in favour of humans exercising free will. Innocent excommunicated Pelagius on 27 January 417.

RAMPAGING VISIGOTHS
King Alaric I of the Visigoths (a Germanic tribe) saw the vulnerability of the Western Roman Empire under its profoundly ineffective young emperor Honorius and invaded Italy in 401. He was defeated by the brilliant Roman general Flavius Stilicho in 402 but moved again after Stilicho was executed by Honorius on suspicion of treachery in 408.

Alaric besieged Rome and would have accepted a negotiated settlement that included a vast ransom except that Honorius, safely ensconced at Ravenna, refused to agree to it – even though a deposition of Romans, including Pope Innocent, went there to try to persuade him to make a deal.

Alaric then besieged Rome again in 409 and for a third time in summer 410, and when on 24 August 410 allies within the city opened the gates, the Visigoth army poured into the city, ransacking, burning and looting.

Right: Innocent I. He reputedly allowed pagan worship in Rome after the city was sacked, but it is said there were few takers. Christianity was secure in Rome.

"WHO WOULD BELIEVE IT?"
This was the first time Rome had been captured by a foreign enemy for almost 800 years, but the damage was not as bad as it might have been since Alaric was a Christian and ordered his men not to damage Christian buildings or hurt any of the devout. St Jerome, in the preface to his *Commentary on the Book of Ezekiel*, bewailed the event as the end of an era: "Who would believe that Rome, built up by the conquering of the entire world, had collapsed, that the mother of all countries had been made their tomb…?"

In the aftermath Alaric led the Visigoths southwards, intending to invade Africa, but he died from a sudden

Left: Visigoth leader Alaric I died after taking Rome. He had given up on plans to invade Sicily and North Africa and then passed away as his army returned northwards.

> **FACT BOX**
> **Original name** Damasus
> **Born** Not known
> **Origin** Italian
> **Date elected pope** 21 December 401
> **Died** 12 March 417
> **Key fact** Promoted papal authority and excommunicated Pelagius

INNOCENT I

> ### PELAGIUS AND THE PELAGIAN HERESY
>
> A British or Irish theologian, Pelagius (c.354–418) took issue with Augustine of Hippo on original sin, predestination and the workings of divine grace, arguing that humans could achieve salvation by their own efforts in exercising free will. He taught in Rome where he emphasized the need for ascetic self-denial and was shocked by the self-indulgence and laxity of many Christians. The fall of Rome in 410 led him to settle with his close supporter, a lawyer named Celestius, in northern Africa and he came into direct conflict with Augustine. After he moved to Palestine in c.412, his work *De libero arbitrio* ("On Free Will", 416) was condemned by two church councils in Africa and the following year he was excommunicated, along with Celestius, by Pope Innocent I. The election of Pope Zosimus would bring respite, and Pelagius was cleared after writing his *Libellus fidei* ("Brief Statement of Faith") but he was again condemned as a heretic at the Council of Carthage in 418. He was expelled from Jerusalem but granted sanctuary by Patriarch Cyril of Alexandria, in Egypt, where he probably died.

Above: Innocent was unable to help John Chrysostom, who was deposed as Patriarch of Constantinople after confronting Empress Aelia Eudoxia over her life of luxury, shown here in a painting by Jean-Paul Laurens.

fever; his army thereafter marched north to Gaul (modern France). Innocent was in Ravenna at the time of the sacking, but he was able to return to Rome in 412.

AUTHORITY OF ROME

The pope had done all that he could to avert the catastrophe. In any case, the principal responsibility for the Sack of Rome lies not with Innocent but with the Western emperor, Honorius, who was reputedly more interested in raising chickens at Ravenna than saving Rome from the barbarian hordes. Despite the terrible events with which his name is associated, Innocent I was a gifted, determined and effective pope, full of energy and zeal, who maintained and strengthened the authority of the papacy and of the Roman Church.

In particular, Innocent sought to exercise the pope's authority as leader of both Eastern and Western churches. For example, he wrote to Archbishop Anysius of Thessalonica confirming papal approval for the archbishop's rights as a vicar of the pope in Illyria (part of the Balkan peninsula) that he said had been granted by previous popes including Damasus and Siricius. In other letters and judgements he demanded absolute papal supremacy, declaring that all ecclesiastical disputes should be submitted to the pope for judgement.

JOHN CHRYSOSTOM

In one celebrated matter Innocent attempted but failed to exert the pope's authority in the East: in 404 he called for a synod at Thessalonica to decide the case of the saintly John Chrysostom. John had been deposed as Patriarch of Constantinople and exiled by the Patriarch Theophilus of Alexandria and the Eastern empress Aelia Eudoxia, who was estranged from her husband and Eastern emperor Arcadius. The bishops he sent to communicate this decision to Arcadius were imprisoned and badly treated and the synod was not held. John Chrysostom remained in exile until his death.

Below: The might and glory of Rome – evidenced by scenes of the looting of Jerusalem in AD 70 on the triumphal Arch of Titus – was no more.

545

ZOSIMUS TO SIXTUS III, 417–40
POPES FIGHT PELAGIANISM – AND OTHER HERESIES

The four popes from Zosimus to Sixtus III committed themselves to maintaining and where possible extending the prestige and authority of the papacy. They were also staunch defenders of orthodoxy who maintained a firm line against heresy.

The first, Zosimus (417–18), was a hasty and somewhat tactless man whose attempts to assert the supremacy of the papacy led the Roman Church into conflict with both French and African bishops in a short and turbulent reign of less than two years. When he declared Bishop Patroclus of Arles to be papal vicar in Gaul this provoked strong opposition from the bishops of Marseille, Vienne and Narbonne, particularly because the decision was made on the grounds that Arles was historically the prime see in Gaul. Outraged at

Below: The core structure of Santa Maria Maggiore remains as built by Sixtus III before 440. Its triumphal arch bears an inscription naming "Sixtus, bishop to the people of God".

the challenge to his authority, Zosimus issued a threat of excommunication but he died before he could carry it through.

The dispute with the African bishops was over Pelagius, who had been condemned by African councils of the church and excommunicated by Innocent I: Zosimus was initially moved to accept Pelagius back into the church and he reprimanded the African bishops for being hasty in their condemnation, but he later changed his mind and confirmed Pelagius's excommunication in his *Epistola tractoria* "Epistolary Sermon").

Zosimus was so unpopular that the announcement of his death on 27 December 418 caused celebrations in the streets of Rome.

STRUGGLE FOR POWER

His successor Boniface I (418–22) faced and overcame the challenge of an antipope, Eulalius. While the candidates were in dispute, Emperor Honorius ordered them to leave Rome and passed the decision on who should take precedence to a church synod scheduled to meet at Spoleto in June, but Eulalius defied the emperor's orders in returning to Rome and so lost the support of the secular authorities.

Above: Celestine contributed to the spread of Christianity in Ireland. Some historians hold that the bishop he sent in 431, Palladius, was confused with St Patrick in some traditions.

Emperor Honorius recognized Boniface as pope on 3 April 419. In a four-year reign, the new pope continued the work of his predecessors

VIRGIN MARY

In Sixtus III's redevelopment the Liberian Basilica, the Roman church now known as Santa Maria Maggiore, was one of the earliest churches to feature images of the Virgin Mary and in this period, following the decree by the Council of Ephesus of 431 that she should be called *Theotokos* ("Bearer of God"), Mary was playing an increasingly important role in Christian worship. Devotion to the Virgin Mary goes back to the 2nd century, and was well established by the 3rd century in Egypt – the earliest surviving prayer to Mary, *Sub Tuum Praesidium* ("Beneath Thy Compassion"), dates to *c.*250 and uses the word *Theotokos*.

ZOSIMUS TO SIXTUS III

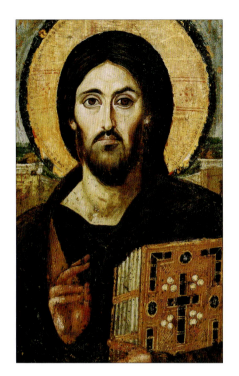

Left: The two facial expressions in this exquisite 6th-century panel from the Monastery of St Catherine, Egypt, perhaps suggest twin natures, divine and human, in Christ – a doctrine propounded by Nestorius.

in defending and exerting the rights of the papacy and in fighting against the beliefs of Pelagianism.

THEOTOKOS – BEARER OF GOD

Celestine I (422–32) was a vigorous defender of orthodoxy. He took a strong line against Nestorianism – the teachings of Nestorius, Patriarch of Constantinople in 428–31, who proposed that Christ has two natures, one human, one divine and argued that the Virgin Mary should be viewed as mother of the human Christ only and should not be celebrated as *Theotokos* ("Bearer of God").

Celestine called a church council in Rome that backed the use of the title *Theotokos* and called on Nestorius to renounce his errors. Then at the Council of Ephesus in 431 Nestorius was condemned as a heretic, deposed as Patriarch and banished.

ENVOYS TO IRELAND AND ENGLAND

Celestine also took an interest in nurturing the growth of Christianity in the British Isles. He sent Palladius, the first bishop to spread the Gospel in Ireland, and carried on the fight against Pelagianism by despatching bishops Germanus of Auxerre and Lupus of Troyes from Gaul to fight the heresy in England, where it was strong.

The Pelagians hoped for better when Sixtus III (432–40) was elected because this Roman priest was thought to be sympathetic to their theology. However, once installed as pope, he followed his predecessors in taking a hard line on orthodoxy and rejected an approach from the Pelagians to re-enter communion with the Church.

SANTA MARIA MAGGIORE

Sixtus set to work rebuilding Rome, which was still suffering from the effects of the Visigoths' three-day rampage through the city in 410. In particular, he rebuilt the Liberian Basilica, which had been constructed by Pope Liberius (352–66) and is now known as Santa Maria Maggiore. This church, which – as rebuilt by Sixtus III – featured exquisite mosaics of the Blessed Virgin Mary, has had a number of names associated with Mary, including Sancta Maria ad Praesepe ("Saint Mary of the Crib"), because it contains a relic of the crib in which Jesus lay as a baby, and Our Lady of the Snows because of the legendary account of its initial foundation according to which the church was built by a Roman named John, together with his wife, after they were instructed by Mary in a vision to build a church on the spot where she made snow fall at the height of summer.

Below: The Blessed Virgin was becoming increasingly important. This mosaic of her coronation was installed by Sixtus III as part of his rebuilding of Santa Maria Maggiore in Rome.

FALL OF THE WESTERN EMPIRE

LEO I, 440–61
FIRST POPE TO WIN ACCOLADE "THE GREAT"

The highly talented Pope Leo I (440–61) proved a courageous leader for the Church, assured in exercise of the authority he saw himself as having inherited directly from St Peter. He was a stern opponent of heresy and defiant of challenges to his position, as well as a fearless protector of Rome who twice confronted invading armies and in so doing greatly enhanced the prestige of the pope as a leading figure in the Western World.

LEO AND ATTILA

In 452 Leo met face to face with Attila the Hun whose army had invaded northern Italy, sacked Aquileia and was preparing to march on Rome. Leo travelled north to meet Attila at Lake Garda, where he persuaded him – one of the sternest enemies of the Roman Empire, both East and West – to retreat and spare Rome.

According to the 6th-century Roman historian Jordanes, Attila was fearful that he would meet the fate of the last man to invade Rome, Alaric of the Visigoths, who had died suddenly shortly after his men attacked the city in 410; in the 8th century Paul the Deacon recorded that Attila had a vision of a great warrior in priestly garb and armed with a naked sword while discussing with Leo – on the strength of which, he decided to abandon his invasion plans. Modern his-

Above: In Raphael's version of the encounter with Attila, Leo is supported by saints Peter and Paul in the sky above. Raphael painted Leo with the face of Leo X (pope 1513–21).

torians suggest that Attila's decision may have been influenced by an outbreak of plague in his army.

No doubt emboldened by this success, Leo again confronted a general three years later when Gaiseric, leader of the Germanic Vandals, had marched to the very gates of Rome. Although

Below: Leo the Great showed courage and profound faith in confronting Attila the Hun.

FACT BOX

Original name Leo
Born Not Known
Origin Tuscan
Date elected pope 29 September 440
Died 10 November 461
Key fact Defined unity of divine and human natures in Jesus Christ

Left; "Thou art Peter, and upon this rock I will build my church." Italian Baroque painter Bernardo Strozzi painted this vision of Christ granting authority to Peter.

his human element had been absorbed into his nature as the Son of God. This undermined the extent to which Jesus could be said to be truly human. After Patriarch Flavian of Constantinople excommunicated Eutyches, Leo issued a forthright response in a celebrated letter to Flavian, emphasizing that Christ had two natures – both human and divine – unmixed and distinct, but not separate.

The Council of Chalcedon (see box) met in 451 and endorsed Leo's statement or *Tome*. The Council noted that they recognized in Leo's words "the voice of Peter" – a notable endorsement of the pope's claim to be operating as Peter's representative and with his authority.

HONOURED FATHER

On his death Leo was buried in the porch of St Peter's but in 668 he was moved and given a monument within the basilica – and he was the first pope to receive this honour. Leo was declared a doctor of the Church by Pope Benedict XIV in 1754.

Leo could not prevent the army taking Rome, he persuaded Gaiseric to stop his men sacking the city.

AUTHORITY OVER BISHOPS

The 432 letters and 96 sermons that survive from Leo's hand assert that the pope has authority over all other Christian bishops and define the legal basis by which the authority of the pope is inherited. He established that Christ gave authority to St Peter alone, and that each new pope drew his authority not from his predecessor but from Peter. If a pope disgraced his position it should have no effect on the authority of the papacy, which derived from Peter and through him, from Christ himself. Bishops had authority over their flocks, but the pope had authority, derived from Peter, over the entire Church.

In 445 Leo won a formal statement of the papacy's ultimate authority over the Church from Emperor Valentinian III. Leo was in dispute with Bishop Hilary of Arles who had exceeded his powers in operating as papal vicar in Gaul (a position granted to the bishops of Arles, amidst much controversy by the ineffectual Pope Zosimus). Valentinian's edict of 8 July 445 stated that the pope had jurisdiction over all Western churches and even allowed for any bishops to be forcibly removed to Rome by secular governors if they refused to attend when summoned by the pope.

CHRIST'S SINGLE NATURE

The major controversy of Leo's reign was over the teachings of Eutyches, a Constantinople monk who held that Christ had only one, divine, nature since

THE NATURE OF CHRIST

The Fourth Ecumenical Council of the Church was called by Emperor Marcian with the backing of Pope Leo I. It met at Chalcedon (at the time a city in the Roman province of Bythnia, but now a suburb of Istanbul) in 451 and accepted Pope Leo's Tome as the basis of the "Chalcedonian Definition" on the nature of Christ: He had two natures (divine and human), both complete, unmixed yet permanently united in hypostasis. The Council's decision led to schisms in the Church between those who supported Chalcedonian orthodoxy and the Monophysites who held Christ had only one (divine) nature.

HILARIUS TO SILVERIUS, 461–537
GELASIUS I DEVELOPS THEORY OF ROYAL AND EPISCOPAL POWER

Hilarius (461–68) built on the achievement of Leo the Great. He had served as a legate for Leo, and carried on where his predecessor had left off in consolidating the authority of the papacy, particularly in relation to churches in Gaul and Spain. In letters to the bishops in the East he underlined the primacy of Rome.

END OF THE WESTERN EMPIRE
In the reign of Pope Simplicius (468–83), the last Roman emperor in the West, Romulus Augustulus, was deposed in 476 by a German warrior, Odoacer, who became the effective ruler of Italy. The Western empire fell apart into principalities. In matters of religion, Simplicius struggled to contain conflict in the Eastern Church between those who accepted the orthodox definition of Christ's dual nature agreed at the Council of Chalcedon and the increasingly troublesome Monophysites (who held that Christ had one – divine – nature).

In 482 the Eastern (Byzantine) Emperor Zeno and Patriarch Acacius of Constantinople tried to make peace with the *Henotikon* ("Statement of Union"), which appeased the Monophysites; but among the first acts of Simplicius's successor Pope Felix III (483–92) was to excommunicate Acacius and so bring about a schism between Rome and Constantinople that was to last until 519.

CHURCH AND STATE
Gelasius I (492–6) was a great writer of treatises and letters, said to be the most prolific writer of any pope in the first 500 years of the papacy, celebrated for his vigorous prose style, although relatively few of his compositions have survived. In a letter to Acacius of 494 he developed the theory of two distinct governmental powers – one royal (held by emperor or king) and one episcopal, the "sacred authority of bishops" (held by the pope) – that would influence Western political theory for centuries.

Anastasius II (496–8) tried to repair relations with the Eastern Church. The pontificate of Symmachus (498–514) never really recovered from the fact that it took him eight years to overcome the challenge of an antipope, Lawrence. His successor Hormisdas (514–23) succeeded in ending the schism with the Eastern Church in 519.

Left: Emperor Justinian I, shown here in a mosaic from Sant'Apollinare Nuovo, Ravenna, retook part of the Western empire and oversaw the rewriting of Roman law. He rebuilt the Hagia Sophia in Constantinople.

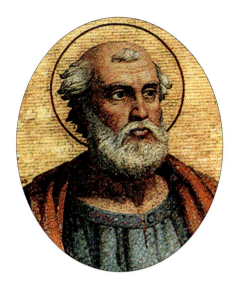  

Above: Gelasius I wrote De duabus in Christo naturis *("On Christ's twofold nature"), which reiterated the orthodox position on the Monophysite controversy.*

Above: Silverius was the legitimate son of Pope Hormisdas, born before his father entered the priesthood. He was deposed in 537, a few months before his death.

Above: John I visited Constantinople at the behest of Theodoric of the Ostrogoths, but failed to convince Emperor Justin to end his persecution of Arian Christians.

FIRST POPE TO VISIT CONSTANTINOPLE

When Byzantine Emperor Justin I began to persecute Arian Christians, it provoked the ire of Theodoric the Great of the Ostrogoths, who had succeeded Odoacer as secular ruler in Italy and was himself an Arian Christian. Theodoric ordered John I (523–6) to Constantinople to seek a solution.

John received a splendid welcome but failed in his mission, much to Theodoric's disgust: on John's return to Italy, Theodoric had him imprisoned and, according to some traditions, executed him.

Felix IV (526–30) had a steady pontificate and built the Basilica of Santi Cosma e Damiano in the Forum of Vespasian, but caused chaos at the end of his reign by nominating archdeacon Boniface as his successor. Roman clergy elected Dioscorus of Alexandria in his place, and both candidates were consecrated in rival ceremonies – but the disagreement ended when Dioscorus died after around a month. Boniface ruled for two years, 530–2, the first pope of Germanic descent.

FIRST PAPAL NAME

A very messy election campaign followed, with corruption and bribery rife in Rome for more than two months, so that King Athalaric, successor to Theodoric the Great, passed a law to stop it happening again. In the end a Roman presbyter named Mercurius was elected John II (533–5) – he was the first pope to change his name, abandoning his birth name because of its associations with the Roman god Mercury and choosing a papal name that honoured Pope John I.

In the pontificate of Agapitus I (535–36), Byzantine Emperor Justinian I drew up plans to invade Italy and reincorporate it into the empire. King Theodahad of the Ostrogoths despatched Agapitus to Constantinople to broker a solution. Agapitus failed to change the emperor's mind but did succeed in ousting the Monophysite Patriarch of the city, Anthimus I, and consecrating Mennas as his successor. This angered Justinian's wife, Empress Theodora, who had Monophysite sympathies and wanted Anthimus restored.

When Agapitus died while still in Constantinople, Silverius (536–7) was elected in Rome and refused to restore Anthimus. Theodora then offered the papal throne to a Roman deacon named Vigilius if he would agree to back Anthimus, and ordered Byzantine general Belisarius to invade Rome and depose Silverius. Vigilius is considered the first pope of the Byzantine Papacy. Belisarius sent Silverius into exile, but when the matter was referred to Emperor Justinian he ordered Silverius back to Rome. Finally Vigilius used force to drive Silverius back into exile – on the island of Palmarola, near Naples – where he died.

> **ST VALENTINE'S DAY**
>
> In 496 Pope Gelasius I succeeded in suppressing the ancient pagan purification festival of Lupercalia and introduced the feast day of St Valentine on 14 February. The original St Valentine may have been a Roman priest who was martyred under Emperor Claudius II Gothicus (268–70) and buried on the Via Flamini. The saint's day became a lovers' festival in the 14th century. According to legend Valentine fell in love with the jailer's daughter while imprisoned and wrote her a letter signed "your Valentine".

ROME AND THE ACQUISITION OF THE PAPAL STATES

A succession of popes worked to make Rome the foremost Christian city and then built up the associated territories of the papal states that survived in various forms until the creation of the Kingdom of Italy in the 19th century.

The papacy established Rome's preeminence over other Christian cities in the course of several centuries. The city's status rested on the pope's spiritual descent from St Peter and his claim that as a result he took precedence over other bishops. Rome was rivalled by Jerusalem and Antioch, as well as Alexandria and from 330 by Constantinople, set up by Emperor Constantine as a new capital for the Roman Empire, but the popes contended that their city could outrank these others because of its association with saints Peter and Paul.

Pope Damasus I (366–84) was the first to claim that Rome was the "Apostolic See" – that is, the See established by the Apostle Peter – and stated that it outranked all other Christian cities because it was the place where saints Peter and Paul died as martyrs. Pope Siricius (384–99) declared that Rome was the head of the Christian body.

After Christianity became the state religion of the Roman Empire, Emperor Theodosius I announced in 380 that the empire's inhabitants must follow the form of the faith "handed down by the Apostle Peter to the Romans"; subsequently in 445 Emperor Valentinian III gave Pope Leo I and his successors as pope authority over all other bishops.

Over centuries this struggle for preeminence continued and there were many more challenges to the status of the pope and of Rome; meanwhile, the city itself had many ups and downs: it was sacked several times, notably by the Visigoths in 410, the Muslims in 846 and the Holy Roman Emperor Charles V in 1527, but was enriched with architectural and artistic jewels in the Renaissance and beautified by the popes of the Counter-Reformation. Yet – save for the period of 1309–77, when the papacy removed to southern France in the "Avignon Exile" – the city of St Peter's martyrdom remained and is still the base for the pope's rule of the Church.

Above: Charlemagne the Great was deeply pious and mourned Pope Hadrian I as "a father". The "Donation of Charlemagne" in 774 consolidated the papal territories.

PAPAL STATES

From as early as the 300s the papacy acquired territory close to Rome – known as the Patrimony of St Peter. Following the collapse of the Roman Empire the popes faced the threat of invasion by northern tribes – not least, from the sixth century onwards, by the Lombards.

The lands held by the papacy in this era were part of the Byzantine Empire, and in theory protected by Constantinople, but the Byzantines failed to defend papal lands against the Lombards: in the 8th century Pope Stephen II (752–7) appealed to the rising

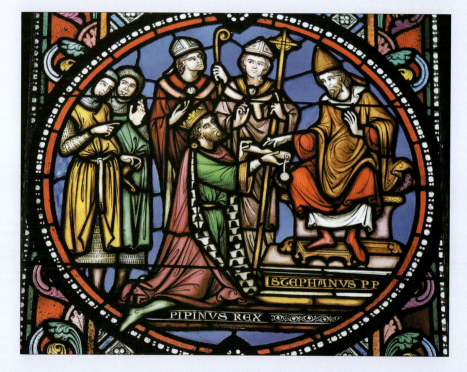

Below: Pope Stephen anoints Pepin III of the Franks, who in return – in the "Donation of Pepin" (754) – granted the lands that formed the basis of the papal states.

Above: Saint Augustine teaching rhetoric in Rome. Many leading figures of the early Church, including Jerome and Tertullian, came to and worked in the seat of the papacy.

power of the Franks for help and from Pepin III, Charlemagne, Louis the Pious and Lothar I the papacy received the basis of what became the papal states – the duchy of Rome, territories around Ravenna and the area known as the Pentapolis.

CONSOLIDATION

In the Middle Ages the papacy maintained control of the papal states and even expanded them with the addition of Spoleto, Benevento and Avignon in southern France; but during the period of the Avignon Exile and the Papal Schism the popes' authority was weak and there were many challenges – including the brief declaration of a republic in Rome in 1347.

Fifteenth-century popes reimposed their authority over the central Italian peninsula and the papal states were further expanded by the warlike Julius II (1503–13), but then as the standing of the papacy declined the popes were increasingly unable to maintain this territory until by the 18th century, international powers felt free – for example in the treaties that ended the War of the Spanish Succession (1701–14) – to dispose of former papal territories as they saw fit.

ANNEXED BY FRANCE

The French Revolution of 1789 and the rise of post-revolutionary France under Napoleon Bonaparte had a major impact. First Avignon was annexed in 1791, then Pius VI (1775) could do nothing as France seized the papal states and declared a Roman Republic. Pius VII (1800–23) made peace with France: Rome along with several of the papal states were restored to the papacy, but the new peace fell apart and Rome was occupied and the papal states annexed once more in 1808.

When Napoleon was defeated, the Congress of Vienna (1814–15) restored Rome and the papal states to the pope. (Napoleon's brief return did not change this.) There were revolts against papal rule in the states in 1830–1 and 1849 when Pius IX (1846–78) could not prevent the brief establishment of another Roman Republic.

RISORGIMENTO

In the end *Risorgimento*, the 19th-century movement for a unified Italy, proved unstoppable. In 1861 the former papal states – apart from Rome and its surrounding area – were made part of the new Kingdom of Italy; in 1870 Italian troops took Rome and it was made the capital of the new kingdom.

Pius IX refused to recognize this new situation: he and his successors declared themselves "prisoners in the Vatican". However, in 1929 Pope Pius XI (1922–39) oversaw the Lateran Treaty under which the papacy renounced its claim to the papal territories (in return for compensation equivalent to £21 million) and the independent ecclesiastical state of Vatican City was set up.

Below: Saints Peter (right, holding key) and Paul. Damasus I said the fact that they were martyred in Rome gave the city its pre-eminent status.

VIGILIUS TO PELAGIUS II, 537–90
POPES DEPENDENT ON BYZANTINE EMPERORS

The reign of Vigilius (537–55) is one of the low points in the history of the papacy. He did not recover from the sordid machinations through which he became pope, when he schemed with the Byzantine Empress Theodora to oust the elected pontiff, Silverius, and took power with the military backing of the Byzantine general, Belisarius.

Thereafter he struggled to assert his independence and proved himself a weak and vacillating leader who seriously damaged the standing of the papacy. He quickly became embroiled in "The Three Chapters controversy" – a clash between the orthodox position that Jesus Christ had a dual human/divine nature and the Monophysite teaching (declared heretical at the 451 Council of Chalcedon) that Christ's nature was divine.

SECOND COUNCIL OF CONSTANTINOPLE

Emperor Justinian issued a pro-Monophysite decree in 544, repudiating the works (the "three chapters") of three writers who supported the orthodox position, and demanded Vigilius ratify it. When Vigilius initially refused, Justinian had him arrested and dragged to Constantinople.

There he vacillated until in 548 Vigilius issued a *Judicatum* ("Verdict") in which he backed the emperor's condemnation, but with some reservations. This caused uproar in the Western Church and Justinian called a general church council to settle the matter, while also repeating his own repudiation of the three chapters.

Then Vigilius snapped. He broke off relations with Justinian and took refuge in a sanctuary, before fleeing to Chalcedon. The Second Council of Constantinople met without him and backed the condemnation of the three chapters. Vigilius first issued a *Constitutum* ("Resolution") on 24 May 553 in which he refused to back the council, then the following February revoked this and issued a new statement backing the council's statement.

Below: Pelagius II (far left) offers his rebuilt Church of San Lorenzo fuori le Mura to Christ and saints Lawrence, Peter and Paul.

Above: The Visigoth king Reccared I who converted from Arian to Roman Christianity in the reign of Pope Pelagius II.

Now Vigilius lost the backing of his loyal nuncio and eventual successor, Pelagius I, whom he excommunicated and who was shortly afterwards imprisoned by Justinian. Finally, ill and dispirited, Vigilius was allowed by

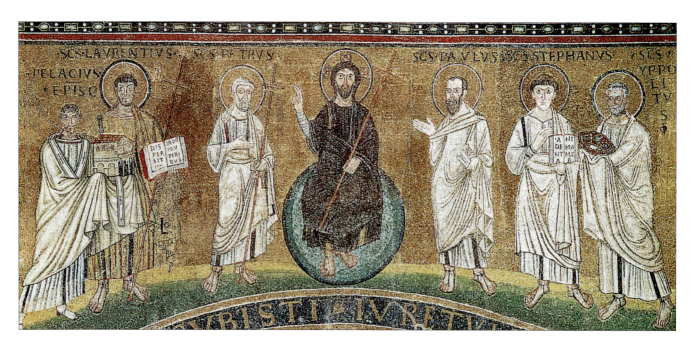

VIGILIUS TO PELAGIUS II

Above: A gold triens (type of coin) minted for King Reccared I of the Visigoths.

Justinian to head back to Rome, but he died en route on 7 June 555 from an attack of gallstones.

On Vigilius's death, Pelagius was released from prison, and with the backing of Emperor Justinian elected pope. He was consecrated Pope Pelagius I in Rome on 16 April 556. A committed opponent of the imperial condemnation of the Three Chapters who even wrote a book in defence of the three denounced authors, he reversed his position once pope and backed the verdict of the Council of Constantinople. This caused a schism within the Western Church with the bishops of Milan and Istria. But Pelagius had considerable success in patching up Rome, which had been ravaged by the Ostrogoths, and in reforming clerical behaviour.

LOMBARD THREAT

John III (561–74) faced invasion by the Lombards and took flight to Naples, where in 571 he asked the former Byzantine general, Narses, to mount a defence of Rome. But the Romans who knew and hated Narses from of old, rose up and John was forced to seek refuge in the catacombs,

Right: Justinian I brooked no opposition in the Three Chapters controversy. This mosaic of the forceful emperor is from San Vitale Cathedral in Ravenna and shows him carrying Eucharistic bread or a symbolic basket for receiving tribute.

from where he conducted his administration until Narses died in 573.

Benedict I (575–9) faced calamity after calamity – plague, famine, the flooding of the Tiber and further southward invasions by the Lombards who laid siege to Rome in 579. He died with Rome in the grip of a severe famine and was succeeded by Pelagius II (579–90), who turned to Constantinople for support against the Lombards. But little help was forthcoming, since the emperor had pressing problems in fighting off attacks by the Persian Sassanian empire.

ENTER THE FRANKS

So Pelagius fixed on a new source of help, a people who would loom large in the history of Western Europe and the papacy: the Franks. He wrote to the Frankish bishop of Auxerre, declaring it the Franks' duty as Christians to defend Rome against the Arian Lombards. The Franks invaded Italy but were then bribed to hold off by the Lombards and Pelagius was forced to appeal to Constantinople again.

The matter was not resolved until 585 when Exarch Smaragdus of Ravenna, the Byzantine representative in Italy, agreed a peace settlement with the Lombards.

> ### THE LOMBARDS
> Originally a tribe from northwestern Germany, the Lombards began to migrate southwards in the 4th century, initially settling in an area that roughly matches that of modern Austria. In 567–8 they invaded Italy, and by the end of 569 had captured all the major cities northwards of the River Po, save Pavia – which survived only until 572. They made several incursions further southwards, and besieged Rome, but eventually established a Lombard Kingdom in Italy further north, with the capital at Pavia. They were defeated by the Frankish king Charlemagne in 774.

VISIGOTHS CONVERT

In around 589 the Visigoths in Spain under King Reccared I were converted from Arian Christianity to the faith of the Roman Church. Then Pelagius came into conflict with the Patriarch of Constantinople who claimed the title "Ecumenical Patriarch", which the pope saw as undermining papal authority. The issue was still undecided when Pelagius died, in February 590 from the plague that had swept Rome after a terrible flooding in the autumn of 589.

ENTER THE FRANKS

GREGORY THE GREAT TO HADRIAN I, 590–795

On Easter Saturday 774 Charlemagne, King of the Franks, was greeted on the steps of St Peter's in Rome by Pope Hadrian I. In the celebrated "Donation of Charlemagne", the Frankish king confirmed the gift of territories made by his father Pepin III to Hadrian's forerunner Stephen II, and greatly expanded the lands to be passed into papal governance.

For much of the 8th century the popes had struggled to extricate the Church from the control of overbearing Eastern Roman (Byzantine) Emperors in Constantinople, while seeking to defend Rome and its earliest associated lands from attack by the Lombards who had invaded northern Italy in the 560s. This momentous encounter between Charlemagne and Hadrian freed the papacy from Constantinople, created the basis of the papal states and established the pope as a worldly prince. Charlemagne went to capture Pavia, crush the Lombards, then overcome the Saxons and Avars to create a great Western empire in opposition to the Eastern Roman Empire of Constantinople.

The consequences for the pope and the Church were significant. While the papacy was increasingly able to operate free of interference from Constantinople, it now had a new secular ruler to deal with. Charlemagne declared his intention to impose unity on the churches in his territories, and was certainly not averse to involving himself in church affairs – he called church councils, instructed clergy on duties and matters of faith and made appointments of abbots and bishops in France. In the short term the papacy certainly did well: Charlemagne was a deeply pious man who was happy to accept the prime position of Rome, but his successors would not all be cooperative in this regard. The seeds were sown that would bear fruit in the tumultuous struggles for precedence between the pope and the Holy Roman Emperor.

Left: Pope Stephen II anoints Frankish king Pepin III "the Short" in July 754. Through an alliance with the Franks, the papacy freed itself from the emperor in Constantinople. Grants of land from Pepin and his son Charlemagne established the papal states.

ENTER THE FRANKS

GREGORY I "THE GREAT", 590–604
THEOLOGIAN AND AUTHOR WHO SENT MISSION TO ENGLAND

The first monk to become pope, Gregory is celebrated as The Great for his prolific and profound writings as well as his papal rule. In the Middle Ages he was known as the "Father of Christian Worship" because of his efforts to revise the forms of worship. He is often seen as standing at the end of the Roman era, looking forward to and playing a significant role in shaping, the Church and Christian faith of the Middle Ages.

Diligent, learned, thoughtful, he was widely and enduringly admired for his qualities: he was acclaimed a saint on his death and is also considered a saint in the Eastern Orthodox Church – where he is known as Gregory Dialogus ("Gregory the Dialogist") on account of his authorship of the *Dialogues* (594), a collection of saints' lives. Even Protestant reformer John Calvin admired Gregory – he declared him the last good pope.

Below: Gregory is traditionally said to have standardized Western plainchant. This 13th-century illuminated manuscript shows him dictating the chant.

> **FACT BOX**
> **Original name** Gregorius
> **Born** 540
> **Origin** Roman
> **Date elected pope** 3 September 590
> **Died** 12 March 604
> **Key fact** Only pope apart from Leo I and Nicholas I to be called "The Great"

FOUNDED A MONASTERY

Gregory came from a wealthy and deeply religious family. He was the great-great grandson of Pope Felix III (483–92); when his father died, his mother Silvia became a nun, and three of his aunts also took monastic vows. Gregory himself retired from the world in 574 – after a good education that may have included legal training. He established a monastery named for St Andrew on his family's land on the Caelian Hill in Rome.

In 579 he became a deacon under Pope Pelagius II, who sent him as a legate to Constantinople. There he tried to drum up military support against the Lombards in Italy.

Back in Rome by 586 he reluctantly agreed to become pope on 3 September 590 after the death of Pelagius II in the plague that swept the city. In traditional accounts, Gregory led a penitential procession through the streets of the city and had a vision of the Archangel Michael that convinced him the city would be spared further suffering; according to some accounts, he wrote seven penitential psalms to be sung on this procession, but in fact these psalms date from the 11th century, around 500 years after his death.

WRITINGS – AND MUSIC

According to historian Gregory of Tours (538–94), Pope Gregory was second to none in rhetoric, grammar and argument; he was well versed in mathematics,

Above: An exquisite 10th-century ivory panel shows Gregory at work on his voluminous writings – with a dove (symbol of the Holy Spirit) dictating at his ear.

music, history, law and natural science and had read the Latin authors. In addition to the *Dialogues* (594), a collection of saints' lives, he wrote: more than 60 homilies, including 40 on the Gospels and 22 on the Book of Ezekiel; *Pastoral Rule* (591), a book of guidance for rulers; and the *Magna Moralia*, a 35-book interrogation of the Book of Job.

In addition Gregory is credited with standardizing Western plainchant, which was known as Gregorian chant. However, the chant was not standardized until the 8th century. Moreover, the first source to attribute this to him is the biography of the pope by John the Deacon written in 873, so nearly 300 years after his death. Historians agree that Gregory did not invent the chant; some suggest that "Gregorian" rightly refers to a later pope and namesake, Gregory II (715–31).

GREGORY I "THE GREAT"

ST AUGUSTINE OF CANTERBURY

Augustine (or Austin) was Prior of the Benedictine monastery of St Andrew in Rome when Pope Gregory chose him to lead a mission of 40 monks to convert pagan England to Christianity. The mission landed in 597 on the Isle of Thanet and was given a place to stay in Canterbury by King Aethelbert of Kent, whose wife Bertha was already a Christian. The mission converted Aethelbert and on Christmas Day 597 thousands of his people. Gregory sent further missionaries with the pallium (symbol of spiritual authority) for Augustine, who founded the Cathedral of Christ Church, Canterbury, and the Benedictine monastery of saints Peter and Paul just outside the city (now known as St Augustine's Abbey). In 604 Augustine consecrated two bishops of the English Church: Mellitus as Bishop of London, and Justus as Bishop of Rochester.

"SERVANT OF THE SERVANTS OF GOD"

Gregory promoted the moral primacy of the pope as descendant of St Peter, but did not argue that the bishop of Rome was above other bishops. When a bishop had done wrong, he should be subject to the pope, but otherwise "all are equal by the law of humility". Like his predecessor, Gregory disputed the right of the patriarch of Constantinople to use the title "ecumenical patriarch". He felt that this title worked against the equality of all bishops and undermined the moral primacy of the pope as the inheritor of the power of St Peter. He was committed to humility and called himself "Servant of the servants of God".

ENGLISH MISSION

According to English monk the Venerable Bede (673–735), Gregory was inspired to send a mission to England by an encounter with fair-skinned Angles (English boys) in the slave market in Rome. He reputedly said *Non Angli, sed angeli* – "they're not Angles, they're angels!"

Above: "They're not Angles, they're angels!" Seeing English boys for sale at the slave market in Rome reputedly inspired Gregory to send Augustine on his mission to England.

Below: According to a medieval legend, while celebrating Mass Gregory was granted a vision in which blood poured directly from Christ's side into his chalice.

559

ENTER THE FRANKS

SABINIAN TO BONIFACE V, 604–25
POPE ADEODATUS I ISSUES FIRST PAPAL BULLS

In these years the papacy in Rome was overshadowed by Constantinople. There were frequent turnovers of pope, with many short reigns: each new elected pontiff had to wait for confirmation of his elevation from the Byzantine emperor before he could be consecrated. Often the confirmation was slow in coming, for frequently the emperor had pressing problems in the East: for example, Boniface V had to wait 13 months for imperial approval in 618–619, because Emperor Heraclius was fighting the Persian Sassanian empire.

Below: The Column of Phocas in the Roman forum once held a gilded statue of Emperor Phocas, erected in 608 in the reign of Boniface IV – probably as a symbol of the emperor's continuing sovereignty over Rome.

Pope Sabinian (604–6) presented quite a contrast to his imposing predecessor Gregory the Great. Where Gregory had promoted monks to key positions, Sabinian gave precedence to secular clergy and while Gregory had been praised for distributing grain at no cost from the papal granaries, Sabinian raised money by selling it at high prices – even in a famine.

His rule was unpopular and the people suffered not only from food shortages but also from southward incursions by the Lombards from their kingdom in northern Italy.

POPE IS "UNIVERSAL BISHOP"
Boniface III had served Gregory I as a deacon and was, according to that great pontiff, "a man of tried faith and character", but he lasted less than nine months in office, from his election on 19 February to his death on 12 November 607. While a deacon he had been sent to Constantinople by Gregory and had established a close relationship with Emperor Phocas; as pope he received from Phocas a decree recognizing Rome as the head of all churches and granting the pope the title of "Universal Bishop".

Boniface also made changes to rules governing papal elections – declaring it illegal, on pain of excommunication, to discuss a pope's successor while the pope was alive, and establishing that the process of finding a new pope should not be started until three days after a pope's death.

SANTA MARIA DELLA ROTONDA
Boniface IV (608–15) took a great interest in the English Church. He convened a council in Rome to restore monastic discipline at which he received the first Bishop of London, Mellitus, and he helped Mellitus settle matters concerning its organization. Boniface also converted

Above: In Rome, Boniface IV oversaw the conversion of the Pantheon into a church dedicated to the Blessed Virgin Mary and martyrs – now Santa Maria della Rotonda.

the Pantheon in Rome into a Church dedicated to the Virgin and Martyrs, now often known as Santa Maria della Rotonda.

In *c.*615 Boniface received a letter from the Irish missionary St Columban challenging him and accusing the papacy of heresy because of its acceptance of the decision of the 553 Second Council of Constantinople against the Three Chapters. This controversy played on and on.

In the tradition of Pope Gregory the Great, Boniface IV lived as a monk

---

SANCTUARY

Pope Boniface V established the right of asylum in churches for criminals, determining that no one who had taken refuge there should be handed over to the authorities until his or her case was heard. This applied at first to the altar and choir but was later extended to the nave and finally the whole church enclosure.

SABINIAN TO BONIFACE V

Above: Coin of Emperor Phocas who gave the Pantheon to Boniface IV.

after his election and appointed many monks to administrative positions. He subsequently converted his house into a monastery and retired there.

FIRST PAPAL BULLS

As Sabinian had reacted against the monastic appointments of Gregory I, so Adeodatus I (615–18) turned against the practice of his predecessor and set out to fill administrative positions with secular clergy rather than monks. Tradition has it that Adeodatus was the first pope to issue papal bulls – documents finished with lead seals (*bullae*). One bull survives from his reign, signed *Deusdedit Papae*, a version of the name Pope Adeodatus. He was an energetic and charitable man who won great admiration for his conduct in helping the victims of an earthquake and outbreak of leprosy that struck Rome in his pontificate.

REBELLION FOILED

In 619, before Boniface V (619–25) was consecrated, the Byzantine regent in Italy (Eleutherius, Exarch of Ravenna) launched a rebellion against Emperor Heraclius. He marched from Ravenna to Rome intending to make the new pope crown him, but was murdered by his own troops en route, at a fort on the Flaminian Way.

Boniface was known and loved for his gentle and mild demeanour and his charity – he distributed his wealth in gifts to the needy. He also carried Adeodatus's practice of preferring clergy to monks for official positions and accounts of his life stress his love for and support of the clergy.

Like his namesake a few years earlier, Boniface was engaged with the English Church. According to the writings of the Northumbrian monk the Venerable Bede (672–735), Boniface wrote to Mellitus, first bishop of London, and to Justus, first bishop of Rochester, when they were successively made Archbishop of Canterbury in 619 and 624 respectively, and also to King Edwin of Northumbria, and Edwin's Christian consort, Ethelburga of Kent, encouraging Edwin and his people to convert to Christianity.

Below: A detail of carving on an altar in the Basilica of San Nicola di Bari, Apulia represents Pope Adeodatus I, reckoned to be the first pope who issued papal bulls.

Above: The Venerable Bede, a monk from Jarrow in the English kingdom of Northumbria, reported that Boniface V urged the English to engage with Christianity.

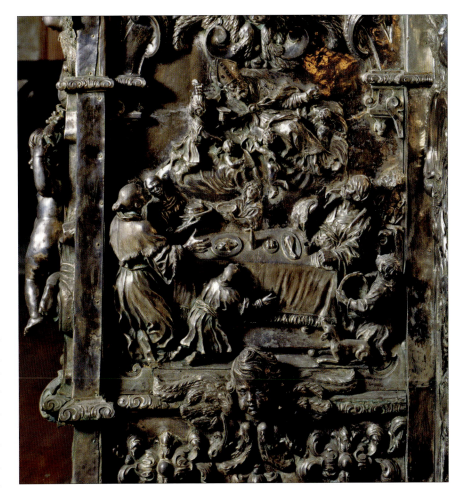

HONORIUS I TO MARTIN I, 625–53
PROLONGED CONTROVERSY OVER MONOTHELITISM

Bitter doctrinal disputes over Monothelitism – the idea that Jesus Christ did not have both divine and human wills, but a single will exercised through his divine and human natures – had a negative impact on relations between the papacy and Constantinople for many years. The controversy was associated with the decades-old disagreements between Monophysiticism (the contention that in Jesus a single, divine nature was dominant) and the orthodox teaching that Jesus had coexistent human and divine natures, separate but not divisible.

SINGLE WILL

Honorius I (625–38) became embroiled in the row when he made a statement apparently showing support for Monothelitism. Honorius issued his controversial teaching in response to a call in 634 from Patriarch Sergius of Constantinople for the Church to unite behind the doctrine that Jesus had one will. Honorius declared that the confession of faith agreed at the Council of Chalecedon of 451 stated that Christ's dual natures could not be divided and that he understood this to mean that Jesus had a single will. Honorius attempted to outlaw further debate on the matter, but the controversy rumbled on.

HOW COULD THE POPE BE WRONG?

In later years Honorius's reputation suffered greatly. The Third Council of Constantinople (680–1), called by Byzantine emperor Constantine IV Pogonatus to try to put an end to the row, denounced Honorius's teaching as being heretical since it appeared to support heretical Monophysiticism. Pope Leo II condemned Honorius in 682, saying his teaching was outside the "apostolic tradition" and was a stain on the "immaculate faith". Many centur-

Above: Honorius I. Was he infallible when he apparently supported Monothelitism? His teaching was later denounced as a "stain" on the Christian faith.

ies later still, Honorius's teaching and its later rebuttal were used by opponents of the idea of papal infallibility – the notion a pope's official announcements were divinely inspired and so could not be mistaken – during the First Vatican Council in 1869–70. Those who defended Honorius attempted to argue that his response to Patriarch Sergius was not an official pronouncement.

ECTHESIS – PRO-MONOTHELITE STATEMENT

In 638 Emperor Heraclius issued a letter, the *Ecthesis*, giving official backing to Monothelitism and refused to endorse the election of the new pope, Severinus, unless the pontiff gave his approval to the letter. When Severinus refused, the Byzantine representative in Italy, the Exarch Isaac of Ravenna, looted

Left: In the imposing Archbasilica of St John, the Lateran Council under Martin I decisively rejected Monothelitism in 649. Martin paid a dear price – humiliated at the hands of Emperor Constans II.

HONORIUS I TO MARTIN I

Right: This mosaic from Ravenna shows the baptism of Christ. The orthodox position was that Christ had dual divine and human wills working in tandem. Supporters of Monothelitism argued he had a single will.

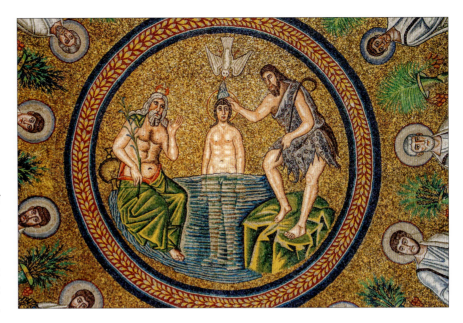

the Lateran Palace to try to force the issue. In the end imperial approval was forthcoming, but as soon as Severinus had been consecrated on 28 May 640, he delivered a ringing endorsement of the orthodox position – that Christ had dual divine/human nature and two wills.

However, the new pope survived the saga of his on/off consecration by just over two months and died on 2 August 640. He was remembered as a kind and mild man, generous to the clergy and to the needy, but clearly also of strong convictions and will.

John IV (640–2) maintained the official line and wrote to the new emperor, Constantine III, in 641 attempting to explain Honorius's apparent lapse from the true faith – claiming that when Honorius spoke of one will in Jesus Christ he meant merely that Jesus was never conflicted, that he had never had two wills working against one another. He also held a synod that reiterated papal condemnation of Monothelitism.

John IV was from Dalmatia (now part of Croatia) and, when he received news of attacks on Christians in that region by invading Slavs, sent an abbot named Martin into the region with substantial funds to help victims. He also arranged for the relics of various Dalmatian saints to be brought back to Rome for safekeeping and to honour them built an oratory, which still stands.

Theodore I (642–9), a Greek who was born in Jerusalem, was noted for his generosity to the needy but otherwise dedicated himself to carrying on the fight against heresy. He put pressure on Emperor Constans II to revoke the *Ecthesis* and excommunicated Pyrrhus and Paul, patriarchs of Constantinople, for their support of the heresy. Enraged, Paul imprisoned the papal nuncios in Constantinople.

IGNOMINIOUS END IN EXILE

Martin I (649–53), a learned and virtuous man who had served as nuncio himself in the past, presided over a Lateran Council in 649 that condemned Monothelitism. Emperor Constans II ordered the pope's arrest and Martin, although he was confined to bed through sickness, was seized in the Lateran Palace and dragged via Greece to Constantinople, where he was tried and flogged and then finally dispatched into exile in Chersonesos Taurica in the Crimean Peninsula (now in southern Ukraine). He died in exile and is celebrated by the Church as a martyr.

Below: Martin I. Arrested by Emperor Constans II in the controversy over Monothelitism, he died in exile in the Crimean Peninsula, although the Roman Church later celebrated him as a martyr.

PATRIARCH OF THE WEST

Theodore I was the first pope to use the title "Patriarch of the West". In the 5th and 6th centuries, while the four established patriarchies of the Eastern Church – Constantinople, Alexandria, Antioch and Jerusalem – were quite clearly demarcated, the territory of the pope was rather harder to delineate. The ecclesiastical system under Emperor Justinian (527–65) listed the pope as patriarch of the West alongside the four Eastern patriarchies given above. After Theodore began the official use of the title, it occurred only intermittently until the 16th–17th centuries, when it became established at a time when the pope was using several official titles. It remained popular until it was dropped by Pope Benedict XVI in 2006. The Pontifical Council for Christian Unity explained that year that the title had become "obsolete and practically unusable".

ENTER THE FRANKS

EUGENIUS I TO AGATHO, 654–81
VITALIAN MAKES PEACE WITH CHURCH IN THE EAST

The controversy over Monothelitism that had brought Pope Martin I to a humiliating end in Crimean exile almost saw to his successor Eugenius I (654–7), also. Initially Eugenius seemed inclined to compromise on the issue, and a letter from Patriarch Peter of Constantinople, a Monothelite, arrived urging reconciliation. But when the letter was read aloud to clergy and people in the Basilica di Santa Maria Maggiore, they were outraged and refused to allow Eugenius to leave the basilica until he pledged to maintain papal opposition to the heresy.

Eugenius subsequently refused to recognize Peter as patriarch. Emperor Constans II threatened him with arrest, but in the event the emperor was busy dealing with attacks by the rampant armies of Islam – who captured Rhodes in 654 and the following year defeated Constans himself at the naval Battle of the Masts fought off Phoenix (modern Finike, Turkey) – and the pope died before the threat was put into force.

Below: This is the underground crypt of the medieval Cathedral of San Leopardo, Osimo, built in 1191 by Mastro Filippo.

PEACE AT A COST
Vitalian (657–72) managed to restore peace between West and East, largely by avoiding direct discussion of controversial doctrinal matters, and Emperor Constans even visited Rome in 663 – the last Eastern emperor to do this for seven centuries. He was very well received, dined with the pope and twice attended Mass in St Peter's Basilica, making a gift to the pope of a pallium (robe) enriched with gold.

However, Constans took the opportunity of being in Italy to make a statement of his power – he confiscated all the bronze artworks and ornaments in Rome (and even the bronze roof tiles of the Pantheon) and ordered that the see of Ravenna, the base for the imperial administration in Italy, be recognized as independent of Rome's control.

ENGLISH DECISIONS
In Vitalian's reign the Synod of Whitby (663–4) in northern England decided that the English Church would follow Roman rather than Celtic Christianity, a decision of the greatest importance for the future of the faith in England. The English sent a priest, Wighard, to

Above: Pope Agatho. Under his rule the Third Council of Constantinople established that Monothelitism was a heresy. He is celebrated as a saint in both Roman and Eastern churches.

Rome for consecration as Archbishop of Canterbury but he died of the plague on arrival and in 668 Vitalian consecrated the learned monk Theodore of Tarsus in his place and sent him to England. Theodore was the seventh Archbishop of Canterbury and the first to govern the whole English church.

Vitalian also attempted to enforce papal authority as a judge of affairs in the Eastern Church. He held a synod in Rome to hear an appeal by Bishop John of Lappa, in Crete, who had been deposed by the Metropolitan Paulus. Vitalian found John innocent and ordered his reinstatement, adding that two monasteries that had been taken from his control should be returned.

CENTURION POPE
Adeodatus II (672–6) was a Roman-born Benedictine monk, and already elderly on his election as pope. Little is known of his pontificate save that he worked to improve monastic discipline and was known for his generous care of the needy – and especially of pilgrims.

Above: Christ delivers a miraculous haul of fish. Pope Agatho reputedly followed his Lord in being a miracle worker.

Below: Agatho's authority did not carry to England. He backed Wilfrid of York in his dispute with Theodore, Archbishop of Canterbury, but on his return Wilfrid was imprisoned, then banished.

His successor Donus (676–8) was celebrated especially for his commitment to restoring churches – including the Basilica Papale di San Paolo fuori le Mura and the Church of St Euphemia on the Appian Way.

Agatho (678–81) was a Sicilian, a Benedictine monk from Palermo, said to have been more than 100 years old when he became pope. He was known for his kindness and friendly nature and was dubbed *Thaumaturgus* ("miracle worker") on account of the many miracles he reputedly performed.

It seems something of a miracle that he also persuaded the Byzantine Emperor Constantine IV to lift the imperial tax levied on the consecration of each new pope. On the matter of the Monothelite controversy, Agatho replied with enthusiasm to a letter sent by Constantine suggesting a church conference to set the matter finally to rest, and sent delegates bearing a statement of orthodox doctrine to the Third Council of Constantinople (the Sixth Ecumenical Council), which met in 680–1.

HONORIUS CONDEMNED

Agatho died on 10 January 681 before the Third Council reached its decision. But it was a momentous ruling since the bishops at the council determined to outlaw Monothelitism as a heresy – and in so doing labelled Pope Honorius, who had made a pro-Monothelite statement, a heretic.

PAPAL OATH

Some traditionalist Catholics believe that Agatho was the first pope to swear an oath on coronation not to change what had been handed down as tradition. According to this argument, popes from Agatho right down to Pope Paul VI (1963–78) swore this oath at their coronation, but there is no concrete evidence that the popes did so. None of the popes after Paul VI – John Paul I, John Paul II, Benedict XVI and Francis – have had a papal coronation, so they could not have sworn the oath.

ENTER THE FRANKS

LEO II TO CONSTANTINE, 682–715
PROLONGED STRUGGLE WITH EMPEROR JUSTINIAN II

Leo II (682–3) was a worthy holder of exalted office: a learned man, fully at home in Greek and Latin, thorough in his knowledge of Scripture and a skilled and eloquent preacher, he was known also for his interest in music and the beauty of his chants and psalmody. Nevertheless he had to wait 19 months for imperial confirmation of his election as the successor to Pope Agatho because he initially resisted ratifying wording in the decrees of the Third Council of Constantinople that denounced Pope Honorius I as a heretic.

In the end Leo accepted the wording and endorsed the council's forthright rejection of the Monothelite position (which held in the Incarnation Jesus Christ had a single will rather than, as explained in orthodox doctrine, human and divine wills working together). Like his predecessor Agatho, Leo was a Sicilian. In his reign the Archbishop of Ravenna, independent since Vitalian's time, returned to Roman control.

Below: Saint Kilian, sent by Pope Conon to Franconia, was killed by soldiers on the orders of a local noblewoman, Geilana. He had offended her by preaching against the widow's marriage to her brother-in-law.

Above: Pope Constantine. He had got to know Justinian, then a prince, during two visits as papal legate to Constantinople. As pope he visited the city again.

Benedict II (684–5) had to wait 11 months for imperial confirmation but in his brief reign got Emperor Constantine Pogonatus to lift the requirement that the election of a new pope must be confirmed in Constantinople. To mark this new harmony between the authorities of Rome and Constantinople Benedict agreed symbolically to adopt Constantine's sons, Heraclius and Justinian – and received in Rome a lock of hair belonging to each of the boys.

EASTERN POPES
John V (685–6) was a Syrian, born in Antioch, and was the first of eleven consecutive popes with a background in the East. He had been a deacon in the service of Agatho at the Third Council, but by the time he was elected pope he was seriously ill and unable to achieve much in his short pontificate.

Conon (686–7), the son of a Thracian soldier, was a compromise candidate for the papacy after the clergy and military factions in Rome disagreed heatedly over who should be John V's successor. But he was well educated and humble, and supported by Emperor Justinian II. He consecrated the Irish missionary Kilian and sent him to preach the Gospel in Franconia (now a region in northern Bavaria, Germany). He was an old man and in poor health when he was elected, and died just 11 months later.

QUINISEXT COUNCIL
Sergius I (687–701) had a murky beginning to his reign in which he finally prevailed over two antipopes, Theodore and Paschal.

In matters of liturgy Sergius introduced the Agnus Dei ("Lamb of God") into the Mass before the eucharistic rite. Some authorities credit him with establishing at Rome the celebration of the festival of Candlemas, held on 2 February and marking the Purification of the Virgin Mary, 40 days after the birth of Jesus.

EMPEROR JUSTINIAN II

Born in c.669, Justinian became emperor aged 16 on the death of his father Constantine IV in 685. He called the Quinisext Council of 692 to agree disciplinary measures related to the second and third councils of Constantinople (553 and 680–1); these were the fifth and sixth ecumenical councils, which explains the name Quinisext. Justinian's attempts to get the papacy to ratify these measures led to conflict with popes from Sergius I to Constantine. Justinian was ousted from power in 695 and his nose was cut off; after a decade in exile he recaptured power in 705. Then in 711 he was deposed a second time and killed: an Armenian named Bardanes took power as Emperor Philippicus.

566

LEO II TO CONSTANTINE

Right: Leo II. Lombard raids forced him to transfer the remains of several martyrs from their burial places in catacombs to churches within the walls of Rome.

In 692 the Quinisext Council called in Constantinople by Emperor Justinian II issued 102 directives, many aimed against practices in the Western Church: these would have put Constantinople on an equal ecclesiastical footing with Rome.

Despite the fact that neither the pope nor any of his representatives were at the council, Justinian demanded that Sergius endorse the directives. When Sergius declined, the emperor ordered his arrest and forcible removal to Constantinople, but the people of Rome and Byzantine troops in Italy stood firm against Justinian, who was deposed shortly afterwards and driven into exile.

John VI (701–5), a Greek, was clearly a good diplomat for he twice maintained the peace when violence threatened, first by intervening in 701 to prevent Exarch Theophylactos of Ravenna, who had marched into Rome, getting into a fight with local soldiers, and second in 705 by persuading Gisulf, the Lombard duke of Benevento, to retreat after he had made a military foray southwards and set up camp within sight of Rome.

Below: Coin of Emperor Justinian II. He had early military success recapturing areas in Thrace and Macedonia that had been taken by Slavs, but he lost imperial possessions in Armenia to Arabs.

DEVOTED TO THE VIRGIN MARY

John VII (705–7), also a Greek, faced a renewed demand from Emperor Justinian II (now restored to power) to endorse the directives of the Quinisext Council to which he responded only by returning the official documents without comment. He was devoted to the Virgin Mary and built an oratory to her as *Theotokos* ("Bearer of God") within the Old St Peter's Basilica – remnants survive in the Vatican grottoes; he also commissioned an icon, Madonna della Clemenza, now in the Basilica di Santa Maria in Trastevere.

Sisinnius, a Syrian, was elected pope on 15 January 708 and died less than three weeks later on 4 February. He suffered terribly from gout. In his short reign he did little except consecrate the Bishop of Corsica and order works to reinforce the walls of Rome.

PAPAL VISIT TO CONSTANTINOPLE

Sisinnius was succeeded by Constantine (708–15), who succeeded in making peace with Emperor Justinian II. He visited Constantinople in 711 – he was to be the last pope to travel to that great city until Pope Paul VI visited in 1967. When Constantine and Justinian met the emperor prostrated himself to kiss the pope's foot and then received communion from his hands.

ENTER THE FRANKS

GREGORY II TO ZACHARIAS, 715–52
CONTROVERSY OVER SACRED USE OF ICONS

In the reign of Gregory II (715–31) a dispute began between Constantinople and Rome over the making and veneration of icons or sacred images that would run on and off until 843, intermittently causing bitter conflict and emphasizing the differences between Eastern and Western churches.

Iconoclasts ("breakers of images") – those who opposed the making and use of icons – believed that the practice was akin to idolatry; those who supported it held that the images were only symbolic. The religious use of images had been opposed in the early church but had become popular in the 6th and 7th centuries.

When Emperor Leo III became a convinced iconoclast and issued an edict against the use of sacred images in 726, Gregory sent a stern rebuttal in which he emphasized that the faithful did not worship the images but used them for "remembrance and encouragement" and declared, "Church dogmas are not a matter for the emperor, but for bishops."

Leo and Gregory had already clashed when Gregory defied the emperor's attempts to increase the taxes lev-

ied on papal territories in Italy. Now Leo planned to have Gregory killed by the imperial representative in Italy, the Exarch of Ravenna; the Exarch, Eutychius, allied himself with the Lombards and marched on Rome. However Gregory was able to break up the alliance and restore peace.

BIRTH OF THE PAPAL STATES
As part of his these negotiations Gregory met the Lombard king, Liutprand, at Sutri outside Rome and received a donation of Lombard-held lands to the papacy. This – known as the Donation of Sutri – was the first expansion of papal lands beyond the Duchy of Rome, and marks the initial establishment of the eventually sizeable and powerful papal states.

Left: Pepin III's likeness is on his tomb in the Basilica of Saint-Denis, France. Pope Zacharias backed his claim to the throne at the expense of the final Merovingian king, Childeric III.

Left: According to tradition, Boniface – sent by Pope Gregory II to convert Germanic tribes – cut down a revered oak tree and used the wood to build a chapel dedicated to St Peter.

MIRACLE AT TOULOUSE
Born in Rome, Gregory carried out refortifications to the walls of the city. There was rising anxiety in this period at the seemingly unstemmable tide of military successes achieved by the armies of Islam (see box), and a fear that they might try to attack Rome herself.

Gregory is associated with a miracle at the Battle of Toulouse in 721 won by a Christian army under Duke Odo of Aquitaine against a Muslim army from Al-Andalus (Islamic Spain). According to this tradition, Gregory sent Odo three baskets of bread to be distributed before the battle and no soldier who ate the bread was killed or even wounded.

SPREAD OF ISLAM
The Prophet Muhammad, founder of the faith of Islam, died in 632 in Medina (now in Saudi Arabia) during the reign of Pope Honorius I. In the hundred-odd years that followed, Islamic warriors created an immense empire that stretched from Spain in the west to parts of China and India in the east, taking in North Africa, Palestine, Syria and Mesopotamia. Rome and Constantinople were left the pre-eminent cities in the Christian world – their historical rivals Antioch, Jerusalem and Alexandria were conquered. Tensions were high between the two centres of power. Constantinople increasingly had to concentrate on defending its eastern possessions. Rome set herself to come to terms with the rising powers of Europe.

GREGORY II TO ZACHARIAS

Above: Pope Zacharias backed the seizing of the Frankish throne by Pepin. His successor Stephen II blessed Pepin and his sons Charlemagne and Carloman in Paris in 754.

Gregory also promoted missionary work in what is now Germany, sending Corbinian and Boniface to work as missionaries there.

Gregory III (731–41), a Syrian by birth, carried on the work of his predecessor both on sacred images – convening a council in Rome in 731 that issued a forthright statement against the iconoclasts – and in missionary work in Germany, in which context he appointed Boniface as metropolitan bishop of Germany.

APPEAL TO THE FRANKS

Then in 739 after the Lombards sacked the Exarchate of Ravenna and appeared set to attack Rome, he appealed for help to the Franks, the Germanic tribe who would later become essential allies of the papacy under their great king Charlemagne. This time, however, the Franks declined to come to the pope's aid on the grounds that the Lombards had been allies in the battles against the Muslim armies of Al-Andalus. Rome was left vulnerable to attack, but survived.

Below: Emperor Leo III. Gregory II survived the trouble that arose after he blocked Leo's efforts to ban the use of sacred images in worship.

LOMBARDS TAKE RAVENNA

Zacharias (741–52), born of Greek descent in southern Italy, was a man of letters and a highly effective diplomat. He made peace with the Lombards although in his reign they captured the remaining Byzantine territories in Italy, the Exarchate of Ravenna, in 751.

He also patched up relations with Constantinople, despite the fact Emperor Constantine V Copronymus was a committed iconoclast, and developed the papal alliance with the Franks. He supported the claim of Pepin III as king of the Franks, and the deposition of the last Merovingian king, Childeric III – so inaugurating the birth of a close relationship between Rome and the new Carolingian royal house.

In Rome he built the church of Santa Maria sopra Minerva on the site of the pagan temple to Minerva and donated it to a group of nuns from Constantinople. He is remembered also for translating the *Dialogues* of Gregory the Great into Greek.

ENTER THE FRANKS

STEPHEN II TO STEPHEN III, 752–72
POPE BECOMES TEMPORAL RULER, HEAD OF THE PAPAL STATES

Two men called Stephen were elected to the papacy in 752. The first, elected on 23 March, survived just three days; a stroke despatched him before he could be consecrated. He is listed as Pope Stephen II in some sources, but was removed from the official listing of popes under Pope John XXIII (1958–63). The second, who ruled from 26 March 752 to 26 April 757, is therefore Stephen II. However, in some books he is listed as Stephen III – or as Stephen II (III).

This pope Stephen II distanced the papacy from Constantinople and moved closer to the Franks. His reign saw a seismic shift: the pope, no longer under imperial authority exercised from Constantinople, established himself as a sovereign prince, ruler of the papal states, with the King of the Franks as his protector.

LOMBARDS THREATEN ROME
The year before Stephen's election, the Lombards had captured Ravenna, capital of the Byzantine territory in Italy, the Exarchate of Ravenna. There was no escaping the conclusion that they were now a threat to Rome.

Stephen could not expect help from Constantinople: relations were strained because of the continuing bitter controversy over iconoclasm, and in any case the Byzantine Empire had its hands full coping with the threats of the Islamic Abbasid Caliphate based in Baghdad.

DONATION OF PEPIN
Stephen tried negotiations, meeting Lombard king Aistulf at Pavia in the autumn of 753, but when this proved fruitless he turned to the Franks, crossing the Alps and travelling to Paris, where he met King Pepin III "the Short" of the Franks. In July 754 Stephen anointed Pepin – and his sons Charlemagne and Carloman – as kings of the Romans. In return Pepin promised to drive off the Lombards and return to the papacy lands in Italy that had been seized by the Lombards. This promise – subsequently known as "the Donation of Pepin" – does not survive in written form but later documents of the 8th century refer to it.

Pepin swept into Italy at the head of his Frankish army and pinned Aistulf back into his capital, Pavia; Pope

Above: Stephen III overcame two rivals amid street fighting to claim the papacy. The establishment of the papal states had made it highly desirable to be pope.

THE FRANKS
The Franks were first known to history as Germanic tribes living near the River Rhine in around the 3rd century AD. After the collapse of the Roman Empire they were ruled by the Merovingian dynasty. The family that gave rise to the great kings Pepin III and Charlemagne were mayors of the palace under the Merovingians – administrators who increasingly were de facto rulers. Pepin III rose to power in alliance with the papacy and was crowned King of the Franks in November 751 by Bishop Boniface with the knowledge and backing of Pope Zacharias: the last Merovingian king, Childeric III, was deposed and despatched to a monastery. Pepin was succeeded by his sons Charlemagne and Carloman ruling side by side. On Carloman's death in 771, Charlemagne annexed his territory and became sole ruler of the Franks.

Below: Pharamond is elected king of the Franks. A legendary figure, he was first mentioned in an eighth-century history that set out to link the Franks to Ancient Troy.

570

STEPHEN II TO STEPHEN III

Stephen travelled back to safety in Rome. But when the Franks returned to their homeland the Lombards marched southwards once more and in January 756 surrounded Rome. Stephen called for aid again and Pepin, Carloman and Charlemagne did not fail him: they led their forces to the rescue a second time. With the Lombards humbled, the Franks bestowed on Pope Stephen the basis of the papal states – lands in the Exarchate of Ravenna, the Duchy of Rome, Istria and Venetia.

Stephen II's younger brother was to succeed him as Pope Paul I in 757. He faced an alliance between the Lombards under their new king Desiderius and Emperor Constantine V Copronymus, who invaded the papal states. Pepin acted as a mediator and most of the pope's territories were safeguarded.

MONKS TAKE FLIGHT
In the Eastern Church, Constantine launched a new wave of iconoclasm; Paul protested strongly and repeatedly. He gave refuge to waves of Greek monks who had fled persecution in Byzantine territories. Paul transferred the bones of several saints from the catacombs damaged by the Lombards in 756 to churches in the city. Among these were the remains of St Petronilla, who was then believed to be the daughter of St Peter.

After Paul died, Pope Stephen III (768–72) was immediately embroiled in a bloody succession crisis. First a Tuscan nobleman, Duke Toto of Nepi, tried to install his brother as pope, and he was briefly in power as antipope Constantine II. Then a Lombard faction had Toto killed and Constantine deposed and installed their own candidate, Philip.

Above: Lands in the Exarchate of Ravenna, site of the beautiful Basilica of Sant'Apollinare Nuovo, were part of the territory transferred to Pope Stephen II. This mosaic shows the Magi guided by a star.

He, too, was ousted and Stephen III was elected by an assembly of clergy, military and the people of Rome.

ALLIANCE IN THE BALANCE
Stephen initially trusted the Franks as his protectors, but was horrified when the Lombards and Franks entered into an alliance in which the Lombard princess Desiderata wed Charlemagne. Stephen made an alliance with the Lombards in 771, and in machinations surrounding this agreement Franks were murdered in Rome. The papacy's relationship with the Franks was hanging by a thread.

571

ENTER THE FRANKS

HADRIAN I, 772–95
POPE WHO FORGED A CRUCIAL ALLIANCE WITH CHARLEMAGNE

When Pope Stephen III chose alliance with the Lombards over loyalty to the Franks the decision could have been disastrous for Rome, but his successor Hadrian I (772–95) – a man of great ability and deep piety – extricated the papacy from these problems and rebuilt the alliance with the Frankish kings. This resulted in Charlemagne crushing the Lombards.

LOMBARD AMBITIONS
At the start of Hadrian's reign, the Lombard king Desiderius was ambitious to extend his rule throughout Italy. He saw that the Frankish king

Below: A momentous encounter. The 15th-century Chronicles of France depicts Hadrian greeting Charlemagne in Rome to cement the alliance between the papacy and Franks.

> **FACT BOX**
> **Original name** Hadrian
> **Also known as** Adrian I
> **Born** 700
> **Origin** Roman
> **Date elected pope** 1 February 772
> **Died** 25 December 795
> **Key fact** Established the papacy as a temporal power

Charlemagne had his hands full fighting the Saxons, and hoped to foster dissension among the Frankish people. The previous year Charlemagne's brother and co-ruler Carloman had died, leading Charlemagne to annexe his brother's lands and set himself up as sole king; Desiderius had Carloman's exiled widow and sons in the Lombard capital, Pavia, and hoped to get Hadrian to back their claim to a share in Frankish power.

But Hadrian would not cooperate and instead ordered the arrest of Desiderius's agent in Rome, Paul Afiarta, and demanded the return of papal territories that the Lombards had seized. Desiderius threatened Rome. Hadrian refortified the city and called on Charlemagne for military help.

FAST AND FURIOUS RESPONSE
At this critical moment there was a lull in the Saxon war that enabled Charlemagne to strike in support of the pope. In autumn 773 he swept across the Alps, captured Verona and besieged Desiderius in Pavia.

Then, leaving his troops to carry on the siege, Charlemagne marched to Rome. He arrived on Holy Saturday at

> **ICONOCLASM**
> The controversy over whether it was permissible to make and venerate images of Jesus Christ and the saints caused bitter division in the 8th and 9th centuries. The religious use of images had been opposed in the early Church but had become popular in the 6th and 7th centuries. Byzantine Emperor Leo III prohibited the use of icons in 730 and persecution of those who revered icons became severe. Then in 787 the Second Ecumenical Council at Nicaea, convened by the Empress Irene, condemned iconoclasm and backed the use of images. Iconoclasm would return in 814 with the accession of Emperor Leo V and the use of icons was to be banned in 815. Finally in 843 Empress Theodora, widow of Emperor Theophilus, would restore the sacred use of icons – an event celebrated as the Feast of Orthodoxy in the Eastern Orthodox Church today.

572

Above: In Rome, Pope Hadrian constructed the Basilica of Santa Maria in Cosmedin on the site of an earlier church, de Schola Graeca, and an ancient food distribution centre.

Easter, was warmly welcomed and solemnly celebrated Easter with Hadrian at St Peter's.

DONATION OF CHARLEMAGNE

For three days the Roman and Frankish parties celebrated Easter, then on the following Wednesday met to settle affairs of state. This was a momentous en-counter that transformed the face of Italy for centuries to come.

In the celebrated "Donation of Charlemagne", the Frankish king gave Hadrian and his successors possession of great swathes of territory in the Italian peninsula. Two months later, Pavia fell to Charlemagne's army. The Lombard era was at a close.

CLASH OVER ICONS

Hadrian also intervened in the bitter rows over iconoclasm (see box), supporting the efforts of Byzantine Empress Irene (widow of Leo IV and co-ruler with her son Constantine VI) to end the dispute. He despatched legates bearing a treatise that explained the doctrinal justification of venerating icons to the Second Council of Nicaea (787), which outlawed iconoclasm. This briefly caused a rift with Charlemagne, who rejected the council's decrees, perhaps because he was suspicious of this revival of co-operation between Rome and Constantinople and also, it is thought, taking offence because he had been invited to send bishops himself. His theologians issued the *Libri Carolini*, which defied Nicaea by declaring in favour of iconoclasm, but the difficulty passed and was explained on the grounds that Charlemagne had seen a poor Latin translation of the council's decrees that wrongly spoke of "adoration" rather than the more restrained "veneration" of images in worship.

Hadrian also fought against the heresy of Adoptionism in the Spanish Church, condemning the teaching of Archbishop Elipandus of Toledo on the dual natures of Jesus Christ. The teaching had this name because Elipandus argued that the human Jesus Christ was the "adopted son" of God while the divine Jesus was God's son by nature.

In Rome, Hadrian rebuilt the churches of Santa Maria in Cosmedin and San Marco and also carried out restoration works on some of the old aqueducts.

LONG SERVICE

Hadrian reigned for 23 years, ten months and 26 days. His papal rule was not surpassed until Pope Pius VI's 24-year reign in 1775–99. In the whole history of the papacy only three other popes – Pius IX (1846–78), Leo XIII (1878–1903) and John Paul II (1978–2005) – have had longer reigns.

When Hadrian died aged 95 on 25 December 795 Charlemagne reputedly wept as if he had lost a close relative, and he celebrated this great pope in a verse epitaph written by the scholar Alcuin and inscribed on a marble monument that he sent to Rome. In the epitaph, which can still be viewed in St Peter's Basilica, Charlemagne called Hadrian "father".

Below: After the negotiations in Rome at Easter 774, Charlemagne returned to Pavia and directed the end of the siege. The citizens opened their gates to the Frankish army.

CONFLICT IN THE CHURCH

LEO III TO LEO IX, 795–1054

The reign of Pope Benedict IX in the mid-11th century is one of the most degrading in the history of the papacy. He was linked to murders and rapes; he even sold the position of pope to his father-in-law John Gratian, who became Pope Gregory VI. Here was the offence of simony writ as large as could be. The papacy's alliance with the Frankish throne brought with it the gift of lands on the Italian peninsula that made the pope a temporal prince. In the 10th and 11th centuries the position of pope was a glittering prize disputed amidst violence, bribery and politicking by the Roman nobility.

Benedict IX was not only put on the throne by his father and briefly succeeded by his father-in-law, but was also the nephew of popes Benedict VIII and John XIX and related to popes Sergius III and John XI. These men were all associated with the Tusculani family, placed in power by various counts of Tusculum (near Rome in central-western Italy). Their bitter rivals were the Crescentii family, who provided one pope in Giovanni Crescentius (John XIII; 965–972) and controlled most of the pontiffs from *c.*950–1012, when their puppet Sergius IV died in the same year as the *patricius* (leader) of the clan.

Increased worldly power and the alliance with Frankish kings and subsequent Western emperors made the papacy independent of its former masters, the Byzantine emperors in Constantinople. In the mid-11th century the reforming pope Leo IX emphasized repeatedly the primacy of the pope over the whole Church. The ensuing conflict with church authorities in Constantinople led to a schism between the Western and Eastern churches that has not been healed to this day.

Left: The old order passeth. By tradition the papacy was established in authority over Rome and the Western Roman Empire by the "Donation of Constantine", here celebrated by Renaissance master Raphael in his work for the Vatican Palace. The alliance with Charlemagne and the Franks set the papacy free from Constantinople.

CONFLICT IN THE CHURCH

LEO III, 795–816
POPE WHO CROWNED CHARLEMAGNE

Pope Leo III consolidated the already highly profitable relationship between the papacy and Franks by crowning Frankish king Charlemagne the first Holy Roman Emperor.

DRIVEN FROM ROME
Pope Hadrian's associates and family members initially made life almost impossible for his successor, Leo III (795–816). Some had perhaps expected to succeed Hadrian, and began to spread rumours to undermine the new pope. Hadrian's nephew Pascalis led a brutal attack on Leo as the pope toured the city on 25 April 799, trying without success to make him unfit for office by blinding him and cutting his tongue out, but Leo escaped intact and fled to Paderborn, Germany, seeking the protection of Charlemagne.

At the same time, Leo's enemies sent messengers to Charlemagne, accusing the pope of perjury and sexual offences. Could Charlemagne pass judgement on an elected pope? However his advisers, who included the learned monk Alcuin of York – the great scholar of Charlemagne's revival of learning – assured him

FACT BOX
Original name Not known; son of Atyuppius and Elizabeth
Born 750
Origin Roman; Greek or possibly Arab ancestry
Date elected pope 27 December 795
Died 12 June 816
Key fact Built key relationship with the Franks

Above: On Christmas Day, 800, Leo III crowns Charlemagne Emperor of the West – "great and pacific emperor, governing the Roman Empire". This view was painted by Raphael in 1516–17.

that there was no precedent for him to do this. He sent the pope back to Rome with a Frankish escort for protection.

Trouble continued in Rome, however, and in the autumn of 800 Charlemagne himself travelled there to attempt to settle matters. On 23 December of that year, Leo solemnly swore his innocence on the Gospels at the high altar of St Peter's before a synod of abbots, bishops and members of the Frankish and Roman nobility that was also attended by Charlemagne himself. The synod duly accepted his word and cleared him of all charges.

IMPERIAL CORONATION

Two days later at Christmas Day Mass in St Peter's, Leo crowned Charlemagne Emperor of the West. Charlemagne is generally viewed as the first Holy Roman Emperor, although he did not use this title – he was styled "most serene Augustus, crowned by God, great and pacific emperor, governing the Roman Empire". The coronation consolidated Leo's still precarious position, and clarified the basis on which Charlemagne had taken a role at the synod that cleared Leo of charges just two days earlier.

According to the Frankish account, Leo prostrated himself in front of Charlemagne, kissing the ground before his feet – the accepted act of adoration due to an emperor. This act of homage was not recorded by the papal chronicler, who stated that Leo anointed Charlemagne.

Afterwards Charlemagne claimed that he had been taken by surprise and would not have entered St Peter's on that day had he known what Leo intended, but it is impossible not to believe that the two men had planned this act of high visual drama in advance, perhaps even as early as their meeting in Paderborn the previous year.

Above: The coronation of Charlemagne. In this unprecedented act, which had no legal basis, Leo attempted to establish the right of the pope to anoint and crown the emperor.

At the Lateran, Leo commissioned two mosaics that provide a commentary on the coronation. In one, Jesus Christ hands St Peter the pallium and gives Constantine the labarum or Chi-Ro symbol of Christ's name; in a second Peter hands Leo the pallium and gives Charlemagne a banner and spear.

FILIOQUE

The ceremony sought to establish Charlemagne as protector of the papacy. The coronation would surely not have taken place if there had been a male emperor ruling in Constantinople. But there was not, for the Empress Irene, widow of Leo IV, was in power, having seized the throne from her son Constantine V with whom she had been co-ruler. In the eyes of many in the West, who believed in a male line of succession, the imperial throne was empty. In this sense the papacy – indeed, the whole Christian world – had no protector.

In 810 these co-rulers came into conflict over Charlemagne's support for adding the word *Filioque* ("and the Son")

Left: At the Lateran, Leo commissioned mosaics that comment on the coronation. In one, Christ hands Leo the pallium (a robe, symbol of spiritual authority) and gives Charlemagne a banner and spear.

to the creed. The proposed addition signified that the Holy Spirit derived from the Father and the Son (Jesus Christ) together, and did not come solely from the Father. Having first appeared in Spain as early as the 6th century, use of the *Filioque* wording had spread widely through the Western Church, but its use was opposed in the Eastern Church.

Leo accepted the doctrine but rejected the notion that the Church of the Franks could make changes to the creed that had been agreed by the ecumenical councils of Nicaea and Constantinople and so was a unifying factor for Eastern and Western churches. "For safeguarding of the true faith", he had the creed (without *Filioque*) engraved in both Latin and Greek on silver panels and attached these to tombs of Saints Peter and Paul in Rome.

CHARLEMAGNE

Charlemagne was King of the Franks (768–814), King of the Lombards (774–814) and Emperor of the West (800–14). When he was born in April 747, his father Pepin was mayor of the palace under the Merovingian kings – notionally an administrator, but in fact a position of great power. With the backing of Pope Zacharias (741–52) Pepin seized the throne and ousted the final Merovingian king, Childeric III, who was despatched to a monastery. On Pepin's death in 768 the kingdom was divided between Charlemagne and his younger brother Carloman, then when Carloman died in 771 Charlemagne became sole ruler of the Franks. He was 24 years old. In alliance with the papacy, he went on to build a great empire, defeating the Lombards, the Saxons and the Avars. He promoted Christianity, education and the arts, commerce and agriculture in his vast realms, building many splendid churches and palaces, and his era is called the "Carolingian Renaissance".

CONFLICT IN THE CHURCH

STEPHEN IV TO SERGIUS II, 816–47
EMPERORS EXERT POWER OVER PAPACY

In the first half of the 9th century the descendants of Charlemagne exercised increasing power over the papacy. Initially popes Stephen IV and Paschal I held quite a strong position and sought to emphasize the papal role in anointing the emperor, but popes from Eugenius II to Sergius II lost ground and had to make concessions regarding imperial approval of and sovereignty over new popes.

Stephen IV (816–17) travelled to Reims to crown and anoint Charlemagne's successor, Louis the Pious, as Holy Roman Emperor. Louis had previously been crowned by his own father, Charlemagne, in 813, but Stephen's action underlined the papacy's role in establishing each new imperial ruler in power. Stephen and Louis confirmed their alliance and the pope's possession of the papal states. Stephen died shortly after his return to Rome, on 24 January 817.

His successor Paschal I (817–24) had his coronation almost immediately after his election, perhaps to prevent any interference in the process by Louis. When Paschal sent news of the event to Louis, he received in return a celebrated document, the *Pactum Ludovicianum,* which congratulated Paschal, recognized his right over the papal states and guaranteed that future popes could be freely elected and need only inform the emperor after being crowned. Some historians doubt the authenticity of this document, however, which was so highly favourable to the papacy.

In 823 Paschal crowned and anointed Louis's son Lothair I as co-emperor with his father in Rome. This was the first coronation ceremony in which the pope handed the emperor a sword as a symbol of temporal power that was to be used to banish evil.

> **SIMONY**
>
> Simony means selling ecclesiastical positions or church sacraments. The name comes from Simon Magus, a sorcerer from Samaria who according to the biblical book Acts of the Apostles (8:18) tried to buy from the Apostles the knowledge of how to transmit the Holy Spirit. The oldest surviving statement against simony is the second canon of the Council of Chalcedon of 451. Simony became a major and widespread problem in the European Church in the 9th–10th centuries.

POPE MUST SWEAR FEALTY TO EMPEROR

Eugenius II (824–7) owed the Holy Roman Emperor gratitude from the first day of his pontificate. He was elected by Roman nobles with imperial support and in opposition to the candidate favoured by the clergy in Rome. As a result Frankish control of the papacy reached a high point in this reign: Eugenius did not resist a new constitution imposed by Lothair I on a visit to Rome in 824, under which the emperor had sovereignty over Rome and each pope elect had to swear fealty before he could be elected.

"FATHER OF THE PEOPLE"

On matters of church discipline and organization, Eugenius established that priests should not wear secular clothing or have secular occupations, and took various measures to promote learning. He was known for humility and

Left: Pope Stephen IV crowns Louis the Pious – as depicted in the 14th-century manuscript "Grandes Chroniques de France". Stephen wanted to restate that the papacy's blessing was necessary for an imperial succession.

STEPHEN IV TO SERGIUS II

love of simplicity, and his generosity to the poor, especially widows and orphans, won him the title "father of the people".

Pope Valentine lasted only 40 days in August–September 827. At the start of the reign of his successor, Gregory IV (827–44), the pope was reprimanded by Louis for having attempted to arrange his consecration before receiving the emperor's approval of the election. Subsequently Gregory attempted to mediate in the quarrels between Lothair and his father Louis in the course of which Lothair led a rebellion and briefly deposed his father in 833. Then, following the death of Louis in 840, war broke out between Lothair and his brothers and in the end the great empire of Charlemagne was broken up by the Treaty of Verdun (843).

CORRUPTION

Sergius II (844–7) was elected by the Roman nobility and had to contend with an antipope, John, popular with the people of Rome. He managed to overcome this challenge but rushed his consecration to end the issue. This

Above: Paschal I honours the Virgin Mary. He built or renovated several churches in Rome as part of the Carolingian Renaissance associated with Charlemagne – a programme of artistic and theological rebirth.

Below: Money could not buy Simon Magus secret knowledge about the Holy Spirit from the Apostles. Italian Renaissance artist Filippino Lippi imagined the scene.

brought on another show of imperial strength, and Lothair sent his son Louis to Rome at the head of an army to punish the pope for having failed to wait for emperor's approval of his election. Sergius was forced to accept that no pope could be elected without the emperor's approval, and that each papal consecration must be in the presence of an imperial representative.

Because he suffered so badly from gout, Sergius delegated much of his power to his brother, Bishop Benedict of Albano. Between them they carried out major rebuilding in Rome, but won an unwanted reputation for financial misdemeanours and simony.

SARACEN ATTACK

For many years, since they had captured Palermo in Sicily in 831, Muslim Arabs had been a force to fear in southern Italy. In 846 a Muslim fleet sailed up the Tiber and unleashed 500 horsemen who sacked Rome, even tearing silver from the doors of St Peter's. Many saw it as a judgement of God on the financial wrongdoing under Pope Sergius.

579

CONFLICT IN THE CHURCH

LEO IV TO LEO V, 847–903
POPE'S CORPSE EXHUMED AND PUT ON TRIAL

Leo IV (847–55) responded with fortitude and energy to the challenge laid down by the Saracens when they sacked Rome in the last days of Pope Sergius II. Leo built a coalition against the common enemy, and himself taking command of a fleet combining the navies of Amalfi, Gaeta and Naples, defeated the Arab navy in a sea battle off Ostia in 849.

LEONINE WALL
He then set several hundred prisoners to work alongside locals to improve Rome's fortifications, raising the great Leonine Wall – 40ft/12m high, 12ft/3.6m thick, 1.8 miles/3km long and with 40 towers – around the Vatican and St Peter's. Another tradition about this great defender of the faith and of Rome holds that when a blazing fire threatened to engulf the Borgo district adjacent to St Peter's Square, Leo stopped the flames by making the sign of the cross.

Benedict III (855–8) was elected after another candidate, Hadrian, had refused to become pope, and faced an antipope, Anastasius, who had the backing of Emperor Louis II. Remarkably, however, the popular backing for Benedict proved too strong for the imperial candidate and after

Above: When Leo IV made the sign of the cross it was sufficient to turn back flames that had threatened the Borgo district. A Vatican Palace fresco by Raphael celebrated the event.

Louis dropped his opposition Benedict was consecrated. He acted with authority in disciplining Frankish bishops and restating the primacy of Rome over Constantinople. In his reign, the Christian King Aethelwulf of Wessex made a pilgrimage to Rome with his son, the future King Alfred the Great.

VIGOROUS AUTHORITY
Nicholas I the Great (858–67) was a more forthright proponent still of papal authority and Rome's jurisdiction over the church; he challenged the Western emperor's right to legislate on ecclesiastical matters, and restated the pope's inheritance of priestly and royal authority from St Peter. This vigorous leader made three great statements of

Left: "Pope Joan" gives birth in mid-procession. An anti-Catholic pamphlet of 1675 imagines the scene, describing Rome as "the whore of Babylon".

papal authority. He refused to accept the deposition of Patriarch Ignatius of Constantinople by Byzantine emperor Michael III and excommunicated his replacement, Photius, causing a new schism between Eastern and Western churches. He excommunicated the archbishops of Cologne and Trier in finding against their decision to allow King Lothair of Lorraine to divorce his first wife and remarry. And he reinstated the Bishop of Soissons, France, overriding the Archbishop of Reims's decision.

A relative of two previous popes, Stephen IV and Sergius II, Hadrian II (867–72) had twice declined to become pope before he finally accepted in 867. He was an ineffective pontiff. His five-year reign included the fourth Council of Constantinople (869–70), which deposed Patriarch Photius of Constantinople.

FIRST POPE TO BE MURDERED
John VIII (872–82) was the first pope to be assassinated – he was poisoned and clubbed to death as a result of a local dispute. This rather sordid end followed an active and effective pontificate in which in alliance with the Franks he

580

defended Italy against Muslim raiders. He clashed with and excommunicated the Bishop of Porto, Formosus, who later became pope.

Marinus I (882–84) was Bishop of Caere (modern Cerveteri) when elected pope – the first bishop of another diocese to be made Bishop of Rome. Among his few acts of note as pontiff was to absolve Formosus and restore him to his bishopric in 883.

Hadrian III (884–5) likewise achieved little. By now Charlemagne's once great empire was in decline, and Pope Stephen V (885–91), finding no help from the Franks, was forced to turn once more to Constantinople in seeking aid against Arab raids on Italy.

Formosus (891–6) was a highly effective pontiff and skilled diplomat, a deeply pious man and a very fine preacher, but one who made many enemies. His

POPE JOAN

Tradition – usually dismissed as legend – has it that a woman held the reins of papal power in 855–7, between Leo IV and Benedict III. According to the story that circulated in chronicles through the Middle Ages, she went by the name of John VIII, and was English by birth; after coming to Rome via Athens and building a great reputation as a master of the liberal arts in the disguise of a man, she was unanimously elected pope. When she became pregnant by a companion, she tried to conceal it but gave birth while in the midst of a procession from St Peter's to the Lateran, in a lane between the Colosseum and St Clement's Church. One version claims she reigned in 1099–1106 between Urban II and Paschal II. It is also said that for 600 years each newly elected pope had to submit to an intimate examination – he sat in a specially designed chair with a section cut away so that a junior cleric could touch the pope's genitals to verify that he was a man.

Above: The infamous "Cadaver Trial". Stephen VI had the corpse of his predecessor Boniface VI dug up to face accusations of wrongdoing while pope.

name means "good-looking" – and he was accused of vanity. He allied with Arnulf of Carinthia, King of the Eastern Franks, against Emperor Guy III of Spoleto and his son Lambert, and crowned Arnulf Emperor in Rome in 896. Arnulf fell ill and became paralysed and the alliance came to nothing, but it earned Formosus the hatred of the House of Spoleto and cast a long shadow over the following years.

THE CADAVER TRIAL

The next two years saw four popes, one of whom was imprisoned and murdered, and a scandalous trial. Boniface VI (896) died after 15 days. His successor Stephen VI (896–7) was one of Formosus's many bitter enemies, and in the gruesome "Cadaver Trial" he had the former pope's body exhumed, dressed in full papal regalia and propped up on the throne to face trial for alleged offences committed while pope. Formosus was found guilty, stripped and had the three fingers of his right hand that he had used for giving blessings cut off; then the corpse was cast into the river Tiber. These events caused a scandal and Stephen was imprisoned and strangled in captivity.

Romanus reigned for four months in August–November 897 but was deposed and ended his life as a monk and Theodore II died after being pope for 20 days in December of the same year. In his very brief reign Theodore had the body of Formosus, which had been recovered by a hermit from the Tiber, reburied.

John IX (898–900) tried to rehabilitate Formosus's reputation and held synods at Rome and Ravenna to this end. Bitter struggles over the memory of Formosus dominated the reign of Benedict IV (900–3) and Leo V (August/September 903). Leo was imprisoned by an antipope, Christopher, and probably murdered in captivity.

Below: Church Triumphant. Defeated pagans are dragged before Pope Leo IV after his victory at sea over the Saracens in the Battle of Ostia (849).

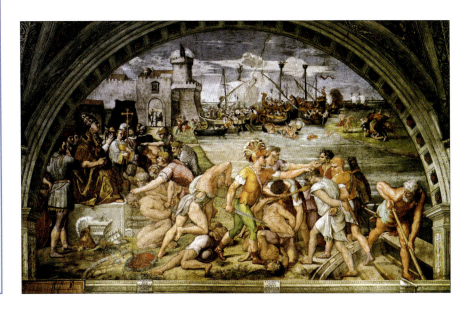

CONFLICT IN THE CHURCH

SERGIUS III TO GREGORY V, 904–99
PAPACY ENDURES A "DARK AGE"

In these years the papacy was a prize bitterly contested by noble families in Italy. Sergius III (904–11) owed his time in the limelight to the support of Count Theophylact of Tusculum and was little more than his puppet. According to one account, Sergius was the lover of Theophylact's daughter Marozia and had an illegitimate son by her who went on to become Pope John XI.

MURDEROUS POWERPLAY
Sergius had in fact been elected pope in 898 by supporters of Stephen VI and enemies of Formosus, but he had been driven from Rome by John IX. When the antipope Christopher ousted John IX's successor Leo V, Sergius moved in with the support of Count Theophylact. He defeated Christopher and seized power for himself. It is said that he ordered the murder by strangling of both Christopher and Leo.

Popes Anastasius III (911–13) and Lando (913–14) were both Count Theophylact's men and did his bidding – indeed, all the popes down to John XII were in the pocket of Theophylact or his descendants. One note of interest about Lando is that he was the last pope – until Pope Francis in 2013 – to use a papal name that had not previously been chosen by a pontiff.

To combat Saracen raids in Italy, John X (914–28) built an anti-Muslim Christian alliance that pointed forward

Above: Pope John X. To combat Saracen raiders, he built an anti-Muslim Christian alliance that pointed forward to the crusader armies of 1096 and afterwards. His army won the Battle of Garigliano (915).

to the crusader armies of 1096 and afterwards. John himself led the army to victory over the Saracens at the Battle of Garigliano in June 915. He rewarded King Berengar of Italy for his participation by crowning him Holy Roman Emperor, with Theophylact's backing, on 3 December 915.

DANGEROUS MISTRESS
John was reputedly the lover of Marozia's mother Theodora, to whom he granted the title *senatrix* (senatoress) of Rome. In 924, following the assassination of Berengar and the death of Theophylact he tested the patience of his noble backers by seeking an alliance with Hugh of Provence. Marozia – now married to Guy, Margrave of Tuscany – had the pope cast in prison and smothered to death.

Leo VI (928) and Stephen VII (928–31) were both Marozia's appointments, and both may have been killed; John XI (931–35/6) was her son by Sergius III. He was loyal to her but was deposed and imprisoned by another of her sons, his half-brother Duke Alberic II of Spoleto.

Leo VII (936–939), Stephen VIII (939–42), Marinus II (942–6) and Agapitus II (946–55) were all appointed by Alberic and entirely dominated by him. They all took an interest, encouraged by Alberic, in reforming Italian monasteries. Leo invited Odo, abbot of the Cluniac order of reforming monks, to Rome.

WHEN THE VATICAN WAS LIKE A BROTHEL
On the death of Agapitus, Alberic's illegitimate son Octavian succeeded as pope John XII (955–64). He may have been as young as 17 years old and was entirely unsuited to lead the Church, for he led a wildly dissolute life – and in his time the Vatican was described as a brothel.

He relied on the support of Otto I of Germany, who had marched into Italy in 951 and declared himself King of the Lombards, and John consolidated his position by crowning Otto and his wife Adelaide as Roman Emperor and Empress on 2 February 962. John and the Roman nobles swore an oath of loyalty to Otto who issued a guarantee of the independence of the papal states.

Below: Benedict V: a medal dated 964. He was pope for just one month, 22 May–23 June, before he was ousted by Emperor Otto I and his preferred candidate, Leo VIII.

POPES OF THE DARK AGE

For half a century from Sergius III in 904 to John XII in 955, popes were under the influence of the Roman Theophylacti family. The Latin name *Saeculum obscurum* ("dark age") was first given to these years by the 16th-century Vatican librarian and papal historian Caesar Baronius.

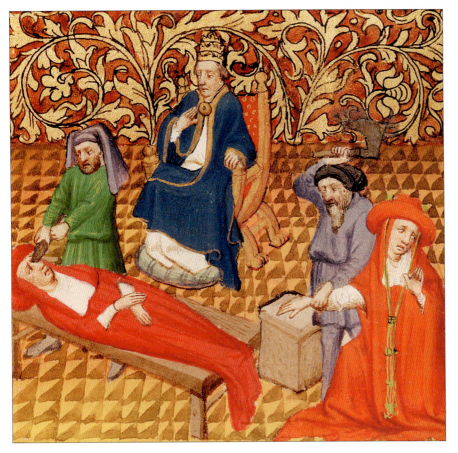

Above: John XII oversees the punishment of those who plotted against him – his confessor, Benedict, is blinded and a deacon has his right hand cut off.

But when Otto left Rome to impose his authority on Berengar II, King of Italy, John began to plot behind his back, provoking the fury of the emperor who replaced him with Pope Leo VIII (963–5). Briefly in 964, after Otto had left Rome, John engineered his own reinstatement but then he died suddenly while having sexual relations with one of his concubines – the word in Rome was that he died after being struck on the head by the devil himself.

On his death the Romans refused to accept Leo and elected Benedict V (964) as their own candidate. But Otto returned to Rome, removed Benedict from the papal throne and reinstalled his own man.

John XIII (965–72), another candidate imposed by Otto, followed Leo. At Christmas 967 he crowned the emperor's 12-year-old son as co-Emperor Otto II. His unpopularity among the Romans was a political matter rather than a judgement on his character, for he was learned and pious, and an expert in canon law. His nickname was "the white hen", on account of his very fair hair.

Otto died shortly after the election of Benedict VI (973–4) and while his son Otto II was distracted imposing himself in Germany, Roman nobles strangled Benedict and replaced him with antipope Boniface VII. Otto II's candidate Benedict VII (974–83) prevailed after a struggle and the antipope Boniface was excommunicated. Benedict and Otto worked well together and kept the peace in Rome for nine years, promoting monasticism and church reform.

On Benedict's death Otto II offered Majolus, abbot of Cluny, the chance to be pope but he declined. One of Otto's ministers, Pietro Canepanova, stepped into the breach as John XIV (983–4).

However, he was left isolated and vulnerable when Otto died on 7 December 983 and the antipope Boniface VII returned from exile and deposed the pope, throwing him in prison where he starved to death. Boniface held power until his death in July 985.

FIRST CANONIZATION

John XV (985–96), another pope controlled by the Roman nobility, was not inactive – in 993 he solemnly canonized Bishop Ulrich of Augsburg (died 973) in the first recorded ritual of this kind. When he died of fever in March 996, the new German king Otto III chose his cousin Bruno of Carinthia as Gregory V (996–9). Within three weeks of his consecration on 3 May 996, Gregory crowned Otto emperor. Then when Otto returned to Germany a revolt in Rome drove Gregory to flee and installed an antipope, John XVI. Furious, Otto marched on Rome, captured the antipope and reinstalled Gregory. However, Gregory died in February 999 after contracting malaria before his 30th birthday.

Below: The Benedictine Abbey of Cluny was widely seen as a leading light of monasticism in Europe. So Leo VIII turned to its abbot, Odo, for advice on monastic reform in Italy.

SYLVESTER II, 999–1003
POPE WHO WAS ACCUSED OF BEING A MAGICIAN

The French-born Gerbert of Aurillac was Archbishop of Ravenna when with the support of Emperor Otto III he was elected to become pope. He chose the name Sylvester II to honour Pope Sylvester I (314–35), who had been pontiff in the era of the great Emperor Constantine I (324–37). He aimed to position himself and Otto as the Sylvester and Constantine of the 10th–11th century, leaders of a renewed Christian empire.

PREMATURE END TO PROMISING PARTNERSHIP
They worked closely together, seeking to consolidate papal–imperial authority and to eliminate abuses in the Church such as simony and the practice of some priests living with women as if married. In 1001 they were driven from Rome

Below: Stephen I, the first king of Hungary, reputedly received his crown from Sylvester. Some historians think this a legend; if it did happen, it must have been with the blessing of Otto.

FACT BOX
Original name Gerbert
Born c.945
Origin French
Date elected pope 2 April 999
Died 12 May 1003
Key fact The first French pope – and a brilliant scholar

by a revolt among the nobility and took refuge in Ravenna. Otto died of malaria the following year, bringing their highly promising cooperation to a premature end. Sylvester was allowed to return to Rome, but died himself not long afterwards.

THE MOST BRILLIANT MAN OF HIS TIME
Sylvester was a very great scholar and author who engaged with and promoted the study of mathematics and astronomy. He reintroduced to Europe the abacus and the armillary sphere (an astronomical instrument), which had been out of use there since the classical era of ancient Greece and Rome.

He was receptive to the learning of the Arabs of Al-Andalus (the Muslim state on the Spanish peninsula), elements of which were drawn from classical texts that had been translated into Arabic but otherwise lost to history. He learned of Hindu–Arabic numerals (the numerals with which we are familiar today) and used them on his abacus at a time when most Europeans were using Roman numerals – I, V, X, C and so on. He was also a gifted teacher, who before he became pope taught at the Cathedral School at Reims and was tutor successively to the young men who became emperors Otto II and Otto III.

MAGUS?
After his death in 1003, many legends circulated about Sylvester and his great learning. While a young man he had studied at the monastery of Santa Maria de Ripoli in Spain and people spread rumours that he had travelled to the Islamic cities of Cordoba and Sevilla.

Below: Sylvester II. The first French pope was so learned that legends sprang up alleging he had made devilish pacts to acquire specialist knowledge.

Right: Sylvester was open to the learning of Arab scholars and brought the armillary sphere (an instrument used in astronomy) back into use in Europe.

William of Malmesbury recounted the story that Sylvester stole an invaluable book of spells from its Islamic keeper and fled through the night; when he was pursued he hid by hanging beneath a wooden bridge over a river and because he was not touching water or land he could not be discovered. Afterwards he fled and reached a beach where he made a pact with the devil to carry him across the sea to safety.

CONTROLLED BY A FEMALE DEMON?

Other sources claimed that Sylvester carried about an artificial head, Meridiana, that gave him the answer "yes" or "no" to any questions he asked; Meridiana told him that he would be seized by the devil if he ever read Mass in Jerusalem. According to this tradition, Sylvester misunderstood the warning. He cancelled a planned trip to Jerusalem, but did not scent danger when he agreed to read Mass in the Church of Santa Croce in Gerusalemme ("The Holy Cross of Jerusalem") in Rome: he was dismembered by the devil who scraped out his eyes and threw them to demons to play with. He was also said to be in alliance with a female demon or was schooled directly by the devil. In one account he won the papacy by playing dice with the pope. Another legend has it that his bones (in a tomb in St John Lateran) rattle to signal when a pope is about to die.

Below: Otto III receives homage. He had a close relationship with Sylvester, who had been his tutor before he became emperor. Sadly, both died prematurely.

ANTICHRIST

At the end of the first millennium people were looking for signs that the Last Days and God's Final Judgement were imminent. A monastic reformer and Benedictine abbot named Adso of Montier-en-Der wrote a treatise on the Antichrist for Queen Gerbera (wife of Louis IV of France) that became widely popular in the Middle Ages. Adso was well connected and, aside from Gerbera, had friendly contact with Sylvester II before he became pope when he was Bishop Gerbert of Aurillac. In Adso's account, which takes the popular form of a saint's life, the Frankish empire would endure to the end of time, which would be ushered in by the Antichrist, born in the Jewish tribe of Dan in Babylon and filled with wickedness by the devil himself. He would travel to Jerusalem, rebuild the Temple and claim to be the Son of God – performing miracles, raising the dead and gaining followers among the world's rulers. For three and a half years he would persecute good Christians. Then in a final battle on the Mount of Olives, Christ (or the archangel Michael) would defeat the Antichrist in a spot opposite where Jesus ascended into heaven, and bring about a time of peace and repentance for the faithful followed by the Last Judgement. This book later circulated under various names, including those of Alcuin and St Augustine.

CONFLICT IN THE CHURCH

JOHN XVII TO DAMASUS II, 1003–48
THE TUSCULANI FAMILY AND THE FIGHT FOR THE PAPACY

John XVII (1003), John XVIII (1003–9) and Sergius IV (1009–12) were candidates elected by and dependent on the Roman Crescentii family. However the influence of this family – which had largely controlled the papacy in the second half of the 10th century – was waning, and Pope Benedict VIII (1012–24) was loyal to their great rivals the Tusculani.

Below: In this miniature, Henry receives his crown from Christ himself. In fact, he was crowned by Pope Benedict VIII in 1014.

EARLY CRUSADING ZEAL

Johns XVII and XVIII and Sergius IV achieved little of note. John XVIII is remembered as a pope who abdicated and ended his life in a monastery, while Sergius IV is linked to a papal bull calling for the forces of Islam to be driven from the Holy Land; he reputedly issued this in 1009 following the destruction of the Church of the Holy Sepulchre in Jerusalem by the Fatimid caliph al-Hakim bi-Amr Allah, but many historians consider it to be a forgery.

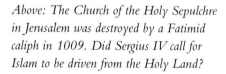

Above: The Church of the Holy Sepulchre in Jerusalem was destroyed by a Fatimid caliph in 1009. Did Sergius IV call for Islam to be driven from the Holy Land?

Benedict VIII was a layman who came to power by force. Initially he was challenged by an antipope, Gregory VI, and was driven from Rome, but he attained power with the backing of King Henry II of Germany and afterwards crowned Henry Holy Roman Emperor on 14 February 1014. But he proved an effective pope.

The two men held a synod at Pavia that passed clauses outlawing simony and lack of self-restraint among the clergy. Benedict also supported his friend Odilo, abbot of Cluny, in his monastic reforms. In Italy the pope built an alliance with Norman settlers against Muslim Saracens in Sardinia and then dealt with the increasing threat of Byzantine troops in southern Italy by travelling to Germany in 1020 to seek the Emperor's military backing.

While there, Benedict consecrated the Cathedral of Bamberg, visited the monastery of Fulda and received from Henry a charter confirming the gifts to the papacy of Charlemagne and Otto I. Then in 1022 the pope and the emperor imposed imperial authority on southern Italy.

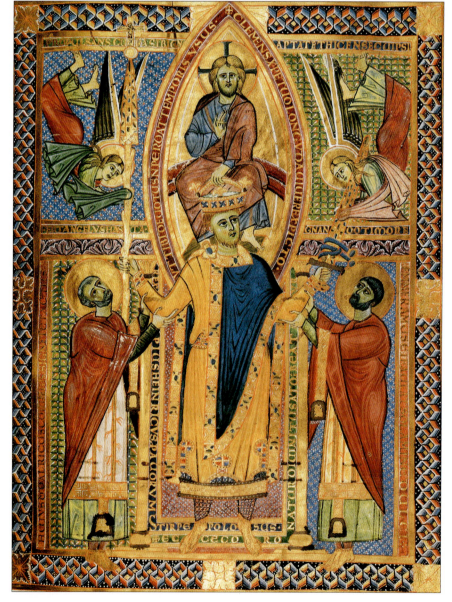

586

Right: Conrad II, crowned by Pope John XIX in 1027, founded the Salian dynasty that – through Conrad, Henry III, Henry IV and Henry V – ruled the Holy Roman Empire until 1125.

FIRST INDULGENCE

Benedict was succeeded by his brother Romanus, who took the name of Pope John XIX (1024–32). Following the death of Emperor Henry II in 1024 he was crowned Emperor Conrad II in a lavish ceremony at St Peter's at Easter 1027. King Canute of Denmark and England was in Conrad's party on this trip. John XIX is also remembered as the first pope to grant an indulgence (statement that a person's sins can be pardoned) in return for money.

FEAST OF IMMORALITY

In these years the papacy was a family affair – and an utterly scandalous one, at that. John XIX's nephew Theophylactus succeeded as Pope Benedict IX; according to some accounts, he was just 12 when he was elected. He had no qualifications as pope apart from the backing of a powerful family: he led a dissolute life and was said by the reforming

Below: Benedict VIII was a highly effective pope. He allied with the Normans against the Saracens in Italy and got imperial support to counter the Byzantines.

monk Petrus Damiani (1007–73) to have feasted on immorality. His reign came in the three parts: 1032–44, 1045 and 1047–8. In 1045 he was briefly replaced by Bishop John of Sabina who took the name Sylvester III, but then Benedict regained power by force. In 1048, either through greed or because he wanted to marry, he sold the papacy to his godfather John Gratian and abdicated. Gratian became Pope Gregory VI (1045–6).

THREE-WAY STRUGGLE

Benedict regretted his resignation and returned to seize the papal throne. At one point in 1046 all three figures – Benedict IX, Sylvester III and Gregory VI – were claiming to be the rightful pope. King Henry III of the Germans declared the first two deposed and stated that Gregory should resign because he had paid for the office of pope. Bishop Suidger of Bamberg was elected as Pope Clement II (1046–7) and on the same day Henry was crowned as Holy Roman Emperor.

Yet this was not the end of the scandals visited on the papacy by Benedict IX. On Clement's death in October 1047, Benedict grabbed power a third time; enraged, Henry III despatched German troops to Rome to remove Benedict. Bishop Poppo of Brixen was elected as Pope Damasus II. But he died after just 23 days (reigning 17 July–9 August); some accounts suggest that Damasus was poisoned by an associate of Benedict, but more reliable sources suggest he died after contracting malaria. He was succeeded by Pope Leo IX (1049–54).

> **SHORTEST PAPAL REIGNS**
>
> The rule of Damasus II, at 23 days, is only the seventh shortest papal reign. He comes after Urban VII (13 days, 15–27 September 1590); Boniface VI (16 days in April 896); Celestine IV (17 days, 25 October –10 November 1241); Theodore II (20 days in December 897); Sisinnius (21 days, 15 January–4 February 708); and Marcellus II (23 days, 9 April–1 May 1555). The shortest reign of the modern era – that of John Paul I (34 days, 26 August– 28 September 1978) is only the 11th shortest across the whole history of the papacy.

THE GREAT SCHISM OF THE TWO CHURCHES

The schism or split between Western and Eastern churches – subsequently known as the Roman Catholic Church and the Eastern Orthodox Church – began in a bitter exchange of excommunications in 1054 and has endured right into the 21st century.

On 16 July 1054 Cardinal Humbert of Silva-Candida dramatically laid a bull of excommunication against Patriarch Michael Cerularius of Constantinople on the high altar of the Cathedral of Hagia Sophia in Constantinople in the middle of the celebration of the Mass. Patriarch Cerularius responded by issuing his own excommunication of Cardinal Humbert and of the pope.

There was no way of knowing at the time that this split would endure, as it has, for more than 900 years, for it was one of many disagreements between the churches in the East and in the West. Over previous centuries there had been theological disputes and ecclesiastical arguments over matters including the pope's claim to have primacy over other bishops, the use by Western churches of unleavened bread in the Eucharist and the relative status of Rome and Constantinople – the city of Constantinople (modern Istanbul, Turkey) had been founded by Emperor Constantine in 330 as a new capital for the Roman Empire, but Rome claimed prime importance as the place in which saints Peter and Paul were martyred and buried and the historic home of the Church.

Many popes including Gregory I "the Great" (590–604) challenged the assumption by the Patriarch of Constantinople of the title "ecumenical patriarch" since they felt it undermined the primacy of the pope as the inheritor of the power of St Peter. Another major matter of dispute was over whether the Holy Spirit derived from God the Father or from God the Father and God the Son together; the Latin word *filioque* ("And from the Son") was widely included in the Creed in Western churches from at least the 8th century in a phrase specifying that the Holy Spirit "proceeds from the Father and the Son", but was strongly opposed in Eastern churches, where the accepted form of the Creed stated that the Holy Spirit proceeds "from the Father".

There had even been schisms before: for example, after Pope Felix III (483–92) excommunicated Patriarch Acacius of Constantinople in 484 a schism between the two churches lasted until 519, when Pope Hormisdas (514–23) and Patriarch John II of Constantinople agreed a reconciliation. A second schism arose in 863 when Patriarch Photius of Constantinople and Pope Nicholas I the Great (858–67) exchanged excommunications after Photius attacked the papal claim to supremacy and the Western churches' use of *filioque*. The schism ended in 867

Above: The Hagia Sophia in what is now Istanbul was the seat of the Patriarch of Constantinople, the counterpart of St Peter's in Rome.

Below: Iconoclasm – the breaking of sacred images – was a major issue. The Eastern Church often viewed images as idolatrous, but popes defended their use in worship. The Theodore Psalter of 1066 shows Nicephorus the Patriarch and the pope examining iconoclasts breaking an image.

Above: Gregory I the Great, third from the left in this carving from the south portal of Chartres Cathedral, emphasized the pre-eminent position of the pope above all other Christian leaders as the inheritor of the authority granted to Saint Peter.

on the death of Nicholas I, the assassination of Byzantine emperor Michael III and the seizing of power by Emperor Basil I who wanted to restore relations with Rome.

IMMEDIATE BACKGROUND TO THE 1054 SCHISM

Pope Leo IX (1049–54) strongly asserted the primacy of the pope over the whole Church. He also provoked the ecclesiastical authorities in Constantinople by intervening in Byzantine territories in southern Italy in an ill-fated campaign against the Normans there that ended with his being in captivity for several months. During this intervention he held a synod and appointed Cardinal Humbert Archbishop of Sicily. In 1053 Patriarch Michael Cerularius of Constantinople ordered the closing of all Latin churches in Constantinople.

In 1054 Leo wrote a forthright letter to the patriarch, in which he cited the Donation of Constantine – a forged document, then thought to be genuine, that was reputedly written in 315 or 317 by Emperor Constantine to give the pope, Sylvester I (314–35), and his successors imperial authority to govern Rome and the Western empire, power over the world's churches and primacy over the bishops of Constantinople, Antioch, Alexandria and Jerusalem. In his letter Leo claimed authority over Constantinople, which he decried as a source of heresy. Patriarch Michael replied with a letter in which he claimed the disputed title of ecumenical patriarch.

Leo sent Cardinal Humbert to Constantinople as his legate, but the patriarch refused to meet him – provoking the excommunication. In the time between Leo sending the legation and Cardinal Humbert making his dramatic gesture, Leo died in Rome; technically the excommunication, which relies on the authority of a reigning pope, was not valid.

MOVEMENTS TOWARDS RECONCILIATION

Over the ensuing centuries there were various attempts at reconciliation between the two churches, but none had a lasting effect. Pope Gregory X (1271–76) and Byzantine Emperor Michael VIII Palaeologus agreed a reunion at the Council of Lyon in 1274 but while the emperor supported the agreement the Eastern clergy would not accept it.

In 1369, also, Byzantine emperor John V Palaeologus submitted to the authority of Pope Urban V (1362–70) and the Latin Church during a visit to Rome, but the initiative came to nothing. Another reconciliation was agreed by Pope Eugenius IV (1431–47) and Byzantine Emperor John VIII Palaeologus at the Council of Ferrara in 1439 but again did not result in a reunion of the churches.

Modern efforts seem to be making genuine progress, however. In January 1964 Pope Paul VI (1963–78) met Ecumenical Patriarch Athenagoras I on the Mount of Olives in Jerusalem. The following year, on 7 December 1965, the two leaders issued a joint statement that withdrew the excommunications exchanged in 1054. The movement towards reconciliation was further strengthened when in 2013 Patriarch Bartholomew I of Constantinople attended Pope Francis's inauguration mass. This was the first time the ecumenical patriarch of Constantinople had attended a papal installation since 1054.

Below: Leo IX justified his position by referring to the "Donation of Constantine", the forged document in which Constantine allegedly gave the papacy imperial authority in the West.

LEO IX, 1049–54
POPE WHO LAUNCHED GREAT REFORM PROGRAMME

During the papacy of Leo IX (1049–54) the Western and Eastern churches came to the brink of the Great Schism or split that began just three months after his death and would last with only brief interruptions right through into the modern era.

BAREFOOT IN ROME
Leo IX was a great reforming pope. His driving desire was to attack and eliminate what he saw as the scourges of the church in the mid-11th century – clerical marriage, simony (the sale of spiritual benefits and church offices) and the practice of lay rulers having control of church appointments. He was himself elevated to the papacy by a lay ruler – Emperor Henry III – but he insisted that he would only accept the position if he were also freely elected by the people and clergy in Rome. He travelled to Rome and, arriving in pilgrim's clothing and barefooted, was acclaimed and elected by the people and crowned pope on 12 February 1049.

BAND OF REFORMERS
His companion on the journey to Rome was Hildebrand, a fellow reformer and a monk from Cluny, better known to history as Pope Gregory VII (1073–85). Leo brought to the centre of church affairs a small band of reformers, all gifted scholars and great administrators. In addition to Hildebrand, these included Humbert of Moyenmoutier, who became Cardinal Humbert of Silva-Candida (see box); Frederick of Lorraine, who became the reforming pope Stephen IX; and Hugh of Remiremont, a significant figure in the reigns of Leo's successors.

One unusual feature of Leo's papacy was that the pope travelled widely as part of his programme of reform, chairing more than ten councils in France, Germany, Sicily and Italy outside Rome to reinforce strictures against simony, the marriage of clergy and other offences. In his first year in office he held a celebrated synod in Rome at Easter 1049 that renewed the requirement of celibacy for priests, then presided in person over further synods and councils at Pavia, Reims in France and Mainz in Germany. He was back in Rome for another Easter synod in 1050. In these travels he maintained contact with local churchmen and gave physical expression to the pope's primacy as leader of Christ's Church.

Left: Leo IX flexed the muscles of the papacy in the clash with Constantinople. He believed the Donation of Constantine, which he cited, to be genuine.

Left: Leo came from Eguisheim – then in Upper Alsace and part of the Holy Roman Empire, now in the Haut-Rhin department in northeastern France. His statue stands in the village square. His father, Count Hugh, was a cousin of Emperor Conrad II.

FACT BOX
Original name Bruno of Egisheim
Born 21 June 1002
Origin German – from Alsace
Date elected pope 12 February 1049
Died 19 April 1054
Key fact Oversaw build-up to Great Schism of 1054

LEO IX

PRISONER OF THE NORMANS

But Leo's itinerant papacy was brought to a shuddering halt when he suffered a humiliating defeat at the hands of the Normans in the Battle of Civitate in southern Italy and was then held as their prisoner for nine months.

The Normans, initially useful allies for the papacy in combatting Byzantine Greeks and Muslim Saracens in southern Italy, had begin to pose a threat to the papal states. Leo had planned to attack them in alliance with Henry III and the Byzantines but when both dropped out was left to face the Norman army with an inadequate force bolstered by Swabian mercenaries. After the battle on 18 June 1053, the pope was captive at Beneveto until March 1054.

Above: Pope Leo IX is taken prisoner by the Normans. He is celebrated as a saint in the Roman Catholic Church. He died before the outcome of his clash with Patriarch Michael Cerularius was known.

THE GREAT SCHISM

Leo's assertion of the primacy of the pope as leader of the whole Church provoked conflict with the Eastern Church, worsened by his military intervention in the Byzantine territories of southern Italy – during which he held a synod and appointed Cardinal Humbert as Archbishop of Sicily.

Patriarch Michael Cerularius of Constantinople closed the Latin (that is, Western) churches in Constantinople and issued a condemnation of points of Western dogma. Leo wrote a forthright letter to Cerularius in 1054 citing the Donation of Constantine, then believed genuine, as showing that the pope should be honoured as spiritual and temporal leader of the empire.

In April 1054 he despatched to Constantinople a legatine mission under Cardinal Humbert of Silva Candida to negotiate over these differences. The pope died in Rome that same month, and did not live to see the dramatic result of the mission. For after unsatisfactory negotiations Humbert took matters into his own hands and placed a bull of excommunication against Patriarch Michael Cerularius on the altar of the Church of Hagia Sophia in Constanti- nople; in retaliation, the Patriarch excommunicated Humbert and his party. The split between Rome and Constantinople was made concrete.

Below: Leo's Easter Synod of 1050 was occupied with the controversial teaching of Berengara of Tours, who denied the doctrine of transubstantiation – according to which the bread and wine of the Mass become the body and blood of Christ.

CARDINAL HUMBERT – THE MAN WHO MADE THE EXCOMMUNICATION

Cardinal of Moyenmoutier was born in *c.*1000 in France. He joined the Benedictine monastery of Moyenmoutier in Lorraine aged 15 and rose to become its abbot. He worked with his friend Bruno of Toul to effect church reform and when Bruno became Pope, Leo IX was summoned to Rome. He was appointed Archbishop of Sicily and then Cardinal-Bishop of Silva-Candida – possibly the first Frenchman to be made a cardinal. After serving Leo IX on a legatine mission to Constantinople – during which he delivered the bull of excommunication of Patriarch Michael Cerularius of Constantinople that effected the Great Schism between Eastern and Western Churches – he returned to Rome and served under popes Victor II and Stephen IX, for whom he was librarian of the Roman Curia. He died in Rome on 5 May 1061.

591

CRUSADING POPES & THE REFORMATION

In almost 500 years from 1054 to 1534 the papacy unleashed the crusades – holy wars principally against Muslim power in the Middle East and heretic Christians in Europe; survived almost three-quarters of a century in exile from Rome during the Avignon papacy of 1309–77; and as patrons brought the Italian Renaissance in art, architecture and learning to its full flowering. The names of Urban II, the pope who launched the First Crusade, Gregory XI, the pope who returned the papacy to Rome in 1377, and papal patrons such as Sixtus IV or Julius II resound through history. Other popes such as Paul II and Alexander VI – notorious for corruption, overweening ambition or licentiousness – demeaned the institution of the papacy and drove the church on to the rocks of the Protestant Reformation.

In this period the papacy was a major patron and had the finest artists of the Italian Renaissance at its disposal. Michelangelo, Raphael and Donato Bramante discuss work on the Vatican and St Peter's Basilica with Pope Julius II, in this painting by Emile Jean Horace Vernet (1789–1863).

BIRTH OF THE CRUSADES

VICTOR II TO CLEMENT III, 1055–1191

The Great Schism of 1054 between Eastern and Western churches looms large in history. Its significance is greatly enhanced for historians by its longevity – the split has lasted with minor interruptions to the 21st century. Yet in the mid-11th century there was little to distinguish this from previous fallings out between Rome and Constantinople and so for the papacy in 1054–5 it was business as usual – which meant initially a continuation of the programme of reform begun by Emperor Henry III and popes Clement II and Damasus II and carried forward with great energy by Leo IX and his successor Victor II.

Political manoeuvrings included the negotiation of a crucial alliance between the pope and the Normans in southern Italy – to protect the independence of the papacy and the Church in the face of the claims of the Holy Roman Empire. One of the greatest reforming popes, Gregory VII, stood up defiantly against Holy Roman Emperor Henry IV in the celebrated "Investiture Controversy". Gregory's reign was transformational in the long term: his assertion of the pope's supremacy laid the groundwork for the development of the papal monarchy in the 12th and 13th centuries. Indeed he gave his name to the whole programme of "Gregorian Reform".

This period also saw the birth of the crusading era: Pope Urban II called the First Crusade, resulting in the establishment of a Christian kingdom of Jerusalem and associated territories in Outremer, and this was followed before 1191 by the less successful Second and Third Crusades. By the end of this period popes were committed to using crusades as an instrument not only of holy war against Muslims in the Holy Land but also of papal policy closer to home.

Left: Entrance of the pope and Emperor Frederick I Barbarossa into Rome. Popes Hadrian IV (1154–59), Alexander III (1159–81) and successors played out their own chapters in the long-running battle between papacy and imperial power.

VICTOR II TO ALEXANDER II, 1055–73
CHURCH REFORM UNDER LEO'S SUCCESSORS

The popes who succeeded Leo IX pressed on with the programme of church reform he had begun in association with Emperor Henry III. Victor II (1055–7) was Henry's choice to succeed Leo: a German noble, he had risen to become Bishop of Eichstatt and then the emperor's chief adviser. After his consecration he shared the top table with the emperor at a council in Florence that took further measures to prevent simony and clerical marriages and he afterwards presided at synods in Lyon and Toulouse in 1055–6. On Henry's death in 1056 Victor became guardian of the infant Henry IV and adviser to the regent, Empress Agnes.

ASSOCIATION OF REFORMERS

Stephen IX (1057–8) was one of the group of reforming churchmen associated with Leo. Known as Frederick of Lorraine before becoming pope, he was the brother of Duke Godfrey of Lorraine and Leo's cousin; he had served

Below: The use of fortified hilltop castles to dominate a region was key to the Normans' success across Europe. They built this castle at Caccamo, Sicily, in 1093.

Right: Norman lord Robert Guiscard, conqueror of southern Italy and Sicily, allied with Pope Nicholas II, who made him Duke of Apulia, Calabria and Sicily.

as papal legate to Constantinople and afterwards become abbot of the major Benedictine abbey of Monte Cassino, then been made cardinal priest by Victor II. He became pope in 2 August 1058 but was already dying and survived only eight months, until 29 March 1058.

In this brief period he zealously opposed simony and clerical marriage. He worked closely with cardinals and fellow reformers Peter Damian, Humbert of Silva-Candida and Hildebrand, a monk from Cluny and important associate of Leo IX who went on himself to become a great reforming pope, Gregory VII.

When he died, the Tusculani family moved to take the papacy back from the reformers, attempting through bribery to install their own candidate John Mincius, Cardinal Bishop of Velletri, as pope. John was in power as antipope Benedict X for nine months, but cardinals loyal to the reform movement elected Gerard of Lorraine, Bishop of

Florence, as pope in his place. The antipope took to his heels and Gerard was consecrated on 24 January 1059.

LATERAN SYNOD

As Pope Nicholas II he had a short but profoundly important papal reign. Among his first acts as pope was to attempt to eliminate bribery and aristocratic manoeuvring from papal elections. He issued a decree at an Easter synod at the Lateran on 13 April 1059 to the

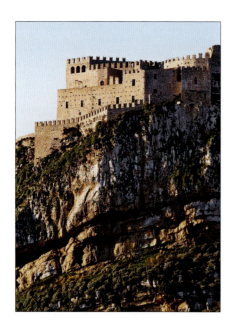

NORMANS IN ITALY

The Normans were originally Vikings (known as "Northmen" and subsequently Normans). After the unsuccessful Viking siege of Paris in 886 their chieftain Rollo or Robert settled in what is now western France and established the feudal Duchy of Normandy.

Rollo's descendants' use of heavy cavalry and fortified castles, together with natural daring, cunning and ruthlessness, made them a supremely effective military force and they spread out through Europe on missions of conquest. They arrived in southern Italy and Sicily in the early 11th century, initially fighting as mercenaries in the service of local Lombard princes against Muslim Arabs and Greek Byzantine troops.

The sons of Tancred de Hauteville established themselves as major landholders in the region – Pope Nicholas II's ally Robert Guiscard was Tancred's sixth son. Guiscard built a great military reputation: he was celebrated in chronicles, and by the poet Dante in *La Divina Commedia* ("The Divine Comedy") as one of the greatest of Christian warriors, with a place in the "Heaven of Mars".

Right: Choral miniature of Pope Alexander II celebrating Mass at the Abbey of Cassino, Italy.

effect that each new pope should initially be chosen by the seven cardinal bishops, then approved by the other cardinals. The clergy and people would then give their assent; the emperor would confirm the election, but his right to do so was not hereditary and was subject to confirmation by each new pope at the start of a new imperial reign.

The same synod also promoted several reforms, banning simony, clerical marriage and clerical concubinage (priests living with a woman as if married); gave papal protection to pilgrims and papal backing to the *Pax Dei* ("Peace of God") movement that sought to protect church property, priests, women, merchants and pilgrims from violence.

NORMAN ALLIANCE

Nicholas's other major engagement was to make an alliance with the Norman leader Robert Guiscard, whom he invested as Duke of Apulia, Calabria and Sicily at the Council of Melfi in August

Below: The papal reign of Alexander II saw William of Normandy invade England. Alexander instructed English clergy to back his claim to the throne of England.

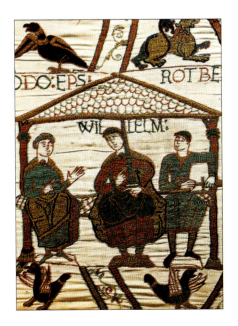

1059. In return Robert swore an oath of fealty to the pope and promised to help Nicholas regain lost papal territories and to maintain Nicholas in power. This new alliance provoked a clash with the German imperial court since it undermined the Emperor's claim to protect the pope and hold these parts of Italy himself. In 1060 German bishops voted that Nicholas's decrees were void and declared that he should be deposed.

The following year Nicholas died, and an antipope, Honorius II, was established in Basel with the support of the Empress Agnes. But in Italy Bishop Anselm of Lucca was elected and consecrated as Pope Alexander II with the backing of Roman troops and the support of Hildebrand. Honorius II marched on Rome but in the end lost the support of the imperial court and was deposed at a council in Mantua. Alexander held power.

NORMAN CONQUEST

As pope Alexander II pressed on with the campaign of reform, he also issued an early papal call for a crusade, against the Islamic Moors in Spain, and in 1066 gave papal blessing to Duke William of Normandy's invasion and conquest of England – issuing an edict to the English clergy that they should back William's claim to the throne.

BIRTH OF THE CRUSADES

GREGORY VII, 1073–85
THE GREAT REFORMER

Remembered as one of the most important popes of the medieval church, Gregory VII gave his papal name to the Gregorian Reform, the improvement programme begun by his close associate and mentor Leo IX (1049–54) aimed at preserving the morality of the clergy and the independence of the Church. In the "Investiture Controversy" – a dispute over the right to appoint abbots and bishops and invest them with the symbols of their office – he twice excommunicated Emperor Henry IV in a bold statement of the papacy's renewed authority.

"HOLY SATAN"
Hildebrand was the son of a Tuscan peasant, short and unprepossessing, with a paunch belly, a thick regional accent and poor verbal delivery. He was not a great theologian or scholar, but he had immense ability and character – he could impose himself on a group by strength of his single-minded purpose. The reforming monk Peter Damian called him a "holy Satan".

On becoming pope he took the name Gregory as tribute to Gregory I. He brought to the position a forthright conception of the authority of the pope and the primacy of the papacy over secular governments as well as archbishops, bishops and other members of the church hierarchy. In his view, the pope could judge all and was answerable only to God. All popes, as spiritual descendants of Peter the Apostle, were saints.

Above: Gregory VII. Before his election as pope he had been a major presence at the papal court through the reigns of Leo IX, Stephen IX, Nicholas II and Alexander II, pursuing their reform programme against simony, clerical marriage and concubinage.

He asserted the primacy of the pope over the kings of countries throughout Europe; many rulers – including William I of England – refused when Gregory demanded they swear an oath of fealty. His determination that he as pope rather than the ruling monarch should have authority over Investiture (appointment) of abbots and bishops brought conflict with Philip I of France and, more seriously and enduringly, with Emperor Henry IV.

CHALLENGE TO PAPAL AUTHORITY
In 1075 after Henry made appointments to the bishoprics of Milan, Fermo and Spoleto, Gregory wrote forcibly to Henry demanding that he undo the appointments and cease contact with five counsellors whom Gregory had earlier excommunicated. In January 1076 a synod in Worms declared that Gregory had forfeited his right to be pope; the bishops renounced their obedience to him and Henry declared Gregory deposed, calling on the Romans to choose a new pope.

Gregory responded by excommunicating and deposing Henry, and declaring Henry's subjects absolved of their oath of fealty. This bold act sent shock waves through the Christian world and had major consequences in Germany, where rebellious nobles met at Tribur to elect a new ruler. In the event they could not agree on a new king so decreed that Henry must promise obedience to the pope and that if he had not reconciled himself to Gregory by the first anniversary of his excommunication his throne would be considered vacant; they invited Gregory to Augsburg to determine the way forward.

PENANCE AT CANOSSA
Henry saw that he needed to act. He travelled in person to Italy and intercepted the pope at the Castle of

Below: Papal supremacy. An 18th-century engraving imagines the moment in which Henry pays homage to Gregory at Canossa.

FACT BOX
Original name Hildebrand
Born c.1025
Origin Tuscan
Date elected pope 22 April 1073
Died 25 May 1085
Key fact First pope to depose a crowned ruler

GREGORY VII

Above: The Castle of Canossa, outside which Henry waited to do penance, is now a ruin. In the 12th century it was one of Italy's most formidable fortresses.

Canossa, where he was staying with Countess Matilda of Tuscany en route to Augsburg. Gregory refused Henry entry to the castle for three full days – and the emperor, according to tradition, waited outside the whole time, barefoot in winter and wearing a penitent's hair shirt.

When he was finally admitted, Henry knelt before Gregory and begged forgiveness; Gregory absolved him and readmitted him to the Church.

INVESTITURE

The central matter in dispute between Henry and Gregory was the right to appoint or invest bishops or abbots. It had become established custom for kings and nobles to make the appointments in question, and church positions – since they often brought with them wealth and possession of land – were commonly sold. As part both of the church reform campaign against simony (the sale of church positions and spiritual benefits) and his own promotion of papal supremacy, Gregory claimed the right of investiture for the pope.

This proved to be nothing more than a brief truce; emperor and pope were soon at each other's throat once more. The rebels in Germany elected Rudolf of Rheinfelden as the new king on 15 March 1077, and he was crowned in May that year; then in 1078 Gregory issued a formal prohibition against lay investiture. In 1080 Gregory excommunicated Henry a second time and recognized Rudolf as his successor, but Rudolf was mortally wounded in the course of defeating Henry in a battle at the Elster river.

Henry hit back against Gregory, presiding as the synod of Brixen in south Tyrol that deposed Gregory a second time in June 1080, and nominated Archbishop Wilbert of Ravenna as the new pope. Henry gathered an army and marched on Rome, and took the city in March 1084. Wilbert was enthroned as antipope Clement III and crowned Henry emperor.

"LOVED RIGHTEOUSNESS"

Gregory, meanwhile, took refuge in Castel Sant'Angelo, from where he was rescued by his Norman ally Robert Guiscard and helped to escape into exile at Salerno. There he died, on 25 May 1085, defiant in what looked like defeat: tradition has it that on his deathbed he paraphrased words from Psalm 44, "I have loved righteousness and hated iniquity, therefore I die in exile." He was buried in the cathedral there.

Below: A kneeling Henry IV asks Matilda and Abbot Hugh of Cluny to intervene on his behalf in his dispute with Gregory VII.

BIRTH OF THE CRUSADES

VICTOR III AND URBAN II, 1086–99
BIRTH OF THE CRUSADING ERA

Popes Victor III and Urban II had to deal with the chaotic aftermath of the era of Gregory VII. After Victor's brief rule, conducted in the face of antipope Clement III, Urban occupied the papal throne for over a decade, a reign remembered most of all for his preaching a holy war to liberate Jerusalem – and the enduring effects of the cycle of crusades that he launched.

NORMAN POWER
Gregory's reign had ended in bloodshed and disorder on the streets of Rome. Threatened by the prospect of Henry IV ensconced in the Eternal City with a puppet pope in the form of antipope Clement III, Robert Guiscard and a formidable Norman army had marched on Rome. Henry fled back to Germany even before Guiscard arrived; the Normans then attacked and took the city – amid scenes of brutal violence in which Rome was badly damaged by fire. Then after Gregory fled, with Guiscard's help, to Salerno and shortly afterwards died there, Desiderius – abbot of Monte Cassino – was elected pope, against his will.

POPE VICTOR III
He did not last long. Driven from Rome by supporters of antipope Clement III, he returned to the Abbey of Monte Cassino, whose development he had made his life's work. Desiderius was an

Right: Before becoming pope, Urban was prior of the Abbey of Cluny in France. He consecrated the third rebuilding of the abbey.

Below: Various preachers took up Urban's crusading call. Peter the Hermit, a priest from the French city of Amiens, electrified his listeners, inspiring crowds of peasants to follow him in the People's Crusade – distinct from the main crusading groups of royals and noblemen.

600

VICTOR III AND URBAN II

MONTE CASSINO

The Abbey of Monte Cassino was founded on a hilltop near the town of Cassino around 80 miles (130km) southeast of Rome by St Benedict of Nursia in 529. It was the cradle of the Benedictine Order. The Lombards sacked the abbey in 581, and the monks fled to Rome for more than 100 years. The abbey was re-established by Abbot Petronax in 718, but sacked by the Saracens in 884. Rebuilt again, it was at the height of its glory under Desiderius (Pope Victor III), who while abbot in 1058–87 presided over manuscript illumination of high quality celebrated throughout the Western World. He also oversaw grand rebuilding and exquisite mosaic work by Byzantine artists. Pope Alexander II consecrated the abbey in 1071. The abbey was again sacked by Napoleon Bonaparte's army in 1799 and severely damaged by Allied bombers in World War II, rebuilt after the war and reconsecrated by Pope Paul VI in 1964.

Below: A 13th-century fresco in the Monastero of San Benedetto in Subiaco honours the founder of the Rule of St Benedict. Benedict's monks began at Subiaco before settling at Monte Cassino.

immensely able man, who had greatly extended the abbey's territory and vastly improved its library (see box) and abbey church, and had also negotiated the highly significant alliance between the papacy and the Normans.

In the second year of his reign he emerged from Monte Cassino in a flurry of activity: he excommunicated the antipope, sent an army to Tunis where it defeated the Saracens, and with the support of the seemingly invincible Norman army marched to Rome, drove Clement III to flight and was crowned. But then he returned hastily to his abbey, where he died on 16 September 1087.

URBAN AND THE FIRST CRUSADE

The continuing struggle with Clement III delayed the election of a successor but eventually a French cardinal, Odo of Châtillon-sur-marne, was elected Pope Urban II on 12 March 1088. For some years Urban had to tread carefully in the face of the emperor's hostility but was finally established in Rome by 1094. Like his predecessors he vigorously pursued the agenda of church reform and in a series of synods passed measures against simony and clerical marriage and to reinforce papal authority in the Investiture Controversy.

One of his concerns was to improve relations with Constantinople and in time restore unity to the church and he invited Byzantine Emperor Alexius I Comnenus to send delegates to the Council of Piacenza in 1095. There Urban and the delegates heard heart-rending tales of the threat to Christian holy places in the east from the Seljuk Turks. These accounts inspired Urban to call for a crusade, a holy war led by the flower of chivalric Europe to protect Christians and sacred sites in the East.

Urban made his dramatic call to arms a few months later, at a different church council, at Clermont in central France. He had originally intended to speak in the cathedral at Clermont, but after he issued a statement that he wished to

Above: Urban's sermon at Clermont unleashed a flood of violence and ushered in the crusading era that transformed relations between East and West.

speak on a matter of importance for all Christendom, the crowd that gathered was too large to fit in and he delivered his epochal sermon in a field outside the city.

On 27 November 1095, he called on the Christian warriors of the west to ride to the aid of the brothers in the east and liberate them from Turks and Arabs; he promised remission of sins (forgiveness) as a reward. According to one account of his sermon, by Robert the Monk, Urban personified the city of Jerusalem: "From you," he declared, "she begs help… Take on this journey for the remission of sins, in confidence of the undying glory of God's kingdom."

"GOD WILLS IT!"

At once a shout went up in the crowd: "God wills it! God wills it!" Adhemar, bishop of Le Puy, stepped forward and knelt before Urban, asking to be allowed to take part in a voyage to the east: Urban appointed him leader of the crusade. Many came forward in response to his example. Thus was launched the First Crusade. Its armies captured Jerusalem on 15 July 1099, a fortnight before Urban's death in Rome.

PASCHAL II AND GELASIUS II, 1099–1119
INVESTITURE CONTROVERSY RUMBLES ON

In the pontificates of Paschal II (1099–1118) and Gelasius II (1118–19) the main issue was the continuing dispute over whether the pope or secular rulers should have the right to appoint or invest abbots and bishops. In addition – following the success of the First Crusade launched by Urban II – there were manoeuvrings over whether Jerusalem and other territories captured in the Holy Land should be papal territory or a secular state.

GENTLE CHARACTER
The antipope Clement III had hung around throughout Urban's reign, but he died shortly after Paschal was elevated to the papacy. Paschal, a gentle and good-natured man but by no means a pushover, then had to face down no fewer than three further antipopes raised by King Henry IV and his supporters – Theodoric in 1100, Aleric in 1102 and Sylvester IV in 1105 – but none of them caused significant trouble. When Henry IV again refused to budge on the

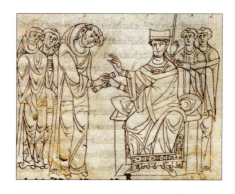

Above: Paschal delivers the papal bull establishing the religious order of the Knights Hospitaller to the order's founder, Gerard Thom, in 1113. The first knights in the order kept a hospital in Jerusalem to care for pilgrims.

investiture issue, Paschal excommunicated him and the emperor died in Liege on 7 August 1106.

PASCHAL FAILS TO HOLD A FIRM LINE
Paschal reached a settlement on investiture with Philip I of France and Henry I of England in 1107 but the matter continued to poison relations with the German crown. The new emperor, Henry V, was every bit as intransigent

> **KINGDOM OF JERUSALEM**
> Archbishop Daimbert of Pisa, papal legate on the First Crusade, tried to claim Jerusalem and associated lands captured in the First Crusade for the papacy. Daimbert was sent to Jerusalem in 1099 to replace the original papal legate, Adhemar of Le Puy, who had perished after contracting the plague in Antioch; he won for himself the position of Patriarch of Jerusalem. The first ruler of Jerusalem, the crusading knight Godfrey of Bouillon, was elected to power by the crusaders on 22 July 1099, but refused to be named king in the city that was the rightful possession of Jesus Christ and took the title of "Defender of the Holy Sepulchre". Daimbert won Godfrey's promise that on his death the territory would pass to the papacy. But when Godfrey unexpectedly died Daimbert was outmanoeuvred by Godfrey's brother Baldwin (formerly of Boulogne, now of Edessa) who seized power. Daimbert had no choice but to crown him King Baldwin I of Jerusalem on Christmas Day 1100.

as his father had been, but equally was determined to be crowned emperor by the pope in Rome.

After Pope Paschal issued a formal condemnation, Henry crossed the Alps with an army and a cadre of lawyers. Pope and emperor met at Sutri, near Rome, and thrashed out an agreement under which Henry renounced his right to investiture, Paschal promised to make the German church return to the emperor all lands and rights they held from the crown and Henry would have his longed-for coronation.

When this agreement was made public there was uproar among German bishops and a popular uprising in Rome.

Below: Pisa Cathedral in Italy. Gelasius II consecrated the cathedral in 1118; later in the century Pope Gregory VIII was buried there.

Above: The knights of the First Crusade capture Jerusalem in July 1099. According to the Gesta Francorum *chronicle, "there was so much killing that the blood came up to our ankles".*

Henry took flight and carried Paschal off as his prisoner; two months in captivity broke Paschal's resolve entirely and he gave in – restoring Henry's rights of investiture and agreeing to the coronation, which was performed in Rome on 13 April 1111.

This settlement, too, provoked a row. A papal council declared it invalid, the emperor was excommunicated by Archbishop Guido of Vienne (later Pope Callistus II) and then in 1112 Paschal tore up the agreement and in 1116 once again issued a condemnation of investiture by secular rulers. But he had lost his authority and the issue rumbled on through the pontificate of Gelasius II and into that of Callistus II (1119–24).

KNIGHTS HOSPITALLER

Amongst all these difficulties, on 15 February 1113, Paschal gave papal backing to the establishment of one of the greatest and most enduring of the chivalric orders, the Knights Hospitaller. The religious order of St John of Jerusalem had been founded under the Benedictine rule in Jerusalem in 1099, immediately after the First Crusade, by a knight or merchant named Gerard Thom – later "Blessed Gerard". Its members were initially guardians of a long-standing hospital for pilgrims to Jerusalem that had been founded in 600, destroyed by the Fatimids in 1010 and rebuilt by merchants from Amalfi and Salerno in 1023.

Paschal decreed that the members of the order – which his papal bull called the Hospitallers of St John of Jerusalem – should be subservient to the papacy not the King of Jerusalem. Its members soon began to offer armed escort to pilgrims and the order was established as a major military force by its second Grand Master, Raymond du Puy of Provence in the years 1120–60.

ALONE IN A COUNTRY FIELD

Gelasius II (1118–19) was never properly established as pope. He had to face an antipope, Gregory VIII, raised by Henry V; he was imprisoned and brutally beaten by Henry's supporter Censius Frangipani and was later forced by another Frangipani attack to flee Rome on horseback – after which he was found sitting alone in a country field, still wearing his papal vestments. Gelasius took to his heels and died in exile at the monastery of Cluny on 29 January 1119.

Below: The ruins of the Hospitallers' castle of Belvoir (known as the "Star of the Jordan") stand near the Sea of Galilee in northern Israel. The castle was built by Grand Master Gilbert of Assailly in the 12th century.

BIRTH OF THE CRUSADES

CALLISTUS II, 1119–24
WELL-CONNECTED ARISTOCRAT WHO TAMED EMPEROR HENRY V

Before his election as Pope Callistus II, Guido was well established as a church reformer and forthright opponent of lay investiture (the claim by lay rulers that they had the right to appoint abbots and bishops) – as Archbishop of Vienne, he had himself excommunicated Emperor Henry V over the issue. The major achievement of his pontificate was to bring the long-running investiture dispute between pope and emperor to a successful conclusion with the signing of the Concordat of Worms in 1122.

WELL CONNECTED
Guido was an aristocrat, born the fourth son of Count William I of Burgundy and related to the German, French, Danish and English royal houses. Nominated by Pope Gelasius as his successor, Guido was elected by the cardinals who had followed the pope into exile at Cluny and then crowned Callistus II at Vienne on 9 February 1119 – and afterwards unanimously approved by the cardinals in Rome.

Below: Callistus issued the bull Sicut Judaeis *("As the Jews") in 1120. Its aim was to protect the Jews in Europe, who in the era of crusading vigour were frequently being attacked and killed.*

Above: Louis VI of France watching the construction of a church. At the start of Callistus's reign, Louis and most of the French barons attended the church council called by the pope at Reims.

HENRY EXCOMMUNICATED
At once Callistus called a Church Council in Reims and sent an embassy to Henry V at Strasbourg: the emperor withdrew his support for the antipope Gregory VIII and agreed to meet Callistus at Mousson in France. But when Henry arrived at Mousson with a large army, Callistus – fearing he would be forced to make concessions – declined to meet, and then excommunicated Henry and the antipope Gregory.

Afterwards he travelled to Rome, where he was joyfully received. The antipope Gregory fled to Sutri, but with the support of a Norman army Callistus dragged the fugitive antipope from hiding and carried him back to Rome, where he was humiliated by being forced to ride through the streets mounted backwards on a camel. Afterwards Callistus imprisoned Gregory near Salerno and used the power of the

---

FACT BOX
Original name Guy/Guido of Burgundy
Born Unknown
Origin Burgundy
Date elected pope 2 February 1119
Died 14 December 1124
Key fact Settled Investiture controversy at Concordat of Worms

604

CALLISTUS II

> **FIRST LATERAN COUNCIL**
>
> Meeting on 18 March 1123 and attended by almost 300 bishops and 600 abbots from many parts of Europe, the First Lateran Council confirmed the Concordat of Worms, then renewed the indulgences granted to crusaders and passed decrees on disciplinary matters – including orders against simony and clerical concubinage (priests living with women as if married). It also passed decrees against those who broke the Truce of God (a general agreement under which churchmen and women, pilgrims and the vulnerable should be protected from violence on Sundays and festival days and at any time in sacred places such as churches, monasteries and cemeteries), those who stole from churches and people who forged church documents.

Above: Indulgences (guarantees that sins would be forgiven) granted to crusaders were renewed by the First Lateran Council in 1123.

Below: Emperor Henry V. Under the compromise of the Concordat of Worms he invested bishops and archbishops with secular authority; their spiritual authority came from the pope.

Normans to eliminate the threat of the Frangipani family, staunch supporters of Henry V and the imperial party.

CONCORDAT OF WORMS

Securely established in Rome, Callistus was happy to reopen negotiations on the investiture issue. These were started at Wurzburg in October 1121 and continued at Worms in September 1122. Callistus sent Cardinal Lambert of Ostia (the future Pope Honorius II) as his legate to Worms, and the papal party won a significant victory in the agreement that was finally signed off as the Concordat of Worms on 23 September 1122: the pope would invest bishops and archbishops with spiritual authority (he would invest them with ring and crosier, symbols of spiritual authority); the emperor would invest them with secular authority (he would invest them with a sceptre, a symbol of secular power). This was derived from a compromise arrangement that had been earlier established in Norman England.

In addition, the emperor guaranteed freedom of election for bishops and archbishops, while the pope granted such elections in Germany should be held in the emperor's presence and the emperor would have the right of arbitration where an election was disputed.

BASILICA OF SANTA MARIA IN COSMEDIN

Callistus called the First Lateran Council to confirm the Concordat of Worms. After this triumph, he worked to restore the territorial holdings of the papacy in Italy and to combat the power of nobles in the Campagna region. In Rome his aim was to restore peace after years of unrest dating back to Gregory VII. He worked on St Peter's and rebuilt the Basilica of Santa Maria in Cosmedin.

He settled a number of disputes in the French church, which he knew and understood so well, and ruled that his own See of Vienne should take primacy over that of Arles, ending an old dispute. He also despatched Gerard of Angouleme as papal legate to Brittany. He imposed his authority on King Henry I of England, forcing Henry under threat of excommunication to accept Thurstan as Archbishop of York.

In Germany he canonized Conrad of Constance, a 10th-century German bishop and ally of Otto I, in 1123, and sent Otto of Bamberg as his papal legate to the churches of Pomerania on the Baltic Sea, where Otto achieved many conversions and founded 11 churches.

BIRTH OF THE CRUSADES

HONORIUS II, 1124–30
SWORD-WIELDING THUGS OVERTURN A PAPAL CORONATION

Honorius II came to power amid uproar. Members of the powerful Frangipani family refused to accept the election of Cardinal Teobaldo Buccapeco, the favoured candidate of their rivals the Pierleoni family, as Celestine II: they burst into his coronation service with swords drawn and forcibly brought about the elevation to the papacy of their own candidate, Cardinal Lamberto of Ostia. Celestine II was injured in the struggle and resigned the papacy on the spot; he is usually counted as an antipope.

The conflict did not end there. There was infighting between the factions, but at length support for Celestine dwindled and Honorius was left the only viable candidate. At this point he resigned, but was unanimously re-elected and acclaimed pope, then consecrated on 21 December 1124.

CONCORDAT OF WORMS
Cardinal Lamberto, the new Pope Honorius II, was no mere puppet candidate but an established churchman who had been made cardinal bishop of Ostia by Pope Paschal II in 1117, and accompanied Pope Gelasius II to Cluny before playing a key role in the negotiations for the Concordat of Worms as Callistus II's envoy.

Above: St Norbert of Xanten by Peter Paul Rubens. Honorius gave approval in 1126 to Norbert's founding of the Premonstratensian order – or "White Canons".

Unlike his aristocratic predecessor, however, he was of peasant origin, having been born in a rural community near modern Imola in the Emilia-Romagna region of Italy. He had risen through the church hierarchy through application and a forceful character, as well as great natural ability – he deserves a great deal of credit for the success of the negotiations that brought about the Concordat of Worms.

GERMAN SUCCESSION
The death of Emperor Henry V on 23 May 1125 led to a power struggle for the succession. Henry, childless, nominated his nephew Frederick Hohenstaufen but a faction of German

---

FACT BOX
Original name Lamberto Scannabecchi
Born 9 February 1060
Origin Romagna
Date elected pope 21 December 1124
Died 13 February 1130
Key fact Backed Lothair of Supplinburg in German succession crisis

HONORIUS II

FRANGIPANI FAMILY

The Frangipani clan who brought about the election of Honorius II was a powerful Roman family, great rivals of the Pierleoni. Their name (meaning "breakers of bread") derives either from Christ's breaking of bread at the Last Supper, as commemorated in the Mass, or an occasion on which a Frangipani ancestor gave out bread during a severe famine. A noble member of the family, Censius, delivered a brutal beating to Pope Gelasius II, whom he grabbed by the throat, punched and kicked and sliced with his spurs. In the early 12th century the Frangipani – in alliance with another baronial family, the Annibaldi – transformed the Colosseum in Rome into a fortress.

Above: Honorius granted papal recognition to the Knights Templar, established by Hugues of Payens and Godfrey of Saint-Omer, at the Council of Troyes in 1129.

princes elected Lothair of Supplinburg, while Frederick's brother Conrad was also put forward for the succession.

Conrad marched over the Alps and was crowned King of Italy by Archbishop Anselm of Milan, but Honorius supported Lothair and backed German bishops in their excommunication of Conrad. In the end both Frederick and Conrad were forced to acknowledge Lothair as emperor.

ROGER II OF SICILY

Another succession struggle in Apulia brought Honorius into military conflict with Duke Roger II of Sicily. On the death of Duke William II of Apulia in July 1127, Roger landed from Sicily and claimed his cousin's lands, declaring that he had been nominated William's heir, but Honorius contested this, saying that William had left his territory to be part of the papal states.

Honorius built an alliance of local nobles and excommunicated Roger and even, on 30 December 1127, preached a crusade against him. In July 1128 Roger's troops and Honorius's army encountered one another on the banks of the river Bradano. Although there was no proper battle it was clear Roger had the victory: amid desertions by his own troops, Honorius secretly agreed to make Roger Duke of Apulia in return for his oath of fealty. The deal was made public the following month at Benevento.

Determined to impose his authority throughout the church, Honorius had significant conflicts with the abbots of Monte Cassino and Cluny. At Cluny he deposed the worldly Pons of Melgueil as abbot and invested the reformer Peter the Venerable in his place.

At Monte Cassino he took on the unruly abbot Oderisio di Sangro, an old enemy who reputedly made fun of Honorius's peasant origins when his back was turned: three times without success he summoned Oderisio to Rome, then finally deposed him in 1126.

TEMPLARS

In 1129 Honorius approved the establishment and rule of another major chivalric brotherhood, the Knights Templar. French knights Hugues of Payens and Godfrey of Saint-Omer had established the brotherhood to protect pilgrims in c.1120 and were given space by King Baldwin II of Jerusalem in the former al-Aqsa mosque on Temple Mount in Jerusalem – because this was then believed to be the site of the biblical Temple of Solomon, they took the name "Poor Knights of Christ and the Temple of Solomon". In 1126 Hugues of Payens came to Europe to seek backing and after drawing up a rule for the brotherhood with the help of Bernard of Clairvaux, received the Church's official blessing at the Council of Troyes in 1129.

Below: The Knights Templar kept Temple Church, near Fleet Street, London, as their headquarters. It was consecrated in 1185.

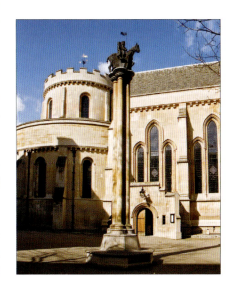

Below: Cluny Abbey. Honorius intervened in the dispute between Pons of Melgueil and Peter the Venerable at Cluny. Peter collected materials on Islam and defended the theologian Peter Abelard.

INNOCENT II TO LUCIUS II, 1130–45
PAPAL SCHISM AS RIVAL POPES DIVIDE EUROPE

The church under Innocent II (1130–43) endured a long and extremely difficult schism, with European monarchs split between backing Innocent and supporting his persistent rival, the antipope Anacletus II who ruled in direct opposition to Innocent in 1130–38.

Innocent – known before he became pope as Gregorio Papareschi, Cardinal-Deacon of St Angelo – was raised to the papacy by the power and manoeuvrings of the Frangipani clan in Rome. On the very night of his predecessor Honorius's death on 13 February 1130, the Frangipani family arranged for him to be elected by a minority of cardinals. But when they tried to present this as a *fait accompli*, the majority of cardinals – as well as many Roman nobles and people – declared it uncanonical and elected their own candidate, Papal Chancellor Cardinal Aimeric, as pope: he took the name Anacletus II.

Anacletus and his supporters – many of whom were associates of the rival Pierleoni clan – took control of the Lateran and St Peter's. Anacletus was consecrated at St Peter's while Innocent II received the same honour at a rival ceremony in the basilica of St Maria Novella. Pierleoni bribes won more and more of the city to Anacletus's side and in the end Innocent had to flee – creeping away to safety in two chartered galleys down the river Tiber.

"WELCOMED BY THE WORLD"

With the help of Bernard of Clairvaux and Norbert of Magdeburg, however, Innocent won the support of the monarchs of France, England and Germany to his cause – in Bernard's words, "expelled from the City, he was welcomed by the world." Anacletus allied himself with Roger II Duke of Apulia, whom he recognized as King of Sicily; he also had backing in Scotland, Aquitaine and the northern Italian cities.

In 1132–3 Innocent and Emperor Lothair invaded Italy and took control of all of Rome save the section occupied by Anacletus. Innocent crowned Lothair Holy Roman Emperor in the Lateran, but when Lothair returned to Germany the pope's support dwindled very quickly and he was forced to flee Rome to Pisa, where he summoned a council to condemn the antipope.

END TO THE SCHISM

Still the schism continued. Lothair invaded southern Italy in 1137 and imposed his authority – in the short term at least – on Roger II of Sicily but then, by now feeling his 71 years and keen to return home, he set off once more for Germany. He died on the way home in a peasant's hut in the Tyrol on 3 December 1137.

Above: Celestine II. In his early life he was a pupil of Peter Abelard. He backed the Knights Templar and Hospitaller, giving the latter control of a Jerusalem hospital.

PETER ABELARD

A great philosopher, theologian, poet and teacher, Peter Abelard provoked great opposition in the Church and his teachings were condemned by Pope Innocent II. Abelard was also celebrated for his involvement in one of history's most resonant and tragic love affairs – his doomed entanglement with his former pupil Heloise. The son of a knight from Brittany, he gave up his inheritance and the chance of a military career to become an itinerant scholar of philosophy and theology. As a teacher in Paris, he fell in love with his pupil Heloise and together they had a son, Astrolabe, and married secretly; but then they were forced by Heloise's family to separate and enter monastic life – Abelard was even castrated. Later he became abbot of the order of nuns Heloise had founded, the Paraclete, and drew up a rule for the nuns; the couple collected their amorous and religious correspondence. Abelard became a celebrated teacher at Mont-Saint-Genevieve near Paris, attracting pupils from all over Europe, and his wide-ranging revisions of traditional theology led to his condemnation.

Above: The remains of doomed lovers Abelard and Heloise were reburied side by side in the Père Lachaise Cemetery, Paris, in the 19th century.

Lothair's death was followed in January 1138 by that of Anacletus himself – and this more than anything brought the schism to a close. For although a replacement was elected in the form of antipope Victor IV, he was persuaded to resign by the formidable Bernard of Clairvaux just weeks later, on 29 May 1138. The Second Lateran Council in April 1139 ended the schism and excommunicated Roger of Sicily.

INNOCENT HUMBLED

But then Innocent, overconfident at these developments, almost threw it all away. After the resignation of Victor IV, Roger of Sicily had recognized Innocent as rightful pope, but Innocent refused to accept reconciliation and marched south to confront Roger in battle. On 22 July Innocent was captured at Galluccio with his cardinals and treasure. Three days later he was forced to recognize Roger as King of Sicily.

Innocent's reign was dominated by the long schism, but he did rebuild the ancient Roman basilica of Santa Maria in Trastevere, incorporating Ionic capitals taken from the ruins of either the Baths of Caracalla or the Ancient Roman Temple of Isis. During the restoration he demolished the recently completed tomb of his foe Anacletus II and replaced it with one for himself. He died in Rome on 24 September 1143.

CELESTINE II AND LUCIUS II

Before his death Innocent had quarrelled with Louis VII of France over Louis's rejection of Pierre de la Chatre as Archbishop of Bourges, and placed an interdict on the French kingdom. His successor Celestine II's brief reign (1143–4) was distinguished chiefly by the end of this difficulty – he lifted the interdict and absolved Louis, who accepted the papal candidate. Lucius II (1144–5) attempted to challenge Roger II of Sicily but was forced to accept a

Below: Innocent rebuilt the ancient Roman basilica of Santa Maria in Trastevere, and appears in this mosaic in the church at the far left.

Above: Lucius II. He backed the cause of the Empress Matilda in the English civil war known as the Anarchy. Closer to home he had to sign a humiliating truce with Roger of Sicily in 1144.

demeaning truce, and as a result of this humiliation faced an uprising in Rome led by the brother of antipope Anacletus II, Giordano Pierleoni, who declared a secular republic independent of the papacy. Lucius took arms against the rebels, but died after being hit by a heavy stone during the fighting.

EUGENIUS III, 1145–53
POPE WHO CALLED THE SECOND CRUSADE

Eugenius III was elected pope on the same day his predecessor Lucius II died, 15 February 1145, with Rome in turmoil as rebels against papal authority attempted to establish a secular republic. He was a surprising choice – a gentle, self-effacing man, a former monk of Clairvaux and pupil of the formidable Bernard of Clairvaux and subsequently abbot of the Cistercian monastery of Saints Vincent and Anastasius near Rome.

"A MERE RUSTIC"?
Bernard of Clairvaux was not impressed: he wrote to the Curia, "May God forgive you for what you have done!" and castigated them for picking "a mere rustic". However, the pope was later to be roundly praised for his character by Peter the Venerable, abbot of Cluny: "Never," wrote Peter, "have I found a truer friend,

> **FACT BOX**
> **Original name** Bernardo da Pisa
> **Born** not known
> **Origin** Pisa
> **Date elected pope** 15 February 1145
> **Died** 8 July 1153
> **Key fact** First Cistercian to become pope

a more sincere brother, a purer father." It is said that throughout his pontificate he wore a Cistercian monk's habit beneath his pontifical robes.

When Eugenius tried to make his way to St Peter's to be consecrated pope he found the route blocked by the secularist rebels. Within three days he had fled Rome and thereafter spent the majority of his eight-year pontificate (1145–53) in exile.

He set about raising a new crusade to the Holy Land. On Christmas Eve 1144 the Turkish general Imad ed-Din Zengi had captured the capital of the crusader state the County of Edessa

Above: Inspiration pours into Hildegard of Bingen from above. Mystic, composer, author and Benedictine abbess, she was at the height of her powers in Eugenius's reign. In October 2012 Pope Benedict XVI declared her a Doctor of the Church.

from its Christian garrison. The news – carried to Rome by Bishop Hugh of Jabala in Syria – stunned the pope and the Christian world.

OUTREMER AND TURKISH RESURGENCE
The First Crusade had resulted in the creation of four crusader states: the County of Edessa, which was based on the city of that name (now Urfa in Turkey) and founded by Baldwin of Boulogne in 1098; the Principality of Antioch, which was founded by Bohemond of Taranto in the same year; the Kingdom of Jerusalem, which was established in 1100 when Baldwin (formerly of Boulogne, now of Edessa) was crowned King of Jerusalem; and, finally, the County of Tripoli, which was formed by Raymond of Toulouse

Below: Louis VII of France receives Eugenius's blessing in the Basilica of St-Denis (Paris) prior to embarking on the Second Crusade. Eugenius called the crusade in 1145.

in 1102. The four states together tended to be known as Outremer, from the French for "overseas".

On 1 December 1145, after less than a year on the papal throne, Eugenius issued a papal bull entitled *Quantum praedecessores* calling on Louis VII of France and his people to wage a holy war against the Turks, offering remission (forgiveness) of sins for those who took up the cross of Christ. That same Christmas Louis announced his intention to lead a crusade and won the pope's enthusiastic blessing: Eugenius reissued his papal bull on 1 March 1146 and authorized his mentor Bernard of Clairvaux to preach the crusade throughout Europe.

"CRUSADERS BEYOND COUNTING"

Bernard preached a famous sermon on 31 March 1146 at Vézelay in central France, whipping the crowd into a frenzy of enthusiasm. He wrote to Eugenius: "I opened my mouth; I preached; and the crusaders have multiplied beyond counting." On Christmas Day 1146 his sermon before Conrad III of Germany reduced the king to tears:

Below: The Cistercian Abbey of Sénanque in Provence, France, was founded in 1148. Eugenius was the first Cistercian to become pope and reputedly wore his monk's habit beneath his papal robes at all times.

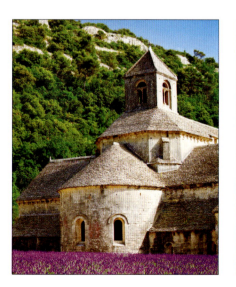

Right: Holy Roman Emperor Frederick I Barbarossa. Eugenius agreed an alliance with him under which the exiled papacy would regain Rome but died before it could be put into effect.

Conrad, Frederick of Swabia (later Emperor Frederick I Barbarossa) and many Germans also took the cross.

Less than a quarter of a century after his death, Bernard was canonized, on 18 January 1174, by Pope Alexander III – he became the first Cistercian saint. Then in 1830 he was declared a "Doctor of the Church" by Pope Pius VIII.

The crusade was a star-studded affair: in addition to Louis VII and Conrad III, Louis's wife Eleanor of Aquitaine (later, after her first marriage had been dissolved, Queen consort of England alongside King Henry II) and brother Robert I of Dreux also travelled along with William of Warennes, 3rd Earl of Surrey, William II, Count of Nevers and other notables. But it ended in humiliating failure, with a botched siege of Damascus, and badly damaged the reputation of Bernard of Clairvaux.

Eugenius was denounced as a "man of blood ... [and] oppressor of the innocent" by religious reformer Arnold of Brescia, a former associate of Peter Abelard and long-term enemy of Bernard of Clairvaux. After many travels, Arnold had allied himself with the secular radicals in Rome and preached

enthusiastically against the pope and cardinals. Eugenius excommunicated him in July 1148.

GERMAN ALLIANCE

Towards the end of his life Pope Eugenius formed an alliance with Emperor Frederick I Barbarossa that promised to restore Rome to the pope. In the Treaty of Constance (1153) Frederick also promised to oppose any attempts by the Byzantines to re-establish a foothold in Italy; in return, Eugenius would crown Frederick emperor in Rome. However Eugenius died, at Tivoli on 8 July 1153, before the emperor could honour his promise.

BERNARD OF CLAIRVAUX

Bernard of Clairvaux was a fervent and energetic French abbot, a major force behind the growth of the Cistercian order, an ally and key supporter of popes Innocent II and Eugenius III and a staunch opponent of what he saw as heresy. He did much to promote a personal Christian faith, with devotion to the Virgin Mary prominent. The son of Burgundian nobles, Bernard joined the Cistercian order aged 19 on the death of his mother Aleth of Montbard.

In 1115 he founded a new abbey in a clearing initially named Claire Vallée (later "Clairvaux"). In 1128 he helped formulate the rule of the chivalric order of the Knights Templar at the Council of Troyes, then in the 1130s was an indomitable force in support of the exiled Pope Innocent II. In 1146 he preached the Second Crusade with the blessing of Pope Eugenius III. Bernard died at the age of 63 on 20 August 1153. He was canonized in 1174.

BIRTH OF THE CRUSADES

HADRIAN IV, 1154–9
THE ONLY ENGLISH POPE

After the brief reign of Anastasius IV (1153–4), the extremely able Englishman Nicholas Breakspear came to the papal throne as Hadrian IV (1154–9). He built an important alliance with Emperor Frederick I and with his help finally eliminated that long-term enemy of the papacy, Arnold of Brescia.

FROM ST ALBANS TO ROME

Hadrian IV (1154–9) is the only English pope to date. Born Nicholas Breakspear, he grew up near St Albans in Hertfordshire, southeast England, and became a canon regular of St Rufus near Arles, southern France, eventually becoming abbot. Known as a strict disciplinarian, he was a very good speaker and also it is said, an extremely good-looking man. Eugenius III appointed him cardinal bishop of Albano in 1150 and then sent him as papal legate to Scandinavia in 1152, where he won such a great reputation that on his return to Rome he was elevated to the papacy.

Once in power he moved quickly against Arnold of Brescia, who remained a thorn in the side of the papacy. He ordered Arnold to leave Rome, then when Arnold ignored the order and

Above: England's only pope – to date. Hadrian IV was born Nicholas Breakspear in Abbots Langley, Hertfordshire. He acted swiftly and ruthlessly against Arnold of Brescia.

Cardinal Guido of Saint Pudenziana was killed by Arnold's followers, placed the city of Rome under an interdict. It was just before Palm Sunday 1155. All the churches of Rome would be closed over Easter, depriving Rome of the income generated by countless pilgrims. The people protested; Arnold and his cronies were expelled; the interdict was lifted. On Easter Sunday Pope Hadrian celebrated Mass at the Lateran.

ALLIANCE WITH FREDERICK

Hadrian next sent legates to Frederick I Barbarossa, who had crossed from Germany into Italy and been crowned King of the Lombards at Pavia. The legates asked for help in apprehending Arnold of Brescia. Frederick delivered the rebel into their hands: Arnold was hung, then his body was burned and his ashes flung into the Tiber.

Hadrian and Frederick then met at Campo Grosso near Sutri. The meeting was almost over before it began: Frederick refused the traditional act of respect, whereby the emperor led the pope's horse by the bridle and held his stirrup while the pope dismounted; in retaliation, Hadrian refused to give Frederick the traditional kiss of peace. A brief stand-off ended when Frederick gave way. They agreed an alliance that essentially reiterated the terms of the Treaty of Constance of 1153: Frederick would defend papal interests; the pope would excommunicate enemies of the empire; neither side would negotiate independently with the Byzantines, Sicily or the Senate of Rome; and Hadrian would crown Frederick Emperor in Rome.

Below: Byzantine Emperor Manuel Comnenus invaded Italy during Hadrian's reign, in 1155. Papal forces allied with the Byzantines against Norman Sicily.

> **FACT BOX**
> **Original name** Nicholas Breakspear
> **Born** c.1100
> **Origin** Abbots Langley, Hertfordshire
> **Date elected pope** 4 December 1154
> **Died** 1 September 1159
> **Key fact** Made alliance with Frederick I

> ### ANASTASIUS IV – PEACEMAKER
> Anastasius IV (1153–4) was already around 80 years old when he was elected pope on the death of Eugenius III. He lasted less than 18 months. He was a peacemaker. Roman-born and formerly the cardinal bishop of Sabina, he had served as Innocent II's vicar in Rome during that pope's long exile; he used his local experience to establish some much-needed amity in relations with the republicans. He spent freely on restoring the Lateran Palace and the Pantheon.

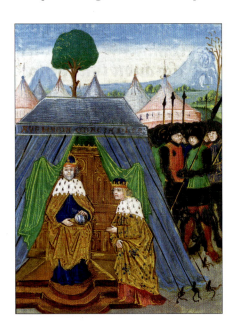

612

HADRIAN IV

Above: Frederick I rides into Rome. Hadrian IV crowned Frederick Holy Roman Emperor on 18 June 1155 in St Peter's Basilica.

CORONATION VIOLENCE

They acted quickly to forestall opposition from the Senate in Rome to the coronation. Hadrian performed it with little fanfare early in the morning of Saturday 18 June 1155. It was followed by brutal fighting between Frederick's German troops and the republicans that left 1,000 Romans dead and 600 captive; even so, parts of the city remained barricaded against the emperor, so Frederick and Hadrian – not prepared to mount a siege – retreated.

FRIENDS NO MORE

Relations between emperor and pope began to sour over the Normans of southern Italy. Hadrian hoped that Frederick would march south to humble King William I "the Bad of Sicily", who had succeeded Roger II in 1154, but Frederick returned to Germany. When Hadrian refused to recognize William as king and then excommunicated him, the Normans flexed their military muscles in the south. The treaty that brought peace, signed at Benevento in June 1156, granted William greatly increased territory and papal recognition of his kingship in return for swearing on oath to acknowledge the pope as feudal suzerain (overlord), and agreeing to pay an annual tribute.

Granting William territories that Frederick viewed as his own further aggravated the imperial-papal relationship, which came almost to breaking point after a letter from Hadrian, read aloud in the emperor's presence at the Diet of Besançon in 1157, appeared to suggest that the emperor held his lands from the pope as a feudal vassal from his lord. Historians disagree as to whether this was deliberate or a slip of the pen; in any case, Hadrian was forced to backtrack – or, at least, explain his meaning more carefully – but the row rumbled on; he even prepared to excommunicate Frederick, but died unexpectedly at Agnani on 1 September 1159 before he could implement his decision.

Below: Arnold of Brescia, a reforming canon who denounced Eugenius III as "an oppressor of the innocent", is viewed as a precursor of the Reformation. Hadrian oversaw his capture and execution. He had Arnold's ashes thrown into the Tiber to prevent his burial place from becoming celebrated.

> ### IRELAND GIVEN TO THE ENGLISH?
> When Pope Hadrian IV was in Benevento prior to agreeing the 1156 treaty with King William I of Sicily, he was visited by the English philosopher John of Salisbury, who was also the Archbishop of Canterbury's secretary. John records that Hadrian granted possession of Ireland to the English king, Henry II, by hereditary right. The so-called "Donation of Hadrian" was reputedly recorded in a papal bull, Laudabiliter, widely believed to be a forgery. Henry invaded Ireland in 1171.

BIRTH OF THE CRUSADES

ALEXANDER III TO CLEMENT III, 1159–91
STRUGGLES AGAINST FREDERICK I AND HIS SON HENRY VI

The poor relationship between the papacy and the Holy Roman Empire caused many difficulties in the reigns of the popes who succeeded Hadrian IV – from Alexander III (1159–81) to Clement III (1187–91).

The first, Alexander III, faced the challenge of a series of antipopes backed by Emperor Frederick I from the start of his reign. He fled to France, where in 1162–5 he won the recognition of Louis VII of France and Henry II of England. Whilst in Paris, he laid the foundation stone for one of the world's greatest and most evocative buildings, the Cathedral of Notre Dame.

LOMBARD LEAGUE

Alexander returned to Rome briefly in 1165, but the following year he was forced into exile again in Benevento; from his base there, he oversaw the formation of the Lombard League, an alliance of northern Italian cities against the emperor. This alliance won a major victory over Frederick at Legnano in 1176, paving the way for the Peace of Venice (1177) under which Frederick finally recognized Alexander as pope.

Above: Pope Lucius III. Lucius took a tough line with heretics in 1184 in Ad abolendam *("On Abolition").*

LAWYER-POPE

In 1179 Alexander presided over the Third Lateran Council (1179) that condemned heresies, promoted education and extended to all cardinals the right to elect popes (see box). Before becoming pope Alexander had been a professor of law at the University of Bologna. He was a shrewd and intelligent diplomat, the first of a series of lawyer-popes.

Lucius III (1181–5) also endured difficult relations with Frederick I and in 1185 refused to crown Henry VI as Frederick's designated successor. Lucius presided over the Synod of Verona in 1184 that imposed excommunication on all heretics and those who protected them.

Under Urban III (1185–7) conflict with the emperor became more open. In 1186 Frederick's son Henry VI married Constance, daughter and heir of Roger II of Sicily, at a stroke undoing the papacy's strategy of building an alliance with Norman Sicily against the empire. The marriage was performed in Milan by the Patriarch of Aquileia, who also afterwards crowned Henry King of Italy; outraged, Urban excommunicated the patriarch and the bishops who had assisted him.

When Urban also clashed with Frederick over elections to the archbishopric of Trier, Frederick sent Henry

Below: In the Battle of Hattin in July 1187 Salah al-Din Yusuf ibn Ayyub (Saladin) delivered a crushing blow to the army of the Kingdom of Jerusalem. In the same year Saladin took Jerusalem herself.

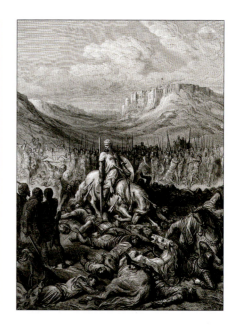

CARDINALS

The name "cardinal" comes from the Latin *cardo*, meaning "pivot", and was first applied to the priests serving the 28 titular churches of Rome, who were also attached to the papal basilicas – of St Peter's, St John Lateran, S Paolo fuori le mura and S Maria Maggiore; they were seen as pivots between the pope and the parishes of Rome. A synod of 769 established that only a cardinal could become pope and then in 1059 under Pope Nicholas II cardinals were granted the right to elect the pope. Under Urban II (1088–99) the cardinals were organized in a college and accepted as second only to the pope in three ranks – cardinal-priests, cardinal-deacons and cardinal-bishops. The right of election – in practice limited to cardinal-bishops – was extended to all cardinals in 1179 at the Third Lateran Council. A two-thirds majority was required. The right to wear a red hat would be granted to cardinals in 1245 by Pope Innocent IV. Only the pope can create a cardinal. Today cardinals are granted the title "Eminence" and are considered to be princes of the church. They are the pope's main counsellors.

614

Above: Alexander III presents a sword representing political power to Sebastiano Ziani Doge of Venice. Ziani hosted Alexander, Frederick I Barbarossa and William II of Sicily for the signing of the Treaty of Venice in 1177.

to invade the papal states. Urban prepared to excommunicate the emperor but died before he could carry it through.

WAR IN THE EAST

Also in Urban's reign, on 4 July 1187, the Christian knights of the Kingdom of Jerusalem suffered a devastating defeat at the hands of the Ayyubid general Salah al-Din Yusuf ibn Ayyub – or Saladin – that effectively wiped out the kingdom's military capability and made inevitable Saladin's capture of Jerusalem later that year. Urban reputedly died of grief on hearing the news.

In the course of his very brief reign (21 October to 17 December 1187) Gregory VIII preached a Third Crusade, issuing on 29 October 1187 the bull *Audita tremendi*. This was in response to the defeat at Hattin and before the news of Saladin's capture of Jerusalem came through.

Under Clement III (1187–91) crusading sermons won the support of Henry II of England, Philip II of France and Frederick I himself for the holy war. Frederick departed first, in May 1189, won a major victory over the Seljuk Turks but then died on 10 June 1190 crossing the river Saleph (now called the Göksu, in Turkey) and the German arm of the crusade petered out. Henry II died before he could honour his vow but Philip II and Henry's son Richard I did embark in July 1190. Richard inflicted a major defeat on the previously invincible Saladin at the Battle of Arsuf, but the crusade ended in a negotiated settlement that did not deliver possession of Jerusalem.

PEACE IN ROME

Clement was a Roman by birth and in his pontificate succeeded in making peace with Roman republicans, ending a decades-long dispute with the papacy. Under the agreement the citizens of Rome elected their own magistrates but the pope could nominate the governor of the city. At the end of his reign, conflict with the empire flared up again after Clement bestowed Sicily on Count Tancred of Lecce, in defiance of Henry VI who claimed the territory through his wife Constance. Henry led an army into Italy but Clement died before the issue could be resolved.

Below: An image from the 15th-century Le Miroir Historial *by Vincent de Beauvais shows Thomas a Becket meeting Alexander III in France. Becket was murdered in Canterbury in 1170 and canonized by Alexander in 1173.*

THE MENDICANT ORDERS

CELESTINE III TO BENEDICT XI, 1191–1304

The Fourth Lateran Council of November 1215 issued no fewer than 72 canons against heresy, while also clarifying crusading privileges, encouraging education and establishing standards for the clergy. The defence of the faith and fight against heresy was at the forefront of papal activity in these years, and lay behind successive popes' enthusiasm for crusading. The fight to maintain orthodoxy also inspired the foundation by Gregory IX of the papal inquisition to combat heresy and the support of Innocent III and Honorius III for the mendicant orders of the Dominicans and the Franciscans.

By the start of Innocent III's pontificate in 1198 the papacy had despatched two crusades to the Holy Land: the First Crusade, called by Urban II, had resulted in the capture of Jerusalem and establishment of the crusader territories known collectively as Outremer; the Second, called by Eugenius III after the capture by Turks of the capital of the crusader territory of the County of Edessa, had been a disastrous failure. Despite this disappointment, Innocent III was committed to the use of crusading as an instrument of papal policy, not only calling the Fourth Crusade but also launching a whole series of crusades within Europe – against Muslims, heretics and even fellow Christians who were opponents of papal policy. Innocent called crusades against Markward of Anweiler who was challenging papal policy in southern Italy and Sicily; against pagans in the Baltic region; against Cathar heretics in southern France; and against the Muslim Almohad caliphs in Spain. Then in 1213 he called a Fifth Crusade to the Holy Land. He reiterated the call at the Fourth Lateran Council in 1215 and when he died in Perugia the following year he was trying to promote the crusade.

Left: Innocent III grants approval of the regula prima *for the new Franciscan order to Francis and his first group of monks in 1210. The fresco by Giotto is in the Upper Church at Assisi.*

THE MENDICANT ORDERS

CELESTINE III, 1191–8
CROWNED THE TROUBLESOME EMPEROR HENRY VI

Like many of his predecessors, Celestine III endured a turbulent relationship with the Holy Roman Emperor – particularly difficult in his case because he was dealing with the ruthless and violent Henry VI. Remarkably, he prevailed upon Henry to support his call for a new crusade, although Henry did not travel on the crusade and it petered out to nothing. However the pope was successful in supporting the chivalric orders and confirmed the new order of the Teutonic Knights.

LONG CHURCH CAREER
The first member of the Orsini family of Rome to become pope, Giacinto Bobo-Orsini had been a cardinal for 47 years when he was elected to the papacy as Celestine III on 30 March 1191. He was in his 85th year. As a young man, he had been a student and friend of that remarkable monk and teacher Peter Abelard, and had then been a legate to Germany, Spain and Portugal.

Above: Celestine grants the Ospedale di Santa Maria della Scala of Siena its independence in 1442. The fresco commemorating the event was painted by Domenico di Bartolo.

Archbishop Thomas a Becket – King Henry II of England's obdurate opponent – held Bobo-Orsini to be his most trustworthy friend in the Roman Curia.

Despite this long ecclesiastical service, Giacinto was only a deacon and so was ordained a priest shortly after his election, on Holy Saturday 13 April 1191, and then was consecrated a bishop on Easter Day 14 April.

CORONATION
He inherited a pressing problem with Emperor Henry VI who had marched into Italy to enforce his claim to Sicily through his wife Constance (daughter and heir of Roger II of Sicily). This was despite the fact that Celestine's predecessor Clement III had granted Sicily to Constance's nephew Count Tancred of Lecce (an illegitimate son of Constance's brother Roger). In Rome on 15 April 1191 Celestine crowned Henry and Constance emperor and empress.

Pressing southwards to put Tancred in his place, Henry besieged Naples, but a revolt in Germany by Henry the Lion,

Below: England's great crusading king: Richard I. Henry VI's imprisonment of Richard caused an international incident and led to Henry's excommunication.

FACT BOX

Original name Giacinto Bobone
Born c.1106
Origin Rome
Date elected pope 30 March 1191
Died 8 January 1198
Key fact Confirmed military order of the Teutonic Knights

CELESTINE III

Above: A miniature from the Liber ad honorem Augusti *("Book in Honour of the Emperor") by Peter of Eboli shows Henry VI entering Rome and being crowned as emperor by Celestine.*

Duke of Saxony and Bavaria, forced him to lift the siege and march home. Henry later got his way: in 1194 after the death of Tancred left the crown of Sicily in the hands of a boy, William III, Henry met scant resistance as he surged into Palermo and was crowned King of Sicily on Christmas Day.

EXCOMMUNICATED

In the interim, Henry went far beyond accepted boundaries of behaviour in imprisoning King Richard I of England who had been captured by Duke Leopold of Austria (an enemy of the English king after a quarrel on the Third Crusade at Acre) as he was making his way home from the Third Crusade. Henry kept Richard in jail for months before ransoming him for the vast amount of 150,000 silver marks. In 1193

Right: Celestine III, seen here consecrating the first bishop of Viterbo, excommunicated both Henry VI and Alfonso IX of Leon.

Celestine excommunicated Henry for this unprecedented act in imprisoning a returning crusader and set about trying to enforce repayment of the ransom.

ENTHUSIASM FOR A CRUSADE

In 1195 Celestine called a new crusade. According to an account by English chronicler Ralph of Diceto, Clementine declared that the limited success of the most recent holy war should not prevent Christians from staying strong in their faith that God would "instruct their hands in battle"; he promised a plenary indulgence (full forgiveness of sins) "and afterwards eternal life".

Surprisingly Henry VI acted on this call. According to some sources, he wanted to win Celestine's favour so that the pope would crown Henry's son Frederick II. Whatever the reason, a German crusade departed – but without Henry – in spring 1197. The troops landed at Acre and occupied Beirut and Sidon but Henry VI did not join them because he died while campaigning in Sicily in 1197, aged 32, and the crusade faded away. This minor campaign is not given a crusade number by historians.

> ### LIBER CENSUUM
> The *Liber Censuum Romanae Ecclesiae* ("Census Book of the Roman Church") was compiled in 1192 by Cencius Camerarius, chamberlain to Celestine III (and later himself Pope Honorius III). It consisted of a list of the papacy's property revenues for the years 492–1192. Historians regard this as a key source of information on the economics of the Church and the papacy in the Middle Ages.

Celestine was forthright in his support of the crusading orders, notably the Knights Templar and the Hospitallers. Moreover in 1192 he approved the establishment of a new military order, the Teutonic Knights, who had established a brotherhood at Acre.

In his last years Celestine attempted to abdicate and to nominate Cardinal Giovanni di San Paolo as his successor but the cardinals would not permit this and Celestine continued as pope until his death in Rome on 8 January 1198 at the age of around 92.

THE MENDICANT ORDERS

INNOCENT III, 1198–1216
THE MOST POWERFUL POPE OF THE MIDDLE AGES

Innocent III was the most important pope of the Middle Ages, a major church reformer who presided over the Fourth Lateran Council of 1215, a notable legal mind who developed significant teachings on papal authority and expanded the pope's power in the papal states, a forthright defender of the faith who called both the Fourth and the Fifth Crusades as well as a series of holy wars against pagans, heretics and Muslims in Europe.

A nephew of Pope Clement III, Lothar of Segni (the future Innocent III) was from an aristocratic Roman family. As a young man he studied in Paris under Peter of Corbeil and Peter the Chanter, the leading theologians of the day, and alongside Englishman Stephen Langton, whom he later appointed Archbishop of Canterbury. Afterwards he studied law at the University of Bologna. He was intelligent, learned, serious-minded and a theologian of some merit. His theological tract *De miseria condicionis humane* ("On the Misery of the Human Condition") was widely popular.

MARKED BY THE HOLY SPIRIT

He was still relatively young, aged 37, when he was elected pope – on the very day that his predecessor, the 92-year-old Celestine III, died. Tradition has it that when he was elected three doves (symbols of the Holy Spirit) were flying around the room, and that the whitest of the three flew to the newly elected pope and landed alongside his right hand.

> **FACT BOX**
> **Original name** Lothar of Segni
> **Born** 1160/61
> **Origin** Campagna di Rome
> **Date elected pope** 8 January 1198
> **Died** 16 July 1216
> **Key fact** Called Fourth and Fifth crusades and holy war against Cathars in southern France

Innocent moved quickly to re-establish papal authority in Rome, building a military fort in the city, the Torre dei'Conti, and asserting his precedence over leading ministers. He also set out to safeguard and expand the papal states, taking advantage of the opportunity presented by the death in 1197 of Emperor Henry VI. He despatched papal legates to cities of central Italy, many of which declared loyalty to him.

SUN AND MOON

A letter he sent in 1198 to the rectors of these cities contained a striking image of papal authority: he likened secular princes to the Moon and the papacy to the Sun. Both are created and maintained by God: in the same way that the Moon reflects the light of the Sun, secular authorities draw their dignity and status from the authority of the pope.

In expanding and consolidating the papal states, Innocent established the pope as a major secular prince in central Italy. Following the death of Henry VI his widow Constance ruled Sicily on behalf of her son and Henry's heir, the

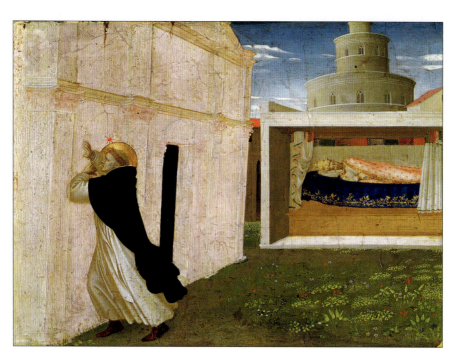

Below: Innocent had a dream in which he saw two men – said to be Francis of Assisi and Dominic Guzman – holding up the Basilica of St John Lateran in Rome. He understood the Franciscan and Dominican orders would support the Church.

Above: Otto of Brunswick is expelled. Innocent withdrew his backing of Otto in the imperial succession dispute and plumped for the eventual emperor, Frederick II.

620

INNOCENT III

Above: This fresco of Innocent III is in the Lower Church of St Benedict's Monastery in Subiaco. Innocent donated funds to the monastery in 1203.

> **POPE IN PURGATORY?**
> Flemish mystic nun (later saint) Lurgadis – or Lutgarda – reportedly had a vision of Innocent III in purgatory on the very day of Innocent's death. He told her he was in purgatory rather than in heaven because of three faults, which he did not specify. He begged her to help him and said he had only won the opportunity to speak to her through the intervention of the Blessed Virgin Mary. He said "It is terrible… and will carry on for centuries if you do not come to my aid… help me!"

four-year-old Frederick II. Constance died in 1198 but before her death appointed Innocent Frederick's guardian. Innocent regained papal rights in Sicily that had been lost to William I of Sicily in the time of Pope Hadrian IV.

Two candidates disputed the succession – Philip of Swabia and Otto of Brunswick. Innocent backed Otto's claim but after Philip was murdered in a feud, Otto backtracked on an earlier agreement with Innocent and attempted to retake former imperial territory in Italy and Sicily. Innocent excommunicated him and gave his full backing to Frederick.

In 1214 Otto's claim evaporated after he and his ally King John of England were defeated in the Battle of Bouvines against King Philip II Augustus of France. Frederick was now the sole candidate. Innocent took advantage of this dispute to make a statement of the pope's right to judge candidates in a disputed imperial election, a statement that became part of canon law.

CRUSADES

The Third Crusade had not resulted in the reconquest of Jerusalem, and in August 1198 Innocent issued a new call to arms, promising a papal indulgence (for the forgiveness of sins) and imposing a tax on clergy of one-fortieth of their annual revenue for a year to help raise funds. But the resulting Fourth Crusade (1202–4) spiralled out of Innocent's control, diverting first to Zara in Hungary (modern Zadar in Croatia) and then to Constantinople. The city was sacked amid degrading scenes of murder, rape and looting in April 1204.

But this did not deter Innocent from crusading. He launched a whole series of crusades within Europe – against opponents of papal policy as well as against heretic Christians and Muslims. In the course of the holy war of 1212 against the Muslim Almohad caliphs in Spain, crusader knights fought alongside the armies of Sancho VII of Navarre, Peter II of Aragon and Alfonso VIII of Castile to win victory over the Muslims at the Battle of Las Navas de Tolosa. Then in 1213 he called a Fifth Crusade.

REFORM

Innocent reformed the curia and the papal judicial system, centralizing church institutions and reinforcing the pope's supremacy within the church hierarchy: he reiterated the subordination of bishops to the pope, and insisted only the pope could agree movements, resignations and removals of bishops. He encouraged the Franciscans and Dominicans. Among the measures of the Fourth Lateran Council of 1215 was one defining the Real Presence in the Mass, another requiring Christians to confess their sins and receive Holy Communion at least once a year and another banning clerics from taking part in trial by ordeal. Less than a year after the close of the Council, Innocent died suddenly, aged just 55, from malaria in Perugia on 16 July 1216.

Below: Francis of Assisi. Innocent gave his backing to Francis's new monastic order – which became the Franciscans – in an audience on 16 April 1210.

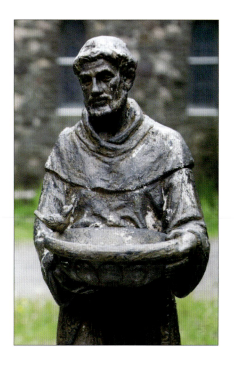

CRUSADES AGAINST ENEMIES OF THE PAPACY

For five centuries, beginning in 1096 and lasting until the end of the 16th century, popes sent Christian armies to battle in crusades (holy wars) against Muslims, pagans and heretic Christians.

Historians number nine crusades, beginning with the First Crusade (1096–9) that resulted in the capture of Jerusalem from Fatimid Muslims, and ending with the Ninth Crusade (1271–2) in which the future King Edward I of England made a few territorial gains. These were principally fought against Muslim power in the region of the Holy Land and in Egypt.

In addition to the nine numbered crusades, there were many other smaller crusades in the years 1096–1271 and several other campaigns promoted as crusades after 1271 – at least until the Battle of Lepanto (1571), a victory for the Christian "Holy League" (of the papal states, Spain, Venice, Genoa, the Duchy of Savoy and the Knights of Malta) over the Ottoman Empire's fleet; the triumph was attributed to the Blessed Virgin Mary and celebrated by Pope Pius V (1566–72) with the declaration of the Feast of Our Lady of Victory.

NINE CRUSADES

When he called the First Crusade at Clermont in France in November 1095, Pope Urban II likened the possession of Jerusalem by Seljuk Turks to the taking "into slavery of the holy city of Christ". (The Seljuk Turks held the city at this time, but in 1098, while the crusaders were en route from Europe, were ousted by Fatimid Muslims so that when the crusaders took Jerusalem it was from the Fatimids.) He personified Jerusalem and declared "from you, she asks for help!" His sermon produced a wildly enthusiastic response – the crowd chanted "God wills it!" "God wills it!" and surged forward to volunteer.

Two expeditions embarked – one popular, known as the People's Crusade; and one noble, the Princes' Crusade, consisting of no fewer than five armies led by (among others) Godfrey, Lord of Bouillon and Raymond, Count of Toulouse. The survivors of these groups joined forces in Constantinople and eventually after many trials, battles and sieges captured Jerusalem.

In the wake of the crusade, four Christian states were established in Palestine and Syria, in what came to be known as Outremer (from the French for "overseas"): the County of Edessa, the Principality of Antioch, the Kingdom of Jerusalem and the County of Tripoli. This territory survived in various forms until 1291 and was the inspiration for a whole series of crusading expeditions to the Holy Land and to North Africa.

SECOND TO NINTH CRUSADES

The Second Crusade (1147–9), called by Pope Eugenius III (1145–53) following the capture of Edessa by Muslim forces, ended with a humiliating failure to capture Damascus. The Third Crusade (1189–92) was called by Pope Gregory VIII (pope 21 October to 17 December 1187) after the army of the Kingdom of Jerusalem suffered a heavy defeat in the Battle of the Horns of Hattin that led to Muslim general Saladin's subsequent capture of Jerusalem. It ended in a negotiated settlement that did not deliver the hoped-for retaking of Jerusalem.

The Fourth Crusade (1202–4) was called by Pope Innocent III (1198–1216) with the intention of assaulting the Holy Land by way of Egypt, but the city of Venice – which provided the crusaders' fleet – diverted the campaign against its enemies in the Christian city of Zara and the campaign afterwards degenerated into the sacking of Constantinople. The Fifth Crusade (1217–21) attacked Muslim power bases in Egypt but achieved little; however, the Sixth Crusade (1228–9) – led by Holy Roman Emperor Frederick II after he had been excommunicated by Pope Gregory IX (1227–41) following a quarrel – succeeded, through diplomacy and

Left: Pope Urban II preaching the First Crusade to Philip I and assembled knights, noblemen and cardinals in France, 1095.

Right: Gregory IX quarrelled with, and indeed excommunicated, Emperor Frederick II at the time of the Sixth Crusade.

not through military campaigning, in regaining possession of Jerusalem, Nazareth and Bethlehem.

Jerusalem fell to the Khwarazmian Turks in 1244, and King Louis IX of France led the Seventh Crusade (1248–54) in response: another attack on Egypt and another desperate humiliation in which Louis was captured and ransomed at vast expense. Louis then led the Eighth Crusade in 1270: embarking for Syria, it diverted to attack Tunis in North Africa and there Louis died either of dysentery or bubonic plague; the crusade petered out. The Ninth Crusade (1271–2) led by Prince Edward of England (the future King Edward I) achieved very little.

CRUSADE INDULGENCES

In calling the First Crusade, Pope Urban II promised those who took part a plenary indulgence that freed them from all temporal punishment for their sins. In the medieval church an individual who had sinned could gain God's forgiveness through genuine repentance and confession but still faced a temporal punishment for the sins; the tradition had developed by which the Church could offer a partial indulgence (waiving part of the punishment) to those who gave money, supported the poor through alms giving or performed a required amount of penance, but Urban's speech now offered a plenary or full indulgence. He said, "Take on this journey for the remission of sins, in confidence of the undying glory of God's kingdom."

In the ensuing centuries, many popes called wars that offered full crusade indulgences for those who took part in a holy war, and a case can be made that all these wars should be counted as crusades. They include campaigns against Muslims in Europe: in the long struggle against Islamic power in the Iberian Peninsula, the Reconquista – which lasted from the arrival in Spain of Muslim Arabs and Berbers in the late 8th century until 1492, when the armies of Ferdinand and Isabella of Aragon and Castile conquered the city of Granada, the last territory in the peninsula held by Muslims – a succession of campaigns were declared crusades.

They include wars against Christians viewed as heretics – Pope Innocent III (1198–1216) called a crusade against the Cathars or Albigensians of southern France and no fewer than five crusades were launched in 1430–2 in Bohemia against the followers of university lecturer and preacher Jan Hus; Pope Sixtus V (1585–90) offered crusading privileges to the sailors of the Spanish Armada of 1588 – since he viewed the war of Roman Catholic Spain against Protestant England as a crusade.

CRUSADES AGAINST PAGANS

Others were called against pagans in northern Europe – in 1147 Eugenius III (1145–53) offered full crusade indulgences to those fighting against the pagan Wends in the Baltic region. Crusades were also called to further papal interests closer to home – for example in 1127 Pope Honorius II (1124–30) called a crusade against King Roger II of Sicily and in 1199 Pope Innocent III (1216–27) declared a crusade against Markward of Anweiler in Sicily.

Right: The city of Carcassonne in southern France was besieged in 1209, early in the Albigensian Crusade against the Cathars.

HONORIUS III, 1216–27
CRUSADING POPE WHO LAUNCHED THE MENDICANT ORDERS

Following the death of Innocent III at Perugia on 16 July 1216 a new pope was quickly elected. Cencio Savelli was consecrated Pope Honorius III in Perugia on 24 July and crowned in Rome on 31 August. Before becoming pope, Savelli had served under Clement III and Celestine III as treasurer of the Roman Church and had compiled in 1192 the *Liber Censuum Romanae Ecclesiae* ("Census Book of the Roman Church"), an eight-volume record of ecclesiastical revenues since the year 492. Historians rely on this as a key resource for the economics of the Church in the Middle Ages. Savelli had served as tutor to the future Holy Roman Emperor Frederick II. He was already elderly and rather weak when elected pope.

CRUSADING FERVOUR
Pope Honorius set about bringing to fruition his predecessor Innocent III's plans for a new crusade to the Holy Land. The first armies, under Leopold VI of Austria and Andrew II of Hungary, departed for Acre on schedule but their campaign achieved little beyond the capture of a few sacred relics, and the main contingent of crusaders diverted to attack the territories of the Muslim Ayyubids – descendants of Saladin – in Egypt in 1218. Meanwhile Honorius was frustrated by the refusal of his former pupil, Frederick, to honour his promise to go on crusade to the Holy Land.

> **FACT BOX**
> **Original name** Cencio Savelli
> **Born** 1148
> **Origin** Roman
> **Date elected pope** 18 July 1216
> **Died** 18 March 1227
> **Key fact** Launched Fifth Crusade; approved Dominicans and Franciscans

The campaign in Egypt got off to a promising start, and at one point Ayyubid sultan al-Kamil offered the crusaders possession of Jerusalem, its associated kingdom and the Relic of the True Cross (on which Christ was said to have been crucified), which had been in Ayyubid hands since Saladin took it in the Battle of the Horns of Hattin (1187). But the crusaders did not accept the offer because the papal legate Pelagius determined Jerusalem could not be bartered over. In the end the campaign petered out in abject failure.

Honorius crowned his former pupil Holy Roman Emperor in Rome in 1220. He continued to put pressure on Frederick to lead a crusade, and in 1223 reached an agreement under which the

Below: Francis was known for his preaching and for demonstrating his faith in the way he lived. He reputedly said "Preach the gospel at all times; when necessary, use words."

Left: Francis of Assisi preaches a sermon to Honorius III. Honorius gave formal approval to the Franciscans' code in 1223. This magnificent Giotto fresco can be seen in the Upper Church of the Papal Basilica of St Francis of Assisi.

Above: Honorius gives his blessing to Dominic Guzman and his newly formed Dominican monastic order, in 1216.

widowed Frederick took the 11-year-old heir to the crown of Jerusalem, Isabella, as his new wife and promised to lead a crusade – as King of Jerusalem – in 1225. Yet still Frederick delayed, and Honorius III died in Rome in March 1227 before he could see his plans bear fruit. Frederick did finally embark for the Holy Land in June 1228 and in the course of the Sixth Crusade regained control of Jerusalem.

COMBATTING ENEMIES

Honorius also carried on his predecessor's crusading work in fighting Muslim Almohads in Spain and heretic Cathars (later called Albigensians) in southern France. In Spain Honorius called a crusade in 1218-19 to build on the success of Innocent III's 1212 crusade. In southern France a military campaign against the Cathars had been under way since 1209, but after initial successes had suffered setbacks at the hands of resurgent rebels; Honorius persuaded the French king, Louis VIII to lead a new campaign in 1226 that recaptured many towns and castles including Avignon.

THE MENDICANT ORDERS

Honorius III engaged a new force in the fight against heresy with his approval of the Order of Preachers (later called the Dominicans), founded by Spanish priest Dominic Guzman to preach the Gospel and combat heretical beliefs. Honorius gave members of the new order, which was officially approved on 22 December 1216 under papal bull *Religiosam vitam*, a place of residence in Rome, first at the convent of San Sisto Vecchio and then at the Basilica of Santa Sabina.

On 29 November 1223 another bull, *Solet annuere*, gave papal approval to the rule of the Franciscans. Francis of Assisi had established the Order of the Friars Minor (Franciscans) and drawn up a primitive code for his early members in 1209; this won the approval of Innocent III. Later, he appealed to Honorius for help and the pope appointed Cardinal Ugolino (later Pope Gregory IX) protector of the order. Francis then drew up a fuller code, which Honorius approved in 1223. Three years later Honorius approved the Carmelite Order under his bull *Ut vivendi normam* of 30 January 1226. The Dominicans, Franciscans and Carmelites were the first of a new breed of monastic organization that did not own property and relied on charity for their survival: the mendicant orders.

AS AN AUTHOR

Renowned as the compiler of the *Liber Censuum Romanae Ecclesiae*, Honorius is also remembered as the author of biographies of popes Celestine III and Gregory VII, 34 sermons and a volume of church ceremonial and ritual, the *Ordo Romanus*. He is also associated with a *grimoire*, or magic textbook.

CATHARS

The Cathars – or Albigensians, from the French town of Albi, which was mistakenly identified as their base – were dualists, who believed in two gods – one higher and purely good, and a lesser second divinity who was evil and had created the material world; they held that the human soul was pure and good but trapped in the material creation, and that humans should seek salvation through a life of chastity, poverty and asceticism. The crusade against the Cathars or Albigensians, launched by Innocent III in 1209, largely ended with a peace treaty in 1229 but the Church's fight against the Cathars' beliefs was carried on by the Dominican Inquisition, established in 1233. Many Cathars fled to Italy and were not heard from after the end of the 14th century. In France, following further intermittent Cathar rebellions, a royal army besieged the Castle of Montségur – said to be the Cathars' final stronghold in 1243–4. Around 220 Cathars were burned at the stake, but a handful reputedly escaped with a treasure that, according to esoteric tradition, had been handed down by the Knights Templar – and may have been the Holy Grail itself.

GREGORY IX, 1227–41
POPE WHO FOUNDED THE PAPAL INQUISITION

Gregory IX was a stern and profoundly spiritual man, friend both of Dominic Guzman and Francis of Assisi and adviser to Clare of Assisi, who founded the Poor Clares. Already over 80 years old on his election to the papacy, he had a harsh side and could be swift to anger, finding it difficult to be patient with those who opposed him. He founded the papal inquisition to fight heresy, but is also remembered for promulgating the *Decretals* in 1234, used by the Church as a legal codebook until after 1918.

STUDENT IN PARIS
Before becoming pope, Ugo di Segni was a student of theology at the University of Paris and had a long career as a highly valued diplomat under his uncle Pope Innocent III and Pope Honorius III. In these years he was on good terms with the young Emperor Frederick II. But after his enthronement as Gregory IX, he quickly fell out with Frederick, whose failure to depart on crusade as promised had already enraged Honorius. Just three days into his reign he ordered Frederick to embark for the Holy Land.

Frederick had taken the cross in 1215 in response to Innocent's call to arms of 1213 and then renewed his vows in 1220 after Honorius III crowned him Holy Roman Emperor. He had repeatedly been on the verge of embarking on the Fifth Crusade, and sent an advance party of his force in 1221, but he himself had not departed – and his absence was a major factor in the abject failure of that crusade in Egypt. He finally departed for the Holy Land in 1227 but then an outbreak of plague on his fleet forced him to turn back to Brindisi.

FREDERICK AND THE SIXTH CRUSADE
Seeing this as further evidence of Frederick's dishonesty and unreliability, Gregory excommunicated the emperor. Frederick issued a condemnation of the pope's actions, then blithely embarked for the Holy Land despite the fact that technically an excommunicate could not lead a crusade. Gregory issued another forthright condemnation of the emperor. In Frederick's eyes he was leading the crusade on his own terms as emperor rather than as an instrument of papal power.

In the Sixth Crusade of 1228–9 Frederick regained possession of Jerusalem under a treaty signed with Ayyubid sultan of Egypt, al-Kamil, on 18 February 1229. Frederick crowned himself Lord

Above: Emperor Frederick II took Jerusalem in 1229. This miniature shows him reaching an agreement with al-Kamil, the Sultan of Jerusalem.

of Jerusalem the following month on 17 March, then returned to Italy, where he defeated papal troops that Gregory had sent into Frederick's Italian territories.

Gregory lifted the excommunication but renewed it in 1239 after Frederick had embarked once more on military activity in Italy. Gregory called a general council of the church for Easter 1241 in Rome, but Frederick forbade bishops to travel to Rome and captured a number of those who did. He invaded the papal states and surrounded Rome – at which point Gregory died, already more than 90 years old. Frederick withdrew his troops.

CHURCH REFORMS
In the 1230s – temporarily at peace with the emperor – Gregory focused on spiritual matters and church organization. He established the papal inquisition

---

FACT BOX
Original name Ugo/Ugolino di Segni
Born c.1145
Origin Roman
Date elected pope 19 March 1227
Died 22 August 1241
Key fact Promulgated *Decretals* (1234), code of canon law

GREGORY IX

INQUISITION

The name Inquisition derives from the Latin *inquiro* ("make enquiries into") and was given to church inquiries designed to combat heresy from the 13th century onwards. Pope Lucius III had ordered bishops to hold judicial inquiries into heresy in 1184 and the Fourth Lateran Council of 1215 reiterated the requirement. Because not all bishops carried this through and those who did had limited regional power, popes took control of the process and Gregory IX then appointed the first inquisitorial judges in 1227. Many were Domini-can and Franciscan friars. The first handbook of inquisitorial practice was later issued under Innocent IV, who also in 1252 authorized inquisitors to use torture against heretics who would not bend to authority.

Below: Because Frederick had been excommunicated, no bishop would crown him in Jerusalem. He performed the ceremony himself.

Above: Cardinal Ugolino di Segni (later Gregory IX) consecrates St Gregory's Chapel at St Benedict's Monastery, Subiaco.

to fight heresy. In 1231 he enacted a law under which heretics should be handed over to secular authorites for due punishment – meaning burning at the stake.

In 1234 he tried to end the Schism with the churches of the East, but despite a series of meetings in Nicaea in January 1234 this attempt came to nothing. The same year he promulgated the *Novo Compilatio decretalium* ("New Collection of Decretals"), a book of canon law drawn up by canon lawyer Raymond of Peñafort on the basis of papal letters and conciliar rulings.

"FATHER OF ALL NATIONS"

Before becoming pope, while Cardinal-Bishop of Ostia, Gregory (then called Ugo) would adopt the monastic robes of a member of the Order of Friars Minor established by Francis of Assisi and walk barefooted with Francis, discussing matters of faith. Francis viewed Ugo as a father, and called him "the bishop of the whole world and the father of all nations"; it was at Francis's request that Honorius III appointed Ugo protector of the order in 1220. Gregory was also a friend of Dominic Guzman and promoted the Dominican movement; on Dominic's death in 1221 Ugo held the funeral service. As pope he canonized both Francis (in 1228) and Dominic (in 1234).

THE MENDICANT ORDERS

CELESTINE IV TO CLEMENT IV, 1241–68
POPES WHO OPPOSED FREDERICK II AND HIS DESCENDANTS

The five popes from Celestine IV to Clement IV (1241–68) fought tirelessly against Frederick II and his Hohenstaufen descendants Conrad IV, Manfred and Conradin. In Clement IV's reign the Hohenstaufens were finally brought low by the papacy in alliance with King Louis IX of France's brother Charles of Anjou, who became King of Naples and Sicily in 1266.

CONCLAVE

Celestine IV (1241) was the first pope to be elected in a conclave. Gregory IX's death had come in the midst of a fierce conflict with Frederick II with the emperor's army encamped near Rome, and the cardinals could not agree on the best candidate to deal with the emperor. After a deadlock of 60 days, a group of cardinals was confined by Roman senator Matteo Rosso Orsini; they elected the elderly and frail Goffredo da Castaglione as pope. Born in Milan, and a nephew of Urban III, he was pope for 17 days from 25 October to 10 November 1241.

RECONCILIATION?

It took the cardinals a year and a half to find a successor, but they finally elected Sinibaldo Fieschi as Innocent IV on 25 June 1243. He was one of the leading authorities on canon law of his day and had taught the subject at the University of Bologna before being called to the Roman Curia in 1226 and made a cardinal in 1227.

He seemed the right man to manage Frederick for the emperor was known to respect Fieschi's learning and the two men had been on good terms – and had remained so after the emperor's excommunication. Frederick joked that he had lost the friendship of a cardinal and gained the enmity of a pope.

Left: Queen Margaret of Scotland was canonized by Pope Innocent IV in 1290 in recognition of her personal holiness and fidelity to the Church.

Above: Innocent IV approved the rule of the Poor Clares, in 1253. The founder of the order, Clare of Assisi, kneels before the pope. This painted wood image is from Nuremberg, c.1360–70.

Innocent and Frederick entered negotiations, principally over lifting Frederick's excommunication and the return of Lombardy to the papal states. But these came to nothing and Innocent, aware imperial agents were instigating plots against him, fled Rome and escaped via his birthplace Genoa to Lyon. The possibility of reconciliation was lost.

There in 1245 he called the First Council of Lyon, which solemnly condemned and deposed Frederick on the grounds of perjury, sacrilege and suspicion of heresy, freeing his subjects from their oath of loyalty to him. Innocent called on German princes to elect a new emperor and they named first Henry

Raspe, landgrave of Thuringia, and then after Henry's death in 1247, William of Holland.

Frederick died on 13 December 1250 but the papal-imperial conflict rumbled on, first against Frederick's son Conrad IV then after Conrad's death in May 1245 against another this time illegitimate son, Manfred, who was regent for Conrad IV's infant son Conradin. Manfred took power in Sicily, despite the fact that Innocent had granted the kingdom to King Henry III of England's nine year-old son, Edmund. Manfred defeated the papal army at Foggia on 2 December 1254.

BEYOND EUROPE

Innocent called for a new crusade after Jerusalem, regained by Frederick II in the Sixth Crusade (1228–9), fell to Khwarazmian Turks in 1244, and King Louis IX of France embarked on the Seventh Crusade in 1248. This was a failure and ended with Louis in chains and facing a ransom demand of 800,000 gold bezants.

Innocent sent a mission to the Mongols in 1245, calling on their leader to convert to Christianity and stop the slaughter of Christians. The Third Great Khan Guyuk, grandson of Genghis Khan, replied demanding that the pope and all other European rulers submit to his authority. The letter, written in Persian, is still in the Vatican Library.

Alexander IV (1254–61) carried on Innocent's policies, excommunicating Manfred and investing Edmund with Sicily. He tried without success to organize a crusade against the Turkic Tatars who had raided Poland.

CORPUS CHRISTI

The French-born pope Urban IV (1261–4) established the Feast of Corpus Christi to celebrate the Real Presence of Christ in the Eucharist, on the Thursday after Trinity Sunday. Urban had been a professor of canon law at Paris and served as Patriarch of Jerusalem under Alexander IV, but had returned to Europe to seek help for the Christians in the East when Alexander died and he was elected to the papacy on 29 August 1261. He tried to solve the problem of Sicily by offering the crown to Charles of Anjou, brother of Louis IX of France, whilst negotiating with both Charles and Manfred to try to launch a new crusade.

His crusading aim was to refound the Latin Empire of Constantinople: this had been established during the Fourth Crusade, but ended when a Byzantine force under Michael VIII Palaeologos retook the city from its last Latin emperor, Baldwin II, in 1261. Urban died in Perugia on 2 October 1264 before Charles arrived to receive the crown or the crusade could be brought about.

Clement IV (1265–8) carried the plan to fruition, crowning Charles who then defeated Manfred and captured and beheaded Conrad IV's son Conradin. His reign also saw the humiliating failure of the Eighth Crusade, again led by Louis IX of France, which got no further than Tunis in North Africa, an action planned as a preliminary to an attack on Egypt prior to a campaign in the Holy Land. Louis died – reputedly crying "Jerusalem!" with his last word – and the crusaders failed to take Tunis.

Above: Pope Clement IV negotiated with the Mongol ruler Abaqa. This illustration shows Abaqa on horseback next to Arghun and his young son Ghazan Khanz.

FISHERMAN'S RING

The earliest known reference to the Fisherman's Ring, which was used until 1842 to seal papal documents, is in a letter written by Pope Clement IV in 1265. Initially the ring was used to seal the pope's private documents and a different seal was used for official letters, but in the course of the 15th century popes began to use the Fisherman's Ring for official letters. A new ring is cast for each pope, who receives his Fisherman's Ring during his papal coronation. Also known as the *Annulus Piscatoris* and "Piscatory Ring", it traditionally bears a relief of the Apostle Peter fishing from a boat; however, the gold-plated silver ring that Pope Francis was given during his installation mass in St Peter's Square in the Vatican on 19 March 2013 bore the image of Peter holding the keys that represent papal authority over the church. It was a design made by Enrico Manfrini for Pope Paul VI but not previously made into a ring.

GREGORY X, 1271–6
POPE WHO ISSUED NEW RULES FOR PAPAL ELECTIONS

Clement IV died at Viterbo on 29 November 1268. The cardinals – split into a French and an Italian camp and unable to reach the necessary two-thirds majority to approve a candidate – took three years to find a successor. In the end they were locked in the papal palace in Viterbo and threatened with having their supplies of food withdrawn; finally, six cardinals were designated to make the decision and lighted on a compromise candidate, Tedaldo Visconti, archdeacon of Liege. Visconti satisfied both camps because, while Italian-born, he had spent most of his career to date outside Italy and so was not caught up in Italian factional disputes.

"IF I FORGET THEE O JERUSALEM…"

Visconti was not a cardinal or even a priest. He had accompanied Cardinal Jacopo of Palestrina on a mission to England, and at the time he was elected he was far away in the Holy Land – in Acre with Prince Edward of England (the future King Edward I), on the Ninth Crusade. Throughout his pontificate he was a keen promoter of crusading and the interests of the Christians in the Holy Land. Famously in his final sermon before departing Acre for Italy to become pope, he quoted Psalm 137: "If I forget thee, O Jerusalem, let my right hand forget her cunning."

Elected on 1 September 1271, Visconti arrived back in Viterbo on 12 February 1272, was ordained a priest in Rome on 13 March 1272 and consecrated Pope Gregory X on 27 March 1272. On the fourth day after coronation Gregory called a general council of the church to meet at Lyon on 1 May 1274. He set to work to organize a new crusade to the Holy Land. The Council of Lyon determined that one-tenth of church benefices for six years be collected to support Christians in the Holy Land and fund a new crusade. The money was collected, but the crusade did not take place.

GERMAN SUCCESSION

In the 1250s Pope Alexander IV had backed Richard, Earl of Cornwall, against Alfonso X of Castile for power in Germany, and following Richard's death in 1272 Gregory resisted Alfonso's attempts to take control, instead advising the German princes to elect a successor, and then backing their chosen candidate Rudolf of Habsburg. Gregory invited Rudolf to Rome to

> **FACT BOX**
> **Original name** Tedaldo/Tebaldo Visconti
> **Born** c.1210
> **Origin** Lombardy
> **Date elected pope** 1 September 1271
> **Died** 10 January 1276
> **Key fact** Promoted rules for papal elections used until the 20th century

Above: A stained glass window in Vienna Cathedral depicts Rudolf I of Habsburg (left), whom Gregory backed in a dispute over the imperial succession.

Below: Maffeo and Niccolo Polo deliver a message to Pope Gregory X from the Mongol emperor, Kublai Khan. Niccolo was the father and Maffeo the uncle of the celebrated Venetian traveller Marco Polo.

630

ALBERTUS MAGNUS AND THOMAS AQUINAS

Albertus Magnus (Albert the Great) was a Dominican bishop and teacher of theology, one of the great scholars of the Middle Ages. He wrote copiously on the Bible and on the works of the Ancient Greek philosopher Aristotle, who had recently been rediscovered by way of Spanish Arab scholars. Albert, who died in 1280 in Cologne and was canonized in 1931, established that nature could legitimately be studied by Christians; in 1941 he was declared patron saint of the natural sciences. His greatest pupil was his fellow Dominican Thomas Aquinas who studied under Albert from 1245 onwards. Aquinas is celebrated as the greatest of the medieval scholastics or "schoolmen" who based their teachings on the Christian Fathers and Aristotle; as author of the masterpieces *Summa theologiae* and *Summa contra gentiles* that systematized theology; and as founder of the school known as "Thomism". Aquinas was taken gravely ill while travelling to the Council of Lyon after receiving a personal invitation from Gregory X. He took refuge in the Cistercian abbey of Fossanova and died there on 7 March. He was canonized in 1323.

Above: The great scholars Albertus Magnus and Thomas Aquinas have a vision of St Paul as they work in their study. Aquinas surpassed his teacher, Albertus, to become the greatest of the medieval scholastics. Painting by Alonso Antonio Villamor.

be crowned emperor. In fact Gregory and Rudolf met at Lausanne in October 1273, where Rudolf swore to defend the Church, renounced imperial claims to possessions in Rome and the papal states and, at Gregory's insistence, took the cross and committed himself to lead the planned crusade.

Gregory invited the Byzantine Emperor Michael VIII Palaeologus to send ambassadors to the council at Lyon and at the fourth sitting on 6 July 1274 they agreed a reconciliation of the Eastern and Western churches, accepting the creed as used in the Western church (with the *Filioque* ("and the Son") clause), as well as the Roman doctrine of purgatory and the pope's supremacy over the whole Christian world. However the Byzantine Emperor found it difficult to implement the agreement and the apparent end of the Great Schism soon came to nothing.

UBI PERICULUM

Another significant result of the Council of Lyon was the agreement of new rules to govern the conclave of cardinals at a papal election, designed to prevent in future the long delay that had blighted the start of Gregory's own reign. Under these rules, gathered in the papal bull *Ubi periculum* ("Where danger"), cardinals would in future be required to gather within ten days of a pope's death at the location of his death and be locked away in conditions growing more and more uncomfortable with reducing food supplies, until they elected a candidate. These rules were in place for more than 700 years until the reforms of Pope Paul VI (1963–78), although in several elections they were suspended or disregarded.

A CITY EXCOMMUNICATED

In Italy, Gregory set out to bring peace between the Guelphs and Ghibellines, factions who had been in conflict in northern Italy all through the 12th and 13th centuries. In the long-running struggle for primacy of the papacy against the German emperor, the Guelphs were supporters of the papacy and the Ghibellines supporters of the emperor. Gregory excommunicated the city of Florence, a hotbed of Guelph/Ghibelline violence, when its leading figures were obstructive of his attempts at pacification.

On the way back from the Council Gregory died at Arezzo on 10 January 1274. He is buried in Arezzo Cathedral.

Right: Thomas Aquinas. As well as writing masterpieces of theology, he was author of a series of profoundly beautiful eucharistic hymns (sung during Mass).

THE MENDICANT ORDERS

INNOCENT V TO BENEDICT XI, 1276–1304
POPES WHO TRIED BUT FAILED TO LAUNCH A NEW CRUSADE

Innocent V, the first Dominican monk to be elected pope, lasted one day over six months as supreme pontiff. He made it the custom for the pope to wear a white cassock, the Dominican habit. He pressed on towards the main aims of Gregory X's pontificate, in particular trying to bring about a new crusade.

Innocent was succeeded by Hadrian V, pope for just five weeks until his death on 18 August 1276. During his pontificate he revoked the conclave measures contained in Gregory X's bull *Ubi periculum*.

Below: Honorius approved the rule of the Carmelites (the Brothers of the Blessed Virgin Mary of Mount Carmel) in 1286. The order is traditionally said to have been founded on Mount Carmel, Israel.

DOCTOR POPE
Pope John XXI (1276–7) was a learned scholar and medical doctor, who wrote a medical textbook *Liber de oculo* ("Concerning the Eye"), the psychological *De anima* ("On the Soul") and a highly prized medieval book on logic *Summulae logicales* ("Small Logical Sums"). Born in Portugal, he had taken a master's degree at the University of Paris and then taught medicine at the newly established University of Siena.

After being elected to the papacy he continued to dedicate himself to his research and writing – working in a study he had constructed at the papal palace at Viterbo – and left the public and political side of being pope to his adviser, Cardinal Orsini (the future Pope Nicholas III). John died of injuries sustained when the makeshift study in which he was working collapsed.

RESIDENT OF THE VATICAN
Cardinal Orsini became pope as Nicholas III (1277–80). In Rome he restored St Peter's Basilica and the Vatican, being the first pope to use it as his official residence. He was not averse to favouring his own family for preferment in the church and was lampooned for nepotism; in *The Divine Comedy*, Dante placed him in the Eighth Circle of Hell for the sin of simony.

Martin IV (1281–5) was more or less a puppet of Charles of Anjou, king of Sicily and Naples. He appointed Charles Roman Senator and in order to facili-

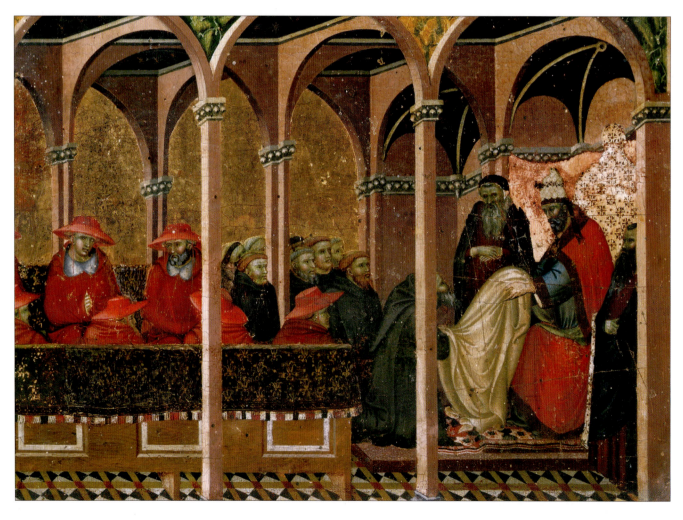

INNOCENT V TO BENEDICT XI

> **UNAM SANCTAM**
> On 18 November 1302 Boniface VIII issued his celebrated papal bull *Unam Sanctam* ("The one holy", a reference to the Church). This declared that spiritual salvation depended on being subject to the Pope. It declared: "outside the Church there is no salvation nor the remission of sins... of the one and only Church there is one body and one head... we declare, we proclaim and we define as a truth necessary for salvation that every human being must be subject to the Roman pontiff.'

tate Charles's plan to recreate the Latin Empire of Constantinople that had been established after the Fourth Crusade, he excommunicated Byzantine Emperor Michael VIII Palaeologus.

PEACE IN ROME

Honorius IV (1285–7) was already around 75 years old and the veteran of a long diplomatic career when he was elected on 2 April 1285. Roman-born and the brother of a Roman senator, Pandulf, he brought peace to the city, which had been in constant uproar under Martin IV.

Below: John XXI was renowned as a scholar. This is the title page of Copulata Omnium Tractatuum, *his treatise on logic.*

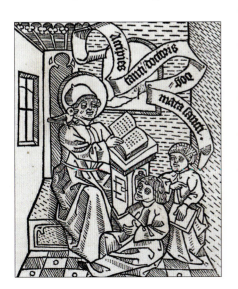

Above: Pope Celestine V resigned on 13 December 1294. He was a Benedictine hermit, Pietro del Morrone, who had been elected only on 5 July that year.

Under Nicholas IV (1288–92) the last Christian territorial holding in Holy Land, Acre, was lost to Sultan Khalil of Muslim Egypt in 1291. Outremer was no more; Nicholas called without success for a crusade. The first Franciscan to be elected to the papacy, he promoted missionary work, notably in China, Serbia, Bulgaria, Armenia and Ethiopia; in 1289 he sent the Franciscan missionary John of Montecorvino to Kublai Khan, the Mongol ruler of China, and John went on to found the first missions in China and India and become Archbishop of Peking.

After Nicholas's death in Rome on 4 April 1292, the papal throne was vacant for 2 years 3 months while cardinals wrangled. Benedictine hermit Pietro del Morrone wrote a letter warning of God's anger if the authorities did not make a quick election – and ended up being elected himself as Pope Celestine V on 5 July 1294. The saintly founder of a monastic order later called the Cel-estines, he proved unequal to the demands of his high office and abdicated after just five months.

BONIFACE VIII

He was succeeded by Benedetto Caetani as Pope Boniface VIII (1294–1303). Dedicated to learning, he founded the University of Rome in 1303 and reorganized the Vatican archives, and was a patron of artists, notably Giotto di Bondone.

Learned, impulsive, quick to anger, Boniface had a very strong sense of his own authority and was drawn into violent conflict with those who challenged him. He fell out seriously with King Philip IV of France over the pope's intervention in a dispute between France and England and Philip's efforts to exercise royal authority in the French church.

He issued the bull *Unam Sanctam* (see box) as a statement of papal power and authority, but was then challenged and even attacked by French minister Guillaume de Nogaret and Sciarra, head of the Colonna clan. Confronting him at Anagni, the pair demanded Boniface resign; when he refused, they struck him in the face and stripped him of his crown and vestments. But then they fell to arguing themselves, allowing the pope to escape and his supporters to drive them off. Boniface died shortly afterwards.

Benedict XI (1303–4) excommunicated Nogaret and the others who had taken part in the attack. He died suddenly on 7 July 1304, after only eight months as pope. Some accused Nogaret of having poisoned him.

Below: In an illustration to Dante's Divine Comedy, *the poet meets Pope Nicholas III. He condemned Nicholas for simony.*

633

AVIGNON EXILE AND PAPAL SCHISM

CLEMENT V TO EUGENIUS IV, 1305–1447

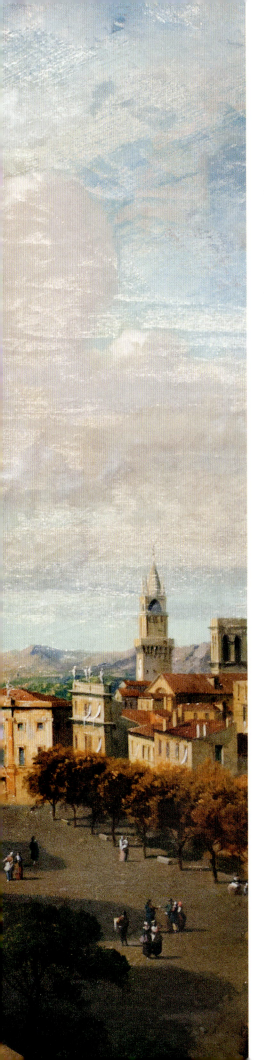

French pope Clement V, who was effectively controlled by King Philip IV of France, began the papacy's long exile from Rome by settling as pope in Avignon in 1309. The "Avignon Exile" lasted more than 67 years, 1309–77. Popes in this period established a splendid court at Avignon, and Clement VI in particular lived in the grandest style of a prince at the Palais des Papes there. Nevertheless several pontiffs looked to return to Rome, and Urban V did achieve a temporary return to the city, in 1367–70, but was driven out by unrest. The papacy was not returned permanently to Rome until the reign of Gregory XI.

The Avignon Exile was followed by the Papal Schism (or Great Western Schism) – the period 1378–1417, in which two and sometimes three popes reigned at the same time and in opposition to one another. This Schism began with the election in 1378 by the same cardinals of two popes – Urban VI, who reigned in Rome, and Clement VII, who established his own papal court and returned to Avignon. It was resolved at the Council of Constance (1414–18), which accepted the resignations of John XXIII and Gregory XII and excommunicated a third pope, Benedict XIII, who refused to stand down, while electing a new pontiff, Oddone Colonna, as Pope Martin V.

The standing of the papacy was at a very low point and the delegates to Constance passed resolutions declaring that the council had superior authority to the pope. Adherents of the "conciliar movement" thereafter posed a major problem for a succession of popes. When the council elected a new antipope Felix V, the recklessness of this action undermined the conciliarists' own authority and restored the standing of the papacy to a significant degree.

Left: Clement VI built a splendid new papal palace in Avignon to replace the older palace of Benedict XII (1334–42). The new building contained a grand chapel 170 feet (52 metres) long. This view was painted by 19th-century French artist Jules Romain Joyant.

CLEMENT V, 1305–14
POPE RESPONSIBLE FOR BEGINNING THE AVIGNON EXILE

In addition to being the pontiff who settled the papacy in Avignon, and began the 67-year "Avignon exile" from Rome, Clement V is remembered as the pope who, at the insistence of Philip IV of France, oversaw the dissolution of the Knights Templar military order in 1312 and the seizure of some of their vast assets.

After the death of Benedict XI from dysentery, cardinals were in dispute for 11 months at Perugia over a suitable successor, and eventually through the machinations of Philip IV selected Archbishop Bertrand of Bordeaux in June 1305. Informed of his election in Bordeaux, he was consecrated on 14 November of that year in Lyon, in a very grand ceremony at which Philip was present. In his whole pontificate Pope Clement V did not once visit Rome.

'SHEPHERD WITHOUT LAW'
For the first four years of his pontificate the papal court moved between Poitiers, Lyon and Bordeaux, but in 1309 pope and courtiers settled in the Dominican priory at Avignon. Throughout his years as pope Clement suffered terribly from stomach cancer. He was a clever

> **FACT BOX**
> **Original name** Bertrand de Got
> **Born** c.1260
> **Origin** French
> **Date elected pope** 5 June 1305
> **Died** 20 April 1314
> **Key fact** Acquiesced in Philip IV's dissolution of the Knights Templar

and adept pope, but lacked the ability to stand up to Philip; he was also guilty of unashamed nepotism in promoting members of his family within the Church and built up a secret hoard of wealth by simony (the sale of ecclesiastical positions and favours) as well as other means. The poet Dante placed him in Hell and denounced him as "a shepherd without law".

From the start of his pontificate Clement did the bidding of Philip IV. At the French king's prompting, he annulled Boniface VIII's *Unam Sanctum*

Below: Consecrated pope in Lyon, France, Clement never made it to Rome. In 1309 he settled the papacy in Avignon, where it would stay for more than 67 years.

bull, which had made such a ringing statement of papal authority, and the same pope's *Clericis Laicos* bull, which had outlawed the payment by clergy of subsidies to secular authorities. He was also swept along by Philip's intense desire to do away with the military order of the Knights Templar, to whom the French king owed very substantial debts.

MOVE AGAINST TEMPLARS
The Templars were under public attack because of the lavish lifestyle of some members and on account of charges of heresy made by former Templar knights. One proposal was for the Templars to merge with the Knights Hospitaller and to this end Clement invited the Grand Masters of the two orders to Poitiers to discuss the matter. The Templar Grand Master, Jacques de Molay, arrived in 1307 but the Grand Master of the Hospitallers, Fulk de Villaret, was delayed.

Philip moved against the order, issuing secret commands by which 5,000 Templars in France – including Jacques de Molay – were seized in dawn raids and arrested on charges of heresy, blasphemy and sodomy. Under torture most

Below: From the start of his pontificate Clement did the bidding of Philip IV of France. In 1305 he created ten cardinals, including nine from France (and four who were his nephews).

CLEMENT V

Above: This letter from Mongol leader Oljeitu to Clement was part of negotiations between the papacy and Mongol empire over a potential alliance against Muslims.

of the Templars admitted to allegations including that they spat on the cross and denied Christ during their initiation rites, that they were not permitted to refuse to have sexual relations with other knights and that they worshipped a pagan idol. (Some historians have argued that the allegation about spitting on the cross, which was widely confessed, may have been true – and been part of an initiation rite that demanded a loyalty to the order so complete that it even overrode religious faith.)

On 22 November 1307 Clement demanded that all Christian rulers arrest Templars and seize their assets. In hearings before a papal committee, senior Templars retracted the confessions they had made under torture but this did not save them.

EDUCATIONAL AND LEGAL LEGACY

Clement was committed to education and founded the universities of Orleans and Perugia, while also establishing chairs of Arabic and other oriental languages at Bologna, Oxford, Paris and Salamanca. He also played a role in the development of canon law: his collected decretals combined with those of the Council of Vienne were promulgated in 1317 by his successor as pope, John XXII.

At the Council of Vienne in 1312 Clement dissolved the Templars and transferred the majority of their assets to the Knights Hospitaller; Philip, however, seized the order's French assets. Then at a trial in Paris on 18 March 1314 Jacques de Molay and leading Templar Geoffrey de Charney again retracted their confessions and were sentenced to death by burning at the stake. According to legend, Jacques cried out as he gave up his spirit that both Pope Clement and King Philip would soon meet him before the Throne of God – and indeed both men were dead before the end of 1314.

MONGOL CONTACT AND CRUSADING INITIATIVE

Clement entered into tentative negotiations with the Mongol empire in the hope of building an alliance against the Muslims in the Holy Land. Mongol embassies in 1305, 1307 and

Above: Last days of the Templars – they make their case before Clement and Philip IV. Clement dissolved the brotherhood in 1312 and Philip seized their assets.

1313 made contact with Clement and European monarchs, but nothing came of them. Then in 1312 at the Council of Vienne, Clement called a crusade to the Holy Land. Philip IV took the cross, but died – in a hunting accident – in November of the same year before he could enact his promise.

STRUCK BY LIGHTNING

Clement himself died at Roquemaure in Provence on 20 April 1314. According to tradition, lightning struck the church in which his body lay on the night after his death, causing a great fire that almost entirely destroyed the body. He was buried, as requested in his will, at Uzeste in southwestern France, close to his birthplace of Villandraut.

JOHN XXII, 1316–34
THE SECOND AVIGNON POPE

There was a delay of more than two years between the death of Clement V on 20 April 1314 and the election of Jacques Duèse as John XXII on 7 August 1316 due to disagreements between factions of cardinals. The election was brokered by Count Philip of Poitiers (later King Philip V of France), who arranged a conclave of 23 cardinals at Lyon. John XXII settled the papacy permanently at Avignon, where he founded the papal library.

A short, thin man with a pale complexion, John was strong-willed and sometimes impetuous, but also serious-minded with a keen intelligence. Aged 67 on his election as pope, he was a fine administrator who, after studying theology and law in Montpellier and Paris, had served as chancellor to Charles II of Naples before being made Cardinal Bishop of Porto in 1312.

FRANCISCAN DISPUTE
John tried to end a long-running and bitter division within the Franciscan order between the majority (the Conventuals) and the *Fraticelli* or Spirituals, who argued that monks should observe absolute poverty on the grounds that Christ and the Apostles had owned nothing. In 1317, after clashes in which Spirituals drove Conventuals out of abbeys and took local control, John condemned the Spirituals and announced that those who continued to resist would be treated as heretics; some were burned at the stake.

> **FACT BOX**
> **Original name** Jacques Duèse
> **Born** 1249
> **Origin** French, born in Cahors
> **Date elected pope** 7 August 1316
> **Died** 4 December 1334
> **Key fact** Restored papal finances and settled papacy permanently in Avignon

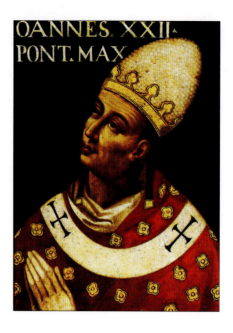

Above: The longest-reigning of the Avignon popes, John XXII consolidated the close links with the French crown. He canonized Thomas Aquinas on 18 July, 1323.

When in 1322 the Franciscan chapter of Perugia declared it a valid position to argue that Christ and the Apostles had no property either individually or collectively, John denounced this position and the following year issued a papal bull that pronounced it "heretical".

ANTIPOPE NICHOLAS V
John clashed with Holy Roman Emperor Louis IV and as a result faced the challenge of an antipope, Nicholas V, set up in Rome by Louis. The trouble began when Louis came to power after overcoming the challenge of Frederick of Austria and John warned him not to act as emperor until he as pope had deliberated on the disagreement.

Louis issued the Sachsenhausen Appellation of 22 May 1324 that denied that the papacy had authority over imperial elections; he also attacked John's denunciation of the Spiritual Franciscans. John then excommunicated Louis and Louis marched into Italy where he set up a Franciscan Spiritual, Pietro Rainalducci, as antipope Nicholas V and had a straw effigy of John XXII burned in the streets of Rome; Michael of Cesena, the general of the Franciscans, argued that a church council should sit in judgement on John.

Thereupon John excommunicated Nicholas V and deposed Michael. Subsequently, after Louis returned to Germany, Nicholas submitted to the pope who allowed him to live out his days in peace, with a small pension, in the palace at Avignon.

DECLINING STATUS
John's close relationship with the French crown contributed to a growing distrust of the papacy. He was guilty – like many of the other Avignon popes – of nepotism and showing favouritism to fellow Frenchmen. He created three of his nephews cardinals and out of the 28 cardinals he created no fewer than 20 were from southern France.

Below: Holy Roman Emperor Louis IV was a difficult opponent for John, who had to face down the challenge of antipope Nicholas V, set up by Louis.

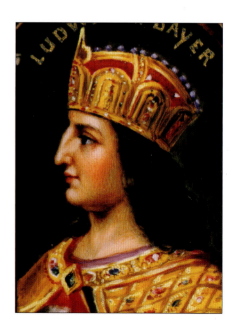

Above: An English friar from Surrey, William of Ockham protested against John's move against the Spirituals, or Fraticelli, backers of absolute poverty, within the Franciscan order.

> **MEISTER ECKHART**
>
> The German philosopher, theologian and mystic Meister Eckhart was condemned by John XXII in a papal bull of 27 March 1329. Johannes Eckhart was born in *c.*1260 in Hochheim, Thuringia (now part of Germany), joined the Dominicans aged 15 and studied – possibly under the great Albertus Magnus – in Cologne, before teaching theology and taking a master's degree in Paris. He held official Dominican positions in his native Thuringia, in Saxony and Bohemia and after 1314 was dedicated to preaching, based in Strasbourg. He viewed God as the inner being of all things – an "uncreated and uncreatable" light in the soul – and gave instructions on how the human soul can establish union with God. He was accused of heresy while a professor in Cologne later in life, and his case was heard before a papal court in Avignon. He told them that his teachings were based on religious experience: "What I have taught is the bare truth." Pope John's condemnation came after Eckhart's death – probably in 1327 or 1328 – in Avignon.

Above: John supported missionary work and created bishoprics as far afield as India. This illustration of building at Jerusalem is from the John XXII Bible in the Palais des Papes.

Yet he also had positive attributes. A great proponent of missionary activity, he established bishoprics in India, Iran, Armenia and Anatolia. He also reorganized church administration and control of finances – in particular, issuing a tax document that set fees for work done by the papal chancery. He established a university at Cahors in France.

BEATIFIC VISION

John was embroiled in a controversy over his views on the blessed soul's encounter with God after death. In sermons in 1331–2 he reiterated the idea, which he had also expressed before becoming pope, that the souls of the blessed would not access full experience of God's glory (the beatific vision) until the Last Judgement – whereas most theologians argued that blessed souls would not have to wait but would be in full communion with God after death. A committee at the University of Paris condemned John's position and Cardinal Napoleone Orsini even tried to establish an ecumenical council to sit in judgement on the pope. John tried to find a common position with his opponents before his death on 4 December 1334, aged 84.

Church historians do not consider John a heretic because the doctrine of the beatific vision was not formally defined at the time of his pontificate. His successor Benedict XII did issue that definition in the encyclical *Benedictus deus* (1336).

EXILE OF THE PAPACY TO AVIGNON

For a period of over 67 years, from 1309 to 1377, the papacy was exiled from Rome in the city of Avignon, southern France. French-born pope Clement V (1305–14) settled the papacy in Avignon under the influence of Philip IV of France. Some of his successors, notably Clement VI (1342–52), lived in fine style there in the Palais des Papes "Palace of the Popes"). Urban V (1362–70) returned to Rome in 1367–70 but was forced by unrest there to retreat to France, before Gregory XI (1370–8) brought the papacy back to Rome in 1377.

Below: Italian poet Petrarch spent much of his youth in Avignon. He called on Urban V to return to Rome.

Right: The Widow of Rome. A 13th-century allegorical image shows Rome mourning the loss of the papacy to southern France.

BACK IN AVIGNON DURING THE PAPAL SCHISM

In the Papal Schism of 1378–1417 that followed the Avignon Exile, two and sometimes three leaders of the Church set themselves up to reign in opposition to one another: a succession of these, starting with antipope Clement VII (1378–94), ruled in Avignon but were opposed by popes resident in Rome. Church historians identify the leaders of the Church in Rome as popes and the others, in Avignon (and later also in Pisa), as antipopes.

The "Avignon Exile" refers to the period 1309–77, when there was a single line of popes, resident in Avignon rather than Rome, and does not include the years in which antipopes ruled in Avignon while popes ruled in Rome.

"A SEWER"

When Clement V settled in Avignon the city belonged to the Duke of Anjou, who was a vassal of the pope. Its appeal lay in the fact that it offered refuge from the highly unsettled situation in Rome and the papal states; it could also be said that it was located more centrally in Christian Europe than Rome; but the main reason Clement settled there was that he was effectively under the thumb of the French king, Philip IV. To begin with, the city was unappealing, especially to Italian courtiers forced to move there. The poet and humanist Petrarch – who spent part of his youth there after his family had to relocate to follow Clement V – was scathing about the place: he called it "a sewer where all the muck of the universe collects".

PALAIS DES PAPES

But over the years in which the popes and the papal court were resident in Avignon, the city was greatly developed. The formidable eight-towered Palais des Papes was raised on a rock some 190 feet (58 metres) above the main city, alongside a 12th-century Romanesque cathedral, Notre Dame des Doms. The cathedral contains the elaborate Gothic tomb of Pope John XXII (1316–34), the second Avignon pope, who added several chapels to the building.

The palace consists of two main parts. The first, the Palais Vieux ("Old Palace") was built in 1334–42 by Pope Benedict XII (1334–42) on the site of the old episcopal palace used by the bishops of Avignon. It was largely plain and heavily fortified, its four wings flanked by towers. The second, the Palais Nouveau ("New Palace"), was erected by pope Clement VI, with additions by Innocent VI (1352–62) and Urban V (1362–70). The building, which contains the vast Grand Chapel (170 feet/52 metres) in length, was lavishly ornamented and

Above: The Palais des Papes dominates the city. Six papal conclaves were held in Avignon, from the election of Benedict XII in 1334 to that of the antipope Benedict XIII in 1394.

decorated with wooden ceilings, stained glass, golden ornamentation, frescoes and paintings, tapestries and sculpture. When finished, the complex covered 118,400 square feet (11,000 square metres).

In 1348 Clement VI purchased Avignon and the surrounding area, the Venaissin, from Queen Joan I of Naples who had come by the land through her husband Andrew, a member of the Hungarian branch of the House of Anjou.

CITY TRANSFORMED

Avignon expanded, its population growing to around 30,000, and became established as a centre not only of religion but also of intellectual life, trade and banking. The School of Theology and the University Law School were internationally renowned. The papal library – with its remarkable collection of 2,000 books including Hebrew, Greek, Latin and Arabic manuscripts – was the largest in Europe at the time, and a treasure trove for the first humanists. The finest musicians and singers came to perform in the Grand Chapel. The merchants of Avignon grew rich catering to a population including bishops and cardinals who lived in great style in mansions and palaces. With such a magnificent headquarters, the Curia or papal administration was expanded during the Avignon period. Avignon remained the property of the papacy until the time of the French Revolution, when it was annexed by the French National Assembly in 1791. The palace was used as a military barracks and its interior was badly damaged.

BLACK DEATH IN AVIGNON

In 1348 the Black Death struck Avignon, killing roughly three-quarters of the people – around 62,000; one-quarter of the papal staff died. Pope Clement VI bought a large field for use as a cemetery and took part in processions to ask God to spare the city, until he decided these increased the risk of infection and cancelled them. People blamed the Jews for this visitation, and there were riots in Narbonne and Carcassonne in which all the local Jews were murdered. Clement issued two bulls condemning these attacks and threatening with excommunication any Christians who continued to attack Jews. He was the first pope to defend the Jews and he welcomed them to Avignon.

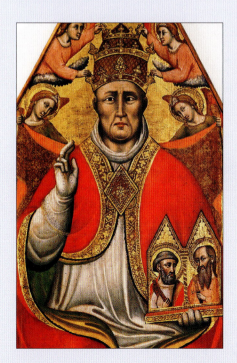

Below: Urban V. He made several additions to the new papal palace begun by his predecessor Clement VI – in particular, completing the palace courtyard.

BENEDICT XII TO URBAN V, 1334–70
POPES BUILD AND EXPAND PAPAL PALACE IN AVIGNON

The popes from Benedict XII to Urban V (1334–70) established the papal court at Avignon and built the grand Palais des Papes there. Clement VI kept a lavish court like a secular prince but the popes to either side of his pontificate, Benedict XII and Innocent VI, were more austere figures dedicated to reform.

Benedict XII (1334–42) was a Cistercian monk, a tall and bulky former Inquisitor known for his loud voice who had built his reputation rooting out the Cathar heresy in the south of France. He was elected on 20 December 1334, within three weeks of the death of John XXII. He was a stern figure, who set to work to root out nepotism and corrupt clerical practices and insisted on stricter observance of monastic rule, drawing up new constitutions for the Benedictines, Cistercians and Franciscans.

He largely failed on the international stage. His attempts to keep the peace between England and France did not succeed, and the long conflict that became known as the Hundred Years' War began in 1337 during his pontificate (see box).

PALAIS DES PAPES

Early in his reign Benedict seemed set on returning to Rome, and spent money on the restoration of St Peter's and the Lateran, but French cardinals and Philip V pressured him to remain in Avignon. He set to work building the Palais des Papes (the Papal Palace) there, on a site south of the cathedral. Alongside a 150ft/45m tower that housed the papal

Below: Benedict XII (right) confirms the rule in Bologna of Taddeo of the Pepoli banking family. As part of his drive to return to Rome, Benedict proposed a move to Bologna. In the end he did not leave Avignon.

HUNDRED YEARS' WAR

The prolonged conflict between England and France known as the Hundred Years' War in fact lasted more than a century, from 1337 to 1453. It began when King Edward III of England – a nephew of Charles IV, who died in 1328 – laid claim to the French throne in opposition to Count Philip of Valois who took power as King Philip VI. The wars included celebrated English victories such as those at Crécy in 1346, Poitiers in 1356 and Agincourt in 1415 as well as famous French triumphs such as relief of the siege of Orléans in 1428 by a force led by Joan of Arc. The conflict is generally said to have ended with the French victory at the Battle of Castillon in 1453. The English were left with possession only of Calais.

Above: Urban V was a reformer and educational patron. Austere and pious, he wore the habit of the Benedictine order to which he belonged even after becoming pope. He was beatified in 1870.

treasury and the pope's own apartments, he built a two-storey chapel and the palace's northern section.

EXTRAVAGANCE AND VICE

Clement VI (1342–52) greatly enlarged the papal palace and lived in great comfort, in the style of a worldly prince with fabulous robes and being extravagantly generous to crowds of hangers-on. He declared, "My predecessors did not understand how to live as pope."

Before becoming pope, as Pierre Roger, he had an astonishing career: with doctorates in canon law and theology, he had been appointed Archbishop of Sens and then of Rouen before the age of 30, and served as Chancellor of France for Philip VI. He was charming, brilliantly intelligent and was said to be the finest preacher of his time. He was not without vices, however, and there were rumours of sexual affairs – most of all with the beautiful Countess Cecile of Turenne. The poet Petrarch claimed that the Avignon churchmen under this pope consorted with prostitutes and misused their wealth to seduce the wives and daughters of indignant local menfolk.

Above: Pope Clement VI – an extravagantly gifted but reportedly worldly man – here delivers to the bishop of Ferrara an ultimatum to the Visconti of Milan.

Not only did he spend lavishly on the papal palace, but in 1348 he also purchased Avignon and its county of Venaissin for 80,000 gold florins. The seller was Queen Joan I of Naples, who was also Countess of Provence and who had fled to Avignon begging for her name to be cleared at a papal trial after she had been accused of murdering her husband Andrew and Naples had been invaded by King Louis I of Hungary. In the trial Clement found her not guilty before buying her local landholdings.

STERN REFORMER

The pontificate of Innocent VI (1352–62) came as a shock in Avignon after the extravagance of Clement VI. Innocent was a stern clerical and monastic reformer. He spent money fortifying the papal palace and city against marauding gangs but was keen to effect a return to Rome and attempted to prepare the ground there for papal governance. But he died before his plans bore fruit.

BRIEFLY BACK IN ROME

Urban V (1362–70) did achieve a temporary return to Rome, in 1367–70. While in residence there – as part of attempts to arrange a crusade against the Ottoman Turks – he received in 1369 a visit from Eastern emperor John V Palaeologus, who submitted to Latin Christianity and to the pope; however, John was not able to win the support of his clergy and the reunion of the churches did not come about.

In the meantime, unrest in Italy arising in part from disputes with the powerful Bernabo Visconti of Milan led Urban to decide to return to Avignon in 1370. Before the end of the year he had died, on 19 December 1370 while standing before the high altar of Avignon Cathedral during Mass.

Below: The reliquary cross of Urban V was said to contain a fragment of the cloth used by St Veronica to wipe Christ's blood-and sweat-stained face on His way to Calvary.

GREGORY XI, 1370–8
THE LAST OF THE AVIGNON POPES

Gregory XI succeeded in returning the papacy to Rome in 1377 and so ending the near-68-year exile in Avignon.

A nephew of Pope Clement VI, Gregory received many benefits from his uncle who created him cardinal deacon in 1348 aged only 19. He was well educated – he studied at the University of Perugia, and gained a reputation as a leading theologian and canon lawyer. He was not a priest when he was elected pope at Avignon on 30 December 1370, but was ordained within a week and then crowned pope on 5 January 1371.

MYSTIC PIETY
Gregory was deeply religious, pious with a mystical strain, known for his purity of heart, ascetic character and humble bearing. He felt that the papacy belonged in Rome, and that the unrest in the papal states must be dealt with. He also knew and liked the Italian peninsula, after his spell in Perugia when he learned the language and became acquainted with many of the leading humanist scholars. Among his first acts was to attempt – without success – to broker peace between

Below: English condottiere or mercenary John Hawkwood fought both for and against the papacy. Italian artist Paolo Uccello painted this mounted portrait of Hawkwood, originally as a fresco.

England and France, for hostilities had broken out again in what was later called the Hundred Years' War. Gregory also tried – again unsuccessfully – to arrange a new crusade and bring about reconciliation between the Eastern and Western churches. He embarked upon church reform.

Early in his pontificate, on 9 May 1372, he announced his intention to return the papacy to Rome. But he knew that this might be a challenging task – not least because fighting against unrest in the papal states and the attempt to move back to Rome under Urban V had severely weakened the papacy's finances. He borrowed from Louis I, Duke of Anjou and King Charles II of Navarre to bridge the gap.

> **FACT BOX**
> **Original name** Pierre-Roger De Beaufort
> **Born** 1329
> **Origin** French, born in Limoges-Fourches
> **Date elected pope** 30 December 1370
> **Died** 26–7 March 1378
> **Key fact** Ended the Avignon papacy, returned to Rome

Left: Born Pierre-Roger De Beaufort in Limoges, Gregory XI was the last French pope and the last to govern the Church from Avignon. In returning the papacy to Rome, he had to face down the opposition of his own country and several cardinals.

ATTEMPTS TO TAME VISCONTI
Then he turned his attention to unrest in Italy. He excommunicated the troublesome Bernabo Visconti of Milan, who had seized papal territory in Reggio and other locations. Visconti was supremely unbothered – and showed it by forcing the legates who carried the excommunication to eat the parchment on which it was written. Gregory declared war on him in 1372. He built an alliance of the Holy Roman Emperor Charles IV, Queen Joan I of Naples and King Louis I of Hungary and sent English condottiere John Hawkwood into battle on behalf of the papacy, but achieved only an unsatisfactory peace signed on 6 June 1374.

ST CATHERINE'S PLEA FOR A RETURN TO ROME
Visconti carried on causing trouble, allying with Florence and stirring up insurrection in the papal states. In response Gregory placed an interdict on the city of Florence, excommunicating all its inhabitants and outlawing their possessions (which could therefore legally be seized) on 31 March 1376. The mystic Dominican nun, Caterina Benincasa – known to history as St Catherine of Siena – travelled to Avignon and called on the pope to arr-ange a new crusade against the Muslims and to return the papacy to its true home, the city of Rome.

DIFFICULT HOMECOMING
The journey to Rome was extremely prolonged and difficult. Gregory and his cardinals departed from Avignon on 13 September 1376 and left France from

Marseilles on 2 October. The voyage at sea was interrupted by severe storms in which several ships were lost. Over several months the papal party reached Corneto, then made their way down to Ostia and sailed up the river Tiber to the monastery of San Paolo. Gregory did not arrive in Rome until 17 January 1377. The pope did not receive a friendly welcome. Feelings were running high against the papacy as a result of prolonged unrest and dissension in the papal states and a massacre in Cesena in February – which was ordered by papal legate Cardinal Robert of Geneva (the future antipope Clement VII) and was carried out by John Hawkwood and his "White Company" of mercenaries – only served to make matters even worse. Riots in Rome forced Gregory to retreat to Anagni in May 1377, but he returned to Rome on 7 November 1377 and died there in March 1378 while negotiations were under way to bring peace to the papal states.

Above: St Catherine of Siena travelled to Avignon to ask Gregory to return the papacy to Rome and call a new crusade against Islam.

JOHN WYCLIFFE

Pope Gregory issued five bulls condemning the work of English church reformer and theologian John Wycliffe on 22 May 1377 – and took energetic measures against the Lollards who were Wycliffe's followers. Born in Yorkshire, northern England, in *c.*1330, Wycliffe studied at Oxford University and gained a doctorate in divinity before becoming a prominent churchman. He called for the Church to abandon its worldly wealth and attacked the doctrine of Transub-stantiation (that the bread and wine in the Mass are transformed into the body and blood of Christ), arguing that the bread remained bread while also containing the Real Presence of Christ. He also translated the Bible into English. He and the Lollards were increasingly attacked in England after the Peasants' Revolt of 1381. Wycliffe was condemned at a synod in London in 1382 and expelled from Oxford University. He died, after suffering a stroke, in December 1384. Wycliffe can be seen as a forerunner of Martin Luther and other thinkers of the Protestant Reformation.

Right: English cleric John Wycliffe, translator of the Bible into English, was an outspoken critic of Transubstantiation, the Requiem Mass and the papacy itself.

URBAN VI TO MARTIN V, 1378–1431
THE PAPAL SCHISM

During the Papal Schism of 1378–1417 a succession of popes and antipopes ruled in opposition to one another, principally in Rome and Avignon. At times there were three rival popes all claiming authority as leader of the Church at once, each one with a college of cardinals and supporting court in tow. The split – caused by political rather then theological disputes – was brought to an end by the Council of Constance of 1414–18.

URBAN VI VS CLEMENT VII

After Gregory XI died in March 1378 – shortly after returning the papacy to Rome from its near-68-year exile in Avignon (1309–77) – an unruly crowd of Romans unhappy at the succession of French popes surrounded the cardinals in conclave and tried to force them to elect a Roman as pope. In the event the cardinals chose an Italian (although not a Roman) – Bartolomeo Prignano, Archbishop of Bari and a native of Naples. He took the name Urban VI.

Below: Coronation of the antipope. The illustrator of this manuscript had no doubt that the powers of evil were behind those who challenged the authority of the papacy.

Above: Pope Martin V (centre) was elected at the Council of Constance in 1417. He backed Sigismund (kneeling) to end the unrest caused by Jan Hus in Bohemia.

Before his election a well-liked and able administrator in the papal chancery, Prignano proved unpredictable and irascible once in power. He did not treat the cardinals well and so, encouraged by the French king, they fled to Anagni and elected a Frenchman, Robert of Geneva, as a rival pope, Clement VII. They annulled the first election on the grounds that it had been made under duress. Antipope Clement VII established his own papal court, returning to Avignon.

A DIFFERENT ANTIPOPE

This was a new development in the history of papal elections. When previous popes and antipopes had been established in power, they had been elected and backed by rival groups, but in this case the same group of cardinals had elected two popes. Neither candidate backed down, and Europe was divided in support of the two popes.

The Holy Roman Empire, Portugal, England, Flanders, Ireland, the Republic of Venice and the northern Italian city-states were among those who supported the Roman pope Urban VI. France, Naples, Burgundy, Savoy, Aragon, Castile, Scotland and others supported the Avignon pope, Clement VII.

The schism was disastrous for the standing of the papacy and undermined peace in Europe. The divisions along national lines tended to foster conflict between countries. There were wars in the Iberian Peninsula over the schism.

POPE AND ANTIPOPE

The split endured after the pontificates of the initial candidates. In terms of papal history the Roman pontiffs are considered popes – Urban VI (1378–89), Boniface IX (1389–1404), Innocent VII (1404–6), Gregory XII (1406–15) and Martin V (1417–31); the others – Clement VII (1378–94), Benedict XIII (1394–1417), Alexander V (1409–10) and John XXIII (1410–15) – are seen as antipopes.

MISSED OPPORTUNITY

There were attempts to end the crisis. On the death of Boniface IX in 1404 eight cardinals in conclave at Rome

---

POPES AND ANTIPOPES OF THE PAPAL SCHISM

Popes
Urban VI 1378–89
Boniface IX 1389–1404
Innocent VII 1404–6
Gregory XII 1406–15
Martin V 1417–31

Antipopes
Clement VII 1378–94
Benedict XIII 1394–1417
Alexander V 1409–10
John XXIII 1410–15

URBAN VI TO MARTIN V

> ### HUS AND THE HUSSITES
> The Council of Constance that effected an end to the Papal Schism condemned and burned as a heretic Czech church reformer Jan Hus. A university lecturer and preacher who was influenced by Englishman John Wycliffe's forthright proposals for church reform, Jan Hus made his name as a church reformer through his sermons in Czech at the Bethlehem Chapel in Prague. He had been excommunicated by Alexander V for defying a papal ban on preaching in private chapels and was summoned to the Council of Constance with a promise of safe conduct. Despite this promise, however, he was condemned as a heretic and burned at the stake on 6 July 1415. Afterwards, no fewer than five crusades were called against his followers, the Hussites, in Bohemia in the years 1420–32.

offered to refrain from electing a successor if Benedict XIII would stand down, but his representatives refused, so the cardinals elected Innocent VII.

Below: Church authorities promised Jan Hus he would be safe at Constance, but he was burned at the stake after being denounced as a heretic.

Above: Duke Frederick IV of Austria smuggled antipope John XXIII away from the Council of Constance along the Rhine in a boat. John later returned to Constance, where he was deposed and imprisoned.

At various points, diplomats and leading churchmen called for a church council to solve the issue, but this solution was initially rejected on the grounds that a church council could not be called by anyone save a reigning pope. As seen in the calls for a council to sit in judgement on John XXII and again here, there was a growing conciliar movement in Europe arguing that a general church council had greater authority than an individual pope.

THIRD RIVAL POPE

In 1409 a third pope was elected. Representatives of Benedict XIII and Gregory XII had come to an agreement that the two popes would meet but when the two pontiffs in fact failed to do so, the cardinals elected Alexander V in Pisa. He reigned briefly in 1409–10 and was succeeded by John XXIII (1410–15).

In 1409–15 Gregory XII in Rome, Benedict XIII in Avignon and first Alexander V then John XXIII in Pisa were all claiming to be pope at the same time.

COUNCIL OF CONSTANCE

In the end the issue was resolved at the Council of Constance (1414–18), called by Pisan pontiff John XXIII and backed by Roman pope Gregory XII. The council accepted the resignations of John and Gregory and excommunicated Benedict XIII, who refused to give way, then elected an Italian, Oddone Colonna, as Pope Martin V (1417–31). This is generally taken as ending the Papal Schism, although Avignon refused to accept the new appointment and continued to recognize Pope Benedict XIII and on his death in 1417 two more antipopes were elected – some archbishops elected Benedict XIV and others elected Clement VIII.

EUGENIUS IV, 1431–47
INITIAL STEPS IN RESTORING PAPAL AUTHORITY

Augustinian monk Gabriele Condulmaro – a tall, thin and good-looking nephew of Pope Gregory XII – was unanimously elected pope by a conclave of cardinals in Rome on 3 March 1431. He was crowned in St Peter's eight days later on 11 March 1431. His pontificate was dominated by issues arising from the reign of his predecessor Martin V – in particular, clashes between the pope and the Council of Basel, which had been called by Martin then postponed, in the course of which the pope's authority faced very serious challenges.

Martin V had been wary of general church councils and the conciliar movement whose adherents argued that a council had greater authority than the pope. Among his first acts had been a condemnation of the "conciliar theory" and a statement that no appeal could be made from the pope's judgement on any matter of faith. He had called a church council at Pavia in 1423 but then arranged its postponement for seven years, and he died in 1431 before the delegates met in Basel. This council loomed over the reign of Eugenius IV.

COUNCIL OF BASEL
Within five months of the council starting, Eugenius attempted to wind it up: on 18 December 1431 he issued a bull dissolving the council and proposing that it should meet again at the end of 18 months, in Bologna. But the delegates refused to disperse, and reissued resolutions made at the Council of Constance in 1414–18 to the effect that a general council had greater authority than the pope. Then they ordered Eugenius to appear before them in Basel.

A compromise was reached through the intervention of Holy Roman Emperor Sigismund, whom Eugenius crowned in Rome on 31 May 1433, under which Eugenius withdrew his order of dissolution and recognized the council while also rejecting the resolutions that elevated its authority above that of the papacy.

Above: Last of the antipopes: Amadeus VIII, Duke of Savoy, was elected as antipope Felix V at Ferrara in 1439. He resigned in 1449, and was a cardinal at the end of his life.

ANTIPOPE FELIX V
Then in 1438 Eugenius called a second council at Ferrara and excommunicated the delegates still sitting in Basel. In retaliation the Basel council suspended him on 24 January 1438 and then denounced him as a heretic and deposed him on 25 June 1439 before in the following November electing Duke Amadeus VIII of Savoy as antipope Felix V.

Further afield the pope's authority was in tatters – in France, Charles VII issued the Pragmatic Sanction of Bourges, which supported freedom for the French church and limitations on papal authority, while in Germany the Diet of Mainz similarly limited the pope's authority in the Holy Roman Empire.

CHURCH UNITY?
However, in Italy Eugenius gained a much-needed boost to his standing when he agreed a reunification of Western and Eastern churches on 5 July 1439 at the council he had called, which had been forced by an outbreak of plague to move from Ferrara to Florence. Byzantine Emperor John VIII Palaeologus was happy to agree to the reunification as part of negotiations for a crusade against the Ottoman Turks. However, it was no more lasting than previous attempts to patch up the Great

Below: Scenes from the life of Eugenius IV were sculpted in the central door of St Peter's Basilica, decorated by Antonio Filarete.

FACT BOX

Original name Gabriele Condulmaro
Born c.1383
Origin Venetian
Date elected pope 3 March 1431
Died 23 February 1447
Key fact Defeated the conciliar movement

Schism of 1054, and the resulting crusade ended in a heavy defeat at the Battle of Varna on 10 November 1444.

In the end antipope Felix V and the remaining delegates at Basel were left isolated. Sigismund's successor as Holy Roman Emperor, Frederick III, backed Eugenius over the antipope and when Eugenius recognized the claim of King Alfonso V of Aragon to the crown of Naples, Alfonso, too, gave his support and so consolidated Eugenius in power.

TROUBLE IN ROME

Early in his reign, Eugenius – a committed opponent of nepotism – had taken on several members of the Colonna family, relatives of Martin V whom that pope had showered with positions, territories and lands. This plunged him into a conflict with the powerful Colonna. In 1434, with the papal states in uproar following attacks against the pope by rebel condottieri, the Colonna set up a republic in Rome, and in June that year Eugenius had to flee in the disguise of a Benedictine monk: he was rowed down the centre of the Tiber while his enemies hurled stones at him from both banks, and escaped to Florence.

Above: Eugenius IV crowned Sigismund – King of Germany, Bohemia and Italy – as Holy Roman Emperor in 1433.

Given a great ovation on arrival, he took refuge in the Dominican convent of Santa Maria Novella, and sent Giovanni Vitelleschi, Bishop of Recanati, to restore order in Rome; Vitelleschi, in consort with the papal condottiere Francesco Sforza, retook most of the papal states.

Before the end of his reign, Eugenius was able to return to Rome after an exile of almost a decade – on 28 September 1443. He died there on 23 February 1447 at the end of a pontificate so clouded by trouble and conflict that he is said to have regretted on his deathbed that he ever left his monastery.

His pontificate went some way to re-establishing the standing of the papacy and reasserting its authority over the conciliar movement. He may have been lacking in tact, but he was genuinely pious and committed to the welfare of the poor: as a young man, he distributed a great part of his inheritance to the needy before entering the Augustinian monastery of St George in Venice. Among his other achievements were the re-establishment of the University of Rome and the consecration of Florence Cathedral, complete with dome by Filippo Brunelleschi, on 25 March 1436.

FRANCESCO SFORZA

Francesco Sforza, an illegitimate mercenary commander's son who rose to become Duke of Milan, was foremost among the condottieri active in Eugenius IV's reign. These were mercenaries who switched sides in conflicts in the papal territories. At different times he fought both for and against the pope and Sforza's on-off patron Filippo Maria Visconti, Duke of Milan. Born in 1401, he married Visconti's only child, the illegitimate Bianca Maria, in 1441. He became Duke of Milan in 1450 after a long struggle following Visconti's death and established a dynasty that remained in power for almost 100 years. He died in Milan on 8 March 1466. He was famed for his ability to bend metal bars with his hands alone. He was mentioned admiringly in Niccolo Machiavelli's *The Prince* (1513).

Left: Francesco Sforza, mercenary, Duke of Milan and dynastic founder. When Renaissance miniaturist Bonifacio Bembo painted this portrait, Sforza insisted on wearing his battered campaigning hat.

RENAISSANCE AND REFORMATION

NICHOLAS V TO CLEMENT VII, 1447–1534

The Renaissance – the period of European history marked by a magnificent flowering of the arts and a new interest in learning, as people rediscovered the values and culture of the classical world – found its first expression in 14th-century Italy. The first of the Renaissance popes to value the arts as an expression of God's glory reigned in the mid-15th century: Nicholas V, who founded the Vatican Library and began the recreation of Rome as a Renaissance city.

Later popes enthusiastically carried this work on. Sixtus IV restored some 30 churches in Rome and began the decoration of the magnificent Sistine Chapel. Perhaps the greatest of papal art patrons, Julius II, began the rebuilding of St Peter's Basilica, and commissioned masterpieces from Raphael in the Vatican and Michelangelo on the Sistine Chapel ceiling. Leo X was a patron of learning who expanded the Vatican Library, reformed the University of Rome and supported printers, scholars and poets. Himself an excellent musician, he invited the finest musicians to Rome and the papal choir became famous. Rome became the centre of the Italian Renaissance.

These years were a high point for the pope as patron of the arts, but also witnessed a nadir in terms of the pontiff's spiritual standing. The Renaissance popes included men who degraded the papacy through their corruption and self-indulgence. Paul II wore extravagant robes with rouge on his face. Alexander VI used any means to advance his four illegitimate children, who included Cesare and Lucrezia Borgia. It could scarcely have been clearer that reform was needed. German theologian Martin Luther's disgust at the sale of indulgences to fund the rebuilding of St Peter's launched the Protestant Reformation.

Left: The Creation of Adam takes centre stage in the Sistine Chapel ceiling, painted in 1508–12 by Michelangelo at the behest of Pope Julius II. Italian painter and historian Giorgio Vasari said it contained "every perfection possible".

RENAISSANCE AND REFORMATION

NICHOLAS V AND CALLISTUS III, 1447–58
NICHOLAS V FOUNDS THE VATICAN LIBRARY

Nicholas V (1447–55) embarked on the architectural regeneration of Rome, was a patron of many artists and humanist scholars and founded the Vatican Library. He also ended the clash with the Council of Basel and the conciliar movement and rebuilt peace in the papal states and throughout Italy. He brought about peace in papal states; rejecting the previous policy of using mercenary armies and instead built strategically placed castles with able governors. His successor Callistus III (1455–8) was the first of a line of Spanish popes, a Borgia from the Kingdom of Valencia.

HUMANIST ENCOUNTER
As a young man the future pope Nicholas V – then called Tommaso Parentucelli – had to break off his studies in Bologna due to lack of money, and found employment as a tutor in the Strozzi and Albizzi families in Florence, where he met many of the

Above: The Transfiguration *by Bellini: "He was transfigured before them … His face did shine as the sun" (Matthew 17). Nicholas V made the Transfiguration (on 6 August) a universal feast.*

leading humanist scholars of the day. He returned to Bologna and took a master's degree in theology before serving Niccolo Albergati, Bishop of Bologna, for 20 years. When elected pope on 6 March 1447 he took the name Nicholas V after the bishop; he is the last pope to date to take the name Nicholas.

Nicholas was cheerful and pious, pale with dark eyes and a piercing gaze. He set out to restore peace in the church, the papal states and throughout Italy and to make Rome, so long neglected and so many times battered and damaged, a city rich in architecture and the arts – and so a worthy centre for the Christian world.

Left: Nicholas V honours the memory of Francis of Assisi. Nicholas established peace in the papal states, moving away from using mercenaries and building castles with able governors.

652

POLITICAL/ECCLESIASTICAL ACHIEVEMENTS

Nicholas ended the schism within the Church by bringing about the resignations of the antipope Felix V on 7 April 1449 and his own recognition as pope by the remnant of the Council of Basel. He called a Jubilee in 1450 and as many as 100,000 pilgrims came to Rome – attracted by the offer of a plenary indulgence (the remission of temporal punishment for their sins); the offerings they made helped pay for the reconstruction of the city. On 19 March 1452 he crowned Holy Roman Emperor Frederick III in St Peter's – a statement of renewed papal authority and the last such coronation to take place there.

He restored peace to the papal states and negotiated the Peace of Lodi in 1454 between Venice, Milan, Florence and Naples. His intention was to organize a crusade against the Ottoman Turks for on 29 May 1453 the one great negative event of his reign had occurred: at the head of an army of around 80,000, 21-year-old Ottoman Sultan Mehmet II captured Constantinople, wiping out the Christian Byzantine Empire. Nicholas tried but without success to generate enthusiasm for a holy war.

VATICAN LIBRARY AND REGENERATION OF ROME

Highly intelligent and a gifted scholar, Nicholas was devoted to learning; he read very widely and collected books – some of his volumes, with marginal notes in his fine handwriting, still survive. He was a Renaissance man in the sense we use that term today – he knew all that was worth knowing; as his friend Aeneas Silvio Piccolomini (later Pope Pius II) said, "what he does not know is outside the scope of human knowledge".

In Rome he founded the Vatican Library containing 1,200 volumes and including rare Greek manuscripts brought by refugees from the Fall of Constantinople. He had a team of 45 copyists at work, and the finest scholars including the humanist Lorenzo Valla set to work making Latin translations of Greek works.

He rebuilt the Leonine Walls, paved several streets, carried out much-needed work on the aqueducts and restored the Castel Sant'Angelo. He rebuilt the Vatican, using architects Leon Battista Alberti and Bernardo Rossellino, and hiring artist Fra Angelico to paint frescos of saints Stephen and Lawrence in his study and chapel.

JOAN OF ARC

Over the course of these two pontificates Joan of Arc was cleared of heresy. After her exploits inspiring the French army against the English during the Hundred Years' War – inspired she claimed by God and the voices of saints Michael, Catherine and Margaret – she had been found guilty of witchcraft and heresy and burned at the stake in Rouen in 1431. In 1449 Nicholas V ordered her retrial and this carried on for seven years and heard 115 witnesses until in 1456 Callistus III declared her innocent. Her rehabilitation would be complete when Pope Benedict XV canonized her on 16 May 1920.

Above: Joan of Arc announces the Liberation of Orléans to Charles VII at Loches. Callistus declared her innocent of the charges of witchcraft that had led to her execution in 1431.

FIRST OF THE BORGIAS

Callistus III, the first Borgia pope, was aged 78 at his election on 8 April 1455. He had gout and spent the great part of his reign in bed. Callistus was notorious for his nepotism, and he appointed several relatives to key positions; in 1456 he raised his nephew Rodrigo Borgia (later the corrupt Pope Alexander VI) to the rank of cardinal.

He did succeed in raising a crusade of sorts – a papal fleet that won a few minor victories. His pontificate also saw the "miracle of Belgrade" – when a makeshift army inspired by the sermons of Italian-born Franciscan friar Giovanni da Capestrano drove off a vast Ottoman besieging force some 70,000 strong, and saved the city of Belgrade from capture. To mark the event, Callistus made the Transfiguration of Jesus a universal feast to celebrate the victory. It is celebrated on 6 August, the day on which news of the Battle of Belgrade – which seemed to evoke the glories of the First Crusade – arrived in Rome.

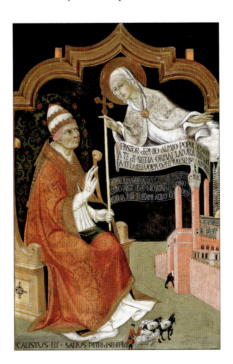

Left: The Virgin Mary appeared to Pope Callistus III to ask him to save Siena from the ravages of famine. Callistus was the first Borgia pope and the uncle of Pope Alexander VI.

PIUS II, 1458–64
POPE WHO PUBLISHED AN EROTIC NOVEL

Pius II rose to the papacy from relatively humble beginnings and by way of a colourful church career in which he was secretary to an antipope, fathered several illegitimate children, was excommunicated and almost lost his life on a secret international mission. He was a humanist and gifted writer of international renown, author of novels, poetry, geography and history, and a skilled diplomat; but he failed in the main endeavour of his pontificate, to call a crusade against the Ottoman Turks who had not only captured Constantinople in 1453 but were posing a threat to the whole of Europe.

Born Aeneas Silvio Piccolomini in the Republic of Siena, he was one of 18 children in a once wealthy family that had fallen on hard times. He managed eight years of humanistic study and embarked on a church career as secretary to cardinals including Cardinal Niccolo Albergati, the Bishop of Bologna for whom Tommaso Parentucelli (Pope Nicholas V) had worked.

> **FACT BOX**
> **Original name** Aeneas Silvio Piccolomini
> **Born** 18 October 1405
> **Origin** Corsignano [now Pienza], Siena
> **Date elected pope** 19 August 1458
> **Died** 14 August 1464
> **Key fact** Unable to launch the crusade he longed for

SAVED BY THE VIRGIN MARY?
In the service of Cardinal Albergati, Piccolomini went on an extraordinary secret mission. His task was to persuade King James I of Scotland to invade England, as part of a scheme to bring the Hundred Years' War to an end. His first attempt was stymied by the refusal of the English, who seemingly suspected skulduggery, to allow him to land; so he returned to Sluys, in Flanders (now in the Netherlands), and took ship again directly to Scotland. This voyage was almost his last, for a great storm sent him towards the coast of Norway; fearing for his life, he vowed that if he survived he would walk barefoot to the nearest shrine of the Blessed Virgin Mary. When he finally landed, in Dunbar, he honoured his promise but nearly lost his feet in tramping without shoes across frozen miles to the nearest shrine, at Whitekirk. He suffered from the effects throughout his life.

EXCOMMUNICATED
Subsequently he became an official of the Council of Basel, the church council that caused such difficulties for Eugenius IV, and then secretary to the antipope Felix V. He was excommunicated. In 1442 he became poet laureate and private secretary in the service of King Frederick IV of Germany (later Holy Roman Emperor Frederick III); the ban of excommunication was lifted. In these years, he lived a dissolute existence and fathered several illegitimate children. He became ill, mended his ways and became a priest in 1446.

Thereafter he played an important role in reconciling Frederick with the papacy. He was made Bishop of Trieste in 1447, Bishop of Siena in 1450 and Cardinal Bishop of Santa Sabina in 1456. He was elected pope on 3 September 1458.

CRUSADING DRIVE
At once he set to work trying to raise a crusade against the Turks. He called a council to this end for Christian rulers at Mantua in June 1459, but it was a failure; indeed, none of his efforts as pope to launch the crusade he had pronounced on 14 January 1460 came to anything. In 1461 he even wrote to the Ottoman Emperor Mehmet II, giving a detailed criticism of the Koran and of Islam and urging him to embrace

Below: As Aeneas Silvio Piccolomini, the future Pius II receives his cardinal's hat in December 1456. He had a long church career before becoming pope in his 50s.

Below: A fresco in Siena Cathedral by Bernardino Pinturicchio shows Pius II's coronation. He launched himself into a campaign to raise a crusade.

PIUS II

Above: Pius, too sick to stand, arrives in Ancona borne on a litter. For all his determination he did not manage to launch the crusade he longed for against the Turks.

THE TALE OF TWO LOVERS

Pius II is unique among popes in having written and published an erotic novel. His *Historia de duobos amantibus* ("Tale of Two Lovers") is one of the first epistolary novels (based around a collection of letters between two characters) and features the interchange between a married woman named Lucretia and one of the Duke of Austria's men in waiting, Euryalus. Piccolomini wrote the book in 1444 before he became pope and when he was in service at the German court. Some scholars identify Euryalus with Gaspar Schlick (to whom the book was dedicated), Chancellor to the Holy Roman Emperor.

He also wrote a 13-book autobiography, *Commentaries*, and made a collection of his letters. The earlier works were written during his dissolute youth, but the *Commentaries* dates from his time as Pius II and as such is the only autobiography written by a reigning pope.

Below: Mehmet II. He tried to claim the Roman title "Caesar" after he captured Constantinople in 1453. Pius wanted him to become Christian ruler of the former Eastern Roman Empire.

Christianity and to become Christian Emperor of the East, but this letter achieved nothing; some historians doubt whether it was ever sent to Mehmet, but it certainly circulated in Europe.

Eventually, in June 1464, Pius took the cross himself and set out in the hope of leading the crusade himself. He declared, "Our call to 'go forth' had not been listened to; perhaps if we say 'Come along with me' this will have more impact". But it was a doomed enterprise: he was already so sick that he had to travel on a litter; and when he arrived at Ancona, from where the crusade was due to embark, he found very few assembled crusaders and the promised Venetian fleet missing. On 12 August a paltry twelve ships arrived in place of the promised fleet. This was too much for Pius and he died at Ancona, his plans in tatters, just two days later on 14 August 1464.

FROM EROTIC VERSE TO PAPAL AUTOBIOGRAPHY

Among Pope Pius II's many writings were several erotic works in Latin: poems, a comedy called *Chrysis* and a novel entitled *The Tale of Two Lovers*.

655

PAUL II, 1464–71
A LOVER OF SHOW – AND MELONS

Celebrated for his love of extravagant show, Paul II (1464–71) wore lavish robes and lived while pope in the magnificent Palazzo San Marco (now called Palazzo di Venezia), which he built at vast expense to the papacy in Rome. He is remembered for dissolving the Roman Academy on the grounds that it promoted the pagan values of the classical world; in doing so, he made enemies of many leading humanists including Bartolomeo Platina, who later wrote *The Lives of the Popes* – and some of the more colourful tales about Paul's misdemeanours can be attributed to this enmity.

"OUR LADY OF PITY"
A nephew of Pope Eugenius IV, he was born Pietro Barbo in a family of wealthy Venetian merchants, and became a cardinal at the age of just 23. He was very ambitious – and free with his money, which made him popular: he once boasted that if he became pope he would buy every cardinal a summer villa.

Before the age of 30 he was archpriest of the Vatican Basilica and was already known for his love of ecclesiastical robes and emotionality. The then pope, Pius II, said of Barbo that he should be called "Our Lady of Pity" because he was quickly reduced to tears when pleading his case; Pius may also have been making a nod towards Barbo's love of fine robes, his wearing of rouge on his face – and perhaps, also, his taste for sexual relations with handsome young men.

By all accounts Barbo thought himself handsome and when he was elected on 30 August 1464 he wanted to call himself Formosus II (the name, used by a handsome pope in 891–6, which means "good-looking"), but the cardinals dissuaded him and he took the name Paul II.

Paul had won the election by agreeing a number of conditions with the cardinals – (a "capitulation"), including that the number of cardinals would not be increased beyond 24, that the creation of new cardinals and certain important church appointments would be made

Below: Bartolomeo Platina, author of The Lives of the Popes, *is installed as director of the Vatican Library. He had a highly troubled relationship with Paul II.*

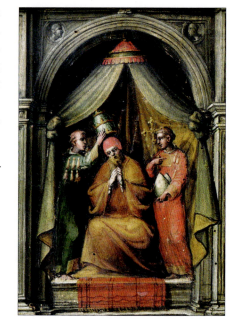

Above: The coronation of Paul II. He won election by agreeing conditions with the cardinals – a "capitulation".

only with the approval of the College of Cardinals and that within three years of taking office he would call an ecumenical council. But once pope he declared that he was not obliged to stand by these commitments.

LEARNING AND ANTIQUITIES
Paul endured a serious falling out with leading humanists, resulting from his dissolution of both the Roman Academy, and the College of Secretaries in the papal chancellery where many found employment. He was not uncultured

> **FACT BOX**
> **Original name** Pietro Barbo
> **Born** 23 February 1417
> **Origin** Venice
> **Date elected pope** 30 August 1464
> **Died** 26 July 1471
> **Key fact** Dissolved the Roman Academy

PAUL II

> ### BARTOLOMEO PLATINA
> Originally known as Bartolomeo Sacchi, he was born in Piadena, near Cremona, in 1421 and came to Rome aged 40. He became a member of the College of Secretaries in the papal chancellery and also wrote the first printed cookbook, *De honesta voluptate et valetuduine* ("On honourable pleasures and good health") in c.1465. He issued an angry response when Pius II wound up the College of Secretaries and was imprisoned for four months in the dungeons of the Castel Sant'Angelo. He was later imprisoned again following the discovery of a plot against the pope's life and then on his release was not offered employment by Pius II. He got his own back by writing a poisonous entry on Paul II in his great works *The Lives of the Popes*, which he wrote in the mid-1470s and gave to Paul's successor Sixtus IV.

ROME RESTORED

Paul restored several ancient monuments in Rome, including the Pantheon, the equestrian statue of Marcus Aurelius (now in the Capitoline Museums) and the arches of Titus and Septimius Severus. As part of Carnival festivities, he allowed the running of a horse race down the Via Lata (subsequently known as the Via del Corso).

He decreed Jubilee Years, in which pilgrims were called to pay their respects at the shrines and churches of Rome, should be held four times a century rather than twice every hundred years.

BOHEMIAN EXCOMMUNICATION

Paul moved against the Hussites (followers of the Bohemian reformer Jan Hus) when he excommunicated the pro-Hussite Bohemian king, George of Podebrady, and called on King Matthias I Corvinus of Hungary to invade. After Matthias conducted a successful campaign, Paul crowned him King of Bohemia in March 1469.

Around this time, in 1468, he tried without success to persuade Holy Roman Emperor Frederick III to launch a crusade against the Ottoman Turks; as part of these negotiations he

Above: In 1466 Paul excommunicated George of Podebrady who supported the Hussites, deposing him as king of Bohemia.

laid on the most lavish of welcomes for Frederick when the emperor made the second visit of his reign to Rome.

Paul died of a stroke at the age of 54, on 26 July 1471. Self-indulgent in all things, Paul was known for his extravagant love of melons, and according to one account his death came as a result of serious overindulgence in the fruit. Another account had it that his stroke hit while he was having sexual relations with a pageboy.

and was a significant patron of scholars; he did a great deal for the advancement of learning by permitting the establishment of the first printing presses in the papal states, first in Subiaco in 1464 and then in Rome in 1467.

He loved fine things, and collected hangings, bronzes and jewels, antiquities and art objects for his palazzo – now known as the Palazzo di Venezia in central Rome. His papal tiara was decorated with diamonds, emeralds, pearls, sapphires, topaz and other gems; when, after Paul's death, Pope Sixtus IV and various cardinals inspected his hoard of jewels they found more than 50 shells filled with pearls, altogether worth more than 300,000 ducats, as well as a single diamond that alone was worth 7,000 ducats. According to some stories he even took fine gems to bed with him.

Right: In 1467 Paul allowed carnival horse racing along the Via Lata in Rome; it became known as the Via del Corso.

RENAISSANCE AND REFORMATION

SIXTUS IV, 1471–84
POPE WHO CHANGED THE FACE OF ROME

Sweeping away medieval alleys and creating elegant piazzas and broad streets, renovating churches and spanning the Tiber with the beautiful Ponte Sisto, Sixtus IV transformed Rome into a fine Renaissance city. He built and began the decoration of the Sistine Chapel, but was also responsible for the establishment of the infamous Spanish Inquisition.

Francesco della Rovere was a Franciscan monk who served as minister general of the order from 1464 and was a highly regarded theologian known for his piety and unworldly character. Made a cardinal in 1467, he was elected pope on 9 August 1471 and straight away embraced extravagance and nepotism.

He spent more than one-third of the papacy's annual income on his coronation tiara, which cost 100,000 ducats. One of his first acts was to raise two of his nephews to be cardinals – one of these, Pietro Riario, was believed actually to be the pope's son by his own sister and lived such a degenerate life that he died of his excesses aged just 28. Among his other appointments were an eight-year-old boy as Bishop of Lisbon and an eleven-year-old boy as Bishop of Milan. There were even allegations that he handed out ecclesiastical positions in return for sexual favours from young men. These may be the work of Protestant propagandists.

PLOT AGAINST THE MEDICI
Sixtus allowed the papacy to become embroiled in a dispute with the Medici of Florence and a rather sordid assassination plot against Lorenzo de'Medici that severely damaged the moral standing of the Holy See. The Medici was a

> **FACT BOX**
> **Original name** Francesco della Rovere
> **Born** 21 July 1414
> **Origin** Republic of Genoa
> **Date elected pope** 9 August 1471
> **Died** 12 August 1484
> **Key fact** Built and named the Sistine Chapel

Above: Sixtus IV was notorious for nepotism. This portrait of the pope in c.1475 is by Joos van Gent (Joos van Wassenhove).

Below: Rome beautified. Sixtus gave his name to the elegant Ponte Sisto and to the Sistine Chapel, both built in his reign.

658

SIXTUS IV

> **SPANISH INQUISITION**
>
> Under a papal bull of 1 November 1478 Sixtus created the notorious Spanish Inquisition at the request of King Ferdinand II and Queen Isabella I, to combat the threat these monarchs believed was posed to Catholicism in Spain by converts from Judaism (Marranos) and from Islam (Moriscos). Isabella's former confessor Tomas de Torquemada was appointed as Grand Inquisitor. Sixtus later sent out a papal brief that reprimanded Spanish inquisitors for failing to follow procedures and being too zealous in treating alleged heretics.

Above: Sixtus was a patron of artists including Perugino, Botticelli and Pinturicchio. The Giving of the Keys to St. Peter, *a fresco in the Sistine Chapel, was painted in 1481 by Perugino.*

celebrated banking family: when they refused to loan Sixtus the money he needed to buy the town of Imola, which he wanted to give to his nephews, he had switched to their great rivals the Pazzi and threatened Lorenzo de'Medici with excommunication. It appears that Sixtus gave his backing to a plot in which agents of Sixtus's nephew Girolamo Riario attacked Lorenzo de'Medici and his brother Giuliano during Mass in Florence Cathedral: they struck blasphemously at the moment when the Host was elevated, stabbing and killing Giuliano and seriously injuring Lorenzo, who escaped to safety in the sacristy. Afterwards Sixtus placed an interdict on Florence and prevailed upon King Ferdinand I of Naples to declare war on the city. This lasted two years.

Sixtus made attempts to raise a crusade against the Turks with very limited success: an expedition in 1472 led by Cardinal Olivero Carafa captured Smyrna but a second attempted crusade in the following year failed. Then in 1480 the Turks captured Otranto on the Italian mainland and Sixtus, fearing that Rome might be next, called again for a crusade – a Christian army led by Alfonso II of Naples besieged the city; the death of Sultan Mehmet II and a disputed succession in Istanbul probably prevented the Ottomans from sending reinforcements and the episode ended with the invaders withdrawing and Otranto restored to freedom.

ROME REMADE

However, in terms of the rebuilding of Rome and endowment of Church buildings and institutions Sixtus's pontificate was a golden one. He built the first bridge across the Tiber since the classical era – the elegant Ponte Sisto, named after him – and laid out the Via Sistina (later called the Borgo Sant'Angelo), which links the Castel Sant'Angelo and St Peter's. He restored 30-odd churches, including Santa Maria del Popolo, San Vitale and Santa Maria della Pace, as well as the Acqua Vergine aqueduct.

SISTINE CHAPEL

He famously built the Sistine Chapel and hired major Renaissance artists including Pietro Perugino, Sandro Botticelli and Domenico Ghirlandaio to decorate it. (Michelangelo's work on the Chapel ceiling was under Pope Julius II in 1508–12.) Sixtus consecrated the chapel and dedicated it to the Virgin Mary on 15 August 1483, on which occasion he celebrated the first mass in the chapel.

He also brought the Roman Academy back to life and restored the foundling hospital, the Ospedale di San Spirito. He made a major investment in the Vatican Library, increasing his size threefold: Bartolomeo Platina recovered from his disgrace under Pope Paul II to be named librarian. A papal bull gave bishops authority to give unidentified corpses and the bodies of executed criminals to doctors to be cut up and studied; this helped make possible the anatomist Vesalius's masterwork *De humani corporis fabrica* ("The Fabric of the Body"), written in 1543 and perhaps the most important anatomy book in history.

He died on 12 August 1484 and is commemorated by one of the finest of all papal tombs, a magnificent bronze in the Vatican by Florentine sculptor, goldsmith and painter Antonio del Pollaiuolo.

Below: Tomas de Torquemada, Grand Inquisitor of the Spanish Inquisition. The seated figure in this painting by Pedro Berruguete is believed to be Tomas.

659

RENAISSANCE AND REFORMATION

INNOCENT VIII, 1484–92
POPE WHO KEPT AN OTTOMAN PRINCE CAPTIVE IN THE VATICAN

A weak and self-indulgent character, Innocent VIII was promoted to the papacy through the influence of Cardinal Giuliano della Rovere (the future Pope Julius II) and throughout his pontificate was under the cardinal's thumb. His reign was a disaster: he failed to impose authority on Rome, where the Orsini and Colonna families competed violently for the upper hand, or on the papal states, which descended into near-anarchy.

PUPPET POPE
Born Giovanni Battista Cibo in Genoa, he was of Greek ancestry. He was made Bishop of Savona under Paul II and – thanks to della Rovere's manoeuvrings – became a cardinal under Sixtus IV. The conclave from which he was elected pope, in 1484, was strongly divided, and was held while the people of Rome were rioting in the streets. Both della Rovere and Cardinal Rodrigo Borgia (the future Alexander VI) had their eye on the main prize, but neither – despite vast bribes – could garner enough support in the Sacred College, and so della Rovere settled in the short term for being the power behind the throne: he brought about the election of the utterly second-rate Cibo, whom he knew he could control.

Once pope, Innocent enthusiastically embraced the nepotism that was now taken for granted by many pontiffs. He already had two children by a mistress from Naples, and these he openly acknowledged and showered with benefits. He arranged the marriage of his son Franceschetto to Maddalena, daughter of Lorenzo de' Medici; Lorenzo's reward was the elevation of his own son Giovanni (the future Pope Leo X) to cardinal at the age of 13.

CAPTIVITY OF PRINCE CEM
Sixtus IV had virtually bankrupted the papacy and Innocent – whose own expenditure was also lavish – was not averse to indulging in simony to try to restore papal finances. He even resorted to inventing new ecclesiastical posts in order to charge large sums for their sale.

He was fortunate in that he chanced upon an unexpected and substantial source of income when he agreed to keep the rival claimant to the Ottoman sultanate, Prince Cem, in captivity in Rome. Following the death of Sultan Mehmet II, his successor Bayezit had

Left: Innocent VIII. An inscription on his tomb suggests the New World was found in his reign; some historians suggest that Columbus's voyage to the Americas took place earlier than generally thought.

Left: End of the Reconquista. An altarpiece in the royal chapel of the Cathedral of Granada depicts the last Muslim ruler of Granada leaving the city in 1492.

FACT BOX

Original name Giovanni Battista Cibo
Born 1432
Origin Republic of Genoa
Date elected pope 29 August 1484
Died 26 July 1492
Key fact Reign saw the end of the 700-year-long Reconquista in Spain

INNOCENT VIII

Above: Turkish sultan Bayezit II. Innocent kept Bayezit's brother Prince Cem in captivity in Rome. From Bayezit he received a relic – the lance that pierced Christ's side at His crucifixion.

Above: Innocent VIII issued a bull in 1487 appointing Tomas de Torquemada Inquisitor General of Spain. Spanish chronicler Sebastian de Olmedo called Torquemada "the hammer of heretics".

been challenged by his brother Cem; when Cem's bid for power failed, he had fled. Cem had then been taken into captivity on the island of Rhodes by the Grand Master of the Knights Hospitaller, Pierre d'Aubusson, who was handsomely remunerated by Bayezit for guarding the prince. Cem was later moved to France and in 1489 came into the care of Pope Innocent. In return for the vast sum of 120,000 ducats, Innocent agreed to keep Cem in Rome; the pope also received the gift of a treasured sacred relic, the Holy Lance that had pierced Christ's side on the cross. Cem and his travelling party were housed in the Vatican in a splendid apartment, where they lived in great comfort.

BULL AGAINST WITCHCRAFT

At a time of some agitation in Western Europe about the presence of witches in communities, Innocent issued a papal bull on 5 December 1484 that gave backing to belief in witchcraft, issued a condemnation of it and supported the activities of Inquisitor Heinrich Kramer in trying to root out witches in Germany. In Italy he was drawn into a conflict with Naples after its king, Ferdinand I, refused to pay papal dues. He excommunicated Ferdinand in 1489, and also condemned Italian philosopher Giovanni Pico della Mirandola, whose *900 Theses* had been published in 1486.

YEAR OF REMARKABLE EVENTS

For the last year of his life, Innocent was seriously ill: he kept to his bed but somehow found the energy to eat large meals when he awoke, and grew very fat; an attempt to give him a blood transfusion shortly before his death sadly resulted in the death of the three blood donors.

Before he died, however, he was cheered to receive the news that Ferdinand and Isabella had driven the Muslim Moors from Granada and so brought to a triumphant conclusion the 700-year holy war of the Reconquista. He survived another six months or so and died on 25 July 1492.

One week later Innocent's compatriot and fellow-Genoan, the explorer Christopher Columbus, set sail from Palos de la Frontera, Andalusia, on a voyage of exploration partly funded by Ferdinand and Isabella that resulted in the European discovery of the Americas.

RECONQUISTA

The Reconquista ("reconquest") was the struggle by Christians to reclaim control of the Iberian Peninsula from Muslims. It lasted over 700 years from the early 8th century when Muslim Arabs and Berbers captured the land from the Visigoths, to 1492, when the armies of Aragon and Castile took Granada, the last Muslim territory. The final stage was a ten-year war waged by Ferdinand and Isabella and financed by crusade taxes and the sale of crusade indulgences. Sultan Boabdil surrendered Granada at the end of 1491 and Ferdinand and Isabella took control on 2 January 1492. They reconsecrated the main mosque as a church; and there were great rejoicings in the Vatican. Innocent, close to death, gave Ferdinand the title of "Catholic Majesty".

ALEXANDER VI AND PIUS III, 1492–1503
RENAISSANCE POPE MOST NOTORIOUS FOR SINFULNESS

The corruption and excess of Pope Alexander VI's pontificate fed calls for the Protestant Reformation. He was vastly ambitious and worldly, openly acknowledging his several illegitimate children, notably the four he had by Roman noblewomen Vannozza dei Cattanei – Juan, Cesare, Goffredo and Lucrezia – and stopped at nothing to advance them through nepotism, marriage and diplomatic intrigue.

Rodrigo de Borgia himself had had a church career of many decades when he was elected pope on 11 August 1492, at around the age of 61. He had received his first ecclesiastical benefices while still a teenager, from his uncle Alonso de Borgia, then Bishop of Valencia and subsequently Pope Callistus III. He served as vice-chancellor of the Church and used the position to build up a vast personal wealth.

Below: Alexander takes a humble position at the feet of the Virgin Mary. His name may be a byword for self-serving corruption but he was deeply read in Holy Scripture.

Above: Rodrigo de Borgia – Pope Alexander VI – at prayer. He was a highly talented man, but not at all pious – happy to use bribery and indulge in nepotism.

Physically impressive and highly intelligent, Rodrigo was a gifted conversationalist, skilled at getting his own way. He loved playing cards. He lived in the expansive – and expensive – style of a Renaissance prince and after scandalous conduct in Siena was reprimanded by Pius II in 1460. He was also undeniably a skilled administrator and good diplomat, as shown by many of his dealings under pressure as pope.

PAPACY FOR SALE
In the papal conclave of 1492 Rodrigo spent freely and lavishly to persuade cardinals to vote for him – in effect, he bought the position of pope; he famously bribed Cardinal Ascanio Sforza, whose vote delivered the required two-thirds majority, with four mule-loads of silver. But his election was popular in Rome and celebrated by the locals with bonfires and torchlit processions and even a bullfight in the square before St Peter's; and on the procession to his coronation he received a great ovation.

He set to work to restore peace and justice in a Rome troubled by squabbles among adherents of noble families, and kept Tuesdays as a day on which those with grievances could make them heard before the pope himself.

FRENCH INVASION
Just two years into his pontificate Alexander faced the crisis of King Charles VII of France's invasion of Italy with a 30,000-strong army. Charles wanted to press his claim to the throne of Naples against that of King Alfonso II, whom Alexander had backed. Alexander's rival Cardinal Giuliano della Rovere (the future Pope Julius II) gave his support to Charles, who threatened to depose Alexander and call an ecclesiastical council.

Fearing for his future, Alexander briefly attempted an alliance with the Ottoman sultan Bayezit II, but in the end used all his diplomacy to negotiate a settlement with Charles in Rome. The French king got his way and crowned himself King of Naples on 12 May 1495.

By that date Alexander had formed a Holy League of the Holy Roman Emperor Maximilian I, Venice, Milan and King Ferdinand of Spain – notionally against the Turks but principally to drive the French from Italy. Charles, alarmed, retreated quickly to France and in due course Alfonso's son Ferdinand II was installed on the throne of Naples.

FACT BOX ALEXANDER VI
Original name Rodrigo de Borgia
Born 1431
Origin Jativa near Valencia
Date elected pope 11 August 1492
Died 18 August 1503
Key fact Libertine pope with six sons and three daughters

ALEXANDER VI AND PIUS III

PAPACY AND AMERICAS

When Alexander VI was asked to arbitrate in disputes between the Portuguese and Spanish over New World territory, his decision favoured Spain. In 1493 he issued the bull *Inter caetera* ("Among other things"), according to which Spain had the right to lands and seas west, and Portugal the right to territories and seas east of a line drawn from north to south 100 leagues (320 miles/515km) west of the Cape Verde islands. In the Treaty of Tordesillas in 1494 between Spain and Portugal the principle was agreed but the line moved to 370 leagues (1,185 miles/1,900km) west of the Cape Verde islands. Pope Julius II agreed this change in 1506.

BORGIA MURDER

In June 1497 Alexander was plunged into mourning when his eldest son, the 20-year-old Juan (or Giovanni) – who had already through his father's machinations married Maria Enriquez, King Ferdinand IV of Castile's cousin, and became Duke of Gandia in Spain – was found murdered in Rome. His body was hauled from the Tiber, his throat cut and showing evidence of nine stab wounds.

Alexander took refuge in the Castel Sant'Angelo and did not eat or drink for three days. The likely murderer was Juan's brother Cesare – according to rumours, they were both pursuing the sexual favours of the same woman, either their own sister Lucrezia or their sister-in-law Sancia, wife of their brother Goffredo.

Alexander was shocked into piety for a short while, and declared, "We loved the Duke of Garcia more than any other person in the world. God has done this as a punishment for our wrongdoings. We on our account are determined to mend our own life and to begin reform of the Church." He drew up a draft bull containing measures to outlaw simony and concubinage (priests living as if married with women) but it was never enforced.

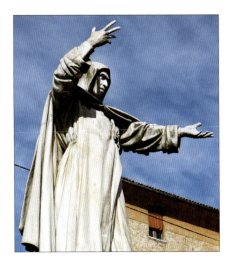

Right: In Florence Dominican friar Savonarola denounced church corruption. Alexander silenced him – he was excommunicated and burnt alive.

Alexander had made his son Cesare a cardinal at the age of 18, but following his brother Juan's assassination, on 17 August 1498 he became the first person to resign from the cardinalate and was named Duke of Valentinois by Louis XII of France. Thereafter Alexander set him up as an Italian prince with territories carved from the papal states. In 1499 he married Charlotte d'Albret, sister of King John III of Navarre.

Alexander died of a fever contracted on 12 August 1503 in a Rome that was in the grip of a heatwave, where malaria and the plague were on the prowl. The story that he died after mistakenly eating the poisoned confectionery he had intended for a cardinal when the plates were switched is probably no more than a legend. But it is true that the pope's body decayed and swelled in the heat, the face discoloured and the nose and tongue swelled horribly – and that when they came to put his body in its coffin the coffin was too small: Alexander's corpse was rolled in a carpet and battered and beaten until it could be squeezed into its final container.

PIUS III – A MAN OF INTEGRITY

Alexander's successor Pius III reigned for just 26 days from his election on 22 September to his death on 18 October 1503. A nephew of Pius II, he was a man of integrity who looked to bring about much-needed reforms but died before he could achieve anything.

Below: Alexander with his daughter Lucrezia Borgia. She was said to be a great beauty. He shamelessly made use of his position to advance his family.

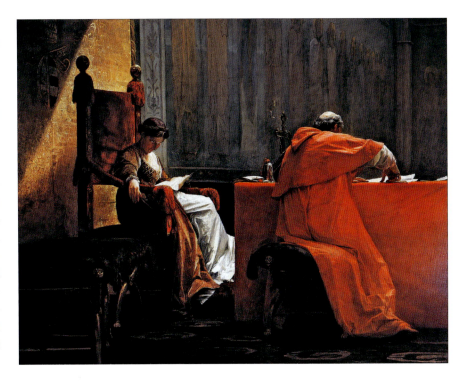

RENAISSANCE AND REFORMATION

JULIUS II, 1503–13
GREATEST OF PAPAL ART PATRONS

The remarkable Julius II is remembered as a warrior pope for his exploits in the field in reuniting the papal states and driving the French out of Italy, but also – and above all – as a patron of the arts, the pontiff who began the rebuilding of St Peter's and commissioned both Raphael's extraordinary frescoes in the Vatican and Michelangelo's immortal ceiling painting in the Sistine Chapel.

A nephew of Pope Sixtus IV – and the third consecutive pope to be the nephew of a previous pontiff – he had an extensive ecclesiastical career and had attempted to manoeuvre and bribe

Above: Raphael painted this moving portrait of Julius in c.1512, around a year before the pope's death. Julius wore a beard in 1511–12 in mourning for the loss of Bologna from the papal states.

FACT BOX
Original name Giuliano della Rovere
Born 5 December 1443
Origin Albisola, Republic of Genoa
Date elected pope 1 November 1503
Died 21 February 1513
Key fact Began rebuilding of St Peter's Basilica

Below: Michelangelo succeeded triumphantly in his commission for the Sistine Chapel ceiling. In four years, 1508–12, he painted more than 300 figures and covered more than 5,000 sq ft (500 sq m).

his way to the papal throne before. He spent most of the reign of his predecessor and enemy Alexander VI in exile at the French court and twice took part in French invasions of Italy with Charles VIII in 1494 and with Louis XII in 1502.

Julius was unscrupulous. Short-tempered and frequently rude, he often leapt into action without full thought for the consequences and was not good at organization or judging character. Yet he was powerful, brave and never gave up – in some ways, as his achievements show, he was an impressive man. The epithet "terrible" was applied to him.

He was devoted over many years to Francesco Alidosi, whom he raised to the cardinalate, defended and protected despite many failures and mourned deeply and extravagantly – to the extent where many have speculated that the men may have been lovers. Alidosi served as go-between for Julius and the artist Michelangelo and signed on the pope's behalf the contract for Michelangelo's paintings of the Sistine Chapel ceiling.

SECOND JULIUS CAESAR
On his election as pope on 1 November 1503 – after another conclave in which bribes flowed like water – he set to work to restore order to the papal states and northern Italy. Often taking to the field at the head of the papal troops in full armour, he regained control of

Above: Artist and patron: Michelangelo explains ideas to Julius. The pope began to commission Michelangelo after seeing the artist's magnificent sculpture of the Pietà.

Above: One of the frescoes Raphael painted for the papal apartments in the Vatican shows Emperor Constantine's victory at the Battle of the Milvian Bridge in 312.

Perugia and Bologna and as part of an Anti-Venetian League of Cambrai (with France, Milan, the Holy Roman Empire and Spain) defeated Venice in 1509. In his vision he was an emperor as well as a pope, a second Julius Caesar.

Formally reconciled with Venice after a ceremony in February 1510 at which he granted the republic absolution, he turned on his former ally, France. In the ensuing war of 1510–12 Julius had many severe setbacks and faced an ecclesiastical council in Milan called by Louis XII of France that denounced him and declared him suspended from office; but he built a new Holy League of Venice, Henry VIII of England, Ferdinand II of Spain and Naples and eventually Holy Roman Emperor Maximilian II, and called in Rome the first Lateran Council, which declared the rulings of the Milan council void and excommunicated all associated with it. This, combined with uprisings in northern Italy against the French, led to the withdrawal of the French army and the gain for the papal states of Piacenza and Parma.

PATRON OF THE ARTS

Even before becoming pope Julius II was a great artistic patron who commissioned the magnificent bronze tomb by Antonio Pollaiuolo for his uncle Sixtus IV. As pope he was patron of the finest artists of his day, including Michelangelo, Donato Bramante and Raphael.

In 1503 Julius determined to rebuild St Peter's Basilica. He appointed one of Italy's leading architects, Donato Bramante, to design it and in 1506 laid the foundation stone of the new basilica. Bramante worked on the new St Peter's from 1506 to his death in 1514 when Raphael succeeded him as principal architect. Bramante also built the Belvedere Courtyard at the Vatican for Julius.

Julius was a friend of Michelangelo, whom he commissioned to paint the extraordinary ceiling of the Sistine Chapel, to design the dome of the new St Peter's and to build Julius's own monument. This tomb was originally intended to be 36ft/11m in height and to contain no fewer than 40 life-size statues; it was to be housed in the new St Peter's – according to the art historian Vasari, one of the principal reasons for rebuilding St Peter's was to create a suitable setting for the tomb. In the end a much-reduced tomb was completed in 1545, 32 years after Julius's death – and stands today in San Pietro in Vincoli, where before becoming pope Julius had been cardinal-priest; only the statue of Moses is by Michelangelo – but that statue is a masterpiece. Julius and Michelangelo had a close and often fiery relationship and Julius had a significant input to masterworks such as the Sistine Chapel ceiling.

Raphael produced exquisite frescoes for the pope's new apartments in the Vatican. Julius famously declared that he would not occupy the same papal apartments as his enemy, the Borgia pope Pope Alexander VI, and declared that all paintings commissioned by the Borgias should be covered with black crepe. Raphael also painted a masterful portrait of Julius as a pensive old man, one of the finest portraits in art history, now in the Uffizi Gallery, Florence.

Another artist to benefit from his patronage was Pinturicchio, who painted the frescoes in the apse of the Church of Santa Maria del Popolo; Julius also commissioned several cardinals' sepulchres for the church from Sansovino.

SWISS GUARD

Julius founded the Pontifical Swiss Guard in 1506. At the time Swiss mercenary regiments served in many armies and before becoming pope Julius II had fought alongside Swiss mercenaries in Charles VIII's invasion of Italy. The first guard consisted of 150 men commanded by Captain Kasparvon Silenen, who were blessed by Julius on 22 January 1506. Julius granted the guards the title "Defenders of the Church's freedom". The Guard is still responsible for the pope's safety.

LEO X AND HADRIAN VI, 1513–23
POPE DENOUNCED BY MARTIN LUTHER

Leo X made Rome the centre of European cultural life and was another very great papal patron of the arts and learning; he famously said "God has given us the papacy, now let us enjoy it." However, he did not make an adequate response to the first stirrings of the Protestant Reformation and so failed to protect the Church from its later dissolution.

Born Giovanni de'Medici, he was the second son of Florentine ruler Lorenzo de' Medici and was made a cardinal-deacon at the age of 13. At the Medici court he had the finest available humanist education – one of his tutors was philosopher Pico della Mirandola – and also studied law and theology at the University of Pisa. After the expulsion of the Medici from Florence in the course of the French invasion of Italy in 1494 he travelled in northern Europe.

He was not good-looking, with a big head and wide, red face, but he was charming and likeable – a sophisticated and highly cultured man, peace-loving and good-natured.

As a patron of the arts he accelerated the rebuilding of St Peter's and built the Church of San Giovanni dei Fiorentini on Via Giulia. He supported Raphael, who worked on papal rooms in the Vatican, and Michelangelo (whom he had known since they were both boys in Florence). Leo chiefly used Michelangelo on projects in their hometown to aggrandize the Medici.

> **FACT BOX LEO X**
> **Original name** Giovanni de'Medici
> **Born** 11 December 1475
> **Origin** Florence
> **Date elected pope** 9 March 1513
> **Died** 1 December 1521
> **Key fact** Humanist education made him great patron of learning

Above: Leo had a big, wide head and unprepossessing looks but he had a sophisticated intelligence. This striking portrait, in chalks, is by early Mannerist artist Giulio Romano.

Above: Leo issued his bull Exsurge Domine *("Arise O Lord!") "against the erroneous Martin Luther and his followers" on 15 June 1520, threatening the German with excommunication.*

He was a great patron of learning who, in addition to expanding the Vatican Library as well as reforming the University of Rome, supported the printer Aldo Manuzio in publishing editions of the Roman and Greek classics and employed one of the great Greek scholars of the Renaissance, Janus Lascaris (who is sometimes called John Rhyndacenus), while encouraging many of the leading writers of the day, especially poets.

Leo is widely believed to have been homosexual and to have enjoyed close relations with some of his chamberlains. His court was colourful, with jesters and panthers – and a pet white elephant named Hanno, which he had received as a gift from King Manuel I of Portugal. He loved to go hunting, accompanied by as many as 300 in his entourage, and gave vast and indulgent banquets.

All this was very expensive – and to defray expenses Leo relied on raising money through the sale of cardinals' hats and in particular the sale of indulgences. In 1517 alone he named 31 new cardinals.

The preaching in Germany of an indulgence to raise money for the construction of St Peter's provoked an attack by the German reformer Martin Luther that led to a bitter dispute in which Luther denounced Leo as "antichrist" and Leo excommunicated Luther – and this is seen as the beginning of the Protestant Reformation.

FAILED DIPLOMACY

Leo had to deal with the ambitions of French kings Louis XII and Francis I in Italy: after Francis won the Battle of Marignano in September 1515 Leo had little choice but to make a peace that allowed the French crown to nominate all the leading bishops, abbots and priors in the French Church. In 1519 Leo then attempted to prevent the accession of Charles I of Spain as Holy Roman Emperor Charles V but in the end allied

LEO X AND HADRIAN VI

> **ERASMUS**
>
> The great Dutch humanist scholar Desiderius Erasmus dedicated his edition of the Greek New Testament in 1516 to Leo X. Born in 1469 in Rotterdam he studied in an Augustinian monastery but left to become Latin secretary to the Bishop of Cambrai. Afterwards he studied theology in Paris and went to England – where for a while he was professor of divinity and Greek at Cambridge University and wrote his satire on church and society, *Encomium Moriae* ("In Praise of Folly", 1511). Later he studied and wrote in Louvain and Basel. He wrote his masterpiece *Colloquia* in 1522–3. He died in Basel in 1536.

with Charles against Francis. His attempts to raise a crusade against the Turks failed.

On 1 December 1521 he died unexpectedly ten days before his 46th birthday. He may have had malaria or bronchopneumonia, but because his corpse became swollen and discoloured, contemporaries whispered that he had been poisoned. He left the Church virtually bankrupt – having spent more than 5 million ducats in his pontificate, and for all his worth as a patron the reputation of the papacy was at a very low ebb.

Left: Desiderius Erasmus by Quentin Massys. His editions of the New Testament were important for the Protestant Reformation, but he never lost his respect for the Roman Catholic Church and the papacy.

Above: Raphael painted this portrait of Leo X, his cousin Giulio de' Medici (left) and Cardinal Luigi de' Rossi in 1518. Giulio de' Medici became Pope Clement VII in 1523.

POPE HADRIAN VI

Born Hadrian Florenszoon Boeyens in Utrecht, Hadrian VI (1522–3) was a former professor of theology at the University of Louvain and tutor to Holy Roman Emperor Charles V; he had even acted as Charles's regent in Spain. Elected pope on 9 January 1522, he was unable to win the backing of the Romans and although he set out to reform the Church and tame the Ottoman Turks he achieved very little towards either goal before his death on 14 September 1523 in Rome.

Hadrian VI is the only Dutch pope to date and the last non-Italian to be pope until the Polish pontiff John Paul II in 1978.

THE PAPACY AND THE PROTESTANT REFORMATION

Beginning in the early 16th century Protestant Reformers denounced the papacy as "antichrist" and established their own religious groups to replace the Church of Rome.

There had been plenty of attempts to reform abuses in the Roman Catholic Church before the advent of the Protestant Reformation. These went all the way back to Peter Waldo or Valdes, founder (c.1140–1218; founder of the Waldensians) and St Francis of Assisi (1181–1226; founder of the Franciscans) and also included Englishman John Wycliffe (1330–84) and Bohemian Jan Hus (1378–1417).

The controversy generally seen as the start of the Reformation was between Pope Leo X (1513–21) and German theologian Martin Luther. It was over the pope's sale of indulgences (granting remission of the temporal penalty for a person's sins), principally to raise money for the construction of St Peter's. Popes had been granting indulgences for many centuries, and abuse of this mechanism

Below: A woodcut shows church discipline being enforced as Leo X supervises the burning of Martin Luther's books after the first Diet of Worms, in 1521.

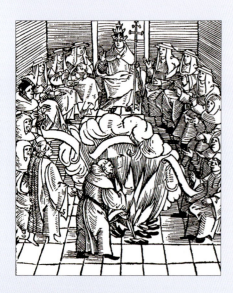

had been strongly criticized before. However, by the early 16th century the time was ripe for reform – and revolt. The Papal Schism of 1378–1417 – a time when two and sometimes even three popes had set up in opposition to one another – had undermined the standing of the papacy and had been followed by a period in which popes such as Innocent VIII (1484–92) and Alexander VI (1492–1503) had through nepotism, self-indulgence, corruption and sexual promiscuity brought their office to its nadir. The spiritual authority of the papacy and the Church was severely weakened.

LEO X UNDER ATTACK

Shortly after becoming pope, Leo X had affirmed a special indulgence previously issued by Julius II (1503–13) to raise money for the construction of St Peter's; the preaching of this indulgence by Dominican friar Johann Tetzel in Germany provoked Luther, a professor at the University of Wittenberg and a pastor, to pin his 95 theses on the door of Wittenberg Cathedral on 31 October 1517. (This is the traditional account, accepted for centuries; modern scholars suggest that while Luther certainly circulated his theses, he did not actually pin them to the cathedral door.)

The theses, which Luther intended as topics for debate on the sale of indul-

Above: The power of the word: Martin Luther's Sermon – a detail from a triptych painted in 1547 by German artist Lucas Cranach, the Elder, a friend of Luther and enthusiastic supporter of the Reformation.

gences – spread quickly throughout Germany and beyond in Europe.

On 15 June 1520 Leo issued a papal bull *Exsurge Domine* ("Arise O Lord") that condemned 41 of Luther's propositions, called on him to recant and threatened excommunication. Luther defied him, burning a copy of the bull and denouncing the pope as "antichrist sitting in the Temple of God"; Leo issued a second bull *Decet Romanum Pontificem* ("It pleases the Roman pontiff") on 3 January 1521 that excommunicated him.

"PROTESTANTS"

In April 1521 Luther appeared before the Diet or Assembly of Worms, in Germany, to answer charges of heresy. He was asked to repudiate his works, but refused unless he could be convinced that he was wrong using reason or Scripture. He declared, "Here I stand; I can do no other." He left Worms and went into hiding; the following month, in the Edict of Worms, the Diet declared him an outlaw whose writings should be forbidden and who should be pursued and handed to the Holy Roman Emperor to be disciplined.

In 1526 the Diet of Speyer determined that each ruler should be free to decide whether or not to enforce the Edict of Worms; in 1529 Emperor Charles V had withdrawn this provision, and at another diet in Speyer, in 1529, six Lutheran princes and 14 cities of Germany made a protest against Charles's decision. They – and supporters of the Reformation protest generally – became known as "Protestants".

SCRIPTURAL AUTHORITY

These Protestants challenged the teaching authority of the Church and declared that each Christian could have an individual relationship with God, reliant only the Word of God as revealed in the Scriptures. They emphasized the importance of translating the Bible into vernacular languages. Luther published a translation of the New Testament into German in 1522; Englishman William Tyndale published a translation of the New Testament into English in 1525.

JUSTIFICATION BY FAITH

Luther attacked the Church's teaching on redemption, the necessity of doing good works to be saved and the action of God's grace. He declared Scripture alone was authoritative, and people were justified (that is freed from sin and made righteous) by God's grace through faith alone – good works were not necessary.

French lawyer John Calvin was converted to Protestantism and, after taking refuge in Basel, Switzerland, wrote the *Institutes of the Christian Religion* (1536), the Protestants' first systematic work of theology. He followed Luther on justification by faith alone, and developed the doctrine of predestination, according to which one group of souls (the Elect) were eternally chosen for salvation while another were eternally marked out for damnation. Like Luther he denounced the pope as "antichrist".

The Reformation spread widely through Europe. By c.1550 northern

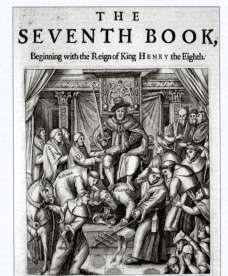

Europe was dominated by Lutheranism. Italy and Spain remained untouched, and they became the centre of the Church's fightback in the Counter-Reformation.

THE CHURCH OF ENGLAND

King Henry VIII of England was initially a friend to the papacy. In 1521 he wrote a pamphlet entitled *A Defence of the Seven Sacraments* in response to Luther and Pope Leo X awarded him the title *Fidei Defensor* ("Defender of the Faith"). But in little over a decade king and pope were at loggerheads

Left: The title page of John Foxe's Seventh Book shows Henry VIII trampling on Pope Clement VII with the help of Cranmer.

and the English Church split from the Church of Rome.

From 1527 Henry VIII pestered Clement VII with requests that Henry's marriage to Catherine of Aragon be annulled; Clement was unwilling to provoke Catherine's nephew Charles V by granting the annulment. Clement said Henry could not marry until a papal verdict had been announced but Henry married Anne Boleyn in 1533 and at a trial in England, Archbishop Thomas Cranmer determined Henry's first marriage was annulled. In 1533 Clement excommunicated Henry and Cranmer. In 1534 the English Act of Supremacy made the king supreme head of the English Church. Henry confiscated for the crown the wealth of the Church in England in the Dissolution of the Monasteries.

Below: Martin Luther in the Circle of Reformers. At the table are John Wycliffe (extreme left), Luther (centre) and Jan Hus (extreme right). Facing the table figures include a cardinal, the pope and a Franciscan.

RENAISSANCE AND REFORMATION

CLEMENT VII, 1523–34
INEFFECTIVE WHILE PROTESTANT REFORMATION GATHERS PACE

Clement's attempts to challenge the authority of Holy Roman Emperor Charles V led to the ignominious Sack of Rome in 1527 by Charles's unpaid, mutinous troops. They also contributed to the unwanted progress of the Protestant Reformation because while the pope and emperor were quarrelling they could not act to defend the Church.

Clement was born Giulio de'Medici in 1478 one month after his father Giuliano's assassination in Florence Cathedral in a plot hatched by Pope Sixtus IV's nephew Girolamo Riario. He was raised by his uncle Lorenzo the Magnificent, then after Lorenzo's death in 1492 by his cousin, Lorenzo's son Giovanni (who became Pope Leo X).

Giulio gained valuable experience in administration and diplomacy: he was vice-chancellor under Leo and a major director of papal policy in Leo's pontificate. He served as cardinal protector of England.

Below: This imperious marble Moses was the only part of the tomb of Julius II that Michelangelo completed. Giorgio Vasari said it was "unequalled by any modern or ancient work".

> **FACT BOX**
> **Original name** Giulio de'Medici
> **Born** 26 May 1478
> **Origin** Florence
> **Date elected pope** 19 November 1523
> **Died** 25 September 1534
> **Key fact** Helpless during Sack of Rome by Emperor Charles V

Elected pope on 19 November 1523 aged 48, he was pious, thin-lipped and rather haughty; and while he was also intelligent, learned and hardworking, he was poor at making decisions. For all his diplomatic experience he failed dismally to find a good line in dealing with the international struggle for power between King Francis I of France and Holy Roman Emperor Charles V.

Clement's frequent shifts of allegiance led eventually to the Sack of Rome by Charles's mutinous troops in May 1527. Having supported Charles up to the Battle of Pavia in 1525, in which Charles triumphed and Francis was taken prisoner, he then allied with Francis (along with Milan, Venice and Florence) in the 1526 League of Cognac against the Empire.

"HELLISH" SACK OF ROME
In 1527 Charles's troops in Italy ran amok after finding that there were no funds available to pay them: they moved on Rome, then after the death of their commander, Duke Charles III of Bourbon, stormed the city. Only the bravery of the Pontifical Swiss Guard, who lost 147 of their number in the fighting, enabled the pope to escape to safety in the Castel Sant'Angelo. Looting, raping and stealing went on for eight terrible days – the greatest indignity suffered by Rome since the invasion of the Visigoths. One stunned eyewitness wrote, "Hell cannot compare to the current condition of Rome".

Above: Portrait of Clement VII: he was pious and haughty, but poor decision-making led to his humbling in the Sack of Rome by Charles V's troops.

Clement surrendered in June, then remained in the Castel Sant'Angelo for six months, until he finally managed to escape by night in the guise of a gardener. He fled to Orvieto and then Viterbo – and was not to return to Rome until October 1528. Under the terms of the peace, agreed in summer 1529, Charles agreed to return Florence to the Medici, who had been expelled again in the fighting. It took a siege of 11 months before the city was taken, in 1530, and Clement made his son Alessandro de'Medici Duke of Florence. Clement did not challenge Charles's authority again; in Bologna on 24 February 1530 Clement crowned Charles Holy Roman Emperor – the last time a pope would crown a Holy Roman Emperor.

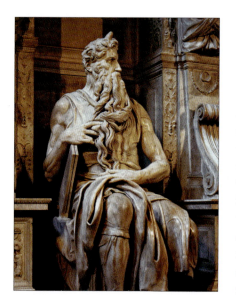

CLEMENT VII

> ### MICHELANGELO
> Sculptor, architect, painter and poet Michelangelo Buonarroti was born in 1475 in Caprese, part of the Republic of Florence. After his sculptures of the *Pietà* (1498) and of *David* (1501–4), he was hired by Julius II to design and make the pope's tomb (only the statue of Moses was completed, 1513–15) and paint the ceiling of the Sistine Chapel (1508–12). For Pope Leo X he worked largely in Florence, particularly on the Medici Chapel in the new sacristy of the Church of San Lorenzo. After 1534 he lived in Rome, working as an architect on the Capitoline Square and the dome of St Peter's Basilica, as well as painting the Sistine Chapel's *The Last Judgement*. He died on 18 February 1564 in Rome.

HENRY VIII AND THE ENGLISH CHURCH

Clement's disastrous pontificate also saw the separation of the English Church from Rome, a major development in the Protestant Reformation. From 1527 onwards Henry VIII was asking the pope to annul his marriage to Catherine of Aragon, widow of his deceased brother Arthur, on the grounds that marrying a brother's wife was forbidden and so the marriage had not been blessed by God with a male offspring. After the humiliation of the Sack of Rome, Clement was no longer willing to risk the anger of Holy Roman Emperor Charles V – and Charles supported Catherine's cause because of their familial connection: she was his aunt.

In March 1530 Clement announced that Henry was forbidden to marry until the papal verdict had been reached. However, Henry would not wait. In January 1533 he married Anne Boleyn and a trial in England at which Archbishop of Canterbury Thomas Cranmer presided found that the king's first marriage was annulled.

In 1533 Clement finally acted – determining that the marriage to Catherine of Aragon was valid and excommunicating Henry and Cranmer. It was too late. The following year saw the English Act of Supremacy, which made the king, not the pope, the head of the English Church.

THE LAST JUDGEMENT

Like his forerunners in the Renaissance papacy, Clement was a lavishly generous patron of the arts and learning. He was a friend of Erasmus and the goldsmith and sculptor Benvenuto Cellini and a patron of Machiavelli and Guicciardini;

Above: This delicate ink drawing by Dutch artist Maarten van Heemskerck shows the interior of the basilica of St Peter's with the new building under construction, c.1532.

from Michelangelo, considered the greatest living artist in his day, Clement commissioned the peerless painting of *The Last Judgement* on the east wall of the Sistine Chapel.

Right: Commissioned by Clement VII, Michelangelo painted The Last Judgement *on the altar wall of the Sistine Chapel in 1536–41. The Risen Christ divides the saved (rising to heaven, left) from the damned (falling to hell, right).*

671

POPES IN THE MODERN ERA

In the mid-16th century Pope Paul III led the Church in the Counter-Reformation – an energetic response to the Protestant revolt. The teaching decrees of the Council of Trent, the outreach of the Jesuits and the severity of the Inquisition in stamping out heresy were supplemented by the glories of Baroque art and architecture as Rome was made beautiful to demonstrate the greatness of God and his Church and by the energy and spiritual force of reformers such as Teresa of Avila, John of the Cross and Francis de Sales. As the political influence of the papacy waned and disappeared, popes focused energy on being teachers and examples. Pontiffs such as John XXIII and John Paul II connected forcefully with the faithful and have both been canonized saints. Their successor, Pope Francis, is the first pope to be appointed from the Americas.

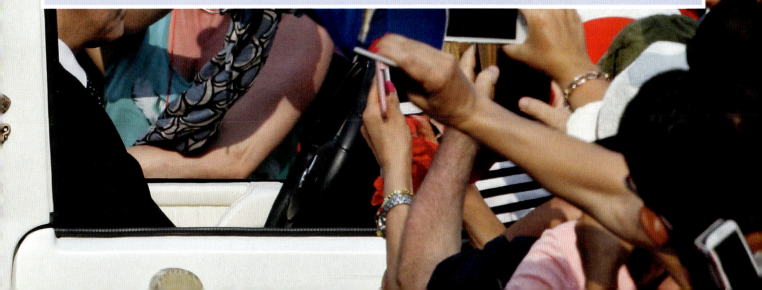

Pope Francis, elected on 13 March 2013, took his papal name to honour St Francis of Assisi, whom he called "the man of poverty, the man of peace, the man who loves and protects creation". Here he is mobbed by the faithful in St Peter's Square on 16 September 2015.

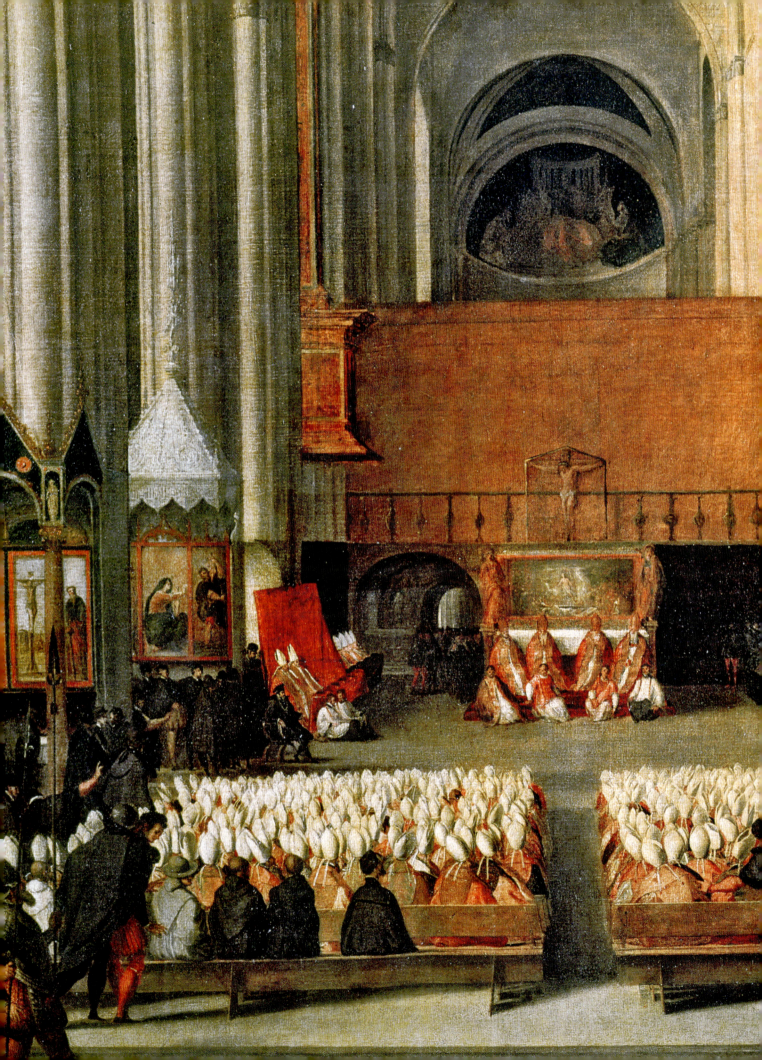

THE COUNTER-REFORMATION

PAUL III TO INNOCENT X, 1534–1655

Pope Paul III is celebrated as the first pope of the Counter-Reformation – the Roman Catholic Church's efforts to renew itself and fight back against the Protestant Reformation. He appointed leading humanist churchmen to a commission tasked with analyzing the Church's problems and devising reforms. Paul drove reform forward. He called the Council of Trent, whose decrees clarified doctrine and brought in many organizational improvements, and approved the establishment of new and revitalizing Catholic orders such as the Jesuits. His successors carried the work on. Julius III approved the creation and founding of the Jesuits' Collegium Romanum for training priests to serve in Germany. The ascetic and authoritarian Paul IV established the Index of Prohibited Books and strongly backed the work of the Roman Inquisition in stamping out heresy. Pius IV, Pius V and Gregory XIII in particular implemented the reforms of the Council of Trent. Various popes also supported military action against the Protestants of northern Europe – notably Pius V and Gregory XIII, who sent aid to French regent Catherine de'Medici in her struggles with the French Huguenots.

Rome was beautified to reflect the greatness of Church and papacy. By the close of the 16th century, 30 new streets had been laid out, three aqueducts splendidly restored and scores of fountains and fine parks created; under Sixtus V the long rebuilding of St Peter's Basilica, begun in 1506, was brought to a triumphant conclusion in 1590. Then in the early 17th century, particularly under the artistic patronage of Urban VIII, the city was further improved with the full and gorgeous flowering of the baroque architectural and sculptural style in Rome.

Left: The Council of Trent (1545–63) embodied the Counter-Reformation. The Tridentine Creed and the Tridentine Mass resulted from its work. It had 25 sessions under three popes, Paul III, Julius III and Pius IV.

THE COUNTER-REFORMATION

PAUL III, 1534–49
FIRST POPE OF THE COUNTER-REFORMATION

Paul III (1534–49) may be the first pontiff of the Counter-Reformation, but in many respects he was also the last of the Renaissance popes. While he was responsible for calling the Council of Trent (1545–63), whose decrees ushered in reform and clarified doctrinal matters, and for approving the formation of reforming Catholic orders such as the Jesuits, he also – like many of his forerunners in the Renaissance papacy – spent lavishly on the arts, lived like a secular prince in fathering four children and enthusiastically embraced nepotism as a way to advance his family interests.

"PETTICOAT CARDINAL"
Alessandro Farnese was a brother of Giulia Farnese, mistress of Pope Alexander VI: Alexander appointed him

Below: Paul spent lavishly on his family's palace, the Palazzo Farnese, in Rome. This allegory of Paul between Peace and Fertility, is from a fresco in the palace by Cecchino Salviati.

> **FACT BOX**
> **Original name** Alessandro Farnese
> **Born** 29 February 1468
> **Origin** Canino, papal states
> **Date elected pope** 13 October 1534
> **Died** 10 November 1549
> **Key fact** Called the Council of Trent

treasurer of the Roman Church and made him a cardinal deacon in 1493. Because he owed his advancement in the Church to his sister's position, he was known as the "petticoat cardinal".

Exploiting his position, he grew wealthy and spent lavishly on the Palazzo Farnese in the Via Giulia. He travelled on diplomatic missions and was known for his love of the hunt and of grand ceremonial. He kept a mistress in Rome and fathered four children – Pierluigi, Paolo, Ranuccio and Costanza.

As pope he was a shameless nepotist – he famously raised his two grandsons to be cardinals at the ages of 14 and 16.

Above: Paul III (Alessandro Farnese) was descended from a family that had served the papacy since the 12th century. His grandfather, Ranuccio the Elder, was a leading condottiere whom Pope Martin V made a Roman senator. This celebrated portrait is by the great Titian.

His son Pierluigi was well known for his wildly dissolute lifestyle and his love of homosexual antics, but this did not stop Paul raising him to be Captain-General of the Church and later in 1545 establishing him as Duke of Parma and Piacenza.

Paul was 67 when elected pope on 13 October 1534. Pageants and chivalric tournaments were held in Rome, as smiles returned to Roman faces following the tragedy of 1527; later, in 1536, Paul announced the revival of the Carnival, and the Romans enjoyed balls, feasts, firework displays, horseraces and bullfights.

Paul commissioned Michelangelo not only to work on the Palazzo Farnese, but also to refashion the Campidoglio and move the equestrian statue of Marcus

Right: Nicolaus Copernicus. He may have felt that dedicating the work to Paul III would give him some protection. This statue is in Warsaw, Poland.

Aurelius to be its centerpiece, to work as architect on the new St Peter's Basilica and to design his tomb – it was erected in St Peter's by Guglielmo della Porta. He also drove the great artist on to finish *The Last Judgement* in the Sistine Chapel and to complete his final frescoes in the Capella Paolina (the Pauline Chapel) in the Vatican.

He was a patron of the artist Titian who made a series of magnificent portraits of the pope – including one, in c.1545–6 of the pope with his grandsons: a symbol of the corruption of a Renaissance papacy that was devoted to nepotism and dynastic politicking.

PIOUS AND CHARMING

Yet for all his extravagance and his many faults, Paul III was also devout and serious about reform of the Church. Sensitive and intelligent, he was very well educated: in his youth, he had a humanist education under

Below: The opening session of the Council of Trent took place in December 1545 – eight years after Paul first proposed it. He did not attend in person; he was represented by a papal legate.

Pomponio Leto and was associated with the Medici in Florence, where he made friends with Giovanni de'Medici, the future Pope Leo X. As pope, Paul was known for his immense charm and shrewdness: he spoke fine Italian and Latin and in negotiations was a wary negotiator, highly skilled at deferring a decision until an issue was fully worked out. Then he acted decisively.

COUNTER-REFORMATION

Shortly after his accession Paul summoned a general church council to meet at Mantua. After many delays it convened in Trent in December 1545. It would meet 25 times over the next 18 years, to 1563, and laid the groundwork for the Church's Counter-Reformation, making practical reforms and issuing definitions on key points of doctrine such as original sin, purgatory, the Seven Sacraments and justification (the means by which people should seek salvation – the principal means usually were either through good works or by faith).

He gave military and financial support to Holy Roman Emperor Charles V in his military campaign of 1546–7 against the Schmalkaldic League of Protestant princes. He also issued a second and final excommunication against King Henry VIII of England in December 1538.

COPERNICUS

Among the fields of learning encouraged at the papal court by Pope Paul III was astronomy and Polish mathematician and astronomer Nicolaus Copernicus dedicated his groundbreaking *De revolutionibus orbium coelestium* ("On the Revolutions of the Heavenly Spheres") to Paul in 1543. Copernicus's understanding that the Sun and not the Earth was at the centre of the solar system and that the Earth, rotating daily on its axis, circuits the Sun paved the way for the scientific revolution of later centuries. Born in Thorn (modern Torun) in Poland in 1473, he studied at the universities of Krakow, Bologna and Padua and visited Rome in the Jubilee year of 1500. He died on 24 May 1543, the year in which his book was published. The Church did not condemn Copernicus until 1616, in the era of Galileo Galilei.

REFORMING ORDERS

Under Paul the establishment and consolidation of new reforming religious orders, which had had its first beginnings under his predecessor, continued apace. The Theatines and Barnabites, given papal approval by Clement VII in 1524 and 1533 respectively, thrived – as did the Capuchins, an offshoot of the Franciscans Clement had approved in 1528. The Ursulines, an order of teaching nuns, were founded in Paul's pontificate in 1535. In 1540 Paul issued his bull *Regimini militantis ecclesiae* ("For government of the militant Church"), which gave formal approval to the Society of Jesus (or Jesuits). In July 1542 he set up the Holy Office of the Inquisition with significant reforming powers effective throughout Europe.

Paul died on 10 November 1549, still devastated after the assassination of his son Pierluigi two years earlier and after a violent row with Pierluigi's successor as Duke of Parma and Piacenza, Paul's own grandson Cardinal Ottavio Farnese.

THE COUNTER-REFORMATION

JULIUS III, 1550–5
CHURCH REFORM CONTINUES DESPITE A WEAK POPE

The Counter-Reformation continued apace through the pontificate of Julius III, almost in spite of the efforts of the dissolute pope himself.

In 1551 Julius did briefly reconvene the Council of Trent, suspended in 1548, but he suspended it again two years later; he reconfirmed the order of the Jesuits and founded their Collegium Germanicum for training priests to defend the Catholic faith in Germany. But he directed most of his energy to his own pleasure, spending vast sums on entertainments devised for him by the Mannerist architect Giacomo Barozzi da Vignola at the pope's country house, Villa Giulia, and scandalizing Rome and the Church by the brazen promotion of his adopted nephew Innocenzo Ciocchi del Monte, a good-looking beggar he had picked up on the streets of Parma.

SKILLED ADMINISTRATOR

For all that he did not bring honour to the papacy once pontiff, Giovanni Maria Ciocchi del Monte was a renowned canon lawyer and an admired administrator before becoming pope. He had an excellent education under the humanist Raffaele Brandolini in Rome and studied law firstly at Perugia and then Siena.

He was twice made governor of Rome and during the Sack of Rome almost lost his life after being given up as a hostage by Pope Clement VII to the

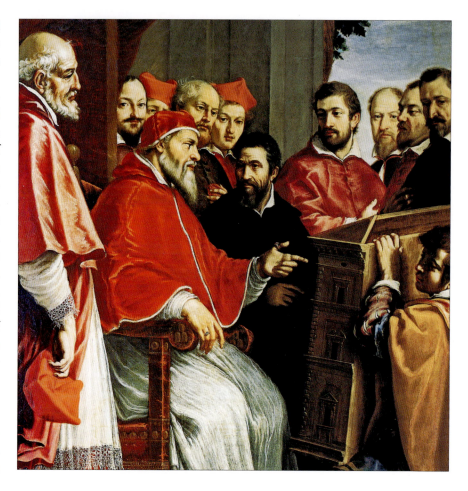

Above: Julius liaised closely with the artists whose patron he was. Here Michelangelo presents a model of a building to the pope in a painting by contemporary artist Fabrizio Boschi.

Below: Julius appointed the great Giovanni Pierluigi da Palestrina, whom he knew from Palestrina's Book of Masses, *singing master to the papal choir. Before his death in 1594, Palestrina composed 105 masses.*

emperor's troops. Under Paul III he was appointed cardinal-bishop of Palestrina and he served as the first president of the Council of Trent. He came to the papacy as a compromise candidate.

INNOCENZO

On his election Pope Julius was already known for his infatuation with Innocenzo, the beggar boy he had selected from the streets of Parma and made his adoptive nephew. His first act as pope was to promote the young man to be a cardinal, and thereafter he was shameless in directing church positions

> **FACT BOX**
> **Original name** Giovanni Maria Ciocchi del Monte
> **Born** 29 February 1468
> **Origin** Rome
> **Date elected pope** 7 February 1550
> **Died** 23 March 1555
> **Key fact** Founded the Germanicum, Jesuit college to train priests for Germany

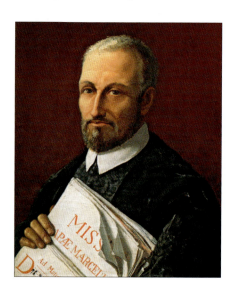

Above: Before becoming pope, Julius had been first president of the Council of Trent. As pope he reconvened the council, which had been suspended in 1548. This statue, in bronze, is in Perugia.

and revenues Innocenzo's way. Wildly infatuated, he refused to change his ways even when cardinals Reginald Pole and Giovanni Carafa warned him that he was abusing his position and that tongues were wagging over the relationship.

These tongues were saying the lavish banquets held at the pope's country dwelling, Villa Giulia, degenerated into homosexual orgies. This of course was food and drink for Protestant pamphleteers and polemic authors such as English clergyman Thomas Beard, Cromwell's schoolmaster, who in his *Theatre of Judgement* described how, when Innocenzo was delayed, the pope waited like an impatient lover for his mistress — and also that he made indecent boasts about the young man's physique and performance.

COUNCIL OF TRENT

The Council of Trent had been suspended in 1548: initially an outbreak of plague in Trent had caused a move to Bologna, but when some prelates refused to leave Trent, Pope Paul had suspended the council rather than risk a schism with two rival councils in session. Julius III reconvened the council to meet on 1 May 1551 and six sessions were held; but it was boycotted by French bishops and, although some Protestant theologians attended, its success was limited and Julius suspended it again on 15 April 1552 against a backdrop of conflict between Emperor Charles V and King Henry II of France over Parma.

On church reform he made various attempts to re-establish reform commissions, reconfirmed the Society of Jesus and in a papal bull of 31 August 1552 founded the Society's Collegium Germanicum and gave it a guaranteed annual income.

ARTS AND LEARNING

Julius brought the composer Giovanni Pierluigi da Palestrina to Rome to serve as *maestro di cappella* (singing master) for the papal choir at St Peter's. Before becoming pope, Julius had been cardinal bishop of Palestrina, near Rome — the composer's native city, from which he took his name; Palestrina had been organist of St Agapito there. Julius had been deeply impressed by Palestrina's first musical publication — a book of Masses, which was the first of its kind by an Italian composer.

Julius pressed on with the building of the new St Peter's. Michelangelo, appointed principal architect under Paul III in 1547, worked on the project until his death in 1564, refusing a fee because he said he was working for the glory of God and the Apostle Peter. The great artist also worked on the pope's country villa, the Villa Giulia, along with painter and architect Giorgio Vasari, author of the celebrated *Lives of the Artists*.

CATHOLICISM IN ENGLAND

In 1553 Catholicism was restored in England with the accession of Queen Mary I. Julius sent English cardinal Reginald Pole as papal legate to England. He served as Archbishop of Canterbury from 1556 to his death in 1558.

Below: Julius took a close interest in the design of his beautiful Villa Giulia on the edge of Rome. It could be reached from the Vatican by boat along the Tiber.

> **VILLA GIULIA**
>
> Originally a country villa situated just outside the city wall, the Villa Giulia is now within Rome and houses the National Etruscan Museum. The house was mostly designed by Giacomo Barozzi da Vignola, with garden structures by Bartolomeo Ammanati — the whole supervised by painter, architect and pioneer art historian Giorgio Vasari. It is celebrated as one of the finest examples of Mannerist architecture. The villa was papal property until 1870 when it was taken over by the Kingdom of Italy and the museum was founded in 1889.

THE COUNTER-REFORMATION

MARCELLUS II TO PIUS V, 1555–72
CHURCH RESURGENT AS COUNCIL OF TRENT RECONVENES

The years 1555–72 saw the reconvening and final sessions of the Council of Trent and the first attempts by the papacy to implement its decrees and decisions.

Cardinal Marcello Cervini, a leading church reformer, was elected to succeed Julius III as pope on 9 April 1555. He took the name Marcellus II. Experienced and well educated, he possessed integrity and was a humanist scholar of no small ability. His pontificate had a very promising start: he took a firm stand against nepotism, cut back the papal court and had an inexpensive coronation. But after only 22 days he died, aged just 53, from a stroke.

NO COMPROMISE
Paul IV (1555–9) was a fiercely ascetic authoritarian and reformer, whose uncompromising hatred of Charles V and Spain led the papacy to a damaging defeat. Before becoming pope, as Cardinal Gian Pietro Carafa, he was Pope Leo X's envoy to England and Spain, then in 1524 with Gaetano da Thiene cofounded the Theatines, an extremely ascetic clerical reform movement. He served on the ecclesiastical reform commission established by Paul III, and as cardinal after 1536 took responsibility for reorganizing the Roman Inquisition. He was 79 on his election, and his pontificate brought conflict at every turn.

Paul knew his mind and would not compromise – or even listen to opposing arguments. In December 1555 he made an alliance with France in the hope of driving Spain from Italy; this provoked war with Spain and led to a heavy defeat in August 1557, so Paul had to make peace from a position of weakness the following month. When Holy Roman Emperor Charles V abdicated and was succeeded by his brother as Ferdinand I, Paul refused to accept either decision on the grounds that he had not been asked for papal approval.

In his dealings with Protestant Europe, he had equally negative effects. He denounced the Peace of Augsburg of September 1555 that proposed an arrangement whereby Catholics and Protestants might live side by side in

Above: Pius V. If he feared one thing, it was being too tolerant rather than too fierce. His reign was an austere period in which the Inquisition stamped out opposition. This insightful portrait is by Spanish artist El Greco (Domenico Theotocopuli).

> **PALESTRINA'S MISSA PAPAE MARCELLI**
>
> Perhaps the most celebrated mass by Giovanni Pierluigi da Palestrina, the *Missae Papae Marcelli* ("Pope Marcellus Mass") was written in honour of Pope Marcellus II, whose highly promising pontificate in 1555 lasted just three weeks. The work was traditionally sung at the papal coronation mass, up to and including the coronation on 30 June 1963 of Paul VI – the last pope to date to be crowned.

Germany on the basis that in each state the ruler would determine the religion. In England he turned against Cardinal Pole and attempted to recall him to Rome on rather unconvincing charges of heresy – and his meddlings there served to pave the way for the return to Protestantism under Elizabeth I.

INDEX

In his rule the Roman Inquisition became a force to be feared – and he faithfully attended every one of its weekly meetings. He approved the drawing up in 1557–8 of the Index of Prohibited Books deemed too dangerous for the faithful to read, which included all the works of Erasmus. He turned ferociously on the Jews, creating a Jewish ghetto in Rome, and requiring Jews to converse only in Latin or Italian and to wear yellow hats on the street – measures that were to remain in force until the 19th century. Only one synagogue per city was permitted – and seven were destroyed in Rome.

On top of all this, Paul IV's reputation was badly damaged by the corruption and cruelty of his nephew Carlo Carafa, whom Paul had created

Below: The Blessed Virgin Mary, a painting by Francesco Zuccarelli. Pius V attributed victory in the Battle of Lepanto to her and declared the Feast of Our Lady of Victory to celebrate the triumph over the Turks.

cardinal. When Paul died on 18 August 1559, the news of his demise caused wild celebrations in Rome – crowds gathered to attack the Inquisition and set its prisoners free, and then felled and decapitated Paul's statue on the Capitol and hurled its head into the Tiber.

TRENT – FINAL SESSIONS

Pius IV (1559–65) retreated from many of these extreme positions – revising the Index, toning down the Inquisition and restoring peaceable relations with Spain. He reconvened the Council of Trent for its final session in 1562–3, and gave papal confirmation to its definitions and decrees in a bull of 26 January 1564, then on 3 November of the same year issued a summary of doctrine, *Professio Fidei Tridentina* ("The Tridentine Statement of Faith") that bishops were required to accept.

In Rome he built the Porta Pia (designed by Michelangelo) and the Villa Pia and rebuilt the church of Santa Maria degli Angeli. He died on 9 December 1565.

Pius V (1566–72) was another stern ascetic, a Dominican and a veteran of the Inquisition who as pope set about implementing the decisions and decrees of the Council of Trent. He often wore a hair shirt under his vestments and walked barefoot in penitential rites. He issued a catechism (1566), revised the

Left: Pius supported Catherine de' Medici against the Huguenots (Calvinist Protestants). This portrait was painted by Catherine's contemporary, the French artist François Clouet.

breviary (book of church services) in 1568 and missal (prayers and responses for celebrating Mass) in 1570, and established the Mass in the form in which it remained until the 20th century.

He excommunicated Elizabeth I in 1570; he sent financial and military aid to French regent Catherine de'Medici to attack the French Huguenots; he complained that Holy Roman Emperor Rudolf II was too tolerant of his subjects' religious behaviour. He joined the Catholic League that pitted Venice, Spain and the papacy against the Turks: this led to a major Catholic victory at the Battle of Lepanto in 1571. He declared the Feast of Our Lady of Victory to celebrate triumph in the Battle of Lepanto. Victory was attributed to the Blessed Virgin Mary.

Pius died in Rome on 1 May 1572 and this time there was no rejoicing. Indeed, he would be canonized on 22 May 1712 – the only pope between Celestine V in 1294 and Pius X (1903–14) to be declared a saint.

Below: This architectural study in brown ink by Michelangelo may be his design for the Porta Pia, which he built for Pius IV in the walls of Rome.

PAPACY AND THE COUNTER-REFORMATION

In the 1540s the papacy of Pope Paul III (1534–49) launched the Counter-Reformation, the Roman Catholic Church's fightback against the Protestant religious revolution.

Encompassing internal reform as well as energetic outreach, the movement was principally carried forward through the doctrinal teaching and decrees of the Council of Trent, through the education and missionary work of new religious orders such as the Jesuits and a hard-hitting fight against heresy in the work of the Roman Inquisition.

This work was accompanied over decades by the redevelopment of the churches, streets and squares of Rome to create a city that would impress upon pilgrims the greatness of God and renewed vigour and glory of His Church. In 1600, Pope Pius IV presided over a Jubilee in which three million pilgrims came to Rome and they can only have been impressed by the major improvements to the city, which would carry on well into the early 17th century.

Below: Pope Paul III launched the Counter-Reformation to revivify the Catholic Church, but his rule had many of the faults of the Renaissance papacy. This 1545 portrait by Titian shows him with his nephews.

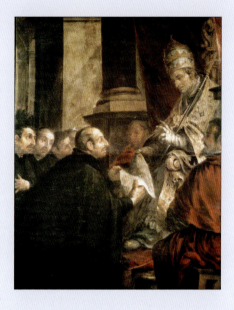

Above: The Jesuits were a driving force of the Counter-Reformation. Loyola received from Paul III the papal bull approving the foundation of the Jesuits in 1540.

ROLE OF PAPACY

In all these endeavours the papacy played a key role. Popes called the sessions of the Council of Trent and forcefully implemented its teachings and decrees, gave unwavering support to the Jesuits and other reforming orders and were energetic patrons and organizers of the improvements.

Despite being a worldly pontiff in many ways, Pope Paul III was the initial driving force of the movement. He called the Council of Trent, which met for its first session in 1545–7, gave papal backing to the formation of the Society of Jesus or Jesuits in 1540 and in 1542 set up the Holy Office of the Inquisition.

The first session of the Council of Trent agreed a whole series of enduringly important decisions. It defined the number of sacraments as seven and the doctrine on original sin. It established the canon of Old Testament and New Testament books. It fixed as authorita-

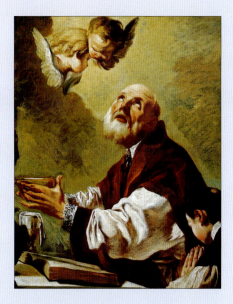

Right: Reformer St Philip Neri founded the Congregation of the Oratory, a society of secular clergy (those who are not monastics), in 1575. They had no formal vows.

tive the creed issued by the Council of Nicaea in 325 and the Council of Constantinople in 381. It rejected Luther's proposed justification by faith, arguing that a person was justified (moved from sin to salvation and righteousness) through the operation of the gratuitously given grace of God.

Julius III (1550–5) convened the second session of the council in 1551–2. This was boycotted by French bishops, but nevertheless defined the doctrine of transubstantiation (according to which the substance of bread and wine becomes wholly transformed into Christ's body and blood at the Eucharist).

Pius IV (1559–65) convened the Council of Trent a third time under a bull of 29 November 1560. The council met from 18 January 1562 to 4 Dec-ember 1563 and agreed further reforms and doctrinal teachings including statements on purgatory, matrimony and the veneration of saints.

BORROMEO
In the preparation for and management of the council, Pius was highly reliant upon his nephew Charles Borromeo, one of the great figures of the Counter-Reformation. Pius had called Borromeo to Rome on his election and made him a cardinal; Borromeo then served as secretary of state to Pius and his principal adviser and afterwards was vital to the implementation of the decrees, which were confirmed in a papal bull of 26 January 1564 and summarized in the *Professio Fidei Tridentina* ("Tridentine Statement of the Faith") that Pius required all bishops to accept. He also played a key role in the development of the catechism brought out by Pius V (1566–72). Borromeo was canonized in 1610 and is celebrated as St Charles Borromeo on 4 November.

IMPLEMENTATION
The implementation of the decrees and teachings of the Council was continued by Pius V. As well as issuing a catechism (1566), he made a revision of the breviary (church service book) in 1568 and issued a missal (responses for Mass) in 1570.

Pope Sixtus V (1585–90) is seen as one of the key figures of the Counter-Reformation because he carried out major reforms of the Church's administrative system, notably establishing 15 congregations or departments in the Curia that remained largely unaltered until after the Second Vatican Council of 1962–5 and which were essential to the effective delivery of the reforms of the Council of Trent.

Sixtus also brought great drive and energy to the rebuilding of Rome intended to glorify God, the Church and the papacy. He was the pope under which the new St Peter's Basilica was completed in 1590, more than 80 years after the foundation stone had been laid by Pope Julius II (in 1506).

ROMAN CATHOLIC MYSTICISM
Another essential part of the Counter-Reformation was the spiritual renewal fostered by the poetic mysticism of Teresa of Avila and St John of the Cross and the devotional writings of Francis de Sales. Spanish nun Teresa of Avila won the backing of Pope Pius IV in order to open the first Carmelite Reform convent (a reformed, more austere strain of the Carmelite order) in 1562.

Her fellow Spaniard John of the Cross opened the first Carmelite reform monastery in 1568. Both wrote classic texts of contemplative faith – Teresa's works include *The Way of Perfection* (1583) and *The Interior Castle* (1588), as well as the autobiographical *Life of the Mother Teresa of Jesus* (1611); John wrote several celebrated poems on the process through which a soul might become united with God, including "The Dark Night of the Soul" and "The Living Flame of Love". Born in what is now France, Francis de Sales served as Bishop of Geneva in 1602–22 and wrote *Introduction to the Devout Life* (1609), which declared that busy members of the laity could achieve spiritual perfection – and that this was not reserved for those who withdrew from the world.

Below: The Church fights back. Religion Overthrowing Heresy and Hatred was carved in c.1697 by Pierre Le Gros the Younger for the Jesuits' home church, the Gesù in Rome.

THE COUNTER-REFORMATION

GREGORY XIII, 1572–85
BACKER OF THE JESUITS AND GREAT BUILDER OF SEMINARIES

Gregory XIII carried on the Counter-Reformation with energy, faith, enthusiasm and force – if anything, perhaps too much force. He took the fight to Protestantism and showed little mercy. But he is remembered above all for his commitment to the education of priests and missionaries, his strong support of the Jesuits and his reform of the Ancient Roman Julian calendar in the Gregorian calendar that he introduced in 1582.

Aged 70 on his election as pope, Ugo Boncompagni was nearing the end of a long and distinguished career as a canon lawyer and papal diplomat. After studying at the University of Bologna, he had taught canon law there for eight years, 1531–9, and was then sent by Pius IV to the Council of Trent. Made a cardinal in 1565, he was Pius's legate to Spain. He was elected pope on 14 May 1572.

EDUCATION AND MISSION
Gregory dedicated his pontificate to combatting Protestantism and to implementing the decrees of the Council of Trent. He established committees of cardinals to stamp out church abuses and revise the Index of Prohibited Books. He did not indulge in nepotism; although among the 24 cardinals he made, two (Filippo Boncompagni and Filippo Vastavillano) were his nephews, these were generally considered worthy of their elevation to the cardinalate.

Above: An enthusiastic promoter of the Counter-Reformation, Gregory XIII was a major supporter of the Jesuits. He is remembered for his reform of the calendar.

Left: The Massacre of St Bartholomew's Day: Gregory called a Te Deum service of thanksgiving in St Peter's to celebrate the events of 24 August 1572, in which 30,000 Huguenots were killed.

FACT BOX
Original name Ugo Boncompagni
Born 7 January 1502
Origin Bologna
Date elected pope 13 May 1572
Died 10 April 1585
Key fact Commissioned the Gregorian Calendar

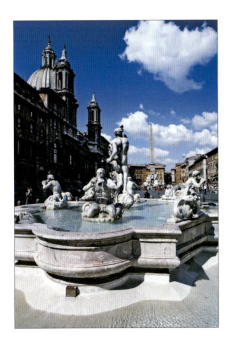

Above: As part of his beautification of Rome, Gregory built fountains in three squares – including the Fontana de Moro, designed by Giacomo della Porta in 1575.

He especially responded to the council's call for the creation of seminaries to train a new generation of priests. In this area Gregory relied mainly on the Jesuits. He gave generously to the Germanicum college for training German priests, enlarged the Jesuit College in Rome, which became known as the Gregorian University, and backed the establishment of more than 20 Jesuit colleges in cities abroad, including Vienna, Douai, Graz, Augsburg and Prague. In Rome, colleges for Armenians, English, Greeks, Hungarians and Maronites were established.

Jesuit missionaries carried the faith out to east and west: to Japan, India, China and Brazil. In Rome, Gregory oversaw the building of the extraordinary Jesuit mother church, the Gesù, a magnificent example of the high Baroque style in architecture designed in 1568 by Giacomo della Porta.

He also gave official approval to a new religious order, the Congregation of the Oratory, founded in 1575 by Philip Neri as a community of priests who did not take monastic vows, but committed themselves to preaching and prayer. He also backed the reform of the Carmelites by St Teresa of Avila in 1580.

ST BARTHOLOMEW'S DAY

Gregory gave his backing to the use of military force against the Protestants of Europe, providing financial support for Roman Catholic rulers. He celebrated the Massacre of St Bartholomew's Day – the events sparked on 24 August 1572 in Paris, when as many as 30,000 French Huguenots (Calvinist Protestants) were killed in mob violence that may have been instigated by Catherine de'Medici – by calling a Te Deum service of thanksgiving in St Peter's. He commissioned Vasari to paint three frescoes in the Vatican commemorating the slaughter and issued a commemorative medal.

He provided troops and equipment to back rebellions in Ireland against the rule of Elizabeth I of England and may have been given his backing to a plot to assassinate her.

PALAZZO DEL QUIRINALE

Gregory built fountains in Rome in the Piazza del Pantheon, Piazza Navona and the Piazza del Popolo. His other building projects in the city included the Palazzo del Quirinale, built from 1574 onwards as a summer palace on the Quirinal Hill, the highest of the city's seven hills, well away from the summer humidity typical in the Lateran Palace. The new palazzo was designed by Ottaviano Mascherino; today it is the official residence of the Italian president.

Gregory also commissioned Giacomo della Porta to complete the magnificent Gregorian Chapel in St Peter's. This contains the extraordinary Altar of Our Lady of Succour (so called from a 12th-century fresco that Gregory had mounted there in 1578), celebrated for its amethysts, alabaster and columns of marble and porphyry. The chapel, sometimes claimed as the most beautiful anywhere in the world, also contains superb mosaics by Marcello Provenzale and Salvatore Monosilio.

> ### GREGORIAN CALENDAR
> Gregory introduced the Gregorian Calendar in 1582. It was devised by Italian astronomer Luigi Lilios. A small inaccuracy in the calculation of a year's length in the Julian calendar, named after Julius Caesar, had caused the date to slip behind the change of seasons. Under papal bull *Inter gravissima* ("A matter of most serious concern") of 24 February 1582, ten days were removed from October 1582: the day after 4 October that year was reckoned as 15 October. Initially only Roman Catholic countries accepted the new calendar; but it was gradually adopted by Protestant and Orthodox countries.

ANARCHY IN THE PAPAL STATES

Gregory's enthusiasm as an artistic and educational patron brought the papacy close to penury. In an attempt to raise funds he attempted to confiscate territories and castles in the papal states, causing great unrest. Gregory died in Rome on 10 April 1585 with the papal states close to anarchy.

Below: Bernini's masterpiece depicts the Ecstasy of St Teresa of Avila. Her mystical work was a key part of the spiritual revival of the Counter-Reformation.

SIXTUS V, 1585–90
POPE SETS ROME ON PATH TO GLORY AS BAROQUE CITY

Sixtus V blew into the Vatican like a whirlwind. Impatient and choleric, he was willing to take draconian measures – and in just five years he reformed the Curia, repaired church finances and with brutal effectiveness restored peace in the lawless papal states. He also carried out major redevelopment in Rome.

He was an able, driven man who had risen on merit. Born in Ancona the son of a farmworker and himself a swineherd as a boy, he became a novice in the Franciscans at the age of 12, was ordained at Siena in 1547 and soon gained a reputation as a fine preacher: his Lenten sermons in Rome in 1552 won him the support of major figures of the Counter-Reformation including Ignatius Loyola, Philip Neri and the future popes Paul IV and Pius V.

His church career was assured, but his uncompromising approach led him into trouble early on: serving Pope Paul IV as inquisitor general in Venice, he was so high-handed in his dealings that he had to be recalled to Rome. Pope Pius V appointed him the Franciscans' vicar general and made him a cardinal in 1570 but, out of favour under Gregory XIII, he retired from church life to edit the works of Bishop Ambrose of Milan and build a villa on the Esquiline. The first volume of his edition of Ambrose was published in 1580, but his scholarship is said to be of indifferent quality.

CENTRALIZING POWER
Fittingly for a man of such personal force, when he was elected pope on 24 April 1585, the vote was unanimous. He set to work to curtail the power of the college of cardinals, under a papal bull of 3 December 1586 setting a limit of 70 on the number of cardinals – this was to remain the maximum until the pontificate of John XXIII (1958–63).

He created 15 congregations to govern the Church and administer its affairs – a set-up that remained largely unchanged until the reforms of the Second Vatican Council (1962–5). These included congregations to oversee the Index of Forbidden Books, the Sapienza (Roman University) and the Vatican Press and implement the Council of Trent.

He made a bold statement of papal authority over bishops: at the Council of Trent there had been some debate as to whether bishops derived spiritual authority from God or the pope, and Sixtus established that all bishops must submit to the pope in Rome and thereafter visit the city to make regular reports to the pope.

He transformed papal finances, cutting back on expenditure, imposing new taxes, extending public loans and raising vast sums through the sale of administrative and bureaucratic positions. Before the end of his short reign he had become immensely rich.

SHOW OF FORCE
Everywhere he acted at breakneck speed. It took him only two years to restore order in the anarchic papal states. No fewer than 7,000 outlaws were publicly executed in the course of his reign of terror; the heads of executed brigands were displayed on spikes on the Pont Sant-Angelo in the first year of his pontificate – and it was said that these outnumbered the melons for sale in the markets of Rome.

In foreign policy he supported military action against Protestant rulers. He pledged major backing for Philip II's planned attack on Protestant England

Above: Sixtus the redeveloper of Rome. Moving the ancient Roman obelisk from the Circus of Nero to the centre of St Peter's Piazza before St Peter's took 800 men, 40 horses and 40 winches.

> ### COMPLETION OF NEW ST PETER'S BASILICA
> The new St Peter's Basilica was completed in 1590, the final year of Sixtus V's pontificate. It had been under construction since Pope Julius II had laid the foundation stone of the new basilica in 1506. Architects on the project included the great Raphael and Michelangelo; the final architects, who completed the building of the basilica's majestic dome, were Giacomo della Porta and Domenico Fontana, appointed by Sixtus in 1585. The lantern would be completed under Gregory XIV (1590–1) and the cross raised by Clement VIII (1592–1605).

> ### FACT BOX
> **Original name** Felice Peretti
> **Born** 13 December 1520
> **Origin** Ancona, papal states
> **Date elected pope** 13 May 1572
> **Died** 27 August 1590
> **Key fact** Oversaw completion of St Peter's Basilica

SIXTUS V

Above: Both the façade of the Church of St John Lateran (background) and the Lateran Palace (left) were rebuilt by Domenico Fontana towards the end of Sixtus's pontificate.

– and renewed the excommunication of Elizabeth I. In the event – after the failure of the Spanish Armada in 1588 – he did not pay. As a result of his support, the Catholic faith made great advances in Poland.

REBUILT TO GOD'S GLORY

Sixtus believed Rome should project the papacy's grandeur and spiritual power. Using his favourite architect, Domenico Fontana, he rebuilt the Vatican and the Lateran Palace, then oversaw the laying out of elegant new avenues and a

superb new aqueduct, the Acqua Felice, that carried fresh water a distance of 20 miles (32km) from Palestrina. Under his direction symbols of the city's pagan past were brought into the service of God and the papacy, as obelisks were raised in front of the Vatican, the Lateran, Santa Maria Maggiore and Santa Maria del Popolo, and statues of Saints Peter and Paul were placed atop the restored

Left: Pope Sixtus V rebuilt Rome to honour God. He used his energy and drive to complete the rebuilding of St Peter's Basilica in 1590.

Above: A gypsy predicts that Felice Peretti, the future Sixtus V, will become pope. Sixtus came from a poor background but showed great promise in his youth.

columns of Trajan and Antoninus Pius. His fierce will drove the long-term rebuilding of St Peter's Basilica to a triumphant conclusion.

Yet, for all this, he was deeply unpopular in Rome and following his death on 27 August 1590 crowds celebrated wildly in the streets and tore down the statue that had been erected in his honour on the Capitol.

THE COUNTER-REFORMATION

URBAN VII TO GREGORY XV, 1590–1623
SUCCESSION OF PONTIFFS DIE AFTER VERY SHORT REIGNS

Seven popes governed the Church from 1590–1623, with three in the 16 months between 15 September 1590 and 30 December 1591 alone.

Urban VII was pope for just 13 days, 15–27 September 1590 – the shortest reign in the history of the papacy. Aged 69 on his election, he had served as papal ambassador to Spain and Inquisitor General and was known for his profound piety. He died before his coronation after contracting malaria on the very day after his election.

Gregory XIV (1590–1) carried on the church reform policies of his forerunners. He was elected with the backing of Philip II of Spain, a pretender to the French throne, and in international affairs promoted Philip's interests in excommunicating the Protestant King Henry IV of France and raising an army for invasion to support the French Catholic League.

Below: Clement VIII suffered from poor health towards the end of his life. He was visited by St. Philip Neri who attempted to cure him.

Curiously Gregory was afflicted with a tendency to laugh at inappropriate times – and this occurred during his coronation. He died of a gallstone that weighed 2.5oz (70g).

Innocent IX was pope for two months, 29 October–30 December 1591. He was 82 and in poor health when he was elected, towards the end of a career in which he had been papal nuncio to Venice and Patriarch of Jerusalem. During the reign of Gregory XIV he was largely in charge of the papal administration, due to Gregory's ill health, and so when he became pope himself policy continued without much change in supporting French Catholics against Henry IV.

KING BECOMES A CATHOLIC

The manoeuvrings over the French throne came to an end when Henry IV became a Catholic on 25 July 1593. The new pope, the able and hard-working Clement VIII (1592–1605), recognized Henry as French king and removed his excommunication in 1595. Clement also, through his papal legate Cardinal Alessandro de' Medici

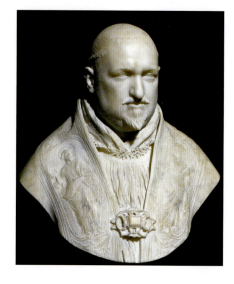

Above: Pope Paul V, by Bernini. Among Paul's acts were the canonization of Charles Borromeo and the beatification of Ignatius of Loyola, Teresa of Avila and Francis Xavier.

(later Pope Leo XI), negotiated peace between France and Spain at the Treaty of Vervins (a town in northern France) signed on 2 May 1598.

Clement committed himself to the work of the Counter-Reformation, expanding the Index of Prohibited Books and backing the Inquisition. In his pontificate the Inquisition condemned and executed the Dominican friar and polymath Giordano Bruno, who was burned at the stake on 17 February 1600 and has been much celebrated since for his original ideas on astronomy, God and the training of the memory. Bruno argued that the Sun is essentially a star as modern scientists understand that, and that the universe is infinite – with countless worlds containing intelligent beings.

That same year, 1600, saw a Jubilee in which as many as three million pilgrims visited Rome to pay their respects at the holy places of the city.

A probably apocryphal story involves Pope Clement in the history of the Western popularization of cof-

BANK OF THE HOLY SPIRIT

The Banco di Santo Spirito was established by Paul V on 13 December 1605. It was the national bank of the papal states – and the first national bank in Europe. After two mergers it became the Banco di Roma in 1992 and after another merger became Capitalia in 2002. Capitalia was taken over by Unicredit in 2007.

fee. According to this tale, Clement approved of the drinking of coffee when he was being urged to denounce it as "the bitter invention of Satan" because of its popularity among Muslims.

Clement suffered from gout and spent the last part of his life in bed. He died on 3 March 1605 in Rome.

THE LIGHTNING POPE

When Cardinal Alessandro de' Medici became Leo XI aged 70, he survived less than a month, 1–27 April. He fell ill immediately after his coronation and was nicknamed "the Lightning Pope" because his reign was so short.

Paul V (1605–21) was drawn into a serious dispute with Venice – principally over the use of a civil court to try priests – that damaged the papacy's prestige. In May 1606 he placed an interdict on the republic with little effect, and the mediation of France was needed to bring the matter to a conclusion in April 1607. This made him cautious in international relations and he did not back German Catholics when violence broke out with Protestants at the start of the Thirty Years' War (1618–48).

In Rome, Paul restored the aqueduct of Trajan, which was renamed Aqua Paola in his honour, and built the Borghese Chapel (so called from his family name) in the Basilica of Santa Maria Maggiore.

SECRET BALLOT IN PAPAL ELECTIONS

Gregory XV (1621–3) carried out two major reforms. Firstly he introduced the procedures for papal elections that are largely still followed today – nota-

Above: Clement VIII appointed Francis de Sales (seated) Bishop of Geneva. Author of Introduction to the Devout Life, *Francis promoted Catholicism in Switzerland. He was canonized in 1665.*

Left: Portrait of Pope Gregory XV and his nephew Ludovico Ludovisi by Domenichino (Domenico Zampieri). Gregory issued the last papal ordinance against witchcraft.

bly, the use of a written secret ballot in an election behind closed doors. These were contained in a papal bull of 15 November 1621. Secondly he established the Congregation for the Propagation of the Faith, a board to control missionary activity around the world. In 1622 he canonized Ignatius of Loyola, Francis Xavier, Philip Neri and Teresa of Avila.

In Rome he was a patron of the celebrated Baroque artist Guercino, who in 1623 painted the altarpiece "The Burial of St Petronilla" for St Peter's Basilica, as well as of Gian Lorenzo Bernini and Alessandro Algardi, both of whom made his bust. He sat with his nephew, Ludovico Ludovisi (whom he made cardinal) for a fine double portrait by Domenichino (Domenico Zampieri).

Gregory died on 8 July 1623 in the Quirinal Palace.

URBAN VIII, 1623–44
FULL FLOWERING OF THE BAROQUE IN ROME

Urban's pontificate saw the fullest and most splendid flowering of the Baroque architectural and sculptural style in Rome. His reign is also remembered for the condemnation and imprisonment of astronomer Galileo Galilei by the Roman Inquisition.

The son of a Florentine nobleman, Maffeo Barberini came to Rome at an early age following his father's death. He was educated by the Jesuits in Rome and studied law at Pisa, then under Clement VIII was sent first as papal legate (1601) and then papal nuncio (from 1604) to Paris, where he became close to King Henry IV. Pope Paul V made him a cardinal in 1606 and he was elected pope, in succession to Gregory XV, on 6 August 1623.

COMBATTING THE HABSBURGS

Urban's pontificate saw the key period of the Thirty Years' War (1618–48) and the ministry of Cardinal Richelieu

Below: Celebration, Baroque style – Glorification of the Reign of Pope Urban VIII is a ceiling painting by Pietro da Cortona in the pope's Roman palace, the Palazzo Barberini.

Above: Pope Urban VIII. He supported missionary work, revised the breviary and officially condemned slavery. He was a major patron of the sculptor Gian Lorenzo Bernini.

FACT BOX
Original name Maffeo Barberini
Born April 1568
Origin Florence
Date elected pope 6 August 1623
Died 29 July 1644
Key fact Did not defend his friend Galileo against investigations by the Inquisition

URBAN VIII

Above: Galileo was put on trial for his heliocentric theory because it challenged the biblical account of Creation. He was sentenced to life imprisonment (commuted to house arrest).

in France. Urban tended to support French interests, partly as a result of his service as papal nuncio at the court of Henry IV but principally through a desire to combat the imperial ambitions of the Habsburgs of Spain and Austria.

He did not support the Habsburg Holy Roman Emperor Ferdinand II against the Swedish Protestant ruler Gustav II Adolf (better known as Gus-tavus Adolphus). After Cardinal Richelieu allied Roman Catholic France with Protestant Sweden and declared war on Roman Catholic Spain in 1635, the war – which had initially been between Catholics and Protestants – was no longer divided on religious lines but became a struggle between the royal houses of Bourbon and Habsburg.

GALILEO CONDEMNED

Italian astronomer, mathematician and natural philosopher Galileo Galilei was condemned by the Inquisition in 1633 and sentenced to life imprisonment (later commuted to house arrest) for advocating the heliocentric theory of the universe (according to which the Earth orbits the Sun) in his book of 1632, *Dialogue Concerning the Two Chief World Systems*. He was forced to recant on his support for the theory, which presented problems for the Church since it could not be reconciled with the biblical account of creation; heliocentrism had been proposed by Copernicus in his 1543 book *On the Revolutions of the Heavenly Spheres*, which was dedicated to Pope Paul III and had drawn no papal condemnation, but it had later been condemned by Paul V in 1616. Urban was a friend of Galileo and had even written a Latin poem celebrating his achievement in identifying sun spots, but he did not defend the condemned man. Galileo was born in Pisa on 15 February 1564. He died aged 77 on 8 January 1642 near Florence.

Right: Galileo Galilei. According to legend, after the Church forced him to recant his theory that the Earth moves around the Sun, he muttered "And yet it moves".

691

THE COUNTER-REFORMATION

Above: Bernini carved this bust of Urban's mother, Camilla Barbadori, and one of his father, Antonio Barberini, for the family vault at Sant' Andrea della Valle, Rome.

At home Urban looked to his defences. In Rome he fortified the Castel Sant'Angelo and built defences along the right side of the Tiber. He developed Civitavecchia as a successful military port, constructed Fort Urbano at Castelfranco and developed an arms manufacturing centre at Tivoli.

MISSIONARY OUTREACH

In church matters Urban gave substantial backing to missionary work. In 1627 he founded in Rome the Collegium Urbanum, a specialist training centre for overseas missionaries. He opened to all missionaries two countries – Japan and China – that Gregory XV had said were open only to Jesuits. Urban revised the breviary and issued a new edition in 1632. He himself wrote the Office of St Elizabeth and composed new hymns for the feasts of St Elizabeth of Portugal,

Left: A miracle in marble. Bernini's celebrated carving of the pope – with its extraordinary rendition in stone of the folds of cloth – is part of Urban's tomb in St Peter's Basilica.

URBAN VIII

Above: Directly beneath the dome of the basilica, St Peter's Canopy ("Baldacchino") covers the high altar. It was commissioned from Bernini by Urban close to the start of his reign in 1623 and completed in 1634.

Francesco Barberini to the cardinalate; he later appointed Francesco librarian of the Vatican. He made a second nephew, Antonio Barberini the Younger, first cardinal in 1627 then commander-in-chief of the papal troops and a third, Taddeo Barberini, Prefect of Rome. He made his own brother, another Antonio, cardinal and later granted him a position at the Vatican Library. Such appointments channelled wealth to the Barberini family.

ROMAN BAROQUE – AND BERNINI

Urban was a major patron of the great Baroque architect and sculptor Gian Lorenzo Bernini, from whom he commissioned the magnificent bronze canopy or baldachin above the high altar in St Peter's and Urban's own very grand papal tomb, also in St Peter's. Urban and Bernini were also responsible for the magnificent Triton Fountain in Piazza Barberini and the superb nearby Palazzo Barberini, the pope's family palace. Some of this work reused the bronze from the pantheon – and the Romans commented satirically, referring to the pope's family name, "What the barbarians didn't manage, the Barberini achieved".

RETURN TO NEPOTISM

His reign saw a return to the nepotism practised so enthusiastically by his predecessors. Only three days after his coronation, he raised his nephew

St Hermenegild and St Martina. He canonized Elizabeth of Portugal and Andrew Corsini and beatified several people, including John of God and Cajetan (Gaetano da Thiene), co-founder of the Theatines.

In Urban's bull of 22 April 1639 he condemned slavery in Paraguay, Brazil and the West Indies. Another bull, which was issued on 6 March 1642, condemned the *Augustinus*, a book on the theology of St Augustine by the late Bishop of Ypres, Cornelius Jansen, whose writings were the source of the movement of Jansenism.

Below: Bernini also worked on the Palazzo Barberini, the pope's magnificently reconstructed family palace in Rione Trevi, Rome. He succeeded Carlo Maderno and Francesco Borromini on the project.

INNOCENT X, 1644–55
POPE DOMINATED BY THE *PAPESSA*

Innocent X reversed most of the policies of his predecessor Urban VIII, supporting the interests of Spain rather than France in international affairs. He is remembered particularly for being dominated by his sister-in-law and perhaps lover Olimpia Maidalchini, who was notorious for her greed and avaricious self-interest.

SPANISH CONNECTION

Giambattista Pamphili studied in Rome and qualified as bachelor of laws. Under Gregory XV he served as papal nuncio to Naples and subsequently to Madrid. He was made cardinal-priest of Sant'Eusebio in 1626. He emerged victorious in 1644 from a troubled papal conclave in which the French and Spanish factions were at loggerheads; after rejecting the principal Spanish candidate, Cardinal Firenzola, the French members of the conclave accepted Pamphili as a compromise despite his known pro-Spanish sympathies.

Almost at once he set about unpicking the work of his predecessor, ordering an enquiry into the way Urban's relatives had enriched themselves and sequestering their wealth. Antonio and Francesco Barberini took to their heels, and sought refuge in Paris with Cardinal Mazarin, an Italian churchman who had succeeded Richelieu as chief minister of France. Innocent initially took a stern approach to this, but was forced to yield when the cardinal began to raise an army to invade Italy.

FACT BOX
Original name Giambattista Pamphili
Born 7 May 1574
Origin Rome
Date elected pope 15 September 1644
Died 7 January 1655
Key fact Adopted pro-Spanish, anti-French policies

EUROPEAN INTERVENTIONS

He supported Spain in refusing to recognize Portugal's independence or accept its king, John IV of Braganza. When the Peace of Westphalia of 1648 brought an end to the Thirty Years' War, Innocent issued a bull declaring null and void any articles in the treaty that would have a negative impact on Catholic interests but his intervention was simply ignored by the parties involved.

In a papal bull of 1653 Innocent issued a further papal condemnation of Cornelius Jansen's *Augustinus*, to complement that issued by Urban VIII. Innocent condemned five propositions concerning God's grace and human free will from the *Augustinus*. The Jansenist controversy in France was to run for many decades.

"LADY POPE"

Although he attacked the relatives of Urban VIII for wrongfully appropriating church funds, Innocent was not above

Left: The finest portrait ever painted? Diego Rodriguez de Silva y Velázquez painted Innocent X in the midpoint of his pontificate, in 1650.

INNOCENT X

Above: Papal power: a bronze statue of Innocent by Alessandro Algardi. In the English Civil War (1642–49) Innocent sent his papal nuncio with troops to support the king and safeguard the Catholic faith in Ireland.

nepotism himself and funnelled wealth to members of his Pamphili family. In particular, he was dominated by his late brother's ambitious and worldly widow, Olimpia Maidalchini-Pamphili, who was in almost constant communication with the pope and appeared to hold a veto on his decisions. Said by a contemporary to be possessed of "nauseating greed", and sometimes described as *papessa* ("lady pope"), she benefited from the sale of military and civil positions and of benefices.

The pope even appointed her Princess of San Martino in 1645, and some accounts claim that she used the expertise of her private pharmacist to poison cardinals in order to open positions that could then be sold for money. Some suggested she must have been Innocent's lover, although he was already 70 on his election and was 80 when he died. Her influence was only challenged by one of Innocent's relatives, Camillo Astalli, whom the pope made a cardinal and secretary of state, but she ousted him and he was removed from office.

PIAZZA NAVONA

In Rome, Innocent was responsible for the Baroque transformation of the Piazza Navona, which lay in front of his family palace, the Palazzo Pamphili. He commissioned the extraordinary "Fountain of the Four Rivers" made in 1651 by Gian Lorenzo Bernini and the church of Sant'Agnese in Agone from father and son architects Girolamo and Carlo Rainaldi, together with Francesco Borromini. Girolamo Rainaldi also designed the magnificent family palazzo (1644–50), with its superb long gallery created by Borromini and decorated with frescoes by Pietro da Cortona.

Innocent was also a patron of the Spanish artist Diego Velázquez. When the artist visited Rome from Madrid in 1649–50 Innocent provided a warm welcome, presented him with a golden chain and medal and commissioned a superb portrait (see box). The picture captured a ruthless glean in Innocent's eyes and some of those at the Vatican were afraid that Innocent would be unhappy with the result, but he reputedly declared "All too true" when he first saw it and showed his appreciation by hanging the picture in the waiting room he kept for visitors.

Above: Archangel Michael tramples a Satan recognizable as Innocent. Guido Reni's painting of c.1636 is in the Capuchin church of Santa Maria della Concezione, Rome.

Innocent died on 7 January 1655 after an illness in which all his worldly wealth was stripped from him by hangers-on, especially his long-term adviser and intimate aide Olimpia Maidalchini-Pamphili. On his death Olimpia showed her true colours by refusing to meet the cost of his burial. The pope's body was left to lie in the corner of the sacristy at St Peter's for three days and was eventually given the simplest of burials, paid for by Innocent's former butler.

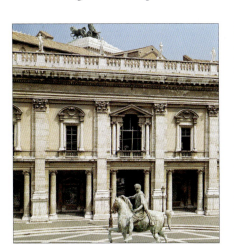

Right: Innocent was a major patron of the arts. The Palazzo Nuovo in the Piazza del Campidoglio was completed in his rule.

> ### VELAZQUEZ PORTRAIT OF INNOCENT X
>
> The portrait of Innocent X painted by Spanish painter Diego Velázquez in 1650 is considered by some to be the finest portrait ever painted. Now held in the gallery of the Palazzo Doria Pamphili, in Rome, it was the model for the "Screaming Popes" series created by Irish artist Francis Bacon in the 1950s–60s.

PAPAL POWER AND INFLUENCE

ALEXANDER VII TO CLEMENT XIII, 1655–1769

In the mid-18th century Pope Benedict XIV won friends and admirers far and wide, even among opponents of the Roman Catholic Church. Voltaire wrote of him, in a couplet penned to accompany a portrait of the pope, "Here is Lambertini, pride of Rome, and Father of the World, who instructs the whole world by his writings and honours all through his virtues." This pope – admired for his moderation, intelligence and his support for the study of history and science – was rare in this era, for generally the popes from Alexander VII to Clement XIII struggled to come to terms with what became known as the age of reason and were unable to make their mark on the European stage.

In these years the pope was increasingly sidelined in international affairs. Clement XI attempted to position himself as a mediator in the War of the Spanish Succession but only succeeded in underlining the fact that the papacy no longer had a major role in the politics of Europe. Clement XIII was a saintly figure but despite being a firm supporter of Jesuits himself was unable to calm the chorus of demands for action against the society from the leaders of European countries and was close to dissolving the order when he died in 1769.

Yet these years also saw another succession of great papal artistic patrons who were responsible for beautifying Rome in the ornate and elaborate Baroque style. Under Alexander VIII, Bernini created the stately colonnade on St Peter's Piazza and the magnificent *Cathedra Petri* ("Chair of St Peter") in St Peter's Basilica. Bernini also reworked several squares. Clement X built the Palazzo Altieri and added a splendid fountain, designed by Bernini, to St Peter's Piazza.

Left: St Peter's Piazza was made elegantly beautiful by popes including Alexander VIII, who commissioned Gian Lorenzo Bernini's colonnade, and Clement X, who added the fountain – also by Bernini. This view is by 18th-century Italian artist Antonio Joli.

PAPAL POWER AND INFLUENCE

ALEXANDER VII, 1655–67
POPE WHO BUILT COLONNADE ON ST PETER'S PIAZZA

Alexander VII's 12-year pontificate saw the building of Gian Lorenzo Bernini's great masterpiece, the colonnade on St Peter's Piazza, and the religious conversion of Queen Christina of Sweden who settled in Rome as a Catholic.

Born into one of the grand families of Siena, Fabio Chigi was the grandnephew of Pope Paul V (1605–21). Despite being unable to go to school as a child because of illness, he studied hard under the finest tutors and was awarded doctorates in theology, law and philosophy from Siena University. In a distinguished church career he served as vice-legate of Ferrara, Inquisitor of Malta and nuncio to Cologne, and attempted to defend the interests of the papacy in the negotiations that resulted in the 1648 Peace of Westphalia.

Thereafter he was made a cardinal by Innocent X (1644–55) and Bishop of Imola in 1652. He served as Innocent's secretary of state and was cardinal priest of the Church of Santa Maria del Popolo.

Below: Early in his rule, when he lived strictly and modestly, Alexander is said to have seasoned his meat with ashes. Later he reacquainted the papacy with the nepotism that had stained the reigns of earlier pontiffs.

The conclave that followed the death of Alexander's predecessor, Innocent X, lasted no less than eighty days because of the initial refusal of the French chief minister, Cardinal Mazarin, to accept Chigi, the preferred candidate, as pope; but in the end Mazarin backed down and the pious and learned Bishop of Imola became Pope Alexander VII.

MEMENTO MORI
Alexander was deeply devout. Initially he took a firm stand against nepotism and in the first year of his pontificate even banned his relatives from coming to Rome; in this period his papacy was

Above: Bernini was one of Alexander's preferred artists and devised a magnificent Baroque tomb (1672–78) for this pope in marble and gilded bronze in the north transept of St Peter's.

FACT BOX

Original name Fabio Chigi
Born 13 February 1599
Origin Siena, Republic of Florence
Date elected pope 1 April 1655
Died 22 May 1667
Key fact Reiterated condemnation of Jansenists

Above: Bernini restored the Scala Regia, the staircase to the Sistine Chapel, in 1663–66 during Alexander's pontificate.

notable for the simple life he led: he reputedly gave audience in a room containing human skulls and a coffin as a *memento mori* (reminder of mortality – from the Latin, "remember you will die").

But in 1656 he reversed his position, seemingly persuaded by advisers that family ties made governance stronger, and appointed relatives to key ecclesiastical and civil positions.

LITERARY INTERESTS

He personally maintained a simple life and focused much of his interest on literature and learning. He published a book of Latin poems in 1656 and expanded the Vatican Library. He also issued a new edition of the Index of Prohibited Books and an apostolic constitution (or decree) stating the doctrine of the Immaculate Conception of the Blessed Virgin Mary.

FRENCH TROUBLE

Alexander had difficulty dealing with France. French king Louis XIV broke off relations, seizing Avignon and the surrounding area; Alexander was forced to acquiesce, and accepted a humiliating settlement in the Treaty of Pisa in 1664. In France the Jansenists claimed that Innocent X's condemnation of their theology in 1653 was not just, since the propositions concerning divine grace and human free will he condemned were not found in the *Augustinus* of Cornelius Jansen; but Alexander, who advised Innocent on the initial document, reconfirmed the condemnation in his 1665 papal bull *Ad Sacram* ("To the Sacred"). He sent to France a "formulary" – a document to be signed by all clergy and used as a means of identifying and disciplining those with Jansenist sympathies.

ROYAL CONVERT

Queen Christina of Sweden converted to Catholicism and abdicated her throne in 1654. She travelled to Rome and entered the city in a splendid sedan chair designed by Bernini that had been despatched to greet her by Alexander VII. On Christmas Morning 1655 Alexander confirmed her in the faith in a ceremony in St Peter's. She lived in exile in Rome in the Palazzo Farnese and then the Palazzo Corsini for the next 35 years, until her death in 1689.

Alexander died on 22 May 1667 in Rome. Gian Lorenzo Bernini designed a magnificent marble tomb for him erected in St Peter's Basilica in 1672–8.

> ### QUEEN CHRISTINA
> Christina succeeded her father Gustavus Adolphus as ruler of Sweden in 1632 at the age of six years. She refused to wed and nominated her cousin Charles Gustavus (later Charles X) as her successor. After secretly converting to Roman Catholicism, she abdicated in 1654 (Catholicism was illegal at the time in Sweden) and travelled to Rome where she was warmly greeted by the pope and took up residence. She was highly intelligent, artistic and unconventional and regularly dressed in men's clothes. She died in Rome on 19 April 1689 and was buried in the Vatican Grotto. In 1702 Pope Clement XI commissioned a marble monument in Christina's honour in St Peter's designed by Carlo Fontana. Greta Garbo famously portrayed her in the 1933 Hollywood movie *Queen Christina* directed by Rouben Mamoulian.

Below: Queen Christina in Sweden by Pierre-Louis Dumesnil the Younger. She converted to Catholicism and made her way to Rome to live as a guest of the papacy.

THE PAPACY AND BAROQUE ART AND ARCHITECTURE

The spectacular Baroque style began as the art of the Counter-Reformation. The popes and other Church patrons set out to create sacred architecture and art that made a direct appeal to the emotions and senses of the faithful.

Under a succession of popes, Rome was transformed, the city's churches made beautiful to the glory of God and in the service of the Counter-Reformation. The city was remodelled, the old huggermugger of medieval alleys and roads replaced with straight streets that terminated in vistas of grand buildings and fine squares with fountains, obelisks and columns. The purpose of Baroque art for the papacy and the ecclesiastical hierarchy was to energize the faithful and impress them with the greatness of God and His Church. Baroque artists made both a sensuous and a spiritual appeal to worshippers, often combining naturalistic and dramatic treatments of a subject.

COLOUR AND DRAMA

In promoting these styles, the papacy and Church were also countering in a dramatic and engaging fashion the call for plainness made by the churches of the Protestant Reformation. While many Protestants denounced religious art as idolatrous, worshipped in plain chapels and even embarked on iconoclastic sprees in which they painted over frescoes with whitewash and destroyed statues and stained glass windows, the art of the Roman Catholic Counter-Reformation embraced the colour, drama and emotion of religious encounter.

Above: Gian Lorenzo Bernini was the pre-eminent Baroque artist. Allegorical figures representing Charity and Justice adorn his tomb for Urban VIII in St Peter's.

EXTRAVAGANT "BAROQUE"

These works of art were not called Baroque at the time. The label "Baroque" was originally a term of abuse in art criticism. It was used to describe painting, sculpture and architecture that was bizarre or extravagant, which did not follow the conventional proportions and rules; right up to the end of the 19th century "Baroque" meant art that was overdone or strange, with too much decoration. The word may derive from the Italian *barocco* (originally a philosophical term that came to mean a convoluted process of thought).

Baroque art generally belongs to the 17th century. In some places – for example, in Germany and in European colonies in South America – some of the finest flowerings of the style grew up in the 1700s. But in Italy, and particularly in Rome – the birthplace of

Below: The drama of space and light that typified Baroque church architecture is on display in the interior of St Peter's, Rome – pictured here in 1750 by Giovanni Paolo Pannini.

the style – Baroque architecture and art began to appear in the second half of the 16th century.

In Rome, the Chiesa dei Gesù (Church of the Gesù), the mother church for the Society of Jesus or Jesuits, was begun in 1568 in the pontificate of Gregory XIII (1572–85) and is widely seen as the first great example of Baroque architecture. The church was begun to plans by architect Giacomo da Vignola; but his designs, largely in the prevailing Mannerist style, were transformed by Giacomo della Porta, with the assistance of Giovanni Tristano.

The Gesù – a single nave without aisles that focuses attention on the high altar, with a great dome above the crossing of the nave with the transepts – was highly influential on the design of churches built throughout the Baroque period. Its interior – completed in the following century – is lavishly decorated, a riot of marble and gilt ornamentation, frescoes, columns and statues.

The nave ceiling vault features one of the great masterpieces of Baroque sacred painting – a fresco entitled *Triumph of the Name of Jesus* by Giovanni Battista Gaulli, painted 1678–9. Another dramatic Baroque sacred painting, *The Burial of St Petronilla*, was made in 1623 by Guercino (Giovanni Fran-cesco Barbieri) for Gregory XV in St Peter's Basilica.

SPECTACLE

Baroque architecture set out to create a dramatic spectacle. The styles – developed by architects including Carlo Maderno (1556–1629), Francesco Borromini (1599–1667) and Gian Lorenzo Bernini (1598–1680) – laid emphasis on monumental size, created drama using space and light and took pleasure in lavish interior decoration using colour, texture and fine materials.

Carlo Maderno was architect to Pope Paul V and worked on St Peter's Basilica. He designed the Church of Santa Maria della Vittoria ("Our Lady of Victory" – the church that contains one of the greatest and most celebrated pieces of Baroque sculpture, Bernini's *Ecstasy of St Teresa*), and worked with his nephew Francesco Borromini on the Palazzo Barberini for Urban VIII (1623–44). Borromini also worked on the Church of Sant'Agnese in Agone, part of Pope Innocent X (1644–55)'s reworking of the Piazza Navone.

THE GENIUS OF BERNINI

But the greatest Baroque architect and sculptor was Gian Lorenzo Bernini, who worked for popes from Urban VIII to Alexander VII (1655–67), creating a long series of masterpieces. Bernini took over the Palazzo Barberini for Urban VIII while still a prodigy in 1629; he also designed the Triton Fountain in the Piazza Barberini before the palazzo. For this pope he additionally created the magnificent baldachin

Above: The altar in the Cornaro chapel of Carlo Maderno's church of Santa Maria della Vittoria. Bernini's exuberant Ecstasy of St Teresa – *one of the greatest pieces of Baroque sculpture – is visible behind.*

or bronze canopy over the high altar in St Peter's and an extravagant tomb, also in St Peter's. For Innocent X he created the extraordinary "Fountain of the Four Rivers" in the Piazza Navona.

He designed another series of great works for Pope Alexander VII (1655–67), including the colonnade on St Peter's Piazza together with the *Cathedra Petri* ("Chair of St Peter") and Alexander's tomb in the basilica. Also under this pope's patronage, Bernini worked on the Chigi Chapel in the Church of Santa Maria del Popolo and restored the Scala Regia, the staircase that links the Vatican to St Peter's, as well as reworking a number of Roman squares.

CLEMENT IX TO INNOCENT XII, 1667–1700
POPES ARE INCREASINGLY MARGINALIZED

The majority of popes from Clement IX to Innocent XII clashed with Louis XIV of France over control of the French church. Some also gave valuable support to campaigns against the Ottoman Turks in Europe. Generally these popes struggled with the consequences of the papacy's ever-declining temporal power.

POET AND LIBRETTIST
Clement IX (1667–9) has a most unusual distinction among popes: he wrote the libretti to several operas – and indeed is credited with having

Above: Cardinal Pietro Ottoboni became Pope Alexander VIII in 1689. One of the acts of his two-year reign was to buy Queen Christina of Sweden's books and manuscripts for the Vatican Library.

created the genres of sacred opera and comic opera. Among his works were the comic opera *Chi soffre Speri* ("The One who suffers also hopes"), where his libretto, based on tales by Giovanni Boccaccio, was set to music by Virgilio Mazzocchi and Marco Marazzoli; he also wrote the sacred opera *Sant'Alessio* (St Alexis), with music by Stefano Landi. Both were written in the 1630s, well before Giulio Rospigliosi (as he was then known) became pope. The future Clement IX was also a notable poet and a patron of French painter Nicolas Poussin, from whom he commissioned the celebrated painting *A Dance to the Music of Time*. He carried on his artistic interests during his pontificate, opening Rome's first public opera house.

As pope he was known for his charity and kindliness, and he brought about a brief respite for the Jansenists in his Peace of Clement IX, signed in January 1669, and also was a mediator in the negotiations between France, Spain, England and the Netherlands that brought about the Peace of Aachen in 1668.

SUCCESS AGAINST OTTOMANS
Clement X (1670–6) was elected in his 80th year and his administration was largely conducted by Cardinal Paluzzi degli Albertoni, to whom he was dis-

Below: This bust of Clement X was one of Gian Lorenzo Bernini's last sculptures. He was 79 when elected pope and initially said "I am too old to bear such a burden".

CLEMENT IX TO INNOCENT XII

> ### LOUIS XIV OF FRANCE
> The king celebrated as *le roi de soleil* ("the Sun King") was on the French throne from 1643 to his death in 1715 and saw no fewer than nine popes – from Urban VIII to Clement XI – occupy the papal throne. He waged a long series of expansionist wars to little effect. He repeatedly clashed with popes over papal authority in France and the right – disputed by king and pope – to make appointments to French bishoprics. The son of Louis XIII, he succeeded to the throne in 1643, at the age of five years; until he became an adult, rule was by Cardinal Mazarin and Louis's mother, Anne of Austria. He took power in 1661 and ruled with absolute authority – famously declaring *L'Etat, c'est moi* ("I am the state"). He transformed the Palace of Versailles built for his father into a vast palace that was celebrated throughout Europe.

tantly connected by marriage after Clement's niece had married the cardinal's nephew. The cardinal channelled wealth shamelessly to his family and the pope's reputation was damaged as a result.

Clement contributed to a major success against the Ottomans, sending financial support to Polish general John Sobieski who defeated the Ottomans in November 1673 and thereafter became King of Poland. The pope also clashed with King Louis XIV of France over Louis's claim that the French king should take control over appointments to and revenues from bishoprics in France.

GALLICAN CHALLENGE TO PAPAL AUTHORITY

Relations with France worsened further under Innocent XI (1676–89). After Innocent warned Louis XIV that his aggressive claims were nothing less than an insult to God, the majority of the French clergy signed up in March 1682 to four Gallican articles, which denied the papacy authority in temporal matters and declared that a general council of the Church was superior to the pope. Innocent rejected these articles and the relationship with Louis continued to deteriorate. In January 1688 Innocent excommunicated Louis and his ministers and in September that year Louis once again occupied Avignon and the surrounding area.

Elsewhere papal support of King John Sobieski of Poland reaped benefits: in 1683 Sobieski drove the Ottomans back from the very gates of Vienna; Innocent put together a Holy League combining Holy Roman Emperor Leopold I, Sobieski, Venice and Russia, which succeeded in forcing the Ottomans out of Hungary in 1686 and freeing Belgrade in 1687.

Innocent was a highly devout man of undoubted integrity who lived a simple, frugal life as pope. He is generally viewed as the finest pontiff of the 17th century. In the penultimate year of his reign Catholicism suffered a setback in England in 1688 when the Catholic King James II was ousted from the English throne and replaced by his Protestant daughter

Below: Spanish mystic St John of the Cross was a key figure of the Counter-Reformation. He was beatified on 26 January 1675 by Clement X and canonized by Benedict XIII in 1726.

Above: The funeral monument of Innocent XI in St Peter's was made by French sculptor Pierre-Etienne Monnot. The tomb features a bas-relief celebrating John Sobieski's defeat of the Turks at Vienna.

Mary and her Dutch husband William of Orange. The following year, on 12 August 1689, Innocent died.

IN DEFENCE OF ORTHODOXY

A former head of the Roman Inquisition, Alexander VIII (1689–91) took a hard line in support of doctrinal orthodoxy. He once again condemned Jansenism, and issued a censure to followers of Spanish mystic and priest Miguel de Molinos, who had been sentenced to life imprisonment in Innocent XI's reign for his teaching of Quietism (which promoted mental tranquillity as a truer means of religion than formal worship).

Innocent XII (1691–1700) was elected after a five-month conclave. His first act as pope was to take a stand against nepotism, issuing a papal bull in 1692 that banned popes from giving offices, revenues or estates to their relatives and did away with the office of cardinal nephew. He declared that the poor were his nephews, and began a programme of charitable care for the needy. He made the Lateran Palace into housing for the unemployed and greatly enlarged the orphanage of the Ospizio di San Michele.

PAPAL POWER AND INFLUENCE

CLEMENT XI, 1700–21
PAPACY HUMBLED IN WAR OF THE SPANISH SUCCESSION

The status and authority of the papacy suffered severely in the War of the Spanish Succession (1701–14). Clement XI was unable to mediate in the conflict, and the treaties that ended the war distributed papal territories to new rulers while the pope could only watch.

Born in Urbino to a noble family, Giovanni Francesco Albani was a brilliant scholar, known by the age of 18 for the elegance of his translations from Greek into Latin, educated in Rome and taken up there by Queen Christina of Sweden and her coterie of men of letters. He became a doctor of canon and civil law, and served successively as Governor of Rieti, Sabina and Orvieto. He later became Vicar of St Peter's, Secretary of Papal Briefs and Cardinal-priest of San Silvestro. During this period he drafted Pope Innocent's condemnation of nepotism.

In contrast to several elderly predecessors, he was only 51 years old when he was elected to the papacy on 23 November 1700. But his relative youth and vigour were not enough to enable him to make a mark on the international stage at a time when the papacy and its political interests were sidelined.

THE SPANISH SUCCESSION

During the 46-day conclave that delivered Pope Clement XI, King Charles II of Spain died. At the close of Innocent XI's reign, the pope had recommended

> **FACT BOX**
> **Original name** Giovanni Francesco Albani
> **Born** 23 July 1649
> **Origin** Urbino, papal states
> **Date elected pope** 23 November 1700
> **Died** 19 March 1721
> **Key fact** Authority challenged by French Jansenists

Above: Clement is represented in procession across St Peter's Square in this painting by Pier Leone Ghezzi. He made improvements to the Piazza del Pantheon.

to Charles II, who had no children, that he should choose as his heir Louis XIV's grandson, Philip of Anjou, rather than Holy Roman Emperor Leopold I's son Charles, Archduke of Austria; Charles II changed his will to this effect.

Now on his death Louis XIV despatched Philip to Madrid to claim the throne as King Philip V of Spain. But naturally enough Leopold contested the will – conflict was inevitable; yet no one could have known that this struggle, the War of the Spanish Succession, would last 13 years from 1701 to 1714.

Before becoming pope Clement had been one of the cardinals who had advised Innocent on his decision; as pope, Clement favoured the accession of Philip – and, indeed, he sent a letter to Madrid congratulating the new Spanish king. At the beginning of the war, however, he attempted to maintain a position of neutrality and to position himself as mediator. In this he failed.

French troops captured Milan but in 1706 the imperial general Eugene of Savoy drove them out. In 1707 the troops of Leopold's son, Holy Roman Emperor Joseph I, invaded the papal states and captured Naples, and Clement was forced to abandon Philip V and

Below: Clement XI was pope for around 20 years and died at the age of 71 in March 1721. He was unable to prevent the loss of papal territories.

704

recognize Leopold's younger son (and Joseph's brother) Charles as the rightful king of Spain. Philip abruptly ended diplomatic relations with Clement.

But then the unexpected death of Joseph I – from smallpox, at the age of just 33 – changed everything. Were Charles to succeed to the Spanish throne and, as was inevitable, also succeed his brother as Holy Roman Emperor, he would become vastly powerful. When a new status quo was thrashed out at the treaties of Utrecht and Rastatt of 1713–14, the papacy was no more than a bystander. Various papal possessions – including Naples, Parma, Sardinia and Sicily – were handed to new rulers in the settlement without regard to papal claims. The pope was not strong enough to intervene and had to accept it.

CONFLICT OVER JANSENISM

Clement issued a stern bull *Unigenitus Dei Filius* ("The Only-begotten Son of God") condemning the Jansenists in France. It provoked an outcry: four bishops challenged it, with the backing of 12 others and some 3,000 clergy. In August 1718 Clement excommunicated the four bishops but the churchmen maintained

Below: St Louis Cathedral, which stands in the French Quarter of New Orleans, is the oldest cathedral in the United States. It was founded in Clement's reign, in 1718.

their opposition and renewed their appeal against the bull in 1720. Gallicanism, which sought to restrict the papacy's power in France, was resurgent and the prestige of the pope was ever-declining. The controversy rumbled on until Clement's death on 19 March 1721.

CHINESE RITES

Clement also provoked major difficulties for Jesuit and Dominican missionaries in China. The Chinese Rites Controversy centred on whether – as a way of easing conversions – it was permissible for missionaries to accept certain local ceremonies in honour of Ancient Chinese philosopher Confucius and ancestors of the Chinese emperors. Clement decreed in 1704 and again in 1715 that this practice was not permissible and after the second ruling many Chinese turned against the missionaries and began to persecute Christians in China. Several missions were closed down.

PATRON OF ARTS

In Rome, Clement founded an academy of painting and sculpture in the Campidoglio and made alterations to the Piazza del Pantheon and the Church of Santa Maria degli Angeli e dei Martiri, where he added a celebrated sundial. A learned and virtuous man, he enriched the collections of the Vatican Library.

Above: The controversy over the Jansenists (followers of Dutch theologian Cornelius Jansen) is represented in this satirical engraving of 1714. Clement made a declaration against the Jansenists.

JANSENISM

The reform movement of Jansenism derived from the writings of Dutch theologian Cornelius Jansen, in particular his four-volume *Augustinus*, published in 1640. In this work Jansen, who served as professor of theology at Louvain in 1630 and Bishop of Ypres in 1636, defended writings of St Augustine of Hippo on free will and divine grace and attacked the teachings of the Jesuits on these issues – and in particular emphasized the necessity of divine redeeming grace for the salvation of a soul damaged by original sin. Jansenism became closely associated with Gallicanism – a movement that sought to restrict the power of the papacy in France. Innocent X (1644–55) and Alexander VII (1655–67) made declarations against the Jansenists, as well as Clement XI. After the promulgation as French law in 1730 of Clement's *Unigenitus* bull, Jansenists mainly took refuge in the Netherlands.

INNOCENT XIII TO CLEMENT XII, 1721–40
POPES BEAUTIFY ROME BUT THEIR PRESTIGE FAILS

From Innocent XIII (1721–4) to Clement XII (1730–40), three elderly popes were unable to prevent the continuing decline in the papacy's prestige and international standing. But in their pontificates the Baroque splendour of Rome was further enhanced, with the addition of the famous "Spanish Steps" and the magnificent Trevi Fountain.

THE CONTI POPES

Innocent XIII (1721–4) was – like his distant predecessors Innocent III (1198–1216), Gregory IX (1227–41) and Alexander IV (1254–61) – a member of the noble Conti family. He was the last pope to take the name "Innocent". Elected pope on 8 May 1721 after a lengthy conclave dominated by disputes between French and imperial cardinals, he was already 66, overweight and in poor health. But he was known also for his kindness and intelligence.

There was no hiding the political weakness of the papacy. Innocent had to invest Holy Roman Emperor Charles VI with sovereignty over Naples and Sicily, recently prized papal possessions, and curried favour with France by making a cardinal of the French councillor of state, the dissolute and highly unsuitable Abbé Guillaume Dubois. Nevertheless Innocent maintained a hard line on Jansenism, firmly refusing a request that his predecessor's *Unigenitus* bull be recalled, and was strict with the Jesuits – in the light of the Chinese Rites Controversy, banning the Jesuits from carrying on their mission in China and from taking in new members.

Above: Clement XII in a painting by Agostino Masucci. He defied old age and poor health, including blindness, to be an energetic and effective pope.

Innocent supported the exiled claimant to the English throne, James Edward Stuart (known as the "Old Pretender"), and allowed Stuart and his court to remain in residence in the Palazzo Muti, which Clement XI had given to the exile.

DEVOUT BUT NAÏVE

The pontificate of Benedict XIII (1724–30) was a political and diplomatic disaster. The Church's new leader had many qualities: scholarly, pious and frugal, he lived as a Dominican friar while pope, visited the sick and cared for the poor. He regularly waited on the poverty-stricken at his table and sought to curb the ostentation of many cardinals, in particular banning the wearing of wigs. But he was also naïve, far too trusting of the man to whom he handed control of other papal business – the corrupt and self-interested Cardinal Niccolò Coscia, who took bribes and sold offices for his own financial gain.

Benedict also caused a diplomatic crisis by refusing when King John V of Portugal sought to nominate candidates

Below: James II of England's Catholic son, James Edward Stuart, lived in Rome as a guest of Clement XI and Innocent XIII.

THE OLD PRETENDER

James Francis Edward Stuart – known as "the Old Pretender" – was the son of King James II of Great Britain. As a Roman Catholic from 1671, James II had been ousted in the revolution of 1688 in which his Protestant daughter Mary and her Dutch husband William of Orange came to the throne as William III and Mary II. After his father's death in 1701 James Francis Edward Stuart was proclaimed his successor in France and recognized as such by King Louis XIV. However, attempts to restore him to the throne, including the Jacobite Rebellion of 1715, all failed – and after Louis's death he came to Rome, where Clement XI gave him the Palazzo Muti as his residence and Innocent XIII granted him a lifetime annuity. He maintained a "Jacobite court" in Rome, where his son Charles was born. This young man – the Young Pretender, also known as "Bonnie Prince Charlie" – failed in his attempt to reclaim his throne in 1745–6 and lived out his life in exile, claiming the title King Charles III of Great Britain after his father's death in 1766.

INNOCENT XIII TO CLEMENT XII

Above: Another of Rome's Baroque masterpieces, the vast Trevi Fountain was designed by architect Nicola Salvi for Pope Clement XII and constructed in 1732–62.

to the Sacred College, as many other European royal courts did; John broke off relations and attempted to stop the paying of Portuguese alms to Rome.

SPANISH STEPS

Benedict's reign also saw the completion and inauguration in 1725 of the Scalinata della Trinità dei Monti, the famous "Spanish Steps" that climb from the Piazza di Spanga to the Piazza Trinità dei Monti in Rome.

ELDERLY BUT ENERGETIC

Clement XII (1730–40) was 78 on his election, and during his pontificate was often bedridden and was completely blind from 1732 onwards – his hand had to be positioned in the correct place for him to sign papal documents. Yet for all his declining physical and mental powers, this elderly man somehow remained full of energy. He arrested, tried and imprisoned for ten years the corrupt Cardinal Niccolò Coscia and took various measures to try to reinvigorate papal finances – including reintroducing the Roman lottery, which Benedict XIII had outlawed.

On the international stage he could do little in the face of the new spirit of indifference to papal territorial and political interests: Holy Roman Emperor Charles VI simply annexed former papal territories and Don Carlos of Spain marched through the papal states and helped himself to Naples and Sicily.

Clement did deliver effective support for missionary work, for example despatching Franciscans to Ethiopia, and issued a papal bull in 1738 condemning Freemasonry and threatening with excommunication any Catholic who joined the masons.

In Rome, Clement was a patron of many fine works – including the new façade for the archbasilica of San Giovanni in Laterano and the superb Corsini Chapel within, both designed by Alessandro Galilei, and the laying out of the Piazza di Trevi and the construction there of the extraordinary Fontana di Trevi (Trevi Fountain): 86 feet (26 metres) high, it is a baroque masterpiece designed by architect Niccola Salvi. Clement also enriched the holdings of the Vatican Library and on the Capitol opened a public museum of antique sculptures, the first of its kind in Europe.

Long a sufferer of gout, he developed a hernia and trouble with his bladder and died on 6 February 1740 at the close of what, given his age, very poor health and the international circumstances, was a remarkably successful pontificate.

Right: St Vincent de Paul helps the plague-ridden in a painting by Antoine Ansiaux. He was canonized by Clement XII in 1737.

PAPAL POWER AND INFLUENCE

BENEDICT XIV, 1740–58
MODERNIZING POPE WHO CORRESPONDED WITH VOLTAIRE

At a time when the Catholic Church was facing severe criticism from philosophers of the European Enlightenment, Benedict XIV was an engaging and learned pope who won widespread admiration for his moderate approach to the difficulties encountered by the papacy and especially for his wit, intelligence and dedicated support for higher learning and the study of science and history. He became popular throughout Europe, liked and praised by Protestants as well as Catholics.

THEOLOGIAN AND LAWYER

A gifted and determined scholar, Prospero Lambertini (the future Benedict XIV) was awarded doctorates in theology, canon law and civil law by the University of Rome at the age of 19. He was made a cardinal in 1728 by Benedict XIII, and served with great distinction as first Bishop of Ancona and then Archbishop of Bologna.

The conclave from which he emerged as pope lasted a full six months following the death of Clement XII on 6 February 1740; finally, Lambertini emerged as a surprise candidate and was elected pope on 17 August, taking the name Benedict in tribute to the pope who had raised him to the cardinalate. He famously said to the cardinals, referring to the two other leading candidates: "If you want to elect a saint, choose Gotti; a statesman, Aldobrandini; a good man, elect me."

Above: Benedict XIV raises his arm to deliver a blessing. He was a great reformer and educational patron. The portrait is by French artist Pierre Subleyras.

Left: Benedict presents an encyclical addressed to the bishops of France to the Comte de Stainville. Painting by Pompeo Girolamo Batoni.

> **FACT BOX**
> **Original name** Prospero Lambertini
> **Born** 31 March 1675
> **Origin** Bologna, papal states
> **Date elected pope** 17 August 1740
> **Died** 3 May 1758
> **Key fact** Highly popular pontiff and a major patron of education

He was a good choice: in addition to being learned and serious-minded, he was kindly and accessible, funny and witty, happy to meet the people of Rome during his regular walks in the city. He engaged with a lively society of intellectuals in Rome and corresponded with many of the leading intellectual figures of the day. These included the French historian-philosopher Voltaire who dedicated his 1741 tragic play *Mahomet* to Benedict.

AUSTRIAN TROUBLES

His papacy was quite effective politically: he improved relations with Spain and Portugal, coming to an agreement in 1740 under which the Portuguese monarch had rights of patronage over all abbeys and bishoprics in his kingdom and another in 1753 under which the Spanish crown gained the right to appoint to some 12,000 church livings. However, he got into some difficulty over the disputed succession to the Holy Roman Empire following the death in 1740 of Emperor Charles VI. His initial refusal to decide and then his support for Charles Albert of Bavaria after he was elected Emperor Charles VII soured relations with Queen Maria Theresa of Austria, daughter of Charles VI and wife of the other candidate, Francis of Lorraine, Grand Duke of Tuscany: in 1742 she announced the seizure of church benefices in Austria. In the event Charles VII died only three years later and Francis succeeded as Holy Roman Emperor Francis I. Relations were restored after Benedict formally recognized him.

PATRON OF LEARNING

Benedict was one of the greatest of papal patrons, but in education rather than architecture and painting. In Rome he created four academies for the study of Christian and Roman antiquities, church history and canon law and liturgy. At the city's university he established professorial chairs of chemistry, physics and mathematics; at the University of Bologna, his native city, he created a chair of surgery. He also initiated the cataloguing of the Vatican Library. He drew up new rules for the Index of Prohibited Books, so that books could only be banned with the pope's approval. His ecclesiastical writings, notably the *Institutiones Ecclesiasticae,* were honoured. He wrote what is still regarded as the standard official work on canonization.

REFORMS

Benedict was an active reformer, setting to work to improve priestly education, the breviary (the Church's book of liturgical rites) and the calendar of feasts. He issued an encyclical in 1745 condemning usury and effectively stamped it out. A bull of 1748 defined the conditions under which mixed marriages between Protestants and Catholics were permissible; these notably included that the children of the marriage should be brought up in the Catholic faith.

To save money he refrained from creating any cardinals for four years. He improved financial revenue from the papal states by introducing changes to agricultural practices and was able to cut taxes. He delivered himself of forthright decisions on the Jesuits and the "Rites

Above: Silvio Valenti Gonzaga was Benedict's secretary of state. He was a devoted art collector, and this painting by Giovanni Paolo Pannini shows his gallery.

Controversy" and the driving of South American peoples into slavery. His popularity across Europe with intellectuals and others of religious backgrounds made Catholics and Romans proud. When he died on 3 May 1758 the city of Rome was plunged into grief.

LAWS ON MISSION

Benedict issued two bulls, *Ex quo singulari* in 1742 and *Omnium sollicitudinum* in 1744, prohibiting the native customs such as ancestor worship that the Jesuits had allowed in missions to native peoples. He required missionaries to take an oath that they would not allow such practices in future; many converts abandoned the Christian faith. In 1741 another of his bulls, *Immensa Pastorum Principis*, spoke out against the enslavement of native peoples in South America.

CLEMENT XIII, 1758–69
POPE OVERWHELMED BY SERIES OF ATTACKS ON JESUITS

The pontificate of Clement XIII was dominated by a major scandal involving the Jesuits, in the course of which they were driven out of Portugal, France, Spain, Naples and Parma. When European rulers then demanded the dissolution of the Society of Jesus, Clement was forced to summon a consistory to bring this about, but he died in February 1769 on the night before it was due to meet.

Clement was in fact a staunch supporter of the Jesuits, in contrast to his predecessor who had had distinctly mixed feelings about the Society. Born in Venice, the future Clement XIII was educated by the Jesuits in Bologna before becoming governor of first Rieti and then Fano. Raised to the cardinalate by Clement XII in 1737, he became Bishop of Padua in 1743 and was elected pope on 6 July 1758 as a compromise candidate after the French had vetoed the conclave's earlier choice.

SAINTLY BUT INDECISIVE
He was not the character needed to deal effectively with the coming storm over the Jesuits. He was by no means the impressive wit and philosophical thinker that his predecessor had been. He lacked imagination and verve – he ordered, as Paul V had done, the covering up or even painting out of some of the more risqué elements of the papacy's Renaissance art, including sections of the Sistine Chapel frescoes.

FACT BOX
Original name Carlo della Torre Rezzonico
Born 7 March 1693
Origin Venice
Date elected pope 16 July 1758
Died 2 February 1769
Key fact Added French *Encyclopédie* to Index of Prohibited Books

Strong in faith, moderate, a lover of justice, he may have had elements of the saint about him – but he was unable to come up with a decisive response to the onslaught of Enlightenment thinkers against the Jesuits and the Church.

Within two months of his election he faced the crisis. King Joseph I of Portugal, believing that members of the Society of Jesus had been involved in a conspiracy to murder him, confiscated their riches and drove them out of his country, sending them to the Roman seaport of Civitavecchia as a "gift" to the pope. Diplomatic relations were broken off.

Above: Rezzonico was educated by the Jesuits in Bologna and once installed as Pope Clement was a supporter of the Society of Jesus.

FRENCH ONSLAUGHT
The flames of anti-Jesuit feeling spread through France, which was primed already by the presence there of the writer and philosopher Voltaire and the *philosophes*, free-thinking intellectuals who increasingly saw the Church (which they privately called the *Infâme* or "infamous one") as ridiculous and dangerous – an enemy of freedom.

CLEMENT XIII

Above: Clement's magnificent marble tomb in St Peter's was commissioned by his nephew, Senator Abbondio Rezzonico, and designed by the neoclassical sculptor Antonio Canova.

Voltaire – despite his open admiration for Benedict XIV – was scathing about religion, the Church and the Jesuits. He wrote to Frederick the Great, "So long as there are rogues and fools in the world, there will always be religion … ours is the most ridiculous, absurd and bloodthirsty that ever infected the earth." He and the philosophes saw an attack on the Jesuits as the first step in bringing down the Church herself – Voltaire wrote to French philosopher Claude Adrien Helvétius, "When we have destroyed the Jesuits, we shall have easy work with the *Infâme*."

The Jesuits came under strong attack and in 1764 Louis XV, influenced by philosophes at court, issued a decree declaring the Society of Jesus abolished in France and expelling all Jesuits from his country.

In Spain, Charles III held the Jesuits responsible for riots and may even have been persuaded that they were plotting against him. He banished them on 27 February 1767, and in the course of that year and 1768 the Jesuits were also expelled from Naples, Sicily, Malta and the Duchy of Parma and Piacenza.

WHAT TO DO WITH THE HOMELESS JESUITS?

Initially Clement, fearing the potential consequences of the influx of so many exiled Jesuits, refused to allow them to come to Rome or the papal states. Many settled in Corsica but had to move on again when the French purchased the island in 1768. Then Clement showed compassion, and allowed the bedraggled and impoverished Jesuits to settle in the papal states.

CLASH WITH PARMA

When the Duke of Parma and Piacenza, a former papal territory, issued a proclamation in 1768 that forbade all appeals to Rome unless with the duke's permission, and banned all papal edicts including bulls, Clement was affronted and pronounced the duke's decree and other earlier anticlerical laws null and void, declaring for good measure that those responsible were to be excommunicated by his bull *In Coena Domini*. This provoked widespread outrage. France took possession of Avignon; Naples seized Benevento. Voltaire even made the statement that it was not fitting for the pope to rule any territory at all.

Above: Charles III of Spain. Clement's bull Quantum ornamentum of 1760 approved his request to invoke the Immaculate Conception as Patroness of Spain.

Then in January 1769 came a demand from the ambassadors of France, Spain and Naples that the Society of Jesus be abolished. Clement never recovered his equanimity. He ordered a consistory to consider the matter on 3 February, but the night before its opening he died in Rome following a stroke.

THE ENCYCLOPÉDIE AND THE ENLIGHTENMENT

The French *L'Encyclopédie, ou dictionnaire raisonné des sciences, des arts ets des métiers* ("The Encyclopedia, or systematically arranged dictionary of arts and crafts") was published in 28 volumes in 1751–72. Edited by Denis Diderot and initially also by Jean le Rond d'Alembert, the work included criticism of the Roman Catholic Church – including attacks on the monastic way of life and clerical celibacy – and Clement XIII had it placed on the Index of Prohibited Books.

Right: Pope Clement XIII had Denis Diderot's "Encyclopedie" placed on the Index of Prohibited Books. "The Art of Writing" is an engraved plate from the encyclopedia.

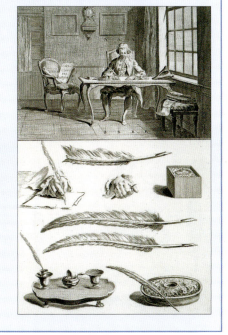

711

POPES IN AN AGE OF REVOLUTION
CLEMENT XIV TO LEO XIII, 1769–1903

Pope Pius VII was crowned on 21 March 1800 with a tiara made of papier-mâché and in the Benedictine monastery on the island of San Giorgio Maggiore, Venice, rather than in Rome. When his predecessor Pius VI died in captivity in France, Rome was not safe due to severe unrest following its occupation by the French in 1798, and the conclave from which Pius VII was elected was held on San Giorgio Maggiore under the protection of Holy Roman Emperor Francis I. Pius was crowned with a papier-mâché tiara because the French had taken possession of the original when they occupied Rome.

At the start of his pontificate Pius set about repairing relations with the French Republic. He signed a concordat in 1801 with Napoleon, at this point First Consul of France. But when the pope travelled by invitation to Napoleon's coronation as emperor, he was a mere spectator – Napoleon crowned himself and his empress Josephine. The relationship soured quickly: Napoleon occupied Rome and annexed the papal states, Pius excommunicated Napoleon in 1809 and was then imprisoned by him from 1809–14. As in the previous century, the papacy was unable to hold its own on the international stage.

At the Congress of Vienna in 1814, the papal states and Rome were restored to the pope. The popes were not yet ready to give up their standing as temporal rulers; they felt they needed worldly power in order to exercise spiritual authority. Yet they were unable to hold on to this worldly power. The establishment of the Kingdom of Italy in 1860 during the pontificate of Pius IX saw the papal states annexed and the pope's temporal power wiped out.

Left: French power, papal humiliation. Rather than performing the coronation himself, Pope Pius VII merely looks on as Napoleon crowns his empress, Josephine, in Notre Dame de Paris on 2 December 1804.

CLEMENT XIV AND PIUS VI, 1769–99
POPES WHO FACED A TIME OF REVOLUTION

After Clement XIV (1769–74) carried out the dissolution of the Jesuits that had been pressed so forcefully on his predecessor, Pius VI (1775–99) ruled for 24 years – the longest pontificate up to this date in the history of the papacy. Pius had to face the consequences of the French Revolution of 1789, not least the invasion of the papal states by French general Napoleon Bonaparte.

At the start of his pontificate Clement XIV managed to hold off international pressure to dissolve the Jesuits for four years. Initially he set out to restore peace, renouncing papal claims to Parma and so regaining control of Avignon and Benevento, then reconnecting with Portugal by appointing as a cardinal Paulo de Carvalho, brother of the Portuguese Secretary of State the Marquis of Pombal, and sending a papal ambassador to the Portuguese royal court.

Clement was intelligent, approachable, frugal and honest. He was well versed in church history and theology and known for his fine speech and educated conversation. But he had no diplomatic experience and was slow to take decisions; he wanted to keep the peace, but lacked the necessary strength of character.

BULL OF DISSOLUTION
Finally, under the threat that unless he wound up the Jesuits Spain and France would break off relations with the papacy, he dissolved the Society of Jesus in his bull *Dominus ac Redemptor noster* ("Our Lord and Saviour") of 16 August 1773. He declared as one of the reasons

Above: A relatively youthful pope, Clement died aged just 68 in 1774. His neoclassical tomb was designed by Antonio Canova and is in the Church of the Santi Apostoli, Rome.

NAPOLEON

Corsican-born French general Napoleon Bonaparte was First Consul in 1799–1804, then Emperor of the French in 1804–15. He was forced to abdicate and exiled on the island of Elba in 1814 then returned to power in March 1815 until he was defeated at the Battle of Waterloo and forced again into exile on St Helena.

Despite his intermittent conflict with the papacy, he was a Roman Catholic throughout his life. In 1796, at the head of the French army, he had orders to invade Rome and depose the pope, but signed a treaty that guaranteed Pius VI safety in Rome. In 1800 as First Consul he declared his interest in achieving reconciliation between France and the Holy See, but his relationship with Pope Pius VII was fiery: Napoleon annexed the papal states, occupied Rome and imprisoned the pope, and for his troubles was excommunicated. When the defeated and captive Napoleon was in exile on St Helena at the end of his life Pius exhibited forgiveness by sending him a chaplain.

Left: Napoleon Bonaparte invades. The French army occupied the papal states, proclaimed a Roman Republic and announced the deposition of the pope as the head of state.

Right: Clement dissolves the Jesuits in 1773. He had tried to resist pressure from France and Spain to wind up the Society.

for his decision that it was impossible to restore "a true and lasting peace" in the Church while the Society was in existence. Many Jesuits found refuge in Russia and Prussia, where the authorities declined to implement the bull.

Being effectively forced to carry out the dissolution hit Clement hard. He had been educated by the Jesuits in his hometown of Rimini, and in his 30s he had dedicated a theological work to the founder of the Jesuits, Ignatius of Loyola.

After signing the bull of dissolution, Clement was filled with remorse, suffered from depression and lived in fear of his life – convinced that he was going to be assassinated. When he died at the relatively young age of 68 on 22 September 1774, there were whispers that he had been poisoned, but an autopsy established that he had died of natural causes.

RETURN OF NEPOTISM

With Pius VI (1775–99), in an era of crisis when an exceptional pope such as Benedict XIV was needed, the papacy fell back into bad, old ways – nepotism and profligacy. Pius was proud and somewhat vain: tall and good-looking, he lacked seriousness and was not profoundly spiritual. He constructed the Palazzo Braschi in Rome for his nephew Luigi Braschi Onesti: a throwback to the Renaissance that proved to be the last such palace financed and built by a pope for his relatives. He spent very freely on the arts, particularly on expanding the Museo Pio-Clementino in the Vatican.

TROUBLE WITH THE EMPIRE

Pius faced a major difficulty with Holy Roman Emperor Joseph II who in 1781 introduced church reforms in the empire under which non-Catholic minorities were granted toleration, seminaries were taken under control of the state and would provide trainee priests with a liberal as well as a religious education,

Below: The French Revolution struck in 1789. Clement is among the powerful brought low in this cartoon depicting "The Electrical Spark of Liberty that will Topple the Thrones of all Corrupt Monarchs", 1793.

some 1,300 monasteries were closed and various church festivals and traditions that were deemed superstitious in the era of the Enlightenment were abolished. Pius attempted to intervene and made a personal trip to Vienna in 1782; he was well received but achieved little.

FRENCH REVOLUTION – PAPACY UNDER ATTACK

When the French Revolution struck in 1789, an effigy of the pope was burned in Paris. The inhabitants of Avignon, still a papal territory, declared themselves citizens of France. The French clergy were made state employees. Pius initially took no action but in 1791 after the clergy were required to take an oath of loyalty to the state, he denounced the Revolution and the Declaration of the Rights of Man.

Then in 1796 the French army under Napoleon Bonaparte invaded northern Italy with the intention of taking the papal states and Pius had to sign a humiliating peace treaty at Tolentino on 19 February 1797. When in December that same year a French general was killed in the course of a riot in Rome, the die was cast: the French occupied the city on 15 February 1798 and a republic was declared. The pope was deposed as head of state. Pius died in humiliation and captivity at Valence, in France, on 29 August 1799.

POPES IN AN AGE OF REVOLUTION

PIUS VII, 1800–23
DIGNIFIED IN DEALINGS WITH NAPOLEON

In the 23-year pontificate of Pius VII, the papacy began to win back lost prestige and international sympathy. After initially making peace with Napoleonic France, Pius acted with courage in challenging and excommunicating Napoleon – and with dignity when he was captured and held in French captivity in 1810–14. He made a triumphant return to Rome following Napoleon's fall from power and regained much of the land lost to French invaders.

Born to a noble family in Cesena in 1742, Barnaba Chiaramonti was related through his mother to the future Pope Pius VI (1775–99). He became a Benedictine aged 16 in 1758 and after working as a professor of theology and philosophy in the order's colleges in Rome and Parma, rose to become cardinal-priest in the basilica of San Callisto and Bishop of Imola in 1785 under his relative Pius VI. He was himself pious and gentle, and proved brave in adversity.

EQUALITY AND DEMOCRACY

While a cardinal, in 1797, Pius had declared in a homily that there was no necessary incompatibility between Roman Catholicism and democracy – stating "equality is an idea not of the philosophers but of Jesus Christ" – and from the start of his pontificate he set out to establish good relations with the French Republic. His representative Ercole Consalvi, whom Pius appointed to the key position of Cardinal Secretary of State, negotiated a concordat in 1801 with Napoleon, at this point First Consul of France, under which dioceses in France were reorganized and Roman Catholicism confirmed as the country's principal religion. However, Pius was forced to protest when additional articles were unilaterally added to the document by Napoleon in 1802; under these, the pope needed the approval of the French government for his rulings in France.

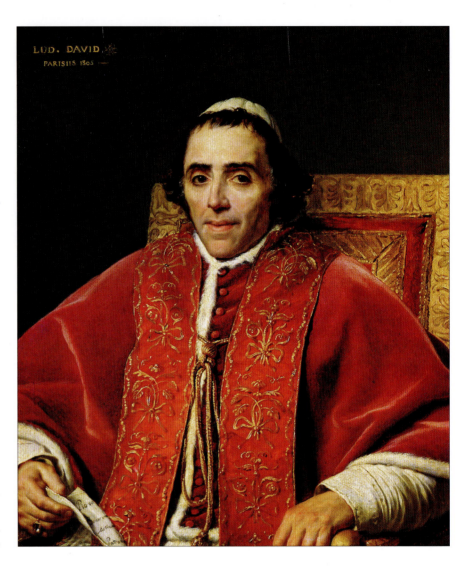

Above: Pius VII initially made peace with France. This portrait by the celebrated French artist Jacques Louis David was made at the Tuileries in 1805.

FACT BOX

Original name Luigi Barnaba Gregorio Chiaramonti
Born 14 August 1742
Origin Cesena
Date elected pope 14 March 1800
Died 20 August 1823
Key fact Showed charity to French leader despite ill treatment

SPECTATOR AT NAPOLEON'S CORONATION

Pius travelled to Paris in 1804 to consecrate Napoleon as Emperor of France. The coronation proved something of a humiliation for the pope: Napoleon not only kept him waiting for a full hour, but also insisted on performing his own coronation, as well as crowning Empress Josephine, while the Pope merely looked on. Pius's role as mere spectator is emphasized in Jacques-Louis David's celebrated painting of the event – with Pius's disgruntlement clear to see.

Relations between pope and emperor were not to recover. Seeking to establish a Kingdom of Italy in his own name,

> **RELATIONS WITH THE USA**
> When the United States won a notable victory over Berber Muslim pirates of northwest Africa in the First Barbary War of 1801–5, Pius declared that in bringing about the defeat of the pirates – who were a scourge of Christian shipping in the Mediterranean – the USA had "done more for the cause of Christianity than the most powerful nations of Christendom have done for ages". Pius also approved the establishment of several dioceses in the USA: Boston, New York, Philadelphia and Bardstown in 1808, Charleston (1820) and Cincinnati (1821).

Napoleon occupied Rome in 1808 and declared the papal states annexed to France in 1809. Pius attempted to fight back: he excommunicated Napoleon on 10 June 1809. But he was afterwards seized from the Quirinal Palace and taken first to Grenoble, France, then to Savona, northern Italy, and in 1812 back to France and captivity at Fontainebleau. There Pius – in very poor health and bullied by Napoleon – signed a draft concordat on 25 January 1813 under which the pope would give up all temporal power and the seat of the papacy would be moved from Rome to France.

RETURN TO ROME

Recovering his mind and health, Pius wrote to Napoleon two months later to repudiate the concordat. By this stage Napoleon had his hands full dealing with the collapse of his empire. Pius was released in 1814 and made a triumphant return to Rome: the horses of his carriage were freed and the carriage drawn into the city by 30 young men from Rome's leading families.

At the Congress of Vienna in 1814, with Napoleon defeated and exiled to Elba, the pope regained possession of the papal states and Rome. Napoleon's return, defeat at Waterloo and final exile to St Helena did nothing to change this.

Above: Jacques-Louis David also painted Pius's discomfiture as a mere onlooker at the coronation of Napoleon in Notre Dame, Paris. Napoleon crowned first himself and then his empress.

By 1815 the international standing of the papacy was significantly restored from the low points of the previous century. Napoleon's harsh treatment of the

Below: Antonio Canova, sculptor of tombs for Clement XIII and XIV, was the most celebrated artist of his age in Europe. This portrait is by English portraitist Thomas Lawrence. Canova died in 1822.

pope, Pius's dignified resistance and his behaviour in captivity had won widespread admiration and restored respect for the pope. In the years that remained to him before his death on 20 July 1823 Pius set to work to adapt the Church to the new conditions of the modern world. He signed 20 concordats with different countries, generally having to cede the long-disputed right of the pope to appoint bishops, but achieving the re-establishment of many monasteries and seminaries that had been closed and regaining control of schools.

REVIVAL OF THE JESUITS

In addition, Pope Pius VII revived the Jesuits in 1801 for Russia, in 1813 for Ireland, England and the United States and elsewhere in 1814. He issued condemnations of Protestant Bible Societies and of Freemasons and in 1817 revised the working of the Congregation of Propaganda.

Given the way he was treated in captivity, Pius showed considerable Christian charity towards Napoleon after the French emperor's downfall. He allowed Napoleon's relatives – including his mother Princess Letitia and brothers Lucien and Louis – to settle in Rome and sent Abbé Vignali to St Helena as a chaplain for Napoleon in his exile.

LEO XII, 1823–9
POPE WHO WORKED TO AGENDA OF CONSERVATIVE CARDINALS

The pious, authoritarian Leo XII largely reversed the reforming policies of his predecessor. His rule in the papal states, where a feudal aristocracy and ecclesiastical courts were re-established, won him a reputation as a tyrant and was denounced as "government by priests".

Della Genga rose to high ecclesiastical position through being private secretary to Pius VI (1775–99), then served as papal nuncio briefly in Lucerne and for 11 years (1794–1805) in Cologne. He gained significant diplomatic experience – although he was sacked from his position in 1814 by Cardinal Consalvi, who held him responsible for failings in the negotiations to regain control of Avignon. Subsequently cardinal-priest of Santa Maria in Trastevere, he was appointed Vicar General of Rome in 1820 by Pius VII (1800–23).

Below: Rome under Leo's rule, *in 1825, by Silvestr Feodosievich Shchedrin. Life was highly regulated, and all residents had to attend instruction in the Catholic faith. Many Jews left Rome and the papal states.*

PASSION FOR SHOOTING BIRDS

Leo XII was tall, handsome and gifted as a speaker – winning great admiration for the well-judged funeral oration he delivered in the Sistine Chapel in 1790 on the death of Holy Roman Emperor Joseph II. He lived simply, with little furniture, not eating much – and was persistently unwell, troubled in particular by piles; although he had a passion for music and for shooting birds, he was generally puritanical. In outlook he was somewhat narrow-minded, a conservative committed to strict tradition rather than compromise and so naturally opposed to the modernizing reforms of Pius VII.

CONSERVATIVE RULE – CLIMATE OF FEAR

His election as pope on 28 September 1823 after a 26-day conclave at the Quirinal Palace came about through the influence of the *zelanti*, a conservative group of cardinals who wanted firm leadership for the Church. He was 63 years old and in very poor health

Above: Leo is carried through St Peter's in Rome. A conservative, he introduced regulations and a strict regime that provoked unrest in the papal states.

– almost at death's door. However, he recovered – in some accounts, due to the intervention of the Bishop of Marittima, who prayed fervently for his restoration to health – and set to work to deliver on the agenda of the zelanti.

He strengthened the work of the Inquisition and introduced a host of regulations governing daily life in Rome and the papal states. He banned the open sale of alcohol, outlawed the playing of games on feast days or Sundays – with offenders subject to a jail sentence; he declared that dressmakers who made low-cut or transparent dresses would be

FACT BOX

Original name Annibale Sermattei Della Genga
Born 22 August 1760
Origin La Genga, near Spoleto
Date elected pope 28 September 1823
Died 10 February 1829
Key fact Hated for tyrannical rule

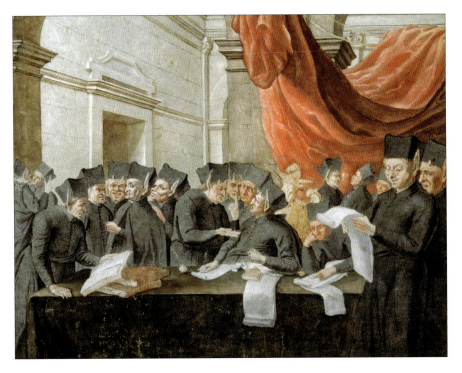

Above: The Jesuits, shown here in conclave discussing their accounts, were a resurgent force under Leo and re-established their Collegio Romano.

excommunicated. He banned encores and great ovations in theatres – and even outlawed the ad-libbing of lines by actors – because he felt these encouraged the expression of seditious ideas.

PERSECUTION OF JEWS

He forbade Jews to own property, gave them a very short time to sell what they owned, banned them from doing business with Christians and forced them once again to live in ghettos behind high walls and locked gates. In Rome, he required 300 Jews to attend a weekly Christian sermon. Many Jews left Rome to settle in Tuscany and Lombardy. The economy of the papal states slowed to a crawl.

These rules and strict forms of government were rigidly enforced by a regime that created a climate of fear and made full use of informers. Life was austere under Leo's rule and he was immensely unpopular. His delegate in the south of Italy, Cardinal Palotta, brought in martial law to tame outlaws, introducing fines for villages found to be harbouring criminals and even abolishing courts of law because he claimed judges might be subject to intimidation. But he was so unpopular that he was made to stand down after a month and the outlaws financed the singing of Masses of Thanksgiving.

EDUCATION AND ECCLESIASTICAL DISCIPLINE

Under Leo the Jesuits were resurgent. The society's education system was revived and the Collegio Romano re-established. By a papal bull of 1824 Leo put all schools in Rome and the papal states under priestly control.

Leo also reiterated his predecessors' pronouncements against Freemasonry and Protestant Bible Societies and in May 1825 issued a condemnation of indifferentism, the argument that all religions were of equal standing.

In international affairs, he was more successful and maintained good relations with both Protestant and Catholic countries. He supported Roman Catholics in Britain who were under the yoke of discriminatory laws and signed concordats with Hanover in 1824 and the Netherlands in 1827.

CARBONARI AND SANFEDISTI

Two popular groups with enduring influence were in opposition in early 19th-century Italy. The carbonari – "charcoal burners" – were members of an anti-clerical revolutionary secret society established in Italy in the early 1800s. Pius VII issued a papal constitution, *Ecclesiam a Jesu Christo*, in 1821 under which carbonari were excommunicated and denounced for plotting against the Church and the primacy of the pope. Later Pius IX would issue an encyclical, *Qui Pluribus*, that was seen as an attack on the movement. Their influence fed into the *Risorgimento* movement that led to the unification of Italy in 1861. Sanfedisti were members of an anti-Republican movement called *Sanfedismo* ("Holy Faith"). Initially the counter-revolutionary movement was founded by Cardinal Fabrizio Ruffo in 1799 to mobilize peasants from the papal states against French occupation of the former Kingdom of Naples. The name was applied more generally to religiously inspired peasant armies and to those who rose up against the House of Savoy in the build-up to Italian unification.

Below: The anticlerical carbonari met in secret. This illustration is from an album on the history of the Risorgimento movement that led to the unification of Italy.

PAPAL MISSIONS TO SPREAD THE GOSPEL AROUND THE WORLD

Spreading the Gospel is a responsibility for all Christians, not least the leader of the Roman Catholic Church – from the preaching of St Peter to the globe-trotting missions of modern popes such as Paul VI (1963–78) and John Paul II (1978–2005).

THE GREAT COMMISSION
The Church's missionary activity has its origin in the command of the Risen Christ to carry his teachings all over the world. As told in Matthew 28:16–20, Jesus appeared to the disciples after his crucifixion and resurrection and told them, "All authority in heaven and earth has been given to me. Go therefore and make disciples of all nations, baptizing them in the name of the Father and the Son and the Holy Spirit, teaching them to observe all that I have commanded you." Missionaries call Christ's command to carry the Gospel around the world "the Great Commission".

Left: The Jesuits arrive by ship on the coast of New Granada, bringing the Christian faith to the Spanish territory in the northern part of South America.

ST PETER THE MISSIONARY
Before becoming leader of the Church in Rome, St Peter himself preached a key sermon to a gathering of Gentiles at Caesarea, as described in the Book of Acts Chapter 10. He declared that God shows no partiality, but accepts those in every nation who fear him and do what is right. He declared himself a witness of all that Jesus did and recalled that Jesus "commanded us to preach to the people and to testify that he is the one appointed by God to be judge of the living and the dead." The account continues, "While Peter was still saying these things, the Holy Spirit fell on all who heard the word. And the believers from among the circumcised who had come with Peter were amazed, because the gift of the Holy Spirit was poured out even on the Gentiles."

Over the centuries many of Peter's successors supported missionary outreach. The report that Pope Eleutherius (c.175–c.189) sent missionaries to Britain at the request of a British king named Lucius is thought to be apocryphal, but Gregory I (590–604) sent missionaries – including St Augustine of Canterbury

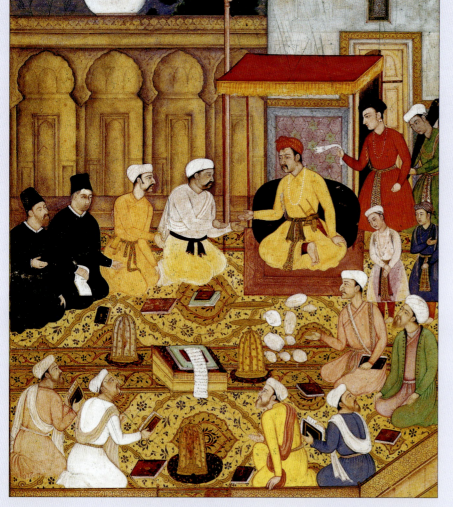

Left: The third Mughal emperor, Akbar the Great, welcomed Jesuit missionaries to India and hosted debates between his visitors and local Muslim scholars.

720

– to England and they reputedly baptized thousands of locals on Christmas Day 597. In the 8th century Gregory II sent the great missionary St Boniface to what is now Germany.

THE RELIGIOUS ORDERS

In the Middle Ages the great religious orders of the Dominicans and the Franciscans were connected to mission from their foundation. The Dominicans were approved by Honorius III (1216–27) to combat heresy and preach the Gospel; their founder, St Dominic Guzman, was inspired to found the order while taking part in a mission to the heretic Albigensians in the south of France. The Franciscans won the support of Innocent III (1198–1216) in their early years as an order ready to preach orthodoxy and combat heresy. Later the Jesuits – established in the pontificate of Paul III (1534–49) – were also dedicated to education and foreign mission.

Members of these orders carried the Gospel around the world. For example, Nicholas IV (1288–92) sent the Franciscan John of Montecorvino as the first Roman Catholic missionary to China; Dominican monk Jordanus Catalani (flourished 1321–30) was a key missionary to India. In the 16th century Franciscan and Dominican missionaries travelled to the New World with European explorers and adventurers.

In this work they were encouraged by popes such as Alexander VI (1492–1503) and Paul III (1534–49). In 1493 Alexander VI gave orders that Spain should establish missions through the New World; in 1537 Paul III commanded that the native peoples of the New World be converted to Christianity "by the preaching of the divine word".

Jesuits led important missions around the world – in Japan and China, in Brazil and Canada – but were also active throughout Europe as part of the Counter-Reformation, winning back Protestants to Roman Catholicism.

PAPAL MISSIONARY JOURNEYS

In the modern era, while there are specially established Roman Catholic missionary orders – including the Missionaries of the Sacred Heart (founded 1854) and Maryknoll (formerly the Catholic Foreign Missionary Society of America, founded 1911), as well as many members of larger religious orders such as Franciscans and Jesuits working in overseas missions – several popes have personally taken up the missionary mantle, travelling tirelessly to encourage the faithful, strengthen the Church and spread the Gospel.

Paul VI visited India, Colombia, the USA, Portugal, Turkey and the Holy Land and made a pastoral journey to Africa in 1969.

John Paul II visited 129 countries in the course of 104 official journeys. He was the first pope to visit Mexico and Ireland, the first pontiff in the modern era to visit Egypt and the first reigning pope to visit the UK; in the USA he was the first pope to visit the White House in Washington, D.C., where he was greeted by President Jimmy Carter in 1979.

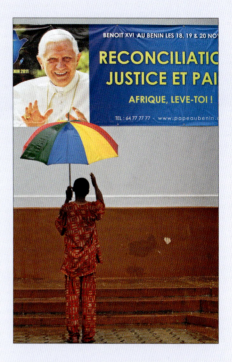

Above: Benedict XVI visited Benin on 18–20 November 2011. It was his second visit to Africa, after an earlier mission to Cameroon and Angola in 2009.

Benedict XVI (2005–13) also travelled widely on apostolic missions. He made visits to Turkey, Austria and the USA; in Brazil in 2007 he canonized an 18th-century Franciscan friar, Antonio Galvao, the first Brazilian-born saint.

As the first South American pope, Benedict's successor Francis visited Brazil on his first overseas trip as pontiff, in July 2013. For Roman Catholic World Youth Day he attracted a crowd of three million – many of whom camped out overnight – to hear him celebrate Mass on Copacabana Beach, Rio de Janeiro. For World Youth Day in 2016, he was in Krakow, Poland, and he later made visits to Colombia in September 2017, Myanmar and Bangladesh in November–December 2017, Ireland in August 2018, the United Arab Emirates in February 2019, Mozambique, Madagascar and Mauritius in September 2019, and Iraq in March 2021. Despite some health issues, he visited the Democratic Republic of the Congo and South Sudan in January 2023 and Hungary in April 2023.

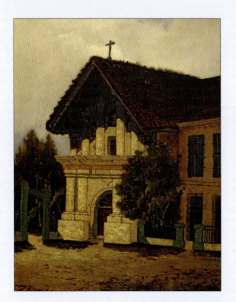

Below: The Mission San Francisco de Asis is the oldest surviving structure in San Francisco. It was established in June 1776 by the Franciscans.

PIUS VIII AND GREGORY XVI, 1829–46
A MODERNIZER FOLLOWED BY AN AUSTERE CONSERVATIVE

Pope Pius VIII (1829–30) and Gregory XVI (1831–46) were starkly contrasting pontiffs. While Pius generally followed in the modernizing footsteps of his mentor Pius VII (1800–23), Gregory reverted to the style of the harsh and authoritarian Leo XII (1823–9). In his 15-year pontificate Gregory fought with little success to turn back the tide of rationalism and the growth of modern developments, even seeking to ban the railroad – which he dubbed *le chemin d'enfer* ("path of hell"), a pun on the French for railroad *le chemin de fer* – from the papal states.

Below: In France Louis Philippe was sworn in as king on 9 August 1830. Pius was quick to back the new regime and grant the title of "Most Christian King".

A MAN OF PRINCIPLE

Born in Cingoli in the papal states in 1761, Pius VIII (original name Francesco Saverio Castiglioni) studied canon law and was appointed Bishop of Montalto by Pius VII in 1800. A man of principle and courage, he endured an eight-year imprisonment during the French rule of Italy after refusing to take the required oath of allegiance to Napoleon. He was made a cardinal in 1816 and appointed grand penitentiary, an important position in the Curia, in 1821.

His pontificate as Pius VIII was notable for the 1829 Catholic Emancipation Act in Britain and the agreement of a concordat with France after the coming to the throne of Louis Philippe, Duc d'Orleans, in the July Revolution of 1830. When events in France forced the

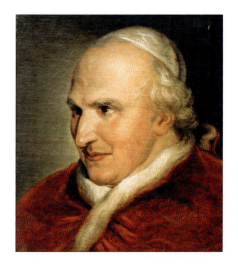

Above: Pius VIII. He backed the first convention of bishops in the United States. His 1829 encyclical Traditi humilitati *condemned efforts to put other branches of the faith on a par with Catholicism.*

PIUS VIII AND GREGORY XVI

abdication of the unpopular Charles X, Pius was quick to support Louis Philippe of Orleans as his successor, granting him the title "Most Christian King" and encouraging French churchmen to back the new regime. Another of Pius's international acts was to issue approval to the statements of the Provincial Council of Baltimore, the first formal convention of bishops in the United States.

Throughout his pontificate he suffered from poor health, in particular from sores on his body and neck. He died on 30 November 1830 in the Quirinal Palace and when an autopsy found no evidence of sickness internally, there were whispers that he had been poisoned. His successor Bartolomeo Alberto Cappellari assumed the papal throne as Gregory XVI, after no fewer than 83 ballots over the course of 64 days, on 2 February 1831.

OPPONENT OF LIBERALISM

Gregory was a Camaldolese monk (an austere version of the Benedictines, who devoted part of their time to living as hermits) from the monastery of San Michele di Murano, on the island of Murano in the lagoon of Venice – the last monk to date to become pope, as well as the last pope to take the name Gregory. Opposed to change, he supported Europe's con-

Below: Gregory XVI's 1839 apostolic letter In supremo apsotolatus *condemned the Atlantic slave trade.*

1829 CATHOLIC EMANCIPATION ACT IN BRITAIN

Under the 1829 Catholic Emancipation Act Roman Catholics were able to sit in the Houses of Parliament at Westminster and hold most public offices. The background to the passing of the act was the winning in 1828 by Irish Catholic lawyer Daniel O'Connell of the seat for Clare, Ireland; under previous law he was forbidden to take his seat, but he waged a lively campaign for change on the issue.

Below: Pius supported British Catholics, who were suffering under discriminatory laws. The Roman Catholic Relief Act of 1829 opened the higher Civil Service and judiciary to middle-class British Catholics.

---

servative monarchies and clamped down very hard on those arguing for democracy, republicanism and liberalism. He condemned the liberal French priest H. F. R. de Lammenais, founder of the newspaper *L'Avenir* ("The Future"), which argued for freedom of conscience and the separation of church and state, and placed his works on the Index of Prohibited Books. In his encyclical *Mirari Vos* ("We think that you wonder…") of August 1832 Gregory denounced the claim of freedom of conscience as an erroneous doctrine, or rather delirium'.

Gregory fiercely put down revolts in the papal states with Austrian help and using execution with sentences of hard labour and exile, and the territory was occupied by foreign troops. When Polish Roman Catholics rose up against the tyrannical rule of Tsar Nicholas I of Russia, to whom they had been subject since the Third Partition of 1795, Gregory did not support them but issued a papal brief in which he condemned them for having used religion as a cover while setting themselves against "the legitimate power of princes". After a brief initial success, the uprising was brutally put down by Nicholas I in 1831.

MISSIONARY ENTHUSIASM

Yet he energetically supported international Roman Catholic missionary work, which he reorganized and placed under papal control, creating near to 200 missionary bishops while establishing 70 new dioceses around the world. In 1839 he condemned slavery in his bull *In Supremo Apostolatus* ("At the summit of Apostolic power"), in which he called the slave trade "a shame" and "absolutely unworthy of the Christian name".

Gregory died on 1 June 1846 in Rome after a very bad attack of erysipelas of the face – the condition, marked by red swellings and lesions accompanied by fever and vomiting, sometimes known as "holy fire" or "St Anthony's fire".

PIUS IX, 1846–78
POPE WHO BEGAN THE FORMATION OF THE MODERN PAPACY

In his 32-year pontificate, the longest papal reign to date, Pius IX oversaw a vast range of changes, including the establishment of the Kingdom of Italy in 1860 and the consequent shrinking of papal territories to what they are today – the Vatican and its immediate surroundings. Pius's period in power also saw the definition of the dogma of the Immaculate Conception and the doctrine of papal infallibility as the papacy attempted to concentrate on matters of faith and spirituality.

Born to a noble family in Senigallia, Giovanni Maria Mastai-Ferretti studied theology in Volterra and Rome. His studies were almost cut short by his epi-lepsy, but with the support and encouragement of Pope Pius VII (1800–23), he continued and in time entered papal service: on behalf of Pius VII he served on a mission to the newly created South American republics – the first pope to visit the Americas.

Under Pope Leo XII he was appointed Archbishop of Spoleto at the age of 35, then in 1839, after being moved to Imola, was made cardinal. At this stage of his life, he was committed to charitable work such as helping street children and visiting prisoners in jail. He gained a reputation as a political liberal that carried over into his first years as pope.

He was elected pope after a conclave of just two days on 16 June 1846. He took the name Pius as a tribute to Pius VII. The election of a liberal pope caused astonishment, for most had expected the triumph of a conservative candidate.

> **FACT BOX**
> **Original name** Giovanni Maria Mastai-Ferretti
> **Born** 13 May 1792
> **Origin** Senigallia, papal states
> **Date elected pope** 16 June 1846
> **Died** 7 February 1878
> **Key fact** Presided over First Vatican Council

Right: Pius IX was the first pope to be photographed. Particularly at the start of his pontificate, he was generally progressive and open to unfamiliar things – such as the new art of photography.

FORWARD-LOOKING
The new pontiff was amicable, warm-hearted, approachable, progressive. While cardinal he had been critical of the rule of Gregory XVI (1831–46), and in the first month of his reign he granted amnesties to more than 1,000 exiles and political prisoners. He embraced the modern conveniences his predecessor had rejected – including gas lighting and the railways. Pius IX took important steps towards creating a free press and also did away with the requirement that Jews must listen to a Christian sermon every week.

Everywhere the new pope went Pius found himself celebrated – the crowds in Rome shouted "A long life

Left: The First Vatican Council was opened on 8 December 1869. The council underlined the pope's authority to rule on dogma and defined papal infallibility.

724

Right: Pius aboard the papal train. He embraced modern inventions Gregory XVI resisted. In a pun on the French for railway ("chemin de fer") Gregory had called it the "chemin d'enfer" ("pathway to hell").

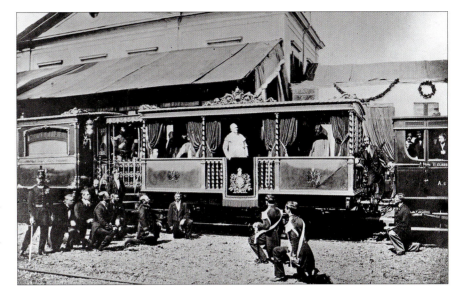

for Pius IX!" Even in Protestant England he was praised for his commitment to freedom.

But his popularity melted away and his reputation as a supporter of freedom was lost amid the revolutions of 1848, as he and the papacy were cast as reactionaries blocking the desires of Italian nationalists for a united country. Amid upheaval in Rome, and after the Swiss Guard was disbanded by local ministers, he fled to Gaeta in the kingdom of Naples. A new assembly in Rome declared the establishment of a democratic republic and the end of the papacy's temporal power. Pius made a formal appeal for international help and with the backing of a French army was reinstalled in Rome on 12 April 1850.

THE CAPITAL OF ITALY

This reprieve was only temporary – even though it lasted 20 years. In 1860 the Kingdom of Italy was created and it annexed the papal states. Then in 1870 the French troops on which Pius relied for security left Rome to fight in the Franco-Prussian War of 1870–1. Italian republicans under the command of Giuseppe Garibaldi forced Pius to agree to a settlement under which the papacy kept the Vatican, which remained independent, but lost Rome.

A plebiscite of 1 October 1870 voted for Rome to become the capital of Italy. Pius was to have full authority within the Vatican and its immediate surroundings and could conduct diplomatic relations with other powers, but elsewhere in Italy, church and state would be separated. Pius did not accept the new situation and regarded himself as a prisoner in the Vatican.

IMMACULATE CONCEPTION

On 8 December 1854 Pius defined the dogma of the Immaculate Conception. According to this, in the moment in which she was conceived by her mother, the Blessed Virgin Mary was made immaculate – was set free from the taint of original sin by which all humankind is touched as descendants of Adam and Eve.

SYLLABUS OF ERRORS

Pius turned away from his early liberalism and became a firm opponent of those pressing for reform in the church. In December 1864 he issued the Syllabus of Errors, which listed 80 of what he identified as the main contemporary errors of thought and notably attacked those who argued that "the Roman pontiff can and should reconcile and harmonize himself with progress, with liberalism and with recent civilization". In 1869 he called the First Vatican Council, which asserted the power of the papacy in its definition of papal infallibility.

Pius died in Rome on 7 February 1878. He was beatified by Pope John Paul II on 3 September 2000.

Left: In this 1860 John Tenniel cartoon from the British magazine Punch, *Garibaldi shows Pius IX the cap of liberty – suggesting that it would be far more comfortable than the heavy papal crown.*

PAPAL INFALLIBILITY

The First Vatican Council of 1869–70 set out the doctrine of papal infallibility: when the pope defines church doctrine concerning faith or morals, speaking ex cathedra and so requiring assent from the whole Church, he cannot be wrong. The pope's authority in this matter derives from the teaching power assigned to the pope as head of the Church by Jesus Christ himself. This was the first formal definition of a position that had been held by many since the medieval period. Papal infallibility lies in the office of pope and is not claimed by the person who happens to be pope.

LEO XIII, 1878–1903
THE "WORKERS' POPE" IN A CHANGING WORLD

Elected pope close to his 68th birthday and in poor health, Leo XIII might have expected a brief pontificate but he remained on the papal throne for more than a quarter of a century until his death in 1903 aged 93. To the end he kept his energy and keen intellect, and in his reign he succeeded in repositioning the Church in its relationship with science and a swiftly changing world, proving the relevance of the papacy to a new century.

JESUIT EDUCATION

Born the sixth of seven sons to a noble family from Carpineto Romano, near Rome, Vincenzo Gioacchino Pecci studied with the Jesuits in Viterbo and Rome, gaining doctorates in theology, civil law and canon law. Full of energy, with a quick intelligence and a gentle manner, he thrived in the papal service and was legate (governor) of first Benevento and then Perugia before being sent as papal nuncio to Belgium. As Archbishop of Perugia in 1846–77, he was known for his charitable work with the homeless and poverty-stricken; he was made a cardinal in 1853.

He was elected pope on 20 February 1878, shortly before his 68th birthday, on only the third ballot. He chose his papal name in honour of Leo XII, whom he had admired for his commitment to education, his non-confrontational

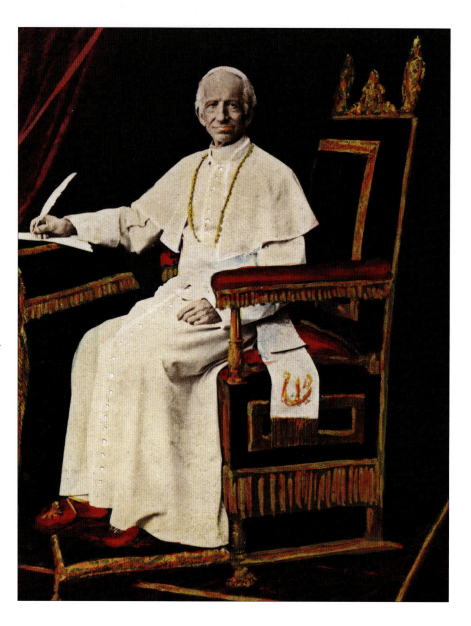

Above: A coloured image of Leo. He was at home in the modern world, the first pope to appear in moving pictures. He was filmed by W. K. Dickson and blessed the movie camera.

dealings with secular governments and his interest in building bridges with non-Catholic Christians.

THE KINGDOM OF ITALY

The new pope inherited a difficult position in the Kingdom of Italy, where the government was hostile to the papacy and the Roman Catholic Church. He was not permitted to bless the faithful from the loggia of St Peter's, as was traditional, and had to hold his coronation in the Sistine Chapel.

His response was measured. His diplomatic experience stood him in good stead and on the international stage he built a good relationship with England, France, Germany, Prussia and Russia, as well as other countries. The expansion of Catholicism begun under his predecessor was continued, with the establishment of dioceses and vicariates around the world.

FACT BOX
Original name Vincenzo Gioacchino Pecci
Born 2 March 1810
Origin Carpineto Romano, papal states
Date elected pope 20 February 1878
Died 20 July 1903
Key fact Wrote 11 encyclicals on using the rosary

He attempted to reposition the Church in a swiftly changing world without compromise on major teaching. He issued condemnations of socialism, communism, secular liberalism and Freemasonry, but offered support to the working classes – many of whom were suffering dire conditions in the wake of industrialization – by backing democracy and the right to form unions (see box).

THE CHURCH AND SCIENCE

Leo was determined the Church should not be seen as an enemy of science. He actively encouraged science and astronomy, re-establishing the Vatican Observatory to make clear to people that the Church was "not opposed to true and solid science", and calling for a return to the study of St Thomas Aquinas's philosophy and theology – both for priests in seminaries and laity in universities. In his encyclical *Aeterni Patris* ("Of the Eternal Father"), he called Aquinas "the special bulwark and glory of the Catholic faith ... a lover of truth for its own sake" and said that "richly endowed with human and divine science, like the sun he heated the world with the warmth of his virtues

Below: Leo dictates a phonograph message to American Catholics – he was the first pope whose voice was recorded.

THE WORKERS' POPE

On account of his 1893 encyclical *Rerum Novarum* ("Of new things"), which accepted the creation of trades unions, Leo gained the nickname of "the workers' pope". The open letter, sent to all bishops, rejected communism and the unrestricted operation of capitalism and defended an individual's right to own private property, but it recognized the right of workers to form unions and expressed the need for improvements in the miserable and wretched conditions that so many members of the working classes were forced to endure.

and filled it with the splendour of his teaching". Leo also backed the study of history and of the Bible, and attempted to reach out to Protestants and Orthodox Christians, calling them "our separated brethren", and inviting them to submit to and unite with Rome.

He did not seem ill at ease in the face of innovation: he was the first pope to make a sound recording and the first to be filmed on a movie camera – film camera pioneer William Kennedy Dickson filmed the pope in the Vatican Gardens in 1898.

Above: Leo XIII. In 1887 the future St Therese of Lisieux met Leo, begging him to authorize her entering the Carmelites aged 15. He said, "You will enter if God wills it."

ROSARY POPE

Leo exhibited a particular devotion to the Sacred Heart of Jesus and to the Blessed Virgin Mary. In 1899 he consecrated the whole world to the Sacred Heart of Jesus. He also promoted Marian devotion, issuing eleven encyclicals on the rosary – and became known, as an alternative byname, as the "Rosary Pope". He began the custom among Roman Catholics of daily rosary prayer during October and established in 1883 the Feast of the Queen of the Holy Rosary.

In these encyclicals Pius was the first pope fully to engage with and promote the concept of the Virgin Mary as *mediatrix* or mediator, the person through whom the prayers of the faithful are channelled to Christ and God the Father and through whom the grace of God is passed to the world.

He also taught that from the moment of the Annunciation (when she was told by the Angel Gabriel that she would conceive and bear Jesus), Mary was co-redemptrix with Christ: she played a role in the mystery of redemption as the mother of Christ and of all people.

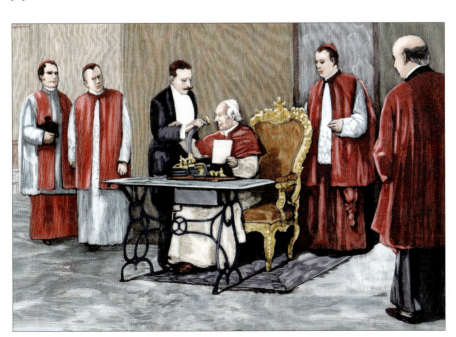

PEACE FOR A TROUBLED WORLD

PIUS X TO FRANCIS, 1903–TODAY

In the first Easter homily of his pontificate, on 31 March 2013, Pope Francis called for peace throughout the world, saying, "We ask the risen Jesus, who turns death into life, to change hatred into love, vengeance into forgiveness, war into peace." Through the 20th century his predecessors dedicated themselves to working and praying for peace. On 1 August 1917 Pope Benedict XV circulated, sadly without success, a peace plan to end the First World War; in 1942, at the height of the Second World War, Pius XII dedicated the entire human race to the Blessed Virgin Mary. In the aftermath of the war John XXIII and Paul VI pressed for peace at the height of the Cold War and John Paul II was on the papal throne when the countries of the communist Eastern bloc saw their hold on power dissolve, and the spectre of Islamic terrorism arose in the 1990s.

In difficult times a succession of popes attempted to return to the original values of the papacy. John XXIII laid far less emphasis on his role as ruler and more on his position as "servant of the servants of God". Pope John Paul I passed up the grandeur of a papal coronation for a simple investiture and chose *Humilitas* ("Humility") as the motto of his papacy. The Lateran Treaty of 1929 saw the papacy renounce its claim to expansive papal territories, and the establishment of the pope as ruler of the small independent state of Vatican City.

In years of increasing materialism after the Second World War and in the early 21st century at a time of financial crisis, popes condemned modern consumerism. Throughout his reign, Pope Francis has opposed irresponsible development, and embraced simplicity, action on climate change and concern for the poor.

Left: A pope for the modern age? Armed with smartphones on "selfie sticks", United Nations peacekeeping troops press around Francis during the Wednesday general audience at Paul VI Audience Hall on 28 January 2015.

PIUS X, 1903–14
TRADITIONALIST POPE WHO LOOKED FOR RENEWAL

Pius X was strongly opposed to liberal and modernist revisions of doctrine, but was not resistant to change in itself and carried through many reforms – recodifying canon law, remodelling the Curia and restructuring seminaries.

Pius performed the duties of a parish priest in his young adulthood and many of his revisions of practice were focused on the daily life of Roman Catholics at the parish level; throughout his pontificate he preached a sermon every Sunday – the only pope of the 20th century to do so. He was canonized by Pius XII on 29 May 1954, the first since his namesake St Pius V (1566–72), to be named a saint.

Above: Pius relaxes in the gardens of the Vatican in 1913. He established the Biblical Institute in Rome to be directed by the Jesuits.

Below: Pius blesses pilgrims at the Vatican in 1903. His family were far from well off, but he sought no favours for them: his brother carried on working as a postal clerk.

Born the son of a postman and a seamstress in Treviso, Venice, Giuseppe Melchiorre Sarto was ordained a priest at the age of 23 and served for eight years as chaplain at Tombolo, performing many of the duties of a parish priest, then was arch-priest of Salzano in the Diocese of Treviso. He filled various other positions before being named Bishop of Mantua in 1884, then cardinal and Patriarch of Venice in 1893.

A decade later he was elected pope with 55 out of a possible 60 votes on 4 August 1903 and was crowned Pius X on 9 August. He was friendly, warm-hearted and practical – as well as being pious and, in the words of his tomb inscription, "meek and humble of heart".

FACT BOX
Original name Giuseppe Melchiorre Sarto
Born 2 June 1835
Origin Treviso
Date elected pope 4 August 1903
Died 20 August 1914
Key fact First pope to be canonized since his namesake Pius V in 1712

"RENEW ALL THINGS IN CHRIST"

His commitment to change was shown when he identified in his first encyclical that the motto of his papacy would be from *Ephesians* 1:10 – "renew all things in Christ". He produced the first code of canon law, which was promulgated by his successor Benedict XV on 27 May 1917. He revised the operation of the Curia, cutting the number of its departments from 37 to 19.

He rewrote the catechism and urged that it should be used with adults as well as children, and that a class should be held in every parish around the world. He himself held catechism classes every week in the courtyard of San Damaso in the Vatican.

Pius reformed the breviary. He placed a new emphasis on the ritual of Holy Communion, which he described as "the shortest and safest way to Heaven", and encouraged the faithful to take communion more frequently – every day or once weekly at the least. He reduced the age of discretion, at which children should take their first communion, from 12 years to 7 years. He decreed that Church music would turn back from the recently popular Baroque and classical styles to plainsong and Gregorian chant.

STERN TRADITIONALIST

Yet Pius was no intellectual and certainly no supporter of "modernists" who wanted to adapt the Church to the new philosophical and psychological ideas of the 19th century.

In 1907 he issued a decree *Lamentabile Sane Exitu* ("On a Deplorable Result") and an encyclical *Pascendi Dominici Gregis* ("'On Feeding the Flocks of the Lord") that condemned this modernism in the Church as a "compendium of all the heresies". In 1910 he issued a decree ordering all seminary teachers and all clerics on ordination to take an oath supporting these two papal documents and denouncing modernism.

As part of a programme to enforce discipline on these matters he endorsed the creation of the "Society of Pius V", which functioned almost like a secret police force using underhand methods – including agents who attempted to trap liberal Catholics into incriminating themselves. His use of this body was brought up as a reason against his canonization in the 1950s and was the cause of some controversy.

RELATIONS WITH ITALY AND FRANCE

Pius X maintained papal opposition to the annexation of the papal states by Italy and criticized French president Emile Loubet for making a visit to the Italian King Victor Emmanuel III. When the French issued in 1905 the Law of Separation under which church and state were separated in France, Pius denounced this development and in the end diplomatic relations with France were broken off. In 1907 the French government confiscated all church property in France. Throughout his pontificate Pius refused to recognize the government of Italy, but he did give Roman Catholics permission to vote in general elections.

Above: This initial "A" in a 13th-century antiphonal depicts St Gregory. Pius brought about a return to plainsong and Gregorian chant in church music.

FIRST WORLD WAR

The outbreak of the First World War crushed Pius. He called on Catholics to turn "to Him from whom alone help can come, to Christ, the prince of peace" and to pray for peace. He was 79 years old, suffered from gout and had had a heart attack in 1913; the news of the war further set him back and he died in the early hours of 20 August 1914. In his will this saintly pope wrote, "I was born poor; I have lived poor; and I wish to die poor."

REFUGEES IN THE APOSTOLIC PALACE

Pius was known for his charity and Christian concern. After a terrible earthquake struck Messina and Reggio Calabria in south Italy on 28 December 1908 he did not wait for the Italian government to act but opened the Vatican to refugees. In his will he left a legacy for 400 children who were made orphans of the earthquake.

Below: Pius watches Andre Beaumont, winner of the Paris-Rome section, fly over the Vatican during the Paris-Rome-Turin air race, in an illustration for Le Petit Journal, *18 June 1911.*

BENEDICT XV, 1914–22
PEACEMAKER IN THE TIME OF WORLD WAR

Benedict XV remained impartial during the First World War and attempted with all his might to bring about an end to hostilities. Afterwards he was very disappointed to be excluded from the peace negotiations in 1919 and in 1920 dedicated the papacy to efforts for reconciliation between nations whilst consolidating the position of the Church in Europe.

Born in Pegli, Genoa, to an aristocratic family, Giacomo della Chiesa was initially refused permission to train for the priesthood by his father, who wanted his son to become a lawyer. However, in 1875 – after acquiring a doctorate in law and at the age of 21 – he did gain his father's permission to enter the Church and began training in Rome, where he was ordained on 21 December 1878.

Below: Il piccoletto *("the little fellow": after being born prematurely, Benedict XV was very short throughout his life. When he became pope there were no robes small enough for him. He had poor eyesight.*

> **FACT BOX**
> **Original name** Giacomo della Chiesa
> **Born** 21 November 1854
> **Origin** Pegli, Genoa
> **Date elected pope** 3 September 1914
> **Died** 22 January 1922
> **Key fact** Spent 82 million lira on war relief

After working in the papal diplomatic service he became Archbishop of Bologna in 1908 and in 1914 was made cardinal, just three months before his election as pope. Benedict had been born extremely prematurely and was very small in stature – in Bologna he had been nicknamed *il piccoletto* ("the little fellow"), and on his election as pope there were no robes small enough for him to wear. He had poor eyesight, one shoulder raised above the other and was not personable or charismatic, but was kind-hearted and very generous – and well loved by those who knew him well.

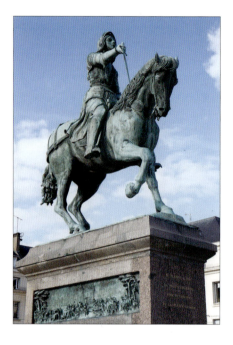

Above: This statue in Orleans honours St Joan of Arc. After Pius X had beatified her in 1909, Benedict canonized her in 1920. Her feast day is 30 May.

Below: Pope Benedict XV in the garden of the Vatican during the Catholic Congress in Rome, 1921.

732

Above: A satirical view: Jesus reads the peace plan issued by Benedict, and says (with a nod to Luke 23:34) "Father, forgive him, for he knows not what he does."

"PROPHET OF PEACE"

In the war, with Catholics fighting on both sides, he had no choice but to maintain impartiality. He did what he could to bring about an end to the fighting. His first encyclical, on 1 November 1914, was a call for peace and he tried to persuade the combatants to revive the medieval tradition of the "Truce of God" on Christmas Day, 1914. In August 1917 he circulated a detailed seven-point plan for peace but his proposals were rejected by the warring countries. When in 2005 Benedict XVI chose his papal name it was to honour this pontiff, whom he called "that courageous prophet of peace".

RELIEF EFFORTS

In 1914 he established an agency for the repatriation of prisoners of war and wounded that brought about the homecoming of 65,000 people. In 1915 he negotiated the exchange of civilians from occupied areas – this led to 20,000 people being sent to unoccupied southern France. In 1916 he achieved an agreement under which 29,000 prisoners with tuberculosis were sent to neutral Switzerland. Through his intervention many prisoners were spared execution. He organized several humanitarian missions, particularly to aid children – in Belgium, Lithuania, Russia and elsewhere. He reputedly spent 82 million lira on humanitarian and relief programmes and left the Vatican reserves empty – it is said that after his death Cardinal Gasparri was forced to raise a bank loan in order to pay for the conclave that selected Pope Pius XI.

The success of these initiatives won the respect and admiration of many countries. When the Turks raised a statue in Benedict's honour in Istanbul they described him as "the benefactor of all peoples, irrespective of nationality or religion". His humanitarian outlook in the war was one reason why an increasing number of states sent diplomatic representative to the Vatican: these included Britain, who sent a chargé d'affaires in 1915 (the first British diplomat at the Vatican since the 1600s), and France. Relations with France improved after Benedict canonized Joan of Arc in 1920.

ITALY AND RUSSIA

Relations with the Italian government, however, remained very tricky. But Benedict made progress towards a solution by giving official backing to

> ### MARIOLOGY
> Benedict – like "the Rosary Pope", Leo XIII before him – enthusiastically promoted devotion to the Blessed Virgin Mary, particularly emphasizing her role as Co-Redemptrix with Christ. Benedict raised 20 Marian shrines to the status of minor basilicas. In May 1917 he placed the whole world under Mary's protection, a few days before the first of the Virgin's reputed appearances at Fatima, Portugal. To the well-known Litany of the Blessed Virgin Mary (often called "the Litany of Loreto" because of its early usage at the Shrine to the Virgin at Loreto in Italy) he added the invocation "Queen of Peace, pray for us".

Above: Benedict was a devoted Marian. He placed the world under the protection of the Blessed Virgin in the First World War. He authorized the Feast of Mary, Mediator of All Graces.

the establishment of the *Partito Populaire* (Italian People's Party) by Sicilian priest Don Luigi Sturzo in 1919. The war raised the prospect of the expansion of Russia and the Orthodox Church but the Russian Revolution of 1917 and the virulently anti-religious policies of the new regime spelled profound trouble for Christianity there. In Rome, Benedict established the Congregation for the Eastern Church and the Pontifical Eastern Institute.

AN EYE FOR TALENT

Benedict promoted two future popes to important positions. He appointed Eugenio Pacelli (the future Pius XII) to lead the work on prisoners of war at the Vatican and afterwards sent him as papal nuncio to Munich. He took the distinguished paleographer Achilles Ratti (the future Pius XI) from his position working as prefect at the Vatican Library and sent him in 1918 as papal representative to Poland; afterwards he was made Archbishop of Milan.

Pope Benedict died unexpectedly young, at the age of just 67 and following an attack of pneumonia, on 22 January 1922.

PEACE FOR A TROUBLED WORLD

PIUS XI, 1922–39
FIRST SOVEREIGN OF THE INDEPENDENT VATICAN CITY

The pontificate of Pius XI saw the establishment of the pope as sovereign ruler of the independent state of Vatican City. The Lateran Treaty that delivered this outcome stated that the papacy would be permanently neutral in diplomatic and military conflicts and recognized the creation of the Kingdom of Italy.

LASTING HATRED OF COMMUNISM

Achille Ratti came to the papacy at the age of 65 after a distinguished career as a palaeographer and a librarian. He was plucked from his position as prefect of the Vatican Library by Benedict XV (1914–22), who in 1919 sent him as papal nuncio to newly independent Poland. There he showed great bravery and won respect by refusing to flee to Rome when the invading Bolsheviks marched on Warsaw in 1920; he remained in place in the Polish capital while Marshal Jozef Pilsudski, Chief of

Below: Pius XI was a distinguished palaeographer and librarian who became the first sovereign ruler of the independent state of Vatican City.

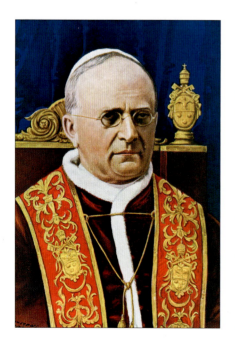

> **FACT BOX**
> **Original name** Ambrogio Damiano Achille Ratti
> **Born** 31 May 1857
> **Origin** Desio, Lombardy
> **Date elected pope** 6 February 1922
> **Died** 10 February 1939
> **Key fact** Initially tolerant of fascist regimes, he later attacked them

State, masterminded "the miracle on the Vistula" and drove the Russians back. These events convinced Ratti that communism was the greatest threat of all those faced by the countries of Christian Europe in these highly troubled times.

Back in Italy in 1921, he was made cardinal and then Archbishop of Milan, and in February 1922 – after what must have seemed a whirlwind three years since he left the Vatican Library – he was pope. Ruling in the era of the Spanish Civil War and the build-up to the Second World War, Pius used as his papal motto the phrase *Pax Christi in Regno Christi* ("The Peace of Christ in the Kingdom of Christ") and attempted to work for international cooperation.

RELATIONS WITH FASCISM

Pius's administration made pacts with the fascists both in Italy and in Germany, but the pope also issued attacks on both in encyclicals of the 1930s. By the Lateran Treaty that established the Holy See as an independent neutral state – signed on 11 February 1929 by Prime Minister Benito Mussolini and Pius's Secretary of State, Cardinal Pietro Gaspari – the pope received financial compensation equivalent to around £21 million for renouncing his claim to papal territories, Roman Catholicism was recognized as the only state religion in Italy, all anticlerical laws were scrapped and canon law was recognized in addition to

Above: Pius offers a blessing. He was an admirer of Thérèse of Lisieux and fast-tracked her path to sainthood. She was beatified in 1923 and canonized in 1925.

state law. The terms were by no means bad, but there was no getting away from the fact that the papacy had implicitly backed fascism.

Then on 20 July 1933 Pius's new secretary of state, Cardinal Eugenio Pacelli (the future Pope Pius XII), signed a concordat with Franz von Papen, Hitler's

> ### CHRIST THE KING
> In 1925 Pius initiated the Feast of Christ the King in his encyclical *Quas Primas* ('In the first'). At first celebrated on the last Sunday in October, in 1969 Paul VI moved it to the last Sunday of the liturgical year. Pius described the Church as "the kingdom of Christ on earth" and said she should "with every token of veneration salute her Author and Founder in her annual liturgy as King and Lord, and as King of Kings". He added that when people recognize that Christ is King they will receive the "great blessings of real liberty, well-ordered discipline, peace and harmony".

PIUS XI

Above: Pius was the first pope to make a radio broadcast. Here he is with radio pioneer Guglielmo Marconi in the Vatican in January 1933.

Vice-Chancellor, in Rome. Under this treaty the Church and its schools gained privileges in Germany but agreed to give up social and political activity in the country, and as a result the Centre Party, the second most powerful in the German Reichstag under the leadership of Monsignor Ludwig Kaas, was terminated – opening the way for the progression of the Nazis.

FORTHRIGHT ENCYCLICALS

Pius issued encyclicals attacking Italian fascism in *Non abbiamo bisogno* ("We need not acquaint you", June 1931) and the rule of the Nazis in *Mit brennender Sorge* ("With Profound Anxiety", 1937). But it is undeniable that the pope issued no condemnation of the Nazis' anti-Semitic Nuremberg race laws of 1935 nor of the terrible events of the *Kristallnacht* pogrom against the Jews of 9–10 November 1938 in which 91 Jews were slain and 30,000 arrested and taken to concentration camps.

A third encyclical, *Divini redemptoris* ("Our Divine Redeemer", 1937), issued a forthright condemnation of communism. Pius prepared a fourth that was to explicitly condemn anti-Semitism and persecution of the Jews but died before he could deliver it in 1939.

MISSION AND LEARNING

Pius was also active in other areas. He oversaw a great expansion in the number of native priests and bishops overseas, notably in China and India. He attempted, with little success, to bring about reconciliation with the Eastern Orthodox Churches. Devoted as he was to learning, he founded several higher education bodies, including the Pontifical Institute of Christian Archaeology in 1925 and the Pontifical Academy of Science in 1936.

He built the Pinacoteca as a home for the Vatican's ever-expanding picture collection and moved the Vatican Observatory to Castel Gandolfo. In 1931 he installed a radio in the Vatican. He became the first pope to make a radio broadcast.

By 1938 Pius's health was very poor. Already suffering badly from diabetes, he had two heart attacks in a single day on 25 November. He struggled on, desperately trying to stay alive to deliver his final encyclical, intended as a denunciation of fascist dictators, but died on 10 February 1939.

Below: Pope Pius XI instituting celebration of the social reign of Jesus Christ, in a drawing by Damblans from the French paper Le Pelerin, *3 January 1926.*

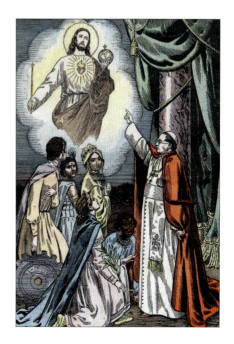

735

PIUS XII, 1939–58
CONTROVERSIAL SILENCE OVER WORLD WAR II ATROCITIES

Pius XII maintained a position of impartiality through the Second World War. For some, the fact that he did not issue a forthright condemnation of the outrages perpetuated by the Nazis against the Jews was a terrible failure. Others emphasize the work he did to help the victims of war and point out that he was celebrated after the war by leading Jewish figures.

DESTINED FOR THE CHURCH

Eugenio Pacelli was born in 1876 to a family with a long and distinguished history of papal service. His great-grandfather was Pope Gregory XVI's minister of finance, his grandfather Pius IX's undersecretary of the interior, his father dean to the lawyers at the Vatican. According to his sister, as a boy he used to dress as a priest and enact his own cele-bration of the Mass in his bedroom.

Below: Pius soon after his coronation in 1939. Only one day long, the conclave that elected him was the shortest for 300 years.

He took degrees in law and theology, was ordained in 1899 at the age of 23 and under Pius X worked on the recodification of canon law. He served as papal nuncio to Germany, and became a lover of that country, before returning to Rome and becoming secretary of state in 1930. He negotiated concordats with Austria and Nazi Germany.

He was elected pope on his 63rd birthday, 2 March 1939, on the very first day of the conclave – the shortest for three centuries.

Pacelli was a cautious figure, highly intelligent and a fine diplomat. He did not issue the encyclical condemning anti-Semitism on which his predecessor had been working, but he set about trying to dissuade the governments of Europe from entering the looming war. He did not condemn the German invasion of Poland on 1 September 1939. He sought to maintain a position not of neutrality (since this might imply indifference to suffering) but of impartiality.

THE SILENCE OF PIUS XII?

Many historians criticize Pius for not denouncing the atrocities committed by the Nazis during the war. When he did make public references to the suffering

Above: As a cardinal, the future Pius XII (at head of table) signs a concordat with Franz von Papen (second from left), Hitler's vice-chancellor, in Rome on 20 July 1933.

he spoke in curiously veiled terms. For example, in his Christmas broadcast in 1942 – at the end of a year in which he had repeatedly rebuffed requests to condemn German massacres of Jews (including one from US President Roosevelt) – he spoke of "persons who, without any fault on their part, sometimes only because of their nationality or race, have been consigned to death or to a slow decline" – not mentioning the Jews or Nazis by name.

FACT BOX

Original name Eugenio Mafria Giuseppi Giovanni Pacelli
Born 2 March 1876
Origin Rome
Date elected pope 2 March 1939
Died 9 October 1958
Key fact Invoked papal infallibility in defining dogma of the Assumption of Blessed Virgin Mary

> **BOTCHED EMBALMING**
>
> Pius died of heart failure on 9 October 1958 at Castel Gandolfo. In his last years his medical treatment had been almost exclusively in the hands of his personal physician Riccardo Galeazzi-Lisi, who now took responsibility for the embalming of the pope's body – claiming that he would rely on the same method used for Jesus Christ himself. Unfortunately this did not work as predicted and the pope's body suffered many indignities, including the loss of fingers and his nose, while his skin turned black.

When the Nazis occupied Rome and began to take away 1,259 of the Jews of Rome to a terrible end in the Auschwitz death camp, still Pius did not issue an open condemnation of their actions, although according to some accounts the Vatican managed to rescue and give refuge to 252 Jews at this time.

Below: The first pope to become familiar to the world through TV and radio, Pius gives a radio broadcast in 1941. His failure to issue outright condemnations of the Nazis in these broadcasts remains controversial.

Those who defend Pius's action argue that he not only wanted to maintain an impartial position, but had a responsibility to avert reprisals against the Church and perhaps feared that denunciation would provoke further and even more savage atrocities against the powerless. They point out, moreover, that he established the Vatican Information Service that discreetly saved the lives of many hundreds of thousands of Jews in the course of the war and he was praised for his actions by prominent Jews after the war – for example, on Pius's death in 1958 Israeli Prime Minister Golda Meir declared, "When fearful martyrdom came to our people in the decade of Nazi terror, the voice of the pope was raised for the victims. The life of our times was enriched by a voice speaking out on the great moral truths, above the tumult of daily conflict. We mourn a great servant of peace."

AFTER THE WAR

A lifelong opponent of communism, Pius issued condemnations of communist expansion in Eastern Europe. In a decree of 1949 he attacked the Soviet Union and threatened excommunication for any Catholics joining the Communist Party or collaborating with communists.

Above: Czeslawa Kwoka, a Polish Catholic girl, was sent to the Nazi-run death camp at Auschwitz in December 1942 and photographed there, aged 14. She and her mother were dead within three months.

Now in his 70s, the pope became increasingly entrenched in traditional doctrinal positions, for example on birth control and marriage relations. He issued a condemnation of the questioning attitudes of a new wave of theology in France in his 1950 encyclical *Humani generis* ("Concerning the Human Race") and in 1953 terminated what had been proving a successful pastoral experiment in which worker priests laboured alongside workers in factories.

ASSUMPTION OF THE VIRGIN MARY

In 1950 he invoked papal infallibility in defining the dogma of the Assumption of the Virgin Mary – the teaching that Mary was taken body and soul into heaven on her death. This was the first use of papal infallibility since the doctrine of infallibility had been proclaimed at the First Vatican Council in 1869–70. One of his final appointments, on 4 July 1958, was of Karol Wojtyla (the future Pope John Paul II) as Auxiliary Bishop of Krakow.

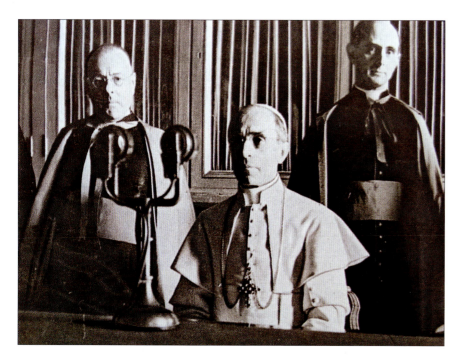

JOHN XXIII AND PAUL VI, 1958–78
TWO POPES WHO CARRIED THROUGH CHANGE

Remembered with affection as "The Good Pope", John XXIII (1958–63) believed strongly in equality and was committed to change. He called the Second Vatican Council (1962–5). Paul VI (1963–78) carried on the work his predecessor called *aggiornamento* ("bringing up to date"), seeing the Council through its latter stages and travelling widely – he was the first pope to travel by aeroplane and helicopter and the first to visit the Holy Land.

John XXIII was born Angelo Giuseppe Roncalli, one of 13 children of a modest tenant farmer in Sotto il Monte, a tiny Lombardy village. He studied in nearby Bergamo and in Rome, eventually taking a doctorate in canon law and becoming secretary to the Bishop of Bergamo. He served as papal diplomat in Bulgaria, Greece and Turkey and then from 1944 in France; he was made a cardinal and Patriarch of Venice by Pius XII in 1953. He was a compromise candidate when he was elected pope on the twelfth ballot on 28 October 1958.

"JOHNNY WALKER"

John reigned at a time of high political tension in the Cold War between West and East and urged nations to live together in peace – in particular, winning the respect of US President Kennedy and Soviet Premier Khrush-chev for his input during the Cuban Missile Crisis of 1962.

Above: Front page news. The front cover of Paris Match, *a weekly news magazine, reported the election of Cardinal Roncalli as Pope John XXIII. He was elected on 28 October 1958.*

He followed Leo XII in stressing the need for the rich to help the poor. He was unaffected, humble and approachable – once he stopped to hold the hand of a peasant woman who had reached up to him as he was being carried through St Peter's, saying to her there was no reason why she should not be allowed as close to him as the King of Jordan had been on a recent encounter. John

Left: Paul VI's meeting with United States President John F. Kennedy at the Vatican on 3 July 1963, was deliberately low key. Paul had good English and the meeting was conducted in that language.

JOHN XXIII AND PAUL VI

liked to go out incognito at night and walk the streets of Rome – and was reputedly nicknamed "Johnny Walker" after the celebrated brand of whisky. He published a diary of spiritual reflections in book form under the title *Journal of a Soul*.

He was also committed to furthering reconciliation among Christians and between faiths. In 1960 he set up a Secretariat for Christian Unity and received a visit in Rome from the Archbishop of Canterbury, the first since the 1300s, and in 1961 he sent brotherly greetings to the Patriarch of Constantinople.

RELATIONS WITH THE JEWS

As papal nuncio in the war years, he saved the lives of thousands of Jews during the Holocaust, for example by facilitating the passage of refugee Jews who had reached Istanbul to Palestine. As pope he removed the word "perfidious" as relating to Jews from the Good Friday liturgy and made a confession for

Below: John XXIII was approachable, humble and committed to equality. He famously said, "We were all made in God's image and thus we are all Godly alike."

the church of the sin of anti-Semitism over the centuries. He prayed in 1965: "We are conscious today that many, many centuries of blindness have cloaked our eyes so that we can no longer see the beauty of Thy chosen people… Forgive us for the curse we falsely attached to their name as Jews. Forgive us for crucifying Thee a second time in their flesh."

SECOND VATICAN COUNCIL

John announced that he would be calling an ecumenical council soon after his election as pope. He was 77 and seen by some as a caretaker pope, and conservative elements in the Curia did what they could to delay the calling of the council in the hope that the pope might pass on and the project be dropped. However, John survived long enough to see the opening session of the Second Vatican Council.

Paul VI (1963–78), original name Giovanni Battista Montini, carried through the reforms of the Second Vatican Council. He introduced changes that provoked fierce opposition among traditionalists – such as the use of vernacular languages rather than universal Latin for most of the liturgy. But he also upset modernizers when he took a firm stand on some issues – for example he insisted that priests must be celibate and in his 1968 encyclical *Humanae vitae* condemned artificial birth control.

Above: President Lyndon Johnson visited the Vatican on 23 December 1967. Paul had previously met him in the US in 1965.

"PILGRIM POPE"

Paul VI, who visited six continents on his travels, was nicknamed the "pilgrim Pope". He travelled to the USA in October 1965, where he met President Johnson, visited the United Nations and celebrated Mass in the Yankee Stadium. He was the first modern pope to visit the Holy Land and to travel to India. He even reached out to the Moon: he sent one of the 73 Goodwill messages carried to the Moon by *Apollo 11* in 1969. After a quote from Psalm 8, it stated, "To the glory of the name of God who gives such power to men, we ardently pray for this wonderful beginning."

> ### IN THE HOLY LAND
> Paul VI was the first modern pope to visit the Holy Land. On his two-day trip in January 1964 he met Ecumenical Patriarch Athenagoras I on the Mount of Olives in Jerusalem. He also met President Shazar of Israel in Megiddo and King Hussein of Jordan, celebrated Mass at the Church of the Holy Sepulchre in Jerusalem and in Bethlehem, and toured the shores of the Sea of Galilee.

THE SECOND VATICAN COUNCIL TO REVITALIZE THE CHURCH

The Second Vatican Council of 1962–5 was a major landmark in the history of the modern Roman Catholic Church, bringing about changes in tone and attitude, in liturgy and the life of the Church. Pope John XXIII (1958–63) called the Council. He was concerned above all to promote Christian unity, and saw the need for a spiritual renewal in the Church, a reform of institutions and structures – a process he characterized in the Italian word *aggiornamento* ("updating" or "revitalization").

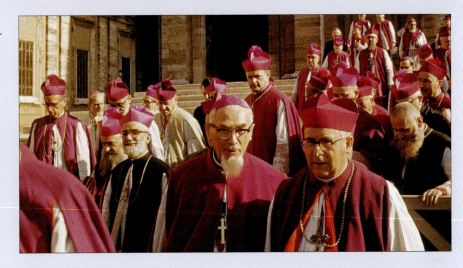

"A NEW ENTHUSIASM"

The pope opened the first session on 11 October 1962. He said, "What is needed … is a new enthusiasm, a new joy and serenity of mind in the unreserved acceptance by all of the entire Christian faith, without forfeiting that accuracy and precision in its presentation which characterized the proceedings of the Council of Trent and the First Vatican Council." He said doctrine was "certain and immutable" and the faithful owed it obedience, but it should be "studied afresh and reformulated in contemporary terms".

The first session ended on 8 December 1962. Pope John XXIII died on 3 June 1963 and the council might have ended with him, for an ecumenical council is

Above: Bishops exit St Peter's during the Second Council session, November 1963.

automatically suspended on the death of the pope who called it; but John's successor Paul VI, elected on 21 June 1963, announced that the council would continue. There were three more sessions: 29 September–4 December 1963; 14 September–21 November 1964; and 14 September–8 December 1965.

The Second Vatican Council was the 21st ecumenical council of the Church. The First Vatican Council was held in 1869–70, under Pius IX (1846–78), and is remembered above all for its definition of papal infallibility. Before that the previous ecumenical council of the Church was the Council of Trent (1545–63).

EFFECTIVE COMMUNICATION

The overall impetus of the Second Vatican Council's work was to try to make the Church more effective at delivering the Gospel in the 20th century. The Church would be more open, there would be a greater role for lay Catholics in the Mass, as well as more use of English and other vernacular languages rather than traditional Latin.

The Council approved 16 documents (see panel). The Constitution on

Below: The council in session. Its Decree on Ecumenism called for the reuniting of Christendom and declared ecumenism should be a matter of concern for all the faithful.

Below: John XXIII is carried through St Peter's. He called the council having discerned the need for spiritual renewal – "a new enthusiasm, a new joy" – in the Church.

the Sacred Liturgy ordered a revision of the liturgy to increase the involvement of lay people in the Mass and other rites, while the Decree on the Ministry and Life of Priests reaffirmed the requirement of celibacy for priests. It presented committing to a life of celibacy as an act of charity on behalf of a priest – which provided "in a special way a source of spiritual fruitfulness in the world".

The Declaration on the Relationship of the Church to Non-Christian Religions spoke out against denunciations of the Jews. It declared: "True, the Jewish authorities and those who followed their lead pressed for the death of Christ; still, what happened in His passion cannot be charged against all the Jews, without distinction, then alive, nor against the Jews of today … the Jews should not be presented as rejected or accursed by God, as if this followed from the Holy Scriptures."

COLLEGE OF BISHOPS

The Decree on the Bishops' Pastoral Office in the Church identified the bishops as a college that succeeded the Apostles in governing and teaching the Church. A note clarified the college did not challenge the authority of the pope.

The Dogmatic Constitution on the Church was a statement on the character and identity of the Roman Catholic Church. It talked of the "common priesthood of the faithful" as interrelated with the ministerial priesthood; the faithful exercise their priesthood by "joining in the offering of the Eucharist"

Above: Chinese cardinal Thomas Tien Ken-sin takes a meal in the Vatican during the first session of the council in October 1952. This photograph appeared in Life *magazine.*

and "in receiving the sacraments, in prayer and thanksgiving, in the witness of a holy life, and by self-denial and active charity".

PAUL VI MASS

In the wake of the Council, Paul VI (1963–78) introduced a revised form of the Mass in 1969. The Mass would be in the vernacular rather than the traditional Latin and the priest would face the congregation while saying it rather than facing the altar as was usual practice. A number of Roman Catholics rebelled against this reform. In particular French Archbishop Marcel Lefebvre led a movement to use the Tridentine Mass, the Latin liturgy approved by the Council of Trent in the 16th century, as contained in the 1962 Missal. Pope John Paul II excommunicated Lefebvre in 1988.

In 2007 Benedict XVI (2005–13) declared celebrating Mass according to the 1962 Missal would be made easier. Previously groups wishing to use the Tridentine Mass had had to ask the permission of their bishop but they could now ask their local priests to allow it. He issued a letter to allay concerns that this move might be seen as undermining the decrees of the Second Vatican Council: he stated that the Mass of Paul VI would remain the norm and that no priest could refuse to use the Paul VI Mass.

FOUR POPES

Four churchmen present at the opening session of the Second Vatican Council went on to become pope: Cardinal Giovanni Battista Montini, later Pope Paul VI; Bishop Albino Luciani, later Pope John Paul I; Bishop Karol Wojtyla, later Pope John Paul II; and Father Joseph Ratzinger, later Pope Benedict XVI. Father Ratzinger was theological consultant to the Archbishop of Cologne at the Council.

Panel Documents approved by the Second Vatican Council
Promulgated 4 December 1963
• Constitution on the Sacred Liturgy (*Sacrosanctum Concilium*).
• Decree on the Instruments of Social Communication (*Inter Mirifica*).

Promulgated 21 November 1964
• Dogmatic Constitution on the Church (*Lumen Gentium*).
• Decree on Ecumenism (*Unitatis Redintegratio*).
• Decree on Eastern Catholic Churches (*Orientalium Ecclesiarum*).
Promulgated 28 October 1965

• Decree on the Bishops' Pastoral Office in the Church (*Christus Dominus*).
• Decree on Priestly Formation (*Optatam Totius*).
• Decree on the Appropriate Renewal of the Religious Life (*Perfectae Caritatis*).
• Declaration on the Relationship of the Church to Non-Christian Religions (*Nostra Aetate*).
• Declaration on Christian Education (*Gravissimum Educationis*).

Promulgated 18 November 1965
• Dogmatic Constitution on Divine Revelation (*Dei Verbum*).
• Decree on the Apostolate of the Laity (*Apostolicam Actuositatem*).

Promulgated 7 December 1965
• Declaration on Religious Freedom (*Dignitatis Humanae*).
• Decree on the Ministry and Life of Priests (*Presbyterorum Ordinis*).
• Decree on the Church's Missionary Activity (*Ad Gentes*).
• Pastoral Constitution on the Church in the Modern World (*Gaudium et Spes*).

JOHN PAUL I, 1978
"SMILING POPE" WHOSE REIGN WAS CUT SHORT

Remembered as *il papa del sorisso* ("the smiling Pope"), John Paul I was an unexpected choice as pontiff. He was a cardinal without diplomatic or curial experience but with warmth and great good humour who seemed determined to sweep away formality and to humanize the office of pope, but who died of a heart attack after just 33 days so that the character of his pontificate was never developed or fully revealed.

Born in Forno di Canale in the Veneto region, northern Italy, Albino Luciani was the son of a bricklayer. He was ordained in 1935 and taught theology, canon law and sacred art at a seminary before gaining a doctorate in theology. He was appointed Bishop of Vittorio Veneto by John XXIII and then made Patriarch of Venice in 1970 and a cardinal in 1973 by Paul VI.

A cardinal Luciani wrote a series of letters to historical and fictional characters, which were later collected in the book *Illustrissimi*, published in 1976. These included letters to Jesus Christ,

Below: Pope Paul VI, his predecessor, with Albino Luciano, the future John Paul I, visiting Venice in 1972.

> **FACT BOX**
> **Original name** Albino Luciani
> **Born** 17 October 1912
> **Origin** Forno di Canale
> **Date elected pope** 26 August 1978
> **Died** 28 September 1978
> **Key fact** Died of heart attack after just 33 days

Right: The smiling pope. John Paul I's inner joy and great good humour are plain in this photograph of his first official ceremony after his election. Cardinal Basil Hume said of him, "he was God's candidate".

Pinocchio, Figaro (the barber in French playwright Pierre Beaumarchais' plays *The Barber of Seville* and *The Marriage of Figaro*) and Mark Twain. He was elected on the fourth ballot of the conclave following the death of Paul VI, on 26 August 1978.

FIRST DUAL NAME

He chose the first dual name in papal history to honour his two immediate predecessors, John XXIII and Paul VI. He announced that he would continue the implementations of the decrees of the Second Vatican Council while upholding traditional discipline. He refused to be crowned – choosing an investiture with the pallium of an archbishop rather than a coronation. He chose as his papal motto *Humilitas* ("Humility").

His decision to forgo the splendour of a papal coronation was popular in some quarters, but may have fuelled doubts about him among more conservative elements in the Church. Moreover, he was known to have had significant concerns about the ban on contraception in his predecessor's encyclical *Humanae vitae* and in 1968 while Bishop of Vittorio Veneto had recommended to Paul VI that use of the contraceptive pill be permitted – a recommendation the then pope rejected.

Some sources suggest that John Paul was not respected as an intellectual within the highest echelons of the Church and was seen as naive and idealistic – one unnamed cardinal is said to have dismissively said "They have elected Peter Sellers", a reference to the British comic actor particularly famous at that time for his portrayal of the bumbling yet inexplicably successful Inspector Clouseau in the *Pink Panther* movies.

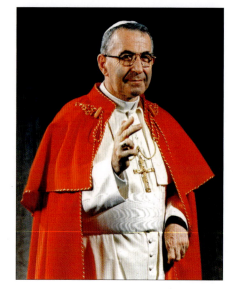

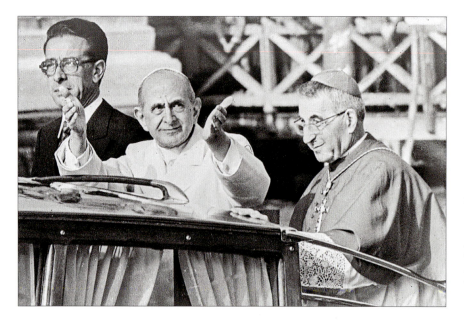

JOHN PAUL I

> **YEAR OF THREE POPES**
>
> Because the pontificate of John Paul I was so short, 1978 was the year of three popes – Paul VI, John Paul I and John Paul II. There have been 12 such years; this was the first since 1605. There was once a year of four popes – Gregory X, Innocent V, Hadrian V and John XXI, who all reigned in 1276.

"GOD'S CANDIDATE"

Yet other voices hailed his election as divinely inspired. English cardinal Basil Hume declared of the conclave in which John Paul I was elected, "Seldom have I had such an experience of the presence of God ... for me he was God's candidate."

John Paul was immediately popular. His friendly manner, humility and warm smile were allied with skill as an orator. He came across extremely well. Mother Teresa of Calcutta said of him, "He has been the greatest gift of God, a sun ray of God's love shining in the darkness of the world."

Below: After John Paul I's sudden death, 111 Cardinals were sealed inside the Sistine Chapel to elect his successor. After eight ballots, they chose Polish cardinal Karol Wojtyla. He chose the name Pope John Paul II.

SUDDEN DEATH

On the morning of 29 September 1978 John Paul was found dead. The previous night the pope had dined quietly in his Vatican apartment with his two secretaries, Father Diego Lorenzi and Father John Magee, then gone to bed just after 9pm. When discovered, he was sitting up in bed still clasping the papers he had been reading.

There were later inconsistencies in the reported facts, which fuelled some conspiracy theories that he had been murdered. The usual details given are that he was discovered by Sister Vincenza Taffarel – who had brought him his morning coffee for decades – just after 4.30am, his normal rising time. She then raised the alarm; Cardinal Jean Villot, Secretary of State, called the papal embalmers; and Dr Renato Buzzonetti, deputy head of the Vatican's health service, determined that Pope John Paul had had a heart attack at 11pm the previous night.

No post-mortem was held and the Vatican, when questioned, declared that post-mortems were not held for popes – despite the fact that they had been performed in previous reigns, such as that of Clement XIV (1769–74). It later

Above: Pope John Paul I with Cardinal Karol Wojtyla, who was to succeed him as pope in October 1978.

emerged that the pope's personal doctor, Giuseppe da Ros, had given John Paul a medical examination less than a week before and concluded that John Paul was not only well, but in robust health.

CONSPIRACY THEORIES

Some conspiracy theorists argue that the pope was about to expose a Mafia-connected financial scheme involving the Vatican Bank, and that those involved, desperate to prevent this, had him murdered; others propose that the pope was planning to demote prominent churchmen who could have been tempted to stop his reforms before they started. However, while there do seem to have been puzzling inconsistencies and departures from normal procedure within the Vatican after John Paul's death, the conspiracy theories have little force and there seems no doubt in truth that he died from natural causes.

After lying in state, John Paul's body was buried on 4 October 1978 in a tomb designed by Francesco Vacchini in the crypt of St Peter's Basilica.

PEACE FOR A TROUBLED WORLD

JOHN PAUL II, 1978–2005
POLISH POPE WHO CONNECTED POWERFULLY WITH THE YOUNG

Pontiff for 26 years and five months, John Paul II was the third longest-reigning pope in history after St Peter (roughly 35 years) and Pius IX (21 June 1846– 7 February 1878, 31 years seven months). Seeking to develop an understanding between nations and faiths, he travelled very widely – visiting more than 129 countries in the course of 104 journeys.

He was the first Polish pope and the first non-Italian pope since the Dutch Hadrian Florenszoon Boeyens who ruled as Hadrian VI in 1522–3; Wojtyla's early years in Poland under first Nazi and then Soviet domination profoundly influenced his attitudes – he helped to inspire the collapse of communist rule in his native country and Eastern Europe.

FACT BOX
Original name Karol Józef Wojtyla
Born 18 May 1920
Origin Wadowice, Poland
Date elected pope 16 October 1978
Died 2 April 2005
Key fact Inspired peaceful resistance to communist rule

Right: Shortly after his death, John Paul II joined Leo I, Gregory I and Nicholas I in being referred to as "the Great". Pope Francis recognized him as a saint in 2014.

Karol Wojtyla lost his mother, his beloved older brother "Mundek" and his father by his early 20s. By this stage the Nazis had invaded Poland and he was forced to take various jobs, including working in a quarry and a chemical factory. He began to train for the priesthood in secret and illegal classes during the war and was ordained in November 1946, by which time the Soviets had taken over from the Nazis as occupiers of Poland.

In his youth Wojtyla played soccer (as a goalkeeper), studied languages and was a playwright. After the war he wrote and anonymously published poetry, taught philosophy and served as professor at the Catholic University of Lublin. Pius XII made him Auxiliary Bishop of Krakow in 1958 and Paul VI appointed him

Below: John Paul II is welcomed by President Lech Walesa to Poland in 1991. This was the pope's fourth pilgrimage to his native land.

Archbishop of Krakow in 1963. Wojtyla was made a cardinal in 1967.

He was elected pope on the third day of the second conclave of 1978. He followed his predecessor in dispensing with the traditional coronation and having a simple investiture instead.

As pope, John Paul II supported the reforms of the Second Vatican Council and otherwise maintained a traditional line in many of his teachings, rejecting calls for the use of artificial contraception, the end of priestly celibacy, and the ordination of women priests, speaking out against abortion, against sex before marriage and against practising as a homosexual – although he made no condemnation of homosexual orientation.

"BE NOT AFRAID" – NON-VIOLENT PROTEST

In his installation Mass on 22 October 1978 John Paul II invoked the biblical phrase "Be not afraid!", a command given in these or similar words by God to Abraham (Genesis 46:3), by Gabriel in the Annunciation (Luke 1:30) and Jesus himself to his disciples (for example, in Matthew 14:27). These words became a byword for his papacy, and notably they looked forward to the peaceful campaigns for political and religious freedom and for human rights that the pope promoted during his pontificate.

744

JOHN PAUL II

JOHN PAUL II AND COMMUNISM

John Paul II visited his native Poland on his second official trip, in June 1979, and declared to vast audiences that they had the right to be free. He repeated the message of his homily at his installation Mass: "Be not afraid!" He was an inspiration for those seeking freedom from communist rule, those who formed the Polish trade union federation Solidarity that forced the first multi-party elections in the Soviet bloc of countries. These brought about the ousting of the communist regime in Poland and the collapse of communist rule across Eastern Europe. Some hold that the Vatican Bank secretly funded Solidarity. Mikhail Gorbachev, the former Soviet leader, said, "The collapse of the Iron Curtain would have been impossible without John Paul II" – a reference to the "curtain" said to divide the capitalist West from the communist East during the Cold War.

Above: John Paul II places a note in the Wailing Wall in Jerusalem, 2000. Israeli prime minister Ehud Barak met him with the words, "Blessed are you in Israel".

He was a strong critic of the apartheid system and called for economic sanctions against South Africa. He opposed the US-led invasion of Iraq in 2003. He taught that "Wars do not in general solve the problems for which they are fought, and therefore prove ultimately futile."

INTERFAITH INITIATIVES

Through his travels and other engagements John Paul worked hard to bring about reconciliation among Christian denominations and between Christianity and other world faiths. In 1982, he prayed in Canterbury Cathedral alongside Archbishop of Canterbury Robert Runcie; in 1983 he was the first pope to visit a Lutheran church; in 1990 he pronounced anti-Semitism a sin against God and humanity and in 1993 he established diplomatic relations between the Holy See and the state of Israel; in 1995, during a visit to Buddhist-majority Sri Lanka, he expressed admiration for Buddhism and its "four great values of … loving kindness, compassion, sympathetic joy and equanimity"; in 2001, during a visit to Damascus in Syria, he became the first pope to set foot in and pray in an Islamic mosque.

ASSASSINATION ATTEMPT – SAVED BY THE VIRGIN?

On 13 May 1981 John Paul survived an assassination attempt. While John Paul was being driven through St Peter's Square, a 23-year-old Turkish man named Mehmet Ali Agca shot and wounded him. He was struck four times and suffered severe blood loss.

John Paul later said that he was saved by the Virgin Mary, who diverted the bullet away from his heart; on the first anniversary of the attack he visited the shrine of the Virgin in Fatima, Portugal, and performed a consecration of the modern world to the Immaculate Heart of Mary.

DECLINING HEALTH

Fit and athletic when he became pope, John Paul enjoyed swimming and even jogging in the Vatican Gardens – in an Irish newspaper article, he was dubbed the "keep-fit pope". But for the last decade or more of his life, he was in declining health.

As early as 1991 there were the first signs that he might be developing Parkinson's disease, although this was not officially confirmed until 2003. Towards the end of his life, he suffered from osteoarthritis and hearing difficulties. He died on 2 April 2005. His final words were "Allow me to depart to the House of the Father".

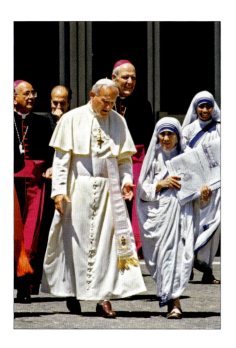

Below: John Paul II walks with Mother Teresa in 1988. He said she found strength and perseverance "in prayer and in the silent contemplation of Jesus Christ".

BENEDICT XVI, 2005–13
FIRST POPE TO ABDICATE SINCE 1415

Benedict XVI is remembered above all for his decision, announced on 11 February 2013, to abdicate as pope. His eight-year pontificate was generally conservative and overshadowed somewhat by a series of sexual abuse scandals involving Roman Catholic clerics.

Born the youngest of three children to a hotel cook and a policeman in Bavaria, Ratzinger was six years old when the Nazis came to power in Germany. His parents were fervent Catholics and were anti-Nazi but after beginning training as a priest the young Joseph Ratzinger was made to join the Hitler Youth in 1941 and then drafted into the German army in 1943. He deserted in April 1945 and was a prisoner of war for a short period after being captured by the Americans.

After the war he was ordained a priest in 1951 and embarked on a distinguished academic career, taking a doctorate in theology and teaching at the universities of Bonn, Munster, Tubingen and Regensburg. He served as the Archbishop of Cologne's expert

Below: Pope Benedict XVI with US President George W. Bush at the White House, Washington, on 16 April 2008, the day the pope celebrated his 81st birthday.

assistant at the Second Vatican Council before in 1977 Paul VI appointed him Archbishop of Munich and elevated him to the cardinalate.

"GOD'S ROTTWEILER"
From 1978 onwards he was a close friend of John Paul II and in 1981 the pope appointed him prefect of the Congregation for the Doctrine of the Faith, the body responsible for enforcing doctrinal orthodoxy and the modern equivalent of the Inquisition. In more than 20 years in this role he won a reputation for being a stern authoritarian and was nicknamed "God's rottweiler", in a reference to the originally German breed of dogs.

A highly intelligent and humble man, Ratzinger certainly had a gentle side – while a cardinal, he was known as a lover of cats, prone to adopting strays from the streets in Rome. In his younger years he was an accomplished pianist, particularly devoted to the works of Bach and Mozart. As his friend John Paul II did, Ratzinger spoke several languages very well.

When he was elected pope on 19 April 2005 he was already 78 and was the oldest new pope since Clement XII, who was the same age on his election in 1730. Benedict indicated that he would

Above: Benedict blesses the faithful in 2005. In his encyclical "God is Love", he declared, "Prayer, as a means of drawing ever-new strength from Christ, is concretely and urgently needed".

follow John Paul II's traditionalist line on matters concerning sexuality and priestly celibacy and intended to continue his predecessor's work to bring Christian denominations and world faiths together.

However, early in his pontificate he faced controversy when a speech in Germany in September 2006 offended many Muslims. In his speech he quoted some words, originally spoken by the Byzantine emperor Manuel II Palaeologus: "Show me just what Muhammad brought that was new and there you will find things only evil and

---

FACT BOX
Original name Joseph Alois Ratzinger
Born 16 April 1927
Origin Marktl am Inn, Germany
Date elected pope 19 April 2005
Abdicated 28 February 2013
Key fact Issued apologies for sexual abuse by priests

BENEDICT XVI

Above: The faithful made a pictorial puzzle to welcome Benedict to the Dos Coqueiros stadium in Luanda, Angola, 2009. He called for further evangelization of Africa.

> **POPE EMERITUS 2013–2022**
>
> As Pope Emeritus Benedict continued to wear white and retained his papal name and the style "His Holiness". He returned his Fisherman's Ring used for sealing papal documents (normally destroyed on the death of a pope). He lived in the renovated Mater Ecclesiae monastery in the grounds of the Vatican with his personal secretary Archbishop Georg Gänswein and four consecrated laywomen. His successor Pope Francis said that having Benedict living in the Vatican posed no difficulty. It is, he said, "like having a grandfather – a wise grandfather – living at home."

inhuman, such as his command to spread by the sword the faith he preached." He apologized for causing offence and later that year visited Turkey, where he prayed inside the celebrated Blue Mosque. He also met the Ecumenical Patriarch of Constantinople, Bartholomew I.

Benedict taught frequently on the need for people to open themselves to friendship with Jesus Christ. In his first homily he declared, "Only in this friendship do we experience beauty and liberation … open wide the doors to Christ – and you will find true life."

"POPE OF AESTHETICS"

Benedict was noted for wearing very fine ecclesiastical vestments; he revived the use of traditional papal garments including red papal shoes, the *camauro* (red velvet cap bordered with white fur) and the wide-brimmed *cappello romano*, also red. He was nicknamed "the pope of aesthetics"; he also revitalized the link between the Church and the world of the arts, holding a meeting with artists in the Sistine Chapel in 2009 "to express and renew the Church's friendship with the world of art" and declaring that "art is like an open doorway to the infinite, towards a beauty and truth that go beyond everyday reality."

APOLOGY FOR PRIESTLY SEXUAL ABUSE

During a visit to the United States in 2008 Benedict met victims of priestly sexual abuse and spoke out condemning perpetrators. In the same year in Australia he apologized for abuse by priests, saying "I would like to … acknowledge the shame which we have all felt as a result of the sexual abuse of minors by some clergy and religious in this country."

ABDICATION

Pope Benedict XVI announced on 11 February 2013 his decision to abdicate as pope with effect from 28 February. He was 85 years old. Benedict said, "My strengths, due to an advanced age, are no longer suited to an adequate exercise of the petrine ministry." His resignation was the first by a pope

Below: Pope Benedict and Ecumenical Orthodox Patriarch Bartholomew I in Istanbul, 2006. They discussed how to bring an end to the Catholic/Orthodox divide.

since Gregory XII in 1415. The move was unexpected as all popes in modern times had held office until death. Benedict was the first pope to resign without external pressure since Celestine V in 1294.

As Pope Emeritus, Benedict did not live a cloistered life, but studied and wrote. He attended many religious ceremones and continued to celebrate mass. However, Benedict's health continued to detoriorate and he died on 31 December 2022. His long-time secretary, Georg Gänswein, reported that his last words were "*Signore ti amo*" ("Lord, I love you"). His funeral took place on 5 January 2023 in St Peter's Square, presided over by Pope Francis. Benedict was then interred in the crypt beneath St Peter's Basilica, in the same tomb originally occupied by John Paul II and John XXIII.

PEACE FOR A TROUBLED WORLD

FRANCIS, 2013–
FIRST LATIN AMERICAN AND FIRST JESUIT POPE

Argentinian cardinal Jorge Mario Bergoglio, the former Archbishop of Buenos Aires, was 76 when he was elected pope on 13 March 2013. His pontificate began with a call for peace and for the Church to embrace the needs of the poor. He chose the name Francis to honour St Francis of Assisi, and at his first media audience, praised his saintly namesake as "the man who gives us this spirit of peace, the poor man."

Pope Francis is known for his humility. On the night of his election he rode back in a bus to his hotel rather than take the papal car. He tends to adopt a "no frills" style, dressing plainly and living simply. He chose to live in the Domus Sante Marthae (St Martha's House), a guesthouse adjacent to St Peter's Basilica rather than in the papal apartments of the Apostolic Palace.

The new leader of the Church was known from his time as Archbishop of Buenos Aires as being committed to social justice. In the first months of his pontificate he called on world leaders to avoid the "cult of money", which he said was making people unhappy, and attacked a "throw away culture"

Below: Pope Francis is the first pope from the Americas and the first Jesuit pope. He met members of sports associations for the 70th anniversary of Centro Sportivo Italiano, Vatican City in June 2014.

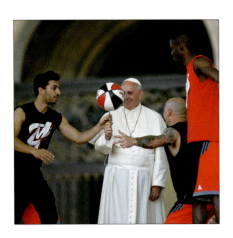

in which "human beings themselves are … considered as consumer goods which can be used and thrown away". He said "in circumstances like these, solidarity, which is the treasure of the poor, is often considered counterproductive, opposed to the logic of finance and the economy."

In his 2013 exhortation *Evangelii gaudium* ("The Joy of the Gospel") he denounced market autonomy and declared, "Just as the commandment 'Thou shalt not kill' sets a clear limit in order to safeguard the value of human life, today we also have to say 'thou shalt not' to an economy of exclusion and inequality. Such an economy kills." In 2015 he declared "Poverty is at the centre of the Gospel."

At the same time he was, like his two predecessors, generally conservative on matters of morality and sexuality, unresponsive to modern calls for the ordination of women or for priests to be allowed to marry. He declared that there would be no going back on the possibility of women priests: "John Paul II made the Church's stance definitive. The door is closed." However, he argued that women had a special role in the Church: "Our Lady was more important than the Apostles, bishops,

Above: Francis greets pilgrims during the 2016 Jubilee of Mercy. He is said to be approachable, informal and reportedly introduces himself on the phone as "Hi, it's Pope Francis here!"

deacons and priests. Women play a role that's more important than that of bishops or priests. How? This is what we have to explain better publicly." In his apostolic letter *Spiritus Domini* ("The Spirit of the Lord") of 10 January 2021, he empowered bishops to appoint women to the roles of acolyte and lector, previously reserved for men.

ENVIRONMENT AND THE "CULTURE OF ENCOUNTER"
On his election Francis said one reason he chose his papal name was because Francis of Assisi "teaches us profound

---

FACT BOX

Original name Jorge Mario Bergoglio
Born 17 December 1936
Origin Buenos Aires, Argentina
Date elected pope 13 March 2013
Key fact Shares Vatican with pope emeritus

> **TWO POPES MEET**
>
> On 23 March 2013 the new pope Francis met the pope emeritus Benedict at Castel Gandolfo, where Benedict began his retirement. They embraced on meeting and prayed together, then shared lunch. Both wore white. The last time such a meeting was possible was in 1294, after Celestine V stood down and was replaced by Boniface VIII. Relations were not so friendly then: Boniface had Celestine imprisoned in the castle of Ferentino, south-east of Rome, where the former pope died.

respect for the whole of creation and the protection of our environment". The pope later argued in favour of using renewable energy sources rather than traditional fuels, but also emphasized that consumerism must be brought under control. On 18 June 2015, Francis published the encyclical, *Laudato si* ("Praise be to You") calling for "swift and unified global action" to counter global warming.

Shortly after becoming pope, Francis called for interreligious dialogue in order to "help to build bridges connecting all people". On 20 March 2013 he reached out to non-believers, saying that people of no religious tradition who were "searching for truth, goodness and beauty" were the Church's "valued allies in the commitment to defending human dignity, in building a peaceful coexistence between peoples and in safeguarding and caring for creation," adding in a homily on 22 May that God "redeemed all of us, with the Blood of Christ: all of us, not just Catholics, Everyone! … even the atheists!" He called for a "culture of encounter': "we must meet one another doing good".

Right: The modern face of the Vatican. Francis is the first pope to create an Instagram account. He gained more than 1 million followers in the first 12 hours.

"ALWAYS CONSIDER THE PERSON…"

In an interview with Jesuit journal *La Civilta Cattolica* on 19 September 2013 Francis called for a less condemnatory attitude in the Church towards divorced people, women who have had an abortion and gays. He said, "We must always consider the person … In life, God accompanies persons, and we must accompany them, starting from their situation."

He remained strongly opposed to gay marriage, which he said in January 2015 would "disfigure God's plan for creation". But on 26 June 2016 he said the Church owed gay people an apology for how it had treated them and added: "they should not be discriminated against, they should be respected, accompanied pastorally."

In his comments on 26 June 2016 Francis suggested that the Church owed an apology to other groups as well: "I think that the Church not only should apologize … to a gay person whom it offended but it must also apologize to the poor as well, to the women who have been exploited, to children who have been exploited by [being forced to] work. It must apologize for having blessed so many weapons."

REFUGEE CRISIS, TERROR ATTACKS, CORONAVIRUS, BLACK LIVES MATTER

In 2016 Francis engaged with the refugee crisis that engulfed Europe, as thousands of migrants fled Syria, Iraq, Afghanistan and African countries. He visited the Moria migrant camp on the Greek island of Lesbos on 16 April.

In 2017 he responded to the wave of terrorist attacks on leading cities, invoking "God's blessings of peace, healing and strength" upon England after the attack in Manchester on 22 May, and on 4 June praying for victims of the previous night's attack on London Bridge:

Francis emphasized mercy as the most powerful part of Jesus's message. He urged people never to give up seeking God's forgiveness. In the COVID-19 pandemic, Francis was forced to cancel his general audiences in St Peter's Squre. On 10 March 2020, with Italy in a nationwide lockdown, he encouraged priests to go out and visit the sick and on 13 March he urged people to remember the needs of the poor during the crisis.

In response to the Black Lives Matter protests that followed the death in police custody of American George Floyd on 25 May 2020, Francis called the death "horrendous" and said protesters were united by "healthy indignation". In a comment that appeared to express frustration that some American Catholics might be concerned less over racism than over other matters, especially abortion, he said on 3 June 2020: "My friends, we cannot tolerate or turn a blind eye to racism and exclusion in any form and yet claim to defend the sacredness of every human life."

Ahead of the World Youth Day in Lisbon, July 2023, Francis responded to prerecorded questions from young people in the Vatican News's newly produced podcast, dubbed the "Popecast". To each he responded with words of encouragement and urged faith in God's love.

Glossary

ABSOLUTION The power of forgiveness that can be exercised by a priest during the sacrament of penance (confession).

ANATHEMA From the Greek word originally meaning an offering to a god, but subsequently coming to mean despised, hated and accursed; excommunicated from or condemned by the Church.

ANNUNCIATION A festival celebrated on 25 March to commemorate the announcement by the archangel Gabriel to Mary of Jesus' coming birth.

ANTICHRIST From the New Testament, the ultimate enemy of Christ who will oppose Christ's teachings and substitute himself for Christ.

APOSTASY A total rejection of the Christian faith by a baptized person.

APOSTLE A messenger with the purpose of spreading the Christian message; specifically, the name given by Jesus to 12 of his faithful followers, who were given the task to spread the Word by preaching the gospels.

APOSTLES' CREED A 1st-century AD formula of Church teachings established by the first pope, St Peter.

APOSTOLIC FATHERS Writers of the Christian faith in the 1st and 2nd centuries AD, thought to have known or been personally influenced by the apostles and their writings.

ASCENSION The elevation of Christ to heaven on the 40th day after his Resurrection, celebrated as a feast day that falls 40 days after Easter.

ASSUMPTION OF MARY The entrance of the body and soul of Mary to heaven after her death, commemorated on 15 August.

ATHANASIAN CREED A formula of Catholic faith, probably drawn up in the 4th or 5th century AD in response to various heretical theories on the nature of Christ.

BAPTISM A sacramental rite involving water that cleanses a person of sin; in Catholic doctrine, due to original sin, baptism is a necessary requirement to gain entry into heaven.

BEATITUDES The blessings due to followers of Christianity listed by Jesus at the beginning of the Sermon on the Mount, recorded in Matthew (5:3–12) and Luke (23:42).

BEATIFICATION A papal declaration of a deceased person as officially "blessed", a stage in the process of canonization.

CANONIZATION The process by which a deceased person who has previously been beatified is formally declared a saint.

CATECHISM An exposition of the doctrines of Catholicism taught in a catechistic, or question and answer, form.

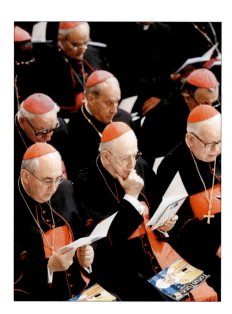

Above: Pope John Paul II moved a step closer to sainthood when he was beatified after a dossier was presented to the Vatican.

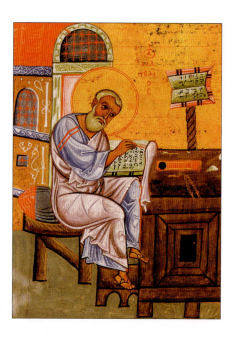

Above: St Matthew the Evangelist, shown in this 12th-century Byzantine evangelistary, was one of the four apostles responsible for the gospels.

COMMUNION The act of celebrating the Eucharist (thanksgiving) through partaking of bread and wine that Catholicism states are the true body and blood of Jesus Christ.

CONFESSION The sacrament of penance, or admission of sins committed after baptism, to a priest in order to obtain forgiveness.

COUNTER-REFORMATION A period of Catholic revival from c.1522 to 1648, during which time attempts were made to stem the rise of Protestantism through reforms in the Catholic Church.

CULT OR CULTUS A system of beliefs and religious observances surrounding a particular saint.

DEUTEROCANONICALS Also known as the Apocrypha, certain Old Testament books and passages that are present in the Catholic Bible but that are not part of the Jewish or Protestant canon.

DOCTRINE An authoritative set of beliefs taught by the Church.

DOGMA Church doctrine that has

GLOSSARY

been revealed by God and therefore is deemed to be indisputable, belief in which is said by the Catholic Church to be necessary for salvation.

EVANGELIST Someone who aims to convert others to their cause; specifically the authors of the four Gospels, Sts Matthew, Mark, Luke and John.

EXCOMMUNICATION The suspension of a person from the possibility of redemption by revoking their membership of the Church community.

FEAST DAY A fixed or movable holy festival designated for giving special honour to God, members of the Holy Family or saints, often commemorating specific events.

HERESY A single belief or set of beliefs at variance with the official or orthodox doctrine of the Church.

INCARNATION The union of the divine and human natures of the Son of God in the person of Jesus Christ.

INDULGENCES The remittance of temporal punishments given to a sinner after the sin has been confessed and absolved, dispensed by the Church.

JUDGEMENT DAY The time at which a final judgement and trial of all mankind will take place after Armageddon, where each person will be rewarded or punished according to his or her merits.

LAST SUPPER The last meal eaten by Jesus before his Crucifixion, where he asked that bread and wine be shared by those at the meal in memory of him, and when he gave his final instructions to his followers.

LIMBO The destination of righteous but unbaptized souls, such as infants who die without baptism or those who died before Christ.

MAGISTERIUM The teaching office or authority of the Catholic Church embodied in the pope and

Above: Some feast days honour the Madonna and child, shown in this 15th-century painting by Giovanni Bellini.

bishops, who are the representatives of the Church.

MASS The church service during which Eucharist is celebrated, which is the central act of worship in Catholic liturgy.

MORTAL SIN A deadly sin that revolts against God and deprives the sinner of their right to enter heaven.

NICENE CREED A formulation of Catholic doctrine first released in AD 325 and revised in AD 381, which outlines the nature of Christ in response to the Arian heresy.

ORIGINAL SIN The state of sin that all of humankind are born into as a result of the fall from grace of Adam and Eve, and which is cleansed through baptism.

PURGATORY The temporary destination for those who have died in a state of grace, where they can atone for their sins before they can enter heaven.

REDEMPTION The salvation of humanity through Jesus Christ, who gave his life in return for the expiation of humanity's debt of sin.

REFORMATION A period of religious, social and political unrest from 1517 to 1648, which resulted in the formation of Protestantism.

RESURRECTION The miracle of Christ's return to life three days after his death and burial, followed by his Ascension to heaven.

REVELATION The disclosure by God of himself and his plan to humanity, for example, through private revelation in the form of visions of the Virgin Mary.

SACRAMENT A formal religious ceremony, during which a specific grace is conferred upon those who receive it, such as Communion and confession.

TRANSUBSTANTIATION The process by which Catholics believe that bread and wine become the body and blood of Christ during the celebration of the Eucharist.

TRINITY, THE HOLY The name used to represent the three distinct persons present in the Christian God: the Father, the Son and the Holy Spirit.

VENIAL SIN A pardonable sin that offends against God but does not on its own deprive the sinner of his or her right to enter heaven.

Above: Limbo is shown in this 14th-century panel from an altarpiece in Santo Sepulchro, a convent in Zaragoza.

INDEX

A
Aachen 63, 67, 204
Abbey of Cluny 583, 600, 607
Abbey of Monte Cassino 596, 597, 600, 601, 607
Abelard, Peter 608, 618
abortion 222, 223
absolution 224, 225, 750
Acacian Schism 550
Acacius 407
Act of Supremacy 669, 671
Acutis, Blessed Carlo 287
Adam and Eve 128–20, 152, 214
Adeodatus I 561
Adeodatus II 564
adultery 221
Advent 209, 241, 245, 246
Aethelbert of Kent, King 559
Aethelwulf of Wessex, King 580
Africa 101, 106–7, 122–3, 196, 197
Agapitus I 551
Agapitus II 582
Agatho 564, 564, 565, 565, 566
Alacoque, Marguerite Marie 233, 273, 509
Alaric I, King 544, 544–5, 548
Albertus Magnus 631, 639
Albigensians see Cathars
Aleric [antipope] 602
Alexander I 524, 525
Alexander II 596, 597–8
Alexander III 103, 595, 611, 614, 615
Alexander IV 191, 629, 630, 706
Alexander V [antipope] 646, 647
Alexander VI 72, 96, 593, 651, 653, 660, 662–3, 664, 665, 668, 721
Alexander VII 697, 698, 698–9, 701, 705
Alexander VIII 696, 697, 702, 703
Alfred the Great, King 580
All Saints' Day 279, 290–1
Almohads 617, 621, 625
altar, the 206-7
    sacrament of 212–13
Americas, the 101, 104–5
    native peoples in 104, 105, 144
Anacletus I 523, 524
Anacletus II [antipope] 608, 609
Anastasius [antipope] 580
Anastasius I 542, 543, 544
Anastasius II 550
Anastasius III 582
Anastasius IV 612

angelus, the 28–9
Anicetus 526
animals, patron saints of 398–9
Annunciation 28, 236, 244, 750
Anterus 528
Apocrypha books 139
Apostles 33, 38–9, 132, 206, 216, 224, 232, 252, 270, 310–11, 312–21
Apostle of the Indies 103
Apostles' Creed 134–5, 236, 270
Apostolic (Vatican) Palace 537, 574, 731, 748
Apostolic See 540, 552
Appian Way 532, 533, 565
Aquinas see St Thomas Aquinas
Arcadius, Emperor 545
Arch of Titus 545, 657
archbishops 53, 107, 114–7, 155, 176
architecture 20, 21, 66–7, 94–5
Arianis 52, 53, 129, 135
Arianism 534, 538, 539, 551
Arius of Alexandria 534, 534, 538
Ascension 36–7, 245, 270
Ash Wednesday 244, 250–1, 252
Asia 101, 103
Asia Minor 102
Association of Papal Orders 199
Assumption, the 143, 241, 245, 750
Athalaric, King 551
Attila the Hun 519, 537, 548
Augustine of Canterbury 276, 339, 348, 368, 377
Augustinians 91, 174, 180, 248
Avars 557, 577
Avellino, Andrew 289, 389, 508
Avignon Annexation 553
Avignon Exile 15, 552, 553, 53, 635, 636, 640–1, 644, 646

B
Bakhita, Josephine 282, 389, 491
baptism 31, 150, 151, 166–7, 214–15, 239, 750
Barat, Madeleine Sophie 276, 467, 470
Barbarigo, Gregorio 509
Barbieri, Clelia 472
Basil I, Emperor 589
Basilica di Santa Maria del Fiore 204
Basilica di Santa Maria Maggiore 540, 546–7, 564, 687, 689
Basilica di Santa Maria, Trastevere 527, 539, 567, 609, 718
Basilica of Our Lady of Peace (Ivory Coast) 205
Basilica of Sant'Apollinare Nuovo 513, 550, 571

Basilica of Santa Maria, Cosmedin 573, 605
Basilica of St Paul Outside the Walls 526, 542, 565
Basilica San Marco, Rome 538
Battle of Agincourt 642
Battle of Belgrade 653
Battle of Bouvines 621
Battle of Castillon 642
Battle of Civitate 591
Battle of Crécy 642
Battle of Garigliano 582
Battle of Hattin 614, 615, 622, 624
Battle of Las Navas de Tolosa 621
Battle of Lepanto 622, 681
Battle of Marignano 666
Battle of Ostia 580, 581
Battle of Pavia 670
Battle of Poitiers 642
Battle of the Masts 564
Battle of the Milvian Bridge 534
Battle of Toulouse 568
Battle of Varna 649
Battle of Waterloo 714, 717
Bays, Marguerite 510
Beatitudes 32–3, 270
Bede, The Venerable 276, 338, 369, 379, 502, 559, 561
Bellarmine, Robert 343, 442
Benedict I 555
Benedict II 566
Benedict III 580, 581
Benedict IV 581
Benedict V 583
Benedict VI 583
Benedict VII 583
Benedict VIII 575, 586
Benedict IX 575, 587
Benedict X [antipope] 596
Benedict XI 70, 632, 633, 636
Benedict XII 70, 156, 159, 635, 639, 641, 642
Benedict XIII [antipope] 635, 646, 647
Benedict XIII 706–7
Benedict XIV [antipope] 647
Benedict XIV 106, 549, 697, 708, 709, 715
Benedict XV 18, 177, 653, 729, 731, 732, 733, 734
Benedict XVI 19, 21, 119, 121, 123, 137–9, 145, 147, 167, 171, 172, 177, 214, 231, 235, 238, 243, 563, 565, 610, 721, 741, 746–7, 749
Benedictines 60, 61, 184, 186, 190, 192, 193, 195, 255, 256, 642, 713, 723
Berchmans, John 488

INDEX

Bernini, Gian Lorenzo 523, 695, 697, 698, 699, 700, 701, 702
Bertoni, Gaspar 469
Bertrand, Louis 388, 436
Billiart, Julie 509
bishops 172, 176, 177, 182, 183, 208, 216, 229, 238
Black Death 641
Blessed Virgin *see* Mary, the Blessed Virgin
blessings 238–9
Bobola, Andrew 509
Bonhoeffer, Dietrich 281
Boniface I 546
Boniface II 551
Boniface III 560
Boniface IV 560–1
Boniface V 560, 561
Boniface VI 581, 587
Boniface VII [antipope] 551
Boniface VIII 70, 72, 146, 633, 636, 749
Boniface IX 646
Bonnie Prince Charlie 706
Borgia, Cesare 651, 662, 663
Borgia, Francis 389, 431
Borgia, Lucrezia 651, 662, 663
Borromeo, Charles 342, 508
Boscardin, Bertilla 485
Bosco, John 348, 476
Botticelli, Sandro 542, 659
Bourgeoys, Marguerite 452
Briant, Alexander 508
brides of Christ 192–3
Byzantium 47, 59

C

Cabrini, Frances 289, 483
Cadaver Trial 581
Cafasso, Joseph 476, 510
Calabria, John 491
Calasanz, Joseph 509
Callistus I 57, 533, 539
Callistus II 603, 604–5
Callistus III 652, 653, 662
Calvin, John 558, 669
Calvinism 69, 91, 93, 133
Campion, Edmund 508
Canisius, Peter 136–7, 437
canon law 177
canonization 146–7, 750
Canterbury 64
  Archbishop of 112, 155
Canterbury Cathedral 26, 65
Canute, King 587
Carbonari 719

Cardinal Humbert 588, 589, 590, 591, 596
Cardinal Richelieu 690, 691, 694
cardinals 139, 145, 167, 176
  College of Cardinals 172, 173, 176
Carlo of Sezze 273
Carloman 750, 571, 572, 577
Carmelites 190, 193, 256, 525, 625, 633, 683, 685
carnival 248–9
Carolingian Renaissance 577, 579
Carthusians 188–90, 256
Cassian, John 154
Castaneda, Hyacinth 460
Catechism, the 136–7, 750
Catedral Metropolitana Nossa Senhora Aparecida (Brasilia) 205
Cathars (Albigensians) 78, 78, 237, 620, 623, 625, 721
Cathedral of San Leopardo 564
Catherine de' Vigri of Bologna 342, 343, 250
Catherine of Genoa 92
Catherine of Racconigi 273
Catholic Emancipation Act (1829) 722, 723
Catholicism: Catholic Calendar 241, 244–5
  Catholic doctrine 10–11, 124–67
  Catholic history 11, 20–1
  Catholic Year 240–55
  in decline 120–3
  medieval Catholicism 56–7
  in the middle ages 54–7
  and pop culture 115
  practising of 10, 168–255
  and the Reformation 90–9
  and the Renaissance 68–89
  as world religion 6, 100–123
  see also Church, the
Celestine I 546, 547
Celestine II [antipope] 606
Celestine II 608, 609
Celestine III 617, 618–9, 620, 624, 625
Celestine IV 587, 628
Celestine V 633, 681, 749
celibacy 178, 179, 180–1
celtic saints 368–9
Champagnat, Marcellin 509
Chanel, Peter 388, 510
Chantal, Jane Frances de 443, 508
Charlemagne 14, 96, 97, 204, 279, 513, 552, 553, 555, 557, 569, 570, 571, 572, 573, 576–7, 578, 586
Charles of Anjou 628, 629, 632
Charles V, Emperor 52, 85, 86, 666, 667,

Above: St Hugo of Grenoble in the Refectory of the Carthusians.

669, 670, 671, 677, 679, 680
Chartres Cathedral 62, 66, 124–5
Chavara, Kuriakose Elias 471
child saints 336–7
Childeric III 568, 569, 577
Chinese Rites Controversy 705, 706, 709
Christ
  as the Redeemer 130–1
  in the wilderness 250
  see also Jesus
Christmas 209, 245, 246–7
Christopher [antipope] 581, 582
Chrysostom, John 545
Church Fathers 50–1
Church of England 21, 90, 91, 118
Church of San Callisto 527, 533
Church of the Holy Sepulchre (Jerusalem) 20, 229, 241
Church of the Holy Sepulchre 586, 739
Church, the
  division of 52–3
  early Church 24–53, 216
  hierarchy of 176–7
  institutions of 170–99
  marriage to 180–1
  power of 56–7, 84–5
  wealth of 56–7
  see also Catholicism
churches and cathedrals 66–7, 202–5, 206–7
Cistercians 20, 61, 189, 193, 256, 642
Clare of Rimini, Blessed 282, 283
Claret, Antony 472

753

INDEX

Above: St Cuthbert.

Claver, Peter 287, 289, 388, 446
Clement 273
Clement I 450, 513, 524
Clement II 587, 595
Clement III [antipope] 599, 600, 602
Clement III 595, 614, 615, 618, 620, 624
Clement IV 628, 629, 630
Clement V 17, 20, 70–1, 635, 636, 637, 638, 640
Clement VI 17, 70, 635, 640, 641, 642, 643, 644
Clement VII [antipope] 21, 71, 85, 91, 96, 635, 640, 646
Clement VII 645, 651, 669, 670, 671, 677, 678
Clement VIII [antipope] 647
Clement VIII 73, 686, 688, 690
Clement IX 702
Clement X 696, 697, 702
Clement XI 697, 699, 704, 705, 706
Clement XII 706, 707, 708, 710, 746
Clement XIII 697, 710, 710, 711
Clement XIV 713, 714, 715, 743
clergy
  decline in 120–1
  married clergy 181
  sexual impropriety of 121
  vestments of 208–9
  see also archbishops; bishops; priests
Clitherow, Margaret 508
Cluny (France) 20, 61
Cold War 729, 738, 745
Colombière, Claude de la 509
Colosseum 524, 607
Columba of Iona 276, 343, 368, 390
Columbus, Christopher 21, 88, 89, 104, 661
Column of Phocas 560
communion 132, 133, 168–9, 210, 213, 217, 219, 232, 750

Communion of Saints 161
communism 110–1, 114, 115, 117
Concordat of Worms 604, 605, 606
confession 121, 224–15, 750
confirmation 216–7
Congress of Vienna 553, 713, 717
Conon 566
Conrad II, Emperor 587
Constans II, Emperor 562, 563, 564
Constantine 566, 567
Constantine I, Emperor (the Great) 16, 46–7, 129, 135, 274, 311, 346, 515, 523, 534, 535, 542, 552, 584, 589
Constantine II [antipope] 571
Constantine III, Emperor 563
Constantine IV, Emperor 562, 565, 566
Constantine V, Emperor 569, 571
Constantinople 20, 47, 53, 59, 129, 142
Constantius II, Emperor 538, 539
contemplative monasticism 188–9
contraception 222–3
Copernicus, Nicolaus 21, 89, 108, 677, 691
Cordero, Miguel 482
Cornelius 316, 317, 399, 450, 528
Cottolengo, Joseph 465
Council of Ariminum 539
Council of Arles 534, 543
Council of Basel 648, 652, 653, 654
Council of Carthage 543, 545
Council of Chalcedon 537, 549, 550, 554, 562, 578
Council of Clermont 58
Council of Constance 635, 646, 647, 648
Council of Constantinople, First 129, 683
Council of Constantinople, Fourth 580
Council of Constantinople, Second 554, 560
Council of Constantinople, Third 562, 564, 565, 566
Council of Ephesus 142, 546, 547
Council of Ferrara 589
Council of Florence 160, 167
Council of Jerusalem 39, 14
Council of Lyon, First 160, 190, 628
Council of Lyon, Second 589, 630, 631
Council of Nicaea 20, 46, 52, 129, 135, 254, 534, 538, 539, 683
Council of Orange 130, 131
Council of Piacenza 601
Council of Pisa 20, 71
Council of Sardica 538
Council of Trent 18, 82–3, 92, 115, 131, 133, 137, 160, 673, 674, 675, 676, 677, 678, 679, 680, 681, 682, 683, 684, 686, 740
Council of Troyes 607, 611
Council of Vienne 637
Counter-Reformation 18–19, 552, 669, 673, 674, 675, 676, 677, 678, 682, 683, 684, 686, 688, 700, 721
Cranmer, Thomas 669, 671
creeds
  Apostles' Creed 134–5, 236, 750
  Athanasian Creed 135, 157, 750
  classic creeds 134–5
  Nicene Creed 20, 53, 128, 129, 134, 135, 221, 751
Crispin and Crispinian 277, 342, 343, 500, 501
crucifixion 42
  Crucifixion of Christ 44–5, 224, 234, 235, 253
crusades 58–9, 88
  Albigensian 20, 79–81
  Eighth 623, 629
  Fifth 617, 620, 622, 626
  First 595, 601, 602, 603, 617, 622, 623
  Fourth 617, 620, 621, 622, 633
  Ninth 622, 623, 630
  Second 610–1, 617, 622
  Seventh 623, 629
  Sixth 622, 623, 625, 626, 629
  Third 615, 619, 621
Cuban Missile Crisis 738
Cunegund 438, 439
Cyricus 407

D

Damasus I 537, 540, 540–1, 545, 552, 553
Damasus II 586, 587, 595
Damian *see* Cosmas and Damian
Damien de Veuster, Father Joseph 286
damnation 162, 164–5
Dante 57
David, King 26, 298
  House of 28, 29
de' Medici, Catherine 675, 681
de' Medici, Lorenzo 658, 659, 660, 666
de Torquemada, Tomas 659, 661
deacons 176–9, 182, 208, 211
Decius, Emperor 528, 532
Delanoue, Jeanne 456
Demetrius 333, 416, 417
Desiderius 571, 572
Deuterocanonical books 139, 750
Diderot, Denis 21, 108
Diego, Juan 275, 285, 507

754

Dierks, Marie Adolphine 475
Diet of Worms 668
Diets of Speyer 669
Diocletian, Emperor 43, 533
Dioscorus [antipope] 551
disciples 38–9, 232
Discipline of the Secret 137
Discovery, Age of 88–8, 103
Dissolution of the Monasteries 98–9, 669
divorce 221
Dogmatic Constitution of the Church 531
Dominicans 75, 79, 80, 104, 190, 191, 199, 256, 617, 624, 625, 627, 705, 721
Domitian, Emperor 524
Donation of Charlemagne 552, 557, 573
Donation of Constantine 535, 574, 589, 590, 591
Donation of Hadrian 613
Donation of Pepin 552, 570
Donation of Sutri 568
Donatism 534, 543
Donato Bramante 593
Donatus Magnus 534, 543
Donus 565
Drexel, Katharine 276, 492
Duchesne, Philippine 308
Duchy of Rome 553
Duomo de Milano 21
Durer, Albrecht 540

E

early saints 264–5
Easter 209, 224, 244, 252–3, 254–5
Easter Synods 589, 590, 591
Eastern saints 268–9
Ecumenical Council of Nicaea, Second 572, 573
Edict of Milan 14, 48, 135, 146, 513, 531, 534
Edward I of England 622, 623, 630
Edward III of England 642
Edward the Confessor 277, 289, 386, 438, 466
Edward the Martyr 384, 439
Edwin of Northumbria, King 561
Eleanor of Aquitaine 611
Eleutherius 526, 720
Elizabeth I of England 681, 685, 687
Elizabeth of Russia, Grand Duchess 281
Elmo 288, 500
Eluvathingal, Euphrasia 471

Empress Theodora 551, 554
England 67, 115, 188
English Bible 90
English Civil War 695
Enlightenment, the 108–9, 708, 711
Erasmus of Rotterdam 82, 83, 667, 667, 671, 681
Escrivá, Josemaría 198, 199, 495
Eucharist, the 132–3, 137, 150, 151, 183, 200–2, 206–210, 212–3, 217, 219, 224, 227, 228–9, 239, 751
Eugene IV 84
Eugenius I 564
Eugenius II 578
Eugenius III 610–1, 617, 622, 623
Eugenius IV 589, 635, 648, 649, 654, 656
Eulalius [antipope] 546
Eusebius, pope 533
Eutychian 532, 533
Evangelists, the 140–1, 751
Evaristus 524
Exarchate of Ravenna 569, 570, 571
extreme unction 227

F

Faber, Peter 517
Fabian 49, 528–9
Faith see St Foy
faith, the mystery of 126–47
Farina, Giovanni Antonio 510
Fascism 21, 112–3
fasting 250–1
Fatima 144–5
feast days 232–3, 244–5, 276–7, 751
Felix I 532, 533
Felix II [antipope] 538, 539
Felix III 550, 558, 588
Felix IV 551
Felix V [antipope] 527, 635, 648, 653, 654
Ferdinand I, Emperor 98
Ferdinand II of Spain 9, 69, 659, 661, 662
Ferdinand III 288, 289, 342, 343
Filioque 577, 588, 631
First World War 729, 731, 732
Fisher, John 425
Fisherman's Ring 629, 747
Formosus 581, 582
Fourteen Holy Helpers 277, 406–7
France 8, 49, 50, 54, 86, 99, 110, 134, 178, 179, 181, 193, 227
French Revolution 21, 108
papacy in 70–1
Francis 10, 15, 16, 18, 19, 530, 565, 582, 589, 673, 672, 721, 728, 729,

747, 748–9
Francis de Sales 673, 683
Francis I, Emperor 110
Franciscans 617, 621, 624, 625, 642, 668, 677, 721
Franciscans 80, 103, 178, 184, 190, 197, 256
Franciscan revolution 74–5
    Secular Franciscans 199
Franco-Prussian War 725
Franks 513, 552, 555, 557, 570–3, 575, 576
Frederick I Barbarossa, Emperor 595, 611, 612, 613, 614, 615
Frederick II, Emperor 59, 619, 620, 621, 622, 623, 624, 626, 628, 629
Frederick III, Emperor 653, 654, 657
Freemasons 717, 719, 727
French Revolution 553, 714, 715
friars 190–1
    Black Friars 190–1
    Friars Minor 74, 190, 256
    Grey Friars 190
    White Friars 191
funeral services 228–9

G

Gabriel, Archangel 237, 245, 289, 295, 296, 298, 303, 342
Gaiseric 548–9
Gaius 52
Galgani, Gemma 481
Galileo Galilei 21, 89, 174–5, 677, 690–1
Gall 288, 389
Gallienus, Emperor 532
Garampi, Giuseppe 287
Garibaldi, Giuseppe 725
Gelasius I 172, 256, 550, 551
Gelasius II 102, 602, 603, 607
Gennaro 243
Gerebernus 334
Germany 21, 63, 67, 90, 97, 112, 113
Gertrude of Nivelles 265
Giuliani, Veronica 273
Gnosticism 144–5
Gnostics 524, 27
Gonzalez, Roque 444
Good Friday 229, 235, 244, 245
Goretti, Maria 289, 336, 337, 511
gospels 37, 140–1
    Holy Gospel 211, 215, 236, 239
    Infancy Gospels 31
    John's Gospel 29, 141, 207, 253
    Luke's Gospel 28–31, 132, 141, 237, 247

INDEX

Mark's Gospel 36, 132, 140, 141, 153
Matthew's Gospel 29, 36, 74, 132, 137, 141, 153, 180, 232, 237, 247, 251, 252
Synoptic Gospels 141
Gothic churches 20, 21, 66–7, 95, 202, 203
grace, a state of 148–67
Gratian, Emperor 250, 541
Great Schism (East-West) 53, 129, 531, 588, 590, 591, 595, 648–9
Great Western (Papal) Schism 553, 635, 640, 646, 647, 668
Gregorian Reform 595, 598
Gregory I (the Great) 20, 50, 51, 76, 154, 160, 199, 246, 250, 256, 267, 277, 289, 343, 376–7, 378, 426, 427, 451, 557, 558–9, 560, 561, 588, 589, 598, 720
Gregory II 451, 558, 568, 569, 721
Gregory III 569
Gregory IV 106, 579
Gregory V 582, 853
Gregory VI [antipope] 586
Gregory VI 755, 787
Gregory VII 451, 590, 596, 598–9, 600, 605, 625
Gregory VIII [antipope] 603, 604
Gregory VIII 602, 615, 622
Gregory IX 80, 617, 622, 623, 625, 626–7, 628, 706
Gregory X 589, 630, 630–1, 632, 743
Gregory XI 20, 71, 593, 635, 640, 644, 645, 646
Gregory XII 635, 646, 647, 648
Gregory XIII 675, 684, 685, 686, 701

Above: Julius II.

Gregory XIV 686, 688
Gregory XV 97, 689, 690, 692, 694
Gregory XVI 722, 723, 724, 736
Guadalupe 144
Guiscard, Robert 596, 597, 599, 600
Guzman, Dominic 620, 625, 626, 627, 721

H

Habsburgs 690, 691
Hadrian I 538, 552, 557, 572, 573, 576
Hadrian II 580
Hadrian III 581
Hadrian IV 595, 612–13, 621
Hadrian V 632, 743
Hadrian VI 666, 667, 744
Hagia Sophia 550, 588, 591
Harding, Stephen 392, 393
heaven 158–9
hell 162–3, 166
hellfire 163
Henry I of England 602, 605
Henry II of England 611, 613, 614, 615, 618
Henry II, Emperor 289, 438, 586, 587
Henry III of England 629
Henry III, Emperor 587, 590, 591, 595, 596
Henry IV, Emperor 15, 595, 596, 598–9, 600, 602
Henry V, Emperor 602, 603, 604, 605, 606
Henry VI, Emperor 614, 615, 618, 619, 620
Henry VIII of England 21, 69, 90, 91, 98, 221, 665, 669, 671, 677
Heraclius, Emperor 560, 561, 562
heresy 78–9, 80, 89, 135, 247, 751
hermitages 188–9
Herod Agrippa I 523
Herod, King 20, 26–7
Hilarius 550
Hilary of Poitiers 356
Hippolytus of Rome [antipope] 527, 528
Holocaust 112–3
Holy days 242–3, 244–5
Holy Family, the 296–7
Holy Father, the 172–3
Holy grail 37
Holy matrimony 218–21

Holy orders 182–3, 238
Holy relics 278–9
Holy See 174, 175, 177
Holy Spirit 128, 129, 153, 214–6, 228, 230
Holy water 211, 215, 238
Holy week 252–3, 254
homosexuality 222
Honorius I 562, 563, 565, 568
Honorius II [antipope] 597
Honorius II 605, 606–7, 623
Honorius III 75, 617, 619, 624–5, 625, 626, 721
Honorius IV 633
Honorius, Emperor 544, 545, 546
Hormisdas 550, 551, 588
Houses of God 478–9
Howard, Philip 508
Hugo of Grenoble 348
Huguenots 675, 681, 685
humanism 82, 83
Hundred Years' War 642, 644, 653, 654
Huron Carol 205
Hus, Jan 21, 80, 81, 123, 647, 657, 668, 669
Hyginus 525

I

Iconoclasm 572, 588
Immaculate Conception 142, 245, 699, 711, 724, 725
incorruptibles 467–7
Index of Prohibited Books 675, 681, 684, 686, 688, 699, 709, 711, 723
India 102, 103, 185, 195, 257
indulgences 72–3, 161, 751
Innocent I 537, 544–5, 546
Innocent II 608, 609
Innocent III 20, 75, 79, 96, 167, 257, 617, 620–1, 622, 623, 624, 625, 706
Innocent IV 73, 81, 628, 629
Innocent V 632, 743
Innocent VI 641, 642, 643
Innocent VII 646, 647
Innocent VIII 81, 660, 661, 668
Innocent IX 688
Innocent X 18, 675, 694, 695, 698, 701, 705
Innocent XI 703, 704
Innocent XII 702, 703
Innocent XIII 706

756

Inquisition 80–1, 89
Investiture Controversy 595, 598, 599, 602
Ireland 53, 120–1, 144, 217, 257
Islam 20, 55, 58–9, 79, 102, 119, 122–3, 568
Israel 20, 21, 26, 119
Italy 110–11, 120, 191

J

Jacobite Rebellion 706
James Edward Stuart 706
James I of Scotland 654
James II of England 703, 706
Jansen, Cornelius 693, 694, 699, 705
Jansenism 693, 698, 799, 702, 703, 704, 705, 706
Jerusalem 20, 31, 41, 59, 64, 65, 72, 118, 202, 229, 241
Jesuits (Society of Jesus) 18, 92–3, 103–5, 185, 203, 256, 673, 676, 677, 679, 682, 684, 685, 690, 701, 705, 709, 710, 711, 714, 715, 719, 720, 721
Jesus 244, 245, 296
   birth of 28–9, 246–7
   death of 21, 34–5, 151, 224, 234, 235, 252–3
   the Jesus Prayer 240
   ministry of 32–3
   Resurrection 35, 36–7, 151, 209, 210, 229, 254–5
   temptation of 31, 250
   see also Christ
Jewish Temple (Jerusalem) 26, 27, 30, 202
Jews 28, 81, 82, 112–3, 118, 119, 230, 681, 724, 735, 736, 737, 739, 741
Joan I of Naples 641, 643, 644
Joan of Arc 642, 653, 732
John [antipope] 759
John I 551, 551
John II 551
John III 555
John IV 563
John V 566
John V, Emperor 589
John VI 567
John VII 567
John VIII 580–1
John VIII, Emperor 589
John IX 581, 852
John X 582

John XI 575, 582
John XII 582, 583
John XIII 575
John XIV 583
John XV 583
John XVI [antipope] 583
John XVII 586
John XVIII 586
John XIX 575, 587
John XXI 632, 633, 743
John XXII 637, 638, 639, 641, 642, 647
John XXIII [antipope] 635, 646, 647
John XXIII 19, 21, 114, 118, 198, 570, 673, 686, 729, 738–9, 740, 742
John of England, King 621
John Paul I 173, 565, 587, 729, 741, 742–3
John Paul II (John Paul the Great) 18, 19, 21, 81, 113, 115, 117, 118–9, 137, 142, 144, 147, 151, 153, 163, 173, 177, 181, 193, 195, 196, 198, 204, 205, 210, 223, 229–31, 234–6, 499, 565, 573, 667, 673, 720, 721, 729, 737, 741, 743, 744–5, 746, 750
John, Esther 281
Judaism 30, 39, 139, 254
Judas Iscariot 34, 35, 132, 235, 249, 252, 253, 310, 311, 316, 317, 371
Judgement Day 151, 156–8, 163, 751
Julius I 538, 539
Julius II 84, 86, 87, 90, 96, 553, 593, 659, 660, 662, 663, 664, 665, 668, 670, 671, 683, 686
Julius III 675, 678, 679, 680, 683
July Revolution 722
Justin I, Emperor 551
Justinian I, Emperor 177, 550, 551, 554, 555, 563
Justinian II, Emperor 566–7
Justus, Bishop of Rochester 559, 561

K

Kalinowski, Raphael 482
Kasper, Maria Katharina 511
Kemble, John 509
Kenelm, Prince 336
Khwarazmian Turks 623, 629
King, Dr Martin Luther, Jr 281
Kingdom of Italy 552, 553, 713, 716, 724, 725, 726, 734

Knights Hospitaller of St John 348, 349, 603, 619, 636, 637, 661
Knights Templar, Order of the 70, 348, 607, 611, 619, 625, 636, 637
Kolbe, Maximilian 277, 281, 343, 489
Kostka, Stanislaus 431, 507
Kowalska, Maria Faustina 488
Krak des Chevaliers 59

L

La Salle, John-Baptist de 276, 343, 454
Labouré, Catherine 467, 469
Labre, Benedict Joseph 289, 461
Lando 582
Lang Fu, Paolo 336, 337
Las Casas, Bartolomé de 104
last rites 226, 227
Last Supper, The 67, 132–3, 141, 206, 210, 234, 245, 254, 275, 525, 533, 607
Lateran Council [synod] 562, 563
Lateran Council, First 605
Lateran Council, Fourth 617, 620
Lateran Council, Second 609
Lateran Council, Third 614
Lateran Palace 534, 563, 612, 685, 687, 703
Lateran Synod 596–7
Lateran Treaty 18, 21, 110, 111, 174, 553, 729, 734
Latin America 21, 114–5, 117, 122, 197, 217
Lavigerie, Archbishop Charles 107
Lawrence [antipope] 550
lay groups 198–9
laying on of hands 183
Laziosi, Peregrine 506
League of Cognac 170
Ledochowska, Maria Teresa 287
Lefebvre, Archbishop Marcel 113
Lent 209, 224, 234, 248, 250–1
Leo I (the Great) 20, 49, 277, 366, 450, 513, 537, 548, 549, 552, 558
Leo II 562, 566, 567
Leo III 204, 531, 568, 572, 575, 576, 577
Leo IV 580–1
Leo V 580, 581, 582
Leo V, Emperor 572
Leo VI 582
Leo VII 582
Leo VIII 583

INDEX

Leo IX 451, 513, 535, 575, 587, 589, 590–1, 595, 596, 597, 598
Leo X 48, 85, 91, 161, 548, 651, 660, 666–7, 668, 669, 670, 671, 677, 680
Leo XI 688, 689
Leo XII 718, 719, 722, 724, 726, 738
Leo XIII 21, 111, 116, 186, 573, 713, 726–7, 733
Leonard of Noblac 288, 289, 343
Leonine Wall 80, 653
Leopold II of Belgium, King 107
Leopold III 388, 504
Lepanto, Battle of 21, 59
Liber Pontificalis 524
Liberius 538, 539, 541, 547
Licinius, Emperor 534, 535
limbo 166–7, 751
Lincoln Cathedral 202, 203
Linus 524
Litany of the Saints 182, 183
Little Sisters of the Poor 194–5, 257
liturgy
    of the Eucharist 212–3, 219
    of the Hours 187–8
    liturgical year 241
    of the requiem Mass 228
    Tridentine 115, 229
    of the Word 210–1
Liverpool Metropolitan Cathedral 115, 203, 205
Lollards 79, 645
Lombard League 614
Lombards 552, 555, 557, 569, 570, 571, 572, 573, 577, 612
Lord's Prayer 237
Loreto, Basilica 278
Lothair I 553, 578, 579, 580
Lothair II 608, 609
Louis II, Emperor 580
Louis IV, Emperor 638
Louis IX of France 289, 342, 343, 439, 622, 628, 629
Louis Philippe I of France 722, 722, 723
Louis the Pious 553, 578, 579
Louis VII of France 609, 610, 611, 614
Louis VIII of France 625
Louis XII of France 663, 664, 665, 666
Louis XIV of France 699, 702, 703, 704, 706

Lourdes 144, 209, 237
Loyola, Ignatius 682, 686, 688, 689, 715
Lucius I 529
Lucius II 608, 609, 610
Lucius III 78, 614
Luther, Martin 21, 69, 90, 95, 136, 139, 140, 141, 275, 280, 427, 645, 651, 666, 668–9
Luwum, Janani 281
Lwanga, Charles 282, 475

M

Machiavelli, Niccolo 649, 671
Magnus Maximus, Emperor 542
Magus, Simon 135
Majella, Gerard 200
Mandic, Leopold 511
Marcellinus 43, 532, 533
Marcellus I 533
Marcellus II 587, 680
Marcian, Emperor 549
Marcionism 525, 526, 527
Marcus Aurelius, Emperor 527, 657, 677
Margaret, Queen of Scotland, 439
Marillac, Louise de 343, 449
Marinus I 581
Marinus II 582
Mark 537, 538
marriage 218–21
    annulment of 221
    married clergy 119, 181
    mixed marriage 219
    same-sex marriage 119
Martin I 562, 563, 564
Martin IV 632, 633
Martin V 71, 635, 646, 647, 648
martyrs 280–1
    20th-century martyrs 281
    child martyrs 336
    of Natal 283
    of Otranto 15, 422–3
    of Tlaxcala 283
    of Uganda 474, 475
Mary Anne of Jesus 273
Mary I of England 679
Mary II of England 703, 706
Mary of the Divine Heart, Blessed 286
Mary, the Blessed Virgin 13, 28–31, 51, 142–3, 166, 188, 212, 219, 235, 236–7, 244–6, 296–7, 274, 277, 284, 285, 288, 289, 298–9, 300–3, 309, 315, 322, 324, 361, 388, 389, 406, 426, 427, 430, 467, 485, 486–7
    Marian apparitions 144–5
    virginity of 142–3
Masemola, Manche 281
Massacre of St Bartholomew's Day 684, 685
Maundy Thursday 244, 253
Maurus 60
Maxentius, Emperor 533, 534
Maximinus Thrax, Emperor 528
Maximus 288, 352
Meister Eckhart 639
Meletian Schism 542
Mellitus, Bishop of London 559, 560, 561
mendicants 74–5, 80, 190–1
Mexico 104, 105, 144
Michael III, Emperor 580, 588
Michael VIII, Emperor 589, 633
Michael, archangel 14, 72, 157, 164, 245, 277, 294, 295, 343, 388, 417, 418
Michelangelo 593, 650, 659, 664, 665, 666, 670, 671, 676, 679, 681, 686
Middle Ages 54–67
Miki, Paul 282
Miltiades 534
miracles 32, 38–9, 63, 133, 141, 272–3
missionaries 196–7
    in Africa 101, 106–7, 186–7
    in the Americas 101, 104–5, 106, 196–7
    in Asia 101, 103
    in the East 102–13
    in India 185
Maryknoll 197
Missionaries of Charity 194–5, 231, 257
Missionaries of La Salette 197
Missionaries of the Poor 196
Missionaries of the Sacred Heart 196
Mkasa, Joseph 474, 475
Modeste Andlauer 431
Molas y Vallve, Mary Rose 510
monasteries 60–1
    Dissolution of 98–9
Mongols 629, 637
Monophysiticism 549, 550, 551, 554, 562

758

INDEX

Monothelitism 562, 563, 564, 565, 566
Montanism 526, 527
Montfort, Louis Grignion de 453
Moors 597, 661
More, Thomas 276, 342, 343, 425
Moscati, Giuseppe 485
Mother Teresa see St Teresa of Calcutta
Mount Carmel 525
Muhammad 568
music, church 76–7
 requiem Masses 229
Mysteries
 Glorious 236, 237
 Joyful 236, 237
 Luminous 236
 Sorrowful 236

N

Napoleon Bonaparte 553, 712, 713, 714, 716, 717, 722
Napoleon I, Emperor 109
Napoleon III, Emperor 111
Nativity, the 129, 246–7
Nazis 21, 112–3, 735, 736, 737, 744, 746
Neri, Philip 276, 289, 437, 683, 685, 686, 688, 689
Nero, Emperor 42, 43, 515, 523
Nestorius, Archbishop 53
Neumann, John 510
New World 88, 104–5, 106
Newman, John Henry 477
Nicene Creed 532, 534, 539
Nicetas of Remesiana 389, 427
Nicholas [antipope] 638
Nicholas I (the Great) 558, 580, 588
Nicholas II 596, 598
Nicholas III 632, 633
Nicholas IV 70, 633, 721
Nicholas V 175, 651, 652, 653, 654
Nonnatus, Raymond 288, 343, 505
Normans 587, 589, 591, 595, 596, 599, 600, 601, 605
North America 105, 106
Novatian [antipope] 528

O

O'Toole, Laurence 397
Odoacer 550, 551
Opus Dei 198–9
orders, religious see religious orders
ordination 179, 182–3
Origen 523, 528, 543
Oriol, Joseph 509
Orthodoxy 20, 52, 53, 71, 113, 118, 119, 134, 143
Ostrogoths 551, 554
Otranto, Martyrs of 422–3
Otto I of Germany 582, 583, 586, 605
Otto II of Germany 583, 584
Otto III of Germany 583, 584, 585
Ottoman Turks 643, 648, 653, 654, 657, 667, 702
Our Lady of Czestochowa 273, 285
Our Lady of Guadalupe 295, 288
Our Lady of Walsingham 274
Outremer 595, 610–11, 617, 622

P

Palais des Papes 635, 639, 640, 641, 642–3
Palamas, Gregory 268, 269
Palatine Chapel 204
Palladius 546, 547
Pallotti, Vincent 510
Palm Sunday 244, 252
Pantheon (Santa Maria della Rotunda) 560, 564, 612, 657
Papczynski, Stanislaus 509
Paschal [antipope] 566
Paschal I 578, 579
Paschal II 581, 602
Passover 235, 254
Patrimony of St Peter 552
patron saints 288–9
 of animals 398–9
 of nations 388–9
 of Professions 342–3
Paul I 571
Paul II 84, 248, 249, 538, 593, 651, 656, 657, 659
Paul III 18, 257, 673, 675, 676, 677, 680, 682, 691, 721
Paul IV 675, 680, 686
Paul V 96, 689, 690, 691, 698, 701, 710
Paul VI 19, 115, 140, 172, 177, 181, 496, 523, 565, 567, 589, 680, 720, 721, 729, 738, 739, 740–1, 742, 743, 744, 746
Pazzi, Mary Magdalene de' 273, 508
Peace of Clement IX 702
Peace of Venice 614

Peace of Westphalia 694, 698
Peasants' Revolt 645
Peckham, Archbishop John 155
Pelagianism 547
Pelagius (monk) 131, 544, 545, 546
Pelagius I 554
Pelagius II 537, 554, 555, 558
penance and reconciliation 224–5
penitence 210
penitential meditations 234–5
Pentecost 37, 38, 134, 209, 216, 233, 241, 245
Pentecostalism 21, 122
Pepin I, King 20, 96
Pepin III, the Short 552, 553, 557, 568, 569, 570, 571, 577
persecution 20
 Great Persecution 20, 42–3
 of Jews 112–3, 118, 119
Peter of Alcantara 388, 434, 435, 455
Pharamond 570
Philip [antipope] 571
Philip I of France 598, 602, 622
Philip II of France 615, 621
Philip II of Spain 99, 165, 686, 688
Philip IV of France 633, 635, 636, 637, 640
Philip V of France 638, 642
Philip VI of France 642, 643
Phocas, Emperor 560–1
pilgrimage 62, 63, 64–5, 72, 237
Pisa Cathedral 602
Pius I 525
Pius II 653, 654–5, 662, 663
Pius III 662, 663
Pius IV 675, 681, 682, 683, 684

Below: Urban II.

759

INDEX

Above: A demon tempts a woman on the exterior of Chartres Cathedral, France.

Pius V 433, 451, 622, 675, 680, 681, 683, 686, 730, 731
Pius VI 553, 573, 713, 714, 715, 716, 718
Pius VII 108, 114, 553, 712, 713, 716–7, 718, 719, 722, 724
Pius VIII 611, 722, 723
Pius IX 21, 110, 111, 199, 233, 234, 243, 533, 553, 573, 713, 719, 724–5, 736, 740, 744
Pius X 219, 451, 458, 681, 729, 730–1, 736
Pius XI 21, 112, 113, 523, 553, 733, 734–5
Pius XII 112–3, 118, 143, 198, 233, 729, 730, 733, 734, 736–7, 738, 744
Pius of Pietrelcina *see* Padre Pio
Platina, Bartolomeo 656, 657, 659
Plunket, Oliver 509
Pontian 528
Pontius Pilate 530
Poor Clares 75, 184, 193, 194, 256
Pope Joan 580, 581
popes 56, 172–3, 176, 512–749
    in Avignon 70–1
    election of 172, 173
    first popes 48–9
    papal infallibility 21, 111, 172–3
    powerful popes 84–5
    rival popes 70–1
    saintly popes 450–1
Poussin, Nicolas 524, 702
prayer 230–1
    Eucharistic Prayer 214–5
Preca, Father George 493

Prester John, King 102
priests 176–7, 178–9, 180–2, 207, 208–9, 211, 224–19, 238
undercover priests (during Reformation) 99
Primaldo, Antonio 422
Protestant Reformation 593, 645, 651, 662, 666, 668, 669, 670, 671, 673, 675, 700
Protestantism 90–1, 94, 95, 97–9, 122, 138, 139, 181, 203
Purgatory 72, 73, 160–1, 751

Q

Queen Christina of Sweden 698, 699, 702, 704
Quinisext Council 566–7
Quirinal Palace 685, 689, 717, 718, 723

R

Raphael 521, 537, 548, 574, 576, 580, 593, 651, 664, 665, 666, 687
Raphael, Archangel 245, 288, 289, 294, 295
Ratzinger, Cardinal Joseph 139, 145, 167
Reccared I, King 554–5
Reconquista 623, 660, 661
redemption 150–1, 751
Reformation 21, 69, 76, 78, 80, 81, 83, 90–99, 136, 138, 139, 150, 751
Counter-Reformation 92–3, 94–5, 97, 103, 203, 750
    in England 98–9
    political consequences of 98–9
Regis, John Francis 289, 343, 508
relics, sacred 62–3, 206
religious orders 61, 184–5, 186–95, 256–7, 348–9
    see also by name of order
Renaissance 68–9, 651, 653, 658, 659, 662, 676, 677, 710, 715
Resurrection 35, 36–7, 151, 209, 210, 229, 254–5, 751
revelations, private 144–5
Ricci, Catherine de' 273, 508
Richard I of England 615, 618, 619
Risorgimento 553, 719
Roger II of Sicily 607, 608, 613, 614, 618, 623
Roman Academy 656, 659
Roman Inquisition 675, 677, 680,

681, 682, 688, 690, 691
Romano, Vincenzo 510
Romanus 581
Rome 21, 44–5, 46–7, 51, 52, 174–5
    Bishop of 172
    catacombs of 44–5
Roman Inquisition 89
Romero, Archbishop Oscar 116, 117, 281, 511
Romulus Augustulus, Emperor 550
Roncini, Amato 505
rosary, the 246–7
Rossi, John Baptist 509
royal saints 438–9
Rubens, Peter Paul 606
Ruiz, Lorenzo 445
rules (of religious orders) 60, 61, 184, 186, 189, 199
Russian Revolution 733

S

Sabinian 560, 561
Sack of Rome 544, 545, 670, 671
sacraments, living the 200–239, 751
Sacred Heart Cathedral (Bendigo) 233
Sacred Heart of Jesus 232–3, 245
Saint-Etienne-du-Mont (Paris) 203
saints 146–7, 258–511
    Alacoque, Marguerite Marie 233, 273, 509
    Avellino, Andrew 289, 389, 508
    Bakhita, Josephine 282, 389, 491
    Barat, Madeleine Sophie 276, 467, 470
    Barbarigo, Gregorio 509
    Barbieri, Clelia 472
    Bays, Marguerite 510
    Bede, The Venerable 276, 338, 369, 379, 502
    Bellarmine, Robert 343, 442
    Berchmans, John 488
    Bertoni, Gaspar 469
    Bertrand, Louis 388, 436
    Bobola, Andrew 509
    Borromeo, Charles 342, 284
    Boscardin, Bertilla 485
    Bourgeoys, Marguerite 452
    Briant, Alexander 508
    Cabrini, Frances 289, 483
    Cafasso, Joseph 476, 510
    Calabria, John 491

INDEX

Calasanz, Joseph 509
Campion, Edmund 508
Canisius, Peter 136–7, 437
Celtic saints 368–9
Chanel, Peter 388, 510
Chantal, Jane Frances de 443, 508
child saints 336–7
Claret, Antony 472
Claver, Peter 287, 289, 388, 446
Clitherow, Margaret 508
Colombière, Claude de la 509
Communion of Saints 161
Cordero, Miguel 482
Cottolengo, Joseph 465
Delanoue, Jeanne 456
Diego, Juan 275, 285, 507
Dierks, Marie Adolphine 475
Drexel, Katharine 276, 492
early saints 264–5
Eastern saints 268–9
Edward the Confessor 277, 289, 386, 438, 466
Edward the Martyr 384, 439
Eric of Sweden 389, 394, 439
Escrivá, Josemaría 198, 199, 495
Faber, Peter 517
Farina, Giovanni Antonio 510
feast days 276–7
Gabriel, Archangel 237, 245, 289, 295, 296, 298, 303, 342
Goretti, Maria 289, 336, 337, 511
Harding, Stephen 392, 393
in art 426–7
incorruptibles 466–7
Kalinowski, Raphael 482
Kasper, Maria Katharina 511
Kemble, John 509
Kolbe, Maximilian 277, 281, 343, 489
Kostka, Stanislaus 431, 507
Kowalska, Maria Faustina 488
La Salle, John-Baptist de 276, 343, 454
Labouré, Catherine 467, 469
Laziosi, Peregrine 506
Leo I (the Great) 20, 49, 277, 366, 450
Leopold III 388, 504
Lwanga, Charles 282, 475
Majella, Gerard 200
Mandic, Leopold 511
Mary, the Blessed Virgin 13, 28–31, 51, 142–3, 166, 188, 212, 219, 235, 236–7, 244–6, 296–7, 274, 277, 284, 285, 288, 289, 298–9, 300–3, 309, 315, 322, 324, 361, 388, 389, 406, 426, 427, 430, 467, 485, 486–7
Michael, archangel 14, 72, 157, 164, 245, 277, 294, 295, 343, 388, 417, 418
Mkasa, Joseph 474, 475
Molas y Vallve, Mary Rose 510
Montfort, Louis Grignion de 453
Moscati, Giuseppe 485
Neri, Philip 276, 289, 437
Neumann, John 510
Newman, John Henry 477
Nonnatus, Raymond 288, 343, 505
O'Toole, Laurence 397
Oriol, Joseph 509
Pallotti, Vincent 510
Papczynski, Stanislaus 509
patron saints 288–9
patron saints of nations 388–9
patron saints of professions 342–3
Pazzi, Mary Magdalene de' 273, 508
Pius V 433, 451
Plunket, Oliver 509
Preca, Father George 493
Raphael, Archangel 245, 288, 289, 294, 295
Regis, John Francis 289, 343, 508
Ricci, Catherine de' 273, 508
Romano, Vincenzo 510
Romero, Archbishop Oscar 116, 117, 281, 511
Roncini, Amato 505
Rossi, John Baptist 509
royal saints 438–9
Ruiz, Lorenzo 445
Serrano, Francis 456
Seton, Elizabeth 276, 284, 463
Solano, Francis 388, 389, 440
Stein, Edith 277, 490
Strambi, Vincent 509
Stylites, Simeon 367
Thresia, Mariam 511
Tomasi, Joseph 509
Vaz, Joseph 509
Vénard, Theophane 510
Vianney, Jean-Baptiste 277, 343, 467, 468, 473
Vigri of Bologna, Catherine de' 507
warrior saints 416–17
Youville, Margaret d', 459
See also individual saint names
saintly popes 450–1
saints' days 209, 241–5
saints in art 426–7
Saladin 615, 622, 624
Sanfedisti 719
Santiago de Compostela 63–5
Saracens 580, 581, 582, 586, 591, 601
Saul 20, 40–1
Saul see Paul
Savio, Dominic 288, 336, 337
Saxons 557, 552, 577
Scholastica 373
Scriptural Way of the Cross 235
Scriptures, the 138–9
Second Temple, Jerusalem 524
Second Vatican Council 531
Second World War 729, 734, 736–7
Seljuk Turks 601, 615, 622
Séntanque Abbey (France) 61
Septimius Severus, Emperor 527, 657
Sergius I 566
Sergius II 578, 579, 580
Sergius III 575, 582
Sergius IV 575, 586
Sermon on the Mount 32
Serrano, Francis 456
Seton, Elizabeth 276, 284, 463
Severinus 562, 563
Sforza, Francesco 649
shrines, holy 62–3
Shrove Tuesday 241, 244, 248
sick, annointing the 236–7
Siege of Orléans 642, 653
sign of the Cross 238, 239
Silverius 551, 554
Simeon 30
Simon of Cyrene 235
Simon Peter see Peter
Simony 574, 578, 579, 584, 586, 590
Simplicius 550
sin 152–3, 166–7, 225
    mortal sins 153, 224, 751
    original sin 131, 142, 150, 166, 751
    purging of sins 160–1
    seven deadly sins 149, 154–5
    sins of the 21st century 155
    venial sins 152, 224, 751
Siricius 542, 543, 545, 552
Sisinnius 567, 587

INDEX

Sistine Chapel 18, 650, 651, 658, 659, 664, 665, 671, 677, 710, 718, 726, 743, 747
Sistine Chapel 69, 85, 86–7, 173, 174
Sithney 399
Sixtus I 513, 524, 25
Sixtus II 450, 532
Sixtus III 546, 547
Sixtus IV 84, 86, 593, 651, 657, 658, 658–9, 660, 663, 665, 670
Sixtus V 249, 623, 675, 683, 686–7
Society of Apostolic Life 185
Society of Jesus 21, 92, 93, 105, 185, 203
Society of our Lady 165
Solano, Francis 388, 389, 440
Soter 526
South America 104–5, 106–7, 122
Spain 65, 81, 98, 111, 113, 120
Spanish Armada 99
Spanish Inquisition 21, 81
Spanish Civil War 734
Spanish Inquisition 658, 673
St Abbo of Fleury 504
St Adalbert of Prague 504
St Agatha 276, 341–3, 355
St Agnes 264, 265, 336, 337, 399
St Agnes of Bohemia 412
St Aidan 368, 390
St Alban 387, 500
St Alberic 504
St Albert the Great 279, 343, 405, 410, 411
St Alexander Nevski 277, 408, 417, 438
St Alexis Falconieri 506
St Aloysius Gonzaga 289, 431, 508
St Alphonsus Liguori 458, 462
St Amand 342, 343, 502
St Ambrose 50–2, 131, 266, 267, 277, 342, 354, 399
St Anastasia 332
St Andrew 277, 310, 316, 319, 342, 389
St Andrew of Crete 503
St Angela Merici 428
St Angela of Foligno 273, 506
St Anne 147, 277, 289, 301, 302, 342, 343, 388
St Anselm 276, 391
St Anskar 388, 503
St Anthony 143, 249
St Antoninus of Florence 507

St Antônio de Sant'Anna Galvâo 464
St Antony of Egypt 267, 276, 289, 342, 348, 350, 399
St Antony of Padua 276, 289, 388, 389, 399, 402
St Apollinare 12
St Apollonia 288, 289, 342, 500
St Asaph Cathedral (Wales) 207
St Athanasius the Aconite 127, 134, 276, 277, 347
St Augustine of Canterbury 558, 558, 721
St Augustine of Hippo 20, 46, 50–3, 78, 127, 130, 131, 153, 158–60, 167, 184, 191, 266, 267, 277, 278, 304, 324, 342, 343, 356, 363, 391, 392, 533, 542, 544, 545, 553, 693, 705
St Babylas 500
St Barbara 271, 342, 343, 352, 389, 407
St Barnabas 316, 318, 320, 388
St Bartholomew 313, 314, 342, 343, 388
St Bartholomew of Farne 505
St Bartholomew of the Martyrs 508
St Bartholomew's Day Massacre 98
St Basil the Great 269, 276, 301, 347, 351, 353
St Benedict 20, 60, 184, 186, 256, 276, 342, 347, 348, 378–9, 382, 383, 450
St Benno of Munich 390
St Bernadette of Lourdes 144, 145, 237, 276, 284, 289, 467, 473
St Bernard of Aosta 289, 399
St Bernard of Clairvaux 61, 251, 257, 342, 388, 392, 393, 396, 398, 399, 607, 608, 609, 610, 611
St Bernard of Montjoux 276, 288, 504
St Bernardino of Feltre 287, 342
St Bernardino of Siena 342, 507
St Beuno 399
St Blaise 289, 342, 343, 359, 399, 407
St Bonaventure 409
St Boniface 276, 342, 343, 381, 388
St Braulio of Saragossa 502
St Brendan the Navigator 289, 368, 371
St Bridget of Sweden 276, 389, 415
St Brigid of Ireland 271, 276, 343, 370, 388, 399

St Bruno 188, 256, 504
St Cajetan 428
St Callistus I 44, 450, 500
St Camillus of Lellis 289, 343, 416, 417, 508
St Canute 387, 388, 439
St Casimir of Poland 388, 389, 424
St Cassian (John Cassian) 348, 501
St Catherine of Alexandria 43, 264, 288, 342, 343, 364, 418, 426
St Catherine of Aragon 407, 425
St Catherine of Genoa 273, 507
St Catherine of Siena 269, 273, 276, 342, 343, 388, 414, 441, 492, 644, 645
St Catherine of Sweden 506
St Cecilia 277, 289, 332, 343, 466
St Celestine V 70, 449, 451, 505
St Christopher 268, 271, 276, 277, 335, 342, 406, 407
St Clare of Assisi 75, 194, 277, 289, 348, 404
St Clare of Montefalco 273
St Clotilde 501
St Colette 273, 507
St Columban 560
St Corentin 500
St Cosmas and Damian 288, 328, 342, 343, 383
St Cuthbert 276, 277, 368, 369, 379, 399
St Cyril 276, 382, 388, 389
St Cyril of Jerusalem 352
St Daniel the Stylite 501
St David of Wales 276, 374, 389, 502
St Denys of Paris 272, 277, 330, 388, 407, 532
St Dismas 288, 306, 342
St Dominic 75, 81, 197, 199, 247, 256, 277, 342, 343, 349, 388, 397, 405
St Dominic of Silos 504
St Dorothy 288, 340, 342, 343
St Dulce of the Poor 498
St Dympna 288, 289, 334
St Ebbe 502
St Elizabeth (wife of Zachary) 303, 324
St Elizabeth of Hungary 277, 342, 403, 439
St Elizabeth of Portugal 413, 439
St Elizabeth of the Trinity 280, 511
St Eloi 289, 343, 502

INDEX

St Erasmus 264, 288, 289, 407, 500
St Eric of Sweden 389, 394, 439
St Eulalia of Mérida 277, 336, 338
St Eustace 288, 325, 343, 398, 399, 407
St Felicitas 329
St Fiacre 342, 502
St Finbar 502
St Florence of Mont Glonne 275
St Florian 501
St Foy 285, 336, 343
St Fra Angelico 421, 653
St Frances of Rome 273, 342, 507
St Francis de Girolamo 509
St Francis of Assisi 12, 20, 74–5, 78, 184, 194, 256, 271, 273, 277, 282, 285, 342, 348, 388, 392, 399, 400–1, 402, 404, 409, 414, 442, 457, 620–1, 624, 625, 627, 652, 668, 672, 748
St Francis of Sales 93, 342, 343, 443, 448, 476
St Francis Xavier 21, 102, 103, 277, 282, 289, 388, 389, 431, 432, 689
St Frideswide 503
St Genesius of Arles 342, 343
St Genevieve 276, 289, 367
St George 268, 271, 276, 289, 333, 343, 388, 407, 416, 417
St Gertrude 273
St Gilbert of Sempringham 505
St Giles 288, 289, 403, 407, 503
St Godric 505
St Gregory of Nazianzus 269, 276, 353
St Gregory of Nyssa 161, 276, 301
St Gregory of Sinai 269
St Hedwig 506
St Helen 274, 276, 342, 346
St Henry of Finland 388, 394
St Hildegard of Bingen 18, 277, 380, 396, 414, 427
St Hippolytus 250, 289, 399, 500
St Homobonus 343, 505
St Honoratus of Arles 501
St Hubert 289, 343, 399, 503
St Hyacinth of Cracow 405
St Ignatius of Loyola 21, 92–3, 95, 185, 257, 277, 289, 349, 430–1, 432, 444
St Irenaeus of Lyons 326, 328
St Irene 265, 336
St Isidore of Seville 276, 291, 373, 378

St Isidore the Farmer 273, 342, 343
St Ives 504
St Ivo of Brittany 288, 289, 343
St James the Great 63, 276, 285, 289, 298, 301, 310, 312, 322, 343, 388, 389, 412, 416, 426
St James the Less 312, 313, 389
St Januarius 243, 264, 272, 273, 466
St Jerome 20, 50, 51, 127, 266, 267, 303, 342, 343, 345, 347, 356, 360–1, 399, 426, 524, 537, 540, 541, 542, 543, 544
St Jerome Emiliani 276, 288, 289, 507
St Joachim 298, 301, 302
St Joan of Arc 265, 272, 276, 388, 418–19
St John 29, 140–1, 172, 207, 216, 235, 253, 268, 276, 277, 284, 289, 309, 310, 312, 322, 326, 342, 373, 379, 386, 388, 389, 488
St John Bosco 191
St John Chrysostom 269, 277, 290, 333, 345, 353, 357, 362, 389
St John Damascene 503
St John of Beverley 503
St John of Capistrano 507
St John of God 273, 288, 289, 343, 417, 429
St John of Nepomuk 389, 415
St John of Sahagun 507
St John of the Cross 277, 343, 430, 435, 436, 455, 490, 673, 683, 703
St John the Almsgiver 276, 375
St John the Baptist 31, 214, 267, 273, 276, 295, 303, 304–5, 313, 319, 323, 325, 161, 399
St Josaphat 389, 508
St Joseph 219, 244, 246, 276, 284, 289, 296–7, 498, 300, 342, 388, 389
St Joseph of Anchieta 508
St Joseph of Arimathea 36, 37, 235, 254, 276, 307, 342
St Joseph of Copertino 288, 289, 342, 447, 473
St Jude 277, 289, 314, 318
St Julian the Hospitaller 342, 343, 500
St Justin 276, 343
St Justus of Beauvais 336, 339
St Kentigern 502
St Kilian 566

Above: Noli me Tangere *by the Master of the Lehman Crucifixion, 1370–5.*

St Lambert 502
St Laurence 342, 343, 500
St Lawrence of Rome 342, 343, 513, 532
St Lazarus of Bethany 309
St Leander 375, 378
St Leonard of Port Maurice 457
St Lidwina 273
St Lioba 503
St Louis of Toulouse 506
St Lucian of Antioch 345
St Lucy 264, 277, 341, 342, 343, 426
St Lucy of Narnia 273
St Ludmilla 383, 504
St Ludovico of Casoria 510
St Luke 277, 285, 295, 300, 306, 324, 342, 343, 427
St Luke 28–31, 132, 140–1, 237, 247
St Lutgardis 273, 505
St Magdalena of Canossa 465
St Magnus of Norway 388
St Malachy 277, 504
St Marcoul 502
St Margaret of Antioch 288, 289, 407, 418, 419, 426
St Margaret of Città de Castello 506
St Margaret of Cortona 273, 289, 506
St Margaret of Scotland 389, 390
St Mariam of Jesus Crucified 510

763

St Marie de l'Incarnation 273, 509
St Mark 31, 36, 62, 132, 140–1, 153, 276, 300, 323, 388
St Mark's Basilica, Venice 532
St Martha 276, 277, 289, 308, 309, 342, 343
St Martin 273, 275, 386
St Martin de Porres 289, 343, 445
St Martin of Tours 277, 289, 343, 348, 356, 405
St Mary Magdalene 33, 36, 254, 255, 276, 289, 308–9, 343, 427
St Matthew 29, 31, 36, 74, 132, 137, 140–1, 146, 153, 180, 232, 237, 247, 251, 252, 277, 310, 314, 322, 342, 343, 362, 750
St Matthias 310, 316
St Maurice 343, 389, 416
St Menas 14, 275
St Methodius 276, 382, 388, 389
St Monica 289, 363
St Moses the Black 501
St Nicholas of Flue 389, 424
St Nicholas of Myra 268, 277, 289, 342, 343, 358, 388, 389
St Nicholas of Tolentino 288, 289, 412
St Nino 501
St Norbert 392
St Odile 273, 503
St Odo of Cluny 383
St Olaf 385, 388, 438
St Osanna of Mantua 273
St Pachomius 267, 276, 347, 349
St Padre Pio 273, 277, 285, 494
St Pancras of Rome 336, 339
St Pantaleon 342, 344, 407
St Paraskeva 14, 268
St Patrick 276, 368, 370, 388

St Patrick's Cathedral (NYC) 206
St Paul 40–1, 46, 140, 142, 180, 243–5, 263, 274, 276, 290, 304, 313, 316–18, 320–1, 324, 325, 342, 343, 362, 366, 388, 460
    Paul's Epistles 41, 210
St Paul of the Cross 461
St Paula 361, 501
St Paulinus of Nola 501
St Pelagia of Antioch 336
St Pelagia the Penitent 263, 342, 357
St Perpetua 329
St Peter 13, 16, 33, 39, 42, 46, 48, 49, 65, 73, 135, 140, 172, 174, 176, 177, 204, 206, 232, 235, 243, 245, 252, 256, 274, 276, 310, 311, 316–17, 319–23, 342, 343, 355, 366, 380, 388, 460, 513, 515, 522–3, 524, 529, 530, 531, 537, 540, 541, 548, 549, 552, 558, 580, 720, 744
St Peter's Basilica 13, 21, 22–3, 47, 84, 95, 90, 97, 114, 170–2, 174, 204, 523, 530, 535, 564, 567, 573, 576, 577, 593, 605, 632, 648, 651, 664, 665, 668, 671, 675, 677, 679, 685, 686, 687, 689, 693, 697, 699, 700, 701, 743, 748
St Peter's Square 523, 580
St Petroc 502
St Petronilla 571
St Philip 307, 312, 213
St Philip of Moscow 507
St Philomena 271, 336
St Phocas of Sinope 342, 343
St Pirmin 289, 503
St Polycarp 326
St Pontian 500
St Raymund of Pennafort 505
St Rita of Cascia 273, 276, 288, 289, 420, 467
St Robert of Molesme 61, 256, 504
St Roch 282, 288, 333, 343, 380, 398, 399, 406, 413
St Rosalia of Palermo 504
St Rose of Lima 299, 342, 388, 389, 441, 445
St Rose of Viterbo 505
St Rupert 380, 388
St Sava of Serbia 276, 389, 505
St Sebastian 43, 276, 342, 343, 500
St Sergius of Radonezh 267, 269, 279, 506
St Sharbel the Maronite 511

St Simon 277, 314, 318, 342
St Stanislaus of Cracow 387, 389
St Stephen 263, 264, 277, 325
St Stephen of Hungary 277, 342, 386, 388, 417, 438, 439
St Teresa of Ávila 145, 277, 434–5, 436, 490, 673, 683, 685, 689
St Teresa of Calcutta 137, 147, 194, 195, 231, 257, 497, 743, 745
St Teresa of Jesus Jornet y Ibars 289, 511
St Teresa of Los Andes 276, 484
St Theodore of Canterbury 502
St Theodore of Sykeon 502
St Theresa of Lisieux 193, 267, 277, 342, 388, 480–1, 484
St Thomas 63, 143, 276, 277, 288, 315, 342, 343, 388, 432
St Thomas Aquinas 20, 57, 127, 149, 154, 155, 167, 276, 298, 343, 391, 405, 410–12, 467, 505, 631, 638, 727
St Thomas Becket 62, 64, 65, 274, 275, 277, 293, 395, 615, 618
St Thomas More 82, 83
St Thomas of Villanova 429
St Thorlac of Skalholt 388, 505
St Turibius of Lima 440, 441
St Ubaldo 288, 289, 505
St Ulric 384
St Urith of Chittlehampton 500
St Ursula 265, 343, 365, 428, 543
St Valentine 271, 276, 288, 331, 342
St Venantius Fortunatus 289, 502
St Veronica 62, 235, 306, 343
St Victor of Marseilles 331, 342
St Vincent de Paul 289, 388, 448–9
St Vincent Ferrer 342, 506
St Vincent Liem 460
St Vincent of Saragossa 340, 343
St Vitus 289, 334, 342, 407
St Vladimir 389, 417, 438, 439, 504
St Walburga 503
St Wenceslas 277, 342, 383, 388, 504
St William of Norwich 271, 504
St William of Rochester 505
St William of Roskilde 504
St Willibrord 388, 503
St Willigis 504
St Wolfgang of Regensburg 385
St Zachary 303, 324
St Zita 342, 343, 505
stained glass windows 479

Above: The seven pilgrim churches of Rome, seen from above in this 1575 copper engraving by Antonio Lafreri.

INDEX

Stations of the Cross 234–5
Stein, Edith 277, 490
Stephen I 529
Stephen II 535, 552, 552–3, 569, 570
Stephen III 557, 557, 570, 571, 572
Stephen IV 578, 580
Stephen V 581
Stephen VI 581, 582
Stephen VII 582
Stephen VIII 582
Stephen IX 590, 596, 598
Strambi, Vincent 509
Strozzi, Bernardo 549
Stylites, Simeon 367
Swiss Guard 165, 670, 725
Syllabus of Errors 21, 111
Sylvester I 47, 199, 515, 534, 535, 584, 589
Sylvester II 584–5
Sylvester III 587
Sylvester IV [antipope] 602
Symmachus 339, 550
Synod of Verona 614
Synod of Whitby 564

T

Tapiedi, Lucian 281
Tekakwitha, Kateri 276
Telesphorus 525
temptation (of Jesus) 31, 250
Tertullian 46, 51, 129, 143
Teutonic Knights 618, 619
Thaddeus 314
Theodore [antipope] 566
Theodore I 563
Theodore II 581, 587
Theodore of Tarsus 564, 565
Theodoric [antipope] 602
Theodoric the Great 551
Theodosius I, Emperor 51, 52, 537, 541, 542, 552
Theophilus of Alexandria 543, 545
Third Partition of Poland 723
Thirty Years' War 21, 96, 97, 689, 690, 694
Thomas Becket see St Thomas Becket
Three Chapters Controversy 554, 555, 560
Thresia, Mariam 511
Titian 677
Titus, Emperor 321, 388, 524
Tlaxcala, child martyrs of 507
Tomasi, Joseph 509

Torres, Camilo 117
Toussaint, Pierre 286, 287
Trajan, Emperor 524, 687
Trappists 189, 257
Trappistines 193
Treaty of Constance 612
Treaty of Pisa 699
Treaty of Rastatt 705
Treaty of Utrecht 705
Treaty of Verdun 579
Treaty of Vervins 688
Trebonianus Gallus, Emperor 528, 529
Trinity, the 128–9, 134, 135, 137, 149, 751
Tsar Nicholas I of Russia 723
Tyndale, William 769

U

United States 122-4, 127, 177, 185, 195, 197, 217, 243
Urban I 527
Urban II 15, 20, 58, 581, 593, 595, 600–1, 617, 622
Urban III 614, 628
Urban IV 629
Urban V 589, 640, 641, 642, 643
Urban VI 71, 635, 646
Urban VII 587, 688
Urban VIII 18, 93, 97, 106, 243, 675, 690–3, 694, 701
Ursinus [antipope] 540

V

Valentine 579
Valentinian I, Emperor 540
Valentinian III, Emperor 537, 542, 549, 552
Valerian, Emperor 529, 532
Vandals 548
Varani, Baptista 273
Vatican 47, 112, 170–1, 174–5, 750
Vatican Council, First 111, 562, 724, 725, 737, 740
Vatican Council, Second 21, 114, 115, 119, 121, 137, 162, 163, 181, 205, 210, 227, 229, 683, 686, 738, 739, 740, 740–1, 742
Vatican Library 175, 629, 651, 652, 653, 656, 659, 693, 699, 702, 705, 707, 709, 733, 734
Vaz, Joseph 509
Velázquez, Diego 694, 695

Vénard, Theophane 510
Venice 62, 96, 248
vestments 208–9
Vianney, Jean-Baptiste 277, 343, 467, 468, 473
Victor I 526–7
Victor II 595, 596
Victor III 600, 601
Victor IV [antipope] 609
Vigilius 551, 554, 555
Vigri of Bologna, Catherine de' 507
Virgin Mary see Mary, the Blessed Virgin
Visigoths 537, 544, 547, 548, 552, 554, 555, 661
Vitalian 564
Voltaire 197, 708, 709, 711
vows 184–6
of celibacy 179
of obedience 179, 183
Vulgate Bible 541

W

Waldensians 78–9
anti-Waldensian Inquisition 80
Waldo, Peter 20, 78
Wang Zhiming 281
War of the Spanish Succession 553, 697, 704
warrior saints 416–17
Western Schism 20, 71
Westminster Abbey 73
White Fathers 21, 107, 257
Wilfred 369
William of Normandy 597, 598
William of Orange 703, 706
William the Pious 61
women in the Church 192–5
Wycliffe, John 79, 645, 668, 669

X

Xavier, Francis see St Francis Xavier

Y

Youville, Margaret d', 459

Z

Zacharias 569, 570, 577
Zeno, Emperor 342, 348, 550
Zephyrinus 527
Zosimus 546, 549
Zwinglians 133

ACKNOWLEDGEMENTS

PICTURE CREDITS
The Publishers are grateful to the agencies listed below for kind permission to reproduce the following images in this book:

CATHOLICISM
akg-images 21bl, 19tl, 33br, 37b, 38tr, 45bl, 48tr, 49br, 50b, 51tr, 51bm, 52tr, 54, 56tr, 60bl, 61tl, 72br, 673bl, 74tr, 77tr, 82tr, 83l, 84tr, 87tr, 90b, 92tr, 93l, 93br, 994tr, 95tm, 100tr, 102bl, 103tr, 112tr, 128tr, 129bl, 132tr, 136tr, 136bl, 139bl, 143bl, 148, 153br, 156tr, 157bl, 159tm, 160bl, 161br, 164tr, 164bl, 165bl, 166bl, 196tr, 102tr, 103br, 214tr, 214b, 224bl, 233br, 245tl.
Alamy 94b, 99tm, 115br, 121tm, 168, 175br, 180bl, 184tr and 184br, 190t, 191b, 193tr, 193br, 194t, 195t, 196bl, 202bl, 203tm, 205br, 206bl, 207br, 208bl, 209rm, 211bl, 213bl, 218tr, 218bl, 223br, 224tr, 226bl, 228tr, 228bl, 233t, 236b, 239bl, 248tr, 253t, 253br, 255tr. **Ancient Art & Architecture** 27b. **ArkReligion.com** 179br, 182r, 182bl, 183tr, 188, 190br, 192bl, 205tl, 207bl, 211tm, 212tr, 216bl, 2017br, 246bm.
The Art Archive 2, 1, 12t, 20tm, 20tl, 21bl, 21b, 22, 24, 26br, 29b, 30tr, 32tr, 34t, 34m, 34b, 35tr, 35b, 36tr, 36b, 37t, 39t, 40bl, 41, 42tr, 42b, 43t, 43b, 45, 47t, 47b, 47br, 49b, 50tr, 52bl, 54tm, 55tm, 56bl, 57b, 57b, 59bl, 63b, 64try, 67b, 70t, 70bl, 71br, 74b, 75, 76t, 76bl, 77b, 678tr, 78bl, 80tr, 81br, 82bl, 83r, 85br, 86tr, 88tr, 88bl, 89dl, 89br, 90tr, 91tr, 91br, 92bl, 96tr, 97tr, 98tr, 101, 103bm, 104tr, 104br, 105tm, 106bl, 106bl, 109tm, 110br, 111br, 116tr, 127tr, 128b, 129tr, 130bl, 131br, 133tm, 133bl, 134tr, 134, 135tm, 1340bl, 141br, 143b, 146bl, 147br, 149tm, 150bl, 151tr, 152bl, 154bl, 158tr, 159br, 160tr, 162t, 165br, 166tr, 167b, 167br, 201tm, 204tr, 205tr, 210bl, 212bl, 216tr, 219tm, 219br, 220bl, 221tr, 221br, 223t, 227b, 230bm, 234bl, br and 235bl, br, 237tr, 237b, 238tr, 241tm, 244tr, 244bm, 246tr, 247b, 239b, 252tr, 254tr, 254bl, 256tr, 256bl, 257tr, 258bl, 258br, 269tl, 260t, 261t, 262bl.
The Bridgeman Art Library 27, 28t, 30, 31b, 32bl, 33, 39b, 41tr, 46tr, 48bl, 48t, 49tr, 62t, 64b, 65t, 65, 68, 71tr, 72t, 73tr, 79b, 79br, 80b, 80br, 81tr, 85tr, 86b, 87br, 89bm, 95br, 96b, 97br, 99tr, 99br, 100, 106tr, 107bl, b, 108tr, 109br, 113bl, 126, 130tr, 132b, 135b, 137tl, 138t, 139b, 140t, 141tr, 142tr, 144tr, 146tr, 152tr, 153t, 154tr, 155t, 156b, 157tr, 161t, 162b, 163t, 163b, 165tr, 186tr, 195br, 206t, 222tr, 225tr, 230ty, 231tr, 232b, 236t, 242t, 242b, 245mr, 247tr, 248by, 250t, 252bl, 261br, 263b **Corbis** 28bl, 29, 44b, 67tr, 84bl, 98b, 111bl, 114t, 115tl, 116b, 117tm, 1018t, 118bl, 120tr, 123br, 124, 142tr, 144bl, 145tm, 145br, 147tr, 150tr, 151br, 155br, 158b, 172b, 173tr, 174bl, 175tr, 176tr, 178tr, bl, 179bl, 180tr, 185br, 186bl, 187tr and bm, 188tr, 189br, 200, 209br, 210tr, 211b, 213tr, 215tr, 217tr, 220tr, 226tr, 229bl, 234tr, 239tm, 240, 253br, 260, 261t, 267tr, 270bl. **Getty Images** 63tl, 110tr, 114bl, 115bl, 118tr, 119tr, 120bl, 121bl, 122tr, 122bl, 123tr, 131tr, 138br, 171tm, 172tr, 173br, 176bl, 177mr, 177br, 181tr, 181bl, 183tl, 185tl, 198tr, 198bl, 199tm, 215tl, 222bl, 225tl, 231bl, 238bl, 243tr, 245tr, 251br, 255br, 259tr. **Courtesy Hayes & Finch** 208tr. **Heritage-Images** 60tr, 62br, 73br. **Kobal Collection** 189tr. **Photoshot** 259bm. **Photolibrary** 13, 170, 191t, 194bl, 204bl, 229tm, 232tr, 245bl, 249t. **Rex Features** 113br, 119br. **Robert Harding** 66tr, 174tr, 192tr, 215br, 245br. **Sonia Halliday Photographs** 38bl, 40tr, 66bl. **TopFoto** 46bl, 112tr, 137br, 197tr and br. **Courtesy Vanpoulles Ltd** 227tl.

SAINTS & SAINTHOOD
akg-images 267b, 277t, 280b, 282b, 283t, 284b, 45b, 60t, 65b, 82t and b, 85b, 86t and b, 91m, 100t, 303b, 381b, 385t, 193t and b, 401, 418bm, 424t, 425t, 437t, 438l, 439tr, 468t, 480t, 489t, 490t, 503, /Amelot 510b, /Orsi Battaglini 386b, /British Library 263b, 301t, 335l, 342r, 352t, 394t, 395b, 439b, /Cameraphoto 286b, 288t, 289, 302bl, 308l, 313t, 354t, 357, 359t, 413b, 457, /Hervé Champollion 473bl, 481t, /Gérard Degeorge 14b, /Stefan Diller 271, /Jean-Paul Dumontier 311t, 336t, 501l and r, /Electa 312r, 314b, 316b, 361tl, 361t, 508t, /Hilbich 274tr, 338t, /Andrea Jemolo 288b, 390b, /Kunstsammlung Böttcherstraße 319r, /Tristan Lafranchis 427l, /Erich Lessing 14, 264t, 280t, 298b, 299t, 309t, 311b, 313t, 317t, 320b, 326t, 328t, 330t, 334b, 336t, 353b, 426l, 435bl, 500, 502, /Joseph Martin 364r, /Gilles Mermet 508, /James Morris 321t, 437b, /Nimatallah 407tr, 442t, 508, /Pirozzi 349t, 382t, 416b, 433, /Rabatti-Domingie 273, 309tl, 317br, 341b, 389br, /Jürgen Raible 439tl, /Gerhard Ruf 342m, /Sambraus 281, /Sotheby's 504, /Michael Teller 380t, /Ullstein Bild 466t, /Yvan Travert 347b, /Phillipe Lissace/Godong 498t. **Alamy** /Peter Adams Photography 481br, /Arkreligion.com 446b, /Alessandro Bianchi 471t /Gary Blake 422b/Chris Caldicott/Axiom–RF 423 /Giuseppe Ciccia 506t/Cubo Images Sri 204b, 485t, /Julio Etchart 444r, /Barbara Gonget/G&B Images 474t, /Tim Graham 497b, 499b, /History of Art Collection 506b /Images of Africa Photobank 475t, /William S Kuta 482b, 492b, /Lonely Planet Images 351t, /Mary Evans Picture Library 468t, 491t, 494t, /Northwind Picture Archives 459b /Pictorial Press 477t, /RealyEasyStar/Fotografia Felizi 499t. **ArkReligion.com** 442t, /Agence Ciric 467tl, tr and b, /Tibor Bognar 469t, 488t, 493b, /Richard Powers 482b, /John Randall 476t, /Helene Rogers 474b. **The Art Archive/ Gianni Dagli Orti** 332bl, 481bl, 487b, /Armenian Museum Isfahan 269, /Chapelle de la Colombiere 446t, /Collection Antonovich 487t, /Domenica del Corriere 476b, /Eglise Saint Laurent Paris 449m, /Missions Etrangères Paris 282t, /Museo della Civiltá Romana, Rome 339t, /Museo Nacional Bogota 283t, /St Julian Cathedral Le Mans 332t. **The Bridgeman Art Library** 256r, 268b, 285b, 293r, 322b, 330b, 331b, 334t, 370t, 389tr, 394b, 400t, 413t, 419bl, 420l and r, 436, 442b, 453t, 461b, 469b, 475b, 486bl, /Agnew's, London 443t, /Alte Pinakothek, Munich 377t, /Archivo Capitular, Spain 411br, /Art Museum of Estonia, Tallinn 331b, /Ashmolean Museum, University of Oxford 346t, /The Barnes Foundation, Pennsylvania 405t, /Biblioteca Nazionale, Turin 383, /Bibliothèque Municipale, Avranches 374r, /Bibliothèque Nationale, Paris 353t, 196b, /Bibliothèque de L'Arsénal, Paris 264b, /Bibliotheque des Arts Decoratifs, Paris 277br, /Bibliotheque de L'Institut de France, Paris 444b, /Bibliotheque Royale de Belgique, Brussels 407b, /Bonhams, London 276t, 426t, 482t, /British Library Board 274t, 368t, /British Library, London 374l, 379t, 4111t, /Cheltenham Art Gallery and Museums, Gloucestershire 370b, /Christie's Images 290b, /Church of Notre-Dame-de-Bonne-Nouvelle, Paris 367b, /Collection of the New York Historical Society 459t, /Duomo, Sicily 347t, 355, /Eglise Saint-Louis-en-L'lle, Paris 443b, /Fitzwilliam Museum, University of Cambridge 434b, /Galleria degli Uffizi, Florence 396b, /Galleria Nazionale delle Marche, Urbino 405b, /Groeningemuseum, Bruges 365t, /Guildhall Library, London 339b, /Held Collection 450t, /Hermitage, St. Petersburg 351b, 398t, 408b, /His Grace the Duke of Norfolk, Arundel Castle 415t, 508, /Kremlin Museums, Moscow 324t, /Kunsthistorisches Museum, Vienna 305bl, /Lambeth Palace Library, London 455t, /Lobkowicz Palace, Prague Castle, Czech Republic 383t, /Louvre, Paris 346r, 356, 450b, /Magyar Nemzeti Galeria, Budapest 386r, /Musee Bonnat, Bayonne 448t, /Musée des Beaux-Arts, Caen 426b, /Musée des Beaux-Arts, Marseilles 302br, 406, 407tl, /Musée des Beaux-Arts, Orléans 419t, /Musée Conde, Chantilly 329r, 375b, 378b, 391b, /Musée de la Ville de Paris 460b, /Musée de l'Oeuvre de Notre Dame, Strasbourg 300, /Musée Guimet, Paris 174b, /Musée Jacquemart-Andre, Paris 333b, /Museo Catedralicio, Castellón 338b, /Museo de Santa Cruz, Toledo 445t, /Museum of History, Moscow 506, /Museumslandschaft Hessen Kassel 364l, /Nationalgalerie, SMPK, Berlin 381t, /National Museum of Ancient Art, Lisbon 267t, /Orihuela Cathedral Museum, Spain 410, /Palazzo Ducale, Venice 327b, /Palazzo Pitti, Florence 424t, 455b, /Piccolomini Library, Siena 270t, /Regional Art Museum, Kaluga 408t, /Richard and Kailas Icons, London 268tl, /Roy Miles Fine Paintings 362b, /Samuel Courtauld Trust, Courtauld Institute of Art Gallery 411bl, 508, /San Diago Museum of Artback 402l, /Sant'Apollinare Nuovo, Ravenna 319b, /Sir Geoffrey Keynes Collection, Cambridgeshire 307, /South West Museum, California 283br, /Staatliche Kunstsammlungen, Dresden 412t, /Universitatsbibliothek, Heidelberg 371, /Ken Welsh 329b, 456b, 460t. **Corbis** 286t, 324b, 452t, /Alinari Archives 305t, 325b, 356b, /Araldo de Luca 377b, 430b, 447t, /Archivo Iconografico, S.A. 304, 322t, 348tl, 354b, 366, 369m, 376t, 388b, 393, 409, 419br, 435t, 451bl, 511, /The Art Archive 301b, 321b, 328b, 346bc, 372t, 387t, 458b, /Arte & Immagini srl 388t, 402r,

Above: Statue of Our Lady of Fatima.

766

ACKNOWLEDGEMENTS

421b, /Atlantide Phototravel 440t, /Austrian Archives 380b, /Bettmann 343tr, 398m, 425b, 463t, 466m, 483t, 499b, 490b, 494b, /Brooklyn Museum 429t, /Burstein Collection 403, /Christie's Images 312b, 320t, 472b, /Elio Ciol 266b, 308t, 312t, 323t, 341t, 348tr, 358b, 398b, 400b, 404t, /Geoffrey Clements 414b, /Richard A Cooke 287bl, /Pablo Corral V 224t and b, /Richard Cummins 183b, /Gianni Dagli Orti 68t, 107b, 191b, /Araldo de Luca 104t, /Leonard de Selva 69t, /EPA 34t, /Fine Art Photographic Library 379b, /Werner Forman 367t, /The Gallery Collection 292, 294b, 309tr, 399r, 417br, 427, 431b, 448b /Gianni Giansanti 352b, /Christian Guy/Hemis 456t, /Lars Halbauer / dpa 485b, /Jon Hicks 268tr, /Historical Picture Archive 337b, 361b, /Hulton-Deutsch Collection 453b, /Andrea Jemolo 397t, /Krause Johansen 428, /Mimmo Jodice 314t, 355b, /David Lees 14, 375t, /Danny Lehman 291, /Massimo Listri 350b, 434t, /Francis G Mayer 363bl, /The National Gallery Collection; by kind permission of the Trustees of the National Gallery, London 294b, 302t, 306t and b, 315, 360b, 373t, 399bl, /Michael Nicholson 275, 367rm, /Fred de Noyelle/Godong 486t, /Hamish Park 383b, /José F. Poblete 382t, /Gérard Rancinan/Sygma

POPES
Alamy: Heritage Image Partnership Ltd 556–7, 569t; John Kellerman 590b; Peter Horree 634–5; REUTERS 746b, 447t, 447b.
Bridgeman Images: 560b, 579t, 690t, 701, 740br; Aachen Cathedral Treasury, Aachen, Germany/De Agostini Picture Library/A. Dagli Orti 605; Alinari 742b, 743t, 743b; Archivio di Stato, Siena, Italy 656t; Archivo General de Simancas, Valladolid, Spain/Index 661r; Art Gallery of New South Wales, Sydney, Australia 559t; Basilique Saint-Denis, France 568b; Bayerische Staatsbibliothek, Munich, Germany/ De Agostini Picture Library 586b; Biblioteca Marucelliana, Florence, Italy 691b; Biblioteca Monasterio del Escorial, Madrid, Spain/Mithra-Index 620r; Biblioteca Nazionale, Turin, Italy/ Index 572; Bibliothèque de la Sorbonne, Paris, France/Archives Charmet 633bl; Bibliothèque Historique de la Ville de Paris, Paris, France/ Archives Charmet 733tl; Bibliothèque Municipale, Amiens, France 636r; Bibliothèque Municipale, Castres, France 577t, 578, 604t; Bibliothèque Municipale, Laon, France 558b, 731t; Bibliothèque Nationale, Paris, France 598b, 700t, 603t, 622, 640t, 705t; Bibliothèque Nationale, Paris, France/Archives Charmet 583t, 724b; Bibliothèque Nationale, Paris, France / De Agostini Picture Library/J. E. Bulloz 630b; Bischöfliches Dom-und Diözesanmuseum, Mainz, Germany/Bildarchiv Steffens/ Bischöfliches Dom-und Diözesanmuseum Mainz 559b; The Bowes Museum, Barnard Castle, County Durham, UK 702t; Brancacci Chapel, Santa Maria del Carmine, Florence, Italy 579b; British Library, London, UK 637r; British Library, London, UK/© British Library Board, All Rights Reserved 588b, 612b, 623b; British Museum, London, UK 181br; Buyenlarge Archive/UIG

473t, /Vittoriano Rastelli 373b, /Reuters 270b, 488b, 493t, /New York Historical Society 287t, / Joel W Rogers 359b, /Bob Sacha 465b /Marcelo Sayao/epa 464t, /Sean Sexton Collection 491b, /Stapleton Collection 390t, /Summerfield Press 262b, 295, 397b, /Sygma 287br, /Sandro Vannini 317bl, 421t, /Nik Wheeler 285t, /Roger Wood 363m. **Getty** 276b, 376b, 384, 396t, 432t, 492t, 495b, /AFP 284t, 466b, 470b, 486br, 510, / Oliver Benn 277bl, /Bridgeman Art Library 263t, 272b, 360t, 389tl, 395t, /Byzantine 417bl, /Matthias Grunewald 416t, /Hulton Archive 299b, 335r, 345, 414t, 429b, 430t, 435br, 451br, 480b, /Francisco Jose de Goya y Lucientes 431t, /Yannick Le Gal 457b, /Lorenzo Lotto 404b, /Petr Mikhailovich Shamshin 417t, /Jim Richardson 368b, /Dante Gabriel Rossetti 424, / Time & Life Pictures 337t, /Travel Ink 415b, /Paolo Uccello 412b, /Vatican Museums and Galleries/Pietro Perugino 372b. **Associazione Amici di Carlo Acutis** 287b. **Andrew Leaney** 385b. **Mary Evans Picture Library** 472t. **Photo12.com** 449t, /Hachédé 447b, 452b, / Oronoz 445b, 495t. **SCALA, Florence** 461t. **Shutterstock** 440b, 454t, 477b.
Sonia Halliday Photographs 262t, 272t, 298t, 305br, 310t and b, 316t, 318b, 325t, 332br,

737t; California Historical Society /Gift of M. Calder 721b; Casa Buonarroti, Florence, Italy 665l; Castello Sforzesco Civiche Raccolte Archeologiche E Numismatiche Museo Della Preistoria E Protostoria, Milan, Italy /De Agostini Picture Library 582b; Catacombs of San Callisto, Rome, Italy 533; Chartres Cathedral, Chartres, France/Photo © Paul Maeyaert 589t; Château de Versailles, France 610b, 699b, 722b; Church of St. Gall, Prague, Czech Republic 643b; Church of St. Luke, Bath, Somerset, UK 568t; Church of St.Marien, Wittenberg, Germany 668t; Church of the Gesù, Rome, Italy 683b; Collection of the Duke of Devonshire, Chatsworth House, UK/© Devonshire Collection, Chatsworth/Reproduced by permission of Chatsworth Settlement Trustees 166l; CSU Archives/Everett Collection 238b; De Agostini Picture Library 9t, 540t, 585b, 619t, 626, 631t, 633t, 647t, 657b, 662b, 693t; De Agostini Picture Library/A. Dagli Orti 512r, 518–19, 524b, 561tl, 561tr, 571, 586r, 602t, 638b, 646b, 678b, 683t, 693b, 710, 717b; De Agostini Picture Library/A. De Gregorio 561b, 632, 677b, 679b; De Agostini Picture Library/F. Ferruzzi 652t; De Agostini Picture Library/ G. Cigolini 581b; De Agostini Picture Library/ G. Dagli Orti, 555t, 583b, 584b, 601b, 604b, 608b, 630t, 641b, 654l, 654r, 655t, 660b, 676b, 692l, 714b, 718t, 722t, 723b, 750; De Agostini Picture Library/G. Nimatallah 621t, 678b; De Agostini Picture Library/L. Pedicini 663b, 687tr; De Agostini Picture Library/L. Romano 596b; De Agostini Picture Library/M. Seemuller 541b, 597t, 639r, 720t; De Agostini Picture Library/ R. Carnovalini 599t; De Agostini Picture Library /S. Vannini 619b, 636l; Detroit Institute of Arts, USA /Gift of Mrs. Edgar R. Thom 700b; Deutsches Historisches Museum, Berlin,

Above: St Helen.

333t, 349b, 350t, 369t, 387b, 389bl, 391t, 438r, / Bibliothèque Nationale, Paris 378t, 451t.
Wiki Images 422t, 471b, 496t, 497t, 498b.

Germany/© DHM 666r, 669b, 670t; © Devonshire Collection, Chatsworth/ Reproduced by permission of Chatsworth Settlement Trustees 719t; Duomo, Florence, Italy 644b; Église Saint-Louis-en-L'Île, Paris, France 689t; Elvehjem Museum of Art, Madison, WI, USA 49; Forum 19t, 521r, 744t, 744b; Galleria Borghese, Rome, Italy 688t; Galleria degli Uffizi, Florence, Italy 664t, 667t, 688b, 753; Galleria Doria Pamphilj, Rome, Italy 694; Galleria Nazionale d'Arte Antica, Rome, Italy/Photo © Stefano Baldini 702b; Galleria Nazionale delle Marche, Urbino, Italy 704t, Gallerie dell'Accademia, Venice, Italy/Cameraphoto Arte Venezia 543; Germanisches Nationalmuseum, Nuremberg, Germany 628t; Godong/UIG 531b, 576, 721t; Gonville and Caius College, University of Cambridge, UK/© Leemage 639l; J. T. Vintage 730b; Koninklijk Museum voor Schone Kunsten, Antwerp, Belgium/© Lukas - Art in Flanders VZW 606; Kunsthistorisches Museum, Vienna, Austria 524t, 558t; Louvre, Paris, France 592–3, 620l, 631b, 658t, 674–5, 712–13, 716, 717t; Maison Jeanne d'Arc, Orléans, France 653t; Minneapolis Institute of Arts, MN, USA/The William Hood Dunwoody Fund 708b; Monastero di San Benedetto, Subiaco, Italy 627t; Mondadori Portfolio/ Archivio Grzegorz Galazka/Grzegorz Galazka 18, 672–3, 728–9, 745t, 745b, 746t, 748t, 748b, 749; Mondadori Portfolio/Electa/Bruno Balestrini 679t; Mondadori Portfolio /Electa/ Sergio Anelli 554b, 714t; Monte Cassino Abbey Museum, Cassino, Italy 597t; Musée Bonnat, Bayonne, France 529b; Musée Calvet, Avignon, France 643tl; Musée Cantonal des Beaux-Arts de Lausanne, Switzerland/De Agostini Picture Library/G. Dagli Orti 684b; Musée Conde, Chantilly, France 615b; Musée Crozatier, Le

ACKNOWLEDGEMENTS

Puy-en-Velay, France 545t; Musée de l'Assistance Publique, Hôpitaux de Paris, France 707b; Musée de la Ville de Paris, Musée Carnavalet, Paris, France 681t, 715b; Musée des Beaux-Arts, Béziers, France 689b, 752; Musée des Beaux-Arts, Marseille, France 709; Musée des Beaux-Arts, Nantes, France 581t; Musée des Beaux-Arts, Orléans, France/Roger-Viollet, Paris 652b; Musei Capitolini, Rome, Italy/Photo © Stefano Baldini 695tl; Museo Civico, Bologna, Italy /Mondadori Portfolio/Electa/Antonio Guerra 642; Museo Correr, Venice, Italy 615t; Museo de Bellas Artes, Seville, Spain/Index 682t; Museo del Risorgimento, Bologna, Italy/De Agostini Picture Library/A. Dagli Orti 715t; Museo e Gallerie Nazionale di Capodimonte, Naples, Italy 676t, 682b; Museo Lazaro Galdiano, Madrid, Spain 711tr; Museum Europaischer Kulturen, Berlin, Germany/De Agostini Picture Library 671t; National Gallery, London, UK 2; Ognissanti, Florence, Italy 542b; Ospedale di Santa Maria della Scala, Siena, Italy/Alinari 618t; Palazzo Barberini, Rome, Italy 667b, 690b; Palazzo Chigi, Ariccia, Italy 698b; Palazzo dei Conservatori, Musei Capitolini, Rome 658b; Palazzo Pubblico, Siena, Italy, 594–5, 613t; Photo © CCI 741; Photo © Everett Collection 739t; Photo © Patrick Morin 740t; Photo © PVDE 526t, 528t, 532t, 542t, 551l, 551m, 551r, 643tr, 735b; Photo © Stefano Baldini, 520, 535, 623t, 665r; Photo © Tallandier 648t, 736t; Photo © Zev Radovan 547t; Piazza del Campidoglio, Rome, Italy 695b; Pictures from History 599b, 629, 637l; Pierluigi Praturlon/Reporters Associati & Archivi/Mondadori Portfolio 511t; Pinacoteca Ambrosiana, Milan, Italy/De Agostini Picture Library 8b, 638t; Pinacoteca di Brera, Milan, Italy 649b; Pinacoteca Nazionale, Siena, Italy 653b; Prado, Madrid, Spain 659b; Private Collection 7b, 565b, 577b, 580b, 1610t, 645t, 645b, 646t, 680, 684t, 686, 691t, 706t, 719b, 724t, 725t, 732bl, 735t, 736b, 738t; Private Collection/Archives Charmet 588t; Private Collection/© Bianchetti /Leemage 584t, 596t; Private Collection/© Coll. Farabola/Leemage 742t; Private Collection/© Costa/Leemage 538l, 538r, 564t, 566t, 570t, 587b, 633br, 660t; Private Collection/De Agostini Picture Library 720b; Private Collection/Index 203b; Private Collection/© Look and Learn 525t, 544t, 562t, 566b, 582t, 587t, 590t, 607t, 608t, 609t, 612t, 614t, 644t, 657t, 730t, 731b, 734b; Private Collection/© Look and Learn/Rosenberg Collection 727t; Private Collection/Photo © Agnew's, London 2707t; Private Collection/Photo © Christie's Images, 659t, 696–7, 704b, 708t; Private Collection/Photo © Ken Welsh 528b, 570b, 649t; Private Collection/Photo © Philip Mould Ltd, London 706b; Private Collection/Photo © Rafael Valls Gallery, London, UK 681bl; Private Collection/Photo © Tarker 7t, 554t, 563t, 567t, 598t, 727b; Private Collection/The Stapleton Collection 569b, 573t, 613b, 627b, 661l, 669t, 687tl, 711b; S. Agostino, San Gimignano, Italy 553t; Saint Louis Art Museum, Missouri, USA/Museum purchase, by exchange 567b; San Clemente, Rome, Italy 525b, 751; San Francesco, Upper Church, Assisi, Italy, 616–17, 624l; San Martino, Monte San Martino, Italy 553b; San Vitale, Ravenna, Italy 555b; Santa Maria della Concezione, Rome, Italy 695tr; Santa Maria della Vittoria, Rome, Italy/De Agostini Picture Library / G. Nimatallah 685b; Santi Giovanni e Paolo, Venice, Italy/Cameraphoto Arte Venezia 625; Scala Regia, Vatican Museums, Vatican City 699t; SeM/Universal Images Group 739b; Sizergh Castle, Cumbria, UK/National Trust Photographic Library 628b; St. Peter's, Vatican City 648b, 698t, 700t, 240bl; St. Peter's Basilica, Vatican City 711tl; Statens Museum for Kunst, Copenhagen, Denmark 692r; SZ Photo/Scherl 591t, 732br; Tino Soriano/National Geographic Creative 703t; Topkapi Palace Museum, Istanbul, Turkey 655b; Tretyakov Gallery, Moscow, Russia 718b; United Archives/Carl Simon 734t; Universal History Archive/UIG 541t, 668b, 725b, 737b; Vatican City 662t; Vatican Library, Vatican City 580t; Vatican Museums and Galleries, Vatican City, 536, 548t, 650–1, 656b; Vatican Museums and Galleries, Vatican City/Artothek 671b; Vatican Museums and Galleries, Vatican City/Photo © Stefano Baldini, 574–5, 589b; Victoria & Albert Museum, London, UK 565c; Yale Center for British Art, Paul Mellon Collection, USA 723t. **Fotolia:** 530t; Pisa Cathedral, Italy 602b. **iStock:** 520r, 600b, 687b; laurent 732t; © HultonArchive 726; AndreaAstes 552t; annavee 640b; bbstanicic 585t; Borisb17 57l, 562b; Brzozowska 611b; Claudiad 62l; clodio 564b; DeniseSerra 527r; duncan1890 64m, 601t, 605t, 614b, 618b; Faabi 607bl; FabrizioBernardi 546b; FilippoBrandini 514l; frankix 539t; Gerardo_Borbolia 18t, 664b; gkuna 603b; Jorisvo 552b; parys 50b; pavlemarjanovic 16, 534b; Peter Zelei 532b; peterspiro 545b; photovideostock 17b, 641t.

Page 1: *Pieta* by Michelangelo.
Page 2: *Crucifixion* by Tommaso Masaccio.
Page 3: *Pope Julius II* by Raphael.
Page 4: *The Wilton Diptych* (right wing), French School.
Front endpaper: *Clement XI in Procession Across St Peter's Square* by Pier Leone Ghezzi.
Back endpaper: *The Miraculous Draft of Fishes* by Raphael.

This edition is published by Lorenz Books an imprint of Anness Publishing Ltd
info@anness.com
www.annesspublishing.com

© Anness Publishing Ltd 2024

Publisher: Joanna Lorenz
Editorial Director: Helen Sudell
Catholicism and *Saints* sections produced for Lorenz Books by Toucan Books (Managing Editor: Ellen Dupont)
Editorial: Theresa Bebbington, Hannah Bowen, Elizabeth Young
Design: Elizabeth Healey, Nigel Partridge
Cover Design: Nigel Partridge
Cartography by Cosmographics, UK
Production Controller: Bob Worley

All rights reserved. No part of this publication may be reproduced, stored in a retrieval system, or transmitted in any way or by any means, electronic, mechanical, photocopying, recording or otherwise, without the prior written permission of the copyright holder.

Previously published in three separate volumes, *The Illustrated Guide to Catholicism*, *The Illustrated Encyclopedia of Saints* and *The Illustrated History of Popes*

PUBLISHER'S NOTE
Although the information in this book is believed to be accurate at the time of going to press, neither the authors nor the publisher can accept any legal responsibility or liability for any errors or omissions that may have been made.

Right: St Benedict, founder of the monastery at Monte Cassino, Italy, wrote his celebrated rule for monastic life in c.AD 535–40.